FUNDAMENTALS OF ADVANCED ACCOUNTING (FINANCIAL ACCOUNTING)

VOLUME–I

FUNDAMENTALS OF ADVANCED ACCOUNTING (FINANCIAL ACCOUNTING)

For the Students of B.Com., M.Com., BBA., CA., ICWA, CAIIB., CS and Various Diploma and Certificate Examinations

VOLUME–I

R.S.N. PILLAI, *M.A., M.Com., LL.B.,*
Prof. & HoD., Commerce Department
Arignar Anna College
Aramboly (Kanyakumari)

BAGAVATHI, *M.A., M.Com.,*
240, Chidambaranagar
Nagercoil (Kanyakumari)

S. UMA, *M.Com., M.Phil*
G-606, Pride Apartments
181, Bannerghatta Road
Bilekkahallai
Bangalore

S. CHAND PUBLISHING

S Chand And Company Limited

(ISO 9001 Certified Company)

S Chand And Company Limited

(ISO 9001 Certified Company)

Head Office: D-92, Sector–2, Noida – 201301, U.P. (India), Ph. 91-120-4682700

Registered Office: A-27, 2nd Floor, Mohan Co-operative Industrial Estate, New Delhi – 110 044, Phone: 011-49731800

www.**schandpublishing.com;** e-mail: **info@schandpublishing.com**

S. CHAND PUBLISHING

Marketing Offices:

Chennai	:	Ph: 23632120; chennai@schandpublishing.com
Guwahati	:	Ph: 2738811, 2735640; guwahati@schandpublishing.com
Hyderabad	:	Ph: 40186018; hyderabad@schandpublishing.com
Jalandhar	:	Ph: 4645630; jalandhar@schandpublishing.com
Kolkata	:	Ph: 23357458, 23353914; kolkata@schandpublishing.com
Lucknow	:	Ph: 4003633; lucknow@schandpublishing.com
Mumbai	:	Ph: 25000297; mumbai@schandpublishing.com
Patna	:	Ph: 2260011; patna@schandpublishing.com

First Edition 2006
Reprint 2007; Second Revised Edition 2008; Reprint 2009
Third Revised Edition 2012; Reprint with Corrections 2013; Reprints 2014, 2015, 2016, 2019, 2020, 2022 (Twice)

Reprint 2024

ISBN: 978-81-219-2662-1 **Product Code:** H8AAC48ACCN10ENAC12O

PRINTED IN INDIA

By Vikas Publishing House Private Limited, Plot 20/4, Site-IV, Industrial Area Sahibabad, Ghaziabad – 201 010 and Published by S Chand And Company Limited, A-27, 2nd Floor, Mohan Co-operative Industrial Estate, New Delhi – 110 044.

PREFACE TO THE THIRD REVISED EDITION

We are happy to place the Third Revised Edition of Advanced Accounting Vol. I before the students and teachers. We also take this opportunity to express our gratitude to the academic community – fellow Professors and students for the unstinted support and encouragement to our books. Of the 33 Chapters of this book, the following topics have completely been re-written and updated.

Chapters : 1. Introduction

8. Errors and their Rectifications

9. Inventory Valuation

11. Depreciation and Reserves

16. Joint Venture Accounts

18. Hire Purchase Accounts

24. Accounts of Non-profit Organisations

26. Farm Accounts

27. Government Accounts

Many new topics have been included, in addition to the thorough revision. The style of presentation is simple and lucid. Many significant changes have been made according to a number of Accounting Standards issued by the Institute of Chartered Accountants of India. The latest amendments of SEBI have also been duly incorporated while solving various problems. The amendments have been high-lighted for the benefit of students.

The book contains 502 solved Illustrations, 863 Objectives Type Questions and their answers, 223 Theoretical Questions and 635 Practical Problems. Detailed answers have been given to the Practical Problems.

Errors which have come to our notice have been rectified. We believe that the blending of our academic and practical experience have made this book a useful guide to students and teachers and the feed-back has been most positive. We have been engaged for quite a long time in the field of teaching, particularly in Accountancy. Hence we are intensely aware of the pulse of the students and their difficulties. So, we have incorporated the maximum number of new problems selected at examinations of different Indian Universities and Professional Institutions to acquaint students with the recent trend of examinations.

Our endeavour has been to make the book more student-oriented and learner-friendly. All the chapters have been dealt with in great depth with suitable illustrations alongwith notes wherever necessary. We have taken sufficient care that the book meets the needs of a variety of students.

A number of colleagues and friends helped us in the preparation of this book. We thank each and every one of them. We will be grateful if mistakes or lacuna are pointed out. Suggestions for further improvement of this book are most welcome and will be acknowledge with thanks.

We are thankful to the Management Team and the Editorial Department of S. Chand & Company Pvt. Ltd. for all help and support in the publication of this book.

Nagercoil
(Kanyakumari)

AUTHORS

PREFACE TO THE FIRST EDITION

Advanced Accounting is a subject of Commerce stream which is attracting more and more students in view of their future prospects in this area. The present book of Advanced Accountancy has been split into 2 Volumes just to facilitate students as well as teachers to carry it with them. The present book, which is the first Volume of the subject dealing with Financial Accounting, is now in your hands which contains about 385 worked out illustrations, 150 theoretical questions and 620 practical problems with answers for the help of both the students and teachers. Latest material available on the subject has been introduced in a simple language with clarity and precision in order to enable the students, to learn and understand the accounting problems without any difficulty. The authors have put all their long teaching experience in developing the material of this textbook and it is expected that it will meet the requirements of the students of B.Com, M.Com, BBA, CA, ICWA, CAIIB, MBA, CS, etc.

Any errors / omissions and suggestions for the improvement of this Volume may kindly be brought to the notice of the authors and publishers in order to make the book error-free and user-friendly.

Our grateful thanks are due to the Editorial Staff and specially to Shri R.K. Gupta, Managing Director of S. Chand & Company Ltd. for bringing out this book in its present form.

AUTHORS

CONTENTS

Chapter 1

Introduction

Introduction – Book-keeping – Book-keeping and Accounting – Origin of Accounting – Meaning of Accounting – Distinction between the two – Objects of Book-keeping – Importance of Accounting – Development of Accounting – Functions of Accounting – Accounting as a Language – Limitations of Accounting – Classifications of Accounting – Accounting and other Disciplines – Accounting Concepts – Accounting Conventions – Accounting Policies – Financial Statements – Accounting Principles – Accounting Standards – Accounting Equation – Accounting Methods – Systems of Accounting – Advantages of Double Entry System – Role of Accountants in the Society – Some Accounting Terminology – Indian Accounting Standards – Objective Type Questions – Theoretical Questions

INTRODUCTION

Book-keeping is as old as money itself. Book-keeping is that branch of knowledge which tells us how to keep a record of financial transactions. The necessity of Book-keeping and Accountancy, in the early periods, arose mainly due to the fact that memory of the human beings is limited. For instance, a person, who receives a monthly salary, spends the amount on various items. At the end of the month, he may find that he owes some amount against a few bills; which remain still unpaid. When he possesses no money, he may recall his memory as to how the money has been spent. He may fail to recall all the transactions, in the absence of written records, he had done. It may also be possible that he will have no correct account for the money he spent or may forget some items for which he had paid. In short, he is in confusion. At the same time, if he had noted down his incomes and expenditures, he can now readily not only command the required information but also regulate the savings and expenditures. Thus people, who are earning and spending, must maintain a note or diary or register in which details of the transactions have been recorded. The fundamental idea behind this record is to show a correct position relating to incomes and expenditures. The need for keeping such records, in a clear and systematic manner, is the basis which gives rise to the subject—book-keeping.

BOOK-KEEPING

L.C.Cropper observes: "Book-keeping may be described as the science of recording transactions in money or money's worth in such a manner that at any subsequent date, their nature and effect may be clearly understood, and that when required a combined statement of their result may be prepared."

R.N. Carter says, "Book-keeping is the science and art of correctly recording in books of account all those business transactions that result in the transfer of money or money's worth."

Book-keeping includes recording of journal, posting in ledgers and balancing of accounts. All the records before the preparation of trial balance is the whole subject matter of book-keeping. Thus, book-keeping may be defined as the science and art of recording transactions in money or money's worth so accurately and systematically, in a certain set of books, regularly, that the true state of businessman's affairs can be correctly ascertained. Here it is important to note that only those transactions related to business are recorded which can be expressed in terms of money.

BOOK-KEEPING AND ACCOUNTING

As discussed in the above paragraph, book-keeping may be defined as the art and science of correctly and systematically recording in the books of account the business transactions of an individual or a concern in a way to show clearly the monetary effect of each such transaction. The work of book-keeping is usually entrusted to junior employees, who maintain various books of accounts—journal, subsidiary books, ledgers etc.—can be called as book-keepers. The books of original record, by themselves, do not give an idea of the company's financial position. When one has to make a judgement regarding the financial position of the firm, the information contained in these books has to be analysed and interpreted. According to American Institute of Certified Public Accountants, "Accounting is the art of recording, classifying and summarising in a significant manner and in terms of money, transactions and events which are of a financial character and interpreting the results thereof."

ORIGIN OF ACCOUNTING

Accounting originated to meet the requirements of exchange of goods and commodities. The need for accounting grew in order to serve the transactions of the business-world. The origin of accounting cannot be exactly located. The value of money or the use of currency, that now we attach to the goods to-day, was unknown to the people of ancient times when barter system existed. Later, innovation of money facilitated to ease exchange of commodities. The credit transactions necessitated to maintain accounts, and accounting is as old as business itself. Accounting was practised in India, from ancient time, as is clear from the book *Arthashastra* written by Kautilya, the minister of King Chandra Gupta. In 1494, the system of book-keeping was first conceived on scientific line in Venice by Luca Pacioli, a Fraciscan monk. The book titled *De Computic at Scripturies* (Italian) dealt with the use of memorandum book, journal and ledgers. This work was translated and published in English by Hugh Old Castle in 1543. Later, James Pule improved the method of book-keeping for the purposes of accounts of debtors and creditors. Thereafter, many works was published. The most important of them was the published work on accounting in 1795 by Edward Jones, who innovated two columns in the journal entries. From time to time, various innovations were introduced. The modern system of accounting based on the principles of Double Entry System owes its origin to Luca Pacioli. The art of accounting has been practised for centuries but only since the late thirties it has been seriously taken up.

MEANING OF ACCOUNTING

The modern system of accounting is based on what is known as the Double Entry principle. Accounting is a science because it has some definite objects to be fulfilled and is an art as it prescribes the process through which the object can be achieved. Non-financial transactions cannot be recorded in accounting, *i.e.*, only transactions of financial nature is the subject-matter of accounting. To be more clear, only those transactions which are expressed in terms of money are recorded. Accounting is an art of recording transactions according to size, nature and type of business transactions— cash transaction, credit transaction, frequent transaction etc. When the recording in journal or subsidiary books is done, they are to be classified by grouping the transactions or entries of one nature at one place. This is done by opening accounts in a book called ledger. Then such ledgers are summarised in order to give useful information to the management or interested parties. This is done by preparing trading and profit and loss account and balance sheet of whole accounting record. Finally, it is an art of interpreting the results of the financial transactions and communicating the result thereof. The aspect of interpretation falls under management accounting.

DISTINCTION BETWEEN BOOK-KEEPING AND ACCOUNTING

Book-keeping should be distinguished from accounting. Book-keeping is a process of accounting concerned with recording transactions and keeping records. Book-keeping is a small and simple part of accounting. It is mechanical and repetitive while dealing with business transactions. As such, this work is usually entrusted to junior employees of accounts department, who are known as Book-keepers. Accounting, on the other hand, aims at designing a satisfactory information system which may fulfil informational needs of different users and decision makers. Accounting primarily focusses on measurement, analysis, interpretation and use of information. It highlights the relevance and relationship of the information produced by the accounting process and effects of different accounting alternatives. Accounting includes budgeting, strategic planning, cost analysis, auditing, income-tax preparation, performance measurement, evaluation, control, preparing managerial reports for decision making etc. The persons who are engaged with these works are known as Accountants. That is why it is rightly said that when book-keeping ends, accounting starts. Accounting is the language of business because it is through accounting that various monetary matters related with business are communicated. In the words of Smith, "Accounting is the science of recording and classifying business transactions and events, primarily of a financial character, and the art of making significant summaries, analysis and interpretation of those transactions and events and communicating the results to persons who must make decisions or form judgement."

Book-keeping is concerned with the recording aspect, while accounting, being comprehensive, includes not only book-keeping but also the activities involved in analysis and reporting of the recorded information, apart from designing a proper and suitable system for recroding.

Distinctions between Book-keeping and Accounting

Book-keeping	Accounting
1. It is the basis of Accounting	1. It is the basis for Business Language.
2. Persons, do book-keeping, are called Book- keepers.	2. Persons, responsible for accounting, are called Accountants.
3. No Financial Statements can be prepared from book-keeping records.	3. Financial Statements can be prepared from the accounting records.
4. It has no branch.	4. It has many branches—Cost Accounting, Management Accounting etc.
5. It is the recording phase.	5. It is the summarising phase.
6. A complete picture of financial condition of a business cannot be known.	6. A complete picture of the financial condition of a business unit can be known.
7. It need not require any special skill or knowledge.	7. It requires special skill and knowledge.
8. Personal judgement of the book-keeper is not required.	8. Personal judgement of the Accountant is essential.
9. It provides no information for taking managerial decisions.	9. It provides information for taking managerial decisions.
10. It does not guide in complying with any legal formality.	10. Legal formalities can be complied with the help of accounting records.

OBJECTS OF BOOK-KEEPING AND ACCOUNTING

By keeping a systematic record of transactions, the following objects are fulfilled:

1. Accounting provides a permanent record of each transaction.
2. Entries related to incomes and expenditures of a concern facilitate to know the profit or loss for a given period.
3. Soundness of a firm can be assessed from the records of assets and liabilities on a particular date.

4. It enables to prepare a list of customers and suppliers to ascertain the amount to be received or paid.
5. Accounting as a method gives opportunities to review the business policies in the light of the past records.
6. Analysis of the accounting entries facilitates a good and proper control over expenses incurred so as to maximise the profits.
7. Amendment of business laws, provision of licences, assessment of taxes etc., are based on accounting records.
8. In the case of the companies to comply the provisions of the Companies Act 1956, it is necessary to maintain accounting records.
9. It provides the most vital information to the management for making and preparing budgets.
10. It provides the most effective way to the management for fixing up the objectives of the business.

Apart from the above, the position of cash and goods can be known, errors and frauds can be detected and the requirements of the business at any time can be known. In short, the object of book-keeping and accounting is measurement of wealth.

IMPORTANCE OF ACCOUNTING

The progress and reputation of any business firm is built upon the sound financial footing. There are a number of parties who are interested in the accounting information relating to business. Accounting is the language employed to communicate financial information of a concern to such parties.

According to Slawin and Reynolds, "Conceptually, accounting is the discipline that provides information on which external and internal users of the information may base decisions that result in the allocation of economic resources in society". That is, users of accounting information may be grouped into two classes, *viz*., Internal users and External users.

(A) Internal Users :

Internal users of accounting information are those persons or groups which are within the organisation. Following are such internal users;

1. **Owners.** The owners provide funds or capital for the organisation. They possess curiosity in knowing whether the business is being conducted on sound lines or not and whether the capital is being employed properly or not. *Owners, being businessmen, always keep an eye on the returns from the investment.* Comparing the accounts of various years helps in getting good pieces of information. Properly kept accounts are good proof in dispute, they determine the amount of goodwill and facilitate in assessing various taxes.

2. **Management.** The management of the business is greatly interested in knowing the position of the firm. The accounts are the basis, the management can study the merits and demerits of the business activity. Thus, the management is interested in financial accounting to find whether the business carried on is profitable or not. *The financial accounting is the "eyes and ears of management and facilitates in drawing future course of action, further expansion etc."*

3. **Employees.** *Payment of bonus depends upon the size of profit earned by the firm.* The more important point is that the workers expect regular income for the bread. The demand for wage rise, bonus, better working conditions etc. depend upon the profitability of the firm and in turn depends upon financial position. For these reasons, this group is interested in accounting.

(B) External Users:

External users are those groups or persons who are outside the organisation for whom accounting function is performed. Following are such external users:

1. **Creditors.** Creditors are the persons who supply goods on credit, or bankers or lenders of money. It is usual that these groups are interested to know the financial soundness before granting credit. The progress and prosperity of the firm, to which credits are extended, are largely watched by creditors from the point of view of security and further credit. *Profit and Loss Account and Balance Sheet are nerve centres to know the soundness of the firm.*

2. **Investors.** The prospective investors, who want to invest their money in a firm, of course wish to see the progress and prosperity of the firm, before investing their amount, by going through the financial statements of the firm. This is to safeguard the investment. *For this, this group is eager to go through the accounting which enables them to know the safety of investment.*

3. **Government.** Government keeps a close watch on the firms which yield good amount of profits. The state and central Governments are interested in the financial statements to know the earnings for the purpose of taxation. *To compile national accounts the accounting is essential.*

4. **Consumers.** *These groups are interested in getting the goods at reduced price.* Therefore, they wish to know the establishment of a proper accounting control, which in turn will reduce the cost of production, in turn less price to be paid by the consumers. Researchers are also interested in accounting for interpretation.

5. **Research Scholars.** Accounting information, *being a mirror of the financial performance of a business organisation*, is of immense value to the research scholar who wants to make a study into the financial operations of a particular firm. To make a study into the financial operations of a particular firm, the research scholar needs detailed accounting information relating to purchases, sales, expenses, cost of materials used, current assets, current liabilities, fixed assets, long-term liabilities and share-holders funds which is available in the accounting records maintained by the firm.

6. **Financial Institutions.** Bank and financial institutions who provide loan to the business are interested to know credit-worthiness of the business. The groups, who lend money need accounting information to analyse a company's profitability, liquidity and financial position before making a loan to the company. Further, *they keep constant watch on the operating results and financial position of the business through accounting data.*

7. **Regulatory Agencies.** Various Government departments such as Company law department, Reserve Bank of India, Registrar of Companies etc. require information to be filed with them under law. By examining these accounting information they ensure that concerned companies are following the rules and regulations.

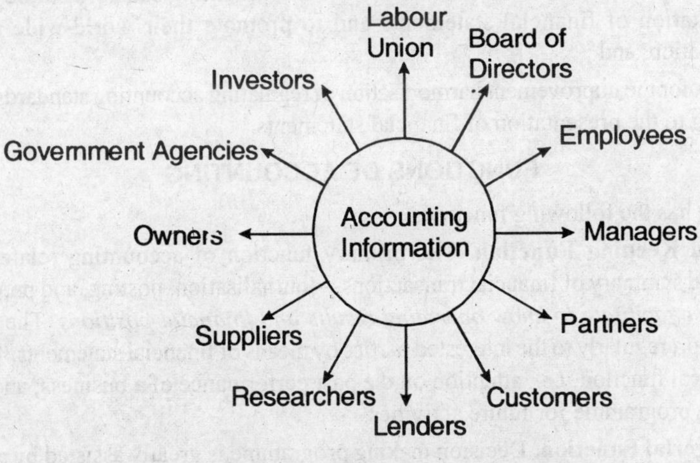

Users of Accounting Information

DEVELOPMENT OF ACCOUNTING

Accounting is as old as money itself. In India, Chanakya in his "Arthashastra" has emphasised the existence and need of proper Accounting and Auditing. The modern system of accounting owes its origin to Pacioli who lived in Italy in the 15th century. Accounting, at its initial stage, tried to meet the need of historical and stewardship functions. The conventional accounting principles and practices prove to be insufficient. The advent of Industrial Revolution has resulted in large scale production, cut-throat competition and widening market. To-day there is greater need for coordination and control. Accounting to-day cannot be the same as it used to be about half a century ago. It has become a very dynamic subject. At present some of the important specialised branches of accounting which are developed are: Cost Accounting, Management Accounting, Responsibility Accounting, Social Accounting or Macro Accounting, Government Accounting, Inflation Accounting, Mechanised Accounting, Human Resource Accounting etc. Needless to mention that some of the said techniques devised are standard Costing, Marginal Costing, Budgetary Control, Statistical and quantitative techniques, Ratio Accounting, Fund and Cash Flow Analysis etc.

To promote world-wide uniformity in published accounts, the International Accounting Standards Committee (IASC) has been set up in 1973 to formulate and publish in the public interest, standards to be observed in the presentation of audited financial statements and to promote their world-wide acceptance and observance. Since then it has issued "Standards" and disclosure of accounting policies, inventory valuation, consolidated financial statements, depreciation accounting, disclosures in financial statements, price-level changes, statement of changes in financial position, unusual items and changes in accounting policies.

International Accounting Standard Committee (*IASC*). It came into being on 29th June 1973 when 16 accounting bodies (*viz*., The Institute of Chartered Accountants from 9 nations, *i.e.*, U.S.A., Canada, U.K., Ireland, Australia, France, Germany, Japan, Mexico and Netherlands), signed the constitution for its formation. Its headquarter is situated at London. The objectives of IASC is to develop accounting standards which are to be observed in the presentation of audited financial statements and to promote their world-wide acceptance. Moreover, its other responsibility is to keep member bodies informed of the latest development and standards by issuing drafts from time to time. Needless to mention that Institute of Chartered Accountants of India and the Institute of Cost and Works Accountants of India are the members of the IASC.

The objectives of IASC which are set out in its revised agreement and constitution are:

(*i*) to formulate and publish in the public interest accounting standards to be observed in the presentation of financial statements and to promote their world-wide acceptance and observation, and

(*ii*) to work for the improvement harmonisation of regulating accounting standards and procedures relating to the presentation of financial statements.

FUNCTIONS OF ACCOUNTING

Accounting has the following functions:

1. **Record Keeping Function.** The primary function of accounting relates to recording, classification and summary of financial transactions—journalisation, posting, and preparation of final statements. *These facilitate to know operating results and financial positions.* The purpose of this function is to report regularly to the interested parties by means of financial statements. Thus accounting performs historical function, *i.e.*, attention on the past performance of a business; and this facilitates decision making programme for future activities.

2. **Managerial Function.** Decision making programme is greatly assisted by accounting. The managerial function and decision making programmes, without accounting, may mislead. The day-to-day operations are compared with some pre-determined standard. *The variations of actual operations with pre-determined standards and their analysis is possible only with the help of accounting.*

3. **Legal Requirement Function.** Auditing is compulsory in case of registered firms. *Auditing is not possible without accounting*. Thus accounting becomes compulsory to comply with legal requirements. Accounting is a base and with its help various returns, documents, statements etc., are prepared.

4. **Language of Business.** Accounting is the language of business. Various transactions are communicated through accounting. There are many parties—owners, creditors, government, employees etc., who are interested in knowing the results of the firm and this can be communicated only through accounting. *The accounting shows a real and true position of the firm or the business.*

ACCOUNTING AS A LANGUAGE

Accounting is often called the "Language of business." It is a means of communicating information about a business. Its responsibility is applying a thorough knowledge of the theory of accounting, that is, generally accepted principles of accounting to the practical field of business in order that income and financial position may be stated fairly. Accounting is the analysis and interpretation of book-keeping records. It includes not only maintenance of accounting records but also the preparation of financial and economical information which involves the measurement of transaction and other events pertaining to a business. To operate a business profitably and to stay solvent, the profitability and solvency of a business should be measured at regular intervals. For that, it is essential to know whether a business is earning sufficient profits or incurring losses and it has sufficiant money to pay off debts. Accounting provides all these pieces of information which enable the management to guide the business on a profitable and solvent course.

After analysing properly the information supplied by the accounting statements, the users of the same take decisions for future activities. Since accounting supplies the necessary information, it performs, in fact, a service function and, at the same time, it is used to represent economic position of an entity. Therefore, it becomes clear that keeping of accounts is not the primary objective of a person or an entity. On the contrary, the primary objective is to take decision on the basis of financial facts presented by accounting statements. Thus, the understanding of accounts is not the basic objective, it only helps to realise a specific objective. As such, accounting is not an end in itself but a means to an end.

We express ourselves through our language. Similarly, the results of the activities are expressed through accounting with the help of financial statements. Accounting measures the performances of the business, that is, profitability and financial position. Thus, the language of accounting expresses the whole story of the undertaking through the various processes of accounting. The progress of the firm can easily be compared and seen with the help of various accounting data.

Yuji Ijiri, observes "As the language of business, accounting has many things in common with other languages. The various business activities of a firm are reported in accounting statements using accounting language, just as news events are reported in newspapers, in English or another Language. To express as event in accounting or in English we must follow certain rules. Without following certain rules diligently, not only does one run the risk of being misunderstood but also risks a penalty for misrepresentation, lying or perjury. Comparability of statements is essential to the effective functioning of a language whether it is in English or in accounting. At the same time, language has to be flexible to adapt to a changing environment."

LIMITATIONS OF ACCOUNTING

Financial accounting is significant for management as it helps them to control the firm activities and in determining appropriate managerial policies in different areas – production, sales, administration, finance etc. However, financial accounting does not provide adequate and useful information. Most of limitations are mainly due to the cumulative effect of recorded facts, accounting conventions and personal judgements on financial statements. Financial accounting suffers from the following limitations which have been responsible for the emergence of Cost and Management Accounting.

1. Transactions of non-monetary nature do not find place in accounting. Accounting is limited to monetary transactions only. It excludes qualitative elements like management reputation, employee morale, labour strike etc.

2. Cost concept is found in accounting. Price changes are not considered. Money value is bound to change often from time to time. This is a strong limitation of accounting.

3. Acceptable alternatives are so broad based that comparisons are likely to be confusing or misleading. For instance, inventory cost may be ascertained by LIFO or FIFO; or stock may be evaluated at cost price or market price.

4. Accounting policies are framed by the Accountant. The figures of balance sheet are largely resulted by personal judgement of accountant hence it is the subjective factor that prevails in accounting and objective factor is ignored.

5. Recording and accounting for wages and labour is not carried out for different jobs, processes, products or departments. This creates problems in analysing the cost associated with different activities.

6. It is difficult to know the behaviour of costs in financial accounting as expenses are not assigned to the product at each stage of production. Expenses are not classified into direct and indirect and therefore, cannot be classified as controllable and uncontrollable. Control of cost which is the most important objective of all business enterprise, cannot be achieved with the aid of financial accounting alone.

7. Financial accounting does not provide information to analyse the losses due to various factors —idle plant and equipment, seasonal fluctuations in volume of business etc. It does not help management in taking important decisions about expansion of business, dropping a product, alternative methods of production, improvement in products etc.

8. Financial accounting does not set up a proper system of controlling materials and supplies. Undoubtedly, if materials and supplies are not controlled in a manufacturing concern, they will lead to losses on account of misappropriation, misutilisation, scrap, defectives etc.

CLASSIFICATION OF ACCOUNTING

Accounting can be classified into the following categories :

(*a*) **Financial Accounting.** The main purpose of this type of accounting is to record business transactions in the books of accounts in such a way that operating results for a particular period and financial condition on a particular date can be known for the information of the various persons.

(*b*) **Cost Accounting.** It relates to the collection, classification, ascertainment of cost and its accounting and cost control relating to the various elements of cost, that is, materials, labour and overheads.

(*c*) **Management Accounting.** It relates to the use of accounting data collected with the help of financial accounting and cost accounting for the purpose of policy formulation, planning, control and decision-making by the management. The accounting which is prepared exclusively for the use of management is called management accounting.

ACCOUNTING AND OTHE DISCIPLINES

In order to appreciate fully the role of accounting in modern society, it is essential to consider the environment in which accounting functions.

1. **Accounting and Statistics.** Both accounting and statistics deal with the collection, classification, summarising, analysis and interpretation of data. Accounting method is statistical in character because its central mechanism consists of accounts, and accounts are classification categories used for compressing and simplifying a mass of enterprise transactions. The chief function of statistical method is to classify, compress and simplify masses of data so that their significance may better be understood. Accounting has the same function. As a matter of fact, accounting is concerned with the

data which can be expressed in terms of money whereas the field of statistics is not so limited. It deals with both quantitative and financial data. With the help of statistical methods, effect of seasonable changes, boom or slump can be forecasted with a fair degree of accuracy.

2. **Accounting and Law.** These two subjects are closely related to each other. Practically without sufficient knowledge in law, an accountant cannot prove his efficiency in his profession. We know that accounting function must be performed in accordance with the internal and external affairs of a firm. Therefore, an accountant should possess sufficient knowledge about the Partnership Act, if he wants to be an accountant of such a firm or if he wants to maintain proper books of accounts of such a firm. Similar principle is also being followed in case of any company accounts, since there is Companies Act, that is, he must know thoroughly the Companies Act while preparing company accounts or else his accounting work may not be valid. An accountant should know the various commerical laws, *viz.*, Company Law, Partnership Law, Sale of Goods Act, Sales Tax and Income Tax Law etc., otherwise he will not be able to solve the problems that may arise. Similarly, a lawyer should possess adequate knowledge in accounting, since in most cases disputes are created out of transactions and tax matters.

3. **Accounting and Economics.** Economics studies those acts of human being which are related with the consumption, production, exchange and distribution of wealth aiming at maximising human satisfaction. Economics can also be defined as a science which studies human behaviour as a relationship between ends and scarce means which have alternative uses. Thus, in all types of economic problems the problem of choice arises. It may be mentioned that the economist limits his study of human behaviour in economics is restricted to only those aspects which can be expressed in terms of money. In accounting too, only those transactions are recorded which can be expressed in terms of money. The accountant can provide meaningful information when he understands the basic concepts of value and wealth as given in economics. In the same way the economist must understand the basic concepts and conventions followed by the accountant in providing information for his use.

4. **Accounting and Engineering.** An engineering firm or the accountant of a production unit – particularly the Cost Accountant and an Engineer, who is associated with the planning and production of such unit, are to work simultaneously in order to solve the day-to-day problems. The figures and values which an engineer uses for preparing his statements, designs etc. are presented frequently in different accounting reports and statements which are prepared by the accountants. Thus, it is clear that in order to perform his duties efficiently, an engineer should possess some knowledge of accountancy and, on the contrary, an accountant should possess sufficient knowledge of different machinery, the effective working life of them, etc. Otherwise, he will not be able to perform his duties in an efficient manner. Accountants and engineers should co-operate each other in arriving at a correct decision because engineers can give judgement on the technical feasibility of the project and accountants can give judgement on the financial feasibility of the project. Both can prove helpful in cost reduction programmes.

5. **Accounting and Management.** Members of the management team perform their management functions only on the basis of accounting information. One of the main functions of accounting is internal reporting and enabling the management personnel to perform their functions efficiently. "Decision-making" is the main function of management. The important function, that is, decision-making is performed only on the basis of accounting information. Accounting provides timely and useful information to the management for planning, control, performance-measurement, and for performing many other activities and functions of a concern. Accounting is the language of the business. Accounting is used to communicate business information to the management for discharging their functions efficiently. Accounting information is used by the management as a basic source tor planning and controlling the activities of the management.

Accounting is the language of business and information about business is communicated to outsiders through accounting statements. In order to make these statements easily understandable and meaningful, it is necessary that accounting should be based on certain uniform scientifically laid down norms, which are called accounting principles. The accounting principles are rules of action or a body of doctrine universally adopted while recording the business transactions. Adopting uniform principles in recording the transactions will ensure uniformity, clarity and understanding. If accounting is to serve its purpose more effectively, it should be based on certain uniform and scientifically laid down principles or postulates, also termed as accounting standards. The accounting principles can be classified into two categories : (1) Accounting Concepts and (2) Accounting Conventions.

ACCOUNTING PRINCIPLES

Accounting Concepts	Accounting Conventions
1. Money Measurement	1. Disclosure
2. Business Entity	2. Consistency
3. Going Concern	3. Conservatism
4. Cost	4. Materiality
5. Dual Aspect	
6. Accounting Period	
7. Matching	
8. Realisation	
9. Objectivity	
10. Accrual	

ACCOUNTING CONCEPTS

There are some assumptions on which accounting is based. Accounting is the language of business. Business firms communicate their affairs and financial positions to the outsiders through the medium of accounting, which is the language of business in the form of financial statements. To make the language convey the same meaning to all interested parties, accountants have agreed on a number of concepts which they try to follow. The meassages so communicated should be easily understood by the people for whom it is intended. Accounting concepts can be described as something which signifies a general notion regarding accounting principle. The assumptions, so made, are most natural and are not forced ones. A concept is a self-evident proposition, *i.e.*, something taken for granted. There is no authoritative list of these concepts. The following are some of the accounting concepts that are quite popular in accounting.

1. Money Measurement Concept

Only those transactions, which can be expressed in monetary terms, are recorded in accounting though their quantitative records may also be kept. All business transactions should be expressed only in money. Thus transactions, which cannot be expressed in money, will not be recorded in accounting books. Thus, labour-management relations, sales policy, labour unrest, effectiveness of competition etc., which are of vital importance to business concern, do not find place in accounting. Another limitation of this concept makes the assumption that the money value is constant. It is contrary to fact as there are fluctuations in the money value. For instance, a land, purchased for Rs 10,000 in 1980, may cost four or five times in 2004. This is because of fall in money value.

2. Business Entity Concept

Business is treated as separate from the proprietor. This concept is important and implies that a business is separate and distinct from the persons who supplied capital to the firm. All transactions of the business are recorded in the books of the firm. If business affairs and private affairs are mixed, the true picture of the business will not be available. The proprietor is treated as a creditor to the extent of his capital. Capital is thus a liability to the firm and the proprietor is the creditor of the business. The proprietors—sole trader, partners of a partnership firm etc.—may draw amount out of the business and this reduces the liability of the firm. Because of this concept, financial position of the business can be easily found out and earning capacity of the firm can be easily ascertained. It is important to note that transactions of the business affairs and private affairs are separated for recording only and in law, no such distinction is recognised except for an incorporated company.

3. Going Concern Concept

This concept relates with the long life of the business. A business is intended to continue for an indefinitely long period. For all practical purposes, a business firm comes under going concern concept, when there is no evidence to the contrary. All firms that continue to operate on a profitable footing are treated as going concerns. Accordingly, continuity of activity is assumed, thus accounting reports are fashioned as a going concern, just as against liquidation. The current disposal value is irrelevant for a continuing business. Thus under this assumption fixed assets are recorded at original cost and are depreciated in a proper manner. In Balance Sheet market price of fixed assets are not considered. While preparing final accounts, record is made for outstanding expenses and pre-paid expenses with the assumption that the business will continue.

4. Cost Concept

Under this concept fixed assets are recorded in the account books at the price at which they are acquired. The price paid to acquire the assets is termed as cost and this cost is the basis for all the subsequent accounting for the asset. When an asset is acquired for Rs 5,000, it is recorded in the account books at Rs 5,000 even though the market value may be different. But the asset is shown in balance sheet year after year, at cost price minus depreciation. This value is called book value. If the business pays nothing for an item it acquired, then this will not appear in the accounting records as an asset. Thus, all such events are ignored which affect the business but have no cost, for example, a favourable location, a good reputation with its customers, market standing etc.

5. Dual Aspect Concept (Accounting Equation Concept)

This concept signifies that every business transaction involves a two-fold aspect — (*a*) the yielding of benefit and (*b*) the giving of the benefit. For an exchange of value, two parties are required — a giver and a receiver. Thus, a firm sells goods worth Rs 100, the two simultaneous implications on the *seller* are (1) forgoing goods worth Rs 100 and (2) receipt of cash Rs 100. And those on the *purchaser* would be (1) receipt of goods for Rs 100 and (2) forgoing cash Rs 100. Every transaction affects two accounts and entails two-fold simultaneous effect on each party. Thus a giver necessarily implies a receiver and receiver necessarily implies a giver and each transaction affects receiving account and giving account equally. Technically speaking, "for every debit, there is a credit". Therefore, we can say that every debit must have a corresponding credit and vice versa. This is the only system of modern account keeping. The underlying principle of Double Entry is very simple but wonderfully effective. "Double Entry book-keeping is a system of accounting by which receiving and giving aspects of each transaction are recorded at a time." As such transaction affects giving account and receiving account equally, the assets of a business entity will always be equal to its equities, *i.e.*,

$$\text{Total Assets} = \text{Total Liabilities}$$
$$\text{Total Assets} = \text{Capital} + \text{Outsiders' liabilities}$$
$$\text{Capital} = \text{Total Assets} - \text{Outsiders' liabilities.}$$

6. Accounting Period Concept

Accounting is a continuous process in any business undertaking. Every businessman wants to know the result of his investment and efforts at frequent intervals. Accountants choose some shorter period to measure the result. Therefore, one year has been, generally, accepted as the accounting period. It may be 3 months, 6 months or 2 years also. This period is called accounting period. Financial period chosen, in this regard, should be neither too long nor too short. Closing day of the accounting period is known as accounting date. At this date, accountant prepares income and position statements, shows the business operations, brings the changes of positions since the construction of last statements. The financial reports prepared facilitate to make good decision, corrective measures, expansion etc. On the basis of income and position statement, financial position and earning capacity of one year can be compared with another. Their comparison helps the business for expansion. The outsiders too draw various conclusions. One year accounting period is recognised by law and the taxation is assessed annually. Reports to the outsiders are provided on this accounting period.

7. Matching Concept

According to this concept, it is necessary to match the expenses incurred during the accounting period with the revenues recognised during the same period. Since profit is an excess of revenue over expenses, it becomes necessary to bring together all revenues and expenses pertaining to a particular period. In other words, expenses incurred in an accounting year should be matched with the revenues recognised in that year. Again, only such expenses as incurred in generating revenues during the period should be deducted from those revenues for deriving the amount of income or profit during the period. The object of accounting is that accounting record be made in such a manner that cost may be compared with revenue. If the accounting method does not facilitate the comparison, then accounting method is considered unsatisfactory. Neither receipt of cash for revenue nor payment of cash for expenses is necessary. What is necessary is this that they must accrue in the current year so that the incurred expenses are matched against the realised revenue. American Institute of Certified Public Accountants' Committee on Accounting Procedure states that "it is plainly desirable to provide, by charging in the current income statement, properly classified, for all foreseeable costs and losses applicable against current revenues, to the extent that they can be measured and allocated to fiscal periods with reasonable approximation." All costs incurred during the period are taken. Similarly, expenses paid in advance are excluded from the total costs incurred to arrive at the expired costs. By application of this concept, proprietor can easily know about the profit/loss and he can make effort to increase earning capacity.

8. Realisation Concept

This concept revolves around the determination of the point of time when revenues are earned. A business firm invests money to purchase or manufacture goods for sale. To earn profit, sales have to be made. There can be no profit without realisation of sale proceeds. According to realisation concept, which is also known as the "revenue recognition concept", revenue is considered as being earned on the date on which it is realised, *i.e.*, the date on which goods and services are transferred to customers either for cash or for credit. "Credit transactions create debtors and the promise of debtors to make payment is sufficient for the purpose of realising revenue. The realisation concept is important in ascertaining the exact profit earned during a period in a business concern. This concept is very important as it prevents firms from inflating their profits by recording sales and incomes that are likely to accrue.

9. Objectivity Concept

This concept implies that all accounting transactions should be evidenced and supported by business documents, *i.e.*, invoices, vouchers etc. The evidence substantiating the business transactions should be objective, *i.e.*, free from the bias of the accountant or others. These supporting documents form the basis for record of entries and of audit. Accounting record based on documentary evidence is readily and objectively verifiable and therefore universally acceptable.

10. Accrual Concept

According to this concept the revenue is recognised on its realisation and not on its actual receipt. Similarly, the costs are recognised when they are incurred and not when payment is made. This assumption makes it necessary to give certain adjustments in the preparation of income statement regarding revenues and costs. But under cash accounting system, the revenues and costs are recognised only when they are actually received or paid. Hence, the combination of both cash and accrual system is preferable to get rid of the limitations of each system.

ACCOUNTING CONVENTIONS

Conventions in accounting have been evolved and developed to bring about uniformity in the maintenance of accounts. Conventions denote customs or traditions or usage which are in use since long. To be clear, these are nothing but unwritten laws. The accountants have to adopt the usage or customs, which are used as a guide in the preparation of accounting reports and statements. These conventions are also known as doctrine. Following are the important accounting conventions in use.

1. Convention of Disclosure

This convention requires that accounting statements should be honestly prepared and all significant information should be disclosed therein. That is, while making accountancy records, care should be taken to disclose all material information. Here the emphasis is only on material information and not on immaterial information. This convention assumes greater importance in respect of corporate organisations where the management is divorced from ownership. That is why forms of Balance Sheet and Profit and Loss accounts are prescribed in Schedule VI of the Companies Act, 1956; so that significant information may not be left out to be disclosed. The purpose of this convention is to communicate all material and relevant facts of financial position and the results of operations, which have material interests to proprietor, creditors and investors. Sometimes, there may be time gap between the preparation of Balance Sheet and its publication and if there are material events — bad debts, destruction of plant or machinery etc., which occurred in the time gap, may also be known to users — proprietors, creditors etc. In short, full disclosure of all relevant facts in accounts is a necessity in order to make accounting record useful. Therefore, full disclosure is a very healthy convention, and is important.

2. Convention of Consistency

Rules and practices of accounting should be continuously observed and applied. In order to enable the management to draw conclusions about the operation of a company over a number of years, it is essential that the practices and methods of accounting remain unchanged from one period to another. Comparisons are possible only if a consistent policy of accounting is followed. If there are frequent changes in the treatment of accounts there is little or no scope for reliability. Comparison of accounting period with that in the past is possible only when the convention of consistency is adhered to. According to Anthony, "the consistency requires that once a company had decided on one method, it will treat all subsequent events of the same character in the same fashion unless it has a sound reason to do otherwise." This convention plays its role particularly when alternative accounting practice is equally acceptable. Moreover, consistency serves to eliminate personal bias. But if a change becomes desirable, the change and its effect should be clearly stated in the financial statements. Accounts should lend themselves easily to comparisons and contrasts. This convention increases accuracy and comparability of accounting information for prediction or decision making. This convention does not prohibit changes. If there is any change, its effect should be clearly stated in the financial statments.

3. Convention of Conservatism

"Anticipate no profit and provide for all possible losses" is the essence of this convention. Future is uncertain. Fluctuations and uncertainties are not uncommon. Conservatism refers to the policy of choosing the procedure that leads to understatement as against overstatement of resources and income. The consequences of an error of understatement are likely to be less serious than that of an error of overstatement. For example, closing stock is valued at cost or market price whichever is lower. This is a convention of caution or playing safe and is adhered to while preparing financial statements. Showing a position better than what it is, is not permitted. Moreover, it is not proper to show a position substantialy worse than what it is. Following are the examples :

(*a*) The value of an asset should not be overestimated.

(*b*) The value of a liability should not be underestimated.

(*c*) The profit should not be overestimated.

(*d*) The loss should not be underestimated.

Such conservatism is generally accepted to present a true and fair value of business in the financial statements.

4. Convention of Materiality

American Accounting Association defines the term materiality as "An item should be regarded as material if there is reason to believe that knowledge of it would influence the decision of informed investor." It refers to the relative importance of an item or event. Materiality of an item depends on its amount and its nature. Theoretically, all items, large or small, should be treated alike. Materiality convention implies that the economic significance of an item will to some extent affect its accounting treatment. Materiality in its essence is of relative significance. In the sense that some of the unimportant items are either left out or included with other items. For instance, acquisition of items like fountain pen, stapler, pin cushion, punching machine etc., can be treated as part of assets, when considering their durability and span of life. But, it is not necesary to maintain separate ledgers. Such low cost items can be treated as expense for the period. Therefore, unimportant items are either left out or merged with other items. The reason for this different treatment lies in the magnitude of their amount. The dividing line between material and immaterial varies according to the company, the circumstances of the transactions and economic significance. It should also be noted that an item considered to be material for one business firm, may be immaterial for another firm. Similarly, an item of material in a year may not be material in the subsequent years. Similarly, most of the companies publish their financial statements in whole rupees—round figures, by ignoring paise. Omission of paise is immaterial, *i.e.*, insignificant when figures appear in lakhs. In short, all material information should be disclosed that is necessary to make the financial statements clear and understandable.

ACCOUNTING POLICIES

Financial statements, in every country, are prepared in accordance with the accounting principles (discussed above) generally followed in each country. Hence they are called by the name "Generally Accepted Accounting Principles", briefly called GAAP. In fact, to be useful, financial accounting information should be collected, classified, summarised and reported objectively. Accounting policies represent choices among different accounting methods that can be used in recording financial transactions and preparing financial statements. To quote International Accounting Standards Committee, "Accounting policies encompass many principles, bases, conventions, rules and procedures adopted by management in preparing and presenting financial statements. There are many different accounting policies in use even in relation to the same subject and judgement is required in selecting and applying those which are appropriate to the circumstances of the enterprises and are best suited to present properly its financial position and the results of its operation". GAAP plays a vital role and financial accounting information can be meaningful only when prepared according to some agreed upon standards and procedures, *i.e.*, Generally Accepted Accounting principles. Generally GAAP are primarily relevant to financial accounting. In management accounting, the main objective of using GAAP is to help management in making decisions and in operating effectively. Therefore, in the area of management accounting it is frequently useful to depart from accounting principles used in financial accounting. On many occasions, financial accounting data are reassambled or altered to be more useful in solving internal business problems and in making decisions.

FINANCIAL STATEMENTS

Financial statements provide useful information to the users. To be useful, financial statements must possess the following qualities:

(a) Reliability: Information provided through financial statement should be reliable. It should contain correct fact and figures for all financial transactions. If there is fraud or misrepresentation, the statements will not be reliable.

(b) Understandability: Financial statement should provide such information which can be understood easily by the users. However, when a business is governed by some statute, such as companies, information required by laws is to be included in the statement.

(c) Relevance: Information provided by the financial statement should be relevant. Relevance depends on the nature and materiality. Any material fact or figure should not be omitted or diluted. Then this may misguide the decision makers.

(d) Comparability: The information provided by financial statements is compared by the management for decision making. Therefore, uniform accounting methods and policies should be following from year to year, for this purpose accounting bodies frame accounting standards, so that all business enterprises follow common methods and policies of accounting.

ACCOUNTING PRINCIPLES

Accounting principles, to secure general acceptance, must have three attributes, namely, relevance, objectivity and feasibility. A principle is said to have relevance if it results in more meaningful and useful information about the enterprise to the users. It is said to be objective when the information furnished is not influenced by the bias or personal judgement of those furnishing the same. It is objective when it is solidly supported by facts. A principle is said to be feasible when the adoption does not create problems of collecting information or increase the cost.

According to the terminology of American Institute of Certified Public Accountants (AICPA), the nature of the generally accepted accounting principles is in the following statements:

"Accountants are generally agreed that accounting principles cannot be derived from or proven by the laws of nature. They are rather in the category of conventions or rules developed by man from experience to fulfil the essential and useful needs and purposes in establishing relaiable financial and operating information control for business activities. In this respect, they are similar to principles of commercial laws and other social disciplines.

AICPA, further states the following as to the meaning of Accounting Principles:

"It is desirable that the accountant conceives of his work as a complex problem to be solved and of his statements as creative works of art, and that he reserves to himself the freedom to do his work with the cannons of art constantly in mind and as his skill, knowledge and experience best enables him. Every art must work according to a body of applicable rules, but is also must reserve the right to depart from the rules, whenever it can thereby achieve a better result."

For correct understanding of the accounting principles, it is necessary to know the several concepts and conventions, discussed above.

ACCOUNTING STANDARDS

The term "Accounting Standard" is defined as written statements issued from time to time by institutions of the accounting professsion or institutions in which there is involvement and which are established expressly for this purpose. Such accounting institutions or bodies are currently found in many countries of the world, for example, Accounting Standards Board (India), Financial Accounting Standards Board (US), Accounting Standards Committee (UK), Accounting Standards Committee (Canada) etc. At the international level, International Accounting Standards Committee (IASC) has been created "to formulate and publish, in the public interest, basic standards to be observed in the presentation of audited accounts and financial statements and to promote their worldwide acceptance and observance".

ACCOUNTING EQUATION

There is an accounting equation based on 'Duality Concept' which explains that at any point of time the assets of any business enterprise are equal in monetary terms to its equities, both internal and external. Internal equities are the amount contributed by proprietor as capital and amount of profit retained in the business. External equities are liabilities (amount payable to outsiders). Internal equities will be termed as 'Equity' and external equities as 'Liabilities'. Thus:

ASSETS = EQUITY + LIABILITIES

Equity plus Liabilities represent source of funds and Assets represent applications of fund. Assets may consist of fixed assets, *i.e.*, assets which are put to long term use in the business such as building, machinery etc. and current assets, which remain constantly changing and remain in flow such as Cash, Bank, Stock, Debtors etc.

Liabilities may consist of short-term liabilities and long-term liabilities. When amount is payable within a period of 12 months, these are known as short-term liabilities. These are also termed as 'Current Liabilities', such as creditors for goods or expenses. When amount is payable beyond a period of 12 months, these are known as 'Long Term Liabilities for example, Bank Loans.

EQUITY = ASSETS – LIABILITIES

EQUITY = (FIXED ASSETS + CURRENT ASSETS)

– (LONG TERM LIABILITIES + CURRENT LIABILITIES)

ACCOUNTING METHODS

There are mainly two recognised methods of accounting :

1. Cash Method of Accounting (Cash Basis of Accounting)

Under this method, all incomes are considered to be earned only when they are actually received in cash. Similarly, expenses are deemed to be incurred only when they are actually paid in cash. In other words, importance is attached to cash receipts and payments but non-cash items, such as Outstandings, pre-paid Expenses, Accrued Incomes or income received in advance are ignored. This method is adopted in those concerns where only cash transactions take place. Generally this system is followed by individuals like Doctors, Lawyers, Auditors, Engineers, Brokers, Small Traders etc.

The advantage of this system of accounting is that it is very simple because it requres no adjustments at the close date. But, the disadvantage is that cash basis of accounting fails to reveal profit or loss accurately in the absence of adjustments at the end of accounting period.

2. Accrual Basis of Accounting (Mercantile Basis of Accounting)

This method is commonly adopted by business concerns. Incomes are recorded or credited to the period in which they are earned irrespective of the fact that whether the same has actually been received or not. Similarly, expenses are charged to the period in which they relate irrespective of the fact that they have actually been paid or not. In other words, all items of incomes and expenditures, both cash items as well as non-cash items such as pre-paid expenses, accrued incomes or income received in advance etc. are taken into account.

This system of accounting reveals profit or loss accurately because of taking adjustments into account. The Final Accounts exhibit a true and fair view of the state of affairs.

HYBRID OR MIXED BASIS OF ACCOUNTING

This system can be considered as a third method. Cash basis of accounting is a simple system whereas the accrual basis of accounting is scientific and reliable. So, accountants have tried to club these advantages of the two systems and have come up mixed or hybrid basis of accounting. Under this method, both cash basis and accrual basis are followed. Incomes are recorded on cash basis whereas expenses are taken on accrual basis. The net income is ascertained by matching expenses on accrual basis with income on cash basis. This is the most conservative basis of ascertaining income because all possible expenses relating to the period whether actually paid or not are considered whereas income only received in cash is taken into consideration. This system is followed by professionals like Doctors, Lawyers, CAs., but not widely used.

SYSTEMS OF ACCOUNTING

There are two systems of Book-keeping—the Single Entry System and the Double Entry System.

1. Single Entry System

The single entry system is not really a system because in some cases record may be one-sided; and in some other cases no record is maintained at all. It is more appropriate to call it an incomplete system of recording transactions. Double effect of every transaction is ignored and only the accounts relating to suppliers and customers and cash account are found. Thus, the system is incomplete, inaccurate and unscientific system of recording business transactions. (The same topic is discussed in deatil under Chapter No. 12).

2. Double Entry System

The modern system of accounting is based on what is known as double entry principle. It refers to that system of book-keeping where each transaction is recorded in both of its aspects, *viz*., (1) receiving of the benefit of the transaction and (2) giving away of the benefit of the transaction. For a complete record of transaction, it should be presented in both the accounts. Business transaction affects two aspects of the account in the opposite direction. If one account receives a benefit there must be another account to give the benefit. It is like the two sides of a coin. Thus, every transaction involves two accounts (1) one which gives the benefit of the transaction and (2) another which receives the same. Normally, the receiver account is debited and the giver account is credited. The system under which both the debit and credit (receiving and giving) aspects are recorded is known as the principle of Double Entry System of book-keeping. Therefore, we can say that every debit must have a corresponding credit and vice versa. It follows that any number of transactions can be recorded in the above manner; the total debit must be equal to total credits and this helps drawing of a trial balance to prove the arithmetical accuracy of the account books.

Answers to the following Questions will bring out the *Importance and Objects of Accounting*

1. What amount of Profit or Loss is made during the year ?
2. What have we earned in the past years ?
3. Is our business improving ?
4. Are the number of customers increasing ?
5. What do we owe to others through business ?
6. What do our customers owe us ?
7. Are the customers prompt in payment ?
8. What is the position of the business ?
9. How much cash do we have ?
10. Is it enough for taking vital decisions ?

Advantages of Double Entry System

The following are the advantages of accounting if double entry system is adopted :

1. It presents a complete record of transactions. Because it records both the aspects of every transaction, which relates to personal or impersonal.

2. Profit and loss account can easily be prepared. The exact reason for profit or loss can be ascertained. The information enables the firm to take action to increase the profit and reduce the losses (or expenses).

3. It gives exact information regarding the amount due to and due by the firm at any time, because the system gives ready reference.

4. Arithmetical accuracy can be tested by preparing a list of balances (Trial Balance) from all ledgers concerned.

5. It provides full particulars of various assets and liabilities of the business, so final financial position can be known by preparing Balance Sheet. A comparative study of the Balance Sheet for various years shows a firm's progress.

6. It reveals the position relating to customers who fail to pay in time, otherwise loss is suffered through bad debts.

7. It provides facility for comparison of sales, purchases, expenditure, income etc. of the present year with those of previous years. Thus the system facilitates to maximise the profit and to reduce the loss.

8. It prevents frauds and errors and makes their detection easier.

9. It has readymade information to be sent to Sales Tax and Income Tax authorities.

10. A proper system of accounts will enable us to have good guidance. This guidance helps us to take new decisions, which will increase our profit and convert losses into profit.

ROLE OF ACCOUNTANTS IN SOCIETY

There are only a few professions in the world which are held in high esteem in the society, accountant's profession is one of them. His primary function is to prepare the financial statements, interpret and analyse such statements and audit at the end. The modern accountant is not like the old book-keeper. At present, he is expected to perform multifarious duties and play a wider role than he was supposed to play earlier. His area of operation, at present, covers the matters relating to productivity, taxation laws, general problems of the management etc. Thus accountant acts as friend, philosopher and guide to the management and helps the management in decision-making.

There is usually an unlimited supply of data available in an enterprise and the accountant has to select for the presentation to the management only useful information. He should develop a system by which there is regular flow of information in detail. He should develop the required communication skills because information supplied by him is taken for granted by the management for decision-making. The information system should be such that comparability of financial statements as between both business and individual years is possible so that it may benefit both management and investors.

A qualified accountant will be able to play an important role in performing important functions of a business relating to accountancy, costing, budgetary control etc. He is, in fact, the person responsible for informing quickly and adequately the facts of a business operations to the management demonstrating in financial terms the plans and measuring achievements, providing essential data to the management for determining industrial policies and enabling the managements to make financial and trading forecasts.

Accountants should largely corcern with bringing about a change in management practices and attitudes by showing the area where excessive expenditures incurred, where saving could be possible and thus costs reduced. It is only the accountants who are able to provide control figures for the management to reduce the loss of production to minimum.

Productivity is related to profitability. Increased productivity will result in higher profits. The accountants stimulate the attention of the management to the problems of increasing productivity by means of labour and machine utilisation reports, production reports and intelligent analysis of various variances under standard costing.

Accountants have social obligation to express their views on broad tax policy, on effect of rates on business and economy in general and on all other aspects of taxation. They should point out limitations of tax structure and tax laws as a result of which there may be loss of revenue.

The systems of financial and budgetary control and of accounting, auditing and reporting has, therefore, become a matter of interest and concern to the nation. It is the duty of accountants that they prepare the accounts and reports of these corporations in such a way that they enable the general public to know how far these corporations justify their existence.

STAGES OF DOUBLE ENTRY SYSTEM OF ACCOUNTING

1. **First Stage** : When a transaction takes place, it is recorded in a Primary Book, Called Journal.
2. **Second Stage** : All entries in the Journal or Books of Original Entry should be posted to the appropriate ledger accounts to find out at a glance the total effect of all such transactions in a particular account.
3. **Third Stage** : Balance of each account in ledger is found out and is transferred to a statement, called "Trial Balance".
4. **Fourth Stage** : Final accounts are prepared from Trial Balance, that is, Trading Account, Profit and Loss Account and Balance Sheet.
5. **Fifth Stage** : After the preparation of final accounts, analysis and interpretation of these accounts are made in order to have true and fair idea about earning capacity and financial position of the concern.

SOME ACCOUNTING TERMINOLOGY

Some of the technical terms used in double entry system of book-keeping are as follows :

Transaction

A business transaction involves exchange of value or benefit between two persons. An exchange means giving and receiving of equal value. Any dealing of a business that involves buying and selling in value is called business transaction. Thus every transaction has two aspects—giving and receiving. The types of transaction are :

(*a*) Cash Transaction and (*b*) Credit Transactions.

(*a*) **Cash Transaction.** Cash transaction involves immediate payment or receipt of cash. A transaction in which there is an immediate payment or receipt of money, is called cash transaction.

(*b*) **Credit Transaction.** Credit transaction is different from cash transaction, because there is .o immediate receipt or payment. They do not involve receipt or payment of money. In credit transaction the payment or receipt is postponed to a future date. When we sell goods on credit to a person, we debit the personal account of that person and cash account is not debited. Why ? Because we have not received the cash—credit transaction. The parties to whom we sell goods on credit become our debtors, because their account is debited.

Characteristics of a transaction

(1) It is concerned with money or money's worth of goods or services.

(2) It arises out of the transfer of exchange of goods or services.

(3) It has dual aspects or sides — *Receiving* and *Giving* of the benefit.

(4) Every transaction must be vouched by supporting documents.

(5) It brings about a change in the financial position (assets and liabilities) of a business firm.

Goods

Commodities bought for the purpose of resale are termed as goods. That is, the things (or service) which a businessman sells are called goods. Thus a cloth merchant deals in cloth, a rice merchant deals in rice; cloth and rice are goods.

Account

An account is a summary of business transactions affecting a person or property or an income or an expense. An account is a brief history of financial dealings of a particular man or in a particular item. An account has two sides — debit and credit. The left side is known as DEBIT and the right side is known as CREDIT. Double entry book-keeping means recording of both the receiving and giving aspects of every transaction. When an account receives a benefit, the account is debited. When an account gives a benefit, the account is credited. These two aspects are denoted by the symbols Debtor (Dr.) and Creditor (Cr.) respectively. The rules for Debit and Credit are formulated according to the types of accounts. The accounts can be divided into three — Personal, Real and Nominal. (For more details, see Chapter 2.)

Journal

Journal is the prime book or books of original entry. Because all transactions are first recorded in the journal. All transactions are entered in the order of their happening *i.e.*, date-wise (chronological order). Journalising is an act of recording the debit and credit aspect of a business transaction in journal. Narration is nothing but a brief explanation which is added after each journal entry.

Entry. Entry is a record of a transaction in account books.

Drawings. Drawings are the withdrawals of money (cash) or money's worth (goods) by the proprietor from the business for his personal use.

Debit. It denotes receiving aspect.

Credit. It denotes giving aspect.

Debtor. A Debtor is one who receives the benefit and he owes money to the business.

Creditor. A Creditor is one who gives the benefit, and to whom the business owes money.

Cash Discount. Cash Discount is an allowance against the amount due.

Trade Discount. Trade Discount is an allowance against the Invoice (Bill) price.

Contra. It is a Latin term which means opposite or on the other side.

Solvent. A solvent is one whose assets are in excess of his liabilities.

Insolvent. If a trader's liabilities are far in excess of his assets, he is said to be an insolvent.

Compound Journal Entry

If two or more transactions of the same nature occur on the same day either debit account and/or credit account are common in them, then instead of passing separate entry for each such transaction, one combined entry may be passed and such type of entry is known as compound journal entry.

Capital

The amount with which the trader starts his business or the amount which is actually invested in the business at any given time is known as capital.

Fixed Assets

Fixed assets are those assets which are acquired only for use and not for resale, for instance, plant, machinery, land, building etc. of a soap manufacturer.

Current Assets

It is also known as floating assets. Current assets are those that are meant to be converted into cash as soon as possible, for instance, stock of goods, book debts, etc.

Liability

Capital of the proprietor and the debts which are due by the firm to other parties are collectively known as liabilities.

Ledger

The ledger is the main, important and the final book of entry. A ledger account may be defined as a summary statement of all the transactions relating to a person, asset, expense or income which have taken place during a given period of time and shows their net effect. It contains all the account of the business in a well arranged form.

Tangible Assets: Assets which have physical existence, that is, they can be seen or felt or touched. are termed as tangible assets. For example, plant, machinery, cash, land etc.

Intangible Assets: Assets which have no physical existence, that is, they cannot be seen or felt or touched, are termed as intangible assets. For example, patent rights, goodwill, copy-right etc.

Fictitious Assets: Items shown alongwith other assets on the assets side of a Balance Sheet, but actually representing unadjusted losses are termed as fictitious assets. For example, Preliminary expense, debit balance of Profit and Loss Account etc.

Wasting Assets: Those assets which certainly lose value with usage, are termed as wasting assets. For example, Mines, becomes waste once the mineral is fully extracted etc.

Purchases: Buying of goods with the intention of resale is called purchases. Purchases may be cash purchase or credit purchase..

Sales: Selling of goods in the normal course of business is termed as sales. It may be cash sales or credit sales.

Stock: It refers to goods lying unsold on a particular date. It may be closing stock (at the end of accounting period) or opening stock (in the beginning of accounting period).

Invoice: It is a statement prepared by a seller of goods to be sent to the buyer. It shows details of the goods.

Voucher: It is a written record and evidence of a transaction, that is, documentary evidence. For example, cash receipts, counterfoils etc.

Current Liability: Those liabilities which are payable within a year, are termed as current liabilities. For example, trade creditors, Bills Payable etc.

Insolvent: A person whose liabilities are more than the realisable value of his assets, is called an insolvent.

INDIAN ACCOUNTING STANDARDS

PREFACE TO THE STATEMENTS OF ACCOUNTING STANDARDS

1. Formation of the Accounting Standards Board

The Institute of Chartered Accountants of India, recognising the need to harmonise the diverse accounting policies and practices at present in use in India, constituted an Accounting Standards Board (ASB) on 21st April, 1977.

2. Scope and Functions of Accounting Standards Board

2.1 The main function of ASB is to formulate accounting standards so that such standards may be established by the Council of the Institute in India. While formulating the accounting standards, ASB will take into consideration the applicable laws, customs, usages and business environment.

2.2 The Institute is one of the Members of the International Accounting Standards Committee (IASC) and has agreed to support the objectives of IASC. While formulating the Accounting Standards, ASB will give due consideration to International Accounting Standards, issued by IASC and try to integrate them, to the extent possible, in the light of the conditions and practices prevailing in India.

2.3 The Accounting Standards will be issued under the authority of the Council. ASB has also been entrusted with the responsibility of propagating the Accounting Standards and of persuading the concerned parties to adopt them in the preparation and presentation of financial statements. ASB will issue guidance notes on the Accounting Standards and give clarifications on issues arising therefrom. ASB will also review the Accounting Standard at periodical intervals.

3. Audited Financial Statements

3.1 For discharging the above functions, ASB will keep in view the purposes and limitations of published financial statements and the attest function of the auditors. ASB will enumerate and describe the basic concept to which accounting principles should be oriented and state the accounting principles to which the practices and procedures should conform.

3.2 ASB will clarify the phrases commonly used in such financial statements and suggest improvements in the terminology wherever necessary. ASB will examine the various current alternative practices in vogue and identify such alternatives which should be preferred.

3.3 The Institute will issue the Accounting Standards for use in the presentation of the general purpose financial statements issued to the public by such commercial, industrial or business enterprises as may be specified by the Institute from time to time and subject to the attest function of its members. The term "General Purpose Financial Statements" includes balance sheet, statement of profit and loss and other statements and explanatory notes which form part thereof, issued for the use of shareholders/ members, creditors, employees and public at large. References to financial statements in this Preface and in the standards issued from time to time will be constituted to refer to General Purpose Financial Statements.

3.4 Responsibility for the preparation of financial statements and for adequate disclosure is that of the management of the enterprise. The Auditor's responsibility is to form his opinion and report on such financial statements.

4. Scope of Accounting Standards

4.1 Efforts will be made to issue Accounting Standards which are in conformity with the provisions of the applicable laws, customs, usages and business environment of our country. However, if due to subsequent amendments in the law, a particular Accounting Standard is found to be not in conformity with such law, the provisions of the said law will prevail and the financial statements should be prepared in conformity with such law.

4.2 The Accounting Standards by their very nature cannot and do not override the local regulations which govern the preparation and presentation of financial statements in our country. However, the Institute will determine the extent of disclosure to be made in financial statements and the related Auditor's reports. Such disclosure may be by way of appropriate notes explaining the treatment of particular items. Such explanatory notes will be only in the nature of clarification and therefore, need not be treated as adverse comments on the related financial statements.

4.3 The Accounting Standards are intended to apply only to items which are material. Any limitations with regard to the applicability of a specific Standard will be made clear by the Institute from time to time. The date from which a particular Standard will come into effect, as well as the class of enterprises to which it will apply, will also be specified by the Institute. However, no standard will have retroactive application, unless otherwise stated.

4.4 The Institute will use its best endeavours to persuade the Government, appropriate authorities, industrial and business community to adopt these standards in order to achieve uniformity in the presentation of financial statements.

4.5 In carrying out the task of formulation of Accounting Standards, the intention is to concentrate on basic matters. The endeavour would be to confine Accounting Standards to essentials and not to make them so complex that they cannot be applied effectively and on a nation-wide basis. In the years to come, it is to be expected that Accounting Standards will undergo revision and a greater degree of sophistication may then be appropriate.

5. Procedure for Issuing Accounting Standards

Broadly, the following procedure will be adopted for formulating Accounting Standards:

5.1 ASB shall determine the broad areas in which Accounting Standards need to be formulated and priority in regard to the selection thereof.

5.2 In the preparation of Accounting Standards, ASB will be assisted by Study Groups constituted to consider specific subjects. In the formation of Study Groups, provision will be made for wide participation by the members of the institute and others.

5.3 ASB will also hold a dialogue with the representatives of the Government, Public Sector Undertakings. Industry and other Organisations for ascertaining their views.

5.4 On the basis of the work of the Study Groups and the dialogue with the organisations referred to in 5.3 above, an exposure draft of the proposed standard will be prepared and issued for comments by members of the Institute and the public at large.

5.5 The draft of the proposed standard will include the following basic points:

5.5.1 A Statement of concepts and fundamental accounting principles relating to the Standard.

5.5.2 Definitions of the terms used in the Standard.

5.5.3 The manner in which the accounting principles have been applied for.

5.5.4 The presentation and disclosure requirements in complying with the Standard.

5.5.5 Class of enterprises to which the Standard will apply.

5.5.6 Date from which the Standard will be effective.

5.6 After taking into consideration the comments received, the draft of the proposed Standard will be finalised by ASB and submitted to the Council of the Institute.

5.7 The Council of the Institute will consider the final draft of the proposed Standard, and if found necessary, modify the same in consuitation with ASB. The Accounting Standard on the relevent subject will then be issued under the authority of the Council.

6. Compliance with the Accounting Standards

6.1 While discharging their attest functions, it will be duty of the members of the Institute to ensure that the Accounting Standards are implemented in the presentation of financial statements covered by their audit reports. In the event of any deviation from the Standards, it will also be their duty to make adequate disclosures in their reports so that the users of such statements may be aware of such deviations.

6.2 In the initial years, the Standards will be recommendatory in character and the Institute will give wide publicity among the users and educate members about the utility of Accounting Standards and the need for compliance with the above disclosure requirements. Once an awareness about these requirements is ensured, steps will be taken, in course of time, to enforce compliance with the accounting standards in the manner outlined in para 6.1 above.

6.3 The adoption of Accounting Standards in our country and disclosure of the extent to which they have not been observed will, over the years, have an important effect, with consequential improvement in the quality of presentation of financial statements.

AS 1

DISCLOSURE OF ACCOUNTING POLICIES*

The following is the text of the Accounting Standard l (AS-1) issued by the Accounting Standards Board, the Institute of Chartered Accountants of India on "Disclosure of Accounting Policies". The Standard deals with the disclosure of significant accounting policies followed in preparing and presenting financial statements.

In the initial years, this accounting standard will be recommendatory in character. During this period, this standard is recommended for use by companies listed on a recognised stock exchange and other large commercial, industrial and business enterprises in the public and private sectors.

Introduction

1. This statement deals with the disclosure of significant accounting policies followed in preparing and presenting financial statements.

2. The view presented in the financial statements of an enterprise of its state of affairs and of the profit or loss can be significantly affected by the accounting policies followed in the preparation and presentation of the financial statements. The accounting policies followed vary from enterprise to enterprise. Disclosure of significant accounting policies followed is necessary if the view presented is to be properly appreciated.

3. The disclosure of some of the accounting policies followed in the preparation and presentation of the financial statements is required by law in some cases.

4. The Institute of Chartered Accountants of India has, in Statements issued by it, recommended the disclosure of certain accounting policies, e.g., translation policies in respect of foreign currency items.

5. In recent years, a few enterprises in India have adopted the practice of including in their annual reports to shareholders a separate statement of accounting policies followed in preparing and presenting the financial statements.

6. In general, however, accounting policies are not at present regularly and fully disclosed in all financial statements. Many enterprises include in the Notes on the Accounts, descriptions of some of the significant accounting policies. But the nature and degree of disclosure vary considerably between the corporate and the non-corporate sectors and between units in the same sector.

7. Even among the, few enterprises that presently include in their annual reports a separate statement of accounting policies, considerable variation exists. The statement of accounting policies forms part of accounts in some cases while in others it is given as supplementary information.

8. The purpose of this statement is to promote better understanding of financial statements by establishing through an accounting standard the disclosure of significant accounting policies and the manner in which accounting policies are disclosed in the financial statements. Such disclosure would also facilitate a more meaningful comparison between financial statements of different enterprises.

Explanation

Fundamental Accounting Assumptions

9. Certain fundamental accounting assumptions underlie the preparation and presentation of financial statements. They are usually not specifically stated because their acceptance and use are assumed. Disclosure is necessary if they are not followed.

10. The following have been generally accepted as fundamental accounting assumptions:

a. *Going Concern*

The enterprise is normally viewed as a going concern, that is, as continuing in operation for the foreseeable future. It is assumed that the enterprise has neither the intention nor the necessity of liquidation or of curtailing materially the scale of the operations.

b. *Consistency*

It is assumed that accounting policies are consistent from one period to another.

c. *Accrual*

Revenues and costs are accrued, that is, recognised as they are earned or incurred (and not as money is received or paid) and recorded in the financial statements of the periods to which they relate. (The considerations affecting the process of matching costs with revenues under the accrual assumption are not dealt within this statement.)

Nature of Accounting Policies

11. The accounting policies refer to the specific accounting principles and the methods of applying those principles adopted by the enterprise in the preparation and presentation of financial statements.

12. There is no single list of accounting policies which are applicable to all circumstances. The differing circumstances in which enterprises operate in a situation of diverse and complex economic activity make alternative accounting principles and methods of applying those principles acceptable. The choice of the appropriate accounting principles and the methods of applying those principles in the specific circumstances of each enterprise calls for considerable judgement by the management of the enterprise.

13. The various statements of the Institute of Chartered Accountants of India combined with the efforts of government and other regulatory agencies and progressive managements have reduced in recent years the number of acceptable alternatives particularly in the case of corporate enterprises. While continuing efforts in this regard in future are likely to reduce the number still further, the availability of alternative accounting principles and methods of applying those principles is not likely to be eliminated altogether in view of the different circumstances faced by the enterprises.

Areas in which Differing Accounting Policies are Encountered

14. The following are examples of the areas in which different accounting policies may be adopted by different enterprises:

- Methods of depreciation, depletion and amortisation
- Treatment of expenditure during construction
- Conversion or translation of foreign currency items
- Valuation of inventories
- Treatment of goodwill
- Valuation of Investments
- Treatment of retirement benefits
- Recognition of profit on long-term contracts
- Valuation of fixed assets
- Treatment of contingent liabilities

15. The above list of examples is not intended to be exhaustive.

Consideration in the Selection of Accounting Policies

16. The primary consideration in the selection of Accounting Policies by an enterprise is that the financial statements prepared and presented on the basis of such accounting policies should represent

a true and fair view of the state of affairs of the enterprise as at the Balance Sheet date and of the profit or loss for the period ended on that date.

17. For this purpose, the major considerations governing the selection and application of accounting policies are:

a. **Prudence**

In view of the uncertainty attached to future events, profits are not anticipated but recognised only when realised though not necessarily in cash. Provision is made for all known liabilities and losses even though the amount cannot be determined with certainty and represents only a best estimate in the light of available information.

b. **Substance over Form**

The accounting treatment and presentation in financial statements of transactions and events should be governed by their substance and not merely by the legal form.

c. **Materiality**

Financial statements should disclose all "material" items, *i.e.*, items the knowledge of which might influence the decisions of the user of the financial statements.

Disclosure of Accounting *Policies*

18. To ensure proper understanding of financial statements, it is necessary that all significant accounting policies adopted in the preparation and presentation of financial statements should be disclosed.

19. Such disclosure should form part of the financial statements.

20. It would be helpful to the reader of financial statements if they are all disclosed as such in one place instead of being scattered over several statements, schedules and notes.

21. Examples of matters in respect of which disclosure of accounting policies adopted will be required are contained in paragraph 14. This list of examples is not, however, intended to be exhaustive.

22. Any change in an accounting policy which has a material effect should be disclosed. The amount by which any item in the financial statements is affected by such change should also be disclosed to the extent ascertainable. Where such amount is not ascertainable, wholly or in part, the fact should be indicated. If a change is made in the accounting policies which has no material effect on the financial statements for the current period but which is reasonably expected to have a material effect in later periods, the fact of such change should be appropriately disclosed in the period in which the change is adopted.

23. Disclosure of accounting policies or of changes therein cannot remedy a wrong or inappropriate treatment of the item in the accounts.

Accounting Standard

Disclosure of Accounting Policies

(The Accounting Standard comprises paragraphs 24-27 of this statement. The standard should be read in the context of paragraphs 1-23 of this statement and of the Preface to the Statements of Accounting Standards.)

24. All significant accounting policies adopted in the preparation and presentation of financial statements should be disclosed.

25. The disclosure of the significant accounting policies as such should form part of the financial statements and the significant accounting policies should normally be disclosed in one place.

26. Any change in the accounting policies which has a material effect in the current period or which is reasonably expected to have a material effect in later periods should be disclosed. In the case of a change in accounting policies which has a material effect in the current period, the amount by

which any item in the financial statements is affected by such change should also be disclosed to the extent ascertainable. Where such amount is not ascertainable, wholly or in part, the fact should be indicated.

27. If the fundamental accounting assumptions, *viz.*, Going Concern Consistency and Accrual are followed in financial statements specific disclosure is not required. If a fundamental accounting assumption is not followed, the fact should be disclosed.

OBJECTIVE TYPE QUESTIONS

I. State whether each of the following statement is "True" or "False".

1. Accounting is as old as money itself.
2. Accounting is the language of the business.
3. Book-keeping and Accounting are synonymous terms.
4. Accounts may be grouped into personal accounts and impersonal accounts.
5. Income is a source of capital.
6. In accoutancy, all business transactions are recorded as having dual aspect.
7. It is on the basis of going concern concept that the assets are always valued at maıket value.
8. Accounting is for the use of owners of business alone.
9. Accounting is concerned with finalising and interpreting accounting data.
10. Accounting records are not accepted as authentic evidence in courts.

(*Ans.* 1. True; 2. True; 3. False; 4. True; 5. True; 6. True; 7. False; 8. False; 9. True; 10. False.)

II. Fill in the blanks.

1. Accounting is the .... of business.
2. In every transaction, atleast .... parties are involved.
3. All those to whom business owes money are ....
4. An obligation of business is ....
5. Withdrawal of money by the owner is not an expense but a reduction of ....
6. The business entity concept implies that a business unit is .... from the persons who supply captial to it.
7. According to the .... concept, it is possible to remove the cost of fixed assets from the accounts altogether by charging depreciation.
8. Changing the accounting policy to show a rosy picture of the state of affairs is called ....
9. The primary objective of a business concern is the production of .... and ....
10. Users of accounting information may be grouped into two classes, *viz.*, ... and ....

(*Ans.* 1. Language; 2. Two; 3. Creditors; 4. Liability; 5. Capital; 6. Separate; 7. Cost; 8. Window-dressing; 9. Goods and Services; 10. External and Internal.

III. Multiple Choice

Choose the correct alternative for each of the following :

1. Revenue is considered as being earned when
   (a) Cash is received. (b) Sales effected.
   (c) Production is done.
2. Which is correct ?
   (a) Capital = Assets + Liabilities (b) Liabilities = Capital – Assets
   (c) Capital – Assets = Liabilities
3. According to Entity Concept, the proprietor is treated as :
   (a) Owner of the business. (b) Creditor for the business to the extent of capital.
   (c) Manager of the business.

4. Business is distinct from the owner. This concept is called
   (a) Business Entity (b) Going concern
   (c) Cost (d) Money Measurement
5. Accounting does not record non-financial transactions because of:
   (a) Entity Concept (b) Accrual Concept
   (c) Money Measurement Concept
6. Find out the correct accounting equation from the following
   (a) Capital = Assets + Liabilities (b) Capital = Assets – Liabilities
   (c) Liabilities = Assets + Capital (d) Liabilities = Cash + Capital
7. According to which concept the owner who provides capital is treated as a creditor of the business :
   (a) Cost Concept (b) Entity Concept
   (c) Realisation concept (d) Money Measurement Concept
8. The Accounting Equation is connected with
   (a) Assets only (b) Liability only
   (c) Asses and Liabilities (d) None of the above
9. The principle of not taking anticipated profit and providing for all estimated losses arising due to:
   (a) Convention of consistency (b) Convention of Disclosure
   (c) Convention of Conservatism (d) None of the above
10. Dual aspect oncept results in the accounting equation :
   (a) Capital + Liabilities = Assets (b) Capital = Assets
   (c) Revenue = Expenses (d) Capital + Profit = Assets + Expenses.
11. Revenue is recognised:
   (a) At the point of sale (b) When the money is received
   (c) At the point, goods are delivered by the seller
12. Historical cost concept requires the recording of an asset:
   (a) At its cost (b) At its market value
   (c) at its net realisable value.

(Answers : 1. (c); 2. (c); 3. (b); 4. (a); 5. (c); 6. (b)
7. (b); 8. (c); 9. (c); 10. (a); 11. (a); 12. (a)

THEORETICAL QUESTIONS

1. Define Book-keeping and Accounting.
2. Describe the advantages of Book-keeping and Accountancy. *(B. Com. MS)*
3. What are accounting conventions ? Explain briefly. *(B. Com. Agra)*
4. What are accounting concepts ? Explain briefly. *(B. Com. Madurai)*
5. What groups of people would be interested in accounting reports and why ? *(B.Com. Kerala*
6. "Every debit has got a credit and vice versa." Explain the significance of this statement. *(B. Com. Kerala)*
7. Explain briefly the true significance of the term "Double Entry" and enumerate the advantages attaching to the system.
8. What do you mean by business transaction ?
9. What is an Account ?
10. Distinguish between Cash System and Mercantile System of Accounting. *(B. Com. Punjab)*
11. How does "book-keeping" differ from "accounting"? *(B. Com. Chennai)*
12. Who are the parties or groups interested in accounting information ? *(B. Com. MS)*
13. Write a note on "Hybrid System of accounting". *(B. Com. Kerala)*

14. "Accounting begins where book-keeping ends". Discuss. *(B. Com. Madurai)*
15. Discuss the limitations of Financial Accounting ? *(B. Com. Kerala)*
16. Accounting is said to be the language of business. What does it try to communicate and how ? *(B.Com. Agra)*
17. In what way Accounting Standards are helpful to Accountants, Auditors and Managers.
18. What are Accounting Standards ? Explain their significance. *(B.Com. Madurai)*
19. Explain the "role of Accountants in the Society". *(M.Com. Bhopal)*
20. What is Accounting Equation ? *(M.Com. Madurai)*

Chapter 2

Recording of Financial Data

Memorandum Book – Business Transactions – Journal – Rules for Debit and Credit – Compound Journal Entry – Advantages of Journal – Ledger – Ledger Account – Ledger Posting – Process of Posting – Balancing of an Account – Significance of Balance – Relation between Journal and Ledger – Advantages of Subsidiary Records– Purchase Book – Sales Book – Purchase Return Book – Sales Return Book – Posting Rules – Debit Note – Credit Note – Journal Proper – Cash Book – Questions – Objective Type Questions – Theoretical Questions – Practical Problems.

Various types of books are used by businessmen for accounting record. Businessman usually maintains the following books :

MEMORANDUM BOOK

Memorandum book, also called Waste Book or Rough Book, is kept by a businessman for noting down the transactions as they take place from time to time, during the course of the day. The recording is only for the sake of memory. So, when any transaction takes place, businessman immediately notes it down in the book so that the transaction may not be forgotten. Maintenance of this book is not necessary. It helps in making records in the journal and ledger.

BUSINESS TRANSACTIONS

Business activities in a business are known as 'events'. A transaction is a business event involving ransfer of money or money's worth. As soon as a business event occurs which can be measured and expressed in terms of money and must be recorded in the books of accounts, it is called a 'transaction'. In a business transaction, there must be some monetary change between the parties. In other words, the meaning of a transaction is to 'receive' and 'give', that is, one party receives and the other party gives. For instance, if X gives Rs. 10 to Y, Y is receiving Rs. 10 whereas X is giving the same and there is a monetary change between the parties. There are two types of business transactions, *viz.*, Cash Transactions and Credit Transactions. Cash transactions involve transfer of money, that is, money flow from one account to another. Credit transactions, on the other hand, do not involve any transfer of money, but only money's worth.

JOURNAL

Journal is a book of 'primary entry' or 'original entry'. Journal records all daily transactions of a business in the order in which they occur. Therefore, a 'journal' may be defined as a book containing a chronological records of transactions. The Journal is, thus, a Book of Prime Entry. It is otherwise known as the Book of Original Entry. These entries are then posted from the Journal into the Ledger. As such, the Ledger is known as the Principal Book or the Main Book. The Ledger is otherwise known as the Book of Final Entry. The Journal merely helps the posting of entries from the journal into the Ledger. Hence, journal is known as Subsidiary Record or Subsidiary Book. Journalising is an act of recording the debit and credit aspects of a business transaction in journal, together with an explanation of the transaction, known as Narration.

Journal

Date (1)		Particulars (2)	L.F (3)	Dr. Amount (Rs) (4)	Cr. Amount (Rs) (5)
Year Month	Date	Name of Account to be Debited To Names of Account to be Credited (Narration)			

1. The date column is meant for recording the date of the transaction.
2. The second column is meant for recording the accounts to be debited and credited.
3. The third column is meant for recording the page number of the ledger, where the entries are posted.
4. In this column, we write the amount to be debited against Dr.
5. In this column, we write the amount to be credited against Cr.

In the second column, within brackets, a brief explanation of the transaction is written, which is known as narration.

RULES OF JOURNALISING

The act of recording the transactions in journal is called Journalising. This recording is made according to certain rules and these rules are called rules of journalising.

The businessman must enter into transactions with a number of persons or firms, possess some property, for example, cash, furniture, machinery etc. to carry on the business, pay certain expenses, for example, rent, salaries, wages etc. and receive certain incomes, for example, interest, commission, dividend etc. through business. Thus, to keep a proper record of all aforementioned transactions, the following accounts are required to be maintained :

(A) The account of a person or of a firm, with whom the business deals, is known as Personal Account.
(B) The account of property in the business, is known as Real Account.
(C) The account of each specific head of expense or income, is known as Nominal Account.

In every transaction, two accounts are affected. Before journalising a transaction, we ask ourselves the following questions :

1. What aspects (accounts) are affected ? Analyse the transaction, find out the receiving aspect and the giving aspect.
2. What class of accounts are they ? Identify the accounts, *e.g.*, Personal, Real or Nominal.
3. Which account is to be debited and which one to be credited ? Apply the golden rules for debit and credit according to the type of accounts.

Types of Accounts

- Personal
  (Ram's Account
  Bank Account
  Dubey's Account
  Mohan's Account)
- Impersonal
  - Real (Property)
    (Plant Account
    Machinery Account
    Cash Account
    Goods Account)
  - Nominal (Fictitious)
    (Salary Account
    Discount Account
    Wages Account
    Postage Account)

Rule: If any word (as a prefix or suffix) is added to a nominal account then it becomes a personal account.

ILLUSTRATION 2.1

Analysis of Transactions

Date	Transactions	Accounts involved	Classification of Accounts	Rules for debit and credit	Explanation	Account to be debited	Account to be credited
2005 Jan 1	Started business with Rs 10,000	Cash Capital	Real Personal	Debit what comes in Credit the giver	Cash comes in the business Proprietor is the giver of cash	Cash – Rs 10,000	Capital – Rs 10,000
2	Received Rs 100 from B	Cash B	Real Personal	Debit what comes in Credit the giver	Cash comes in the business B is the giver of cash	Cash – Rs 100	B – Rs 100
3	Received Rs 500 as Commission	Cash Commission	Real Nominal	Debit what comes in Credit all incomes and gains	Cash comes in the business Commission is income	Cash – Rs 500	Commission – Rs 500
4	Paid rent Rs 100	Rent Cash	Nominal Real	Debit the expenses and losses Credit what goes out	Rent is an expense Cash goes out of the business	Rent – Rs 100	Cash – Rs 100
5	Purchased a machine for Rs 1000	Machine Cash	Real Real	Debit what comes in Credit what goes out	Machine comes in Cash goes out of the business	Machine – Rs 1,000	Cash – Rs 1,000
6	Purchased a machine from AB & Co. for Rs 2,000	Machine AB. & Co.	Real Personal	Debit what comes in Credit the giver	Machine comes in AB & Co. is the giver of machine	Machine – Rs ,2000	AB & Co. – Rs 2,000
7	Proprietor withdrew Cash Rs 100	Drawings Cash	Personal Real	Debit the receiver Credit what goes out	Proprietor is the receiver of cash Cash goes out of business	Drawings – Rs 100	Cash – Rs 100
8	Goods returned to Ramesh for Rs 200	Ramesh Goods	Personal Real	Debit the receiver of goods Credit what goes out	Ramesh is the receiver of goods Goods go out of the business	Ramesh – Rs 200	Goods – Rs 200
9	Goods worth Rs.100 returned by Ram	Goods Ram	Real Personal	Debit what comes in Credit the giver	Goods come in the business Ram is the giver of goods	Goods – Rs 100	Ram – Rs 100

Notes : 1. In a Cash Transaction omit the Personal Account.
2. In a Credit Transaction, omit the Cash Account.

Rules for Debit and Credit

1. Personal Accounts	Debit the Receiver Credit the Giver
2. Real Account	Debit what comes in Credit what goes out
3. Nominal Account	Debit all losses and expenses Credit all gains and incomes

Alternatively

Put the rules in another way :

Classes of account	*Debit*	*Credit*
Personal	The Receiver	The Giver
Real (Property)	What comes in	What goes out
Nominal (Fictitious)	Expenses and Losses	Incomes and Gains

COMPOUND JOURNAL

When many transactions of the same nature occur on a particular day, such transactions can be entered in the journal by means of combined (composite) journal entries, known as Compound Journal Entry. Make sure that the amount in the debit column equals to the amount in the credit column, based on the double entry system of book-keeping. One amount in the debit column must be equal to two or more amounts in the credit column or one amount in the credit column equals to two or more amounts in the debit column or under compound entry, a few debits will be equal to a few credits. The rule for journalising is the same as that of simple journal.

ILLUSTRATION 2.2

2005

Jan. 1 Purchased goods on credit from Ram For Rs 2,000
Purchased goods on credit from Gopi for Rs 1,500
Purchased goods on credit from Balu for Rs 3,000
Purchased goods on credit from Seth for Rs 500
Pass (*a*) simple, and (*b*) compound journal.

SOLUTION

(*a*) Simple Journal Entry

Date	*Particular*		*L.F.*	*Dr. Amount Rs*	*Cr. Amount Rs*
2005	Purchase Account	Dr.		2,000	
Jan. 1	To Ram Account				2,000
	(Being credit purchase)				
"	Purchase Account	Dr.		1,500	
	To Gopi Account				1,500
	(Being credit purchase)				
"	Purchase Account	Dr.		3,000	
	To Balu Account				3,000
	(Being credit purchase)				
"	Purchase Account	Dr.		500	
	To Seth Account				500
	(Being credit purchase)				

(*b*) **Compound Journal**

Date	*Particulars*		*L.F.*	*Dr.* Amount *Rs*	*Cr.* Amount *Rs*
2005	Purchase Account	Dr.		7,000	
Jan 1	To Ram Account				2,000
	To Gopi Account				1,500
	To Balu Account				3,000
	To Seth Acount				500
	(Being credit pruchase)				

Advantages of Journal

The following advantages can be had from a journal :

1. It provides a date-wise information.
2. The history of each transaction can be known.
3. Errors can easily be located and prevented.
4. Omissions are minimised.

LEDGER

As we know that first, all business transactions are recorded in the journal, separately and date-wise. The transactions relating to persons, assets, expenses and income are journalised chronologically *i.e.*, date-wise. But, one cannot find similar transaction at one place in the journal. Therefore, to have a consolidated view, we have to prepare different accounts in the ledger. No transaction gets into the ledger unless it appears first in the journal. The source of information for the ledger is the journal. Thus, journal is subsidiary to the ledger and the ledger is the principal or main book of account. The method of writing from journal to the ledger is called posting or ledger posting. Ledger contains accounts. Accounts are generally kept in a book called ledger. It contains accounts related to business transactions. Ledger is a register, having a number of pages, which are numbered consecutively. One page in the ledger is usually allotted to one account. An index to various accounts in the ledger is given at the beginning of the ledger for easy reference.

Dr. **Specimen of Ledger** Cr.

Date	*Particulars*	*J.F.*	*Amount* *Rs*	*Date*	*Particulars*	*J.F.*	*Amount* *Rs*

LEDGER ACCOUNT

An account is a summary of business transactions affecting a person or property or an income or an expense. An accoount is a brief history of financial dealings of a particular man or a particular item. An account has two sides—Debit and Credit. The left side is known as DEBIT and the right side is known as CREDIT. Double entry book-keeping, means recording of both the receiving and giving aspects of every transaction. When an account receives a benefit, the account is debited. When an account gives a benefit, the account is credited. These two aspects are denoted by the symbols Debtor (Dr.) and Creditor (Cr.) respectively. So, for every debit there will be a corresponding credit. The rules for Debit and Credit are formulated according to the types of accounts. The accounts can be divided into three types—Personal, Real and Nominal.

1. Personal Account

These are accounts of persons, firms, and other associations with which we have business dealings. The rule is to debit the account of the person, who receives something and credit the account of the person, who gives something. That is, *Debit the receiver and Credit the giver*.

2. Real or Property Account

Real accounts are the accounts of things. *i.e.*, lifeless things. It is an account relating to properties or assets, such as Land, Machinery etc. Debit the account of the things which come in and credit the account of the things which go out. That is, *Debit what comes in and Credit what goes out*.

3. Nominal or Fictitious Account

This type of accounts relate to the accounts of income, expenses, profit and losses. Many items of expenses like, salary, wages, rent etc. are incurred in the business. Similarly, many items of income, *i.e.*, discount, commission etc. are earned in the business. The rule is that *Debit all losses and expenses and Credit all gains and incomes*.

LEDGER POSTING

As soon as a transaction takes place, the same is recorded in the journal in the form of a journal entry. This entry is posted again in the respective ledger accounts under the double entry principle from the journal. This is called ledger posting.

PROCESS OF LEDGER POSTING

The following procedures are followed for posting :

First part of the Account :

1. Locate in the ledger, the first Account named in the journal.
2. Write the date of the transaction, in the date column, in debit-side of that account.
3. Enter in the debit-side of the ledger, in particulars column, the name of the Account credited with prefix "To".
4. Write in folio column on the debit-side of the account, the page number of journal from which the entry is being posted.
5. Enter the amount, on the debit column of the ledger as per journal.
6. Similarly, write the ledger page number in the folio column of the Journal.

Second part of the other Account :

1. Locate in the ledger, the second Account named in the Journal.
2. Write the date of the transaction, in the date column on credit side of that Account.
3. Enter in the credit-side of the ledger, in particulars column, the name of the Account debited with prefix "By".

4. Write in the folio column of the ledger, the page number of the journal from which the entry is being posted.
5. Enter the amount on the credit side of the ledger as per the journal.
6. Similarly, write the ledger page number in the folio column of the journal.

Example : Record the following transaction and post them into ledgers :

On 1st Dec. 2004, Ram started business with a capital of Rs. 50,000.

Journal Entries

Date	*Particulars*	*L.F.*	*Debit Rs*	*Credit Rs*
2004				
Dec. 1	Cash A/c Dr.	15	50,000	
	To Capital A/c	11		50,000
	(Being business started)			

Ledger Posting

Dr. **Cash Account** Cr.

Date	*Particulars*	*JF*	*Amount Rs*	*Date*	*Particulars*	*JF*	*Amount Rs*
2004							
Dec. 1	To Capital A/c	1	50,000				

Dr. **Ram's Capital Account** Cr.

Date	*Particulars*	*JF*	*Amount Rs*	*Date*	*Particulars*	*JF*	*Amount Rs*
				2004 Dec. 1	By Cash A/c	1	50,000

BALANCING OF AN ACCOUNT

Debit side of the journal entry is posted to the debit side of the account and credit side of the journal entry is posted to the credit side of the account. After the ledger posting, accounts are closed and their balances are found out. There are three possibilities while striking the balance in an account:

1. The two sides of the account are equal.

or 2. The debit total is greater than the credit total.

or 3. The credit total is greater than the debit total.

If the two sides of an account are equal, it indicates the equality of benefits received and given by that account. The account can be closed as there is no balance in that account. If debit side total of an account is greater than the credit total, then the account indicates a "Debit Balance". If the credit side of an account is greater than the debit total, then that account indicates a "Credit Balance". The procedure to balance an account is :

A. Total both the sides of the account, on rough sheet of paper.
B. Find out the difference between the total, *i.e.*, credit side and debit side. The difference is called "Balance".
C. Enter (write) the difference (balance) in the lesser side as Balance c/d (carried down) as the last item, and on the last date of the month.

D. Now, both the sides are equal in total. Write the totals which are equal and close the account.

The balance is afterwards taken to the opposite side and entered as Balance b/d (brought down) on the first day of the next month.

SIGNIFICANCE OF BALANCES

The word "Balance" which is the difference between the two sides of an account or the difference between total debits and total credits, indicates the net effect of all transactions relating to that account during a given period. In case an account in the ledger shows the same totals on either side, there will not be any balance at all.

If a personal account shows a debit balance, the person is a debtor to business, that is, he owes money equal to the amount of debit balance. On the other hand, if the personal account shows a credit balance, it means that the person is a creditor to the business to the extent of the amount of credit balance.

Real accounts being accounts of properties, always show debit balances. Such balances signifying the value of properties of the business.

Nominal account should not be balanced and are transferred to Trading Account or Profit and Loss Account.

Capital Account always shows credit balance indicating that capital is a liability to the business, that is, the proprietor has invested money in the business and is a creditor of the business. Drawing Account always shows debit balance. It shows that the proprietor has withdrawn money during the accounting period.

RELATION BETWEEN JOURNAL AND LEDGER

1. Transactions are entered first in the journal and then these entries are posted to appropriate accounts in the ledger.
2. The journal is subsidiary book, while the ledger is the main book of accounts.
3. The journal shows the transaction in chronological order, that is, journal is a daily record. Posting from the journal is done periodically, may be weekly or fortnightly etc.
4. Entering the transactions in the journal is called journalising and the act of recording in the ledger is called posting.
5. Journal is the book of prime entry, while ledger is the book of final entry.

CLASSIFICATION OF JOURNAL

Journal is classified into (1) General Journal and (2) Special Journal. Special journal is further subdivided as shown below :

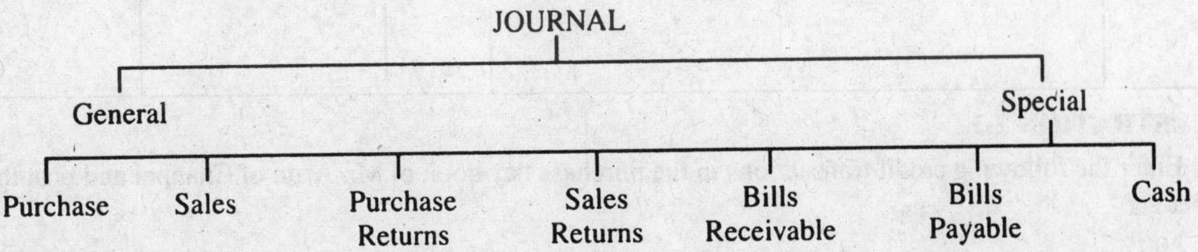

General journal is the simplest type of journal, which is capable of recording any kind of transaction. When the transactions are few, they are recorded in general journal by a clerk. But, when the business grows bigger, transactions are numerous and one man cannot do all the work himself. Thus, there is a need for sub-division of journal into various books. Transactions relating to one head or similar transactions are recorded in one book. All the sub-divided books are called *subsidiary books* or *books of original entry* or *special purpose subsidiary books.* The number of subsidiary books differs from firm to firm, according to its requirements and objects.

A medium size business generally maintains the following types of journals:

1. Cash Book — to record cash transactions;
2. Sales Day Book — to record credit sales;
3. Purchases Day Book — to record credit purchases;
4. Sales Return Day Book — to record sales returns;
5. Purchases Return Day Book — to record purchases returns;
6. Bills Recoivable Book — to record bills receivable:
7. Bills Payable Book — to record bills payable;
8. Petty Cash Book — to record petty cash payments; and
9. Journal Proper — to record residuary transactions. It is also used for rectifying errors.

ADVANTAGES OF SUBSIDIARY RECORDS

1. When similar type of transactions are recorded through subsidiary books, much time is saved and thus, clerical labour is saved. It is a labour-saving method. For instance, on a particular day, there are 10 transactions of sales. If these transactions are entered through the subsidiary book, *i.e.*, Sales Day Book, then there will be only one entry in the sales account, instead of ten entries.

2. There is division of labour, further it speeds up the work.

3. More effective internal check is possible and further reference becomes easy, because transactions of similar nature are in separate books. Moreover, postings are also easy.

PURCHASE BOOK

The purchase book is also known as Purchase Journal, Bought Book, Purchase Day Book or Invoice Book. This book is recorded with credit purchases of goods, meant for resale. Cash purchases are not recorded in this book. Cash purchases are entered in the Cash Book. At the same time, credit purchases of assets, meant for the firm, are entered in the journal. The form of Purchase Book is as follows :

Purchase Book

Date	*Name of the Supplier*	*L.F.*	*Inward Invoice No.*	*Amount Rs*
(1)	(2)	(3)	(4)	(5)

ILLUSTRATION 2.3

Enter the following credit transactions in the purchase day book of Mr. Arun of Channai and post them in the ledger.

2005

Jan. 1 Bought goods from Ram for Rs 5,000

10 Purchased goods from Shyam for Rs 10,000

17 Purchased goods from Mohan for Rs 9,000

25 Purchased goods from Raja for Rs 8,000

SOLUTION

Purchase Book

Date		Name of Suppliers	L.F.	Inward Invoice No.	Amount Rs
2005					
Jan.	1	Ram			5,000
	10	Shyam			10,000
	17	Mohan			9,000
	25	Raja			8,000
				Purchase A/c Dr.	32,000

LEDGER ACCOUNTS

Dr. **Ram Account** Cr.

Date	Particulars	JF	Amount Rs	Date	Particulars	JF	Amount Rs
				2005			
				Jan. 1	By Purchase Account		5,000

Dr. **Shyam Account** Cr.

Date	Particulars	JF	Amount Rs	Date	Particulars	JF	Amount Rs
				2005			
				Jan. 10	By Purchase Account		10,000

Dr. **Mohan Account** Cr.

Date	Particulars	JF	Amount Rs	Date	Particulars	JF	Amount Rs
				2005			
				Jan. 17	By Purchase Account		9,000

Dr. **Raja Account** Cr.

Date	Particulars	JF	Amount Rs	Date	Particulars	JF	Amount Rs
				2005			
				Jan. 25	By Purchase Account		8,000

Dr. **PurchaseAccount** Cr.

Date	Particulars	JF	Amount Rs	Date	Particulars	JF	Amount Rs
2005							
Jan. 31	To Sundries as per Pruchase Book		32,000				

SALES BOOK

This book is also called "Sales Journal" or "Sold Book" or "Sales Day Book". Only credit sales are recorded in this book. Cash sales are not entered in it. At the same time, sales of any asset of the firm is also not entered in this journal. The form of this book is as follows :

Sales Book

Date	*Name of Customers*	*L.F.*	*Outward Invoice No.*	*Amount Rs*
(1)	(2)	(3)	(4)	(5)

ILLUSTRATION 2.4

Write the following transactions of credit sales in the Sales Book of Chennai Company and post them in the ledger.

2005

Jan. 1 Sold goods to Mohan Rs 100

11 Sold goods to Gopal Rs 300

20 Sold goods to Balu Rs 250

SOLUTION

Sales Book

Date	*Name of Customers*	*L.F.*	*Outward Invoice No.*	*Amount Rs*
2005				
Jan. 1	Mohan			100
11	Gopal			300
20	Balu			250
			Sales A/c Dr.	650

LEDGER ACCOUNT

Dr. **Mohan Account** Cr.

Date	*Particular*	*JF*	*Amount Rs*	*Date*	*Particulars*	*JF*	*Amount Rs*
2005							
Jan. 1	To Sales Account		100				

Dr. **Gopal Account** Cr.

Date	*Particulars*	*JF*	*Amount Rs*	*Date*	*Particulars*	*JF*	*Amount Rs*
2005							
Jan. 11	To Sales Account		300				

Dr. **Balu Account** Cr.

Date	Particulars	JF	Amount Rs	Date	Particulars	JF	Amount Rs
2005 Jan. 20	To Sales Account		250				

Dr. **Sales Account** Cr.

Date	Particulars	JF	Amount Rs	Date	Particulars	JF	Amount Rs
				2005 Jan. 31	By Sundries as per Sales Book		650

PURCHASE RETURNS BOOK

This book is also called "Purchase Return Journal" or "Return Outward Book". Goods, which are purchased on credit, may be returned to the supplier by the purchaser, if they are defective. The purpose of this book is to record only the transactions relating to the return of goods. The form of Purchase Returns Book is given below :

Purchase Returns Book (Returns Outward Book)

Date	Name of Suppliers	Debit Note No.	L.F.	Amount Rs
(1)	(2)	(3)	(4)	(5)

ILLUSTRATION 2.5

Enter the following transactions in the Purchase Returns Book :

2005

Jan. 1 Returned goods to Balu Rs 150

9 Returned goods to Ram Rs 100

26 Returned goods to Hari Rs 50

SOLUTION

Purchase Returns Book

Date	Name of Suppliers	L.F.	Debit Note No.	Amount Rs
2005				
Jan. 1	Balu			150
9	Ram			100
26	Hari			50
			Purchase Returns A/c Cr.	300

LEDGER ACCOUNT

Dr. **Mohan Account** Cr.

Date	Particulars	JF	Amount Rs	Date	Particulars	JF	Amount Rs
2005 Jan. 1	To Purchase Returns Account		150				

Dr. **Ram Account** Cr.

Date	Particulars	JF	Amount Rs	Date	Particulars	JF	Amount Rs
2005 Jan. 9	To Purchase Returns Account		100				

Dr. **Hari Account** Cr.

Date	Particulars	JF	Amount Rs	Date	Particulars	JF	Amount Rs
2005 Jan. 26	To Purchase Returns Account		50				

Dr. **Purchase Returns Account** Cr.

Date	Particulars	JF	Amount Rs	Date	Particulars	JF	Amount Rs
				2005 Jan. 31	By Sundries as per Purchase Returns Book		300

SALES RETURNS BOOK

This book is also called "Returns Inwards Book" or "Sales Returns Journal". After the goods have been sold, they may be returned by the purchaser, if they are defective. Such particulars of goods returned by the customers are recorded in this book. The form of this book is as follows :

Sales Returns Book

Date	Name of Customers	L.F.	Credit Note No.	Amount Rs
(1)	(2)	(3)	(4)	(5)

ILLUSTRATION 2.6

Enter the following transactions in the sales returns book.

2005

Jan. 1	Mohan returned goods worth	Rs 25
10	Gopal returned goods worth	Rs 50
28	Balu returned goods worth	Rs 75

SOLUTION

Sales Returns Book

Date	*Name of Customers*	*L.F.*	*Credit Invoice No.*	*Amount Rs*
2005				
Jan. 1	Mohan			25
10	Gopal			50
28	Balu			75
			Sales Returns A/c Dr.	150

LEDGER ACCOUNTS

Dr. **Mohan Account** Cr.

Date	*Particulars*	*JF*	*Amount Rs*	*Date*	*Particulars*	*JF*	*Amount Rs*
				2005			
				Jan. 1	By Sales Returns Account		25

Dr. **Gopal Account** Cr.

Date	*Particulars*	*JF*	*Amount Rs*	*Date*	*Particulars*	*JF*	*Amount Rs*
				2005			
				Jan. 10	By Sales Returns Account		50

Dr. **Balu Account** Cr.

Date	*Particulars*	*JF*	*Amount Rs*	*Date*	*Particulars*	*JF*	*Amount Rs*
				2005			
				Jan. 28	By Sales Returns Account		75

Dr. **Sales Returns Account** Cr.

Date	*Particulars*	*JF*	*Amount Rs*	*Date*	*Particulars*	*JF*	*Amount Rs*
2005							
Jan. 31	To Sundries as per Sales Returns Book		150				

POSTING RULES

Purchase Book :	(A) Purchase Account is debited with TOTAL.
	(B) Personal Accounts are credited individually.

Sales Book :	(A) Sales Account is credited with TOTAL. (B) Personal Accounts are debited individually.
Purchased Returns Book :	(A) Purchase Returns Account is credited with TOTAL. (B) Personal Accounts are debited individually.
Sales Returns Book :	(A) Sales Return Account is debited with TOTAL. (B) Personal Accounts are credited individually.

It is to be carefully noted that Personal Accounts are posted individually, whereas Goods Account (*i.e.*, Purchase Account, Sales Account, Purchase Returns Account and Sales Returns Account) must be posted only in totals periodically.

In business, after the goods are bought, they may be returned because :

(*a*) Goods may be defective ;
or (*b*) they have been damaged in transit ;
or (*c*) the price charged is high ;
or (*d*) the goods might have been received late ;
or (*e*) the goods supplied are of bad quality ;
or (*f*) unsuitable terms and conditions on dealings etc.

DEBIT NOTE

When goods are returned to suppliers, a statement is sent to them informing about the debit given to their account. This statement is called Debit Note. It is so called (Debit Note), because of the Debit given to the concerned Party's account. The Purchase Returns Book is written up the details from the duplicate copy of the Debit Note.

CREDIT NOTE

Our customers may return goods to us. On receipt of the goods returned by the customers, a credit note is sent to them, by us, intimating the credit given to their account. This statement is called Credit Note. The Sales Returns Book is written up the details from the duplicate of the Credit Note.

(Refer Chapter 4 for Bills Receivable Book and Bills Payable Book)

ILLUSTRATION 2.7

Enter the following transactions in proper subsidiary records.

April 1 Purchased goods from Anand for Rs 800 less 20% Trade Discount.
2 Purchased goods from Baskar for Rs 700 less 20% Trade Discount.
4 Returned Anand goods worth Rs 100.
5 Returned Baskar goods worth Rs 80.
8 Sold goods to Chandar for Rs 500 less 10% Trade Discount.
11 Chandar returned us goods worth Rs 100.
16 Sold goods to David for Rs 300 less 10% Trade Discount.
19 David returned us goods worth Rs 50.
21 Bought goods from Easwar for Rs 300.
22 Sold goods to Farook for Rs 150.
25 Bought goods from Gopal for Rs 150 less 20% Trade Discount.
28 Returned goods worth Rs 50 to Gopal. (*B.A., Madurai*)

SOLUTION

Purchase Book

Date	Name of Suppliers	L.F.	Inward Invoice No.	Amount Rs
April 1	Anand			640.00
2	Baskar			560.00
21	Easwar			300.00
25	Gopal			120.00
			Purchase Account Dr.	1620.00

Sales Book

Date	Name of Customers	L.F.	Outward Invoice No.	Amount Rs
April 8	Chandar			450.00
16	David			270.00
22	Farook			150.00
			Sales Account Cr.	870.00

Purchase Returns Book

Date	Name of Suppliers	L.F.	Debit Note No.	Amount Rs
April 4	Anand			80.00
5	Baskar			64.00
28	Gopal			40.00
			Purchase Returns A/c Dr.	184.00

Sales Returns Book

Date	Name of Customers	L.F.	Credit Note No.	Amount Rs
April 11	Chandar			90.00
19	David			45.00
			Sales Return A/c Cr.	135.00

Note : In all the books, entries are made after deducting the amount of Trade Discount. Trade discount is not recorded in account books.

JOURNAL PROPER

There are certain transactions, which cannot be entered in through any subsidiary books and such transactions are entered in the form of journal, called Journal Proper. From this journal proper, further postings are made as usual. Examples of such transactions are :

1. Opening entries
2. Transfer entries
3. Adjusting entries

4. Closing entries
5. Rectification journal entries
6. Credit purchase/Sales of assets
7. Bad debts
8. Other entries not made in any other subsidiary books.
   (These topics are dealt with under Chapter 7)

CASH BOOK

One of the most important books maintained in any business concern is the cash book. The cash book records transactions connected with cash. The object of cash book is to keep a daily record of transactions relating to receipts and payment of cash. When the business is large, the number of transactions relating to cash are also usually large. Since, cash transactions form the major portion of the transactions of a business, it is necessary to keep a separate book for cash transactions. If every transaction is entered in the journal, it will be a tremendous job. Thus, it becomes necessary to have a cash book to record only the cash transactions.

Cash book is a book of prime (original) entry. Besides being a book of original entry, the cash book also serves as a ledger account. The cash book and cash account in the ledger being the same, there is no need to open separate Cash Account in the ledger. At the same time, the accounts, which are affected by the cash payments and cash receipts are posted in the ledger. That is, the entries from the debit side of cash book should be posted to the credit side of individual accounts opened in the ledger; and the entries from the credit side should be posted to the debit side of the account concerned.

The following are the different types of cash book maintained in business firms :

1. Simple Cash Book.
2. Cash Book with Discount and Cash Columns.
3. Cash Book with Discount and Bank Columns.
4. Cash Book with Discount, Cash and Bank Columns.
5. Analytical Petty Cash Book.

1. Simple Cash Book

This type of cash book makes a record of all the receipts and payment of cash — coin, notes, cheques, bank drafts, postal orders etc. The following is a specimen of Simple Cash Book.

Dr. **Cash Book** Cr.

Date	*Receipts*	*R. No.*	*L.F.*	*Amount Rs*	*Date*	*Payments*	*V.No.*	*L.F.*	*Amount Rs*

R. No. : Receipt No.

V. No. : Voucher No.

A Simple Cash Book is ruled exactly like a ledger. When cash is received, it is entered on the debit side of the book, and similarly cash payment is entered on the credit side. When cash is received by the cashier, usually a cash receipt is issued against the cash; the cash receipt possesses a number (R.No.) which is written on the debit side, in column R.No. Similarly, cash is paid against the voucher and the number on it is entered on credit side, in column V.No. The difference between the total received including opening balance (Dr. side) and total payment (Cr. side) represents the balance, *i.e.*, the amount of cash in hand. The Cash Book should always show a debit balance, because total cash paid will never exceed opening balance plus cash received.

ILLUSTRATION 2.8

Enter the following transactions in a Cash Book.

2005			Rs
March	1	Balance of cash in hand	200
	1	Cash Sales	3,000
	2	Paid for cash purchases	1,500
	4	Received from Ramu	2,500
	7	Deposited into bank	1,000
	9	Bought goods	250
	13	Paid Taxi charges	140
	15	Paid wages	100
	20	Cash sales	1,300
	21	Received from Gopal	2,000
	24	Paid auto charges	40
	28	Bought goods	1,500
	29	Bought furniture	1,000
	30	Paid salaries	1,500
	30	Paid wages	470
	31	Paid rent	1,000
	31	Paid to Mahesh	250

SOLUTION

Dr. **Cash Book** Cr.

Date	Receipts	R. No.	L.F.	Amount Rs	Date	Payments	V. No.	L.F.	Amount Rs
2005					2005				
March 1	To Balance b/d			200	March 2	By Purchase A/c			1,500
1	To Sales A/c			3,000	7	By Bank A/c			1,000
4	To Ramu A/c			2,500	9	By Purchase A/c			250
20	To Sales A/c			1,300	13	By Taxi Charges A/c			140
21	To Gopal A/c			2,000	15	By Wages A/c			100
					24	By Auto Charges A/c			40
					28	By Purchase A/c			1,500
					29	By Furniture A/c			1,000
					30	By Salaries A/c			1,500
					30	By Wages A/c			470
					31	By Rent A/c			1,000
					31	By Mahesh's A/c			250
					31	By Balance c/d			250
				9,000					9,000
April 1	To Balance b/d			250					

2. Cash Book with Discount and Cash Column

Sometimes cash book is provided with an additional column of 'Discount' on each side. This type of cash book is known as Cash Book with Discount and Cash Column or two columns Cash Book.

Discount. Generally, it may not be possible to conduct business only on cash transactions. Businessmen sell their goods on credit, in order to increase the sales. Purchase may also be done on credit. Such credit transactions are settled against payments, in future. In order to induce prompt payment of credit transactions a concession is allowed to pay lesser amount than what they are to pay. This concession is known as discount. For instance, Mr. A sold goods to Mr. B on 1.1.2005 for Rs 500 for a period of one month. B paid Rs 475 on 15.1.2005, in full settlement of account. Here Rs 25 is the amount of discount, a concession allowed by A.

There is an other type of discount, known as *Trade Discount*. This type of trade discount arises at the time of transactions and is a concession given by the wholesale dealer to the retailer to enable the latter to sell the goods at catalogue price. For instance, A makes a purchase of goods worth Rs 1,000 at 10% trade discount. The amount of trade discount is adjusted in the invoice itself. Thus, A has to pay only Rs 900 (Rs 1,000 – 100), that is, after deducting the amount of trade discount. The amount of trade discount is deducted in the invoice itself. And the amount of trade discount does not appear in the account books.

Allowing cash discount is conditional, *i.e.*, we allow discount, when our debtors settle their accounts within the period of credit and we receive discount when we pay our creditors promptly. However, there is no question of cash discount unless payment is received from our customers and no cash discount is received unless payment is made to suppliers. Cash discount accompany cash receipts from debtors and payment to creditors. Therefore, it is convenient to record discount allowed or discount received alongwith cash receipt or cash payment. The column on the debit side records discount allowed to debtors and the column on the credit side records the discount received from creditors.

Posting of cash column is similar to simple cash book. After posting, the cash columns are balanced like other ledger accounts, but discount columns are totalled but not balanced. That is, on balancing the cash book, the discount columns are added up. The total of Discount Allowed (Dr.) column is then posted to debit of Discount/Discount Allowed Account and the total of discount received (Cr.) column is posted to the credit of Discount/Discount Received Account in the ledger. The discount column in the cash book is only a memorandum column and does not stand for Discount Account.

Distinction between Cash Discount and Trade Discount are given below in brief :

Cash Discount	*Trade Discount*
1. Cash discount is recorded in the account books.	1. Trade discount is not recorded in account books.
2. It is allowed by a creditor to the debtor.	2. It is allowed by the manufacturers or wholesale dealers to the retailers.
3. It is reduction in the amount due by a creditor, if the account is cleared within the stipulated time.	3. It is adjusted in the invoice and is not subjected to the time of payment.
4. It is an incentive for prompt discharge of the debit within specified period.	4. The object of trade discount is to enable the retailers to make profit, even if he sells at catalogue price.
5. It is conditional, because cash discount is enjoyed, if payment is made within the period.	5. It is unconditional.
6. No question of returning the cash.	6. It is deducted from any goods returned.
7. Rate of cash discount is almost same in all kinds of trade.	7. The rate of trade discount differs from business to business.

ILLUSTRATION 2.9

Enter the following transactions in a cash book with Discount and Cash columns.

2005

Jan. 1 Balance of Cash in hand Rs 12,000.

2 Received from Prem Rs 1,200 and allowed him discount Rs 40.

6 Bought typewriter for Rs 900.

9 Purchased goods for cash Rs 13,000

12 Paid Govindan Rs 800 and was allowed a discount Rs 80.

15 Received for cash sales Rs 3,800.

18 Paid towards printing Rs 150.

20 Murugan who owed Rs 1,500 settled his account by paying Rs 1,360.

25 Received from Kannan Rs 1,600 and allowed him discount Rs 80.

31 Paid salaries Rs 800.

SOLUTION

Dr. **Cash Book with Discount and Cash Column** Cr.

Date	*Receipts*	*R. No.*	*L.F.*	*Discount Rs*	*Amount Rs*	*Date*	*Payments*	*V. No.*	*L.F.*	*Discount Rs*	*Amount Rs*
2005						2005					
Jan. 1	To Balance b/d			–	12,000	Jan. 6	By Typewriter A/c			–	900
2	To Prem's A/c			40	1,200	9	By Purchase A/c			–	13,000
15	To Sales A/c			–	3,800	12	By Govindan's A/c			80	800
20	To Murugan's A/c			140	1,360	18	By Printing A/c			–	150
25	To Kannan's A/c			80	1,600	31	By Salaries A/c			–	800
						31	By Balance c/d				4,310
				260	19,960					80	19,960
Feb. 1	To Balance b/d				4,310						

Note. Discount allowed, *i.e.*, Rs 260 to be transferred to the debit of Discount Allowed A/c and discount received, *i.e.*, Rs 80 to be transferred to the credit of Discount Received A/c

3. Cash Book with Discount and Bank Columns

In big firms, transactions are not done in cash. All cash receipts are deposited with the bank and payments are made only through cheques. This type of cash book is similar to the above cash book, *i.e.*, cash book with discount and cash columns, but the only difference is that bank is there instead of cash. Procedure of closing the cash book is similar to the above cash book.

ILLUSTRATION 2.10

Enter the following transactions in a Cash Book with discount and Bank columns, assuming that all payments are made by cheques and all receipts are immediately banked.

2004

Nov. 1 Paid into bank Rs 5,000

3 Purchased goods Rs 2,000

7 Sold goods for cash Rs 1,700

9 Purchased goods Rs 1,500

10 Sold goods to Raju on credit Rs 500

13 Purchased goods from Gopi for Rs 1,000 on credit

14 Paid electricity charges Rs 45

15 Received from Raju Rs 490 in full settlement

16 Paid office Rent Rs 150
17 Withdrawn from bank for petty payments Rs 50
18 Paid to Gopi Rs 975 in full settlement
19 Sold goods for Rs 750
20 Sold goods to Chatterji on credit Rs 450
21 Purchased goods from Gopal for Rs 1,100 on credit
24 Received cash from Chatterji Rs 440 in full settlement
25 Paid to Gopal on account Rs 600
26 Paid salaries Rs 175
27 Withdrawn for personal use Rs 300
28 Paid to Gopal Rs 485 in full settlement
29 Sold goods for cash Rs 400
30 Purchased goods by cheque Rs 300
30 Paid telephone charges Rs 55.

(B.Com., Madurai)

SOLUTION

Dr. **Cash Book with Bank and Discount Columns** Cr.

Date	*Receipts*	*L.F.*	*Discount Rs*	*Bank Rs*	*Date*	*Payments*	*L.F.*	*Discount Rs*	*Bank Rs*
2004					2004				
Nov. 1	To Cash A/c			5,000	Nov. 3	By Purchase A/c			2,000
7	To Sales A/c			1,700	9	By Purchase A/c			1,500
15	To Raju A/c		10	490	14	By Electricity Charge A/c			45
19	To Sales A/c			750	16	By Office Rent A/c			150
24	To Chatterjee A/c		10	440	17	By Petty Cash A/c			50
29	To Sales A/c			400	18	By Gopi A/c		25	975
					25	By Gopal A/c			600
					26	By Salaries A/c			175
					27	By Drawings A/c			300
					28	By Gopal A/c		15	485
					30	By Purchase A/c			300
					30	By Telephone A/c			55
					30	By Balance c/d			2,145
			20	8,780				40	8,780
Dec. 1	To Balance b/d			2,145					

(**Note :** All credit transactions have been omitted.)

4. Cash Book with Discount, Cash and Bank Columns

This book is also known as three Columnar Cash Book or Triple Column Cash book, which has three columns on either side, *viz.*, Discount, Cash and Bank. In modern days and with the development of banks, many receipts and payments are made through cheques. Here, the cash column and bank column represent Cash Account and Bank Account respectively. But, the discount column is only a memorandum column and such separate Discount Account has to be opened.

Method of Recording in Three Columnar Cash Book. All cash receipts are entered on debit side of the Cash Book in the cash column and all payments are entered on the credit side of the cash book in cash column.

All cheques received are entered in the cash column on the debit side. Then, these cheques are sent to bank for collection and the treatment is similar to *cash paid into bank*, which is explained below. If the cheque received from a customer is sent to the bank on the same day, the amount is entered in the bank column on the debit side.

Cash Paid into Bank. When cash is paid into bank, Bank Account receives and Cash Account gives the benefit and the double entry is complete by debiting the Bank Account and crediting the Cash Account. An Account cannot receive and give both at the same time. An Account that receives is debited and the Account that gives is credited. Since here, the Cash Book contains two Accounts — Cash Account and Bank Account, the credit and the debit may be found in the two Accounts, in the same book. Thus, when cash is paid into bank, the entry is Bank Account Dr. to Cash Account. This means, on the debit side of Cash Book, that amount is written, in Bank Column as "To Cash" and on the credit side of cash book, the amount is written in Cash Column as "By Bank". Since, both the entries appear in Cash Book, letter "C" is written in L.F. column. C stands for contra and contra means opposite or against, which indicates that the other aspect of the transaction is found on the opposite side.

Cash withdrawn from Bank. It is possible that a businessman withdraw some amount from the bank for office. Bank Account gives the benefit and Cash Account receives the benefit. Since, Cash Account and Bank Account appear in Cash Book, both the aspects can be entered in the cash book. When cash is drawn, cash comes in and is debited in the cash book in cash column as "To Bank" and credit in cash book in Bank Column as "To Cash". This is a contra entry.

Remember the following points when writing a three column Cash Book :

Transactions	*Debit/Credit*	*The column in which the amount is entered*
1. Received a cheque	Debit side	Cash column
2. Received a cheque and sent the same to bank for collection	Debit side	Bank column
3. Paid Mr. Ram by cheque	Credit side	Bank column
4. Cheque has been drawn for personal use	Credit side	Bank column
5. Draw a cheque for office use	Credit side	Bank column
	Debit side	Cash column
6. Paid into the bank	Credit side	Cash column
	Debit side	Bank column
7. Amount directly paid into the bank	Debit side	Bank column

Note : S. No. 5 and 6 are contra entries.

ILLUSTRATION 2.11

From the following transactions, write up the cash book with three columns and bring down the balance.

2004			Rs
July	1	Commenced business with cash	15,000
	2	Incurred opening expenses	500
	2	Paid into the bank	13,500
	3	Paid Raman by cheque	3,450
		Discount allowed by him	50
	4	Paid carriage on goods	85
	5	Bought furniture by cheque	700
	8	Received cheque from Kannan	3,300
		Discount allowed	60
	8	Cash sales	2,500
	9	Deposited into the bank	2,400
	10	Cheque purchases	5,000
	12	Received commission	150

15	Advertising expenses	120
18	Withdrew cash from bank	500
20	Received cheque from Murugan	1,250
	Discount allowed	50
25	Drew for private use	500
28	Office expenses	125
31	Salaries paid by cheque	500
31	Paid rend by cheque	1,000
31	Purchased a typewriter by cheque	3,200

(*B.Com., Madurai*)

SOLUTION

Cash Book with Discount, Cash and Bank Columns

Dr. Cr.

Date	Receipts	R. No.	L.F.	Dis. Rs	Cash Rs	Bank Rs	Date	Payments	V. No.	L.F.	Dis. Rs	Cash Rs	Bank Rs
2004							2004						
July 1	To Capital A/c				15,000	—	July 2	By Expenses A/c				500	—
2	To Cash A/c		C		—	13,500	2	By Bank A/c		C		13,500	—
8	To Kannan's A/c			60	3,300	—	3	By Raman's A/c			50	—	3,450
8	To Sales A/c				2,500		4	By Carriage A/c				85	—
9	To Cash A/c		C		—	2,400	5	By Furniture A/c				—	700
12	To Commission A/c				150	—	9	By Bank A/c		C		2,400	—
18	To Bank A/c		C		500	—	10	By Purchase A/c				—	5,000
20	To Murugan's A/c			50	1,250	—	15	By Advertising A/c				120	—
							18	By Cash A/c		C		—	500
							25	By Drawings A/c				—	500
							28	By Office Expenses				125	—
							31	By Salaries A/c				—	500
							31	By Rent A/c				—	1,000
							31	By Typewriters A/c				—	3,200
							31	By Balance c/d				5,970	1,050
				110	22,700	15,900					50	22,700	15,900
Aug. 1	To Balance b/d				5,970	1,050							

ILLUSTRATION 2.12

Enter the following transactions of the Premier Trading Company in Cash Book with three columns—Discount, Cash and Bank and balance the accounts as on 31st December 2004.

2004

Dec. 1 Cash in hand Rs 4,000
1 Bank Rs 1,000 (Cr.)
3 Received a cheque from A Rs 290 and allowed him discount of Rs 40
7 A's cheque deposited into the bank
10 Withdrew from bank for office use Rs 800
12 Paid B/P by cheque Rs 600
15 B/R from Ram, Rs 2,500 ; Discounted it, crediting with bank Rs 2,400
20 Issued a cheque for Petty Cashier Rs 100
25 Paid to Gupta by cheque Rs 920 ; discount received Rs 30
28 Made cash sales Rs 900.

SOLUTION

Cash Book with Discount, Cash and Bank

Date	Receipts	L.F.	Dis. Rs	Cash Rs	Bank Rs.	Date	Payments	L.F.	Dis. Rs	Cash Rs.	Bank Rs
2004						2004					
Dec. 1	To Balance b/d			4,000	—	Dec. 1	By Balance b/d				1,000
3	To A's A/c		40	290	—	7	By Bank A/c	C		290	—
7	To Cash A/c	C		—	290	10	By Cash A/c	C		—	800
10	To Bank A/c	C		800	—	12	By B/P A/c			—	600
15	To B/R A/c		100	—	2,400	20	By Petty Cashier A/c			—	100
28	To Sales A/c			900	—	25	By Gupta's A/c		30	—	920
31	To Balance c/d			—	730	31	By Balance c/d			5,700	—
			140	5,990	3,420				30	5,990	3,420
2005						2005					
Jan. 1	To Balance b/d			5,700		Jan. 1	By Balance b/d				730

Cash Book with two bank coloumns

ILLUSTRATION 2.13

Mr. Lal operates two bank accounts both of which are maintained in the columnar cash book itself. You are required to prepare a proforma of the Cash Book, record the following transactions therein and draw the closing balances as on 30th June.

20th June	Opening Balance—Cash	Rs 1,180	
	Progressive Bank	Rs 19,040	(Dr.)
	Goodwill Bank	Rs 6,460	(Cr.)

20th June Received cheque for Rs 1,800 from X and deposited in Goodwill Bank. The Bank credited the amount on 23rd June and debited Rs 4 to the account as its collection charges.

21st June Purchased goods for Rs 18,210 and a cheque issued on Progressive Bank.

22nd June Paid Office expenses Rs 410 and Rs 80 for stationery in cash.

23rd June Deposited a cheque for Rs 21,090, being sale proceeds of goods, in Progressive Bank. The Bank credited the amount on the same day and debited Rs 21 as discounting charges.

23rd June A cheque for Rs 8,000 drawn by Mr. Lal himself on Progressive Bank was deposited in his account with Goodwill Bank.

25th June Cash drawn from the account with Progressive Bank Rs 600 for office expenses.

25th June A cheque for Rs 1,100 received from Mr. Arun and earlier deposited in the account with Goodwill Bank on 14th June was returned unpaid and the Bank debited Rs 10 towards its charges. Mr. Lal received the amount of returned cheque and bank charges in cash from Arun.

28th June Deposited cash Rs 1,500 in the account with Goodwill Bank.

29th June Purchased postal stamps for Rs 200 and paid in cash. *(CAIIB)*

SOLUTION

See on the next page.

5. Analytical Petty Cash Book

Petty means small. In big business firms, all payments are made by cheques and all receipts are banked. There are numerous small payments on account of expenses like stationery, cartage, coolie hire, refreshments to guests etc. which cannot be paid through cheques. Moreover, the main cashier will be over-burdened if he makes these small as well as frequent payments. To avoid this inconvenience, such items of expenditure of frequent occurrence are removed to a separate book, known as Petty Cash Book, which is maintained by a Petty Cashier. Petty Cashier is a person, who maintains the Petty Cash Book. Petty cash book is maintained in a columnar form. In this book, separate columns are provided for usual head of expenditure. A Petty Cashier makes a detailed analysis of petty payments and records under suitable heads, *i.e.*, column. Petty cash book is similar to cash book. The amounts received by Petty Cashier from the main Cashier is debited in petty cash book and all petty payments are credited. Periodic total of each column is posted to respective nominal account in the ledger. The book may be considered as the book of original entry or memorandum book. If treated as a part of double entry, then no separate Petty Cash Account is needed. When the Petty Cashier needs further cash, he makes up the petty cash book and presents it to the Chief Cashier, who verifies the accounts and gives further amount.

Imprest System of Petty Cash Book. Under this system, a round sum of money estimated as necessary for the possible needs of the business to meet petty expenses for the week or fortnight is handed over to the Petty Cashier. At the end of the fixed period or earlier, when petty cashier needs further cash, he submits the petty cash book, alongwith vouchers. The Chief Cashier examines the cash book with the vouchers. Then, Chief Cashier gives money/cheque for the exact amount, which he actually spent during the period. Thus, he starts for the next period with the same sum as held previously. That is, the Petty Cashier will have again the fixed sum in the beginning of the next period. This system is known as Imprest System of Petty Cash Book. For instance, a business estimates

Cash Book with Discount, Cash and Two Bank Columns

Date	Receipts	R. No.	L.F.	Discount	Cash Rs	Progressive Bank Rs	Goodwill Bank Rs	Date	Payments	V. No.	L.F.	Discount	Cash Rs	Progressive Bank Rs	Goodwill Bank Rs
June 20	To Balance b/d				1,180	19,040	—	June 20	By Balance b/d				–	–	6,460
20	To X's Account				–	–	1,800	21	By Purchase A/c				–	18,210	–
23	To Sales A/c				–	21,090	–	22	By Office Expenses A/c				410	–	–
	To Progressive Bank A/c		C		–	–	8,000	22	By Stationery A/c				80	–	–
25	To Bank A/c		C		600	–	–	23	By Bank Charges A/c				–	21	–
	To A's A/c				1,110	–	–	”	By Bank Charges A/c				–	–	4
28	To Cash A/c		C		–	–	1,500	”	By Goodwill Bank A/c		C		–	8,000	–
								25	By Cash A/c		C		–	600	–
									By Arun A/c (Rs 1,100 + Rs 10)				–	–	1,110
								28	By Goodwill Bank A/c		C		1,500	–	–
								29	By Postage A/c				200	–	–
								30	By Balance c/d				700	13,299	3,726
					2,890	40,130	11,300						2,890	40,130	11,300
July 1	To Balance b/d				700	13,299	3,726								

that a sum of Rs 500 is required to meet small expenses in the business for one week. This amount is given to the Petty Cashier. At the week end or earlier, the Petty Cashier spent Rs 480 and needs more cash. Therefore, Petty Cashier completes the records and hands over the petty cash book alongwith vouchers to Chief Cashier, who examines the entries. Then, the Chief Cashier gives a cheque for an exact amount he spent *i.e.*, Rs 480. This sum *i.e.*, Rs 480 plus the unspent balance *i.e.*, Rs 20 would restore him the original sum with which he has started in the beginning of the last period *i.e.*, Rs 500.

Advantages of Imprest System of Petty Cash Book

1. It relieves the cash book and the Chief Cashier of the burden of recording tiny and frequent payments.
2. Commission of fraud is reduced as the Chief Cashier verifies petty cash book alongwith vouchers and the Petty Cashier is more responsible.
3. This method is very scientific and labour saving. The total expenditure under each column can easily be ascertained and only the periodical totals of each column need be posted to the ledger.

ILLUSTRATION 2.14

Mr. Mohan maintains a Columnar Petty Cash Book on the Imprest system. The imprest amount is Rs 700. From the following information show how his petty cash book would appear for the week ended on 18th December.

December	13	Balance in hand	Rs 78.00
	13	Received cash to make up the imprest.	
	14	Postage	120.00
	14	Stationery	75.00
	14	Entertainment	35.00
	15	Travelling expenses	41.00
	15	Miscellaneous expenses	26.00
	15	Entertainment	19.00
	16	Repairs	31.00
	16	Postage stamps	18.00
	16	Entertainment	10.00
	17	Entertainment	8.00
	18	Stationery	51.00
	18	Postage stamps	12.00
	18	Repairs	10.00

(*B.Com. MS*)

SOLUTION

Dr. **Columnar Petty Cash Book** Cr.

Amount Received Rs	Date	V.No.	Particulars	Total Payments Rs	ANALYSIS OF PAYMENTS Postage & Telegrams Rs	Printing & Stationery Rs	Travelling & Conveyance Rs	Repairs Rs	Entertainment Rs	Mis. Expenses
78.00	Dec. 13		To Balance b/d							
622.00	13		To Cash A/c							
	14	1	By Postage A/c	120.00	120.00					
	14	2	By Stationery A/c	75.00		75.00				
	14	3	By Entertainment A/c	35.00					35.00	
	15	4	By Travelling and Conveyance A/c	41.00			41.00			
	15	5	By Miscellaneous A/c	26.00						26.00
	15	6	By Entertainment A/c	19.00					19.00	
	16	7	By Repairs A/c	31.00				31.00		
	16	8	By Postage A/c	18.00	18.00					
	16	9	By Entertainment A/c	10.00					10.00	
	17	10	By Entertainment A/c	8.00					8.00	
	18	11	By Stationery A/c	51.00		51.00				
	18	12	By Postage A/c	12.00	12.00					
	18	13	By Repairs A/c	10.00				10.00		
				456.00	150.00	126.00	41.00	41.00	72.00	26.00
	18		By Balance c/d	244.00						
700.00				700.00						
244.00	18		To Balance b/d							
456.00			To Cash A/c							

OBJECTIVE TYPE QUESTIONS

I. State whether each of the following statement is "True" or "False".

1. Sales returns Journal is also known as Return Inwards Journal.
2. Totals of Returns Outward Book is debited to Returns Outward Account.
3. A contra entry in the Cash Book does not require posting to the ledger.
4. The balance of Petty Cash is a liability.
5. Purchases of merchandise on credit are recorded in the Purchase Book.
6. Sales Book is used to record all sales of goods.
7. When a customer returns goods a debit note is sent to him.
8. Purchase of fixed asset on credit is recorded in Journal Proper.
9. Allowance made for prompt payment is called Trade Discount.
10. Cash Book is both a Journal and a Ledger.
11. Bank column of the Cash Book shows only a debit balance.
12. Discount received is recorded on the debit side of Three column Cash Book.
13. Journal is a book of Secondary entry.
14. Ledger is a book of Secondary entry.
15. A sale of goods to "X" for cash debited to "X" Account.
16. Cash sales and credit sales are recorded in the Sales Book.
17. Cash discount appears in Cash Book.
18. Debit Note is a document prepared at the time of purchase returns.
19. Trade discount is not shown in the accounts.
20. A withdrawal of cash by the proprietor from the business is credited to Drawings Accounts.

(***Ans.*** 1. True 2. False 3. True 4. False 5. True 6. False 7. False 8. True 9. False 10. True 11. False 12. False 13. False 14. True 15. False 16. False 17. True 18. True 19. True 20. False)

II. Fill up the blanks.

1. .... Discount is a reduction in catalogue price.
2. Goods destroyed by fire should be credited .... Account.
3. Purchase Book records only .... purchase of goods.
4. Building Account will indicate a .... balance.
5. A .... is sent to a customer when he returns the goods.
6. Debit balance in a nominal account shows .... or ....
7. Goods sold on credit will be primarily recorded in .... book.
8. Journal is the book of .... entry, while a ledger is the book of .... entry.
9. The word "By" is used with an account while making posting on the .... side of an account.
10. The tatal of the Sales Book is .... to Sales Account.

(*Ans.* : 1. Trade 2. Trading 3. Credit 4. Debit 5. Credit Note 6. Expense or Loss 7. Sales 8. Original. Secondary 9. Credit 10. Credited)

III. State the nature of the following accounts (Personal, Real and Nominal)

1. Goodwill Account
2. Trade Mark Account
3. Patents Account
4. Salary Prepaid Account
5. Rent Account
6. Salary Outstanding Account
7. Furniture Account
8. Cash Account
9. Bank Account
10. Unexpired Insurance Account
11. Proprietor Account
12. Bad Debts Account

(*Ans.* : 1. Real 2. Real 3. Real 4. Personal 5. Nominal 6. Personal 7. Real 8. Real 9. Personal 10. Personal 11. Personal 12. Nominal)

IV. Select the most appropriate answer: (Multiple Choice)

1. The amount broght in by the Proprietor in the business should be credited to
   (a) Cash Account (b) Capital Account
   (c) Drawings Account
2. The cash discount allowed to a debtor should be credited to
   (a) Discount Account (b) Customer's Account
   (c) Sales Account
3. Salary paid to Mohan should be debited to
   (a) Mohan's Account (b) Cash Account
   (c) Salaries Account.
4. Rent paid to the landlord should be credited to
   (a) Landlord's Account (b) Rent Account
   (c) Cash Account
5. The return of goods by a customer should be debited to
   (a) Customer's Account (b) Sales Returns Account
   (c) Goods Account
6. In case of a debt becoming bad, the amount should be credited to
   (a) Debtor's Account (b) Bad Debts Account
   (c) Sales Account
7. Which of the following books should be used to record purchase of furniture on credit ?
   (a) Cash Book (b) Journal Proper
   (c) Purchase Book
8. The credit balance in the Bank Account is
   (a) An Asset (b) A liability
   (c) An expense
9. Asset Account is a
   (a) Personal Account (b) Real Account
   (c) Expense Account
10. Double entry means
    (a) Entry in two sets of books (b) Entry in two pages
    (c) Entry for two aspects of a transaction
11. Wages paid to worker "A" should be
    (a) Debited to Wages Account (b) Debited to "A" Account
    (c) None of the above
12. Outstanding salaries Account are shown as
    (a) An expenditure (b) A Liability
    (c) An asset
13. Interest on Drawings is
    (a) Expenditure for the business (b) Income to the Proprietor
    (c) Gain for the business
14. In Double Entry system of book-keeping every transaction affects
    (a) Two sides of the same account (b) The same account on two different dates
    (c) Two or more accounts.
15. The return of goods to a supplier should be credited to
    (a) Supplier Account (b) Goods Account
    (c) Purchase Returns Account

16. Prepaid Insurance Account is a
    (a) Personal Account (b) Nominal Account
    (c) Real Account
17. Goods taken for personal use of own should be debited to
    (a) Drawing Account (b) Proprietor's Account
    (c) Purchases Account.
18. Patent Right Account is of the nature of
    (a) Nominal Account (b) Personal Account
    (c) Real Account.
19. Goods given as charity should be credited to
    (a) Purchase Account (b) Charity Account
    (c) Sales Account
20. Interest on Capital is
    (a) Expenditure for the business (b) Expense for the proprietor
    (c) Gain for the business.

(*Ans:* 1. (b) 2. (b) 3. (c) 4 . (c) 5. (b) 6. (a) 7. (b) 8. (b) 9. (b) 10. (c) 11. (a) 12. (b) 13. (c) 14. (c) 15. (c) 16. (a) 17. (a) 18. (c) 19. (a) 20. (a)

THEORETICAL QUESTIONS

1. What do you mean by Journal ?
2. Define a Ledger.
3. Distinguish between Ledger and Journal.
4. Define ledger and explain the method of posting.
5. Explain the meaning and purpose of subsidiary books.
6. Explain what is meant by Debit Note and Credit Note.
7. What is journal proper ?
8. Define a Cash Book. Is it a subsidiary book or principal book of accounts ? Give reasons.
9. What do you mean by Contra Entry ?
10. How should a cheque received be treated in three column cash book ?
11. What purpose does an analytical petty cash book serve ?
12. Define and distinguish "Trade Discount" and "Cash Discount". (*B.Com., Kerala*)
13. Explain the "Imprest System of Petty Cash Book". (*B.Com., Madras*)
14. Explain the advantages of Journal. (*B.A., Punjab*)
15. What do you mean by posting ? (*B.A., Madurai*)

PRACTICAL PROBLEMS

1. Enter the following transactions in cash book with Discount, Cash and Bank columns :

2005

Jan. 1 Muthu commenced business with Rs 10,000.
2 Remitted into current account Rs 9,000.
6 Paid to Kannan by cheque Rs 4,000 and discount allowed Rs 100.
10 Cash Sales Rs 4,000.
11 Paid into Bank Rs 3,000.
15 Moni paid into our bank account Rs 1,000.
19 Issued a cheque to Lilly for furniture Rs 2,000.
20 Received from Gopal Rs 500 and discount allowed Rs 50.
22 Withdrew from bank Rs 200.
25 Cash purchase paid by cheque Rs 800.

31 Paid salaries by cheque Rs 1,200. (*B.Com., Madurai*)

[**Ans.** Discount Rs 50 (Dr.) and Rs 100 (Cr.) ; Cash in hand Rs 2,700 ; Cash at bank Rs 4,800]

2. Enter the following transactions in cash book with Discount, Cash and Bank columns :

2004

Dec. 1 Cash in hand Rs 16,000.

2 Opened a bank account with Rs 7,000.

3 Cash purchases Rs 600.

4 Received a cheque of Rs 400 from Prabhakar and gave him a discount of Rs 25. Cheques deposited with bank.

6 Cash sales Rs 1,200.

7 Received a cheque of Rs 100 from Venu for interest.

9 Salary paid to the manager by cheque Rs 450.

11 Withdrew from bank for personal use Rs 300.

15 Purchased a bicycle for office use Rs 300.

18 Paid office rent Rs 80.

20 Sold goods for cash Rs 900.

22 Purchased Government Bonds for Rs 700.

25 Paid travelling allowance to the manager Rs 150.

27 Received Commission Rs 175.

28 Gave a cheque to Ajantha for advertisement Rs 50.

29 The cheque received from Prabhakar on 4th Dec. was dishonoured.

31 Cash in excess of Rs. 2,000 was paid into the bank. (*B.Com,, Madras, Marathwada*)

[**Ans.** Discount Rs 25 (Dr.) Rs 25 (Cr.) ; Cash deposited on 31st Dec. Rs 7,545 ; Cash in hand Rs 2,000 ; Cash at Bank Rs 13,745]

3. From the following particulars, prepare a Three-Column Cash Book of Ram Prasad.

2004

Sept. 1 Cash in hand Rs 2,500 and at Bank Rs 1,700.

3 Received Cash from Lal Rs 290 ; discount allowed Rs 10.

4 Deposited into bank Rs 1,100.

5 Paid Ramlal Rs 395 ; discount received Rs 5.

6 Received a cheque from Janata Store Rs 400 and deposited with bank.

7 Bought goods Rs 375 and paid by cheque.

8 Cash sales Rs 900 of which Rs 800 were banked.

9 Drew from bank for office use Rs 175.

11 Paid municipal taxes in cash Rs 160.

12 Sent a cheque to Moonlight Brothers for Rs 375.

14 Received from Verma Stores Rs 1,450 ; discount allowed Rs 50.

17 Purchased an office safe for cash Rs 325.

19 Paid to Trivedi Sons Rs 970 ; discount received Rs 30.

25 Bought goods for cash Rs 1,000.

25 Bought goods by cheque Rs 750.

29 Sold goods to Ram for Rs 500 for which received a draft. Draft sent to bank.

30 Paid salaries in cash Rs 150.

30 Paid rent by cheque Rs 125.

30 Paid wages in cash Rs 25. (*B.Com., Madurai*)

[**Ans.** Discount Rs 60 (Dr.) ; Rs 35 (Cr.) ; Cash in hand Rs 390 ; Cash at bank Rs 2,700]

4. Following particulars are available for the month of December 2004 of Ram Seth & Sons. Enter the transactions in Three-Column Cash Book.

2004

Dec. 1 Cash in hand Rs 700 ; Bank overdraft Rs 900.
3 Received Cash from Prasad Rs 790 ; discount allowed Rs 10.
4 Deposited into bank Rs 800.
5 Paid to Lal Rs 675 in full settlement of his account for Rs 700.
6 Cash Sales Rs 900.
7 Purchased and paid for the same by cheque Rs 500.
9 Deposited into the bank Rs 600.
11 Received from Mohan a cheque for Rs 400 and deposited into the Bank.
13 Received cash from Ram Rs 695 ; discount allowed Rs 5.
17 Sold goods to Shyam for Rs 1,000 and received a cheque for the same and sent it on the same day to bank.
19 Purchased furniture for Rs 150 and issued a cheque for the same.
20 Cash sales Rs 900.
21 Cash purchases Rs 700.
23 Drew from bank for office use Rs 500.
30 Paid for advertisement in cash Rs 530.
30 Paid to Sohan Rs 650 by cheque ; discount received Rs 20.
31 Paid for postage in cash Rs 15. (*B.Com., Madurai*)

[**Ans.** Discount : Rs 15 (Dr.) and Rs 45 (Cr.) ; Cash Rs 1,165 (Dr.) ; Bank Rs 100 (Dr.)]

5. Write down the following transactions in a cash book with Discount, Cash and Bank columns.

2004

July 1 Cash balance Rs 5,600.
Bank balance Rs 11,800.
2 Cash sales Rs 3,800.
3 Deposited into the bank Rs 4,000.
4 Issued a cheque to A for Rs 2,920 in full settlement of Rs 3,000.
5 Purchased from B for Rs 1,500 for which issued a cheque.
6 Sold goods to C for Rs 2,000 for which received cash Rs 700, a cheque for Rs 900 and for the remaining drew a bill for Rs 400. Cheque sent to Bank.
7 Paid D by cheque Rs 500.
9 Received a cheque from E for Rs 1,100 in full settlement of Rs 1,200.
10 Drew from the bank for office use Rs 200.
12 The cheque of E was deposited into the bank.
13 Paid F by cheque Rs 475 ; discount allowed Rs 25.
14 The bill of C was discounted at the bank for a discount of Rs 35 and cash deposited into the bank.
17 Paid sundry expenses Rs 20.
18 E's cheque was returned by the bank dishonoured and the discount disallowed.
19 Cash sales paid into the bank Rs 740.
23 Purchased stationery Rs 100.
25 Withdrew from the bank for personal use Rs 600.
27 Received from G a cheque of Rs 460 ; discount allowed Rs 40.
28 Bought goods for cash Rs 800.
29 Drew from bank for office use Rs 500.

30 Paid rent Rs 250.

31 Paid into Bank Rs 5,000. *(B. Com. Jabalpur)*

[**Ans.** Discount Rs 175 (Dr.) and Rs 205 (Cr.) ; Cash in hand Rs 1,090 ; Cash at bank Rs 16,110]

6. Mr. Ram operates two Bank Accounts which are maintained in the columnar Cash Book itself. You are required to draw up a proforma of the Cash Book and record therein the following transactions relating to 29th February and close the Cash Book for the day.

1. Opening Balances :
   Cash Rs 150
   National Bank Rs 11,240 (Overdraft)
   Overseas Bank Rs 35,460
2. Received cheque for Rs 1,250 in respect of sales for realising which the National Bank charged Rs 12 and credited the balance.
3. Purchased goods for Rs 13,210 and a cheque issued on the Overseas Bank. The Bank charged Rs 13 for collection of the cheque to the concerned party.
4. Paid Rs 45 for office expenses and Rs 16 for stationery.
5. Out of cash sales of Rs 13,265 a sum of Rs 10,000 was deposited in the National Bank.
6. A purchase of Rs 15,000 was made from Mr. Martin, who sent the documents relating to the goods through the Overseas Bank for 90% of their value. The Bank charged Rs 115 for releasing the documents.
7. Withdrew Rs 5,000 from the Overseas Bank.
8. A Bill Receivable for Rs 10,000 was discounted with the Overseas Bank which charges 1% towards discounting.
9. Deposited Rs 5,000 in National Bank.
10. A demand draft was purchased for Rs 3,000 from a bank after paying Rs 2 towards their charges and paid to the Electricity Department as deposit.
11. An amount of Rs 1,500 was withdrawn from the Overseas Bank and paid salaries.
12. Manager's salary of Rs 1,000 was paid by cheque drawn on National Bank.
13. Interest of Rs 122 and Rs 50 was credited and debited respectively by the Overseas Bank and National Bank.
14. Overseas Bank collected dividends of Rs 1,250 and sent a credit note.
15. An amount of Rs 1,500 was transferred from Overseas Bank to the National Bank. *(C.A.)*

[**Ans.** Cash in hand Rs 352 ; Cash at National Bank Rs 5,448 ; Cash at Overseas Bank Rs 11,907]

7. Enter the following transactions in a Cash Book with Discount, Cash and Bank Columns and Balance the Cash Book on 30th September :

Sept. 1 Balance of cash on hand Rs 400 and Bank Overdraft Rs 5,000.

4 Introduced cash Rs 10,000 as further capital of which Rs 5,000 was deposited into Bank.

5 Sold goods for cash Rs 3,000.

6 Collected from Xaviour Rs 8,000 by cheque and allowed him a discount of Rs 200. Deposited the same on the day.

10 Purchased goods for cash Rs 2,000 and by cheque Rs 3,000.

11 Paid Ram Rs 2,500 by cheque and discount received Rs 100.

12 Paid commission to an agent Rs 500.

15 Purchased office furniture by cash Rs 2,000.

16 Paid Rent Rs 100.

17 Drew a cheque for personal use Rs 1,000.

18 Cash Sales Rs 5,000.

20 Collected from Yogi Rs 4,000 in cash and deposited into the Bank on the same day.

23 Dividend received by cheque Rs 100 and deposited into the Bank.

28 Paid office salaries by cheque Rs 2,000.

29 Deposited cash into the Bank Rs 7,000. *(CAIIB)*

[Ans. Discount Rs 200 (Dr.) Rs 100 (Cr.) ; Cash in hand Rs 1,800 ; Cash at Bank Rs 10,600]

8. Prepare columnar Petty Cash Book of Ram Ltd. for the month of January under the Impress system. The Petty Cash limit fixed was Rs 250 and the cashier draws money under the Imprest cash system as and when the balance available with him is below Rs 50. The Petty Cash transactions for the month of January are given below :

Jan.	1	Paid Opening balance	Rs 250.00
	2	Paid towards conveyance charges	Rs 42.00
	3	Purchase of stationery	Rs 83.00
	3	Wages to sweeper	Rs 21.00
	5	Paid towards conveyance charges	Rs 62.00
	7	Postage stamps purchased	Rs 110.00
	9	Wages to sweeper	Rs 42.00
	10	Telegram charges paid	Rs 9.50
	16	Conveyance charges paid	Rs 22.50
	19	Postage stamps purchased	Rs 49.00
	19	Wages to sweeper	Rs 81.00
	19	Telegram charges paid	Rs 14.00
	22	Entertainment expenses	Rs 31.00
	25	Wages to sweeper	Rs 63.00
	28	Postage stamps purchased	Rs 36.00
	28	Taxi charges paid	Rs 27.50
	31	Entertainment expenses	Rs 31.00
	31	Wages to sweeper	Rs 42.00

(CAIIB)

[Ans. Cash in hand Rs 149.50]

9. Record the following transactions in their proper subsidiary books, post them to ledger and prepare the trail balance :

			Rs
Sept.	1	Sold to Raman at 10% trade discount	5,000
	3	Kesavan sold us goods at 20% trade discount	3,000
	4	Sold to Narayanan	1,000
	6	Purchased goods from Madhavan at a trade discount of 15%	2,000
	9	Goods returned by Raman	500
	10	Purchased goods from Govindan	1,700
	12	Returned goods to Kesavan	300
	14	Sold to Narayanan at 10% trade discount	1,500
	15	Purchases from Kesavan (Net value)	1,000
	18	Narayanan returned a part of the goods sold to him on 14th Sept.	300
	22	Returned goods to Kesavan (a part of 15th Sept. purchases)	100
	27	Goods purchased from Madhavan	400
	29	Sold to Narayanan (at 10% trade discount)	500
	30	Returned goods to Madhavan	40

(B.A., Madurai)

[Ans. Trail Balance Rs 14,500]

10. Write up a Triple Column Cash Book from the following transactions :

July 1 Cash in hand Rs 450 and cash at Bank Rs 6,500.

2 Received a cheque from Krishna (in full settlement of a debt of Rs 650) Rs 620

3 Cash sales Rs 250.

3 Paid for advertising by cheque Rs 350.

3 Paid wages Rs 435.

4 Amount drawn from Bank for office Rs 600.

5 Drawn cash by Proprietor Rs 200.

6 Issued a cheque to Rao (discount received Rs 25) Rs 1,000.

8 Received a cheque from Mohan (discount allowed Rs 20) Rs 800.

10 Sale of machine, settlement by cheque Rs 2,500.

12 Bank returns cheque of Mohan.

15 New machine purchased and cheque issued Rs 10,000
Paid installation expenses by cash Rs 500
Bank charges as per pass book Rs 10. (*B.Com., Madurai*)

[**Ans.** Discount Rs 50 (Dr.) Rs 45 (Cr.) ; Cash in hand Rs 165 ; Cash at Bank Rs 2,340 (OD)]

Chapter 3

Trial Balance

Objects – Method of Preparing Trial Balance – How to Locate Errors – Hints for the Preparation of Trial Balance – Questions – Objective Type Questions – Theoretical Questions – Practical Problems.

The fundamental principle of the double entry system of accounting is that for every debit entry there must be a corresponding credit entry. In the preparation of journals as well as ledgers, both aspects of a transaction are taken into account. Thus, for every debit or a series of debits given to one or several accounts, there is a corresponding credit or a series of credits of an equal amount given to some other account or accounts and vice versa. This implies that in case of journal, the total of the debit amount column must be equal to the total of the credit amount column. If journal entries are correctly posted to different ledger accounts, the total of all debit postings in the ledger must be equal to the total of all credit postings in the ledger. Instead of taking the totals of debit and credit entries in the ledger, if we take only the debit and credit balances of all the ledger accounts, the two totals must agree. If the debit totals or balances do not tally with the credit totals or balances, it means that some mistake has crept in. For instance, all the entries from the prime book might not have been correctly transferred into the ledger accounts or one aspect of the journal entry might not have been posted into the ledger or if posted, wrong amount might have been posted in the amount column. Efforts must be made to locate the error and to rectify it.

Books of accounts of a firm are closed at the end of the year, but they may be closed at any time according to the requirements of the proprietor. Whenever books are closed, balances are found out in various accounts and then, these balances are recorded in a statement which has four columns, *viz.*, Particulars, L.F., Debit Balances and Credit Balances and this statement is called TRIAL BALANCE. Thus, *Trial Balance is a statement in which the debit and credit balances of all accounts are recorded with a view to ascertain the arithmetical accuracy of the books of accounts*. The only condition is that accounts must be balanced in order to draw a Trial Balance. Trial Balance is not a part of journal or ledger. *It is only a list or statement.* No posting can ever be made to a trial balance. Note that although its disagreement always signals the presence of an error, its agreement does not assure a conclusive proof as to the absolute accuracy of the books.

OBJECTS

The objects of the preparation of Trial Balance are as follows :

1. A Trial Balance provides a good check on the accuracy of the work done in preparing the ledger accounts. *When the total of the debit balances agrees with the total of credit balances, it is quite a good proof that the ledger accounts have been correctly written up*. If the trial balance totals do not agree, then it shows that there are some errors which must be detected and rectified, before final accounts are prepared.

2. It brings together the balances of all the accounts at one place and thus facilitates the preparing of trading acount and Profit and Loss Account, which is the result of the business ; and the Balance Sheet to ascertain the financial position of the firm. In short, *Trial Balance is the basis to prepare the final accounts.*

3. The balance of any account can be easily and conveniently known by a trial balance.

4. It serves as a summary of what is contained in the ledger.

METHOD OF PREPARING TRIAL BALANCE

A trial balance refers to a list of the ledger balances, as on a particular date. It can be prepared in the following manners :

1. The Total Method

According to this method, debit total and credit total of each account of ledger are recorded in the trial balance.

2. The Balance Method

According to this method, only the balances of the accounts either debit or credit, as the case may be, are recorded against their respective accounts.

The second method is the most common and is considered to be better, because a trial balance prepared according to this method supplies ready figures for final accounts. The illustration explains the methods :

Trial balance can be prepared on a loose sheet having four columns. A specimen is given below:

Trial Balance of .... as on ....

S.No.	*Name of Account*	*Dr. Balance Rs.*	*Cr. Balance Rs.*

ILLUSTRATION 3.1

Journalise the following transactions, post them into ledger and prepare the Trial Balance.

2013

July	1	Started business with Rs 50,000 of which Rs 20,000 is deposited into bank.
	2	Bought furniture for cash Rs 5,000 and machinery for Rs 8,000.
	4	Purchased goods for cash Rs 14,000.
	6	Sold goods for cash 8,000.
	8	Purchased goods from Mahesh & Co., for Rs 11,000 on credit.
	9	Paid telephone rent for the year by cheque Rs 500.
	10	Bought one typewriter for Rs 2,000 from Typewriter Company on credit.
	11	Sold goods to Ram for Rs 12,000.
	12	Sold goods to Kumar for Rs 2,000 for cash.
	13	Amount withdrawn for personal use Rs 2,000.
	15	Withdrew from Bank for office use Rs 3,500.
	18	Received from Ram cash Rs 11,900 and allowed him discount of Rs 100.
	20	Paid into the bank Rs 5,900.
	25	Goods worth Rs 1,000 returned to Mahesh & Co., and the balance settled by issuing a cheque.
	28	Bought goods worth Rs 3,000 from Ram and supplied them to Babu for Rs 3,500.
	30	Babu returned goods worth Rs 350, which in turn is returned to Ram.
	30	Paid cash for stationery Rs 500 and postage Rs 325.

SOLUTION

Journal Entries

Date	*Particulars*		*L.F.*	*Debit Amount Rs*	*Credit Amount Rs*
2013	Cash Account	Dr.		50,000	
July 1	To Capital Account				50,000
	(Being Cash brought in as Capital)				
1	Bank Account	Dr.		20,000	
	To Cash Account				20,000
	(Being Cash deposited into the bank)				

Date	Particulars		L.F.	Debit Amount Rs	Credit Amount Rs
2	Furniture Account	Dr.		5,000	
	Machinery Account	Dr.		8,000	
	To Cash Account				13,000
	(Being Furniture and machinery purchased)				
4	Purchase Account	Dr.		14,000	
	To Cash Account				14,000
	(Being Goods purchased for cash)				
6	Cash Account	Dr.		8,000	
	To Sales Account				8,000
	(Being Goods sold for cash)				
8	Purchase Account	Dr.		11,000	
	To Mahesh & Co. Account				11,000
	(Being Goods purchased on credit)				
9	Telephone Rent Account	Dr.		500	
	To Bank Account				500
	(Being Telephone rent paid by cheque)				
10	Typewriter Account	Dr.		2,000	
	To Typewriter Co. A/c				2,000
	(Being Purchased a typewriter on credit)				
11	Ram Account	Dr.		12,000	
	To Sales Account				12,000
	(Being Goods sold on Credit)				
12	Cash Account	Dr.		2,000	
	To Sales Account				2,000
	(Being Goods sold for Cash)				
13	Drawings Account	Dr.		2,000	
	To Bank Account				2,000
	(Being Amount withdrawn from bank for personal use)				
15	Cash Account	Dr.		3,500	
	To Bank Account				3,500
	(Being Amount drawn for office use)				
18	Cash Account	Dr.		11,900	
	Discount Account	Dr.		100	
	To Ram Account				12,000
	(Being Cash received and discount allowed)				
20	Bank Account	Dr.		5,900	
	To Cash Account				5,900
	(Being Cash deposited into the bank)				
25	Mahesh & Co. Account	Dr.		11,000	
	To Purchase Return Account				1,000
	To Bank Account				10,000
	(Being Goods returned for Rs 1,000 and balance settled by cheque)				

Date	Particulars		L.F.	Debit Amount Rs	Credit Amount Rs
28	Purchase Account	Dr.		3,000	
	To Ram Account				3,000
	(Being Goods bought from Ram)				
28	Babu Account	Dr.		3,500	
	To Sales Account				3,500
	(Being Goods sold on credit)				
30	Sales Returns Account	Dr.		350	
	To Babu Account				350
	(Being Goods returned by Babu)				
30	Ram Account	Dr.		300	
	To Purchase Returns A/c				300
	(Being Goods returned at cost)				
30	Stationery Account	Dr.		500	
	Postage Account	Dr.		325	
	To Cash Account				825
	(Being cash paid for Stationary and Postage)				

LEDGER

Dr. **Cash Account** Cr.

Date	Particulars	L.F.	Amount Rs	Date	Particulars	L.F.	Amount Rs
2004				2004			
July 1	To Capital A/c		50,000	July 1	By Bank A/c		20,000
6	To Sales A/c		8,000	2	By Furniture A/c		5,000
12	To Sales A/c		2,000	2	By Machinery A/c		8,000
15	To Bank A/c		3,500	4	By Purchase A/c		14,000
18	To Ram A/c		11,900	20	By Bank A/c		5,900
				30	By Stationery A/c		500
				30	By Postage A/c		325
				31	By Balance c/d		21,675
			75,400				75,400
Aug. 1	To Balance b/d		21,675				

Dr. **Capital Account** Cr.

Date	Particulars	L.F.	Amount	Date	Particulars	L.F.	Amount
2004			Rs	2004			Rs
July 31	To Balance c/d		50,000	July 1	By Cash A/c		50,000
			50,000				50,000
				Aug. 1	By Balance b/d		50,000

Dr. **Bank Account** Cr.

Date	Particulars	L.F.	Amount	Date	Particulars	L.F.	Amount
2004			Rs	2004			Rs
July 1	To Cash A/c		20,000	July 9	By Telephone Rent A/c		500
20	To Cash A/c		5,900	13	By Drawings A/c		2,000

Date	Particulars	J.F.	Rs	Date	Particulars	J.F.	Rs
				15	By Cash A/c		3,500
				25	By Mahesh & Co. A/c		10,000
				31	By Balance c/d		9,900
			25,900				25,900
Aug. 1	To Balance b/d		9,900				

Dr. **Furniture Account** Cr.

Date	Particulars	J.F.	Rs	Date	Particulars	J.F.	Rs
2004			Rs	2004			Rs
July 2	To Cash A/c		5,000	July 31	By Balance c/d		5,000
			5,000				5,000
Aug. 1	To Balance b/d		5,000				

Dr. **Machinery Account** Cr.

Date	Particulars	J.F.	Rs	Date	Particulars	J.F.	Rs
2004			Rs	2004			Rs
July 2	To Cash A/c		8,000	July 31	By Balance c/d		8,000
			8,000				8,000
Aug. 1	To Balance b/d		8,000				

Dr. **Purchase Account** Cr.

Date	Particulars	J.F.	Rs	Date	Particulars	J.F.	Rs
2004			Rs	2004			Rs
July 4	To Cash A/c		14,000	July 31	By Balance c/d		28,000
8	To Mahesh A/c		11,000				
28	To Ram A/c		3,000				
			28,000				28,000
Aug. 1	To Balance b/d		28,000				

Dr. **Sales Account** Cr.

Date	Particulars	J.F.	Rs	Date	Particulars	J.F.	Rs
2004			Rs	2004			Rs
July 31	To Balance c/d		25,500	July 6	By Cash A/c		8,000
				11	By Ram A/c		12,000
				12	By Cash A/c		2,000
				28	By Babu A/c		3,500
			25,500				25,500
				Aug. 1	By Balance b/d		25,500

Dr. **Mahesh & Co. Account** Cr.

Date	Particulars	J.F.	Rs	Date	Particulars	J.F.	Rs
2004			Rs	2004			Rs
July 25	To Purchase Return A/c		1,000	July 8	By Purchase A/c		11,000
25	To Bank A/c		10,000				
			11,000				11,000

Dr. **Telephone Rent Account** Cr.

Date	Particulars	J.F.	Rs	Date	Particulars	J.F.	Rs
2004			Rs	2004			Rs
July 9	To Bank A/c		500	July 31	By Balance c/d		500
			500				500
Aug. 1	To Balance b/d		500				

Dr. **Typewriter Account** Cr.

Date	Particulars	J.F.	Rs	Date	Particulars	J.F.	Rs
2004			Rs	2004			Rs
July 10	To Typewriter Co. A/c		2,000	July 31	By Balance c/d		2,000
			2,000				2,000
Aug. 1	To Balance b/d		2,000				

Dr. **Typewriter Co. Account** Cr.

Date	Particulars	J.F.	Rs	Date	Particulars	J.F.	Rs
2004			Rs	2004			Rs
July 31	To Balance c/d		2,000	July 10	By Typewriter A/c		2,000
			2,000				2,000
				Aug. 1	By Balance b/d		2,000

Dr. **Ram Account** Cr.

Date	Particulars	J.F.	Rs	Date	Particulars	J.F.	Rs
2004			Rs	2004			Rs
July 11	To Sales A/c		12,000	July 18	By Cash A/c		11,900
30	To Purchase Returns A/c		300	18	By Discount A/c		100
31	To Balance c/d		2,700	28	By Purchase A/c		3,000
			15,000				15,000
				Aug. 1	By Balance b/d		2,700

Dr. **Drawings Account** Cr.

Date	Particulars	J.F.	Rs	Date	Particulars	J.F.	Rs
2004			Rs	2004			Rs
July 13	To Bank A/c		2,000	July 31	By Balance c/d		2,000
			2,000				2,000
Aug. 1	To Balance b/d		2,000				

Dr. **Discount Account** Cr.

Date	Particulars	J.F.	Rs	Date	Particulars	J.F.	Rs
2004			Rs	2004			Rs
July 18	To Ram A/c		100	July 31	By Balance c/d		100
			100				100
Aug. 1	To Balance c/d		100				

Dr. **Purchase Returns Account** Cr.

Date	Particulars	J.F.	Rs	Date	Particulars	J.F.	Rs
2004			Rs	2004			Rs
July 31	To Balance c/d		1,300	July 25	By Mahesh & Co. A/c		1,000
				30	By Ram A/c		300
			1,300				1,300
				Aug. 1	To Balance b/d		1,300

Dr. **Babu Account** Cr.

Date	Particulars	J.F.	Rs	Date	Particulars	J.F.	Rs
2004			Rs	2004			Rs
July 28	To Sales A/c		3,500	July 30	By Sales Returns A/c		350
					By Balance c/d		3,150
			3,500				3,500
Aug. 1	To Balance b/d		3,150				

Dr. **Sales Returns Account** Cr.

Date	Particulars		Amount	Date	Particulars		Amount
2004			Rs	2004			Rs
July 30	To Babu A/c		350	July 31	By Balance c/d		350
			350				350
Aug. 1	To Balance b/d		350				

Dr. **Stationery Account** Cr.

Date	Particulars		Amount	Date	Particulars		Amount
2004			Rs	2004			Rs
July 30	To Cash A/c		500	July 31	By Balance c/d		500
			500				500
Aug. 1	To Balance b/d		500				

Dr. **Postage Account** Cr.

Date	Particulars		Amount	Date	Particulars		Amount
2004			Rs	2004			Rs
July 30	To Cash A/c		325	July 31	By Balance c/d		325
			325				325
Aug. 1	To Balance b/d		325				

Trial Balance as on 31st July, 2004

	Ledger Account	Total Method		Balance Method	
		Debit Total	Credit Total	Debit Total	Credit Total
		Rs	Rs	Rs	Rs
1.	Cash Account	75,400	53,725	21,675	–
2.	Capital Account	–	50,000	–	50,000
3.	Bank Account	25,900	16,000	9,900	–
4.	Furniture Account	5,000	–	5,000	–
5.	Machinery Account	8,000	–	8,000	–
6.	Purchase Account	28,000	–	28,000	–
7.	Sales Account	–	25,500	–	25,500
8.	Mahesh & Co. Account	11,000	11,000	–	–
9.	Telephone Rent Account	500	–	500	–
10.	Typewriter Account	2,000	–	2,000	–
11.	Typewriter Co. Account		2,000		2,000
12.	Ram Account	12,300	15,000		2,700
13.	Drawings Account	2,000	–	2,000	–
14.	Discount Account	100	–	100	–
15.	Purchase Returns Account	–	1,300	–	1,300
16.	Babu Account	3,500	350	3,150	–
17.	Sales Returns Account	350	–	350	–
18.	Stationery Account	500	–	500	–
19	Postage Account	325	–	325	–
		1,74,875	1,74,875	81,500	81,500

Is Trial Balance a conclusive proof of the accuracy of books of accounts ? *The agreement of a trial balance is not a conclusive proof as to the absolute accuracy of the books.* There is always the possibility of some mistakes being committed while writing up the books of accounts. Although a trial balance gives a prima facie evidence that the accounts are correct from the arithmetical point of view, it does not necessarily mean that the books of accounts are free from errors, *i.e.*, *agreement of trial balance itself is not the conclusive proof that everything in the accounts is alright*. We explain below what errors are disclosed, and what errors are not disclosed by a trial balance.

Advantages of Drawing up Trial Balance

1. *It summarises the result of all transactions* during a period.
2. *It proves the arithmetical accuracy* of accounting entries in the ledger.
3. It supplies in one place *ready reference of all the balances* of all the ledger accounts.
4. If any error is found, *it can easily be rectified.*
5. It is a basis, on which *the final accounts of a firm can be prepared.*

A Trial Balance will not disclose the following errors

The Trial Balance is not absolute proof of the accuracy of ledger accounts. It is a proof only of the arithmetical accuracy of the postings. The total of debits may be equal to the total of credits yet still there may be errors. Such errors are not disclosed by a trial balance ; and they are:

1. Errors of Principle. An error of principle is an error which violates the fundamentals of book-keeping. For instance, purchase of furniture is debited to Purchase Account, instead of Furniture Account ; Wages paid for the erection of plant is debited to Wages Account, instead of Plant Account; the amount spent on extension of building is debited to Repairs Account instead of Building Account etc. These types of errors do not affect the total debits and total credits but affect the principle of book-keeping.

2. Errors of Omission. If a transaction is completely omitted, there will be no effect on the Trial Balance. When a transaction goes completely unrecorded in both aspects or a transaction after being recorded in the books of primary entry is not at all posted in the ledger, the error is an error of omission. For instance, if a credit purchase is omitted to be recorded in the Purchase Day Book, then it will be omitted to be posted both in the Purchase Account and the Supplier's Account. This error will not, however, result in the disagreement of Trial Balance.

3. Posting to Wrong Account. Posting an item to wrong account, but on the correct side. For instance, if a purchase of Rs 200 from Ramu has been credited to Raman, instead of Ramu and this error will not affect the agreement of Trial Balance. Thus, Trial Balance will not detect such an error.

4. Error of Amounts in Original Book. If an invoice for Rs 632 is entered in Sales Book as Rs 623, the Trial Balance will come out correctly, since the debit and credit have been recorded as Rs 623. The arithmetical accuracy is there, but in fact there is an error.

5. Compensating Errors. If one account in the ledger is debited with Rs 500 less and another account in the ledger is credited Rs 500 less, these errors cancel themselves. That is, one error is neutralised by similar error on the opposite side.

A Trial Balance will disclose the following errors

If the Trial Balance does not agree, there must have been some error or errors somewhere in our working. The following are some of the errors, which cause the Trial Balance to disagree, in brief :

1. Wrong Totalling of Subsidiary Books. If the total of any subsidiary book is wrongly cast, it would cause a disagreement in the Trial Balance. For instance, Sales book has been undercast by Rs 100. From the Sales book, all the personal accounts have been debited correctly but mistake occurred only in Sales Account, to the extent of Rs 100 (Less). Thus, the Trial Balance disagrees to the extent of Rs 100 ; credit side falls short of the amount.

2. Posting of the Wrong Amount. If a wrong amount is posted in one of the two accounts, the Trial Balance disagrees. For instance sales made to Ram for Rs 570, wrongly debited to Ram's Account with Rs 750, instead of Rs 570. Ram's account has been overdebited by Rs 180. Thus, the debit side of the Trial Balance will exceed by Rs 180, *i.e.*, 750 – 570 = 180.

3. Posting an Amount on the Wrong side of the Account. For instance, a credit sales made to a customer for Rs 500 has been credited to the customer account, instead of debit. As a result of this error, the credit side of the Trial Balance will exceed by Rs 1,000 (double the amount of the error) because there are two credits—one in Sales Account and another in Personal Account and no debit for the transaction.

4. Posting Twice to a Ledger. For instance, salary of Rs 500 paid has been debited to Salary Account twice by mistake. This will cause disagreement of Trial Balance in debit side by excess of Rs 500.

Apart from the above, the following are some of the common errors, by which Trial balance totals disagree.

5. Omission of an Account from the Trial Balance (Cash, Bank etc.)
6. Wrong additions or balancing of ledger accounts.
7. Balance of account written to the wrong side of the Trial Balance.
8. Errors made in preparing the list of Debtors and Creditors.
9. Errors made in carrying forward the total from one page to another page.
10. There may be some items to which double entry is incomplete.
11. Wrong totals of the Trial Balance.

How to Locate Errors

Some errors are disclosed by a Trial Balance while some errors are not. If the Trial Balance does not agree, it is an indication of some error or errors in the books of account. The checking usually begins from the Trial Balance itself. The following steps should be taken to locate the errors and the step may be taken one after another until the errors that cause the difference are located.

(1) Retotal the debit and credit columns of the Trial Balance. Find out the amount of difference by the two columns, divided by 2 and see similar amount appears in the Trial Balance. If similar figure exists, see whether it is in the correct column. It is also possible that such a balance might have been recorded on the wrong side, causing a difference of double the amount.

(2) See that Cash balance and Bank balance are properly listed in the Trial Balance.

(3) If still the difference exists, divide the difference by 9. If the difference is evenly divisible by 9, the error is likely to occur from the transposition or transplacement of figures. Disarrangement of figures is transposition and transplacement means the digits of the numbers are moved to the left or right.

	Transposition Error		Transplacement Error	
If	6418		67.180	
is written as	4618		6.718	
Difference is	1800		60.462	
A Complete division is possible, thus,	$\frac{1800}{9}$	= 200	$\frac{60.462}{9}$	= 6.718

If such a difference exists, search the figures, where such errors might have been made.

(4) Confirm that the opening balances have been correctly brought forward in the current year, from the previous year.

(5) Recheck the amounts listed in the Trial balance and confirm that all the ledger balances have been copied down.

(6) Check the totals in the lists of Sundry Debtors and Sundry Creditors.

(7) Recompute the Account balances.

(8) Check the casting and carry forward of all subsidiary books.

(9) Verify the postings of individual items from the subsidiary books.

(10) After making complete checking of journal, ledger and subsidiary books, if the errors cannot be located, then transfer the difference to a Suspense Account and when the mistake is found out the Suspense Account is closed.

Hints for the Preparation of Trial Balance

When all transactions for a particular period are entered in subsidiary records and posted to their respective accounts in the ledger, they are balanced by casting their two sides by striking the difference. Then, a list of these balances is prepared by grouping all debit balances on the left-hand side and credit balances on the right-hand side and both sides are totalled. It is important to note that transactions for a period may be numerous, vouchers relating to them may heap up into huge files, the entries and postings may run into hundreds of pages, but the essentials (balances) are comprised into a small list of balances and the list of balances is called *trial balance.*

The parties to whom we sell out goods on credit are our debtors. In business, credit purchases and credit sales are common. Thus, when we sold goods on credit to our customers and, if not yet settled, their accounts show a debit balance. If these debit balances are shown individually, it is cumbersome and unwieldy as the individual debits run into a number of pages. In order to avoid this, the amount of such personal (debtors) accounts, which shows a debit balance, are totalled and this consolidated total figure is shown in trial balance as *Sundry Debtors*, as a single item. Similarly, the parties from whom we have bought goods on credit are our creditors. If we have not paid off, their accounts show a credit balance. The amount of such personal accounts, which shows credit balances are totalled and this consolidated total figure is shown in trial balance as *Sundry Creditors* as a single item.

A Trial Balance is a summary of all the ledger balances outstanding as on a particular date. The debit balances of the accounts are to be written in debit column whereas credit balances of the accounts are to be written in the credit column. Dr. and Cr. have been given within brackets in the following chart which are of great help in preparing Trial Balance.

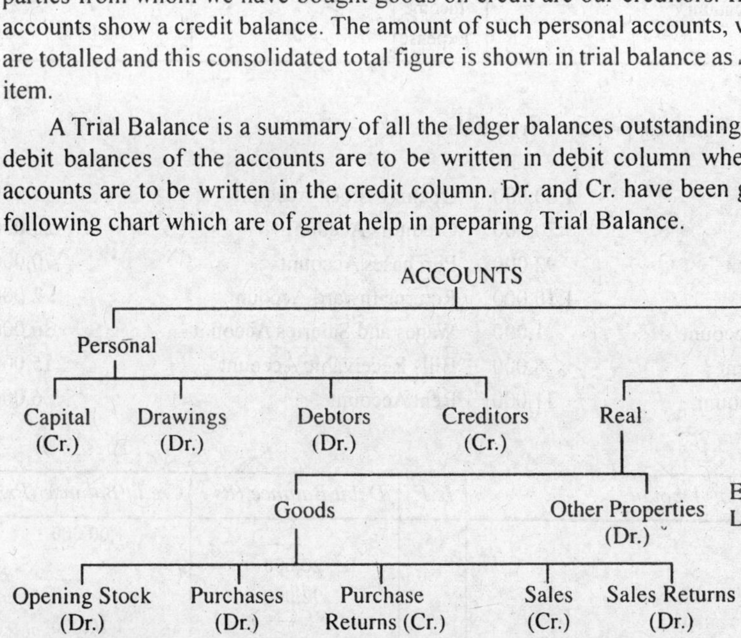

The following principles may also be followed :

1. **Debit Side.** (*a*) Assets, (*b*) Expenses, (*c*) Losses, (*d*) Drawings, (*e*) Debtors
2. **Credit Side.** (*a*) Liabilities, (*b*) Incomes, (*c*) Gains, (*d*) Creditors.

ILLUSTRATION 3.2

State whether the balances of the following accounts should be placed in debit column or credit column of the Trial Balance.

1. Plant and Machinery
2. Fumiture
3. Salary
4. Discount Allowed

5. Bank Overdraft
6. Cash in hand
7. Creditors
8. Sundry Debtors
9. Carriage Inwards
10. Carriage Outwards
11. Sales
12. Purchases
13. Discount Received
14. Interest Paid

SOLUTION

Sl. No.	*Heads of Account*	L.F.	*Debit Balance (Rs.)*	*Credit Balance (Rs.)*
1.	Plant and Machinery Account	Asset	✓	
2.	Furniture Accout	Asset	✓	
3.	Salary Account	Expense	✓	
4.	Discount Allowed Account	Expense	✓	
5.	Bank Overdraft Account	Liability		✓
6.	Cash in Hand Account	Asset	✓	
7.	Creditors Account	Liability		✓
8.	Sundry Debtors Account	Asset	✓	
9.	Carriage Inward Account	Expense	✓	
10.	Carriage Outward Account	Expense	✓	
11.	Sales Account	Income		✓
12.	Purchases Account	Expense	✓	
13.	Discount Received Account	Income		✓
14.	Interest Pail Account	Expense	✓	

ILLUSTRATION 3.3

From the following list of balances, prepare a Trial Balance.

	Rs		Rs
Capital Account	1,00,000	Opening Stock Account	15,000
Debtors Account	20,000	Creditors Account	20,000
Fixed Assets Account	92,000	Purchases Account	70,000
Sales Account	1,10,000	Returns Inward Account	2,000
Returns Outward Account	1,000	Wages and Salaries Account	30,000
Bills Payable Account	8,000	Bills Receivable Account	15,000
Bank Overdraft Account	11,000	Rent Account	6,000

SOLUTION

Sl. No.	*Heads of Account*	*L.,F.*	*Debit Balance (Rs.)*	*Credit Balance (Rs.)*
1.	Capital Account		—	1,00,000
2.	Debtors Account		20,000	—
3.	Fixed Assets Account		92,000	
4.	Sales Account		—	1,10,000
5.	Returns Outward Account		—	1,000
6.	Bills Payable Account		—	8,000
7.	Bank Ovewrdraft Account			11,000
8.	Opening Stock Account		15,000	
9.	Creditors Account			20,000
10.	Purchases Account		70,000	
11.	Returns Inward Account		2,000	
12.	Wages and Salaries Account		30,000	
13.	Bills Receivable Account		15,000	
14.	Rent Account		6,000	
	Total		2,50,000	2,50,000

ILLUSTRATION 3.4

The following Trial Balance for the year ended 31st December 2004 has been prepared by a non-commerce man. You are asked to re-draft the same by pointing out the mistakes, if any, in each case.

Ledger Balances	*Debit* *Rs*	*Credit* *Rs*
Capital	—	10,000
Discount Allowed	—	1,300
Purchase Returns	1,300	—
Bad Debts Reserve	—	800
Commission Received	2,000	—
Loan Secured	—	10,000
Sales	17,000	—
Insurance Paid	—	1,000
Purchase	11,900	—
Carriage Outward	—	700
Carriage Inward	200	—
Goodwill	—	4,000
Reserve Fund	—	3,000
Miscellaneous Receipt	—	2,400
Deposit with Kumar	12,700	—
Bank Overdraft	5,000	—
Accrued Rent	900	—
General Reserve	—	4,800
Outstanding Salary	—	500
Pre-paid Insurance	—	300
Rent Recoverable	1,000	—
Provision for Discount on Debtors	—	400
Opening Stock	—	15,800
Interest Paid	6,800	—
Interest Received	—	1,000
Bad Debts	—	600
Bad Debts Recovered	—	600
Cash in hand	—	1,600
Total	58,800	58,800

SOLUTION

The correct Trial balance as on 31st Dec. 2004

Ledger Balances	*Debit* *Rs*	*Credit* *Rs*
Capital A/c	—	10,000
Discount Allowed A/c (*a*)	1,300	—
Purchase Returns A/c (*b*)	—	1,300
Bad Debts Reserve A/c	—	800
Commission Received A/c (*c*)	—	2,000
Loan Secured A/c	—	10,000
Sales A/c (*d*)	—	17,000
Insurance Paid A/c (*e*)	1,000	—
Purchases A/c	11,900	—

Carriage Outward A/c (*f*)	700	—
Carriage Inward A/c	200	—
Goodwill A/c (*g*)	4,000	—
Reserve Fund A/c	—	3,000
Miscellaneous Receipt A/c	—	2,400
Deposit with Kumar A/c	12,700	—
Bank Overdraft A/c (*h*)	—	5,000
Accrued Rent A/c	900	—
General Reserve A/c	—	4,800
Outstanding Salary A/c	—	500
Pre-paid Insurance A/c (*i*)	300	—
Rent Recoverable A/c	1,000	—
Provision for Discount on Debtors A/c	—	400
Opening Stock A/c (*j*)	15,800	—
Interest Paid A/c	6,800	—
Interest Received A/c	—	1,000
Bad Debts A/c (*k*)	600	—
Bad Debts Recovered A/c	—	600
Cash in hand A/c (*l*)	1,600	—
Total	58,800	58,800

		Side of T.B.	Reasons
Hints :	(*a*)	Debit	Expenses
	(*b*)	Credit	Goods go out
	(*c*)	Credit	Income
	(*d*)	Credit	Goods go out
	(*e*)	Debit	Expenses
	(*f*)	Debit	Expenses
	(*g*)	Debit	Asset
	(*h*)	Credit	Liability
	(*i*)	Debit	Asset
	(*j*)	Debit	Asset
	(*k*)	Debit	Loss
	(*l*)	Debit	Asset

ILLUSTRATION 3.5

Mr. Gopal is not an export in accounting. He prepared the following trial balance. Capital Account is missing. You are required to correct the trial balance and also find out the Capital Account, which is missing.

S.No.	*Name of Account*	*L.F.*	*Debit Balance Rs*	*Credit Balance Rs*
1.	Capital A/c		–	?
2.	Sales A/c		–	27,560
3.	Sales Returns A/c		–	980
4.	Drawings A/c		5,640	–
5.	Sundry Debtors A/c		–	5,300
6.	Freehold Premises A/c		7,410	–
7.	Purchases A/c		12,680	–
8.	Ruturns Outwards A/c		2,640	–

9.	Loan from Sharma A/c		–	2,500
10.	Sundry Creditors A/c		5,280	–
11.	Administration Expenses A/c		7,840	–
12.	Cash in hand		1,420	–
13.	Bills Payable A/c		1,000	–
14.	Wages A/c		5,980	–
15.	Opening Stock A/c		–	2,640
16.	Factory Expenses A/c		4,650	–
			54,540	54,540

SOLUTION

Corrected Trial Balance

S.No.	*Name of Account*	*L.F.*	*Debit Balance Rs*	*Credit Balance Rs*
1.	Capital A/c (Balancing figure)		–	15,560
2.	Sales A/c		–	27,560
3.	Sales Returns A/c		980	–
4.	Drawings A/c		5,640	–
5.	Sundry Debtors A/c		5,300	–
6.	Freehold Premises A/c		7,410	–
7.	Purchases A/c		12,680	–
8.	Ruturns Outwards A/c		–	2,640
9.	Loan from Sharma A/c		–	2,500
10.	Sundry Creditors A/c		–	5,280
11.	Administration Expenses A/c		7,840	–
12.	Cash in Hand		1,420	–
13.	Bills Payable A/c		–	1,000
14.	Wages A/c		5,980	–
15.	Opening Stock A/c		2,640	–
16.	Factory Expenses A/c		4,650	–
			54,540	54,540

QUESTIONS

OBJECTIVE TYPE QUESTIONS

I. Indicate whether the following statements are True or False :

1. Every kind of error affects the agreement of Trial Balance.
2. A trial balance will not tally if a transaction is omitted.
3. Trial Balance contains various ledger balances on a particular date.
4. Trial Balance is a ledger.
5. The trial balance serves as a summary of what is contained in the ledger accounts.

(*Ans.* 1. False; 2. False; 3. True; 4. False; 5. True.)

II. Choose the correct answer for the following:

1. Errors of carry forward affect:

   (a) Personal Account (b) Impersonal Accounts

   (c) Nominal Account

2. Errors which affect one account can be:

   (a) Errors of omission (b) Errors of principle

   (c) Errors of posting

3. Sales to "A", not recorded in the books. This will affect
   (a) Sales Account (b) "A" Account
   (c) Both the accounts.
4. Trial balance is
   (a) A revenue Statement (b) Ledger Account
   (c) Statement of Ledger Balances
5. Any difference in Trial balance is normally transferred to:
   (a) Capital Account (b) Suspense Account
   (c) Sundry Expense Account

(*Ans.* 1. (b); 2. (c); 3. (c); 4. (c); 5. (b)

THEORETICAL QUESTIONS

1. What is a Trial Balance ?
2. What is the object of preparing a Trial Balance ?
3. What type of errors does a Trial Balance disclose ?
4. Define "Trial Balance". "The mere agreement of Trial Balance does not mean that everything is alright with Accounts." Discuss
5. Enumerate the various kinds of errors committed in writing up a set of books.

PRACTICAL PROBLEMS

1. From the following ledger accounts of Poddar, draw Trial Balance as on 31st December.

	Rs		Rs
House Property	45,000	Repairs	1,200
Furniture	5,000	Rent Received	4,800
Utensils	6,000	Medical Expenses	1,200
Ornaments	25,000	School Fee	1,800
Cash	630	Conveyance	1,350
Bank Balance :		Cosmetics	1,150
Fixed Deposits	20,000	Interest Received	3,000
Savings Bank	3,500	House Building Loan from Govt.	20,000
Shares & Govt. Securities	12,000	Interest paid	1,870
Claims against persons	1,500	Municipal Taxes	3,000
Salary (Income)	24,000	Income-tax	2,500
Servants wages	1,200	Accumulated Fund	88,300
Food and Drink	3,750		
Dress and Clothings	2,450		

(*Tripura H.S.*)

[Ans. Total of Trial Balance : Rs 1,40,100]

2. The following Trial Balance was extracted from the books of a Merchant, although the columns are agreed, yet they are incorrect. You are required to correct and redraft it.

Trial Balance

	Dr.		Cr.
	Rs		Rs
Premises	30,000	Capital	36,800
Machinery	8,500	Fixtures	2,800
Bad Debts	1,400	Sales	52,000
Returns Outwards	1,300	Debtors	30,000

Cash	200	Interest Received	1,300
Discount Received	1,500		
Bank Overdraft	5,000		
Creditors	25,000		
Purchases	50,000		
	1,22,900		1,22,900

[Ans. T.B. Rs 1,22,900]

3. Correct the following Trial balance :

	(Dr.) Rs		(Cr.) Rs
Return Outwards	16,000	Debtors	15,000
Opening Stock	34,200	Carriage Outwards	5,000
Salaries	12,000	Capital	55,200
Creditors	28,000	Machinery	18,000
Bank	45,000	Returns Inward	3,000
Carriage Inwards	6,000	Discount Received	4,000
Rent Received	3,000	Trade Expenses	6000
Discount allowed	2,000	Building	20,000
Purchases	1,00,000	Sales	1,40,000
Bills Payable	20,000		
	2,66,200		2,66,200

(H.S.)

[Ans. Correct Total of Trial Balance Rs 2,66,200]

4. Mr. Blank, a client of yours with whom book-keeping is not a strong point, asks you to audit his accounts for the year ended 31st December 2004, upon which data his Closing Stock was valued at Rs 574.

As a basis for your audit Blank furnishes you with the following statements :

	Dr.	Cr.
	Rs	Rs
Blank Capital	—	1,556
Blank Drawings	564	—
Leasehold Premises	741	—
Sales	—	2,756
Due from Customers	—	530
Purchases	1,268	—
Purchases Return	264	—
Loan from Bank	—	250
Creditors	528	—
Trade Expenses	784	—
Cash at Bank	142	—
Bills Payable	100	—
Salaries & Wages	598	—
Stock (1st January)	—	264
Rent, Rates, etc.	465	—
Sales Return	—	98
	5,454	5,454

If you do not approve this statement, amend it. *(C.A.)*

[Ans. Correct total of the Trial Balance Rs 5,454]

5. Set out below is the Trial Balance of Mr. Baby drawn on 31st December 2004. Redraw it correctly :

Dr.	Rs		Cr. Rs
Capital	80,000	Debtor	75,800
Bad Debts Recovered	2,500	Bank Deposit	27,500
Creditors	12,500	Discounts Allowed	400
Returns Outwards	3,500	Drawings	6,000
Bank Overdraft	15,700	Returns Inwards	4,500
Rent	3,600	Sales	1,46,900
Salaries	8,500	Bills Payable	13,500
Trade Expenses	3,000		
Cash in hand	2,100		
Stock Jan. 2004	24,500		
Purchases	1,18,700		
	2,74,600		2,74,600

(*H.S.*)

[Ans, Corrected T.B. Rs 2,74,600]

6. From the undermentioned balances extracted from the books of a sole trader on 31st December, prepare a Trial Balance as on 31st Dec.

	Rs		Rs
Cash in hand	2,400	Plant & Machinery	1,20,000
Capital	2,00,000	Sales	4,00,000
Purchases	2,40,000	Furniture	30,000
Bills Payable	44,000	Bad Debts Reserve	2,000
Stock (Opening)	70,000	Bills Receivable	40,000
Sundry Debtors	1,00,000	Rent & Taxes	20,000
Sundry Creditors	48,000	Salaries	40,000
Wages	32,000		

(*H.S.*)

[Ans. Total Trial Balance Rs 6,94,400]

7. Prepare a Trial Balance from the following as on 31st Dec. 2004

	Rs		Rs
Cash	370	Land & Buildings	28,000
Opening Stock	5,700	Rent Received	5,000
Debtors	3,200	Electricity	6,500
Sales	63,900	Bills Receivable	1,700
Wages	13,200	Travelling expenses	2,300
Creditors	5,200	Insurance	3,600
Bad Debts Reserve	400	Purchases	12,000
Carriage	300	Purchase Returns	500
Trade Marks	5,300	Discounts (Dr.)	300
Advertising	1,250	Bad debts	700
Salaries	10,900	Bank	8,500
Machinery	28,900	Capital	?

[Ans. Capital Rs 57,720; Trial Balance Total Rs 1,32,720]

8. Prepare a Trial Balance as on 31 Dec., 2004

	Rs		Rs
Stock Jan. 2004	46,000	Sundry Debtors	36,000
Purchases	1,50,200	Sundry Creditors	29,670
Purchase Returns	600	Wages	25,000
Cash in hand	3,400	Salaries	14,000
Bank Balance	22,660	Capital	1,14,000
Freehold Premises	38,600	Income Tax	1,600
Trade Expenses	840	Discount Allowed	6,300
Printing & Stationery	1,640	Discount Received	4,600
Professional Charges	280	Sales Returns	550
Commission Received	3,300	Sales	2,08,950
Investments	4,000	Bills Receivable	3,200
Interest thereof	200	Office Furniture	3,050
		Rent & Rates	4,000

[**Ans.** Trial Balance Total Rs 3,61,320]

9. The following are the balances extracted from the books of Mr. Ram as on 31st August 2004. Prepare a Trial Balance as on 31st Aug., 2004

	Rs		Rs
Capital	20,000	Cash in hand	300
Buildings	15,000	Cash at Bank	4,700
Machinery	10,000	Salaries	14,000
Furniture	1,000	Rent	4,000
Motor Car	8,000	Commission (Dr)	1,400
Opening Stock	16,000	Rates & Taxes	600
Purchases	74,000	Bad Debts	200
Purchase Returns	1,000	Insurance	400
Sales	1,40,000	Discounts earned	500
Sales Returns	500	Discounts allowed	700
Sundry Debtors	15,000	General expenses	800
Sundry Creditors	4,800	Reserve for Bad Debts	300

[**Ans.** Trial Balance Total Rs 1,66,600]

10. Prepare a Trial Balance from the following as on 31st Dec., 2004.

	Rs		Rs
Stock (Jan.)	12,000	Electricity	40
Furniture & Fittings	4,000	Salaries	1,250
Loan from Ram	5,600	Discount Allowed	230
Capital	18,000	Discount Received	180
Drawings	2,120	Sundry Expenses	160
Motor Car	6,000	Postage & Telegrams	76
Sales	12,350	Stationery	200
Sales Returns	250	Carriage	24
Purchases	10,320	Sundry Debtors	3,350
Purchase Returns	280	Sundry Creditors	12,920
Rent	80	Cash at Bank	7,460
Wages	980	Cash in hand	600
Loan Interest	80	Petty Cash in hand	110

[**Ans.** Trial Balance Total Rs 49,330]

11. The undermentioned balances were extracted from the books of Sri Kumar as on 31st March 2005. You are asked to prepare a Trial Balance as on that date.

	Rs
Capital	78,000
Stock 1.4.2004	5,000
Leasehold Premises	46,000
Furniture & Fittings	13,500
Plant & Machinery	35,000
Purchases	78,900
Sales	1,30,620
Discount Received	470
Discount Allowed	540
Carriage Inwards	120
Carriage Outwards	230
Returns Inward	1,500
Returns Outward	380
Wages and Salaries	17,680
Rates and Taxes	1,370
Rent Received	530
Sundry Expenses	1,660
Trade Creditors	22,760
Book Debts	34,000
Drawings	3,000
Bills Payable	1,140
Cash in hand	1,200
Bank Loan	5,800
Closing Stock	3,900

(*H.S.*)

[Ans. Total of Trial Balance Rs 2,39,700]

12. The following Trial Balance for the year ended on 31st December 2004 has been prepared by the accountant of a firm. Re-draft the same and mention the nature of mistake in each case :

	Dr. Rs	Cr. Rs
Closing Stock	10,100	—
Capital Accounts :		
A (Overdrawn)		3,000
B	5,450	—
Cash in Hand	1,400	—
Bank Overdraft	9,320	—
Sales	—	1,26,400
Purchases	76,400	—
Returns Inward	—	3,400
Returns Outward	2,900	—
Carriage	2,300	—
Discount Allowed	—	4,200
Salaries	9,540	—
Wages	3,720	—

Sundry Debtors	16,500	—
Sundry Creditors	—	26,500
Opening Stock	—	12,120
Land and Building	35,900	—
Trade Expenses	2,090	—
	1,75,620	1,75,620

(*H.S.*)

[**Ans.** Correct Total of Trial Balance Rs 1,70,570]

13. The clerk of a businessman wrongly prepared the following Trial Balance. You are required to draw up the Trial Balance correctly stating reasons in brief :

	Dr. Rs.	Cr. Rs.
Capital		80,000
Stock at commencement	25,000	—
Discount Allowed	—	500
Commission Received	—	700
Fixed Assets	—	60,000
Sales	90,000	—
Purchases	—	50,000
Returns Outwards	—	1,000
Returns Inwards	2,000	—
Carriage Inwards	—	600
Carriage Outwards	—	700
Wages and Salaries	27,000	—
Bill Receivable	5,000	—
Debtors	10,000	—
Bills Payable	—	8,000
Rent	3,000	—
Interest Paid	—	2,000
Cash	800	—
Creditors	6,900	—
Stock at end	33,800	—
	2,03,500	2,03,500

(*H.S.*)

[**Ans.** Correct Total of Trial Balance Rs 1,86,600]

Chapter 4

Bills of Exchange

Bills of Exchange – Essentials of a Bill of Exchange – Other Types of Negotiable Instruments – Kinds of Bills – Endorsement – Retiring a Bill – Holder – Holder in Due Course – Renewal of a Bill – Dishonour of Bill – Notice of Dishonour – Noting and Protesting – Insolvency – Advantages of Bill of Exchange – Bill Books – Treatment of Bills in the Books of Account – Drawing, Accepting and Discharging of a Bill, Discounting the Bill – Endorsing the Bill – Sending the Bill for Collection – Dishonouring the Bill – Renewal of the Bills – Retiring a Bill under Rebate – Accommodation Bill – Questions – Objective Type Questions – Theoretical Questions – Practical Problems.

Business transactions are, as we saw earlier, either cash transactions or credit transactions. When a person buys goods, on credit, for a smaller amount, the seller relies on him for the recovery of the debt (dues from the buyer) and no security or evidence is necessary because of the small transactions. But, at the same time, when the amount involved in the transaction is large, the seller needs security and evidence over the dealings. Here, the Bill of Exchange solves the problems of the seller. Moreover, when one wanted to increase the business transactions, credits may be allowed and are paid after some time. In such cases, it becomes necessary that the dealings be reduced in writing so that there is no possibility of misunderstanding between the seller and the buyer, besides, the amount may be paid punctually as agreed upon. Thus, commercial practices have developed these written promises into the valuable instruments of credit. If they are in proper form, the buyer and the seller, who concluded a credit transaction, are in sound position. Even these written promises can be passed on from person to person—Bills of Exchange and Promissory Notes. However, these instruments come under the Negotiable Instruments. Negotiable Instruments are divided into three main classes—Bills of Exchange, Promissory Notes, and Cheques. Our purview is focused on Bills of Exchange and Promissory Notes.

BILLS OF EXCHANGE

According to the Indian Negotiable Instruments Act of 1881, under section 5, "A Bill of Exchange is an instrument in writing containing an unconditional order, signed by the maker, directing a certain person to pay a certain sum of money only to, or to the order of, a certain person or to the bearer of the instrument."

Essentials of a Bill of Exchange

1. A Bill of Exchange must be in writing.
2. It must be dated and stamped.
3. It must be signed by the maker or drawer.
4. The name of the drawer must be clearly mentioned.
5. The order must be an unconditional one.
6. It must contain an order to pay money and not goods.

7. The sum payable must be specified.
8. The money must be payable to a definite person or to his order or to the bearer.
9. The amount should be paid within a stipulated time.
10. It must have adequate stamp duty at the prescribed rate.

Specimen of a Bill of Exchange

Rs 4,000

KALANIKETAN, CHENNAI
1st August 2004

STAMP

Three months after date, pay to me or my order the sum of Rupees Four Thousand only, for value received.

RAMU

To
Mr. Ram Prasad,
Moor Market, Chennai

Ram Prasad is a: Debtor (Acceptor) (Drawee)

Ramu is a: Creditor (Maker) (Drawer) (Payee)

Drawer : The person who draws the Bill.
Drawee : The person on whom the Bill is drawn.
Payee : The person to whom the amount of the bill is payable

OTHER TYPES OF NEGOTIABLE INSTRUMENTS

Promissory Note

"A Promissory Note is an instrument in writing (not being a bank note or currency note) containing an unconditional undertaking, signed by the maker, to pay a certain sum of money only to, or to the order of, a certain person, or to the bearer of the instrument." [Sec. 4]

Essentials of a Promissory Note:

In order to be a valid one, a promissory note must have the following :

1. The instrument must be in writing.
2. The instrument must be signed by its maker.
3. The instrument must contain a promise to pay.
4. The promise to pay must be conditional.
5. The maker of the instrument must be certain and definite.
6. It must be stamped.
7. The sum of money to be paid must be certain.
8. The payment must be in legal tender money of India.
9. The money must be payable to a definite person or according to his order.
10. The Promissory note must be payable on demand or after a certain definite period of time.

Cheque

"A cheque is a Bill of Exchange drawn on a specified banker and not expressed to be payable otherwise than on demand."

Essential features of a Cheque

1. A cheque must have to fulfil all the essential elements of a Bill of Exchange.
2. It must be payable to the bearer or to order, but in either case, it must be payable on demand.

3. The banker, named, pay it when it is presented for payment.
4. The signature must tally with the specimen signature of the drawee in the bank.
5. A cheque must be dated.
6. A cheque drawn with a future date is valid, but the same is payable on and after such specified date.

Difference between a Bill of Exchange and a Cheque

Cheque	*Bill of Exchange*
1. A cheque is always drawn on a printed form.	1. A bill need not be drawn on a printed form.
2. A cheque does not require any acceptance.	2. A bill of exchange requires acceptance.
3. A cheque is always supposed to be drawn against the funds in the hands of a banker.	3. There is no such supposition.
4. A cheque is always payable on demand.	4. Acceptor is allowed 3 days of grace after the date of maturity.
5. A cheque is free from stamp duty.	5. A bill of exchange must be stamped (except in certain cases)
6. A cheque may be crossed to ensure safety.	6. It cannot be crossed.
7. A cheque may be countermanded.	7. The payment of a bill cannot be countermanded.
8. Notice of dishonour is not necessary.	8. Notice of dishonour is necessary.
9. It is not protested or noted on dishonour.	9. It is usually protested and noted for dishonour.

Distinction between Bill of Exchange and Promissory Note

Bill of Exchange	*Promissory Note*
1. It is drawn by the creditor.	1. It is drawn by the debtor.
2. It has three parties, *i.e.*, the drawer, drawee and payee.	2. It has two parties, *i.e.*, the maker and the payee.
3. It contains an order to pay.	3. It contains a promise to pay.
4. It is used in settlement of trade debts.	4. It is used to borrow money.
5. Drawer is a creditor.	5. Drawer is a debtor.
6. It needs acceptance by the drawee.	6. It does not need acceptance.
7. Drawee or acceptor is primarily liable.	7. Maker (debtor) is primarily liable to honour his promises.
8. Demand bill of exchange does not require stamp.	8. Both demand and time promissory note require stamp duty.
9. Foreign bills are drawn in sets and inland bill is drawn one copy.	9. Only one copy is prepared whether it is foreign or inland.
10. It is widely circulated in business.	10. Not so common in circulation.

The important points in a Bill of Exchange are :

1. Date. Whenever a bill is drawn, it is usual for the drawer to specify the date of the bill, on the top right-hand corner. The date is important for the purpose of calculation of the due date of the bill. In the above specimen bill, the due date of the bill is calculated by adding, to the date of the bill, the period of the bill. It is a general practice to give to the drawee three days of grace (extra days) over and above the period of the bill. Thus, the due date of the specimen bill (given above) is 1st August plus three months plus three days, *i.e.*, 4th November 2004. Due date is the date of payment. It is also known as the date of maturity.

2. Term. It is the period after which the sum mentioned in the bill is to be paid. In the specimen given above, the term of the bill is three months. The term is agreed upon by the parties.

3. Amount. The sum payable is specified both in figures and words. This is done with a view to minimise the possibility of alteration.

4. Stamp. The stamp is affixed on every bill of exchange, except bill payable on demand. The value of stamp depends on the amount of the bill. Usually the stamp is affixed on the top left-hand corner of the bill.

5. Parties. There are three parties to a bill of exchange:

(*a*) *Drawer.* The person who draws or writes the bill is called Drawer, who is also called the Maker. Maker is the creditor. The Creditor or Maker of the bill will receive the amount, mentioned in the bill, on the due date.

(*b*) *Drawee.* Drawee is the person on whom the bill is drawn. Drawee is a debtor. He is the person who is ordered by the Drawer to pay the amount. When the bill is accepted by the drawee, he becomes the Acceptor. That is, when the drawee gives his consent by writing the word "Accepted" duly signed on the bill, the drawee becomes an Acceptor.

(*c*) *Payee.* The person, who has the right to receive the amount of the bill, is called payee. The payee may be a third person or the drawer himself. When the drawer has made the bill payable to himself, the drawer is the payee. In such case, the number of parties is reduced to two. In some cases, the drawer may make the bill payable to a third party, then the drawer and the payee will be different persons.

6. Acceptance. A bill requires "Acceptance" by the drawee. But, a bill drawn and payable at sight or on demand, does not require acceptance. Acceptance is the assent by the drawee to the order of the drawer. Unless the drawee gives his acceptance by writing the word "Accepted" and also putting his signature alongwith date, the bill does not become a legal document. After the acceptance the bill is returned to the drawer. Before the acceptance the bill is called a Draft and after the acceptance, it is termed an Acceptance. The effect of an acceptance is to bind the drawee to honour the bill on the due date. The acceptance may be General Acceptance or Qualified Acceptance. A general acceptance is an unconditional assent to the order of the drawer. It means that the drawee accepts the contents of the bill without any change. When the drawee makes material alterations in the wordings of the bill, and then accepts it, it is a qualified acceptance.

Acceptance is given across the face of the Bill as:

Accepted
Signature of Ram Prasad
Date

KINDS OF BILLS

There are two types of Bills :

(*a*) *Inland Bill :* An inland bill is drawn and payable in the same country. The specimen given above is an example of inland bill. The due date is counted from the date given in the bill.

(*b*) *Foreign Bill :* Foreign bill is drawn in one country, but payable in another country. A foreign bill is always drawn in a set of three, each of which is called "VIA". The drawee has to accept and make payment of only one Bill. After the acceptance of one bill, the other two sets become inoperative. The due date of the foreign bill is to be counted from the date, when it is seen and accepted by the drawee.

Liabilities of Parties

The liability of the Acceptor is primary and absolute. The acceptor is liable to pay the amount on the due date to the holder. On endorsement of the bill, the drawer also become liable.

ENDORSEMENT

An endorsement is the process by which a bill is transferred from one person to another. He may use the bill to settle his debt with another person. The endorsement is done by signing by the holder, on the face or back of the bill and thus transfers the right to someone else. The person who makes the endorsement is called the "Endorser". The person to whom the bill is transferred is known as the "Endorsee".

When the maker retains the Bill till maturity, it involves only two parties *viz*., the drawee and the drawer, since the latter is payee also. Whereas, endorsement implies three parties *viz*. the drawee, drawer (endorser) and endorsee (payee).

RETIRING A BILL

Retiring a bill means honouring it before its due date. The drawee, who does so, is allowed a rebate. It is an allowance for early payment. Whenever the payment of an amount which is less than the face value of the bill is made, before the due date by the acceptor and accepted by the drawer, it is known as retirement of a bill under rebate.

HOLDER

According to Sec. 8 of the Negotiable Instruments Act, a holder is "any person entitled in his own name to the possession thereof and to receive or recover the amount due there on from the parties thereto." That is, the person who is legally entitled to receive the money due on the instrument is called the holder.

HOLDER IN DUE COURSE

According to Sec. 9 of the Negotiable Instruments Act, "the holder in due course is a particular kind of holder. The holder of a negotiable instrument is called the holder in due course, if he satisfies the following conditions :

(*a*) He obtained the instrument for valuable considerations;

(*b*) He became holder of the instrument before its maturity;

(*c*) He had no cause to believe that any defect existed in the title of the person from whom he derived his title.

RENEWAL OF A BILL

When the acceptor finds it difficult to meet his acceptance on the due date, he approaches the drawer and requests him for an extension of time. If the drawer agrees to his request, the old Bill is cancelled and a fresh Bill is drawn for the amount stated in the old Bill plus interest for the extended period. The process is referred as Renewal of Bill.

DISHONOUR OF BILL

On maturity if the Bill is not paid by the Acceptor, it is said to be dishonoured. A Bill may be dishonoured either by non-acceptance or by non-payment. Dishonour makes the drawer and endorsers liable to compensate the subsequent parties. Each endorsee may look to his transferror for payment.

NOTICE OF DISHONOUR

When a Bill is dishonoured, the holder of the Bill must give notice of dishonour to the drawer and each endorser. Failure to do so will discharge them from their obligations. The notice must be given within a reasonable time to warn the parties of their obligations.

NOTING AND PROTESTING

After acceptance of the bill, the Acceptor becomes liable to pay the amount to the Payee on maturity. If the payment is duly made, the Bill is said to be honoured or discharged. If the Acceptor fails to pay off, the Bill is dishonoured by non-payment. On the Bill being dishonoured by the Acceptor, the holder hands it over to a Notary Public. Notary Public is a Public Officer authorised to certify deeds and other documents. He represents the bill, again, to the Drawee and notes down the particulars of dishonour in his register. This process is known as Noting a Bill. Then, the Notary Public issues a note of the dishonour of the bill and it is an authentic proof, which is attached to the bill. This record of dishonour is called protest. The charge payable for the services of the Notary Public is called Noting Charges.

The holder of a Bill of Exchange is said to be the *holder in due course*. The holder of the Bill can *hold* the Bill till its due date to realise the amount, or if he is in need of cash before maturity, he may *discount* it with his banker or he may *endorse* it over to anyone in settlement of his debt. A Bill can be endorsed any number of times, till the due date.

INSOLVENCY

It is common that a few of the acceptors become bankrupt before their acceptances mature. These acceptances then be treated as dishonoured by the holder or drawer and the relevant entries recorded. On the adjudication of a person as insolvent, his estate vests with the Officer Receiver who realises the bankrupt's properties and proportionately pays the creditors out of the realised sum. The payment by the Official Receiver to the insolvent's creditors is called 'Dividend'. Generally, the dividend is expressed as so many paise in the rupee. The dividend is usually below 100 paise a rupee. Hence, the entire claim is rarely discharged. In order to close off the personal accounts, the unsatisfied balance is debited to Bad Debts Account in the creditor's book.

ADVANTAGES OF BILLS OF EXCHANGE

A Bill of Exchange is a very useful instrument. The following are the main advantages :

1. It facilitates movement of capital, because it is an instrument of credit.
2. It is a valid evidence of debt. It is a full proof of indebtedness.
3. Since the date of payment is fixed, debtor knows when he has to pay and the creditor knows when to expect his money.
4. The creditor can allow credit and at the same time capital is not locked up.
5. Since it is a negotiable instrument, it can easily be transferred in settlement of debts.
6. It is easy and convenient for remitting money from one place to another place.
7. Free transfer facility of bills enhances commercial transactions.
8. If the Drawer is in need of money, the Bill can be converted into cash, by discounting it with a bank, at a very nominal expense.

BILL BOOKS

Where numerous bills are drawn and received, it is cumbersome to make journal entries. Therefore, it is advisable to record them, separately in a special subsidiary book.

ILLUSTRATION 4.1

Enter the following transactions in Bills Receivable Book and Bills Payable Book:

Mohan's debtors and creditors on 1st Jan., 2004 were :

DEBTORS	CREDITORS
A – Rs 1,000	D – Rs 1,000
B – Rs 1,000	E – Rs 500
C – Rs 1,900	F – Rs 600

The following bill transactions took place in January 2004:-

Jan.	10	Mr. A's acceptance for Rs 1,000 at 3 months payable at Punjab Bank (No. 103)
Jan.	15	Acceptance of Mr. X for Rs 1,100 dated 20th Dec., 2003 for 2 months sent by B, payable at Indian Bank (No. 104)
Jan.	18	Mr. C's acceptance for Rs 1,900 at 2 months payable at Canara Bank (No. 105)
Jan.	19	Mr. A's acceptance sent to Mr. D
Jan.	20	Bill No. 104 and 105 discounted with bankers.
Jan.	21	Mohan's acceptance for two months for Rs 500 sent to E (No. 51)
Jan.	21	Mohan's acceptance for three months for Rs 600 sent to F (No. 52)

SOLUTION

Bills Receivable Book

S.No.		*Date*	*From whom received*	*Name of Acceptor*	*Date of Bill*	*Terms of Bill*	*Date of Maturity*	*Where payable*	*Amount Rs*	*L.F.*	*Disposal*
		2004					2004				
1.	103	Jan. 10	A	A	10.1.2004	3 Months	13.4.2004	Punjab Bank	1,000		Endorsed to D
2.	104	Jan. 15	B	X	20.12.2003	2 Months	23.2.2004	Indian Bank	1,100		Discounted
3.	105	Jan. 18	C	C	18.1.2004	2 Months	21.3.2004	Canara Bank	1,900		Discounted

Bills Payable Book

S.No.		*Date of Bill*	*Name of Drawer*	*Payee*	*Terms of Bill*	*Date of Maturity*	*Amount Rs*	*L.F.*	*Payable at*	*Disposal*
1.	51	21.1.2004	E	E	2 Months	24.3.2004	500			
2.	52	21.1.2004	F	F	3 Months	24.4.2004	600			

Posting Rules

Bills Receivable Book :	(*a*) Bills Receivable Account debited with total. (*b*) Personal Accounts are credited individually.
Bills Payable Book :	(*a*) Bills Payable Account credited with total. (*b*) Personal Accounts are debited individually.

BILLS OF EXCHANGE

Bills Receivable	**Bills Payable**
In the Books of Drawer	*In the Books of Acceptor*
1. *When a Bill Receivable is received.* Debit: *Bills Receivable Account,* because it is an asset. Credit: *Personal Account* of the party, who gives the Bill.	1. *When a Bill is accepted.* Debit: *Personal Account* of the Drawer, because he receives the Bill. Credit: *Bills Payable Account,* since the Bill goes out.
2. *When Bills Receivable is honoured* Debit: *Cash Account,* since cash comes in. Credit: *Bills Receivable Account,* since it goes out.	2. *When a Bill payable is duly honoured.* Debit: *Bills Payable Account,* since it receives the benefit. Credit: *Cash Account,* since cash goes out.

3. *When Bills Receivable is discounted.* Debit: Cash since cash comes in Debit : Discount, since it is a loss Credit: B/R, since it goes out.	NO ENTRY
4. *When a Bill is endorsed* Debit: Receiver A/c. Credit: Bills Receivable A/c, since it goes out.	NO ENTRY
5. *When a bill is retired.* Debit: Cash A/c, since cash comes in. Debit: Rebate A/c, since it is a loss. Credit: Bills Receivable A/c, since it goes out.	5. *When a bill is retired.* Debit: Bills Payable A/c with full amount. Credit: Cash A/c. Credit: Rebate A/c, since it is an income.
6. *When a bill is dishonoured* Debit: Acceptor A/c, since the amount is due from him. Credit: Bills Receivable A/c, since it goes out.	6. *When a bill is dishonoured* Debit: Bills Payable A/c, to cancel it. Credit: Drawer A/c, since liable to him.
7. *When a bill is sent for collection.* Debit: Bank A/c for collection of bills. Credit: Bills Receivable A/c, since it goes out.	NO ENTRY
8. *When a bill is renewed* (*a*) Debit: Acceptor A/c Credit: Bills Receivable A/c (Being cancellation of old bill)	8. *When a bills payable is renewed.* (*a*) Debit: Bills Payable A/c Credit: Drawer A/c (Being cancellation of old bill)
(*b*) Debit: Acceptor A/c Credit: Interest A/c (Being the amount of interest)	(*b*) Debit Interest A/c Credit: Drawer A/c (Being the amount of interest)
(*c*) Debit: Bills Receivable A/c Credit: Acceptor A/c (Being drawal of new bill)	(*c*) Debit: Drawee A/c Credit: Bills Payable A/c (Being drawal of new bill)
9. *When a bill is noted.* Debit: Acceptor A/c, with the amount of Bills Receivable plus noting charges. Credit: Cash A/c for noting charges. Credit: Bills Receivable A/c, since it is cancelled.	9. *When a bill is noted.* Debit: Bills Payable A/c, since it comes in. Debit: Noting Charges A/c, since it is a loss. Credit: Drawer A/c, with Bills Payable and noting charges payable to the Drawer.

TREATMENT OF BILLS IN THE BOOKS OF ACCOUNT

Bills of Exchange and Promisory Notes are treated alike for accounting purposes. That is, both are treated and recorded under the common account "Bills of Exchange". We come across four parties to a Bill : (*a*) Drawer, (*b*) Drawee (Acceptor), (*c*) Endorser, and (*d*) Endorsee. When a drawer endorses a Bill, which he received from the Acceptor, he becomes Endorser. Endorsee is a person to whom the Bill is transferred. When the endorsee, again, endorses the Bill, he becomes an Endorser and the receiver of the endorsed Bill is an Endorsee.

A Bill of Exchange or Promissory Note may be treated as Bills Receivable, when payment has to be received against it. Thus, a Bill of Exchange is Bills Receivable for the drawer as he has to receive the amount. A Bill of Exchange or Promissory Note may be treated as a Bill Payable, when payment has to be made against it. Thus, a Bill of Exchange is a Bill Payable for the drawee (Acceptor). Thus, it is clear that Bills of Exchange or Promissory Notes can be Bills Receivable to one party and Bills

Payable to another party. The Bill in the possession of the Creditor may be dealt with in any one of the following ways :

(1) One can keep the Bill till the date of maturity and realise the payment against it.

(2) One can discount the Bill with a bank before its maturity, if he is in need of money.

(3) One can transfer the Bill, against a debt, to his Creditor by endorsing it.

(4) One can send the Bill to the bank for collection of amount against it.

We shall discuss the accounting treatment of transactions :

Terms used in Bill Transactions

1. One who draws a Bill is called *Drawer or Maker.*
2. One who accepts the Bill is known as *Acceptor.*
3. The Drawer is concerned, the Bill is a *Bills Receivable.*
4. To the Acceptor, the same bill is *Bills Payable.*
5. The person, endorses the Bill, is known as *Endorser.*
6. The person to whom the Bill is endorsed is *Endorsee.*
7. Failure to pay the Bill on the due date is *Dishonour.*
8. To pay the Bill before the due date is *Retiring.*
9. The person, who is entitled to receive the sum, is *Payee.*
10. The date, on which a Bill falls due, is known as *Maturity.*

Let us take examples of transactions dealing with Bills of Exchange between two parties, with all possible situations.

DRAWING, ACCEPTING AND DISCHARGE OF A BILL

ILLUSTRATION 4.2

On March 10th, A sold goods to B and draws on B a Bill at three months for Rs 800, which B accepts immediately and returns it to A. The Bill is honoured on the due date. Pass entries in the books of both A and B.

SOLUTION

A's Journal				B's Journal		
		Rs	*Rs.*		*Rs*	*Rs*
March 10	B Account Dr.	800		Purchase Account Dr.	800	
	To Sales Account		800	To A Account		800
	(Being credit sales made to B)			(Being credit purchase)		
March 10	Bills Receivable Account Dr.	800		A Account Dr.	800	
	To B Account			To Bills Payable Account		800
	(Being acceptance received)			(Being acceptance given)		
June 13	Cash Account Dr.	800		Bills Payable Account Dr.	800	
	To Bills Receivable Account		800	To Cash Account		800
	(Being amount received)			(Being acceptance met)		

DISCOUNTING THE BILL

ILLUSTRATION 4.3

A accepted a four months' draft for Rs 1,000 drawn on him by B on 15th April. The Bill was discounted with the bankers on the next day at 12%. On maturity the Bill was met. Make journal entries in the books of A and B.

SOLUTION

A's Journal

		Rs	Rs
April 15	B Account Dr. To Bills Payable Account (Being acceptance given)	1,000	 1,000
April 16	NO ENTRY		
Aug. 18	Bills Payable Account Dr. To Bank Account (Being acceptance met)	1,000	 1,000

B's Journal

	Rs	Rs
Bills Receivable Account Dr. To A Account (Being acceptance given)	1,000	 1,000
Bank Account Dr. Discount Account Dr. To Bills Receivable Account (Being the Bill discounted)	960 *40	 1,000
NO ENTRY		

$$*1,000 \times \frac{12}{100} \times \frac{4}{12} = 40.00$$

ENDORSING THE BILL

ILLUSTRATION 4.4

On 1st June Ram drew a bill upon Krishna for Rs 500 at four months date. This was duly accepted and payable at Canara Bank. After the acceptance, the Bill was endorsed to Gopal. On the due date, the Bill was honoured. Pass the journal entries in the books of all parties.

SOLUTION

Ram's Journal

			Rs	Rs
June 1	Bills Receivable Account To Krishna Account (Being acceptance received)	Dr.	500	 500
June 1	Gopal Account To Bills Receivable Account (Being Krishna's acceptance endorsed to Gopal)	Dr.	500	 500

Krishna's Journal

			Rs	Rs
June 1	Ram Account To Bills Payable Account (Being acceptance given)	Dr.	500	 500
Oct. 4	Bills Payable Account To Cash Account (Being acceptance met)	Dr.	500	 500

Gopal's Journal

			Rs	Rs
June 1	Bills Receivable Account To Ram Account (Being Krishna's acceptance endorsed)	Dr.	500	 500
Oct. 4	Cash Account To Bills Received Account (Being cash received)	Dr.	500	 500

SENDING THE BILL FOR COLLECTION

ILLUSTRATION 4.5

A four months Bill for Rs 500 was returned duly accepted by Natesh on 1st February, to the drawer, Mahesh, who sent it to his banker for collection. On maturity, the banker informed Mahesh that the Bill was honoured. Pass journal entries in both the books.

SOLUTION

	Mahesh's Journal			**Natesh's Journal**		
		Rs	*Rs.*		*Rs*	*Rs*
Feb. 1	Bills Receivable Account Dr. To Natesh's Account (Being acceptance received)	500	500	Mahesh Account Dr. To Bills Payable Account (Being acceptance given)	500	500
Feb. 1	Bills Sent for Collection A/c Dr. To Bills Receivable A/c (Bill sent to bank for collection)	500	500	NO ENTRY		
June 4	Bank A/c Dr. To Bills Sent for Collection A/c (Cash received on the honour of the Bill)	500	500	Bill Payable A/c Dr. To Cash A/c (Being acceptance met)	500	500

DISHONOURING THE BILL

(a) When Drawer is the Holder of the Bill

ILLUSTRATION 4.6

Mr. Ravi draws a Bill for Rs 2,000 on Gopal on 15th September for three months. On maturity, Gopal failed to honour the Bill. Pass the necessary journal entries in the books of Ravi and Goipal, if he had retained the Bill with him till maturity. *(Calicut)*

SOLUTION

	Ravi's Journal			**Gopal's Journal**		
		Rs	*Rs.*		*Rs*	*Rs*
Sept. 15	Bills Receivable A/c Dr. To Gopal A/c (Being acceptance received)	2,000	2,000	Ravi's A/c Dr. To Bills Payable A/c (Being acceptance given)	2,000	2,000
Dec. 18	Gopal A/c Dr. To Bills Receivable A/c (Being Bill dishonoured at maturity)	2,000	2,000	Bills Payable A/c To Ravi A/c (Being acceptance dis-honoured at maturity)	2,000	2,000

(b) When Banker is the Holder of the Bill

ILLUSTRATION 4.7

On 15th June, Niranjan sold goods to Prema, valued at Rs 2,000. He drew a Bill at 3 months for the amount and discounted the same with his bankers at Rs 1,960. On the due date, the Bill was dishonoured and Niranjan paid the bank the amount due plus the noting charges of Rs 10.

Pass the journal entries in the books of the two parties. *(B. Com., Mysore)*

SOLUTION

Date	Niranjan's Journal		Rs	Rs.	Prema's Journal		Rs	Rs
June 15	Prema Account	Dr.	2,000		Purchases Account	Dr.	2,000	
	To Sales Account			2,000	To Niranjan Account			2,000
	(Being goods sold on credit)				(Being goods purchased on credit)			
June 15	Bills Receivable Account	Dr.	2,000		Niranjan Account	Dr.	2,000	
	To Prema Account			2,000	To Bills Payable A/c			2,000
	(Being acceptance received)				(Being acceptance given)			
June 15	Bank Account	Dr.	1,960		NO ENTRY			
	Discount Account	Dr.	40					
	To Bills Receivable Account			2,000				
	(Being the bill discounted)							
Sept. 18	Prema Account	Dr.	2,010		Bills Payable Account	Dr.	2,000	
	To Bank Account			2,010	Noting Charges Account	Dr.	10	
	(Being the amount of the bill plus Noting charges of Rs. 10, paid)				To Niranjan Account			2,010
					(Being the amount of the Bills plus Noting Charges)			

(*c*) *When Endorsee is the Holder of the Bill*

ILLUSTRATION 4.8

On 1st January, A drew a Bill on B for Rs 1,000 payable after three months. B accepted the Bill and returned it to A. After 10 days A endorsed the Bill to his Creditor C. On the due date, the Bill was dishonoured and C paid Rs 5 as noting charges.

Record the transactions in the journals of A, B and C. (*Madurai*)

SOLUTION

A's Journal

			Rs	Rs
Jan. 1	Bills Receivable Account	Dr.	1,000	
	To B Account			1,000
	(Being acceptance received)			
Jan. 10	C Account	Dr.	1,000	
	To Bills Receivable Account			1,000
	(Being the acceptance endorsed to C)			
April 4	B Account	Dr.	1,005	
	To C Account			1,005
	(Being dishonour of Bill and Noting charges paid by C)			

B's Journal

			Rs	Rs
Jan. 1	A Account	Dr.	1,000	
	To Bills Payable Account			1,000
	(Being acceptance given)			
April 4	Bills Payable Account	Dr.	1,000	
	Noting Charges Account	Dr.	5	
	To A Account			1,005
	(Being the bill dishonoured and Noting charges paid)			

C's Journal

			Rs	Rs
Jan. 10	Bills Receivable Account	Dr.	1,000	
	To A Account			1,000
	(Being B's acceptance endorsed by A)			
April 4	A Account	Dr.	1,005	
	To Bills Receivable Account			1,000
	To Cash Account			5
	(Being the dishonour of the bill and paid Noting charges)			

(*d*) *When the Bill is sent for collection*

ILLUSTRATION 4.9

On 1st January, A drew a Bill on B for Rs 1,000, payable after three months. Immediately after its acceptance, A sent the Bill to his Bank for collection. On the due date, the Bill was dishonoured.

Record the transactions in the journals of A and B.

SOLUTION

	A's Journal				**B's Journal**			
			Rs	Rs			Rs	Rs
Jan. 1	Bills Receivable A/c	Dr.	1,000		A A/c	Dr.	1,000	
	To B A/c			1,000	To Bills Payable A/c			1,000
	(Being acceptance received)				(Being acceptance given)			
Jan. 1	Bills Sent for Collection A/c	Dr.	1,000					
	To Bills Receivable A/c			1,000	NO ENTRY			
	(Being Bill sent to bank for collection)							
April 4	B A/c	Dr.	1,000		Bills Payable A/c	Dr.	1,000	
	To Bill Sent for Collection A/c			1,000	To A A/c			1,000
	(Being Bill dishonoured)				(Being acceptance dishonoured)			

RENEWAL OF THE BILLS

ILLUSTRATION 4.10

On 1st May, Merchant & Company sold goods to A B & Co. for Rs 500 and drew upon him a Bill at three months for the amount. A B & Co. accepted the draft and returned to Merchant & Co. On the due date A B & Co. expressed their inability to meet the Bill and offered Rs 300 in cash and to accept a new Bill for the balance plus interest at 12% p.a. for three months. Merchant & Co. agreed to the proposal. On maturity, the Bill was duly met by A B & Co.

Pass entries in the books of the parties to record the above transactions. (*B. Com., Karnataka, Madras*)

SOLUTION. Solution see next Page.

Effects of Dishonour of a Bill

(1) When a bill is dishonoured, it becomes valueless and the original position of debtor and creditor is restored between the drawee and the drawer.

(2) Upon its dishonour, the holder of a bill has a right of action against the drawee or any previous endorser.

(3) When an endorser makes the payment to the endorsee, he can sue any previous endorser or the drawer.

(4) Upon dishonour, to avoid confusion and multiplicity of legal actions, generally the drawer takes up the bill and exercises his rights upon the drawee.

(5) Expenses incurred for establishing the fact of dishonour of a bill (noting charges) are generally paid by the holder, but ultimately these are recoverable from the drawee.

Merchant & Co.'s Journal

Date	Particulars		L.F.	Rs	Rs.
May 1	A B & Co. Account To Sales Account (Being sale of goods on credit)	Dr.		500	500
"	Bills Receivable Account To A B & Co. Account (Being acceptance received)	Dr.		500	500
Aug. 4	A B & Co. Account To Bills Receivable Account (Being cancellation of old Bill)	Dr.		500	500
"	Cash Account To A B & Co. Account (Being the receipt of part payment)	Dr.		300	300
"	A B & Co. Account To Interest Account (Being interest on Rs 200 at 12% for three months)	Dr.		6	6
"	Bills Receivable Account To A B & Co.. Account (Being new acceptance received)	Dr.		206	206
Nov. 7	Cash Account To Bills Receivable Account (Being amount received on Bill)	Dr.		206	206

A B & Co.'s Journal

Date	Particulars		L.F.	Rs	Rs
May 1	Purchase Account To Merchant & Co. Account (Being purchase of goods on credit)	Dr.		500	500
"	Merchant & Co. Account To Bills Payable Account (Being acceptance given)	Dr.		500	500
Aug. 4	Bills Payable Account To Merchant & Co. Account (Being cancellation of acceptance)	Dr.		500	500
"	Merchant & Co. Account To Cash Account (Being payment of part payment)	Dr.		300	300
"	Interest Account To Merchant & Co. Account (Being interest on Rs 200 at 12% for three months)	Dr.		6	6
"	A B & Co. Account To Bills Payable Account (Being new acceptance given)	Dr.		206	206
Nov. 7	Bills Payable Account To Cash Account (Being acceptance honoured)	Dr.		206	206

RETIRING A BILL UNDER REBATE

ILLUSTRATION 4.11

On 1st January, A sold goods to B for Rs 1,000 and drew upon him a Bill at three months for the amount. B accepted the Bill and returned it to A. On 4th March, B returned the Bill under rebate of 12% p.a.

Record these transactions in the journals of A and B.

SOLUTION

A's Journal				B's Journal		
		Rs	*Rs*		*Rs*	*Rs*
Jan 1.	B Account Dr.	1,000		Purchase Account Dr.	1,000	
	To Sales Account		1,000	To A Account		1,000
	(Being goods sold on credit)			(Being purchase of goods on credit)		
Jan. 1	Bills Receivable Account Dr.	1,000		A Account Dr.	1,000	
	To B Account		1,000	To Bills Payable Account		1,000
	(Being acceptance received)			(Being acceptance given)		
March 4	Cash Account Dr.	990		Bills Payable Account Dr.	1,000	
	Rebate Account Dr.	10		To Cash Account		990
	To Bills Receivable Account		1,000	To Rebate Account		10
	(Being Bill honoured under rebate)			(Being acceptance met under rebate)		

ILLUSTRATION 4.12

On 1st February, Ram received from Hari three acceptances for Rs 6,000, Rs 8,000 and Rs 10,000 for two months.

The first Bill for Rs 6,000 was endorsed to Mohan; the second Bill for Rs 8,000 was held till due date; and the third Bill for Rs 10,000 was discounted for Rs 50.

At maturity all the Bills were dishonoured. Give journal entries in the books of Ram and the ledger accounts in the books of Hari, in respect of these transactions. (*CA*)

SOLUTION

Journal (Ram's Book)

			Rs	*Rs*
Feb. 1	Bills Receivable Account	Dr.	6,000	
	To Hari Account			6,000
	(Being Bill accepted by Hari for 2 months)			
"	Bills Receivable Account	Dr.	8,000	
	To Hari Account			8,000
	(Being Bill accepted by Hari for 2 months)			
"	Bills Receivable Account	Dr.	10,000	
	To Hari Account			10,000
	(Being Bill accepted by Hari for 2 months)			
"	Mohan Account	Dr.	6,000	
	To Bills Receivable Account			6,000
	(Being B/R endorsed to Mohan)			
"	Bank Account	Dr.	9,950	
	Discount Account	Dr.	50	
	To Bi'ls Receivable Account			10,000
	(Being Bill discounted by the Bank)			

April 4	Hari Account Dr. To Mohan Account (Being Bill endorsed to Mohan dishonoured by Hari)		6,000	6,000
"	Hari Account Dr. To Bills Receivable Account (Being Bill dishonoured by Hari)		8,000	8,000
"	Hari Account Dr. To Bank Account (Being Bill discounted by Bank dishonoured by Hari)		10,000	10,000

In the Books of Hari

Ram's Account

		Rs			Rs
Feb. 1	To Bills Payable A/c	6,000	Feb. 1	By Balance b/d	24,000
"	To Bills Payable A/c	8,000	April 4	By Bills Payable A/c	6,000
"	To Bills Payable A/c	10,000		By Bills Payable A/c	8,000
	To Balance c/d	24,000		By Bills Payable A/c	10,000
		48,000			48,000
			April 5	By Balance b/d	24,000

ACCOMMODATION BILL

As stated above, Bills are accepted and endorsed for the benefit received. Generally, an acceptance is made to settle a trade debt, which is due to the Drawer by the Drawee and such a Bill is called *Trade Bill.* Moreover, in such a Bill, we come across the words "for value received". This means, Bills are accepted and endorsed for value (benefit) received. Thus, it is clear that Bill of Exchange is usually used in the businesses for discharging of mutual indebtedness arising from genuine trading activities.

As contrasted with the Trade Bill, Accommodation Bills are drawn and accepted with no consideration passed or received. *The Bill, which is drawn just to oblige a friend, who is in need of money, of course without any trading activities, with sole intention of raising funds required for ready cash is known as Accommodation Bill.* The accommodating party, *i.e.,* the drawee accepts the Bill drawn by the accommodated party (drawer). That is the Drawer of the accommodation bill can be called accommodated party and drawee can be called accommodating party. After the Bill is accepted, the drawer discounts it with a bank and obtains the cash. Before the due date of the Bill, Drawer provides funds to the Acceptor, who honours the Bill. Since the acceptance is given without consideration and to help the accommodated party to raise the funds, the accommodated party has to discharge the Bill by himself or provide funds to accommodating party. Thus, there is always a mutual understanding between the parties and hence, these bills are called Accommodation Bills. The language of an Accommodation Bill is the same as that of an ordinary Trade Bill. The mode of drawing, accepting, discounting, honouring etc. are similar to that of any Trade Bills. A banker cannot make distinction between a genuine Trade Bill and Accommodation bill. These Bills are also called "Kites" or "Finance Bills".

However, there is following distinction between the two :

Trade Bill	*Accommodation Bill*
1. It is a real Bill.	1. It is an imaginary Bill.
2. Rightly used for financing trade.	2 Misused for raising a loan.
3. Drawer is a creditor.	3. Drawer is pretended creditor. (Really creditor is the real debtor.)

4. Drawee is a debtor.	4. Drawee is a pretended debtor. (Really a creditor)
5. Valuable consideration is there by backing real transactions.	5. No valuable consideration is there because there is no backing of real transaction.
6. Bankers are willing to buy such documents.	6. Bankers are reluctant or unwilling to buy accommodation bills.
7. Documents of title to goods are attached to the Bill.	7. No documents are attached because of no transactions existed.

From accounting point of view, there is no difference between the Trade Bill and Accommodation Bill. Therefore, the rules and procedure of Accommodation Bill is the same as for a Trade Bill, except the reimbursement to the accommodating party by the accommodated party as their relation is that of lender and borrower.

There are three common methods of dealing with accommodation Bills and they are :

(*a*) *When one party accepts a Bill to accommodate the drawer only.*

When a party, who is in urgent need of cash, approaches a business friend to raise funds through a Bill of Exchange. In such situation, the party, who needs cash, draws a Bill which is accepted by his friend, without any valuable consideration. The drawer can discount the Bill with a bank and the proceeds are used by him alone. At the time of maturity, the drawer pays the amount to the Acceptor, who honours the Bill.

ILLUSTRATION 4.13

Mr. A accepted a bill for Rs 20,000 drawn by B to enable the latter to raise funds at three months on 1st October 2004. The bill was duly discounted by B at their Bank at 6% per annum. On the due date B remitted the amount to the acceptor and the Bill was duly met.

Pass journal entries in the books of both the parties.

SOLUTION

	B's Journal			A's Journal		
		Rs	*Rs*		*Rs*	*Rs*
2004	Bills Receivable Account Dr.	20,000		B Account Dr.	20,000	
Oct. 1	To A Account		20,000	To Bills Payable Account		20,000
	(Being Bill drawn on A for 3 months)			(Being acceptance of Bill drawn by B)		
Oct. 2	Cash Account Dr.	19,700				
	Discount on Bills Account Dr.	300		NO ENTRY		
	To Bills Receivable		20,000			
	(Being Bill discounted at 6% p.a.)					
2005	A Account Dr.	20,000		Cash Account Dr.	20,000	
Jan. 4	To Cash Account		20,000	To B Account		20,000
	(Being amount paid to A to meet the Bill on the due date)			(Being cash received from B to honour the Bill)		
Jan. 4				Bills Payable Account Dr.	20,000	
	NO ENTRY			To Cash Account		20,000
				(Being bill honoured on maturity)		

Discount : 20,000 × 6/100 × 3/12 = Rs 300

(*b*) *Where a Bill is drawn for mutual benefit of both the parties.*

Sometimes an accommodation Bill is drawn and accepted for mutual benefit of the Drawer and Drawee. The Drawer draws a Bill and Drawee accepts it. The same Bill is discounted by the Drawer and an agreed portion of the proceeds is remitted to the Acceptor. The discounting charge is also shared by both the parties in the same proportion in which the collection proceeds of the Bill were shared. Before the due date, the Drawer pays his share to the Acceptor, who meets the Bill by adding his share of money.

ILLUSTRATION 4.14

Mr. Ram draws a Bill for Rs 15,000 on Mr. Gopal on 1st January payable three months after the date at Canara Bank, Ernakulam. The Bill after acceptance is discounted by Ram at 6% p.a. and he remits 1/3 of the proceeds to Gopal. On the due date, Ram sends the necessary amount to Gopal who meets the Bill.

Record these transactions in the journal of both the parties.

SOLUTION

	Ram's Journal			**Gopal's Journal**		
		Rs	*Rs*		*Rs*	*Rs*
Jan. 1	Bills Receivable Account Dr.	15,000		Ram Account Dr.	15,000	
	To Gopal Account		15,000	To Bills Payable Account		15,000
	(Being acceptance received from Gopal)			(Being Ram's bill accepted)		
"	Cash Account Dr.	14,775				
	Discount on Bills Account Dr.	225				
	To Bills Receivable Account		15,000	NO ENTRY		
	(Being Bill discounted at 6% p.a.)					
"	Gopal Account Dr.	5,000		Cash Account Dr.	4,925	
	To Discount on Bills Account		75	Discount on Bills Account Dr.	75	
	To Cash Account		4,925	To Ram Account		5,000
	(Being 1/3 of proceeds and 1/3 of discount charges transferred)			(Being 1/3 of proceeds and 1/3 of discount charges transferred)		
April 4	Gopal Account Dr.	10,000		Cash Account Dr.	10,000	
	To Cash Account		10,000	To Ram Account		10,000
	(2/3 of the Bill sent to Gopal, who met the Bill)			(Being 2/3 contribution received from Ram)		
"				Bills Payable Account Dr.	15,000	
	NO ENTRY			To Cash Account		15,000
				(Being Bill paid on maturity)		

(c) *Where the two parties, each drawing a Bill*

There are two parties to a Bill–the Drawer and the Drawee. Both these parties draw each a Bill of equal amount or different amount on the other. Both the parties are in need of money. For instance, Mr. A draws a Bill on Mr. B for Rs 1,000 and Mr. B draws a Bill on Mr. A for Rs 1,000. Both A and B discount their Bills with a Bank to meet their financial needs. They bear charges of their respective Bills. Both the parties honour their acceptances on the due date.

ILLUSTRATION 4.15 (Two Bills of equal value)

Mr. A drew a Bill on B on November 1st, 2004 for an amount Rs 4,000 payable three months after that date. On the very same date Mr. A accepted a Bill for Rs 4,000 drawn by B for a period of three months. Both the parties discounted their Bills at 12% p.a. On the due date both the Bills were honoured. Make journal entries in the books of both the parties.

SOLUTION

Date	A's Journal	Rs	Rs.	B's Journal	Rs	Rs
2004 Nov. 1	Bills Receivable A/c Dr. To B A/c (Being acceptance of B received)	4,000	4,000	A A/c Dr. To Bills Payable A/c (Being acceptance given to A)	4,000	4,000
"	B A/c Dr. To Bills Payable A/c (Being acceptance given to B)	4,000	4,000	Bill Receivable A/c Dr. To A A/c (Being acceptance received from A)	4,000	4,000
"	Cash A/c Dr. Discount on Bills A/c To Bills Receivable A/c (Being discounting of Bill at 12% p.a.)	3,880 120	4,00	NO ENTRY		
"	NO ENTRY			Cash A/c Dr. Discount on Bills A/c Dr. To Bills Receivable A/c (Being discounting of Bill at 12% p.a.)	3,880 120	4,000
Feb. 4	Bills Payable A/c Dr. To Cash A/c (Being the Bill is met)	4,000	4,00	NO ENTRY		
"	NO ENTRY			Bills Payable A/c Dr. To Cash A/c (Being the bill is met)	4,000	4,000

DISHONOUR OF ACCOMMODATION BILLS

ILLUSTRATION 4.16

Balan draws a three months Bill on Sekhar for Rs 4,000 on 1st April 2004. Sekhar accepts the Bill and sends it to Balan, who gets it discounted with his bank for Rs 3,940. Balan immediately remits Rs 985 to Sekhar. On the due date, Balan being unable to remit the amount due, accepts a Bill for Rs 4,500 for three months which is discounted by Sekhar for Rs 4,440. Sekhar sends Rs 330 to Balan. Before the maturity of the second Bill Balan becomes insolvent and his estates paying 40 paise in the rupee.

Give journal entries in the books of Balan and Sekhar. Also, show the ledger accounts. *(B.Com., Madurai)*

SOLUTION

Date	Journal of Balan	Dr. Rs	Cr. Rs	Journal of Sekhar	Dr. Rs	Cr. Rs
2004 April 1	Bills Receivable Account Dr. To Sekhar Account (Being acceptance received)	4,000	4,000	Balan Account Dr. To Bills Payable Account (Being acceptance given)	4,000	4,000
"	Bank Account Dr. Discount on Bill Account Dr. To Bills Receivable A/c (Being Bills discounted)	3,940 60	4,000	NO ENTRY		
"	Sekhar Account Dr. To Discount Account To Bank Account (Being remittance of amount less discount)	1,000	15 985	Bank Account Dr. Discount Account Dr. To Balan Account (Being share received from Balan less discount)	985 15	1,000

Date	Particulars			Particulars		
July 4	Sekhar Account Dr. To Bills Payable Account (Being acceptance given)	4,500	 4,500	Bills Receivable Account Dr. To Balan Account (Being acceptence received)	4,500	 4,500
"	NO ENTRY			Bank Account Dr. Discount on Bills Account Dr. To Bills Receivable Account (Being acceptance discounted)	4,440 60	 4,500
"	NO ENTRTY			Bills Payable Account Dr. To Bank Account (Being own acceptance honoured)	4,000	 4,000
"	Bank Account Dr. Discount on Bills Account Dr. To Sekhar Account (Being receipt of share on discounting of bill)	330 45	 375	Balan Account Dr. To Discount on Bills Account To Bank Account (Being remittance of share of proceeds to Balan)	375	 45 330
Oct. 7	Bills Payable Account Dr. To Sekhar Account (Being Bill dishonoured by Sekhar)	4,500	 4,500	Balan Account Dr. To Bank Account (Being dishonour of Bill by Balan)	4,500	 4,500
"	Sekhar Account Dr. To Bank Account To Deficiency Account (Being cash paid to Sekhar 40 paise in the rupee)	3,375	 1,350 2,025	Bank Account Dr. Bad Debts Account Dr. To Balan Account (Being cash received at 40 paise in the rupee)	1,350 2,025	 3,375

Sekhar Account

Dr. *Cr.*

Date	Particulars	JF	Amount Rs	Date	Particulars	JF	Amount Rs
2004				2004			
April 1	To Discount A/c		15	April 1	By Bill Receivable A/c		4,000
"	To Bank A/c		985	July 4	By Bank A/c		330
July 4	To Bills Payable A/c		4,500	"	By Discount on Bills A/c		45
Oct. 7	To Bank A/c		1,350	Oct. 7	By Bills Payable A/c		4,500
"	To Deficiency A/c		2,025				
			8.875				8,875

Balan Account

Dr. *Cr.*

Date	Particulars	JF	Amount Rs.	Date	Particulars	JF	Amount Rs.
204				2004			
April 1	To Bills Payable A/c		4,000	April 1	By Bank A/c		985
July 4	To Discount on Bills A/c		45	"	By Discount on Bills A/c		15
"	To Bank A/c		330	July 4	By Bills Receivable A/c		4,500
Oct. 7	To Bank A/c		4,500	Oct. 7	By Bank A/c		1,350
				"	By Bad Debts A/c		2,025
			8,875				8,875

ILLUSTRATION 4.17

On 1st January 2004, A draws a Bill on B at four months for Rs 1,000 and B draws on A for similar amount and term. Both the Bills are accepted and discounted at 6% p.a. A meets his own acceptance at maturity, but B's acceptance is dishonoured. B then accepts a new Bill at three months for the amount due by him plus interest at 8% p.a. which is duly met at maturity.

Journalise the above transactions in the books of A and B. *(B.Com. Madurai)*

SOLUTION

	In the books of A			In the books of B		
		Rs	*Rs*		*Rs*	*Rs*
2004 Jan. 1	Bills Receivable Account Dr. To B's Account (Being acceptance received)	1,000	 1,000	A Account Dr. To Bills Payable Account (Being acceptance given to A)	1,000	 1,000
"	B Account Dr. To Bills Payable Account (Being acceptance given)	1,000	 1,000	Bills Receivable Account Dr. To A Account (Being acceptance received)	1,000	 1,000
"	Bank Account Dr. Discount on Bills Account Dr. To Bills Receivable Account (Being discounting the bill at 6% p.a.)	980 20	 1,000	NO ENTRY		
"	NO ENTRY			Bank Account Dr. Discount on Bills Account Dr. To Bills Receivable Account (Being discounting the bill at 6% p.a.)	980 20	 1,000
May 4	Bills Payable Account Dr. To Bank Account (Being honouring the bill at maturity)	1,000	 1,000	NO ENTRY		
"	B Account Dr. To Bank Account (Being B's acceptance met)	1,000	 1,000	Bills Payable Account Dr. To A Account (Being dishonour of acceptance given)	1,000	 1,000
"	Bills Receivable Account Dr. To B Account To Interest Account (Being acceptance received plus interest at 8% p.a.)	1,020	 1,000 20	A Account Dr. Interest Account Dr. To Bills Payable Account (Being acceptance given)	1,000 20	 1,020
Aug. 7	Bank Account Dr. To Bills Receivable Account (Being honour of B's bill)	1,020	 1,020	Bills Payable Account Dr. To Bank Account (Being honouring own acceptance)	1,020	 1,020

ILLUSTRATION 4.18

X draws a Bill for Rs 1,500 and Y accepts the same for the mutual accommodation of both of them to the extent of X–2/3 and Y–1/3. X discounts the same for Rs 1,410 and remits 1/3rd of the proceeds to Y. Before the due date, Y draws another Bill for Rs 2,100 on X, in order to provide funds to meet the first Bill. The second Bill is discounted for Rs 2,040 with the help of which the first Bill is met and Rs 360 is remitted to X. Before the due date of the second Bill X becomes insolvent and Y receives a dividend of 50 paise in the Rupee in full satisfaction.

Pass necessary entries in the books of X and Y. *(B.Com., Madurai, Delhi)*

SOLUTION

In the books of X		Rs	Rs.	In the books of Y		Rs	Rs
Bills Receivable Account	Dr.	1,500		X Account	Dr.	1,500	
To Y Account			1,500	To Bills Payable Account			1,500
(Being acceptance received from Y)				(Being acceptance given to X)			
Bank Account	Dr.	1,410		NO ENTRY			
Discount on Bills Account	Dr.	90					
To Bills Receivable Account			1,500				
(Being Y's acceptance discounted)							
Y Account	Dr.	500		Bank Account	Dr.	470	
To Bank Account			470	Discount on Bills Account	Dr.	30	
To Discount on Bills Account			30	To X Account			500
(Being 1/3rd of the proceeds remitted to Y)				(Being 1/3rd of the proceeds received from X)			
Y Account	Dr.	2,100		Bills Receivable Account	Dr.	2,100	
To Bills Payable Account			2,100	To X Account			2,100
(Being acceptance given)				(Being acceptance received from X)			
NO ENTRY				Bank Account	Dr.	2,040	
				Discount on Bills Account	Dr.	60	
				To Bills Receivable Account			2,100
				(Being acceptance discounted)			
NO ENTRY				Bills Payable Account	Dr.	1,500	
				To bank Account			1,500
				(Being own acceptance honoured)			
Bank Account	Dr.	360		X Account	Dr.	400	
Discount on Bills Account	Dr.	40		To Discount on Bills Account			40
To Y Account			400	To Bank Account			360
(Being amount received plus 2/3 of discount)				(Being amount remitted plus 2/3rd of discount)			
Bills Payable Account	Dr.	2,100		X Account	Dr.	2,100	
To Y Account			2,100	To Bank Account			2,100
(Being entry for dishonour of own acceptance)				(Being dishonour of X's acceptance)			
Y Account	Dr.	1,400		Bank Account	Dr.	700	
To Bank Account			700	Bad Debts Account	Dr.	700	
To Deficiency Account			700	To X Account			1,400
(Being 50 paise in the rupee paid)				(Being 50 paise in the rupee received)			

ILLUSTRATION 4.19

Latika for mutual accommodation draws a Bill for Rs 3,000 on Sumita. Latika discounted the Bill for Rs 2,925 and remits Rs 975 to Sumita. On the due date Latika is unable to remit her dues to Sumita to enable her to meet the Bill. She, however, accepts a Bill for Rs 3,750 which Sumita discounts for Rs 3,525. Sumita sends Rs 175 to Latika. Latika becomes insolvent and a dividend of 80 paise in the rupee is received from her estate.

Pass journal entries and show the accounts of Sumita in the books of Latika. (*ICWA Inter*)

SOLUTION

In the books of Latika

Journal Entries

Date	Particulars		L.F.	Dr. Rs	Cr. Rs
	Bills Receivable Account	Dr.		3,000	
	To Sumita Account				3,000
	(Being acceptance received)				
	Bank Account	Dr.		2,925	
	Discount Account	Dr.		75	
	To Bills Receivable Account				3,000
	(Being bills discounted)				
	Sumita Account	Dr.		1,000	
	To Bank Account				975
	To Discount Account				25
	(Being remittance of amount less discount)				
	Sumita Account	Dr.		3,750	
	To Bills Payable Account				3,750
	(Being acceptance given)				
	Bank Account	Dr.		175	
	Discount Account	Dr.		138*	
	To Sumita Account				313
	(Being amount received and discount chargeable)				
	Bills Payable Account	Dr.		3,750	
	To Sumita Account				3,750
	(Being dishonour of acceptance)				
	Sumita Account	Dr.		2,313	
	To Bank Account				1,850.40(1)
	To Deficiency Account				462.60@
	(Being cash paid to Sumita 80 paise in the Rupee)				

Sumita Account

Dr.		Rs			Cr. Rs
	To Bank A/c	975		By Bills Receivable A/c	3,000
	To Discount A/c	25		By Bank A/c	175
	To Bills Payable A/c	3,750		By Discount A/c	138
	To Bank A/c	1,850.40		By Bills Payable A/c	3,750
	To Deficiency A/c	462.60			
		7,063			7,063

Discount: $\frac{225}{3525} \times (2000 + 175) =$ Rs. 138*

(1) $2313 \times \frac{80}{100} =$ Rs. 1850.40

@Rs. $2313 \times \frac{20}{100} =$ Rs. 462.60

MISCELLANEOUS

ILLUSTRATION 4.20

Rao owed Mohan Rs 10,000 on 2.1.2004. Rao accepted four bills of exchange drawn by Mohan to discharge the whole debt. The first for Rs 1,000 at one month, the second for Rs 2,000 at two months, the third for Rs 3,000 at three months and the last one for Rs 4,000 at four months. On 15th Jan. Mohan sent the first bill to bank for collection. On 17th Jan., he endorsed the second bill in favour of X. On 1st Feb. he got the fourth bill discounted with the bank @ 8% p.a. The first three bills were duly honoured but the fourth one, *i.e.*, the discounted one, was dishonoured on the due date noting charges being Rs. 50.

Show the entries in the books of Rao and Mohan. *(CS, B.Com., Madurai, Kerala, Agra)*

SOLUTION

In the Books of Mohan

				Rs	*Rs*
2004 Jan. 2	Bills Receivable A/c	Dr.		1,000	
	To Rao A/c				1,000
	(Being the bill accepted for one month)				
"	Bills Receivable A/c	Dr.		2,000	
	To Rao A/c				2,000
	(Being the bill accepted for two months)				
"	Bills Receivable A/c	Dr.		3,000	
	To Rao A/c				3,000
	(Being the bill accepted for three months)				
"	Bills Receivable A/c	Dr.		4,000	
	To Rao A/c				4,000
	(Being the bill accepted for four months)				
Jan. 15	Bank for Collection A/c	Dr.		1,000	
	To Bills Receivable A/c				1,000
	(Being the first bill sent to bank for collection)				
17	X A/c	Dr.		2,000	
	To Bills Receivable A/c				2,000
	(Being the second bill endorsed to X)				
Feb. 1	Bank A/c	Dr.		3,920	
	Discount A/c	Dr.		80	
	To Bills Receivable A/c				4,000
	(Being the fourth bill discounted at 8% p.a. for 3 months)				
Feb. 4	Bank A/c	Dr.		1,000	
	To Bank for collection A/c				1,000
	(Being the first bill honoured at maturity)				
April 4	Cash A/c	Dr.		3,000	
	To Bills Receivable A/c				3,000
	(Being the third bill honoured at maturity)				
May 4	Rao A/c	Dr.		4,050	
	To Bank A/c				4,050
	(Being the fourth bill dishonoured at maturity and noting charges Rs. 50)				

In the Books of Rao

				Rs	Rs
2004	Mohan A/c	Dr.		1,000	
	To Bills Payable A/c				1,000
	(Being the bill accepted for one month)				
"	Mohan A/c	Dr.		2,000	
	To Bills Payable A/c				2,000
	(Being the bill accepted for two months)				
"	Mohan A/c	Dr.		3,000	
	To Bills Payable A/c				3,000
	(Being the bill accepted for three months)				
"	Mohan A/c	Dr.		4,000	
	To Bills payable A/c				4,000
	(Being the bill accepted for 4 months)				
Feb. 4	Bills Payable A/c	Dr.		1,000	
	To Cash A/c				1,000
	(Being the first bill honoured at maturity)				
March 4	Bills Payable A/c	Dr.		2,000	
	To Cash A/c				2,000
	(Being the second bill honoured at maturity)				
April 4	Bills Payable A/c	Dr.		3,000	
	To Cash A/c				3,000
	(Being the third bill honoured at maturity)				
May 4	Bills Payable A/c	Dr.		4,000	
	Noting Charges A/c	Dr.		50	
	To Mohan A/c				4,050
	(Being the fourth bill dishonoured at maturity,. noting charges being Rs 50)				

ILLUSTRATION 4.21

Ravi accepted on April 1, 2007 bill for Rs. 10,000 drawn by Kapil at three months. Kapil, on 4th April, discounted the bill with his banker at 6% p.a. Ravi failed to meet the bill on the due date and at his request Kapil agreed to renew the bill for three more months for which he demanded collateral security. Ravi endorsed two of his customers bills for Rs. 7,000 and Rs. 5,400 due on August, 20 and September 20, 2007 respectively as collateral security. Kapil discounted all the three bills at 6% p.a. on 10th July with the bankers; but on the due date the second customer's bill was dishonoured, Ravi became bankrupt on 1st September, 2007 and nothing was realized from his estate.

Pass the necessary Journal Entries and Ravi Account in the books of Kapil.

SOLUTION

In the Books of Kapil

Journal

Date	Particulars		L.F.	Dr. Rs	Cr. Rs
2007					
April 1	Bills Receivable A/c	Dr.		10,000	
	To Ravi A/c				10,000
	(Being a bill drawn on Ravi for 3 months)				

Date	Particulars		Dr. (Rs.)	Cr. (Rs.)
April 4	Bank A/c	Dr.	9,850	
	Discount on Bills A/c	Dr.	150	
	To Bills Receivable A/c			10,000
	(Being the bill discounted with the bank @ 6% p.a.)			
July 4	Ravi A/c	Dr.	10,000	
	To Bank A/c			10,000
	(Being the bill dishonoured at maturity)			
July 4	Bills Receivable A/c	Dr.	10,000	
	To Ravi A/c			10,000
	(Being a new bill drawn for 3 months)			
	Bills Receivable A/c	Dr.	12,400	
	To Ravi A/c			12,400
	(Being two bills endorsed in favour of us by Ravi for Rs. 5,400 and Rs. 7,000 respectively)			
July 10	Bank A/c	Dr.	22,139	
	Discount on Bills A/c	Dr.	261	
	To Bills Receivable A/c			22,400
	(Being the bill discounted with the bank @ 6% p.a)			
Sept. 1	Ravi A/c	Dr.	10,000	
	To Bank A/c			10,000
	(Being the new bill dishonoured due to Ravi's insolvency)			
Sept. 20	Ravi A/c	Dr.	5,400	
	To Bank A/c			5,400
	(Being the second customer's bill dishonoured at maturity)			
	Bad Debt A/c	Dr.	3,000	
	To Ravi A/c			3,000
	(Being the amount written-off as bad debt)			

Working: Calculation of discount:

		Rs.
1.	Net bill (due date 7th Oct. 2007) = Rs. 10,000 × 6/100 × 3/12 =	150
	1st customer's bill (due date Aug. 20) = Rs. 7,000 × 6/10 × 41/365 =	47
	2nd customer's bill (due date Sept. 20) = Rs. 5,400 × 6/100 × 72/365 =	64
		261

Dr. **Ravi Account** Cr.

Date	*Particulars*	*Rs*	*Date*	*Particulars*	*Rs*
1.4.07	To Balance b/f	10,000	1.4.07	By Bills Receivable A/c	10,000
7.7.07	To Bank A/c (dishonoured)	10,000	7.7.07	By Bills Receivable A/c (New bill)	10,000
1.9.07	To Bank A/c (New bill dishonoured)	10,000	7.7.07	By Bills Receivable A/c (Customer's Bill)	12,400
20.9.07	To Bank A/c (2nd customer's bill dishonoured)	5,400	20.9.07	By Bad Debt A/c	3,000
		35,400			35,400

ILLUSTRATION 4.22

On 1st January 2007, X owes Y Rs. 10,000 for which Y draws on X two bills for Rs. 4,000 and Rs. 6,000 payable after 3 months and 4 months respectively.

Both the bills are drawn on 1st January 2007. Y discounts both the bills with his bankers on 3rd January, at 12% p.a.

Before the due date of the 1st bill, X requests Y to assist him by providing with Rs. 4,000 cash and drawing a 3rd bill on him (X) for the amount plus interest @ 12% p.a. for 3 months. Y agrees to this proposal and pays the money after discounting the third bill with his banker @ 12% p.a.

A week before the 2nd bill for Rs. 6,000 falls due, X again asks Y to assist him by providing Rs. 5,000. Y however is not in a position to pay any cash but he arranges with X to draw on him (Y) two bills for Rs. 2,000 and Rs. 3,000 at 2 months and 3 months respectively from the due date of the 2nd bill (Rs. 6,000).

Y accepts these two bills and X discounts them with his bankers at 12% p.a. and assisted by the proceeds, duly meets the 2nd bill on the due date.

Y fails to meet his own acceptances. On 10th June 2007, X becomes bankrupt, before meeting his third bill.

On 1st September 2007, a first and final dividend of 50 paise in the rupee is received from X's estate.

Pass journal entries and the account of X in the books of Y. *(B.Com. MS, MK)*

SOLUTION

In the books of Y

Journal

Date	*Particulars*		*L.F.*	Dr *Rs*	Cr. *Rs*
2007					
Jan. 1	Bills Receivable A/c	Dr.		10,000	
	To X A/c				10,000
	(Being two bills drawn on X for Rs. 4,000 and 6,000 payable after 3 months and 4 months respectively)				
Jan. 3	Bank A/c	Dr.		9,640	
	Discount on Bills A/c (1)	Dr.		360	
	To Bills Receivable A/c				10,000
	(Being the bills discounted with the banker @ 12% p.a.)				
April 3	X A/c	Dr.		4,000	
	To Cash A/c				4,000
	(Being cash paid to X)				
April 3	X A/c (2)	Dr.		120	
	To Interest A/c				120
	(Being Interest on Rs. 4,000 @ 12% p.a. for 3 mnoths debited to X)				
April 3	Bills Receivable A/c	Dr.		4,120	
	To X A/c				4,120
	(Being a new bill drawn on X for Rs. 4,000 plus interest, payable after 3 months)				
April 3	Bank A/c	Dr.		3,996	
	Discount on Bills A/c (3)	Dr.		124	
	To Bills Receivable A/c				4,120
	(Being the bill discounted with the banker @ 12% p.a.)				
May 4	X A/c	Dr.		5,000	
	To Bills Payable A/c				5,000
	(Being two bills accepted for financing X for Rs. 2,000 and 3,000 payable after 2 and 3 months respectively)				

July 6	X A/c Dr.		4,120	
	To Bank A/c			4,120
	(Being the dishonour of 3rd bill)			
July 7	Bills Payable A/c Dr.		2,000	
	To X A/c			2,000
	(Being the dishonour of our acceptance given to X)			
Aug. 7	Bills Payable A/c Dr.		3,000	
	To X A/c			3,000
	(Being dishonour of our acceptance at maturity)			
Sept. 1	Bank A/c Dr.		2,060	
	Bad Debt A/c Dr.		2,060	
	To X A/c			4,120
	(Being 50 paise in a rupee received from the estate of X as final dividend)			

Dr. **Ravi Account** Cr.

Date	Particulars	Rs	Date	Particulars	Rs
1.1.07	To Balance b/d	10,000	1.1.07	By Bills Receivable A/c	10,000
3.4.07	To Cash A/c	4,000	3.4.07	By Bills Receivable A/c	4,120
3.4.07	To Interest A/c	120	7.7.07	By Bills Payable A/c	2,000
4.5.07	To Bills Payable A/c	5,000	7.8.07	By Bills Payable A/c	3,000
6.7.07	To Bank A/c	4,120	1.9.07	By Bank A/c	2,060
			1.9.07	By Bad Debt A/c	2,060
		23,240			23,240

1. 1st bill: Rs. 4,000 × 12% × 3 months = Rs. 120
   2nd bill : Rs. 6,000 × 12% × 4 months = Rs. 240
   Total : = Rs. 360
2. Rs. 4,000 × 12% × 3 months = Rs. 120
3. Rs. 4,120 × 12% × 3 months = Rs. 123.60 or Rs. 124

QUESTIONS

OBJECTIVE TYPE QUESTIONS

I. State whether each of the following statement is True or False.

1. An accommodation bill is drawn and accepted for genuine trade transactions.
2. There are only two parties in case of a bill of exchange.
3. A bill of exchange contains an unconditional order to a ceratin person to pay a certain sum of money.
4. There is no difference between a holder and a holder in due course.
5. A bill of exchange payable otherwise than on demand can be made payable to the bearer.
6. Retiring of a bill is different from dishonour of a bill.
7. A bill drawn in India on a person residing outside India but payable in India is an inland bill.
8. Amount of noting charges paid by the drawer is a loss to the drawee.
9. Promissory note contains an unconditional order.
10. Interest on renewal of a bill is a gain to the drawer and loss to the drawee.

(**Ans.** 1. False; 2. False; 3. True; 4. False; 5. True; 6. True; 7. True; 8. True; 9. False; 10. True)

II. Indicate whether the following statements are True or False.

1. Accommodation bills are backed by business transactions.
2. In order to renew a bill, the original bill need not be cancelled.
3. No cancellation entry is required, when one party in accommodation bill becomes insolvent.
4. No entry is passed in the books of the drawee when a bills receivable is either discounted with the bank or endorsed to some party.
5. The creditor is the person on whom the bill is drawn.
6. A bill of exchange is one kind of a post-dated cheque.
7. A promissory note must be accepted by the drawee.
8. Accommodation bills are always discounted.
9. Discount on bills is a loss for the drawer and a gain for the drawee.
10. Days of grace is not allowed when the bill is payable on demand.

(**Ans.** 1. False; 2. False; 3. False; 4. True; 5. False; 6. True; 7. False; 8. True; 9. False; 10. True.)

II. Fill in the blanks.

1. A bill of exchange payable after a certain period is known as .... bill.
2. A bill which is not an Inland Bill is .... bill.
3. Noting charges are paid in the event of .... of a bill.
4. At the time of renewal of a bill, interest account is .... in the books of the drawee.
5. A person who draws a bill of exchange is known as the ....
6. A bill of exchange has .... parties.
7. When a Bill is dishonoured .... Account is debited in the books of the drawee.
8. When the endorsed bill is dishonoured, ... Account is credited in the books of the drawer.
9. Bills Receiveable Account is a .... Account.
10. A bill of exchange is drawn by a ....
11. Noting charges are paid in the event of .... of a bill.
12. .... days of grace allowed in case of time bills for calculating date of maturity.

(**Ans.** 1. Time; 2. Foreign; 3. Dishonour; 4. Debited; 5. Drawer; 6. Three; 7. Bills Payable; 8. Creditor; 9. Real; 10. Creditor; 11. Dishonour; 12. Three.)

III. Select best choice to complete each statement given below:

1. A Bill of Exchange is also known as:
   (a) Accommodation Bill (b) Cash Bill
   (c) Trade Bill
2. A bill drawn and accepted for mutual accommodation is known as:
   (a) Trade Bill (b) Finance Bill
   (c) Cash Bill
3. When a new acceptance is received by cancelling the old bill, it is called:
   (a) Renewal (b) Discounting
   (c) Dishonour
4. A bill of exchange is an acknowledgement of:
   (a) Debt (b) Goods received
   (c) Credit extended
5. When a bill is endorsed, credit is given to:
   (a) Bills Receivable Account (b) Endorsee's Account
   (c) Acceptor's Account
6. At the time of endorsement of a bill, the drawer credits:
   (a) The Drawee's Acount (b) The Endorsee's Account
   (c) Bills Receivable Account

7. When a bill is discharged, the acceptor debits
   (a) Creditor's Account (b) Cash Account
   (c) Bills Payable Account
8. A bill of exchange cannot be:
   (a) Endorsed (b) Accepted
   (c) Crossed.
9. The person on whom the bill is drawn is called the :
   (a) Drawer (b) Drawee
   (c) Payee
10. A bills of exchange is renewed generally at the request of :
   (a) Drawer (b) Bank
   (c) Drawee
11. A bill of exchange is dishonoured by
   (a) Drawer (b) Drawee
   (c) Bank
12. Discount allowed on a retired bill is a :
   (a) Gain for the Drawer (b) Loss for the Drawee
   (c) Gain for the Debtor

(**Ans.** 1. (c); 2. (b); 3. (a); 4. (a); 5. (a); 6. (c); 7. (c); 8. (c); 9. (b); 10. (c); 11. (b); 12. (c))

THEORETICAL QUESTIONS

1. What is a Bill of Exchange ? State its characteristics.
2. Distinguish between a Bill of Exchange and Promissory Note.
3. Discuss the advantages of a Bill of Exchange.
4. Explain the terms "Drawing a Bill" and "Accepting a Bill" with suitable examples.
5. Give journal entries :
   (*a*) When a Bill is drawn and accepted.
   (*b*) When a Bill is endorsed..
   (*c*) When a Bill is encashed.
   (*d*) When a Bill is discounted.
   (*e*) When a Bill is dishonoured.
6. What is an Accommodation Bill ? How does it differ from the Trade Bill ?

PRACTICAL PROBLEMS

TRADE BILLS

1. A Bill for Rs 1,000 is drawn by A on B and accepted by the latter payable at the Bank of India. Show what entries should be passed in the books of A under each of the following circumstances :
   (*i*) If A retained the Bill till the due date and then realised it on maturity.
   (*ii*) If he discounted it with his bankers for Rs 950.
   (*iii*) If he sent it to his bankers for collection.
   (*iv*) If he endorsed it to his creditor C in full settlement of his debt.
   Also, give the necessary entries in each of the cases, if the Bill is dishonoured. (*Hr. Sec. Delhi*)
2. Anand purchased goods worth Rs 1,000 from Kiran on 1st January 2005 and accepted a Bill for one month drawn by Kiran for same. Being unable to meet the Bill on the due date, Anand requested Kiran to accept cash Rs 250 and drew a new Bill for 2 months for the balance amount plus interest of Rs 10. Kiran accepted this proposal and drew on Anand another Bill. The Bill was duly met on the due date. Pass journal entries in the books of both the parties. (*Inter Andhra*)

3. Hari sells goods for Rs 1,000 to Mohan on 1st January 2005 and on the same day draws a Bill on Mohan at three months for the amount. Mohan accepts it and returns it to Hari, who discounts on January 5th with his bank at 6% p.a. The acceptance is dishonoured on the due date, the noting charges paid by the bank being Rs 60.

   On April 5th, 2005, Mohan accepts a new bill at three months for the amount due to Hari together with interest at 12% p.a.

   Make a journal entries to record these transactions in the books of Hari.

4. Amarnath sells goods to Bholanath for Rs 10,000 and draws upon him a Bill for the amount payable three months after the date. The Bill is accepted by Bholanath. Amarnath discounted the Bill with his bankers at a discount of Rs 150. Bholanath fails to meet the Bill on maturity. Amarnath pays off his banker and his expenses amount to Rs 100. Bholanath gives a fresh Bill for two months for Rs 10,250 which he met at maturity.

   Show the necessary journal entries in Amarnath's book. *(B. Com., Delhi)*

5. On January 1st 2005, Julie supplied goods to Vikram of the value of Rs 9,000 and settled the account by means of three bills of Rs 3,000 each due after two, three and four months respectively.

   A week later Julie discounted the first Bill at a discount of Rs 60. The other two Bills were held till maturity.

   The first two bills were duly met on maturity. On the maturity of the third bill, however, Vikram arranged to retire the Bill paying Rs 1,000 in cash and giving Julie a fresh Bill for four months to cover the balance together with 12% interest p.a. Julie discounted this bill for Rs 2,000. The Bill was met on maturity.

   Pass the necessary journal entries in the books of Julie and Vikram. *(CAIIB)*

6. On 1st January 2005, Bimal drew on Chetan three Bills of Exchange in full settlement of claims; the first Bill for Rs 14,000 for one month, the second Bill for Rs 16,000 for two months and the third Bill for Rs 18,000 for three months. These Bills were duly accepted by Chetan.

   The first Bill was endorsed by Bimal to his creditor Tarun on 3rd January, the second Bill was discounted on 15th January for Rs 15,000 and the third Bill was sent to bank for collection on 4th February. All the Bills were duly met on maturity except the second Bill which was dishonoured, noting charges being Rs 240. Bimal charged Chetan Rs 300 for interest and drew on a fourth Bill for two months for the amount due. The fourth Bill was duly met on maturity.

   Pass journal entries in the books of Bimal. *(CAIIB)*

ACCOMMODATION BILLS

7. Mr A for mutual accommodation of himself and Mr B draws upon the latter a Bill at 3 months date for Rs 800 on 1st January. The Bill is discounted by Mr A at 5% and half the proceeds are remitted to Mr B.

   Mr B at the same time draws a Bill at 3 months on Mr A for Rs 400. After securing A's acceptance, the Bill is discounted at 6% by Mr B who remits half the proceeds to Mr A. Mr B becomes a bankrupt on 31st March and 25 paise in the Rupee is received on 15th May as first and final dividend from his estate.

   Write up journal and Mr B's account in Mr A's books. *(B.Com., Madras)*

   [Ans. Bad Debts Rs 450]

8. For mutual accommodation of themselves Patel and Murty draw Bills on each other. On January 2nd, Patel draws a Bill on Murty for Rs 1,000 payable three months and on 3rd January, Murty draws a Bill on Patel for Rs 500 payable three months. As arranged, both the Bills are immediately discounted @ 5% p.a. and the proceeds are shared equally. On maturity of the first Bill, Murty becomes insolvent and is unable to honour the Bill. A dividend of 50%, however, is realised from his estate on 30th June.

   Show the relevant accounts in the books of Patel who closes his books on 30th June. *(CA Inter)*

   [Ans. Bad Debts Rs 375]

9. A draws a Bill on B for Rs 3,000 for mutual accommodation of both (A—2/3 and B—1/3). B accepts the same and returns it to A. A discounts the Bill for Rs 2,820 and remits 1/3 of the proceeds to B. Before the due date, not having funds to meet the Bill, B draws a Bill for Rs 4,200 on A on the same terms as to mutual accommodation. The second Bill is discounted for Rs 4,080. The first Bill is met on

the due date a net amount of Rs 720 is remitted to A by B. Before the due date of the second Bill A becomes bankrupt and B is obliged to meet the obligation on this Bill to the discounting banker. He receives a dividend of 60 paise in the rupee in full satisfaction.

Pass journal entries in the book of A and B. (*B.Com., Calcutta Co. Secretary*)

[Ans. Bad Debts Rs 1,120]

10. Inder drew upon Mohan a Bill for Rs 9,000 on 1st April... for 3 months for mutual accommodation. Mohan accepted the draft and Inder got it discounted at 6% and remitted one-third of the proceeds to Mohan. On the due date Inder was not able to send the required sum and asked Mohan to receive a two months Promissory Note for Rs 6,090 which Mohan did. Mohan got the Note discounted for Rs 6,000 and met his acceptance. Inder became insolvent just before his Promissory Note was due for payment. Only 50% was received from his estate.

    Give journal entries in the books of both Inder and Mohan and prepare Inder's account in the books of Mohan. (*B.Com., Punjab*)

    [Ans. Bad Debts Rs 3,045]

11. For mutual benefit, A accepted a Bill for Rs 5,000 drawn by B on 1.7.2005 at three months. They agreed to share the benefit in the ratio of 2 : 3. B discounted the Bill at 12% p.a. on the same day and remitted two-fifth of the share to A on the due date A drew a Bill at three months for Rs 10,000 on B in order to provide funds to meet the first Bill. The second Bill was discounted for Rs 9,850 on the same day. The first Bill was met and the remaining amount was shared between both the parties in the agreed ratio. Before the maturity of the second Bill A became bankrupt and B honoured the Bill and recovered 30 paise in the rupee from the bankruptcy proceeds of A.

    Make necessary journal entries in the books of both the parties and also open personal ledgers in their respective books. (*B.Com., Madurai*)

    [Ans. Bad Debts Rs 2,800]

12. P and R were in need of funds. Therefore, on 1st June 2004, P accepted a Bill for Rs 5,000 drawn by R for three months. R got the bill discounted at 8% p.a. from Punjab Bank and remitted half of the proceeds to P. On the due date, however, R was not in a position to send the remaining half of the amount to P. On 29th August 2004, however, he agreed to accept a Bill for Rs 2,520 (inclusive of interest) drawn by P for three months, which P discounted for Rs 2,500. On the due date, R honoured the Bill.

    Give journal entries in the books of P and R. (*B.Com., Punjab*)

13. R owed Rs 2,000 to S. On 1st October 2004, R accepted a Bill drawn by S for the amount at 3 months. S got the Bill discounted with his bank for Rs 1,900. Before due date, R approached S for renewal of the Bill. S agreed on the conditions that Rs 1,000 be paid immediately together with interest on the remaining amount at 12% p.a. for 3 months and for the balance, R accepted a new Bill at three months. These arrangements were carried out. But, afterwards, R became insolvent and 40% of the amount could be recovered from his estate.

    Pas journal entries in the books of S and R. (*CAIIB*)

    [Ans. Bad Debts Rs 600]

14. On 1st July 2005, Mr S, for mutual accommodation of himself and Mr R drew on the other a Bill for Rs 5,000 payable at three months. The Bill was discounted with the bank at 5% and half of the proceeds were remitted to R on 2nd July 2005.

    On 2nd July, Mr R drew a Bill on Mr S for Rs 2,000 payable at 3 months date. He discounted the Bill with his bankers at 10% and remitted half of the proceeds to Mr S.

    Mr R became insolvent on 31st August 2005 and only 25% was received by Mr S on 15th Sept. 2005 as the first and dinal dividend from his estate.

    Write the journal entries and the ledger account of Mr R in the books of Mr S. (*CA Inter*)

    [Ans. Bad Debts Rs 2,625]

15. On 1st April 2005, Mr A accepts a three months Bill drawn by his creditor Mr B for Rs 10,000. On 5th May 2005, B discounts the same at 15% p.a. Mr A being unable to meet at the Bill at maturity, requests Mr B to accept Rs 4,000 in cash and to draw another Bill for three months for the balance amount plus

interest @ 18% p.a. and Mr B agrees. But, before the second Bill matures, Mr A becomes insolvent and is unable to pay any amount whatsoever.

Show the entries in the books of both the parties. **[Ans.** Bad Debts Rs 6,270]

16. On 1st July 2004, Salil for mutual accommodation of himself and Sunil drew on the other a Bill for Rs 10,000 payable at 3 months date. The Bill was discounted with Central Bank of India at 5% and half of the proceeds were remitted to Sunil on 2nd July.,

    On 2nd July Sunil drew a Bill on Salil for Rs 4,000 payable at 3 months date. He discounted the Bill with Bank of India at 10% and remitted half of the proceeds to Salil.

    Sunil became bankrupt on 31st Aug. 2004 and only 25% was received by Salil on 15th Sept. 2004 as the first and final dividend from his estate. Write the journal entries in the books of Salil. (*ICWA*)

    [Ans. Bad Debts Rs 5,250]

17. X draws on Y a Bill for Rs 15,000 on 1st April 2005 for 3 months. Y accepts the Bill and sends back to X who gets it discounted for Rs 14,400. X immediately remits Rs 4,800 to Y. On the due date, X being unable to remit the amount due, accepts a Bill for Rs 21,000. for three months which is discounted by Y for Rs 20,055. Y sends Rs 3,370 to X. Before the maturity of the Bill X becomes bankrupt, his estate paying 50 paise in the rupee.

    Give journal entries in the books of X and Y. (*B.Com., M.S.*)

    [Ans. Bad Debts Rs 7,000]

18. On 1st January 2005, A drew a Bill on B for Rs 10,000 due for payment on 30th April 2005, plus the days of grace. The Bill was accepted by B. On 4th January 2005, A discounted the bill with his bank and realised a sum of Rs 9,500. He remitted half of the amount, *i.e.,* Rs 4,750 on the same day to B by cheque.

    On 1st March 2005, B drew a Bill on A for Rs 12,000 due for payment on 31st May 2005, without days of grace. On the same day, A accepted the Bill. On 2nd March 2005, B discounted the Bill with his bank for Rs 11,500 and remitted half of the proceeds to A. Both of them agreed to share the discount charges on the two bills equally.

    B failed to honour the Bill drawn on him on the due date. A, therefore, paid the Bill amount in cash to his bank on 15th May 2005 alongwith interest amounting to Rs 75. On the same day, A drew a Bill for the original amount of the dishonoured Bill plus Rs 350 towards interest. The Bill duly accepted by B was payable on 15th July 2005 without days of grace. A paid the Bill drawn on him on its due date by cheque. Before the second Bill drawn on B was due for payment, the drawee became insolvent. The Bill was, therefore, dishonoured on its due date and A received in cash on 1st August 2005, a sum of Rs 4,000 towards full and final settlement of the amount due to him from B.

    Pass journal entries to record the above transactions in the books of A and also prepare B's account in A's books. (*CAIIB*)

    [Ans. Bad Debts Rs 7,350]

Chapter 5

Bank Reconciliation Statement

Introduction – Debit/Credit Balances – Reasons for Discrepancies – Omission of Entry – Procedure – Usefulness – Overdraft – Adjustment of Cash Book – Questions – Objective Type of Questions – Theoretical Questions – Practical Problems.

There is hardly any business firm worth its name today that does not have a bank account of its own. Generally, at present, a business firm maintains several accounts with several banks. Many transactions involving receipts and payments of money take place every day, during the course of business. To avoid such a tedious work of cash dealings every businessman opens a current account with banks. All payments are made through cheques and all receipts are banked. For this purpose, the businessman maintains a Cash Book with bank column. All transactions relating to bank deposits and withdrawals are recorded in the bank column of the Cash Book.

At the same time, the bank also maintains the accounts of the individual customers in their personal ledgers, *i.e.,* the customers' account in the bank ledger. A copy of the personal account of the customer, kept by the banker, is handed over to the customer and this copy of the personal account or the statement is known as Pass Book. Thus, Pass Book is a copy of customer's accounts as it appears in the bank ledger. For the purpose of verification of the bank balance of the customers, the bank issues the Pass Book, where the customers' transactions are copied down from the bank ledgers.

DEBIT/CREDIT BALANCES

Balance as per Cash Book means the balance as per the Bank column of the Cash Book, which is maintained by the trader or Bank's client. This Cash Book is maintained and entered by the trader himself. When the total of debit column of the Cash Book (Bank column) is more than the total credit column of Cash Book (Bank column), it is known as *debit* balance. That is, there is a favourable balance of cash deposited at the bank. When Cash Book balance is given, it is treated as debit balance. When credit balance as per Cash Book is given, it is treated as overdraft.

Bank keeps account for its customer. The amount deposited by its customer are credited to his account in Bank's ledger and the amounts withdrawn by customer are debited in his account. When credit balance is more than the debit balance, it is called *credit* balance as per the Pass Book. When debit balance is more than the credit balance, it is a debit balance/overdraft as per Pass Book.

Cash Book Shows Debit Balance = Favourable Balance
Pass Book Shows Credit Balance = Favourable Balance
Cash Book Shows Credit Balance = Unfavourable/Overdraft
Pass Book Shows Debit Balance = Unfavourable/Overdraft
Bank Balance means favourable balance unless otherwise stated.

All the entries in the Cash Book (Bank column) are made by the customer/trader and all entries in the Pass Book are made by the bank. Periodically, the customer verifies the entries of the Pass Book with the entries made in the Cash Book (in bank column). When the customer deposits any amount into the bank, his bank balance increases, *i.e.,* Cash Book (bank column) shows a debit balance. At the same time, when the bank receives the deposit, the customer's Account is credited, thus the Pass Book shows a credit balance. The balances of Cash Book and the Pass Book must tally. Theoretically speaking, these two balances must agree with each other, because the same transactions are recorded in both the books—Cash Book and Pass Book. But it very often happens that the bank balance as shown by the Cash Book does not tally with the balance shown by the bank Pass Book, as written by the bank. The reasons are obvious. (Discussed later in this Chapter).

Specimen of Pass Book

Name_________ Account No.

Address_________

Current Account with_________Bank

Date	Particulars	Withdrawals Dr.	Deposits Cr.	Balance Dr./Cr.	Acctt's initials

REASONS FOR DISCREPANCIES

Theoretically speaking, when the same transactions are entered in both the books, the balances must agree each other. But practically looking, the two balances disagree. This may happen because some entries made in the Pass Book do not appear in the Cash Book because the cashier has no knowledge of such entries; similarly, some entries made in the Cash Book do not appear in the Pass Book because the bank has not received such intimation. For instance, a cheque issued to a party is credited in the Cash Book, on the date it is issued, thus the balance reduces the bank balance for that date in the trader's Cash Book. But, in the Pass Book, the balance will not be reduced till the cheque is paid by the bank. It may be encashed after a few or many days. Thus discrepancies arise between the balances of two accounts. We mention some of the reasons which cause a difference between the two, are as follows:

Let us look at the pattern of entries made in Pass Book and Cash Book:

Summary of Factors Affecting Balances (Under Favourable Balance)

Causes of Disagreement	What to do if it is started from Cash Book	What to do if it is started from Pass Book	Withdrawal or Deposit
1. Cheques issued but not presented for payment	+	–	Withdrawal
2. Cheques paid into Bank but not credited by the Bank	–	+	Deposit
3. Bank charges, for services rendered by bank, debited in the Pass Book but not in the Cash Book	–	+	Withdrawal
4. Dividend, Interest etc. collected by the Bank, entered in the Pass Book but not entered in Cash Book	+	–	Deposit
5. When Banker allows interest on bank balance but not entered in the Cash Book	+	–	Deposit
6. Amount directly deposited into Bank, but not entered in the Cash Book	+	–	Deposit
7. Subscriptions, premium etc. paid by the Banker under standing orders.	–	+	Withdrawal
8. Dishonour of cheques not entered in the Cash Book	–	+	Withdrawal
9. Credit, if any in the Pass Book	+	–	Deposit
10. Debit, if any in the Pass Book	–	+	Withdrawal

Alternatively

Factors Affecting Balances

Information	Cash Book Shows Debit Balance *i.e.* Pass Book Shows Credit Balance		Cash Book Shows Credit Balance *i.e.* Pass Book Shows Debit Balance	
	CB to PB	PB to CB	CB to PB	PB to CB
Cheques issued but not presented in the Bank	ADD	LESS	LESS	ADD
Cheques paid into Bank but not collected and credited by Bank	LESS	ADD	ADD	LESS
Credit, if any in the Pass Book	ADD	LESS	LESS	ADD
Debit, if any in the Pass Book	LESS	ADD	ADD	LESS

A short-cut formula for Bank Reconciliation Statement is given below :

"IF THE GIVEN BALANCE IS LESS, THEN THE FIND-OUT BALANCE WILL BE MORE, SO ADD THE DIFFERENCE TO IT. IN THE SAME WAY, IF THE GIVEN BALANCE IS MORE, THEN THE FIND-OUT BALANCE WILL BE LESS, SO DEDUCT THE DIFFERENCE FROM IT."

Alternatively :

If C.B. Balance is the starting point	If P.B. Balance is the starting point
Add : Item which makes the C.B. balance smaller than the one in the P.B.	Add : Item which makes the P.B. Balance lesser than the C.B. Balance
Deduct : Item which makes the C.B. Balance larger than the one shown in the P.B. (See Illustration 14)	Deduct : Item which makes the P.B. Balance larger than the one in the C.B. Balance.

OMISSION OF ENTRY

Trader may receive cheques. It is possible that some cheques might have been entered in the Cash Book but omitted to be banked. It means there is no entry in the Pass Book. Because of this omission, Cash Book balance is greater than Pass Book balance. This causes the difference. Similarly, it is also possible that some cheques might have been banked but without entry in the Cash Book. Therefore, balances as per Pass Book is greater than the balance as per the Cash Book. Hence the difference.

It is also possible that the ledger clerks at the bank may commit mistakes in posting, totalling or carrying over totals from one page to another. The trader may also commit similar mistakes.

All these items cause a difference between the balance as shown by the Cash Book and the balance as shown by the Pass Book. The various items, mentioned above, responsible for the disagreement are listed in the form of a statement. This statement is called Bank Reconciliation Statement. Thus a Bank Reconciliation Statement is prepared at periodical intervals with a view to indicate the items that cause disagreement between the balance as per the bank column of the Cash Book and the bank Pass Book, on any given date.

Procedure

The procedure for the preparation of Bank Reconciliation Statement is as follows:

1. Select the date (usually last day of the previous month) and start with Pass Book (or Cash Book) balance.
2. Look into the Pass Book and Cash Book. Tally and tick off the common items of the two books over the same period upto the selected date. Then Unticked or Unmarked items are sorted out which are responsible for the disagreement.
3. For the purpose of Reconciliation Statement, the balance appearing in the Cash Book (or the balance appearing in the Pass Book) should be taken as the starting point; and necessary

adjustments (addition or subtractions) should be made in this balance. The final amount should be the same as shown by the Pass Book (or the Cash Book). The two balances are thus reconciled with each other.

"A Bank Reconciliation statement is a statement prepared periodically, in order to reconcile the balance as shown by the Cash Book with the balance shown by Pass Book, by showing various causes of difference between the two balances."

According to Kohler, "Bank Reconciliation Statement is a statement displaying the items of difference between the balance of an account reported by a Bank and the account appearing on the book of the Bank's customer".

ILLUSTRATION 5.1

Prepare a Bank Reconciliation Statement as on 31st Jan., 2004 from the following extracts from the Cash Book (bank column) and the Bank Pass Book. *(CAIIB)*

Pass Book

Date	Particulars	Withdrawals	Deposits	Dr./Cr.	Balance
2004		Rs	Rs		Rs
Jan. 1	By Cash		4,000		4,000
4	To Furniture Dealers	600			3,400
4	To Dass & Co.	1,250			2,150
10	By Johnson & Co's cheque		350		2,500
12	To Roy & James	1,000			1,500
15	By Babu & Co's cheque		760		2,260
16	By Cash		300		2,560
20	To Cash	500			2,060
26	By J. Rai & Brothers cheque		430		2,490
31	To Premium paid (standing order)	250			2,240
31	To bank Charges	10			2,230
31	By Interest collected on Bonds		200		2,430

SOLUTION

Dr. **Cash Book (Bank Column)** Cr.

Date	*Particulars*	*Amount Rs*	*Date*	*Particulars*	*Amount Rs*
2004			2004		
Jan. 2	To Cash	4,000	Jan. 1	By Furniture Dealers	600
8	To Johnson & Co.	350	2	By Roy and James	1,000
10	To Babu & Co.	760	4	By Dass & Co.	1,250
16	To Cash	300	17	By Nagpal & Co.	730
20	To Rai & Brothers	430	20	By Cash	500
22	To Mohan & Co.	1,050	25	By Babu & Co.	780
31	To Nandy & Sons	340	31	By Balance c/d	2,370
		7,230			7,230
Feb. 1	To Balance b/d	2,370			

Solution : When such a problem is given, we may start solving the problem either from the Pass Book balance or Cash Book balance. It means when we start solving the problem from the Pass Book balance, the final amount should be the same as shown by the Cash Book balance and vice versa. We solve the problem in both the ways. Let us see how the Cash Book (Bank column) and the Pass Book should be compared.

Here the Cash Book shows a balance of Rs 2,370 whereas the Pass Book shows a balance of Rs 2,430. Look on the debit side of Cash Book and deposit column of the Pass Book, check item by item, one can find that two cheques have been deposited into bank but were not credited in the Pass Book because there is no entry in the Pass Book till 31st January 2004.

Cheque from Mohan & Co. Rs 1,050

Cheque from Nandy & Sons Rs 340

They appear only in the Cash Book and not in the Pass Book.

Had the cheques been credited in the Pass Book, then the Pass Book balance would have been 2,430 + 1,050 + 340 = Rs. 3,820. Similarly, looking on the credit side of the Cash Book and the withdrawals column of the Pass Book, we can find that the following cheques issued, have not been presented for payment, *i.e.,* the bank has not debited in the Pass Book.

Cheque issued to Nagpal & Co. Rs 730

Cheque issued to Babu & Co. Rs 780

The total of the two cheques comes to Rs 1,510. Had the cheques been paid, it would have been debited in the Pass Book. Then the balance would be Rs 3,820 – 1,510 = 2,310.

Further, we find that the Pass Book shows debit of Rs 250 towards premium and Rs 10 towards bank charges, totalling Rs 260. These are only in the Pass Book and not in the Cash Book. Had this amount Rs 260 ignored in the Pass Book, then the balance would be as in the Cash Book, *i.e.,* Rs 2,310 + Rs 260 = Rs 2,570.

Further, in the Pass Book, under deposit column, Rs 200 appears but not in the Cash Book. Thus balance increases only in Pass Book and not in Cash Book. To get the Cash Book balance, deduct the amount of Rs 200 from Rs 2,570, *i.e.,* 2,370 which agrees with the Cash Book balance.

The above problem can also be solved from Pass Book balance.

Bank Reconciliation Statement
as at 31st January 2004

		Rs	Rs
Bank Balance as per Pass Book			2,430
Add: Cheques paid in but not collected by the bank:			
Mohan & Co.	1,050		
Nandy & Sons	340	1,390	
" Premium paid by bank, but not credited in Cash Book		250	
" Bank charges debited in Pass Book but not credited in Cash Book		10	(+) 1,650
			4,080
Less: Cheques issued but not presented for payment at bank:			
Nagpal & Co.	730		
Babu & Co.	780	1,510	
" Interest collected on Bonds but not entered in Cash Book		200	(–) 1,710
BANK BALANCE AS PER CASH BOOK			2,370

Alternatively, the same problem can also be solved starting from the Cash Book:

Bank Reconciliation Statement
as at 31st January 2004

		Rs	Rs
Bank Balance as per Cash Book			2,370
Add: Cheques issued but not presented:			
Nagpal & Col.	730		
Babu & Co.	780	1,510	
" Interest collected on Bonds but not entered in Cash Book		200	(+) 1,710
			4,080

Less:	Cheques paid in but not collected:			
	Mohan & Co.	1,050		
	Nandy & Sons	340	1,390	
"	Premium paid by bank, but not credited in Cash Book		250	
"	Bank charges debited in Pass Book but not credited in Cash Book		10	(–) 1,650
	BANK BALANCE AS PER PASS BOOK			2,430

Alternatively, this problem can also be solved in a different method. There are two columns—Plus and Minus, indicating Positive balance and Overdraft balance. Here all the items to be added are put in the Plus column and items to be deducted are put in the Minus column. Then a balance is struck. The balance is the balance as per the Cash Book or Pass Book. Let us see:

Bank Reconciliation Statement
as on 31st January 2004

		Plus *Rs*	*Minus* *Rs*
Bank Balance as per Cash Book		2,370	
Cheques issued but not presented:			
Nagpal & Co.	730		
Babu & Co.	780	1,510	
Interest collected on Bonds but not entered in Cash Book		200	
Cheques paid in but not collected:			
Mohan & Co.	1,050		
Nandy & Sons	340		1,390
Premium paid by bank, but not credited in Cash Book			250
Bank charges debited in the Pass Book but not credited in Cash Book			10
BALANCE AS PER PASS BOOK			2,430
	Total	4,080	4,080

Alternatively :

Bank Reconciliation Statement
as on 31st January 2004

		Plus *Rs*	*Minus* *Rs*
Balance as per Pass Book		2,430	
Cheques paid in but not collected:			
Mohan & Co.	1,050		
Nandy & Sons	340	1,390	
Premium paid by bank, but not credited in the Cash Book		250	
Bank charges debited in the Pass Book but not credited in Cash Book		10	

Cheques issued but not presented:		
Nagpal & Co.	730	
Babu & Co.	780	1,510
Interest collected on Bonds, but not entered in the Cash Book		200
BALANCE AS PER CASH BOOK		2,370
	4,080	4,080

Usefulness

The important of Bank Reconciliation Statement can be judged on the basis of the following facts:

1. By the preparation of Bank Reconciliation Statement, *errors or mistakes can be corrected.*
2. *Misappropriation*, by Bank Staff or depositors' staff, *can be checked.*
3. *Delay in collection of cheques or non-payment of cheques can be brought into light.*
4. Reconciliation Statement is prepared to ascertain the *correct bank balance* which is shown in Balance Sheet.
5. Chances of *embezzlement are reduced.*
6. There is a moral check on the staff of organisation *to keep the cash records always up-to-date.*

Finding out Pass Book balance on the basis of Cash Book balance

ILLUSTRATION 5.2

From the following particulars of a business concern, prepare a Bank Reconciliation Statement as on 31st March 2004 :

(*i*) Bank balance as per Cash Book Rs 9,400.

(*ii*) During the month, total amount of cheques for Rs 12,400 was deposited into Bank, out of which one cheque for Rs 1,860 had been entered in the Pass Book on 2nd April 2004.

(*iii*) During the month, cheques for Rs 14,930 were drawn in favour of creditors. Of them, one creditor for Rs 6,430 encashed on 4th April, whereas another creditor for Rs 720 had not encashed his cheque.

(*iv*) As per instruction, the Bank on 26th March had paid Rs 4,400 to a creditor, but my mistake, the same has not been recorded in the Cash Book.

(*v*) According to agreement, on 24th March, a debtor had deposited directly into the Bank Rs 9,000, but the same has not been recorded in the Cash.

(*vi*) In the month of March, the Bank without any intimation had debited the account of the business for a sum of Rs 180 as bank charges and credited the same for Rs 300 as interest.

(*B.Com. Bombay, Kerala Ms.*)

SOLUTION

Bank Reconciliation Statement as on 31st March 2004

	Particulars	*Amount* Rs	*Amount* Rs
Bank Balance as per Cash Book			9,400
Add:	Cheque drawn but not presented for payment (Rs 6,430 + Rs 720)	7,150*	
Add:	Direct deposit made by a debtor, not entered in Cash Book	9,000	
Add:	Interest credited by Bank, not entered in Cash Book	300	(+) 16,450
			25,850
Less:	Cheque deposited but not credited	1,860	
Less:	Bank paid to a creditor, not recorded in Cash Book	4,400	
Less:	Bank charges debited by Bank not entered in Cash Book	180	(–) 6,440
	Bank Balance as per pass Book		19,410

*Alternatively, apply the short-cut formula. The Given Balance, *i.e.*, Cash Book balance shows reduced balance because Rs 6,430 + Rs 720 = Rs 7,150 have already been credited in Cash Book. But these two cheques have not been paid and thus there is no debit entry in the Pass Book in respect of Rs 6,430 + Rs 720 = Rs 7,150. Therefore, Given Balance, *i.e.,* Cash Book balance is less, then find out balance (Pass Book) will be more. Therefore, add Rs 6,430 + Rs 720 = Rs 7,150 to the Cash Book balance so as to get the Pass Book Balance. Similarly, the students are advised to apply the formula when a Bank Reconciliation Statement is prepared.

Finding out Cash Book balance on the basis of Pass Book balance

ILLUSTRATION 5.3

From the following particulars, prepare a bank reconciliation statement as on 28th February 2005. The Bank Pass Book showed a credit balance of Rs 9,436 on that date.

1. Out of the total cheques amounting to Rs 1,536 issued during the month, cheques of Rs 496 were presented for payment in March 2005. One cheque of Rs 50 issued to an upcountry party was lost in transit.
2. The Bank had in accordance with the standing instructions of the account holder, paid life insurance premium of Rs 427, for which no entry is recorded in his books.
3. One of his customers directly deposited in the Bank Rs 1,000 for which no entry is recorded in his books.
4. A cheque for Rs 579 was deposited in the Bank on 15th February and the same was not recorded in the Cash Book.
5. The Cash Book (bank column) did not show the bank charges debited by the bank amounting to Rs. 12. *(B.Com., Bombay)*

SOLUTION

Bank Reconciliation Statement
as on 28th February 2005

		Rs	*Rs*
Bank Balance as per Pass Book			9,436
Add:	Life Insurance Premium paid by the Bank but not entered in Cash Book	427	
"	Bank charges debited in the Pass Book, but not in Cash Book	12	(+) 439
			9,875
Less:	Cheques issued but not presented	496	
"	Cheque lost in transit	50	
"	Amount directly deposited by a customer, but not entered in Cash Book	1,000	
"	Cheque deposited and credited by the bank but not entered in Cash Book	579	(–) 2,125
	Bank Balance as per Cash Book		7,750

OVERDRAFT

So far we were assuming that the Cash Book shows a debit balance or the Pass Book shows a credit balance, that is, the Bank owes an amount to the trader. Generally, a bank allows its customer to draw from his account over and above its balance upto a limit as agreed upon. The facility is known as over-draft. Suppose, Mr A has a deposit of Rs 500 but he draws Rs 800. Then, his Pass Book shows debit balance of Rs 300 and such a balance (Rs 300) is technically known as Overdraft. Overdraft means overdrawing of a bank account. It is the nature of a loan granted by the bank.

When there is overdraft the situation will just opposite to that when there is a favourable balance. Hence, reverse steps would, of course, be taken while preparing Bank Reconciliation Statement. When there is an overdraft, the bank Pass Book shows a debit balance and the Bank Account in the Cash Book shows a credit balance. The reasons for the discrepancies mentioned earlier are the same, under overdraft, but in opposite direction. The following examples clarify:

Finding out Overdraft on the basis of Cash Book balance

ILLUSTRATION 5.4

From the following particulars, ascertain the balance by means of a statement, that would appear in the pass Book of Ramlal and Sons, as on 31st December.

1. Overdraft as per Cash Book on 31st December Rs 10,540.
2. Interest on overdraft for six months ending Dec. Rs 240.
3. Interest on investments collected by bank Rs 300.
4. Bank charges for the above period Rs 60.
5. Cheques drawn but not cashed by the customers, prior to December Rs 2,500.
6. Cheques paid into the bank, but not cleared before 31st December Rs 4,200.
7. A Bill Receivable for Rs 1,000 (discounted with the bank in Nov.) was dishonoured on December 31st. *(B.Com., Madurai, Kerala)*

SOLUTION

Ramlal & Sons
Bank Reconciliation Statement
as on 31st December

		Rs	*Rs*
Overdraft as per Cash Book			10,540
Add:	Interest on overdraft	240	
"	Bank charges	60	
"	Cheques paid in but not cleared	4,200	
"	Bills Receivable disonoured	1,000	(+) 5,500
			16,040
Less:	Cheques drawn but not cashed	2,500	
"	Interest on investments	300	(–) 2,800
	Overdraft as per Pass Book		13,240

Finding out Cash Book Overdraft on the basis of Pass Book Overdraft

ILLUSTRATION 5.5

Prepare a bank Reconciliation Statement on 31st December 2004.

(*a*) A's overdraft as per Pass Book was Rs 12,000 on that date.

(*b*) On 30th December cheques had been issued for Rs 7,000 of which cheques worth Rs 3,000 only had been encashed upto 31st December.

(*c*) Cheques amounting to Rs 3,500 had been paid into the bank for collection but of these only Rs 500 had been credited in the Pass Book.

(*d*) The bank charged Rs 500 as interest on overdraft, the intimation of which has been received on 2nd January 2005.

(*e*) The bank Pass Book shows a credit for Rs 1,000 representing Rs 400 paid by a debtor of A direct into the bank and Rs 600 collected direct by the bank in respect of interest on A's investments. A had no knowledge of these items.

(*f*) A cheque for Rs 200 had been debited in bank column of Cash Book by A, but it had not been sent to Bank. *(B.Com. Madurai, Madras)*

SOLUTION

Bank Reconciliation Statement
as on 31st December 2004

		Rs	Rs
Debit balance as per Pass Book (overdraft)			12,000
Add:	Cheques issued but not presented for payment	4,000	
"	Direct payment received by bank from A's debtor	400	
"	Interest on investment directly received by the bank	600	(+) 5,000
			17,000
Less:	Cheques sent for collection but not collected	3,000	
"	Interest on overdraft	500	
"	Cheque entered in Cash Book but not sent to bank	200	(–) 3,700
	Credit Balance as per Cash Book (overdraft)		13,300

ADJUSTMENT OF CASH BOOK

Usually, when a trader looks into his Cash (Bank column) Book and the Pass Book, there may be differences. At the end of financial year, it is ncessary to show the correct financial statements. Thus, it is implied that the entries ought to be made, should be made. Thus the trader tries to adjust his Cash Book by incorporating the entries or items like–Bank charges, Interest, direct deposit etc. in Pass Book. He will also try to rectify the error in his Cash Book, if any. With these adjustments, reconciliation is done with the remaining items, say, cheques issued but unpresented, cheques deposited but uncredited, Pass Book error, etc. The following example will clarify the adjustment.

It is important to note that the result of the Bank Reconciliation Statement must be the same whether it is prepared under (a) without adjustment in Cash Book or (b) with adjustment in Cash Book methods. It must also be remembered that those items which had already been recorded in the amended Cash Book will not appear any more in the Bank Reconciliation Statement.

The following illustration will clarify the adjustments.

ILLUSTRATION 5.6

From the following particulars, ascertain the Bank balance as per Pass Book as on 31st December.

1. The Bank balance as per Cash Book on the date was Rs 11,500.
2. Cheques issued but not cashed before that date amounted to Rs 1,750.
3. Cheques paid into Bank, but not cleared before December amounted to Rs 2,150.
4. Interest on Investments collected by the Bank but not entered in the Cash Book amounted to Rs 275.
5. Local cheque paid in but not entered in the Cash Book Rs 300.
6. Bank Charges debited in the Pass Book Rs 25. *(B.Com., Madurai)*

SOLUTION

(a) Without adjustment in Cash Book:

Bank Reconciliation Statement
as on 31st December

		Rs	Rs
Bank Balance as per Cash Book			11,500
Add:	Cheques issued not cashed	1,750	
"	Interest on Investments collected by the Bank but not entered in the Cash Book	275	
"	Cheques paid in but not entered in Cash Book	300	(+) 2,325
			13,825
Less:	Cheques paid in but not cleared	2,150	
"	Bank charges not entered in Cash Book	25	(–) 2,175
	Bank Balance as per Pass Book		11,650

(b) With adjustment in Cash Book:

If the balance at Bank, as per the Cash Book adjusted, it will be Rs 12,050, thus:

Dr. **Cash Book (Bank Col.)** *Cr.*

		Rs			*Rs*
Dec. 31	To Balance b/d	11,500	Dec. 31	By Bank Charges	25
"	To Interest on Investment	275	"	By Balance c/d	12,050
"	To Cheques omitted	300			
		12,075			12,075

BANK RECONCILIATION STATEMENT will then appear as follows:

Bank Reconciliation Statement
as on 31st December

	Rs	*Rs*
Bank balance as per Cash Book		12,050
Add: Cheques issued but not presented	1,750	(+) 1,750
		13,800
Less: Cheques paid in but not collected	2,150	(–) 2,150
Bank Balance as per Pass Book		11,650

ILLUSTRATION 5.7

Sri Balan maintained two separate Banking Accounts, one with Union Bank and the other with State Bank. On 31st December 2004, the bank balance as per Union Bank Statement and the State Bank statement were Rs 556 and Rs 1,308 respectively. But the bank balance in Balan's books on that date were Rs 2,870 (Dr.) and 4,680 (Dr.) respectively. On verification of these records the following information was ascertained:

(*a*) A cheque of Rs 250 from Roy which was directly remitted to the Union Bank was not entered in Balan's books.

(*b*) A cheque for Rs 700 drawn on State Bank and paid to Sen & Co. was entered in Union Bank Account in Balan's book.

(*c*) Payment of Rs 1,020 by Union Bank to Life Insurance Corporation of India under a standing order was not recorded in Balan's book.

(*d*) Cheques lodged but not yet credited Rs 212 for Union Bank and Rs 1,600 for State Bank.

(*e*) A cheque for Rs 57 paid in State Bank was returned dishonoured but this was not recorded in Balan's books.

(*f*) Bank charges of Rs 32 and Rs 45 for Union Bank and State Bank respectively were not accounted for by Balan.

(*g*) Rs 350 recorded to be deposited into State Bank on 31st Dec. 2004 was actually credited by Bank on 4th Jan. 2005.

(*h*) There were no unpresented cheques except one for Rs 620 drawn on State Bank.

Ascertain actual Bank balances of Sri Balan on 31st December 2004 and prepare a Bank Reconciliation Statement. (*B.Com., Calcutta, Bombay*)

SOLUTION

Balan
Cash Book

		Union Bank Rs.	*State Bank Rs.*			*Union Bank Rs.*	*State Bank Rs.*
2004				2004			
Dec. 31	To Balance b/d	2,870	4,680	Dec. 31	By Union Bank		700
	To Roy (Cheque directly deposited)	250			(Cheque drawn on State Bank but recorded in Union		

Date	Particulars	Union Bank	State Bank	Particulars	Union Bank	State Bank
	To State Bank (Cheque drawn on State Bank but recorded in Union Bank)	700		Bank Insurance Premium	1,020	
				By Party's A/c (Cheque dishonoured)		57
				By Bank Charges	32	45
				By Balance c/d	2,768	3,878
		3,820	4,680		3,820	4,680
Jan. 1	To Balance b/d	2,768	3,878			

Bank Reconciliation Statement as on 31st Dec. 2004

	Union Bank *Rs.*	*State Bank* *Rs.*
Bank Balances as per Cash Book (Dr.)	2,768	3,878
Add: Cheque issued but not presented for payment		(+) 620
	2,768	4,498
Less: Cheque lodged but not credited	(–) 212	1,600
	2,556	2,898
Less: Amount recorded in the Cash Book as being deposited but not credited by the Bank until 31st Dec. 2004		(–) 350
Bank Balance as per Pass Book	2,556	2,548

ILLUSTRATION 5.8

From the following particulars prepare a Bank Reconciliation Statement of Govil as on 31st December 2004:

1. Balance as per Pass Book on 31st Dec. 2004 Rs 8,500.
2. Cheques for Rs 5,100 were issued during the month of December but of these cheques for Rs 1,200 were presented in the month of January 2005 and one cheque for Rs 200 was not presented for payment.
3. Cheques and cash amounting to Rs 4,800 were deposited in Bank during December but credit was given for Rs 3,800 only.
4. A customer has deposited Rs 800 into the Bank directly.
5. The Bank has credited the merchant for Rs 200 as interest and has debited him for Rs 30 as bank charges, for which there are no corresponding entries in the Cash Book.

SOLUTION

Bank Reconciliation Statement
as on 31st December 2004

		Plus items	*Minus items*
		Rs	Rs
1.	Balance as per Pass Book	8,500	
2.	Cheques issued but not presented Rs 1,200 + 200		1,400
3.	Cheques deposited, but not cleared	1,000	
4.	Direct payment		800
5.	Interest allowed by bank		200
6.	Bank Charges	30	
	BALANCE AS PER CASH BOOK		7,130
		9,530	9,530

ILLUSTRATION 5.9

Ranganath has two accounts with Hanuman Bank, styled Account No. 1 and Account No. 2 On 31st December 2004, his Cash Book showed balances of Rs 5,400 and Rs 2,70,400 in the two accounts respectively. On an examination of Bank's statement, the following were noticed :

(*a*) Rs 27,000 has been transferred from Account No. 2 to Account No. 1 by the Bank without advice to Ranganath.

(*b*) Rs 10 has been Bank's incidental charges in respect of each account which was also not advised.

(*c*) Cheques for Rs 5,421 issued in Account No. 1 late in December have not yet been presented to the Bank.

(*d*) A cheque for Rs 4,272 deposited by Ranganath into Account No. 2 has been credited by the Bank into Account No. 1.

You are required to prepare Reconciliation Statement showing the balance as per Bank Statements.

(CA Entrance, B.Com., Madurai; MS., Bhopal

SOLUTION

Ranganath
Bank Reconciliation Statement (Account No. 1)
as on 31st December 2004

		Rs	*Rs*
Bank Balance as per Cash Book			5,400
Add:	Amount transferred from Account No. 1	27,000	
"	Cheques issued but not presented	5,421	
"	Wrong credit to this Account	4,272	(+) 36,693
			42,093
Less:	Incidental charges debited	10	(–) 10
	Bank Balance as per Pass Book		42,083

Ranganath
Bank Reconciliation Statement (Account No. 2)
as on 31st December 2004

		Rs	*Rs*
Bank Balance as per Cash Book			2,70,400
Less:	Transfer from Account No. 2	27,000	
"	Incidental charges debited	10	
"	Wrong Crtedit to Account No. 1	4,272	(–) 31,282
	Bank Balance as per Pass Book		2,39,118

ILLUSTRATION 5.10

A firm has two Accounts with State Bank of India. The Accounts were known as Account No. I and Account No. II. As at 31st December 2004, the balance as account books reflected the following:

Account No. I Rs 1,25,000 good balance

Account No. II Rs 1,11,250 Overdraft balance.

The Accountant failed to tally the balance with the Pass Book and the following information was available:

(*a*) The Bank has charged interest on Account No. II Rs 11,375 and credited interest on Account No. I Rs 1,250. These were not recorded by the Accountant.

(*b*) Rs 12,500 drawn on 10th December 2004, from Account No. I was recorded in the books of Account No. II.

(*c*) Bank charges of Rs 150 and Rs 1,125 for Account No. I and Account No. II were not recorded in the books.

(*d*) A deposit of Rs 17,500 in Account No. I was wrongly entered in Account II in the books.

(*e*) Two cheques of Rs 12,500 and Rs 13,750 deposited in Account No. I, but entered in Account No. II in the books, were dishonoured. The entries for dishonoured cheques were entered correctly in Account No. II.

(*f*) Cheques issued for Rs 1,50,000 and Rs 15,000 respectively from Account No. I and Account No. II were not presented until 5th January 2005.

(*g*) Cheques deposited for Rs 1,25,000 and Rs 1,17,500 in Account No. I and Account No. II respectively were credited by the Bank only on 2nd February 2005.

You are required to prepare Bank Reconciliation Statement for Account No. I and Account No. II.

(*ICWA*)

SOLUTION

Bank Reconciliation Statement for Account No. 1
as on 31st December 2004

	Particulars	*Amount* Rs	*Amount* Rs
Bank Balance as per Cash Book			1,25,000
Add:	Interest earned but not recorded in the Cash Book	1,250	
Add:	Deposits not entered in Cash Book	17,500	
Add:	Cheques deposited but not entered (Rs. 12,500 + Rs. 13,750)	26,250	
Add:	Cheques issued but not presented for payment	1,50,000	(+) 1,95,000
			3,20,000
Less:	Withdrawals not entered in Cash Book	12,500	
Less:	Bank charges debited in Pass Book but not entered in Cash Book	150	
Less:	Cheques dishonoured but not entered in Cash Book (Rs 12,500 + Rs 13,750)	26,250	
Less:	Cheques deposited but not credited by the Bank	1,25,000	(–) 1,63,900
	Bank Balance as per Pass Book		1,56,100

Bank Reconciliation Statement of Account No. II
as on 31st December 2004

		Rs	Rs
Overdraft balance as per Cash Book			1,11,250
Add:	Interest charged by the Bank but not recorded in the Cash Book	11,375	
"	Bank charges debited only in the pass book, but not in Cash Book	1,125	
"	Wrong debit in the Cash Book—Account No. II for deposit made in Account No. I	17,500	
"	Cheques paid into but not credited in the Pass Book	1,17,500	(+) 1,47,500
			2,58,750
Less	Wrong credit in the Cash Book Account No. II for amount withdrawn for Account No. I	12,500	
"	Cheques issued but not presented for payment	15,000	(–) 27,500
	OVERDRAFT BALANCE AS PER PASS BOOK		2,31,250

ILLUSTRATION 5.11

The pass Book of John shows a debit balance of Rs. 500 on 31st October 2006.

On comparison of the Pass Book with the Cash Book, it is observed that :

(i) Cheques issued by John in October 2006 amounted to Rs. 4,535 of which cheques amounting to Rs. 3,535 were paid by the bank by 31st October 2006.

(ii) John deposited cheques amounting to Rs. 5,000 on 31st October 2006 and these cheques were realised by the Bank on 1st November 2006.

(iii) Yogi a customer of John had directly deposited a sum of Rs. 3,000 on 24th October 2006 to the credit of John account with the Bank. John recorded this receipt on 4th November 2006.

(iv) The bank had debited John's account with Rs. 1,520 on 31st October 2006 on account of a dishonoured bill. No entry for the same has been made in the account books.

(v) On 31st October 2006 John's account was credited with Rs. 130 being dividend collected by the bank. On the same day, his account was debited with Rs. 10 being bank charges. Both these entries were recorded by John only on 5th November 2006.

Prepare a Bank Reconciliation Statement as on 31st October 2006.

(CAIIB; B.Com. Osmania Gurunanak, Jabalpur)

SOLUTION:

BANK RECONCILIATION STATEMENT

as on 31st October 2006

Particulars	*Amount Rs*	*Amount Rs*
Overdraft balance as par Pass Book		500
Add: Cheque issued but not presented for payment	1,000	
Add: Cheque directly deposited by a customer, not recorded in the Cash Book	3,000	
Add: Dividend credited in Pass Book and not recorded in Cash Book	130	(+) 4,130\
		4,630
Less: Cheque deposited not credited by the bank	5,000	
Less: Dishonoured bill not recorded in Cash Book	1,520	
Less: Bank charges debited not recorded in Cash Book	10	(–) 6,530
BANK BALANCE AS PER CASH BOOK (Dr.)		1,900

ILLUSTRATION 5.12

From the following particulars ascertain the bank balance as per bank pass book of Ramnath as on 31st December 2006.

(a) Bank overdraft as per Cash Book on 31st December 2006, Rs. 6,000.

(b) Interest on overdraft for six months ending 31st December 2006 Rs. 200 is debited in the Pass Book.

(c) Cheques issued but not cashed before 31st December 2006 amounted to Rs. 1,500.

(d) Cheques deposited into bank but not cleared and credited before 31st December 2006 amounted to Rs. 2,500.

(e) Interest on investments collected by bank and credited only in Bank pass book amounted to Rs. 1,800.

(f) Bills receivable which was discounted with the bank in November 2006, was dishonoured on 31st December 2006 and bank had debited Rs. 1,050 including bank charges Rs. 50.

(g) The bank col. of cash Book receipt side was over cast by Rs. 1,000 in December 2006.

(h) Bank had wrongly debited Mr. Ramnath for Rs. 500 on 10th December, on account of dishonour of cheque pertaining to Mr. Ramgopal but rectified the said mistake on 31st December 2006.

(B.Com. Bharathier, CAIIB)

Solution:

BANK RECONCILIATION STATEMENT

as on 31st December 2006

Particulars		*Amount Rs*	*Amount Rs*
Overdraft as per Cash Book			6,000
Add:	Interest on overdraft not entered in the Cash Book	200	
Add:	Cheques deposited into bank but not yet credited	2,500	
Add:	Bills receivable dishonoured and bank charges of Rs. 50, not entered in Cash Book	1,050	
Add:	Overcasting of bank Col. of the receipt side of the Cash Book	1,000	(+) 4,750
		1,500	10,750
Less:	Cheques issued but not cashed		
Less.	Interest on investment collected by bank, but not entered in Cash Book.	1,800	
	Cash Book		(–) 3,300
	OVERDRAFT AS PER BANK PASS BOOK		7,450

NB: (h) has no effect on BRS.

ILLUSTRATION 5.13

Prepare bank reconciliation statement from the following data as on 30th October 2006:

(a) Balance as per Pass Book on 30th October 2006 overdrawn Rs. 18,408.

(b) Cheques drawn on 30th October 2006 but not cleared till November 2006, Rs. 6,450, Rs. 1,490 and Rs. 1,852.

(c) Bank overdraft interest charged on 28th October not entered in Cash Book Rs. 3,220.

(d) Cheque received on 29th October 2006 entered in Cash Book but not deposited to bank till November 3, 2006, Rs. 22,644 and Rs. 3,460.

(e) Cheque received amounting to Rs. 70 entered in Cash Book twice.

(f) Bills receivable due on 29th October 2006 sent to Bank for collection on 28th October 2006 and entered in Cash Book forthwith but the proceeds were not credited in the Pass Book till 3rd November 2006, Rs. 5,960.

(g) A periodic payment by bank of Rs. 160 under standing instructions not entered in the cash book.

(h) Cheque deposited on 30th October 2006 dishonoured but the entry thereof was not made in the Cash Book Rs. 3,780.

(M.Com. B.Com. Madras)

SOLUTION:

BANK RECONCILIATION STATEMENT

as on 30th October 2006.

	Particulars	*Amount Rs*	*Amount Rs*
	(a) Overdraft as per Pass Book (Dr.)		18,408
Add:	(b) Cheques drawn but not cleared till November 2006	9,792	(+) 9,792
			28,200
Less:	(c) Bank overdraft interest not entered in Cash Book	3,220	
Less:	(d) Cheque received and entered in the Cash Book but not banked (Rs. 22,644 + Rs. 3,460)	26,104	
Less :	(e) Cheque received and entered twice in the Cash Book	70	
Less:	(f) Bills receivable sent to Bank for collection but not credited	5,960	
Less:	(g) Periodic payment by the bank not entered in the Cash Book	160	
Less:	(h) Cheque deposited and dishonoured but not entered in the Cash Book	3,780	(–) 39,294
	BANK BALANCE AS CASH BOOK (Dr.)		11,094

ILLUSTRATION 5.14

Prepare a Bank Reconciliation statement as on 30th November 2006 from the following information:

1. Balance as per Pass Book on 30th November 2006, overdrawn Rs. 40,000
2. On 5th October 2006, Mr. Ram deposited a cheque for collection of Rs. 2,000 and made entry in the Cash Book which appears in the Pass Book on 6th December 2006, at Rs. 1,980.
3. Cheques issued to parties but not presented for payment till 30th November 2006 are of Rs. 1,050, Rs. 1670 and Rs. 1,800.
4. Cheques deposited for collection but collected by bankers till 30th November 2006 Rs. 17,520 and Rs. 820.
5. Interest on investment collected by Bankers on 30th November 2006 Rs. 1,910 entered in Cash Book on 4th December 2006 on receipt of Bank intimation.
6. Bank charges Rs. 180 of 27th November 2006, not entered in Cash Book.
7. Cheque deposited for collection on 30th November 2006 but returned dishonoured on 6th December 2006 Rs. 1,890.
8. Bankers have made a mistake in balancing by showing overdrawn balance in excess by Rs. 2,000 on 30th November 2006 which was rectified in bank pass book on 7th December 2006.

(B.Com. Madurai)

SOLUTION:

BANK RECONCILIATION STATEMENT
as on 30th November 2004

		Particulars	*Amount* *Rs*	*Amount* *Rs*
OD as per CB is more, so such item are added.		(1) Overdraft as per Pass Book		40,000
	Add:	(3) Cheques issued but not presented for payment till 30th November (Rs. 1,050 + Rs. 1,670 + Rs. 1,800)	4,520	
	Add:	(5) Interest on investment collected by the Bank entered in Cash Book after 30th November.	1,910	(+) 6,430
				46,430
OD as per CB is less, so such item are deducted	Less:	(2) Cheque deposited but collected by the bank after 30th November	2,000	
	Less:	(4) Cheques deposited but not collected by the bank till 30th November. (Rs. 17,520 + Rs. 820)	18,340	
	Less:	(6) Bank charges not recorded in Cash Book	180	
	Less:	(7) Cheque deposited but dishonoured	1,890	
	Less:	(8) Bank's mistake in balancing the account and showing it in excess	2,000	(–) 24,410
		OVERDRAFT AS PER CASH BOOK		22,020

ILLUSTRATION 5.15

Titan Ltd. received its bank statement for the period ended 30th June 2004 but this does not agree with the balance shown in the Cash Book of Rs. 2,972 in Company's favour.

Examination of the two records, revealed the following:

1. A deposit of Rs. 492 paid in on 29th June 2006 had not been credited by the bank until 1st July 2006.
2. Bank charges amounting to Rs. 17 had not been entered in the Cash Book.
3. A debit of Rs. 42 appeared on the bank statement for an unpaid cheque, which had been returned marked "Out of date". The cheque had been re-dated by the customer of Titan Ltd. and paid into the bank again on 3rd July 2006.
4. A standing order for payment of an annual subscription amounting to Rs. 10 had not been entered in the Cash Book.
5. On 25th June, the Managing Director had given the cashier a cheque for Rs. 100 to pay into his personal account at the bank. The cashier had paid it into the company's account by mistake.
6. On 27th June, two customers of Titan Ltd. had paid direct to the company's bank account Rs. 499 and Rs. 157 for goods supplied. The advices were not received by the company until 1st July and were entered in the Cash Book under that date.
7. On 30th March 2006, the company had entered into a hire purchase agreement to pay by Banker's order a sum of Rs. 26 on the 10th day of each month commencing from April. No entries had been made in the Cash Book.
8. Rs. 364 paid into the Bank had been entered twice in cash book.
9. Cheque issued amounted to Rs. 4,672 had not been presented to the bank for payment until after 30th June.

10. A customer of the company, who received a cash discount of 2.5% on his account of Rs. 200, paid the company a cheque on 10th June. The Cashier, in error, entered the gross amount in the bank col. of the cash book.

You are required:

(a) to show the necessary adjustments in the Cash Book of Titan Ltd. bringing down the correct balance on 30th June 2006.

(b) to prepare a reconciliation statement.

SOLUTION:

In the Books of Titan Ltd.

Dr. CASH BOOK Cr.

Date	Particulars	Amount Rs	Date	Particulars	Amount Rs
2006 June 30	To Balance b/d	2,972	2006 June 30	By Bank Charges A/c	17
	To Debtors A/c (Direct Deposit) (Rs. 499 + 157)	656		By Subscription A/c	10
				By Hire Purchase A/c (26 × 3)	78
				By Cheque's wrong entry	364
				By Discount Allowed A/c (Rs. 200 × 2.5%)	5
				By Balance c/d	3,154
		3,628			3,628

NB: There will be no entry in the amended Cash Book for the wrong deposit of Rs. 100, by the Cashier, because it is assumed that it was not recorded in the Cash Book previously.

BANK RECONCILIATION STATEMENT

as on 30th June 2006

Particulars	Amount Rs	Amount Rs
Balance as per Cash Book (amended)		3,154
Add: Cheque issued but not presented	4,672	
Add: Cheque not presented (Managing Director)	100	(+) 4,772
		7,926
Less: Amount deposited but not credited by the Bank	492	
Less: Cheque re-presented	42	(–) 534
BALANCE AS PER PASS BOOK		7,392

ILLUSTRATION 5.16

Prepare the Bank Reconciliation Statement from the following data as on 30.11.06

(i) Balance as per the Pass Book 30.11.06 (Dr.) Rs. 9,204.

(ii) Cheques drawn on 30.11.06 but not cleared till December 2006 Rs. 3,225 Rs. 745 and Rs. 926.

(iii) Bank interest on overdraft not entered in the Cash Book Rs. 1,610.

(iv) Cheque received on 29.11.06 entered in the Cash Book but not deposited to bank till December 2006 Rs. 11,322 and Rs. 1,730.

(v) Cheque received amounting to Rs. 35 entered in the Cash Book twice.

(vi) B/R due on 29.11.06 was sent to the bank for collection on 28.11.06; it was entered in the Cash Book forthwith but the proceeds were not credited by bank till 3rd December, 2006 Rs. 2,980.

(vii) A periodic payment by Bank for Rs. 80 under standing instructions not entered in the Cash Book.

(viii) Cheque deposited on 30.11.06 dishonoured but not entered in the Cash Book Rs. 1,890.

[I.C.W.A (Inter)

SOLUTION:

Bank Reconciliation Statement as on 30.11.2006

		Particulars	*Amount Rs*	*Amount Rs*
Bank Overdraft as per the Pass Book (Dr.)				9,204
Add:	(ii)	Cheques drawn on 30.11 06 but not cleared till Dec. 06 (Rs. 3,225 + Rs. 745 + Rs. 926)	4,896	(+) 4,896
				14,100
Less:	(iii)	Bank interest on Overdraft not entered in the Cash Book	1,610	
	(iv)	Cheques received on 29.11.06 entered in Cash Book but not deposited to the Bank (Rs. 11,322 + Rs. 1,730)	13,052	
	(v)	Cheque received amounting to Rs. 35 entered twice in the Cash Book	35	
	(vi)	B/R sent to Bank for collection entered in the cash book but the proceeds were not credited by the bank till 3.12.06	2,980	
	(vii)	Periodic payment of Rs. 80 not entered in the Cash Book	80	
	(viii)	Cheque deposited and dishonoured but not entered in the Cash Book	1,890	(–) 19,647
		Bank balance as per the Cash Book (Dr.)		5,547

ILLUSTRATION 5.17

The Cash Book of Gupta showed an overdraft of Rs. 30,000 on 31.12.2006. The scrutiny of the entries in the Cash Book and the Pass book revealed that :

(i) On 22nd December, cheques totalling Rs. 6,000 were sent to bankers for collection, out of which a cheque for Rs. 1,000 was wrongly recorded on the credit side of the Cash Book and cheques amounting to Rs. 300 could not be collected by the bank within the year.

(ii) A cheque for Rs. 4,000 was issued to a supplier on 28th December, 2006. The cheque was presented to the bank on 4th January, 2007.

(iii) There were debits in the Pass Book for interest Rs. 2,000 on overdraft and bank charges Rs. 600 not recorded in the Cash Book.

(iv) A credit side of the Bank Column of the Cash Book was undercast by Rs. 100.

(v) A cheque for Rs. 1,000 was issued to a creditor on 27th December but unfortunately, the same was not recorded in the Cash Book. The cheque was, however, duly encashed within 31st December.

(vi) As per standing instructions, the banker collected dividend of Rs. 500 on behalf of Gupta and credited the same to his account within 31st December, 2006. The fact was, however, intimated to Gupta on 3rd January, 2007.

You are required to prepare a Bank Reconciliation Statement as on 31st December, 2006

(B.Com. Ujjain Punjab)

SOLUTION.

Gupta

Bank Reconciliation Statement as on 31.12.2006

	Particulars	*Amount Rs*	*Amount Rs*
	Bank Overdraft as per the Cash Book (Cr.)		30,000
Add:	(i) Cheques deposited but not collected	300	
	(iii) Debits in the Pass Book for interest on overdraft and the bank charges not recorded in the Cash Book	2,600	
	(iv) The credit side of the Bank column of the Cash Book was undercast	100	
	(v) Cheque issued to a creditor not recorded in the Cash Book, but it was duly encashed within 31.12.2006	1,000	(+) 4,000
			34,000
Less:	(i) Cheque wrongly recorded on the credit side of the Cash Book (Rs. 1,000 × 2)	2,000	
	(ii) Cheque issued but not presented for payment	4,000	
	(vi) Dividend collected by the Bank not recorded in the Cash Book	500	(–) 6,500
	Bank balance as per the Pass Book (Dr.)		27,500

QUESTIONS

Objective Type Questions

I. State whether each of the following statements is True or False.

1. Cheques issued but not presented for payment will reduce the balance as per the Pass Book.
2. Bank balance as per bank statement is shown in the Balance Sheet at the end of the year.
3. Bank Reconciliation Statement is prepared at the end of the year only.
4. The Bank Pass Book enables the customer to know the state of his account with the bank.
5. Bank charges as well as interest on deposit are shown in the Pass Book as credit items.

(*Ans.* 1. (F) 2. F; 3. (F); 4. (T) 5. (F))

II. Fill in the blanks

1. For reconciliation purposes only the .... column of the Cash Book are to be considered.
2. When money is withdrawn from the bank, the bank .... the account of the customer.
3. Bank charges increase .... balance in Pass Book.
4. When Pass Book shows a debit balance, it means ....
5. When a customer opens a bank account, he becomes a .... to the bank to the extent of his deposit.

(*Ans.* 1. Bank; 2. Debit; 3. Debit; 4. OD as per PB; 5. Creditor.)

III. Indicate the correct alternative in each of the following cases

1. Bank Reconciliation Statement is prepared to know the correctness between:
   (a) Cash Book and Petty Cash Book balances.
   (b) Petty Cash Book and Pass Book balances.
   (c) Pass Book and Cash Book balances.
2. Unfavourable bank balance means
   (a) Credit balance in the Cash Book. (b) Credit balance in the Pass Book.
   (c) None of the above.

3. Bank Reconciliation Statement is a
   (a) Ledger Account (b) a Statement
   (c) Subsidiary record.
4. A customer's bank Pass Book contains a copy of:
   (a) The bank col. of the customer's Cash Book.
   (b) The customer's account in the bank's books.
   (c) The Cash col. of the customer's Cash Book.
5. The credit balance of Bank Account in Cash Book indicates:
   (a) Amount payable by the Bank (b) Amount payable to the Bank
   (c) None of the above.
6. The receipt side of the Cash Book is overcast by Rs. 500. When overdraft as per Pass Book is the starting point:
   (a) Rs. 500 will be deducted (b) Rs. 1,000 will be deducted
   (c) Rs. 500 will be added.
7. A Bank Reconciliation Statement is prepared by:
   (a) A Bank (b) The Firm
   (c) Creditors
8. A Bank Reconciliation Statement is prepared with the help of:
   (a) Bank Statement and Bank col. of the Cash Book.
   (b) Pass Book and Cash col. of the Cash Book
   (c) None of these.
9. When the overdraft as per cash book is the starting point, a cheque of Rs. 10,000 deposited into bank but not recorded in Cash Book will be:
   (a) Added by Rs. 10,000 (b) Deducted by Rs. 10,000
   (c) Added by Rs. 20,000.
10. When preparing a Bank Reconciliation Statement, if you start with a debit balance as per the Cash Book, cheques issued but not presented within the period should be:
   (a) Added (b) Deducted
   (c) None of these

(*Ans.* 1 (c); 2. (a); 3. (b); 4. (b); 5. (b) 6. (a); 7. (b) 8. (a); 9. (b); 10. (a))

THEORETICAL QUESTIONS

1. What is a Bank Reconciliation Statement ? How is it prepared ?
2. Give reasons for the difference between the Balance as per Cash Book and that as per Pass Book on a particular day.
3. What is "adjusted Cash Book" ?
4. Distinguish between Cash Book and Pass Book.
5. What is the purpose of preparing Bank Reconciliation Statement ?

PRACTICAL PROBLEMS

1. On 31st December 2004, the Cash Book of Prakash showed a balance of Rs 2,000 at bank. He had deposited cheques worth Rs 10,000 in the bank before 31st December, but cheques worth Rs 4,000 only had been credited before that date. Similarly, out of cheques for Rs 5,000 issued during December cheques for Rs 2,500 were presented and paid in January 2005. The Pass Book also showed a payment of Rs 320 as Insurance premium and Rs 2,000 against a Promissory Note as per instructions. There was a credit in the Pass Book for Rs 600 for interest on Investments collected and a debit of Rs 50 for interest and Rs 20 for bank charges.

   Prepare a Bank Reconciliation Statement as on 31st December 2004. (*B.Com., Madurai*)

   [Ans. Overdraft as per Pass Book Rs 3,290]

2. Sunderlal and Sons find that the Bank Balance shown by their Cash Book on 31st December, 2004 is Rs 10,500 (Credit), but the Pass Book shows a difference due to the following reasons :
   (*a*) Cheque No. 51 for Rs 540 in favour of Amar has not yet been presented.
   (*b*) A post-dated cheque for Rs 300 has been debited to the bank account in the Cash Book, but it could not be presented for payment.
   (*c*) Four cheques totalling Rs 1,200 sent to the Bank for collection have not yet been credited while a fifth cheque for Rs 400 deposited in the account has been dishonoured.
   (*d*) Fire insurance premium amounting to Rs 50 paid by the Bank understanding instructions has not been entered in the Cash Book.
   (*e*) A Bill for Rs 1,000 was retired by the Bank under a rebate of Rs 15, but the full amount of the Bill was credited in the Cash Book.

   Prepare a Bank Reconciliation Statement. (*B.Com., Kerala, Delhi, Allahabad*)

   [**Ans.** Overdraft as per Pass Book Rs 11,895]

3. Raghunath's Cash Book showed a credit balance of Rs 8,800 on 31st December 2004. On examining entries with the Pass Book, it was found that :
   (*a*) Out of the two cheques issued to Rajaram on 27th December one for Rs 860 and another for Rs 680, the cheque for Rs 680 was cashed only on 2nd January 2005.
   (*b*) Out of the three cheques deposited in the Bank for collection on 26th December for Rs 300, Rs 400 and Rs 500 respectively, the cheque for Rs 400 only was collected by 31st December.
   (*c*) There was a credit in the Pass Book for Rs 75 towards interest collected directly by the banker on behalf of Raghunath and a debit in the Pass Book for Rs 15 towards collection charges but not corresponding entries were found in the Cash Book.
   (*d*) A cheque for Rs 250 being entered in the Cash Book was omitted by oversight to be deposited in the bank for collection.
   (*e*) A wrong credit for Rs 225 relating to some other account was found in the Pass Book.

   Prepare a Bank Reconciliation Statement as on 31st December showing the Pass Book.

   (*B.Com., Madurai, Madras*)

   [**Ans.** Overdraft as per Pass Book Rs 8,885]

4. On 31st December 2004, Atmaram's Pass Book showed an overdraft of Rs 9,700. From the following further particulars, prepare a Bank Reconciliation Statement :
   (*a*) Cheques paid into Bank but not cleared and credited before 31st December amounted to Rs 1,700.
   (*b*) Cheques issued prior to 31st December but presented for payment after that date, amounted to Rs 900.
   (*c*) Interest on Overdraft amounting to Rs 175 debited in the Pass Book is not entered in the Cash Book.
   (*d*) Rs 600, interest on investment collected by the bankers and credited in the Pass Book remains to be entered in the Cash Book.
   (*e*) Bank charges Rs 12.50 appear in the Pass Book but not in the Cash Book.
   (*f*) Rs 800 in respect of dishonoured cheque appears in the Pass Book and not in the Cash Book.

   (*B.Com., Kerala, MS*)

   [**Ans.** Overdraft as per Cash Book Rs 8,512.50]

5. On 31st December 2005, the Bank Pass Book of Naresh & Co. showed an overdraft of Rs 10,700. From the following particulars, prepare a Bank Reconciliation Statememt.
   (*a*) Cheques issued before 31.12.2005 but presented for payment after that date amounted to Rs 900.
   (*b*) Cheques paid into the Bank but not collected and credited until 31.12.2005 amounted to Rs 2,200.
   (*c*) Interest on Overdraft amounting to Rs 1,200 did not appear in the cash book.
   (*d*) Rs 5,000 being interest on investments collected by the Bank and credited in the Pass Book were not shown in the Cash Book.
   (*e*) Bank charges of Rs 50 were not entered in the Cash Book.

(*f*) Rs 800 in respect of a dishonoured cheque were entered in the Pass Book but not in the Cash Book. (*B.Com. Jabalpur*)

[**Ans.** Overdraft as per Cash Book Rs 12,350]

6. Prepare Bank Reconciliation Statement from the following:
   (*a*) Balance as per Pass Book on 31st December 2004 Rs 10,266.
   (*b*) Cheques drawn on 31st December 2004 but not cleared till 3rd January 2005, Rs 10,212, Rs 981 and Rs 1,128.
   (*c*) Interest on Overdraft not entered in the Cash Book Rs 1,510.
   (*d*) Outstation cheques Rs 21,000 lodged in the bank on 13th December 2004 but collected and credited in January 2005.
   (*e*) A B/R for Rs 2,500 due on 31st December 2004 was sent to the Bank for collection two days before and entered in the Cash Book forthwith, the proceeds were credited on 1st January 2005.
   (*f*) Rs 100 Insurance Premium paid by the Bank under standing order on 31st December 2004 had not been entered in the Cash Book. (*B.Com., Punjab*)

[**Ans.** Cash Book Balance Rs 23,055]

7. On examining the Bank Pass Book of a firm, it is found that the balance shown on 31st March 2005, the close of the firm's financial year, differs from the Bank balance of Rs 23,650 shown by the Cash Book on the date. From a detailed comparison of the entries it is found that :
   (*a*) Rs 2,860 is entered in the Cash Book as paid into Bank on 31st March, but not credited by the Bank until the following day.
   (*b*) Bank charges Rs 70 on 31st March, are not entered in the Cash Book.
   (*c*) A bill for Rs 5,500 discounted with the bank is entered in the Cash Book without recording the discount charge of Rs 270.
   (*d*) Cheques totalling Rs 16,720 was issued by the Company and duly recorded in the Cash book before 31st March but had not been presented at the Bank for payment until after that date.
   (*e*) On 25th March, a debtor paid Rs 1,000 into the Company's Bank in settlement of his acount, but no entry was made in the Cash Book of the Company in respect of this.
   (*f*) No entry has been made in the Cash Book to record the dishonour on 15th March, of a cheque for Rs 550 received from a party.

   Your are asked to prepare a statement Reconciling Cash Book balance as amended with the balance which should appear in the Bank Pass Book. (*B.Com., Colcutta, Kerala*)

[**Ans.** Bank Balance as per Pass Book Rs 37,620]

8. On 31st December 2004, the Cash Book of a firm showed a bank balance of Rs 3,000. From the following information, prepare a Bank Reconciliation Statement showing the balance as per the pass Book :
   (*a*) Cheques had been issued for Rs 2,500, out of which cheques worth Rs 2,000 only were presented for payment.
   (*b*) Cheques worth Rs 700 were paid on 28th December but had not been credited by the Bank. One cheque for Rs 250 was entered in the Cash Book on 30th December but was banked on January 3rd.
   (*c*) A cheque from Mohan for Rs 200 was paid on 26th December but was dishonoured and the advice was received on 2nd January 2005.
   (*d*) The Pass Book showed bank charges of Rs 10 debited by the Bank. It also showed Rs 400 collected by the Bank as interest.
   (*e*) One of the debtors deposited a sum of Rs 250 in the account of the firm on 20th December; intimation in this respect was received from the Bank on 2nd January 2005. (*B.Com., Punjab*)

[**Ans.** Bank Balance as per Pass Book Rs 2,990]

9. On checking Ram's Cash Book with the Bank Statement of his Overdraft current account for the month November 2004, you find the following :
   (*a*) Cash Book showed an Overdraft of Rs 4,500.

(*b*) A cheque for Rs 750 drawn on his saving account has been shown as drawn on Current Account.

(*c*) The payment side of the Cash Book had been undercast Rs 150.

(*d*) Cheques amounting to Rs 7,000 drawn and entered in the Cash Book had not yet been presented.

(*e*) Cheques amounting to Rs 6,000 sent to the Bank for collection though entered in the Cash Book, had not been credited by the bank.

(*f*) Bank charges of Rs 75 as per bank Statement of account had not been taken into the Cash Book.

(*g*) Dividends of the amount of Rs 2,500 had been paid direct into the bank and not entered in the Cash Book.

You are required to prepare the Bank Reconciliation Statement on 30th November 2004.

(*B.Com., Kurukshetra*)

[**Ans.** Overdraft as per pass Book Rs 475]

10. On the basis of the following information available from the books and records of M/s Rajesh & Sons, you are required to prepare a Bank Reconciliation Statement as on 31st March 2004 :

(*a*) Overdraft balance as per Pass Book Rs 14,360.

(*b*) Cheques amounting to Rs 24,450 were deposited by the firm in its bank account on or before 31st March 2004, but the bank cleared them and credited the account on 4th April excepting one cheque for Rs 980 which was returned unpaid on 6th April 2004.

(*c*) The bank debited Rs 11 on 6th April 2004 towards its charges on the aforesaid cheque.

(*d*) Cheques aggregating Rs 4,110 issued by the firm on or before 31st March 2004 were presented and debited to the account on 2nd April 2004.

(*e*) A cheque dated 26th March 2004 issued by the firm for Rs 3,080 was returned unpaid on 29th March 2004 on account of technical defect therein. The firm received the intimation about the return of cheque on 3rd April 2004.

(*f*) A cheque for Rs 1,415 deposited by another firm was wrongly credited by bank to the account of this firm on 26th March and the entry was reversed on 3rd April 2004.

(*g*) Interest on overdraft amounting to Rs 181 was debited by the bank on 31st March 2004 but the advice thereof was received by the firm on 2nd April 2004.

You are required to arrive at the balance as per Cash Book as on 31st March 2004. (*CAIIB*)

[**Ans.** Overdraft as per Cash Book Rs 1,666]

11. Bank pass Book of Mr Ghosh shows an overdraft balance of Rs 2,005 as on 30th June 2004. On checking with his books, he found the following differences ;

(1) Cheques worth Rs 5,000 were deposited in bank account on 29th June, however, no credit was given until 30th June. On 1st July, the bank gave credit of Rs 5,000 and debited Rs 1,000 on 3rd July, being return of one cheque.

(2) Bank charges amounting to Rs 250 were debited by Bank on 27th June. However, the same could not be accounted for by Ghosh before 30th June.

(3) Bank credited the account by Rs 125 on 22nd June being interest for the half year, which was accounted for by Ghosh in July.

(4) Annuity refund of Rs 710 was directly received by the bank on 29th June, without any knowledge of Ghosh.

(5) On 1st June, Bank wrongly credited his account by Rs 500 instead of Ghosh Industries Ltd.

(6) Cheques worth Rs 1,500 were issued by Ghosh, however, none of these cheques was presented for payment prior to 30th June.

(7) As per standing instructions, Bank paid Life Insurance premium of Rs 750 and car taxes of Rs 120, during last week of June. However, corresponding entries were made by Ghosh on 4th July.

From the above particulars, prepare a Bank Reconciliation Statement as on 30th June 2004.

(*ICWA Inter*)

[**Ans.** Debit balance as per Cash Book Rs 1,280]

12. From the following particulars, you are required to ascertain the Bank balance as would appear in the Cash Book of Ram Prasad as at 31st December 2004 :
    (1) Bank Pass Book showed an Overdraft of Rs 6,500 on 31st Dec., 2004.
    (2) Interest on Overdraft for six months ending December 2004, Rs 250 debited in Pass Book, but is not entered in the Cash book.
    (3) Bank charges for the above period also debited in the Pass Book but not entered in the Cash Book amounted to Rs 35.
    (4) Cheques issued, but not cashed till 31st Dec., amounted to Rs 1,500.
    (5) Cheques paid into Bank, but not cleared and credited before 31st December were for Rs 2,500.
    (6) Interest on Investments collected by the Bankers and credited in the Pass Book amounted to Rs 1,800. *(B.Com., Delhi)*

[**Ans.** Overdraft as per Cash Book Rs 7,015]

13. On 31st January 2005, the Pass Book of Ram Prasad shows a debit balance of Rs 41,000. Prepare a Bank Reconciliation Statement with the following information :
    (1) Cheques amounting to Rs 15,600 were drawn on 27th January of which Rs 11,000 were cashed upto 31st January.
    (2) A wrong debit of Rs 800 has been given by the Banker in Pass Book.
    (3) A cheque of Rs 200 was credited in the Pass Book but was not recorded in the Cash Book.
    (4) Cheques amounting to Rs 21,000 were deposited for collection. But cheques for Rs 7,400 have been credited in the Pass Book on 2nd February 2005.
    (5) A cheque for Rs 1,000 returned dishonoured and was debited in Pass Book only.
    (6) Interest and Bank charges amounted to Rs 100 were debited in Pass Book only.
    (7) A cheque of Rs 500 debited in the Cash Book omitted to be banked.

(B.Com., Ravi Shanker, MS)

[**Ans.** Overdraft as per Cash Bōok Rs 36,000]

14. From the following particulars prepare a Bank Reconciliation Statement as on 31st March 2004 :
    (1) Bank balance as on 31st March 2004 as per Pass Book Rs 15,200.
    (2) Bank charges debited Rs 130 in the Pass Book.
    (3) Cheques issued but not presented to Bank for payment Rs 2,000.
    (4) Cheques deposited to Bank but not credited in the Pass Book Rs 7,000.
    (5) A cheque entered as a deposit in the Cash Book instead of a payment Rs 220.
    (6) Rs 364 paid into Bank had been entered twice in the Cash Book.
    (7) The receipt column of the Cash Book has been overcast by Rs 1,000.
    (8) A cheque drawn for Rs 9 had been incorrectly entered in the Cash Book as Rs 99.

(B.Com., Calcutta, Kerala)

[**Ans.** Bank Balance as per Cash Book Rs 22,044]

15. From the following particulars, ascertain in the Bank Balance as per Pass Book as on 31st December 2004.
    (1) The Bank balance as per Cash Book was Rs 11,500 on 31st Dec. 2004.
    (2) Cheques issued but not cashed before that date amounted to Rs 1,750.
    (3) Cheques paid into bank, but not cleared before 31st December 2004 amounted to Rs 2,150.
    (4) Interest on investments collected by the bank not entered in the Cash Book amounted to Rs 275.
    (5) Local cheque paid in but not entered in the Cash Book Rs 300.
    (6) Bank charges debited in the Pass Book Rs 25.
    (7) Interest on Current account credited in the Pass Book Rs 95. *(B.Com., Madurai)*

[**Ans.** Bank Balance Rs 11,745]

16. Prepare Bank Reconciliation Statement as on 31st March 2004 from the following information :

(1) Bank Balance as per Banker's record is Rs 1,000.

(2) Cheques worth Rs 5,000 were deposited in Bank account, but bank has cleared cheques worth Rs 2,000 only.

(3) Interest on Overdraft Rs 100 debited in the Pass Book has been shown in the Cash Book as interest given by bank on deposit.

(4) Bank charges Rs 25 entered in the Pass Book only.

(5) Cheques issued for Rs 10,000 to a creditor not presented to the Bank.

(6) Cheque issued for Rs 200 to Smith has been wrongly entered in the Cash Column on the payment side of the Cash Book. The same has not been presented to the Bank.

(7) Bank has credited our account in the Pass Book for a cheque worth Rs 1,000 though the same has not been deposited by us. *(B.Com., Agra, Bombay)*

[Ans. Overdraft as per Cash Book Rs 6,775]

17. From the following information given by the Accountant, prepare a bank Reconciliation Statement as on 31st December 2004 :

(1) Cash book balance Rs 5,000 (Dr).

(2) The following cheques were issued but not yet presented for payment :

Cheque in favour of Mr. Ram for Rs 300 on 29th Dec.

Cheque in favour of Mr. Rahim for Rs 750 on 31st Dec.

(3) The following cheques were paid into the Bank, cleared and credited by the Bank as below :

(*a*) Cheque from John Rs 1,000 cleared on 1st January 2005.

(*b*) Cheque from Singh Rs 750 cleared on 5th January 2005.

(4) The Bank has, as per standing instructions, paid insurance premium for Rs 300 on 28th December and the Bank intimation was received on 5th January 2005.

(5) The Bank received from clients Rs 3,500 being the collection on account on 26th December 2004 but credit intimation was received on 10th January 2005 only.

(6) Bank charged Rs 50 towards collection charges on 30th Dec.

(7) The Bank wrongly credited the Pass Book with Rs 10,000 on 28th Dec. 2004 which is due to some other client and reversed it on 28th January 2005. *(CAIIB)*

[Ans. Pass Book balance Rs 17,450]

18. From the following particulars, prepare a Bank Reconciliation Statement of Mr Samy :

(1) Overdraft as per Pass Book March 31st, 2004 was Rs 12,900.

(2) Cheques issued before that date but presented for payment after the date amounted to Rs 1,200.

(3) Cheques paid into the Bank but not cleared and credited before 31.3.2004 amounted to Rs 3,200.

(4) Interest on Overdraft amount to Rs 175 debited in the pass Book but not entered in the Cash Book.

(5) Interest on Investment amounting to Rs 700 was collected by the bank and credited in the Pass Book but not entered in Cash Book.

(6) Bank charges of Rs 22 not entered in the Cash Book.

(7) Rs 950 in respect of a dishonoured cheque entered in the Pass Book but not in the Cash Book.

[Ans. Overdraft as per Cash Book Rs 10,453]

19. Mr Bharat has two accounts with Union Bank, account No. I and Account No. II. On 31st December 2004, his Cash Book shows balance of Rs 5,400 and Rs 2,70,400 in the two accounts respectively.

On checking the Bank Statements the following was noticed :

(*i*) Rs 27,000 was transferred from Account No. II to Account No. I by the Bank without advice to Bharat.

(ii) Bank has charged Rs 10 as incidental charges in respect of each account.

(iii) Cheques amounting to Rs 15,421 issued in Account No. I in the last week of December were not yet presented to Bank.

(iv) A cheque for Rs 14,272 deposited by Mr Bharat into Account No. II has been credited by the Bank in Account No. I.

(v) Credit balance of Rs 2,100 in Account No. I on 31st October 2004 was wrongly carried forward as debit balance in the Bank statement.

(vi) Income tax refund order for Rs 1,640 deposited in Account No. I has been cleared and credited to the account in the first week of January 2005.

You are required to prepare Bank Reconciliation Statement showing the balance as per Bank Statements. *(CAIIB)*

[**Ans.** Bank Balance as per Pass Book Rs 56,243 (A/c No. I)
Bank Balance as per Pass Book Rs 2,29,118 (A/c No. II)]

20. From the following particulars taken on 31st Dec. 2004, you are required to prepare Bank Reconciliation Statement to reconcile the bank balance shown in the Cash Book with that shown in the Pass Book.

(1) Balance as per Pass Book on 31st Dec. 2004 (O.D.) Rs 1,027.

(2) Four cheques drawn on 31st December but not cleared till Jan 2005 : Rs 12; Rs 1,021; Rs 98 and Rs 113.

(3) Interest on Overdraft not entered in the Cash Book Rs 51.

(4) Three cheques received on 30th December and entered in the bank column of the Cash Book but not lodged in bank for collection till 3rd Jan. 2005 : Rs 1,160; Rs 2,100 and Rs 2,080.

(5) Cost of cheque book, Pass Book etc. Rs 1.50 entered twice in the Cash Book, by mistake, in Nov. 2004.

(6) B/R for Rs 250 due on 29th Dec. was passed to the Bank for collection on 28th December and entered in the Cash Book forthwith whereas the proceeds were credited in the Pass Book only on January 2005.

(7) Chamber of Commerce subscription Rs 10 paid by the Bank on 1st December had not been entered in Cash Book.

(8) Bank charges of Rs 5 had been debited in the Pass Book by error. *(B.Com. Madras)*

[**Ans.** Debit balance as per pass Book Rs 3,383.50]

21. From the following particulars, prepare a Bank Reconciliation Statement of a firm as at 30th September:

	Rs.
(1) Overdraft balance on 30th September as per Bank Statement.	13,095
(2) Cheque deposited in Bank not recorded in Cash Book	105
(3) Cheque received and recorded in the Bank column but not sent to Bank for collection	1,015

(4) Several cheques were drawn in the last week of September totalling Rs 15,075; of these cheques totalling Rs 9,074 were encashed.

(5) Several cheques totalling Rs 9,400 were sent to Bank for collection. Of these cheques of the value of Rs 1,500 were credited on 5th October and Rs 2,050 were credited on 7th October, the remaining were credited before 30th September.

(6) On 11th September the credit side of the Bank column of the Cash Book was cast Rs 1,000 short and on 15th September the credit balance of Rs 2,600 was brought forward on 16th September as Debit balance of Rs 2,600.

(7) Chamber of Commerce fee of Rs 250 was paid by the Bank but was not recorded in the Cash Book.

(8) In the Cash Book a bank charge of Rs 30 was recorded twice while another bank charge of Rs 45 was not recorded at all.

(9) Interest of Rs 1,400 was charged by the Bank but was not recorded in the Cash Book.

(CA Inter)

[Ans. Overdraft as per Cash Book Rs 6,771]

22. According to the Cash Book of Arun, there was a balance of 1,050 in his favour on 30th June. But according to Pass Book, this account was overdrawn. On investigation, you find that :

(*i*) The receipt column of the Cash Book have been overadded by Rs 1,100.

(*ii*) Cheques drawn and entered in the Cash Book in June, amounted to Rs 1,670 were not presented for payment until July.

(*iii*) Discount received from a supplier of Rs 100 had been included with the cheque entered in the Bank column of the Cash Book in April.

(*iv*) An amount of Rs 750 paid directly into Arun's account by a customer in May, had not yet been entered in Cash Book.

(*v*) A cheque payment of Rs 1,230 in April, had been entered in the Cash Book as Rs 1,320.

(*vi*) The Bank had charged in business account with a chque for Rs 2,200 in February which should have been passed through Arun's private account.

(*vii*) Bank charges of Rs 80 at 31st December last and Rs 100 at 30th June, had not yet been entered in the Cash Book.

(*viii*) Cheques to the value of Rs 3,780 received from customers were recorded in the Cash Book on 20th June, but not found in the Pass Book till 2nd July.

You are asked to prepare statement (*i*) adjusting Arun's Cash Book balance as at 30th June, (*ii*) reconciling the adjusted Cash Book balance with the balance shown by the Bank Statement at 30th June.

(CA Inter)

[Ans. Overdraft as per Pass Book Rs 3,600]

23. On 31st December, the Bank column of the Cash Book shows a debit balance of Rs 922. On examination of the Cash Book and Bank statement you find that :

(*a*) Cheques amounting to Rs 1,260 issued before 31st Dec. and entered in the Cash Book were not presented for payment till after that date.

(*b*) Cheques amounting to Rs 500, entered in the Cash Book as sent to the Bank on 31st Dec., were entered in the Bank Statement after that date.

(*c*) A cheque from a debtor for Rs 146 had been dishonoured prior to 31st December, but no record appeared in the Cash Book.

(*d*) A dividend warrant for Rs 76 was paid direct to the Bank and nothing appeared in the Cash Book.

(*e*) Bank interest and charges amounting to Rs 84 were not entered in the cash book but appeared in the pass Book.

(*f*) There was no entry in the Cash Book for a club membership subscription Rs 20 paid by Bank.

(*g*) Bank's charges for a cheque book received Rs 2 was entered in the Cash Book twice.

(*h*) A cheque for Rs 54 drawn by a customer had been charged to this account, in error, during September.

Make appropriate adjustments into the Cash Book to bring down the correct balance and prepare a Bank Reconciliation Statement reconciling the corrected Cash Book balance.

(B.Com. Hons Delhi)

[Ans. Bank balance as per Pass Book Rs 1,456]

24. The following are the Cash Book and Bank Pass Book of Mr. Ghosh for the month of April.

Cash Book (Bank Column)

Date	*Particulars*	*Amount Rs.*	*Date*	*Particulars*	*Amount Rs.*
2004			2004		
April 1	To Balance b/d	12,500	April 1	By Salaries A/c (Cheque No. 182)	4,000
4	To Sales A/c	8,000	6	By Purchase A/c (Cheque No. 184)	3,200
8	To Prem A/c	1,500	11	By Machinery A/c (Cheque No. 185)	6,000
13	To Mohan A/c	3,400	15	By Prakash A/c (Cheque No. 186)	1,000
18	To Kamal A/c	4,600	19	By Drawings A/c (Cheque No. 187)	800
21	To Furniture A/c	1,200	23	By Komal A/c (Cheque No. 188)	2,000
25	To Sales A/c	3,800	27	By Sahu A/c (Cheque No. 189)	1,000
30	To Arun A/c	3,000	30	By Printing A/c (Cheque No. 190)	500
			30	By Balance c/d	19,500
		38,000			38,000

Pass Book

Date	*Particulars*	*Cheque No.*	*Debit Rs.*	*Credit Rs.*	*Dr. or Cr.*	*Balance*
2004 April						
1	By Balance b/d					12,500
2	To Cheque	183	4,000			8,500
6	By Cheque			8,000		16,500
6	To Cheque	184	3,200			13,300
10	By Cheque			1,500		14,800
16	By Cheque			3,400		18,200
17	To Cheque	187	800			17,400
20	By Cheque			4,600		22,000
24	By Cheque			3,800		25,800
28	To Cheque	185	6,000			19,800
28	To Cheque	189	1,000			18,800
30	By Interest			100		18,900
30	By Deposit			3,000		21,900
30	To Charges		10			21,890

You are required to prepare a Bank Reconciliation Statement as at 30th April 2004. (*CAIIB*)

[Ans. Bank Balance as per Pass Book Rs 21,890]

25. Prepare a bank Reconciliation Statement from the following data as on 30th Nov. 2004.

(*i*) Balance as per Pass Book on 30th Nov. 2004 overdrawn Rs 9,204.

(*ii*) Cheques Drawn on 30th Nov. 2004 but not cleared till December 2004 Rs 3,225, Rs 926 and Rs 745.

(*iii*) Bank overdraft interest charged on 28th Nov. not entered in the Cash Book Rs 1,610.

(*iv*) Cheques received on 29th Nov. entered in the Cash Book but not deposited to Bank till 3rd December 2004 Rs 11,322 and Rs 1,730.

(*v*) Cheque received amounting to Rs 35 entered in the Cash Book twice.

(*vi*) Bills Receivable due on 29th Nov. 2004 was sent to Bank for collection on 28th Nov. and was entered in the Cash Book forthwith but the proceeds were not credited in Pass Book till 3rd December Rs 2,980.

(*vii*) A periodic payment by the Bank for Rs 80 understanding instruction not entered in Cash Book.

(*viii*) Cheque deposited on 30th Nov. 2004 dishonoured but the entry thereof was not made in the Cash Book Rs 1,890. (*ICWA*)

[Ans. Bank Balance as per Cash Book Rs 5,547]

26. From the following particulars, prepare a Bank Reconciliation Statement showing the balance as per the Cash Book on 31st March 2004 :

	Rs
(1) Balance as per Pass Book	8,000
(2) Cheques deposited but not credited by the Bank	1,000
(3) Cheques deposited into Bank without recording in the Cash Book	500
(4) Cheques deposited into Bank without recording in the Cash Book	600
(5) Cheques issued to Creditors but not recorded in Cash Book	700
(6) Dividend collected by the Bank not recorded in Cash Book	100
(7) Debtors directly deposited into Bank not recorded in the Cash Book	2,000
(8) Debit side of the Cash Book was undercast by	1,000
(9) Bank charges debited in the Pass Book, not recorded in Cash Book	50
(10) Bank met a Bills Payable for Rs 1,000 on 31st March under advice to the firm on 2nd April 2004	
(11) A Bill for Rs 2,000 discounted for Rs 1,900 returned dishonoured by the Bank, noting charges being Rs 10	
(12) A Bill for Rs 1,000 discounted with the Bank is entered in the Cash Book without recording the discount charges	100

(*B.Com., Madras, Calcutta*)

[Ans. Bank Balance as per pass Book Rs 8,660]

27. On 30th June, the pass book of Messers Thin and Short showed a balance of Rs 2,000 at the bank. They had sent cheques amounting to Rs 10,000 to the bank before 30th June, but it appears from the pass book that cheques worth Rs 9,000 had been credited before that date. Similarly out of cheques for Rs 5,000 issued during the month of June, cheques for Rs 4,000 were presented and paid in July. The pass book also showed the following payments :

(*a*) Rs 320 as premium according to standing instructions and

(*b*) Rs 2,000 against a promissory note as per instructions. The pass book showed that the bank had collected Rs 1,800 as interest on Government securities. The bank had charged as interest Rs 50 and incident expenses Rs 20. There was no entry in the cash book for the payment of interest etc. A bill sent for collection was returned dishonoured on 28th June amounting to Rs 600.

Prepare the Bank Reconciliation statement as on 30th June. (*B.Com. Madurai*)

[Ans. Overdraft as per Cash Book Rs 410]

28. From the following particulars, find out adjusted Bank Balance as per Cash Book and prepare thereafter a Bank Reconciliation Statement as on 31st December 2004 of a sole trader.

(1) Bank overdraft as per Cash Book	80,000
(2) Cheque deposited as per Bank Statement but not entered in Cash Book	3,000
(3) Cheques recorded for collection but not sent to Bank	10,000
(4) Credit side of Bank column Cash short	1,000
(5) Premium on proprietor's Life Insurance Policy said on standing orders	5,000
(6) Bank charges recorded twice in Cash Book	100
(7) Customer's cheque returned as per Pass Book	4,000
(8) Cheques issued but dishonoured on technical grounds	3,000
(9) Bills collected by Bank directly	20,000
(10) Cheques for Rs 50,000 deposited but collection as per Bank Pass Book	49,980
(11) Cheque received entered twice in Cash Book	5,000

(*ICWA*)

[Ans. Overdraft as per Pass Book Rs 78,920]

29. Prepare a Bank Reconciliation statement from the following details :
   (1) Bank Overdraft as per Cash Book Rs 8,000.
   (2) Cheques deposited into bank but no entry was passed in the Cash Book Rs 300.
   (3) Cheques received but not sent to bank Rs 1,000.
   (4) Credit side of Bank column (Cash Book) cast short Rs 100.
   (5) Insurance Premium paid directly by Bank Rs 500.
   (6) Bank charges entered in the Cash Book twice Rs 10.
   (7) Cheques received returned by bank but not entered in Cash Book Rs 400.
   (8) Cheques issued returned on technical grounds Rs 300.
   (9) Bills directly collected by the Bank Rs 2,000.
   (10) Bank charges debited by the Bank Rs 12.
   (11) Cheques received entered twice in Cash Book Rs 500.
   (12) Bills discounted dishonoured Rs 4,000. (*M.Com., Calcutta, Institute of Bankers*)

[Ans. Bank Overdraft as per Pass Book Rs 11,902]

30. Mr Jones is having two Accounts "A" and "B" with Central Bank of India. On 31st December 2004, his ledger shows a balance of Rs 5,000 in Account "A" and an overdraft of Rs 2,250 in Account "B". On verifying the ledger entries with the respective Bank statements, the following facts were discovered :
   (1) The deposit of Rs 1,500 made into Account "A" on 20th Dec. 2004 has been entered in the ledger in Account "B".
   (2) A withdrawal of Rs 500 from Account "A" on 2nd Nov. 2004 has been entered in the ledger in Account "B".
   (3) Two cheques of Rs 500 and Rs 750 deposited in the Account "A" on Ist December 2004, and entered in the books in "B" account, have been dishonoured by the Bankers. The entries for the dishonour of these cheques have been entered in the books in "B" Account.
   (4) On the account "A" and "B" Mr Jones has issued on 29th Dec. 2004 cheques for Rs 10,000 and Rs 1,000 respectively and these have not been cashed till 31st Dec. 2004.
   (5) Incidental charges of Rs 10 and Rs 25 charged in the Accounts "A" and "B" respectively have not been entered in the Cash Books.
   (6) The Bank has credited an intertest of Rs 50 for Account "A" and has charged interest of Rs 275 for account "B" which have not been recorded in the books.

(7) The deposits of Rs 5,000 and Rs 3,500 made into the Accounts "A" and "B" both on 30th Dec. 2004 have not been given credit to by the Bank till 31st December 2004.

Draw up the Bank Reconciliation Statement for the above two accounts. *(CA Inter)*

[**Ans.** Bank Balance as per Pass Book (Cr.) Rs 11,040—Account 'A'
Bank Balance as per Pass Book (Dr. Rs. 6,050—Account 'B']

31. From the following details make out a Reconciliation Statement of Ram Seth & Sons, on 31st December 2004 relating to No. 1 Account.
    (1) Balance as per Pass Book (overdraft) Rs 10,000 on 31st Dec. 2004.
    (2) Out of cheques of Rs 6,000 issued on No. 1 Account prior to this date,
        (*a*) A cheque for Rs 700 was dishonoured.
        (*b*) A cheque for Rs 800 was reported as lost.
        (*c*) A cheque for Rs 900 was torn off.
        (*d*) A cheque for Rs 1,000 was encashed but the Banker has entered it wrongly in the account of another customer.
        (*e*) A cheque for Rs 1,200 was paid out of No. 2.
        (*f*) Other cheques have been presented.
    (3) Out of cheques of Rs 7,000 sent to bank for collection,
        (*a*) A cheque for Rs 1,400 was dishonoured.
        (*b*) A cheque for Rs 1,500 did not reach the Bank as Ram Seth and Sons' peon has absconded with the cheque.
        (*c*) A cheque for Rs 1,600 though collected, was credited wrongly to some other account.
        (*d*) A cheque for Rs 400 was lying with the bank as the Bank staff had been careless and not collected it in time.
        (*e*) A cheque for Rs 500 was collected but bank has wrongly entered the amount twice.
        (*f*) Other cheques have been collected and credited.
    (4) Interest on Overdraft of Rs 250 and Bank charges of Rs 150 were entered in the Pass Book.
    (5) Bank has collected Dividends of Rs 1,900 and entered in Pass Book only.
    (6) Bank had paid subscription of Rs 750 and Insurance Premium of Rs 650. *(CA)*

[**Ans.** Overdraft as per Cash Book Rs 10,300]

32. On checking Surendra's Cash Book with Bank Statement of his current account for the month of March 2004, you find the following :
    (*a*) Cash Book showed an overdraft of Rs 4,500.
    (*b*) The payment side of the Cash Book had been undercast by Rs 150.
    (*c*) A cheque for Rs 750 drawn on his saving deposit account has been shown as drawn on current account.
    (*d*) Under instructions from Surendra the Bank had transferred interest Rs 900 from his deposit account to his current account on 3rd April 2004. This amount had, however, been taken in the Cash Book before 31st March 2004.
    (*e*) Cheques amounting to Rs 7,500 drawn and entered in the Cash Book had not been presented.
    (*f*) Cheques amounting to Rs 6,000 sent to the Bank for collection though entered in Cash Book had not been credited by the Bank.
    (*g*) Bank charges of Rs 75 as per Bank Statement of Account had not been taken in the Cash Book.
    (*h*) Dividends of the amount of Rs 3,000 had been paid direct to the Bank and not entered in the Cash Book.
    (*i*) A cheque issued to Mr A for Rs 200 was replaced when out of date. But it was entered in the Cash Book again and no other entry having been recorded. Both cheques were also included in the totals of cheques issued but not presented as shown above.

You are required to arrive at the balance as it would appear in the Bank Statement as on 31st March 2004. *(C.S. Inter)*

[**Ans.** Bank Overdraft as per Pass Book Rs 375]

33. On 31st March 2004, the Cash Book of Mr Subramaniam shows a Bank Overdraft of Rs 15,500. On verification with the Bank Pass Book, it is observed that the adjustments regarding the following are to be made :

(*a*) Following cheques were not presented in the Bank before 31st March :

(*i*) Ram Rs 400
(*ii*) Krishna Rs 250
(*iii*) Somu Rs 125
(*iv*) Salim Rs 225
(*v*) Mohan Rs 150

(*b*) Cheques sent in for collection were not credited in the Bank before 31st March :

(*i*) Gopal Rs 250
(*ii*) Kannan Rs 300
(*iii*) John Rs 175
(*iv*) Thomas Rs 125

(*c*) Mr A has paid into Bank directly a sum of Rs 300 on 28th March which has not been entered in Cash Book.

(*d*) The Bank has charged Rs 10 towards Incidental charges and Rs 250 towards Interest on overdraft on 31st March.

(*e*) A cheque received from Padma for Rs 500 taken in Cash Book on 31st March, but remitted in Bank on 2nd April 2004.

Prepare a Bank Reconciliation Statement and find out the Bank Overdraft as shown by the Bank Pass Book. (*B.Com., MS, Kerala, Bhopal*)

[**Ans.** Overdraft as per Pass Book Rs 15,660]

34. From the following particulars ascertain the balance that would appear in the Pass Book of Mr Ram as on 31st December 2004.

(1) The Cash Book showed a credit balance of Rs 18,500.
(2) Out of the cheques worth Rs 30,000 issued prior to this date, it was found that the Bank had paid only cheques worth Rs 14,500.
(3) There was also a credit in the Pass Book for an amount paid by our customer direct into the Bank Rs 11,610.
(4) The Bank had also collected the Bill for Rs 8,200 which fell due on 31st December 2004.
(5) Rs 950 in respect of a cheque paid in but dishonoutred appear in the Pass Book only.
(6) Cheques paid in before 31st December 2004 amounted to Rs 23,000 but the bank had collected and credited cheques worth Rs 9,000.
(7) Interest on Investments collected by Bank and credited in the Pass Book amount to Rs 95.
(8) There was an entry on the debit side in the Pass Book for bank charges Rs 25.

(*B.Com., MS., Kerala, Agra*)

[**Ans.** Bank Balance as per Pass Book (Cr.) Rs 1,930]

35. Prepare the Bank Reconciliation Statement as on 30th November, 2006, from the following information:

1. Balance as per the Pass Book on 30.11.2006 (Dr.) Rs. 20,000.
2. On 5.10.2006, deposited a cheque for collection of Rs. 1,000 and made entry in Cash Book, appears in the Book on 6.12.2006 at Rs. 990.
3. Cheques issued to parties but not presented for payment till 30.11.2006, are of Rs. 525, Rs. 835 and Rs. 900.
4. Cheques deposited for collection but not collected by the bankers till 30.11.2006, Rs. 8,760 and Rs. 410.
5. Interest on investment collected by the Bankers on 30.11.2006, Rs. 955 entered in the Cash Book on 4.12.2006, on receipt of Bank intimation.

6. Bank charges Rs. 90 dated 27.11.2006 not entered in the Cash Book.
7. Cheque deposited for collection on 30.11.2006 but returned dishonoured on 6.12.2006 of Rs. 945.
8. Bankers have made a mistake in balancing by showing overdrawn balance in excess by Rs. 1,000 on 30.11.2006, which was rectified in the Bank Pass Book on 7.12.2006 when notified.

(ICWA Inter, B.Com. MS)

(**Ans.** Overdraft balance as per Cash Book : Rs. 11,010)

36. The Pass Book of Bank Account No. 1 of Ghose and Co. Calcutta shows an overdraft of Rs. 17,950 on July 31, 2006 but this does not agree with the bank balance as shown by the Cash Book of the firm. On scrutiny, the following discrepancies are revealed:

(i) Out of cheques amounting to Rs. 4,350 drawn by the firm on July 27, cheques amounting to Rs. 2,650 only are cashed up to July 31.

(ii) The firm paid Rs. 7,000 into the bank, but the bank credited the same to Account No. 2 in the name of the firm.

(iii) Interest and bank charges amounting to Rs. 1,200 debited by the bank to the Firm's account have not been entered in the firm's books.

(iv) Out of Rs. 11,300 paid in by the firm in cash and by cheques on July 31, cheques amounting to Rs. 4,750 are credited to the firm's account on August 4, 2006.

(v) A cheque of Rs. 900 credited in the Pass Book on July 28 being dishonoured is debited to the firm's account on August 2.

(vi) Bankers have credited the firm's account with Rs. 16,000 for interest collected by them on Government papers held by them but the same has not been entered in the firm's books.

(vii) A payment of Rs. 250 from Account No. 2 has been wrongly debited by the bankers to Account No. 1.

Prepare the Bank Reconciliation Statement as at 31st July, 2006 for Bank Account No. 1.

(**Ans.** Overdraft as per Cash Book Rs. 23,350)

(ICWA B.Com, Madras)

Chapter 6

Final Accounts

Trading Account - Individual Items Posted to the Debit of Trading Account - Individual Items Credited to Trading Account - Advantages of Trading Account - Profit and Loss Account - Advantages of Profit and Loss Account - Manufacturing Account - Balance Sheet - Classification of Assets and Liabilities - Questions - Objective Type Questions - Theoretical Questions - Practical Problems.

A Trial Balance marks a definite stage in the preparation of accounts. It indicates that all the transactions for a particular period have been duly entered, posted and balanced. But this itself is not the end of book-keeping work. It is a means to an end, the end being (*a*) to find out the profit or loss made by the business firm in a given period and (*b*) to understand the financial position of the business as on a given date. A businessman can ascertain these by preparing the Final Accounts, which is prepared on the basis of the Trial Balance. The preparation of Final Accounts is the last step in the accounting circle. The Final Account includes Manufacturing Account, Trading Account, Profit and Loss Account and Balance Sheet. Even though the Balance Sheet is a statement, for all practical purposes, it is treated as a part of Final Accounts. We are concerned with Trading and Profit and Loss Account and Balance Sheet and the same are discussed in this chapter.

TRADING ACCOUNT

Trading account is prepared mainly to know the profitability of 'goods' bought or manufactured and sold by the businessmen. The difference between the selling price and cost price of the goods is the gross result. The term 'goods' means the goods bought for resale. It does not include assets. If sale proceeds are more than the cost of goods sold, gross profit is made. If sale proceeds are less than the cost of the goods sold, gross loss is incurred. Cost of goods sold can be ascertained as follows :

	Rs
Opening Stock	–
Add : Purchases less returns	–
Add : Direct Expenses	–
	–
Less : Closing Stock	–
Cost of goods sold	–

The Trading and Profit and Loss Account may be prepared separately or they may be shown as one account headed as Trading and Profit and Loss Account, with two sections. The first part of this section which is relating to the study of the result of Trading transactions alone, is known as the Trading Account. Trading Account may be defined as an Account which discloses the result of buying and selling goods. Trading Account is a ledger account. It contains the result of operations over a period. It is shown on next page.

INDIVIDUAL ITEMS POSTED TO THE DEBIT OF TRADING ACCOUNT

Opening Stock

This is the stock of goods in hand. This figure is available from Trial Balance. Generally, when Trading Account is prepared, stock is taken on the last day of the trading period, by actual counting and fixing value. The valuation is usually done at cost price or market price whichever is lower. The current year's closing stock of goods will be the opening stock of the next year. A firm, which is started newly, has no opening stock. Opening stock consists of raw materials, work-in-progress and finished goods.

A proforma of a Trading Account is given below:

Name of the Firm
Trading Account
for the year ended on 31st December .....

Dr.	Rs		*Cr.* Rs
To Opening Stock	–	By Sales less Returns	–
To Purchases less Returns	–	By Closing Stock	–
To Wages	–		
To Carriage	–		
To Freight	–		
To Dock Charges	–		
To Excise Duty	–		
To Octroi	–		
To Import Duty	–		
To Fuel, Power etc.	–		
To Stores consumed	–		
To Royalty (Production basis)	–		
To Manufacturing Expenses	–		
To Profit and Loss A/c (Balancing figure) (Gross Profit transferred)	–		

Opening Stock is always debited to Trading Account.

Purchases

Traders generally purchase goods on cash or on credit. The purchases are debited to the Trading Account after deducting Purchase Returns, if any. The deductions are shown in the inner column and net purchases are shown in outer column. Purchases of assets are separated from the purchases of goods. It is possible that the proprietor may use goods for his own use and this amount of goods taken by the proprietor should be deducted from the purchase. In certain cases adjusted purchases are seen in the Trial Balance. It means, there is an adjustment of opening stock and closing stock through purchases. In its simple meaning the cost of goods sold is accounted for better comparison with sales. Thus adjusted purchase means, Opening Stock + Purchase – Closing Stock. Thus, there will be no Opening Stock in the Trial Balance. In the Trial balance adjusted Net Purchase and Closing Stock appear and Net Purchases is taken to the debit of Trading account and Closing Stock is taken to Balance Sheet. To adjust the purchases for Opening and Closing Stocks, the following two entries are passed:

(*a*) Purchases Account Dr.
To Opening Stock Account
(Closing of Opening Stock Account and thereby purchases increase)

(*b*) Closing Stock Account Dr.
To Purchases Account
(Opening a new account for unsold stocks :) Thus the Net Purchases are debited to Trading Account and Closing Stock is shown in Balance Sheet.

Direct Expenses

Direct expenses are those expenses which have been incurred to bring the goods or making the goods ready for sale. All such expenses are debited to Trading Account. A few examples are given below :

Wages/Direct Wages/Productive Wages : Wages paid to workers, who are directly engaged in the production are direct expenses. Workers may be employed to manufacture a merchandise or make it more saleable. Similar types of items are debited to Trading Account.

Carriage/Freight/Carriage Inward : These items fall under direct expenses. These are transportation expenses met for bringing the goods purchased to the business place. Whether such expenses are paid or outstanding does not matter; if they have been incurred must be debited to Trading Account.

Import Duty/Customs Duty : In case of goods imported from abroad, import duty, customs duty or dock charges etc. have to be paid. Since these are related to purchase of goods for resale purposes, these expenses are shown in the debit side of the Trading Account.

Fuel/Power/Lighting etc. : Machines are used in the production process with the help of coal or electricity. Such charges are direct and are debited to Trading Account.

Packaging Charges : Sometimes, it is necessary to pack the goods in a special type of packages in order to protect the goods or attract the customers. In these circumstances, the cost of packaging is a direct expense and is debited to Trading Account. At the same time, the ordinary packing of goods at the time of sales are not direct and these expenses are debited to Profit and Loss Account.

INDIVIDUAL ITEMS CREDITED TO TRADING ACCOUNT

Sales

Both cash and credit sales of goods are included under this item. From this figure, Sales Returns, if any, should be deducted in the inner column and net sales amount shown in the outer column. Sales of assets are not credited to Trading Account.

Closing Stock

The Closing Stock is credited to the Trading Account. It is nothing but unsold stocks. The closing stock is valued at Cost Price or Market price whichever is less. Closing Stock is shown in Balance Sheet.

In the credit side of the Trading Account, sales, closing stock etc. are shown.

ADVANTAGES OF TRADING ACCOUNT

Trading Account provides the following advantages:

1. The result of trading can be known separately.
2. The various items of trading account of different periods can be compared.
3. The adjustment in the selling price can be made by knowing the percentage of gross profit on net sales.
4. Over-stocking/under-stocking can be known in order to act wisely.
5. If gross loss is discolosed, the business can be closed immediately because the loss will further increase when the indirect expenses are added to it.
6. The progress can be studied on the basis of gross Profit ratio, year after year.

TRADING ACCOUNT EQUATION

Trading account is prepared for calculating gross profit or gross loss. Gross profit or gross loss is the difference between the 'cost of goods sold' and 'sales'. In accounting terms gross profit is the excess of revenue over cost of sales. This statement can be expressed in the form of an equation.

Gross Profit = Sales – Cost of goods sold

(or) Gross Profit + Cost of goods sold = Sales

ILLUSTRATION 6.1

A firm had opening stock of Rs. 5,000 on 1st April 2005. The following transactions took place during year. Find Gross Profit.

Purchases	Rs. 25,000
Sales	Rs. 40,000
Purchase Returns	Rs. 100
Sales Returns	Rs. 250
Carriage in	Rs. 300
Duty	Rs. 500
Stock on 31st Dec.'06	Rs. 1,000

SOLUTION:

Gross Profit = Net Sales – Cost of goods sold

(Net Sales = Rs. 40,000 – Rs. 250 = Rs. 39,750

Cost of goods sold = Rs. 5,000 + Rs. 24,900 + Rs. 800 – Rs. 1,000) = 29,700

Gross Profit = Rs. 39,750 – Rs. 29,700

= Rs. 10,050.

ILLUSTRATION 6.2

The following balances were extracted from the books of a Sole Trader on 30th June 2004. Prepare Trading Account by giving necessary entries :

	Rs		*Rs*
Opening Stock Account	2,000	Sales Account	7,000
Closing Stock Account	1,500	Freight Account	100
Returns Inward Account	300	Carriage Account	75
Returns Outward Account	200		
Wages Account	350		
Purchases Account	4,000		

SOLUTION

Closing Entries

2004			*Rs*	*Rs*
June 30	Sales Account	Dr.	300	
	To Returns Inwards Account			300
	(Being transfer of Returns)			
	Returns Outwards Account	Dr.	200	
	To Purchase Account			200
	(Being transfer of returns)			
	Trading Account	Dr.	6,325	
	To Opening Stock Account			2,000
	To Purchases Account			3,800
	To Wages Account			350
	To Freight Account			100
	To Carriage Account			75
	(Being of various accounts to Trading Account)			
	Sales Account	Dr.	6,700	
	To Trading Account			6,700
	(Being transfer of net sales)			
	Trading Account	Dr.	1,875	
	To Profit and Loss Account			1,875
	(Being transfer of gross profit to Profit & Loss Account)			
	ADJUSTMENT ENTRIES			
	Closing Stock Account	Dr.	1,500	
	To Trading Account			1,500
	(Being unsold stock brought into account)			

Trading Account
for the year ended on 30th June

Dr.	Rs	Rs	Cr.	Rs	Rs
To Opening Stock Account		2,000	By Sales Account	7,000	
To Purchases Account	4,000		Less: Returns Account	300	6,700
Less: Returns Account	200	3,800	By Closing Stock Account		1,500
To Wages Account		350			
To Freight Account		100			
To Carriage Account		75			
To Profit and Loss Account (Gross Profit transferred)		1,875			
		8,200			8,200

PROFIT AND LOSS ACCOUNT

By preparing the trading account, it is possible to find out the gross profit or gross loss made during the given period. The next step is the preparation of the Profit and Loss Account to ascertain net profit earned or net loss suffered during a given period of time. The balance of Trading Account is brought down to Profit and Loss Account. Then, the Profit and Loss Account is credited with other incomes and debited with all indirect expenses. Then the Profit and Loss Account may be balanced and the balance is (net profit/net loss) to be transferred to Capital Account, in case of sole trading or partnership firms.

The following items are debited in the Profit and Loss Account :

1. *Administrative expenses/Management expenses :* Office salaries, Office Rent, Office Lighting, Printing, Stationary, Telephone Rent, Directors' fees, Auditor's fee, Legal Expenses, Postage, Insurance, Repairs, Interest and other similar expenses connected with the office.

2. *Financial expenses :* Interest on loan, Discount Allowed, Interest on Capital, Bad Debts, Bank Expenses, Discount on Bills etc.

3. *Sales Expenses :* Salesmen Salaries, Travelling Expenses, Advertising, Selling Commission, Brokerage, Free Samples, Trade Expenses etc.

4. *Distribution expenses :* Carriage out, Warehouse expenses, Warehouse Insurance, Warehouse rent, Delivery Van Expenses, packing expenses etc.

5. *Depreciation* of assets, various provisions etc.

A proforma of a Profit and Loss Account is given below:

Profit and Loss Account
for the year ended 31st December

Dr.		Rs	Cr.		Rs
To Gross Loss b/d			By Gross Profit b/d		
To Management Expenses :			By Interest Received		
Office Salaries			By Discount Received		
Rent of office building			By Commission Received		
Office Lighting			By Income from Investment		
Office, Rent, Rates and Taxes			By Apprenticeship Premium		
Printing and Stationery			By Rent from Tenants		
Telephone Charges			By Reserve for Discount on Creditors		
Postage			By Interest on Renewal of Bills		
Legal Expenses			By Miscellaneous Income		
Audit Fees			By Net Loss, transferred to Capital		

Insurance General Expenses etc.		Account	
To Selling Expenses : Salesmen Salaries Travelling Expenses Advertising Bad Debts Selling Commission Brokerage Free Samples			
To Distribution Expenses Carriage Out Warehouse Rent Warehouse Insurance Delivery Van Expenses Packing Expenses			
To Depreciation : Depreciation of Assets Maintenance Expenses			
To Finance Expenses : Discount Allowed Interest on Loan Interest on Capital Discount on Bills Loss by Fire			
To Net Profit, transferred to Capital Account			

ADVANTAGES OF PROFIT AND LOSS ACCOUNT

It provides the following advantages :

1. Various *expenses can be effectively controlled* by comparing various expenses, year after year.
2. *The net result* - profit or loss, revealed by the Profit and Loss Account is an index by which progress can be measured.
3. Profitability is the basis and *helps in planning future course of action.*

ILLUSTRATION 6.3

From the following figures, prepare Profit and Loss Account of Madanlal, as it would appear at the one year ended on 30th June.

	Rs		*Rs*
Salaries and Wages	3,000	Advertising	1,000
Commission paid	200	Discount Allowed	1,800
Postage & Telegram	150	Rent Received	1,700
Insurance	300	Interest on Investment	1,500
Interest paid	400	Bad Debts	900
Carriage out	500	Brokerage paid	95

The gross profit was 45% of sales, which amounted to Rs 65,000.

Closing Entries

Date	Particulars		L.F.	Rs	Rs
June 30	Profit and Loss Account	Dr.		8,345	
	To Salaries and Wages A/c				3,000
	To Commission Paid A/c				200
	To Postage & Telegrams A/c				150
	To Insurance A/c				300
	To Interest Paid A/c				400
	To Carriage Out A/c				500
	To Advertising A/c				1,000
	To Discount Allowed A/c				1,800
	To Bad Debts A/c				900
	To Brokerage A/c				95
	(Being transfer of above nominal Accounts to Profit & Loss Account)				
	Rent Received A/c	Dr.		1,700	
	Interest on Investment A/c	Dr.		1,500	
	To Profit & Loss A/c				3,200
	(Being transfer of above nominal Accounts to Profit and Loss A/c				
	Profit and Loss Account	Dr.		24,105	
	To Capital Account				24,105
	(Being transfer of Net Profit to Capital Account)				

SOLUTION

Profit and Loss Account of Madanlal for the year ended on 30th June...

Dr.	Rs		*Cr.* Rs
To Salaries A/c	3,000	By Gross Profit 45% of Rs 65,000	29,250
To Commission A/c	200	By Rent Received A/c	1,700
To Postage & Telegrams A/c	150	By Interest on Investment A/c	1,500
To Insurance A/c	300		
To Interest A/c	400		
To Carriage Out A/c	500		
To Advertising A/c	1,000		
To Discount Allowed A/c	1,800		
To Bad Debts A/c	900		
To Brokerage A/c	95		
To Capital A/c (net profit transferred)	24,105		
	32,450		32,450

Difference between Trading and Profit and Loss Account

Trading Account	*Profit and Loss Account*
1. The first section of revenue account is known as Trading Account.	1. The second section of revenue account is known as the Profit and Loss Account.
2. It is prepared to know only the result of trading.	2. It is prepared to know the ultimate result of the business.
3. It deals with purchasing and manufacturing costs of goods.	3. It deals with administration, selling, distribution expenses etc.
4. Balance of this account is transferred to Profit and Loss Account.	4. Balance of this account is transferred to Capital Account.

MANUFACTURING ACCOUNT

A businessman purchases finished goods for resale whereas a manufacturer buys raw materials, converts them into finished goods, by incurring certain expenses, and then sells them. Thus, Trading Account is splitted into two—Manufacturing Account and Trading Account. Manufacturing account is the account employed to show the cost of manufacture or production. On the debit side, opening stock of raw materials, work-in-process, purchases of raw materials, carriage, manufacturing expenses and all other expenses relating to factory are entered. On the credit side, closing stock of raw materials, work-in-process are shown and the balance, representing the cost of production of finished goods, is transfered to Trading Account. If one wants to know the cost of manufacturing, then an Account—Manufacturing Account—will have to be prepared. The following example illustrates it.

ILLUSTRATION 6.4

From the following particulars prepare Manufacturing Account and Trading and Profit and Loss Account :

	Rs		*Rs*
Purchase of Raw Materials	13,195	Interest on Bank Loan	600
Returns Inward	70	Stock : 1st Jan. 2004	
Stock on 31st Dec. 2004		Raw Materials	400
Raw Materials	1,210	Work-in-progress	300
Work-in-progress	1,000	Finished Goods	410
Finished goods	1,370	Sales	19,500
Productive wages	2,000	Returns Outward	85
Factory Expenses	1,840	Carriage Outward	105
Office Expenses	300	Carriage Inward	100
Salaries	600	Discount Allowed	10
Distributing Expenses	100	Sale of Scrap	20
Selling Expenses	700	Depreciation of Machinery	500
Purchase Expenses	600	Reparings to Machinery	100
Export Duty	300	Depreciation of office furniture	40
Import Duty	200		

SOLUTION

Manufacturing Account
for the year ended on 31st December 2004

Dr. *Cr.*

			Rs		*Rs*
To Work-in-progress			300	By Sale of Scrap	20
To Materials Consumed:				By Work-in-progress	1,000
Opening Stock		400		By Cost of Finished goods, transferred	
Purchases :	13,195			to Trading Account	16,920
Less: Returns	85	13,110			
		13,510			
Less: Closing Stock		1,210	12,300		
To Wages			2,000		
To Factory Expenses			1,840		
To Purchase Expenses			600		
To Import Duty			200		
To Carriage Inward			100		
To Depreciation of Machinery			500		
To Repairs to Machinery			100		
			17,940		17,940

Trading & Profit and Loss Account
for the year ended on 31st December 2004

Dr.	Rs			Rs Cr.
To Opening Stock A/c	410	By Sales A/c	19,500	
To Manufacturing A/c	16,920	Less: Returns	70	19,430
To Gross Profit c/d	3,470	By Closing Stock A/c		1,370
	20,800			20,800
To Office Expenses A/c	300	By Gross Profit b/d		3,470
To Salaries A/c	600			
To Distributing Expenses A/c	100			
To Selling Expenses A/c	700			
To Export Duty A/c	300			
To Carriage Outward A/c	105			
To Discount Allowed A/c	10			
To Interest on Loan A/c	600			
To Depreciation on Furniture A/c	40			
To Net Profit, transferred to Capital Account	715			
	3,470			3,470

BALANCE SHEET

A Balance Sheet is a statement of the financial position of a firm at a given date. The given date is the date at which the final accounts are prepared. Transactions are first recorded in journal. Entries in the journal are posted to ledgers. Ledger accounts are balanced and the balances are recorded in a Trial Balance. Trial Balance consists of all Accounts—Personal, Real and Nominal. From the Trial Balance, nominal accounts are transferred to Trading or Profit and Loss Account and the remaining balances are taken to Balance Sheet. However, Balance Sheet is a summary of whole of the accounting record. This is because the nominal accounts are transferred to Revenue Accounts, and Revenue account is closed by shifting the balance to the Balance Sheet. Balance Sheet is also known as a statement of Assets and Liabilities. Balance Sheet is the last and the most important link in the chain of Final Accounts and Statements. It describes the financial position of a business in a systematic standard form. It is a mirror of a business. When the assets exceed the liabilities, one can conclude that the business is sound and solvent. The function of the Balance Sheet is to show the true picture of the business on a particular date.

Difference between a Trial Balance and a Balance Sheet

Balance Sheet	*Trial Balance*
1. Balance Sheet columns are headed by Liabilities and Assets.	1. Trial balance columns are headed by Dr. and Cr.
2. It is a statement showing closing balances of Personal and Real Accounts.	2. It is a codified summary of all ledger balances–Personal, Real and Nominal accounts.
3. It is the last step in final accounts.	3. It is the first step in the final accounts.
4. It contains only closing stock.	4. It contains opening stock.
5. It reveals the true and financial position of a firm.	5. It establishes the arithmetical accuracy of the accounting work.
6. It is prepared after the preparation of revenue accounts.	6. It is prepared before the preparation of revenue accounts.
7. Stock taking is essential for the preparation of Balance Sheet.	7. Stock taking is not necessary for a Trial Balance.
8. The arrangement of assets and liabilities are made in order of liquidity or permanence.	8. There is no order as to the arrangement of ledger balance in a Trial Balance.
9. To complete the accounting circle, Balance Sheet is essential.	9. To complete the accounting circle, Trial Balance is not necessarily prepared.
10. It gives a clear picture of the trend of the firm.	10. It will not give any guidance to understand the trend of the firm.

Form of Balance Sheet

It has two sides—left hand side (liabilities) and right hand side (assets). It is not an account. It is a statement. 'To' and 'By' should not be used in the Balance Sheet. The left hand side contains the credit balances of all personal accounts while right hand side contains debit balances of real and personal accounts. The two sides of the Balance Sheet must always agree.

Functions of a Balance Sheet

1. A Balance Sheet *exhibits the true financial position of a firm* at a particular date.
2. *Financial position can be ascertained* clearly with the help of Balance Sheet.
3. It provides valuable information to the management for *taking better decision* through ratio analysis.
4. Balance Sheet helps in knowing past and present position of an enterprise. It may be called the *horoscope of the concern.*
5. It is a *mirror of a business.*

Limitations of Balance Sheet

1. It is prepared on a historical cost basis. Changes in prices are not considered.
2. Window-dressing may be done in Balance Sheet.
3. Historical Cost of Balance Sheet does not convey fruitful information.
4. Different assets are valued according to different rules.
5. It cannot reflect the ability or skill of staff.
6. It is measured in terms of money or money's worth. That is, only those assets are recorded in it which can be expressed in money.
7. In inflationary trend, if the readers are not expert may mislead.
8. Balance Sheet has some fictitious assets, which have no market value. Such items are unnecessarily inflate the total value of assets.

CLASSIFICATION OF ASSETS AND LIABILITIES

Assets

Assets are the properties possessed by an undertaking. Assets are what the business owns, *i.e.,* its property and possessions such as Cash, Book-debts, Debtors, Stock, Land, Building etc. The classification is done as follows :

1. Fixed Assets : Fixed Assets are durable in nature, acquired and held permanently in the business and are used for the purpose of earning profits. And are not intended for sale. For instance, Plant and Machinery, Land, Buildings, Furniture, Fixture etc.

Fixed assets may be tangible or intangible. Tangible assets are those assets which have existence or concrete things—can be seen, touched and felt; like Building, Machinery etc. Intangible assets are those assets which cannot be seen and touched. They are non-visible, like Goodwill, patent, Trade Mark etc.

2. Current Assets : Current assets or Floating assets are in the form of cash or that can be converted into cash within a short period of time. Cash in hand, Cash at Bank, Debtors, Bills Receivable, Investment etc. are the examples. This type of asset is also known as circulating assets, because their amounts are subject to constant change.

3. Fictitious Assets : These are not real assets and are fictitious in nature. These are unwritten lossses or non-recoupable costs. For instance, underwriting commission, Brokerage, Discount on Issue of Shares or Debentures, heavy advertisement expenses, etc. Fictitious assets although intangible are unrealisable and hence are worthless items. All such expenses have debit balances and are to be written off through Profit and Loss Account, slowly during future years and unwritten off portion of such expenses appear in the Balance Sheet.

4. Wasting Assets : Generally speaking assets that lose value through wear and tear or constant use, for instance, mines, quarries etc. Natural resources like timber-land, mineral deposits, oil reserves etc. can be called wasting assets by effluxion of time or use etc. Further, coal existing in coal mines, and if the coal has been taken out, fresh coal cannot be created, therefore mine is treated as wasting assets.

Liquid Assets

Liquid assets are those assets, which can be readily converted into cash. Liquidty does not mean mere convertibility. It means convertibility without any appreciable loss of value. For instance, Cash, Cash at Bank, Stocks, Bills Receivable etc. These can also be called circulating assets.

Liabilities

Liabilities are the amounts which a business has to pay. They are generally classified according to the period for which they are contracted. Certain liabilities are repayable within a short period of time while certain other liabilities are repayable only after a long time.

1. Fixed Liabilities : All long period liabilities are treated as fixed liabilities whether they are payable to the proprietor or to the outsiders. For instance, Debentures, mortgages, long term loans etc.

2. Current Liabilities : These are to be redeemed in the near future, usually within a year. That is all short period liabilities which are payable within one year are termed as current liabilities. Trade Creditors, Bank loans, Bills Payable etc. are examples of current liabilities.

3. Contingent Liabilities : The liabilities which are not the liabilities of the firm on the date of the Balance Sheet but may become liabilities in future on happening of an uncertain event, are all called contingent liabilities. In other words, they would become liabilities in the future provided the contemplated event occurs. If the event does not occur, no liability is incurred. For instance, a suit which is pending in the court of law, if lost, may create a liability. Bills discounted with a bank are also a contingent liability, if the acceptor fails to meet the bill.

There are two ways in which assets and liabilities are arranged in the Balance Sheet. Balance Sheet items may be set out in order of either liquidity or permanence. Under the order liquidity, the assets and liabilities are arranged according to their realisability and payment preferences. In the order of permanence or fixity, the order is reversed from that what is followed in liquidity order.

The specimen proforma of a Balance Sheet is given below:

Balance Sheet (Liquidity Order)

Liabilities	*Rs*	*Assets*	*Rs*
Current Liabilities		*Liquid Assets*	
Bills Payable		Cash in hand	
Sundry Creditors		Cash at Bank	
Bank Overdraft			
Long Term Liabilities		*Floating Assets*	
Loan from Bank		Sundry Debtors	
Debentures		Investments	
		Bills Receivable	
Fixed Liabilities		Stock in trade	
Capital		Prepaid Expenses	
		Fixed Assets	
		Plant and Machinery	
		Buildings	
		Furniture & fixtures	
		Land	

		Fictitious Assets	
		Advertisement	
		Miscellaneous Expenses	
		Profit & Loss	
		Intangible Assets	
		Goodwill	
		Patents	
		Copyright	

Balance Sheet (Order of permanence)

Liabilities	*Rs*	*Assets*	*Rs*
Fixed Liabilities		Intangible Assets	
Long Term Liabilities		Fictitious Assets	
Current Liabilities		Fixed Assets	
		Floating Assets	
		Liquid Assets	

ILLUSTRATION 6.5

From the following particulars, prepare a Balance Sheet as on 31st December 2004

	Dr. *Rs*	*Cr.* *Rs*
Capital		40,000
Drawings	4,400	—
Creditors and Debtors	6,400	4,200
Cash in hand	360	—
Cash at Bank	7,200	—
Furniture	3,700	—
Plant	10,000	—
Net Profit	—	1,660
General Reserve	—	1,000
Closing Stock	14,800	—
	46,860	46,860

SOLUTION

Balance Sheet
as on 31st December 2004
(Liquidity Order)

Liabilities		*Rs*	*Assets*	*Rs*
Sundry Creditors	*Rs*	4,200	Cash in hand	360
General Reserve		1,000	Cash at Bank	7,200
Capital :	40,000		Sundry Debtors	6,400
Add: Profit	1,660		Stock	14,800
			Furniture	3,700
	41,660		Plant	10,000
Less: Drawings	4,400	37,260		
		42,460		42,460

Alternatively

BALANCE SHEET
(Order of Permanence)
As on 31st December 2004

Liabilities		*Rs*	*Assets*	*Rs*
Capital	40,000		Plant	10,000
Add: Profit	1,660		Furniture	3,700
	41,660		Stock	14,800
Less: Drawings	4,400	37,260	Sundry Debtors	6,400
General Reserve		1,000	Cash at Bank	7,200
Sundry Creditors		4,200	Cash in hand	360
		42,460		42,460

QUESTIONS

Ojective Type Questions

I. State whether each of the following statement is True or False.

1. The term 'current assets' and 'liquid assets' have synonymous meanings.
2. All intangible assets are fictitious assets.
3. "Salary paid in advance" is not an expense because it neither reduces assets nor increases liabilities.
4. Stock at the end, if appears in the Trial Balance, is taken only to the Balance Sheet.
5. Captial Account is a liability Account.
6. All accounts with credit balances are either liabilities or incomes or gains.
7. Bad debts recovery is credited to Debtors Account.
8. Gross Profit = Sales – Cost of goods sold.
9. Capital is the excess of assets over liabilities.
10. Fixed assets are shown in the Balance Sheet at their market value.

(*Ans:* 1. False; 2. False; 3. True; 4. True; 5. True; 6. True; 7. False; 8. True; 9. True; 10. False.)

II. Fill in the blanks.

1. If outstanding salary appears in the Trial Balance, it is taken only to the ....
2. Salary outstading is a .... Account.
3. Outstanding expense is a ....
4. Closing Stock is valued at cost price or market price which is ....
5. Assets, meant for permanent use in business, are called .... assets.

(*Ans:* 1. Balance Sheet; 2. Personal; 3. Liability; 4. Less; 5. Fixed)

III. Select the most appropriate answer:

1. Sales are equal to:
   (a) Cost of goods sold + Profit (b) Cost of goods sold – Gross Profit.
   (c) Gross Profit – Cost of goods sold.
2. Outstanding salaries are shown as:
   (a) An expense. (b) A Liability.
   (c) An Asset.
3. Goods given as samples should be credited to :
   (a) Advertisement Account. (b) Sales Account.
   (c) Purchase Account.

4. Final Accounts are prepared with the help of:
   (a) Journal Entries. (b) Cash Book.
   (c) Trial Balance.
5. Loss by theft is debited to:
   (a) Manufacturing Account. (b) Profit and Loss Account.
   (c) Trading Account.
6. Goodwill is:
   (a) A current asset. (b) A tangible asset.
   (c) An intangible asset. (d) A fictitious asset.
7. Which one of the following is intangible asset:
   (a) Machinery. (b) Goodwill.
   (c) Stock.
8. Stock is valued at:
   (a) Cost Price. (b) Market Price.
   (c) Cost price or Market Price whichever is less.
9. Unearned income account is:
   (a) An Asset. (b) A Liability.
   (c) An Expanse.
10. Assets convertible into cash easily are:
   (a) Floating Assets (b) Current Assets.
   (c) Fixed Assets. (d) Liquid Assets.

(Ans: 1. (a) 2. (b); 3. (c); 4. (c); 5. (b); 6. (c); 7. (b); 8. (c); 9. (b); 10. (d).)

THEORETICAL QUESTIONS

1. State the objects of Trading Account.
2. How does the Profit and Loss Account differ from Trading Account ?
3. Define a Balance Sheet.
4. State the object of preparing a Balance Sheet.
5. How is a Balance Sheet different from a Trial Balance ?
6. Briefly explain the purpose of preparing Final Accounts. (*B.Com. Madurai*)
7. What do you understand by "Liquidity Order" and "Permanency Order" of preparing Balance Sheet? (*B.Com. MS*)

PRACTICAL PROBLEMS

1. Preparing Trading and Profit and Loss Account for the year ended 31st December 2004 from the following :

	Rs		*Rs*
Opening Stock	3,600	Rent (office)	500
Purchase	18,260	Sales Returns	700
Wages	3,620	Purchase Returns	900
Closing Stock	4,420	General Expenses	900
Sales	32,000	Discount to Debtors	300
Carriage	500	Interest from Bank	200
Carriage Out	400		
Rent (Factory)	400		

[Ans. Gross Profit Rs 10,240; Net Profit Rs 8,340**]**

2. Prepare Trading and Profit and Loss Account for the half year ended 30th June 2004, from the following Trial Balance :

	Rs	Rs
Capital	—	15,000
Purchase	20,000	—
Wages	1,200	—
Sales	—	30,000
Furniture	800	—
Travelling Expenses	700	—
Salaries	900	—
Commission	300	—
Cash	1,000	—
Bank	3,400	—
Repairs	500	—
Buildings	16,000	—
Returns	500	700
Debtors & Creditors	4,500	4,000
Bills Payable and Bills Receivable	600	800
Telephone	52	—
Interest	48	—
	50,500	50,500

Stock at the end Rs 6,500. [**Ans.** Gross Profit Rs 15,500; Net profit Rs 13,000]

3. From the following information, prepare Balance Sheet of Mr John as at 31st December 2004, arranging the assets and liabilities (*i*) in order of permanence and (*ii*) in order of liquidity :

	Rs		*Rs*
Goodwill	10,000	Land and Buildings	30,000
Capital	90,000	Bank	10,000
Outstanding Expenses	600	Sundry Creditors	31,500
Cash in hand	500	Bills Receivable	6,500
Investments	10,000	Plant and Machinery	20,000
Net Profit	46,300	Bills Payable	5,350
Sundry Debtors	25,000	Bad Debts Provision	1,250
Drawings	15,000	Closing Stock	40,000
		Furniture	8,000

[**Ans.** Balance Sheet Rs 1,58,750]

4. From the following balances, prepare a Trial Balance and Balance Sheet as on 31st December 2004 :

	Rs		*Rs*
Capital	32,500	Furniture	1,250
Bank (Cr)	3,000	Loan from Mr. A	3,000
Profit & Loss (Cr.)	500	Drawings	2,500
Bills Payable	4,000	Motor Van	4,000
Bills Receivable	3,500	Machinery	8,500
Sundry Debtors	11,000	Buildings	10,000
Sundry Creditors	7,500	Stock	6,000
Patents	3,750		

[**Ans.** Trial Balance Total : Rs 50,500; Balance Sheet Rs 48,000]

5. Prepare Trading and Profit and Loss Account and Balance Sheet from the following Trial Balance :

Trial Balance as on 31st December 2004

	Dr. *Rs*	*Cr.* *Rs*
Prem's Capital	—	40,000
Prem's Drawing	5,000	—
Leasehold land	25,000	—
Freehold Premises	20,000	—
Goodwill	7,000	—
Trade Mark	13,000	—
Machinery and Plant	15,000	—
Fixtures and Fittings	2,000	—
Stock at beginning	18,000	—
Bills Payable and Receivable	4,000	6,000
Sundry Debtors and Creditors	16,000	24,000
Purchases and Sales	80,000	1,50,000
Returns	1,000	2,000
Carriage Inward	1,500	—
Carriage Outward	500	—
Freight, Duty etc.	1,200	—
Manufacturing Wages	22,000	—
Coal, Fuel, Gas etc.	800	—
Factory Expenses	4,500	—
Salaries	18,000	—
Rent, Taxes, Insurance	6,000	—
Commission	2,500	—
Interest	—	3,000
Discount	4,000	6,000
Stationary and Printing	500	—
Trading Expenses	1,800	—
Cash in hand	700	—
Bankers	—	39,000
	2,70,000	2,70,000

[**Ans.** Gross Profit Rs 23,000; Net Loss Rs 1,300; Balance Sheet Rs 1,02,700]

6. From the following Trial Balance, prepare Manufacturing, Trading and Profit & Loss Accounts and a Balance Sheet as on 31st December 2004.

	Rs	*Rs*
Stock on 1st Jan. 2004		—
Raw Materials	2,000	—
Work-in-progress	5,000	—
Finished Goods	10,000	—
Manufacturing wages	10,000	—
Factory Rent	5,000	—
Purchase of Raw Materials	30,000	—
Carriage of Raw Materials	3,000	—
Salary of works manager	2,000	—
Office Rent	2,000	—
Printing and Stationary	1,000	—
Bad Debts	1,000	—
Sales	—	60,000

Land and Buildings	30,000	—
Plant and Machinery	20,000	—
Depreciation of Plant	2,000	—
Sundry Debtors and Creditors	5,000	30,000
Cash in hand	5,000	—
Capital	—	43,000
	1,33,000	1,33,000

Closing Stocks on 31st December 2004

Raw Materials	Rs 5,000
Work-in-process	Rs 4,000
Finished Goods	Rs 10,000

[**Ans.** Cost of Production Rs 50,000; Gross Profit Rs 10,000; Net Profit Rs 6,000 and Balance Sheet Rs 79,000]

Chapter 7

Final Accounts with Adjustments

Introduction – Closing Stock – Outstanding Expenses – Unexpired or Pre-paid Expenses – Accrued Income – Income Received in Advance – Depreciation – Additional Bad Debts – Provision for Doubtful Debts – Provision for Discount on Debtors – Interest on Capital – Interest on Drawings – Provision for Discount on Creditors – Creation of Various Reserves – Deferred Revenue Expenditure – Commission Payable as a Percentage on Net Profit – Accidental Loss – Goods Used as Free Samples – Work Sheet – Questions – Objective Type Questions – Theoretical Questions – Practical Problems.

INTRODUCTION

In the early chapters we have seen how the Final Accounts—Trading Account, Profit and Loss Account and Balance Sheet are prepared with the help of Trial Balance. After the agreement of the Trial Balance, steps are taken for the preparation of Final Accounts, which helps the trader to know the exact financial position of the business and to know the trend of the business. The Trial Balance is only a summary of the transactions which have already been recorded in the books of accounts during a given period. Trial Balance gives the particulars of goods bought and sold, expenses paid and incomes derived and also the amount of assets and liabilities. The actual transactions done are revealed by the Trial Balance. It does not include the information connected with pending transactions. The object of book-keeping is to present a true and fair view of the Profit and Loss Account and present the state of the business. If there is any item stated incorrectly in the final accounts, then the books of accounts will not fulfil the object of presenting a true and fair view of the business. In the preceding chapters, the Final Accounts are prepared without taking into consideration items like Outstanding expenses and income, prepaid expenses and incomes, Depreciation, etc. Then, naturally Final Accounts cannot reveal the true financial position. To ensure that the Final Accounts disclose the true trading result, it is necessary to take into account all items of income and expenditure pertaining to the period of accounting irrespective of the fact whether they are received or not, paid or not, received in advance or paid in advance, etc. For instance, a trader employs salesman at a salary of Rs 8,000 per month on 1st January. Salary of January is paid at the beginning of February; salary of February paid at the beginning of March and so on. Thus salary for the month of December 2004 will be paid at the beginning of January 2005. Trial Balance as on 31st December 2004 shows Rs 88,000 (Rs 8,000 × 11). But the salary for December 2004 remains unpaid on 31st December 2004. The Trial Balance shows Rs 88,000 under salary account. If this amount is taken into account, without making the adjustment of salary (unpaid) for December 2004, the profit would be overstated. Similarly, if a businessman has paid 15 months rent, during a particular year, the Trial Balance shows 15 months rent and thus three months rent is overpaid. If this is not considered at the stage of preparation of Final Accounts, the profit will be understated. Therefore, all such outstanding expenses and outstanding incomes should properly be adjusted through adjusting entries. Adjustment entries are made before the accounts are closed and Final Account is prepared.

When the accrual basis of accounting is used, adjusting entries are required at the end of the period to record any previously unrecognised changes in assets, liabilities or revenue items. The adjusting entries have the following features:

(1) Every adjusting entry affects both Profit and Loss Account and Balance Sheet.

(2) It does not directly affect cash.

(3) It is recorded at the end of the accounting period.

(4) There is a change in income or expense.

(5) There is a change in Balance Sheet item.

WHEN ADJUSTMENT ENTRY IS PASSED, IT AFFECTS MINIMUM TWO ACCOUNTS
1. TRADING AND PROFIT AND LOSS ACCOUNT
or 2. TRADING ACCOUNT AND BALANCE SHEET
or 3. PROFIT AND LOSS ACCOUNT AND BALANCE SHEET

Some of the common items that need adjustment to be made at the end of accounting period are discussed and are as follow:

1. Closing Stock

The closing stock is the unsold goods lying in the concern. Generally, the firm takes out a list of all stocks, remaining unsold alongwith their value. The stock is always valued at cost or market price whichever is lower. Generally, the closing stock will not appear in the Trial Balance and it lies in the adjustment. When it lies in the adjustment, adjustment entry has to be passed before the preparation of Final Accounts. For instance, the value of the closing stocks is Rs 10,000, then the following entries are to be passed :

		Rs	*Rs*
Closing Stock Account	Dr.	10,000	
To Trading Account			10,000
(Being adjustment entry for unsold goods)			

It affects two accounts and appears in the ledgers as follows :

Closing Stock A/c

Dr.	*Rs*		*Rs* *Cr.*
To Trading A/c	10,000	By Balance c/d	10,000
To Balance b/d	10,000		

Trading Account

			Cr. *Rs*
		By Closing Stock	10,000

Again, the two fold aspects are as follows :

1. Closing Stock is shown on the Credit Side of Trading Account.
2. Closing Stock is shown on the Asset Side of Balance Sheet.

But, sometimes in the Trial Balance, Adjusted Purchase are given and this means Opening Stock and Closing Stock are adjusted through purchases. Then both Adjusted Purchases A/c and Closing

Stock Account appear in the Trial Balance. Then, Adjusted Purchases amount may be taken to the debit side of Trading Account and Closing Stock appear on the Asset side of Balance Sheet. It should be noted that under this circumstance, Closing Stock will not appear in Trading Account. In the following year, the Closing Stock becomes Opening Stock. For this, a reverse entry is made as follows :

Trading Account	Dr.
To Opening Stock A/c	
(Being the Opening Stock brought into current year Trading Account)	

2. Outstanding Expenses

There are certain expenses incurred but not paid. They are called Outstanding expenses. Such Outstanding expenses relate to a given accounting period but are not paid. Expenses like salaries, rent etc. of each month are paid in the following months. Such expenses, which are due for payment in given accounting year but the payment will be made in future accounting year, *i.e.*, payment of such items is postponed, are Outstanding or unpaid expenses. In order to bring a true result, it is necessary to account the expenses in that year in which they are incurred, irrespective of the fact whether they are paid or not. That is, all such Outstanding expenses which are liability account must be recorded in the accounting period, if they relate to the accounting year.

For instance, Trial Balance, shows Salary of Rs 15,000 but salary of Rs 1,000 for the month of December 2004 has not been paid till 31.12.2004. This Outstanding expenses must be brought into account before the preparation of the Final Accounts by means of adjusting entry :

		Rs	Rs
Salary Account	Dr.	1,000	
To Outstanding Salary Account			1,000
(Being unpaid salary brought into account)			

Dr. **Salary Account** Cr.

	Rs		Rs
Balance c/d	15,000	By Profit & Loss A/c	16,000
Outstanding Salary A/c	1,000		
	16,000		16,000

Dr. **Outstanding Salary A/c** Cr.

	Rs		Rs
To Balance c/d	1,000	By Salary A/c	1,000
		By Balance b/d	1,000

Dr. **Profit & Loss A/c**

		Rs	
To Salary A/c	15,000		
Add: Outstanding	1,000	16,000	

Balance Sheet

Liabilities	Rs	
Outstanding Salary A/c	1,000	

That is, the double effect of the adjustment is :

1. Outstanding Salary of Rs 1,000 is added to Salary Account and is debited to Profit and Loss Account.
2. Outstanding Salary is a liability and shown in Balance Sheet (liability).

When Outstanding salary is paid, we pass entry as follows :

		Rs	Rs
Outstanding Salary A/c	Dr.	1,000	
To Cash A/c			1,000

3. Unexpired or Prepaid Expenses

When we have paid any expense and its benefit is to be availed in future, it is termed as unexpired or prepaid expenses. For instance, when insurance premium is paid upto 31.3.2005 and if we prepare the Final Accounts for the year ended 31.12.2004, then the premium from 1.1.2005 to 31.3.2005, paid is unexpired or prepaid expenses. Thus, when the Final Accounts is prepared, the amount of premium is deducted in Profit and Loss Account and the same is shown in Balance Sheet asset side. The following entry is made :

Prepaid Expenses A/c	Dr.	
To Expenses A/c		

For instance, Trial balance as on 31.12.2004 shows a sum of Rs 1,000 paid on Rates. In the adjustment, it has been mentioned that Rates has been prepaid to the extent of Rs 150 on the date :

Prepaid Rates A/c	Dr.	150	
To Rates A/c			150

Dr. **Rates Account** Cr.

	Rs		Rs
To Cash A/c	1,000	By Prepaid Rates A/c	150
		By P & L A/c	850
	1,000		1,000

Dr. **Prepaid Rate Account** Cr.

	Rs		Rs
To Rates A/c	150	By Balance c/d	150
To Balance c/d	150		

Dr. **Profit and Loss A/c**

	Rs		
To Rates A/c	1,000		
Less: Prepaid	150	850	

Balance Sheet

	Asset side	Rs.
	Prepaid Rates	150

Thus, the two effect of the adjustment are :

1. The amount of prepaid expense is deducted in the Profit and Loss A/c from the expense.
2. The amount will appear in the Asset side of Balance Sheet.

4. Accrued Income

Accrued income is an amount earned but not actually received during the accounting period or till the date of preparation of Final Accounts for the period concerned. Such an income receivable is also called *income earned but not received* or *income accrued* or *income due and outstanding*. For instance, interest on investments, rent from sub-letting, commission on sales etc., earned by the business during a particular accounting period but might not have been received so far. Thus such outstanding income need adjustment when Final Accounts are prepared.

For instance, commission has been earned but not received Rs 100.

The adjustment entry is :

		Rs	Rs
Outstanding Commission A/c	Dr.	100	
To Commission A/c			100
(Being outstanding commission brought into account)			

Outstanding Commission Account

Dr.	Rs		Cr. Rs
To Commission A/c	100	By Balance c/d	100
To Balance b/d	100		

Commission Account

Dr.	Rs		Cr. Rs
To Profit and Loss A/c	100	By Outstanding Commission A/c	100

Profit and Loss Account

Dr.			Cr. Rs
		By Commission A/c	100

Balance Sheet

		Assets side	*Rs*
		Commission Outstanding	100

The double effect of accrued income is :

1. It is credited to the Profit & Loss Account
2. It is shown in the asset side of the Balance Sheet.

5. Income Received in Advance (Income Received but not Earned)

Income received during a particular trading period for the work to be done in future is termed as unearned income. When income is received in advance, for the work not done yet, the trader is liable. That is such income though received is not the income for the current trading period, but services will be rendered in the next year. Entries for such income are :

Concerned Income Account	Dr.
To Income Received in Advance A/c	

The unearned income is deducted from the concerned income, in the credit side of Profit and Loss Account and also shown in the liability side of the Balance Sheet.

For instance, a trader received rent @ Rs 200 per month for a full year ending on 31st March 2005 but his Final Accounts are prepared for the year ending on 31st December 2004. Then, the entries are :

		Rs	Rs
Rent Received Account	Dr.	600	
To Rent Received in Advance A/c			600

Rent Received Account

Dr.	Rs		*Cr.* Rs
To Rent Received in Advance A/c	600	By Cash A/c	2,400
To Profit and Loss A/c	1,800		
	2,400		2,400

Rent Received in Advance Account

Dr.	Rs		Rs Cr.
To Balance c/d	600	By Rent Received A/c	600
		By Balance b/d	600

Profit and Loss Account

Dr.			Rs	Rs Cr.
		By Rent Received A/c	2,400	
		Less: Received in Advance	600	1,800

Balance Sheet

Liability side	*Rs*	
Rent Received in Advance	600	

The double effect in the Final Account is :

1. The unearned income, is deducted from Rent Received Account.
2. The deducted amount, is shown in the liability side of the Balance Sheet.

6. Depreciation

When an asset is purchased, it does not long continue to be worth that amount. It gradually decreases in value. The asset may lose its value due to its constant use or due to its non-use (merely by passage of time). When the value of asset decreases because of wear and tear due to use or passing of time, it is termed as Depreciation. The amount of Depreciation is operation expenses of the business. If the Depreciation is not accounted, the net profit for the period will be overstated. Even in Balance Sheet, the value of assets should not be shown at proper value. Depreciation is a loss. Depreciation is debited to Depreciation Account which is a Nominal Account and transferred to Profit and Loss Account. The adjusting entries are :

Depreciation Account To Asset Account (Being depreciation charged on asset)	Dr.
Profit and Loss Account To Depreciation Account (Being transfer of Depreciation Account)	Dr.

The double effect of depreciation is :

1. Depreciation is shown on the debit side of Profit & Loss Account.
2. The amount of depreciation is deducted from the concerned asset, in the asset side of the Balance Sheet.

For instance, a machine costing Rs 10,000 purchased on 1.1.2004. Charge Depreciation @ 15% p.a. How this will be dealt in the Final Accounts ending on 31st December 2004.

		Rs	Rs
Depreciation Account To Asset Account (Being depreciation on asset)	Dr.	1,500	 1,500
Profit and Loss Account To Depreciation Account (Being closing entry for Depreciation	Dr.	1,500	 1,500

Depreciation Account

Dr.	Rs		Cr Rs
To Asset Account	1,500	By Profit and Loss A/c	1,500

Machine Account

Dr.	Rs		Cr. Rs
To Balance b/d	10,000	By Depreciation A/c	1,500
		By Balance c/d	8,500
	10,000		10,000

Profit and Loss Account

Dr.	Rs		Cr. Rs
To Depreciation A/c	1,500		

Balance Sheet as on 31st Dec. 2004

Dr			Rs	Cr. Rs
		Asset: Machine	10,000	
		Less: Depreciation	1,500	8,500

7. Additional Bad Debts

Credit transactions are common in business. The customers to whom we sell goods on credit become our Debtors and they are liable to pay their dues. But it is not uncommon that some of the Debtors fail to pay their dues because of insolvency or dishonesty. Thus, the amounts due from such Debtors are irrecoverable and represent loss to us. This loss is known as Bad Debts. Thus Bad Debts are debts which are definitely known to be irrecoverable.

During the accounting year, the Bad Debts that occur are recorded as :

Bad Debts Account	Dr.
To Debtors Account	

At the end of the accounting period, when the Trial Balance is drawn, these two account, *i.e.*, Bad Debts and Sundry Debtors appear in the Trial Balance and both show debit balances. The Sundry Debtors appear in the Trial Balance is the net balance after deduction of Bad Debts, during the year. In such case, Bad Debts are debited to Profit and Loss Account and Sundry Debtors, as per Trial Balance, appear in Balance Sheet.

ILLUSTRATION 7.1 (Bad Debt within Trial Balance)

Trial Balance as on 31.12.2004

Sundry Debtors	Rs 10,000
Bad Debts	Rs 500

SOLUTION

These will appear in the Final Accounts as follows :

Profit and Loss Account

Dr.	Rs	
To Bad Debts A/c	500	

Balance Sheet

	Asset side	Rs.
	Sundry Debtors	10,000

But after the preparation of Trial Balance, before the Final Accounts are drawn, a trader may have additional Bad Debts or further Bad Debts. This additional or further Bad Debts are recorded by the following entry before the preparation of Final Accounts :

Bad Debts Account To Sundry Debtors Account (Being further Bad Debts)	Dr.
Profit and Loss Account To Bad Debts Account (Being transfer of Bad Debts to Profit & Loss Account)	Dr.

To the extent of additional Bad Debts, the Sundry Debtors are reduced in the Balance Sheet. See the following examples :

ILLUSTRATION 7.2 (Bad Debt given outside Trial Balance)

Sundry Debtors as per Trial Balance Rs 10,000.

Adjustments : Write off Bad Debts amounting to Rs 300.

Show the entries and Open Ledger accounts. Also show how these appear in the Final Accounts.

SOLUTION

		Rs	Rs
Bad Debts Account	Dr.	300	
To Sundry Debtors Account			300
(Being Bad Debts written off)			

In the final Accounts, it appears as follows :

Dr. **Profit and Loss Account**

	Rs		
To Bad Debts A/c	300		

Balance Sheet

Asset side		
	Rs	Rs
Sundry Debtors :	10,000	
Less: Bad Debts	300	
		9,700

ILLUSTRAITON 7.3 (Bad Debt appears both inside and outside Trial Balance)

Sundry Debtors as per Trial Balance Rs 10,000

Bad Debts as per Trial Balance Rs 500

Adjustment : Additional Bad Debts amounted to Rs 300

Show the adjustment entries, ledger accounts and Final Accounts

SOLUTION

		Rs	Rs
Bad Debts Account	Dr.	300	
To Sundry Debtors Account			300
(Being Additional Bad Debts written off))			

Dr. **Bad Debts Account** *Cr.*

	Rs		*Rs*
To Balance b/d	500	By Profit & Loss A/c	800
To Sundry Debtors	300		
	800		800

Dr. **Profit & Loss A/c** *Cr.*

	Rs	*Rs*
To Bad Debts A/c	500	
Add: Additional Bad Debts	300	
		800

Dr. Closing Debtors A/c Cr.

	Rs		Rs
To Balance b/d	10,000	By Bad Debts A/c	300
		By Balance c/d	9,700
	10,000		10,000

Balance Sheet as on...

	Asset side	Rs	Rs
	Debtors	10,000	
	Less: Additional Bad debts	300	9,700

8. PROVISION FOR DOUBTFUL DEBTS

Book debts from customers may be categorised as good, bad and doubtful. Good debt is fully recoverable but bad debt is totally irrecoverable. In between these lie, doubtful debts which may prove bad, and are at the most partially recoverable.

As and when bad debts occur, the same should be adjusted by debiting bad debts account and crediting sundry debtors' account. Since bad debts are written off at the time of occurrence during the accounting period, bad debts account appears inside the trial balance. In such case, all that is to be done is to transfer bad debts account to the debit side of Profit and Loss Account.

Sometimes, bad debts may occur at the end of accounting period after the accounts are balanced and the trial balance is prepared. In such a case, bad debts should be brought into account by passing the adjusting entry, that is, debiting bad debts account and crediting sundry debtors's account. The amount of bad debts is transferred to Profit and Loss Account and to complete the dual aspect, the same amount is deducted from sundry debtors in the balance sheet.

Besides Bad Debts, there may be certain debts whose recovery may seem to be doubtful. A Bad Debt is different from Doubtful Debts. The Bad Debt is definitely irrecoverable and a Doubtful Debt may or may not be recoverable. A Bad Debt is a known loss. But a Doubtful Debt is only an expected loss. An expected loss need not be treated as a loss before it actually occurs. Such Debts cannot be written off as Bad Debt because non-recovery of such an amount is not certain. For such loss, as expected, some provision is made in the form of Provision for Doubtful Debts.

This is done for the purpose of showing the Debtors on the Balance Sheet at their true value. This provision is created by debiting the Profit and Loss Account for the period. The nature of various debts decides the amount of Doubtful Debts. The amount so debited in the Profit and Loss Account and an Account named "Provision for Doubtful Debts Account" is credited with the amount. The adjustment entry is :

Profit and Loss Account Dr.

To Provision for Doubtful Debts Account

The double effect of Provision for Bad Debt is :

1. It is debited in the Profit & Loss Account.
2. It is shown as a deduction from Debtors, in the Balance Sheet.

Provision for bad debts is the amount earmarked or set apart from out of the profits of an accounting period. The amount to be earmarked is based on a percentage of the amount due from sundry debtors. The amount of sundry debtors for this purpose is the balance left on the account after deducting bad debts.

If bad debts occur during the next accounting period, the same are charged to the provision account, instead of Profit and Loss Account. The entry for this is to debit the Provision Account and credit bad debts account. If the provision is insufficient, the balance of provision together with any additional provision created for the next period, suitably adjusted, is debited to Profit and Loss Account and the additional provision is deducted from sundry debtors in the balance sheet.

BAD DEBTS RECOVERED

Sometime bad debts once written off might be recovered in a subsequent period. An important point to remember in this case is that the amount thus realised should not be credited to the customer's personal account as his account has already been closed. As bad debts recovered is a business income it must be credited to Profit and Loss Account. Therefore, when the amount is received, debit Cash Account and credit Bad Debts Recovered Account by transferring to Profit and Loss Account. Alternatively, bad debts recovered may be credited to Bad Debts Account itself so that only the balance of the bad Debts Account is transferred to the Profit and Loss Account at the end of the year.

ILLUSTRATION 7.4

A portion of the Trial Balance (31.12.2004) is as follows :

Sundry Debtors	Rs 10,000
Bad Debts	Rs 300

It is estimated that 5% of the Sundry Debtors is doubtful as to recovery. The entries are :

			Rs	*Rs*
2004	Profit and Loss Account	Dr.	500	
Dec. 31	To Provision for Bad & Doubtful Debts A/c			500
	(Being provision for Doubtful Debts created)			

SOLUTION

Dr. **Profit and Loss A/c** *Cr.*

	Rs	*Rs*	
To Bad Debts A/c	300		
To Provision for Doubtful Debts A/c	500	800	

Balance Sheet as on 31st Dec. 2004

		Asset side	*Rs*	*Rs*
		Sundry Debtors	10,000	
		Less: Provision for Doubtful Debts	500	9,500

By making a provision, Personal accounts of the Debtors are not touched and no amount is written off as Bad Debts until it is definitely known to be irrecoverable. The Doubtful Debts, actually proves Bad, is set off against the Provision for Doubtful Debts account. That is, when the Bad Debts actually take place, the amount of Bad Debts shall be transferred to Provision for Doubtful Debts Account and not to Profit and Loss Account directly.

ILLUSTRATION 7.5

Trial Balance as on 31st December 2004

	Dr.	*Cr.*
	Rs	*Rs*
Sundry Debtors	30,000	
Bad Debts	5,000	

Additional Information :

1. After the preparation of Trial Balance, we come to know that a Debtor has become insolvent and therefore, the entire amount of Rs 3,000 due from him was irrecoverable.
2. Create 10% Provision for Bad and Doubtful Debts.

You are required to pass necessary adjusting entries and show how the items appear in the Balance Sheet.

(B.Com., MS)

SOLUTION

2004			*Rs*	*Rs*
Dec. 31	Bad Debts Account	Dr.	3,000	
	To Sundry Debtors Account			3,000
	(Being amount written off as Bad Debts)			
	Profit and Loss Account	Dr.	2,700	
	To Provision for Doubtful Debts Account			2,700
	(Being Provision for Doubtful Debts created Rs. 27,000 × 10/100)			

Profit and Loss A/c
for the year ended 31st December 2004

Dr. *Cr.*

	Rs	*Rs*	
To Bad Debts A/c	5,000		
Add: Additional Bad Debts	3,000		
Provision for Doubtful Debts	2,700	10,700	

Balance Sheet as on 31st December 2004

	Asset side		*Rs*
		Rs	
	Sundry Debtors	30,000	
	Less: Additional Bad Debts	3,000	
		27,000	
	Less: Provision for Doubtful Debts	2,700	24,300

ILLUSTRATION 7.6

A portion of Trial Balance as on 31st Dec. 2004 is as follows :

	Dr.	*Cr.*
	Rs	*Rs*
Sundry Debtors	50,000	
Provision for Doubtful Debts		5,000
Bad Debts	3,000	

Additional Information :

1. Additional Bad Debts amounted to Rs 3,000.
2. Create a Provision for Doubtful Debts @ 10% on Debtors.

You are required to pass the necessary journal entries, prepare Provision for Doubtful Debts Account and show how the different items appear in the Final Accounts. *(B.Com., Madurai)*

SOLUTION

2004			Rs	Rs
Dec. 31	Bad Debts Account	Dr.	3,000	
	To Sundry Debtors Account			3,000
	(Being additional Bad Debts written off)			
	Provision for Doubtful Debts Account	Dr.	6,000	
	To Bad Debts Account			6,000
	(Being Rs 3,000 (TB) and Rs 3,000 additional Bad Debts transferred to Provision for Doubtful Debts Account)			
	Profit and Loss Account	Dr.	5,700	
	To Provision for Bad Debts Account			5,700
	(Being amount charged from Profit and Loss Account to keep Provision for Doubtful Debts at 10% on Debtors)			

Provision for Bad Debts Account

Dr. Cr.

	Rs		Rs
To Bad Debts A/c	6,000	By Balance b/d	5,000
To Balance c/d	4,700	By Profit and Loss A/c	5,700
Rs., 50,000 – Rs. 3,000 = 47,000			
= 47,000 × 10% = 4,700			
	10,700		10,700

Profit and Loss A/c
for the year ended 31st December 2004

Dr. *Cr.*

	Rs	Rs		
To Bad Debts (TB)	3,000			
Add: Additional Bad Debts	3,000			
Add: Provision required	4,700			
	10,700			
Less: Existing Provision	5,000	5,700		

Balance Sheet as on 31st December 2004

	Asset side		*Rs*
		Rs	
	Sundry Debtors	50,000	
	Less: Additional Bad Debts	3,000	
		47,000	
	Less: Provision for Doubtful Debts	4,700	42,300

ILLUSTRATION 7.7

On December 2004, Mr Ram closes his books when his Debtors amounted to Rs 25,000. On January 2004, the Provision for Doubtful Debts Account shows a Credit balance of Rs 1,000. During the year he incurred a bad debt of Rs 1,300. He maintains 5% provision on Debtors.

Pass journal entries and show the necessary account and Balance Sheet.

SOLUTION

Date	Particulars		Rs	Rs
2004				
Dec. 31	Provision for Doubtful Debts A/c	Dr.	1,300	
	To Bad Debts A/c			1,300
	(Being Bad Debts transferred to Doubtful Debt Provision account			
	Profit and Loss Account	Dr.	1,550	
	To Provision for Doubtful Debts			1,550
	(Being adjustment to bring the balance to 5% on Debtors)			

Dr. **Bad Debts Account** *Cr.*

Date	Particulars	Rs	Date	Particulars	Rs
2004			2004		
Dec. 31	To Balance b/d	1,300	Dec. 31	By Provision for Doubtful Debts A/c	1,300

Dr. **Provision for Doubtful Debts Account** *Cr.*

Date	Particulars	Rs	Date	Particulars	Rs
2004			2004		
Dec. 31	To Bad Debts A/c	1,300	Dec. 31	By Balance b/d	1,000
"	To Balance c/d	1,250		By Profit and Loss A/c	1,550
		2,550			2,550
				By Balance b/d	1,250

Profit and Loss Account
for the year ended 31st Dec. 2004

Dr. *Cr.*

Particulars	Rs	Rs	
To Bad Debts A/c	1,300		
Add: Bad Debts Provision (new)	1,250		
	2,550		
Less: Existing Provision	1,000	1,550	

Balance Sheet as on 31st Dec. 2004

	Asset side	*Rs*	*Rs*
	Sundry Debtors	25,000	
	Less: Bad Debts Provision	1,250	
			23,750

ILLUSTRATION 7.8

A part of the Trial Balance as on 31st March 2005 is as follows :

	Rs	*Rs*
Sundry Debtors	50,000	
Bad Debts	4,000	
Provision for Doubtful Debts		4,000

Additional Information :

1. Write off further bad debts Rs 1,000.
2. Provide for Doubtful Debates at 7% on Debtors.

Write journal entries, open ledgers and show them in final accounts.

SOLUTION

Date	Particulars		Rs	Rs
2005 March 31	Bad Debts A/c	Dr.	1,000	
	To Sundry Debtors A/c			1,000
	(Being additional Bad Debts written off)			
	Provision for Doubtful Debts A/c	Dr.	5,000	
	To Bad Debts A/c			5,000
	(Being Bad Debts transferred to Provision Accounts)			
	Profit and Loss A/c	Dr.	4,430	
	To Provisional for Bad Debts A/c			4,430
	(Being adjustment to bring the balance to 5% on Debtors)			

Dr. **Bad Debts Account** *Cr.*

2005		Rs	2005		Rs
March 31	To Balance b/d	4,000	March 31	By Provision for Doubtful Debts A/c	5,000
"	To Sundry Debtors A/c	1,000			
		5,000			5,000

Dr. **Provision for Doubtful Debts Accounts** *Cr.*

2005		Rs	2005		Rs
March 31	To Bad Debts A/c	5,000	March 31	By Balance b/d	4,000
"	To Balance c/d	3,430	"	By Profit & Loss A/c	4,430
		8,430			8,430
			April 1	By Balance b/d	3,430

Dr. **Profit and Loss Account** *Cr.*
for the year ended 31st March 2005

		Rs	
To Bad Debts A/c	4,000		
Add: Additional Bad Debts	1,000		
Add: Provision Required (7% on Rs 49,000)	3,430		
	8,430		
Less: Existing Provision	4,000	4,430	

Balance Sheet as on 31st March 2005

	Asset side	Rs	Rs
	Sundry Debtors	50,000	
	Less: Additional Bad Debts	1,000	
		49,000	
	Less: Provision for Doubtful Debts	3,430	45,570

9. Provision for Discount on Debtors

Discount is allowed when our Debtors settle their accounts promptly. If the Debtors of the current period settle their accounts promptly in the succeeding period, discount will have to be allowed by us. The amount of discount is an expected loss and a provision has to be made for it in the Final Accounts of the current year. The Accounting procedure for this provision is similar to that of Provision for Doubtful Debts discussed above. So, the discount that might be allowed on debts whose debts fall in the succeeding year is estimated. The adjusting entry is :

Profit and Loss Account	Dr.
To Provision for Discount on Debtors Account	

The discount payable on Debtors is only a contingent loss and not a loss already incurred. The discount is to be given only to those Debtors who make prompt payment, thus the amount of provision for Discount on Debtors is to be calculated on good debts. The Account–Provision for Discount on Debtors is carried forward next year. By doing so, Profit and Loss Account and Balance Sheet disclose true financial position. When discount is allowed, the entry is :

Discount Account	Dr.
To Debtors Account	

At the end of accounting year, the firm also estimates the amount of discount which it may have to give to the Debtors outstanding at the end of the accounting period in the course of next year. This is done by creating a Provision for Discount on Debtors and journal entry is :

Profit and Loss Account	Dr.
To Provision for Discount on Debtors Account	

Discount is allowed to prompt Debtors, but not to bad and doubtful debtors. Therefore, before making the Provision for Discount, the amount of Bad and Doubtful Debtors must first be estimated and deducted from the amount of Debtors as per the ledger. On the balance of Debtors, *i.e.* on the good debtors only, the Provision for Discount on Debtors must be created.

The double effect of Provision for Discount on Debtors is :

1. It is shown on the debit side of Profit and Loss Account.
2. It is shown as deduction from Debtors in Balance Sheet. But remember the amount of Provision is calculated only after deducting the amount of additional Bad Debts.

ILLUSTRATION 7.9

From the following figures, you are required to prepare:

(*a*) Bad Debts Account
(*b*) Profit and Loss Account
(*c*) Provision for Bad Debts Account

		Rs.			*Rs.*
2003			Dec. 2004		
Jan.	Provision for Bad Debts	1,800		Bad Debts	1,850
Dec. 31	Bad Debts (Dr.)	980		Debtors	30,000
	Bad Debts (Cr.)	120		Discount allowed to Debtors	270
	Debtors	20,000			

Information:

1. Further Bad Debts Rs. 200
2. Make a provision for Bad Debts at 5% on Debtors.

Information:

1. Make a Provision for Bad Debts at 5% on Debtors.
2. Make Provision for Discount on Debtors at 2%.

(*CS B.Com. MS*)

SOLUTION

Dr. Bad Debts Account Cr.

		Rs.			Rs.
2003			2003		
Dec. 31	To Balance b/d	980	Dec. 31	By Balance b/d	120
"	To Debtors A/c	200	"	By Provision for Bad Debts A/c	1,060
		1,180			1.180

Dr. Provision for Doubtful Debts Account Cr.

		Rs.			Rs.
2003			2003		
Dec. 31	To Bad Debts A/c	1,060	Jan. 1	By Balance b/d	1,800
"	To Balance c/d	990	Dec. 31	By Profit & Loss A/c	250
	(Rs. 20,000 – Rs. 200) × 5% = 990.	2,050			2,050
			2004		
			Jan. 1	By Balance b/d	990

Dr. Profit and Loss Account for the year ended 31st December 2003 Cr.

	Rs.	Rs.	
To Bad Debts A/c	980		
Add: Additional Bad Debts	200		
	1,180		
Less: Bad Debts Recovered	120		
	1,060		
Add: Reserve Required	990		
	2,050		
Less Existing Provision	1,800	250	

Dr. Bad Debts Account Cr.

		Rs.			Rs.
2004			2004		
Dec. 31	To Balance b/d	1,850	Dec. 31	By Provision for Doubtful debts	1,850

Dr. Provision for Doubtful Debts Account Cr.

		Rs.			Rs.
2004			2004		
Dec. 31	To Bad Debts A/c	1,850	Jan. 1	By Balance b/d	990
"	To Balance c/d	1,500	Dec. 31	By Profit & Loss A1/c	2,360
	Rs. 30,000 × 5% = Rs. 1,500.				
		3,350			3,350
				By Balance b/d	1,500

Profit and Loss Account

Dr. **for the year ended 31st December 2004** Cr.

	Rs.	Rs.	
To Bad Debts A/c	1,850		
Add: Provision Required	1,500		
	3,350		
Less: Existing Provision	990	2,360	
To Provision for Discount on Debtors A/c		570	

Dr. **Provision for Discount on Debtors** Cr.

		Rs.			Rs.
2004			2004		
Dec. 31	To Balance c/d Rs. 30,000 – Rs. 1,500×2% = Rs. 570	570	Dec. 31	By Profit & Loss A/c	570
				By Balance b/d	570

ILLUSTRATION 7.10

From the following information, write up the relevant ledger account, Profit and Loss Account and show the Debtors in the Balance Sheet.

2004		Rs.
Jan. 1	Provision for Doubtful Debts	800
	Provision for Discount on Debtors	150
2004	Sundry Debtors	13,000
Dec. 31	Bad Debts writen off	700
	Discounts allowed	200

You are required to write off further bad debts Rs. 300, make provision for Doubtful Debts at 5% on Debtors and for discount on Debtors at 2%. *(B.Com., Madurai)*

SOLUTION

Dr. **Bad Debts Account** Cr.

		Rs.			Rs.
2004			2004		
Dec. 31	To Balance b/d	700	Dec. 31	By Provision for Doubtful Debtors A/c	1,000
"	To Sundry Debtors A/c	300			
		1,000			1,000

Dr. **Provision for Doubtful Debts Account** Cr.

		Rs.			Rs.
2004			2004		
Dec. 31	To Bad Debts A/c	1,000	Jan. 1	By Balance b/d	800
"	To Balance c/d Rs. 13,000 – Rs. 300 = Rs. 12,700 × 5% = Rs. 635	635	Dec. 31	By Profit & Loss A/c	835
		1,635			1,635
				By Balance b/d	635

Discount Account

Dr.		Rs.			Cr. Rs.
2004			2004		
Dec. 31	To Balance b/d	200	Dec. 31	By Provision for Discount on Debtors A/c	200

Provision for Discount on Debtors Account

Dr.		Rs.			Cr. Rs.
2004			2004		
Dec. 31	To Discount A/c	200	Jan. 1	By Balance b/d	150
"	To Balance c/d Rs. 13,000 – (Rs. 300 + Rs. 635) = Rs. 12,065 × 2% = Rs. 241	241	Dec. 31	By Profit & Loss A/c	291
		441			441
			1993		
			Jan. 1	By Balance b/d	241

Profit and Loss Account
for the year ended 31st December 2004

Dr.	Rs.	Rs.		Cr.
To Provision for Doubtful Debts Account:				
Bad Debts	700			
Additional Bad Debts	300			
New Provision	635			
	1,635			
Less: Existing Provision	800	835		
To Provision for Discount on Debtors Account:				
Discount Allowed	200			
New Provision	241			
	441			
Less: Existing Provision	150	291		

Balance Sheet as on 31st March 2004

	Asset side	Rs	Rs
	Sundry Debtors (TB)	13,000	
	Less: Additional Bad Debts	300	
		12,700	
	Less: Provision for Doubtful Debts	635	
		12,065	
	Less: Provision for Discount	241	11,824

ILLUSTRATION 7.11

A firm maintain a Provision for Bad Debts at 5% and a Provision for Discount at 2% on total Debtors. From the following particulars, write up the Provision Account for all the years:

Provision for Doubtful Debts	Rs. 450
Provision for Discount on Debtors	Rs. 400

On 31.12.2002: Sundry Debtors Rs. 10,000 after writing off Bad Debts Rs. 250 and allowing discounts Rs. 300.

On 31.12.2003: Sundry Debtors Rs. 6,000 after writing off Bad Debts Rs. 150 and allowing discounts Rs. 175.

On 31.12.2004: Sundry Debtors Rs. 8,000 after writing off Bad Debts Rs. 300 and allowing discounts Rs. 350.

(*B.Com., Madurai, MS*)

SOLUTION

Dr. **Provision for Discount on Debtors Account** *Cr.*

		Rs.			Rs.
2002			2002		
Dec. 31	To Discount A/c	300	Jan. 1	By Balance b/d	400
"	To Balance c/d (Rs. 9,500 at 2%)	190	Dec. 31	By Profit & Loss A/c	90
		490			490
2003			2003		
Dec. 31	To Discount Allowed A/c	175	Jan. 1	By Balance b/d	190
"	To Balance c/d (Rs. 5,700 at 2%)	114	Dec. 31	By Profit and Loss A/c	99
		289			289
2004			2004		
Dec. 31	To Discount Allowed A/c	350	Jan. 1	By Balance b/d	114
"	To Balance c/d (Rs. 7,600 at 2%)	152	Dec.31	By Profit & Loss A/c	388
		502			502
			2005		
			Jan. 1	By Balance b/d	152

Dr. **Provision for Doubtful Debtors Account** *Cr.*

		Rs.			Rs.
2002			2002		
Dec. 31	To Bad Debts A/c	250	Jan. 1	By Balance b/d	450
"	To Balance c/d (Rs. 10,000 × 5%)	500	Dec. 31	By Profit & Loss A/c	300
		7,50			750
2003			2003		
Dec. 31	To Bad Debts A/c	150	Jan. 1	By Balance b/d	500
"	To Profit & Loss A/c	50			
	To Balance c/d (Rs. 6000× 5%)	300			
		500			500
2004			2004		
Dec. 31	To Bad Debts A/c	300	Jan. 1	By Balance b/d	300
"	To Balance c/d (Rs. 8000× 5%)	400	Dec. 31	By Profit & Loss A/c	400
		700			700
			2005		
			Jan. 1	By Balance b/d	400

ILLUSTRATION 7.12

On 31st December 2003, the item Sundry Debtors appeared in the Balance Sheet is as follows :

Asset side of Balance Sheet	Rs.	Rs.
Sundry Debtors	60,300	
Less: Provision for Bad Debts A/c –	3,165	
	57,135	
Less: Provision for Discount on Debtors	3,006	54,129

During the year 2004, Bad Debts amounted to Rs. 2,160 and Discount allowed to Rs. 2,955. At the end of the year the total of balance on Debtors Account amounted to Rs. 78,600. The profit for the year, before allowing for likely Bad Debts and Discounts on Debtors, was Rs. 49,800. Provision for both Bad Debts and Discount are to be 5% of the book debt outstanding on the date.

Give the necessary ledger accounts, the Profit and Loss Account and the position of Debtors in the Balance Sheet as on 31st December 2004 *(B.Com., Madurai, Rajasthan)*

SOLUTION

Dr. **Bad Debts Account** Cr.

		Rs.			Rs.
2004			2004		
Dec. 31	To Balance b/d	2,160	Dec. 31	By Provision for Doubtful Debts A/c	2,160

Dr. **Provision for Doubtful Debts A/c** Cr.

		Rs.			Rs.
2004			2004		
Dec. 31	To Bad Debts A/c	2,160	Jan. 1	By Balance b/d	3,165
"	To Balance c/d Rs. 78,600 × 5% = Rs. 3,930.	3,930	Dec. 31	By Profit & Loss A/c	2,925
		6,090			6,090
			2005		
			Jan. 1	By Balance b/d	3,930

Dr. **Discount Account** Cr.

		Rs.			Rs.
2004			2004		
Dec. 31	To Balance b/d	2,955	Dec. 31	By Provision for Discount on Debtors A/c	2,955

Dr. **Provision for Discount on Debtors Account** Cr.

		Rs.			Rs.
2004			2004		
Dec. 31	To Discount A/c	2,955.00	Jan. 1	By Balance b/d	3,006.00
"	To Balance c/d Rs. 78,600 – Rs. 3,930 = Rs.. 74,670 × 5% = Rs. 3,733.50	3,733.50	Dec. 31	By Profit & Loss A/c	3,682.50
		6,688.50			6,688.50
			2005		
			Jan. 1	By Balance b/d	3,733.50

Profit and Loss Adjustment Account
for the year ended on 31st Dec. 2004

Dr.	Rs.	Rs.		Cr. Rs.
To Provision for Doubtful Debts A/c :			By Profit and Loss A/c	49,800
Bad Debts	2,160			
New provision	3,930			
	6,090			
Less: Existing Provision	3,165	2,925		
To Provision for Discount on Debtors A/c :				
Discount Allowed	2,955.00			
New Provision	3,733.50			
	6,688.50			
Less: Existing Provision	3,006.00	3,682.50		
To Net Profit, transferred to Capital		43,192.50		
		49,800.00		49,800

Balance Sheet as on 31st Dec. 2004

Liability side	*Rs.*	*Asset side*	*Rs.*	*Rs.*
Profit	43,192.50	Sundry Debtors	78600.00	
		Less: Provision for Doubtful Debts	3,930.00	
			74,670.00	
		Less: Provision for Discount	3,733.50	70,936.50

ILLUSTRATION 7.13

The following particulars are extracted from the books of Kalyani.

		Rs.
Jan. 1	Provision for bad & doubtful debts	12,000
	Provision for discount on debtors	5,600
Dec. 31	Discounts allowed during the year	9,300
	Bad debts written off during the year	4,700
	Bad debts recovered during the year	250
	Debtors	1,00,600

Write off further bad debts Rs. 2,400. Provision for doubtful debts @ 10% and for discount @ 2% are to be maintained.

Show how the relevant items would appear in ledger, Profit and Loss Account and Balance Sheet as on 31st December 2006. *(B.Com. Osmania M.S. Madras)*

SOLUTION

Bad Debts Account

Dr.		Rs.			Cr. Rs.
2006			2006		
Dec. 31	To Balance b/d	4,700	Dec. 31	By Provision for Bad Debts A/c	7,100
Dec. 31	To Sundry Debtors	2,400			
		7,100			7,100

Provision for Bad and Doubtful Debts A/c

Dr.		Rs.			Cr. Rs.
2006			2006		
Dec. 31	To Bad debts A/c	7,100	Jan 1	By Balance b/d	12,000
	To Balance c/d	9,820	Dec. 31	By P & L A/c (Bal. fig.)	4,920
		16,920			16,920
			1-1-2007	By Balance b/d	9,820

Bad debts Recovered A/c

Dr.		Rs.			Cr. Rs.
2006			2006		
Dec. 31	To Profit & Loss A/c	250	Dec. 31	By Balance b/d	250
		250			250

Discount on Debtors A/c

Dr.		Rs.			Cr. Rs.
2006			2006		
Dec. 31	To Balance b/d	9,300	Dec. 31	By Provision for Discount on debtors A/c	9,300
		9,300			9,300

Provision for Discount on Debtors A/c

Dr.		Rs.			Cr. Rs.
2006			2006		
Dec. 31	To Discount on debtors A/c	9,300.00	Jan. 1	By Balance b/d	5,600.00
	To Balance c/d	1,767.60	Dec. 31	By P & L A/c	5,467.60
		11,067.60			11.067.60
			1.1.2007	By Balance b/d	1,767.60

Working Note:

	Debtors	1,00,600
Less:	Further bad debts	2,400
		98,200
Less:	Provision at 10% =	9,820
		88,380

Provision for Discount $\text{Rs. } 88,380 \times \frac{2}{100} = \text{Rs. } 1,767.60$

Profit & Loss A/c for the year ended 31st December 2006

Dr.	Rs.	Rs.		Cr. Rs.
To Provision for Bad debts A/c :				
Provisions required	9,820		By Bad debts recovered	250
Add: Bad debts	7,100			
	16,920			
Less: Existing provision	12,000	4,920.00		

To Provision for Discount on Debtors:				
Provisions required	1,767.60			
Add: Discount Allowed	9,300.00			
	11,067.60			
Less: Existing provision	5,600.00	5,467.60		

Balance Sheet as on 31st December 2006

Liabilities	*Rs.*	*Assets*		*Rs.*
		Sundry Debtors	1,00,600.00	
		Less: Bad debts	2,400.00	
			98,200.00	
		Less: Provision for bad debts	9,820.00	
			88,380.00	
		Less: Provision for discount	1,767.60	86,612.40

10. Interest on Capital

Interest is charged at an agreed rate on the Capital of a Sole Trader or a Partnership firm. It is helpful to know the true earning of a firm. Real profits are the profits left after charging interest on capital. Interest is a loss to the business and it is a gain to the Proprietor. Entries for such interest is:

Interest on Capital Account	Dr.
To Capital Account	

The interest on Capital Account is transferred to Profit and Loss A/c

Profit and Loss Account	Dr.
To Interest on Capital Account	

A single entry can also be passed, instead of the above two entries:

Profit and Loss Account	Dr.
To Capital Account	

For instance, Ram has invested Rs. 1,00,000 in a business. He wants to adjust 8% interest on his capital, then the entry is:

		Rs	*Rs*
Profit and Loss Account	Dr.	8,000	
To Ram's Capital Account			8,000
(Being 8% interest on capital charged)			

The two-fold effect is: Rs. 8,000 is debited to Profit and Loss Account

Rs. 8,000 is credited to Capital Account.

However, the interest is not paid in cash to the Proprietor but the amount of interest is adjusted to Capital Account. Thus, the interest on capital is always considered as an adjustment.

11. Interest on Drawings

When the Proprietor withdraws money from the business for personal use, it is treated as a temporary loan to the Proprietor by the business. This loan may be treated on par with the loan to an outsider. So business charges interest on such drawings: It is a gain to the business and loss to the proprietor. The adjustment entry is:

Drawings Account To Interest on Drawing Account (Being interest on Drawings)	Dr.		
Interest on Drawing Account To Profit and Loss Account (Being interest on Drawing Transferred to Profit & Loss A/c)	Dr.		

The double effect of interest on Drawings is:

1. It is credited to the Profit & Loss Account.
2. It is added to the Drawings and then deducted from Capital, in Balance Sheet (liability side).

ILLUSTRATION 7.14

Mr. A has Rs. 30,000 as Capital on 1st January 2004 and his drawings during 2004 comes to Rs. 2,500. Charge interest on Capital at 10% and interest on Drawing at Rs. 100. Make necessary entries.

SOLUTION

2004			Rs.	Rs.
Dec. 21	Interest on Capital Account To Capital Account (Being interest on Capital @ 10% p.a.)	Dr.	3,000	3,000
	Drawing Account To Interest on Drawings A/c (Being interest on Drawings charged)	Dr.	100	100
	Profit and Loss Account To Interest on Capital A/c (Being closing entry for the interest on Capital Account)	Dr.	3,000	3,000
	Interest on Drawings Account To Profit and Loss Account (Being Closing entry for the interest on Drawings Account)	Dr.	100	100
	Capital Account To Drawings Account (Being closing entry for the transfer of Drawings Account)	Dr.	2,600	2,600

Profit and Loss Account

Dr. **for the year ended on 31st December 2004** *Cr.*

	Rs.		Rs.
To Interest on Capital A/c	3,000	By Interest on Drawings A/c	100

Balance Sheet as on 31st Dec. 2004

Liability side	Rs.	Rs.	
Capital Account:			
Balance	30,000		
Add: Interest	3,000		
	33,000		
Less: Drawings: 2500			
Interest thereon 100	2,600	30,400	

12. Provision for Discount on Creditors

Sound business firms settle their accounts with the Creditors at the proper and scheduled time. This will earn goodwill for them. Thus, this prompt payment to creditors helps the business to earn discount. Discount received from Creditors is a profit. When a businessman receives regular income on discount from creditors, he makes a provision for the same by crediting the Profit and Loss Account. The entry is:

Reserve/Provision for Discount on Creditors A/c	Dr.
To Profit and Loss A/c	

The double effect is: (1) Credit the amount in Profit and Loss Account.

(2) In Balance Sheet (liability side) it is shown as a deduction from Sundry Creditors.

13. Creation of various Reserves

A portion of the new profit is kept aside by most of the firms as a Provision for unforeseen contingencies. They are charged to Profit and Loss Account. The entry is

Profit and Loss Account	Dr.
To Reserve Fund A/c	
To Reserve for Repairs A/c	

Such Reserves are shown in the Liability side of the Balance Sheet.

The double effect of reserves is:

1. It is debited to the Profit and Loss Account.
2. It is shown in the Liability side of the Balance Sheet.

14. Deferred Revenue Expenditure

Many a time, there may be heavy expenditure on Research Projects, Advertisements, Sales Campaign, etc. These expenditures are incurred in the initial stage or during the financial year. But the effects of such heavy expenses are enjoyed for many years to come i.e. the effects are spread over a long period. So, such heavy expenditure is written off over a period depending upon the amount and the effect it may produce. Such expenditure is called Deferred Revenue Expenditure. For instance, a firm spent Rs. 20,000 on Advertisement and the firm may decide to write off over a period of 5 years, then an amount of Rs. 4,000 only be debited to Profit and Loss Account and the balance Rs. 16,000 is shown in asset side of the Balance Sheet.

The double effect of this expenditure is:

1. A portion of such expenditure is debited to Profit and Loss A/c.
2. The balance of such expenditure is shown in the Asset side of Balance Sheet.

15. Commission Payable as a Percentage on Net Profit

Many a time, officers of a firm are entitled to commission out of Net Profit earned by the firm. This commission may be fixed percentage on Net Profit, before charging such commission or as a fixed percentage on Net Profit after such commission. The commission payable is taken to the debit side of the Profit and Loss and credited to the concerned officer.

ILLUSTRATION 7.15

The Net Profit of a firm is Rs. 2,200.

The Manager of the firm is entitled to 10% commission on net profit (*a*) before charging such commission (or) (*b*) after charging such commission. Calculate the amount of commission.

SOLUTION

(*a*) Before charging the commission, the Net Profit is Rs. 2,200

The amount of commission = $2,200 \times \frac{10}{100}$ = Rs 220

(*b*) Commission payable = 10% on Net Profit (after charging the commission)

If Net Profit is Rs. 100, Commission payable = Rs. 10

Thus profit before charging the commission = 100 + 10 = 110

Of Rs. 110, Rs. 10 is commission payable and the balance Rs. 110 – Rs. 10 = Rs. 100 is the profit, left after charging the commission.

Here Rs. 2,200 is eqal to 110%

Therefore 10% = $\frac{2,200}{110} \times 10$ = Rs. 200

On verification, the manager gets 10% commission on Net profit, after charging such amount:

Thus percentage of commission = $\frac{200}{2,000} \times 100 = 10\%$

16. Accidental Loss

A business may suffer loss due to accidents like fire, earthquake, white ants etc. The amount of Stock Destroyed Account is debited and Trading Account is credited. It is immaterial whether its amount is recoverable or non-recoverable. If the amount of Stock Destroyed or Stock Damaged Account is not recoverable, the amount may be transferred to Profit and Loss Account. If the amount is recoverable from Insurance Company, then the amount of Stock Destroyed Account is transferred to Insurance Company Account. The whole journal entry is as follows:

1. For the value of Stock Destroyed	Stock Destroyed Account To Trading Account	Dr.
2. When the Stock Destroyed amount is not recoverable	Profit and Loss Account To Stock Destroyed Account	Dr.
3. When the amount is fully recoverable from Insurance Company	Insurance Company Account To Stock Destroyed Account	Dr.
4. When the loss is partly recoverable	Insurance Company Account Profit & Loss Account (Balancing figure) To Stock Destroyed Account	Dr. Dr.

17. Goods used as Free Samples

Distribution of Free Samples of goods is an expenditure on Advertisement. The Free Samples Account is debited which is ultimately transferred to Profit and Loss Account. Corresponding credit entry is made either to Purchase Account or Trading Account.

WORK SHEET

Passing of the necessary adjusting entries in the books are essential so that the Final Accounts represent a true position of the business. When adjusting entries are made and posted them in the ledger, there arises the necessity of opening new accounts and even the existing accounts are got changed. In order to avoid errors, a preliminary draft incorporating all the balances of all accounts are done so as to fecilitate the preparation of Final Accounts. Such a draft is known as work sheet. Work Sheet is not a substitute for the Final Accounts. But it is a record to incorporate the adjustments to the prepared Trial balance and is a base for the preparation of Final Accounts. It contains a number of columns.

ILLUSTRATION 7.16

Consider the following balances extracted from the books of Jain as on 31st December 2004. Prepare a Work Sheet for the Final Accounts:

	Rs.		*Rs.*
Capital	20,000	Office Salaries	6,600
Debtors	8,000	Rent	3,900
Creditors	10,000	Trade Expenses	2,300
Purchases	60,000	Furniture	10,000
Sales	80,000	Cash in hand	2,400
Opening Stock	12,000	Drawings	4,800

Adjustments

1. Salaries outstanding for December 2004 amounting to Rs. 600.
2. Rent paid in advance for January 2005 Rs. 300.
3. Depreciation on Furniture @ 10% p.a.
4. Provide interest on Capital for the year @ 5% p.a.
5. Stock on 31st December 2004 Rs. 14,000.

Also prepare the Final Accounts.

SOLUTION

Adjustment Journal Entries

			Rs.	*Rs.*
2004				
Dec. 31	Salaries Account	Dr.	600	
	To Outstanding Salaries Account			600
	(Being salary for the Month of Dec. due)			
	Pre-paid Rent Account	Dr.	300	
	To Rent Account			300
	(Being rent paid for Jan. 2005)			
	Depreciation Account	Dr.	1,000	
	To Furniture Account			1,000
	(Being depreciation @ 10% on furniture *i.e.* Rs. 10,000)			
	Profit and Loss Account	Dr.	1,000	
	To Capital Account			1,000
	(Being interest on Capital @ 5% p.a. on Rs. 20,000)			
	Closing Stock Account	Dr.	14,000	
	To Trading Account			14,000
	(Being value of closing stock account)			

Work Sheet

Particulars	Trial Balance		Adjustments		Adjusted Trial Balance		Trading Account		Profit & Loss		Balance Sheet	
	Dr. Rs	Cr. Rs	Dr. Rs	Cr. Rs	Dr. Rs	Cr. Rs	Dr. Rs	Cr. Rs	Dr. Rs	Cr. Rs	Dr. Rs	Cr. Rs
Capital		20,000		1,000 (d)		21,000						16,200
Debtors	8,000				8,000						8,000	
Creditors		10,000				10,000						10,000
Purchases	60,000				60,000		60,000					
Sales		80,000				80,000		80,000				
Opening Stock	12,000				12,000		12,000					
Office Salaries	6,600		600 (a)		7,200				7,200			
Rent	3,900			300 (b)	3,600				3,600			
Trade Expenses	2,300				2,300				2,300			
Furniture	10,000			1000 (e)	9,000						9,000	
Cash in hand	2,400				2,400						2,400	
Drawings	4,800				4,800							
Salary Outstanding				600 (a)		600						600
Rent paid in Advance			300 (b)		300						300	
Depreciation			1,000 (c)		1,000				1,000			
Interest on Capital			1,000 (d)		1,000				1,000			
Closing Stock			14,000 (e)		14,000			14,000			14,000	
Trading Account				14,000 (e)		14,000						
Gross Profit							22,000			22,000		
Net Profit									6,900			6,900
	1,10,000	1,10,000	16,900	16,900	1,25,600	1,25,600	94,000	94,000	22,000	22,000	33,700	33,700

Trading and Profit and Loss Account
for the year ended 31st December 2004

Dr.		Rs.		Cr. Rs.
To Opening Stock A/c		12,000	By Sales A/c	80,000
To Purchase A/c		60,000	By Closing Stock A/c	14,000
To Gross Profit c/d		22,000		
		94,000		94,000
To Salaries A/c	6,600		By Gross Profit b/d	22,000
Add: Outstanding	600	7,200		
To Rent A/c	3,900			
Less: Prepaid	300	3,600		
To Trade Expenses A/c		2,300		
To Depreciation on Furniture A/c		1,000		
To Interest on Capital A/c		1,000		
To Net Profit, transferred to Capital Account		6,900		
		22,000		22,000

Balance Sheet of Mr. Jain
as on 31st December 2004

Liability side		Rs.	*Asset side*		Rs.
Creditors		10,000	Furniture	10,000	
Salary Outstanding		600	*Less*: Depreciation	1,000	9,000
Capital:	20,000		Debtors		8,000
Add: Interest	1,000		Cash		2,400
Add: Net Profit	6,900		Rent paid in Advance		300
	27,900		Stock		14,000
Less: Drawings	4,800	23,100			
		33,700			33,700

ILLUSTRATION 7.17

The following Trial Balance was extracted from the books of V. Bal as on 31st December 2004:

	Rs.		Rs.
Debit Balances:			
Plant and Machinery	20,000	Motor Car	12,000
Manufacturing Wages	34,500	Purchases	1,02,000
Salaries	15,850	Sales Returns	3,100
Furniture	10,000	Bad Debts	1,400
Freight on Purchases	1,860	Interest and Bank charges	400
Freight on Sales	2,140	Cash at Bank	4,200
Building	24,000	Cash in Hand	1,120
Manufacturing Expenses	9,500	*Credit Balances*:	
Insurance and Tax	4,250	Capital	80,000
Goodwill	25,000	Sundry Creditors	44,560
General Expenses	8,200	Bank Loan	15,000
Factory Fuel and power	1,280	Purchase Returns	1,740
Sundry Debtors	78,200	Sales	2,50,850
Factory Lighting	950	Provision for Bad Debts	2,000
Opening Stock	34,200		

Prepare Trading and Profit and Loss Account for the year ended 31st December 2004 and the Balance Sheet as on that date taking into consideration the following information:

(*a*) Stock in hand on 31st December 2004 was valued at Rs. 30,500.

(*b*) Depreciate Plant and Machinery by 10%.
Furniture by 5%
Motor Car by Rs. 1,000.

(*c*) Bring Provision for Bad Debts to 5% on Sundry Debtors.

(*d*) A commission of 1% on the gross profit is to be provided for Works Manager.

(*e*) A commission of 2% on net profit (after charging the Works Manager's commission) is to be credited to the General Manager.

(*CA Entrance*)

SOLUTION

Trading and Profit and Loss Account of Mr. V. Bal for the year ending 31st December, 2004

Dr.	Rs.	Rs.		Rs.	Rs. Cr.
To Opening Stock		34,200	By Sales	2,50,850	
To Purchases	1,02,000		*Less*: Returns	3,100	2,47,750
Less: Returns	1,740	1,00,260	By Closing Stock		30,500
To Freight on Purchases		1,860			
To Manufactring Wages		34,500			
To Factory Fuel and Power		1,280			
To Factory Lighting		950			
To Manufacturing Expenses		9,500			
To Gross profit c/d		95.700			
		2,78,250			2,78,250
To Salary		15,850	By Gross Profit b/d		95,700
To Freight on Sales		2,140			
To Insurance and Tax		4,250			
To General Expenses		8,200			
To Bad Debts	1,400				
Add: Provision (5% on 78,200)	3,910				
	5,310				
Less: Old Provision	2,000	3,310			
To Interest and Bank Charges		400			
To Depreciation:					
Plant and Machinery	2,000				
Furniture	500				
Motor Car	1,000	3,500			
To Works Manager's (95,700 × 1%) Commission		957			
To General Manager's Commission 2% on Rs. 57,093) (*i.e.* Rs. 95,700 – 38,607)		1,142			
To Net Profit Transferred to Capital Account		55,951			
		95,700			95,700

Balance Sheet of Mr.V. Bal
as on 31st December, 2004

Liabilities	*Rs.*	*Rs.*	*Assets*	*Rs.*	*Rs.*
Sundry Creditors		44,560	Cash in hand		1,120
Bank Loan		15,000	Cash at Bank		4,200
Outstanding Commission:			Sundry Debtors	78,200	
Works Manager		957	*Less*: Provision for Bad Debts	3,910	74,290
General Manager		1,142	Closing Stock		30,500
Capital	80,000		Furniture	10,000	
Add: Net Profit	55,951	1,35,951	*Less*: Depreciation	500	9,500
			Motor Car	12,000	
			Less: Depreciation	1,000	11,000
			Plant and Machinery	20,000	
			Less: Depreciation	2,000	18,000
			Buildings		24,000
			Goodwill		25,000
		1,97,610			1,97,610

ILLUSTRATION 7.18

From the following Trial Balance of Mr. Seth, prepare Trading and Profit and Loss Account for the year ended 31st December 2004 and a Balance Sheet as on that date, after giving effect to the undermentioned adjustments:

	Rs.		*Rs.*
Debit Balances:		Bad Debts	400
		Patents and Patterns	500
Drawings	3,250	Cash	62
Stock (opening)	17,445	Discount	330
Returns Inwards	554	Wages	754
Deposit with Gupta	1,375	Carriage Inward	1,240
Carriage Outward	725	*Credit balances*:	
Loan to Ashok @ 5% given on 1st Jan. 2004	1,000	Capital	15,000
		Returns Outwards	840
Rent	820	Interest on Loan to Ashok	25
Purchases	12,970	Rent Outstanding	130
Debtors	4,000	Creditors	3,000
Goodwill	1,730	Provision for Doubtful Debts	1,200
Advertisement	954	Sales	27,914

Adjustments:

1. The Manager of Seth is entitled to commission of 10% of the net profit calculated after charging such commission.
2. Increase Bad Debts by Rs. 600.
3. Make Provision for Doubtful Debts at 10% and Provision for Discount on Debtors at 5%.
4. Stock valued at Rs. 1,500 destroyed by fire on 25th Dec. 2004 but the Insurance Company admitted a claim for Rs. 950 only and paid it in January 2005
5. Rs. 200 out of the Advertisement are to be carried forward to the next year.
6. The value of closing stock is Rs. 18,792. *(B.Com., Guru Nanak, MS)*

SOLUTION

Trading and Profit and Loss Account of Mr. Seth for the year ended 31st December 2004

Dr.	Rs.	Rs.		Rs.	Cr. Rs.
To Opening Stock		17,445	By Sales	27,914	
To Purchases	12,970		*Less*: Returns	554	27,360
Less: Returns	840	12,130	By Stock-in-Trade		18,792
To Wages		754	By Stock Destroyed by fire		1,500
To Carriage Inward		1,240			
To Gross Profit c/d		16,083			
		47,652			47,652
To Rent		820	By Gross Profit b/d		16,083
To Advertisement Expenses	954		By Interest on Loan	25	
Less: Prepaid	200	754	*Add*: Accrued Interest	25	50
To Bad Debts	400				
Add: Additional Bad Debts	600				
Add: New Provision for Doubtful Debts	340				
	1,340				
Less: Old Provision for Doubtful Debts	1,200	140			
To Discount		330			
To Loss on Stock by fire		550			
To Carriage Outward		725			
To Provision for Discount on Debtors		153			
To Commission to Manager ($\frac{10}{110}$ × Rs. 12,661)		1,151			
To Net Profit transferred to Capital Account		11,510			
		16,133			16,133

Balance Sheet of Mr. Seth as at 31st December 2004

Liabilities	*Rs.*	*Rs.*	*Assets*	*Rs.*	*Rs.*
Outstanding Rent		130	Cash		62
Commission Payable to Manager		1,151	Deposit with Gupta		1,375
Creditors		3,000	Loan to Ashok	1,000	
Capital	15,000		*Add*: Interest Accrued	25	1,025
Add: Net Profit	11,510		Insurance Company		950
	26,510		Debtors	4,000	
Less: Drawings	3,250	23,260	*Less*: Further Bad Debts	600	
				3,400	
			Less: Provision for Doubtful Debtors	340	
				3,060	
			Less: Provision for Discount on Debtors	153	2,907

		Stock	18,792
		Prepaid Advertisement	200
		Patents and Patterns	500
		Goodwill	1,730
	27,541		27,541

ILLUSTRATION 7.19

The following is the Trial Balance of M/s Kasturi Agencies as on 31st March 2004. Prepare Trading and Profit and Loss Account for the year ended 31st March 2004 and a Balance Sheet as on that date:

	Rs.	Rs.
Capital	—	1,00,000
Buildings	15,000	—
Drawings	18,000	—
Furniture and Fittings	7,500	—
Motor Van	25,000	—
Loan from Mr. A @ 12% Interest	—	15,000
Interest paid on above	900	—
Sales	—	1,00,000
Purchases	75,000	—
Opening Stock	25,000	—
Establishment Expenses	15,000	—
Wages	2,000	—
Insurance	1,000	—
Commission	—	7,500
Sundry Debtors and Creditors	28,100	10,000
Bank Balance	20,000	—
	2,32,500	2,32,500

Adjustments:

(*a*) The value of closing stock on 31st March 2004 was Rs. 32,000.

(*b*) Outstanding Wages Rs. 500.

(*c*) Prepaid Insurance Rs. 300.

(*d*) Commission received in advance Rs. 800.

(*e*) Allow interest on Capital @ 10% p.a.

(*f*) Depreciate Building by 2.5%, Furniture and Fittings by 10% and Motor Van by 10%.

(*g*) Charge interest on Drawings Rs. 500.

(*h*) Balance of interest due on the loan is also to be provided for. (*C.A. Inter, B.Com. Madurai*)

SOLUTION

Kasturi Agencies
Trading and Profit and Loss Account
for the year ended 31st March 2004

Dr. *Cr.*

	Rs.	Rs.		Rs.	Rs.
To Opening Stock		25,000	By Sales		1,00,000
To Purchases		75,000	By Closing Stock		32,000
To Wages	2,000				
Add: Outstanding	500	2,500			
To Gross Profit c/d		29,500			
		1,32,000			1,32,000

Particulars	Rs.	Rs.	Particulars	Rs.	Rs.
To Insurance	1,000		By Gross Profit b/d		29,500
Less: Prepaid	300	700	By Interest Drawings		500
To Interest on Loan	900		By Commission	7,500	
Add: Outstanding	900	1,800	*Less*: Received in Advance	800	6,700
To Establishment Expenses		15,000			
To Depreciation:					
Buildings	375				
Furniture and Fittings	750				
Motor Van	2,500	3,625			
To Interest on Capital		10,000			
To Net Profit transferred to Capital		5,575			
		36,700			36,700

Balance Sheet
as on 31st March 2004

Liabilities			*Amount* *Rs.*	*Assets*		*Amount* *Rs.*
Outstanding Wages			500	Cash at Bank		20,000
Commission Received in Advance			800	Sundry Debtors		28,100
Sundry Creditors			10,000	Closing Stock		32,000
Loan from A		15,000		Prepaid Insurance		300
Add: Interest Outstanding		900	15,900	Buildings	15,000	
				Less: Depreciation	375	14,625
Capital		1,00,000		Furniture & Fittings	7,500	
Add: Net profit		5,575		*Less*: Depreciation	750	6,750
Add: Interest on Capital		10,000				
		1,15,575		Motor Van	25,000	
				Less: Depreciation	2,500	22,500
Less: Drawings	18,000					
Interest thereon	500	18,500	97,075			
			1,24,275			1,24,275

ILLUSTRATION 7.20

From the following Trial Balance prepared from the books of Laxmi Narayan on 30th June 2004, prepare Trading and Profit and Loss Account and a Balance Sheet as on that date:

	Dr. Rs.	Cr. Rs.
Laxmi Narayan's Capital and Drawings	10,550	1,19,400
Bills Receivable	9,500	—
Purchases and Sales	2,56,590	3,56,430
Returns Inwards	2,780	—
Opening Stock	89,680	—
Commission	—	5,640
Plant and Machinery	28,800	—
Salaries	11,000	—
Travelling Expenses	1,880	—
Debtors (including Mohan for dishonoured cheque of Rs. 1,000)	62,000	—
Stationery	2,000	—

Telephone Charges	1,370	—
Interest and Discount	5,870	—
Bad Debts	3,620	—
Fixtures and Fittings	8,970	—
Creditors	—	56,630
6% Loan	—	20,000
Wages	40,970	—
Cash in hand	530	—
Cash at Bank	18,970	—
Insurance (including premium of Rs. 300 p.a. paid upto 31st Dec. 2004)	400	—
Rent and Taxes	5,620	—
	5,61,100	5,61,100

Adjustments:

1. Stock in trade on 30th June 2004 was Rs. 1,28,960.
2. Write off half of Mohan's cheque.
3. Create provision of 5% on Debtors.
4. Manufactring wages include Rs. 1,200 for erection of machine purchased last year.
5. Depreciate Plant and Machinery by 5% and Fixture and Fittings by 10% per year.
6. Commission accrued Rs. 600.
7. Interest on loan for the last two months is not paid. (*CAIIB*)

SOLUTION

Trading and Profit and Loss Account of Mr. Laxmi Narayan for the year ending 30th June, 2004

Dr.	*Rs.*	*Rs.*		*Rs.*	*Rs.* *Cr.*
To Opening Stock		89,680	By Sales	3,56,430	
To Purchases		2,56,590	*Less*: Returns	2,780	3,53,650
To Wages	40,970		By Closing Stock		1,28,960
Less: Last year Machine Erection Charge	1,200	39,770			
		96,570			
To Gross Profit c/d		4,82,610			4,82,610
To Salaries		11,000	By Gross Profit b/d		96,570
To Travelling Expenses		1,880	By Commission	5,640	
To Rent and Taxes		5,620	*Add*: Commission Accrued	600	6,240
To Stationery		2,000			
To Telephone Charges		1,370			
To Insurance	400				
Less: Unexpired	150	250			
To Interest and Discount	5,870				
Add: Interest Due	200	6,070			
To Bad Debts (Rs. 3,620 + Rs. 500)		4,120			
To Provision on Debtors (5% on 61,500)		3,075			
To Depreciation:					
Plant and Machinery	1,500				
Fixtures and Fittings	897	2,397			
To Net Profit Transferred to Capital Account		65,028			
		1,02,810			1,02,810

Balance Sheet of Mr. Laxmi Narayan
as on 30th June, 2004

Liabilities	*Rs.*	*Rs.*	*Assets*	*Rs.*	*Rs.*
Creditors		59,630	Cash in Hand		530
6% Loan		20,000	Cash at Bank		18,970
Outstanding Interest		200	Bills Receivable		9,500
Laxmi Narayan's Capital:			Debtors	61,500	
Balance	1,19,400		*Less*: Provision	3,075	58,425
Add: Profit	65,028				
	1,84,428		Furniture & Fittings	8,970	
Less: Drawings	10,550	1,73,878	*Less*: Depreciation	897	8,073
			Plant and Machinery	30,000	
			Less: Depreciation	1,500	28,500
			Closing Stock		1,28,960
			Unexpired Insurance		150
			Commission Accrued		600
		2,53,708			2,53,708

ILLUSTRATION 7.21

From the following Trial Balance of Mr. Ram, prepare Trading and Profit and Loss Account for the year ended 31st December 2004 and Balance Sheet as at that date taking into consideration the following adjustments:

(*a*) Closing Stock Rs. 9,500.
(*b*) One quarter of insurance premium falls in next year.
(*c*) Provide 10% depreciation on furniture.
(*d*) Loan to X carries 8% interest per year.
(*e*) Loan from Y carries 6% interest per year.
(*f*) Goods worth Rs. 500 have been taken by the proprietor for private use.
(*g*) Provide 5% for bad and doubtful debts.
(*h*) Salaries include salary to the Proprietor @ Rs. 200 per month.

Debit Balances	*Rs.*	*Credit Balances*	*Rs.*
Stock on 1.1.2004	6,000	Capital	40,000
Salaries	6,000	Return Outwards	500
Drawings	6,000	Loan from Y	5,000
Carriage Inwards	1,000	Rent Outstanding	100
Carriage Outwards	500	Creditors	13,000
Return Inwards	800	Outstanding Expenses	1,900
Loan to X	3,000	Bad Debts Provision	1,000
Rent	1,200	Discount	300
Goodwill	5,000	Sales	73,700
Wages	100	Rent by subletting	500
Insurance Premium	600		
Bank	8,500		
Purchases	60,000		
Debtors	30,000		
Advertisements	3,000		
Bad Debts	500		
Discount	600		
Cash	200		
Furniture	3,000		

(*CS Inter, B.Com. Madurai*)

SOLUTION

Trading and Profit and Loss Account of Mr. Ram
for the year ending 31st December, 2004

Dr.	Rs	Rs		Rs	Rs *Cr.*
To Opening Stock		6,000	By Sales	73,700	
To Purchases	60,000		*Less*: Returns	800	72,900
Less: Returns	500		By Closing Stock		9,500
	59,500				
Less: Drawings	500	59,000			
To Wages		100			
To Carriage Inwards		1,000			
To Gross Profit c/d		16,300			
		82,400			82,400
To Salaries	6,000		By Gross Profit b/d		16,300
Less: Paid to Proprietor	2,400	3,600	By Discount		300
To Salaries to Proprietor		2,400	By Rent by Subletting		500
To Carriage Outwards		500	By Interest accrued		240
To Rent		1,200			
To Bad Debts	500				
Add: Provision for Bad Debts	1,500				
	2,000				
Less: Old Provision	1,000	1,000			
To Advertisement		3,000			
To Discount		600			
To Insurance Premium	600				
Less: Unexpired	150	450			
To Outstanding Interest		300			
To Depreciation on Furniture		300			
To Net profit transferred to capital		3,990			
		17,340			17,340

Balance Sheet
as on 31st December, 2004

Liabilities		Rs.	Rs.	*Assets*	Rs.	Rs.
Creditors			13,000	Cash		200
Y's Loan			5,000	Bank		8,500
Liability for other Expenses			1,900	Debtors	30,000	
Rent Outstanding			100	*Less*: Provision for		
Interest Outstanding			300	Doubtful Debts	1,500	28,500
Capital		40,000		Loan to X		3,000
Add: Salary Credited		2,400		Closing Stock		9,500
Add: Net Profit		3,990		Unexpired Insurance Premium		150
		46,390		Interest accrued		240
Less: Drawings	6,000			Furniture	3,000	
Salary	2,400			*Less*: Depreciation	300	2,700
Goods taken	500	8,900	37,490	Goodwill		5,000
			57,790			57,790

LIMITATIONS OF FINANCIAL STATEMENTS

The conventional financial statements - Profit and Loss Account and Balance Sheet, have been criticised by expert-accountant for the following reasons:

1. Profit disclosed by Profit and Loss Account is not real profit. This is because many items shown in the Profit and Loss Account are just estimated.
2. Items shown in the Balance Sheet are not in their real values as there is possibility of window-dressing in the statements.
3. Financial position of a concern is affected by many factors - such as, social, economic, financial factors etc. But only financial factors are considered in the statements.
4. Balance Sheet, sometimes, contains worthless items, such as preliminary expenses, and such items has no real value at all.
5. Data contained in the statements are dumb and they do not speak themselves.
6. Certain valuable qualitative elements, such as reputation, etc. are omitted from the statements.

ILLUSTRATION 7.22

From the following Trial Balance and other particulars given prepare Trading and Profit and Loss Account for the year ended 31st December 2004 and a Balance Sheet as on that date:

	Rs.	*Rs.*
Capital and Drawings	1,00,000	10,00,000
Personal Debts	1,000	
Balance at Bank	1,76,000	
Motor Vehicle at cost less Depreciation	1,48,000	
Debtors and Creditors	2,96,000	
Printing and Stationery	6,600	—
Purchases and Sales	24,00,000	31,60,000
Opening Stock	2,40,000	
Bad Debts Provision	—	5,000
Bad Debts	11,400	—
Freehold Premises at cost	8,00,000	—
Repairs to Premises	47,600	—
General Reserve	—	2,00,000
Proprietor's Remuneration	20,000	—
Wages and Salaries	2,29,000	—
Delivery Expenses	99,000	—
Administration Expenses	1,31,400	—
Rates and Taxes	15,000	—
Profit & Loss (Last Year)	—	1,24,000
	47,21,000	47,21,000

Adjustments:

1. Stock in hands as on 31st December 2004 Rs. 2,80,000.
2. Depreciate motor vehicles by Rs. 74,000.
3. Sundry Creditors include a claim for damages of Rs. 20,000 made last year and during this year settled for Rs. 15,100.
4. Unpaid wages Rs. 1,600.
5. Rates paid in advance Rs. 3,000.
6. Provision for bad debts is to be reduced to Rs. 3,500.

7. The item of repairs to Premises includes Rs. 20,000 which has to be capitalised.
8. Stock of stationery in hand Rs. 2,200. *(CAIIB)*

SOLUTION

Trading and Profit and Loss Account
for the year ending 31st December 2004

Dr.	Rs.	Rs.		*Cr.* Rs.
To Opening Stock		2,40,000	By Sales	31,60,000
To Purchases		24,00,000	By Closing Stock	2,80,000
To Wages and Salaries	2,29,000			
Add: Outstanding	1,600	2,30,600		
To Gross Profit c/d		5,69,400		
		34,40,000		34,40,000
To Printing and Stationery	6,600		By Gross Profit b/d	5,69,400
Less: Stock	2,200	4,400	By Discount on Creditors	4,900
To Bad Debts	11,400			
Add: New Provision	3,500			
	14,900			
Less: Old Provision	5,000	9,900		
To Repairs to Premises	47,600			
Less: Capitalised	20,000	27,600		
To Proprietor's Remuneration		20,000		
To Motor and Delivery Expenses		99,000		
To Administration Expenses		1,31,400		
To Rates and Taxes	15,000			
Less: Prepaid	3,000	12,000		
To Depreciation on Motor		74,000		
To Net Profit transferred to Capital Account		1,96,000		
		5,74,300		5,74,300

Balance Sheet as on 31st December 2004

Liabilities	Rs.	Rs.	*Assets*	Rs.	Rs.
Creditors	2,32,000		Cash at Bank	1,76,000	
Less: Settled	20,000	2,12,000	*Less*: Paid to creditors	15,100	1,60,900
General Reserve		2,00,000	Motor Vehicles	1,48,000	
Outstanding Wages		1,600	*Less*: Depreciation	74,000	74,000
Capital	10,00,000		Debtors	2,96,000	
Add: Profit	1,96,000		*Less*: Provision for Bad		
Add: Last year profit	1,24,000		Debts	3,500	2,92,500
	13,20,000		Stationery Stock		2,200
Less: Drawing 1,00,000			Closing Stock		2,80,000
Personal Debt 1,000	1,01,000	12,19,000	Prepaid Rates		3,000
			Freehold Premises	8,00,000	
			Add: Addition	20,000	8,20,000
		16,32,600			16,32,600

ILLUSTRATION 7.23

From the following Trial Balance of Sri. Narayanan, you are required to prepare a Trading and Profit & Loss A/c for the year ended 31st December 2006 and a Balance Sheet as on that date.

Debit Balances	*Rs.*	*Credit Balances*	*Rs.*
Stock on 1st Jan. 2006	70,000	Capital	2,00,000
Plant & Machinery	50,000	Wages outstanding	4,000
Rent	3,000	Sales	5,00,000
Depreciation on Plant & Machinery	5,000	Creditors	45,000
Drawings	40,000	Bills Payable	16,000
Wages	40,000	Discount (Cr.)	12,000
Income tax	2,000	Bank Overdraft	9,000
Salary for 11 months	11,000	Commission (Cr.)	8,000
Cash	5,000	Purchase returns	5,000
Buildings	1,60,000		
Depreciation on Buildings	8,000		
Purchases	3,00,000		
Debtors	80,000		
Bills Receivable	30,000		
Discount (Dr.)	2,000		
Carriage Inwards	4,000		
Bad debts	6,000		
Sales returns	3,000		
	7,99,000		7,99,000

Adjustments:

(i) Stock on 31st Dec. 2006 was Rs. 96,000.

(ii) Stock destroyed by fire was Rs. 6,000 and the Insurance company accepted a claim for Rs. 3,600.

(iii) Rs. 1,600 paid as rent of the office was debited to Landlord account and was included in the list of Debtors.

(iv) Goods invoiced Rs. 10,000 was sent to customers on sale or return basis on 28th December 2006, the customers still having the right to return the goods. The rate of gross profit was 1/5 of sale.

(v) Write off further bad debts Rs. 4,000 was maintain 5% provision for bad debts on debtors.

(vi) One month's salary was outstanding. *(B.Com. Mysore)*

SOLUTION

Trading and Profit & Loss A/c of Sri. Narayanan for the year ended 31st Dec. 2006

		Rs.			*Rs.*
To Opening Stock		70,000	By Sales	5,00,000	
To Purchases	3,00,000		*Less*: Returns	3,000	
Less: Returns	5,000	2,95,000		4,97,000	
To Carriage Inwards		4,000	*Less*: Goods sent on		
To Wages		20,000	sale or return	10,000	4,87,000
To Gross Profit c/d		2,08,000	By Closing Stock	96,000	
			Add: Stock with customers	8,000	
			Add: Stock destroyed	6,000	1,10,000
		5,97,000			5,97,000

To Salaries	11,000		By Gross Profit b/d		2,08,000
Add: Outstanding	1,000	12,000	By Discount		12,000
To Rent	3,000		By Commission		8,000
Add: Debited to Landlord	1,600	4,600			
To Discount		2,000			
To Bad debts	6,000				
Add: Further bad debts	4,000				
	10,000				
Add: Net provision for Bad debts	3,220	13,220			
To Depreciation on:					
Plant & Machinery		5,000			
Buildings		8,000			
To Loss on stock destroyed		2,400			
To Net Profit transferred to Capital A/c		1,80,780			
		2,28,000			2,28,000

Balance Sheet of Sri. Narayanan as on 31st December 2006.

Liabilities		*Rs.*	*Assets*		*Rs.*
Bills Payable		16,000	Cash		5,000
Bank Overdraft		9,000	Bills Receivable		30,000
Creditors		45,000	Debtors	80,000	
Outstanding Expenses:			*Less*: Rent included	1,600	
Salary	1,000			78,400	
Wages	4,000	5,000	*Less*: Goods on sale or return	10,000	
Capital	2,00,000			68,400	
Less: Drawings	40,000		*Less*: Bad debts	4,000	
	1,60,000			64,400	
Less: Income tax	2,000		*Less*: Provision for B.D.	3,220	61,180
	1,58,000		Insurance Company		3,600
Add: Net Profit	1,80,780	3,38,780	Stock		96,000
			Stock with customers on sale or return		8,000
			Plant & Machinery		50,000
			Buildings		1,60,000
		4,13,780			4,13,780

ILLUSTRATION 7.24

From the following particulars presented by Mr. S.Tendulkar, prepare a Trading A/c, Profit & Loss A/c for the year ended 31st Dec. 2006 and Balance Sheet as on that date.

Debit Balances	*Rs.*	*Credit Balances*	*Rs.*
Plant & Machinery	1,00,000	Sales (Net)	4,00,000
Drawings	36,000	Capital	1,00,000
Purchases	1,20,000	Creditors	40,000
Sundry Debtors	80,000	Bank Overdraft	20,000
Wages	20,000	Provision for Bad debts	4,000
Carriage	6,000	Cash credit	20,000
Salaries	14,000	Bills Payable	16,000

Particulars	Rs.	Particulars	Rs.
Rent	12,000		
Repairs	6,000		
Insurance	10,000		
Opening Stock	24,000		
Land & Buildings	80,000		
Furniture	20,000		
Discount	40,000		
Suspense A/c	32,000		
	6,00,000		6,00,000

Adjustments:

(*i*) Closing Stock Rs. 60,000.

(*ii*) Purchases include purchase of materials used for the constructions of building Rs. 10,000.

(*iii*) Sales include sale of furniture at a selling price of Rs. 2,000 (book Value Rs. 4,000).

(*iv*) Purchased a plant for Rs. 10,000, wrongly debited to purchase A/c.

(*v*) A sale of goods to a customer not debited to customers account Rs. 32,000.

(*vi*) Stock destroyed by fire amounted Rs. 20,000. Insurance Company admitted only Rs. 16,000 as its liability.

(*vii*) Wages include Rs. 6,000 incurred for the erection of a machinery.

(*viii*) The proprietor Mr. S. Tendulkar took goods for his own use from the business amounted to Rs. 2,000.

(*ix*) Rent included Rs. 2,000 paid for Mrs. S. Tendulkar's residential portion.

(*x*) Purchase of stationery for Rs. 200 was debited to repairs A/c.

(*xi*) A customer's cheque returned dishonoured wrongly debited to Discount A/c Rs. 2,000.

(*M.Com. Madurai, Kolkata Jabalpur*)

SOLUTION:

Trading and Profit & Loss A/c of S.Tendulkar for the year ended 31st December 2006.

Particulars		*Rs.*	*Particulars*		*Rs.*
To Opening Stock		24,000	By Sales	4,00,000	
To Purchases	1,20,000		*Less*: Furniture	2,000	3,98,000
Less: Building	10,000		By Closing Stock		60,000
	1,10,000		By Stock destoryed by fire		20,000
Less: Drawings	2,000				
	1,08,000				
Less: Plant & Machinery	10,000	98,000			
To Wages	20,000				
Less: Plant & Machiery	6,000	14,000			
To Carriage		6,000			
To Gross profit c/d		3,36,000			
		4,78,000			4,78,000
To Salaries		14,000	By Gross Profit b/d		3,36,000
To Rent	12,000				
Less: Drawings	2,000	10,000	By Provision for bad debts		4,000
To Repairs	6,000				
Less: Stationery	200	5,800			
To Insurance		10,000			
To Discount	40,000				
Less: Cheque Dishonour	2,000	38,000			
To Loss on sale of furniture		2,000			

Particulars	Rs.	Particulars	Rs.
To Stationery	200		
To Loss of stock by fire	4,000		
To Net Profit transferred to Capital A/c	2,56,000		
	3,40,000		3,40,000

Balance Sheet of Mr. S. Tendulkar as on 31st December 2006.

Particulars			*Rs.*	*Assets*		*Rs.*
Capital		1,00,000		Plant & Machinery	1,00,000	
Add: Net Profit		2,56,000		*Add*: Wages	6,000	
		3,56,000			1,06,000	
Less: Drawings	36,000			*Add*: Additions	10,000	1,16,000
Purchases	2,000			Land & Building	80,000	
Rent	2,000	40,000	3,16,000	*Add*: Additions	10,000	90,000
Creditors			40,000	Furniture	20,000	
Bank Overdraft			20,000	*Less*: Sale of furniture	4,000	16,000
Cash Credit			20,000	Stock		60,000
Bills Payable			16,000	Sundry Debtors	80,000	
				Add: Cheque Dishonoured	2,000	
					82,000	
				Add: Suspense	32,000	1,14,000
				Suspense A/c	32,000	
				Less: Debtors	32,000	Nil
				Insurance claim		16,000
			4,12,000			4,12,000

ILLUSTRATION 7.25

From the following particulars of Ajay Sharma, prepare the Manufacturing Trading & Profit and Loss A/c for the year ended 31st Dec. 2006 and a Balance Sheet as on that date:

Debit Balances	*Rs.*	*Credit Balances*	*Rs.*
Capital A/c (1-1-2006)	7,32,000	Factory Buildings	2,00,000
Drawings A/c	1,00,000	Furniture & fixtures	51,500
Purchases	21,05,000	Plant & Machinery	95,000
Rates & Taxes	25,000	Sundry Debtors	1,87,000
Salaries	1,00,000	4% Govt. Promissory Notes	
Carriage	20,000	(Subscribed on 1-1-2006)	20,000
Fuel & Coal	14,000	Sundry creditors	1,05,000
Factory Insurance	6,000	Sales	25,33,000
Advertisement	20,000	Cash in hand	45,500
Factory power	16,000	Cash at Bank	1,94,500
Bad debts written off	10,000		
Cash Discount allowed	2,000		
Sundry Expenses	3,500		
Opening Stock:			
Raw Materials	60,000		
Finished goods	50,000		
Patents	12,000		
Postage & Telegrams	13,000		
Wages	35,000		
Cash Discount received	15,000		

Additional Information:

(*i*) Depreciation to be provided at the following rates:
Plant & Machinery – 10%; Patents – 10%; Buildings – 2.5%; Furniture 5%.

(*ii*) Provide 2.5% on debtors for doubtful debts.

(*iii*) Purchases invoices aggregating Rs. 25,000 were omitted to be entered in the purchase day book.

(*iv*) Debtors include Rs. 5,000 due from the proprietor.

(*v*) An amount of Rs. 5,000 received in respect of a private loan advance by the proprietor which was wrongly credited to sundry debtors A/c.

(*vi*) Purchase invoices of the value of Rs. 75,000 were entered in the purchase day book on 29th December 2006 but the goods in respect there of were received on 3rd January 2007.

(*vii*) An amount of Rs. 3,500 received from a debtor was wrongly credited to Sales A/c.

(*viii*) The annual interest on Government Promissory Notes accrued due on 31st Dec. 2006 but was collected only in 2007.

(*ix*) Carriages include Rs. 8,000 towards outwards charges.

(*x*) Stock in trade as on 31-12-2006.
Raw materials Rs. 50,000; Finished goods Rs. 40,000

(*C.A.Inter*)

SOLUTION:

Manufacturing Trading and P & L A/c of Ajay Sharma for the year ended 31st December 2006

		Rs.		*Rs.*
To cost of Material Consumed:			By Cost of finished goods A/c	
Opening Stock	60,000		transferred to trading A/c	21,63,700
Add: Purchases	21,05,000			
Add: Purchases (Omitted)	25,000			
Add: Carriage				
(Rs. 20,000 – Rs. 8,000)	12,000			
	22,02,000			
Less: Closing Stock	1,25,000			
		20,77,000		
To Wages		35,000		
To Factory Expenses:				
Fuel & Coal		14,000		
Factory Insurance		6,000		
Factory Power		16,000		
To Depreciation on:				
Plant & Machinery	9,500			
Patents	1,200			
Factory Buildings	5,000	15,700		
		21,63,700		21,63,700
To Opening Stock		50,000	By Sales (25,33,000–3,500)	25,29,500
To Cost of finished goods		21,63,700	By Closing Stock	40,000
To Gross Profit c/d		3,55,800		
		25,69,500		25,69,500
To Rent, Rates & Taxes		25,000	By Gross Profit b/d	3,55,800
To Salaries		1,00,000	By Discount	15,000
To Carriage outwards		8,000	By Interest on Govt.	
To Advertisement		20,000	Promissory Notes	800

Particulars	Rs.	Rs.	Particulars	Rs.
To Bad debts	10,000			
Add: Provision for B.D	4,588	14,588		
To Depreciation on Furniture		2,575		
To Discount		2,000		
To Sundry Expenses		3,500		
To Postage & Telegrams		13,000		
To Net Profit – transferred to capital A/c		1,82,937		
		3,71,600		3,71,600

Balance Sheet of Ajay Sharma as on 31st December 2006.

Liabilities		*Rs.*	*Assets*		*Rs.*
Capital	7,32,000		Factory Buildings	2,00,000	
Add: Additional Capital	5,000		*Less*: Depreciation	5,000	1,95,000
Add: Net Profit	1,82,937		Plant & Machinery	95,000	
	9,19,937		*Less*: Depreciation	9,500	85,500
Less: Drawings	1,05,000		Furniture & fittings	51,500	
(1,00,000 + 5,000)		8,14,937	*Less*: Depreciation	2,575	48,925
Sundry Creditors		1,30,000	Patents	12,000	
(1,05,000 + 25,000)			*Less*: Depreciation	1,200	10,800
			4% Govt. Promissory Notes		20,000
			Stock-in-trade:		
			Raw materials (50,000 + 75,000)		1,25,000
			Finished goods		40,000
			Sundry Debtors (1,87,000 – 5,000 + 5,000 – 3,500)	1,83,500	
			Less: Provision for B.D.	4,588	1,78,912
			Accrued Interest on Govt. Promissory Notes		800
			Cash at Bank		1,94,500
			Cast in hand		45,500
		9,44,937			9,44,937

Illustration 7.26

From the following particulars, prepare Trading and Profit and Loss Account of Mr. Pran for the year ended 31-3-2006 and a Balance Sheet as on 31-3-2006:-

	Dr.	*Cr.*
Building	5,00,000	—
Machinery	2,00,000	—
Furniture	1,00,000	—
Cash at Bank	90,000	—
Cash on hand	10,000	—
18% p.a. Loan obtained by Mr. Pran on 1-6-2005 on mortgage of his building	—	3,00,000
Pran's Capital	—	5,20,000
Sundry Debtors and Creditors	5,00,000	4,00,000
Stock on 1-4-2005	1,20,000	—

Purchases and Sales	25,00,000	32,20,000
Sales returns and Purchases returns	1,20,000	1,00,000
Rent	60,000	
Establishment expenses	1,80,000	—
Electricity charges	15,000	—
Telephone charges	10,000	—
Commission on sales	30,000	—
Insurance premium	10,000	—
Bad debts	20,000	—
Bills Receivable	75,000	—
	45,40,000	45,40,000

You are required to provide for depreciation on Buildings at 5% p.a.; on Machinery at 25% p.a.; on Furniture at 10% p.a.; provision for bad and doubtful debt is to be made at 5% on sundry debtors.

Mr. Pran's manager is entitled to a commission of 10% on the net profit after charging his commission.

Closing stock was not taken on 31.3.2006 but only on 7.4.2006.

Following transactions has taken place during the period from 1.4.2006 to 7.4.2006.

Sales Rs. 2,50,000, purchases Rs. 1,50,000, stock on 7th April was Rs. 1,80,000 and the rate of gross profit on sales was 20%.

Insurance premium mentioned in the trial balance was in respect of building and machinery.

Interest on mortgage loan to be provided up to 31.3.2006.

(C.A.)

Solution.

TRADING AND PROFIT AND LOSS ACCOUNT OF MR. PRAN

Dr. *for the year ending 31st March, 2006.* Cr.

Particulars		*Rs.*	*Particulars*		*Rs.*
To Stock on 1-4-2005		1,20,000	By Sales	32,20,000	
To Purchases	25,00,000		*Less*: Returns	1,20,000	
Less: Returns	1,00,000				31,00,000
		24,00,000	By Stock on 31-3-2006		2,30,000
To Gross Profit		8,10,000			
		33,30,000			33,30,000
To Establishment Expenses		1,80,000	By Gross Profit b/d		8,10,000
To Rent		60,000			
To Electricity charges		15,000			
To Telephone charges		10,000			
To Commission on sales		30,000			
To Insurance premium		10,000			
To Bad debts		20,000			
To Provision for bad debts		25,000			
To Interest on Loan		45,000			
To Depreciation:					
Building 5%		25,000			
Machinery 25%		50,000			
Furniture 10%		10,000			
To Commission to Manager		30,000			
To Net Profit		3,00,000			
		8,10,000			8,10,000

BALANCE SHSEET OF MR. PRAN

as at 31st March, 2006

Particulars		*Rs.*	*Particulars*		*Rs.*
Capital	5,20,000		Building	5,00,000	
Net profit	3,00,000		Less: Depreciation	25,000	
		8,20,000			4,75,000
18% Mortgage Loan		3,00,000	Machinery	2,00,000	
Interest accrued		45,000	Less: Depreciation	50,000	
Sundry Creditors		4,00,000			1,50,000
Commission to Manager due		30,000	Furniture	1,00,000	
			Less: Depreciation	10,000	
					90,000
			Stock		2,30,000
			Debtors	5,00,000	
			Less: Provision for Doubtful Debts	25,000	
					4,75,000
			Bills Receivable		75,000
			Bank		90,000
			Cash		10,000
		15,95,000			15,95,000

Closing Stock:

Value of stock on 7-4-2006		Rs. 1,80,000
Sales during the intervening period	2,50,000	
Less: Gross profit @ 20%	50,000	
Cost of Sales		2,00,000
		3,80,000
Less: Purchases during the same period		1,50,000
Value of stock on 31-3-2006		2,30,000

Interest on Loan: Rs. $3,00,000 \times \frac{18}{100} \times \frac{10}{12} = \mathbf{45,000}$

Illustration 7.27

The following is the Trial Balance of Kesavan as at March 31, 2006

	Rs.		*Rs.*
Fixed Assets	3,00,000	Creditors	1,00,000
Opening Stock	75,000	Bills Payable	5,600
Debtors	2,05,000	Loan from Bank	4,000
Bills Receivable	10,000	Capital Account	5,00,000
12% Investments (purchased on 1-7-2005)	50,000	Sales	6,30,000
Cash in hand	5,000	Purchase returns	5,000
Drawings	10,000	Discount earned	1,000
Cash at Bank	10,000	Bad debts recovered	3,500
Purchases	5,25,000	Interest	3,000
Sales returns	10,000		
Carriage inwards	5,000		
Carriage outwards	2,000		

Rent	3,000		
Insurance	3,600		
Office and Administration Expenses	13,200		
Discount allowed	2,000		
Bad debts	5,000		
Interest	2,500		
Selling and Distribution Expenses	15,800		
	12,52,100		12,52,100

The following additional information is also available:

(a) Closing Stock as on 31st March, 2006 was Rs. 42,000.
(b) Rent is payable at Rs. 300 per month.
(c) Insurance premium was paid for the year ending 30th June, 2006.
(d) Interest on investments is payable half-yearly on 30th June and 31st December.
(e) Write off further Rs. 5,000 as bad.
(f) Create provision for discount on debtors at 2%.
(g) Create provision for bad and doubtful debts at 10%.
(h) Create a reserve for discount on creditors at 2%.
(i) Provide for depreciation on fixed assets at 10% p.a.

Prepare Trading and Profit and Loss Account for the year ended 31st March, 2006 and Balance Sheet as on that date. *(B.Com. Hons. Delhi)*

SOLUTION:

TRADING AND PROFIT AND LOSS ACCOUNT OF KESAVAN
for the year ended 31st March, 2006

Dr. Cr.

		Rs.			Rs.
To Stock 1-4-2005		75,000	By Sales	6,30,000	
To Purchases	5,25,000		*Less*: Returns	10,000	
Less: Returns	5,000				6,20,000
		5,20,000	By Stock, 31-3-2006		42,000
To Carriage inwards		5,000			
To Gross profit		62,000			
		6,62,000			6,62,000
To Office and Administration expenses		13,200	By Gross profit b/d		62,000
To Rent	3,000		By Discount earned		1,000
Add: Outstanding	600		By Interest	3,000	
		3,600	*Add*: Outstanding	1,500	
To Carriage outwards		2,000			4,500
To Insurance	3,600		By Reserve for Discount on Creditors		2,000
Less: Prepaid	900		By Bad debts recovered		3,500
		2,700	By Net loss		32,400
To Discount allowed		2,000			
To Bad debts		10,000			
To Provision for bad & doubtful debts		20,000			
To Provision for discount on debtors		3,600			
To Interest		2,500			
To Selling & Distribution expenses		15,800			
To Depreciation		30,000			
		1,05,400			1,05,400

BALANCE SHEET OF KESAVAN

as at 31-3-2006

		Rs.			*Rs.*
Sundry Creditors	1,00,000		Cash in hand		5,000
Less: Provision for			Cash at Bank		10,000
discount	2,000		Stock		42,000
		98,000	Debtors	2,05,000	
Bills Payable		5,600	*Less*: Bad debts	5,000	
Loan from Bank		4,000		2,00,000	
Outstanding rent		600	*Less*: Provision for bad debts	20,000	
Capital	5,00,000			1,80,000	
Less: Drawings	10,000		Less: Provision for discount	3,600	
	4,90,000				1,76,400
Less: Net loss	32,400		Bills Receivable		10,000
		4,57,600	Investments	50,000	
			Add: O/s interest	1,500	
					51,500
			Prepaid insurance		900
			Fixed Assets	3,00,000	
			Less: Depreciation	30,000	2,70,000
		5,65,800			5,65,800

QUESTIONS

Ojective Type Questions

I. State whether each of the following statement is True or False.

1. Wages paid for installing a new machine are debited to Wages Account.
2. Profit and Loss Account shows the financial position of the concern.
3. If stock is destroyed by fire, Trading Account is to be credited.
4. Fixed Assets are stated in the Balance Sheet at their market value.
5. Capital is the excess of assets over liabilities.
6. Manufacturing Account is closed by transferring its balance to the credit side of the Trading Account.
7. Outstanding wages appearing in Trial Balance are shown on the debit side of Profit and Loss Account.
8. Gross Profit is the difference between sales and purchases.
9. Closing stock is recorded in the Balance Sheet only, if it has already been adjusted against purchase account.
10. Gross Profit = Sales – Cost of goods sold.
11. Sales are equal to (a) Cost of goods sold + Gross Profit.
12. Goods taken over for personal use should be credited to Sales Account.
13. Goods lost by fire are credited to Profit & Loss Account.
14. Carriage inwards is an income and carriage outwards is an expense.
15. Balance Sheet is only a statement and not an account.
16. Revenue is recognised at the point of sale.
17. Carriage outwards is to be debited to Profit & Loss Account.
18. The Balance Sheet is prepared accordingly to entity principle.
19. Profit and Loss Account is a point statement whereas Balance Sheet is a period statement.

20. Patent Rights is in the nature of Nominal Account.

(**Ans:** 1. False; 2. False; 3. True; 4. False; 5. True; 6. False; 7. False; 8. False; 9. True; 10. True; 11. True; 12. False; 13. False; 14. False; 15. True; 16. True; 17. True; 18. True; 19. False; 20. False.

II. Fill in the blanks.

1. Goodwill is an .... asset.
2. The two sides of a Balance Sheet always shows the .... amount.
3. Prepaid expenses appearing in Trial Balance will appear in ....
4. Various assets of a concern should be shown in the Balance Sheet under two heads, viz .... and ....
5. Provision for bad debts will be shown as .... from Sundry Debtors in Balance Sheet.
6. If adjustment related to bad debts is given outside the Trial Balance, then they are adjusted by debiting .... and crediting ....
7. Bank overdraft is a .... liability.
8. If stock is destroyed by fire, ... Account is to be credited.
9. Unearned income account is a ....
10. Loss by theft is debited to .... Account.

(**Ans:** 1. Intangible; 2. Same; 3. Balance Sheet; 4. Fixed. Current; 5. Deduction; 6. Bad Debts Account, Sundry Debtors Account; 7. Current; 8. Trading; 9. Liability; 10. Profit and Loss.

III. Select the most appropriate answer:

1. Goods given as samples should be credited to:
   (a) Advertisement Account (b) Sales Account.
   (c) Purchase Account.
2. Income Tax paid by a proprietor on his business income should be:
   (a) Debited to Trading Account. (b) Debited to Profit & Loss Account.
   (c) Deducted from the Capital A/c in Balance Sheet.
3. Heavy expenditure to launch a new product is a:
   (a) Capital Expenditure. (b) Deferred Revenue Expenditure.
   (c) Revenue Expenditure.
4. Non-trading income is:
   (a) Credited to Profit & Loss A/c (b) Debited to Trading A/c
   (c) Debited to Profit & Loss A/c.
5. Value of scrap material must be:
   (a) Debited to Manufacturing A/c. (b) Debited to Profit & Loss A/c.
   (c) Credited to Manufaturing A/c.
6. Adjusted Purchases means adjustment of :
   (a) Opening stock and closing stock with purchases.
   (b) Cash purchases and credit purchases.
   (c) Purchase minus purchase return.
7. Current liabilities are such obligations which are to be satisfied:
   (a) Within a year. (b) Within two years.
   (c) Within three years.
8. Accrued income is an item of :-
   (a) Asset. (b) Liability.
   (c) Liquid asset.
9. Which one of the following is intangible asset.
   (a) Machinery (b) Goodwill.
   (c) Stock.

10. Material consumed during the year is:
    (a) Opening Stock + Purchases – Closing Stock.
    (b) Opening Stock + Closing Stock – Purchases.
    (c) Opening Stock – Purchases – Closing Stock

(Ans: 1. (c); 2. (c); 3. (b); 4. (a) 5. (c) 6. (a); 7. (a); 8. (a); 9. (b); 10. (a).

THEORETICAL QUESTIONS

1. What are adjustment entries? What is the need of making adjustments while preparing Final Accounts? *(B. Com. Madras)*
2. Give adjustment entries for the following:
   (*a*) Income Received in advance
   (*b*) Prepaid Expenses
   (*c*) Closing Stock
   (*d*) Provision for Doubtful Debts
   (*e*) Outstanding Income
   (*f*) Outstanding Expenses
   (*g*) Provision for Discounts on Debtors
3. What is meant by Bad Debts? Is it necessary to make provision for Doubtful Debts? *(B. Com. Madras)*
4. Is it necessary to pass double entry for every adjustment? If so, why?
5. What are adjustment entries ? Why they are needed ? *(B.Com. MS)*
6. "The accrual concept is the basis for final accounts." Explain. *(B.Com. Kerala)*
7. What are closing entries ? Why are they needed ? *(B.Com. Agra)*

PRACTICAL PROBLEMS

Provisions for Doubtful Debts and Discounts

1. The following is the extract from the Trial Balance of Mr. A as on 31st December 2004:

	Dr. Rs.	Cr. Rs.
Bad Debts	4,000	—
Sundry Debtors	1,50,000	—
Provision for Doubtful Debts	—	6,000

It is desired to maintain a provision of 5% for Bad and Doubtful Debts.

Give the necessary journal entries. Prepare Bad Debts Account and Provision for Bad and Doubtful Debts Account. Also show how the relevant items would appear in the Profit and Loss Account and Balance Sheet. *(B.Com., Madurai)*

[**Ans.** Rs. 5,500 to be debited to Profit & Loss A/c]

2. On Ist July 2003, M/s Purohit and Company had a Provision for Bad Debts of Rs. 6,067 against their book debts. During the year ended 30th June 2004, Rs. 6,524 proved to be bad and they desire to maintain the provision for Bad Debts at 4% on book debts which stood at Rs. 1,93,560 without any adjustment for Bad Debts.

Show the Journal entries on 30th June 2004 in the books of the firm to record these adjustments. *(B.Com., Madras)*

[**Ans.** Rs. 7,938 to be debited to Profit and Loss A/c]

3. On 31st December 2003, the Trial Balance of Das showed the following ledger balances:

	Rs.
Reserve for Bad and Doubtful Debts (1.1.2003)	1,000
Reserve for Discount on Debtors Account (1.1.2003)	475

Sundry Debtors Rs. 40,400 (of the Debtors, 400 are bad and should be written off

On 31st December 2004, the Sundry Debtors were Rs. 20,500 of which Rs. 500 are bad and should be written off.

It is desired to maintain the Reserve for Bad and Doubtful debts at 5% on Sundry Debtors and the Reserve for Discount on Debtors at 2.5%.

Show the Reserve for Bad and Doubtful Debts Account and the Reserve for Discount on Debtors Account as they would appear in the years 2003 and 2004. *(CA Inter)*

[**Ans.** Closing provision for Doubtful Debts Rs. 1,000.
Closing provision for Discount on Debtors Rs. 475]

4. A Company makes a Provision for Doubtful Debts of 5% on Debtors and a Provision at the rate of 2.5% for discount on Debtors.

   On Ist January 2004, the balances standing in the relevant accounts were Provision for Doubtful Debts Rs. 1,440 and Provision for Discount on Debtors Rs. 684.

   During the year, *i.e.*, 2004 the Company incurred bad debts Rs. 1,300 and allowed discounts Rs. 750. On 31st December 2004 debtors amounted to Rs. 32,400.

   Show the appropriate Accounts.

   [**Ans.** Provision for Bad Debts (Closing) Rs. 1,620 and transfer from Profit and Loss Account Rs. 1,480. Provision for Discount (Closing) Rs. 769.50 and transfer from Profit and Loss Account Rs. 835.50]

5. The following items have been given in the Balance Sheet as on 31st December 2003:

	Rs.	*Rs.*
Debtors	20,000	
Less: Reserve for Bad debts	1,000	
	19,000	
Less: Reserve for Discount on Debtors	570	18,430

   The Debtors were for Rs. 36,000 on 31st December 2004. Bad debts incurred in 2004 were Rs. 300 and discounts allowed Rs. 200.

   It is the practice to maintain provisions for bad debts and for discounts on debtors at 5 per cent and 3 per cent respectively.

   Prepare the Provision for Bad Debts a/c and also Provision for Discounts on Debtors account, showing how such items appear in the Profit & Loss Account and the Balance Sheet. *(B.Com., Madurai)*

   [**Ans.** Debit Profit & Loss A/c Rs. 1,100 for provision for Doubtful Debts
   Debit Profit and Loss A/c Rs. 656 for provision for Discount on Debtors]

6. On 1st January 2003, the Provision for Bad Debts Account showed a credit balance of Rs. 3,600. During the year, the bad debts amounted to Rs. 2800. The Debtors on 31st December 2003 amounted to Rs. 96,000 and a provision of 5% for Doubtful Debts was maintained.

   In 2004, the Bad Debts amounted to Rs. 1,200 and the Debtors at the end of the year amounted to Rs. 50,000, on which a provision of 5% for Bad Debts was to be maintained. Show for the years 2003 and 2004: (*i*) provision for Bad Debts Account, and (*ii*) How the relevant items will appear in the Profit and Loss Account and Balance Sheet. *(CAIIB)*

   [**Ans.** Rs. 4,000 debited in P & L A/c in 2003
   Rs. 1,100 credited in P & L A/c in 2004]

7. On 1st January 2003 a firm had a Bad Debt Provision of Rs. 650 at credit. On 31st December 2003 the total debts amounted to Rs. 18,400 of which Rs. 400 were bad and had to be written off. The firm wants to maintain the Bad Debts Provision at 5% of the Debtors.

   On 31st December 2004 total Debt amounted to Rs. 10,320, out of which Rs. 320 had to be written off as bad debt. The Provision to be maintained at 5% of the Debtors.

   Show the Bad Debt Provision Account and Bad Debts Account for 2003 and 2004.

   [**Ans.** Bad Debts Provision Rs. 900 in 2003 and Rs. 650 debited to P & L A/c
   Bad Debts Provision Rs. 500 in 2004 and Rs. 80 credited to P & L A/c]

8. Pass journal entries to incorporate the following at the time of preparing final accounts:

   (*a*) Provide 2.5% for discount on Debtors and a Bad Debts Provision at 10% of Debtors. (Debtors Rs. 30,000).

(*b*) Closing stock was valued at Rs. 43,000.

(*c*) Wages Owing Rs. 2,500.

(*d*) Insurance paid in advance Rs. 1,500.

(*e*) Included in Debtors is Rs. 1,000 owing by the Proprietor.

(*f*) Plant which stood Rs. 75,000 in the books on the 1st day of the year was disposed of for Rs. 30,000 in part exchange for a new machine costing Rs. 60,000. A net invoice of Rs. 30,000 passed through Purchase Book.

(*g*) Purchase invoices amounting Rs. 15,000 had been omitted from the books.

(*h*) A neon sign costing Rs. 7,500 was included in advertising.

(*i*) The Debits for two dishonoured cheques for Rs. 4,500 and Rs. 3,000 respectively had not been entered in the Cash Book. In the case of the second cheque for Rs. 3,000 it was expected that the Debtors would be in a position to pay a dividend of 75 paise in the rupee.

(*j*) Private purchases amounting to Rs. 15,000 had been included in Purchase Book. *(CAIIB)*

9. From the following particulars, prepare the Trading and Profit and Loss A/c for the year ended June 30, 2004 and the Balance Sheet as on that date.

Trial Balance as on 30th June 2004

Debit Balances:	*Rs.*	*Credit Balances:*	*Rs.*
Land	30,000	Loan on Mortgage	20,000
Plant and Machinery	40,000	Sundry Creditors	15,500
Office Furniture	2,000	Sales	1,10,000
Loose tools (1.7.2003)	4,000	Discount Received	300
Sundry Debtors	18,000	Purchase Returns	800
Drawings	2,000	Capital	40,000
Purchases	50,000		
Cash in Hand	300		
Cash at Bank	17,000		
Insurance	400		
Bad debts	850		
Stock (1-7-2003)	8,150		
Rent and Rates	1,200		
Interest on Loan	800		
Trade Expenses	450		
Wages	7500		
Salaries	1,500		
Carriage	450		
Factory Power	1,800		
Discount Allowed	200		
	1,86,600		1,86,600

The following is a list of liabilities not yet been brought in the books,

Wages Rs. 500; Salaries Rs. 100; Factory Power Rs. 200; Interest on loan Rs. 150.

Depreciate Plant and Furniture at 10%. Make provision for Discount on Debtors and Creditors at 2% and provision for Doubtful Debts at 5%. Allow interest on capital at 5%. Insurance prepaid Rs. 100. Stock on 30th June 2004 Rs. 10,500 and Loose Tools Rs. 2,800. *(B.Com., Madurai)*

[Ans. G.P. = Rs. 52,700, N.P. = Rs. 39,118, B/S = Rs. 1,15,258]

10. Below is the trial balance of Arumugam as at Dec. 31, 2004

Debit Balances:	*Rs.*	*Credit Balances:*	*Rs.*
Arumugam's current account	1,500	Capital Account	50,000
Adjusted purchases	6,99,200	Loan from K @ 9%	
Salaries	4,200	(taken on 1-1-2004)	20,000
Carriage on purchase	400	Sales	7,20,000
Carriage on Sale	500	Discount	500
Lighting	300	Sundry creditors	20,000
Rates and Insurance	400		
Buildings	27,000		
Furniture	6,000		
Sundry Debtors	8,000		
Cash on Hand	250		
Cash at Bank	1,500		
Stock (31-12-2004)	61,250		
	8,10,500		8,10,500

Prepare Trading and Profit and Loss Account for the year December 31, 2004 and the Balance Sheet as at that date after taking into consideration the following :

Rates have been prepaid to the extent of Rs. 175.

Bad debts totalling Rs. 500 have to be written off.

A provision for doubtful debts @ 5% on debtors is necessary.

Buildings have to be depreciated at 2% and furniture at 10%.

The manager is entitled to a commission of 5% of net profits before charging such commission.

(B.Com., Madurai)

[Ans. G.P. = Rs. 20,400, N.P. = Rs. 11,267, B/S = Rs. 1,02,160]

11. The following list of balances are given to you as on 31st March 2004, from the account books belonging to Mr. Suresh, who carried on business as a stationery merchant. You are reqired to prepare the Trading and Profit and Loss Account for the year ended 31st March 2004 and a Balance Sheet as on that date.

	Rs.		*Rs.*
Suresh's Capital	1,00,000	Manufacturing Wages	31,250
Furniture and Fittings	3,420	Discount Allowed	2,640
Land and Buildings	21,720	Discont Received	1,990
Drawings	4,200	Bank Charges	70
Cash at Bank	2,430	Office Salaries	4,280
Loan from Ramesh	10,000	Purchase Returns	970
Purchases	1,32,720	Cash in hand	150
Opening Stock	40,170	Sales	1,87,670
Returns Inwards	1,250	General Expanses	2,410
Carriage Outwards	3,450	Bad Debts Provision	3,100
Plant and Machinery	14,430	Sundry Creditors	12,450
Rent and Taxes	2,420	Sundry Debtors	43,830
Bad Debts	920	Bills Receivable	1,240
Insurance	470	Advertising	2,710

Adjustments:

1. 10% depreciation to be written off Plant and Machinery.
2. A new Machine had been installed on 1st Jan. 2004 for Rs. 2,500, but was not paid for, and no entry has been passed in the books of accounts.

3. 5% depreciation is to be written off Furniture & Fittings.
4. The Reserve for Doubtful debts is to be brought upto Rs. 5,000.
5. The unexpired insurance amounted to Rs. 120.
6. Rs. 150 was due to Ramesh against interest.
7. Stock at 31st March 2004 was Rs. 42,470. (*B.Com., Madurai*)

[Ans. G.P. Rs. 25,720; N.P. Rs. 4,733.50; B/S Rs. 1,25,633.50]

12. Mr. Balan carries on the business as a retailer. He extracted the following balances from his books of account as on 31st Dec. 2004.

	Dr. *Rs.*	*Cr.* *Rs.*
Capital and Drawings	18,000	7,50,000
Buildings	5,00,000	—
Furniture and Fixtures	20,000	—
Opening Stock	2,25,000	—
Sales and Purchases	13,37,000	18,00,000
Sundry Debtors and Creditors	5,00,000	2,00,000
Office Expenses	24,000	—
Salaries	18,000	—
Rent	6,000	—
Travelling Conveyance	4,000	—
Insurance	1,000	—
Motor Car Expenses	15,000	—
Postage and Telephones	3,600	—
Electricity Charges	2,400	—
Fixed Deposit with Bank @ 10% interest	50,000	—
Cash in Hand	1,000	—
Cash at Bank	10,000	—
Loan from Society @ 12% interest	—	25,000
Motor Car	40,000	—
Printing and Stationery	5,000	—
Bad Debts Provision	—	5,000
	27,80,000	27,80,000

You are required to prepare Trading and Profit and Loss Account for the year ended 31st December 2004 and a Balance Sheet as on that date after taking into consideration the following adjustments:

1. Closing stock on 31st December 2004 is valued Rs. 64,800.
2. A customer returned goods on 31st December 2004 amounting to Rs. 4,000 which was not accounted for but already included in the closing stock at selling price. The cost price of the sale goods was Rs. 3,200.
3. Annual insurance premium of Rs. 1,000 is valid upto 31.3.2005.
4. Provision for Bad and Doubtful Debts is to be kept 1½% on Sundry Debtors.
5. Interest on Fixed Deposit with Bank and payable to Society is to be provided.
6. Provide Depreciation on Buildings at 2.5%, Furniture and Fixtures at 10% and Motor Car at 20%.
7. Proprietor has used goods for his personal use costing Rs. 2,000 for which adjustment is necessary. (*CAIIB*)

[Ans. G.P. = Rs. 3,00,000, N.P. = Rs. 2,03,270, B.S. = Rs. 11,61,270]

13. From the following balances, prepare Trading and Profit and Loss Account for the year ended 31st December 2004 and a Balance Sheet as on that date:

	Rs.		*Rs.*
Capital	30,000	Trade charges	460
Cash at Bank	3,418	Debtors	17,078
Purchases	35,640	Sales	29,360
Creditors	3,920	Returns outwards	1,756
Rent & Tax	700	Drawings	2,600
Bills payable	2,690	Rent owing (Dr.)	160
Furniture (including purchase of	500	Interest & Discount (Dr.)	270
Rs. 200 on 30th June		Salaries	1,200
Bills Receivable	3,560	Returns inwards	2,460

Information:

1. Stock at the end was valued at Rs. 12,800 (Market value Rs. 13,100).
2. Rs. 300 paid to X against our acceptances were debited by mistake to Y's A/c and from there it was included in the list of Sundry Debtors.
3. Travelling expenses paid to our Sales Representative Rs. 250 per month were debited to his personal account.
4. Depreciate furniture at 10% p.a.
5. Provide for Doubtful debts to the extent of 5% on debtors.
6. Goods costing Rs. 500 were used by the proprietor. *(B.Com., Madurai)*

[**Ans.** G.P. = Rs. 6,316, N.L. = Rs. 43, B/S = Rs. 33.327]

14. From the following trial balance extract from the books of Mr. Subramaniam, prepare his Trading and Profit and Loss Accounts and Balance Sheet as on 31st December 2004.

	Dr. *Rs.*		*Dr.* *Rs.*
Stock (on 1-1-2004)	36,000	Sundry Creditors	30,000
Furniture	2,000	Loan	14,000
Cycle	600	Capital	50,000
Lorry	60,000	Sales	2,60,000
Sundry Debtors	32,000	Return outwards	4,000
Cash in Hand	1,200	Discount earned	2,200
Cash at Bank	4,800	Bills payable	16,600
Purchases	1,80,000		
Bad Debts	1,000		
Return Inwards	10,000		
Salaries	16,000		
Wages	22,000		
Rent	7,200		
Discount allowed	1,800		
Commission	1,400		
Postage	800		
	3,76,800		3,76,800

Take into account the following adjustments:

(*a*) Depreciate Furniture at 10% Cycle at 5% and Lorry at 20%.

(*b*) Create a Reserve of 5% on Sundry debtors for bad and doubtful debts and 1% Reserve for discount on Sundry Creditors.

(*c*) Outstanding Salaries Rs. 3,000.

(*d*) Closing Stock was valued at Rs. 48,000.

(*e*) Provide for 5% interest on capital. *(B.Com., Madurai)*

[**Ans.** G.P. = Rs. 64,000, N.P. = Rs. 18,970, B/S = Rs. 1,34,770]

15. From the following Trial Balance of a trader you are required to prepare trading and profit and loss account for the year ending 31st December 2004 and a Balance Sheet as on that date:

	Dr. Rs.	Cr. Rs.
Cash in hand	1,000	—
Stock	3,500	—
Creditors	—	3,900
Debtors	19,200	—
Drawings	5,130	—
Sales	—	92,800
Purchases	81,200	—
Wages	7,200	—
General Expenses	5,170	—
Furniture	4,000	—
Goodwill	3,000	—
Capital	—	32,700
	1,29,400	1,29,400

Adjustment:

1. Furniture (book value on 1st January 2004 Rs. 400) was sold on 30th June 2004 for Rs. 450 and was passed through the Sales Book.
2. Depreciate furniture at 10% p.a.
3. Private purchase amounting to 100 were passed through the purchase day book.
4. Sales book was overcast by Rs. 50.
5. Wages outstanding Rs. 50 though included in the wages Account, was not included in the Trial Balance.
6. Stock at the end was valued at Rs. 4,500. In view of the constant fall in prices, it has been decided to write off stock by 10%. *(B.Com., Mysore)*

[Ans. G.P. Rs. 4,550; N.L. Rs. 930; B/S Rs. 30,490]

16. Prepare a Trial Balance, Trading and Profit and Loss Account for the year ending 30th June 2004 and a Balance Sheet as on that date:

	Rs.		Rs.
Cash	370	Land and Buildings	28,000
Opening Stock	5,700	Rent Received	5,000
Debtors	3,200	Electricity (factory)	6,500
Sales	63,900	Bills Receivable	1,700
Wages	13,200	Travelling Expenses	2,300
Creditors	5,200	Insurance	3,600
Bad Debts provision	400	Purchases	12,000
Carriage	300	Purchase Returns	500
Trade Mark	5,300	Bad Debts	700
Advertising	1,250	Discounts (Dr.	300
Salaries	10,900	Bank	8,500
Machinery	28,900	Capital	??

Adjustments:

(1) Closing Stock valued at Rs. 3,200, included damaged goods worth Rs. 200 which had to be written off.

(2) Depreciate Machinery by 20% and Land and Building by 10%.

(3) Insurance was prepaid Rs. 600.

(4) Rent Received included Rs. 300 relating to July 2004.

(5) Provide for Bad Debts Reserve at 5% on Debtors. *(B.Com., Kerala)*

[Ans. T.B. = Rs. 1,32,720, Capital Rs. 57,720, G.P. = Rs. 29,900, N.P. = Rs. 7,610, B/S = Rs. 70,830]

17. From the following Trial Balance, extracted from the books of Rakhaldas Ramji, prepare a Trading and Profit and Loss account for the year ended 30th September 2004 and a Balance Sheet as on that date:

	Rs.	Rs.
R.R.'s Capital Account	—	90,000
R.R.'s Drawing Account	6,480	—
Land and Buildings	25,000	—
Plant and Machinery	14,270	—
Furniture and Fixtures	1,250	—
Carriage Inwards	4,370	—
Wages (Maufacturing)	21,470	—
Bad debts Reserve (1 Oct. 2003)	—	2,470
Sales	—	91,230
Sales Return	1,760	—
Bank Charges	140	—
Coal, Gas and Water	720	—
Rates and Taxes	840	—
Discount (Balance)	—	120
Purchases	42,160	—
Purchase Returns	—	8,460
Bills Receivable	1,270	—
Trade Expenses	1,990	—
Sundry Debtors	37,800	—
Sundry Creditors	—	12,170
Stock (1 Oct. 2003)	26,420	—
Apprentice Premium	—	500
Fire Insurance	490	—
Cash at Bank	13,000	—
Cash in hand	850	—
Salaries	14,670	—
	2,04,950	2,04,950

Charge Depreciation on Land and Building at 2½%.
on Plant and Machinery at 10%,
and on Furniture and Fixtres at 10%.

Make a reserve of 5% on Sundry debtors for Bad debts. Carry forward the following unexpired amounts:

(*a*) Fire Insurance 125
(*b*) Rates and Taxes 240
(*c*) Apprentice Premium 400

Charge 5% interest on capital but not on Drawings

The value of stock as on 30th Sept. 2004 was at Rs. 29,390. (*B.Com., Madurai; MS Madras*)

[**Ans.** G.P. = Rs. 32,180, N.P. = 18,538, B/S = Rs. 1,19,128]

18. Ram Chander's Trial Balance appeared as follows on 31st December 2004

	Rs.		Rs.
Capital	92,000	Cash at Bank	14,534
Creditors	18,852	Bills Receivable	5,844
Bills Payable	6,930	Purchases	85,522
Sales	1,21,850	Carriage Inwards	1,291

Reserve for Doubtful Debts	1,320	Carriage Outwards	800
Interest (Cr.)	340	General Expenses	6,085
Buildings	70,000	Insurance	783
Motor Trucks	12,000	Bad debts	613
Furniture	1,640	Audit Fees	400
Debtors	15,600	Travelling Expenses	325
Opening Stock	15,040	Discount (Dr.)	620
Cash in Hand	988	Sales Returns	285
		Investments	8,922

Prepare the Trading and Profit and Loss Account for the year ending 31st December 2004 and a Balance Sheet as on that date after making the following adjustments:

1. Stock on 31st December 2004 was valued at Rs. 15,500.
2. Depreciation has been provided for Motor Trucks by 10% and Furniture by 5%.
3. Write off a further Rs. 140 as Bad Debts and maintain reserve at 5% on Debtors.
4. Insurance Rs. 150 is still unexpired.
5. Interest on investment outstanding Rs. 120. *(B.Com., Calicut)*

[**Ans.** G.P. = Rs. 35,212, N.P. = Rs. 25,321, B/S = Rs. 1,43,103]

19. The Trial Balance of Mr. X as on 31st December 2004 was as follows:

	Dr. *Rs*	*Cr.* *Rs*
Purchases	1,62,505	—
Sales	—	2,52,400
Reserve for Doubtful Debts	—	5,200
Sundry Debtors	50,200	—
Sundry Creditors	—	30,526
Bills Payable	—	3,950
Opening Stock	26,725	—
Wages	23,317	—
Salaries	5,575	—
Furniture	7,250	—
Postage	4,226	—
Power and Fuel	1,350	—
Trade Expenses	5,831	—
Bad Debts	525	—
Loan at 10% p.a. to Ram (1.9.2004)	3,000	—
Cash on hand & Bank	10,000	—
Outstanding wages	—	2,000
Trade Expenses accrued but not paid	—	700
Drawings	4,452	—
Capital	—	10,000
	3,04,776	3,04,776

Prepare the Trading and Profit and Loss Account for the year ended 31st December 2004 and the Balance Sheet as on date taking into account the following information:

1. Depreciation on furniture to be charged at 10% p.a.
2. Sundry Debtors include an item of Rs. 500 due from a customer who has become insolvent.
3. Reserve for Doubtful Debts is to be maintained at 5% on debtors.
4. Goods to the value of Rs. 1,500 have been destroyed by fire and the Insurance Company has admitted the claim for Rs. 1,000.

5. Stock as at 31st December 2004 was Rs. 12,550. (*B.Com., Madurai*)

[**Ans.** GP = 52,733; N.P. = Rs. 37,666; B/S = Rs. 80,390]

20. From the following Trial Balance of Somu as at 31st December 2004 prepare Trading and Profit and loss Account and Balance Sheet.

	Rs.	*Rs.*
Purchases	66,000	—
Discount	3,300	—
Productive Wages	16,500	—
Sales	—	1,30,000
Salaries	12,000	—
Travelling Expenses	5,000	—
Carriage Inward	2,250	—
Insurance	5,550	—
Commission	1,325	—
Rent & Rates	5,000	—
Cash in Hand	2,500	—
Cash at Bank	27,275	—
Repairs	1,950	—
Sundry Expenses	550	—
Mortgage 6% p.a.	—	30,000
Mortgage Interest	1,500	—
Buildings	45,000	—
Machinery	15,000	—
Stock (1-1-2004)	57,500	—
Horses & Carts	5,000	—
Capital	—	1,23,200
Sundry Debtors	31,000	—
Sundry Creditors	—	21,000
	3,04,200	3,04,200

Make provision for the following:

(*a*) Depreciation : Building at 2½%

Machinery at 5%

Horses & Carts at 6%

(*b*) Bad debts Rs. 1,100

(*c*) Reserve 5% on sundry debtors for bad and doubtful debts

(*d*) Rent and Rates unexpired Rs. 300

(*e*) Mr. Somu has taken goods from stock worth Rs. 1,200 for personal use. (*B.Com., Madurai*)

[**Ans.** G.L. = Rs. 11,050; N.L. = Rs. 51,995; B/S = Rs. 1,21,305]

21. From the following Trial Balance of Apareep prepare the Trading and Profit and Loss Account for the year ended 31st March 2004 and Balance Sheet as at that date:

	Rs.		*Rs.*
Stock Opening	45,000	Capital A/c	90,000
Plant & Machinery	85,000	Sundry creditors	40,000
Fixtures & Fittings	7,500	Discount Received	3,500
Freehold premises	75,000	Bank overdraft	20,000
Purchases	1,50,000	Provision for Bad debts	3,000

Salaries	14,000	Purchase Returns	1,500
Sundry Debtors	55,000	Sales (Net)	3,37,070
Manufactring Expenses	15,000		
Manufacturing Wages	30,000		
Carriage in	2,000		
Carriage out	2,100		
Factory Expenses	10,000		
Bad Debts	750		
Interest and Bank charges	625		
Discount	750		
Insurance	1,500		
Cash at Bank	695		
Cash in Hand	150		
	4,95,070		4,95,070

The following adjustments are required:

1. Closing Stock Rs. 57,000.
2. Depreciation: Plant & Machinery @ 7½%.
   Fixtures & fittings @ 10%.
3. Insurance (Unexpired) Rs. 500.
4. Salary includes advances for next period Rs. 600.
5. Outstanding Interest on overdraft Rs. 1,000.
6. Bad Debts provision to be reduced to 5% on Sundry Debtors. *(B.Com., Madurai)*

[Ans. G.P. = Rs. 1,43,570, N.P. = Rs. 1,20,570, B/S = Rs. 2,71,570]

22. From the following balances extracted from the books of Abraham, prepare a Trading Account, Profit & Loss Account and a Balance Sheet.

Ledger Balance as on 31-12-2004

	Rs.		*Rs.*
Purchases (Materials)	16,000	Cash in Hand	175
Discount (Dr.)	1,300	Cash at Bank	2,725
Wages (Productive)	6,500	Stable Expenses	195
Sales	30,000	Repairs	105
Salaries	2,000	Sundry Expenses	55
Travelling Expenses	500	Mortgage and interest to the date (Cr.)	3,050
Carriage	275	Building	4,000
Insurance	150	Horses & Carts	500
Commission	325	Stock (1-1-2004)	5,750
Rent & Rates	500	Capital	10,625
Sundry Debtors	3,250	Sundry creditors	2,100
Machinery	1,500		

Adjustments:

1. Make a provision for Rent & Rates unexpired Rs. 30.
2. Depreciation on Building at 2.5% p.a. Machinery at 5%, Horses and carts at 7.5%.
3. Bad debts Rs. 150
4. Liability for insurance Rs. 20.
5. Discount on Sundry Debtors and creditors at 2.5%.
6. Stock on hand (31.12.2004) Rs. 6075. *(B.Com., Saugar)*

[Ans. G.P. = Rs. 7,550, N.P. = Rs. 2,042, B/S = Rs. 17,814]

23. From the undermentioned particulars of Asha, prepare the Trading and Profit and Loss Account for the year ended 31.3.2004 and Balance Sheet as at the date after making the necessary adjustments:

	Rs.		Rs.
Capital	25,000	Buildings	15,000
Drawings A/c	7,000	Purchases	30,230
Sundry Creditors	8,000	Sundry Debtors	11,000
Mortgage (Cr.)	5,000	Wages	6,000
Discount Received	702	Rent	5,000
Allahabad Bank (Cr.)	4,000	Carriage inward	400
Provision for Bad Debts	600	Carriage outward	420
Purchases Returns	530	Bad Debts	150
Sales	67,500	Salaries	2,800
Stock at start	9,000	Interest & Bank Charges	126
Plant & Machinery (including Mach. for Rs. 5,000 purchased on 1-1-2004)	17,000	Discount Allowed	150
		Insurance (Dr.)	300
		Bank of Bikaner (Dr.)	5,140
Furniture	1,500	Cash in hand	30
Sales Returns	86		

Adjustments:

Provide for

(*a*) Interest on capital at 10% p.a. (no interest is to be provided to drawings)

(*b*) Outstanding expenses:

1. Salaries Rs. 100
2. Wages Rs. 50
3. Interest on Bank Loan Rs. 100

(*c*) Depreciation on:

1. Machinery at 10% p.a.
2. Furniture at 10% p.a.
3. Buildings at 2½% p.a.

(*d*) Prepaid expenses:

1. Insurance Rs. 100
2. Salary Rs. 50

(*e*) Provision for bad and doubtful debts at 10% on debtors.

(*f*) Closing stock Rs. 7,550.

Furniture costing Rs. 500 was sold for Rs. 350 at the commencement of accounting year and this latter amount was credited to furniture account.

(*C.A. Inter*)

[**Ans.** G.P. = R. 29,814, N.P. = Rs. 16,535, B/S = Rs. 54,285]

24. The following are the balances taken on 31st December 2004, from the books of Mr. Mujib:

	Rs.		Rs.
Capital	35,000	Printing & Stationery	325
Drawings	2,400	Bad debts	150
Bills Receivable	8,200	Purchases	50,600
Plant & Machinery	19,600	Sales	84,870
Advertising	1,200	Sales Tax	1,875
Commission (Cr.)	360	Sundry debtors	24,200
Wages	11,600	Sundry creditors	15,300
Discount allowed	160	Stock (1.1.2004)	7,965
Freight on purchases	340	Trade Expenses	190

Returns Inwards	930	Rent	1,650
Cycles	375	Insurance	400
Salaries	7,500	Cash in hand	180
Rates and Taxes	250	Typewriter	1,200
		Bank Overdraft	5,760

Prepare Trading and Profit and Loss account for the year ended 31st Decemer 2004 and a Balance Sheet as on that date, after taking into consideration the following :

1. Depreciation is to be charged as follows:
   Plant & Machinery 5% and Typewriter 10%
2. Commission earned but not received Rs. 140.
3. Provide for the following outstanding items:
   (1) Printing Rs. 75 and (2) Rent Rs. 150.
4. Charge 5% interest on capital.
5. Stationery on hand at the end of the year Rs. 50.
6. Stock on 31st December 2004 was valued at Rs. 12,666.

[Ans. G.P. = Rs. 26,101, N.P. = Rs. 9,876, B/S = Rs. 65,511]

25. From the following Trial Balance of Ram on Decemer 31, 2004, prepare the Final Accounts:

Debit Balances:	*Rs.*		*Rs.*
Drawings	6,000	Postage & Telegrams	3,800
Wages	15,500	Land and Buildings	25,000
Stock	12,800	Plant and Machinery	10,000
Loan to Krishna	4,000	Sundry Debtors	16,500
Rent	5,000	Packing charges	400
General Expenses	1,480	Bad Debts	1,280
Investments	60,000		
Purchases	1,60,000	*Credit Balances:*	
Freight and Carriage	2,100	Bank Overdraft	25,000
Goodwill	40,000	Interest on Investments	5,800
Bills Receivable	6,200	Bills Payable	4,600
Rates and Taxes	1,800	Interest on Loan to Krishna	320
Sales Returns	2,100	Capital	1,00,000
Insurance	900	Doubtful Debts Provision	250
Cash in Hand	2,500	Sales	2,30,000
Savings Bank	1,200	Sundry Creditors	12,590

Adjustments:

1. Closing stock as on 31st December 2004 Rs. 16,000.
2. Goods worth Rs. 700 were sent on 25th December as "Sale on Approval basis" for Rs. 810 and approval was not received before the end of the month.
3. 20% of the Goodwill should be written off.
4. Further Bad Debts was estimated at Rs. 350.
5. Increase Reserve for Bad and Doubtful debts to the extent of Rs. 1,500.
6. Depreciate Land and Buildings by 3% and Plant and Machinery by 10%.
7. Goods worth Rs. 800 were distributed as free samples. *(B.Com., Madras)*

[Ans. G.P. = Rs. 54,190; N.P. = 33,500; B/S = Rs. 1,69,690]

26. From the following Trial Balance of Ramesh as at 31st Dec. 2004 prepare a Trading and Profit and Loss Account for the year ended 31.12.2004 and a Balance Sheet as at that date after making necessary adjustments.

Dr. Balances:	*Rs.*	*Cr. Balances*	*Rs.*
Drawings	3,000	Capital	40,000
Plant & Machinery (1-1-2004)	10,000	Sundry Creditors	5,000
Plant & Machinery (addition on 1-7-2004)	2,500	Sales	60,000
		Return outwards	500
Stock	7,500	Reserve for Doubtful Debts	200
Purchases	41,000	Discounts	400
Returns Inwards	1,000	Rent Received	600
Sundry Debtors	10,300		
Furniture & Fixtures	2,500		
Freight & Duty	1,000		
Carriage outwards	250		
Rent, Rates & Taxes	2,300		
Printing & Stationery	400		
Trade Expenses	200		
Postage & Telegrams	400		
Insurance charges	350		
Salaries & Wages	10,650		
Cash on Hand	3,100		
Cash at Bank	10,250		
	1,06,700		1,06,700

Adjustments:

1. Stock 31.12.2004 was valued at Rs. 7,300.
2. Write off Rs. 300 as bad debts.
3. The Reserve for doubtful debts is to be maintained at 5% on debtors.
4. Create a reserve for discounts on debtors and creditors at 2%.
5. Depreciate Furniture and Fixtures at 5% p.a. and Plant and Machinery at 20% p.a.
6. Insurance prepaid was Rs. 50.
7. A fire occurred on 26th Dec. 2004 in the godown and stock of the value of Rs. 2,500 was fully insured and the Insurance Company admitted the claim in full. (*B.Com., Madurai*)

[**Ans.** G.P. = Rs. 19,800; N.P. = Rs. 3,235, B/S = Rs. 45,135]

27. You are required to prepare the Trading and Profit and Loss Account for the year ended 31st March 2004 and a Balance Sheet as at that date :

Trial Balance

Dr. Balances:	*Rs.*	*Cr. Balances*	*Rs.*
Stock (1-4-2003)	95,280	Capital	1,46,900
Purchases	2,62,590	Loan (Interest @ 6%)	35,000
Manufacturing Wages	45,970	Sundry creditors	86,270
Plant and Machinery	34,800	Sales	3,62,030
Fixtures & Fittings	13,970	Provision for Doubtful Debts	8,500
Sundry Debtors	67,500	Commission Received	10,640
Bills Receivable	15,000	Purchase Returns	13,360
Sales Returns	8,780		
Salaries	16,000		
Bad debts	8,620		
Repairs & Renewals	9,370		
Rent and Taxes	11,120		
Travelling Expenses	6,880		
Insurance	6,400		

Drawings	16,050		
Cash in Hand	8,030		
Cash at Bank	24,970		
Interest & Discount	11,370		
	6,62,700		6,62,700

Adjustments:

(*a*) Closing Stock is valued at Rs. 1,27,000.

(*b*) Depreciate (1) Plant & Machinery by 5%.

(2) Fictures & Fittings by 10% p.a.

(*c*) Outstanding Interest on Loan is Rs. 350.

(*d*) Sales include Rs. 1,030 worth of goods taken by the proprietor for his private use.

(*e*) The Manager is entitled to a commission of 10% on the net profit after charging such commission.

(*B.Com., Madurai*)

[**Ans.** G.P. = Rs. 89,770, N.P. = Rs. 24,694, B/S = Rs. 2,78,603]

28. From the following ledger balances of X, prepare a Trading and Profit and Loss Account for the year ended 31st December 2004 and a Balance Sheet as on that date, after making the necessary adjustments:

	Rs.		*Rs.*
X's Capital	80,000	Printing & Stationery	400
X's Drawings	6,000	Rent, Rates & Taxes	4,600
Plant & Machinery (1-1-2004)	20,000	Sundry Creditors	10,000
Plant & Machinery	5,000	Sales	1,20,000
(Additions on 1-7-2004)		Returns outward	1,000
Stock 1-1-2004	15,000	Postage & Telegrams	800
Purchases during the year	82,000	Reserve for Doubtful debts	800
Returns inwards	2,000	Rent from sublet	1,600
Furniture & Fixtures	5,000	Insurance charges	700
Sundry Debtors	20,600	Salaries & Wages	21,300
Carriage outward	500	Cash in Hand	6,200
Freight & Duty	2,000	Cash at Bank	20,500
Trade Expenses	800		

The items for adjustments are :

1. Stock on 31st Dec. 2004 was valued Rs. 14,000.
2. Write off Rs. 600 as bad debts.
3. The reserve for doubtful debts is to be maintained at 5% on Sundry Debtors.
4. Provide depreciation on furniture and fixtures at 5% p.a., and on plant and machinery at 20% p.a.
5. Insurance prepaid was Rs. 100.
6. A fire occurred on 5th December 2004 in the godown and stock of the value of Rs. 5,000 was destroyed. It was insured and the insurance company admitted the claim in full.

(*B.Com., Delhi*)

[**Ans.** G.P. = Rs. 39,000, N.P. = 6,050, B/S = Rs. 90,050]

29. The following is the Trial Balance of Mr. Mohan as on 31st December 2004, prepare Trading Account, Profit and Loss Account and Balance Sheet.

	Dr. Rs.	Cr. Rs.
Capital and Drawings	20,000	2,00,000
Debtors and Creditors	1,00,000	48,000
Goods Purchased and Sold	2,40,000	4,00,400
Returns of Goods	20,000	30,000
Bills Receivable & Payable	30,000	44,000
Cash in Hand	10,000	—
Office Lighting	10,000	—
Factory Wages	20,000	—
General Expenses	2,000	—
Machinery	1,00,000	—
Machinery Purchased on 1st Oct. 2004	20,000	—
Furniture and Fixtures	30,000	—
Salaries	40,000	—
Loan to Nair	20,000	—
Dividend Received	—	2,000
Stock of Goods (opening)	62,400	—
	7,24,400	7,24,400

Adjustments:

1. Stock on 31st December 2004:
   Goods Rs. 80,000
   Stationery Rs. 400
2. Goods destryed but covered by Insurance amounted to Rs. 10,000 but the amount not yet received.
3. General Expenses include stationery purchased for Rs. 900.
4. Interest on loan to Nair @ 3% p.a. is due.
5. Depreciation on Machinery and Furniture and Fixtures by 10% p.a.
6. Included in Sales is Rs. 5,000 being sale of fixture (book value is Rs. 8,000). Depreciation thereon to the date of sale Rs. 400.
7. The Manager is entitled to get a commission of 10% on the Net Profit before charging such commission.
8. Bad Debts during the year comes to Rs. 1,200. (*B.Com. Bangalore*)

[**Ans.** G.P. = Rs. 1,73,000, N.P. = Rs. 96,390, Commission = Rs. 10,710, B/S = Rs. 3,79,100]

30. From the following Trial Balance of Deepak, you are required to prepare a Trading and Profit and Loss Account for the year ended on 31st December 2004 and a Balance Sheet as on that date after making the necessary adjustments:

	Dr. Rs.	Cr. Rs.
Capital and Drawings	10,000	2,00,000
Purchases and Sales	84,000	2,10,000
Returns	2,000	1,000
Freehold Property	60,000	—
Plant and Machinery	1,00,000	—
Salaries	14,000	—
Printing and Stationery	2,000	—
Furniture and Fixtures	4,000	—
Discount	1,500	—
Bills Payale	—	5,700

Opening Stock	30,000	—
Wages	37,000	—
Sundry Debtors and Creditors	25,000	40,000
Insurance Charges	3,000	—
Gas and Fuel	2,700	—
Bad Debts	600	—
Office Rent	2,600	—
Freight and Duty	5,000	—
Loose Tools 1st Jan.	2,000	—
Factory Lighting	2,600	—
Provision for Doubtful Debts 1st Jan.	—	800
Loan to Prem @ 5%	40,000	—
Interest on Loan to Prem	—	1,000
Cash at Bank	25,000	—
Cash in Hand	5,500	—

Adjustments:

1. Wages Rs. 1,500 and Salaries Rs. 700 were outstanding.
2. Insurance prepaid Rs. 400.
3. A new machinery was installed on 30th Sept. 2004, costing Rs. 15,000 but it was not recorded in the books and no payment was made for it. Wages Rs. 1,000 paid for its erection have been debited to wages.
4. Loose Tools were valued at Rs. 1,500 on December 2004.
5. Depreciate Plant and Machinery by 10% and Furniture and Fixtures by 5%.
6. Drawings account balance includes an item of Rs. 200 drawn in cash for the purchase of stationery which was used in business.
7. Maintain a provision of 5% on Sundry Debtors for doubtful debts and 2% for discount on Debtors and 2% discount on Creditors.
8. Stock on 31st December 2004 was Rs. 70,000.
9. Stock of the value of Rs. 5,000 was destroyed by fire on 25th December 2004 and the Insurance Company admitted to claim of Rs. 4,000. *(B. Com., Mangalore)*

[**Ans.** G.P. = Rs. 1,22,200; N.P. = Rs. 88,075; B/S = Rs. 3,40,075]

31. The following figures have been extracted from the records of Fancy stores, a proprietorship concern, as at 31st December 2004.

	Rs.		*Rs.*
Furniture	15,000	Insurance	6,000
Capital Account	54,000	Rent	22,000
Cash in Hand	3,000	Sundry Debtors	60,000
Opening Stock	50,000	Sales	6,00,000
Fixed Deposits	1,34,600	Advertisements	10,000
Drawings	5,000	Postage & Telegrams	3,400
Pro. for Bad debts	3,000	Bad Debts	2,000
Cash at Bank	10,000	Printing & Stationery	9,000
Purchases	3,00,000	General Charges	13,000
Salaries	19,000	Sundry Creditors	40,000
Carriage Inwards	41,000	Deposit from Customers	6,000

Prepare Trading Profit and Loss Account and Balance Sheet after taking into consideration the following further information:

1. The closing stock as on 31st December 2004 was Rs. 10,000.
2. A sale of Rs. 25,000 made for cash had been credited to Purchases Account.

3. Salary of Rs. 2,000 paid to an employee had been entered in the Cash Book as Rs. 1,000.
4. Charge depreciation of furniture at 10%.
5. Furniture had been sold during the year for Rs. 10,000 and the proceeds had been credited to Furniture Account. The written down value of furniture sold was Rs. 5,000.
6. A sum of Rs. 10,000 received from a party which had purchased some stocks belonging to a separate business of the proprietor was credited to the Sundry Debtors A/c.
7. The proceeds of a matured fixed deposit amounting to Rs. 25,400 had been credited to the Fixed Deposits Account. The original amount of the deposit was Rs. 20,000.
8. There was an outstanding liability for rent of Rs. 2,000.
9. An advance of Rs.1,000 paid to an employee against his salary of January 2005 had been debited to Salaries A/c.
10. The office premises were sub-let from December 2004 for monthly rental of Rs. 1,000 but the rent for December has not yet been received. *(C.A. Inter)*

[Ans. G.P. = Rs. 2,19,000, N.P. = Rs. 1,42,000, B/S = Rs. 2,49,000]

32. Mr. X, a trader, has extracted the following Trial Balance from his books as on 31st March 2004.

Debit Balances:	*Rs.*		*Rs.*
Purchases	4,00,000	Furniture & Fittings	23,000
Sundry Debtors	1,50,000	Deposit with Supplier	6,000
Cash in Hand	4,000	Office Equipment	10,000
Cash at Bank	8,000	Bills Receivable	6,000
Rent, Rates & Taxes	3,000	Bad Debts	4,000
Insurance Premium	9,000	Opening Stock	30,000
Salaries	42,000	Electricity Expenses	2,000
Carriage Outwards	21,000		
Carriage Inwards	18,000	*Credit Balances:*	
Claims recoverable	5,000	Sundry Creditors	50,000
Advertisement Suspense	9,000	Sales	7,00,000

(T.B.; 7,50,000)

The following further information is provided:

1. A purchase invoice for Rs. 15,000, received from a Sundry creditor, has not been entered through over-sight.
2. The claim recoverable has been settled with the insurance company for Rs. 2,000.
3. 50% of the Advertisement Suspense Account is to be written off this year. The amount represents the cost of an advertising campaign conducted this year.
4. Depreciation is to be provided on straight line method on furniture and fittings and office equipment at 5%. The original costs were:

   Furniture & Fittings Rs. 30,000

   Office Equipment Rs. 15,000
5. Goods costing Rs. 5,000 were despatched out on 29th March. The sale, however, took place on 2nd April 2004, when an invoice for Rs. 7,500 was raised against the customer.
6. Insurance premium includes a prepaid amount of Rs. 1,000.
7. The deposit with a supplier was made on 1st October 2003. It carries interest @ 12% p.a.
8. Two bills receivable from customers, of Rs. 700 and Rs. 1,300, were dishonoured on 30th March. These had earlier been discounted with the bank.
9. Provide 2% on Sundry Debtors for doubtful debts.
10. Physical stock of goods on hand on 31st March 2004 at cost was Rs. 1,00,000.

Prepare Trading, Profit and Loss Account and Balance Sheet from the above information.

(C.A. Inter)

[Ans. G.P. = Rs. 3,42,000, N.P. = Rs. 2,49,570, B/S = Rs. 3,14,570]

33. Mr. Ram has extracted the following Trial Balance from his books on 31st March 2004.

	Dr. Rs	Cr. Rs
Drawings and Capital	16,000	34,000
Cash	6,760	—
Petty Cash	1,000	—
Leasehold Land	20,000	—
Opening Stock (Market value)	50,000	—
Salary	12,000	—
Sundry Debtors and Creditors	56,000	35,000
Wages	40,000	—
Bank	21,000	—
Rent	9,000	—
Electricity	6,000	—
Motor Car	10,240	—
Advertising	9,000	—
Purchases and Sales	4,00,000	6,00,000
Postage and Telephone	3,000	—
Discounts	11,400	—
General Charges	4,000	—
Petty Expenses	9,600	—
Suspense	—	10,000
	6,79,000	6,79,000

You are required to prepare a Trading and Profit and Loss Account and a Balance Sheet using the following additional information:

1. Closing stock at market value as on 31st March 2004 was Rs. 80,000 (cost Rs. 75,000)
2. The Petty cash balance represents the month and imprest account. As on the closing the Petty Cashier has vouchers totalling to Rs. 400 for which he had not received reimbursement from the Main Cashier.
3. Discount Allowed amounting to Rs. 1,000 had been posted to the debit of Sundry Debtors.
4. Cash withdrawn from bank Rs. 4,000 had not been entered in the bank column of the cash book.
5. Sales Account had been undercast by Rs. 4,000.
6. The motor car which had been purchased in 2000-2001 was being depreciated at 20% on the Reducing Balance Method. The original cost of the car is Rs. 20,000. It is now decided to charge depreciation at 6% on the straight line method and to make this charge effective from the year of purchase of the car.
7. Leasehold land was purchased during the year. On the date of purchase the unexpired period of the lease was 5 years.
8. No entry had been passed in the books for stock withdrawn from the business by the proprietor valued at Rs. 10,000.
9. Advertising includes cost of campaign done during the year Rs. 6,000. It is expected that the effect of the campaign will be felt for atleast three years.
10. Telephone bills amounting to Rs. 1,000 remained unpaid. *(CA)*

[Ans: G.P. = Rs. 1,99,000; N.P. = Rs. 1,38,560; B/S = Rs. 1,82,960]

34. Mr. Abraham, a shop-keeper, had prepared the following Trial Balance from his ledger as on 31st March 2004:

	Dr. Rs	Cr. Rs
Purchases and Sales	3,10,000	4,15,000
Stock of goods on 1.4.2003	50,000	—
Cash in hand	2,100	—
Cash at Bank	12,000	—
Abraham Capital and Drawings	4,000	2,88,600
Rates and Taxes	5,000	—
Salaries	32,000	—
Postage and Telephone	11,500	—
Salesmen's Commission	35,000	—
Insurance	9,000	—
Advertising	17,000	—
Furniture and Fittings	22,000	—
Printing and Stationery	3,000	—
Motor Car	48,000	—
Bad Debts	2,000	—
Cash Discounts	4,000	—
General Expenses	14,000	—
Carriage Inwards	10,000	—
Carriage Outwards	22,000	—
Wages	20,000	—
Outstanding liability for Expenses	11,000	—
Sundry Creditors and Debtors	1,00,000	40,000
	7,43,600	7,43,600

You are required to prepare Trading and Profit and Loss Account for the year ended on 31st March 2004 and a Balance Sheet as on that date: You are also given the following further information:

(*a*) Cost of goods in stock on 31st March 2004, Rs. 1,45,000.

(*b*) Abraham had withdrawn goods worth Rs. 5,000 during the year.

(*c*) Printing and Stationery expenses of Rs. 11,000 relating to previous accounting year had not been provided in that year but is paid in this year by debiting outstanding liability.

(*d*) Purchases include purchase of furniture worth Rs. 10,000.

(*e*) Debtors include Rs. 5,000 bad debts.

(*f*) Creditors include a balance of Rs. 4,000 to the credit of a Private Company in respect of which it has been decided and settled with the party to pay only Rs. 1,000.

(*g*) Sales include goods worth Rs. 15,000 sent out to a party on approval and remaining unsold as on 31st March 2004. The cost of the goods was Rs. 10,000.

(*h*) Provision for bad debts is to be created at 5% of Sundry Debtors.

(*i*) Depreciate furniture and fittings by 10%, Motor Car by 20%.

(*j*) The salesman are entitled to a commission of 10% on total sales. (*CA Inter*)

[Ans: G.P. = Rs. 1,80,000; N.P. = Rs. 1,700; B/S = Rs. 3,12,300]

35. From the following balances, prepare Trading and Profit and Loss Account for the year ended 31st December 2004 and Balance Sheet as on that date:

	Dr. Rs	Cr. Rs
Discount	300	150
Land & Buildings	50,000	—
Rent Received	—	4,000
Commission	—	13,000
Bills Payable & Receivable	6,000	17,200
Insurance	600	—
Opening Stock	35,000	—
Rent paid	3,000	—
Trade Expenses	1,200	—
Debtors and Creditors	25,000	56,400
Sales and Purchases	60,500	90,300
Machinery	30,000	—
Loose Tools	2,300	—
Wages	2,700	—
Stationery	800	—
Return of Goods	400	650
Capital and Drawings	6,000	56,000
Cash	1,700	—
Carriage	300	—
Salary	1,900	—
Bank	10,000	—
	2,37,700	2,37,700

Adjustments:

1. Closing on 31st December valued at Rs. 15,400.
2. Rent was unpaid to the extent of Rs. 500.
3. Liability for Trade Expenses Rs. 700.
4. Write off Rs. 500 as Bad Debts.
5. Make a provision of Doubtful Debts at 5% on Sundry Debtors.
6. Provide 2% discount on Debtors.
7. Sales Returns of Rs. 400 has been entered wrongly in purchases.
8. Loose tools valued at Rs. 1,800.
9. Wages include Rs. 500 spent on installation of a new machine.
10. Stationery worth Rs. 150 was consumed by the Proprietor.
11. The Sales Book overadded by Rs. 300.
12. Private purchases of Rs. 200 included in purchases.
13. Debtors account overadded by Rs. 300.

[Ans: G.P. = Rs. 7,850; N.P. = Rs. 13,480; B/S = Rs. 1,37,930]

36. Prepare Trading and Profit and Loss Account for the year ended 31st December 2004 and a Balance Sheet as on that date.

	Dr. Rs	Cr. Rs
Stock on 1st Jan. 2004	10,000	—
Capital and Drawings	5,000	20,000
Telephone	3,000	—
Bank Overdraft	—	1,000
Machinery	10,000	—
Sundry Debtors and Creditors	10,000	3,700
Sales Returns	1,000	—
Premises	21,000	—
Sales and Purchases	20,000	48,000
Mortgage	—	12,000
Bills Payable and Receivable	1,500	2,200
Petty Cash	50	—
Fittings	550	—
Trading Expenses	400	—
Bad Debts	400	—
Wages	4,000	—
	86,900	86,900

Adjustments:

1. Mr. Ramdas, who deals in electrical goods, used electrical goods worth Rs. 3,000 for the shop.
2. Goods worth Rs. 200 returned by a customer were included in purchases.
3. Machine worth Rs. 1,000 has not been entered in the books and no payment has been paid for.
4. The telephone was obtained, under Own Your Telephone Scheme and free of rent for 5 years.
5. Stock on 31st December 2004 valued at Rs. 11,000.
6. Included among the debtors Rs. 1,000 to Mahesh and included in creditors list Rs. 1,000 to him.
7. Ramdas's wife works in the firm and is allowed a salary of Rs. 100 per month. This amount has been included in Drawings.
8. It was discovered that stock on 1st Jan. 2004 was overcast by Rs. 2,000.
9. Further bad debts Rs. 200.
10. A commission of 10% on the net profit is due to the Manager after charging such commission.

[**Ans:** G.P. = Rs. 29,000, N.P. = Rs. 23,818, Commission to Manager Rs. 2,382, B/S = Rs. 59,300]

37. From the following particulars extracted from the books of Mr. Somu, you are required to prepare a Trading and Profit and Loss Account for the year ended 31st December 2004 and a Balance sheet as on that date, after making the necessary adjustments:

	Rs.		Rs.
Capital Account	2,08,000	Bills Payable	5,000
Drawings Account	12,000	Stock (1 Jan.)	35,000
Purchases	90,000	Wages	32,000
Returns Inwards	2,000	Sundry Creditors	40,000
Land & Buildings	60,000	Postage & Telegrams	1,400
Plant & Machinery	1,00,000	Insurance Charges	1,600
Sales	2,10,000	Gas and Fuel	2,700
Returns Outwards	1,000	Bad Debts	600
Salaries	12,000	Office Rent	2,600
Office Expenses	2,500	Freight & Duty	9,000
Office Furniture & Fixtures	5,000	Loose Tools	2,000
Discount A/c (Dr.)	1,200	Factory Lighting	1,600
Sundry Debtors	26,600	Provision for doubtful debts	800
Investments	40,000	Interest on Investments	4,000
Cash at Bank	26,600	Cash on Hand	2,400

1. Stock on 31st December 2004 was valued at Rs. 66,000.
2. Wages Rs. 1,600 and salaries Rs. 600 were outstanding.
3. Insurance prepaid was Rs. 400.
4. A new machine was installed on 30th September 2004 costing Rs. 14,000, but it was not recorded in the books and no payment was made for it. Wages Rs. 1,000 paid for its erection have been debited to Wages Account.
5. Loose Tools were valued at Rs. 1,600 on 31st December 2004.
6. Depreciate Plant and Machinery by 10% p.a., Furniture and Fixtures by 5% p.a., and Land & Buildings by 2% p.a.
7. Of the Sundry Debtors Rs. 600 are bad and should be written off.
8. Maintain a provision of 5% on Sundry Debtors for doubtful debts.
9. Stock valued at Rs. 1,500 was destroyed by fire on 25.12.2004 but the Insurance Co. admitted a claim for Rs. 1,000 only. *(B. Com., Madurai)*

[Ans. G.P. = Rs. 1,05,600, N.P. = Rs. 73,675, B/S = Rs. 3,30,875]

38. From the following Trial Balance, prepare Trading and Profit and Loss Account for the year ended 31st December 2004 and a Balance Sheet as on the date:

	Dr. *Rs*	*Cr.* *Rs*
Stock on 1st Jan., 2004	65,000	—
Cash in hand	2,150	—
Cash at Bank	80,000	—
Returns of Goods	6,000	5,000
Investments	30,000	—
Insurance	2,000	—
Sundry Debtors and Creditors	10,000	84,700
Discounts Allowed and Received	1,000	1,100
Bad Debts	3,000	—
Carriage	1,500	—
Bills Receivable and Payable	40,000	34,000
Rent	5,500	—
Furniture	11,000	—
Repairs	150	—
Lighting	400	—
Interest on Loan	1,200	—
Drawings and Capital	8,000	1,50,000
Postage and Telegram	800	—
Printing and Stationery	900	—
Trading Expenses	2,100	—
Salaries and Wages	35,000	—
Purchases and Sales	4,80,000	5,50,000
Commission	—	900
Loan from baby	—	50,000
	8,75,700	8,75,700

Adjustments:

1. Stocks on 31st December 2004 was valued Rs. 98,000.
2. Outstanding Liabilities:

   Rent Rs. 500

   Salaries Rs. 1,000

3. Interest due to Baby Rs. 150
4. Commission earned but not received Rs. 300.
5. Interest accrued on Investments Rs. 900.
6. Insurance unexpired Rs. 200.
7. Depreciate Furniture by 5%.
8. Make provision for Discount on Debtors at 2%.
9. Make provision for Bad and Doubtful Debts at 5%.
10. Calculate interest on Capital at 5%
11. Charge interest on Drawings Rs. 400.
12. Opening stock overvalued by Rs. 2,000.
13. Goods worth Rs. 500 taken by the Proprietor for private use.

[Ans: G.P. = Rs. 1,03,000; N.P. = Rs. 38,150; B/S = Rs. 3,55,100]

39. The following is the Trial Balance of Mr. X at 31st Decembber 2004 and it is desired to prepare Final Accounts showing the results of the transactions for the year:

Debit Balances:	*Rs.*		*Rs.*
Plant & Machinery	5,000	Insurance	30
Office Furniture & Fittings	260	Advertising	565
Opening Stock	4,800	General Expenses	100
Motor Vans	1,200	Bad Debts	250
Sundry Debtors	4,570	Discount Allowed	650
Cash in Hand	40		
Cash at Bank	650	*Credit Balances:*	
Wages: Factory	15,000		
Office	1,400	Capital	4,000
Purchases	21,350	Sales	48,000
Bills Receivable	720	Bills Payable	560
Returns Inwards	930	Sundry Creditors	5,200
Drawings	700	Doubtful Debt Reserve	250
Rent	600	Returns Outwards	550
Factory Lighting & Heating	80	Discount Received	370
Telephone	35		

The following adjustments are to be made:

1. Stock on 31st December 2004 valued at Rs. 5,200.
2. Rent due, but not paid till 31st Dec. 2004 Rs. 200.
3. 3 Months factory lighting and heating due but not paid Rs. 30.
4. Insurance paid in advance Rs. 10.
5. 10% depreciation to be written off Plant and Machinery.
6. 5% depreciation to be written off Furniture.
7. 25% depreciation to be written off motor van.
8. Write off further bad debts Rs. 70.
9. The Provision for Doubtful Debts to be increased to Rs. 300.
10. Discounts of 2.5% on Debtors and Creditors are to be anticipated.
11. Bills Receivable Rs. 400, not yet due, were discounted on 31st Dec. 2004.

(*B. Com., Madurai*)

[Ans. G.P. = Rs. 11,560, N.P. = Rs. 7,202, B/S = Rs. 16,362]

40. The following is the schedule of balances as on 31st Dec. 2004 extracted from the books of Mr. Ram, who carries on business under the name and style of Ram Shankar Enterprises at Bombay:

	Dr. Rs	Cr. Rs
Cash in hand	1,400	—
Cash at Bank	2,600	—
Sundry Debtors and Creditors	86,000	43,000
Stock on 1st Jan. 2004	62,000	43,000
Furniture and Fixtures	21,400	—
Office Equipment	16,000	—
Buildings	60,000	—
Motor Car	20,000	—
Loan from Viswanath	—	30,000
Reserve for Bad Debts	—	3,000
Purchases and Purchase Returns	1,40,000	2,600
Sales and Sales Returns	4,200	2,30,000
Salaries	11,000	—
Rent for godown	5,500	—
Interest on Loan (Viswanath)	2,700	—
Rates and Taxes	2,100	—
Discount allowed to Debtors	2,400	—
Discount received from Creditors	—	1,600
Freight on Purchases	1,200	—
Carriage outwards	2,000	—
Drawings and Capital	12,000	1,62,000
Printing and Stationery	1,800	—
Electric Charges	2,200	—
Insurance Premium	5,500	—
General Office Expenses	3,000	—
Bad Debts	2,000	—
Bank Charges	1,600	—
Motor Car Expenses	3,600	—
	4,72,200	4,72,200

Prepare Trading and Profit and Loss Account for the year ended 31st December 2004 and the Balance Sheet as at that date after making provision for the following:

1. Depreciate:
   (*a*) Buildings by 5% p.a.
   (*b*) Furniture and Fixtures by 10% p.a. One steel table purchased during the year for Rs. 1,400 was sold for same price but the sale proceeds were wrongly credited to Sales Account.
   (*c*) Office Equipment by 15%. Purchases of a type-writer during the year for Rs. 4,000 has been wrongly debited to Purchase Account.
   (*d*) Motor Car by 20%.
2. Value of stock at the close of the year Rs. 44,000.
3. One month's rent for godown is outstanding.
4. One month's salary is outstanding.
5. Interest on loan from Viswanath is payable @ 12% p.a. This Loan was taken on 1st Feb. 2004.
6. Reserve for bad debts is to be maintained at 5% on Sundry Debtors.
7. Insurance premium includes Rs. 4,000 paid towards proprietor's Life Insurance Policy and the balance of the insurance charges cover the period from 1.1.2004 to 31.3.2005.

8. Half of the buildings are used for residential purposes of Ram. *(C.A. Entrance)*

[Ans: G.P. = Rs. 71,800; N.P. = Rs. 18,400; B/S = Rs. 2,38,000]

41. Mr. Ram started a business in Madras. He invested Rs. 1,20,000 in his business, on 1st April 2004. He draws Rs. 1,000 for his personal expenses every month from 30th April 2004.

The following figures are extracted from his books on 31st Dec. 2004

	Rs.		*Rs.*
Purchases	3,10,000	Bad Debts	2,000
Cartage	5,000	Sundry Debtors	45,000
Salaries and Wages	24,000	Bills Receivable	30,000
Electricity Charges	4,500	Cash in hand	8,997
Travelling	8,900	Sales	3,00,000
Telephone	4,300	Income from personal Investment	20,000
Advertisement	10,000		
Repairs and Renewals	3,30	Creditors	85,000
Plant and Machinery	1,50,000	Bank Overdraft	80,000
		Building (Cr.)	10,000

You are required to prepare a Trading and Profit and Loss Account for the period ended 31st December 2004, and also the Balance Sheet as on that date after taking into consideration the following further information:

(1) Purchase include Rs. 10,000 representing the value of furniture purchased.

(2) Rs. 4,000 representing erection wages on Plant and Machinery are debited to Salaries and Wages Account.

(3) Electricity charges include Rs. 2,500 paid as deposit to Electric Supply Company. There are bills outstanding to the extent of Rs. 500.

(4) Advertisement includes Rs. 4,000 representing the cost of a neon sign.

(5) A dishonoured bill of Rs. 5,000 stands debited to the Debtors. 50% thereof considered doubtful and has to be provided accordingly.

(6) A debtor for Rs. 1,000 was declared insolvent on 30th December 2004, and it is expected that nothing would be recovered from his estate.

(7) Provide 5% discount on net realisable debtors.

(8) Ram received Rs. 25,000 in respect of a business with Gopal. The sum received stood credited to Sundry Creditors. It is noted that a sum of Rs. 5,000 was due to Ram as his share of profit from that business.

(9) During the period there was a fire damaging stock costing Rs. 50,000. The damaged goods were sold for Rs. 20,000. This sum of Rs. 20,000 is included in sales. The insurance company paid Rs. 25,000 towards the loss of stock. The godown containing the stock was also damaged to the extent of Rs. 15,000 which has also been paid by the insurance Company. The total amount received from the Insurance Company was credited to Building Account.

(10) The bank overdraft was given on the hypothecation of stock-in-trade. You are informed that the bank had a margin of 33-1/3% and the overdraft balance on 31st Dec. 2004 was the maximum which could have been drawn on the basis of this margin.

(11) The manager of the firm entitled to a commission of 5% on Gross profit.

(12) Provide depreciation on Plant and Machinery by 10% p.a., Furniture and Fittings by 10% p.a. and Buildings by 5% p.a. Depreciation to be provided on closing balance.

[Ans: G.P. = Rs. 1,45,000; N.P. = Rs. 72,009; B/S = Rs. 3,70,759]

42. You are required to prepare the Trading and Profit and Loss Account for the year ended 31st Dec. 2004 and a Balance Sheet as on that from the following Trial Balance of Mr. Prem:

	Dr. Rs	Cr. Rs
Capital and Drawings	10,000	1,08,000
Stock on 1st Jan. 2004	46,800	—
Sales and Sales Returns	8,600	2,89,600
Purchases and Purchase Returns	2,43,100	5,800
Freight and Carriage	18,600	—
Rent and Taxes	5,700	—
Salaries and Wages	9,300	—
Sundry Debtors and Creditors	24,400	14,800
Bank Loan @ 6% from 2004	—	20,000
Interest on Bank Loan	900	—
Printing and Advertising	14,600	—
Income from Investment	—	340
Cash at Bank	8,000	—
Discount Received	—	4,190
Investments	5,000	—
Furniture and Fittings	1,800	—
Discount Paid	7,450	—
General Expenses	3,910	—
Audit Fees	700	—
Insurance	600	—
Travelling Expenses	2,330	—
Postage and Telegram	470	—
Cash in hand	380	—
Deposit with Bank	30,000	—
	4,42,730	4,42,730

Make the following adjustments:

1. Stock on 31st Dec. 2004 was Rs. 78,600.
2. Included among the debtors is Rs. 3,000 due from Amin and included among the creditors is Rs. 1,000 due to him.
3. The effect of advertising being not yet expired, a quarter of printing and advertising is to be carried forward to next year.
4. Make a provision of 2% for discount on Debtors and Creditors and 5% for Doubtful Debts.
5. A depreciation of 10% is to be written off on furniture and fitting.
6. Wages owing on 31st Dec. 2004 Rs. 300, Salaries owing Rs. 500; and carriage owing Rs. 100.
7. Insurance paid in advance on 31st Dec. 2004 Rs. 80.
8. Furniture which stood at Rs. 600 in the books on 1st Jan. 2004 was disposed of at Rs. 290 on 30th June 2004, in part exchange of new furniture costing Rs. 520. A net invoice Rs. 230 was passed through the Purchase Day Book.
9. Purchase invoice amounting to Rs. 400 had been omitted from books.
10. A new sign costing Rs. 100 included in advertising.
11. Two dishonoured cheques for Rs. 200 and Rs. 300 had not been entered in the Cash Book. The first for Rs. 200 is known to be bad and is to be written off. In the case of the second cheque for Rs. 300, it is expected that the debtor would be in a position to pay dividend of 75 paise in the rupee.
12. Private purchase amounting to Rs. 600 had been included in the purchase Day Book.
13. Charge full year's interest on Deposit with the Bank @ 10% p.a.

14. Provide for outstanding interest on Bank loan for the last quarter. *(B. Com., Calcutta)*

[**Ans:** G.P. = Rs. 57,230; N.P. = Rs. 19,313; B/S = Rs. 1,51,829]

43. The following Trial Balance relates to the business of Mr. Patnaik as on 31st March 2004:

	Dr. *Rs.*		*Dr.* *Rs.*
Purchases	5,20,000	Capital account	1,20,000
Buildings	70,000	Sales	7,90,000
Machineries	90,000	Hire Vendors Account	30,000
Travelling Expenses	4,200	Sundry Creditors	96,000
Printing Charges	1,800	Bills Payable	12,000
Miscellaneous Expenses	76,600	Bank Loan (taken on 1.10.91)	60,000
Consignment	84,000	Discount Received	2,400
Sundry Debtors	80,000	Furniture (Cr. Balance)	10,000
Bills Receivable	15,000		
Opening Stock	92,000		
Salaries	18,900		
Cash in hand	1,600		
Cash at Bank	31,600		
Insurance	3,500		
Advertisements	6,000		
Discounts Allowed	1,200		
Drawings	20,000		
Addition to Furniture	4,000		
	11,20,400		11,20,400

Additional Information given:

1. The Miscellaneous expenses include Rs. 1,000 given to his son in connection with his education.
2. A fire occurred on 1st April 2003 and as a result a large part of the building worth Rs. 40,000 was destroyed. Furniture worth Rs. 5,000 was also destroyed. A sum of Rs. 30,000 was recovered from Insurance Company and was credited to Furniture Account. It was observed that the policy of Insurance did not cover furniture.
3. Consignment Account represents goods costing Rs. 80,000 sent on consignment and consignor's expenses thereon. The consignee sold 3/4 of the goods at a profit of 20% on sales. He was allowed a commission of 4% on actual collections which amounted to Rs. 65,000. There was a bad debt of Rs. 1,500. None of the consigner's transactions has been entered in the books and no remittance was made by the consignee till date.
4. Purchase include Rs. 30,000 for a new machinery acquired on Hire Purchase system. Upto 31st March 2004, two quarterly instalments of Rs. 5,000 each became due but remained unpaid. Interest is chargeable at 5% p.a.
5. The value of stock at cost on 31st March 2004 as per physical verification amounted to Rs. 70,000 including goods costing Rs. 6,000 despatched on 12th April 2004 though sales invoice dated 28th March 2004 was into account during the year.
6. Depreciation is to be provided on Buildings at 5% p.a., on Machinery at 10% p.a. and on furniture 10% p.a.
7. Interest on Bank loan to be provided at 12% p.a.
8. It is desired to show Profit or Loss on consignment in the Profit and Loss Account.

You are required to prepare the Trading and Profit and Loss Account for the year ended 31st March 2004 and a Balance Sheet as on that date after taking into consideration the above mentioned information. *(CA)*

[**Ans:** G.P. = Rs. 2,72,000; N.P. = 1,38,050; B/S = Rs. 4,39,400]

Chapter 8

Errors and Their Rectification

Classification of Errors – Types of Errors – How to Correct Errors as They are Found – Pre-Suspense and Pre-Final Account Stage – Post-Trial Balance and Pre-Final Account Stage – Post-Suspense and Post-Final Account Stage – Questions – Objective Type of Questions – Theoretical Questions – Practical Problems.

Before entering into this chapter, go back to Chapter 3 which explains the kinds of errors in details. In this chapter, we discuss, the adjustment of errors discovered. An error is a mistake and rectification means correcting the mistakes that have occurred. A firm is primarily interested in finding out its true profit and financial position, at every period of closing the trading year. The staff in-charge of the account section put best effort to be careful and most accurate in recording the transactions. But due to human element present in the work and in spite of the best efforts, occurring of mistakes or errors is not unlikely. Errors, committed in the recording of the transactions, affect the final accounts of the concern. Therefore, the book-keeper and Accountant should be keen to locate such errors and rectify them and thus the correct profit or loss and financial position of the firm can be ascertained.

We have explained the preparation and presentation of Final Accounts. The basic information for these Final Accounts is supplied by the Trial Balance. It determines to a great extent the accuracy of books of accounts. However, the Trial Balance provides only a proof of the arithmetical accuracy of the books of accounts. It simply assures that for every debit there is an equivalent credit entry. Inspite of the agreed Trial Balance, it is not possible to say that there are no errors in the books of accounts. For instance errors of principle, errors of complete omission etc. do not affect the agreement of the Trial Balance. If such errors happen, the Trial Balance will tally, but the books of account cannot be taken as accurate. We have already learned the Trial Balance, errors disclosed and not disclosed by Trial Balance and the location of errors in the books of accounts. Refer to Chapter 3.

It may be mentioned that already classification of errors have been dealt with in the Chapter 3. However, they are discussed for the purpose of rectification.

CLASSIFICATION OF ERRORS

Effors can be classified into the following:

1. Errors of Omission
2. Errors of Commission
3. Errors of Principle
4. Errors of Wrong Posting
5. Compensating Errors

(For details, refer to Chapter 3)

Before discussing the errors with their rectifications, it becomes necessary to know the impact on Trial Balance. Thus, it is studied under two categories of errors:

Errors

Affect the Trial Balance (A)	Do not affect the Trial Balance (B)

(A) The following errors affect the Trial Balance :

(1) Wrong totalling of subsidiary books

(2) Posting of the wrong amount

(3) Posting an amount to wrong side of an Account

(4) Errors of partial omission

(5) Wrong balancing of ledger accounts

(6) Posting twice to a ledger

(7) Omission of any accounts from the Trial Balance, etc.

(B) The following errors do not affect the Trial Balance.

(1) Errors of principle

(2) Errors of omission

(3) Posting to wrong Account

(4) Errors of recording in subsidiary books

(5) Compensating errors

All those points have been discussed, in detail, in Chapter 3.

TYPES OF ERRORS

For rectification of errors, the errors can be divided into two types: (1) One sided error, that is, errors affecting one account only; and (2) Two sided error, that is, errors affecting two or more accounts.

HOW TO CORRECT ERRORS AS THEY ARE FOUND

If a posting of an item is omitted, then the amount should be posted immediately. But if a wrong posting is made, it can be corrected by passing an adjusting entry. It is important to note that erasing or striking of figures should be avoided. Erasing or striking of figures tend to discredit the records and gives chances for fraud. It also reduces the legal value of the books of accounts, apart from giving a dirty look. Thus erasing or striking off the figures in the books of accounts are strictly avoided.

The method of rectification varies with the type of errors and the time of detection. A Trial Balance is not disturbed by undisclosed errors, for instance, omission of a transaction. A Suspense Account does not appear for such rectification. But Trial Balance disagrees with the disclosed errors. If such mistakes or errors are known, after the preparation of Trial Balance but before the preparation of Final Accounts, errors are to be located and rectified, then revised Trial Balance is prepared (which now agrees because of rectification) and then proceed for the Final Accounts. In case of a rectification, we may first see "What is actually done ?" that is, what errors have been done. Secondly, we may see "what should have been done ?" that is finding the correct entry, which should have been made. Thirdly, make the entry for the correction of error. Consider the following:

Correct the following errors :

1. The purchase of machinery for Rs. 5,000 has been entered in Purchase Day Book.
2. Received Rs. 1,000 from Mahesh but credited to Mohan's Account.
3. A sale of old machinery for Rs. 7,000 has been entered in Sales Account.
4. Rs. 500 paid as wages for erection of a machine has been charged to Repairs Account.
5. Rs. 100 received from Gopal, previously written off, has been credited to Gopal Account.

SOLUTION:

1. What is actually done ? *i.e.* wrong entry:

   What should have been done ? *i.e.* correct entry:

   What should be done now to rectify the error ? Rectification entry:

			Rs	Rs
1. Wrong entry made:	Purchase A/c	Dr.	5,000	
	To Creditors A/c			5,000
Correct entry:	Machinery A/c	Dr.	5,000	
	To Creditors A/c			5,000
Rectification entry:	Machinery A/c	Dr.	5,000	
	To Purchase A/c			5,000

There is no mistake in the Creditors' Account as it has been credited correctly. Purchase Account is wrongly debited instead of Machinery Account. To rectify the error, the debit entry in the Purchase Account has to be transferred to Machinery Account. That is, the wrong debit in the Purchase Account is cancelled by giving a credit entry.

			Rs	Rs
2. Wrong entry made:	Cash Account	Dr.	1,000	
	To Mohan A/c			1,000
Correct entry:	Cash A/c	Dr.	1,000	
	To Mahesh's A/c			1,000
Rectification entry:	Mohan's A/c	Dr.	1,000	
	To Mahesh's Account			1,000

Cash Account is correct. The mistake is that Mohan's account is wrongly credited and Mahesh Account has been omitted to be entered. To rectify the error, we have to cancel the wrong credit by giving an equal debit and credit in Mahesh Account.

			Rs	Rs
3. Wrong entry made:	Customer's A/c	Dr.	7,000	
	To Sales A/c			7,000
Correct entry:	Customer's A/c	Dr.	7,000	
	To Machinery A/c			7,000
Rectification entry:	Sales A/c	Dr.	7,000	
	To Machinery Account			7,000

Customer Account is debited correctly. But Sales Account has been credited instead of crediting Machinery Account. To rectify the error one has to cancel the wrong credit by giving an equal amount of debit in Sales Account and credit Machinery Account.

			Rs	Rs
4. Wrong entry made:	Repairs A/c	Dr.	500	
	To Cash A/c			500
Correct entry:	Machinery A/c	Dr.	500	
	To Cash A/c			500
Rectification entry:	Machinery A/c	Dr.	500	
	To Repair A/c			500

Cash account is correctly credited. But wrongly the debit entry is made to Repairs Account instead of Machinery Account. To rectify the error, debit the Machinery Account and credit the Repairs Account.

			Rs	Rs
5. Wrong entry made:	Cash A/c	Dr.	100	
	To Gopal A/c			100
Correct entry:	Cash A/c	Dr.	100	
	To Bad Debts Recovered A/c			100
Rectification entry:	Gopal A/c	Dr.	100	
	To Bad Debts Recovered A/c			100

Cash Account is correctly debited. Bad Debts Recovered Account must be credited. But by mistake, Gopal Account has been credited. Now the wrong credit given to Gopal Account has to cancel and a credit entry is to be made to Bad Debts Recovered Account.

RECTIFICATION IN DIFFERENT STAGES

Rectification of errors is done in three different stages. From the accounting point of view, the rectification of errors may be classified as under:

RECTIFICATION OF ERRORS (Based on time)

- Stage I (Pre-Trial Balance Stage)
- Stage II (Post TB and Pre-final Account stage)
- Stage III (Post Suspense and Post Final Account Stage)

These stages have been explained below, in details:

(*a*) Errors detected during the book-keeping process and before a Trial Balance is extracted – PRE-TRIAL BALANCE AND PRE-FINAL ACCOUNT STAGE.

(*b*) Errors detected after preparing Trial Balance but before drawing up Final Accounts – POST-TRIAL BALANCE AND PRE-FINAL ACCOUNT STAGE.

(*c*) Errors detected and rectified after preparing Final Accounts – POST-SUSPENSE AND POST-FINAL ACCOUNT STAGE.

Pre-Trial Balance Stage = Pre-Suspense Account Stage

I. PRE-SUSPENSE AND PRE-FINAL ACCOUNT STAGE

This is a stage where the final Trial Balance is not prepared. Rough Trial Balance is drawn and totals are done. If the totals of the Trial Balance disagree, then we have to take steps which have been explained in Chapter 3. If still the Trial Balance is not agreed, the errors are to be found out. The errors are rectified in the Rough Trial Balance and final Trial Balance is made for the preparation of Final Accounts. Consider the following examples :

Example : Purchase of furniture from Mahesh & Company for Rs. 1,000 entered in the Purchase Book.

This is an error of principle. Here debit is wrongly given to Purchase Account, instead of Furniture Account. WHAT IS DONE AND WHAT IS NOT DONE ARE ERRORS. What is done, that is, Purchase Account is debited (which should not have been debited) and it is an error. What is not done, that is, Furniture Account is not debited and it is an error. Mahesh & Company are credited with Rs. 1,000 and is correct. Now what should we do? The Furniture Account which is not debited, is to be debited and Purchase Account, which is wrongly debited is to be credited. Thus the Rectification Entry is :

		Rs.	Rs.
Furniture Account	Dr.	1,000	
To Purchase Account			1,000

(Here missing debit is debited and wrong debit is credited. This is, purchase of furniture wrongly debited to Purchase Account instead of Furniture Account, now rectified).

Example : A credit purchase of goods for Rs. 500 from Babulal & Company was omitted to be recorded in the Day Book.

This is an error of omission. What is done, that is, the omission. What is not done (i.e. not entered) is an error of omission here. The transaction is left out. Now pass the entry for the transaction, which have been omitted. Then the entry is :

		Rs.	Rs.
Purhase Account	Dr.	500	
To Babulal & Company A/c			500

(Omission of purchases of goods now recorded)

Example : A credit sale for Rs. 200 to John & Company has been entered in the Sales Book but John & Co. have been debited wrongly with Rs. 20.

This is an error of commission. The Sales Account is correct as the total of Sales Book have been credited to Sales Account. The error is that John & Company have been short debited by Rs. 180. When the error is known before the preparation of the final Trial Balance, no journal entry is required. To make the account correct, debit John & Company Account further with Rs. 180.

ILLUSTRATION 8.1

Rectrify the following errors :

1. Purchase Book is overcast by Rs. 700.
2. Sales Book has been undercast by Rs. 300.
3. Purchase Returns Book has been overcast by Rs. 400.
4. Sales Returns Book has been undercast by Rs. 200.

SOLUTION :

S.No. *Effect of Error*	*Rectification Entry*
1. Purchase Book is overcast, Excess debit of Rs. 700 in the Purchase Account is an error of commission. Credits to different accounts from the Purchase Day Book are correctly made. There is no journal entry. It is one-sided error.	Credit the Purchase Account with Rs. 700 to rectify the error of overcast.
2. Sales Book is undercast. Under-credit of Rs. 300 in the Sales Account is an error of commission. Debit to different accounts from the Sales Book is correctly made. It is an one-sided error. There is no journal entry.	Credit the Sales Account further with Rs. 300 to rectify the error of undercast.
3. Purchase Returns Book is overcast. The excess credit of Rs. 400 in the Purchase Returns Account is an error of commission. Debit to different accounts from the Purchase Returns Book is correctly made. It is an one-sided error. There is no journal entry.	Debit the Purchase Returns Account with Rs. 400 to rectify the error of overcast.
4. Sales Returns Book is undercast. Under-debit of Rs. 200 in the Sales Return Account is an error of commission. Credit to different Accounts from the Sales Returns Book is correctly made.	Give a further debit of Rs. 200 to Sales Returns Account to rectify the error.

One-sided Error

The problem, we have solved in Illustration 8.1, is one-sided error. It is possible that the mistake might have been committed on only one-side–Debit or Credit–of an Account. This type of errors can be rectified by passing an additional entry either in the debit side or credit side of the Account. (See the above illustration.)

Two-sided Error

We may come across errors affecting two accounts simultaneously. In such cases, rectification journal entry has to be passed. It has the effect of debiting one account and crediting another account. See the illustration.

ILLUSTRATION 8.2

Rectify the following errors without opening a Suspense Account:

1. A sale to Baba for Rs. 261 has been entered in Sales Book as Rs. 216.
2. The total of the Discount Column on the debit side of the Cash Book is short added by Rs. 50.
3. A typewriter purchased for Rs. 3,000 has been entered in the Purchase Book.
4. An old machine sold for Rs. 800 was entered in the Sales Book.
5. Goods worth Rs. 1,500 sold to Ramlal has been entered in the Purchase Book.

SOLUTION :

			Rs	*Rs*
1.	Baba Account	Dr.	45	
	To Sales Account			45
	(Being sales of Rs. 261 to Baba entered in the Sales Book as Rs. 216. The error now rectified. Rs. 261 – 216 = Rs. 45 which is less than the actual sales amount)			
2.	Because of the error, there is an under-debit of Rs. 50. Therefore, debit the Discount Account further with Rs. 50. This will rectify the error.			

			Rs	Rs
3.	Typewriter Account	Dr.	3,000	
	To Purchase Account			3,000
	(Being purchase of type-writer wrongly entered in the Purchase Account, now rectified) What is done is that wrong debit is given to Purchase Account. There is no entry in the Typewriter Account. Now the debit in the Purchase Account has to be cancelled and Typewriter Account has to be entered.			

			Rs	Rs
4.	Sales Account	Dr.	800	
	To Machinery Account			800
	(The wrong entry made to Sale Account is not rectified. The sales of machine should not have been entered in the Sales Account. Therefore, debit the Sales Account to cancel the wrong entry and credit the Machinery Account, which has not been entered.)			

			Rs	Rs
5.	Ramlal Account	Dr.	3,000	
	To Purchase Account			1,500
	To Sales Account			1,500
	(Being sales made to Ramlal wrongly entered in the purchase book, now corrected.) What is done is that instead of giving a debit to Ramlal Account, credited him with Rs. 1,500. Therefore his account is debited with Rs. 1500 to cancel the credit entry and, again debit with Rs. 1,500 for the sales made to him. Thus total of Rs. 3,000 (1,500 + 1,500) is debited to his account. Then Purchase Account is credited with Rs. 1,500 to cancel the wrong debit entry. Then Sales Account is credited with Rs. 1,500 which has not been credited earlier			

ILLUSTRATION 8.3

Show how you will rectify the following errors :

(1) A credit sale of Rs. 450 to Banker was debited to Bundel.

(2) A purchase of goods for Rs. 750 from Sen was debited to his Account.

(3) An office Almirah purchased for Rs. 750 was debited to Repairs Account.

(4) A sum of Rs. 350 received from a debtor was debited to his Account.

(5) Purchases of goods for the consumption of the proprietor were debited to Purchase Account Rs. 1,000.

(6) Discount Allowed Rs 75 was credited to Discount Receivable A/c

SOLUTION :

			Dr.	Cr.
			Rs	*Rs*
(1)	Banker Account	Dr.	450	
	To Bundel Account			450
	(Being sales made to Banker wrongly debited to Bundel now rectified)			
(2)	Credit Sen's Account with Rs 1,500 (Rs 750 + 750). That is the wrong debit in Sen's Account is cancelled by crediting Rs 750 + credit his account with Rs 750 (which has not been credited).			
			Rs	Rs
(3)	Office Furniture Account	Dr.	750	
	To Repairs Account			750
	(Being the purchase of office furniture wrongly debited to Repairs Account, now rectified)			
(4)	Credit the Debtor's Account with Rs. 700 (Rs 350 + 350) (as in 2)			
			Rs	Rs
(5)	Drawing Account	Dr.	1,000	
	To Purchase Account			1,000
	(Being the purchase of goods for personal consumption wrongly debited to Purchase Account, now rectified)			
(6)	Debit the Discount Allowed Account with Rs. 75, which has not been debited. Debit Discount Receivable Account with Rs. 75, which has been wrongly credited.			

Rectification of error is further simplified :

Steps:

1. First, find out the reversal of the wrong entry already passed.
2. Then, find out the correct entry that should have been passed.
3. After the second step, cancel the common debits and credits of first step and second step. The remaining items represent the rectification entry. See example given on page no. 204.

II. POST-TRIAL BALANCE AND PRE-FINAL ACCOUNT STAGE

When the Trial Balance disagrees, efforts are made to locate the errors and to rectify them. When the errors cannot be located, and the preparation of the Final Accounts is urgent, the difference in the Trial Balance is made good by writing it temporarily in the smaller side of the Trial Balance, under the name of SUSPENSE account. The Suspense Account is only a temporary device which should not be allowed to remain in the books for long. In the next Accounting period, attempts must be made to discover the errors which caused the difference in the Trial Balance. Again if the credit side of the Trial Balance is shorter, the Suspense Account is credited and if the debit side of the Trial Balance is shorter, the Suspense Account is debited. Thus, the Trial Balance is artificially tallied and the Final Accounts are prepared. The Suspence Account is shown in the Balance Sheet. If the Suspense Account shows a debit balance, it appears on the asset side and if it shows a credit balance, it appears on the liability side. For every kind of error–one-sided or two-sided errors–there will be journal entry. The following illustrations clarify the situation.

Example:

	Transactions	Reversal of entry already passed		Rs	Rs	Entry that should have been passed		Rs	Rs	Rectification entry		Rs	Rs
1.	The Purchase of Machinery for Rs 5,000 wrongly entered in the Purchase Day Book.	Creditors A/c	Dr.	5,000		Machinery A/c	Dr.	5,000		Machinery A/c	Dr.	5,000	
		To Purchase A/c			5,000	To Creditors A/c			5,000	To Purchase A/c			5,000
2.	Rs 500 paid as wages for erection of plant has been debited to Repairs Account.	Cash Account	Dr.	500		Plant A/c	Dr.	500		Plant A/c	Dr.	500	
		To Repairs A/c			500	To Cash A/c			500	To Repairs A/c			500
3.	An item of Rs 53 debited to Personal account as Rs 35.	Suspense Account	Dr.	35		Personal A/c	Dr.	53		Personal A/c		18	
		To Personal A/c			35	To Suspense A/c			53	To Suspense A/c			18
4.	A Bills Receivable for Rs 155 was passed through Bills Payable Book. Bill was given by Prem.	Bills Payable A/c	Dr.	155		Bills Receivable	Dr.	155		Bills Receivable	Dr.	155	
		To Prem A/c			155	To Prem. A/c			155	Bills Payable	Dr.	155	
										To Prem. A/c			310
5.	A sale of old furniture amounting to Rs 75 credited to Sales Account.	Sales A/c	Dr.	75		Cash A/c	Dr.	75		Sales A/c	Dr.	75	
		To Cash A/c			75	To Furniture A/c			75	To Furniture A/c			75

ILLUSTRATION 8.4

The Trial Balance of Mr Chandra did not agree and the difference was temporarily put to Suspense Account. Later on the following errors were located. Pass the entries to rectify them.

1. The total of debit side of an Expense Account has been cast in excess by Rs 50.
2. The Sales Account has been totalled short by Rs 100.
3. One item of purchase of Rs 25 has been posted from the Day Book to ledger as Rs 250.
4. The Sale Return of Rs 100 from a party has not been posted to that Account, though the party's Account has been credited.
5. A cheque of Rs. 500 issued to the Supplier's Account (shown under Sundry Creditors) towards his dues has been wrongly debited to the Purchase Account.
6. A credit sale of Rs. 50 has been credited to the Sales and also credited to Sundry Debtors Account.

(B.Com. Bhopal, Allahabad)

SOLUTION :

In this problem, the difference has been placed in the Suspense Account. But only one-sided errors require the use of Suspense Account. Two sided errors are rectified by just passing usual entries in the journal proper.

			Dr.	Cr.
			Rs	*Rs*
1.	Suspense Account To Expense Account (Being the error in totalling of an Expense Account, now rectified)	Dr.	50	50
2.	Suspense Account To Sales Account (Being the mistake in totalling of Sales Account now rectified)	Dr.	100	100
3.	Supplier Account To Suspense Account (Being the wrong excess debited to Supplier Account (Rs. 250 – 25 = Rs. 225), now rectified. There is no error in the Purchase Account as the Purchase Account is debited with the total Purchase Book)	Dr.	225	225
4.	Sales Returns Account To Suspense Account (Being the entry to the Sales Returns Account, which has not been entered)	Dr.	100	100
5.	Sundry Creditors Account To Purchase Account (Being the wrong debit given to Purchase Account, is now rectified)	Dr.	500	500
6.	Sundry Debtors Account To Suspense Account (Being the sales wrongly credited to Debtor's Account, is now rectified)	Dr.	100	100

ILLUSTRATION 8.5

The following mistakes were located in the books of a concern after its books were closed and a Suspense Account was created in order to get the Trial Balance agreed:

1. Sales Day Book was overcast by Rs. 200.
2. A sale of Rs. 500 to Xavier was wrongly debited to the Account of John Xavier.
3. Repair Expenses of Rs. 180 was posted as Rs. 810.
4. A Bill Receivable received from Poppy for Rs. 300 was passed through Bills Payable Books.
5. Legal expenses of Rs 900 paid to advocate Mr. Mohan was debited to his personel account.
6. Cash received from Das was debited to Dasan Account as Rs. 150.
7. While carrying forward the total of one page of the Purchase Book to the next, the amount of Rs. 2,345 was written as Rs. 3,245. *(B.Com. Madras, M.S. Jabalpur)*

(*i*) Find out the amount of the difference in Trial Balance.
(*ii*) Prepare Suspense Account.
(*iii*) Show their effect on last year profit.
(iv) Show the effect of rectification of errors in profit.

SOLUTION :

			Dr. Rs	Cr. Rs
1.	Sales Account	Dr.	200	
	To Suspense Account			200
	(Being overcast in Sales Day Book now rectified)			
2.	Xavier Account	Dr.	500	
	To John Xavier Account			500
	(Being sales made to Xavier wrongly debited to John Xavier Account, now rectified)			
3.	Suspense Account	Dr.	630	
	To Repairs Account			630
	(Being Repairs Account debit of Rs. 810 in place of Rs. 180, is now rectified)			
4.	Bills payable Account	Dr.	300	
	Bills Receivable Account	Dr.	300	
	To Poppy Account			600
	(Being Bills Receivable passed through Bills payable Book, now rectified)			
5.	Legal Expenses Account	Dr.	900	
	To Mohan Account			900
	(Being legal expenses paid, wrongly debited to Mohan Account, now rectified)			
6.	Suspense Account	Dr.	300	
	To Dasan Account			150
	To Das Account			150
	(Being cash received from Das wrongly debited to Dasan Account, now rectified)			
7.	Suspense Account	Dr.	900	
	To purchase Account			900
	(Being excess amount of Rs. 900 (Rs. 3245 – Rs. 2345) debited in Purchase Account, now rectified)			

Statement to Ascertain the Difference in Trial Balance

		Debit Rs	Credit Rs
1.	This will result in excess credit	–	200
2.	This will not affect the Trial Balance	–	–
3.	This will result in excess debit	630	–
4.	This will not affect the Trial Balance	–	–
5.	This will not affect the Trial Balance	–	–
6.	This will result in excess debit	300	–
7.	This will result in excess debit	900	–
	Difference in Trial Balance (Balancing figure)		1,630
		1,830	1,830

Suspense Account

Dr.	Rs		Cr. Rs
To Repairs Account	630	By Difference in Trial Balance (Balancing figure)	1,630
To Dasan Account	150	By Sales Account	200
To Das Account	150		
To Purchase Account	900		
	1,830		1,830

Statement Showing Effect of Errors on Profit
(That is before the rectification)

1. Profit increased by Rs 200
2. No effect on profit
3. Profit decreased by Rs 630
4. No effect on profit
5. Profit increased by Rs 900
6. No effect on profit
7. Profit decreased by Rs 900

Therefore last year's profit was decreased by Rs. 430

The effect on Profit after the rectifications

1. Profit decreases by Rs 200
2. No effect on profit
3. Profit increases by Rs 630
4. No effect on profit.
5. Profit decreases by Rs 900
6. No effect on profit.
7. Profit increases by 900

Therefore, after the rectifications the profit increases by Rs. 430.

ILLUSTRATION 8.6

How do you rectify the following errors through a Suspense Account?

1. Furniture purchased for Rs 700 was taken to the Purchase Account.
2. Goods sold on credit to A for Rs. 6,000 were debited to B's Account.

3. Goods worth Rs. 1,000 returned by C were not passed through the Sales Returns Book.
4. A purchase of goods worth Rs. 1,000 from D was entered in the Purchase Book as Rs. 100.
5. An amount of Rs. 2,600 incurred for repairs to Machinery was debited to the Machinery Account.
6. Goods worth Rs. 2,700 purchased from E were posted to the debit side of the Personal Account.
7. An amount of Rs. 500 received in cash from F towards Rent was not posted to Rent Account.
8. An amount of Rs. 600 received from G for cash sales was debited to H's Account.

(*B. Com., Madurai; Madras, MS Allahabad*)

SOLUTION :

				Dr.	Cr.
				Rs	*Rs*
1.	Furniture Account	Dr.		700	
	To Purchase Account				700
	(Being the furniture purchased wrongly debited to Purchase Account, now rectified)				
2.	A's Account	Dr.		6,000	
	To B's Account				6,000
	(Being the wrong debit to B's Account, now rectified)				
3.	Sales Returns Account	Dr.		1,000	
	To C's Account				1,000
	(Being the omission of entry, now rectified)				
4.	Purchase Account	Dr.		900	
	To D's Account				900
	(Being the wrong entry made in the Purchase Book is rectified.) (1,000 – 100 = 900)				
5.	Repairs Account	Dr.		2,600	
	To Machinery Account				2,600
	(Being the rectification of wrong entry made in Machinery Account)				
6.	Suspense Account	Dr.		5,400	
	To E's Account				5,400
	(Being the wrong debit in E's Account, now rectified)				
7.	Suspense Account	Dr.		500	
	To Rent Account				500
	(Being the Rent Account, which is not credited, is now rectified)				
8.	Suspense Account	Dr.		600	
	To H's Account				600
	(Being the wrong debit made to H's account, now rectified).				

ILLUSTRATION 8.7

A Book-keeper having failed to agree the Trial balance, opened a Suspense Account and transferred the difference of Rs. 1709 to the credit of Suspense Account. The following errors were later discovered. Give journal entries and show the Suspense Account:

1. Sales Book was undercast by Rs. 2000.
2. Purchase of Machinery for Rs. 3,000 was passed through the Purchase Book.
3. Goods sold to Raj for Rs. 45 was posted to his account as Rs. 54.
4. Purchase Returns Book was overcast by Rs. 200.
5. The total of the Sales Book page 10 was carried forward as Rs. 1,222 instead of Rs. 1,122.

(B.Com., MS)

SOLUTION :

In the case of those errors which affect only one account introduce Suspense Account to make a journal entry.

			Dr.	Cr.
			Rs	*Rs*
1.	Suspense Account To Sales Account (Being undercasting of sales rectified)	Dr.	2,000	2,000
2.	Machinery Account To Purchase Account (Being the debit given to Purchase Account instead of Machinery Account, now rectified)	Dr.	3,000	3,000
3.	Suspense Account To Raj Account (Being the excess debit given to Raj, now rectified)	Dr.	9	9
4.	Purchase Returns Account To Suspense Account (Being the overcasting of Purchase Returns Book, rectified)	Dr.	200	200
5.	Sales Account To Suspense Account (Being excess carry forward of the total of Sales Book, now rectified)	Dr.	100	100

Suspense Account

Dr.			Cr.
	Rs		*Rs*
To Sales Account	2,000	By Difference in Books Account	1,709
To Raj Account	9	By Purchase Returns Account	200
		By Sales Account	100
	2,009		2,009

ILLUSTRATION 8.8

The Trial Balance of Balan on 31st December 2004, showed a difference of Rs. 580 (excess debit). It was put to a Suspense Account and the books were closed. On going through the books in January 2005, the following errors were discovered. You are required to pass rectifying journal entries and prepare the Suspense Account.

1. Rs. 540 received from Mehta was posted to the debit of his account.
2. Rs. 100 being Purchase Returns was posted to the debit of Purchase Account.
3. Discount Rs. 200 received, entered in the Cash Book was not posted to the ledger.
4. Rs. 574 paid for repairs to motor car was debited to the motor car account as Rs. 174.
5. A sale of Rs. 350 to Sethi was entered in the Sales Book as of Rs. 530.

6. While carrying forward total of one page in Karnal Account, the amount of Rs. 250 was written on the credit side instead of debit side.
7. The purchase of machinery on 1st January 2004 for Rs. 6,000 was entered in the Purchase Account.

(*B.Com., Madurai, Kerala, MS*)

SOLUTION :

			Dr.	Cr.
			Rs	*Rs*
1.	Suspense Account To Mehta Account (Being Rs. 540 received from Mehta wrongly debited to him, now rectified)	Dr.	1,080	1,080
2.	Suspense Account To Purchase Account To Purchase Returns A/c (Being purchase returns of Rs. 100 wrongly debited to Purchase account and omission in Purchase Returns, now rectified)	Dr.	200	100 100
3.	Suspense Account To Discount Account (Being omission in Discount account, now rectified)	Dr.	200	200
4.	Repairs Account To Motor Car Account To Suspense Account (Being repairs to motor car Rs. 574 wrongly debited to Motor Car as Rs. 174, now rectified)	Dr.	574	174 400
5.	Sales Account To Sethi Account (Being sales of Rs. 350, wrongly entered in Sales Book as Rs. 530, now rectified)	Dr.	180	180
6.	Kamal Account To Suspense Account (Being Kamal Account credited with Rs. 250 instead of being debited Rs. 250, now rectified)	Dr.	500	500
7.	Machinery Account To Purchase Account (Being purchase of machinery wrongly debited to purchase account, now rectified).	Dr.	6,000	6,000

Suspense Account

Dr.	*Rs*		Cr. *Rs*
To Mehta Account	1,080	By Balance b/d	580
To Purchase Account	100	By Repairs Account	400
To Purchase Returns Account	100	By Kamal Account	500
To Discount Account	200		
	1,480		1,480

ILLUSTRATION 8.9

The following mistakes were located in the books of a concern after its books were closed and a Suspense Account was opened in order to get the Trial Balance agreed.

1. Sales Day Book was overcast by Rs. 100.
2. A sale of Rs 50 to X was wrongly debited to the Y Account.
3. General expenses of Rs. 18 was posted in the General Ledger as Rs. 80.
4. A Bill Receivable for Rs. 155 was passed through Bills Payable Book. The bill was given by P.
5. Legal expenses of Rs 119 paid to Duftry was debited to his Personal A/c.
6. Cash received from C. Das was debited to G. Das, Rs. 150.
7. While carrying forward the total of one page of the Purchase Book to the next, the amount of Rs. 1,235 was written as Rs. 1,325,

Find out the nature and amount of the Suspense Account and pass entries for the rectification of the above errors in the subsequent year's books.

(B.Com., Madurai, Punjab, Agra)

SOLUTION

			Dr.	Cr.
			Rs	*Rs*
1.	Sales Account	Dr.	100	
	To Suspense Account			100
	(Being Sales Book overcast, now rectified)			
2.	X Account	Dr.	50	
	To Y Account			50
	(Being sales to X, wrongly debited to Y A/c, now rectified)			
3.	Suspense Account	Dr.	62	
	To General Expenses Account			62
	(Being general expenses of Rs. 18, debited as Rs. 80, now rectified)			
4.	Bills Payable Account	Dr.	155	
	Bills Receivable Account	Dr.	155	
	To P Account			310
	(Being Bills receivable from P wrongly entered in Bills Payable Book, now rectified)			
5.	Legal Expenses Account	Dr.	119	
	To Daftry Account			119
	(Being legal expenses paid to Duftry wrongly debited to his account, now rectified)			
6.	Suspense Account	Dr.	300	
	To G. Das Account			150
	To C. Das Account			150
	(Being cash received from C. Das, wrongly debited to G. Das, now rectified)			
7.	Suspense Account	Dr.	90	
	To Purchase Account			90
	(Being carry forward of Rs. 1,325, instead of Rs. 1,235, now corrected)			

Suspense Account

Dr.	Rs		Cr. Rs
To General Expense Account	62	By Difference in Books, on the basis of Trial Balance (balancing figure)	352
To C. Das Account	150	By Sales Account	100
To G. Das Account	150		
To Purchase Account	90		
	452		452

Note: Before the recovery of errors in the books, the Suspense Account showed a Credit Balance of Rs. 352.

III. POST-SUSPENSE AND POST-FINAL ACCOUNT STAGE

This is a stage where the preparation of Trial Balance and Final Accounts is completed. That, if the errors in the accounts are not readily traceable, then the difference in the Trial Balance is placed in the Suspense Account and the Final Accounts – Trading and Profit and Loss Account and Balance Sheet, are prepared. Since the Suspense Account is entered in the Trial Balance it has to be incorporated in the Final Accounts. If the Suspense Account is placed in the Balance Sheet, Suspense Account should be reopened in the next financial year and as and when errors committed in the previous year are located, rectification entry should be made. Thus finally, Suspense Account should completely be closed when all such errors committed in previous year are located and rectified. An error in a nominal account and some real accounts affects the trading result. After the preparation of Final Accounts, nominal account must not be rectified through the concerned nominal accounts. Moreover, the profits disclosed in the previous year differ from the true profits. Therefore, such errors are rectified through Profit and Loss Adjustment Account. It should be remembered that only those rectifying entries are made through Profit and Loss Adjustment Account which are normally related with the items of Trading and Profit and Loss Account. Similarly, after the rectification of errors, the balance of the new Profit and Loss Adjustment Account are transferred to Capital Account.

ILLUSTRATION 8.10

A Trader has agreed his Trial balance by putting the difference in a Suspense Account and has prepared a Trading and Profit and Loss Account and the Balance Sheet. On subsequent scrutiny, the books disclosed several errors as detailed below. Rectify these errors and ascertain the amount carried to Suspense Account.

1. A sale of goods to X for Rs 350 has been credited to his account.
2. Goods purchased from Y amounting to Rs. 750 were entered in the Purchase Day Book but were omitted from Y's account in the Creditors Ledger.
3. An office typewriter purchased for 500 has been passed through the Purchase Account.
4. Goods returned to S. Sen valued Rs. 75 were debited to P. Sen's Account.
5. Repairs to office car of Rs. 750 were debited to the Car Account.
6. Goods sold to Banerji values Rs. 730 have been posted into his account as Rs. 370.

Will the above rectification affect profit figure ? If so, to what extent?

(B. Com., Madurai, Calcutta)

SOLUTION :

			Dr. Rs	Cr. Rs
1.	X Account (Rs 350 × 2) To Suspense Account (Being sales to X Rs. 350, wrongly credited to his account, now rectified)	Dr.	700	700
2.	Suspense Account To Y Account (Being purchase from Y, omitted to be posted, now rectified)	Dr.	750	750

3.	Office Equipment Account To Profit & Loss Adjustment A/c (Being purchase of typewriter, wrongly entered to Purchase Book, now rectified)	Dr.	500	500
4.	S. Sen Account To P. Sen Account (Being goods returned to S. Sen wrongly debited to P. Sen, now rectified)	Dr.	75	75
5.	Profit and Loss Adjustment A/c To Car Account (Being repairs to car wrongly debited to Car, now rectified).	Dr.	750	750
6.	Banerji Account (Rs. 730 – Rs. 370 = Rs. 360) To Suspense Account (Being sales to Banerji Rs. 730, wrongly posted to his account as Rs 370, now rectified)	Dr.	360	360
7.	Capital Account To Profit & Loss Adjustment A/c (Being the balance of Profit and Loss Adjustment Account transferred to Capital Account)	Dr.	250	250

Dr. **Suspense Account** Cr.

	Rs		Rs
To Difference in T.B. (Balancing figure)	310	By X Account	700
To Y Account	750	By Banerji Account	360
	1,060		1,060

Dr. **Profit and Loss Adjustment Account** Cr.

	Rs		Rs
To Car Account	750	By Office Equipment	500
		By Capital Account–transferred	250
	750		750

Note: Account carried to Suspense Account was Rs. 310.

Rectification of the errors results in a decrease of Rs. 250 in the profit for the year.

ILLUSTRATION 8.11

The following errors were discovered in the books of Slack on 31st December 2004. The difference in the Trial Balance had been entered in a Suspense Account and on correction of the errors the Suspense Account was eliminated.

1. The total of the Purchase Day Book had been undercast by Rs 100.
2. The Discount column on the debit side of the Cash Book had been posted to the credit of Discount Received Account as Rs. 20.
3. Rs 76 for repairs to Motor van had been taken to the Motor Van A/c.
4. A cheque received from Quick Rs. 39 had been debited in the Cash Book, but the double entry had not been completed.
5. The Returns Outward Book had been overcast by Rs. 50.

   (*a*) Show by means of Journal entries how these errors would be corrected.

(*b*) Show the Suspense Account bringing out the original difference.

(*c*) The Final Accounts to 31st December 2004 had been prepared on the basis of the incorrect figures. The Net Profit disclosed by these accounts was Rs. 4,320. Show your calculation of the correct Net Profit for the year. (*B. Com., Calcutta, Bombay*)

SOLUTION :

			Dr.	Cr.
			Rs	*Rs*
1.	Profit & Loss Adjustment Account	Dr.	100	
	To Suspense Account			100
	(Being the rectified entry for undercasting the Purchase Day Book)			
2.	Profit & Loss Adjustment Account	Dr.	40	
	To Suspense Account			40
	(Being Discount allowed wrongly credited to Discount Received Account, now rectified)			
3.	Profit & Loss Adjustment Account	Dr.	76	
	To Motor Van Account			76
	(Being repairs to motor van, wrongly debited to motor van, now rectified)			
4.	Suspense Account	Dr.	39	
	To Quick Account			39
	(Being cheque received from Quick not posted from Cash Book, now rectified)			
5.	Profit & Loss Adjustment Account	Dr.	50	
	To Suspense Account			50
	(Being error caused by overcasting in Returns Outward book, now rectified)			

Dr. **Suspense Account** Cr.

	Rs		*Rs*
To Difference in T.B. (Balancing figure)	151	By Profit & Loss Adjustment A/c	100
		By Profit & Loss Adjustment A/c	40
To Quick Account	39	By Profit & Loss Adjustment A/c	50
	190		190

Dr. **Profit and Loss Adjustment Account** Cr.

	Rs		*Rs*
To Suspense Account	100	By Net Profit transferred	4,320
To Suspense Account	40		
To Motor Van Account	76		
To Suspense Account	50		
To Balance, being adjusted as profit	4,054		
	4,320		4,320

EFFECT OF ERRORS ON FINAL ACCOUNTS

Suspense Account is opened to tally the Trial Balance, when accounting errors cause disagreement of Trial Balance. The mistake may be rectified after the preparation of final accounts. In such a case Suspense Account is carried forward to the next accounting year.

If the errors affect the nominal accounts, then the profit will be increased or decreased. This is because all nominal accounts are transferred to Trading and Profit and Loss Account. The profit is increased or decreased on account of errors in nominal accounts. However, Balance Sheet will also be affected by the errors of nominal accounts, because the profit is finally transferred to Capital Account, which appears in Balance Sheet. If errors lie in personal and real accounts, then Balance Sheet is affected and not the profit or loss.

After the preparation of final accounts, nominal accounts should not be rectified through the concerned nominal accounts. Therefore, it is necessary to rectify the errors of the preceding year in such a way that the trading result of the succeeding year in which the errors are rectified, is not affected. Accordingly, rectification of amounts relating to nominal accounts is to be done through a special account styled "Profit and Loss Adjustment Account". After the rectification of errors, the balance in the Profit & Loss Adjustment Account is transferred to Capital Account.

ILLUSTRATION 8.12

The books of Mr. Anandi for the year ending 31st March 2004 were closed with a difference in books carried forward. The following errors were detected subsequently and you are required to pass the necessary rectification entries in the books of 2004-2005.

(*a*) Returns Outward Book was cast Rs. 10 short.

(*b*) The total of the Discount column on the debit side of the Cash Book for March 2004, amounting to Rs. 150, was not posted to the General Ledger.

(*c*) Rs 600 paid for purchase of Office Furniture was posted to the Purchase Account.

(*d*) A credit sale of Rs. 76 was wrongly posted to the Sales Ledger as Rs. 67.

(*e*) The Sales Account was understated by Rs. 1,000 because of wrong carry over in the Sales Day Book.

(f) Closing stock was overstated by Rs. 1,000 by a wrong casting the Inventory.

(*B.Com., Madurai, Kerala, Madras, C.A. Inter*)

SOLUTION :

				Dr.	Cr.
				Rs	*Rs*
(*a*)	Suspense Account To Profit & Loss Adjustment Account (Being the error caused by undercasting in Returns Outward Book, rectified)	Dr.		10	10
(*b*)	Profit & Loss Adjustment Account To Suspense Account (Being total of Discount column not debited, now rectified)	Dr.		150	150
(*c*)	Office Furniture Account To Profit & Loss Adjustment Account (Being the office furniture, wrongly debited to Purchase Account, now rectified)	Dr.		600	600
(*d*)	Customer's Account (76-67) To Suspense Account (Being credit sales of Rs. 76, wrongly debited to customer account as Rs. 67, now rectified)	Dr.		9	9
(*e*)	Suspense Account To Profit & Loss Adjustment A/c (Being Sales Account wrongly understated, now rectified).	Dr.		1,000	1,000
(*f*)	Profit & Loss Adjustment Account To Opening Stock Account (Being closing stock wrongly overstated, now rectified).	Dr.		1,000	1,000
	Profit & Loss Adjustment Account To Capital Account (Being the increase in the profit due to rectification is transferred to Capital Account) (Rs. 10 + 600 + 1,000 – 150 – 1,000)	Dr.		460	460

ILLUSTRATION 8.13

Write the rectification entries of the following in (*a*) Pre-Suspense stage (*b*) Post-Suspense and Pre-Final Account Stage and (*c*) Post-Suspense and Post-Final Account Stage:

SOLUTION:

Errors (1)	*Rectification Entries* Pre-Suspense & Pre-Final Account Stage (2)	Rs	Rs	Post-Suspense & Pre-Final Account Stage (3)	Rs	Rs	Post-Suspense & Post-Final Account Stage (4)	Rs	Rs
1. Sales of goods to X for Rs 100 remains unrecorded	X Account Dr. To Sales Account	100	 100	X Account Dr. To Sales Account	100	 100	X Account Dr. To P & L Adj. A/c	100	 100
2. Depreciation of Rs 1000 on plant remains unrecorded	Depreciation A/c Dr. To Plant A/c	1,000	 1,000	Depreciation A/c Dr. To Plant A/c	1,000	 1,000	P & L Adj. A/c Dr. To Plant A/c	1,000	 1,000
3. Sales Book undercast by Rs 10	Credit Sales A/c with Rs. 10			Suspense A/c Dr. To Sales A/c	10	 10	Suspense A/c Dr. To P & L Adj. A/c	10	 10
4. Bills Payable Book overcast by Rs 30	Debit Bills Payable A/c with Rs 30			Bills Payable A/c Dr. To Suspense A/c	30	 30	Bills Payable A/c Dr. To Suspense A/c	30	 30
5. Purchase Returns Book total Rs 430 unticked	Credit Purchase Returns A/c with Rs 430			Suspense A/c Dr. To Purchase Returns A/c	430	 430	Suspense A/c Dr. To P & L Adj. A/c	430	 430
6. Sales of old furniture for Rs 500 credited to Machinery Account	Machinery A/c Dr. To Furniture A/c	500	 500	Machinery A/c Dr. To Furniture A/c	500	 500	Machinery A/c Dr. To Furniture A/c	500	 500
7. Purchase of Machinery from Ram for Rs 5000 entered in Purchase book	Machinery A/c Dr. To Purchase A/c	5,000	 5,000	Machinery A/c Dr. To Purchase A/c	5,000	 5,000	Machinery A/c Dr. To P & L Adj. A/c	5,000	 5,000
8. Wages of 200 spent on the constructions of Building charged to Wages A/c	Building A/c Dr. To wages A/c	200	 200	Building A/c Dr. To Wages A/c	200	 200	Building A/c Dr. To P & L Adj. A/c	200	 200

	(1)	(2)				(3)				(4)			
				Rs	Rs			Rs	Rs			Rs	Rs
9	Repairs to furniture Rs	Repairs A/c	Dr.	300		Repairs	Dr.	300		P & L Adj. A/c	Dr.	300	
	300 debited to Furniture A/c	To Furniture A/c			300	To Furniture A/c			300	To Furniture A/c			300
10.	Rs 100 paid as freight to	Debit Plant A/c	100			Plant A/c	Dr.	100		Plant A/c	Dr.	100	
	plant debited to freight	Credit Freight A/c	110			Suspense A/c	Dr.	10		Suspense A/c	Dr.	10	
	A/c Rs 110					To Freight A/c			110	To P & L Adj. A/c			110
11	Sales to X Rs 200 debited	Debit X A/c with Rs 180				X account	Dr.	180		X Account	Dr.	180	
	to his account as Rs 20					To Suspense A/c			180	To Suspense A/c			180
12.	Sales of Rs 500 made to A	Debit A with Rs 500				Debit A with Rs 500				A A/c	Dr.	500	
	entered against B, in the	Debit B with Rs 50				Debit B with Rs 50				B A/c	Dr.	50	
	Purchase Book as Rs 50	Credit Purchase A/c with Rs 50				Credit Purchase A/c with 50				To P & L Adj. A/c			550
		Credit Sales A/c with Rs 500				Credit Sales A/c with Rs 500							
13.	Goods sold to A for Rs	A's A/c	Dr.	2,000		A's A/c	Dr.	2,000		A's A/c	Dr.	2,000	
	1000 entered in Purchase	To Purchase A/c			1,000	To Purchase A/c			1,000	To P & L A/c			2,000
	Book	To Sales A/c			1,000	To Sals A/c			1,000				
14.	Purchase Returns Book	Debit Purchase Returns A/c				Purchase Returns A/c	Dr.	70		P & L Adj. A/c	Dr.	70	
	overcast by Rs 70	with Rs 70				To Suspense A/c			70	To Suspense A/c			70
15.	Private purchases Rs 500	Drawings A/c	Dr.	500		Drawings A/c	Dr.	500		Drawings A/c	Dr.	500	
	included in the Purchases A/c	To Purchase A/c			500	To Purchase A/c			500	To P & L Adj. A/c			500

ILLUSTRATION 8.14

The following errors were committed by the Accountant of a firm :

(*a*) Cash Rs. 350 paid to Triman Company posted as Rs. 530.

(*b*) Purchase of stationary worth Rs. 150 remained unposted from Cash Book.

(*c*) Rs. 260 paid for purchase of new office furniture was charged to office expense account (ignore depreciation).

(*d*) Credit sale to Trivedi of Rs. 300 was posted to the credit of his account.

(*e*) A purchase of Rs. 420 from Mantri was passed through the Sales Day Book as Rs. 240.

How would you rectify the errors assuming that :

(*i*) They were detected before preparing Trial Balance.

(*ii*) They were detected after preparing Trial Balance, but before preparing final accounts (the difference being taken to Suspense Account).

(*iii*) They were detected after preparing Final Accounts.

(CAIIB) (B.Com. Madurai Madras)

SOLUTION :

Journal Entries

	Pre-Trial Balance Stage	*Post Trial Balance & Pre-Final Account Stage*				*Post-Trial Balance & Post-Final Account Stage*			
				Rs	Rs			Rs	Rs
(*a*)	The error is one-sided. To rectify the error, credit Triman Company with Rs. 180 (530 – 350). No journal entry is required	Suspense Account To Triman Company	Dr.	180	 180	Suspense Account To Triman Company	Dr.	180	 180
(*b*)	The error is one-sided. To rectify the error, debit Stationery Account with Rs. 150. No journal entry is required	Stationery Account To Suspense Account	Dr.	150	 150	Profit & Loss Adj A/c To Suspense A/c	Dr.	150	 150
(*c*)	This is a two-sided error. Entry is — Rs. Rs. Office Furniture A/c Dr. 260 To Office Expenses A/c 260	Office Furniture A/c To Office Expenses A/c	Dr.	260	 260	Office Furniture A/c To Profit & Loss Adj A/c	Dr.	260	 260
(*d*)	The error is one-sided. Trivedi Account credited instead of being debited. To rectify the error, debit his account with Rs. 600	Trivedi Account To Suspense A/c	Dr.	600	 600	Trivedi Account To Suspense A/c	Dr.	600	 600
(*e*)	This is a two-sided error. Credit purchase is passed through Sales Book and the amount entered is also wrong. Sales Account Dr. 240 Purchase Account Dr. 420 To Mantri Account 660	Sales Account Purchase Account To Mantri Account	Dr. Dr.	240 420	 660	Profit & Loss Adj A/c To Mantri A/c	Dr.	660	 660

ILLUSTRATION 8.15

The following is the Balance Sheet as on 31st December 2004.

Balance Sheet as on 31st December 2004

	Rs		Rs
Capital	98,500	Furniture & other fixed Assets	59,500
Net Profit	45,700	Stock	61,000
Loan	55,710	Debtors	38,190
Creditors	22,150	Fixed Deposits	25,750
		Bank	19,820
		Drawings	14,200
		Suspense A/c	3,600
	2,22,060		2,22,060

On scrutiny the following errors were discovered:

(*a*) Closing stock was overvalued by Rs. 4,000.

(*b*) A sale of Rs 2,300 was recorded in Sales Day Book as Rs 3,200 though it was rightly posted in Sales Account.

(c) The total of one page of Purchase Day Book was carried forward as Rs 3,800 instead of Rs 8,300.

(d) Outstanding telephone bill of Rs 510 was not recorded in the books.

(*e*) A collection of Rs 2,000 from a customer was posted in the creditors Account.

(*f*) Rent of one month of Rs. 2,500 was recorded in the books as rent of the residential house of the proprietor.

(*g*) Some old furniture were purchased at Rs 2,000 for resale but they were recorded in the books as fixed assets and depreciation was charged at 10% p.a.

(*h*) A fixed Deposit of Rs 5,000 matured and Rs 7,500 was realised. But the entire amount was creditired to Fixed Deposit Account

Show necessary journal entries to rectify the errors, prepare a Profit and Loss Adjustment Account and the Balance Sheet after the rectification.

(B.Com. (Hons.) Calcutta)

SOLUTION :

Journal

			Dr. Rs	Cr. Rs
(*a*)	Profit and Loss Adjustment A/c	Dr.	4,000	
	To Stock A/c.			4,000
	(Being rectification made for over valuation of closing stock)			
(*b*)	Suspense A/c	Dr.	900	
	To Sundry Debtors A/c			900
	(Being sale of 2,300 posted to Debtors account as Rs 3,200, now rectified)			
(*c*)	Profit and Loss Adjustment A/c	Dr	4,500	
	To Suspense A/c			4,500
	(Being wrong carry forward of Rs. 8,300–3,800, in Purchase Account Book, now rectified)			
(*d*)	Profit and Loss Adjustment A/c	Dr.	510	
	To O/S Telephone Bill A/c			510
	(Being omission of entry, now made)			

(e)	Sundry Creditors A/c Dr. To Sundry Debtors A/c (Being wrong credit made to creditors account, now rectified)	2,000	2,000
(f)	Profit and Loss Adjustment A/c Dr. To Drawings A/c (Being office rent wrongly recorded now rectified)	2,500	2,500
(g)	Stock A/c Dr. To Fixed Assets A/c (Being purchase of furniture wrongly entered in Fixed Assets, now rectified)	2,000	2,000
	Fixed Assets A/c Dr. To Profit and Loss Adjustment A/c (Being depreciation charged thereon is now cancelled)	200	200
(h)	Fixed Deposit A/c Dr. To Profit and Loss Adjustment A/c (Being interest credited to Fixed Deposit A/c, now rectified)	2,500	2,500

Dr. Profit and Loss Adjustment Account Cr.

	Rs		Rs
To Stock A/c	4,000	By Net profit	45,700
To Suspense A/c	4,500	By Stock A/c	200
To O/S Telephone Bill A/c	510	By Fixed Deposit A/c	2,500
To Drawings A/c	2,500		
To Capital (correct net profit)	36,890		
	48,400		48,400

Dr. Suspense Account Cr.

	Rs		Rs
To Difference in TB	3,600	By Profit & Loss Adjustment A/c	4,500
To Sundry Debtors A/c	900		
	4,500		4,500

Balance Sheet as on 31st Dec. 2004

		Rs		Rs
Capital Account	98,500		Furniture and Fixed	
Add: Net Profit	36,890	1,35,390	Assets (59,500 – 1,800)	57,700
Loan A/c		55,710	Stock A/c	
			(Rs. 61,000 + 2,000 – 4,000)	59,000
Sundry Creditors			Sundry Debtors	
(Rs 22,150 – 2,000)		20,150	(Rs 38,190 – 2000 – 900)	35,290
O/S Telephone Bill		510	Fixed Deposit (Rs 25,750 + 2,500)	28,250
			Bank	19,820
			Drawings (Rs. 14,200 – 2,500)	11,700
		2,11,760		2,11,760

MISCELLANEOUS

ILLUSTRATION 8.16

The Trial Balance of Ramco, Madras, did not tally as on 31st Dec. 2005. The following errors were detected as a result of checking the books of accounts. Pass the necessary entries to rectify the errors and find out the differences in the Trial Balance :

(*a*) Rs. 60 received from M & Co. on 31.12.2005 was entered in the cash book on 2nd Jan. 2006.

(*b*) The Returns Inward Book for December showed Rs. 200, less in totals.

(*c*) The purchase of a typewriter for Rs. 800 was entered in the Purchase Journal.

(*d*) Wages of workers engaged in construction of Building amounting to Rs. 500, was debited to Wages Account.

(*e*) A purchase of Rs. 671 had been posted to the debt of suppliers Mr. D. Das as Rs. 617.

(*f*) Goods amounting to Rs. 100, had been returned by Mr. Shah and were taken into stock, but no entry was passed for the transaction.

(*g*) Rs. 2,000, paid for purchase of a Motor Cycle for Mr. S (proprietor) had been charged to Miscellaneous Account.

(*h*) A sale of Rs. 300, to Mr. A was credited to his account.

(*i*) A sale of Rs. 1,000, has been passed through Purchase Journal. The customers' account has, however, been correctly debited.

(*I.C.W.A*)

SOLUTION:

In the Books of Ramco.

Journal

Date	*Particulars*		*L.F.*	*Debit*	*Credit.*
2005				*Rs.*	*Rs.*
Dec. 31					
(*a*)	Cash A/c	Dr.		60	
	To M & Co. A/c				60
	(Cash received from M & Co. on 31.12.2005 but wrongly recorded on 2.1.2006, now rectified)				
(*b*)	Returns Inward A/c	Dr.		200	
	To Suspense A/c				200
	(Returns Inward Book was cast short by Rs. 200, now rectified)				
(*c*)	Office Equipment A/c	Dr.		800	
	To Purchases A/c				800
	(Office equipment purchased, but wrongly debited to Purchase Account, now rectified)				
(*d*)	Building A/c	Dr.		500	
	To Wages A/c				500
	(Wages paid for the construction of Building, but wrongly debited to Wages Account, now rectified)				
(*e*)	Suspense A/c	Dr.		1,288	
	To Mr. D.Das A/c				1,288
	(Goods purchased from D.Das for Rs. 671, but wrongly debited to his account by Rs. 617, now rectified)				

(f)	Returns Inward A/c	Dr.	100	
	To Shah A/c			100
	(Goods returned by Shah, but not recorded in the books, now rectified)			
(g)	Drawings A/c	Dr.	2,000	
	To Miscellaneous Expenses A/c			2,000
	(Motor Cycle purchased for the proprietor, but wrongly debited to Miscellaneous Expenses Account, now rectified)			
(h)	A.A/c	Dr.	600	
	To Suspense A/c			600
	(Goods sold to A. but wrongly credited to his account, now rectified)			
(i)	Suspense A/c	Dr.	2,000	
	To Purchase A/c			1,000
	To Sales A/c			1,000
	(Goods sold to customers, but wrongly passed through the Purchase Account, now rectified)			

Dr. **Suspense Account** *Cr.*

	Rs		*Rs*
To Das A/c	1,288	By Difference in Trial balance (*bal. fig*)	2,488
To Purchase A/c	1,000	By Returns Inward A/c	200
To Sales A/c	1,000	By A.A/c	600
	3,288		3,288

ILLUSTRATION 8.17.

Rectify the following errors by way of journal entries and work out their effect on the Profit and Loss Account of the concern:

(*a*) Returns Inwards Book for December was short-totalled by Rs. 100.

(*b*) Rs. 5,810 being cash paid to Hira Chand was debited to Ram Chand as Rs. 5,010.

(*c*) Rs. 1,500 worth of furniture purchased on credit was debited to Purchases Account.

(*d*) A purchase made for Rs. 500 was posted to the Purchases Account as Rs. 50.

(*e*) Wages paid for the erection of machinery amounting to Rs. 700 was debited to Wages Account.

(*f*) Goods purchased for proprietor's use for Rs. 1,000 was debited to Purchases Account.

(*g*) A sum of Rs. 1,000 written-off from machinery had not been posted to Depreciation Account.

(*h*) Rs. 100 received from Raghu had been debited to Sunder.

(*i*) Rs. 1,150 received from Radhey Mohan was debited to his account.

(*j*) Purchase returns worth Rs. 980 to Shri Hari Kishan were not recorded in the books.

[*C.A. Entrance*]

SOLUTION:

Journal

Date	Particulars	L.F.	Debit	Credit.
?				
(a)	Returns Inward A/c Dr.		100	
	To Suspense A/c			100
	(Return Inward book was undercast by Rs. 100, now rectified)			
(b)	Hira Chand A/c Dr.		5,810	
	To Ram Chand A/c			5,010
	To Suspense A/c			800
	(Cash paid to Hira Rs. 5,810 was wrongly debited to Ram Chand A/c as Rs. 5,010, now rectified)			
(c)	Furniture A/c Dr.		1,500	
	To Purchases A/c			1,500
	(Purchase of furniture was wrongly debited to Purchase A/c, now rectified)			
(d)	Purchase A/c Dr.		450	
	To Suspense A/c			450
	(Purchase of Rs. 500 was wrongly posted as Rs. 50 to the Purchases A/c, now rectified)			
(e)	Machinery A/c Dr.		700	
	To Wages A/c			700
	(Wages paid for erection of machinery was wrongly debited to Wages A/c, now rectified)			
(f)	Drawings A/c Dr.		1,000	
	To Purchases A/c			1,000
	(Goods purchased for personal use wrongly debited to Purchases A/c, now rectified)			
(g)	Depreciation A/c Dr.		1,000	
	To Suspense A/c			1,000
	(Depreciation on machinery was not posted to Depreciation A/c, now rectified)			
(h)	Suspense A/c Dr.		200	
	To Sunder A/c			100
	To Raghu A/c			100
	(Cash received from Raghu wrongly debited to Sunder's A/c, now rectified)			
(i)	Suspense A/c Dr.		2,300	
	To Radhey Mohan (Rs. 1,150 × 2)			23000
	(Cash received from Radhey Mohan wrongly debited to his account, now rectified)			
(j)	Hari Kishan A/c Dr.		980	
	To Purchases Return A/c			980
	(Purchases return to Hari Kishan were not recorded in the book, now rectified)			

Effect on Profit

	Entries	*Increase Rs.*	*Decrease Rs.*
(*a*)		—	100
(*b*)	No effect	—	—
(*c*)		1,500	—
(*d*)		—	450
(*e*)		700	—
(*f*)		1,000	—
(*g*)		—	1,000
(*h*)	No effect	—	—
(*i*)	No effect	—	—
(*j*)		980	—
		4,180	1,550
	∴ Increase in Profit		2,630
		4,180	4,180

ILLUSTRATION 8.18.

The difference of Trial Balance of a Trader of Rs. 1,118 has been transferred to Suspense Account. Later on the following errors were discovered. Pass the necessary rectifying entries. Open Suspense Account and show the effect of rectifying entries on profit or loss.

(*i*) Depreciation of Rs. 200 was charged on Machinery but it was not recorded in depreciation account.
(*ii*) A discount of Rs. 82 was allowed to Rajesh, but in his account only Rs. 28 was recorded.
(*iii*) A Sale of Rs. 344 was recorded in Sales Account as Rs. 434.
(*iv*) A Machinery of Rs. 4,000 was purchased, but was recorded in purchases book.
(*v*) Instead of crediting Rs. 1,024 in Madan's Account Rs. 430 were debited in his account.
(*vi*) Total of Sales Returns Book was undercast by Rs. 100. [*B.Com. Madurai*]

SOLUTION:

Rectifying Journal Entries

Errors	*Particulars*		*L.F.*	*Debit Rs.*	*Credit Rs.*
(*i*)	Depreciation A/c	Dr.		200	
	To Suspense A/c				200
	(Being omission of posting to depreciation account, now rectified)				
(*ii*)	Suspense A/c	Dr.		54	
	To Rajesh A/c				54
	(Being wrong posting to Rajesh A/c now corrected)				
(*iii*)	Sales A/c	Dr.		90	
	To Suspense A/c				90
	(Being wrong posting to Sales A/c now rectified)				
(*iv*)	Machinery A/c	Dr.		4,000	
	To Purchases A/c				4,000
	(Being wrong record of purchases now corrected)				
(*v*)	Suspense A/c	Dr.		1,454	
	To Madan A/c				1,454
	(Being rectifying entry made for wrong posting)				
(*vi*)	Sales Returns A/c	Dr.		100	
	To Suspense A/c				100
	(Being under casting of sales returns now rectified)				

Suspense Account

	Rs		Rs
To Rajesh A/c	54	By Balance b/d	1,118
To Madan A/c	1,454	By Depreciation A/c	200
		By Sales A/c	90
		By Sales Returns A/c	100
	1,508		1,508

Effect on Gross Profit and Net Profit

Entries	*Gross Profit* *Rs.*	*Net Profit* *Rs.*
(i)	Nil	(–) 200
(ii)	Nil	Nil
(iii)	(–) 90	(–) 90
(iv)	(+) 4,000	(+) 4,000
(v)	Nil	Nil
(vi)	(–) 100	(–) 100
	(+) 3,810	(+) 3,610

On rectification of entries, gross profit is increased by Rs. 3,810 and net profit is increased by Rs. 3,610.

ILLUSTRATION 8.19.

The book-keeper of a Trading concern, having failed to agree the Trial Balance, opened a Suspense Account and entered the difference in the Trial Balance therein. The following errors were then subsequently discovered:

(*a*) A cheque for Rs. 75 received from Jones and Co. having been dishonoured was wrongly debited to Allowances Account.

(*b*) The discount column of the Cash Book representing discount allowed to customers for the month of December was over added by Rs. 30.

(*c*) The total of the Purchase Book for December was undercast by Rs. 100.

(*d*) An item of Rs. 50 representing Returns Inwards from P. Basin and Co., was omitted to be credited to their account from the Returns Inwards Book.

(*e*) The credit side of R.Roy's Account in the Ledger had been overcast by Rs. 10.

(*f*) A sale of old furniture amounting to Rs. 75 had been credited to Sales Account.

(*g*) A Bill Receivable accepted by S. Sampat & Co. for Rs. 200 which had been sent to the bank for collection, having been dishonoured and returned by the bank had been debited to Bills Receivable Account.

You are required to make journal entries and ascertain the total amount of difference in the Trial Balance. Show the Suspense Account as opened by the book-keeper and the subsequent adjusting entries made therein. You are further required to explain how the rectification of the above errors would affect the profit already disclosed by the accounts.

[*B.Com. Bharathiar*]

SOLUTION:

JOURNAL ENTRIES

			Rs.	Rs.
(a)	Jones and Co. Dr. To Allowances Account (Being a cheque for Rs. 75 received from Jones & Co. dishonoured debited to Allowances Account instead of Jones & Co., now corrected)		75	75
(b)	Suspense Account Dr. To Discount Account (Being discount allowed column of the Cash Book over-added by Rs. 30 and accordingly excess debit given to Discount Account, now corrected)		30	30
(c)	Purchases Account Dr. To Suspense Account (Being less debit of Rs. 100 given to Purchases Account due to undercasting of the Purchases Book, now corrected)		100	100
(d)	Suspense Account Dr. To P.Basin & Co. (Being returns inwards from P.Basin & Co. omitted to be credited to their account, now credited)		50	50
(e)	R Roy's Account Dr. To Suspense Account (Being credit side of Roy's Account overcast by Rs. 10, now corrected)		10	10
(f)	Sales Account Dr. To Furniture Account (Being sale of old furniture credited to Sales Account instead of Furniture Account, now corrected)		75	75
(g)	S.Sampat & Co. Account Dr. To Bills Receivable Account (Being the acceptance of S.Sampat & Co. sent to the bank for collection dishonoured debited to Bills Receivable Account instead of S. Sampat & Co., now corrected)		200	200

SUSPENSE ACCOUNT

	Rs		Rs
To Difference in Books as per Trial Balance (Balancing figure)	30	By Purchases Account	100
To Discount Account	30	By R. Roy	10
To P.Basin and Co.	50		
	110		110

Suspense Account shows a debit balance of Rs. 30 in the Trial Balance before the discovery of errors. Therefore, credit side of the Trial Balance exceeded the debit side by Rs. 30 before the discovery of the errors.

Effect of the rectification of errors on profit:

(*a*) Profit increased by Rs. 75.00

(*b*) Profit increased by Rs. 30.00

(*c*) Profit decreased by Rs. 100.00

(*d*) No effect on profit.

(*e*) No effect on profit

(*f*) Profit decreased by Rs. 75.

(*g*) No effect on profit.

The net combined effect of the rectification of all the errors is that profit will decrease by Rs. 70 that is Rs. 70 = $(c + f) - (a + b)$; that is;

Rs. 70 = (Rs. 100 + Rs. 75) – (Rs. 75 + Rs. 30).

(*d*), (*e*) and (*g*) have no effect on profit, already disclosed by the books of accounts as these do not involve any nominal account.

ILLUSTRATION 8.20

The following errors committed by accountant of M/s Das & Co.:

(*a*) Cash paid to Ram Rs. 520, was posted to his account as Rs. 250

(*b*) Sales Day Book was undercast by Rs. 1000

(*c*) Purchase of stationery of Rs. 200, was not posted to the Stationery Account.

(*d*) Goods returned by M. Banerjee Rs. 1,500 posted to his account from Returns Inwards Books as Rs. 5,100.

(*e*) Purchased goods from S. Talukdar for Rs. 1,000, was entered in the Purchase Day Book as Rs. 100.

(*f*) Rs. 500, paid for furniture was charged to Office Expense Account.

(*g*) A Sale of Rs. 500 to P.K. Sen was passed through the Purchase Day Book.

(*h*) Salary paid to Mr. X–Rs. 500, wrongly debited to his Personal Account.

Rectify the above errors by suitable journal entries whenever necessary assuming that they were detected:

(*a*) Before preparation of Trial Balance.

(*b*) After preparation of Trial Balance and taking the difference to a Suspense Account but before preparing Final Accounts.

(*c*) After preparation of Final Accounts. [*B.Com. MS. Modified*]

SOLUTION: (*Solution See Next Page*)

PROBLEM 8.21.

Give journal entries to correct the following errors and show clearly what would be the effect of such rectifications on the Profit and Loss Account and the Balance Sheet of the firm:

(*i*) There were three compensating errors:

(*a*) Discount received was undercast by Rs. 40;

(*b*) The debit side of Mr. Bali (a customer) was overcast by Rs. 250;

(*c*) A payment of Rs. 290 for legal expenses was not posted from the Cash Book.

(*ii*) Rs. 55 of the total of the Returns Inwards Book, was posted to the credit of the Returns Outwards Account.

(*iii*) A sum of Rs. 75 was received from Suraj Prasad, and was duly entered in the Cash Book but was posted to his account as Rs. 57.

(*iv*) A sum of Rs. 1,000 written off as depreciation of building was not posted to Depreciation Account.

(*v*) An item of Rs. 25 having entered in the Returns Inwards Book was debited to the account of the customer who had returned the goods.

(*vi*) An item of sale for Rs. 49 was posted in the Sales Account as Rs. 94.

(*Contd. on page 281*)

SOLUTION.

In the books of M/s Das & Co.
Journal *(without narration)*

Before preparation of Trial Balance			*After preparation of Trial Balance but before preparation of Final Accounts*			*After preparation of Final Accounts*		
				Dr. *Rs.*	*Cr.* *Rs.*		*Dr.* *Rs.*	*Cr.* *Rs.*
(*a*) Ram A/c will be debited with Ram 270			(*a*) Ram A/c Dr.	270		(*a*) Ram A/c Dr.	270	
(*i.e.*, 520 – 250)			To Suspense A/c		270	To Suspense A/c		270
(*b*) Sales Account will be credited with			(*b*) Suspense A/c Dr.	1,000		(*b*) Suspense A/c Dr.	1,000	
Rs. 1,000			To Sales A/c		1,000	To Profit and Loss		
						Adjustment A/c		1,000
(*c*) Stationery Account will be debited with			(*c*) Stationery A/c Dr.	200		(*c*) Profit and Loss		
Rs. 200.			To Suspense A/c		200	Adjustment A/c Dr.	200	
						To Suspense A/c		200
(*d*) Banerjee account will be debited with			(*d*) Banerjee A/c Dr.	3,600		(*d*) Banerjee A/c Dr.	3,600	
Rs. 3,600 (*i.e.*, 5,100 – 1,500)			To Suspense A/c		3,600	To Suspense A/c		3,600
(*e*) Purchase A/c Dr.	900		(*e*) Purchase A/c Dr.	900		(*e*) Profit & Loss		
To S.Talukdar A/c		900	To S.Talukdar		900	Adjustment A/c Dr.	900	
						To S.Talukdar A/c		900
(*f*) Office Furniture A/c Dr.	500		(*f*) Office Furniture A/c Dr.	500		(*f*) Office		
To Office Exp. A/c		500	To Office Exp. A/c		900	Furniture A/c Dr.	500	
						To Profit & Loss Adjustment A/c		500
(*g*) P. K. Sen A/c Dr.	1,000		(*g*) P.K. Sen A/c	1,000		(*g*) P. K. Sen A/c Dr.	1,000	
To Purchases A/c	500		To Purchases A/c		500	To Profit & Loss		
To Sales A/c		500	To Sales A/c		500	Adjustment A/c		1,000
(*h*) Salary A/c Dr.	500		(*h*) Salary A/c Dr.	500		(*h*) Profit & Loss		
To X A/c		500	To X A/c		500	Adjustment A/c Dr.	500	
						To X A/c		500

Note: Balance of Profit and Loss Adjustment Account should be transferred to Capital Account.

(*vii*) During the year Plant and Machinery was purchased for Rs. 790. It was entered in the Purchases Book.

(*viii*) A debit balance of Rs. 65 in Telephone Account was entered on the wrong side in the Trial Balance.

[*B.Com Hons. Calcutta*]

SOLUTION:

JOURNAL ENTRIES

			Rs.	Rs.
(*i*)	(*a*) Suspense Account Dr. To Discount Account (Being discount received undercast, now corrected)		40	40
	(*b*) Suspense Account Dr. To Mr. Bali (Being the debit side of Mr. Bali overcast previously)		250	250
	(*c*) Legal Expenses Account Dr. To Suspense Account (Being amount paid for legal expenses not posted to Legal Expenses Account, now posted)		290	290
(*ii*)	Returns Outwards Account Dr. Returns Inwards Account Dr. To Suspense Account (Being total of the Returns Inwards Books wrongly credited to the Return Outwards A/c, now corrected)		55 55	110
(*iii*)	Suspense Account Dr. To Suraj Prasad (Being a sum of Rs. 75 received from Suraj Prasad wrongly credited to his account as Rs. 57, now corrected)		18	18
(*iv*)	Depreciation Account Dr. To Suspense Account (Being depreciation on building not posted to Depreciation Account, now posted)		1,000	1,000
(*v*)	Suspense Account Dr. To Customer's Account (Being goods worth Rs. 25 returned by a customer wrongly debited to his account instead of being credited, now corrected)		50	50
(*vi*)	Sales Account Dr. To Suspense Account (Being an item of sale of Rs. 49 wrongly credited to Sales Account as Rs. 94, now corrected)		45	45
(*vii*)	Plant and Machinery Account Dr. To Purchase Account (Being purchase of plant and machinery wrongly entered in the Purchases Book, now corrected)		790	790
(*viii*)	Telephone Account Dr. To Suspense Account (Being a debit balance of Rs. 65 on Telephone Account wrongly entered on the credit side in the Trial Balance, now corrected)		130	130

Error	*Effect on Profit and Loss Account*	*Effect on Balance Sheet*
(i) (a)	Net profit will increase by Rs. 40 because discount received was previously undercast.	Capital will increase by Rs. 40 because of increase in profit and credit balance of Suspense Account will reduce by Rs. 40.
(b)	No effect as it does not affect any nomial account	Mr. Bali's debit balances will reduce by Rs. 250 and credit balance of Suspense Account will reduce by Rs. 250.
(c)	Net profit will reduce by Rs. 290 because previously amount of legal expenses was not debited to the Profit and Loss Account.	Capital will reduce by Rs. 290 because of decrease in profit and debit balance of Suspense Account will reduce by Rs. 290.
(ii)	Net Profit will reduce by Rs. 110.	Capital will decrease by Rs. 110 and debit balance of Suspense Account will reduce by Rs. 110.
(iii)	No effect as it does not involve any nominal account	Suraj Prasad's debit balance will reduce by Rs. 18 and Suspense Account's credit balance will reduce by Rs. 18.
(iv)	Net profit will reduce by Rs. 1,000 because of posting of depreciation to Depreciation Account.	Capital will reduce by Rs. 1,000 because of decrease in profit and debit balance of Suspense Account will reduce by Rs. 1,000.
(v)	No effect as it does not affect any nominal account.	Debit balance of Customer's Account will reduce by Rs. 50 and credit balance of Suspense Account will reduce by Rs. 50.
(vi)	Net profit will reduce by Rs. 45 because of decrease in the figure of sales.	Capital will decrease by Rs. 45 because of decrease in profit and debit balance of Suspense Account will reduce by Rs. 45.
(vii)	Net profit will increase by Rs. 790 because of decrease in the figure of purchases.	Capital will increase by Rs. 790 because of increase in profit and plant and Machinery Account's balance will increase by Rs. 790.
(viii)	Net profit will reduce by Rs. 130 because of debit to Telephone Account.	Capital will reduce by Rs. 130 and debit balance of Suspense Account will reduce by Rs. 130.

QUESTIONS

OBJECTIVE TYPE QUESTIONS

I. Mention whether the following statements are right or wrong

1. Errors of carry forward affect two accounts.
2. Omission of a transaction from a subsidiary book affects two accounts.
3. Errors of omission does not affect the agreement of the Trial Balance.
4. All errors affect the agreement of the Trial Balance.
5. If the two sides of the Trial Balance tally, the books of account can be taken as absolutely accurate.
6. Errors of principles affect the agreement of the Trial Balance.
7. Suspense Account representes consolidated result of all the errors.
8. Rectification of errors is necessary to tally the Trial Balance.
9. Rectification of errors will not necessarily balance a Trial Balance.
10. Suspense account is usually closed when all the errors are rectified.

(*Ans:* 1. Wrong; 2. Right; 3. Right; 4. Wrong; 5. Wrong; 6. Wrong; 7. Right; 8. Right; 9. Right; 10. Right.

II. Fill in the blanks.

1. Errors of posting affects .... account.
2. Errors of balancing affects .... account.

3. Errors which affect one account can be errors of ....
4. Errors which affect Profit & Loss relate to .... accounts.
5. Errors which affect one account can be errors of ....

(*Ans:* 1. One; 2. One; 3. Posting; 4. Nominal; 5. Posting.)

III. Choose the appropriate answer:

1. A suspense account is opened when:
   (*a*) Business owes money. (*b*) Trial Balance does not balance.
   (*c*) Pass Book and Cash Book differ.
2. Casting errors are the result of :
   (*a*) Wrong totalling. (*b*) Wrong Balancing.
   (*c*) Wrong carry forward.
3. Errors which affect one account can be :
   (*a*) Errors of omission. (*b*) Errors of principle.
   (*c*) Errors of posting.
4. When purchase of a computer is debited to purchase account, it will:
   (*a*) Inflate the profit (*b*) Decrease the profit
   (*c*) No effect on profit
5. Suspense account is usually closed when :
   (*a*) Accounts are audited. (*b*) Accounts are finalised.
   (*c*) All the errors are rectified.

(*Ans*: 1. (*b*); 2. (*a*); 3. (*c*); 4. (*b*); 5. (*c*).

THEORETICAL QUESTIONS

1. The existence of certain errors will not make the Trial Balance disagree. Discuss such errors with suitable examples.
2. What do you mean by Suspense Account? Why is it opened?
3. How do you rectify the errors of the last year so that current year's profit may not be affected?
4. "Some errors affect the agreement of the Trial Balance and some others do not". Explain. (*B.Com. Madurai*)
5. How do you ascertain the effect of rectification of errors on Net Profit ? (*B.Com. Madras, Kerala*)
6. What is Profit and Loss Adjustment Account ? When do you prepare such an account ? (*B. Com. Jabalpur, Gwalior*)

PRACTICAL PROBLEMS

1. Give journal entries to rectify the following errors:
   (*a*) A purchase of goods from Mahesh amounting to Rs. 150 has been wrongly entered through the Sales Book.
   (*b*) A credit sale of goods, Rs 120 to Ramnath has been wrongly passed through the Purchase Book.
   (c) On 31st December 2004, goods of the value of Rs 300 were returned by S. Dutt and were taken into stock on the same date but no entry was passed in the books.
   (*d*) An account of Rs. 200 due from Lal which had been written off as Bad Debts in a previous year was unexpectedly recovered and had been posted to the personal account of Lal.
   (*e*) A cheque for Rs. 100 received from Manoharan was dishonoured and had been posted to the debit of Sales Returns Account.
   (*f*) Furniture purchased for Rs. 1,000 was debited to Purchase Account.
   (*g*) Salary paid to Mohan Rs 2,000 was wrongly debited to his personal account.

(h) Machinery costing Rs 800 had been debited to Purchase Account.

(B.Com., Madurai Modified)

2. Anand Company closed their books on 31st December 2004. On that date you find that:
   (*a*) Materials from stores Rs 700 and wages Rs 250 had been used in making tools and implements for use in own factory, but no adjustments were made in the books.
   (*b*) Rs 50 paid in instalments to an injured worker, pending the settlement of workman's compensation claim against the insurance company, was debited to the wages account.
   (c) Goods for Rs. 2,600 purchased from Ratibhai on 29th December 2004, had been entered in the purchase book, but the delivery of the goods was not received until 4th January 2005.
   (*d*) Goods (cost price Rs. 7,200; minimum sale price Rs. 9,000) had been consigned to an agent, but were still, unsold.
   (*e*) Goods worth Rs 500 returned by Govind were recorded in the sales book.
   (*f*) Interest received Rs 300, was credited to Commission Account.

   Pass Necessary Journal Entries

(B.Com., Madurai; M.S., Kerala)

3. Pass journal entries to rectify the following errors:
   (*a*) A cheque of Rs. 750 received for loss of stock by fire had been deposited in the proprietor's private bank account.
   (*b*) An item of purchase of Rs. 151 was entered in the purchases book as Rs 15 and posted to the supplier's account as Rs. 51.
   (*c*) A sales return of Rs 500 was not entered in the financial accounts though it was duly taken in the stock book.
   (*d*) An amount of Rs 300 was received in full settlement from a customer after he was allowed a discount of Rs 50 but while writing the books, the amount received was entered in the discount column and discount allowed was entered in the amount column.
   (*e*) Bill receivable from Mr A of Rs 1,000 was posted to the credit of bills payable account and also credited to the account of Mr A. *(C.A. Inter)*

4. Pass necessary journal entries to rectify the following errors:
   (*a*) An item of Rs 53 has been debited to a personal account as Rs 35.
   (*b*) A sum of Rs 100 written off as depreciation on furniture was not debited to Depreciation account.
   (*c*) The total of Purchase Book was added Rs 60 short.
   (*d*) A machine bought for Rs. 5,000 has been debited to purchase account.
   (*e*) Sale of old machine for Rs 500 to Mahesh has been entered in Sales Book.
   (*f*) Total of Return Outwards book was Rs 100 short.
   (*g*) A sale of Rs 359 to Ramu has been entered correctly in Sales Book but credited to Ramu's account as Rs 395.
   (*h*) Repairs of Rs 680 to Motor Truck has been debited to Motor Vehicle account as Rs. 860.
   (*i*) Cash received from Joseph Rs 300 has been debited to Jose's A/c.
   (*j*) Furniture purchased for Rs 3,000, but there is no entry in books.

(B.Com., Kerala, Madras, Delhi)

5. How do you rectify the following errors after the preparation of the Trial Balance?
   (*a*) An item of Rs. 1,000 paid for purchase of an engine has been debited to cash purchase account from the cash book.
   (*b*) A credit sale of Rs 100 to C duly entered in the sales book has been credited to C's Account.
   (*c*) An item of Rs 1,500 for the purchase of furniture has been wrongly passed through the purchase book.
   (d) Rs 150 posted to debit of stationery, instead of Ram, in payment of his account.

(*e*) An amount of Rs 400 withdrawn by the proprietor for his personal use has been debited to Trade Expense Account.

(*f*) Rs 45, cost of repairing building, has been charged to Building account.

(*g*) A sum of Rs 100 paid to Mani has been debited to Gani Account.

(*B.Com., MS, Kerala*)

6. The Trial Balance of Patel & Co. Ltd. having disagreed, the difference was temporarily placed on a Suspense Account. Subsequently the following errors were discovered and you are required to pass the rectifying entries:

(*a*) A sale of Rs 30 was wrongly entered in the Sales Returns Book, but the posting therefrom was correctly made to the debit of the customer's account.

(*b*) A sale of Rs 12.58 was posted to the customer's account as Rs. 9.78.

(*c*) The addition of the Sales Day Book for the month was undercast by Rs. 100.

(*d*) An item of Rs 40 was wrongly credited to the supplier's account from the Returns Outwards Book.

(*e*) An item of Rs 105.62 was posted to supplier A/c as Rs 110.31 from the purchase book.

(*f*) A cash discount of Rs 20 had remained unposted to the customers account from the receipt side of the cash book.

(*B.Com., Madras*)

7. The account books of Messrs Hari Ram Sita Ram were closed on 31st December 2004. On that date there was a difference of Rs. 360 in their Trial Balance. The Trial Balance was totalled by transferring Rs 360 on the debit side of the Suspense account. Afterwards the following mistakes were found out:

(*a*) In the Cash Book, total of the discount column on the debit side was overcast by Rs. 60.

(*b*) The Purchases Book was undercast by Rs. 200.

(*c*) Bhola Nath had returned goods worth Rs 100 but no entry was made in his account.

(*d*) Credit total of Harinath's account was overcast by Rs. 20.

(*e*) There was a debit balance of Rs 300 in Hiral's account but this was not included in the Total Debtors' list.

Pass necessary entries in the journal to rectify the above errors. Open a Suspense account and point out the effect of each entry on the Profit & Loss Account.

(*B.Com., Bombay*)

[Ans: Suspense Account Total Rs. 520]

8. A book-keeper finds that his Trial Balance debit side is short by Rs. 308 and so for the time being he balances the sides by putting the difference to Suspense Account. Subsequently the following errors were discovered:

(*a*) An entry for the goods sold for Rs 102 to Madhav was posted to his account as Rs 120.

(*b*) Rs 100 being the monthly total of discount allowed to customers were credited to Discount account in the Ledger.

(*c*) Rs 275 paid by Madhav were credited to Jadav's Account.

(*d*) Rs 26 appearing in the Cash Book as paid for the purpose of stationery for office use has not been posted to Ledger.

(e) The debit side of Purchases account was undercast by Rs 100.

You are required to make the necessary Journal entries and the Suspense Account.

(*B.Com., Bombay*)

[Ans: Suspense Account Total Rs 326]

9. An accountant while balancing his books found that there was a difference of Rs 1669.37 in the Trial Balance on its debit side which was short by the above amount. The difference was for the time being placed in the Suspense Account. Subsequently, the following errors were traced out:

(*a*) Goods worth Rs 100 as returned by Mohan were not posted to his account, although they were duly entered in the Sales Returns Book.

(*b*) The total discount received was overcast by Rs 100.37.

(*c*) The credit balances of Interest Account, Rs 200 was placed on the debit side of the Trial Balance.

(*d*) An account of Rs 130 instead of being debited to Ram's account was debited to Hari's account.

(*e*) An amount of Rs. 734.50 appearing in the Cash book as paid to Dayalbagh Stores was credited to the latter's account.

(*f*) Furniture Account as standing in the books at Rs 400 was not incorporated in the Trial Balance.

(*g*) The Purchases Book was undercast by Rs 100.

(*h*) Salary Account standing in the books at Rs. 4,100 was entered in the Trial Balance as Rs. 4,000.

(*i*) Rs. 2,000 received from the sale of a machinery were credited to Sale Account.

Give journal entries to correct the above errors, and prepare the Suspense Account.

(*B.Com., Madurai*)

[Ans: Suspense Account Total Rs 2,169.37]

10. The Trial Balance of A prepared on 31st December 2004 did not tally. As he wanted to close his books and prepare the final accounts he placed the difference to a newly opened Suspense Account which was carried forward to the next year. In the next year the following errors were discovered:

(*a*) An amount of Rs 80 owed by a debtor was omitted to be included in the schedule of Sundry Debtors.

(*b*) A sum of Rs 270 paid for repairs to Furniture and Fixtures was found to be debited to Furniture and Fixtures Account as Rs. 720.

(*c*) The purchase Returns Book for the month of May was cast Rs 50 short.

(*d*) A Bills Receivable received from P for Rs 1,200 was found entered in the Bills Payable Day Book at Rs 2,100.

(*e*) An amount of Rs 300 received from the estate of an insolvent debtor was found to be credited to his account which was already written off last year as bad.

(*f*) Old machinery sold on credit for Rs 700 was passed through the Sales Book.

(g) A payment of Rs 500 to a creditor in full settlement of Rs 540 was found credited to his account.

Pass journal entries to rectify the above errors and prepare the Suspense Account, showing also how would you find out the difference in the Trial Balance.

(*B.Com., Madras*)

[Ans: Difference in Trial Balance Rs 620
Suspense Account total Rs 1,120]

11. The Trial Balance of a firm is out by Rs 2,788 (excess debit). The following errors were found, subsequently, to have been committed. Prepare journal entries and suspense account:

(*a*) An amount of Rs 100 was received from D. Das on 31st December 2003, but had been entered in the cash book on 3rd January 2004.

(*b*) The returns inward book for December had been cast Rs 100 short.

(c) A purchase of Rs 671 had been posted to the debit of the creditor's account as Rs 617. The creditor is Panna & Co.

(d) A cheque for Rs 200 received from Joshi had been dishonoured on maturity and was passed to the debit of allowances account.

(*e*) Goods amounting to Rs 100 had been returned by a customer and were taken into stock, but no entry in respect thereof was made in the books.

(*f*) Rs 2,000 paid for the purchase of a motor cycle for Dutt (a partner) had been charged to Miscellaneous Expenses account.

(*g*) A sale of Rs 200 to Singh and Company was credited to their account.

(h) A sale of Rs 1,000 has been passed through the Purchase Day Book. The customer's account has, however, been correctly debited.

(*B.Com., Madurai*)

[Ans: Suspense Account Total Rs 3,288]

12. In taking out trial balance a book keeper finds that he is out by Rs 38.04 excess debit. Being desirous of closing his books, he places the diffeence to a newly opened suspense account which is carried forward. In the next period he discovers that :

(*a*) A credit item of 97.43 has been debited to a personal account as Rs 79.34.

(*b*) A sum of Rs 95 written off as depreciation has not been posted to the depreciation account.

(*c*) Rs 1,500 paid for furniture purchased has been charged to ordinary purchase account.

(*d*) A discount of Rs 37.41 allowed to a customer has been credited to him as Rs 36.14.

(e) The total of the inwards return book has been added Rs 9 short.

(*f*) An item of sale for Rs 59 was posted as Rs 95 in the sales account. Give the correcting entries and prepare suspense A/c.

(*B.Com., Punjab*)

[Ans: Suspense Account Total Rs 178.04]

13. A book-keeper failed to balance his trial balance, the credit side exceeding the debit side by Rs 175. This amount was entered in a Suspense account. Later, the following errors were discovered:

1. The total of the credit side of Ramesh's account was overcast by Rs 100.
2. The Sales Book was undercast by Rs 100.
3. Goods worth Rs 100 purchased from Chandra were wrongly entered in the Sales Book. The account of Chandra was correctly credited.
4. The total of returns outward book amounting to Rs 200 was not posted to the ledger.
5. A credit balance of Rs 755 of rent receivable account was shown as Rs 570.
6. Goods worth Rs 620 sold to Raj were correctly entered in the Sales Book, but posted to Raj's account as Rs 260.

Give the journal entries to rectify the above errors and prepare the Suspense account.

(*B.Com., Calicut*)

[Ans: Suspense Account Total Rs 660]

14. The Trial Balance of a book keeper shows an excess of debits over credits by Rs 261. This difference is placed in a suspense account to facilitate closing of the books. Later on the following errors were discovered:

(*a*) A credit item of Rs. 349 has been debited to a personal account as Rs 439.

(*b*) A sum of Rs 625 written off fixtures as depreciation has not been posted to depreciation account.

(*c*) Rs 9,000 paid for furniture bought have been charged to the purchase account.

(*d*) A discount allowed to a customer has been credited to him as Rs. 145 in place of 154.

(*e*) A sale of Rs 594 was posted as Rs 495 in sales account.

(f) The total of Returns Inward Book has been added Rs 10 short.

Give journal entries to correct these errors and prepare the Suspense account.

(*B.Com., Madurai*)

[Ans: Suspense Account Total Rs 896]

15. The Trial Balance of Hopeless Ltd., having disagreed, the difference of Rs 147.12 excess debit was temporarily placed in a "Suspense Account" and carried forward. In the next year the following errors in connection with the previous year were discovered:

(*a*) A credit item of Rs 190.06 was debited to K. Ramu's account.

(b) Rs 1,650 for addition to Machinery was debited to repairs account.

(c) The total of Returns Inward Account was undercast by Rs 10.

(*d*) Rs 160 written off Machinery as depreciation was not posted to depreciation account.

(*e*) An item of sale for Rs 18 was posted as Rs 81 in the sales account.

Pass journal entries to rectify the errors and show the Suspense account. State also the effect of these correcting entries on the Profit & Loss a/c.

(*B.Com., Calicut*)

[**Ans:** Suspense Account Total Rs 380.12
Net increase in profit Rs 1,417]

16. Rectify the following errors. Calculate the difference in the Trial balance. Prepare Suspense Account and find out the effect of these errors on the net profit of last year.
    (*i*) Goods of the value of Rs 2,100 purchased from Ram were recorded through Sales Book.
    (*ii*) Received final dividend of Rs 200 from Roy whose account had already been written off as bad debts, was credited to his new opened account.
    (*iii*) An item of Rs 2,000 relating to prepaid rent was omitted to be brought forward.
    (*iv*) Bills received from Vasu for repairs done to furniture for Rs 100 and furniture supplied for Rs 1,000 was entered in the invoice book as Rs 1,100.
    (*v*) A sale of Rs 347 to Kishore was entered in the Sales Book as Rs 437. Kishore was, however, debited with Rs 743.

(*B.Com., Madurai*)

[**Ans:** Suspense Account total: Rs 2,000.
Difference in books Rs 1,694.
Last year's Profit & Loss overstated by Rs 5,090]

17. The book keeper of a trading concern having failed to agree the trial balance, opened a Suspense account and entered the difference in the trial balance therein. The following errors were then subsequently discovered:
    1. A cheque for Rs 75 received from Jones & Co. having been dishonoured was wrongly debited to allowance account.
    2. The discount column of the cash book representing discount allowed to customers for the month of December was over added by Rs 30.
    3. The total of Purchases Book for December was undercast by Rs 100.
    4. An item of Rs 50 representing return inwards from P Basu & Co. was omitted to be credited to their account from the returns inward book.
    5. The credit side of R. Roy's account in the ledger had been overcast by Rs 10.
    6. A sale of old Furniture amounting to Rs 75 had been credited to sales account.
    7. A bill receivable accepted by S. Sampat & Co. for Rs 200 which had been sent to the bankers for collection, having been dishonoured and returned by the bank, had been debited to bills receivable account.
    8. A balance of Rs 150 owing by B. Jijibhoy, a customer, had been omitted from the list of sundry debtors.

    You are required to ascertain the total amount of difference in the trial balance. Show the Suspense account as opened by the book keeper and subsequent adjusting entries made therein. You are further required to explain how the rectification of the above errors would affect the profit already disclosed by the accounts.

(*B.Com, Punjab*)

[**Ans:** Difference in Trial Balance Rs 180 (Dr.)
Before rectification, profit is decreased by Rs 70.
After rectification, profit is increased by Rs 70]

18. Rectify the following errors and show their effects on Trial Balance and on profit or loss; before rectification and after:
    1. The Sales day book is totalled Rs 10 short.
    2. Payment of Trade Expenses Rs 55 not posted.
    3. Goods bought from H. for Rs 100 is wrongly posted to the debit of his account.

4. Commission Rs 25 paid has been posted twice to that account.
5. Discount Col. on the receipt side of cash book totalling Rs 123.12 has been added up to show Rs 143.12.
6. An amount of Rs 200 withdrawn by the proprietor for his personal use has been debited to Trade Expenses Account.
7. A purchase of goods from Nathan amounting to Rs 300 has been wrongly entered through the sales book.
8. Rs 50 received from Shaw & Co. have been credited to Sen & Co.
9. Rs 175 paid on account of salary to the cashier Govind stands debited to his personal account.
10. Installation charges of Machinery, Rs 570 have been debited to Installation expenses account.

(B.Com, Karnataka)

[Ans: 1 to 5 are one-sided errors and 6 to 10 are two-sided errors]

19. The Profit and Loss Account of Cardamom for the year ended 31st December 2004 showed a net profit of Rs 1.400 after taking into account closing stock of Rs 2360.

On scrutiny of the books the following information could be obtained:

1. Cardamom has taken goods valued Rs 750 for his personal use without making entry in the books.
2. Purchase of the year included Rs 300 spent on acquisition of a ceiling fan for his shop.
3. Invoices for goods amounting to Rs 2.000 have been entered on 29th December 2004, but such goods were not included in stock.
4. Rs 250 have been included in closing stock in respect of goods purchased and invoiced on 28th December 2004 but included in purchase for January 2005.
5. Sale of goods amounting to Rs 305 sold and delivered in December has been entered in January 2005. You are required to ascertain the correct amount of closing stock as on 31st December 2004 and adjusted net profit for the year ended on that date.

(C.A. Inter)

[Ans: Closing Stock Rs 4,360, Adjusted net profit Rs 4,505]

20. Modern Chemicals were unable to agree the Trial Balance on 30th June 2004 and have raised a Suspense Account for the difference.

Later the following errors were discovered and rectified and the Suspense account was balanced:

(*a*) The addition of the sundry purchases column in the Tabular purchases journal was short by Rs 150 and other totals were in order.

(*b*) A Bill of exchange (received from Gupta) for Rs 2,000 had been returned by the Bank as dishonoured and had been credited to the Bank and debited to Bills Receivable Account.

(c) Goods to value of Rs 105 returned by a customer, Thomas, had been posted to the debit of Thomas and also to Sales returns.

(*d*) Sundry items of furniture sold for Rs 3.000 had been entered in the Sales Day Book, the total of which had been posted to Sales Account.

(*e*) An account of Rs 600 due from Vaz, a customer. had been omitted from the schedule of Sundry Debtors.

(*f*) Discounts amounting to Rs 30 allowed to a customer had been duly posted in his account, but not posted to Discount account.

(*g*) Insurance Premium of Rs 450 paid on 30th June last year for the current year ended 30th June had not been brought forward.

1. Pass journal entries to rectify the above mistakes.

2. Draw up the Suspense Account after rectifying the above mistakes and prepare a statement showing the effect of the above errors on the book profits for the year ended 30th June 2004

Assume that the relevant books have not been finally closed.

(C.A. Inter)

[Ans: Suspense Account Difference Rs 1,020.
Suspense Account Total Rs 1,230.
Profit is reduced by Rs 3,630.]

21. A book-keeper placed the difference in his figures to a Suspense Account. Later on the following errors were discovered. Pass journal entries and raise the Suspense Account showing the balance before the discovery of errors:
    1. Cash Rs 2,532 paid by Sanjay was posted as Rs 2,352.
    2. Sale to Swadesh of Rs 550 was not posted to his account.
    3. The account of a creditor, Jagan was overadded on the credit side by Rs 100 and the balance taken out was in excess to that extent.
    4. The balance of Petty Cash in hand of Rs 150 was placed on the credit side of the trial balance.
    5. A debit balance of Rs 370 in Ravindra's Account was omitted from the trial balance.
    6. Goods returned by Sanjay of Rs 85 were credited to him but were not recorded in the Sales Returns Book.
    7. Sales Book was overcast by Rs 100.
    8. The discount column on the debit side of the Cash Book was underadded by Rs. 50.

(B.Com., Bombay)

[Ans: Suspense Account Difference Rs 1,375
Suspense Account Total Rs 1,555]

22. An Accountant could not tally the Trial Balance. The difference was temporarily placed to Suspense Account for preparing the final account. The following errors were later discovered:
    1. The Sales Book was undercast by Rs 350.
    2. Entertainment expenses Rs 95, though entered in the Cash Book were omitted to be posted in the ledger.
    3. Discount column of the receipt side of the Cash Book wrongly added as Rs 140 instead of Rs 120.
    4. Commission of Rs 25 paid was posted twice, once to Discount Account and once to Commission Account.
    5. A sale of Rs 139 to Ramnath though correctly entered in Sales Book, was posted wrongly to his account as Rs 193.
    6. A purchase from Neelakandan of Rs 92, though correctly entered in the purchases book, was wrongly debited to his personal account.

You are required to pass (*i*) Necessary rectifying entries, (*ii*) prepare Suspense Account, and (iii) State the effect of each of the rectification on the profit. What would be the correct profit if the profit originally arrived at was Rs 10,000?

(CAIIB)

[Ans: Difference in T.B. Rs 538
Suspense Account total Rs 633
Profit increased by Rs 300.]
Correct Profit Rs. 10,000 + Rs. 300 = Rs. 10,300

23. The following errors were located in the Books of Kapil after the same were closed for the year ended 31st December 2004 and the Balance Sheet was prepared as on that date by showing the difference in Suspense Account:
    (*a*) The balance of Furniture Account on 1.1.2004 was carried forward from previous year as Rs 3,500 instead of Rs 5,300. A depreciation of 15% p.a. was charged on written down value.

(*b*) A credit sale of Rs 4,000 to Patil was correctly recorded in the Sales Day Book but was posted to the credit of Patil. A reserve for Doubtful Debts at 5% was raised in the books.

(*c*) Rs. 560 paid for freight on Machinery was debited to Freight Account as Rs 650.

(*d*) Goods bought on credit from Binny for Rs 750 were entered in the Sales Book as Rs 570.

Pass necessary rectification entry and close Suspense Account assuming that the profit of last year transferred to Capital Account.

(*ICWA Inter*)

[**Ans:** Difference in T.B. Rs 10,850
Suspense Account total Rs 10,940
Profit decreased by Rs 1.340]

24. Parekh found that his books for the last year contained some errors inspite of an agreed Trial Balance. The errors were:

(*a*) An invoice for Rs 50 for goods purchased from B was entered in Sales Returns Book in the ledger and this was debited to the account of B.

(*b*) Goods bought on credit from Kishan for Rs 150 were entered in the Sales Book as Rs 105. Kishan's account was credited with this amount of Rs 105.

(*c*) The Sales Book for the (last year's) April was overcast by Rs 133.

(*d*) A sale of Rs 257 to Dutta was entered in the Sales Book as Rs 527. Dutta was debited with Rs 752.

(*e*) Rs 79 paid for freight on Machinery was debited to Freight Account as Rs 97.

Give journal entries to rectify the errors using a Suspense Account where necessary.

(*CA*)

[**Ans:** Suspense Account Total Rs 343
Profit decreased by Rs 561]

25. The following errors were committed by the Accountant Geeta Dyechem:

(*a*) Cash of Rs 350 paid to Triman posted as Rs 530.

(*b*) Purchase of stationery worth Rs 150 remained unposted from the Cash Book.

(*c*) Rs 260 paid for purchase of new office furniture was charged to office expenses account.

(*d*) Credit sales to Trivedi of Rs 300 was posted to the credit of his account.

(*e*) A purchase of Rs 420 from Mantri was passed through the Sales Day Book as Rs 240.

How would you rectify these errors assuming that:

(*i*) They were detected before preparing the Trial Balance.

(*ii*) They were detected after preparing Trial Balance, but before preparing Final Account, the difference being taken to Suspense Account.

(*iii*) They were detected after the preparation of Final Accounts.

(*CAIIB*)

26. Some mistakes were committed in the books of Careless Brothers for the year ended 31st December 2004 and the Final Accounts were completed taking the difference in Suspense Account shown in the Balance Sheet:

The following mistakes were detected in March, 2005 on scrutiny of the books of the earlier year:

1. Sales Day Book was undercast by Rs. 500.
2. Credit sale of Rs 450 was debited to Party's Account as 540;
3. Credit purchase of Rs 215 was wrongly debited to Supplier's Account as Rs 250.
4. An old furniture having a book value of Rs 400 was taken over by the Furniture Supplier at an agreed value of Rs. 300 as part exchange for a new furniture of Rs 500 supplied. The bill for the net amount was passed through Return Inward Day Book.
5. White-washing and repairing charges of Building amounting to Rs 320 were charged to Building Account on which depreciation was charged @ 2.5%.

You are required to pass the journal entries to rectify the above mistakes and to draw the Suspense Account and Profit and Loss Adjustment Account.

(*B.Com. Bombay*)

[**Ans:** Difference in T.B. Rs 1,063
Profit will increase by Rs 288.]

27. The books of accounts of a Company for the year ending 31st March 2004 were closing with difference in books carried forward. The following errors were detected subsequently:
    (*a*) Return Outward Book was undercast by Rs 100.
    (*b*) Rs 1,500 being the total of the Discount column on the Credit side of the Cash Book was not posted.
    (*c*) Rs 6,000 being the cost of purchase of office furniture was debited to Purchase Account.
    (*d*) A credit sale of Rs 760 was wrongly posted as Rs 670 to the Customers account in the Sales Ledger.
    (*e*) The Sale Account was understated by Rs 10,000 being casting the carry-over mistake in the Sales Day Book.
    (*f*) Closing stock was overstated by Rs 10,000 being casting error in the Schedule of Inventory.

    Pass rectification entries in the next year. Prepare Suspense Account and state effect of the errors on determination of net profit of the last year.

(*B.Com. Madras, Madurai*)

[**Ans:** Difference in T.B. Rs 11,510
Profit will increase by Rs 7,600]

28. Rectify the following errors by way of journal entries and work out their effect on the profit and loss account of the firm:
    1. Returns Inward Book for December was short totalled by Rs 100.
    2. Rs 5,810 being cash paid to Hira Chand was debited to Ram Chand as Rs 5,010.
    3. Rs 1,500 worth of furniture purchased on credit was debited to goods Account.
    4. A purchase made for Rs 500 was posted to the Purchase Account as Rs 50.
    5. Wages paid for erection of machinery amounting to Rs 700 was debited to Wages Account.
    6. Goods purchased for proprietor's use for Rs 1,000 was debited to Goods Account.
    7. A sum of Rs 1,000 written off to machinery has not been posted to Depreciation Account.
    8. Rs 100 received from Raghu has been debited to Sunder.
    9. Rs 1,150 received from Radha Mohan was debited to his account.
    10. Purchase Returns worth Rs 980 to Hari Kishan were not recorded in the books.

(*CA Entrance*)

[**Ans:** Profit will increase by Rs 2,630]

29. The Trial Balance of A was short by Rs 3,380 on the credit side. The difference was made good by creating a Suspense Account. The following errors were detected and rectified subsequently.
    (a) An amount of Rs 1,100 incurred towards Plant and Machinery was not posted.
    (*b*) The Purchase Book was overcast by Rs 2,000.
    (c) The sale of old machinery for Rs 1,600 was taken to the Cash Book as sales.
    (*d*) Commission paid Rs 400 was taken to the credit side of the Account.
    (e) Purchases of stationery for Rs 108 was entered in the Purchase Book.
    (*f*) Purchases made for Rs 1,550 from B were debited to his account even though it was properly recorded in the Purchase Book.
    (*g*) Goods returned by C amounting to Rs 350 were not taken to Returns Inwards Book.
    (*h*) The discount of Rs 180 received from D was not posted to Discount Account.
    (*i*) Rs 250 cash received from E was posted to F's Account.

Pass necessary rectification journal entries, prepare the Suspense Account and also show the effects of these errors on the Profit and Loss Account.

(*B.Com., Madurai*)

[**Ans:** Suspense Account Total Rs 5,280

Net profit increased Rs 2,750 – Rs 2,180 = Rs 570]

30. The Trial Balance of Atmaram for the year ended 31st December 2004 did not agree and he introduced a Suspense Account of Rs 1,500 under credit balance. Efforts were made to locate the errors and only a few of the following errors were noticed and rectified in the Final Accounts. Show how the errors were rectified and adjusted in the preparation of Final Accounts and also the balance in the Suspense Account remaining unadjusted in the Balance Sheet as on 31.12.2004.

(*a*) Purchase Day Book was overcast by Rs 1,000 during May 2004.

(*b*) Goods purchased on credit for Rs 7,000 were not posted to the personal ledger of the supplier.

(*c*) Credit sales effected for Rs 3,000 on 19.5.2004 were passed through Purchase Day Book.

(*d*) Sales Returns Book was undercast by Rs 100 during September 2004.

(*e*) Cash Purchases made on 30.9.2004 for Rs 20,000 by issue of a cheque were treated as cash as well as credit purchases.

(*f*) Wages paid as Rs 4,000 was posted to the Salary Account on the credit side as Rs 400.

(*g*) A Bill Receivable for Rs 3,000 endorsed to a creditor was dishonoured and the Personal Accounts of both debtors and creditors were debited by Rs. 300.

(*h*) Income tax paid Rs 500 was wrongly posted to the credit side of General Expenses account as Rs 50.

(*i*) Goods sold to a debtor for Rs 600 were posted to Creditor's Account as Rs 600 on the debit side.

(*j*) The total in the bank column of the Cash Book was overcast by Rs 100 on the debit side.

[**Ans:** Suspense Account balance 1.1.2005 Rs 2,150

Suspense Account Total on 31.12.2004 Rs 8,700]

31. The following errors were discovered in the books of Mr Hopeless on 31st December 2004. The difference in the Trial Balance had been entered in a Suspense Account and on correction of the errors the Suspense was eliminated.

1. An item of Rs 1,000 relating to prepaid Rent Account was omitted to be brought forward.
2. A sale of Rs 589 to Mr Ram entered in Sales Day Book as Rs 859 but Ram's account is debited with Rs 958.
3. Rs 97 paid for freight on Machinery was debited to Freight Account as Rs 79.
4. Rs 100 discount allowed to a customer debited to his account.
5. Rs 1,000 which was written off as bad debts during the last year and is now received and credited to party's account.
6. Goods purchased from Gopi for Rs 1,000 was passed through Sales Book.
7. Credit sales of Rs 500 to Bobby was posted to the credit of his account.
8. Cash paid to Ram Rs 500 was credited to Ramesh Account.
9. Goods bought on credit from Kishore for Rs 750 were entered in Sales Day Book as Rs 570 and Kishore was credited with Rs 570.
10. Goods of the value of Rs 230, returned by Swamy were entered in the Purchase Book and credited therefrom to Sanker Account as Rs 320.

Give journal entries to correct these errors and prepare the Suspense Account.

[**Ans:** Difference in Trial Balance: Rs 3,949 (Dr.)

Suspense Account Total Rs 4,248]

Chapter 9

Inventory Valuation

Meaning of Inventory – Objective of Inventory Valuation – Inventory System – Inventory Valuation – Historical Cost – Net Realisable Value – Stock-taking for Balance Sheet – Accounting Standard (AS-2) Questions – Objective Type Questions – Theoretical Questions – Practical Problems.

MEANING OF INVENTORY

Inventory includes tangible property that (*i*) is held for sale in the normal course of business, or (*ii*) will be used in producing goods or services for sale. Inventories are current assets and reported on the Balance Sheet. As current assets they can be used or converted into cash within one year or within the next operating cycle of the business, whichever is longer. The term 'inventory' is understood to mean a list or a schedule of different items comprising stock-in-trade on hand at the end of the accounting period. Kohlet defines the term as "Raw materials and supplies, goods finished and in process of manufacture, and merchandise on hand, in transit and owned, in storage, or consigned to others at the end of an accouting period." Thus, inventory constitutes raw materials, work-in-progress, finished goods and consumable stores to be used in the production process.

Accounting Standard (AS - 2) issued by the Council of the Institute of Chartered Accountants of India and revised in the year 1999, defines the term as "assets (*a*) held for sale in the ordinary course of business, (*b*) in the process of production for such sale, or (*c*) in the form of materials or supplies to be consumed in the production process or in the rendering of services".

In case of a trading concern, inventory includes only stock-in-trade or finished goods, while in case of manufacturing concern, inventory comprises of raw matarials, work-in-progress, finished goods and consumable stores and spare parts.

OBJECTIVES OF INVENTORY VALUATION

The Balance sheet of a concern must show true and fair view of the financial position of the concern. For this purpose assets including inventory should be properly valued to exhibit a true and fair view. True profits cannot be calculated unless assets are properly valued. The measurement of inventory has a significant effect on income determination and financial position of a business enterprise. The American Institute of Certified Public Accountants (US) states:

"A major objective of accounting for inventories is the proper determination of income through the process of matching appropriate costs against revenues."

It is significant to observe that a direct relationship exists between cost of goods sold and closing inventory. Cost of goods sold is measured by deducting closing inventory from cost of goods available for sale. Because of these relationships, it may be said that the higher the cost of closing inventory, the lower the cost of goods sold will be and higher the resulting net income. On the contrary, the lower the value of closing inventory, the higher the cost of goods sold and the lower the net income.

Closing inventory influences net income of not only the current period but it also influences the net income of the next accounting period because closing inventory of the current period becomes the opening inventory for the next period and thus becomes cost of goods sold.

Inventory of the business should be valued correctly and properly. Valuation of inventory is necessary due to following reasons:

(1) INCOME DETERMINATION: To calculate accurate profit or loss for a certain period, it is necessary to value inventory properly. Profit is the excess of sales over cost of sales. Cost of Sales is equal to Opening stock plus Purchases Plus Direct Expenses Minus Closing stock. Hence, if stock is not valued correctly, profit will not be accurate.

Cost of goods sold can be calculated by the inventory equation:

Opening Stock + Purchases – Closing Stock = Cost of goods sold.

Opening Stock + Purchases – Cost of goods sold = Closing Stock.

In the case of a manufacturing concern, the equation is:

{Opening Stock of Finished goods} + Production – (Closing stock of Finished goods}
= {Cost of goods sold}

Survival of a business depends upon its capacity to earn income. The process of matching costs against revenue enables a business to determine its income. Cost is ascertained by the inventory equation. This cost, which is the cost of goods sold, is deducted from sales revenue. The resultant figure is business income, which is also known as gross profit. The process of matching is accomplished by preparing the Trading Account. Proper determination of gross profit, therefore, necessitates correct valuation of closing inventory.

(2) Presentation of Financial Position : At the end of the accounting period, position of various assets and liabilities is presented in the Balance Sheet. Inventory is one of the items of assets shown in Balance Sheet. If inventory is not valued properly, correct financial position of the business will not be reflected in Balance Sheet.

(3) Location of Wastage: Proper maintenance of inventory records helps a business firm to locate deficiencies, wastages, pilferages etc. Periodical checking of inventory records will enable the business to ascertain any difference between actual physical stock and stock as per books.

(4) Liquidity Position: As inventory is classified as current asset, it is one of the constituents of net working capital which reveals the liquidity position of a business. Current ratio which reveals the relationship between current assets and current liabilities is significantly affected by value of inventory. Further, the value of inventory will help the investor and other users to predict the future cash flow of the firm. This can be accomplished from two points of view. First, the amount of inventory resources available will support the inflow of cash through their sale in the ordinary course of business. Secondly, the amount of inventory resources available will, under normal circumstances, have an effect on the amount of cash required during the subsequent period to acquire the merchandise that will be sold during the period.

INVENTORY SYSTEM

Stock-taking or physical inventory is the process whereby all items of stock are physically counted and then valued. Records pertaining to quantity and value of inventory-in-hand can be maintained according to any of the following two systems:

(1) Periodical Inventory System

(2) Perpetual Inventory System (Continuous Stock-Taking)

(1) Periodical Inventory System

Under this system all purchases and purchase returns of inventories are recorded. But issues of materials are not recorded on regular basis. Physical inventory is taken at the end of the year. Therefore, the inventory used during the year will be calculated by adding opening stock to purchases and deducting closing stock of inventory. For example, opening stock of inventory is Rs. 2,000. Purchases during the year are Rs. 15,000 and closing stock is Rs. 3,000. Inventory used in production will be Rs. 14,000 (Rs. 2,000 + 15,000 – Rs. 3,000). The system does not provide the information regarding quantity and value of materials in hand on a continuous basis. It is assumed that materials not in stock have been used. No accounting is done for theft, shrinkage, losses, wastages etc.

(2) Perpetual Inventory System

Perpetual inventory system is a system of records which is maintained by the controlling department. It reveals the physical movement of stocks and their current balance. Store balances are recorded whenever any receipt or issue is made, that is, upto-date recording is maintained. Under this system, an inventory account is opened which reveals the cost of goods sold during an accounting cycle whenever is required. A perpetual inventory system, is usually checked by a programme of continuous stock taking. This system is intended as an aid to material control. In short, when the upto-date record is maintained the balance shown by store ledger must agree with the physical balance. If any discrepancies arise, proper investigation must be made and a report also will have to be submitted.

ADVANTAGES OF PERPETUAL INVENTORY SYSTEM:

The following are the advantages:

1. It is not necessary to stop production to carry out stock-taking.
2. The long and costly stock-taking (periodic) is avoided.
3. Discrepancies are detected easliy and quickly.
4. Bin cards and stock register give ready figures.
5. It facilitate the preparation of final accounts, even at short notice.
6. Stock levels can be revised from time to time in order to avoid under or over-stocking.
7. A detailed and reliable check on the stores is facilitated.
8. Since it is a regular work, experts can be appointed.
9. Deterioration, obsolescence etc. can be avoided.
10. The balance of stock is always correct.

Distinction between the two:

Continous Stock taking	*Periodic stock taking*
1. Permanent personnels are required.	1. Persons from other departments or temporary committee can be appointed.
2. Held throughout the year.	2. Generally held once in a year.
3. Normal and routine work will not be affected.	3. All work will be paralysed.
4. Discrepancies can be rectified without delay	4. There is delay in taking actions.
5. All items are not checked. Items are selected at random and selection of items is kept secret.	5. All items are checked.
6. It is a costly affair.	6. It is a cheaper method.

METHOD OF INVENTORY VALUATION:

Valuation of inventory is based on the **principle of conservatism.** Under this principle, expected losses from transactions already entered or events that have already occurred have to be recognised during the accounting year. But anticipated profits should not be recognised until profits are acutally realised or become due.

Further, inventory valuation is also based on the **Realisation concept** of accounting. If realisable value of inventory falls below cost price, inventory should be valued at net realisable value. Even if it has become absolutely certain that goods will be sold at a profit, inventory will be valued at cost price.

Thus the most generally accepted accounting principle for the valuation of inventory is that is should be valued at **cost or market value (net realisable value) whichever is lower.**

The meaning of 'cost' is the expenditure incurred in bringing the inventory to the place and condition in which the goods concerned are to be sold. "Market Price" means net "realisable value" in the case of finished goods (in normal course and "replacement price" in the case of raw materials and main items of stores.

According to International Accounting Standard: 2 (IAS:2), the inventories should be valued at the lowest of "Historical cost" and "Net Realisable value".

HISTORICAL COST

"Historical cost of inventories is the aggregate of cost of purchase, cost of conversion, and other costs incurred in bringing the inventories to their present location and condition." Thus, Historical Cost includes not only the price paid for acquisition of inventories but also all costs incurred for bringing and making them fit for use in production or for sale., examples, transportation costs, duties paid, insurance, manufacturing expenses, wages, or manufacturing expenses incurred for converting raw materials into finished products etc. Selling expenses should not be included.

The various methods for assigning historical costs to inventory and goods sold are being explained below:

(1) First In First Out (FIFO) Method

Under this method, materials are issued in the order in which they are received in the store. That is, the materials received first will be issued first. "First come first served". In other words, old stocks are issued first and new stocks will be issued afterwards. As a result of this method, when we value the closing stock of materials, that will be at the latest price.

Advantages:

1. The method is simple and easy to operate.
2. Closing stock of material will reflect at current price.
3. This systm is good for slow moving materials.
4. When prices are falling, this method gives better result.
5. "First come first served" is a logical system.
6. Deterioration and obsolescence can be avoided.

Disadvantages:

1. When price fluctuate, calculation becomes complicated.
2. Complicated calculation will invite clerical errors.
3. Under fluctuating prices, materials charged to different but similar jobs vary, leading to non-competitive.
4. When prices fall, job are charged with higher price of earlier materials; the quotations are less competitive.
5. When materials are returned to the store, they are treated as new purchases for the purpose of next issue.

(2) Last In First Out (LIFO) Method

This method is opposite to FIFO. Here, materials received last are issued first. Issues are made from the latest purchases. The issues are prices at the unit cost of the latest lot or the most recent purchase. The issues are not in chronological order, and cost of the material reflects current market price.

Advantages:

1. Material cost represents current price.
2. It facilitates complete recovery of material cost.
3. It is most suitable when prices are rising.
4. There is better matching of cost and revenue.

Disadvantages:

1. It involves considerable clerical work.
2. Due to variation of prices, comparison of cost of similar job is non-comparable.
3. Stock of materials shown in Balance Sheet will not reflect market price.
4. This system is not accepted by Income Tax authorities.

(3) Specific Identification Method

According to this method, each item of inventory is identified with its cost. The total of various costs so constitutes the value of inventory. This method is generally used when the materials or goods have been purchased for a specific job or customer. Such materials or goods are earmarked for the job and sold to that particular job or customer whenever demanded.

Advantages:

1. This method is realistic and objective since it adheres to the actual flow of goods.
2. Inventory is valued at actual cost instead of an assumed cost.
3. Because the cost is specially identified with the sale prices this method provides an accurate and ideal matching of costs and revenues.

Disadvantages:

1. This method is impracticable for a manufacturing process where inventory units lose their identity.
2. Cost of keeping different lots separately solely for the purpose of inventory valuation may be prohibitive which probably cannot be justified.
3. Profit manipulation by management is possible.

(4) Highest In First Out (HIFO)

Under this method materials of the highest price are issued first. According to this method the closing stock will be of the minimum price or as low as possible. In short, materials purchased at the highest price will be first issued, irrespective of the order of purchase; when the whole lot of the highest price is exhausted, materials purchased at the next higher price are issued. This method is suitable for cost plus contracts, but is not common. It rather operates similar to FIFO and LIFO.

(5) Base Stock Method

In almost all concerns, a minimum quantity of stock is always kept in store. A fixed minimum stock of the material is always maintained and is known as "safety" or "base stock". This stock is valued at a price at which the first lot of materials is received. The stock should not be issued until emergency arises. The quantity in excess of this base stock may be valued either on FIFO or LIFO method.

Since the system operates in conjunction with FIFO and LIFO, the advantages and disadvantages relating to FIFO and LIFO are applicable.

(6) Average Method

Average may be of two types - simple and weighted. In case of simple average, the prices are added and then divided by number of purchases. If 100 units are purchased at Rs. 8 and 50 units at Rs. 9, then the simple average will be (Rs. 8 + Rs. 9) ÷ 2 = Rs. 8.50.

In case of weighted average quantities are also taken into account. The price paid is multiplied by the quantity and the products are added. The total of the products is divided by total number of units involved. In the above case the weighted price will be :

$$\frac{100 \times \text{Rs. } 8 + 50 \times \text{Rs. } 9}{150} = \text{Rs. } 8.33$$

Weighted average is definitely better than simple average. The weighted average arrived at will be used to evaluate the stock in hand.

ILLUSTRATION 9.1

At the beginning of October, a Tin Private Company had 10,000 units @ Rs. 2 per unit. Further purchase were made during the month as follows:

4th Oct. 2,000 units @ Rs. 2.50 per unit.
10th Oct. 5,000 units @ Rs. 3.00 per unit
20th Oct. 10,000 units @ Rs. 3.50 per unit

The issues to the manufacture were as follows:

12th Oct. 16,000 units
28th Oct. 10,000 units

(*a*) Prepare a Bin Card

(*b*) What would be the value of the closing stock at the end of the month if the materials were issued according to:

1. First in first out method
2. Last in first out method
3. Weighted average method
4. FIFO under Base stock method
5. LIFO under Base stock method

} Base Stock 500 units

SOLUTION:

(*a*) **Bin Card**

Bin Card No. .... Maximum Level ....
Name of Material .... Minimum Level ....
Material Code No .... Ordering Level ....
Stores Leder Folio No. .... Unit ....

Date	*Receipts*		*Issues*		*Balance*	*Verification*		
	GRN No.	*Qty.*	*RS No.*	*Qty.*	*Qty.*	*Date*	*Remark*	*Initial*
Oct. 1	—	—	—	—	10,000			
Oct. 4	—	2,000	—	—	12,000			
Oct. 10	—	5,000	—	—	17,000			
Oct. 12	—	—	—	16,000	1,000			
Oct. 20	—	10,000	—	—	11,000			
Oct. 28	—	—	—	10,000	1,000			

(*b*) (1) **STORE LEDGER ACCOUNT (FIFO Method)**

Bin Card No. ....
Name of Meterial ....
Material Code No ....

Folio No. ....
Maximum Stock Level ....
Minimum Stock Level ....
Ordering Level ....
Ordering Quantity ....
Unit ....

		Receipts			*Issues*			*Balance*		
Date	*Particulars*	*Qty.*	*Rate Rs.*	*Amount Rs.*	*Qty.*	*Rate Rs.*	*Amount Rs.*	*Qty*	*Rate Rs.*	*Amount Rs.*
Oct. 1	Balance b/d	—	—	—	—	—	—	10,000	2.00	20,000
Oct. 4	G.N. No.	2,000	2.50	5,000	—	—	—	10,000	2.00	
								2,000	2.50	25,000
Oct. 10	G.R. No.	5,000	3.00	15,000				10,000	2.00	
								2,000	2.50	
								5,000	3.00	40,000
Oct. 12	R.S. No.	—	—	—	10,000	2.00				
					2,000	2.50				
					4,000	3.00	37,000	1,000	3.00	3,000
Oct. 20	G.R. No.	10,000	3.50	35,000	—	—	—	1,000	3.00	
								10,000	3.50	38,000
Oct. 28	R.S. No.	—	—	—	1,000	3.00				
					9,000	3.50	34,500	1,000	3.50	3,500

Value of Stock: 1,000 units @ Rs. 3.50 = Rs. 3,500.

(*b*) (2) **STORE LEDGER ACCOUNT (LIFO Method)**

Bin Card No............
Name of Material:...........
Material Code No............

Folio No...........
Maximum Stock Level:...........
Minimum Stock Level:...........
Ordering Level :...........
Ordering Quantity ....
Unit:...........

		Receipts			*Issues*			*Balance*		
Date	*Particulars*	*Qty.*	*Rate Rs.*	*Amount Rs.*	*Qty.*	*Rate Rs.*	*Amount Rs.*	*Qty*	*Rate Rs.*	*Amount Rs.*
Oct. 1	Balance b/d	—	—	—	—	—	—	10,000	2.00	20,000
Oct. 4	G.R. No.	2,000	2.50	5,000	—	—	—	10,000	2.00	
								2,000	2.50	25,000
Oct. 10	G.R. No.	5,000	3.00	15,000	—	—	—	10,000	2.00	
								2,000	2.50	
								5,000	3.00	40,000
Oct. 12	R.S. No.	—	—	—	5,000	3.00				
					2,000	2.50				
					9,000	2.00	38,000	1,000	2.00	2,000
Oct. 20	G.R. No.	10,000	3.50	35,000				1,000	2.00	
								10,000	3.50	37,000
Oct. 28	R.S. No.	—	—	—	10,000	3.50	35,000	1,000	2.00	2,000

Value of Stock : 1,000 units @ Rs. 2.00 = Rs. 2,000

(*b*) (3) **STORE LEDGER ACCOUNT (Weighted Average Method)**

		Receipts			*Issues*			*Balance*		
Date	*Particulars*	*Qty.*	*Rate Rs.*	*Amount Rs.*	*Qty.*	*Rate Rs.*	*Amount Rs.*	*Qty*	*Rate Rs.*	*Amount Rs.*
Oct. 1	Balance b/d	—	—	—	—	—	—	10,000	2.00	20,000
Oct. 4	G.R. No.	2,000	2.50	5,000	—	—	—	12,000	2.08	25,000
Oct. 10	G.R. No.	5,000	3.00	15,000	—	—	—	17,000	2.35	40,000
Oct. 12	R.S. No.	—	—	—	16,000	2.35	37,600	1,000	2.35	2,350
Oct. 20	G.R. No.	10,000	3.50	35,000	—	—	—	11,000	3.40	37,350
Oct. 28	R.S. No.	—	—	—	10,000	3.40	34,000	1,000	3.40	3,400

Value of stock : 1,000 units @ 3.40 = Rs. 3,400

(*b*) (4) **STORE LEDGER ACCOUNT (Base Stock (FIFO) Method)**

Base Stock 500

		Receipts			*Issues*			*Balance*		
Date	*Particulars*	*Qty.*	*Rate Rs.*	*Amount Rs.*	*Qty.*	*Rate Rs.*	*Amount Rs.*	*Qty*	*Rate Rs.*	*Amount Rs.*
Oct. 1	Balance b/d	—	—	—	—	—	—	10,000	2.00	20,000
Oct. 4	G.R. No	2,000	2.50	5,000	—	—	—	10,000	2.00	
								2,000	2.50	25,000
Oct. 10	G.R. No.	5,000	3.00	15,000	—	—	—	10,000	2.00	
								2,000	2.50	
								5,000	3.00	40,000
Oct. 12	R.S. No.	—	—	—	9,500	2.00				
					2,000	2.50				
					4,500	3.00	37,500	500	2.00	
								500	3.00	2,500
Oct. 20	G.R. No.	10,000	3.50	35,000	—	—	—	500	2.00	
								500	3.00	
								10,000	3.50	37,500
Oct. 28	R.S. No.	—	—	—	500	3.00				
					9,500	3.50	34,750	500	2.00	
								500	3.50	2,750

Value of Stock: 1,000 units (500 × Rs. 2 + 500 × Rs. 3.50) = Rs. 2,750

(*b*) (5) **STORE LEDGER ACCOUNTS (Base Stock (LIFO) Method)**

Base Stock 500

		Receipts			*Issues*			*Balance*		
Date	*Particulars*	*Qty.*	*Rate Rs.*	*Amount Rs.*	*Qty.*	*Rate Rs.*	*Amount Rs.*	*Qty*	*Rate Rs.*	*Amount Rs.*
Oct. 1	Balance b/d	—	—	—	—	—	—	10,000	2.00	20,000
Oct. 4	G.R. No.	2,000	2.50	5,000	—	—	—	10,000	2.00	
								2,000	2.50	25,000
Oct. 10	G.R. No.	5,000	3.00	15,000	—	—	—	10,000	2.00	
								2,000	2.50	

								5,000	3.00	40,000
Oct. 12	R.S. No.	—	—	—	5,000	3.00				
					2,000	2.50				
					9,000	2.00	38,000	1,000	2.00	2,000
Oct. 20	G.R. No.	10,000	3.50	35,000	—	—	—	1,000	2.00	
								10,000	3.50	37,000
Oct. 28	R.S. No.	—	—	—	10,000	3.50	35,000	1,000	2.00	2,000

Value of stock : 1000 @ Rs. 2 = Rs. 2000

ILLUSTRATION 9.2.

Prepare Store Ledger Account from the following information.

Jan. 1 Purchased 500 kg. at Rs. 20 per kg.
10 Purchased 300 kg. at Rs. 21 per kg.
15 Issued 600 kg.
20 Purchased 400 kg at Rs. 22 per kg.
25 Issued 300 kg.
27 Purchased 500 kg at Rs. 21 per kg.
31 Issued 200 kg.

Adopt the Base Stock Method of issue and ascertain the value of closing stock. Base Stock 200 kg.

(B.Com. Bangalore, Madurai)

SOLUTION:

STORES LEDGER ACCOUNT (Base Stock — FIFO)

Name of Article: .... Folio: ....
Code: .... Maximum Level: ....
Bin Card No .... Minimum Level: ....
Units: .... Reordering Level: ....
Reordering Quantity: ....

		Receipts			*Issues*			*Balance*		
Date	*Particulars*	*Qty.*	*Rate Rs.*	*Amount Rs.*	*Qty.*	*Rate Rs.*	*Amount Rs.*	*Qty*	*Rate Rs.*	*Amount Rs.*
Jan. 1	Goods Receeved Note No.	500	20	10,000	—	—	—	500	20	10,000
Jan. 10	Goods Received	300	21	6,300	—	—	—	500	20	
	Note No.							300	21	16,300
Jan. 15	Requisition Slip	—	—	—	300	20				
	No.				300	21	12,300	200	20	4,000
Jan. 20	Goods Received	400	22	8,800	—	—	—	200	20	
	Note No.							400	22	12,800
Jan. 25	Requisition Slip	—	—	—	300	22	6,600	200	20	
	No.							100	22	6,200
Jan. 27	Goods Received	500	21	10,500				200	20	
	Note No.							100	22	
								500	21	16,700
Jan. 31	Requisition Slip				100	22				
	No.				100	21	4,300	200	20	
								400	21	12,400

Value of closing stock: 600 Kg of Rs. 12,400
(or) 200 Kg × Rs. 20 + 400 Kg × Rs. 21 = 12,400

ILLUSTRATION 9.3.

By solving illustration No. 2, under Base Stock: LIFO method.

STORE LEDGER ACCOUNT (Base Stock: LIFO)

Name of Article.......	Folio:.......
Code:.......	Maximum Level:.......
Bin Card No........	Minimum Level:.......
Units:.......	Reordering Level:.......
	Reordering Quantity ....

		Receipts			*Issues*			*Balance*		
Date	*Particulars*	*Qty.*	*Rate Rs.*	*Amount Rs.*	*Qty.*	*Rate Rs.*	*Amount Rs.*	*Qty*	*Rate Rs.*	*Amount Rs.*
Jan. 1	Goods Received Note No.	500	20	10,000	—	—	—	500	20	10,000
Jan. 10	Goods Received Note No.	300	21	6,300				500 300	20 21	16,300
Jan. 15	Requisition Slip No.	—	—	—	300 300	21 20	12,300	200	20	4,000
Jan. 20	Goods Received Note No.	400	22	8,800				200 400	20 22	12,800
Jan. 25	Requisition Slip No.	—	—	—	300	22	6,600	200 100	20 22	6,200
Jan. 27	Goods Received Note No.	50	21	10,500	—	—	—	200 100 500	20 22 21	16,700
Jan. 31	Requisition Slip No.	—	—	—	200	21	4,200	200 100 300	20 22 21	12,500

Value of Closing stock: 600 Kg of Rs. 12,500

(or) 200 Kg × Rs. 20 + 100 Kg × Rs. 22 + 300 Kg × Rs. 21 = 12,500

NET REALISABLE VALUE

According to International Accounting Standard : 2 (IAS:2), the net realisable value means "the estimated selling price in the ordinary course of business less costs of completion and less costs necessarily to be incurred in order to make the sale". Thus, net realisable value is to be calculated after taking into consideration all expenses which might have to be incurred for making sales. For example, if a seller has to pay a commission of 20% on sales, the net realisable value of an article having a selling price of Rs. 10 should be taken as only Rs. 8.

Inventories are to be valued at cost or net realisable value, whichever is less. The ascertainment of net realisable value of different items and its comparision with the historical costs can be done by any of the following methods.

(A) Aggregate or Total Inventory Method:

According to this method, the total cost prices of the different items of inventories are calculated and the total, so calculated, is compared with the total of net realisable value of the different items of inventory. Inventory is valued at a price which is the least of the two.

(B) Group Method:

According to this method, groups are formed to homogeneous items of inventory. The cost and the net realisable value of each group so formed are found out. The least of the two, cost or net realisable value of each group of items, is taken for valuation of inventory.

(C) Item by Item Method:

According to this method, the cost and net realisable prices of each item of inventory are found out. Each item is valued at a price of the cost or net realisable value whichever is the least. IAS:2 has recommended the use of "group" or "item by item" method for valuation of inventory. The "Aggregate or total inventory method" has not found favour with the International Accounting Standard Committee.

STOCK TAKING BEFORE OR AFTER THE DATE OF BALANCE SHEET.

It may happen, sometimes, that the work of physical stock taking cannot be accomplished on the date of the Balance Sheet and, as such, it may have to be taken up and completed a few days after the Balance Sheet date. It may also happen that the work of inventory valuation might have been completed a few days earlier than the date of financial close. In either case, it is necessary to effect certain adjustments for those transactions that have taken place in the interval between the date on which stock is valued and the Balance Sheet date. This is true even if the value of stock is given after the date of the Balance Sheet.

ADJUSTMENTS REQUIRED

The following adjustments become necessary if the value of stock given is ***prior to the closing date:***

(*a*) Add purchases made during the interval between the date of stock-taking and the date of Balance Sheet:

(*b*) Deduct purchase returns during the same period:

(*c*) Deduct sales at cost between the two dates:
(cost = Sales – Margin of profit on sales)

(*d*) Add sales returns at cost:

(*e*) Add any overcasting in the stock sheets:

(*f*) Deduct any undercasting in the stock sheet:

(*g*) Adjust goods held on consignment basis, goods-in-transit, goods sent on approval or sale or return.

In the case, the value of stock given is **after the closing date**, the above adjustments will have to be **reversed.**

When stock is valued after the closing date of financial year.

ILLUSTRATION 9.4

Mr. X who was closing his books on 31st March, 2006 failed to take the actual stock which he did only on 9th April, 2006, when it was ascertained by him to be worth Rs. 25,000.

It was found that sales are entered in the sales book on the same day of despatch and return inwards in the return book as and when the goods are received back. Purchases are entered in the purchases day book once the invoices are received.

It was found that sales between 31-3-2006 and 9-4-2006 as per the sales day book are Rs. 1,720. Purchases between 31-3-2006 and 9-4-2006 as per purchases day book are Rs. 120. Out of these, goods amounting to Rs. 50 were not received until after the stock was taken.

Goods invoiced during the month of March, 2006 but good received only on 4th April, 2006 amounted to Rs. 100. Rate of gross profit is $33\frac{1}{3}$ on cost.

Ascertain the value of physical stock as on 31-3-2006.

(C.A. Foundation)

SOLUTION.

STATEMENT OF STOCK VALUATION

as on 31st March, 2006

			Rs.
Value of stock on 9th April, 2006			25,000
Less:	Purchase from 1-4-2006 to 9-4-2006	Rs. 120	
	Goods not received	50	70
			24,930
Add:	Cost of goods sold from 1-4-2006 to 9-4-2006		
	Sales	Rs. 1,720	
Less:	Gross profit, $33\frac{1}{3}$% on cost, *i.e.*, $\frac{100}{3}\times\frac{3}{400}\times 1{,}720$	= 430	
			1,290
			26,220
Less:	Goods received on 4-4-2006		100
	Stock on 31st March, 2006		26,120

NB: $33\frac{1}{3}$ of Cost = 25% of Sales

That is : Rs. 1,720 × 25% = Rs. 430

When stock is valued earlier than the date of financial year.

ILLUSTRATION 9.5.

Determine the value of stock to be taken for Balance Sheet purposes as on 31st March, 2006 from the following information:

The stock was verified on 25th March, 2006 and was valued at Rs. 10,00,000. The following transactions took place between 25th March, 2006 and 31st March, 2006.

(*a*) Out of goods sent on consignment, goods worth Rs. 40,000 (at cost) were unsold.

(*b*) Sales were for Rs. 2,50,000. This includes goods worth Rs. 75,000 sent on approval basis. One-third of these were returned before 31st March. 2006. As regards the remaining, no intimation is received.

(*c*) Purchases were of Rs. 2,50,000. Out of this, goods worth Rs. 50,000 were delivered after 31st March, 2006.

(*d*) The selling price is fixed by having a 20% margin on sales value. However, to one customer, goods costing Rs. 20,000 were sold for Rs. 15,000. (*I.C.W.A. Final*)

SOLUTION.

STATEMENT OF STOCK VALUATION

as on 31-3-2006.

		Rs.	*Rs.*
Value of stock as on 25th March, 2006			10,00,000
Add:	Goods sent on approval:		40,000
	Sales value of goods sent	50,000	
Less:	Profit at 20% on sales	10,000	
			40,000
Add:	Purchases:		
	Good received	2,00,000	
	Goods in transit on 31-3-2006	50,000	
			2,50,000
			13,30,000

Less:	Cost of normal goods sold:		
	Sales	2,50,000	
	Less: Sale of abnormal goods	15,000	
		2,35,000	
	Less: Goods sent on approval but returned	25,000	
		2,10,000	
	Less: Profit at 20% of sales	42,000	
		1,68,000	
	Add: Cost of abnormal sale	20,000	
			1,88,000
	Value of stock on 31st March, 2006		11,42,000

ILLUSTRATION 9.6.

From the following information, ascertain the value of stock as on 31.3.2006:

	Rs.
Value of Stock on 1.4.2005	70,000
Purchase during the period from 1.4.2005 to 31.3.2006	3,46,000
Manufacturing expenses during the above period	70,000
Sales during the same period	5,22,000

At the time of valuing stock on 31.3.2005, a sum of Rs. 6,000 was written off a particular item which was originally purchased for Rs. 20,000 and was sold for Rs. 16,000. But for the other transactions the gross profit earned during the year was 25% on cost. (C.A)

Solution:

Statement showing the Valuation of Closing Stock as at 31 March 2006

		Rs.
Normal Sales [Rs. 5,22,000 – Rs. 16,000]		5,06,000
Less: Gross Profit @ 20% on Sales		1,01,200
Cost of Goods sold		4,04,800
Opening stock of normal goods [Rs. 70,000 – Rs. 14,000]	56,000	
Purchases	3,46,000	
Manufacturing Expenses	70,000	4,72,000
Value of stock as on 31.3.2006.		67,200

Illustration 9.7

A trader prepared his accounts to 31st March, each year. Due to some unavoidable reasons, no stock taking could be possible till following 15th April, on which date the total cost of goods in his godown came to Rs. 60,500. The following facts were established in between 31st March and 15th April.

(*a*) Sales: Rs. 45,590 [Including cash sales Rs. 10,120]

(*b*) Purchases : Rs. 16,710 [Including cash purchases Rs. 5,990]

(*c*) Sales Returns Rs. 1,200

(*d*) Collections from Debtors Rs. 14,600

(*e*) Payment to Creditors – Rs. 7,816

(*f*) On 15th March, goods of the sale value of Rs. 6,800 were sent on return basis to a customer, the period of approval being four weeks. He returned 40% of the goods on 10th April, approving the rest; the customer was billed on 16th April.

(*g*) The trader had received goods costing Rs. 8,000 in March for sale on consignment basis: 20% of the goods had been sold by 31st March, and another 40% by 15th April. These sales are not included in (*a*) above.

Goods are sold by the trader at a profit of 20% on sales. You are required to ascertain the value of stock on hand on 31st March.

Solution: **Statement showing valuation of Stock on 31st March.**

	Amount (Rs.)	*Amount (Rs.)*
Value of stock as on 15th April		60,500
Add: Sales *Less* returns during 31st March to 15th April (45,590 – 1,200)	44,390	
Less: Gross Profit @ 20%	8,878	35,512
		96,012
Add: 60% of Goods sent on approval basis	4,080	
Less Gross Profit @ 20%	816	3,264
		99,276
Less: Purchase (from 1st April to 15th April)	16,710	
Less: 40% of stock on consignment	3,200	19,910
Stock as on 31st March		79,366

Notes: Collection from debtors, payment to creditors, cash purchases and cash sales have no relevance for calculating value of stock.

Illustration 9.8. S.Ltd. keeps no running records but a physical inventory of stock is made at the end of each quarter and evaluated at cost. The company's year ends on 31st March, 2007 and draft accounts have been prepared to that date. The stock inventory taken on 31st March, 2007 was accidently destroyed before the items had been evaluated, the closing stock figure used in the draft accounts being that shown by the inventory taken on 31st December, 2006. The gross margin earned by the company is 25% of cost. During your audit you discovered the following:

(*a*) The cost of the stock on 31st December, 2006 as shown by the inventory was Rs. 40,525.

(*b*) On 31st December, 2006 stock sheets showed the following discrepancies:

(*i*) A page total of Rs. 5,059 had been carried to the summary as Rs. 5,509.

(*ii*) The total of a page had been undercast by Rs. 98.

(*iii*) 100 items which had cost Rs. 5 each had been taken at 25 paise each.

(*c*) Invoice for purchases entered in the purchases book during the month of January, February and March, 2007 totalled Rs. 38,560. Of this total Rs. 2,800 related to goods received on or prior to 31st December, 2006. Invoices entered in April, 2007 relating to goods received in March, 2007 totalled Rs. 3,700.

(*d*) Sales invoiced to customers in January, February and March, 2007 totalled Rs. 51,073. Of this total, Rs. 3,824 related to goods despatched on or before 31st December, 2006. Goods despatched to customers before 31st March, 2007 but invoiced in April 2007 totalled Rs. 5,241.

(*e*) During the final quarter to the company's year, credit notes at invoiced value of Rs. 1,280 have been issued to customers in respect of goods returned during that period.

You are required to prepare a statement showing the amount of the stock at cost on 31st March, 2007. [*C.A.*]

Solution.

STATEMENT OF STOCK VALUATION

as on 31st March, 2007

	Rs.	Rs.
Stock as on 31st December, 2006		40,525
Less: Error in carry forward (Rs. 5,509 – Rs. 5,059) =		450
		40,075
Add: Error of undercasting		98
Add: Cost of 100 items taken at 25 paise each (Rs. 500 – Rs. 25)		475
		40,648
Add: Purchases from 1-1-2007 to 31-3-2007	38,560	
Add: Goods purchased before 31st March, 2007	3,700	
	42,260	
Less: Goods received prior to 31st Dec., 2006	2,800	
		39,460
		80,108
Less: Cost of goods sold:		
Sales from 1-1.2007 to 31-3-2007	51,073	
Add: Goods despatched before 31-3-2007 but invoiced in April 2007	5,241	
	56,314	
Less: Goods despatched before 31-12-2006	3,824	
	52,490	
Less: Goods returned by customers	1,280	
	51,210	
Less: Profit margin 25% on cost or 20% on 51,210	10,242	
		40,968
Value of stock as on 31st March, 2007		39,140

Illustration 9.9. Mr. Vijay's finiancial year ends on 30th June, but actual stock is not taken until the following 8th July, when it is ascertained at Rs. 7,425.

You find that:

(1) Sales are entered in the Sales Book on the same day as despatched and returns inward in the Return Inward Book the day the goods are received back.

(2) Purchases are entered in the Purchases Day Book as the invoices are received.

(3) Sales between 30th June and 8th July as per the Sales Day Book and Cash Book are Rs. 8,600.

(4) Purchases between 30th June and 8th July as per the Purchases Day Book are Rs. 660 but of these goods amounting to Rs. 60 are not received until after the stock was taken.

(5) Goods invoiced during June (before 30th June), but not received until after 30th June amounted to Rs. 500 of which Rs. 350 worth are received between 30th June and 8th July.

(6) Rate of gross profit is $33^1/_3$ on cost.

Ascertain the value of stock on 30th June. [*C.A.*]

Solution:

Calculation of Stock as on 30th June.

	Rs.	Rs.
Stock as on 8th July		7,425
Add: Sales value of goods sold	8,600	
Less: Gross Profit 25% on Sales	2,150	6,450
		13,875
Less: Purchase entered (30th June to 8th July)	660	
Less: Received after 8th July	60	600
		13,275
Add: Purchases invoiced before 30th June, 1987 not received upto 8th July (500 – 350)		150
Stock on 30th June		13,425

Illustration 9.10. The financial year of Mr X ends on 31st March 2007 but the stock on hand was physically verified only on 7th April 2007. You are required to ascertain the value of closing stock (at cost) as on 31st March 2007 from the following information:

(*a*) The stock (valued at cost) as verified on 7th April 2007 was Rs. 1,54,000.

(*b*) Sales have been entered in the Sales Day Book only after the despatch of goods and sales returns only on receipt of the goods.

(*c*) Purchases have been entered in the Purchases Day Book on receipt of the purchase invoice irrespective of the date of receipt of the goods.

(*d*) Sales as per Sales Day Book for the period 1st April 2007 to 7th April 2007 before the actual verification) amounted to Rs. 68,800 of which goods of sale value of Rs. 12,000 had not been delivered at the time of verification.

(*e*) Purchases as per Purchases Day Book for the period 1st April 2007 to 7th April 2007 (before the actual verification) amounted to Rs. 58,000 of which goods for purchases of Rs. 15,000 had not been received at the date of verification and goods for purchases of Rs. 20,000 had been received prior to 31st March 2007.

(*f*) In respect of goods costing Rs. 50,000 received prior to 31st March 2007, invoices had not been received until the date of verification of stocks.

(*g*) The gross profit is 25% on sales. (*ICWA, Inter*)

Solution:

Statement Showing the Value of Stock
on March 31, 2007

Particulars		Rs.	Rs.
Stock on April 7, 2007			1,54,000
Add: Cost of goods sold and despatched during the period 1st to 7th April sales		68,800	
Less: Goods not despatched at the time of verification		12,000	
Less: Gross Profit @ 25%		56,800	
		14,200	42,600
			1,96,600
Less: Goods purchased and received during the period 1st to 7th April		58,000	
Less: Goods received after 7th April	15,000		
Goods received before 1st April	20,000	35,000	23,000
			1,73,600

Less: Goods received before 31st March but invoice received after wards and not included in purchase of last Accounting period:		
Invoice received before 7th April	20,000	
Invoices received after 7th April	50,000	70,000
		1,03,600
Value of physical stock	1,73,600	
Value of stock on March 31st, 2007 for Final Accounts	1,03,600	

Illustration 9.11. Raghunath made up his annual accounts to Nov. 30 2006. All purchases and sale invoices and credit notes dated Nov. 2006, had been duly entered in the books, but all such documents dated Dec. 2006, had been treated as relating to the year commencing Dec. 1, 2006.

Stock was taken on December 7, 2006 when the total stock was found to be Rs. 1,50,000 valued at cost. The rate of Gross Profit earned was 30% on Sale Price.

Further:

(*a*) Goods were received from suppliers during the five days from Dec. 1 to Dec. 5 (Dec. 6 was Sunday). The connected invoices dated Nov. 2006, amounted to Rs. 1,800 and those dated Dec. 2006 to Rs. 9,180.

(*b*) Sales and sales returns for the period from Dec. 1 to Dec. 5, 2006, were respectively Rs. 12,600 and Rs. 1,440.

(*c*) The stock included goods valued at Rs. 2,100 held by Raghunath on sale or return for which no entries had been made in the books.

(*d*) A sub-total of Rs. 29,000 on one of the Stock Sheets had been carried to the summary of Stock Sheet as Rs. 29,900.

(*e*) One Stock Sheet has been overcast by Rs. 2,000.

(*f*) One item of a number of articles costing Rs. 1,875 had been shown as Rs. 875.

Prepare a statement showing the value of the stock to be included in the accounts on the 30th Nov. 2006.]

SOLUTION:

Statement Showing the Value of Stock on 31.11.2006

		Rs.	*Rs.*
Value of stock on Dec. 8, 2006			1,50,000
Less: Goods received in December relating to invoices dated December			9,180
			1,40,820
Add: Net Cost of Sales:			
Sales in December	12,600		
Less: Sales returns	1,440	11,160	
Less: Gross Profit @ 30%		3,348	7,812
			1,48,632
Less: Goods held on sale or return basis			2,100
			1,46,532
Less: Excess total carried in stock sheet (29,900 – 29,000)			900
			1,45,632
Less: Stock sheet overcast			2,000
			1,43,632
Add: Error in showing one item (1875 – 875)			1,000
Value of stock on 30.11.2006			1,44,632

Illustration 9.12. The Directions of Quality Machineries Ltd. request you to ascertain the amount at which the inventory should be included in the financial statements for the year 2006-07. The value of the inventory as shown in books is Rs. 12,50,000.

To determine the net realisable value of the inventory (on a test check basis), you had selected several items whose book value was Rs. 3,50,000. You ascertain that except for the items (i) to (iii), mentioned below, the cost was in excess of the realisable value by Rs. 29,532.

The following items require special treatment:

(*i*) One machine (Cost Rs. 1,30,000) can now fetch Rs. 1,15,000. It was priced at Rs. 70,000 and was written down to the same figure at the end of 2006-07

(*ii*) A Pump (Cost Rs. 50,000) was expected to realise Rs. 35,000. A special commission of 15% would have to be paid to the broker.

(*iii*) 6 units of product No 15710 were in stock valued each at Rs. 5,520; the selling price was Rs 4,500 per unit; selling expenses are 10% of the selling price.

Taking into consideration only the above mentioned items requiring special treatment, compute the value of the inventory as at 31st March 2007 you would consider reasonable.

(*C.A.*)

Solution.

Statement of Inventory Valuation

			Rs.	Rs.
Total Value of Inventory as per books				12,50,000
Less: Book value of selected items				3,50,000
Book value of the remaining items selling				9,00,000
Less: Deduction @ 15% for realisable value being less than cost (*see working note*)				1,35,000
				7,65,000
Add: Realisable value of selected items except special items				1,67,348
Add: Special items:			Rs.	
(*i*)	Machine (realisable value)		1,15,000	
(*ii*)	Pump (realisable value less 15%)		29,750	
(*iii*)	Product No. 15710:			
	Realisable value	27,000		
	Less: 10% expenses	2,700	24,300	1,69,050
Value of Inventory				11,01,398

Working Note:

			Rs.
Book value of selected items			Rs. 3,50,000
Less: Book value of special items	(*i*)	70,000	
	(*ii*)	50,000	
	(*iii*)	33,120 (5,520 × 6)	1,53,120
Book value of the remaining items	(*a*)		1,96,880
Excess of cost over realisable value	(*b*)		29,532
Realisable value			1,67,348

Percentage of (*b*) to (*a*): 100 × 29,532/1,96,880 = 15%

Illustration 9.13. Determine the value of stock to be taken for Balance Sheet as at 31st March, 2006, from the following information:

The stock was physically verified on 23rd March 2006 and was valued at Rs. 6,00,000. Between 23rd March 2006 and 31st March 2006, the following transactions had taken place:

1. Purchase of Rs. 50,000 of this, goods worth Rs. 20,000 were delivered on 5th April, 2006.
2. Out of goods sent on consignment, goods worth Rs. 30,000 (at cost) were unsold.

3. Sales was of Rs. 1,70,000. This includes goods worth Rs. 40,000 sent on approval, half of these were returned before 31st March. As regards remaining, no intimation is received.
4. Normally firm sells goods on cost plus 25%. However, a lot of goods costing Rs. 30,000 was sold for Rs. 15,000.

[I.C.W.A.]

Solution:

Statement Showing Value of Stock
as on 31st March 2006.

		Rs.	Rs.
Stock as on 23rd March			6,00,000
Add: Purchased between			
23rd and 31st March			
Rs. 50,000 – Rs. 20,000		30,000	
In Transit		20,000	
Goods in the hands of Consignee (at cost)		30,000	
		80,000	
Goods on approval:			
Goods sent	40,000		
Less: ½ Returned	20,000		
	20,000		
Less: Profit thereof 20%	4,000	16,000	96,000
			6,96,000
Less: Cost of Sales between 23rd and 31st March:			
Goods Sold		1,70,000	
Less: Sent on Approval		20,000	
		1,50,000	
Less: Abnormal Sales		15,000	
		1,35,000	
Less: Profit thereof 20%		27,000	
		1,08,000	
Add: Cost of Abnormal Sales		30,000	1,38,000
Value of Stock on 31st March 2006			5,58,000

20% on Cost = 25% on Sales.

ACCOUNTING STANDARD (AS-2) AND INVENTORY VALUATION

The Accounting Standard pertaining to valuation of inventories, issued in 1981, was revised in the year 1999. The revised standard has come into effect in respect of accounting periods commencing on or after 1-4-1999. The standard is also mandatory in nature.

Objective. Parts I and II of Schedule VI to the Companies Act, 1956 have laid down inventory valuation and the requirement of disclosure in the financial statements of companies registered under the said Act. Accounting Standard (AS-2) issued by the Institute of Chartered Accountants of India has elaborated the aspects of inventory valuation and disclosure requirements thereby supplementing the legal requirements. The main purpose of this accounting standard is thus the determination of the value at which inventories are to be carried in the financial statements until the related revenues are recognised, and any write-down thereof to net realisable value.

Meaning of invntory. Paragraph 3 of the Statement defines inventories as assets (*a*) held for sale in the ordinary course of business, (*b*) in the progress of production for such sale, or (*c*) in the form of materials or supplies to be consumed in the production process or in the rendering of services.

Definition (*a*) above covers finished goods. Accordingly, goods produced for sale, merchandise purchased by a retailer and held for resale, computer software held for the same purpose, land and other property meant for sale fall under this part of the definition. Raw materials and work-in-progress are covered under part (*b*) and consumable stores and supplies fall under part (*c*).

Applicability. Th scope of this standard is confined to inventories as defined in paragraphs (3) and (4) of the Statement. However, paragraph (1) of the statement excludes the following from the purview of the standard:

(*i*) work-in-progress arising under construction contracts, including directly related service contracts to which AS-7 is applicable;

(*ii*) work-in-progress arising in the ordinary course of business of service providers;

(*iii*) shares, debentures and other finanacial instruments held as stock-in-trade; and

(*iv*) producers' inventories of livestock, agricultural and forest products, and mineral oils, ores and gases to the extent that they are measured at net realisable value in accordance with well established practices in those industries.

Basis of valuation. Paragraph 5 of this Statement requires that inventories should be valued at cost or net realisable value, whichever is lower. Cost of inventories comprise cost of purchases, cost of conversion and other costs incurred in bringing the inventories to their present position and location

The cost of purchase comprises purchase price including duties and taxes (excluding taxes subsequently recoverable from taxing authorities) freight and carriage inwards as well as those expenditure directly attributable to acquisition. In determining the cost of purchase it is necessary to deduct trade discount, duty drawback and such other items.

Conversion cost includes costs directly related to units of production such as direct labour. It also includes a system allocation of fixed and variable production overheads that are incurred in the process of conversion of materials into finished goods. Fixed production overheads comprise depreciation and maintenance of factory buildings and the cost of factory management and administration. Variable production overheads, on the other hand, comprise indirect costs of production that vary directly or nearly directly with the volume of production.

Cost of inventories may include other costs also if and to the extent they are incurred in bringing inventories to their present location and condition. Interest and borrowing costs are not included.

Exclusion of costs. In determination the cost of inventories, it is usual to exclude the following costs and treat them as expenses in the period in which they are incurred:

(*a*) Abnormal amounts of waste materials, labour or other production costs;

(*b*) Storage costs, unless those costs are necessary in the production process prior to a further production stage;

(*c*) Administrative overheads that do not contribute to bringing the inventories to their present location and condition; and

(*d*) Selling and distribution costs.

Cost Formulae. Cost of inventories of items that are not ordinarily interchangeable, and goods or services produced and segregated for specific projects, should be assigned by specific identification of their individual costs. Specific identification of cost means that specific costs are attributed to identified items of inventory.

A number of cost formulae are used to determine the cost of inventories other than those for which specific identification of individual costs is necessary and appropriate. The cost formula used should provide the fairest possible approximation to the cost incurred in bringing the item to its present location and condition. In order to prevent any under or over-valuation of inventories, this standard does not permit the LIFO method of valuation.

Paragraph 16 of the Statement lays down that the cost of inventories, other than those identified items of inventory referred to in paragraph 14, should be assigned by using the FIFO or Weighted Average Cost formula.

Techniques for measurement of cost. The technique of standard costing may be used for the measurement of the cost of inventories if the results approximate the actual cost. Standard costs take into account normal levels of consumption of materials and supplies, labour, efficiency and capacity utilisation. These are reviewed regularly and, if necessary, reviewed in the light of current conditions.

Apart from standard costing, the retail trade for measuring inventories of large numbers of rapidly changing items and for which it is impracticable to use other methods of costing. The cost of inventories is determined by deducting from the sales value of the inventories the appropriate gross margin.

Net Realisable Value. The practise of writing down inventory to net realisable value which may be below cost, is consistent with the view that assets should not be carried in excess of amounts expected to be realised from their sale or use. The cost of inventories may not be recoverable if the inventories are damaged, if they have become wholly or partially obsolete, or if their selling prices have fallen. Recovery of cost may not also be possible if the estimated costs of completion or the estimated costs necessary to make the sale have increased.

Inventories are usually written down to net realisable value on an item-by-item basis. In some circumstances, similar or related items may be put together as a group. This may be the case with items of inventory relating to the same product line that have similar purposes or end uses and are produced in the same geographical area and cannot be evaluated separately from other items in that product line.

Materials and supplies held for use in the production of inventories are not written down below cost if the finished products in which they will be incorporated are expected to be sold at or above cost. However, when there is a fall in the price of materials and it is estimated that the cost of the finished product will exceed the net realisable value, the materials are written down to net realisable value. In such a case, the replacement cost may be the best available measure of net realisable value.

Disclosure. It is necessary to disclose in the financial statements:

(*a*) the accounting policies adopted in measuring inventories, including the cost formula used; and

(*b*) the total carrying amount of inventories and its classification appropriate to the enterprise.

QUESTIONS

Objective Type Questions.

I. State whether each of the following statements is "true" or "false".

1. The valuation of inventory only affects the income statement.
2. FIFO method correlates the current costs with the current market prices.
3. Periodic inventory gives a continuous balance of stock in hand.
4. Under FIFO method, the closing stock is valued at the rate of last consignment.
5. If the closing inventory is understated, the net profit of the period will be overstated.
6. Stock should be valued at cost or market price whichever is lower.
7. Inventory valuation affects only the position statement.

8. Perpetual inventory system enables management to ascertain stock at any time.
9. Inventory also includes work-in-progress.
10. The need for valuation of inventory arises for determining the true income of a business.

(*Ans*: True – 1, 4, 6, 8, 9, 10. False – 2, 3, 5, 7.)

II. Choose the correct answer:

1. The system which gives continuous information regarding quantum and value of inventory is known as:
   (*a*) Continuous stock taking. (*b*) Periodic Inventory.
   (*c*) Perpetual Inventory.
2. LIFO method matches:
   (*a*) Current costs with current revenues. (*b*) Fixed assets with fixed liabilities.
   (*c*) Pre-determined costs with current revenues.
3. Inventory is recorded in the books of accounts at its:
   (*a*) Market value. (*b*) Cost.
   (*c*) Net realisable value.
4. Inventory is valued at lower of the cost or net realisable value on account of the accounting principles of:
   (*a*) Consistency. (*b*) Realisation
   (*c*) Conservatism.
5. Closing inventory is shown in the Balance Sheet under:
   (*a*) Fixed Assets (*b*) Current Assets.
   (*c*) Current Liabilities.
6. Which inventory pricing method assumes that the goods most recently purchased are sold first ?
   (*a*) FIFO (*b*) LIFO
   (*c*) Simple Average.
7. Cost of sales is equal to:
   (*a*) Opening Stock – Purchases. (*b*) Opening + Purchases.
   (*c*) Opening stock + Closing Stock – Purchases.
   (d) Opening Stock + Purchases – Closing Stock.
8. If merchandise inventory is being valued at cost and the price level is steadily rising, the method of costing that will yield the highest net income is:
   (*a*) LIFO (*b*) FIFO
   (*c*) Average (*d*) Periodic
9. Which inventory pricing method reflects the most recently incurred purchase costs in the ending inventory:
   (*a*) FIFO (*b*) LIFO
   (*c*) Weighted Average.
10. "Lower of cost or market rule" is an example of which concept:
    (*a*) Consistancy (*b*) Conservatism
    (*c*) Matching

(*Ans*: 1. (*c*); 2. (*a*); 3. (*b*); 4. (*c*); 5. (*b*); 6. (*b*); 7. (*d*); 8. (*b*); 9. (*a*) 10. (*b*)).

THEORETICAL QUESTIONS

1. What are the relative advantages and disadvantages of FIFO and LIFO from management point of view.
2. Define inventory. Why proper valuation of inventory is important ?
3. What are the objectives of inventory valuation ?

4. Compare LIFO and FIFO as methods of valuing inventories ?
5. Discuss briefly the perpetual and periodic system of stock-taking?
6. What are various methods of inventory valuation ?
7. What are various methods of valuing the issue of materials.
8. What is inventory ? What is the importance of correct valuation of inventory.
9. Write short notes on Bass Stock method of stock valuation.
10. Discuss the different method of valuation of inventories.
11. What are the usual adjustments needed when stock is valued:
    (*a*) On a date later than the date of closing of accounts;
    (*b*) On a date earlier than the date of closing of accounts.

PRACTICAL PROBLEMS

1. Raja makes up his annual accounts to 31st December each year. He was unable to take stock of physical inventory till 9th January, 2007 on which date the physical stock at cost was valued at Rs. 75,200.

You are required to ascertain the value of physical stock at cost on 31st Dec. 2006, from the following information regarding the period from 1st January, 2007 to 9th January, 2007:-

(*a*) Purchases of goods amounted to Rs. 25,600 of which goods worth Rs. 4,700 had been received on 28.12.2006 and goods worth Rs. 5,900 had been received on 12.1.2007.

(*b*) Sales of goods amounted to Rs. 38,400 of which goods of a sale value of Rs. 3,600 had not been delivered at the time of verification and goods of a sale value of Rs. 6,000 had been delivered on 29.12.2006.

(*c*) Sales return amounted to Rs. 1,800 which included a return of Rs. 720 relating to the goods sold and delivered between 1.1.2007 to 9.1.2007.

(*d*) A sub-total of Rs. 12,000 on one of the stock sheets had been carried to the summary of stock sheet as Rs. 21,000.

(*e*) In respect of goods costing Rs. 4,000 received prior to 31st December, 2006, invoices had not been received up to the date of verification of stock.

(*f*) The rate of gross profit was 20% on the cost price.

(*I.C.W.A.*) (*Ans*: Value of Stock Rs. 74,300)

2. Moon Ltd. keeps no stocks records, but a physical inventory of Stock is made at the end of quarter and the valuation is taken at Cost. The Company's year ends on 30.9.06 and Draft Accounts have been prepared to that date. The Stock Inventory taken on 30.9.06 was, however, misled and you have been advised to value the Closing Stock as on 30.9.06 with the Stock figure as on 30.6.06 and some other information as available to you are:

(*i*) The Cost of Stock on 30.6.06 as shown by the inventory was Rs. 80,000.

(*ii*) On 30th June, Stock sheets showed the following discrepancies:

(*a*) A page total of Rs. 5,000 had been carried to the summary as Rs. 6,000.

(*b*) The total of a page had been undercast by Rs. 200.

(*iii*) Invoice of purchase entered in the Purchases Book during the months from July to September, 2006 totalled Rs. 70,000. Of this Rs. 3,000 related to goods received prior to 30th June, 2006. Invoices entered in October, 2006 relating to goods received on September, 2006 totalled Rs. 4,000.

(*iv*) Sales invoiced to customers from July to September, 2006 totalled Rs. 90,000. Of this, Rs. 5,000 related to goods despatched on or before 30.6.06. Goods despatched to customers before 30.9.06 but invoiced on October, 2006 totalled Rs. 4,000.

(*v*) During the final quarter, credit notes at invoiced value of Rs. 1,000 had been issued to customers in respect of goods returned during that period.

(*vi*) The Gross margin earned by the Company is 25% of cost.

You are required to prepare a statement showing the amount of stock at cost as on 30.9.2006. **[I.C.W.A.]**

(*Ans*: Value of Stock Rs. 79,800)

3. A firm had to take complete stock on 21st June, 2006 because of a deal for sale of business which fell through only at the later stage. As a result, stock was not again taken on 30th June, 2006, when accounts for 2006 were closed for the year. The stock on 21st June, 2006 was Rs. 67,460. The following information is supplied to you regarding transactions in stock between 21st June, and 30th June, 2006.

(1) Goods purchased from 21st June to 30th June amount to Rs. 4,820 out of which goods worth Rs. 1,900 were received on 2nd July, 2006.

(2) Sales during the said period amounted to Rs. 16,800 including Rs. 3,600 for goods sent on approval, half of which was still returnable on 30th June, 2006. The firm sells goods at cost plus 25%, but there was one lot of goods which had cost Rs. 2,800 but had to be sold for Rs. 1,200 due to damage caused by rain. The stock as on 21st June, 2006, included these goods at cost.

(3) Unsold goods in the hand of a consignee on 30th June, 2006, were valued at Rs. 3,200.

Prepare a statement showing the actual value of stock as on 30th June, 2006

(*C.A.*) (*Ans*: Value of Stock Rs. 59,740)

4. Mr. R. prepares accounts annually on 31st Dec., but the stock-taking takes place on the following week end.

The stock-taking for the year ended 31.2.2006 was made on 6th Jan. 2007 on which date the value of stock found in the premises was Rs. 35,970. You are given the following further particulars:

(*a*) Sales during the period from 1st Jan. to 6th Jan. 2007 was Rs. 3,000 and goods sent to approval at selling price Rs. 2,000.

(*b*) Purchases during the same period as per Purchase Day Book was Rs. 6,000.

(*c*) Included in the above purchases were goods worth Rs. 2,000 which were not actually delivered but the invoice was received and entries made accordingly in the Purchase Day Book.

(*d*) The average rate of gross profit on turnover is 30%.

You are required to ascertain the value of stock on 31st Dec. 2006. (*I.C.W.A.*)

(*Ans*: Value of Stock Rs. 35,470)

5. A Head office sends goods to its Branch @ 20% profit on cost; freight and duties amounting to 10% on invoice value being paid by Branch. Branch sells at 20% G.P. on selling price.

The Branch is sold with effect from 31-12-2006 but stock was taken on 10-1-2007. The price for stock was agreed to be the cost to head office to be increased by actual expenses incurred by the Branch less Rs. 12,000. Stock on 10-1-2007 (at Branch cost) amounted to Rs. 1,29,200, Rs. 12,000 stock (invoice value) was received from Head office after 31-12-2006 but before 10-1-2007. Sales in this period amounted to Rs. 20,000.

Ascertain the value of stock as on 31-12-2006, as agreed to with the buyers. [*C.A. Inter*]

(*Ans:* Value of Stock Rs. 1,00,000)

6. Calculate the value of stock on 31-3-2006 from the following details:

(*i*) On 21-3-2006 the storekeeper valued stock at Rs. 1,34,940.

(*ii*) Goods purchased from 21-3-2006 to 31-3-2006 amounted to Rs. 9,640 out of which goods worth Rs. 3,800 were received on 4-4-2006.

(*iii*) Unsold stock in the hands of consignee on 31-3-2006 was valued at Rs. 6,400. It was supplied to him on 1-3-2006.

(*iv*) Sales during the period 21-3-2006 to 31-3-2006 amounted to Rs. 33,600 including Rs. 7,200 for goods sent on approval half of which were still returnable on 31-3-2006.

The firm sells goods at cost plus 25% but there was one lot of goods which had cost Rs. 5,600 but had to be sold at a loss of Rs. 3,200 due to damage. The stock as on 21-3-2006 included these goods at cost.

[*B.Com. Madurai*] (*Ans:* Value of Stock Rs. 1,26,180)

7. Sundaram closed his books of accounts on 31st March, 2006, but due to certain difficulties, it was not possible for him to conduct physical stock taken on that date, physical stock was taken on 7th April when it was valued at Rs. 45,000.

An examination of the records of inventories from 1st to 7th April revealed the following:

(*a*) Net sales during the period were Rs. 10,200. These goods were sold at the usual rate of gorss profit of 15% on cost except goods which realised Rs. 1,200 on the basis of 20% profit on cost.

(*b*) Purchases during the period were Rs. 8,000 of which Rs. 1,000 worth of goods were delivered on 9th April only.

(*c*) Sales return during the period were Rs. 1,200 of which 50% were out of the sales at 20% gross profit mentioned above.

(*d*) On 5th April, Sundaram received certain goods costing Rs. 5,000 to be sold by him on consignment basis.

You are required to prepare a statement showing clearly the value of the stock, to be taken into account in Sundaram's final accounts for the year ended 31st March, 2006.

(*C.A.*) (*Ans*: Value of Stock Rs. 40,220)

8. A trader prepared his accounts to 31st March, each year. Due to some unavoidable reasons no stock taking was possible till 15th April on which date the total cost of goods in his godown came to Rs. 60,500. The following facts were established in between 31st March and 15th April:

(*a*) Sales Rs. 45,590 (including cash sales Rs. 10,120)

(*b*) Purchases of Rs. 16,710 (including cash purchases Rs. 5,990)

(*c*) Sales returns Rs. 1,200

(*d*) Collections from debtors Rs. 14,600

(*e*) Payment to creditors Rs. 7,816.

(*f*) On 15th March, goods of the sale value of Rs. 6,800 were sent on sale or return basis to a customer, the period of approval being four weeks. He returned 40% of the goods on 10th April, approving the rest; the customer was billed on 16th April.

(g) The trader has received goods costing Rs. 8,000 in March for sale on consignment basis; 20% of the goods had been sold by 31st March, and another 40% by 15th April.

These sales are not included in (*a*) above.

Goods are sold by the trader at a profit of 20% on sales. You are required to ascertain the value of stock on hand on 31st March.

[*C.A.Inter*] (*Ans*: Value of stock Rs. 79,366)

9. From the following data, calculate the cost of goods sold and closing inventory under weighted average cost of inventory using (*i*) Periodic system; (*ii*) Perpetual system.

2006

May 1 Stock in hand - 300 units @ Rs. 4.50 each

Receipts:

May 7 Purchase 400 units @ Rs. 5 each

May 15 Purchase 1,000 units @ Rs. 5.50 each

May 23 Purchases 700 units @ Rs. 4.80 each

Issues:

May 3 Issue 300 units

May 8 Issue 100 units

May 17 Issue 700 units

May 26 Issue 700 units

(*B.Com Bombay*)

(*Ans*: (*i*) Cost of goods sold : Rs. 9,157.50. Value of Stock : Rs. 3,052.50

(*ii*) Cost of goods sold : Rs. 9,168.50, Value of Stock Rs. 3,042)

10. Calculate the value of closing stock and cost of sales according to FIFO, LIFO and weighted average methods as on Mar. 31, 2006 using periodic inventory system:

Mar. 1 Stock 10,000 units @ Rs. 8 per unit

7 Purchased 15,000 units @ Rs. 10 per unit

12 Purchased 17,000 units @ Rs. 12 per unit

21 Purchased 18,000 units @ Rs. 15 per unit

28 Purchased 24,000 units @ Rs. 11 per unit

Thy physical stock-taking completed on 31-3-2006 revealed a closing stock of 7,000 units.

Assuming that sale price is Rs. 15 per unit, calculate the gross profit

(*B.Com MS*)

(*Ans:*	FIFO	LIFO	Weighted
	Rs.	*Rs.*	*Rs.*
Value of Stock	77,000	56,000	80,668
Cost of Sales	8,91,000	9,12,000	8,87,332
Gross Profit	2,64,000	2,43,000	2,67,668

11. From the following data, calculate the cost of goods sold and the value of closing inventory according to FIFO method on 15th Oct. 2006 using:

(*i*) Periodic inventory system, and

(*ii*) Perpetual inventory system.

Sep. 1 Stock in hand 500 units @ Re. 1 each.

	Purchases	*Issues*
6-9-2006	100 units at Rs. 1.10	9-9-06 - 500 units
20-9-2006	700 units at Rs. 1.20	22-9-06 - 500 units
27-9-2006	400 units at Rs. 1.30	30-9-06 - 500 units
13-10-2006	1,000 units at Rs. 1.4.	15-10-06 - 500 units

(B.Com Madras)

(*Ans*: Value of Stock (*i*) Rs. 980 (*ii*) Rs. 980)

12. From the following data, calculate the value of inventory according to LIFO method on 31st January using:

(*i*) Periodic Inventory system, and

(*ii*) Perpetual Inventory system.

Receipts:

Jan. 1	Inventory in hand	400 units @ Rs. 7	2,800
Jan. 8	Purchases	2.200 units @ Rs. 8	17,600
Jan. 25	Purchases	600 units @ Rs. 9	5,400
Jan. 31	Purchases	800 units @ Rs. 10	8,000

Issued for sale:

Jan. 6	200 units	Jan. 15	800 units
Jan. 9	400 units	Jan. 27	1,200 units

(*B.Com MS*)

(*Ans*: Value of Stock (*i*) Rs. 10,800 (*ii*) Rs. 12,600)

Chapter 10

Capital and Revenue

Capital and Revenue Items – Capital Expenditure – Revenue Expenditure – Deferred Revenue Expenditure or Capitalised Expenditure – Exception to the General Rules – Distinction between Capital Expenditure and Revenue Expenditure – Questions – Objective Type Questons – Theoretical Questions – Practical Problems.

It is very important to know the distinction between capital and revenue. We prepare the Final Accounts at the end of the year, which consists of Trading and Profit and Loss Account and Balance Sheet. We know from the previous chapters that all accounts in the Trial Balance are taken either to Trading Account or Profit and Loss Account or Balance Sheet. In this Final Accounts all the revenue items are included in the Revenue Account *i.e.*, Trading and Profit and Loss Account and all capital items are included in Balance Sheet. Hence it is necessary to know the principles that govern the proper allocation of capital items and revenue items. Proper distinction between the capital and revenue is essential for correct accounting systems. Any incorrect allocation of Capital and Revenue items will affect the Final Accounts and falsify the whole of the accounting results. Charging a capital item to an expense account or charging a revenue item to an asset account, then the Revenue Accounts and Balance Sheet will be inaccurate and misleading. For instance, when a typewriter is purchased for Rs 2,000 and is debited to Office Expense Account, this is clearly an error of principle where capital expenditure has been treated as revenue expenditure.

CAPITAL AND REVENUE ITEMS

The proper allocation of capital items and revenue items are important for the fundamental principles of correct accounting. It is not easy to give a correct rule to allocate capital items and revenue items. In order to understand them, one should know the correct principles governing the allocation between capital and revenue.

A. Capital Expenditure
B. Revenue Expenditure
C. Capital Receipts
D. Revenue Receipts
E. Capital Profits
F. Revenue Profits
G. Capital Losses
H. Revenue Losses

(A) Capital Expenditure

Capital Expenditure is that expenditure which results in the acquisition of permanent asset or fixed asset which is used continuously in the business for the purpose of earning revenue. Any amount spent on the asset which will result in increasing the production or reducing the cost of production may also be treated as Capital Expenditure.

According to Kohler, "Capital Expenditure is an expenditure intended to benefit future periods, in contrast to a revenue expenditure, which benefits a current period, an addition to a capital asset. The term is generally restricted to expenditures that add fixed asset units or that have the effect of increasing the capacity, efficiency, life span, or economy of operation of an existing fixed asset."

Rules for Determining Capital Expenditure

1. Expenditure incurred for acquiring Land, Building, Machinery, Investments, Patents or Furniture etc. are permanent or fixed assets. The fixed asset is used in the business for earning profit and not for resale, is called a Capital Expenditure. For instance, when we purchase furniture, it is a capital expenditure and at the same time to the Furniture Shop, who is engaged in buying and selling of furniture, it is not capital expenditure.
2. Expenditure incurred for putting an old asset in working condition or for putting a new asset to use, is capital expenditure. For instance, an old machine is purchased for Rs. 10,000 and Rs. 2,000 is spent for its repairs and installation and the total expenditures are capital expenditure.
3. Expenditure incurred on an existing asset which results in the improvement or extension of the business by increasing the earning capacity of the asset or by reducing the cost of production are also called capital expenditure. For instance, installation of machine or additions to buildings or plant etc. are capital expenditure.
4. When benefit of an expenditure is not fully consumed in one period but spread over several periods, it is called capital expenditure. For instance, expenditure met for massive advertisements.
5. Expenditure which increases the earning capacity in any way of a fixed asset can be called capital expenditure. For instance, amount spent on cinema theatre for air conditioning.
6. Expenditure spent on raising the capital required for earning profit is called capital expenditure. For instance, underwriting commission, brokerage etc.

Items of Capital Expenditure

1. Cost of Land, Building, Plant and Machinery.
2. Cost of lease hold Land and Building.
3. Cost of manufacture or purchase of furniture and fixtures.
4. Cost of office Cars, Vans, Lorries or Vehicles.
5. Cost of installation of lights, fans etc.
6. Cost of erection of Plant and Machinery.
7. Cost of Trade Mark, Patents, Copy rights, Patterns and Designs.
8. Preliminary Expenses.
9. Cost of Goodwill.
10. Cost of addition to and extension of existing fixed assets.
11. Cost of development in case of Mines and Plantations.
12. Cost of invention.
13. Cost of increasing capacity of fixed asset.
14. Cost of administration in industrial enterprises incurred during the period of construction.

(B) Revenue Expenditure

Revenue Expenditure is that expenditure which is not a capital expenditure. According to Kohler "It is an expenditure charged against operation; a term used to contrast with capital expenditure". Revenue expenditure is incurred in the current period or in one period of account. The benefit of the revenue expenditure is utilised in that period itself. Revenue expenditure is incurred for the following purposes:

(*a*) All establishment and other expenses incurred in the normal course of business. For instance, Administration expenses of a business, expenses incurred in manufacturing and selling products.

(*b*) Expenses incidental to the carrying of a business, the benefit of which is consumed within the accounting period. For instance, Rent, Wages, Salaries, Advertising, Taxes, Insurance etc.

(*c*) Expenditure on goods purchased for resale. For instance, cost of goods purchased or cost of raw materials etc.

(*d*) For maintaining fixed assets in working order. For instance, repairs, renewals and replacement of existing assets, depreciation etc.

These revenue expenditure items appear in Trading and Profit and Loss Account.

Items of Revenue Expenditure

1. Expenditure on Rent, Wages, Carriage, Salaries, Postage, Insurance, Advertising etc.
2. Interest on loan borrowed for running business.
3. Cost of goods bought for resale.
4. Cost of raw materials consumed in the course of manufacturing.
5. Expenses incurred for maintenance of various assets by way of repairs, renewals and replacement on building, plant, machinery, tools, fixtures, van, car etc. to keep them in the good condition.
6. Depreciation of fixed assets.
7. Taxes and legal expenses.
8. Loss arising from sale of fixed assets.
9. Maintenance of lights and fans.
10. All expenses incurred in the manufacturing and distribution of the products handled.
11. Wages paid for sale of goods.
12. Loss of goods by fire or other reasons.
13. Discounts and allowances.

DEFERRED REVENUE EXPENDITURE (OR) CAPITALISED EXPENDITURE

A large sum of revenue expenditure incurred in some cases, the benefit of such expenditure may extend to a number of years. Such expenditure is called Deferred Revenue Expenditure. Hence this expenditure is not charged straightly to Profit and Loss Account, but a portion of it is charged every year to Profit and Loss Account for the prescribed number of years. The amount which remains uncharged at the end of any particular year is "Deferred Revenue Expenditure or Capitalised Expenditure", which is put as an asset in the Balance Sheet.

Items of Deferred Revenue Expenditure

1. Preliminary Expenses, Brokerage on Shares, Cost of issue of Debentures or Discount on issue of Debentures etc.
2. Underwriting Commission.
3. Heavy Advertisement Expenses paid on contract for a few years.
4. Research Expenses and Development Expenses.
5. Cost of changing the business to a more convenient place.

6. Exceptional repairs.
7. Special types of losses.

EXCEPTION TO THE GENERAL RULES

The following are the exceptions to the general rules i.e. Revenue expenditure becoming Capital expenditure:

1. Legal Costs and Architect's Fees

Legal charges and stamp duty paid for conveyancing on acquisition of a property, or supervisory charges of construction of a property, etc. Such expenses are additional cost of the asset acquired.

2. Brokerage and Stamp Duty

Brokerage paid for the purchase of a property or for purchase of shares, stocks or other securities, and the stamp duty paid etc. are additional cost of the purchase. Hence they are capitalised.

3. Productive Wages

During the commencement of a manufacturing firm, expenses are incurred in factory building, erecting plant or manufacturing tools. Wages paid for these purposes are capitalised.

4. Preliminary or Formation Expenses

Initial expenses are incurred for the formation of a public company to obtain share capital. These expenses are capitalised.

5. Freight and Carriage

Freight or carriage paid on newly acquired fixed asset is an additional cost of the asset and is a capital expenditure.

6. Advertising

If a company or newspaper concern spends a heavy amount for advertising in the beginning stage and will have the effect of creating a goodwill: it is capitalised.

7. Interest

Interest paid on subscribed capital by Public Utility concerns during construction works of buildings or plant, is capitalised.

8. Development Expenses

Concerns like Collieries, Mines, Tea, Rubber and other plantations incur expenses during the period of development and upto the time they begin to earn: such expenses are capitalised.

9. Repairs

If an old machine is bought at a cheaper rate and the expenses incurred to make it in workable condition, then the repair charges are added to the machine cost.

10. Transport Expenses

The transport expenses on machine and plant are added to its cost.

(C) Capital Receipts

Capital Receipts is the amount received in the form of additional Capital (by issuing shares) loans or by the sale proceeds of any fixed assets. Capital Receipts are shown in Balance Sheet.

(D) Revenue Receipts

Revenue Receipts are the amount received in the ordinary course of a business. It is the incomes earned from selling merchandise, or in the form of discount, commission, interest, transfer fees etc. Income received by selling waste paper, packing cases etc. is also a revenue receipt. Revenue Receipts are shown in the Profit and Loss Account.

(E) Capital Profit

Capital profits are earned as a result of selling some fixed assets or in connection with raising capital for the firm. For example a land purchased by a business for Rs 2,00,000 is sold for Rs. 2,50,000. Rs 50,000 is a profit of capital nature. Another example, suppose a company issues its shares of the face value of Rs 100 for Rs 110 each, i.e. issue of shares at premium, the premium on shares i.e. Rs 10 is capital profit. Such profits are (a) transferred to Capital Account or (b) transferred to Capital Reserve Account. This amount is utilised for meeting Capital losses. Capital Reserve appears in the Balance Sheet as a liability.

(F) Revenue Profits

Revenue Profits are earned in the ordinary course of business. Revenue profits appear in the Profit and Loss Account. For example, profit from sale of goods, income from investments, discount received, Interest Earned etc.

(G) Capital Losses

Capital losses occur when selling fixed assets or raising share capital. A building purchased for Rs 2,00,000 is sold for Rs 1,50,000. Rs 50,000 is a capital loss. Shares of the face value of Rs 100 issued at Rs 95, i.e. discount of Rs 5. The amount of discount is a capital loss.

Capital Loss is not shown in the Profit and Loss Account. They are shown in the asset side of Balance Sheet. When Capital Profit arises, Capital losses are gradually written off against them. If capital losses are huge, it is common to spread them over a number of years and a proportionate amount is charged to Profit and Loss Account every year. Balance amount is shown in the Balance Sheet as an asset and it is written off in future years. If the loss is manageable, they are debited to Profit and Loss Account of the same year.

(H) Revenue Losses

Revenue losses arise during the normal course of business. For instance, sale of goods, loss may incur. Such losses are debited in the Profit and Loss Account.

DISTINCTION BETWEEN CAPITAL EXPENDITURE AND REVENUE EXPENDITURE

1. Capital expenditure is incurred in acquiring or improving permanent assets which are not meant for resale. But the revenue expenditure incurred in the normal course of business, and includes the cost of sales as also upkeep of the fixed assets.

2. Capital expenditure seeks to improve the business but revenue expenditure aims at maintaining the earning capacity of business.

3. Capital expenditure produces benefits over several years, hence a small part is charged to revenue account as depreciation and the rest appears in the Balance Sheet. But the revenue expenditure is consumed within the accounting year and the entire amount is charged to the revenue account. Hence, it does not appear in Balance Sheet. Deferred revenue expenditure is, however, an exception to this rule.

To decide an expense,–capital or revenue, one should ask whether the expenses result in the acquisition of fixed assets to increase the earning capacity. If the answer is "Yes", then the expenditure is a capital. If the answer is "No", it is a revenue. However, the rule is not rigid as the distinction depends upon the nature and policy of the business.

ILLUSTRATION 10.1

Classify the following items of expenditure giving brief reasons in each case

1. Cost of Rs 30,000 for dismantling, removing and reinstalling plant by a Sugar Mill incurred in connection with the removal of works to more suitable locality.
2. A sum of Rs 10,000 spent for alteration of existing plant incorporating thereby new devices which could effect substantial reduction in power consumption.
3. Imported goods worth Rs 25,000 confiscated by customs authority for non-disclosure of material fact.
4. Transportation charges of Rs 100 spent on acquiring furniture.
5. Legal expenses incurred in an action for violation of its Trade Mark.

SOLUTION :

1. The expenditure of Rs 30,000 in dismantling, removing and installing the plant to a suitable place may be treated as deferred revenue expenditure. The amount will spread over years. The expended amount will not increase the earning capacity. If it is small amount, it can be treated as revenue expenditure.
2. The sum of Rs 10,000 spent on alteration of existing plant, thereby reducing the power consumption will be capitalised, as it is a capital expenditure.
3. It is revenue loss. Since it is a heavy loss it may be treated as deferred revenue expenditure.
4. Cost to the acquisition of a fixed asset is a capital expenditure.
5. Legal expenses incurred in an action for violation of its trade are revenue expenditure, because expenses are incurred for the maintenance of a fixed asset.

ILLUSTRATION 10.2

State with reasons whether these expenses are capital or revenue:

1. Rs. 500 spent on repairing a second hand machine and Rs 25 paid on carriage.
2. A heavy advertising expenditure of Rs 5,000 incurred in connection with a new product.
3. Rs 400 spent on repairing of machines and Rs 35 spent in adding a new part to a machine, during the year.
4. Spent Rs 1,000 in raising temporary huts for the workers during the construction of a factory building and Rs 40 on demolishing the huts.
5. Rs 2,000 spent on painting and redecorating a cinema hall and Rs 1,000 in enhancing the seating accommodation.

SOLUTION :

1. The expenditure in connection with repairing a second hand machine is a capital expenditure. Because it is necessary to bring the machine into good working condition. The expenditure of Rs. 25 paid on carriage is also of capital nature.
2. The benefit of the expenditure will run for many years, therefore it is a capital expenditure. However, it can be treated as deferred revenue expenditure and be written off against profit and loss account over a number of years.
3. Rs 400 spent on repairing is a revenue expenditure because this amount is the maintenance cost of a machine. But Rs 35 spent on adding a new part to a machine is of capital expenditure. Because, it will increase the earning capacity.
4. They are capital expenditure. Both the sum of Rs 1,000 and Rs 40 spent in building and demolishing the temporary huts should be capitalised. They have been spent for the construction of factory building. Therefore this amount of Rs 1,000 and Rs 40 will be added to the cost of factory building.
5. Painting and re-decoration will not amount to enhancing the earning capacity. Therefore, Rs 2,000 is a revenue expenditure. However, if the amount is large, it can be treated as deferred revenue expenditure, spreading over a few years. The amount of Rs. 1,000 spent on enhancing the seating facilities would increase the earning capacity. Therefore, Rs 1,000 be capitalised.

ILLUSTRATION 10.3

Show, by giving reasons, whether the following items of expenditure are capital or revenue:

1. Carriage paid on goods purchases.

2. Repairs to furniture purchased second hand.
3. Wages of workmen employed for setting up a new plant.
4. Replacement cost of a worn out part of plant.
5. Legal expenses incurred to raise a loan for the business.

SOLUTION :

1. It is a revenue expenditure. Carriage paid on goods purchased is a revenue expenditure, because the goods purchased are meant for resale (merchandise) commodities.
2. It is a capital expenditure. In order to bring the furniture, in a serviceable condition, if any amount spent on repairing will be capitalised.
3. It is a capital expenditure because the earning capacity will be increased. The expenses are necessary to put the asset into use.
4. It is a revenue expenditure. The expenditure is the cost of maintenance of earning capacity. They add nothing to the original value of the plant. And they do not cause any increase in the earning capacity but keep the machine in running order.
5. It is a capital expenditure. Legal expenses incurred in connection with raising a loan, to be used in the business, is a capital expenditure.

ILLUSTRATION 10.4

State, giving reasons, whether you will consider the following items as capital, revenue or deferred revenue.

1. An old machine costing Rs. 3,000 (or WDV Rs. 1,800) was sold for Rs. 1,000.
2. The expenses incurred for white-washing the factory building amounted to Rs. 4,000.
3. Cost of repainting the factory building of Rs. 1,000.
4. Imported goods worth Rs. 20,000 confiscated by customs authority for non-disclosure of material facts.
5. Cost of conversion of gas plant to oil fuel plant for the generation of electricity amounted to Rs. 20,000.
6. Incurred Rs. 4,000 in redecorating a cinema hall and Rs. 12,000 in enhancing the sitting accommodation.
7. A sum of Rs. 2,000 spent on a machine comprises Rs. 400 for replacement of worn out parts and Rs. 1,600 for additions to new devices which enable the output to be doubled.
8. Visit of Sales Manager to USA cost of which was Rs. 40,000 for promoting export sales and is a successful trip.
9. Legal and other expenses incurred in connection with the issue of share capital.
10. Cost of replacement of defective part of machinery.
11. Wages paid for construction building extension.
12. Compensation of Rs. 90,000 paid for termination of services of three workers who were disturbing industrial peace in the factory.
13. A sum of Rs. 3,000 previously written off as bad debts now recovered in this year.
14. Commission on issue of Debentures.
15. Amount received from Insurance Company for loss of stock.
16. Cost incurred in replacing worn out but costly spare parts of a machine.
17. Replace of wooden roof with a guarantee of 20 years.
18. Repainting the building.
19. Renewal of factory licences.
20. Cost in relation to mortgage.
21. Profit on sale of investments.
22. Rs. 1,50,000 received by tenant for surrendering his tenancy right in favour of the builder who has purchased premises.
23. Old items of machinery disposed at a loss.

24. Stock transferred from one factory to another one where there is shortage.
25. Cost of alteration to a cinema theatre in accordance with Corporation Law.
26. Cost of acquisition of copy rights.
27. Loss due to change in exchange rate for purchase of materials.
28. Rs. 15,000 spent on renovation and overhauling a machine which resulted in extension of the life of the plant.
29. Expenditure incurred in preparing a project report.
30. Amount paid for purchase of goodwill of a similar business.

SOLUTION :

1. The loss on sale of old machine amounting to Rs. 800 (i.e., 1,800 – Rs. 1,000) is a revenue loss and selling price amounting to Rs. 1,000 is a capital receipt as it reveals the proceeds of a sale of fixed asset.
2. The expenses which are incurred for white-washing the factory building amounted to Rs. 4,000 may be considered as a regular expenditure in order to maintain the factory and as such, the same should be treated as revenue expenditure.
3. It is a revenue expenditure in order to maintain the building. It is a regular expenditure.
4. Imported goods amounted to Rs. 20,000 which were confiscated by customs authorities for non-disclosure of material facts is an abnormal revenue loss and non-recurring in nature, which are incurred in the regular course of the business. It may be treated as deferred revenue expenditure.
5. The purpose of conversion is not known. The conversion may increase the efficiency or the conversion may arise because of non-availability of gas supply. It may be treated as deferred revenue expenditure.
6. Redecoration of a cinema hall amounting to Rs. 4,000 is a revenue expenditure as it does not enhance the earning capacity. However, if the amount is heavy, it may be treated as deferred revenue expenditure and may be spread over two or three years. But the enhancement of sitting accommodation increases the earning capacity therefore the expendutre (i.e., Rs. 12,000) is capital expenditure.
7. Rs. 400 which is incurred by replacing worn-out parts is a revenue charge since it is a routine expenditure for maintaining the existing earning capacity of the firm. Rs. 1,600 which is incurred for additions to a new device is a capital expenditure since it results in an increase in the earning capacity.
8. Visit of the Sales Manager to USA for promoting export sales is an expenditure in the nature of advertisement campaign. The trip is successful. The expenditure may be treated as deferred revenue expenditure and may be written off against Profit and Loss Account over two or three years.
9. Legal and other expenses in connection with issue of share capital may be treated an deferred revenue expenditure because long term assets is created.
10. Cost of replacement of defective part of a machinery is a revenue expenditure. The expenditure is for maintenance of asset.
11. Wages for building extension is a capital expenditure.
12. It is a normal business expenditure as such it is a revenue expenditure.
13. Bad debts and bad debts recovery are common items in business. It is a normal business receipt. As such it is a revenue receipt.
14. The benefit will last over many years. The expenditure can be treated as deferred revenue expenditure.
15. Amount received in lieu of a revenue item lost. It is revenue receipt.
16. Maintenance cost of an asset is revenue expense. It is revenue expenditure.
17. It is a mainenance expenditure, *i.e.*, it is a revenue expenditure.
18. It is revenue expenditure and is a normal recurring expenditure.
19. Renewal of factory licences are recurring nature. It is a revenue expenditure.
20. It is a revenue expenditure. It is normal business expenditure.
21. Profit on sale of investments is a normal business income and as such it is revenue income.
22. Amount received by tenant for surrendering tenancy right is capital receipt.

23. The loss on sale of old machine is a revenue loss. The loss can be transferred to the Profit and Loss Account.
24. Cost of transferring stock from one factory to another is a normal business expenditure. It is a revenue expenditure.
25. Cost of alteration of cinema theatre in accordance with Corporation law is revenue expenditure. It does not enhance the earning potential or value of the asset.
26. A new asset is accquired and is a capital expenditure.
27. Loss, due to change in exchange rate, is a common item is business and is normal. It is revenue loss.
28. There is an increase in the life of the plant. It is capital expenditure.
29. It is a capital expenditure. Expenditure in preparing project report are common in business.
30. The amount paid for the goodwill of another similar business is a capital expenditure. The expenditure is acquiring an intangible long-term asset.

QUESTIONS

Objective Type Questions.

I. State whether the following statements are "true" or "False".

1. Expenses incurred to keep the machine in working condition is a capital expenditure.
2. An expenditure intended to benefit current period is a revenue expenditure.
3. Amount paid for acquiring goodwill is deferred revenue expenditure.
4. Overhaul expenses of a second hand machinery purchased are revenue expenses.
5. Purchases of a table by a furniture dealer is a capital expenditure.
6. Money spent on transporting new machinery purchased is a revenue expenditure.
7. Legal fees to acquire property is capital expenditure.
8. Amount paid for removal of stock to a new site is revenue expenditure.
9. Interest paid on borrowings is a capital expenditure.
10. Compensation for breach of contract to acquire stock in trade is revenue expenditure.

(*Ans:* True – 2, 7, 8, 10, False – 1, 3, 4, 5, 6, 9)

II. Indicate whether the following are true or false statements.

1. Sale of stock in trade is a capital receipt.
2. Capital expenditure is any expenditure benefiting a future period.
3. Premium received on issue of share is a revenue receipt.
4. Revenue expenditure is not intended to benefit future period.
5. Carriage paid on purchase of a new machine is an example of revenue expenditure.
6. Loan taken from bank is a capital receipt.
7. Amount obtained on sale of fixed assets is a revenu receipt.
8. The redecoration expenditure is a capital expenditure.
9. Premium given for taking a lease is a revenue expenditure.
10. Expenditure which results in acquisition of a permanent asset is a capital expenditure.

(*Ans*: True : 2, 3, 4, 6, 10; False: 1, 5, 7, 8, 9)

III. Choose the most suitable alternative for the following:

1. State an example for capital expenditure:
   (*a*) Goods purchased for sale (*b*) Repairs to furniture
   (*c*) Machinery purchased.
2. Preliminary expenses are example of:
   (*a*) Revenue expenditure (*b*) Deferred revenue expenditure
   (*c*) Capital expenditure.

3. Discount allowed on issue of shares is an example of:
   (*a*) Capital expenditure (*b*) Revene expenditure
   (*c*) Deferred revenue expenditure
4. Repairs incurred before using a second-hand car purchased recently is:
   (*a*) A capital expenditure (*b*) A revenue expenditure
   (*c*) Deferred revenue expenditure.
5. Revenue expenditure is intended to benefit:
   (*a*) Current period (*b*) Past period
   (*c*) Future period
6. Maintenance expenses are:
   (*a*) Revenue items (*b*) Capital items
   (*c*) None of the above.
7. Expenditure incurred as advertising is a :
   (*a*) Capital expenditure (*b*) Revenue expenditure
   (*c*) Nominal expenditure
8. Sale of fixed asset is:
   (*a*) Capital receipt (*b*) Revenue receipt
   (*c*) None of the above
9. When a firm makes investment in Govt. Bonds, it is:
   (*a*) An asset. (*b*) Liability
   (*c*) Revenu expenditure
10. Depreciation of fixed asset is an example of:
   (*a*) Revenue expenditure. (*b*) Capital expenditure.
   (*c*) Deferred revenue expenditure.

(*Ans*: 1. (*c*); 2. (*b*); 3. (*c*); 4. (*a*); 5. (*a*); 6. (*a*); 7. (*b*); 8. (*a*); 9. (*a*); 10. (*a*))

THEORETICAL QUESTIONS

1. State the meaning of Capital Expenditure and Revenue Expenditure. What is the difference between them?
2. Give at least ten examples of Capital Expenditure and Revenue Expenditure.
3. What do you understand by Deferred Revenue Expenditure?
4. State the consideration which would guide you in deciding whether any particular item should be regarded as of a Capital or of Revenue nature.
5. Why is the distinction between capital and revenue is of great important in accounting?

PRACTICAL PROBLEMS

1. A firm incurred the following expenses upon its plant:
   (*a*) Purchase price of second-hand machinery Rs 20,000.
   (*b*) Cost of complete overhauling Rs 9,000.
   (*c*) Carriage and Installation charges Rs 500.
   (*d*) Ordinary repairs Rs 300.
   (*e*) Special repairs necessitated by accidental damage Rs 2000.
   (*f*) Cost of removal and installation Rs 700.

(*B.Com., Madurai*)

[**Ans:** (*a*) Capital; (*b*) Capital; (*c*) Capital; (*d*) Revenue; (e) Capital (*f*) Revenue]

2. Explain with reasons whether the undermentioned items appearing in the books of a manufacturing concern are Capital or Revenue.

(*a*) Legal expenses incurred in raising a debenture loan.

(*b*) Legal expenses incurred in an action for infringement of its Trade Mark.

(*c*) Profit realised on the sale of investments.

(*d*) Labour welfare expenses.

(*e*) Subsidy received from Government.

(*B.Com., Madurai*)

[**Ans:** (*a*) Capital; (*b*) Revenue Expenditure; (*c*) Capital Receipt; (*d*) Revenue Expenditure; (*e*) Revenue Receipt]

3. State with reasons which of the items would be charged to Capital and which to Revenue.
   1. Cost of Rs 30,000 for dismantling, removing and re-installing plant in connection with removal of works to a more suitable place.
   2. Rs 300 paid for removal of stock from the old works to the new place.
   3. A sum of Rs 1,000 spent for alteration of existing plant incorporating thereby new devices which could effect substantial reduction in power consumption.
   4. Imported goods worth Rs 25,000 confiscated by Custom Authority for non-disclosure of material facts.

(*CA Inter*)

[**Ans:** (1) Deferred Expenditure (2) Revenue Expenditure (3) Capital Expenditure (4) Deferred Revenue Expenditure]

4. State which of the expenses stated below are Capital Expenditure and which are Deferred Revenue Expenditure.

(*a*) Demolition of an old building, book value of Rs 10,000 and construction of a new building on its site, costing Rs 1,50,000.

(b) Replacement of vital part, cost Rs 9,900 for the one damaged in transit of a newly purchased machine.

(c) Visit of Sales Manager abroad, total cost Rs 16,000 for promoting export sales—visit is quite successful.

(*CA Iner*)

[**Ans:** (*a*) Rs. 10,000 is Deferred Revenue Expenditure and Rs 1,50,000 is Capital Expenditure (*b*) Deferred Revenue Expenditure (*c*) Deferred Revenue Expenditure]

5. State with reasons whether the following expenditure are Capital or Revenue.

(1) Sale of old plant (depreciated value in books Rs 1,500) for Rs 500 and purchase of new plant Rs 4,750 in place of it.

(2) Freight and carriage on the new plant Rs 300 and wages paid to own workmen for its erection Rs 250.

(3) Purchase of a Patent Right Rs 3,000 and renewal fee for the next year Rs 400.

(4) Repairs to furniture Rs 200.

(5) Purchase of a second-hand pump Rs 2,500, cost of immediate repairs and painting to make it efficient Rs 500.

(6) Cost of repainting the factory shed Rs 700.

(7) Compensation of Rs 1,000 paid to a retrenched worker for loss of employment.

(8) Purchase of new tyres of Rs 800 for an old lorry.

(*B.Com., Madurai*)

[**Ans:** (1) Rs 500 Capital Receipt, Rs 4,750 Capital Expenditure (2) Rs 300 and Rs 250 are Capital Expenditure (3) Rs 3,000 Capital Expenditure, Rs 400 Revenue Expenditure (4) Rs 200 Revenue Expenditure (5) Rs 2,500 and Rs 500 are Capital Expenditure (6) Rs 700 Revenue Expenditure (7) Rs 1,000 Revenue Expenditure (8) Rs 800 Revenue Expenditure]

Chapter 11

Depreciation and Reserves

Definition of Depreciation – Causes – Need – Method of Recording – Calculation – Methods – Change in the Methods – Depreciation Policy – Objectives of Policy – Requirements of Companies Act – Depreciation distinguished from other Terms – Choice of Suitable Method – Depreciation on Replacement Cost – Provisions – Reserves – Accounting Standard – Questions – Objective Type Questions – Theoretical Questions – Practical Problems.

Assets are necessary to run a business. Assets are purchased either for immediate use or for prolonged use. When assets are acquired for immediate use, they are known as current assets; for example, Cash, Debtors, Bills Receivables, stock etc. When assets are acquired for prolonged use, they are known as fixed assets; for example, Plant, Machinery, Building etc. These fixed assets, not meant for resale, having a long life, are kept in the business. When the value of a fixed asset gets diminished due to one reason or the other, the assets are said to have depreciated in value. As the value of the asset in terms of its purchase price gets reduced every year, the business incurs losses by way of depreciation.

Depreciation means decrease or decline in value of assets. Fixed assets are liable to loss of their value once they begin to be used in the productive process. Depreciation is the gradual and permanent reduction in the value of an asset. Depreciation is that part of the cost of the asset which is not recoverable when the asset is finally put out of use. Depreciation, therefore, refers to permanent, continuing and gradual shrinkage in the book value of the asset. Since the asset shrinks in the value from year to year, it is also necessary that the book value will also be written down; otherwise balance sheet will not reveal the correct position. Such a loss will take place as time passes, till the asset becomes unfit for future use and reduced to zero or to a very nominal value (residual value or scrap or break up value or junk value). Since it is a permanent loss or fall in value of an asset, provision should be made in Profit and Loss Account.

DEFINITIONS OF DEPRECIATION

"Depreciation may be defined as the permanent decrease in the value of an asset through wear and tear in use or the passage of time."

"The Primary meaning of the word depreciation is loss of value through wear and the tear or some other form of material deterioration. The secondary sense of depreciation is the operation of adjusting the book values of assets. As the machines or other assets get old, it is the practice of the Accountant to reduce their values in the books of accounts and it is usual to call this as depreciation."

"Depreciation is an expense or loss involved in using machinery, motor vehicles, tools and other fixed assets in the process of production and has to be provided for; this is done by estimating the amount to be written off the value of a particular asset each year and setting this amount against the profits for that year."

"The term depreciation represents loss or diminution in the value of an asset consequent upon wear and tear, obsolescence, effluxion of time or permanent fall in market value."

CAUSES OF DEPRECIATION

1. Wear and Tear

Some assets physically deteriorate due to wear and tear in use. When an asset is constantly used for production, the asset wears out. More and more use of an asset, the greater would be the wear and tear. Physical deterioration of an asset is caused from movement, strain, friction, erosion etc. For instance, building, machineries, furniture, vehicles, plant etc. The wear and tear is general but primary cause of depreciation.

2. Lapse of Time

There are certain assets like leasehold property, patents, copy-right etc. that are acquired for a particular period. After the expiry of the period, they are rendered useless i.e. their value ceases to exist. Thus, their cost is written off over their legal life.

3. Obsolescence

Appearance of new and improved machines result in discarding of old machines. Thus new inventions, change in fashions and taste, market condition, Government policies etc. are the causes to discard the value of an asset. But this is not the cause of depreciation and not depreciation in real sense. A new machine performs the same function more quickly and cheaply than the existing machine. As such, existing machine may become out of date or outmoded or obsolete.

4. Exhaustion

Some assets are of wasting nature. For instance, quarries, mines, oil-well etc. It is the reduction in the value of natural deposits as resources have been extracted year after year. As such these assets are known as wasting assets. The coalmine or oil well gets physically exhausted by the removal of its contents.

5. Non-use

Machines which are idly lying, become less and less useful with the passage of time. Certain types of machines exposed to weather conditions, may have more depreciation from not using it than from its use.

6. Maintenance

A good maintenance of machine will naturally increase its life. When there is no maintenance, there is more depreciated value. When there is good maintenance, there is longer life to the machines. The long life of machine depends upon good and skilled maintenance.

7. Market Trend

The market price may fluctuate in case of certain assets, for instance, investments in gilt-edged securities. When the prices go down, the concerned asset may depreciate its value. In certain cases, accident causes diminution in the value of assets.

NEED FOR DEPRECIATION

Depreciation is provided for the assets with a view to achieve the following results:

1. To ascertain the True Working Result

Asset is an important tool in earning revenues. Huge amounts are spent for acquisition of assets which are worn out in the process of earning income. Thus, the assets get depreciated in their value, over a period of time due to many reasons explained above. When the value of assets decreases, this loss must be brought into account; otherwise a true working result cannot be known. Depreciation is an operating expense of a physical asset, the same should be considered in arriving the true profit earned during each year.

The basic need of depreciation is to ascertain the true income. If depreciation is ignored, the loss that is occurring in respect of fixed assets will be ignored. So, depreciation should be debited to Profit and Loss Account before profit is ascertained.

2. To ascertain True Value of Asset

The function of the Balance Sheet is to show the true and correct view of the state of affairs of a business. If no depreciation is charged and when assets are shown at the original cost year after year, Balance Sheet will not disclose the correct state of affairs of a business.

3. To Retain Funds for Replacement

Assets used in the business need replacement after the expiry of their service. It is always not possible to determine the useful life of assets. But, in certain cases, machine often becomes, obsolete long before it wears out because of rapid changes in tastes and technology. It is a permanent loss in value of the asset. When an asset is continuously used, a time will come when the asset is to be given up and hence its replacement is essential. Therefore, if no depreciation is charged against the profit, during the life time of the asset, it will be very difficult to find cash to replace the asset and if replaced it may cripple resources. Therefore, it is necessary to make provision and create funds to replace such assets, in proper time.

4. To Reduce Tax Liability

Depreciation is a tax deductible expenses. As such, it is permitted by the prevailing taxation laws to be deducted from profit. Consequently, the owner of a business may avail himself of this benefit by charging depreciation to his profit and reducing his tax liability.

5. To present True Position

Financial position can be studied from the Balance Sheet and for the preparation of the Balance Sheet fixed assets are required to be shown at their true value. If assets are shown in the Balance Sheet without any charge made for their use, (that is, depreciation) then their value must have been overstated in the Balance Sheet and will not reflect the ture financial position of the business. Therefore, for the purpose of reflecting true financial position, it is necessary that depreciation must be deducted from the asset and then at such reduced value may be shown in the Balance Sheet.

If depreciation is not accounted for, the profit of the company is overstated, in turn, it is distributed among the shareholders. Thus there is no provision for replacement of machine. It must be pointed out that depreciation by itself does not create funds, it merely draws attention to the fact that out of gross revenue receipts a certain amount should be retained to replace the asset used for carrying on activities. The Companies Act of 1956 now makes it compulsory to write off depreciation on fixed assets before declaring dividend.

CONSEQUENCES OF NOT PROVIDING FOR DEPRECIATION

If depreciation is not provided for, the Income Statement and the Balance Sheet will not exhibit a true or fair view of the business. Ultimately, it affects the following:

1. Profit will be overstated.
2. Capital employed will be overstated.
3. Valuation of assets will be incorrect.
4. Cost of production will be understated.
5. Periodic expenses will be understated.

6. Capital depletion will take place.
7. Net worth will be overstated.
8. Correct sale price of products cannot be fixed.
9. No provision for replacement of assets.
10. A true working result cannot be known.

METHODS OF RECORDING DEPRECIATION

There are two methods of recording depreciation in the books of accounts.

(1) Direct Method (No provision for Depreciation account is maintained)

Depreciation is charged by debiting Depreciation Account and crediting the Asset Account. The Depreciation is closed by transferring to Profit and Loss Account at the end of the year. The asset account appears in the Balance Sheet at its written down value, that is, cost less depreciation at the end of the year.

Journal entries under this method are :

Entry		Narration
(1) Depreciation Account	Dr.	
To Asset Account		For the amount of depreciation
(2) Profit & Loss Account	Dr.	
To Depreciation Account		To close the Depreciation Account
(3) Asset Account	Dr.	
To Bank Account		Further purchase of asset
(4) Bank Account	Dr.	
To Asset Account		When the asset is sold
(5) Asset Account	Dr.	
To Profit & Loss Account		To transfer the profit on sale
(6) Profit and Loss Account	Dr.	
To Asset Account		To transfer the loss on sale

(2) Indirect Method (Provision for Depreciation account is maintained)

The amount of depreciation is debited to Depreciation Account and credited to Provision for Depreciation Account (or Accumulated Depreciation Account). The amount of depreciation is transferred to Profit and Loss Account at the end of the year. However, the Asset Account will appear at cost and the accumulated depreciation is either shown as a deduction from the asset or the same may be shown in the liability side of the Balance Sheet.

Journal entries under this method are :

Entry		Narration
(1) Depreciation Account	Dr.	
To Provision for Depreciation Account		For the amount of depreciation
(2) Profit & Loss Account	Dr.	
To Depreciation Account		To close Depreciation Account
(3) Bank Account	Dr.	
To Asset Account		When the asset is sold
(4) Provision for Depreciation A/c	Dr.	
To Asset Account		To close both the accounts

(5) Asset Account To Profit & Loss Account	Dr.	To transfer the profit on sale
(6) Profit and Loss Account To Asset Account	Dr.	To transfer the loss on sale

CALCULATION OF DEPRECIATION AMOUNT

In order to calculate the amount of depreciation to be charged on assets, the following factors should be considered:

1. Original cost of the asset which includes installation, addition, improvement etc.
2. The estimated working of the asset *i.e.* the effective service of an asset to the business, in number of years or product units.
3. The causes of depreciation such as wear and tear, obsolescence, etc. may be considered in deciding the economic life.
4. Residual value of the asset at the end of the estimated working life.
5. Amount spent periodically for repairs and renewals. Repairs are necessary to keep an asset in good condition, through which its life increases.

Methods of Depreciation

There are various methods of providing depreciation. It is to be written off during economic life of an asset. The various fixed assets differ from each other in their nature and therefore no single method of providing depreciation can be applied to all types of assets. The following are the various methods of providing depreciation.

1. Fixed Instalment Method
2. Diminishing Balance Method
3. Annuity Method
4. Depreciation Fund Method
5. Insurance Policy Method
6. Depreciation Reserves and Repairs Fund Method
7. Revaluation Method
8. Machine Hour Rate Method
9. Depletion Method
10. Kilometer Method
11. Sum of Years Digit Method

1. Fixed Instalment Method or Equal Instalment Method or Straight Line Method or Fixed Percentage on Original Cost Method

In this method a fixed or equal amount of depreciation written off as depreciation at the end of each year, during the life time of the asset. Thus the book value of the asset will become zero or its residual value. This method is suitable for patent, furniture, short-lease etc.

The amount of depreciation may be found out thus:

(*a*) *When the asset has no residual value:*

$$\text{Each Year's Depreciation} = \frac{\text{Original Cost of Asset}}{\text{Estimated life of asset in years}}$$

(*b*) *When the asset has residual value:*

$$\text{Each Year's Depreciation} = \frac{\text{Original Cost of Asset} - \text{Estimated Scrap Value}}{\text{Estimated life of asset in years}}$$

Under this system, the amount of depreciation can be calculated easily. Thus the system is simple. However, when asset becomes old, its repair and maintenance charges would be more but the amount of depreciation remains the same every year.

ILLUSTRATION 11.1 (Depreciation by Fixed Instalment Method)

A company whose accounting year is the calendar year, purchased on 1st April 2003, machinery costing Rs 30,000.

It purchased another machine on 1st October 2003, costing Rs 20,000 and on 1st July 2004, costing Rs 10,000.

On 1st Jan. 2005, one-third of the machinery which was installed on 1st April 2003 became obsolete and was sold for Rs 3,000.

Show how the Machinery Account would appear in the books of the Company. The machinery was depreciated by the Fixed Instalment Method @ 10% p.a. *(CA Inter)*

(B.Com., Madurai, Manonmonian)

SOLUTION

Dr. **Machinery Account** Cr.

		Rs			Rs
2003			2003		
April 1	To Bank Account	30,000	Dec. 31	By Depreciation Account	
Oct. 1	To Bank Account	20,000		(Rs 2,250 + 500)	2,750
			Dec. 31	By Balance c/d	47,250
		50,000			50,000
2004			2004		
Jan. 1	To Balance b/d	47,250	Dec. 31	By Depreciation Account	
July 1	To Bank Account	10,000		(Rs 5,000 + 500)	5,500
			Dec. 31	By Balance c/d	51,750
		57,250			57,250
2005			2005		
Jan. 1	To Balance b/d	51,750	Jan. 1	By Bank Account	3,000
			Jan. 1	By Profit and Loss A/c	5,250*
			Dec. 31	By Depreciation Account	5,000
			Dec. 31	By Balance c/d	38,500
		51,750			51,750
2006					
Jan. 1	To Balance b/d	38,500			

*Loss on Sale of Machine:

	Rs
Cost of Machinery	10,000
(Rs 30,000 × $\frac{1}{3}$)	
Less: Depreciation for 2003 (9 months)	750
	9,250
Less: Depreciation for 2004 (1 year)	1,000
Book Value on 1-1-2005	8,250
Less: Sale Proceeds	3,000
	5,250

ILLUSTRATION 11.2 [Depreciation by Fixed Instalment Method (Scrap value being given)]

Plant costing Rs 32,000 purchased on 1st Jan. 2003 and its estimated life is 8 years.

Further purchases of plant are as follows:

1. On 31st March 2003, plant costing Rs 15,000 and its estimated life is 10 years.
2. On 30th Sep. 2004, plant costing Rs 12,000 and its estimated life is 6 years.
3. On 30th April 2005, plant costing Rs 20,000 and its estimated life is 8 years.

Out of the original plants purchased on 1st Jan. 2003 one machine costing Rs 5,000 was sold for Rs 4,700 on 30th June 2005.

Residual value of each asset is 10% of its original cost.

Prepare the Plant Account for the first three years. *(B.Com., Madurai)*

SOLUTION:

Plant Account

Dr. Cr.

Date	Particulars	Rs	Date	Particulars	Rs
2003			2003		
Jan. 1	To Cash Account	32,000	Dec. 31	By Depreciation A/c	4,613[A]
Mar. 31	To Cash Account	15,000	Dec. 31	By Balance c/d	42,387
		47,000			47,000
2004			2004		
Jan. 1	To Balance b/d	42,387	Dec. 31	By Depreciation A/c	5,400[B]
Sep. 30	To Cash Account	12,000		By Balance c/d	48,987
		54,387			54,387
2005			2005		
Jan. 1	To Balance b/d	48,987	June 30	By Depreciation A/c	281
Apr. 30	To Cash Account	20,000	June 30	By Cash Account	4,700[D]
June 30	To Profit on sale of machinery Account	1,105[C]	Dec. 31	By Depreciation A/c	7,688
			Dec. 31	By Balance c/d	57,423
		70,092			70,092
2006					
Jan. 1	To Balance c/d	57,423			

Workings:

(A) Depreciation on Rs 32,000 for one year

that is, $\frac{32{,}000 - 3{,}200}{8} = \text{Rs } 3{,}600$

Depreciation on Rs 15,000 for 9 months

that is, $\frac{15{,}000 - 1{,}500}{10} \times \frac{9}{12} = \text{Rs } 1{,}013$

Rs 4,613

(B) Depreciation on Rs 32,000 for 12 months = Rs 3,600

Depreciation on Rs 15,000 for 12 months = Rs 1,350

Depreciation on Rs 12,000 for 3 months

that is,

$\frac{12,000-1,200}{6}\times\frac{3}{12}$		=	Rs 450
			Rs 5,400

(C) Profit on sale of Machinery:

Book value on 1.1.2003		Rs 5,000
Less: Depreciation for 2003	562	
Depreciation for 2004	562	
Depreciation (for 6 months) for 2005	281	Rs 1,405
Book value on 30.6.2005		Rs 3,595
Sales Price	Rs 4,700	
Less: Book Value	Rs 3,595	
	Rs 1,105	

(D) Depreciation on Rs 27,000 for one year	=	Rs 3,038
Depreciation on Rs 15,000 for one year	=	Rs 1,350
Depreciation on Rs 12,000 for one year	=	Rs 1,800
Depreciation on Rs 20,000 for 8 months	=	Rs 1,500
Total		Rs 7,688

Merits (Fixed Instalment)

1. The method is very simple and easy.
2. There is no complicated calculations.
3. The value of asset can be reduced to zero.
4. There is realistic matching of cost and revenue.
5. It facilitates easy comparison from year to year.

Demerits

1. When additions made to asset, calculation becomes difficult.
2. Depreciation remains the same every year, but maintenance cost increases as the asset growing older and older.
3. The method does not make any provision for interest on capital invested in fixed assets.
4. It may not be possible for the correct calculation of effective working life of any asset.

ILLUSTRATION 11.3 (Depreciation by Straight Line Method)

Depreciation in a factory is provided by the Straight Line Method at the rate of 10% p.a.

The balance standing on Plant and Machinery Account on 31st December 2003, after writing off depreciation for that year, was Rs 19,515. (Total cost price of the plant was Rs 35,800, including plant purchased in 1995, Rs 8,900.)

During January 2004 new plant was purchased at the cost of Rs 2,950 and one machine which had cost Rs 550 in 1980 was sold as scrap for Rs 35.

During January 2005, there was additions costing Rs 1,800 and a machine which had cost Rs 700 in 2001 was sold for Rs 350.

You are required to write up the Machinery Account for 2004 and 2005. All calculations are to be shown.

(CA Inter)

(B.Com., MK, Bharathdasan, Calcutta, Calicut)

SOLUTION:

Dr. **Machinery Account** Cr.

Date	Particulars	Rs	Date	Particulars		Rs
2004			2004			
Jan. 1	To Balance b/d	19,515	Jan. 1	By Bank Account		35
Jan. 1	To Bank Account	2,950	Dec. 31	By Depreciation at 10%		
Jan. 1	To Profit and Loss A/c	35		Total Cost	35,800	
				Less: Purchased	8,900	
					26,900	
				By Depreciation at 10%		2,690
				on Rs 2,950		295
				By Balance c/d		19,480
		22,500				22,500
2005			2005			
Jan. 1	To Balance b/d	19,480	Jan. 1	By Bank A/c (Sale)		350
Jan. 1	To Bank Account	1,800		By Profit and Loss A/c		70*
				By Depreciation:		
				(on 26,900 – 700)	2,620	
				on Rs 2,950	295	
				on Rs 1,800	180	3,095
			Dec. 31	By Balance c/d		17,765
		21,280				21,280
2006						
Jan. 1	To Balance b/d	17,765				

Note: Rs 35 is a gain because the cost of machinery was Rs 550 and within 10 years its book value is Nil.

	Rs
Cost of Plant in 2001	700
Less: 4 years Depreciation	280
Book Value	420
Less: Sale Price	350
Loss:	70

2. Diminishing Balance Method (Reducing Balance Method)

Under this method, the amount of depreciation is calculated as a fixed percentage of the reducing or diminishing value of the asset standing in the books at the beginning of the year, so as to bring down the book value of the asset to its residual value. The amount of depreciation goes on decreasing every year. That is, the amount of depreciation charged in each period is not fixed but is a gradually decreasing sum. This method is similar to the Fixed Instalment Method with the exception that depreciation is charged every year at a fixed percentage, and not on the original cost of the asset but on the reduced opening balance of the asset as brought forward from the previous year. Therefore, the system is called Reducing Balance Method.

This method is suitable in case of those assets whose repair charges increase as they become old. This method is also simple in calculating the amount of depreciation. Elimination of major portion of cost in early years also minimises the impact of obsolescence. Under this method, the asset can never be reduced to zero. This method is suitable for assets like Plant, Machinery, Boiler, Buildings, etc.

ILLUSTRATION 11.4 (Depreciation by Diminishing Balance Method)

On 1st Jan. 2003 machinery was purchased for Rs 80,000. On 1st Jan. 2004 additions were made to the machinery of Rs 40,000. On 31st March 2005, machinery purchased on 1st January 2004, costing Rs 12,000 was sold for Rs 11,000, and on 30th June 2005, machinery purchased on 1st Jan. 2003 costing Rs 32,000, was sold for Rs 26,700. On 1st Oct. 2005 additions were made to the amount of Rs 20,000. Depreciation was provided at 10% p.a. on the Diminishing Balance Method.

Show the Machinery Account for the three years from 2003 to 2005 December 31st.

(ICWA Inter Agra, Allahabad, Poona)

Dr. **Machinery Account** Cr.

		Rs			Rs
2003			2003		
Jan. 1	To Bank Account	80,000	Dec. 31	By Depreciation Account	8,000
			Dec. 31	By Balance c/d	72,000
		80,000			80,000
2004			2004		
Jan. 1	To Balance b/d	72,000	Dec. 31	By Depreciation Account	11,200
Jan. 1	To Bank Account	40,000	Dec. 31	By Balance c/d	1,00,800
		1,12,000			1,12,000
2005			2005		
Jan. 1	To Balance b/d	1,00,800	Mar. 31	By Depreciation A/c (for 3 months)	270
	To Profit and Loss Account	470[1]	Mar. 31	By Bank Account	11,000
Oct 1	To Profit and Loss A/c	2,076[2]	June 30	By Depreciation A/c (for 6 months)	1,296
June 30	To Bank Account	20,000	June 30	By Bank A/c	26,700
			Dec. 31	By Depreciation A/c	5,908[3]
			Dec. 31	By Balance c/d	78,172
		1,23,346			1,23,346
2006					
Jan. 1	To Balance c/d	78,172			

Notes:

	Rs
Profit on Sale of Machinery:	
(1) Cost of Machinery (1-1-2004)	12,000
Less: Depreciation for 2004	1,200
	10,800
Less: Depreciation for 2005 (3 months)	270
Book Value on 31-3-2005	10,530
Sale Proceeds Rs 11,000	
Profit = Rs 11,000 – 10,530	470
(2) Cost of Machinery (1-1-2003)	32,000
Less: Depreciation for 2003	3,200
	28,800
Less: Depreciation for 2004	2,880
	25,920

Less: Depreciation for 2005 (6 months)	1,296	
Book Value on 30-6-2005	24,624	
Sale Proceeds Rs 26,700		
Profit = Rs 26,700 – 24,624	2,076	
(3) Depreciation for the remaining Assets:		Rs
Book Value of Machinery on 1-1-2004		1,00,800
Book Value of Machinery sold		
Rs 10,800 + Rs 25,920		36,720
		64,080
Depreciation for 2005		6,408
Depreciation for the Machinery Purchased on 1-10-2005 (3 months)		500
		5,908

Distinction between Straight Line and Diminishing Balance Methods :

Straight Line	*Dinimishing Balance*
1. Depreciation is calculated on the original cost each year	1. Depreciation is calculated on written down value.
2. Amount of depreciation is equal each year.	2. Amount of depreciation declines each year.
3. The system is simple but not scientific.	3. The system is simple and scientific.
4. The system is not accepted by law.	4. The system is accepted by law.
5. At the end of the life of the asset, the value of the asset will be zero.	5. At the end of the life of the asset, the value of the asset can never be zero.

ILLUSTRATION 11.5 (Changes in Depreciation Methods)

A company purchased a second-hand machine on 1st January 2002 for Rs 37,000 and immediately spent Rs 2,000 on its repairs and Rs 1,000 on its erection. On 1st July 2003, it purchased another machine for Rs 10,000 and on 1st July 2004, it sold off the first machine purchased in 2002 at Rs 28,000. On the same date it purchased machinery for Rs 25,000. The second machine purchased for Rs 10,000 was also sold off on 1st July 2005 for Rs 2,000.

Depreciation was provided on machinery at the rate of 10% on the original cost annually on 31st December. In 2003, however, the Company changed the method of providing depreciation and adopted the written down value method, the rate of depreciation being 15%.

Give the Machinery Account for four years commencing from 1st January 2002.

(*B.Com., Jabalpur, Calcutta, Poona, Bhopal, MS. Mysore*)

SOLUTION

Dr. **Machinery Account** Cr.

		Rs			Rs
2002			2002		
Jan. 1	To Cash Account–Cost	37,000	Dec. 31	By Depreciation Account Rs 40,000 @ 10% for one year	4,000
Jan. 1	To Cash Account–Expenses (Rs 2,000 + Rs 1,000)	3,000	Dec. 31	By Balance c/d	36,000
		40,000			40,000

Date	Particulars	Rs	Date	Particulars	Rs	Rs
2003			2003			
Jan. 1	To Balance b/d	36,000	Dec. 31	By Depreciation Account		
July 1	To Cash Account	10,000		Rs 36,000 @ 15%		
				for one year	5,400	
				Rs 10,000 @ 15%		
				for 6 months	750	6,150
			Dec. 31	By Balance c/d		39,850
		46,000				46,000
2004			2004			
Jan. 1	To Balance b/d	39,850	July 1	By Cash Account		28,000
July 1	To Cash Account	25,000	Dec. 31	By Depreciation Account		
				Rs 30,600 @ 15% for		
				6 months		2,295
			Dec. 31	By Profit and Loss A/c		
				Loss on Sale of Machinery		305*
			Dec. 31	By Depreciation Account		
				Rs 9,250 @ 15% for		
				one year	1,388	
				Rs 25,000 @ 15%		
				for 6 months	1,875	3,263
			Dec. 31	By Balance c/d		30,987
		64,850				64,850
2005			2005			
Jan. 1	To Balance b/d	30,987	July 1	By Cash Account		2,000.00
				By Depreciation Account		
				Rs 7,862 @ 15% for		
				6 months		589.65
				By Profit and Loss A/c		
				Loss on Sale of second		
				machine		5,272.35**
			Dec. 31	By Depreciation Account		
				Rs 23,125 @ 15% for		
				one year		3,468.75
			Dec. 31	By Balance c/d		19,656.25
		30,987				30,987.00
2006						
Jan. 1	To Balance b/d	19,656.25				

Loss on Sale of Machinery:

		Rs	Rs
* Written Down Value on 1st Jan. 2004			30,600
Less:	Depreciation	2,295	
	Sale Price	28,000	30,295
			305
** Written Down value on 1st Jan. 2005			7,862.00
Less:	Depreciation	589.65	
	Sale Price	2,000.00	2,589.65
			5,272.35

Merits (Diminishing Balance Method)

1. The amount of depreciation to be charged reduces with the reduction in the effective life of the asset.
2. This method is recognised by the Income Tax authorities.
3. As the probability of services to be received from the asset reduces, the amount of depreciation also reduces.
4. Elimination of a major portion of cost in earlier years minimises the impact of obsolescence.

Demerits

1. The value of asset can never be zero.
2. When additions or disposal take place, computation of depreciation becomes difficult.
3. This method puts too much emphasis on the historical cost.
4. Interest on capital invested is not considered.

CHANGE IN THE METHOD OF DEPRECIATION

Of the various methods of charging depreciation, the Straight Line Method is the most popular, although some concerns may adopt the diminishing Balance Method. The other methods, sometimes advocated accountants, are partly for taxation purposes and partly owning to the nature of assets.

Sometimes the method is changed either from Straight Line Method to Diminishing Balance Method or from Diminishing Balance Method to Straight Line Method, with effect from the current year or with retrospective effect. Thus, the changes are of two types:

(*a*) *Change with Immediate Effect :* If the change is from the current year, then there will be no problem but simply to change the method of depreciation.

(*b*) *Change with Retrospective Effect:* This requires necessary adjustments to be made in the current year for any extra or less depreciation charged in the earlier years. In such a case, the best course would be to compute the amount of depreciation which has already been charged according to the old method and the amount of depreciation that is to be charged according to the new method. The difference, if any, should be credited (or debited) to the Asset Account in the current year and should be shown as a separate charge (or income) in the Profit and Loss Account of the current year of the firm. (See Illustration : 5 and 6).

ILLUSTRATION 11.6 (Changes in Method of Depreciation and Rate)

A manufacturing firm purchased on 1st January 2001, certain machinery for Rs 1,00,000 and spent Rs 2,000 on its erection. On 1st July in the same year additional machinery costing Rs 50,000 was acquired. On 1st January 2003, the machinery purchased on 1st January 2001 (having become obsolete) was auctioned for Rs 40,000 and on the same date fresh machinery was purchased at a cost of Rs 25,000.

Depreciation was provided annually on 31st December at 10% p.a. on original cost of the asset. In 2003, however, this method was changed and that of writing of 15% p.a. on the written down value method was adopted.

Give the Machinery Account as it would stand at the end of each year from 2001 to 2005, making your calculations to the nearest rupee. (*B.Com., Madurai, Bangalore, Mysore, Agra*)

SOLUTION

Dr. **Machinery Account** Cr.

		Rs			Rs
2001			2001		
Jan. 1	To Cash Account–Cost	1,00,000	Dec. 31	By Depreciation A/c	
Jan. 1	To Cash Account–Expense	2,000		(Rs 10,200[1] + 2,500[2])	12,700
July 1	To Cash Account	50,000	Dec. 31	By Balance c/d	
				(91,800 + 47,500)	1,39,300
		1,52,000			1,52,000

Date	Particulars	Rs	Date	Particulars	Rs
2002			2002		
Jan. 1	To Balance b/d (91,800 + 47,500)	1,39,300	Dec. 31	By Depreciation A/c (10,200[3] + 5,000[4])	15,200
			Dec. 31	By Balance c/d (81,600 + 42,500)	1,24,100
		1,39,300			1,39,300
2003			2003		
Jan. 1	To Balance b/d (81,600 + 42,500)	1,24,100	Jan. 1	By Cash Account	40,000
Jan. 1	To Cash Account	25,000	Jan. 1	By Profit and Loss A/c Loss on Sale of Machinery	41,600[5]
			Dec. 31	By Depreciation A/c (6,375[6] + 3,750[7])	10,125
			Dec. 31	By Balance c/d (36,125 + 21,250)	57,375
		1,49,100			1,49,100
2004			2004		
Jan. 1	By Balance b/d (36,125 + 21,250)	57,375	Dec. 31	By Depreciation A/c (5,418.75[8] + 3,187.50[9])	8,606.25
			Dec. 31	By Balance c/d	48,768.75
		57,375			57,375.00
2005			2005		
Jan. 1	To Balance b/d	48,768.75	Dec. 31	By Depreciation A/c	7,315.31[10]
			Dec. 31	By Balance c/d	41,453.44
		48,768.75			48,768.75
2006					
Jan. 1	To Balance b/d	41,453.44			

Notes:

1. Rs 1,02,000 × 10/100 = Rs 10,200
2. Rs 50,000 × 10/100 × 6/12 = Rs 2,500
3. Rs 1,02,000 × 10/100 = Rs 10,200
4. Rs 50,000 × 10/100 = Rs 5,000
5. Loss on sale of 1st Machinery:

	Rs	Rs
Cost of Machine on 1-1-2001		1,02,000
Less: Depreciation for 2001	10,200	
Depreciation for 2002	10,200	
Sale Price	40,000	60,400
		41,600

6. Rs 42,500 × 15/100 = Rs 6,375
7. Rs 25,000 × 15/100 = Rs 3,750
8. Rs 36,125 × 15/100 = Rs 5,418.75
9. Rs 21,250 × 15/100 = Rs 3,187.50
10. Rs 48,768.75 × 15/100 = Rs 7,315.31

3. Annuity Method

Under this method, it is assumed that the amount spent in the purchase of the asset is an investment which should yield interest. The amount spent in acquiring an asset assumed as an investment and interest is charged at a certain rate on the diminishing balance of the asset and is debited to Asset Account and credited to Interest Account which is transferred to Profit and Loss Account. The asset is credited every year with a fixed amount of depreciation. The amount of depreciation to be charged every year is such that in spite of asset being debited with interest every year, the asset is reduced to zero or its residual value. The amount of depreciation is calculated from the ready Annuity Tables. The amount of depreciation will be different according to the rate of interest and the life time of the asset.

The net burden on the Profit and Loss Account goes on increasing year after year. This is because depreciation that is debited to Profit and Loss Account is constant and the interest being credited goes on decreasing year after year. When additions are made to the asset account, calculations have to be revised. This method is used in the case of leases having large amounts spread over a number of years.

Journal entries are:

1. When the asset is purchased	Asset Account To Bank Account	Dr.
2. For charging interest	Asset Account To Interest Account	Dr.
3. For charging depreciation	Depreciation Account To Asset Account	Dr.

ILLUSTRATION 11.7 (Depreciation by Annuity Method)

A five year lease worth Rs 30,000 is to be depreciated by Annuity system, the unwritten balance of the asset bearing interest at 5%. The annual amount to be written off as shown by the Annuity table is Rs 6,929.24.

Show the working of the Lease Account for the five years. (*B.Com., Madurai, Calicut, Andhra, Poona*)

SOLUTION

Dr. **Lease Account** Cr.

		Rs			Rs
1st Year			1st Year		
Jan. 1	To Bank Account	30,000	Dec. 31	By Depreciation Account	6,929.24
Dec. 31	To Interest Account	1,500	Dec. 31	By Balance c/d	24,570.76
		31,500			31,500
IInd Year			IInd Year		
Jan. 1	To Balance b/d	24,570.76	Dec. 31	By Depreciation Account	6,929.24
Dec. 31	To Interest Account	1,228.54	Dec. 31	By Balance c/d	18,870.06
		25,799.30			25,799.30
IIIrd Year			IIIrd Year		
Jan. 1	To Balance b/d	18,870.06	Dec. 31	By Depreciation Account	6,929.24
Dec. 31	To Interest Account	943.50	Dec. 31	By Balance c/d	12,884.32
		19,813.56			19,813.56
IVth Year			IVth Year		
Jan. 1	To Balance b/d	12,884.32	Dec. 31	By Depreciation Account	6,929.24
Dec. 31	To Interest Account	644.22	Dec. 31	By Balance c/d	6,599.30
		13,528.54			13,528.54
Vth Year			Vth Year		
Jan. 1	To Balance b/d	6,599.30	Dec. 31	By Depreciation Account	6,929.24
Dec. 31	To Interest Account	329.94			
		6,929.24			6,929.24

Merits (Annuity Method)

1. The amount of depreciation to be charged is ascertained from Annuity Tables. Therefore, this method is scientific.
2. This method provides for recovery of invested capital alongwith interest. This is a great advantage.
3. This method is most suitable to such assets which requires heavy initial investment.

Demerits:

1. Calculation of depreciation becomes very difficult when additions are made to assets.
2. Calculation of interest is arbitrary.
3. This system is not at all suitable for those assets which are of small value.
4. Depreciation and interest taken together are not uniform.

4. Depreciation Fund Method (Sinking Fund Method)

This method not only takes depreciation into account but also makes provision for the replacement of asset when it becomes useless. Under this method a fixed amount is debited every year to Depreciation Account or Profit and Loss Account and is credited to Depreciation Fund Account, instead of Asset Account. The asset is shown at its original cost, in the books, in every year. The amount, which is credited in the Depreciation Fund, is invested in gilt-edged securities. The interest on such investment is also invested in similar securities. The securities are readily convertible into cash. Investments are purchased every year. When the asset becomes useless, the investments are sold away and thus new asset can be acquired without disturbing the financial position. This method is adopted specially when it is desired not merely to write off an asset but also to provide enough funds to replace an asset at the end of its working life. The amount set aside as depreciation is such that this, with compound interest, will be sufficient to meet the cost of a new asset, less scrap value, if any, for replacement.

This method of depreciation is suitable for costly but wasting assets. The depreciation, under this method, can be calculated with the help of a Sinking Fund table for a particular period at a given rate of interest.

The Accounting entries are as follows:

First Year

1. When the asset is purchased	Asset Account To Bank Account	Dr.
2. When Depreciation is provided	Depreciation Account To Depreciation Fund Account	Dr.
3. When Depreciation is transferred	Profit and Loss Account To Depreciation Account	Dr.
4. When the amount of depreciation is invested	Depreciation Fund Investment A/c To Bank Account	Dr.

Second and Subsequent Years

1. When Depreciation is provided	Depreciation Account To Depreciation Fund Account	Dr.
2. When the Depreciation is transferred	Profit and Loss Account To Depreciation Account	Dr.
3. When Interest on Depreciation Fund investment is received	Bank Account To Interest on Depreciation Fund Investment Account	Dr.
4. When Interest is transferred	Interest on Depreciation Fund Investment Account To Depreciation Fund Account	Dr.
5. When investment is made with Depreciation and interest Amount	Depreciation Fund Investment A/c To Bank Account	Dr.

Last Year

1. When Depreciation is provided	Depreciation Account Dr. To Depreciation Fund Account
2. When the Depreciation is transferred	Profit and Loss Account Dr. To Depreciation Account
3. When Interest on Depreciation Fund Investment is received	Bank Account Dr. To Interest on Depreciation Fund Investment Account
4. When Interest is transferred	Interest on Depreciation Fund Investment Account Dr. To Depreciation Fund Account
5. When Investments are sold	Bank Account Dr. To Depeciation Fund Investment A/c
6. Profit or loss on investment is transferred: If Profit	Depreciation Fund Investment A/c Dr. To Depreciation Fund Account
If Loss	Depreciation Fund Account Dr. To Depreciation Fund Investment A/c
7. When the old asset written of	Depreciation Fund Account Dr. To Asset Account
8. Balance, if, any in the Depreciation Fund Account may be transferred to Profit and Loss Account	
9. When new asset is purchased	New Asset Account Dr. To Bank Account

ILLUSTRATION 11.8 [Depreciation by Depreciation Fund Method (without scrap value)]

A firm acquires a four-year lease on 1st January 2002 for Rs 40,000. The firm decides to establish a Depreciation Fund for its replacement. Interest is expected to be earned at 5%.

On 31st December 2005, the balance at Bank, before the receipt of interest on Depreciation Fund Investmen vas Rs 26,000. Investments were sold for Rs 29,000. New lease was acquired for Rs 45,000.

Give journal entries and ledger accounts relating to the above.

Note: The Sinking Fund tables show that Re 0.232012 has to be invested every year to produce Re 1 at the end of four years @ 5%. *(B.Com., Madurai)*

SOLUTION

Note: The Sinking Fund tables show that Re 0.232012 has to be invested every year to produce Re 1 at the end of four years @ 5%. For Rs 40,000, the sum required is Rs 9,280.48. This is the annual depreciation.

Journal

			Dr.	Cr.
2002			*Rs*	*Rs*
Jan. 1	Lease Account To Bank Account (Being Purchase of lease for four years)	Dr.	40,000.00	40,000.00
Dec. 31	Depreciation Account To Depreciation Fund Account (Being Annual Depreciation on Lease, credited to Depreciation Fund)	Dr.	9,280.48	9,280.48

Date	Particulars		Dr. Amount	Cr. Amount
Dec. 31	Depreciation Fund Investment Account	Dr.	9,280.48	
	To Bank Account			9,280.48
	(Being Purchase of investments against Depreciation Fund)			
2003				
Dec. 31	Bank Account	Dr.	464.02	
	To Interest on Depreciation Fund Investment A/c			464.02
	(Being Interest received on D.F. Investments)			
Dec. 31	Interest on Depreciation Fund Investment Account	Dr.	464.02	
	To Depreciation Fund Account			464.02
	(Being transfer of interest on D.F.I. to Depreciation Fund)			
Dec. 31	Depreciation Account	Dr.	9,280.48	
	To Depreciation Fund Account			9,280.48
	(Being Annual Depreciation credited to Depreciation Fund)			
Dec. 31	Depreciation Fund Investments Account	Dr.	9,744.50	
	To Bank Account			9,744.50
	(Being Purchase of investments against Depreciation Fund)			
2004				
Dec. 31	Bank Account	Dr.	951.25	
	To Interest on Depreciation Fund Investment A/c			951.25
	(Being interest on D.F. Investments)			
Dec. 31	Interest on Depreciation Fund Investment Account	Dr.	951.25	
	To Depreciation Fund Account			951.25
	(Being transfer of D.F.I. to Depreciation Fund)			
Dec. 31	Depreciation Account	Dr.	9,280.48	
	To Depreciation Fund Account			9,280.48
	(Being Annual Depreciation credited to Depreciation Fund)			
Dec. 31	Depreciation Fund Investment Account	Dr.	10,231.73	
	To Bank Account			10,231.73
	(Being Purchase of investments for the annual depreciation and interest)			
2005				
Dec. 31	Bank Account	Dr.	1,462.84	
	To Interest on Depreciation Fund Investment Account			1,462.84
	(Being receipt on D.F. Investments)			
Dec. 31	Interest on Depreciation Fund Investments Account	Dr.	1,462.84	
	To Depreciation Fund Account			1,462.84
	(Being transfer of D.F.I. to D.F.)			

Dec. 31	Depreciation Account Dr. To Depreciation Fund Account (Being annual depreciation credited to Depreciation Fund)		9,280.48	9,280.48
Dec. 31	Bank Account Dr. To Depreciation Fund Investment Account (Being sale proceeds of D.F. Investments)		29,200.00	29,200.00
Dec. 31	Depreciation Fund Account Dr. To Depreciation Fund Investments Account (Being transfer of loss on D.F.I. to D.F.)		56.71	56.71
Dec. 31	Depreciation Fund Account Dr. To Lease Account (Being transfer of Lease A/c to D. Fund A/c)		40,000.00	40,000.00
Dec. 31	Profit and Loss Account Dr. To Depreciation Fund Account (Being transfer of Depreciation Fund A/c to Profit and Loss A/c)		56.68	56.68
Dec. 31	New Lease Account Dr. To Bank Account (Being new Lease purchased for Rs 45,000)		45,000.00	45,000.00

Dr. **Lease Account** Cr.

		Rs			Rs.
2002 Jan. 1	To Bank A/c	40,000	2002 Dec. 31	By Balance c/d	40,000
2003 Jan. 1	To Balance b/d	40,000	2003 Dec. 31	By Balance c/d	40,000
2004 Jan. 1	To Balance b/d	40,000	2004 Dec. 31	By Balance c/d	40,000
2005 Jan. 1	To Balance b/d	40,000	2005 Dec. 31	By Depreciation Fund A/c Transfer	40,000

Dr. **Depreciation Fund Account** Cr.

		Rs			Rs.
2002 Dec. 31	To Balance c/d	9,280.48	2002 Dec. 31	By Depreciation Account	9,280.48
2003 Dec. 31	To Balance c/d	19,024.98	2003 Jan. 1	By Balance b/d	9,280.48
			Dec. 31	By Interest on D.F. Investment Account	464.02
			Dec. 31	By Depreciation A/c	9,280.48
		19,024.98			19,024.98

Date	Particulars	Rs	Date	Particulars	Rs
2004			2004		
Dec. 31	To Balance c/d	29,256.71	Jan. 1	By Balance b/d	19,024.98
			Dec. 31	By Interest on D.F. Investment A/c	951.25
			Dec. 31	By Depreciation Account	9,280.48
		29,256.71			29,256.71
2005			2005		
Dec. 31	To Lease Account–Transfer	40,000.00	Jan. 1	By Balance b/d	29,256.71
Dec. 31	To Loss on D.F. Investments A/c	56.71	Dec. 31	By Interest on D.F. Investment A/c	1,462.84
			Dec. 31	By Depreciation A/c	9,280.48
			Dec. 31	By Profit and Loss Account	56.68
		40,056.71			40,056.71

Dr. Depreciation Account Cr.

Date	Particulars	Rs	Date	Particulars	Rs
2002			2002		
Dec. 31	To Depreciation Fund A/c	9,280.48	Dec. 31	By Profit and Loss A/c	9,280.48
2003			2003		
Dec. 31	To Depreciation Fund A/c	9,280.48	Dec. 31	By Profit and Loss A/c	9,280.48
2004			2004		
Dec. 31	To Depreciation Fund A/c	9,280.48	Dec. 31	By Profit and Loss A/c	9,280.48
2005			2005		
Dec. 31	To Depreciation Fund A/c	9,280.48	Dec. 31	By Profit and Loss A/c	9,280.48

Dr. Depreciation Fund Investment Account Cr.

Date	Particulars	Rs	Date	Particulars	Rs
2002			2002		
Dec. 31	To Bank Account	9,280.48	Dec. 31	By Balance c/d	9,280.48
2003			2003		
Jan. 1	To Balance b/d	9,280.48	Dec. 31	By Balance b/d	19,024.98
Dec. 31	To Bank Account (Rs 9,280.48 + Rs 464.02)	9,744.50			
		19,024.98			19,024.98
2004			2004		
Jan. 1	To Balance b/d	19,024.98	Dec. 31	By Balance b/d	29,256.71
Dec. 31	To Bank Account	10,231.73			
		29,256.71			29,256.71
2005			2005		
Jan. 1	To Balance b/d	29,256.71	Dec. 31	By Bank Account	29,200.00
			Dec. 31	By Depreciation Fund A/c	56.71
		29,256.71			29,256.71

Interest on Depreciation Fund Investments Account

Dr.		Rs		Cr.	Rs
2003			2003		
Dec. 31	To Depreciation Fund A/c Transfer	464.02	Dec. 31	By Bank Account	464.02
2004			2004		
Dec. 31	To Depreciation Fund A/c Transfer	951.25	Dec. 31	By Bank Account	951.25
2005			2005		
Dec. 31	To Depreciation Fund A/c Transfer	1,462.84	Dec. 31	By Bank Account	1,462.84

Bank Account

Dr.		Rs		Cr.	Rs
2005			2005		
Dec. 31	To Balance b/d	26,000.00	Dec. 31	By New Lease A/c	45,000.00
Dec. 31	To Investment on D.F. Investment A/c	1,462.84	Dec. 31	By Balance c/d	11,662.84
Dec. 31	To D.F. Investment A/c Sale Proceeds	29,200.00			
		56,662.84			56,662.84
2006					
Jan. 1	To Balance b/d	11,662.84			

New Lease Account

Dr.		Rs		Cr.	Rs.
2005					
Dec. 31	To Bank Account	45,000			

Merits (Depreciation Fund)

1. This method provides liquid funds at the end of economic life of the existing asset to replace it with a new asset.
2. This method is useful for wasting assets.
3. The amount of depreciation, charged to Profit and Loss Account, is invested in outside securities in order to earn compound interest. Thus, the system is beneficial to the business.
4. This is a method which gives advantages from the point of veiw of recovery of capital invested.

Demerits :

1. This method is complicated and involves numerous calculations.
2. Marketable securities always have some kind of uncertainty in terms of price fluctutations.
3. Profit and Loss Account is burdened heavily by fixed amount of depreciation together with the cost of increasing repairs every year.
4. This method will be difficult to be used where frequent additions, replacements or extensions take place.
5. This system works on the basis of original historical cost. The price changes are not considered.

ILLUSTRATION 11.9 [Depreciation by Depreciation Fund Method (with scrap value)]

On 1.1.2001, a Company purchased a machinery at a cost of Rs 50,000. The machinery is expected to run for 5 years at the end of which the estimated scrap value is Rs 10,000. In order to provide sufficient fund for the replacement of the machinery at the end of its life it is decided to create a Sinking Fund and to invest the amount of gilt edged securities yielding 4% interest.

On 31.12.2005 the machinery is sold off as scrap for Rs 8,500. On the same date investments are realised at Rs 31,500. A new machinery is purchased for Rs 75,000 on the following date. Show the necessary accounts in the books of the company for 5 years.

(Re 0.1846 at 4% will produce Re 1 in 5 years) *(B.Com., Madurai, Sambalpur, Usmania, MK)*

SOLUTION

To write off Re 1 at 4% interest annual depreciation will be Re 0.1846.

So to write off Rs 40,000 (Rs 50,000 – 10,000) annual depreciation will be

$0.1846 \times 40,000 = \text{Rs } 7,384$

Dr. **Sinking Fund Account** Cr.

		Rs			Rs
2001			2001		
Dec 31	To Balance c/d	7,384	Dec. 31	By Profit and Loss A/c	7,384
2002			2002		
Dec. 31	To Balance c/d	15,063	Jan. 1	By Balance b/d	7,384
			Dec. 31	By Bank A/c–Interest	295
			Dec. 31	By Profit and Loss A/c	7,384
		15,063			15,063
2003			2003		
Dec. 31	To Balance c/d	23,050	Jan. 1	By Balance b/d	15,063
			Dec. 31	By Bank A/c–Interest	603
			Dec. 31	By Profit and Loss A/c	7,384
		23,050			23,050
2004			2004		
Dec. 31	To Balance c/d	31,356	Jan. 1	By Balance b/d	23,050
			Dec. 31	By Bank A/c–Interest	922
			Dec. 31	By Profit and Loss A/c	7,384
		31,356			31,356
2005			2005		
Dec. 31	To Machinery Account Transfer	40,138	Jan. 1	By Balance b/d	31,356
			Dec. 31	By Bank A/c–Interest	1,254
			Dec. 31	By Profit and Loss A/c	7,384
			Dec. 31	By Sinking Fund Investment A/c–Profit	144
		40,138			40,138

Dr. **Sinking Fund Investment Account** Cr.

		Rs			Rs
2001			2001		
Dec. 31	To Bank Account	7,384	Dec. 31	By Balance c/d	7,384

Date	Particulars	Rs	Date	Particulars	Rs
2002			2002		
Jan. 1	To Balance b/d	7,384	Dec. 31	By Balance c/d	15,063
Dec. 31	To Bank Account Rs 295 + 7,384	7,679			
		15,063			15,063
2003			2003		
Jan. 1	To Balance b/d	15,063	Dec. 31	By Balance c/d	23,050
Dec. 31	To Bank Account Rs 603 + 7,384	7,987			
		23,050			23,050
2004			2004		
Jan. 1	To Balance b/d	23,050	Dec. 31	By Balance c/d	31,356
Dec. 31	To Bank Account Rs 922 + 7,384	8,306			
		31,356			31,356
2005			2005		
Jan. 1	To Balance b/d	31,356	Dec. 31	By Bank Account Sale Proceeds	31,500
Dec. 31	To Sinking Fund Account Profit on sale	144			
		31,500			31,500

5. Insurance Policy Method

In this method, instead of purchasing securities, an insurance policy is purchased for an amount equal to the cost of replacement of asset. The Insurance Company agrees to pay a lump sum in return for a sum known as premium to be paid at the beginning of every year. Under this method, it not only provides funds for the replacement but also provides security to the asset. When the policy is taken, the asset is secured against any loss. The system is applicable to costly wasting assets. The asset account remains at its original cost.

The advantage of this method is that a definite amount is received on maturity. Under Depreciation Fund Investment, there may be loss when the investments are sold and this risk is avoided here. There is also more security. However, Profit and Loss Account is overburdened with Depreciation together with repairs.

Accounting Entries

First and Subsequent Years		
On Payment of Premium (Beginning of the year)	Depreciation Insurance Policy A/c To Bank Account	Dr.
When Depreciation is provided (End of the year)	Profit and Loss Account To Depreciation Reserve Account	Dr.
Last Year		
When Policy amount is received on maturity	Bank Account To Depreciation Insurance Policy Account	Dr.
When writing off old asset	Depreciation Reserve Account To Asset Account	Dr.
For transfer of Profit on Insurance Policy	Depreciation Insurance Policy A/c To Depreciation Reserve Account	Dr.
On purchase of new asset	New Asset Account To Bank Account	Dr.

ILLUSTRATION 11.10 (Depreciation by Insurance Policy Method)

On 1st January 2002, a merchant purchased a four years' lease of premises costing Rs 50,000. It has been decided to provide for its replacement by means of an Insurance Policy, the annual premium on which amounts to Rs 12,000. Show the necessary accounts recording the depreciation and replacement of the lease.

(*B.Com., Madurai*)

SOLUTION

Dr. **Leasehold Premises Account** Cr.

		Rs			*Rs*
2002			2002		
Jan. 1	To Bank Account	50,000	Dec. 31	By Depreciation Fund Account	50,000

Dr. **Depreciation Fund Account** Cr.

		Rs			*Rs*
2002			2002		
Dec. 31	To Balance c/d	12,000	Dec. 31	By Depreciation Account	12,000
2003			2003		
Dec. 31	To Balance c/d	24,000	Jan. 1	By Balance b/d	12,000
			Dec. 31	By Depreciation Account	12,000
		24,000			24,000
2004			2004		
Dec. 31	To Balance c/d	36,000	Jan. 1	By Balance b/d	24,000
			Dec. 31	By Depreciation Account	12,000
		36,000			36,000
2005			2005		
Dec. 31	To Leasehold Premises Account	50,000	Jan. 1	By Balance b/d	36,000
			Dec. 31	By Depreciation Account	12,000
			Dec. 31	By Depreciation Fund Policy Account	2,000
		50,000			50,000

Dr. **Depreciation Fund Policy Account** Cr.

		Rs			*Rs*
2002			2002		
Jan. 1	To Bank Account	12,000	Dec. 31	By Balance c/d	12,000
2003			2003		
Jan. 1	To Balance b/d	12,000	Dec. 31	By Balance c/d	24,000
Jan. 1	To Bank Account	12,000			
		24,000			24,000
2004			2004		
Jan. 1	To Balance b/d	24,000	Dec. 31	By Balance c/d	36,000
Dec. 1	To Bank Account	12,000			
		36,000			36,000

2005			2005		
Jan. 1	To Balance b/d	36,000	Dec. 31	By Bank Account	50,000
Jan. 1	To Bank Account	12,000			
Dec. 31	To Depreciation Fund Account	2,000			
		50,000			50,000

Note: (1) The premium on an Insurance Policy is payable in advance when the policy is taken.

(2) The Depreciation Fund Policy Account can also be maintained at the annual surrender value of the policy, if so desired, by adjusting the amount of the Depreciation Fund Policy Account through the Depreciation Fund Account.

Merits (Insurance Policy Method)

1. It provides adequate funds for replacement of assets.
2. Better security is provided to the investors by assumption of risk by Insurance Companies.
3. The Insurance Company will pay a stipulated amount with which replacement of asset can be made.

Demerits

1. This method is more expensive since Insurance Company keeps its own margin.
2. When policy is surrendered for one reason or other, there is greater loss.
3. The method is unsuitable, where additions are made to assets during the period.

6. Depreciation Reserve and Repairs Fund Method

In this system, the fund or provision method not only equalises the burden on profit and loss account but also provides for replacement of asset and repairs too. Depreciation Reserve and Repairs Fund method is a provision one step further than the Depreciation Fund Method. Under this system an annual provision is made by adding the cost of the asset plus probable cost of repairs (less scrap value, if any) and then divided by the life of the asset. Such an amount is charged to Profit and Loss Account every year. Whenever, any repairs or renewals are effected the expenses will be debited to Depreciation and Repairs Fund Account, instead of Profit and Loss Account. The balance of Fund is ultimately closed by transferring to Asset Account. This system of Depreciation is applicable to all cases where repairs and renewals charges are high:

Journal Entries

1. When the Fund is created	Profit and Loss Account Dr. To Depreciation Reserve and Repairs Fund Account
2. When payment made for repairs	Repairs and Renewals Account Dr. To Bank Account
3. When the repairs expenses are transferred	Depreciation Reserve and Repairs Fund Account Dr. To Repairs and Renewals Account
4. On closing the Depreciation Reserve and Repairs Fund Account	Depreciation Reserve and Repairs Fund Account Dr. To Asset Account

5. If there is any difference in Fund Account, it will be transferred to Profit and Loss Account.

ILLUSTRATION 11.11 (Depreciation by Reserve for Repairs and Renewals Method)

A Company decided to create and maintain a Repairs and Renewals Fund by charging to revenue each year with a fixed amount of Rs 2,000. The actual repairs and renewals for the three years are Rs 1,000; 850 and Rs 950. Open ledger account for three years.

Dr. **Reserve for Repairs and Renewals** Cr.

		Rs			Rs
Ist Year			Ist Year		
Dec. 31	To Repair Account	1,000	Dec. 31	By Profit and Loss Account	2,000
Dec. 31	To Balance c/d	1,000			
		2,000			2,000
IInd Year			IInd Year		
Dec. 31	To Repairs Account	850	Jan. 1	By Balance b/d	1,000
Dec. 31	To Balance c/d	2,150	Dec. 31	By Profit and Loss Account	2,000
		3,000			3,000
IIIrd Year			IIIrd Year		
Dec. 31	To Repairs Account	950	Jan. 1	By Balance b/d	2,150
Dec. 31	To Balance c/d	3,200	Dec. 31	By Profit and Loss Account	2,000
		4,150			4,150
			IVth Year		
			Jan. 1	By Balance b/d	3,200

7. Revaluation Method

This is the most simple method. With the help of experts, compare the value of the assets at the end of the year with the value in the beginning of the year. The loss on revaluation is debited to Profit and Loss Account or Depreciation Account and credited to Asset Account. This method is used for small items like livestock, loose tools, packages etc.

ILLUSTRATION 11.12 (Revaluation Method)

On Ist July 2003, a firm has loose tools worth Rs 10,000. During the year they purchased tools of Rs 6,000. On December 2003, the loose tools valued at Rs 13,500.

On Ist June 2004, loose tools of Rs 8,000 were purchased. During the year, tools worth Rs 1,000 were stolen by the workers. The remaining tools valued at Rs 20,000.

During the year 2005, tools worth Rs 800 were broken and sold as scrap for Rs 150. In the same year tools for Rs 800 purchased. Dec. 2005, tools were valued at Rs 18,500.

Prepare Loose Tools Account and Depreciation Account for three years.

SOLUTION

Dr. **Loose Tools Account** Cr.

		Rs			Rs
2002			2003		
July 1	To Balance b/d	10,000	Dec. 31	By Depreciation Account	2,500
	To Bank Account	6,000	Dec. 31	By Balance c/d	13,500
		16,000			16,000
2004			2004		
Jan. 1	To Balance b/d	13,500		By Profit and Loss A/c	
Jan. 1	To Bank Account	8,000		(Loss by theft)	1,000
			Dec. 31	By Depreciation Account	500
			Dec. 31	By Balance c/d	20,000
		21,500			21,500

		Rs			Rs
2005			2005		
Jan. 1	To Balance b/d	20,000		By Bank Account	150
	To Bank Account	800	Dec. 31	By Depreciation Account	2,150
			Dec. 31	By Balance b/d	18,500
		20,800			20,800
2006					
Jan. 1	To Balance b/d	18,500			

Dr. **Depreciation Account** Cr.

		Rs			Rs
2003			2003		
Dec. 31	To Loose Tools Account	2,500	Dec. 31	By Profit and Loss A/c	2,500
2004			2004		
Dec. 31	To Loose Tools Account	500	Dec. 31	By Profit and Loss A/c	500
2005			2005		
Dec. 31	To Loose Tools Account	2,150	Dec. 31	By Profit and Loss A/c	2,150

8. Machine Hour Rate Method

Under this method, hourly rate of depreciation is calculated. The cost of the asset (less residual value if any) is divided by the estimated working hours. The actual depreciation for any given period depends upon the working hours during that year. The special feature is that the life of the machine is found out not in years but in hours. This system is useful to textiles, jute mills etc.

$$\text{Depreciation per hour} = \frac{\text{Original cost of machine} - \text{Scrap Value, if any}}{\text{Estimated life of the machine in hours}}$$

ILLUSTRATION 11.13 (Machine hour rate method)

A Machine was purchased on Ist January 2004 at a cost of Rs 50,000 and the cost of installation being Rs 8,000. It is expected that its total working life will be 1,00,000 hours. The scrap value may be Rs 3,000. During the year 2004, the machine worked for 1,200 hours and in 2005 for 1,350 hours. Calculate the depreciation for 2004 and 2005.

SOLUTION

Expected Working Life of Machine = 1,00,000 hours

Cost of Machine = Rs 58,000
(Rs 50,000 + 8,000)

Scrap Value = Rs 3,000

$$\text{Hourly Rate of Depreciation} = \frac{\text{Original Cost} - \text{Scrap Value}}{\text{Life of Asset in hours}}$$

$$= \frac{\text{Rs } 58{,}000 - 3{,}000}{1{,}00{,}000}$$

= 0.55 paise per hour

Depreciation for 2004 = 1200 × 0.55
Rs 660

Depreciation for 2005 = 1350 × 0.55
= Rs 742.50

9. Kilometre Method

In transport undertakings, this method is used to calculate depreciation because kilometre run is the main factor causing depreciation. Therefore, lorries, tractors, buses and similar other transportation machines are depreciated by this method. To find out the amount of depreciation, we need the following factors:

1. Estimated life in kilometres
2. Total cost of vehicle
3. Scrap value, if any

$$\text{Depreciation per Kilometre} = \frac{\text{Cost of vehicle} - \text{Scrap Value}}{\text{Estimated life (in kilometres)}}$$

ILLUSTRATION 11.14

A secondhand lorry is purchased for Rs 80,000 and further spent Rs 35,000 to put it in good working condition. It is estimated that the lorry may cover 1,00,000 kilometres. Find out the depreciation per kilometre.

SOLUTION

$$\text{Depreciation per Kilometre} = \frac{\text{Cost of vehicle} - \text{Scrap Value}}{\text{Estimated life (in kilometres)}}$$

$$= \frac{80{,}000 + 35{,}000}{1{,}00{,}000}$$

$$= \text{Rs } 1.15.$$

10. Depletion Method

Depletion means the exhaustion of natural resources, for example, oil well, mineral deposit, timber etc. Here the purchase price is paid for the acquisition of a natural resource. Depreciation is calculated on one unit of the output by dividing the total value of the acquisition of asset by the number of units expected to be produced. The method is similar to production unit method.

ILLUSTRATION 11.15 (Depreciation under Depletion Method)

In 2003, a Company acquired a mine at a cost of Rs 3,00,000. The estimated reserve of minerals in tons is 30,00,000 of which 80% is expected to be raised. The first three years raisings are:

2003–1,60,000 tons,

2004–2,24,000 tons,

2005–2,00,000 tons.

Show the Mines Account charging depreciation under the Depletion method.

SOLUTION

Total Quantity expected to be extracted:

80% of 30,00,000 tons = 24,00,000 tons

Cost of the mine = Rs 3,00,000

$$\text{Charge per ton} = \frac{\text{Rs } 3{,}00{,}000}{24{,}00{,}000} = \frac{1}{8}$$

Dr. **Mines Account** Cr.

		Rs			Rs
2003			2003		
Jan. 1	To Bank Account	3,00,000	Dec. 31	By Depreciation Account (1,60,000 × 1/8)	20,000
			Dec. 31	By Balance c/d	2,80,000
		3,00,000			3,00,000
2004			2004		
Jan. 1	To Balance b/d	2,80,000	Dec. 31	By Depreciation Account (2,24,000 × 1/8)	28,000
			Dec. 31	By Balance c/d	2,52,000
		2,80,000			2,80,000
2005			2005		
Jan. 1	To Balance b/d	2,52,000	Dec. 31	By Depreciation Account (2,00,000 × 1/8)	25,000
			Dec. 31	By Balance c/d	2,27,000
		2,52,000			2,52,000
2006					
Jan. 1	To Balance b/d	2,27,000			

11. Sum of the Years' Digits Method

This method, like diminishing balance, is based on the assumption that the reduction in the value of the fixed asset will be greater initially and will go on decreasing gradually with the decrease in the life of such asset. The amount of depreciation is calculated by using the following formula:

$$\text{Depreciation} = \text{Amount to be written off} \times \frac{\text{Remaining life of Asset}}{\text{Total of all digits representing the life of the assets}}$$

ILLUSTRATION 11.16

An asset has been purchased for Rs 50,000, its effective life being 5 years. The scrap value is estimated at Rs 5,000. Depreciation for the years is calculated as follows:

SOLUTION:

Amount to be written off = Rs 50,000 – 5,000 = 45,000

The sum of all digits is 15 i.e. 1 + 2 + 3 + 4 + 5 = 15

First year depreciation	= Rs 45,000 × 5/15	=	Rs 15,000
Second year depreciation	= Rs 45,000 × 4/15	=	Rs 12,000
Third year depreciation	= Rs 45,000 × 3/15	=	Rs 9,000
Fourth year depreciation	= Rs 45,000 × 2/15	=	Rs 6,000
Fifth year depreciation	= Rs 45,000 × 1/15	=	Rs 3,000
	Total:	=	Rs 45,000

DEPRECIATION POLICY

Now-a-days, a huge amount is spent for acquiring modern machines. For the purpose of such acquisition, the management must have to take some concrete decision. Thus, the policy must include the following:

(1) To select the appropriate method of depreciation:

(2) To review of the current provision for depreciation whether there is any under provision for depreciation or over provision for depreciation:

(3) To evaluate the existing policy of depreciation from the stand point of tax consideration:

(4) To constitute a committee for "Depreciation Policy":

(5) To ascertain the proper amount of depreciation and its recording procedure:

(6) To disclose the policy of depreciation in the published annual report for the benefit of share-holders, outsiders etc.

The depreciation policy to be followed in an organisation is decided at the top level. Depreciation policy, in fact, relates to the choice of the method of depreciation and its suitability for the organisation. Various methods can be evaluated in the light of many factors, such as, effect of obsolescence, repairs and maintenance, future operating efficiency of the asset in use, service cost of the asset, etc.

OBJECTIVES OF DEPRECIATION POLICY

The management has to consider the following objectives while framing a proper depreciation policy.

(*a*) To recover the cost of fixed assets before its effective life.

(*b*) Creating funds to replace the asset in future.

(*c*) To take advantages of tax benefit.

(*d*) To determine the correct profit.

(*e*) Following a uniform rate of return.

(*f*) Sometimes to create a source of fund for working capital.

REQUIREMENT OF COMPANIES ACT 1956

Sec. 205 (2) of the Compaines Act deals with the provision of depreciation. The Companies Act 1988 has delinked depreciation under the Companies Act from that under the Income Tax Act. The Act now provides the rates of depreciation in schedule XIV to the Act. Every company has the following alternatives with respect to provision for depreciation. They are :

(*a*) Provide depreciation on the written down value at the rates specified in Schedule XIV to the Act, at the end of the each financial year.

(*b*) Provide depreciation by dividing 95% of the original cost of each depreciable asset by the specified period in respect of such asset.

(*c*) Any other method with the prior consent from the Central Government which would ensure writing off at 95% of the original cost during specified period.

(*d*) For assets for which schedule XIV does not provide rates on basis approved by Central Government by any general or special order published in official Gazette.

Schedule XIV provides separate rates of depreciation for WDV basis and Straight Line basis. Rates are also specified for single shift, double shift and three shifts. Companies Act also stipulates that in the event an asset is sold, discarded, demolished or destroyed before the new provision of depreciation, the difference between the book value and sale proceeds of the asset must be written off in the financial year in which the asset is sold, discarded, demolished or destroyed.

DEPRECIATION DISTINGUISHED FROM OTHER TERMS

The term 'Depreciation' is to be distinguished from other terms such as, depletion, amortization etc. though they are often used interchangeably.

DEPLETION: Depletion implies removal of an available but irreplaceable resource such as extracting coal from a Coal Mine, or oil out of an Oil Well.

AMORTIZATION: The process of writing off intangible assets is termed as amortization. some intangible assets like patents, copy-rights, leaseholds etc. have a limited useful life. Hence, their cost must be written off over such period.

The American Institutue of Certified Public Accountants (AICPA) has put the difference between depreciation, depletion and amortization in the following words:

"Depreciation can be distinguished from other terms with specialised meanings by accountants to describe assets cost allocation procedures. Depreciation is concerned with charging the cost of man-made fixed assets to operations (and not with determination of asset value for the Balance Sheet). Depletion referes to cost allocations for natural resources such as oil and mineral deposits. Amortization relates to cost allocation for intangible assets such as patents and leaseholds. The use of the term depreciation should also be avoided in connection with the valuation procedures for securities and investments."

DILAPIDATIONS: The term 'dilapidation' refers to the damage done to a building or other property during tenancy. When a property is taken on lease and later returned to the landlord, the lessee may be asked as per the agreement to put the property in a good condition as it was at the time it was leased out. In order to meet the cost of such dilapidation, a provision may be created by debiting the property account with the estimated amount of dilapidation and crediting the provision for dilapidation account. Depreciation may then be charged on the total cost of the asset so arrived at. Any payment made later on dilapidation may be debited to the provision for dilapidation account. The balance, if any, may be transferred to Profit and Loss Account.

CHOICE OF A SUITABLE METHOD:

Each method has its own merits and demerits. It is not possible to choose a method, considered to be the best, on the basis of relative merits. Selection of method depends upon managerial policy. A wrong choice will have its own effect on the financial statements and fails to reflect a true and fair view of the affairs of business.

The choice of the appropriate method of depreciation depends upon many factors such as the nature of the asset, tax implication, maintenance cost during later years, rate of obsolescence, matching cost and revenue, management policy etc. The problem of choice of an appropriate depreciation method need not bother business enterprises in our country since the concerned statutes such as the Companies Act and Income Tax Act have prescribed the method of depreciation to be followed.

Depreciation on Replacement Cost:

There is an important question as to whether depreciation should be calculated or charged on the basis of actual (or historical) cost or of replacement cost, that is the amount required to replace the asset by a new one. Since one of the most important functions of depreciation is to collect funds for replacement of the asset concerned, it would be logical to charge depreciation on the replacement cost. Suppose, a machine costing Rs. 1,00,000 is depreciated on the basis of historical cost. At the end of its life, Rs 1,00,000 would be collected but if it now costs Rs. 1,50,000 to purchase the new machine, it would not be possible to replace the asset. It would have been better to charge depreciation on the basis of Rs. 1,50,000, the replacement price. One may also argue that goods produced with the help of the machine should bear depreciation charge on the basis of Rs. 1,50,000 because that is the value of the machine. If we buy a pen for Rs. 30 and lose it and have to spend Rs. 50 for buying a new pen of the same type, we lose Rs. 50 and not Rs. 30. Hence, depreciation on the basis of replacement price is quite logical from the point of view of cost also.

But there are practical difficulties in adopting this course. The chief ones are the following:—

(*i*) Replacement price cannot be known in the beginning and really not till replacement is due.

(*ii*) Such new assets are rarely of the same type and quality as old assets—they are always much better. Hence, the higher price paid is for an improved asset and to the extent of the improvement at least, depreciation should not have been provided for previously.

(*iii*) Income-tax authorities do not allow depreciation except on strict cost basis.

(*iv*) Under the Companies Act also, depreciation has to be charged on cost basis—any excess over the amount thus calculated is to be treated as accumulated profit and is to be shown as such.

(*v*) Industrialists like to charge depreciation on replacement price when prices are rising. It is very doubtful whether they would agree to these of the method when prices are falling. Their attitude towards this question is mostly governed by the possibility of saving income-tax. When prices are rising, depreciation on replacement basis would be higher and that would reduce the amount of tax payable.

Taking the above-mentioned points into consideration, it is clear that depreciation should be charged on historical cost. If it is desired that funds should be available for replacement of the asset (at the higher price), one of the following courses may be adopted:

(*i*) An estimated amount required for replacement over and above the amount provided by depreciation should be transferred to "Replacement Reserve", as an appropriation of profit.

(*ii*) The accumulated balance in the provision for depreciation should be credited each year with interest at the current rate of interest. The provision will then automatically amount to much more than the original cost and may be quite sufficient to provide for replacement.

It should be noted that if any excess of amount is provided as depreciation over the amount properly chargeable on historical cost basis, it should be shown as reserve (accumulated profit in the balance sheet. This applies particularly to companies.

A few cases have come to notice in India in which companies have revalued their assets upward, crediting Capital Reserve by the profits thus arising but in reality charging depreciation only on the basis of historical costs. First, depreciation is calculated on the basis of the revalued figure but the amount pertaining to the revaluation profit is debited to Capital Reserve and not to the Profit and Loss Account. The Institute of Chartered Accountants of India has stated clearly in AS-6 (Revised) that if assets are revalued, depreciation should be on the basis of the revalued figures.

PROVISION AND RESERVE

Provision means the setting aside of certain amount to meet some contingencies which may be expected but not yet incurred. The Companies Act 1956 states that "Provision usually means any amount written off or retained by way of providing depreciation renewal or diminution in the value of assets or retained by way of providing for any known liability of which the amount cannot be determined with substantial accuracy". The provision is a charge to the Profit and Loss Account and is created to meet any depreciation in the value of an asset or to provide for any known liability, the amount of which cannot be ascertained. If the amount of a known liability can be ascertained, it must be treated as liability and not as a provision. Thus a provision may be created either (*i*) for a known reduction in the value of an asset or (*ii*) for a known liability, the amount of which cannot be ascertained accurately. Provision is a charge on profits. That is provisions are usually created by debiting the Profit and Loss Account.

Reserve or Reserve Fund consists of sums set aside out of divisible profits for the purpose of strengthening the financial position of the business. It is an appropriation of profits and is not a charge to Profit and Loss Account. Reserve is the amount set aside out of undivided profits and other surpluses in order to strengthen the financial position of the business, but not designed to meet any liability or contingency known to exist at the date of the Balance Sheet. In other words, it is used to mean profits retained in the business, it consists of undistributable profits or surplus assets. It increases the working capital of the business. A provision in excess of the amount actually needed for the purpose for which it is created is to be considered as a reserve.

Undistributed profits which are used within the business without being invested outside, are called "reserves". On the other hand, undistributed profits which are represented by earmarked investments outside the business, are called "reserve fund". For example, General Reserves, Dividend Equalisation Reserve, Capital Redemption Reserves are examples of reserves. While Sinking Fund for replacement of an asset or for redemption of a liability is example of reserve fund.

Reserve created for a particular purpose is called a *Specific Reserve*, for example, Debenture Redemption Reserve Fund (which is meant for redemption of debentures), Dividend Equalisation Reserve (which is created for maintaining a steady rate of dividend) etc. Reserve created not for any particular purpose but for increasing working capital and strengthening financial position of the business is called *General Reserve.*

A Reserve which is not available for distribution as dividend through the Profit and Loss Account is a *Capital Reserve.* Examples for Capital Reserves are the profits on revaluation of fixed assets, Profit on re-issue of forfeited shares, Profits earned prior to incorporation. It may be carefully noted that capital reserve is different from reserve capital. Reserve capital means uncalled share capital retained. A Reserve which is free for distribution of dividend through the Profit and Loss Account or otherwise is a Revenue Reserve. Examples of Revenue Reserve are General Reserve, Dividend Equalisation Reserve etc.

"Reserve is the amount set aside out of undivided profits and other surpluses in order to strengthen the financial position of the business, but not designed to meet any liability or contingency known to exist at the date of Balance Sheet". – Williams

"Reserve is used to mean profits retained in the business, it consists of undistributable profits or surplus assets. Reserves may be classified as Capital Reserve or Revenue Reserve. The difference between the two is that Capital Reserve is accumulated in a certain way and is not available for distribution through the Profit and Loss Account, whereas a revenue reserve consists mainly of undistributed profits." – Mckechnie

DISTINCTION BETWEEN RESERVE AND PROVISION

Reserve	*Provision*
1. Reserve is an appropriation of profits.	1. A provision is a charge against profits.
2. Reserves are created to strengthen the financial resources of a concern.	2. Provision is created to meet some known liability, the amount of which is not certain.
3. It is shown always on the liability side of the Balance Sheet.	3. It can be shown on the liability side of the Balance Sheet or shown as a deduction from the asset concerned on the asset side.
4. It can be invested outside the business.	4. It cannot be invested elsewhere.
5. It is not created when there is no profit.	5. It is credited even if there is no profit.
6. Creation of reserve depends on the decisions of the Directors.	6. Creation of provision is a must for redemption of liability and this does not depend upon the decision of Directors.
7. It helps the inner worth or intrinsic value of the business to increase.	7. It helps to meet and adjust future losses or expenses.
8. In case of need, it may be distributed to shareholders as dividend.	8. Provision cannot be distributed to shareholders as dividend.

Secret Reserve

A Secret Reserve can be explained as a surplus the existence of which is not disclosed in the Balance Sheet. Under such a situation, the financial position of the concern is definitely better than what appears from the Balance Sheet. Such reserves are usually maintained by Banks, Insurance Companies, Financial Houses etc. The creation of such secret reserves are in the following manner:

1. By providing excessive depreciation
2. By undervaluing assets

3. By charging capital expenditure to revenue account
4. By overvaluing liabilities
5. By making excessive provisions for losses

Advantages of Secret Reserves

In brief, it can be mentioned as follows:

1. It increases the working capital of the Company and thus strengthens its financial position without disclosing such strength to public.
2. Even in bad times, dividend rate can be equalised.
3. Exceptional losses can be met out of secret reserves.
4. Working capital is always available.
5. It conceals the large profits made by the Company in that particular line of business and thus keeps off competition.

The Indian Companies Act has prohibited the creation of Secret Reserve.

DISADVANTAGES OF SECRET RESERVE

1. Profit and Loss Account does not show true and fair position.
2. The main object of Balance Sheet, i.e., showing true and fair financial position, is defeated.
3. Market value of the shares of such companies is reduced.
4. Directors may mis-use the secret reserves.
5. Secret reserves may be harmful to the interests of employees, customers etc.

Accounting Standard-6

AS 6 (Revised) is reproduced below. It should be read carefully. The requirements of disclosure should be noted for a proper presentation of accounts.

AS 6 (REVISED) : DEPRECIATION ACCOUNTING

Accounting Standard (AS) - 6, Depreciation Accounting was issued by Institute of Chartered Accountants of India in November 1982. Subsequently in the context of insertion of Schedule XIV (prescribing rates of depreciation) in the Companies Act in 1988, the Institute brought out a Guidance Note on Accounting for Depreciation in companies. The Guidence Note differed from AS-6 on a few points. But in May 1994 the Council of the Institute, on the recommendation of the Accounting Standards Board, decided to bring AS-6 in line with the Guidance Note. Accordingly, paragraphs 11, 15, 22 and 24 were modified and paragraph 19 was deleted. Also, in view of delinking of rates of depreciation under the Companies Act from those under the Income-tax Act/rules by the Companies (Amendment) Act, 1988, paragraph 13 was also modified.

AS 6 is mendatory in respect of accounts for periods commencing on or after 1.4.1995.

From the date of Accounting Standard (AS) 26, 'Intangible Assets' becoming mandatory for the concerned enterprises, this standard stands withdrawn insofar as its relates to the amortisation (deprectiation) of intangible assets.

The complete text of the revised AS-6 is given below :—

Introduction

1. This Statement deals with depreciation accounting and applies to all depreciable assets, except the following items to which special considerations apply:

   (*i*) forests, plantations and similar regenerative netural resources;

   (*ii*) wasting assets including expenditure on the exploration for the extraction of minerals, oils, natural gas and similar non-regenerative resourcs;

   (*iii*) expenditure on research and development;

(*iv*) goodwill, and

(*v*) livestock.

This statement also does not apply to land unless it has a limited useful life for the enterprise.

2. Different accounting policies for depreciation are adopted by different enterprises. Disclosure of accounting policies for depreciation followed by an enterprise is necessary to appreciate the view presented in the financial statements of the enterprise.

Definitions

3. The following terms are used in the statement with the meanings specified:

3.1. *Depreciation* is a measure of the wearing out, consumption or other loss of a value of a depreciable asset arising from use, effluxion of time or obsolescence through technology and market changes. Depreciation is allocated so as to charge a fair proportion of the depreciable amount in each accounting period during the expected useful life of the asset. Depreciation includes amortisation of assets whose useful life is predetermined.

3.2. *Depreciable assets* are assets which

(*i*) are expected to be used during more than one accounting period; and

(*ii*) have a limited useful life; and

(*iii*) are held by an enterprise for use in the production or supply of goods and services, for rental to others, or for administrative purposes and not for the purpose of sale in the ordinary course of business.

3.3. *Useful life* is either (*i*) the period over which a depreciable asset is expected to be used by the enterprise; or (*ii*) the number of production or similar units expected to be obtained from the use of the asset by the enterprise.

3.4 *Depreciable amount* of a depreciable asset is its historical cost, or other amount substituted for historical cost[1] in financial statements, less the estimated residual value.

Explanation

4. Depreciation has a significant effect in determining and presenting the financial position and results of operations of an enterprise. Depreciation is charged in each accounting period by reference to the extent of the depreciable amount, irrespective of an increase in the market value of the assets.

5. **Assessment of depreciation and the amount to be charged in respect thereof in an accounting period are usually based on the following three factors :**

(*i*) historical cost or other amount substituted for the historical cost of the depreciable asset when the asset has been revalued;

(*ii*) expected useful life of the depreciable asset; and

(*iii*) estimated residual value of the depreciable asset.

6. Historical cost of a depreciable assets represents its money outlay or its equivalent in connection with its acquisition, installation and commissioning as well as for additions to or improvement thereof. The historical cost of a depreciable asset may undergo subsequent changes arising as a result of increase or decrease in long-term liability on account of exchange fluctuations, price adjustments, changes in duties or similar factors.

7. The useful life of a depreciable asset is shorter than its physical life and is .

(*i*) pre-determined by legal or contractual limits such as the expiry dates of related leases;

(*ii*) directly governed by extraction or consumption;

(*iii*) dependent on the extend of use and physical deterioration on account of wear and tear which again depends on operational factors, such as, the number of shifts for which

1. This statement does not deal with the treatment of the revaluation difference which may arise when historical costs are substituted by revaluations.

the asset is to be used, repair and maintenance policy of the enterprise etc.; and

(*iv*) reduced by obsolescence arising from such factors as:

(*a*) technological changes;

(*b*) improvement in production methods;

(*c*) change in market demand for the product or service output of the asset; or

(*d*) legal or other restrictions.

8. Determination of the useful life of a depreciable asset is a metter of estimation and is normally based on various factors including experience with similar types of assets. Such estimation is more difficult for as asset using new technology or used in the production of a new product or in the provision of a new service but in nevertheless required on some reasonable basis.

9. Any addition or extension to an existing asset which is of a capital nature and which becomes an integral part of the existing asset is depreciated over the remaining useful life of that asset. As a practical measure, however, depreciation is sometimes provided on such addition or extension at the rate which is applied to an existing asset. Any addition or extension which retains a separate identity and is capable of being used after the existing asset is disposed of, is depreciated independently on the basis of an estimate of its own useful life.

10. Determination of residual value of an asset is normally a difficult matter. If such value is considered as insignificant, it is normally regarded as nil. On the contrary, if the residual value is likely to be significant, it is estimated at the time of acquisition/installation, or at the time of subsequent revaluation of the asset. One of the bases for determining the residual value would be the realisable value of similar assets which have reached the end of their useful lives and have operated under conditions similar to those in which the asset will be used.

11. The quantum of depreciation to be provided in a accounting period involves the exercise of judgement by management in the light of technical, commercial, accounting and legal requirments and accordingly may need periodical review. If it is considered that the original estimate of useful life of an asset requires any revision, the unamortised depreciable amount of the asset is charged to revenue over the revised remaining useful life.

12. There are several methods of allocating depreciation over the useful life of the assets. Those most commonly employed in industrial and commercial enterprises are the straight line method and the reducing balance method. The management of a business selects the most appropriate method(s) based on various important factors *e.g.* (*i*) type of asset, (*ii*) the nature of the use of such asset, and (*iii*) circumstances prevailing in the business. A combination of more than one method is sometimes used. In respect of depreciable assets which do not have material value depreciation is often allocated fully in the accounting period in which they are acquired.

13. The statute governing an enterprise may provide the basis for computation of the depreciation. For example, the Companies Act, 1956 lays down the rates of depreciation in respect of various assets. Where the management's estimate of the useful life of an asset of the enterprise is shorter than that envisaged under the provisions of the relevent statute, the depreciation provision is appropriately computed by applying a higher rate. If the management's estimate of useful life of the asset is longer than that envisaged under the statute, depreciation rate lower than that envisaged by the statute can be applied only in accordance with the requirements of the statute.

14. Where depreciable assets are disposed of, discarded, demolished or destroyed, the net surplus or deficiency, if material, is disclosed separately.

15. The method of depreciation is applied consistently to provide comparability of the results of the operations of the enterprise from period to period. A change from one method of providing depre-

ciation to another is made only if the adoption of the new method is required by statute or for compliance with an accounting standard or if it is considered that the change would result in a more appropriate preparation or presentation of the financial statements of the enterprise. When such a change in the method of depreciation is made, depreciation is recalculated in accordance with the new method from the date of the asset coming into use. The deficiency or surplus arising from restrospective recomputation of depreciation in accordance with the new method is adjusted in the accounts in the year in which the method of depreciation is changed. In case the change in the method results in deficiency in depreciation in respect of past years, the deficiency is charged in the statement of profit and loss. In case the change in the method results in surplus, the surplus is credited to the statement of profit and loss. Such a change is treated as a change in accounting policy and its effect is quantified and disclosed.

16. Where the historical cost of an asset has undergone a change due to circumstances specified in para 6 above, the depreciation of the revised unamortised depreciable amount is provided prospectively over the residual useful life of the asset.

Disclosure

17. The depreciation methods used, the total depreciation for the period for each class of asset, the gross amount of each class of depreciable assets and the related accumulated depreciation are disclosed in the financial statements along with the disclosure of other accounting policies. The depreciation rates or the useful lives of the assets are disclosed only if they are different from the principal rates specified in the statute governing the enterprise.

18. In case the depreciable assets are revalued, the provision for depreciation is based on the revalued amount on the estimate of the remaining useful life of such assets. In case the revaluation has a material effect on the amount of depreciation, the same is disclosed separately in the year in which revaluation is carried out.

19. A change in the method of depreciation is treated as a change in an accounting policy and is disclosed accordingly.

Accounting Standard

(The Accounting Standard comprises paragraphs 20—29 of the Statement. The Standard should be read in the context of paragraphs 1—19 of this. Statement and of the Preface to the Statements of 'Accounting Standards).

20. The depreciable amount of a depreciable asset should be allocated on a systematic basis to each accounting period during the useful life of the asset.

21. The depreciation method selected should be applied consistently from period to perid. A change from one method of providing depreciation to another should be made only if the adoption of the new method is required by statute or for compliance with an accounting standard or if it is considered that the change would result in a more appropriate preparation or presentation of the financial statements of the enterprise. When a change in the method of depreciation is made, depreciation should be recalculated in accordance with the new method from the date of the asset coming into use. The deficiency or surplus arising from retrospective recomputation of depreciation in accordance with the new method should be adjusted in the accounts in the year in which the method of depreciation is changed. In case the change in the method results in deficiency in depreciation in respect of past years, the deficiency should be charged in the statement of profit and loss. In case the change in the method results in surplus, the surplus should be credited to the statement of profit and loss. Such a change should be treated as a change in accounting policy and its effect should be quantified and disclosed.

22. The useful life of a depreciable asset should be estimated after considering the following factors:

(*i*) expected physical wear and tear,

(*ii*) obsolescence; and

(*iii*) legal or other limits on the use of the asset.

23. The useful lives of major depreciable assets or classes of depreciable assets may be reviewed periodically. Where there is a revision of the estimated useful life of an asset the unamortised depreciable amount should be charged over the revised remaining useful life.

24. Any addition or extension which becomes an integral part of the existing asset should be depreciated over the remaining useful life of the asset. The depreciation on such addition' or extension may also be provided at the rate applied to the existing asset. Where an addition or extension retains a separate identity and is capable of being used after the existing asset is disposed of, depreciation should be provided independently on the basis of an estimate of its own useful life.

25. Where the historical cost of a depreciable asset has undergone a change due to increase or decrease in long-term liability on account of exchange fluctuations, price adjustments, changes in duties or similar factors, the depreciation on the revised unamortised depreciable amount should be provided prospectively over the residual useful life of the asset.

26. Where the depreciable assets are revalued, the provision for depreciation should be based on the revalued amount and on the estimate of the remaining useful lives of such assets. In case the revaluation has a material effect on the amount of depreciation, the same should be disclosed separately in the year in which revaluation is carried out.

27. If any depreciable asset is disposed of, discarded, demolished or destroyed, the *new surplus* **or deficiency, if material, should be disclosed separately.**

28. The following information should be disclosed in the financial statements:

(*i*) the historical cost or other amount substituted for historical cost of each class of depreciable assets;

(*ii*) total depreciation for the period for each class of assets; and

(*iii*) the related accumulated depreciation.

29. The following information should also be disclosed in the financial statements along with the disclosure of other accounting policies:

(*i*) depreciation methods used; and

(*ii*) depreciation rates or the useful lives of the assets, if they are different from the principal rates specified in the statute governing the enterprise.

QUESTIONS

Objective Type Questions

I. State whether each of the following statements in "True" or "False"

1. Land is the only fixed asset that is not depreciated.
2. A well maintained asset need not be depreciated.
3. Goodwill is never depreciated.
4. Depreciation is a measure of the exact loss in the intrinsic value of an asset.
5. Reducing Balance Method of depreciation is best suited for assets with a long working life.
6. If the value of land increases, such an appreciation of value should be recorded.
7. The loss of value from the time of purchase to the time of disposal of a fixed asset is called depreciation.
8. Depletion method is suitable for charging depreciation in case of live stocks or loose tools.
9. Under straight line method, the depreciation charge is constant every year.
10. The main objective of providing depreciation is to show true profit.

11. Depreciation is a process of valuation.
12. Depreciation is a loss and not an expense.
13. Machine Hour rate $= \frac{\text{Acquisition Cost} - \text{Residual Value}}{\text{Estimated life in hours.}}$
14. Depreciation is an amortised expenditure.
15. The expression – "Depreciation is to be charged at 10% and at 10% p.a. on machinery carry the same meaning.
16. Depreciation cannot be provided in case of loss in a financial year.
17. Fixed assets are stated in the Balance Sheet at their market value.
18. Providing depreciation in the accounts reduce the amount of profit available for dividend.
19. Providing depreciation ensure sufficient cash for asset replacement.
20. The term depreciation, deplation and amortization are synonymous.

(**Ans. True:** 1, 3, 5, 7, 9, 10, 13, 14, 18, 20; **False:** 2, 4, 6, 8, 11, 12, 15, 16, 17, 19)

II. Fill in the blanks.

1. The amount of depreciation charged on machinery will be debited to ________.
2. The mothod of depreciation suitable for mines is ________ .
3. Deprociation is charged only on the ________ assets of a business.
4. Depreciation account is closed at the end of the year by transfor to the ________.
5. The amount of ________ is deducted from the value of respective assets in the Balance Sheet.

(**Ans.** 1. Profit and Loss A/c; 2. Depletion Method; 3. Fixed; 4. Profit & Loss A/c; 5. Depreciation)

III. Choose the appropriate answer from the given alternatives;

1. Under diminishing balance method, depreciation is calculated on:
   (*a*) Original Cost. (*b*) Written Down Value.
   (*c*) The Scrap Value.
2. Deplotion method is most suitable of ;
   (*a*) Mines and quarries. (*b*) Buildings.
   (*c*) Machines.
3. Depreciation is apportioned on the basis of:
   (*a*) Value of machinery. (*b*) Horse power of machinery.
   (*c*) Running hourse of machines.
4. The profit on depreciation policy is transferred to:
   (*a*) Depreciation Fund Account (*b*) Asset Account
   (*c*) Profit & Loss Account.
5. Sinking Fund is also known as:
   (*a*) Depletion method. (*b*) Annuity method.
   (*c*) Depreciation Fund method.
6. The amount of depreciation charged on a machinory will be debited to:
   (*a*) Depreciation Account. (*b*) Mechinery Account.
   (*c*) Provision for Depreciation Account.
7. Under ennuity mothod, the amount of depreciation is:
   (*a*) Reducing every year. (*b*) Increasing every year.
   (*c*) Constant for all the years.
8. The term 'depreciation' refers to a fall in:
   (*a*) Cost Price. (*b*) Market Price.

(*c*) Book value. (*d*) Intrinsic value.

9. Where an asset is sold, discarded or destroyed during the accounting period, depreciation should be calculated:
   (*a*) For the whole year.
   (*b*) For the portion of the period during which the asset is used.
   (*c*) For only six months.
10. For providing depreciation on leasohold property, the appropriate method of depreciation is the:
   (*a*) Replacement Method. (*b*) Revaluation Method.
   (*c*) Fixed Instalment Method.

(**Ans.** 1. (*b*); 2. (*a*); 3. (*c*); 4. (*a*); 5. (*c*); 6. (*a*); 7. (*c*); 8. (*c*); 9. (*b*); 10. (*c*);)

THEORETICAL QUESTIONS

1. What are the causes of depreciation? (*B. Com. MK.*)
2. Why is depreciation charged? (*B. Com. Calicut*)
3. What is deplation? (*B. Com. MS.*)
4. What is the procedure for changing the method of depreciation with retrospective effect? (*B. Com. Kerala.*)
5. What are the factors affecting the amount of Depreciation?
6. What is reserve fund? How does it differ from Reserve?
7. What is secret reserve? How is it created ? What are its merits and demerits? (*B. Com. Madras*)
8. What is 'Provision for Repairs and Renewals'? (*B. Com. MS.*)
9. What are the effects of not providing for Depreciation on assets? (*B. Com. MK.*)
10. Is depreciation a charge against profit or an appropriation of profit? Discuss. (*B. Com. Poona*)
11. Is there any difference between Provision and Reserve?
12. Is it desirable to charge depreciation on replacement cost basis? (*B. Com. Kerala*)
13. Elucidate the objectives of depreciation policy? (*B. Com. Mysore*)
14. What do you mean by Depreciation?
15. What are the contributing factors for Depreciation in the value of fixed assets?
16. Bring out the necessity of providing adequate depreciation for assets.
17. Explain, in brief, the various methods adopted for assessing Depreciation.
18. Differentiate between Fixed Instalment method and Reducing Balance method of Depreciation.
19. For which type of assets can the Revaluation method be suitable?
20. Explain the following:
   (*a*) Machine Hour Rate
   (*b*) Depletion Method
   (*c*) Annuity Method
21. What do you mean by Reserve? How is it created in business?

PRACTICAL PROBLEMS

1. Tempo Dairy Industries Ltd. purchased a Plant worth Rs 1,00,000 on Ist January 2001. They decided to write off at 10% by Straight Line Method. After 2 years they decided to change the method of depreciation to that of diminishing balance method by charging 15% p.a. from 2001. The difference due to this change in the method is to be adjusted by transferring to Profit and Loss Account for the third year. Show the Plant Account for 4 years. (*B.Com., Madras*)

   [**Ans:** Balance Rs 52,200 (1-1-2005)]
2. On Ist January, 2001, machinery was purchased for Rs 25,000. On Ist June, 2002 additions were made

to the amount of Rs 5,000. On Ist March, 2003 additions were made to the amount of Rs 3,200. On 30th June, 2004, machinery of which the original value on Ist January, 2001 was Rs 4,000 was sold for Rs 3,000. Depreciation is charged at 10% on original cost. Show the Machinery A/c for the four years from 2001 to 2004. (*B.Com., Calcutta*)

[Ans: Balance Rs 18,921 (1.1.2005)]

3. A manufacturing concern, whose books are closed on 31st December every year, purchased machinery for Rs 50,000 on 1.1.2000. Additional machinery was acquired for Rs 10,000 on 1.7.2001 and for Rs 16,061 on 1.1.2004. Certain machinery purchased for Rs 10,000 on 1.1.2000 was sold for Rs 5,000 on 30.6.2003.

   Give the Machinery Account for 5 years writing off depreciation at 10% p.a. on written down value.

   (*B.Com., Vikram, Madurai, Madras*)

   [Ans: Balance Rs 45,295)

4. A company whose accounting year is the calendar year, purchased on 1.1.2010 a machine for Rs. 40,000. It purchased further machinery on 1st Oct. 2010 for Rs. 20,000 and on 1st July 2011 for Rs. 10,000. On 1.7.2012 1/4th of the machinery installed on 1.1.2010 become obsolete and was sold for Rs. 6,800.

   Show how the machinery account in the books of the company for all the three years under diminishing balance method. Depreciation is to be provided at 10% p.a.

   (*B.Com MS. Agra. Mysore, Bharathiar*)

   Ans: Balance of Machinery A/c on 2013 Jan. 1 Rs. 46,215)

5. Messrs Mill and Wright commenced business on Ist January, 2000 when they purchased plant and equipment of Rs 7,00,000. They adopted a policy of (i) Charging depreciation at 15% per annum on diminishing balance basis and (ii) Charging full years' depreciation on additions:

Date	Amount Rs
1.8.2001	1,50,000
30.9.2004	2,00,000

   On 1.1.2004 it was decided to change the method and rate of depreciation to 10% on straight line basis with retrospective effect from 1.1.2000, the adjustment being made in the accounts for the year ending 31st December, 2004.

   Calculate the difference in depreciation to be adjusted in the Plant and Equipment A/c on 1.1.2004, and show the ledger amount for the year 2004. (*C.A. Entrance*)

   [Ans: Excess depreciation credited to P & L Account Rs 67,478

   Depreciation for 2004 Rs 1,05,000

   Plant and Equipment Account Rs 6,20,000 (1.1.2005)]

6. On Ist October 2002 Timestar Ltd. purchased a Machine costing Rs 60,000 and spent Rs 10,000 for erection and overhauling. On Ist April 2003, a part of the machine was purchased for Rs 30,000.

   On Ist July 2003, machinery purchased on Ist October 2002 was sold for Rs 56,000 as it was absolute.

On Ist January 2004, a new machine was purchased for Rs 15,000.

Depreciation was provided annually on 31st December at the rate of 10% p.a. on the original cost of the assets.

Show the Machinery Account for 3 years in the books of the company. *(B.Com., Madurai)*

[Ans: Balance Rs 38,250 (1.1.2005)]

7. On Ist January, 2002, a Limited Company purchased machinery for Rs 12,000 and on 30th June 2003 it acquired additional machinery at a cost of Rs 2,000. On 31st March 2004 one of the original machines which had cost of Rs 500 was found to have become obsolete and was sold as scrap for Rs 50. It was replaced on that date by a new machine costing Rs 800.

   Depreciate the machinery at the rate of 15% p.a. on the written down value. Show the ledger accounts for the first 3 years. *(B.Com., Bombay)*

   [Ans: Balance Rs 9,345 (1.1.2005)]

8. X Ltd. which depreciates its machinery at 10% on Diminishing Balance Method had on Ist January 2004, Rs 4,86,000 to the debit of Machinery Account.

   During 2004 part of the Machinery purchased on Ist Jan. 2002 for Rs 60,000 was sold for Rs 40,000 on Ist July 2004 and a new machinery at a cost of Rs 70,000 was purchased and installed at the same date, installation charges being Rs 5,000.

   The Company wanted to change its method of depreciation from Diminishing Balance Method to Straight Line Method with effect from Ist January 2002 and adjust the difference before 31st December 2004. The rate depreciation remains the same as before.

   Show the Machinery Account for 2004. *(B.Com., Madras)*

   [Ans: Balance Rs 4,49,250 (1.1.2005)]

9. A Plant was purchased for Rs 20,000 on 1.1.2001. On 1.1.2002, another plant was purchased for Rs 40,000. On 1.7.2003, one more plant was purchased for Rs 20,000, including the cost of installation of Rs 1,000 by disposing of the Plant which was purchased on 1.1.2001, for Rs 7,000. On 1.4.2004, another plant was purchased for Rs 50,000 by disposing of the Plant which was purchased on 1.1.2002 for Rs 35,000.

   Show the Plant Account upto 31.12.2004 assuming that the rate of Depreciation was @ 10% on Diminishing Balance Method. *(B.Com., Bombay, Punjab, Kerala)*

   [Ans: Balance Rs 63,350 (1.1.2005)]

10. A manufacturing company purchased on Ist January 2001, a second hand plant for Rs 30,000 and immediately spent Rs 20,000 on overhauling it. On Ist July 2001, additional machinery costing Rs 25,000 was purchased. On Ist July 2003, the plant purchased on Ist January 2001 became obsolete and was sold for Rs 10,000. On that date a new machine was purchased at a cost of Rs 60,000.

    Depreciation was provided for annually on 31st December, at the rate of 10% p.a. on the original cost of asset. On 2004, however, the company changed this method of providing depreciation and adopted the method of writing off 15% on Diminishing value.

    Show the Machinery Account as it would appear in the books of the Company for the years 2001 to 2004. *(B.Com. Hons., Delhi)*

    [Ans: Rs 64,388 (1.1.2005)]

11. On Ist January 2002 Hari Om purchased 6 machines for Rs 15,000 each. His accounting year ends on 31st December. Depreciation at the rate of 10% on initial cost has been charged to profit and loss account and credited to a separate depreciation provision account.

    On Ist January 2003 one machine was sold for Rs 12,500 and on Ist January 2004 a second machine was sold for Rs 12,500. An improved model which cost Rs 28,000 was purchased on Ist July, 2003. The same rate of depreciation was decided for the new machine as well. You are required to show:

    (1) The asset account.

    (2) The asset disposal account.

    (3) The depreciation provision Account. *(Institute of Bankers, London)*

    [Ans: Machinery Account Balance Rs 88,000 (1.1.2005)

    Depreciation Provision Account Balance Rs 22,200 (1.1.2005)

    Machinery Disposal Account (2003) Loss Rs 1,000

Machinery Disposal Account (2004) Gain Rs 500)

12. X Y Ltd.'s financial year closing is 31st December each year. It purchased the following machinery:

		Rs
On 1-4-2002	Machines costing	30,000
On 1-10-2002	Machines costing	20,000
On 1-7-2003	Machines costing	10,000

On 1.1.2004, one-third of the machinery which was installed on 1.4.2002 became obsolete and was sold for Rs 3,000. The machinery to be depreciated by Fixed Instalment Method at 10 per cent per annum. Show how the Machinery Account would appear in the Company's Ledger for the years 2002, 2003 and 2004. *(I.C.W.A.)*

[Ans: Machinery Account Balance Rs 38,500 (1.1.2005)]

13. A Company writes off 10% of the original cost of Plant and Machinery in every year till the whole cost of a particular piece of Machinery is wiped off. Full depreciation is written off even if the Machinery is in use for part of a year. Accounts are made upto 31st December annually.

On Ist January 2003 the balance in the Plant and Machinery Account was Rs 1,95,150. The original cost of the various items in use was as follows:

	Rs
Items bought in 1992 or earlier	58,000
Items bought in 1993	31,000
Items bought in 1994	17,000
Items bought in 1995 or later	2,52,000
	3,58,000

During 2003 new Plant was bought at a cost of Rs 29,500 and one machine which had cost Rs 5,500 in 1988 was sold for Rs 350. During 2004 there were additions costing Rs 18,000 and a machine which had cost Rs 7,000 in 1996 was sold for Rs 1,500.

Write up the Plant and Machinery Account for 2003 and 2004. *(B.Com. Hons., Calcutta)*

[Ans: Plant and Machinery Account Balance Rs 1,82,150 (1.1.2005)

Depreciation for 2003 Rs 29,850

Depreciation for 2004 Rs 29,950]

14. Mr Amarnath has acquired mines on payment of Rs 1,00,000 on Ist April 1999. The lease period is five years. He proposes to provide for its replacement by means of an Insurance Policy for Rs 1,00,000. The annual premium is Rs 9,750. On Ist April 2004, the lease is renewed for a further period of 5 years for the same amount.

Show the necessary ledger accounts. *(CA Inter)*

[Ans: Annual Contribution Rs 9,750]

15. On January 1, 2000, R acquired for Rs 3,00,000 the lease of some factory premises of which five years were unexpired. To amortise the lease over the five years and to provide for renewal, it was decided to set up a sinking fund by taking annual instalments out of profits and investing cash of the same amount at five per cent compound interest.

Taking Re 0.180975 as the annual instalment required to produce Re 1 in five years at 5 per cent, write up the Sinking Fund Account for the entire period of five years. *(B.Com. Hons., Calcutta)*

[Ans: Annual Contribution Rs 54,292.50]

16. A combined provision for depreciation and repairs and renewals was made every year at 15% of the original cost of a machine purchased at Rs 50,000. The 'Provision for Depreciation and Maintenance

Account' that was opened for the purpose was, therefore, debited with the actual costs of repairs and renewals which were as stated below:

Cost of Repairs and Renewals

Year	Rs
Year 1	1,500
Year 2	1,600
Year 3	2,100
Year 4	3,000
Year 5	4,200

At the end of the fifth year the machine was sold out at Rs 20,000 after utilising a few of its minor parts valued at Rs 4,000, in installing in its place a new machine purchased at Rs 75,000. The resulting loss in the disposal of the old machine was debited to revenue.

Write up 'Provision for Depreciation and Maintenance Account' for the five years and the 'Old and the New machine Account' at the end. *(B.Com., Calcutta)*

[Ans: Old Machinery (Loss on sale) Rs 900
New Machinery Opening balance Rs 79,000 (6th Year)]

17. Bright Ltd. issued Rs 6,00,000 debentures during 1987 on the following terms and conditions:
    (1) A Sinking Fund to be created by yearly appropriation of profit and similar amount to be invested outside.
    (2) The Company will have the right to purchase for cancellation debentures from the market if available below par value.
    (3) The debentures are to be redeemed on 31st December 2004 at a premium of 2%.
    The following balances appeared in the books of the Company as on Ist January 2004:

		Rs
(*a*)	Sinking Fund Investment	4,43,250
(*b*)	Sinking Fund	4,43,250
(*c*)	Debentures Account	4,50,000

The following transactions took place during the subsequent twelve months:

(*a*) On Ist July 2004 Rs 30,000 Debentures were purchased for Rs 26,664 and cancelled immediately, the amount being provided out of proceeds of investments of the book value of Rs 34,800 made at Rs 33,900.

(*b*) The income from Sinking Fund Investment, Rs 22,200 received on Ist July 2004 was not invested.

(*c*) On 29th December 2004, Rs 4,23,000 was received on sale of the remaining Sinking Fund Investments.

(*d*) On 31st December 2004, the remaining debentures were redeemed.

You are required to show for the year ended 31st December 2004:

(*i*) Debentures A/c. (*ii*) Sinking Find A/c. (*iii*) Sinking Fund Investment A/c. (*iv*) Debentures Redemption A/c. *(C.A. Inter)*

[Ans: Loss on sale (1.7.2004) Rs 900
Profit on sale (31.12.2004 Rs 14,550]

18. A company has acquired a lease of a cinema building for a term of 5 years by payment of Rs 4,00,000. It is proposed to depreciate the lease by the Annuity Method, charging 5% p.a. Show the ledger account of asset during the period of the lease.

    Reference to the Annuity Table shows that the amount for Re 1 for 5 years at 5% is Re 0.230975. Calculations are to be made to the nearest rupee. *(B.Com., Madurai, Bombay)*

[Ans: Annual Amount Rs 92,390]

19. A firm purchased a lease for Rs 10,000 to be depreciated over a period of four years under Annuity

System. The rate of interest is 5% p.a. The Annuity Table shows that the annual amount required to write off rupee one in four years at 5% p.a. is Re 0.282012.

Prepare the Lease Account for four years. (*B.Com., Mangalore*)

[Ans: Annual Amount Rs 2,820]

20. On Ist July 2,000, Wise Ltd. purchased a machine for Rs 1,10,000 and spent Rs 6,000 on its installation. The expected life of the machine is 4 years at the end of which the estimated scrap value will be Rs 16,000. Desiring to replace the machine on the expiry of its life, the company establishes a Sinking Fund. Investments are expected to realise 5% interest.

    On 30th June 2004, the machine sold off as scrap for Rs 18,000 and the investments were realised at 5% less than the book value. On Ist July 2004, a new machine is installed at a cost of Rs 1,25,000.

    Sinking Fund table shows that Re 0.2320 invested each year will produce Re 1 at the end of 4 years at 5%.

    Show the necessary ledger accounts in the books of Wise Ltd. for all the years. (*ICWA*)

    [Ans: Annual Amount Rs 23,200]

21. The Indian Minerals Ltd., leased on June 30, 2001, a manganese ore mine for a sum of Rs 5,00,000. It is estimated that the total quantity of ore in the mine is 1,00,000 tonnes. The annual output is as follows:

Year	Tonnes
2001	5,000
2002	20,000
2003	16,000
2004	21,000

Using the depletion method of depreciation, show the Mine Account for the above four years.

(*B.Com., Madras*)

[Ans: Mine Account Balance Rs 1,90,000 (1.1.2005)]

Chapter 12

Single Entry

(Accounts from Incomplete Records)

Salient Features – Limitations of Single Entry – Differences between Double Entry and Single Entry – Ascertainment of Profit – Net Worth Method – Step to prepare Statement of Affairs – Differences between Balance Sheet and Statement of Affairs – Conversion Method – Questions – Objective Type Questions – Theoretical Questions – Practical Problems.

"Every debit must have a credit" is the fundamental principle of the Double Entry System which records the two-fold effect of every business transaction. Double Entry System is based and designed for the perfect maintenance of accounts of all kinds of business organisations through specific rules and procedures. In contrast to this, Single Entry is that practice which falls short of Double Entry. In Single Entry System, businessman do not follow any uniform system or scientific principles and the records maintained are mostly incomplete. It is more appropriate to call it an incomplete system of recording transactions. The double effect of every transaction is ignored. In certain transactions, double entry may be complete; for instance, when cash is received from Debtors, it is recorded in the Cash Book and in the Debtors Account. In certain cases, only one aspect of the double entry is recorded; for instance when assets are purchased, entry is made in the Cash Book but no account is opened for the assets. In certain cases, no entry is made at all; for instance, stock destroyed by fire depreciation, accrued income etc.

Again small shopkeepers or hawkers keep their books under Pure Single Entry System, where only personal accounts are maintained; under Simple Single Entry System, personal accounts and Cash Books are maintained and under Quasi Single Entry System, personal accounts, Cash Books and a few subsidiary books are maintained. This form of book keeping is followed by Sole Proprietors of small business concerns, where the volume of business may not be big ones. The maintenance of accounts is done by the proprietor himself and no qualified accountant is appointed. Small traders extensively use this system of accounting because of simplicity and flexibility. They maintain Cash Book and personal accounts of Debtors and Creditors. No real accounts or nominal accounts are kept. No accounts of expenses or gains are found in the books. Thus, it is a system of book-keeping in which, as a rule, only records of cash and of personal accounts are maintained; it is always incomplete double entry varying with the circumstances.

SALIENT FEATURES

1. The system is adopted by sole traders, who keep only personal accounts and ignore all other accounts.
2. It has a Cash Book which contains both business transactions as well as personal transactions, mixing of both transactions.
3. In a business concern, there may be purchases and sales. To know the total purchases and sales, one has to depend on original vouchers.

4. This system does not follow uniformity and differ from firm to firm because of individual requirements and convenience.
5. This system gives only partial information.
6. It needs less number of books and is suitable only to petty traders.

Limitations of Single Entry*

1. Full information about the business cannot be obtained because incomplete records are maintained.
2. The arithmetical accuracy of the accounts (i.e., Trial Balance) cannot be tested in the absence of Double Entry.
3. In the absence of arithmetical test, the risk of fraud and errors and their non-discovery is increased.
4. It is not possible to prepare a Profit and Loss Account as nominal accounts are not maintained and so the source of profit or loss cannot be ascertained.
5. To know the profit or loss, Statements of Affairs at the beginning and at the end are prepared. But the reasons for the profit or loss are not known.
6. Balance Sheet cannot be drawn up because real account is not maintained. Therefore, true financial position cannot be known.
7. Comparison of business from year to year is not possible because statistical data are absent.
8. Errors are quite common. Errors happened cannot be traced out easily.
9. At the time of disposal of business, problems arise in proper valuation of intangible assets e.g., Goodwill.
10. Counter check is not at all possible, as in Double Entry System.

DIFFERENCE BETWEEN DOUBLE ENTRY AND SIGNLE ENTRY

Double Entry System	*Single Entry System*
1. The two-fold aspects, on all transactions, are recorded.	1. No such system is followed.
2. All accounts - Personal, Real and Nominal, are prepared.	2. Only Personal and Cash accounts are kept.
3. Trial Balance can be prepared to check the arithmetical accuracy.	3. Trial Balance cannot be prepared. Thus, there is no scope to check the arithmetical accuracy.
4. Final Accounts can be prepared.	4. No Trading and Profit and Loss A/C and Balance Sheet can be prepared.
5. This system is accepted by all	5. It is not accepted by all.
6. The system follows scientific basis.	6. There is no scientific basis.
7. Reliable financial position can be known.	7. Rough financial position is available.
8. This system is suitable for all types of business of any size-big or small.	8. This system is suitable and followed by only in small businesses.
9. Planning and decision-making are possible.	9. Nothing is possible.
10. Internal check up is possible.	10. No such check up is possible.

ASCERTAINMENT OF PROFIT

In Single Entry System, the nominal accounts are not maintained and hence trading results cannot be known by preparing Trading and Profit and Loss Account, as in Double Entry System. More-

* Single Entry System may be defined as "any method of book-keeping which does not follow the scientific principles of the Double Entry System".

over, every person keeps the accounts in his own way. Every businessman wishes to know the amount of profit or loss during any year. There are two methods by which the profit or loss can be ascertained and they are :

1. **Net Worth Method** (Statement of Affairs Method) (or Net Asset Method)
2. **Conversion Method.**

1. Net Worth Method

Under this system, *i.e.*, Net Worth Method, a trader has to prepare two Statements of Affairs, one at the beginning and the other at the end. From these Statements, the amount of Capital at the beginning as well as at the end is ascertained. Then the comparisons of the Capitals reveals the profit or loss made during the period. This system is also known as Capital Comparison Method.

The following is the procedure to be adopted and through which the profit or loss can be ascertained from the books, which are written under Single Entry System.

Step 1. A Statement of Arrairs at the beginning of the period is prepared to find out the amount of capital invested in the beginning. This is done when the capital is not given; because the purpose of preparing the Statement of Affairs is to know the Capital or Net Worth.

Step 2. In the same manner, a Statement of Affairs at the closing period is prepared to ascertain the Capital or Net Worth at the end.

Step 3. The Capital derived at the step 2 may be adjusted by adding back the drawings, if any, by the proprietor. That is, the amount of drawings are to be added to the closing Capital. Because, the Capital would have been more to that extent of amount drawn by the proprietor. For instance a proprietor has withdrawn Rs 5,000 from the business and this means the closing Capital would have been less by Rs 5,000. Had he not withdrawn Rs 5,000, then the Capital at the end would have been more by Rs 5,000.

Step 4. In addition to the initial Capital, it is possible that a trader might have invested fresh amount of Capital in the business during the course of the year. The closing Capital would have been less, in the absene of additional Capital. That is, additional Capital will increase the Capital of the proprietor at the end of the accounting period. Therefore, it is necessary to reduce the amount of fresh Capital from the amount of Capital at the end. This is because the closing Capital would have been less, in the absence of additional Capital during the accounting period.

Step 5. The beginning Capital as ascertain (in Step 1) should be deducted from the adjusted Capital. Adjusted Capital means Closing Capital (as in Step 2) is added to the amount of Drawals (as in Step 3) then from this, the amount of Additional Capital (as in Step 4) is deducted. In other words, Adjusted Capital = Closing Capital (as in Step 2) + Drawings (as in Step 3) – Additional Capital (as in Step 4).

The Comparison of the Capital (adjusted Capital) at the end and the Capital at the beginning shows some difference, which is either gain or loss. If the adjusted Capital at the close is more than the Capital in the beginning, the trader has made a profit to the extent of excess. If, on the other hand, the adjusted Capital is less than the initial Capital, there is a loss. Then the Profit or Loss so arrived may further be adjusted for Depreciation, Interest on Capitals, Interest on Drawings, Provision for Doubtful Debts etc.; the resultant figure is net Profit or Net Loss.

Steps to prepare Statement of Affairs

When the books maintained by the Single Entry System, it is not possible to draw a Balance Sheet. Therefore, to know the financial position of the business, a Statement of Affairs, showing various liabilities and assets of the business, on a particular date is prepared, from available information. The Statement of Affairs is without any adjustment – depreciation on assets, outstanding or pre-paid incomes and expenses etc. A Statement of Affairs is just like a Balance Sheet. When preparing a Statement of Affairs, the following points may be given attention, (in brief);

1. Find out the correct Cash and Bank balances.
2. Record correct stock through physical stock taking.
3. Value of assets should be ascertained from vouchers and other sources. Depreciation on assets should be provided.
4. Summarise the amount payable and receivable–Sundry Debtors and Sundry Creditors.
5. Verify all the accounts of expenses and incomes outstanding and paid in advance.

All these items to be entered in the statements. The difference between the liability side and the asset side is the amount of capital.

STATEMENT OF PROFIT

Statement of Profit or loss for the year ....

Capital at the end	....
Add: Drawings	....
	....
Less: Additional Capital introduced	....
	....
Less: Capital at the beginning	....
Profit or Loss subject to adjustment	....

Alternatively:

$$\text{Net Income} = \left[\text{Closing Capital} + \text{Drawings} - \text{Further Capital introduced}\right] - \text{Opening Capital}$$

Difference between Balance Sheet and Statement of Affairs

Balance Sheet	*Statement of Affairs*
1. It is prepared on the basis of those books which are maintained in Double Entry.	1. It is prepared on the basis of those books which are maintained partly on the basis of Double Entry and partly on the basis of Single Entry.
2. It is possible to prepare a Trial Balance, on the basis of books. Thus the arithmetical accuracy can be verified.	2. It is not possible to prepare a Trial Balance, on the basis of books. Therefore, arithmetical accuracy cannot be verified.
3. Capital is taken from the Capital Account maintained in the ledger.	3. Capital Account is not maintained. Excess of assets over liabilities is treated as Capital.
4. The purpose of Balance Sheet is to find out the financial position of the firm.	4. The purpose of Statement of Affairs is to find out Capital.
5. The value of assets and liabilities in a Balance Sheet are based on ledger balances, which are backed by transactions maintained under Double Entry.	5. Value of Assets and liabilities in a Statement of Affairs are prepared on the basis of estimates, except the figures of Debtors, Creditors, Cash and Bank.
6. Omission of assets or liabilities can easily be found out when Balance Sheet disagrees.	6. It is difficult to trace out omission of assets or liabilities in a Statement of Affairs.

ILLUSTRATION 12.1

From the following information, calculate the profit earned by a petty trader during the year 2004 :

	Rs
Capital as on 31.12.2004	66,000
Capital as on 1.1.2004	65,000
His Drawings during 2004	12,000
Further Capital introduced by him	7,000

SOLUTION

Statement of Profit for the year 2004

	Rs
Capital as on 31st December 2004	66,000
Add: Drawings during 2004	12,000
	78,000
Less: Further Capital introduced in 2004	7,000
Adjusted Capital	71,000
Less: Capital as on 1.1.2004	65,000
Profit made during the year (2004)	6,000

ILLUSTRATION 12.2

Mr Ram informs you that he had started a business on 1.1.2004 with a capital of Rs 20,500 and on 31.12.2004 his capital was Rs 32,800. Further, he informs you that he gave his son Rs 2,000 and he withdraws Rs 500 every month for personal purpose. He had a scooter, which had been sold for Rs 5,000 and invested the same into the business. Further, there is no other information.

Calculate the amount of profit made by him during the year 2004.

SOLUTION

		Rs
Capital at the end (given)		32,800
Add: Withdrawals:		
Expenses for his son	2,000	
Withdrawals @ Rs 500 per month	6,000	8,000
		40,800
Less: Further Capital Introduced		5,000
Adjusted Capital at the end		35,800
Less: Capital in the beginning (1.1.2004)		20,500
Profit made for the year 2004		15,300

Note: In this problem, his closing capital would have been Rs 8,000 (Rs 2,000 + Rs 6,000) more, had he not withdrawn money from his business.

Similarly, had he not introduced fresh capital of Rs 5,000, his closing capital would have been Rs 5,000 less than what it is now.

ILLUSTRATION 12.3

Mr Gopal started a business with Rs 30,800 on 1.1.2004. The drawings during the year amounted to Rs 16,400 and further Capital of Rs 9,600 was introduced on 1st July 2004. Prepare statement to show profit or loss made during the year from the following particulars, as on 31st December 2004

	Rs
Creditors	34,800
Debtors	24,600
Furniture	4,800
Machinery	6,600
Cash	1,800
Investments	23,600
Bills Payable	10,800
Stock	22,200
Bank Overdraft	7,600

Write off Rs 1,200 towards Bad Debts and a further of 5% is to be made towards Doubtful Debts. Depreciate Furniture by 5% and Machinery by 10%

Outstanding salaries Rs 480 and prepaid Rent Rs 320. (*Karnataka*)

SOLUTION

Statement of Affairs
as on 31st December 2004

Liabilities	*Rs*	*Assets*	*Rs*
Creditors	34,800	Cash	1,800
Bank Overdraft	7,600	Debtors	24,600
Bills Payable	10,800	Prepaid Rent	320
Salary Outstanding	480	Stock	22,200
Capital (Balancing figure)	30,240	Investments	23,600
		Furniture	4,800
		Machinery	6,600
	83,920		83,920

Statement of Profit
for the year ended 31st Dec. 2004

		Rs
Capital as on 31st Dec. 2004		30,240
Add: Drawings		16,400
		46,640
Less: Additional Capital Introduced		9,600
Adjusted Capital	Rs	37,040
Less: Capital as on 1st January 2004		30,800
Profit before Adjustments:		6,240
Less: Bad Debts	1,200	
Reserve for Doubtful Debts	1,170	
Depreciation: Furniture	240	
Depreciation Machinery	660	3,270
Profit for the year 2004		2,970

Adjusted Statement of Affairs
as on 31st December 2004

Liabilities		*Rs*	*Assets*		*Rs*
Creditors		34,800	Cash		1,800
Bank Overdraft		7,600	Debtors:	24,600	
Bills Payable		10,800	Less: Bad Debts	1,200	
Salaries: Outstanding		480		23,400	
Capital (1.1.2004)	30,800		Less: Provision for		
Add: Net Profit	2,970		doubtful debt	1,170	22,230
	33,770		Rent Prepaid		320
			Stock		22,200
Add: Additional Capital	9,600		Investments		23,600
	43,370		Furniture	4,800	
			Less: Depreciation	240	4,560
Less: Drawings	16,400	26,970	Machinery	6,600	
			Less: Depreciation	660	5,940
		80,650			80,650

Notes: 1. Opening Statement of Affairs is not prepared because the opening capital is given in this problem.

2. Adjusted Statement of Affairs incorporates all adjustments.

ILLUSTRATION 12.4.

A retail merchant, commenced business with a capital of Rs. 12,000 on 1st January 2006. Subsequently, on 1st May, 2006, he invested further capital of Rs. 5,000. During the year, he has withdrawn Rs. 2,000 for his personal use. On 31st December 2006 his assets and liabilities were as follows:

	Rs.
Cash at Bank	3,000
Debtors	4,000
Stock	16,000
Furniture	2,000
Creditors	5,000

Calculate profit or loss made during the year 2006. *(M.Com. Madras)*

Solution:

STATEMENT OF AFFAIRS
as on 31st Dec. 2006

Liabilities	*Rs*	*Assets*	*Rs*
Creditors	5,000	Cash at Bank	3,000
Capital (Balancing figure)	20,000	Debtors	4,000
		Stock	16,000
		Furniture	2,000
	25,000		25,000

STATEMENT OF PROFIT
for the year ended 31st December 2006.

	Rs.
Capital at the end (31.12.2006)	20,000
Add: Drawings	2,000
	22,000
Less: Additional Capital	5,000
	17,000
Less: Capital in the beginning (1.1.2006)	12,000
Profit for the year	5,000

ILLUSTRATION 12.5

Find the Opening Capital from the following information:

Closing Capital	Rs. 8,000
Profit made during the year	Rs. 2,400
Capital introduced during the year	Rs. 2,000
Drawings	Rs. 1,200

(B.Com. Periyar)

SOLUTION:

STATEMENT SHOWING OPENING CAPITAL

	Rs.
Closing Capital	8,000
Add: Drawings	1,200
	9,200
Less: Additional Capital	2,000
	7,200
Less: Opening Capital (Balancing figure)	4,800
Profit for the year	2,400

Alternatively:

Closing Capital + Drawings – Further Capital – Opening Capital = Profit

(OR)

Closing Capital + Drawings – Further Capital – Profit = Opening Capital

Rs. 8,000 + Rs. 1,200 – Rs. 2,000 – Rs. 2,400 = **Rs. 4,800**

ILLUSTRATION 12.6

Mr Ram had Rs 3,00,000 in Bank on 1st January 2004, when he started his business. He closed his accounts on 31st March 2005. His single entry book (in which he did not maintain any accounts for the banks) showed his position as follows:

	On 31.3.2004 Rs	On 31.3.2005 Rs
Cash in Hand	2,000	3,000
Stock	19,000	29,000
Debtors	1,000	2,000
Creditors	5,000	3,000

On 1st February 2004 he began drawing Rs 800 per month for his personal expenses from the cash box of the business:

	Deposits Rs	Withdrawals Rs
1-1-2004	3,00,000	–
1-1-2004 to 31.3.2004	–	2,23,000
1-4-2004 to 31.3.2005	2,30,000	2,70,000

The above withdrawals included payment by cheques of Rs 2,00,000 and Rs 60,000 respectively during the periods from 1st January 2004 to 31st March 2004 and from 1st April 2004 to 31st March 2005 for the purchase of machinery for the business: and the deposits after 1st January 2004 consisted wholly of sale price received from customers by cheques.

Draw up Ram's Statement of Affairs as at 31st March 2004 and 31st March 2005 respectively and work out his profit or loss for the year ended 31st March 2005. *(CS, B.Com MS)*

SOLUTION

Statement of Affairs of Ram as on 31st March 2004

Liabilities	*Rs*	*Assets*	*Rs*
Creditors	5,000	Cash in Hand	2,000
Capital (Balancing figure)	2,94,000	Cash at Bank (3,00,000 – 2,23,000)	77,000
		Stock	19,000
		Debtors	1,000
		Machinery	2,00,000
	2,99,000		2,99,000

Statement of Affairs of Ram as on 31st March 2005

Liabilities	*Rs*	*Assets*		*Rs*
Creditors	3,000	Cash in Hand		3,000
Capital (Balancing figure)	3,28,000	Cash at Bank		
		On 1.4.2004	77,000	
		Add: Deposit	2,30,000	
			3,07,000	
		Less: Withdrawals	2,70,000	37,000
		Stock		29,000
		Debtors		2,000
		Machinery:	2,00,000 + 60,000	2,60,000
	3,31,000			3,31,000

Statement of Profit of Ram
for the year ended 31st March 2005

	Rs
Capital at the end of the year (31.3.2005)	3,28,000
Add: Drawings during the year @ Rs 800	9,600
	3,37,600
Less: Capital in the beginning of the year (1.4.2004)	2,94,000
Profit made during the year	43,600

ILLUSTRATION 12.7

Following balances are extracted from the books of Joseph, who keeps incomplete records of his transactions:

	1st Jan. 2004	31st Dec. 2004
	Rs	Rs
Stock	2,400	3,000
Debtors	4,000	3,200
Creditors	1,700	3,900
Cash in Hand	2,000	3,800
Bank Overdraft	2,400	
Furniture and Fittings	800	1,000
Motor Bike	9,500	9,500
Bills Receivable	2,000	4,300

Drawings during the year amounted to Rs 2,800. Depreciate Furniture and Fittings @ 5% and write off Rs 500 on Motor Bike. Rs 100 is irrecoverable and a further provision of 5% for Doubtful Debts are to be provided. Further, a provision of Rs 200 in respect of bills are also to be provided.

Ascertain the profit or loss for the year ended 31st December 2004 and prepare a Statement of Affairs as on that date. (*B.Com., Madurai*)

SOLUTION

Statement of Affairs
as on 1st Jan., 2004

Liabilities	*Rs*	*Assets*	*Rs*
Bank Overdraft	2,400	Cash in Hand	2,000
Creditors	1,700	Stock	2,400
Capital (Balancing figure or excess of assets over liabilities)	16,600	Bills Receivable	2,000
		Debtors	4,000
		Furniture and Fittings	800
		Motor Bike	9,500
	20,700		20,700

Statement of Affairs
as on 31st Dec., 2004

Liabilities	*Rs*	*Assets*	*Rs*
Creditors	3,900	Cash in Hand	3,800
Capital (Balancing figure)	20,900	Stock	3,000
		Bills Receivable	4,300
		Debtors	3,200
		Furniture and Fittings	1,000
		Motor Bike	9,500
	24,800		24,800

Statement of Profit or Loss
for the year 2004

		Rs
Capital at the end (31.12.2004)		20,900
Add: Drawings during the year		2,800
Adjusted Capital		23,700
Less: Capital at the beginning (1.1.2004)		16,600
Profit, subject to adjustments:		7,100
Less: Bad Debts	100	
Provision for Doubtful Debt	155	
Provision (B/R)	200	
Depreciation:		
Furniture	50	
Motor Bike	500	1,005
Profit for the year 2004		6,095

Adjusted Statement of Affairs
as on 31st December 2004

Liabilities		*Rs*	*Assets*		*Rs*
Creditors		3,900	Cash in Hand		3,800
Capital:	16,600		Stock		3,000
Less: Drawings	2,800		Bills Receivable:	4,300	
	13,800		Less: Provision	200	4,100
Add: Profit	6,095	19,895	Debtors:	3,200	
			Less: Bad Debts	100	
				3,100	
			Less: Provision for Doubtful Debts	155	2,945
			Furniture and Fittings	1,000	
			Less: Depreciation	50	950
			Motor Bike	9,500	
			Less: Depreciation	500	9,000
		23,795			23,795

ILLUSTRATION 12.8

A retail trader had not kept proper books of accounts but from the following details you are required to ascertain the profit or loss for the year ended 30th June 2004 and also to prepare a statement of affairs as at that date:

	1-7-2003	30-6-2004		1-7-2003	30-6-2004
	Rs.	Rs.		Rs.	Rs.
Stock in Trade	16,700	18,500	Bank Overdraft	20,200	19,400
Sundry Creditors	15,400	14,000	Bills Receivable	15,050	14,200
Sundry Debtors	11,200	10,500	Fixtures, Fittings etc.	1,500	1,500
Cash in Hand	250	1,200	Motor Van	1,900	1,900

The drawings during the year amounted to Rs 2,600. Depreciate Fixtures etc. by 10 per cent and write Rs 300 off Motor Van. As regards the debtors, it is ascertained that Rs 500 are irrecoverable and further reserve of 5 per cent should be made. Also reserve Rs 700 in respect of Bills Receivable. (*B.Com., Madurai*)

SOLUTION

Statement of Affairs
as at 1st July 2003

Liabilities	*Amount*	*Assets*	*Amount*
	Rs		*Rs*
Bank Overdraft	20,200	Motor Van	1,900
Sundry Creditors	15,400	Fixture & Fittings	1,500
Capital, (being excess of assets over		Stock	16,700
liabilities)	11,000	Sundry Debtors	11,200
		Bills Receivable	15,050
		Cash	250
	46,600		46,600

Statement of Affairs
as at 30th June 2004

Liabilities	*Amount*	*Assets*	*Amount*
Bank Overdraft	19,400	Motor Van	1,900
Sundry Creditors	14,000	Fixtures & Fittings	1,500
Capital (being excess of assets over		Stock	18,500
liabilities)	14,400	Sundry Debtors	10,500
		Bills Receivable	14,200
		Cash	1,200
	47,800		47,800

Statement of Profit or Loss
for the year ended 30th June 2004

		Rs
Capital as at 30th June 2004		14,400
Add: Drawings		2,600
		17,000
Less: Capital as at 30th June 2003		11,000
Profit, subject to adjustments:		6,000
Less: Adjustment:		
Depreciation on Fixtures and Fittings	150	
Depreciation on Van	300	
Bad Debts	500	
Bad Debts Provision	500	
Provision for Bills Receivable	700	2,150
Net Profit		3,850

Adjusted Statement of Affairs
as at 30th June 2004

Liabilities		*Amount*	*Assets*		*Amount*
		Rs			*Rs*
Sundry Creditors		14,000	Motor Van	1,900	
Bank Overdraft		19,400	Less: Depreciation	300	1,600
Capital as on 1-7-2003	11,000		Fixtures & Fitting	1,500	
Add: Net Profit	3,850		Less: Depreciation	150	1,350
	14,850		Stock		18,500

Less: Drawings	2,600	12,250	Sundry Debtors	10,500	
			Less Bad Debts	500	
				10,000	
			Less: Reserve for Doubtful debts at 5%	500	9,500
			Bills Receivable	14,200	
			Less reserve for doubtful bills	700	13,500
			Cash		1,200
		45,650			45,650

2. CONVERSION METHOD

The Net Worth Method explained above does not provide a clear operational results of a firm. It does not provide the needed accounting information with which the business can be improved. Moreover, the available figures from the existing books may not be enough to have a meaningful analysis to know the soundness of the business. In the absence of complete records, the correct profit and financial position cannot be known. Therefore, a trader may wish to convert the Single Entry system into Double Entry so that he can prepare final accounts, which reveal the exact financial position of the business, apart from knowing the correct profit. The work involved in the conversion of Single Entry into Double Entry will vary with the set of books maintained. The following procedure may be followed for conversion:

1. A Statement of Affairs at the beginning period (at the end of the previous period) should be prepared and open all those assets and liabilities account which have not been already opened. It is possible that some of the items, for the Statement of Affairs, are missing, such as, Debtors or Creditors or Cash-in-hand or any other items at the beginning. If it is so, one has to find them out by preparing ledger accounts (explained below).
2. Cash Book should be verified and the unposted items, from the debit side and credit side of the Cash Book, should be posted to respective accounts, because generally Nominal Accounts and Real Accounts might not have been opened under Single Entry. Cash balance shown by the Cash Book with Cash-in-hand should be compared. In certain cases, opening balance, closing balance, etc. (explained below).
3. Impersonal accounts (mainly Sales Account, Purchase Account etc.) must be verified to know the correct figure of sales or purchases. These figures might not have been given in Single Entry. Thus, Credit Sales or Credit Purchases may be found out by preparing Total Debtors Account or Total Creditors Account (explained below).
4. Similarly, verify the Cash Book entries relating to discount, allowances, commission etc. to be posted to respective accounts, if not posted already, or open such account if not opened already.
5. Even if no records are kept in respect of certain transactions, such transactions must be journalised and posted. In fact, conversion of Single Entry into Double Entry involves the complete process of journalising, postings and preparation of Trial Balance. Theoretically, it is possible but practically it is a tedious process and consumes a lot of time.

Therefore, one should search out the figures which are needed for the preparation of final accounts. The pieces of information may be scattered in the problem or they may be missing. If such information is missing, it should be got by preparing necessary accounts, before proceeding to prepare final accounts i.e. Trading Account, Profit and Loss Account and Balance Sheet. The following figures are needed :

FOR TRADING ACCOUNT (Dr. side)	Opening Stock Purchases Direct Expenses Manufacturing Expenses
FOR TRADING ACCOUNT (Cr. side)	Sales Closing Stock
FOR PROFIT & LOSS A/C (Dr. side)	Indirect Expenses and Losses Depreciation etc.
FOR PROFIT & LOSS A/C (Cr. side)	Gross Profit Gains and Incomes etc.
FOR BALANCE SHEET (Asset side)	Cash in hand and Bank Sundry Debtors/Bills Receivable Fixed Assets Closing Stock
FOR BALANCE SHEET (Liability side)	Sundry Creditors/Bills Payable Capitals Net Profit/Loss Drawings etc.

How to search out the missing or required information? They are in brief:

Items	*From where to find out*
Opening Stock	Statement of Affairs Or Memorandum Trading Account
Cash Purchases	Cash Book (Credit side)
Credit Purchases	Total Creditors Account Or Other information
Manufacturing Expenses	Cash Book or other information
Buying Expenses	Cash Book or other information
Purchase Returns	Other information
Cash Sales	Cash Book or other information
Credit Sales	Total Debtors Account or other information
Sales Returns	Other information
Closing Stock	Closing Balance of Stock Account or other information
Gross Profit/Loss	Trading Account

	Items	*From where to find out*
Profit & Loss A/c (Dr. Side)	Discount Allowed, Bad debts etc.	Total Debtors Account or other information given
	Selling Expenses Gross Loss	Payment side of the Cash Book and Adjustments or through information given Trading Account
Profit & Loss A/c (Cr. Side)	Gross Profit Incomes Received Incomes Receivable	Trading Account Cash Book Given information.
Balance Sheet (Asset)	Cash/Bank Balance	Opening Statement of Affairs or other information given
	Closing Debtors	Total Debtors Account or given information

	Closing Bills Receivable	Bills Receivable Account or given information
	Assets (New)	Cash Book or given information
	Assets (Old)	From Opening Statement of Affairs
	Additions made to assets	Cash Book
Balance Sheet (Liability)	Bank Overdraft	Cash Book
	Sundry Creditors (Closing)	Total Creditors Account or given information
	Bills Payable (Closing)	Bills Payable Account or given information
	Capital (Opening)	Statement of Affairs (Beginning)
	Additional Capital	Cash Book
	Net Profit/Loss	Profit and Loss Account
	Drawings	Cash Book (Payment side)
	Interest on Capital	Other information.

Some practical approach to find out missing figures are explained below:

ILLUSTRATION 12.9 (Missing value of Opening Stock)

During the year 2004, the following transactions took place:

	Rs
Purchases during the year	75,000
Sales during the year	1,25,000
Closing Stock on Dec. 2004	15,000
Manufacturing Expenses	10,000

Rate of Gross Profit was 25% on cost. Find out the Opening Stock.

SOLUTION

When opening stock is missing, it can be found out by preparing a Memorandum Trading Account.

Dr. **Memorandum Trading Account** Cr.

	Rs		*Rs*
To Opening Stock (Balancing figure)	30,000	By Sales	1,25,000
		By Closing Stock	15,000
To Purchases	75,000		
To Manufacturing Expenses	10,000		
To Gross Profit	25,000		
	1,40,000		1,40,000

25% on cost = 20% on sales

Therefore gross profit = 20% of Rs 1,25,000 = Rs 25,000

Many a time, a number of difficult points arise while solving a single entry problem. The required information may be in scattered form or they may be got by preparing ledger accounts or drawing statements of affairs etc. Generally, credit purchases, credit sales, Debtors Balance (Opening or closing), Creditors Balance (opening or closing), etc. may be missing. Credit purchase or Credit sales can be known by preparing Total Creditors Account or Total Debtors Account. One should recall those transactions connected with purchases or sales and their journal entries.

Total Debtors Account is to be prepared to find out either the missing CREDIT SALES or CLOSING BALANCE OF DEBTORS or OPENING BALANCE OF DEBTORS, in the following manner.

Total Debtors Account

Dr.	Rs		Cr. Rs
To Opening Balance (either given or Balancing figure)		By Cash Received	
To Bills Receivable Dishonoured		By Bills Receivable	
To Credit Sales (either given or Balancing figure)		By Discount Allowed	
		By Returns Inwards	
		By Bad Debts	
		By Transfer to Creditors	
		By Balance (either given or Balancing figure)	

Total Creditors Account is to be prepared to find out either the missing CREDIT PURCHASES or CLOSING BALANCE OF CREDITORS or OPENING BALANCE OF CREDITORS, in the following manner.

Total Creditors Account

Dr.	Rs		Cr. Rs
To Cash Paid		By Balance b/d (either given or Balancing figure)	
To Bills Payable		By Bills Payable Dishonoured	
To Return Outwads		By Credit Purchase (either given or Balancing figure)	
To Discount Received			
To Transfer to Debtors			
To Balance c/d (either given or Balancing figure)			

Bills Receivable Account: It is prepared to find out either to know the Bills Receivable received from Debtors or to know the closing balance.

Bills Receivable Account

Dr.	Rs		Cr. Rs
To Opening Balance (either given or Balancing figure)		By Cash (on Bills)	
To Sundry Debtors (Bills Receivable received) (either or Balancing figure)		By Sundry Debtors (Bills dishonoured)	
		By Balance c/d (either or Balancing figure)	

Bills Payable Account: It is to be prepared to find out either to know Bills Payable accepted or to know the closing balance.

Bills Payable Account

Dr.	Rs		Cr. Rs
To Cash (against Bills)		By Balance b/d	
To Sundry Creditors (Bills dishonoured)		By Sundry Creditors (Bills Accepted)	
To Closing Balance (either given or Balancing figure)			

ILLUSTRATION 12.10 (Missing value of Credit purchase)

During the year 2004, the following transactions took place and you are required to find out the amount of Credit purchase made during the year.

	Rs
Balance of Creditors on Jan. 2004	16,000
Cash paid to Creditors during the year	30,000
Bills Payable accepted during the year	8,000
Purchase Returns	1,000
Balance of Creditors on Dec. 2004	17,000

SOLUTION

When the credit purchases are missing, we have to prepare the Total Creditors Account to know the amount of credit purchase.

Dr. **Total Creditors Account** Cr.

	Rs		*Rs*
To Cash Paid	30,000	By Balance b/d	16,000
To Bills Payable Accepted	8,000	By Purchases	
To Purchase Returns	1,000	(Balancing figure)	40,000
To Balance c/d	17,000		
	56,000		56,000

Thus the credit purchases during the year is Rs 40,000.

There may arise occasions where Bills Payable Accepted during the year may be missing. In such a situation, first the Bills Payable Account is to be prepared to find out the amount of Bills accepted during the year; and then the Total Creditors Account is prepared to find out the Credit Purchases.

ILLUSTRATION 12.11 (Missing value of Bills Accepted during the year and Credit Purchases)

From the following facts supplied by A who keeps his books on Single Entry, you are required to calculate total purchases:

	Rs
Opening Balance of Bills Payable	5,000
Opening Balance of Creditors	6,000
Closing Balance of Bills Payable	7,000
Closing Balance of Creditors	4,000
Cash paid to Creditors during the year	30,200
Bills payable discharged during the year	8,900
Returns Outwards	1,200
Cash Purchases	25,800

(*B.Com. M.K*)

SOLUTION

Dr. **Bills Payable Account** Cr.

	Rs		*Rs*
To Cash	8,900	By Balance b/d	5,000
To Balance c/d	7,000	By Creditors (Bills Accepted during	
		the year)	10,900
		(Balancing figure)	
	15,900		15,900
		By Balance b/d	7,000

Dr. **Total Creditors Account** Cr.

	Rs		Rs.
To Cash	30,200	By Balace b/d	6,000
To Returns	1,200	By Purchases (Credit)	
To Bills Payable	10,900	(Balancing figure)	40,300
To Balance c/d	4,000		
	46,300		46,300
		By Balance b/d	4,000

Total Purchases:	
Cash Purchases	25,800
Credit Purchases	40,300
Total Purchases	66,100

ILLUSTRATION 12.12 (Missing value of Credit Sales)

From the following information, find out the credit sales:

	Rs
Cash Received from Debtors	53,000
Discount Allowed to them	800
Return Inwards	1,500
Balance of Debtors on Jan. 2004	10,000
Balance of Debtors on Dec. 2004	9,500
Bills Receivable from Debtors	13,000
Bad Debts during the year 2004	700
Bills Receivable Dishonoured	950

SOLUTION

Dr. **Total Debtors Account** Cr.

	Rs		Rs
To Balance b/d	10,000	By Cash	53,000
To Bills Dishonoured	950	By Discount	800
To Credit Sales	67,550	By Returns Inwards	1,500
(Balancing figure)		By Bills Receivable	13,000
		By Bad Debts	700
		By Balance c/d	9,500
	78,500		78,500

Sometimes, the Bills Receivable received during the year may not be available in the problem. In such cases first prepare the Bills Receivable Account so that the amount of Bills Receivable received during the year can be known. This figure appears on the credit side of the Total Debtors Account. Then the Total Debtors Account is prepared.

ILLUSTRATION 12.13 [Finding (*i*) Bills Receivable received during the year and (*ii*) Credit sales]

From the following find out the amount of credit sales made during the year 2004.

	Rs
Bills Receivable encashed during 2004	19,000
Cash Received from Debtors during the year	15,000
Balance of Bills Receivable on Jan. 2004	6,000
Balance of Bills Receivable on Dec. 2004	7,000
Balance of Debtors on Jan. 2004	19,500
Bad Debts written off	200
Returns Inwards	300
Bills Receivable Dishonoured	1,000
Balance of Debtors on Dec. 2004	15,000

SOLUTION

Bills Receivable Account

Dr.	Rs		Cr. Rs
To Balance b/d	6,000	By Cash	19,000
To Sundry Debtors	21,000	By Sundry Debtors	1,000
(Bills Received)		(Bills dishonoured)	
(Balancing figure)		By Balance c/d	7,000
	27,000		27,000

Total Debtors Account

Dr.	Rs		Cr. Rs
To Balance b/d	19,500	By Cash	15,000
To Bills Dishonoured	1,000	By Bad Debts	200
To Credit Sales	31,000	By Bills Receivable Received	21,000
(Balancing figure)		By Returns Inwards	300
		By Balance c/d	15,000
	51,500		51,500

ILLUSTRATION 12.14. (Finding Credit Purchases and Credit Sales)

Ascertain credit purchase and credit sales from the following:

	Rs
Sundry Debtors on 1.1.2004	12,800
Sundry Debtors on 31.12.2004	9,800
Sundry Creditors on 1.1.2004	7,600
Sundry Creditors on 31.12.2004	9,030
Cash Received from Debtors	6,400
Cash Paid to Creditors	1,750
Discount Allowed	350
Discount Received	250
Bill Received from Debtors	2,500
Acceptance given to Creditors	5,870
Bad Debts	300
Bills Dishonoured by Debtors	400

(*Karnataka*)

SOLUTION

Total Debtors Account

Dr.	Rs		Cr. Rs
To Balance b/d	12,800	By Cash	6,400
To Bills Receivable Dishonoured	400	By Discount	350
To Sales (Credit		By Bad Debts	300
(Balancing figure)	6,150	By Bills Receivable	2,500
		By Balance c/d	9,800
	19,350		19,350
To Balance b/d	9,800		

Dr. **Total Creditors Account** Cr.

	Rs		Rs
To Cash	1,750	By Balance b/d	7,600
To Discount	250	By Purchases (Credit)	
To Bills Payable	5,870	(Balancing figure)	9,300
To Balance c/d	9,030		
	16,900		16,900
		By Balance b/d	9,030

ILLUSTRATION 12.15 (Finding Credit Sales and Credit Purchases)

From the following prepare total debtors and total creditors account and find out credit purchases:

	Rs		Rs
Debtors on 1st Jan.	5,000	Bad debts written off	1,200
Creditors on 1st Jan.	4,000	Bad debts recovered	300
Debtors as on 31st December	4,000	B/R endorsed to creditors	4,000
Creditors as on 31st December	6,000	B/R dishonoured	1,000
B/R received during the year	10,000	Endorsed B/R dishonoured	500
B/P issued during the year	8,000	B/R discounted	2,000
Cash received from customers	30,000	Discounted B/R dishonoured	700
Cash returned to customers	500	Sales returns	600
Cash paid to suppliers	20,700	Purchases returns	200
Discount allowed by Suppliers	270		
Discount allowed to Customers	150		

SOLUTION

Dr. **Total Debtors Account** Cr.

	Rs		Rs
To Balance b/d	5,000	By B/R	10,000
To Cash returned	500	By Cash	30,000
To B/R dishonoured	1,000	By Discount	150
To Creditors	500	By Bad Debts	1,200
To Bank	700	By Sales returns	600
To Credit Sales (Balancing figure)	38,250	By Balance c/d	4,000
	45,950		45,950

Dr. **Total Creditors Account** Cr.

	Rs		Rs
To B/P	8,000	By Balance b/d	4,000
To Cash	20,700	By Debtors (Bills endorsed &	
To Discount	270	dishonoured)	500
To B/R (endorsed)	4,000	By Credit purchases	
To Purchases returns	200	(Balancing figure)	34,670
To Balance c/d	6,000		
	39,170		39,170

Note: Bad Debts Recovered and Bills Receivable discounted will not appear in Total Debtors Account

Illustration 12.16.

Prepare Total Debtors Account and Bills Receivable Account for the year ended 31st March 2006 from the following:

	Rs.
Total sales during the year	1,12,500
Cash sales during the year	29,450
Returns inward during the year	450
Discount during the year	150
Cash received during the year	68,750
Cash received against B/R during the year	2,900
Provision for bad debts made during the year	650
Debtors on 31st March 2005	39,250
Provision for Bad Debts on 31st March 2005	850
Debtors on 31st March 2006	49,850
Bills Receivable on 31st March 2005	1,900
Provision for Bad Debts on 31st March 2006	600

(*B.Com. Bangalore*)

Solution:

TOTAL DEBTORS ACCOUNT

	Rs		*Rs*
To Balance b/d (31.3.2005)	39,250	By Returns Inward	450
To Credit Sales	83,050	By Cash received	68,750
(Rs. 1,12,500 – Rs. 29,450)		By Discount Allowed	150
		By Bad Debts	900
		By Bills Receivable (Balancing figure)	2,200
		By Balance c/d (31.3.'06)	49,850
	1,22,300		1,22,300

BILLS RECEIVABLE ACCOUNT

	Rs		*Rs*
To Balance b/d (31.3.2005)	1,900	By Cash received	2,900
To Debtors	2,200	By Balance c/d (31.3.'06) (Balancing figure)	1,200
	4,100		4,100

PROVISION FOR BAD DEBTS ACCOUNT

	Rs		*Rs*
To Bad Debts (Balancing figure)	900	By Balance b/d (31.3.2005)	850
To Balance c/d (31.3.'06)	600	By Profit & Loss A/c -Provision made	650
	1,500		1,500

Illustration 12.17 (Finding the amount of sales)

From the following information, find out the amount of total sales:

	Rs.
Opening Stock	8,000
Purchases	40,000
Stock at the end	7,000
Rate of Gross Profit on Sale = 1/6	

(*B.Com. Madras*)

Solution:

TRADING ACCOUNT

	Rs		*Rs*
To Opening Stock	8,000	By Sales (Balancing (figure)	49,200
To Purchases	40,000	By Stock at the end	7,000
To Gross Profit	8,200*		
	56,200		56,200

Workings:

* When cost is 5/6, Profit = 1/6

Cost = Opening Stock + Purchases – Closing Stock
= Rs. 8,000 + Rs. 40,000 – Rs. 7,000 = Rs. 41,000

When 5/6 = Rs. 41,000, $1/6 = \text{Rs. } 41,000 \times \frac{6}{5} \times \frac{1}{6} =$ **Rs. 8,200**

Illustration 12.18 (Finding Opening Stock)

Calculate the stock in the beginning:

	Rs.
Sales	80,000
Purchases	60,000
Stock at closing	8,000
Gross Loss on Cost	1/6

(*B.Com. Madras*)

Solution:

TRADING ACCOUNT

	Rs		*Rs*
To Opening Stock (Balancing fugure)	44,000	By Sales	80,000
		By Stock at close	8,000
To Purchases	60,000	By Gross Loss	16,000
	1,04,000		1,04,000

Workings:

Cost of Goods sold – Gross Loss = Sales
5/6 = Sales = Rs. 80,000

$1/6 = \text{Rs. } 80,000 \times \frac{6}{5} \times \frac{1}{6} =$ **Rs. 16,000 Gross Loss**

ILLUSTRATION 12.19. (Finding (*i*) Sales Amount, (*ii*) Purchased Amount, (*iii*) B/R Closing Balance and (*iv*) B/P Closing Balance)

You are required to ascertain credit sales effected and credit purchases made during the year 2004:

	Rs
Sundry Debtors on 1st January	4,000
Sundry Creditors on 1st January	7,600
Bills Receivable on 1st January	15,000
Bills Payable on 1st January	18,600
Bills Accepted	14,000
Acceptance Received	20,000
Bad Debts written off	700
Discount Allowed	1,000
Discount Earned	800
Bills Discounted	10,000
Bills Discounted Dishonoured	10,000

Bills Receivable Endorsed to Creditors	4,000
Bills Receivable Dishonoured	7,000
Acceptance not met	8,400
Bad Debts Recovered	500
Payments to Creditors	34,100
Cash Received from Debtors	30,000
Returns Inwards	6,000
Returns Outwards	1,400
Bills Payable Honoured	10,000
Bills endorsed Dishonoured	2,000
Endorsements Received	2,000
Sundry Debtors on 31st December	11,000
Sundry Creditos on 31st December	3,100

Sundry Debtors Account

Dr.	Rs		Cr. Rs
To Balance b/d	4,000	By Bills Receivable (Acceptance Received)	20,000
To Bank (Bill discounted dishonoured)	10,000	By Bad Debts	700
To Bills Receivable (Bills Dishonoured)	7,000	By Discount Allowed	1,000
To Sundry Creditors (Bills endorsed Dishonoured)	2,000	By Cash	30,000
To Credit Sales (Balancing figure)	47,700	By Return Inwards	6,000
		By Bills Receivable (Endorsement Received)	2,000
		By Balance c/d	11,000
	70,700		70,700
To Balance b/d	11,000		

Bills Receivable Account

Dr.	Rs		Cr. Rs
To Balance b/d	15,000	By Bank (Bills Discounted)	10,000
To Sundry Debtors (Acceptance Received)	20,000	By Sundry Creditors (Bills Receivable Endorsed)	4,000
To Sundry Debtors (Endorsement Received	2,000	By Sundry Debtors (Bills Dishonoured)	7,000
		By Balance c/d (Balancing figure)	16,000
	37,000		37,000
To Balance b/d	16,000		

Sundry Creditors Account

Dr.	Rs		Cr. Rs
To Bills Payable (Bills Accepted)	14,000	By Balance b/d	7,600
To Discount Earned	800	By Bills Payable (Acceptance not met)	8,400
To Bills Receivable (Endorsed)	4,000	By Sundry Debtors (Endorsed Bills Dishonoured)	2,000
To Cash	34,100	By Credit Purchases (Balancing figure)	39,400
To Returns Outwards	1,400		
To Balance c/d	3,100		
	57,400		57,400
		By Balance c/d	3,100

Bills Payable Account

Dr.	Rs		Cr. Rs
To Sundry Creditors (Acceptance not met)	8,400	By Balance b/d	18,600
To Bank (Bills Payable Honoured)	10,000	By Sundry Creditors (Bills Accepted)	14,000
To Balance c/d (Balancing figure)	14,200		
	32,600		32,600
		By Balance b/d	14,200

ILLUSTRATION 12.20 (Solving the problem under both the methods)

Mr Manoharan kept no books of account for his business. An analysis of his rough Cash Book for the year 2004 showed the following particulars:

Receipts	*Rs*	*Payments*	*Rs*
Received from Debtors	60,000	Overdraft (Jan. 2004)	7,400
Further Capital	5,000	Paid to Creditors	25,000
		Business Expenses	10,000
		Wages Paid	15,500
		Drawings	3,000
		Balance at Bank	4,000
		Balance of Cash in Hand	100
	65,000		65,000

Further, the following information is also available:

	31.12.2003 Rs	31.12.2004 Rs
Debtors	53,000	88,000
Creditors	15,000	19,500
Stock-in-trade	17,000	19,000
Plant	20,000	20,000
Furniture	1,400	1,400

All his sales and purchases were on credit. From the above particulars, prepare Trading and Profit and Loss Account for the year ended 31st December 2004 and a Balance Sheet as on that date after providing for depreciation on Plant at 10% and on Furniture at 5% p.a. (*B.Com., Madurai, Mangalore*)

SOLUTION

Let us solve the problem in both the ways. That first we solve it under Capital Comparison Method and then under Conversion Method.

(*a*) Capital Comparison Method: (Net Worth Method)

Statement of Affairs

Liabilities	*As on* 31.12.2003 Rs	*As on* 31.12.2004 Rs	*Assets*	*As on* 31.12.2003 Rs	*As on* 31.12.2004 Rs
Creditors	15,000	19,500	Cash at Bank	–	4,000
Bank Overdraft	7,400	–	Cash in Hand	–	100
Capital (Balancing figure)	69,000	1,13,000	Sundry Debtors	53,000	88,000
			Stock-in Trade	17,000	19,000
			Plant	20,000	20,000
			Furniture	1,400	1,400
	91,400	1,32,500		91,400	1,32,500

Statement of Profit or Loss
for the year ended 31st Dec. 2004

		Rs
Capital as on 31st Dec. 2004		1,13,000
Add: Drawings during the year		3,000
		1,16,000
Less: Further Capital		5,000
Adjusted Capital		1,11,000
Less: Capital as on 31st Dec. 2003		69,000
Profit:		42,000
Less: Depreciation: Plant	2,000	
Furniture	70	2,070
Final Profit		39,930

Statement of Affairs with Adjustments
as on 31st December 2004

Liabilities		*Rs*	*Assets*		*Rs*
Creditors		19,500	Cash in Hand		100
Capital:	69,000		Cash at Bank		4,000
Add: Net Profit	39,930		Debtors		88,000
Add: Additional Capital	5,000		Stock		19,000
	1,13,930		Furniture	1,400	
Less: Drawings	3,000	1,10,930	Less: Depreciation	70	1,330
			Plant	20,000	
			Less: Depreciation	2,000	18,000
		1,30,430			1,30,430

(*b*) **Conversion Method:** We have to find out credit purchases, credit sales and Opening Capital. Thus, we have to prepare Total Creditors Account, Total Debtors Account and Statement of Affairs as on 31.12.2004

Trading and Profit and Loss Account
for the year ended 31st Dec. 2004

Dr. Cr.

	Rs		*Rs*
To Stock on 1.1.2004	17,000	By Sales	95,000
To Purchases	29,500	By Stock on 31.12.2004	19,000
To Wages	15,500		
To Gross Profit c/d	52,000		
	1,14,000		1,14,000
To Business Expenses	10,000	By Gross Profit b/d	52,000
To Depreciation:			
Plant	2,000		
Furniture	70		
To Net Profit, transferred to Capital A/c	39,930		
	52,000		52,000

Balance Sheet as on 31st December 2004

Liabilities		*Rs*	*Assets*		*Rs*
Creditors		19,500	Cash in Hand		100
Capital:	69,000		Cash at Bank		4,000
Add: Net Profit	39,930		Debtors		88,000
Add: Additional Capital	5,000		Stock		19,000
	1,13,930		Furniture	1,400	
Less: Drawings	3,000	1,10,930	Less: Depreciation	70	1,330
			Plant	20,000	
			Less: Depreciation	2,000	18,000
		1,30,430			1,30,430

Working Note:

1. CALCULATION OF CREDIT PURCHASES:

Dr. **Total Creditors Account** Cr.

	Rs		Rs
To Cash	25,000	By Balance b/d (Dec. 2003)	15,000
To Balance c/d (Dec. 2004)	19,500	By Purchases (Balancing figure)	29,500
	44,500		44,500

Alternative method to find out Credit Purchases

		Rs
	Closing Balance of Creditors (Dec. 2004)	19,500
Add:	The amount paid during the year	25,000
		44,500
Less:	Opening Balance of Creditors (Dec. 2003) (i.e., the amount outstanding against previous years' purchase)	15,000
	The amount of Credit purchase during the year 2004 (Jan. to Dec.)	29,500

2. CALCULATION OF CREDIT SALES:

Dr. **Total Debtors Account** Cr.

	Rs		Rs
To Balance b/d (Dec. 2003	53,000	By Cash	60,000
To Sales (Balancing figure)	95,000	By Balance c/d (Dec. 2004)	88,000
	1,48,000		1,48,000

Alternative method to find out Credit Sales

		Rs
	Closing Balance of Debtors (Dec. 2004)	88,000
Add:	The amount received during the year	60,000
		1,48,000
Less:	Opening Balance of Debtors (Dec. 2003) (i.e. the amount outstanding against previous years' sales)	53,000
	The amount of Credit sales during the year 2004 (Jan. to Dec.)	95,000

3. FIND OUT THE OPENING CAPITAL:

Statement of Affairs
as on 31st December 2003

Liabilities	*Rs*	*Assets*	*Rs*
Creditors	15,000	Debtors	53,000
Bank Overdraft	7,400	Stock	17,000
Capital (Balancing figure)	69,000	Furniture	1,400
		Plant	20,000
	91,400		91,400

ILLUSTRATION 12.21

Mr Kumar does not keep his books on Double Entry System. From the following information, prepare his final accounts for the year ended 30th June 2004

His position on 1st July 2003 was as follows:

	Rs		*Rs*
Stock	12,500	Debtors	27,500
Buildings	20,000	Creditors	9,500
Furniture	5,000		

Cash Book analysis revealed the following facts:

	Rs		*Rs*
Bank Overdraft	5,500	Cash Purchases	8,250
Interest on above	375	Salary	1,500
Receipt from Debtors	35,000	Sundry Expenses	3,250
Cash Sales	12,500	Rent and Rates	600
Payment to Creditors	20,000	Drawings	1,500

From the analysis of personal accounts, it was found that the trader allowed discount Debtors amounted to Rs 1,750 and received discount from Creditors amounted to Rs 1,000. Gopi, a Debtor, from whom Rs 300 were due, paid only Rs 150, balance being treated as Bad Debt.

On 30th June 2004 he had Balance at Bank Rs 6,525, Stock valued at Rs 20,000; Debtors Rs 33,050; Bills Receivable Rs 1,500; Creditors Rs 9,500 and Bills Payable Rs 2,000. Provide depreciation on Building at 10%, interest on Capital at 5% and create provision for Doubtful Debts of Rs 1,200.

(B.Com., Bombay)

SOLUTION

In this problem the missing figures are (1) Credit Sales (2) Credit Purchases and (3) Opening Capital. See working notes:

Dr. **Trading and Profit and Loss Account** Cr.

		Rs			*Rs*
To Stock		12,500	By Sales:		
To Purchases:			Cash	12,500	
Cash	8,250		Credit	43,950	56,450
Credit	23,000	31,250	By Stock (Closing		20,000
To Gross Profit c/d		32,700			
		76,450			76,450
To Salaries		1,500	By Gross Profit b/d		32,700
To Sundry Expenses		3,250	By Discount Received		1,000
To Rent and Rate		600			

	Rs		Rs
To Interest	375		
To Discount Allowed	1,750		
To Bad Debts	150		
To Provision for Doubtful Deb	1,200		
To Depreciation on Buildings	2,000		
To Interest on Capital	2,500		
To Net Profit, transferred to Capital A/c	20,375		
	33,700		33,700

Balance Sheet as on 30th June 2004

Liabilities		*Rs*	*Assets*		*Rs*
Bills Payable		2,000	Cash at Bank		6,525
Creditors		9,500	Stock		20,000
Capital:			Bills Receivable		1,500
on 1.7.2003	50,000		Debtors	33,050	
Add: Interest	2,500		Less: Provision	1,200	31,850
Add: Net Profit:	20,375		Buildings:	20,000	
	72,875		Less: Depreciation	2,000	18,000
Less: Drawings	1,500	71,375	Furniture		5,000
		82,875			82,875

Working Note:

(1) Credit Sales is found out by preparing Total Debtors Account

Dr. **Total Debtors Account** Cr.

	Rs		Rs
To Balance b/d	27,500	By Cash	35,000
To Sales (Balancing figure)	43,950	By Discount Allowed	1,750
		By Bad Debts	150
		By Bills Receivable	1,500
		By Balance c/d	33,050
	71,450		71,450

(2) Credit Purchases is found out by preparing Total Creditors Account.

Dr. **Total Creditors Account** Cr.

	Rs		Rs
To Cash	20,000	By Balance b/d	9,500
To Bills Payable	2,000	By Purchases (Balancing figure)	23,000
To Discount	1,000		
To Balance c/d	9,500		
	32,500		32,500

(3) Capital is found out by preparing Statement of Affairs.

Statement of Affairs
as on 1st July 2003

Liabilities	*Rs*	*Assets*	*Rs*
Bank Overdraft	5,500	Stock	12,500
Creditors	9,500	Debtors	27,500
Capital (Balancing figure)	50,000	Furniture	5,000
		Building	20,000
	65,000		65,000

ILLUSTRATION 12.22

Mr George started a business as cloth merchant on 1st January 2004, with a Capital of Rs 10,000. On the same day, he purchased furniture for cash Rs 3,000. From the following information obtained from the books kept by single entry, prepare a Trading and Profit and Loss Account for the year ending 31st December 2004 and Balance Sheet as on that date:

	Rs
Sales (inclusive of cash sales Rs 7,000)	17,000
Purchases (inclusive of cash purchases Rs 4,000)	15,000
Mr George's Drawings	1,200
Salaries to staff	2,000
Bad Debts written off	500
Business Expenses	700

Mr George took cloth worth Rs 500 from the shop for private use, and paid Rs 200 to his son but omitted to record these transactions in his books. On 31st Decemer 2004, his Sundry Debtors were Rs 5,200 and Sundry Creditors Rs 3,600. Stock in hand valued on 31st December 2004 was Rs 6,500. (*B.Com., Madras*)

SOLUTION

In this problem, the following amounts are not known:

1. The amount received from Sundry Debtors
2. The amount paid to Sundry Creditors
3. Closing cash balance

All these values have been found out before solving the problem. See working note.

Trading and Profit and Loss Account
for the year ended 31st Dec. 2004

Dr. Cr.

		Rs		*Rs*
To Purchase: (given)	15,000		By Sales (given	17,000
Less: Drawings	500	14,500	By Closing Stock	6,500
To Gross Profit		9,000		
		23,500		23,500
To Salaries		2,000	By Gross Profit	9,000
To Business Expenses		700		
To Bad Debts		500		
To Net Profit		5,800		
		9,000		9,000

Balance Sheet as on 31st December 2004

Liabilities		*Rs*	*Assets*	*Rs*
Capital:	10,000		Furniture	3,000
Add: Net Profit	5,800		Sundry Debtors	5,200
	15,800		Closing Stock	6,500
Less: Drawings	1,900	13,900	Cash	2,800
Sundry Creditors		3,600		
		17,500		17,500

Working Note:

1. The Total Debtors Account has to be prepared to know the amount received from Sundry Debtors:

Dr. **Total Debtors Account** Cr.

	Rs		Rs
To Sales	10,000	By Bad Debts	500
		By Bank/Cash (Balancing figure)	4,300
		By Balance c/d	5,200
	10,000		10,000

2. The Total Creditors Account has to be prepared to know the amount paid to them:

Dr. **Total Creditors Account** Cr.

	Rs		Rs
To Cash (Balancing figure)	7,400	By Purchases	11,000
To Balance c/d	3,600		
	11,000		11,000

3. Cash Account has to be prepared to know the Cash Balance:

Dr. **Cash Account** Cr.

	Rs		Rs
To Capital A/c	10,000	By Furniture A/c	3,000
To Sales A/c	7,000	By Purchases A/c	4,000
To Debtors A/c (cash received)	4,300	By Drawings A/c	1,200
		By Drawings A/c	200
		By Salaries A/c	2,000
		By Business Expenses A/c	700
		By Creditors A/c (cash paid)	7,400
		By Balance c/d (Balancing figure)	2,800
	21,300		21,300

ILLUSTRATION 12.23

Given below are:

1. Balance Sheet of A and B on 1st April 2003.
2. Cash transactions for 12 months upto 31st March 2004.
3. A summary of the remaining transactions for the year.

			Rs		Rs
(1)	Bank Overdraft		5,000	Cash in Hand	700
	Sundry Creditors		36,000	Bills Receivable	25,000
	Bills Payable		16,000	Sundry Debtors	39,000
	Capital:	A	1,10,000	Stock of Goods	75,300
		B	90,000	Plant	47,000
				Land and Buildings	70,000
			2,57,000		2,57,000

		Rs		Rs
(2)	Balance in Hand (1.4.2003)	700	Bank Overdraft (1.4.2003)	5,000
	Receipt from Debtors	2,90,000	Salaries	12,000
	Bills Receivable	1,00,000	Wages	15,800
			Bills Payable	1,43,000
			Payments to Creditors	1,47,000
			Office Expenses	8,000
			Drawings by A	25,000
			Drawings by B	20,000
			Balance of Cash	2,400
			Balance at Bank	12,500
		3,90,700		3,90,700

		Rs
(3)	Sales	4,07,000
	Discounts to Customers	2,000
	Purchases	3,00,000
	Discount received from suppliers	1,000
	Bills Receivable received during the year	1,09,000
	Bills Payable issued during the year	1,50,000
	Stock of goods on 31st March 2004	53,000

Reserve for doubtful debts 5% on Debtors Outstanding. Provide Depreciation on Plant at 5% on Land and Buildings at 2.5%.

From the above particulars, prepare a Trading and Profit and Loss Account for the year ended 31st March 2004 and Balance Sheet as on that date. *(B.Com., Madras)*

SOLUTION

Trading and Profit and Loss Account
for the year ended 31st Dec. 2004

Dr. | Cr.

		Rs		Rs
To Stock		75,300	By Sales	4,07,000
To Purchases		3,00,000	By Closing Stock	53,000
To Wages		15,800		
To Gross Profit		68,900		
		4,60,000		4,60,000
To Salaries		12,000	By Gross Profit	68,900
To Discounts		2,000	By Discount	1,000
To Office Expenses		8,000		
To Reserve for Doubtful Debts		2,250		
To Depreciation:				
Plant	2,350			
Land and Buildings	1,750	4,100		
To Net Profit:				
A	20,775			
B	20,775	41,550		
		69,900		69,900

Balance Sheet as on 31st March 2004

Liabilities		*Rs*	*Assets*		*Rs*
Sundry Creditors		38,000	Cash in Hand		2,400
Bills Payable		23,000	Cash at Bank		12,500
Capitals:			Bills Receivable		34,000
A:	1,10,000		Sundry Debtors:	45,000	
Add: Profit	20,775		Less: Reserve for Doubtful Debts	2,250	42,750
	1,30,775		Stock		53,000
Less: Drawings	25,000	1,05,775	Plant:	47,000	
B:	90,000		Less: Depreciation	2,350	44,650
Add: Profit	20,775		Land and Buildings	70,000	
	1,10,775		Less: Depreciation	1,750	68,250
Less: Drawings	20,000	90,775			
		2,57,550			2,57,550

Note: A and B share the profit equally in the absence of any information

The following items are missing:

1. Closing Balance of Total Debtors Account
2. Closing Balance of Total Creditors Account
3. Closing Balance of Bills Receivable Account
4. Closing Balance of Bills Payable Account

Dr. **Total Debtors Account** Cr.

	Rs		*Rs*
To Balance b/d	39,000	By Bank	2,90,000
To Sales	4,07,000	By Discounts	2,000
		By Bills Receivable	1,09,000
		By Balance c/d (Balancing figure)	45,000
	4,46,000		4,46,000

Dr. **Total Creditors Account** Cr.

	Rs		*Rs*
To Bank	1,47,000	By Balance b/d	36,000
To Bills Payable	1,50,000	By Purchases	3,00,000
To Discounts	1,000		
To Balance c/d (Balancing figure)	38,000		
	3,36,000		3,36,000

Dr. **Bills Receivable Account** Cr.

	Rs		*Rs*
To Balance b/d	25,000	By Bank	1,00,000
To Total Debtors	1,09,000	By Balance c/d (Balancing figure)	34,000
	1,34,000		1,34,000

Dr. **Bills Payable Account** Cr.

	Rs		*Rs*
To Bank	1,43,000	By Balance b/d	16,000
To Balance c/d (Balancing figure)	23,000	By Creditors	1,50,000
	1,66,000		1,66,000

ILLUSTRATION 12.24

Mr Krishna, a retail trader, did not keep complete record of his transactions as per Double Entry System. But he is able to provide the following information from which you are required to prepare Trading and Profit and Loss Account for the year ended 30th September 2004 and a Balance Sheet as at that date.

All cash received during the year was deposited into Bank Account and all payments were made by cheques. The transactions were summarised as under:

	Rs
Bank Balance as on 1st October 2003	524
Cash Sales Proceeds	33,312
Paid for new Machine	2,000
Miscellaneous Expenses	3,252
Wages paid	5,334
Loan from Canara Bank	2,800
Amount drawn for personal use	4,160
Rent and Rates paid	1,800
Received from customers on account	14,324
Amount paid to Trade Creditors	32,032

The assets, liabilities, claims and commitments as at the beginning and end of the period were stated to be as follows:

	1st Oct. 2003	30th Sept. 2004
	Rs	Rs
Machines	9,000	10,100
Sundry Debtors	3,256	3,720
Outstanding Expenses	240	300
Stock in Hand	4,320	4,930
Trade Creditors	1,720	1,848
Rent Owing	–	500

Upon scrutiny of book debts it was found that Rs 840 were unrealisable. Discounts received from Creditors and allowed to Debtors, on cash transactions amounted to Rs 1,308 and 630 respectively. *(B.Com., Delhi)*

SOLUTION

Missing figures are:

1. Closing Balance of Bank Account
2. Credit Sales
3. Credit Purchases
4. Capital at the beginning

Dr. **Trading and Profit and Loss Account** Cr.

for the year ended 30th Sept. 2004

		Rs			*Rs*
To Opening stock		4,320	By Sales: Cash	33,312	
To Purhases		33,468	Credit	15,418	48,730
To Wages		5,334	By Stock		4,930
To Gross Profit c/d		10,538			
		53,660			53,660
To Miscellaneous Expenses	3,252		By Gross Profit b/d		10.538
Less: Paid to last year	240		By Discounts		1,308
	3,012				
Add: Outstanding	300	3,312			

		Rs		Rs
To Rent & Rates	1,800			
Add: Outstanding	500	2,300		
To Discount		630		
To Bad Debts		840		
To Depreciation on Machine		900		
To Net Profit		3,864		
		11,846		11,846

Balance Sheet as on 30th Sept. 2004

Liabilities		*Rs*	*Assets*		*Rs*
Creditors		1,848	Bank		2,382
Expenses Outstanding		300	Debtors	3,720	
Rent Outstanding		500	Less: Bad Debts	840	2,880
Canara Bank Loan		2,800	Stock		4,930
Capital:	15,140		Machine:	9,000	
Add: Net Profit	3,864		Add: Purchases	2,000	
	19,004			11,000	
Less: Drawings	4,160	14,844	Less: Depreciation	900	10,100
		20,292			20,292

Working Note:

Dr. **Bank Account** Cr.

	Rs		*Rs*
To Balance b/d	524	By Machine	2,000
To Canara Bank (Loan)	2,800	By Miscellaneous Expenses	3,252
To Cash (Rs 33,312 + 14,324)	47,636	By Wages	5,334
		By Drawings	4,160
		By Rent and Rates	1,800
		By Creditors	32,032
		By Balance c/d (Balancing figure)	2,382
	50,960		50,960

Dr. **Total Debtors Account** Cr.

	Rs		*Rs*
To Balance b/d	3,256	By Bad Debts	840
To Sales (Balancing figure)	15,418	By Discounts	630
		By Cash	14,324
		By Balance c/d (Rs 3,720 – 840)	2,880
	18,674		18,674

Note: It is presumed that the bad debts amounting to Rs 840 are to written off. Thus the closing balance must be Rs 3,720 – 840 = 2,880.

Dr. **Total Creditors Account** Cr.

	Rs		*Rs*
To Discount	1,308	By Balance b/d	1,720
To Bank	32,032	By Purchases (Balancing figure)	33,468
To Balance c/d	1,848		
	35,188		35,188

Statement of Affairs as on 1st Oct. 2003

Liabilities	*Rs*	*Assets*	*Rs*
Expenses Outstanding	240	Machine	9,000
Creditors	1,720	Debtors	3,256
Capital (Balancing figure)	15,140	Stock	4,320
		Bank	524
	17,100		17,100

ILLUSTRATION 12.25

Mr Marcar does not maintain proper books of account or Bank Account. From the following information, prepare Trading and Profit and Loss Account for the year ended 31st December 2004 and a Balance Sheet as on that date:

Assets and Liabilities:	On 31.12.2003	31.12.2004
	Rs	Rs
Debtors	9,000	12,500
Stock	4,900	6,600
Furniture	500	750
Creditors	3,000	2,250

Analysis of other transactions are:

	Rs
Cash collected from Debtors	30,400
Cash paid to Creditors	22,000
Salaries	6,000
Rent	750
Office expenses	900
Drawings	1,500
Fresh Capital introduced	1,000
Cash Sales	750
Cash Purchases	2,500
Discount received	350
Discount allowed	150
Returns Inward	500
Returns Outward	400
Bad Debts	100

He had Rs 2,500 cash at the beginning of the year. (*ICWA*)

SOLUTION

Trading and Profit and Loss Account
for the year ended 31st Dec. 2004

Dr. Cr.

		Rs			*Rs*
To Stock		4,900	By Sales		
To Purchases:			Cash	750	
Cash	2,500		Credit	34,650	
Credit	22,000			35,400	
	24,500			500	34,900
Less: Returns	400	24,100	By Stock		6,600
To Gross Profit		12,500			
		41,500			41,500
To Salaries		6,000	By Gross Profit		12,500

To Rent	750	By Discount Received	350
To Office Rent	900		
To Discount Allowed	150		
To Bad Debts	100		
To Net Profit	4,950		
	12,850		12,850

Balance Sheet as on 31st December 2004

Liabilities		*Rs*	*Assets*	*Rs*
Sundry Creditors		2,250	Cash	1,000
Creditors for Furniture		250	Debtors	12,500
Capital (1.1.2004)	13,900		Stock	6,600
Add: Additional Capital	1,000		Furniture	750
Add: Net Profit	4,950			
	19,850			
Less: Drawings	1,500	18,350		
		20,850		20,850

Workings:

Dr. **Total Debtors Account** Cr.

	Rs		*Rs*
To Balance b/d	9,000	By Cash	30,400
To Sales (Balancing figure)	34,650	By Discount Allowed	150
		By Returns Inward	500
		By Bad Debts	100
		By Balance c/d	12,500
	43,650		43,650

Dr. **Total Creditors Account** Cr.

	Rs		*Rs*
To Cash	22,000	By Balance b/d	3,000
To Discount received	350	By Purchases (Balancing figure)	22,000
To Returns Outward	400		
To Balance c/d	2,250		
	25,000		25,000

Statement of Affairs as on 31st January 2004

Liabilities	*Rs*	*Assets*	*Rs*
Creditors	3,000	Cash	2,500
Capital (Balancing figure)	13,900	Debtors	9,000
		Stock	4,900
		Furniture	500
	16,900		16,900

Cash Account

Dr.	Rs		Cr. Rs
To Balance b/d	2,500	By Sundry Creditors	22,000
To Sundry Debtors	30,400	By Salaries	6,000
To Capital	1,000	By Rent	750
To Sales	750	By Office Expenses	900
		By Drawings	1,500
		By Purchases	2,500
		By Balance c/d (Balancing figure)	1,000
	34,650		34,650

Note: Since, the Furniture Account shows Rs 500 on 31.12.2003 and shows Rs 750 on 31.12.2004, it means that there was a purchase of furniture for Rs 250 during the period. It did not appear in the cash transactions. Therefore, Creditors for furniture for Rs 250 is outstanding.

ILLUSTRATION 12.26

Prem is a small trader. He maintains no books but only an account with a bank in which all takings are lodged and in which all payments for business purchase are passed through:

You are required to ascertain his trading result for the year ended 31st March 2004 and Balance Sheet as on that date from the following information:

1. The bank statement shows deposits during the year of Rs 12,020 and withdrawals of Rs 11,850.
2. The assets and liabilities on 31st March 2004 were:

Stock	1,100
Book Debts	1,150
Bank Balance	320
Furniture	2,000
Trade Creditors	400

3. In the absence of reliable information, Estimates are supplied on the following matters:

(*a*) The Stock and Book Debts have each increased by Rs 100 during the year. There was no purchase or sale of furniture during the year.

(*b*) Trade Creditors were Rs 200 on 1st April 2003.

(*c*) During the year, the personal expenses amounted to Rs 800 and business expenses Rs 700.

(*B.Com. (Hons.) Calcutta*)

Trading and Profit and Loss Account for the year ended 31st March 2004

	Rs		Rs
To Stock (opening)	1,000	By Sales	(A)13,620
To Purchases	12,050	By Stock (closing)	1,100
To Gross Profit	1,670		
	14,720		14,720
To Business Expenses	700	By Gross Profit	1,670
To Net Profit	970		
	1,670		1,670

Balance Sheet as on 31st March 2004

		Rs		Rs
Capital	4,000		Furniture	2,000
Add: Net Profit	970		Stock	1,100
	4,970		Book Debts	1,150

Less: Drawings	800	4,170	Bank	320
Sundry Creditors		400		
		4,570		4,570

Workings:

Sundry Debtors Account

	Rs		Rs
To Balance b/d (Rs 1150 – Rs 100)	1,050	By Bank (collection)	(A)13,520
To Sales (Balancing figure)	13,620	By Balance c/d	1,150
	14,670		14,670

(A) Total Collection = Rs 12,020 + 800 + 700 = Rs 13,520

Sundry Creditors Account

	Rs		Rs
To Bank-payment	11,850	By Balance b/d	200
To Balance c/d	400	By Purchase (Balancing figure)	12,050
	12,250		12,250

Balance Sheet as on 31st March 2003

	Rs		Rs
Creditors	200	Furniture	2,000
Capital (Balancing figure)	4,000	Sundry Debtors	1,050
		Stock	1,000
		Bank @	150
	4,200		4,200

@	Amount deposited during the year	Rs 12,020
	Less: Withdrawal	Rs 11,850
		170
	But actual balance	320
	Opening Balance	150

Illustration 12.27

Mr. Srinivas did not maintain his books of accounts properly. From the following data supplied to you, prepare final accounts for the year ended 31-12-2006:

	Rs.
Opening stock	10,000
Creditors on 1-1-2006	4,000
Cash in hand 1-1-2006	6,000
Furniture on 1-1-2006	2,000
Salaries	6,800
Rent	2,400
Other expenses	4,800
Cash sales	8,000
Credit sales	80,000
Cash received from debtors	64,000
Cash paid to creditors	36,000
Cash purchases	4,000
Credit purchases	60,000

Closing stock	8,000
Debtors on 31-12-2006	24,000
Debtors on 1-1-2006	10,000
Drawings	10,000
Discount allowed to debtors	2,000

(B.Com., Bangalore, Agra, Madras)

Solution.

TRADING AND PROFIT AND LOSS ACCOUNT OF SRINIVAS
for the year ended 31st Decemeber, 2006

Cr.		Rs			Cr. Rs
To Stock, 1-1-2006		10,000	By Sales:		
To Purchases:			Cash	8,000	
Cash	4,000		Credit	80,000	
Credit	60,000	64,000			88,000
To Gross Profit c/d		22,000	By Stock, 31-12-2006		8,000
		96,000			96,000
To Salaries		6,800	By Gross profit b/d		22,000
To Rent		2,400			
To Other expenses		4,800			
To Discount allowed		2,000			
To Net profit		6,000			
		22,000			22,000

BALANCE SHEET OF SRINIVAS
as at 31st December, 2006

		Rs		Rs
Creditors		28,000	Cash	14,000
Capital	24,000		Debtors	24,000
Less: Drawings	10,000		Stock	8,000
	14,000		Furniture	2,000
Add: Net profit	6,000	20,000		
		48,000		48,000

Workings:

CASH ACCOUNT

Dr.	Rs		Cr. Rs
To Balance b/d	6,000	By Salaries	6,800
To Sales	8,000	By Rent	2,400
To Debtors	64,000	By Other expenses	4,800
		By Creditors	36,000
		By Purchases	4,000
		By Drawings	10,000
		By Balance c/d 31-12-2006 (balancing figure)	14,000
	78,000		78,000
To Balance b/d	14,000		

Dr. TOTAL CREDITORS' ACCOUNT Cr.

	Rs		Rs
To Cash	36,000	By Balance b/d	4,000
To Balance c/d—Balancing figure	28,000	By Credit purchases	60,000
	64,000		64,000
		By Balancing b/d	28,000

BALANCE SHEET OF SRINIVAS
as at 31st Dec. 2005

	Rs		Rs
Creditors	4,000	Cash	6,000
Capital—Balancing figure	24,000	Debtors	10,000
		Stock	10,000
		Furniture	2,000
	28,000		28,000

Illustration 12.28.

A trader keeps his books of account under single entry system. On 31st March, 2005, his statement of affairs stood as follows:

Liabilities	Rs	*Assets*	Rs
Trade Creditors	5,80,000	Furniture, Fixtures and Fittings	1,00,000
Bills Payable	1,25,000	Stock	6,10,000
Outstanding expenses	45,000	Trade Debtors	1,48,000
Capital Account	2,50,000	Bills Receivable	60,000
		Unexpired Insurance	2,000
		Cash in hand and at Bank	80,000
	10,00,000		10,00,000

The following was the summary of Cash Book for the year ended 31st March, 2006:

Receipts	Rs	*Payments*	Rs
Cash in hand and at Bank on		Payments to Trade Creditors	75,07,000
1st April, 2005	80,000	Payments for Bills Payable	8,15,000
Cash Sales	73,80,000	Sundry expenses paid	6,20,700
Receipts from Trade Debtors	15,10,000	Drawings	2,40,000
Receipts for Bills Receivable	3,40,000	Cash in hand and at Bank on	
		31st March, 2006	1,27,300
	93,10,000		93,10,000

Discount allowed to trade debtors and received from trade creditors amounted to Rs. 36,000 and Rs. 28,000 respectively. Bill endorsed amounted to Rs. 15,000. Annual Fire Insurance Premium of Rs. 6,000 was paid every year on 1st August for the renewal of the policy. Furniture, Fixtures and Fittings were subject to depreciation @ 15% per annum on diminishing balances method.

You are also informed about the following balances as on 31st March 2006.

	Rs.
Stock	6,50,000
Trade Debtors	1,52,000
Bills Receivable	75,000
Bills Payable	1,40,000
Outstanding expenses	5,000

The trader maintains a steady gross profit ratio of 10% on sales. Prepare Trading and Profit and Loss Account for the year ended 31st March, 2006 and Balance Sheet as at that date.

(*C.A. Inter*) (*B.Com (Hons) Kolkata*)

Solution.

TRADING AND PROFIT AND LOSS ACCOUNT
for the year ended 31st March, 2006

Dr.		Rs			Cr. Rs
To Stock, 1-4-2005		6,10,000	By Sales:		
To Purchases (balancing figure)		84,10,000	Cash	73,80,000	
To Gross Profit:			Credit	19,20,000	
10% on sales		9,30,000			93,00,000
			By Stock, 31st March, 2006		6,50,000
		99,50,000			99,50,000
To Sundry expenses:			By Gross profit b/d		9,30,000
Amount paid	6,20,700		Discount received		28,000
Less: Insurance prem.	6,000				
	6,14,700				
Less: Last years' O/s	45,000				
	5,69,700				
Add: O/s	5,000				
		5,74,700			
To Insurance	6,000				
Add: Prepaid last year	2,000				
	8,000				
Less: Prepaid	2,000	6,000			
To Discount allowed		36,000			
To Depreciation on Furniture @ 15%		15,000			
To Net Profit		3,26,300			
		9,58,000			9,58,000

BALANCE SHEET
as at 31st March, 2006

		Rs			Rs
Sundry Creditors		6,10,000	Cash in hand and at Bank		1,27,300
Bills Payable		1,40,000	Sundry Debtors		1,52,000
Outstanding expenses		5,000	Bills Receivable		75,000
Capital	2,50,000		Stock		6,50,000
Less: Drawings	2,40,000		Prepaid insurance		2,000
	10,000		Furniture	1,00,000	
Net Profit	3,26,300	3,36,300	*Less*: Depreciation	15,000	85,000
		10,91,300			10,91,300

Workings:

Ascertainment of credit sales:

TOTAL DEBTORS' ACCOUNT

Dr.	Rs		Cr. Rs
To Balance b/d 1-4-2005	1,48,000	By Cash received	15,10,000
To Credit sales (balancing figure)	19,20,000	By Discount allowed	36,000
		By Bills Receivable	3,70,000
		By Balance c/d, 31st March, 2006	1,52,000
	20,68,000		20,68,000
To Balance b/d	1,52,000		

Ascertainment of Bills drawn:

Dr. BILLS RECEIVABLE ACCOUNT *Cr.*

	Rs		*Rs*
To Balance b/d, 1st April 2005	60,000	By Cash	3,40,000
To Debtors (bills drawn, balancing figure)	3,70,000	By Creditors (bills endorsed)	15,000
		By Balance c/d, 31st March, 2006	75,000
	4,30,000		4,30,000
To Balance b/d	75,000		

Ascertainment of closing creditors:

Dr. TOTAL CREDITORS' ACCOUNT *Cr.*

	Rs		*Rs*
To Cash	75,07,000	By Balance b/d, 1st April, 2005	5,80,000
To Bills Receivable	15,000	By Purchases (balancing figure in trading account)	84,10,000
To Bills Payable	8,30,000		
To Discount	28,000		
To Balance c/d, 31st March, 2006 (balancing figure)	6,10,000		
	89,90,000		89,90,000
		By Balance b/d	6,10,000

Ascertainment of Bills Accepted:

Dr. BILLS PAYABLE ACCOUNT *Cr.*

	Rs		*Rs*
To Cash	8,15,000	By Balance b/d, 1st Apri, 2005	1,25,000
To Balance c/d, 31st March, 2006	1,40,000	By Creditors (bills accepted, balancing figure)	8,30,000
	9,55,000		9,55,000
		By Balance b/d	1,40,000

Illustration 12.29

From the information supplied below by Vinay Ventures, prepare Profit and Loss Account for the year ended 31-12-2006 and a Balance Sheet as on that date:

	1-1-2006	31-12-2006
	Rs.	Rs.
Sundry Fixed Assets	1,80,000	2,00,000
Stock-in-hand	1,40,000	1,90,000
Cash in hand	82,000	48,000
Cash at Bank	22,000	80,000
Sundry Debtors	?	2,60,000
Sundry Creditors	1,20,000	98,000
Outstanding expenses	10,000	6,000

During the year, the following transactions took place:

	Rs.
(1) Collection from Debtors and discount allowed to them	24,50,000
(2) Return inward	60,000

(3)	Bad debts	10,000
(4)	Sales (cash and credit)	30,00,000
(5)	Return outward	30,000
(6)	Paid to suppliers by cheque	23,62,000
(7)	Collection from debtors and deposited into bank	24,30,000
(8)	Cash purchases	1,00,000
(9)	Salaries and wages paid by cheque	1,80,000
(10)	Miscellaneous cash expenses	50,000
(11)	Drawings in cash	94,000
(12)	Assets purchased by cheque	20,000
(13)	Cash withdrawals from bank	2,10,000
(14)	Cash sales deposited into bank	?
(15)	Discount received	40,000

(*I.C.W.A. Inter*)

Solution.

Vinay Ventures
PROFIT AND LOSS ACCOUNT
for the period ending 31-12-2006

		Rs			*Rs*
To Stock, 1-1-2006		1,40,000	By Sales:		
To Purchases:			Cash sales	4,00,000	
Cash	1,00,000		Credit sales	26,00,000	
Credit	24,10,000			30,00,000	
	25,10,000		*Less*: Returns	60,000	
Less: Returns	30,000				29,40,000
		24,80,000	By Stock, 31-12-2006		1,90,000
To Salaries and Wages		1,80,000	By Discount received		40,000
To Misc. expenses	50,000				
Less: O/s, 2005	10,000				
	40,000				
Add: O/s, 2006	6,000				
		46,000			
To Discount allowed		20,000			
To Bank debts		10,000			
To Net Profit		2,94,000			
		31,70,000			31,70,000

BALANCE SHEET OF VINAY VENTURES
as at 31-12-2006

		Rs			*Rs*
Sundry Creditors		98,000	Cash		48,000
Outstanding expenses		6,000	Bank		80,000
Capital	14,74,000		Stock		1,90,000
Less: Drawings	94,000		Debtors		2,60,000
	3,80,000		Fixed Assets	1,80,000	
Add: Net profit	2,94,000		Additions	20,000	
		6,74,000			2,00,000
		7,78,000			7,78,000

Workings:

BALANCE SHEET OF VINAY VENTURES
as at 31-12-2005

	Rs		Rs
Sundry Creditors	1,20,000	Cash	82,000
Outstanding expenses	10,000	Bank	22,000
Capital (balancing figure)	4,74,000	Stock	1,40,000
		Debtors	1,80,000
		Fixed Assets	1,80,000
	6,04,000		6,04,000

CASH BOOK

Receipts	*Cash Rs.*	*Bank Rs.*	*Payments*	*Cash Rs.*	*Bank Rs.*
To Balance b/d	82,000	22,000	By Suppliers		23,62,000
To Debtors		24,30,000	By Purchases	1,00,000	
To Bank	2,10,000		By Salaries & Wages		1,80,000
To Sales deposited into bank (balancing figure)		4,00,000	By Misc. expenses	50,000	
			By Drawings	94,000	
			By Assets		20,000
			By Cash		2,10,000
			By Balance c/d	48,000	80,000
	2,92,000	28,52,000		2,92,000	28,52,000
To Balance b/d	48,000	80,000			

TOTAL DEBTORS' ACCOUNT

	Rs		Rs
To Balance b/d (balancing figure)	1,80,000	By Cash collection	24,30,000
To Credit sales	26,00,000	By Return inward	60,000
		By Discount	20,000
		By Bad debt	10,000
		By Balance c/d	2,60,000
	27,80,000		27,80,000

TOTAL CREDITORS' ACCOUNT

	Rs		Rs
To Payments	23,62,000	By Balance b/d	1,20,000
To Discount	40,000	By Credit Purchases	24,10,000
To Returns	30,000	(Balancing figure)	
To Balance c/d	98,000		
	25,30,000		25,30,000

ILLUSTRATION 12.30

Mr. Kumar desires you to prepare accounts for the year ended 31st March 2004. No books have been kept, but the following facts are ascertained:

1. The Bank pass book showed lodgements during the year Rs 60,100 and withdrawals of Rs 59,250.
2. Rs 5,000 had been placed on deposit account on 31st Dec. 2002 at 8% p.a. and withdrawn with interest on 30th June 2003.
3. Rs 10,000 3½% National Defence Certificate (Interest due dates, 31st March and 30th Sept. each year) had been purchased on 1st April 2003. Interest was collected on due date.
4. The foregoing transactions and all payments for business purchases passed through the bank account. The takings were banked after meeting business expenses Rs 3,500 and personal expenses Rs 4,000.
5. The assets and liabilities on 31st March 2004 were:

Stock	5,500
Book Debts	5,750
Bank Balance	1,600
Freehold Cottage	10,000
Trade Creditors	2,000

6. On 1st April 2003, the stock and book debts were Rs 5,000 and Rs 5,250 respectively and creditors Rs 1,000.

From the above information, Kumar requests you to help him to prepare his Profit and Loss Account for the year ended 31st March 2004 and Balance Sheet as on that date. (*B.Com., Bombay, Madras*)

Trading and Profit and Loss Account
for the year ended 31st March 2004

	Rs		*Rs*
To Stock	5,000	By Sales	62,550
To Purchases	50,250	By Closing Stock	5,500
To Gross Profit	12,800		
	68,050		68,050
To Business Expenses	3,500	By Gross Profit	12,800
To Net Profit	9,750	By Interest (Rs 350 + Rs 100)	450
	13,250		13,250

Balance Sheet as on 31st March 2004

		Rs		*Rs*
Capital (Opening	25,100		3½% N.D. certificate	10,000
Add: Net Profit	9,750		Stock	5,500
	34,850		Debtors	5,750
Less: Drawings	4,000	30,850	Freehold Cottage	10,000
Creditors		2,000	Bank	1,600
		32,850		32,850

Workings:

Balance Sheet as on 31st March 2003

	Rs		*Rs*
Capital (Balancing figure)	25,100	3½% N.D. certificate	10,000
Creditors	1,000	Stock	5,000
		Book Debts	5,250
		Deposit Account	5,000
		Interest O/S (3 months)	100
		Cash at Bank	750
	26,100		26,100

Bank Account

	Rs		Rs
To Balance b/d (Balancing figure)	750	By Cash (Withdrawals)	59,250
To Cash (Deposits)	60,100	By Balance c/d	1,600
	60,850		60,850

Sundry Debtors A/c

	Rs		Rs
To Balance b/d	5,250	By Bank (Collection)	(*)62,050
To Sales (Credit) (Balancing figure)	62,550	By Balance c/d	5,750
	67,800		67,800

(*)			
	Amount Collected from Debtors		Rs 60,100
	Less: Amount from deposit account alongwith interest:		
	Rs 5,000 + $\left(5000 \times \frac{8}{100} \times \frac{6}{12}\right)$ =		5,200
			54,900
	Less: Interest on N.D. certificate (Rs 10,000 × 3.5%)		350
			54,550
	Add: Business Expenses	3,500	
	Drawings	4,000	7,500
			62,050

Sundry Creditors A/c

	Rs		Rs
To Bank Payment (Rs 59,250 – Rs 10,000)	49,250	By Balance b/d	1,000
To Balance c/d	2,000	By Purchase (Balancing figure)	50,250
	51,250		51,250

ILLUSTRATION 12.31

The following balances are available from the books of a small trader, as on 31st December 2003 and 2004:

	31st December 2003	31st December 2004
Building	60,000	60,000
Equipments	1,20,000	1,34,000
Furniture	10,000	10,000
Debtors	?	48,000
Creditors	32,000	?
Stock	?	34,000
Bank Loan	20,000	16,000
Cash	32,000	22,000

The transactions during the year ended 31st Dec. 2004 were the following:

	Rs
Collection from Debtors	1,86,000
Payment to Creditors	1,22,000
Cash Purchases	32,000
Expenses	20,000

Sale of Equipment (Book value Rs 10,000)	6,000
Drawings	20,000

Cash sales amounted to 10% of total sales.

Credit sales amounted to Rs 1,80,000.

Credit purchases were 80% of total purchases.

He sells goods at cost plus 33 1/3%.

His suppliers allowed him discount of Rs 2,000.

Equipments and Furniture to be depreciated by 10% p.a. and building by 2%.

You are required to prepare the Trading and Profit and Loss Account of the trader for the year ended 31st December 2004 and a Balance Sheet as on that date. *(B.Com. (Hons.) Calcutta)*

Trading and Profit and Loss Account
for the year ended 31st Dec. 2004

		Rs		Rs
To Stock (Opening)	(1)	24,000	By Sales	2,00,000
To Purchases	(2)	1,60,000	By Stock (Closing)	34,000
To Gross Profit		50,000		
		2,34,000		2,34,000
To Loss on sale of equipment		4,000	By Gross Profit	50,000
(Rs 10,000 – Rs 6,000)			By Discount Received	2,000
To Depreciation on:				
Building		1,200		
Furniture		1,000		
Equipment	(3)	12,200		
To Expenses		20,000		
To Net Profit		13,600		
		52,000		52,000

Balance Sheet as on 31st Dec. 2004

		Rs		Rs
Creditors	(4)	36,000	Building 60,000 – 1,200	58,800
Bank Loan		16,000	Equipment 1,34,000 – 12,200	1,21,800
Capital	(5) Rs 2,48,000		Furniture 10,000 – 1,000	9,000
Add: Profit	13,600		Debtors	48,000
	2,61,600		Stock	34,000
Less: Drawings	20,000	2,41,600	Cash	22,000
		2,93,600		2,93,600

Workings:–

(1) Sales and Opening Stock:

Cash Sales = 10% of Total Sales.

So, Credit Sales = 90% of Total Sales

$$\text{Total Sales} = \frac{1,80,000}{90} \times 100 = \text{Rs } 2,00,000$$

Cash Sales = 10% of Rs 2,00,000 = Rs 20,000

Profit is $\frac{1}{4}$ of sales = Rs 50,000

Cost of Goods Sold = Opening Stock + Purchases – Closing Stock

Rs 1,50,000 = X + (Rs 1,28,000 + 32,000) – Rs 34,000

Rs 1,50,000 = X + Rs 1,60,000 – Rs 34,000

Rs 1,50,000 = X + Rs 1,26,000

∴ X = Rs 24,000 (Opening Stock)

(2) Cash purchases given Rs 32,000, which is 20%

$$\therefore \text{ Total purchases} = \frac{32,000}{20} \times 100 = \text{Rs } 1,60,000$$

Credit purchase = 80% of Rs 1,60,000 = Rs 1,28,000

(3) **Equipment Account**

	Rs		Rs
To Balance b/d	1,20,000	By Sales	10,000
To Cash (Purchase)	24,000	By Balance c/d	1,34,000
	1,44,000		1,44,000

Depreciation:

10% on Rs 1,10,000	11,000
10% on Rs 24,000 for half year	1,200
	12,200

(4) **Creditors Account**

	Rs		Rs
To Cash	1,22,000	By Balance b/d	32,000
To Discount	2,000	By Purchase A/c (2)	1,28,000
To Balance c/d (Balancing figure)	36,000		
	1,60,000		1,60,000

(5) **Balance Sheet as on 31st Dec. 2003**

	Rs			Rs
Bank Loan	20,000	Building		60,000
Creditors	32,000	Equipments		1,20,000
Capital (Balancing figure)	2,48,000	Furniture		10,000
		Debtor	(6)	54,000
		Stock	(1)	24,000
		Cash		32,000
	3,00,000			3,00,000

(6) **Debtors Account**

	Rs		Rs
To Balance b/d (Balancing figure)	54,000	By Cash	1,86,000
To Sales	1,80,000	By Balance c/d	48,000
	2,34,000		2,34,000

Cash Account

	Rs		Rs
To Balance b/d	32,000	By Creditors A/c	1,22,000
To Debtors A/c	1,86,000	By Purchase A/c	32,000
To Equipment (Sale)	6,000	By Expenses	20,000
To Sales A/c	20,000	By Drawings	20,000
		By Loan (paid)	4,000
		By Equipment (purchase)	24,000
		By Balance c/d	22,000
	2,44,000		2,44,000

ILLUSTRATION 12.32

Mr. Manohar submits you the following figures relating to his business for the year ended 31st December, 2004. You are required to prepare a Trading and Profit and Loss Account for the year ended 31st December, 2004 and a Balance Sheet as on that date. Any difference in Cash Book balance is to be taken as his personal drawings.

	Rs
Deposits into Bank	26,070
Personal Dividend deposited into business cash	600
Personal Payments out of Bank	2,250
Payments to Trade Creditors	23,850
Withdrawn from Bank	23,250
Received from Debtors	35,100
Paid for wages	3,900
Paid for delivery charges	1,800
Paid for salaries	600
Paid for rent and rates	405
Paid for general charges	750
Interest credited by Bank	30

The Assets and Liabilities were as follows:

	1.1.2004	31.12.2004
	Rs	Rs
Stock	1,800	2,250
Bank Balances	2,400	3,000
Cash in hand	90	60
Trade Debtors	2,250	3,150
Trade Creditors	3,600	4,200

(*ICWA*)

SOLUTION

Trading and Profit and Loss Account for the year ended 31st Dec. 2004

Dr. Cr.

	Rs		Rs
To Stock (1.1.2004)	1,800	By Sales	36,000
To Purchases	24,450	By Stock (31.12.2004)	2,250
To Wages	3,900		
To Gross Profit	8,100		
	38,250		38,250
To Salary	600	By Gross Profit	8,100
To Rent and Rates	405	By Bank Interest	30
To General Charges	750		
To Delivery Charges	1,800		
To Net Profit	4,575		
	8,130		8,130

Balance Sheet as on 31st December 2004

Liabilities		*Rs*	*Assets*	*Rs*
Trade Creditors		4,200	Cash in Hand	60
Capital (1.1.2004)	2,940		Cash at Bank	3,000
Add: Additional Capital	600		Trade Debtors	3,150
Add: Net Profit	4,575		Stock	2,250
	8,115			
Less: Drawings	3,855	4,260		
		8,460		8,460

ILLUSTRATION 12.33

Doll and Dolly are in partnership sharing profits and losses equally. They keep their books by Single Entry System. No ready figures are available for total sales but they maintain a steady gross profit @ 25% on sales.

An abstract of their cash transactions for the year 30th June 2004 is given below:

Receipts	*Rs*	*Payments*	*Rs*
Cash in Hand	10,800	Salaries	22,000
Receipts from Customers	2,70,000	Rent	4,400
Cash Sales	32,000	Advertising	1,800
		Printing	1,600
		General Expenses	19,100
		Payment to Trade Creditors	2,24,000
		Doll's Drawings	4,000
		Cash in Hand	35,900
	3,12,800		3,12,800

The following balances are available from their books as on 30th June 2004:

	as on 30.6.2003	as on 30.6.2004
	Rs	Rs
Stock-in-Trade	44,000	50,000
Sundry Debtors	?	70,000
Sundry Creditors	46,800	37,000
Furniture	6,000	?

Other information:

(*a*) Discount allowed Rs 2,800;

(*b*) Discount earned Rs 2,400;

(*c*) Outstanding printing Rs 500;

(*d*) Capital of Doll as on 30th June 2003 was Rs 4,000 more than Capital of Dolly.

(*e*) Provide depreciation on Furniture @ 10% p.a.

From the above, prepare:

(*i*) The Trading and Profit and Loss Account for the year ended on 30th June 2004.

(*ii*) The Balance Sheet as on that date. (*ICWA*)

SOLUTION

Trading and Profit and Loss Account for the year ended 30th June 2004

Dr.		Rs	Cr.		Rs
To Opening Stock		44,000	By Sales		
To Purchases (1)		2,16,600	Cash	32,000	
To Gross Profit c/d		70,200	Credit (2)	2,48,800	2,80,800
			By Closing Stock		50,000
		3,30,800			3,30,800
To Salaries		22,000	By Gross Profit b/d		70,200
To Rent		4,400	By Discount Received		2,400
To Advertising		1,800			
To Discount Allowed		2,800			
To General Expenses		19,100			
To Printing	1,600				
Add: Outstanding	500	2,100			
To Depreciation on Furniture @ 10% on Rs 6,000		600			
To Net Profit transferred to Capital Account:					
Doll	9,900				
Dolly	9,900	19,800			
		72,600			72,600

Balance Sheet As on 30th June 2004

Liabilities		*Rs*	*Assets*		*Rs*
Sundry Creditors		37,000	Cash in Hand		35,900
Outstanding Printing		500	Sundry Debtors		70,000
Capital Accounts:			Closing Stock		50,000
Doll	56,000		Furniture	6,000	
Add: Net Profit	9,900		Less: Depreciation	600	5,400
	65,900				
Less: Drawings	4,000	61,900			
Dolly	52,000				
Add: Net Profit	9,900	61,900			
		1,61,300			1,61,300

1. Calculation of Credit Purchases:

Total Creditors Account

Dr.	*Rs*	Cr.	*Rs*
To Cash	2,24,000	By Balance b/d	46,800
To Discount Received	2,400	By Credit Purchases	
To Balance c/d	37,000	(Balancing Figure)	2,16,600
	2,63,400		2,63,400

2. Calculation of Credit Sales:

Dr. **Total Debtors Account** Cr.

	Rs		Rs
To Balance b/d	94,000	By Cash	2,70,000
To Credit Sales		By Discount Allowed	2,800
(Balancing Figure)	2,48,800	By Balance b/d	70,000
	3,42,800		3,42,800

3. Calculation of Opening Capital:

Balance Sheet
as on 30th June 2003

Liabilities		Rs	*Assets*	Rs
Sundry Creditors		46,800	Cash	10,800
Capital*			Debtors	94,000
(Balancing Figure)			Stock	44,000
Doll	56,000		Furniture	6,000
Dolly	52,000	1,08,000		
		1,54,800		1,54,800

* Capital of Doll and Dolly

	Rs
Total Capital	1,08,000
Less Difference	4,000
	1,04,000

Doll Capital = 1,04,000 × 1/2 = Rs 52,000 + Rs 4,000
= Rs 56,000

Dolly Capital = 1,04,000 × 1/2 = Rs 52,000

ILLUSTRATION 12.34

Ram kept his account books by Single Entry System. From the particulars given below, prepare Trading, Profit and Loss Account and a Balance Sheet for the year ended on 31st December 2004

(a)	Cash and Bank Transactions:	Rs
	Cash in Hand on 1st January	600
	Cash Purchases	27,000
	Cash Sales	28,000
	Cash Payments to Creditors	38,000
	Cash Received from Debtors	41,000
	Cheques issued to Creditors	27,000
	Cheques Received from Debtors	30,000
	Interest and Bank Charges	1,500
	Bills honoured by issued of cheques	17,000
	Bills Receivable discounted and banked	25,000
	Cash receipts of Bills Receivable	10,000
	Salaries	3,000
	Wages	1,200
	Rent	1,800
	Carriage	300
	Commission paid	100
	Discount for Bills discounted	600

General Expenses	700
Interest collected by the banker on investments	900
Bank Overdraft on 1st January	10,000
Investments (Bank)	2,000
Withdrew from Bank for personal use	1,500
Income Tax (Cash)	300

(*b*) Statement of Affairs

	Jan. 2004	Dec. 2004
	Rs	Rs
Bills Receivable	6,000	7,400
Bills Payable	2,000	1,000
Sundry Debtors	26,000	27,000
Sundry Creditors	15,000	13,000
Land and Buildings	50,000	49,000
Plant and Machinery	31,000	29,500
Furniture	4,000	3,500
Investments	17,000	19,000
Provision for Bad Debts	2,000	3,000
Stock on Hand	15,600	18,400

(*c*) Adjustments:

During the year an amount of Rs 700 written off as bad debts

Goods worth Rs 200 were distributed as free samples.

Outstanding Expenses were :

(*i*) Wages Rs 100

(*ii*) Salaries Rs 400

(*iii*) Rent Rs 150 (*M.Com., Kolkatta*)

Trading and Profit and Loss Account
for the year ended 31st December 2004

Dr. Cr.

		Rs			*Rs*
To Opening Stock		15,600	By Sales:		
To Purchases:			Cash	28,000	
Cash	27,000		Credit (4)	1,09,700	1,37,700
Credit (6)	79,000	1,06,000	By Samples		200
To Wages	1,200		By Closing Stock		18,400
Add: Outstanding	100	1,300			
To Carriage		300			
To Gross Profit c/d		33,100			
		1,56,300			1,56,300
To Salaries	3,000		By Gross Profit b/d		33,100
Add: Outstanding	400	3,400	By Interest on Investments		900
To Rent	1,800				
Add: Outstanding	150	1,950			
To Interest and Bank Charges		1,500			
To Discount for Bills Discounted		600			
To Commission		100			
To General Expenses		700			
To Bad Debts		700			
To Free Samples		200			

To Provision for Bad Debts:					
Required:	3,000				
Less: Existing:	2,000	1,000			
To Depreciation:					
Furniture	500				
Plant and Machinery	1,500				
Land and Building	1,000	3,000			
To Net Profit transferred to					
Capital Account		20,850			
		34,000			34,000

Balance Sheet
as on 31st December 2004

Liabilities		*Rs*	*Assets*		*Rs*
Sundry Creditors		13,000	Cash in Hand (1)		7,200
Bills Payable		1,000	Cash at Bank (2)		900
Outstanding Expenses:			Bills Receivable		7,400
Wages	100		Sundry Debtors	27,000	
Salaries	400		Less: Reserve	3,000	24,000
Rent	150	650	Closing Stock		18,400
Capital Accounts:			Investment		19,000
As on 1st Jan. 2004 (7)	1,21,200		Furniture	4,000	
Add: Capital Introduced	4,000		Less: Depreciation	500	3,500
	1,25,200		Plant and Machinery	31,000	
Add: Net Profit	20,850		Less: Depeciation	1,500	29,500
	1,46,050		Land and Building	50,000	
Less: Drawings	1,500		Less: Depreciation	1,000	49,000
	1,44,550				
Less: Income Tax	300	1,44,250			
		1,58,900			1,58,900

Working Notes:

1. Calculation of Closing Balance

Cash Account

Dr. Cr.

	Rs		*Rs*
To Balance b/d	600	By Purchases	27,000
To Sales	28,000	By Creditors	38,000
To Debtors	41,000	By Salaries	3,000
To Bills Receivable	10,000	By Wages	1,200
		By Rent	1,800
		By Carriage	300
		By Commission	100
		By General Expenses	700
		By Drawings (Income Tax)	300
		By Balance c/d (Balancing Figure)	7,200
	79,600		79,600

2. Calculation of Closing Balance

Bank Account

Dr.	Rs		Rs Cr.
To Debtors	30,000	By Balance b/d	10,000
To Bills Receivable	25,000	By Creditors	27,000
To Interest on Investment	900	By Bills Payable	17,000
To Capital (Additional)	4,000	By Interest and Bank charges	1,500
		By Investments	2,000
		By Drawings	1,500
		By Balance c/d (Balancing Figure)	900
	59,900		59,900

3. Calculation of Bills Receivable Received

Bills Receivable Account

Dr.	Rs		Rs Cr.
To Balance b/d	6,000	By Bank	25,000
To Debtors (Balancing Figure)	37,000	By Cash	10,000
		By Discount	600
		By Balance c/d	7,400
	43,000		43,000

4. Calculation of Credit Sales

Total Debtors Account

Dr.	Rs		Rs Cr.
To Balance b/d	26,000	By Cash	41,000
To Credit Sales (Balancing Figure)	1,09,700	By Bank	30,000
		By Bad Debts	700
		By Bills Receivable (3)	37,000
		By Balance c/d	27,000
	1,35,700		1,35,700

5. Calculation of Bills Payable Accepted

Bills Payable Account

Dr.	Rs		Rs Cr.
To Bank	17,000	By Balance b/d	2,000
To Balance c/d	1,000	By Creditors (Balancing Figure)	16,000
	18,000		18,000

6. Calculation of Credit Purchases

Total Creditors Account

Dr.	Rs		Rs Cr.
To Cash	38,000	By Balance b/d	15,000
To Bank	27,000	By Credit Purchases (Balancing Figure)	79,000
To Bills Payable (5)	16,000		
To Balance c/d	13,000		
	94,000		94,000

7. Calculation of Opening Capital

Balance Sheet

As on 1st January 2004

Liabilities	*Rs*	*Assets*		*Rs*
Sundry Creditors	15,000	Cash in Hand	Rs	600
Bills Payable	2,000	Debtors	26,000	
Bank Overdraft	10,000	Less: Reserve	2,000	24,000
Capital (Balancing Figure)	1,21,200	Bill Receivable		6,000
		Closing Stock		15,600
		Investments		17,000
		Furniture		4,000
		Plant and Machinery		31,000
		Land and Building		50,000
	1,48,200			1,48,200

ILLUSTRATION 12.35

Suresh runs a circulating library and his accounts are unsatisfactory. One Bank account has been used for both the business as well as his personal transactions. After looking into his records and questioning him you gather the following information:

(1) Payments for Magazines in the year ended 31.3.2004 9,700

(2) Payments of Delivery peon's wages for the year ended 31.3.2004 2,200

(3) Payments of other expenses for the year ended 31.3.2004 3,080

(4) Subscriptions collected 21,695

(5) He has taken Rs 500 per month in cash from the subscriptions collections to pay to his wife for their household and personal expenses, depositing the balance of the collections into the Bank.

(6) During the year bought a second hand scooter, not used for business, from a friend for Rs 4,000. However, as the friend owed him Rs 250 for subscription, the matter was settled by a cheque for the difference.

(7) As assurance policy on his life matured during the year and realised Rs 7,000.

(8) Suresh cashed a cheque for Rs 1,200 for a friend, which cheque was dishonoured. The friend is repaying by instalment, and owes Rs 500 on 31st March 2004.

(9) Other personal payments by cheque total Rs 2,350.

(10) Magazine subscription for the year amounting to Rs 400 had to be written off by Suresh as irrecoverable.

(11) The cash collected includes Rs 600 in respect of magazine subscriptions written off as irrecoverable in a previous year.

(12) Suresh runs the business from his flat for which a rent of Rs 90 per month is included in the payments for other expenses Rs 3,080. The living accommodation may be regarded as two-thirds of the whole.

(13) The following balances may be accepted as correct:

	31st March 2003	31st March 2004
	Rs	Rs
Cash in Hand	115	70
Bank Balance	4,720	5,880
Subscriptions Receivable (Debtors) Considered good	1,830	2,105
Creditors for purchase of Magazines	900	840
Stock of Magazines at cost	2,450	830

You are required to prepare:

(*i*) A Cash and Bank Summary Account for the year;

(*ii*) Suresh (Proprietor) Account for the year;

(*iii*) An Income and Expenditure Account for the Circulating Library for the year.

(*iv*) A Balance Sheet of the business as at 31st March 2004 (*C.A., B.Com., Madras*)

Solution:

Summary of Cash and Bank Transaction

Dr.	Cash	Bank		Cash	Bank Cr.
	Rs	Rs		Rs	Rs
To Balance b/d	115	4,720	By Sundry Creditors –		
To Sundry Debtors–Subscription	21,695	–	–Purchase of magazines	–	9,700
			By Wages	–	2,200
To Cash (C)	–	15,695	By Other Expenses	–	3,080
To Suresh–Insurance Policy	–	7,000	By Bank (C)	15,695	–
To Cash–Friend's Cheque	–	1,200	By Drawings	6,000	–
To Suresh	700	–	By Suresh–Car	–	3,750
To Bank (Balancing Figure) (C)	455	–	By Bank–Friend's Cheque	1,200	–
			By Suresh–Friend's Cheque dishonoured	–	1,200
			By Suresh	–	2,350
			By Cash (Balancing Figure) (C)		455
			By Balance c/d	70	5,880
	22,965	28,615		22,965	28,615

Suresh Capital Account

Dr.	Rs		Rs Cr.
To Cash Drawings	6,000	By Balance b/d (3)	8,215
To Bank–Car	3,750	By Bank–Insurance Policy	7,000
To income and Expenditure Account–Subscription adjusted towards payment of car	250	By Income and Expenditure Account–Excess of Income over Expenditure	6,400
To Bank–other personal payments	2,350	By Cash–Cash received from friend	700
To Income and Expenditure Account–2/3rd of Rent	720		
To Bank–Friend's Cheque Dishonoured	1,200		
To balance c/d	8,045		
	22,315		22,315

Income and Expenditure Account of Suresh
for the year ended 31st March 2004

Dr.		Rs			Rs Cr.
To Stock of Magazines		2,450	By Sales–Subscription(1)	21,770	
To Purchases (2)		9,640	Add: Subscription adjusted		
To Wages		2,200	towards payment of car	250	22,020
To Other Expenses	3,080		By Bad Debts Recovered	600	
Less: 2/3rd of Rent			Less: Bad Debts	400	200
Charge to Suresh	720	2,360	By Stock		830
To Net Profit transferred to Capital Account		6,400			
		23,050			23,050

N.B. Subscription collected included Rs. 600 in respect of earlier year.

Balance Sheet
As on 31st March 2004

Liabilities	*Rs*	*Assets*	*Rs*
Creditors	840	Cash	70
Capital Account*	8,045	Bank	5,880
		Subscription Outstanding	2,105
		Stock	830
	8,885		8,885

Working Notes:

Dr. **1. Total Debtors Account** Cr.

	Rs		*Rs*
To Balance b/d	1,830	By Cash	21,095
To Credit Sales (Balancing Figure)	21,770	By Bad Debts	400
		By Balance c/d	2,105
	23,600		23,600

Dr. **2. Total Creditors Account** Cr.

	Rs		*Rs*
To Bank	9,700	By Balance b/d	900
To Balance c/d	840	By Purchases (Balancing Figure)	9,640
	10,540		10,540

3. Balance Sheet of Suresh
as on 31st March 2003

Liabilities	*Rs*	*Assets*	*Rs*
Sundry Creditors	900	Cash	115
Capital (Balancing Figure)	8,215	Bank	4,720
		Subscription Outstanding	1,830
		Stock	2,450
	9,115		9,115

* Refer Suresh Capital Account.

QUESTIONS

Objective Type Questions

I. State whether each of the following statements are "True" of "False".

1. The amount of credit sales is determined by preparing a Total Creditors Account.
2. Trial Balance cannot be prepared under the Single Entry Method.
3. Sales – Gross Profit = Cost of goods sold.
4. Cash Sales are ascertained by preparing Total Debtors Account.
5. Single Entry is the exact opposite of double entry.
6. A Trading and Profit & Loss Account can be prepared under single entry system.
7. 20% profit on sales equals 25% profit on cost.
8. The balancing figure in a statement of affairs is the amount of profit for the accounting period.

9. Profit = Closing Capital + Drawings – Additional Capital – Opening Capital.
10. Gross Profit = Sales – Cost of Goods sold.

(*Ans*: True – 2, 3, 7, 9, 10, False – 1, 4, 5, 6, 8)

II. Indicate the correct alternative in each of the following:

1. Credit purchases are ascertained by preparing:
   (*a*) Total Debtors Account (*b*) Total Creditors Account
   (*c*) Purchase Account
2. The amount of credit sales is ascertained by:
   (*a*) Preparing Total Debtor A/c (*b*) Preparing Trading A/c
   (*c*) Preparing Statement of Affairs.
3. Under single entry, normally the following are recorded:
   (*a*) Personal Accounts only. (*b*) Cash Transactions only.
   (*c*) Both (*a*) and (*b*).
4. Sales can be calculated by adding:
   (*a*) Cash sales and cash received from Debtors. (*b*) Cash sales and credit sales.
   (*c*) Credit sales and cash received from Debtors.
5. Bills Receivable endorsed are debited to:
   (*a*) Bills Receivable A/c (*b*) Debtors Account
   (*c*) Creditors Account
6. Closing Capital + Drawings – Opening Capital = ?
   (*a*) Profit and Loss Account (*b*) Additional Capital
   (*c*) Opening Creditors
7. Profit for an accounting year equals:
   (*a*) Opening Capital + Additional Capital – Drawings – Closing Capital
   (*b*) Opening Capital – Additional Capital + Drawings – Closing Capital
   (*c*) Closing Capital – Additional Capital + Drawings – Opening Capital
8. Opening balance of creditors can be ascertained by preparing:
   (*a*) Debtors Account (*b*) Balance Sheet
   (*c*) Creditors Account
9. Total Creditors Account shows:
   (*a*) Credit Purchases (*b*) Cash Purchases
   (*c*) Total Purchases
10. The figure of opening capital is ascertained from:
   (*a*) Cash Account (*b*) Total Debtors Account
   (*c*) Opening Statement of Affairs.

(*Ans*: 1. (*b*); 2. (*a*); 3. (*c*); 4. (*b*); 5. (*c*); 6. (*a*); 7. (*c*); 8. (*c*); 9. (*a*); 10. (*c*).)

THEORETICAL QUESTIONS

1. What are the disadvantages of Single Entry System of accounting.
2. Distinguish between Single Entry System and Double Entry System.
3. What is Single Entry System of book-keeping ? (*B.Com. MK*)
4. What do you understand by the Single Entry System of Book-keeping? What are its disadvantages?
5. How is profit or loss found out under Single Entry System?
6. Explain the steps to be taken to convert the Single Entry System into Double Entry System.
7. What is a Statement of Affairs? How does it differ from a Balance Sheet?

PRACTICAL PROBLEMS

Capital Comparison Method

1. X keeps his book on the Single Entry System and the following information is available:

	1.1.2004	31.12.2004
	Rs	Rs
Furniture	200	200
Stock	2,800	3,050
Debtors	2,100	3,400
Cash	150	200
Creditors	1,750	1,900
Bills Payable		300
Loan	–	500
Investments	–	1,000

He has drawn out of the business Rs 500 during the year. Prepare a Statement showing his profit for the year ended 31st December 2004 after writing off 10% depreciation on Furniture and making a provision for bad debts at 10% on Sundry Debtors. *(B.Com., Punjab, Madurai)*

[**Ans:** Capital on 1.1.2004 Rs 3,500
Capital on 31.12.2004 Rs 4,790
Profit for the year 2004 Rs 1,790]

2. Mr Ram keeps his books by Single Entry System. His assets and liabilities were as under:

	1.1.2004	31.12.2004
	Rs	Rs
Cash at Bank	4,000	–
Sundry Debtors	2,000	3,000
Bank (Overdraft)	–	2,000
Office Equipment	2,000	2,000
Sundry Creditors	1,400	2,800
Furniture	4,000	2,000
Cash in Hand	5,000	500
Expenses Outstanding	–	400

Ram has withdrawn Rs 500 per month for personal use. He had introduced Rs 2,000 as additional capital on 14th August 2004. Provision for Doubtful Debts @ 5% on Sundry Debtors is to be provided. Charge depreciation @ 10% on Furniture and Office Equipment. Ascertain the profit or loss for the year. *(B.Com., Madurai)*

[**Ans:** Statement of Affairs (1.1.2004) Total Rs 15,000
Capital (1.1.2004) Rs 13,600
Statement of Affairs (31.12.2004) Total Rs 6,950
Capital (31.12.2004) Rs 1,750
Loss: Rs 7,850]

3. A Retail Trader had not kept proper books of accounts, but from the following details, you are required to ascertain the Profit or Loss for the year ended 30th June 2004 and also to prepare his Statement of Affairs as at that date:

	1st July 2003	30th June 2004
	Rs	Rs
Stock	16,700	18,100
Sundry Creditors	15,400	16,200
Sundry Debtors	11,200	10,600

Cash in Hand	250	1,400
Bank Overdraft	19,200	Nil
Bills Receivable	16,000	5,000
Fixtures & Fittings	1,500	1,500
Scooter	1,900	Nil
Bank Balance	Nil	2,900

The drawings during the year amounted to Rs 2,400. Depreciate Fixtures and Fittings by 10%. Rs 600 is irrecoverable from Debtors. Provide 5% Reserve for Doubtful Debts and a Reserve of Rs 200 in respect of Bills Receivable. *(B.Com., Karnataka)*

[**Ans:** Statement of Affairs (1.7.2003) Total Rs 47,550. Capital Rs 12,950.
Statement of Affairs (30.6.2004) Total Rs 39,500. Capital Rs 23,300.
Net Profit Rs 11,300.
Adjusted Statement of Affairs (30.6.2004) Rs 38,050]

Conversion Method:

4. Find out Credit Purchases from the following:

	Rs
Balance of Creditors on 1st January	7,600
Returns Outward	2,400
Cash paid to Creditors	20,000
Bills Accepted	4,600
Discount allowed by them	500
Balance of Creditors on 31st December	9,500

[**Ans:** Credit Purchases Rs 29,400]

5. Find out Credit sales from the following:

	Rs
Balance of Debtors on 1st Jan.	12,000
Returns Inward	5,000
Cash received from Customers	45,000
Discount allowed to them	3,000
Bills Receivable received from Customers	17,000
Bad Debts	1,500
Bills Receivable Dishonoured	3,500
Balance of Debtors on 31st December	10,000

[**Ans:** Credit Sales Rs 66,000]

6. Ascertain the amount of Bills Payable on 1st January:

	Rs
Bills Payable issued during the year	30,000
Bills Payable paid during the year	20,000
Bills Payable dishonoured during the year	5,000
Bills Payable on 31st December	10,000

[**Ans:** Bills Payable on 1st January Rs 5,000]

7. Find out the amount of Bills Receivable received during the year:

	Rs
Bills Receivable on 1st January	10,000
Bills Receivable dishonoured	5,000
Bills Receivable discounted	10,000

Cash Received against the Bills	5,000
Bills Receivable endorsed to Creditors	5,000
Balance of Bills Receivable on 31st December	25,000

[**Ans:** Bills Receivable received during the year Rs 40,000]

8. From the following figures drawn from the books of a trader, who maintains his accounts as per Single Entry System, you are required to calculate total sales:

	Rs
Bills Receivable in the beginning of the year	7,800
Debtors in the beginning of the year	30,800
Bills Receivable encashed during the year	20,900
Cash Received from debtors	70,000
Bad Debts written off	2,800
Returns Inwards	8,700
Bills Receivable Dishonoured	1,800
Bills Receivable at the end of the year	6,000
Debtors at the end of the year	25,500
Cash Sales as per Cash Book	28,156

(B.Com., Delhi, Madurai)

[**Ans:** Credit Sales Rs 95,300; Total Sales Rs 1,23,456
Bills received during the year Rs 20,900]

9. Find out the amount of Balance of Debtors on 1st January

	Rs
Sales during the year (Including cash sales of Rs 10,000)	40,000
Bills Receivable received from Debtors during the year	10,000
Cash receive from Debtors	30,000
Discount allowed to the Debtors	5,000
Bad Debts	3,000
Returns Inward	5,000
Bad Debts previously written off, now received	2,000
Bills Receivable Dishonoured	5,000
Balance of Debtors on 31st December	15,000

[**Ans:** Balance of Debtors on 1st January Rs 33,000]

10. Find out the amount paid to Creditors and the amount received from Sundry Debtors from the following:

	Rs
Sundry Debtors on 30th June 2004	32,800
Sundry Creditors on 30th June 2004	36,805
Total Sales	1,99,900
Total Purchases	1,79,400
Discount Earned	5,200
Discount Allowed	4,800
Return Outwards	7,440
Returns Inwards	6,444
Bills Received	26,400
Bills Accepted	39,800
Bad Debts	4,480
Bills Receivable Dishonoured	3,800

	Rs
Bills Endorsed to Creditors	5,200
Cash Sales	34,000
Cash Purchases	28,000
Debtors as on 1.7.2003	28,680
Creditors as on 1.7.2003	41,810

(*Karnataka*)

[**Ans:** Cash Received from Sundry Debtors Rs 1,23,456;
Cash paid to Sundry Creditors Rs 98,765]

11. From the following particulars extracted from the books of Mr Lazy kept under Single Entry System, you are required to find out the figures for credit sales and credit purchases by showing the Total Debtors Account and Total Creditors Account. Show also the Bills Receivable Account and Bills Payable Account.

	Rs
Total Debtors on 1st January	4,425
Total Creditors on 1st January	2,691
Bills Receivable on 1st January	1,600
Bills Payable on 1st January	500
Cash Received from Debtors	17,235
Discount allowed to customers	174
Bad Debts written off	255
Returns Inward	345
Bills Receivable accepted by customers	2,880
Cash paid to Creditors	8,934
Discount allowed by Creditors	129
Cash Received against Bills Receivable	3,000
Returns to Suppliers	156
Bills Payable accepted	1,920
Payments made against Bills Payable	1,400
Total Debtors on 31st December	4,167
Total Creditors on 31st December	2,835

(*I.C.W.A.*)

[**Ans:** Bills Receivable Account Balance on 31st Dec. Rs 1,480
Bills Payable Account Balance on 31st Dec. Rs 1,020
Credit Sales Rs 20,631
Credit Purchases Rs 11,283]

12. Mr Amarnath kept his books under the Single Entry System. The following are the particulars available therefrom. You are required to determine the following figures:
    (*a*) Total Sales for 2004
    (*b*) Total Purchases for 2004

    Show also the Bills Payable Account and Bills Receivable Account as well as any other accounts necessary for the purpose of your computations.

	Rs
Total Debtors on 1.1.2004	55,252
Total Creditors on 1.1.2004	39,275
Bills Receivable on 1.1.2004	27,322
Bills Payable on 1.1.2004	9,345
Cash Received from debtors (not including a sum of Rs 325 Received from Swamy & Co., being the amount due from them but written off as bad debts last year)	23,288

Discount earned from suppliers	1,455
Bad debts written off	3,224
Return Inwards	2,397
Discounts allowed to customers	3,049
Cash Sales	3,398
Cash Purchases	4,245
Bills Receivable accepted by customers	32,500
Cash paid to creditors (including payment to a supplier of a sum of Rs 1,800 being the cost of typewriter purchased for office use on credit during this year)	23,532
Cash Received against Bills Receivable	27,500
Return Outwards	1,156
Bills Payable accepted	19,000
Payments made against Bills Payable	14,000
Total Debtors on 31.12.2004	62,500
Total Creditors on 31.12.2004	33,000

(*I.C.W.A.*)

[**Ans:** Credit Sales Rs 71,706 and Cash Sales Rs 3,398 (Total: Rs 75,104)
Credit Purchases Rs 37,068 and Cash Purchases Rs 4,245 (Total: 41,313)
Bills Receivable A/c Balance on Dec. 2004 Rs 32,322
Bills Payable A/c Balance on Dec. 2004 Rs 14,345]

13. Ram had not kept proper books of accounts. From the following particulars extracted from his books of accounts ascertain the credit purchases made and also the credit sales effected during the year 2004:

	Rs
Sundry Debtors on 1st January	4,000
Sundry Debtors on 31st December	6,000
Sundry Creditors on 1st January	3,000
Sundry Creditors on 31st December	4,000
Cash Received from Debtors	12,000
Cash Paid to Creditors	10,000
Discount Received	400
Discount Allowed	300
Bills Receivable on 31st December	7,000
Bills Payable on 31st December	5,000
Returns Inwards	500
Returns Outwards	600
Bad Debts	100

[**Ans:** Credit Sales Rs 21,900 and Credit Purchases Rs 17,000]

14. From the following information, find out credit sales and credit purchases of Mr Harsha, who keeps his books under Single Entry System:

(*a*) An analysis of cash book for the year reveals the following:

	Rs
Payment to Creditors	1,05,550
Receipts from Debtors	52,050
Cash Sales	65,460
Bills Payable	16,000
Bills Receivable	15,000

Note: Discounts allowed Rs 550 and discounts earned Rs 350.

(*b*) Other Information:

	As on 1.1.2004	on 31.12.2004
	Rs	Rs
Sundry Creditors	4,570	25,640
Sundry Debtors	20,000	15,620
Bills Receivable	25,400	30,450
Bills Payable	22,470	13,240

(*B.Com., Bangalore*)

[Ans: Credit Sales Rs 68,270 and Credit Purchases Rs 1,33,740]

15. The books of Mr Idle on 1st January 2004, disclosed the following position:

	Rs		Rs
Capital	8,000	Furniture	2,000
Sundry Creditors	7,500	Sundry Debtors	9,000
		Stock	4,000
		Cash at Bank	500
	15,500		15,500

During the year 2004, the books were very imperfectly kept, but an analysis of the bank transactions revealed the following:

	Rs
Receipts from Debtors	35,000
Drawings for personal expenses	6,000
Payment of Salaries	3,000
Payment to Creditors	22,000
Payment for Rent	1,500
Miscellaneous expenses	400

Closing Debtors on 31.12.2004 was Rs 9,500 and Closing Creditors Rs 6,400. No inventory of the Stock on 31st December 2004 was taken, but it was stated that a Gross Profit at uniform rate of 40% on turnover was made during the year.

Prepare a Bank Account, Trading Account, Profit and Loss Account for the year ended 31st December 2004 and a Balance Sheet as on that date. (*I.C.W.A.*)

[Ans: Sales during the year Rs 35,500
Purchase during the year Rs 20,900
Closing Stock Rs 3,600
Bank Balance Rs 2,600
Gross Profit Rs 14,200
Net Profit Rs 9,300
Balance Sheet Total Rs 17,700]

16. A Trader, who has not kept a complete set of books, asks you to prepare his final accounts for the year ended 31st December 2004. You are, however, able to obtain the following information:

Summary of his cash Transactions:

	Rs
Balance of Cash on 1st January 2004	5,170
Takings	42,050
Personal Drawings	3,000
Purchases	32,400
Salaries	2,500
Rent	1,200

Electricity Charges		350
Printing and Stationery		350
Advertising		450

His other assets and liabilities were:

	Jan. 2004	Dec. 2004
	Rs	Rs
Debtors	3,350	5,100
Creditors	1,400	3,500
Rent Outstanding	100	100
Electricity Outstanding	20	15
Advertising Outstanding	–	250

The stock on 31st December 2004 was valued at Rs 4,500, but the trader has no record of the stock on 1st January 2004. He informs you, however, that he invariably sells his goods at cost plus 33 1/3%.

Prepare his Profit and Loss Account for the year ended 31st Dec. 2004 and a Balance Sheet as on that date. *(B.Com., Madurai; Jabalpur)*

[**Ans:** Credit Purchase Rs 2,100
Credit Sales Rs 1,750
Stock on January 2004 Rs 2,850
Initial Capital Rs 9,850
Gross Profit Rs 10,950
Net Profit Rs 5,855
Cash Balance on Dec. 2004 Rs 6,970
Balance Sheet Total Rs 16,570]

17. From the information given below, prepare Trading and Profit and Loss Account for the year ended 30th June 2004 and a Balance Sheet as at that date:

	1st July 2003	30th June 2004
	Rs	Rs
Debtors	8,000	7,400
Creditors for purchases	3,000	2,400
Rent Payable	50	30
Cash	750	3,250
Stock	7,500	8,000
Plant	5,000	6,000

Cash transactions:
Receipts: Cash sales Rs 500 Debtors Rs 35,500
Payments: Purchase of plant Rs 1,000
Rent Rs 620
Cash Purchases Rs 1,000
Payment to Creditors Rs 15,600
Salaries Rs 10,000
Wages Rs 3,000
Electricity Rs 1,000
Shortage of Cash to be treated as drawings.
Bad Debts already written off Rs 100
Depreciation on Plant had to be provided at 10%. *(B.Com., Kolkatta)*

[**Ans:** Credit Purchases Rs 15,000
Credit Sales Rs 35,000
Initial Capital Rs 18,200
Gross Profit Rs 16,000
Net Profit Rs 4,700
Balance Sheet Total Rs 24,050
Drawings Rs 1,280]

18. Mr Joseph carries on a small business, but he does not maintain a complete set of account books. He banks all receipts and makes all payments by cheques. From such records you are able to gather the following facts:

	Rs
Receipts for the year ended 31st December, 2004:	
Cash from Debtors	35,250
Cash Sales	8,250
Paid in by Mr. Joseph, from the sales proceeds of his scooter	5,000
Payments made during the year ending 31st December, 2004:	
Furniture purchased	1,250
Drawings	3,000
Wages	13,450
Salaries	2,650
Rent	2,400
Sundry Expenses	5,200
Paid to Creditors	15,250

Assets and Liabilities:

	As at 1.1.2004	As at 31.12.2004
	Rs	Rs
Furniture	15,000	15,500
Sundry Debtors	7,500	12,250
Stock	12,500	6,250
Bank	1,250	?
Sundry Creditors	5,050	4,800

Rs 250 reserve for doubtful debts is to be provided.

From the above particulars prepare trading and profit and loss account for the year ended 31st December 2004 and the Balance Sheet as on that date. (*B.Com., Bangalore*)

[**Ans:** Bank Balance on 31.12.2004 Rs 6,550
Credit Sales Rs 40,000
Credit Purchases Rs 15,000
Initial Capital Rs 31,200
Gross Profit Rs 13,550
Net Profit Rs 2,300
Balance Sheet Total Rs 40,300
Depreciation on Furniture Rs 750]

19. The books of Hemu showed the following figures:

	Dec. 31, 2003	Dec. 31, 2004
	Rs	Rs
Cash in Hand and at Bank	3,400	19,950
Stock in Trade	20,000	25,000
Trade Debtors	?	35,000
Trade Creditors	?	18,500
Sundry Assets	3,000	–

The Cash Book showed the following figures:

	Rs
Receipts from Debtors	1,36,000
Private dividends paid in	2,000
Indirect Expenses	19,650
Drawings	4,600
Payments to Creditors	1,12,000
Discount allowed by them	1,200

Additional information :

(*i*) Cost of goods sold during the year Rs 1,05,300.

(*ii*) Hemu maintains a steady gross profit at the rate of 25% on sale.

(*iii*) Bad debts written off during the period Rs 400 and past bad debts (already written off) recovered Rs 200.

You are required to prepare:

(*a*) Trading and Profit and Loss Account for the year ending 31.12.2004.

(*b*) Balance Sheet as on that date. (*B.Com., Mysore*)

[**Ans:** Missing figures are:
(1) Purchases: Rs 1,10,300
(2) Cash Sales Rs 14,600
(3) Credit Sales Rs 1,25,800
(4) Cash Purchase Nil
(5) Opening Balance of Debtors Rs 45,600
(6) Opening Balance of Creditors Rs 21,400
(7) Capital on 31.12.2003 Rs 50,600
(8) Gross Profit Rs 35,100
(9) Net Profit Rs 16,450
(10) Balance Sheet Total Rs 82,950]

20. Sankaran keeps his books on Single Entry System. He gives you the following information:

	Dec. 31, 2003	Dec. 31, 2004
	Rs	Rs
Furniture and Fittings	5,000	6,000
Stock of materials	3,000	1,000
Sundry Debtors	6,000	7,000
Sundry Creditors	2,000	–
Prepaid Expenses	–	200
Unpaid Expenses	600	1,000
Cash in Hand	1,100	300

Receipts and payments during the year:

	Rs
Receipts from debtors	21,000
Paid to creditors	10,000
Cartage	2,000
Drawings	12,000
Sundry Expenses	16,000
Furniture purchased for cash	1,000

Prepare a Trading and Profit and Loss Account for the year ended 31st December 2004 and a Balance Sheet after providing for bad debts at 10%. There was a considerable amount of cash sales.

(*B.Com., Madurai*)

[**Ans:** Credit Sales Rs 22,000
Cash Sales Rs 19,200
Credit Purchases Rs 8,000
Cash Book Total Rs 41,300
Gross Profit Rs 29,200
Net Profit Rs 12,300
Balance Sheet Total Rs 13,800]

21. You are required to prepare Trading and Profit and Loss Account for the year ended 31.12.2004 and the Balance Sheet as on that date together with workings, if any, in respect of Mr Adam's business from the following information:

(*a*) The Assets and Liabilities as on 31.12.2003 and 31.12.2004 were as under:

	As on 31.12.2003	As on 31.12.2004
	Rs	Rs
Bank Balance	Not available	20,000
Sundry Debtors	15,000	16,000
Sundry Creditors	5,000	8,000
Stock in Trade	15,000	20,000
Fixed Assets	30,000	30,000

(*b*) Sundry Debtors as on 31.12.2004 include Bad Debts of Rs 1,000.

(*c*) Fixed Assets include property rented out for which rent of Rs 500 was received for the year and utilised for personal use.

(*d*) Repairs to premises, etc. amount to Rs 600 which remained unpaid as on 31.12.2004.

(*e*) All sales receipts were banked after meeting business expense of Rs 5,000 and personal expenses of Rs 3,000.

(*f*) Cash purchases and cash sales amounted to Rs 1,000 and Rs 2,000 respectively.

(*g*) His account with bankers reveals that withdrawals amounted to Rs 70,000 and deposits Rs 90,000 for the year. (*I.C.W.A., B.Com., Madurai*)

[**Ans:** Bank Balance on 31.12.2003 Nil
Amount Received from Customers Rs 98,000
Total Sales Rs 99,000
Total Purchases Rs 73,000
Capital on 31.12.2003 Rs 55,000
Gross Profit Rs 31,000
Net Profit Rs 24,900
Balance Sheet Total Rs 85,000]

22. Prepare the Balance Sheet as at 31st December, 2004 and the profit and loss account for the year ended on that date of Mr Arun Ghose's business from the following information for the year 2004 supplied by him:

(*a*) Balance as at 1st January 2004:

	Rs
Cash in Hand	4,000
Cash at Bank	28,000
Sundry Creditors	15,000
Sundry Debtors	23,000

Stocks		35,000
Fixed Assets		20,000
Arun Ghose's:		
Capital Account	75,000	
Current Account	20,000	95,000

(*b*) During the year creditors were paid Rs 26,000 in cash and Rs 1,55,000 by cheques while Debtors paid Rs 55,000 in cash and Rs 1,90,000 by crossed cheques. The balances at close stood as:

Sundry Debtors Rs 27,000 and Sundry Creditors Rs 35,000.

(*c*) All expenses debitable to Profit and Loss Account were disbursed by cheques except petty expenses amounting to Rs 7,500 paid in cash. Outstanding expenses at close were Rs 2000.

(*d*) Net profits for the year were Rs 41,000 after allowing 10 per cent depreciation on Fixed Assets.

(*e*) Closing stocks were Rs 75,000.

(*f*) His drawing during the year were Rs 10,000 in cash and Rs 14,000 by cheques.

(*Co. Secy. Inter*)

[**Ans:** Credit Sales Rs 2,49,000
Credit Purchases Rs 2,01,000
Cash Balance Dec. 2004 Rs 15,500
Bank Balance Dec. 2004 Rs 13,500
Gross Profit Rs 88,000
Net Profit Rs 41,000
B/S Total: Rs 1,49,000]

23. Thomas does not maintain his books in the Double Entry System and Bank Accounts. From the following information, prepare Profit and Loss Account and Balance Sheet as at June 30, 2004:

(*a*) Assets and Liabilities

	30.6.2003	30.6.2004
	Rs	Rs
Stock	19,800	1,13,200
Creditors	31,000	14,500
Debtors	1,18,000	1,25,000
Premises	90,000	90,000
Furniture	11,000	11,500
Air Conditioner	15,000	15,000

(*b*) Creditors as at 30.6.2003 includes Rs 15,000 for purchase of Air conditioners.

(*c*) Cash Transactions:

	Rs
Cash as at July 1, 2003	15,000
Collections from customers	1,60,800
Payments to Creditors (Trade)	1,44,000
Rent, Rates and Taxes	11,500
Salaries	1,12,000
Sundry Expenses	18,000
Sundry Income	16,500
Drawings by Thomas	30,000
Loan from Mrs. Fernandes	23,000
Capital Introduced	12,000

Cash Sales	11,500	
Cash Purchases	15,000	
Paid to creditor for air-conditioner	15,000	
(*d*) Bad debts written off	1,200	(*I.C.W.A., Inter*)

[**Ans:** Credit Sales Rs 1,69,000
Credit Purchases Rs 1,42,500
Bank Overdraft (30.6.2004) Rs 1,07,200
Initial Capital Rs 2,37,800
Gross Profit Rs 1,16,400
Net Loss Rs 9,800
Balance Sheet Total Rs 3,54,700]

24. Mr Umesh carries on a grocery business and does not keep his books on Double Entry Basis. The following particulars have been extracted from his books:

	1.7.2003 Rs	30.6.2004 Rs
Plant and Machinery	25,000	25,000
Stock	22,000	19,500
Sundry Debtors	8,000	25,500
Sundry Creditors	12,500	10,000 (Cr.)
Cash in Hand	400	800
Bank Balance	6,250	7,000

The following cash transactions took place during the year ending 30th June, 2004:

	Rs		Rs
Received on account of Cash Sales	31,250	Payment for purchases	28,850
Received from sundry debtors	1,60,000	Payment to sundry creditors	1,32,000
		General expenses of business	21,450
		Wages	15,000
		Drawings	6,800

During the year Umesh had taken goods from the business for his own consumption which amounted to Rs 1,950 for the whole year and had not paid any money into the business for them.

You are required to prepare (1) the Trading and Profit and Loss Account for the year ending 30th June, 2004 after charging 10% depreciation on Plant and Machinery and, also (2) the Balance Sheet as at 30th June, 2004. (*B.Com., Bangalore*)

[**Ans:** Total Net Purchases Rs 1,56,400
Total Sales Rs 2,08,750
Initial Capital Rs 49,150
Gross Profit Rs 34,850
Net Profit Rs 10,900
Balance Sheet Total Rs 68,300]

25. Mr Ram has a small trading business for which the following procedures are followed:

(*a*) All collections are deposited with the bank each day.

(*b*) All payments except petty expenses are made by cheques.

(*c*) To meet petty expenses a cheque of Rs 500 is withdrawn from bank on 1st day of each month.

(*d*) Mr Ram makes personal drawings from the bank.

The following figures are available from his records:

	Rs
Cash in Hand as on 1.1.2004	320
Cash in Hand as on 31.12.2004	200

Balance in Bank as on 1.1.2004	2,500
Balance in Bank as on 31.12.2004	5,000 (Overdraft)
Debtors as on 1.1.2004	20,000
Debtors as on 31.12.2004	30,000
Creditors as on 1.1.2004	20,000
Creditors as on 31.12.2004	30,000
Stock of goods on 1.1.2004	10,000
Stock of goods as on 31.12.2004	30,000
Payments made to creditors during the year	20,000
Sales made during the year	30,000

Mr Ram spent during the year Rs 200 from the office cash for his personal expenses.

Prepare Profit and Loss Account for the year ended on 31st December 2004 and a Balance Sheet as on that date from the above information. *(C.A. Inter)*

[**Ans:** Amount Received from Debtors Rs 20,000
Credit Purchases Rs 30,000
Petty expenses Rs 5,920 debited to Profit and Loss A/c
Drawings amounted to Rs 1,700
Capital as on 1.1.2004 Rs 12,820
Gross Profit Rs 20,000
Net Profit Rs 14,080
Balance Sheet Total Rs 60,200]

26. The following information is supplied from which you are required to prepare the Trading and Profit and Loss Account for the year ended 31st December 2004 and a Balance Sheet as at the date:

Assets and Liabilities	1.1.2004	31.12.2004
	Rs	Rs
Sundry Assets	18,000	20,000
Cash in Hand	8,200	4,800
Stock	14,000	19,000
Cash at Bank	2,200	8,000
Debtors	?	26,000
Creditors	12,000	9,800
Sundry Expenses Outstanding	1,000	600

Further transactions relating to the year are:

	Rs
Receipts in the year and discounts credited to Debtors A/c	2,45,000
Returns from Debtors	6,000
Bad Debts	1,000
Sales–Cash and Credit	3,00,000
Returns to Creditors	3,000
Payments to Creditors by Cheque	2,36,200
Complete amounts from Debtors deposited into bank	2,43,000
Cash Purchases	10,000
Salary and wages paid out of Bank	18,000
Sundry Expenses paid by Cash	5,000
Drawings by Cash	9,400
Purchase of sundry assets by cheque	2,000

Cash withdrawn from Bank	21,000
Cash Sales deposited into Bank	?
Discount allowed by creditors	4,000

(C.A. Inter., M.Com., Madurai)

[Ans: Cash Sales Rs 40.000
Credit Sales Rs 2,60,000
Opening Balance of Debtors Rs 18,000
Credit Purchases Rs 2,41,000
Opening Capital Rs 47,400
Gross Profit Rs 51,000
Net Profit Rs 29,400
Balance Sheet Total Rs 77,800]

27. Mr Body keeps his books by Single Entry, furnishes the following information:

1. The Statement of Affairs as on 1st January 2004:

	Rs			Rs
Loans	12,000	Debtors	40,000	
Creditors	27,000	Less: Provision	750	39,250
Bills Payable	1,500	Bills Receivable		10,000
Capital:	1,40,000	Stock		45,000
		Plant		30,000
		Buildings		55,000
		Cash		1,250
	1,80,500			1,80,500

2. A summary of Cash Transaction for 2004:

	Rs		Rs
To Balance 1.1.2004	1,250	By Payments to Creditors	1,10,000
To Amount from Debtors	1,72,000	By Cash Purchases	35,000
To Bills Receivable	35,000	By Bills Payable	35,000
To Cash Sales	24 500	By Loans paid	12,000
		By Salaries	10,000
		By Rent	8,400
		By Interest	450
		By General Charges	800
		By Boby's Drawings	17,000
		By Balance 31.12.2004	4,100
	2,32,750		2,32,750

3. A list of remaining transactions for 2004:

	Rs
Total Purchases	2,15,000
Total Sales	2,35,000
Discount allowed to Customers	1,500
Discount allowed by Creditors	1,850
Bills Receivable received during the year	60,000
Bills Payable issued during the year	50,000
Stock on 31st December 2004	90,000

Owing for outstanding Expenses 2,500

Owing for commission earned by the firm 2,200

Provide 5% Reserve for Doubtful Debts and 2% for discount on debtors and depreciate Buildings by 5% and Plant by 10% p.a.

Prepare Trading and Profit and Loss Account and a Balance Sheet from the above for the period 2004.

(*B.Com., Hons.*)

[**Ans:** Closing Balance of Debtors Account Rs 17,000
Closing Balance of Creditors Account Rs 45,150
Closing Balance of Bills Receivable Rs 35,000
Closing Balance of Bills Payable A/c Rs 16,500
Gross Profit Rs 65,000
Net Profit Rs 39,227
Balance Sheet Total Rs 2,26,377]

28. The following details are given:

(1) Balance Sheet as on 1st January 2004

	Rs		Rs
Bills Payable	800	Cash at Bank	1,950
Creditors	1,800	Bills Receivable	750
Capital: A	5,050	Debtors	2,000
B	5,050	Stock	3,000
		Plant	2,000
		Land & Buildings	3,000
	12,700		12,700

(2) Cash Transactions during 2004

	Rs		Rs
Balance 1.1.2004	2,000	Salaries	600
Debtors	13,500	Wages	740
Bills Receivable	4,500	Bills Payable	3,660
		Creditors	7,350
		Office Expenses	400
		Drawings: A	750
		B	750
		Balance	5,750
	20,000		20,000

(3) Summary of Other Transactions

	Rs		Rs
Purchases	15,000	Discount allowed off sales	100
Discount allowed off purchases	50	Bills Received during 2004	4,550
Sales	19,000	Bills Payable given in 2004	7,750
		Stock on 31st Dec. 2004	3,500

Depreciate Plant by Rs 200 and Land and Buildings by Rs 150. Make a provision of Rs 100 for discount on Debtors.

Prepare Trading and Profit and Loss and a Balance Sheet for 2004. A and B Share profits and losses equally.

(*B.Com., Kerala, Madurai, Madras*)

[**Ans:** Closing Debtors Balance Rs 2,850
Closing Creditors Balance Rs 1,650
Closing Balance of Bills Payable A/c Rs 4,890

Closing Balance of Bills Receivable A/c Rs 800
Gross Profit Rs 3,760
Net Profit Rs 2,310 (Rs 1,155 and B Rs 1,155)
Balance Sheet Total Rs 17,450]

29. Mr. Gopal does not keep his books on Double Entry System. He maintained a Cash Book during the year 2004 from which the following information is obtained:

	Rs
Receipts from Debtors	10,000
Additional Capital (1.9.2004)	2,000
Loan from Mohan at 5% (on 1.7.2004)	5,000
Bank Overdraft (1.1.2004)	1,600
Payment to Creditors	7,400
General Expenses	2,200
Salaries	800
Drawings	1,800
Balance at Bank (31.12.2004)	3,200

Assets and liabilities:

	1.1.2004 Rs	31.12.2004 Rs
Debtors	10,600	12,000
Creditors	3,800	4,000
Buildings	5,000	5,000
Stock	3,800	?

On 31st December 2004, stock could not be taken due to some unavoidable circumstances. During the past years, the rate of gross profit was 40% on turnover.

After providing depreciation on Buildings at 5% and Interest at 6% on Capital and Drawings, prepare final accounts for the year ended 31st December 2004. *(B.Com., Madurai)*

[Ans: Credit Purchases Rs 7,600
Credit Sales Rs 11,400
Closing Stock Rs 4,560
Capital on 1.1.2004 Rs 14,000
Gross Profit Rs 4,560
Net Profit Rs 413
Balance Sheet Total Rs 24,510]

30. The following is the Statement of Affairs as on 1st October 2004, of Shri Haphazard, who maintains his books of account under Single Entry System:

Liabilities	*Rs*	*Assets*	*Rs*
Capital	1,05,000	Stock	27,000
Sundry Creditors	24,000	Sundry Debtors	66,000
Bank Overdraft	12,000	Furniture	3,000
		Building	45,000
	1,41,000		1,41,000

The abstract of his Cash Book for the year is as under:

Receipts	*Rs*	*Payments*	*Rs*
Opening Balance	Nil	Bank Overdraft	12,000
Sundry Debtors	75,000	Interest for Bank Overdraft	225
Cash Sales	45,000	Personal Drawings	6,000
		Salaries	25,500
		General Expenses	23,775

		Sundry Creditors	45,000
		Balance (Closing)	7,500
	1,20,000		1,20,000

At the close of the year he had the following balances:

Stock-in-hand	30,660
Sundry Debtors	90,000
Furniture	3,000
Building	45,000
Sundry Creditors	16,500

From the above particulars, you are requested to prepare a Trading and Profit and Loss Account for the year ended 30th September, 2005, and a Balance Sheet as on that date, after providing for depreciation on Furniture @ 5 per cent per annum, Rs 3,000 for Doubtful Debts and Interest @ 5 per cent per annum on Capital. *(I.C.W.A.)*

[**Ans:** Credit Purchases Rs 37,500
Credit Sales Rs 99,000
Gross Profit Rs 1,10,160
Net Profit Rs 52,260
Balance Sheet Total Rs 1,73,010]

31. Mr Sharma who keeps his books by Single Entry System instructs you to prepare his Balance Sheet an on 31st December, 2004 together with the Trading and Profit and Loss Account for the year ended on that date.

Upon analysing his cash book for that year you find the following:

	Rs
Balance of Cash at Bank 1.1.2004	8,700
Cash received from Debtors	76,800
Cash received on Bills Receivable	24,000
Commission received	3,000
Cash Sales	17,200
Payment to Creditors	54,200
Drawings	15,040
Paid Bills Payable	18,600
Wages	24,000
Salaries	13,000
Rent, Rates and Taxes	11,560

Particulars of his other assets and liabilities are as follows:

	1.1.2004	31.12.2004
	Rs	Rs
Capital	83,300	–
Stock	37,400	46,800
Debtors	24,000	28,000
Creditors	18,000	3,000
Bills Receivable	8,000	10,000
Bills Payable	2,000	400
Furniture	1,200	1,200
Buildings	24,000	24,000
Bank	8,700	?

Reserve Rs 2,000 for Doubtful Debts and write off 5% depreciation on Buildings and Furniture. Rs 3,000 are outstanding wages. (*B.Com., Bangalore*)

[**Ans:** Closing Bank Overdraft Rs 6,700
Credit Sales Rs 1,06,800
Credit Purchases Rs 56,200
Bills Receivable Drawn Rs 26,000
Bills Payable Accepted Rs 17,000
Gross Profit Rs 50,200
Net Profit Rs 25,380
Balance Sheet Total Rs 1,06,740]

32. Mr Ram Gopal keeps his books on Single Entry System. His position at the beginning and end of the year were as follows:

	As on 31.12.2003	As on 31.12.2004
	Rs	Rs
Cash	3,908	1,963
Stock	7,900	8,800
Debtors	9,361	8,355
Investments	1,000	1,000
Machinery	2,000	2,000
Bills Receivable	4,000	2,400
Creditors	9,400	8,350
Loan from Babu	1,000	1,000
Bills Payable	3,471	5,051

From his Cash Book following information was available·

		Rs
Receipts:	Bills Receivable	4,300
	Sales	1,200
	Received from Debtors	2,450
	Commission received	930
Payments:	Wages	700
	Carriage	300
	Insurance	800
	Interest on Loan	200
	Printing	500
	Payments to Creditors	1,425
	Purchases	600
	Personal Expenses	1,500
	Salaries	800
	Investments	1,000
	Bills Payable	3,000

Other information relating to his business:

Discount Allowed	400
Discount Received	355
Bad Debts	560
Bills Receivable Dishonoured	300

You are asked to prepare final accounts for the year 2004. (*B.Com., Madurai, Bombay*)

[**Ans:** Credit Sales Rs 5,104
Bills Receivable received during 2004 Rs 3,000
Bills Payable issued during 2004 Rs 4,580
Credit Purchases Rs 5,310
Gross Profit Rs 294
Net Loss Rs 1,681
Balance Sheet Total Rs 25,518]

33. Mr Chandran keeps his books on Single-Entry System. You are required to prepare his Trading and Profit and Loss Account for the year ended 31st December, 2004 from the following information:

(1) An analysis of Cash Book reveals the following:

	Rs
Bank Overdraft as on 1.1.2004	8,560
Interest and Bank charges	240
Drawings A/c of Mr. Chandran	5,200
Salaries	6,400
Payment to Creditors	1,05,550
Receipts from Debtors	52,050
Cash Sales	65,460
Insurance Charges	600
Rent	750
Receipt of fire claim from Insurance Co.,	54,000
Stationery	440
Freight Duty etc.	1,250
Carriage Inward	2,500
Carriage Outwards	1,550
Machinery Repairs	1,240
Income Tax Refunds	1,250
Bills Payable	16,000
Bills Receivable	15,000

Note: The Bills were all relating to purchases or sales only.

(2) Mr Chandran had allowed Rs 550 as discounts and earned Rs 450 as discounts.

(3) A scrutiny of the various large accounts reveals the following:

	As on 1.1.2004	As on 31.12.2004
	Rs	Rs
Stock-in-Hand	3,550	4,560
Sundry Creditors	4,570	15,640
Sundry Debtors	20,000	25,620
Furniture	5,000	5,000
Machinery	25,600	25,600
Motor Car	35,400	35,400
Cash in Hand	650	750
Bills Receivable	25,400	30,450
Bills Payable	22,470	13,240

(4) There was Provision for Doubtful debts at 5 per cent of the Debtors at the beginning of the year and the same percentage is desired to be maintained.

(5) Only 75 per cent of the cost of stock lost in fire was recovered.

(6) Depreciation has to be provided at 5 per cent on Machinery, 10 per cent on Furniture and 20 per cent on vehicle. *(C.A., Inter)*

[**Ans:** Credit Sales Rs 78,270: Credit Purchases: Rs 1,23,840
Bills Receivable received Rs 20,050
Bills Payable issued Rs 6,770
Gross Profit Rs 24,350, Net Profit Rs 2,089
Bank Overdraft Rs 11,220
Balance Sheet Total Rs 1,17,239]

Chapter 13

Account Current and Average Due Date

Account Current – Methods – Calculation of Number of Days – Red Ink Interest – Periodic Balance Method – Average Due Date – Calculations – Utility – Questions – Objective Type Questions – Theoretical Questions – Practical Problems.

ACCOUNT CURRENT

When a business grows, customers also increase. When the businessman gets confidence on his customers, he often sells goods on credit and payments are received according to convenience of customers or as agreed upon. Similarly one businessman sells goods to another businessman and also makes purchases from him. Similar is the case with (*i*) Supplier with customers, (*ii*) Lender to its borrower, (*iii*) Agent to his principal, (*iv*) Banker to his client, (*v*) A co-venturer to another co-venturer etc. Under these circumstances, each party opens each other's account in their books of account, which is called running account. The customers purchase goods and make the payments from time to time.

An Account Current is a statement in Debtor and Creditor form containing various transactions that have taken place between two parties during a particular period. Interest is charged on debit items and allowed on credit items at an agreed rate. It is a statement of account which is sent by one person to another after a prescribed period. It contains entry for purchases, sales, receipts and payments made between them during the period. Record of interest is made for various periods and ultimately its balance indicates the amount which one party has to receive from or pay to another.

An Account Current is a copy of the ledger account of other party. In the heading of this Account Current, the name of the party to whom it is rendered is first mentioned while the name of the sender appears last. For instance, when Gopal renders an Account Current to Ramu, the heading is RAMU IN ACCOUNT CURRENT WITH GOPAL. That is, Receiver's name appears first and sender's name appears last.

To facilitate computation of interest on each transaction a special column adjacent to the usual amount on each side of the ledger is employed on a purely memorandum basis. The net interest – excess of chargeable or allowable interest or vice versa, is, however, charged or allowed as usual on double entry basis.

Account Current and Current Account

Account Current is a statement when entered in the form of an account, sent by one party to another, duly setting out in chronological order the details of the transactions together with interest, is termed as Account Current while Current Account is opened with a banker in which at any time amount may be deposited or withdrawn: a copy of his account is sent to the customer for his information, it is called Current Account.

Methods used in Computing the Periods

The following are the methods employed in computing the relevant period in terms of days or months, as may be appropriate in a given case:

1. Interest Table Method
2. Product Method
3. Interest Number Method
4. Epoque Method

1. Interest Table Method

Interest is calculated by using interest tables. Such tables are available for ready reference. With the help of interest table, one can calculate interest of different amounts at different rates for different periods. When interest on each item has been calculated and entered, the interest columns are balanced and the balance of interest is entered in the Amount column on the side where it belongs. Now it is ready to be sent to other party. The following example will clarify.

ILLUSTRATION 13.1

On Ist January 2005, Mr Arun owed Rs 3,000 to Babu on account. During the six months ended 30th June 2005, the following transactions took place:

		Rs
Jan. 1	Goods sold to Arun	4,000
Feb. 1	Amount received from Arun	3,000
March 1	Goods sold to Arun	5,000
April 1	Arun sold goods to Babu	3,500
May 1	Goods sold to Arun	2,500
June 1	Cash received from Arun	4,000
June 30	Cash received from Arun	1,000

Prepare Account Current to be rendered to Arun on 30th June 2005, interest to be calculated at 12% p.a. (in months).

SOLUTION:

Dr. **Arun in Account Current with Babu as on 30th June 2005** Cr.

Date	Particulars	Months	Interest	Amount	Date	Particulars	Months	Interest	Amount
			Rs	Rs				Rs	Rs
2005					2005				
Jan. 1	To Balance b/d	6	180	3,000	Feb. 1	By Cash A/c	5	150	3,000
Jan. 1	To Sales A/c	6	240	4,000	Apr. 1	By Purchases A/c	3	105	3,500
March 1	To Sales A/c	4	200	5,000	June 1	By Cash A/c	1	40	4,000
May 1	To Sales A/c	2	50	2,500	June 30	By Cash A/c			1,000
June 30	To Interest A/c (as per contra)			375	" "	By Transfer (Contra)		375	
						By Balance c/d			3,375
			670	14,875				670	14,875
July 1	To Balance b/d			3,375					

Interest is calculated by using Ready Reckoner Interest Tables.

2. Product Method

Under the Interest table method, interest columns are provided on both sides of Account Current and the interest, from the interest table, is entered. Under Product method, interest columns are replaced with "Product" columns. Product, in this case, is the amount multiplied with the number of days for which the interest is to be calculated. The "Product", so obtained, is entered in the Product

Columns. The interest is calculated on the different of total of debit product and total of credit product columns. The interest is calculated as under:

$$\frac{\text{Difference in Products} \times \text{Rate of Interest}}{100 \times 365}$$

This method is based on the simple principle that interest on the amount for a number of days is the same as interest for one day on the product. For instance, interest for Rs 1,000 for 73 days @ 18% p.a. (Rs 36) is equal to interest for Rs 73,000 for one day @ 18% p.a. (Rs 36). In other words, it is based on the logic that at a given rate, interest on Rs 100 for one year is the same as on Rs 36,500 (i.e. Rs 100 × 365) for one day.

Steps

1. Compute the number of days from the (due) date of each transaction to the closing date of statement/settlement.
2. The products are obtained by multiplying the amount of each transaction with the number of days.
3. The products obtained (under Step 2) are written in the product columns for every transaction.
4. Find out the balance of products on the two sides. The balance so calculated is entered in the deficit side.
5. Calculate interest on the balance of products at the given rate "for one day".
6. The interest amount so calculated is entered in the amount column of the side where the product is heavier.
7. Finally the amount columns is balanced and the balance arrived at represents the net amount, inclusive of interest, receivable or payable on the settlement date.

Instead of the number of days, number of months may be taken and in that case, interest is calculated on the balance of the product "for one month"

Calculation of Number of Days (Guidance)

1. The date of transaction is left out of calculations. For instance, from 5th to 25th of Nov. = 20 days.
2. When an Account Current commences with brought forward balance, the opening date is also counted.

   For instance, Balance b/d on Ist Jan. to 31st March

   Number of days = Jan. 31 + Feb. 28 + March 31 = 90 days
3. When the sales have been made and the date of settlement has been fixed, the number of days must be counted from the date of settlement and not from the date of transaction.

   For instance, Purchased goods on Ist January, payable on 15th January and closing date of Account Current is 31st March, then the number of days:

   Jan. 16 + Feb. 28 + March 31 = 75
4. In case of Bills, the days will be counted from the date after adding the grace period.

   When the day on which a promissory note or Bill of Exchange is at maturity (after including days of grace) is a public holiday, the instrument shall be deemed to be due on the preceding business day. The expression "public holiday" includes Sundays and other days declared by the Central Government by notification in the official gazette, to be a public holiday. But if the holiday happens to be the emergency or unforeseen holiday then the due date shall be the next following day.
5. Leap year will be given attention.

ILLUSTRATION 13.2

Mr B had the following transactions with A during the year 2005

		Rs
July 1	Balance due from A	600
July 15	Sold goods to A	1,900
Aug. 10	Received cash from A	1,100
Aug. 19	Purchased goods from A	700
Sept. 3	Returned goods to A	300
Sept. 16	Received cash from A	500

Prepare an Account Current to be rendered by B to A as on 30th September 2005 calculating interest at 10% p.a. (*B.Com., Andhra*)

SOLUTION:

Dr. **A in Account Current with B as on 30th September 2005** Cr.

Date	Particulars	Amount Rs	Days	Products	Date	Particulars	Amount Rs	Days	Products
2005					2005				
July 1	To Balance b/d	600	92	55,200	Aug. 10	By Cash A/c	1,100	51	56,100
July 15	To Sale A/c	1,900	77	1,46,300	Aug. 19	By Purchase A/c	700	42	29,400
Sep. 3	To Purchases returns A/c	300	27	8,100	Sep. 16	By Cash A/c	500	14	7,000
Sep. 30	To Interest on Balance of products $\frac{1,17,100 \times 10 \times 1}{100 \times 365}$	32			Sep. 30	By Balance of products			1,17,100
					Sep. 30	By Balance c/d	532		
		2,832		2,09,600			2,832		2,09,600
Oct. 1	To Balance b/d	532							

No. of days:

	July	Aug.	Sept.	
July 1 to Sept. 30	31	31	30	= 92
July 15 to Sept. 30	16	31	30	= 77
Aug. 10 to Sept. 30	–	21	30	= 51
Aug. 19 to Sept. 30	–	12	30	= 42
Sept. 3 to Sept. 30	–	–	27	= 27
Sept. 16 to Sept. 30	–	–	14	= 14

Red Ink Interest

In some cases, it may happen that the due date of a transaction falls after the closing date of Account Current. Generally, interest is computed on the amount of a transaction, in an Account Current, from the due date to the closing date of the period. But in case of Bills, the due dates may fall either within the accounting period or outside the accounting period. In such a situation, ordinary procedure is followed, in the former case (*i.e.* date falls within the accounting period) and in the case of later (*i.e.* date falls outside the accounting period), the interest is written in RED INK. Hence the interest is known as RED INK INTEREST.

The number of days and the products of such transactions are written in Red Ink by way of warning to the Accountant that the products of such transactions should be deducted from the total of products. In such situations, the following methods are adopted:

(*i*) BY USING RED INK FIGURES. The days and the products of such transactions are written in Red-Ink. Then while totalling the product column, the red-ink products are deducted from the total of other ordinary ink products (in the same side) (See Illustration No. 13.3)

(*ii*) BY WRITING PRODUCTS ON OPPOSITE SIDE. To avoid the confusion of red-ink figures in totalling the products, the product of such red-ink transactions are written in the ordinary ink on the opposite side, usually as last item. That is, the credit red-ink products are added to the debits and debit red-ink products are added to the credit. (See Illustration 13.4)

ILLUSTRATION 13.3

Santosh had the following transactions with Kantan

		Rs
2005 Jan. 1	Balance due from Kantan	1,000
Feb. 16	Purchased goods from him	6,000
Feb. 28	Sold goods to him	10,000
Mar. 16	Received a cheque	3,000
Apr. 20	Sold him goods (invoiced on May 3)	10,000
June 16	Purchased goods from him (Invoiced on July 16)	15,000
Sept. 23	Paid him cash	3,000
Oct. 24	Accepted his Bill for 3 months	5,000
Nov. 26	Received his acceptance for 2 months	8,000

You are asked to prepare an Account Current of Kantan completed upto 31st December 2005 as will appear in the books of Santosh reckoning 10% interest on the balance due. (*CA*)

3. Interest Numbers or Index Number Method

This method is similar to product method. But the difference is that the Index Number Column is there instead of Product Column. The product (*i.e.* Amount × Number of days) is divided by 100 and the resultant figure is written in Index Number Column.

$$\text{Interest} = \frac{\text{Balance of Numbers} \times \text{Rate of Interest}}{365}$$

In case of leap year:

$$\text{Interest} = \frac{\text{Balance of Number} \times \text{Rate}}{366}$$

In case the period is calculated in months:

$$\text{Interest} = \frac{\text{Balance of Numbers} \times \text{Rate}}{12}$$

Solution (Illustration 13.3)

Kantan in Account Current with Santosh as on 31st December 2005

Dr. | Cr.

Date	Due Date	Particulars	Amount	Days to 31st Dec.	Products	Date	Due Date	Particulars	Amout	Days to 31st Dec.	Products
			Rs						Rs		
2005						2005					
Jan. 1	Jan. 1	To balance b/d	1,000.00	365	3,65,000	Feb. 16	Feb. 16	By Purchases A/c	6,000	318	19,08,000
Feb. 28	Feb. 28	To Sales A/c	10,000.00	306	30,60,000	March 16	March 16	By Bank A/c	3,000	290	8,70,000
April 20	May 3	To Sales A/c	10,000.00	242	24,20,000	June 16	July 16	By Purchases A/c	15,000	168	25,20,000
Sept. 23	Sept. 23	To Cash A/c	3,000.00	99	2,97,000	Nov. 26	2006Jan. 29	By Bills Receivable A/c	8,000	(–) 29	(–) 2,32,000
Oct. 24	2006 Jan. 27	To Bills Payable A/c	5,000.00	(–) 27	(–) 1,35,000	Dec. 31	Dec. 31	By Balance of product as per contra			9,41,000
Dec. 31	Dec. 31	To Interest on balance of products (9,41,000 × 10/100 × 1/365)	257.80	–	–						
"	"	To Balance c/d	2,742.20								
			32,000.00		60,07,000				32,000		60,07,000
						2006 Jan. 1		By Balance b/d	2,742.20		

Calculation of days:

	Jan.		Feb.		Mar.		April		May		June		July		Aug.		Sept.		Oct.		Nov.		Dec.		Total
Jan. 1 to Dec. 31	31	+	28	+	31	+	30	+	31	+	30	+	31	+	31	+	30	+	31	+	30	+	31	=	365
Feb. 16 to Dec. 31	0	+	12	+	31	+	30	+	31	+	30	+	31	+	31	+	30	+	31	+	30	+	31	=	318
Feb. 28 to Dec. 31	0	+	0	+	31	+	30	+	31	+	30	+	31	+	31	+	30	+	31	+	30	+	31	=	306
Mar. 16 to Dec. 31	0	+	0	+	15	+	30	+	31	+	30	+	31	+	31	+	30	+	31	+	30	+	31	=	290
May 3 to Dec. 31	0	+	0	+	0	+	0	+	28	+	30	+	31	+	31	+	30	+	31	+	30	+	31	=	241
Jul. 16 to Dec. 31	0	+	0	+	0	+	0	+	0	+	0	+	15	+	31	+	30	+	31	+	30	+	31	=	168
Sept. 23 to Dec. 31	0	+	0	+	0	+	0	+	0	+	0	+	0	+	0	+	7	+	31	+	30	+	31	=	99

For those transactions whose due dates fall beyond 31st Dec. 2005

Dec. 31 to Jan. 27th 2006 = 27 Days

Dec. 31 to 29th Jan. 2006 = 29 Days

When the effective date of a transaction falls beyond the date of closing, the number of days from the date of closing upto the effective date are taken into consideration and the product is placed in the opposite side. Sometimes, the product is placed in the same side but in RED INK to denote that it really belongs to the opposite side.

ILLUSTRATION 13.4

The above Problem (13.3) is solved in alternative method.

Kantan in Account Current with Santosh
as on 31st December 2005

Dr. Cr.

Date	Due Date	Particulars	Amount	Days to 31st Dec.	Products	Date	Due Date	Particulars	Amout	Days to 31st Dec.	Products
			Rs						Rs		
2005						2005					
Jan. 1	Jan. 1	To balance b/d	1,000.00	365	3,65,000	Feb. 16	Feb. 16	By Purchases A/c	6,000	318	19,08,000
Feb. 28	Feb. 28	To Sales A/c	10,000.00	306	30,60,000	March 16	March 16	By Bank A/c	3,000	290	8,70,000
April 20	May 3	To Sales A/c	10,000.00	242	24,20,000	June 16	July 16	By Purchases A/c	15,000	168	25,20,000
Sept. 23	Sept. 23	To Cash A/c	3,000.00	99	2,97,000	Nov. 26	2006 Jan. 29	By Bills Receivable A/c	8,000	(–) 29	
Oct. 24	2006 Jan. 27	To Bills Payable A/c	5,000.00	(–) 27	–						
Dec. 31	Jan. 29	To Product on B/P as per contra (Rs 8,000 × 29 (days)			2,32,000	Dec. 31	Jan. 27	By Product on B/P as per contra (Rs 5,000 × 27 days)	–	–	1,35,000
		To Interest on balance of products (9,41,000 × 10/100 × 1/365)	257.80			Dec. 31		By Balance of product as per contra			9,41,000
		To Balance c/d	2,742.20								
			32,000.00		63,74,000				32,000		63,74,000
						2006 Jan. 1		By Balance b/d	2,742.20		

NB: Red ink products appearing on the opposite side.

ILLUSTRATION 13.5

The following transactions took place between Sohan and Mohan between Jan. 1 to June 30, 2005:

		Rs
Jan. 1	Sold goods to Sohan	1,120
Jan. 10	Received Sohan's acceptance (due 2 m/d)	500
Feb. 15	Received cash from Sohan	600
Mar. 2	Bought goods from Sohan	2,750
Mar. 3	Accepted Sohan's Bill one m/d	1,000
April 11	Paid cash to Sohan	1,000
April 30	Sold goods to Sohan	
	(Payable on 31st May)	1,200
May 11	Bought goods from Sohan	750
May 31	Sold goods to Sohan	
	(Payable on 10th June)	1,100
June 15	Bought goods from Sohan	1,500

Prepare the Account Current to be sent by Mohan on 30th June 2005. The rate of interest is 10%.

(B.Com., Kerala, Mysore, MK)

SOLUTION:

Number of days:

	Jan.		Feb.		March.		April		May		June		Total
Jan. 1 to June 30	30	+	28	+	31	+	30	+	31	+	30	=	180
Feb. 15 to June 30	0	+	13	+	31	+	30	+	31	+	30	=	135
Mar. 2 to June 30	0	+	0	+	29	+	30	+	31	+	30	=	120
Mar. 13 to June 30	0	+	0	+	18	+	30	+	31	+	30	=	109
Apr. 6 to June 30	0	+	0	+	0	+	24	+	31	+	30	=	85
Apr. 11 to June 30	0	+	0	+	0	+	19	+	31	+	30	=	80
May 11 to June 30	0	+	0	+	0	+	0	+	20	+	30	=	50
May 31 to June 30	0	+	0	+	0	+	0	+	0	+	30	=	30
June 10 to June 30	0	+	0	+	0	+	0	+	0	+	20	=	20
June 15 to June 30	0	+	0	+	0	+	0	+	0	+	15	=	15

4. Epoque (Backward) Method

This is quite reverse of product method. The following points are worthy to be noted:

1. The number of days are counted from the beginning of the accounting period upto the date of transaction but not from the date of transaction to the date of preparation of account current.
2. If there is any opening balance, it does not carry interest as number of days is zero; while closing balance covers the entire period of statement.
3. Interest on the closing balance, before charging interest, must be charged for the whole period of the account current. That is, if product method is followed, then this balance is multiplied with the total number of days of the accounting period and the product is recorded in the product column.
4. The products on each side are totalled and the difference is ascertained. Then, interest is calculated for one day at an agreed rate for the difference.
5. The interest so calculated is entered, in the amount column, on the side which is shorter. There is no question of Red Ink Interest.

SOLUTION:

Sohan in Account Current with Mohan as on 31st December 2005

Dr. Cr.

Date	Due Date	Particulars	Amount	Days to June 30	Index Numbers	Date	Due Date	Particulars	Amout	Days to June 30	Index Number
			Rs						Rs		
2005						2005					
Jan. 1	Jan. 1	To Sales A/c	1,120.00	180	2,016	Jan. 10	March 13	By Bills Receivable A/c	500.00	109	545
Mar. 3	April 6	To Bills Payable A/c	1,000.00	85	850	Feb. 15	Feb. 15	By Cash A/c	600.00	135	810
April 11	April 11	To Cash A/c	1,000.00	80	800	Mar. 2	Mar. 2	By Purchases A/c	2,750.00	120	3,300
April 30	May 31	To Sales A/c	1,200.00	30	360	May 11	May 11	By Purchases A/c	750.00	50	375
May 31	June 10	To Sales A/c	1,100.00	20	220	June 15	June 15	By Purchases A/c	1,500.00	15	225
June 30		To Balance of Products			1,009	June 30		By Interest on Balance of Products (1009 × 10 × 1/365)	27.65		
June 30		To Balance c/d	707.65								
			6,127.65		5,255				6,127.65		5,255
						July 1		By Balance c/d	707.65		

ILLUSTRATION 13.6

On Ist January 2005, Prem owed Rs 5,400 to Kamal. Prepare an Account Current to be rendered by Kamal for the period upto 30th June 2005. The following transactions have taken place between them during the period of six months.

		Rs
Jan. 1	Sold goods to Prem	800
Jan. 16	Received from Prem	2,000
Jan. 25	Sold to Prem, goods on credit for one month	1,000
Feb. 10	Received three months acceptance from Prem	2,000
March 1	Bought goods from Prem	1,500
April 20	Sold goods to Prem	500
May 7	Prem bought goods	1,200
June 9	Remitted by Prem	800
June 14	Received from Prem	900

Interest is to be charged at an agreed rate of 6% p.a. (*B.Com., Madurai*)

SOLUTION:

Calculation of Days: (Forward Method)

	Jan.		Feb.		March.		April		May		June		Total
Jan. 1 to June 30	31	+	28	+	31	+	30	+	31	+	30	=	181
Jan. 16 to June 30	15	+	28	+	31	+	30	+	31	+	30	=	165
Feb. 25 to June 30	0	+	3	+	31	+	30	+	31	+	30	=	125
March 1 to June 30	0	+	0	+	30	+	30	+	31	+	30	=	121
April 20 to June 30	0	+	0	+	0	+	10	+	31	+	30	=	71
May 7 to June 30	0	+	0	+	0	+	0	+	24	+	30	=	54
May 13 to June 30	0	+	0	+	0	+	0	+	18	+	30	=	48
June 9 to June 30	0	+	0	+	0	+	0	+	0	+	21	=	21
June 14 to June 30	0	+	0	+	0	+	0	+	0	+	16	=	16

Calculation of Days: (Epoque Method)

	Jan.		Feb.		March.		April		May		June		Total
Jan. 1 to Jan. 1	0												0
Feb. 25 to Jan. 1	31	+	25										56
March 1 to Jan. 1	31	+	28	+	1								60
April 20 to Jan. 1	31	+	28	+	31	+	20						110
May 7 to Jan. 1	31	+	28	+	31	+	30	+	7				127
May 13 to Jan. 1	31	+	28	+	31	+	30	+	13				133
June 8 to Jan. 1	31	+	28	+	31	+	30	+	31	+	8	=	159
June 14 to Jan. 1	31	+	28	+	31	+	30	+	31	+	14	=	165
June 30 to Jan. 1	31	+	28	+	31	+	30	+	31	+	30	=	181

When Rates of interest are Different

If the rates of interests are different for the debit items and the credit items as it happens in Bank and Partnership firms then interest is calculated separately on the total of debit items and credit items. Then the balance of interest is recorded. The following two different methods explain the calculations:

SOLUTION: 13.6 (Solved under Product Method)

Dr. **Prem in Account Current with Kamal as on 30 June 2005** (*Product Method*) Cr.

Date	Due Date	Particulars	Amount Rs	Days to June 30	Products	Date	Due Date	Particulars	Amout Rs	Days to June 30	Products
2005						2005					
Jan. 1	Jan. 1	To Balance b/d	5,400	181	9,77,400	Jan. 16	Jan. 16	By Cash A/c	2,000	165	3,30,000
Jan. 1	Jan. 1	To Sales A/c	800	180	1,44,000	Feb. 10	May 13	By Bills Receivable A/c	2,000	48	96,000
Jan. 25	Feb. 25	To Sales A/c	1,000	125	1,25,000						
April 20	April 20	To Sales A/c	500	71	35,500	March 1	March 1	By Purchases A/c	1,500	121	1,81,500
May 7	May 7	To Sales A/c	1,200	54	64,800	June 9	June 9	By Bank A/c	800	21	16,800
June 30		To Interest on Balance of product (7,08,000 × 6 × 100 × 1/365)	116			June 14	June 14	By Bank A/c	900	16	14,400
						June 30		By Balance of product	–	–	7,08,000
						June 30		By Balance c/d	1,816		
			9,016		13,46,700				9,016		13,46,700
July 1		To Balance b/d	1,816								

SOLUTION: 13.6 (Solved Under Epoque Method)

Dr. **Prem in Account Current with Kamal as on 30 June 2005** (*Epoque Method*) Cr.

Date	Due Date	Particulars	Amount Rs	Days to June 30	Products	Date	Due Date	Particulars	Amount Rs	Days to June 30	Products
2005						2005					
Jan. 1	Jan. 1	To Balance b/d	5,400	0	0	Jan. 16	Jan. 16	By Cash A/c	2,000	16	32,000
Jan. 1	Jan. 1	To Sales A/c	800	0	0	Feb. 10	May 13	By Bills Receivable A/c	2,000	133	2,66,000
Jan. 25	Feb. 25	To Sales A/c	1,000	56	56,000						
April 20	April 20	To Sales A/c	500	110	55,000	March 1	March 1	By Purchases A/c	1,500	60	90,000
May 7	May 7	To Sales A/c	1,200	127	1,52,400	June 9	June 9	By Bank A/c	800	159	1,27,200
June 30		To Balance of product A/c			7,08,000	June 14	June 14	By Bank A/c	900	656	1,48,500
June 30		To Interest A/c (7,08,000 × 6 × 100 × 1/365)	116			June 30		By product of Balance of principal amount (Rs 8,900 – 7,200 = 1,700)	–	181	3,07,700
						June 30		By Balance c/d	1,816		
			9,016		9,,71,400				9,016		9,71,400
July 1		To Balance b/d	1,816								

Periodic Balance Method

Under this method interest is calculated after each transaction. Banks and Post Offices adopt this method. After every entry, balance amount as well as the number of days are recorded. The days are counted from the date of one transaction to the date of next transaction. Alternatively, find out the debit totals and credit totals of Product Columns, then multiply the products by their respective rates of interest. Interest is calculated for a day or a month @ 1% on the balance. Write the interest on the larger product side. Follow the two illustrations explained below:

ILLUSTRATION 13.7

Mr Mohan opened a current account with the Indian Bank on Ist January 2005 and deposited Rs 7,000.

His deposits during the period were:

Jan. 25	Rs 1,500
April 15	Rs 2,500
May 26	Rs 800
June 20	Rs 2,000

His withdrawals were:

Jan. 20	Rs 4,000
Feb. 10	Rs 3,000
March 5	Rs 2,000
May 20	Rs 1,800
June 8	Rs 2,750

Calculate interest @ 10% p.a. on the customer's debit balances and 6% p.a. on credit balances and close the account on 30th June 2005.

SOLUTION:

Mr Mohan in Account Current with the Indian Bank

Date	Particulars	Deposits Rs	with-drawals Rs	Dr./Cr.	Balance Rs	Days	Dr. Balance	Cr. Balance
2005								
Jan. 1	By Cash	7,000	–	Cr.	7,000	19	–	1,33,000
Jan. 20	To Cheque No.	–	4,000	Cr.	3,000	5	–	15,000
Jan. 25	By Cash	1,500	–	Cr.	4,500	16	–	72,000
Feb. 10	To Cheque No.	–	3,000	Cr.	1,500	24	–	36,000
Mar. 5	To Cheque No.	–	2,000	Dr.	500	41	20,500	–
Apr. 15	By Cash	2,500	–	Cr.	2,000	35	–	70,000
May 20	To Cheque No.		1,800	Cr.	200	6	–	1,200
May 26	By Cash	800	–	Cr.	1,000	13	–	13,000
June 8	To Cheque No.		2,750	Dr.	1,750	12	21,000	–
June 20	By Cash	2,000	–	Cr.	250	10	–	2,500
June 30	To Interest*	86.83						
June 30	To Balance		336.83					
		13,886.83	13,886.83				41,500	3,42,700

* $\frac{3,42,700 \times 10 \times 1}{100 \quad 366} = 93.63\ (-)$

$\frac{41,500 \times 6 \times 1}{100 \quad 366} = 6.80$

$= 86.83$

ILLUSTRATION 13.8

From the following prepare an Account Current by A to B charging interest on debits @ 12% and on credits @ 8% p.a.

		Rs
2004 Jan. 1	Balance due from B	600
10	Sold goods to B	520
17	B returned goods	125
Feb. 10	B Paid by cheque	400
14	B accepted A's draft for one month	300
April 29	Goods sold to B	615
May 15	Received cash from B	700
June 5	B accepted A's Bill for 3 months	500

Note : Solution of this illustration is given on pages 467 & 468.

AVERAGE DUE DATE

Average Due Date is the date on which several debts due on different dates can be paid by a single payment without any loss of interest either to debtor or creditor. Average Due Date or Equated Due Date is the arithmetic average of several due dates. When a person owes various amounts on different dates to another person, it may be desired to discharge the debts on a single date by a lump sum payment without any loss of interest to either party. Such an equated date of payment is called the Average Due Date. The application of the average due date comes into use in settlement of accounts, such as, Bill transactions, payment of credit transactions, calculation of interest on drawings by partners etc.

Calculation of Average Due Date

Procedure for calculation of Average Due Date varies according to the type of the problem involved, viz.

1. Lending in instalments but repayment in one lump sum.
2. Lending in lump sum but repayment in instalments.

FIRST METHOD

Procedure for calculation of Average Due Date, when lending in instalments but repayment in one lump sum, is as follows:

1. Take any convenient date (preferably the first due date) as the Starting Point or Zero Date or Start Date or Focal Date or Base Date.
2. Count the number of days of each transaction from the base date.
3. Multiply the amount of each transaction with the number of days thus calculated.
4. Add all the products so obtained.
5. Add the amount of all transactions.
6. Divide the total products by total amount (of all items)
7. The result of (6) is the number of days by which AVERAGE DUE DATE is away from the Base Date:

$$\text{Average Due Date} = \text{Base Date} \pm \frac{\text{Total of Product}}{\text{Total of Amounts}}$$

SOLUTION: (Solution of illustration 13.8)

B in Account Current with A as on 30th June 2004

Date	Due Date	Particulars	Amount Rs	Days to 30th June	Products	Date	Due Date	Particulars	Amout Rs	Days to 30th June	Products
2004						2004					
Jan. 1	Jan. 1	To Balance b/d	600	182	1,09,200	Jan. 17	Jan. 17	By Sales Return A/c	125	165	20,625
Jan. 10	Jan. 10	To Sales A/c	520	172	89,440	Feb. 10	Feb. 10	By Bank A/c	400	141	56,400
April 29	April 29	To Sales A/c	615	62	38,130	Feb. 14	March 17	By B/R A/c	300	105	31,500
June 30		To Interest on Total of debit Products $\frac{236770 \times 12 \times 1}{100 \times 366}$	77.62			May 15	May 15	By Cash A/c	700	46	32,200
						June 5	Sept. 8	By B/R A/c	500	(–) 70	(–) 35,000
						June 30		By Interest on Total of credit product $\frac{1,05,725 \times 8 \times 1}{100 \times 366}$	23.10		
June 30		To Balance c/d	235.48								
			2,048.10		2,36,770				2,048.10		1,05,725
						July 1		By Balance b/d	235.48		

The above problem is solved in another method.

B in Account Current with A as on 30th June 2004

Dr. Cr.

Date	Due Date	Particulars	Amount Rs	Days to 30th June	Products	Date	Due Date	Particulars	Amout Rs	Days to 30th June	Products
2004						2004					
Jan. 1	Jan. 1	To Balance b/d	600	182	1,09,200	Jan. 17	Jan. 17	By Sales Return	125	165	20,625
Jan. 10	Jan. 10	To Sales A/c	520	172	89,440	Feb. 10	Feb. 10	By Bank A/c	400	141	56,400
April 29	April 29	To Sales A/c	615	62	38,130	Feb. 14	March 17	By B/R A/c	300	105	31,500
						May 15	May 15	By Cash A/c	700	46	32,200
						June 5	Sept. 8	By B/r	500	(–) 70	(–) 35,000
					2,36,770						1,05,725
		To Rate of Interest			12			By Rate of Interest			8
					28,41,240						8,45,800
June 30		To Interest on Balance of product	54.52*			June 30		By Balance of Product			19,95,440
June 30		To Balance c/d	235.48								
			2,025		28,41,240				2,025		28,41,240
						July 1		By Balance b/d	235.48		

* $\frac{19{,}95{,}440 \times 1}{366 \times 100}$ = Rs 54.52

ILLUSTRATION 13.9

Mr Komal had accepted the undermentioned Bills payable to Suman:

Date of Acceptance	Term	Amount Rs
15th Sept. 2004	2 months	200
10th Oct. 2004	2 months	400
30th Nov. 2004	3 months	500
10th Dec. 2004	3 months	600
30th Jan. 2005	2 months	300

Komal desires to pay the aggregate amount of all these Bills on such a date as would involve no profit or loss to either of them and Suman agrees. Find out the date of this proposed payment.

(*B.Com., Madurai, Calicut, Jiwaji*)

SOLUTION:

1. Three days of grace are added in all the Bills whether they are in months or days.
2. If the amount of a Bill is payable in instalments then in the period of each instalment, days of grace are added.

	Nov.	Dec.	Jan.	Feb.	Mar	April	Total
18th Nov. to 18th Nov. 2004	0	–	–	–	–	–	0
18th Nov. to 13th Dec. 2004	12	13	–	–	–	–	25
18th Nov. to 3rd Mar. 2005	12	31	31	28	3	–	105
18th Nov. to 13th Mar. 2005	12	31	31	28	13	–	115
18th Nov. to 2nd April 2005	12	31	31	28	31	2	135

Calculation of Average Due Date (Base Date: 18th Nov. 2004)

Due Date	Amount Rs	No. of Days from 18th Nov. 2004	Products (2 × 3)
18th Nov. 2004	200	0	0
13th Dec. 2004	400	25	10,000
3rd March 2005	500	105	52,500
13th March 2005	600	115	69,000
2nd April 2005	300	135	40,500
	2,000		1,72,000

$$\text{Average Due Date} = \text{Base Date} \pm \frac{\text{Total of Products}}{\text{Total of Amounts}}$$

$$= \text{18th Nov. 2004} + \frac{1,72,000}{2,000}$$

= 18th Nov. 2004 + 86 days

= 12th February 2005

Due Dates of Bills

15th Sept. 2004 + 2 Months + 3 days = 18th Nov. 2004

10th Oct. 2004 + 2 Months + 3 days = 13th Dec. 2004

30th Nov. 2004 + 3 Months + 3 days = 3rd March 2005

10th Dec. 2004 + 3 Months + 3 days = 13th March 2005

30th Jan. 2005 + 2 Months + 3 days = 2nd April 2005

Note: It should be noted that it is not necessary that one should always take the first due date as the base date for the calculation of Average Due Date. We can take any date as base date. Though any due date can be selected as a base, the earliest or first due date as starting point is most preferable and to avoid minus figures.

ILLUSTRATION 13.10

Kumar, a partner in a firm has drawn the following amounts for the half year ended 30th June 2004:

Jan. 8	Rs 440	April 10	Rs 480
Feb. 12	Rs 400	May 6	Rs 400
Mar. 15	Rs 500	June 8	Rs 400

Interest is charged at 10% p.a. Ascertain average due date and the amount of interest.

(B.Com., Madurai, Mysore, Madras)

SOLUTION:

Calculation of Average Due Date

Due Date	Amount Rs	No. of Days from 8th Jan. 2004	Products
8th Jan. 2004	440	0	0
12th Feb. 2004	400	35	14,000
15th Mar. 2004	500	67	33,500
10th April 2004	480	93	44,640
6th May 2004	400	119	47,600
8th June 2004	400	152	60,800
	2,620		2,00,540

$$\text{Average Due Date} = \text{8th Jan.} + \frac{2,00,540}{2,620} = 76.5 \text{ days or 77 days}$$

= 8th Jan. 2004 + 77 days

= 25th March 2004

The date of settlement is 30th June 2004. Thus interest is to be calculated from 25th March 2004 to 30th June 2004, *i.e.* for 97 days (March 6 days + April 30 + May 31 and June 30 days = 97 days) at 10% p.a.

$$\text{Interest} = \frac{2,620 \times 97 \times 10}{366 \times 100} = \text{Rs } 69.44$$

No. of days:

J		F		M		A		M		J	
23	+	12		–		–		–		–	35
23	+	29	+	15	+	+	+				67
23	+	29	+	31	+	10		–		–	93
23	+	29	+	31	+	30	+	6		–	119
23	+	29	+	31	+	30	+	31	+	8	152

SECOND METHOD

Procedure for calculation of Average Due Date when lending in lump sum but repayment in instalments, is as follows:

1. The basic day is the lending date. Calculate the number of days (or months or years) from the date of lending to the date of each payment.
2. Find out the total number of days/months/years as calculated above.
3. Divide the total as calculated by number of instalments to repay the loan.
4. Add the result (obtained above) to the date of loan to get Average Due Date.

Formulae:

$$\text{Average Due Date} = \text{Date of Loan} + \frac{\text{Total of number of days/months/years calculated from the date of loan to the repayment of instalments}}{\text{Number of instalments}}$$

ILLUSTRATION 13.11 (Repayable in equal instalments)

Mr A had lent Rs 5,000 to B on Ist Jan. 2002. Loan is repayable in 5 half-yearly instalments commencing from Ist Jan. 2003 Interest is charged at 12%. Calculate Average Due Date.

SOLUTION:

Instalments	Due Dates	Months since Jan. 1st 2002
1st	Jan. 1 2003	12 months
2nd	July 1 2003	18 months
3rd	Jan. 1 2004	24 months
4th	July 1 2004	30 months
5th	Jan. 1 2005	36 months
		120 months

Average Due Date = 1st Jan. 2002 + 120/5
= 1st Jan. 2002 + 24 months
= 1st Jan. 2004

Interest @ 12% p.a. Rs 5,000 × $\frac{12}{100} \times \frac{24}{12}$ = Rs 1,200

ILLUSTRATION 13.12 (Repayable in unequal instalments)

Rs 15,000 let on Ist January 2000 is repayable as below:

Rs 1,000 on Ist January 2001

Rs 3,000 on Ist January 2003

Rs 5,000 on Ist January 2004

Rs 6,000 on Ist January 2005

Determine the Average Due Date for settling all the above instalments by single payment and compute interest at 6% p.a. (*B.Com., Madurai*)

SOLUTION:

Due Date	Amount Rs	No. of months from 1.1.2000	Products
1st Jan. 2001	1,000	12 months	12,000
1st Jan. 2003	3,000	36 months	1,08,000
1st Jan. 2004	5,000	48 months	2,40,000
1st Jan. 2005	6,000	60 months	3,60,000
	15,000		7,20,000

Average Due Date = 1st Jan. 2000 + 7,20,000/15,000
= 1st Jan. 2000 + 48 months
= 1st Jan. 2000 + 4 years
= 1st January 2004

Interest for four years = $\frac{15,000 \times 4 \times 6}{100}$ = Rs 3,600

ILLUSTRATION 13.13

Mr Kapoor had the following Bills Receivable and Bills Payable against Mr Ramanathan.

Calculate the Average Due Date when the payment can be made or received without any loss of interest to either party.

Bills Receivable			*Bills Payable*		
Date	Amount	Tenure (months)	Date	Amount	Tenure (months)
1.5.2005	2,000	4	10.5.2005	1,000	2
12.6.2005	1,500	2	29.5.2005	3,000	4
15.6.2005	3,000	3	6.6.2005	2,000	2
7.7.2005	1,000	2	17.6.2005	1,500	3
10.7.2005	2,500	1	30.6.2005	500	1

Gazetted Holidays intervening in the period:

15th Aug. 2005

2nd October 2005

18th September 2005 (Emergency Holiday) *(CA) (B.Com., Madurai, Mysore)*

SOLUTION:

Calculation of Average Due Date

Bills Receivable					*Bills Payable*				
Date	Due Date	Amount	No. of Days (from July 13)	Product	Date	Due Date	Amount	No. of Days (from) July 13)	Product
		Rs					Rs		
1.5.2005	4.9.2005	2,000	53	1,06,000	10.5.2005	13.7.2005	1,000	0	–
12.6.2005	14.8.2005	1,500	32	48,000	29.5.2005	1.10.2005	3,000	80	2,40,000
15.6.2005	19.9.2005	3,000	68	2,04,000	6.6.2005	9.8.2005	2,000	27	54,000
7.7.2005	10.9.2005	1,000	59	59,000	17.6.2005	20.9.2005	1,500	69	1,03,500
10.7.2005	13.8.2005	2,500	31	77,500	30.6.2005	2.8.2005	500	20	10,000
		10,000		4,94,500			8,000		4,07,500

$$\text{No. of Days} = \frac{\text{Difference in Products}}{\text{Difference in Amounts}} = \frac{4{,}94{,}500 - 4{,}07{,}500}{10{,}000 - 8{,}000} = \frac{87{,}000}{2{,}000} = 44 \text{ days}$$

Average Due Date = Starting Date + No. of Days

= 13th July 2005 + 44 days = 26th August 2005

Note: When the due date of a bill after adding three days of grace falls on a public holiday, then due date will be on the working day preceding the public holiday.

When due date of a bill after adding three days of grace falls on such a day which has been suddenly declared a public holiday, then its due date will be on the succeeding working day after the emergency holiday.

ILLUSTRATION 13.14

Ram drew upon Vijayan several bills of exchange due for payment on different dates as under:

Date of the Bill	Amount Rs.	Tenure of the Bill
1st June	1,200	3 Months
19th June	1,600	2 Months

10th July	2,000	3 Months
27th July	1,500	3 Months
7th Aug.	1,800	1 Month
15th Aug.	2,400	2 Months

Find out Average Due Date on which payment may be made in one single amount. *(B. Com. MS)*

Solution.

Computation of Average Due Date

Due Date (1)	Amount Rs. (2)	No. of days from Base Date : 22n Aug. (3)	Product Rs. (4) (2 × 3)
4th Sept.	1,200	13	15,600
22nd Aug.	1,600	0	0
13th Oct.	2,000	52	1,04,000
30th Oct.	1,500	69	1,03,500
10th Sept.	1,800	19	34,200
18th Oct.	2,400	57	1,36,800
Total	10,500		3,94,100

$$\text{Average Due Date} = \text{Base Date} + \frac{\text{Total of Products}}{\text{Total of Amounts}}$$

$$= \text{22nd Aug.} + \frac{3,94,100}{10,500} = \text{22nd Aug.} + 38 \text{ days}$$

Average Due Date = **29th September.**

UTILITY OF AVERAGE DUE DATE

Average Due Date is useful in the following types of accounting problems:

1. Problems relating to calculation of interest on drawings by partners, on different dates.
2. Problems relating to settlement of accounts by a series of bills of exchange due on different dates.
3. Problems of settlement of accounts between principal and an agent.
4. Problems involving settlement of accounts between one trader and another or a trader and his customers.
5. Problems relating to piece-meal distribution of amount, during dissolution of partnership firms.

QUESTIONS

Objective Type Questions.

I. State whether each of the following statements is "True" or "False".

1. Account Current and Current Account are synonymous terms.
2. Average Due Date is the date on which accounts are actually settled by the parties.
3. Account Current is the account opened by a banker when a person deposits money.
4. Account Current is a statement of transactions between two parties during a specified period.
5. If payment is made on the average due date, it results in loss of interest to the creditor.
6. Zero date is the date on which no transactions taken place between the debtor and creditor.
7. Average due date is the mean of due date of various transactions.
8. Average due date is also termed as equated date.
9. Average due date is the mean date on which a single payment can be made.

10. If payment is made before average due date, the party entitled to interest is the creditor.

(Ans : True : 4, 7, 8, 9, False : - 1, 2, 3, 5, 6, 10.

II. Select the most appropriate answer:

1. The account maintained by a businessman with his banker is known as :
   (*a*) Current Account. (*b*) Account Current.
   (*c*) Savings Bank Account.
2. The number of days is calculated from the date of the transaction to the date of settlement in case of:
   (*a*) Forward Method. (*b*) Epoque Method.
   (*c*) Daily Balance Method.
3. In case of running account between traders, the due date for transaction is :
   (*a*) Date of delivery of goods. (*b*) Date of the transaction.
   (*c*) Date of collecting cash.
4. When due date of transaction falls on a public holiday, the due date will be:
   (*a*) the same. (*b*) One day after that holiday.
   (*c*) One day before that holiday.
5. Due date of a bill payable one month after sight should be computed:
   (*a*) From the date of transaction. (*b*) From the date of acceptance of the bill.
   (*c*) From the date of drawing the bill.
6. Epoque method is used:
   (*a*) In Account Current. (*b*) In Average Due Date.
   (*c*) In Savings Account.
7. Red Ink Interest is associated with :
   (*a*) Average Due Date. (*b*) Current Account.
   (*c*) Account Current.
8. The number of days are calculated from the date of the transaction to the date of settlement in case of :
   (*a*) Forward method. (*b*) Epoque method.
   (*c*) Daily Balance method.

(*Ans* : 1. (*a*); 2. (*a*); 3. (*b*); 4. (*c*); 5. (*b*); 6. (*a*); 7. (*c*); 8. (*a*).

THEORETICAL QUESTIONS

1. What do you mean by Account Current? (*B.Com., MK*)
2. What is an average due date? Why is it necessary to find out average due date? (*B.Com., Madras*)
3. Who are the parties involved in the preparation of Account Current? (*B.Com., Madras*)
4. How is the Average Due Date calculated? (*B.Com., Kerala*)
5. What are the methods used for calculating the days for computing interest in Account Current.

PRACTICAL PROBLEMS

Account Current

1. The following are the particulars of transactions that have taken place between A and B for a period of six months. In the books of A

		Rs
July 1	Balance (Dr.)	4,000
10	Purchased goods from B	3,000
25	Paid cash by B	1,000
August 10	Sold goods to B	10,000
25	Given two months acceptance to B	5,000
Sept. 10	Paid cash to B	3,000
20	Purchased goods from B	7,000

You are required to prepare an Account Current to be rendered by A to B for the period upto Dec. 31, 2004. Interest is to be charged at an agreed rate of 12% p.a. (*B.Com., Madurai, Bangalore*)

[Ans: Interest Rs 467.87]

2. The following is the account of Anand in the ledger of Kamlesh:

2003		Rs	2003		Rs
Jan. 1	To Balance b/d	15,000	Mar. 25	By Returns	1,000
Mar. 9	To Sales	30,000	Apr. 10	By Cash	15,000
May 25	To Sales	7,000	June 3	By Cash	20,000
			June 30	By Balance c/d	16,000
		52,000			52,000

Calculate average due date and the amount of interest payable or receivable by Anand at 6% p.a. to 30th June, 2003. (*B.Com., Kurukshetra*)

[Ans: Average Due Date = 22nd September 2002
Interest Rs 739]

3. On Ist January 2004, X owed Rs 5,000 to Y on account. During the three months ended 31st March 2004, the transactions were as follows in the books of Y:

		Rs
Jan. 10	Received two Bills for 2 months and 3 months respectively from X (Rs 2,000 each)	4,000
20	Mat a Bill for 2 months (due this day) drawn by X on November 17, 2003	1,000
Feb. 9	Paid Cash to X	1,000
19	Received cash from X	1,000
Mar. 1	Sold goods to X	1,000
13	X's acceptance due this day dishonoured	

Prepare Account Current to be rendered to X on 31st March 2004, interest to be reckoned at 9% p.a. (*B.Com., Punjab, MS*)

[Ans: Interest Rs 128.12
Amount Due : Rs 4,128.12]

4. Mehra owed Rs 3,000 on Ist Jan. 2004 to Somesh. The following are the transactions that took place between them during 2004. It is agreed between the parties that interest @ 12% per annum is to be calculated on all transactions.

2004		Rs
Jan. 16	Somesh sold goods to Mehra	2,000
Jan. 29	Somesh purchased goods from Mehra	1,500
Feb. 10	Somesh pays cash	1,500
Mar. 7	Mehra accepts a bill drawn for one month	2,000

They desire to settle their accounts by one single payment on 15th March 2004. Ascertain the amount to be paid to the nearest rupee. Ignore days of grace. (*B.Com., Madurai*)

[Ans: Amount to be paid Rs 3,123.60]

5. Mr A had the following transactions with B:

2004		Rs
January 1	Balance (Dr.)	1,000
January 10	Goods sold	600
February 20	Cash received	900
March 5	Goods purchased	1,200

April 25	Cash paid	400
May 16	Goods sold	500
May 16	Received a Bill for Rs 300 at one month and discounted for	290

Make out an Account Current to be submitted by A to B on 30th June 2004 charging interest @ 16% p.a. on debit items and allowing interest @ 12% on credit items. (*B.Com., Andhra*)

[Ans: Amount due Rs 160.33]

6. Santharam had the following transactions with Kantilal:

2004		Rs
Jan. 1	Balance due from Kantilal	1,000
Feb. 16	Purchased goods from him	6,000
Feb. 28	Sold goods to him	10,000
Mar. 16	Received a cheque	3,000
Apr. 20	Sold him goods (invoiced on May 3)	10,000
June 16	Purchased goods from him (invoiced on July 16)	15,000
Sep. 23	Paid him cash	3,000
Oct. 24	Accepted his bill for 3 months	5,000
Nov. 26	Received his acceptance for 2 months	8,000

You are asked to prepare an Account Current of Kantilal completed upto 31st December 2004 as will appear in the books of Santharam reckoning 12% interest on the balance due.

(*CA*) (*B.Com., Agra, Poona*)

[Ans: Interest Rs 310.16
Balance Amount Rs 2,689.84]

7. Santosh had the following transactions with Kamal:

2004		Rs
Jan. 1	Balance due from Kamal	600
Feb. 6	Purchased goods from him	600
Feb. 28	Sold goods to him	2,000
Mar. 7	Received a cheque from him	300
April 20	Sold him goods (invoice on May 5th)	1,000
May 17	Purchased goods from him (Invoiced on 17th June)	500
May 22	Accepted his bill for 2 months	500
June 1	Received his acceptance for 2 months	800
June 15	He returned goods (Out of the goods sold on April 20)	200

Prepare an Account Current upto 30th June 2004 to be rendered by Santosh to Kamal charging interest at 10% p.a. (*B.Com., Delhi*)

[Ans: Interest Rs 75
Balance Amount Rs 775]

8. Rajeev owes Anil Rs 2,000 on Ist July, 2004. He has accepted the following bills drawn upon him by Anil:

Bills for Rs 800 drawn on 12th July, payable one month after date.

Bill for Rs 1,400 drawn on Ist Aug. payable 2 month after date.

Rajeev has also received the following acceptances from Anil:

Bill for Rs 500 drawn on 28th July payable three months after date.

Bill for Rs 400 drawn on 29th July payable 2 months after date.

Bill for Rs 600 drawn on 10th Aug. payable after 2 months.

Bills for Rs 1,000 drawn on 13th Aug. payable after 3 months.

Rajeev wants to settle the account with Anil by one single payment on the equated date. Calculate the equated date and the amount to be paid on that date. Holidays during the period are:

Gazetted holiday: 15th Aug., 2nd Oct., and 31st Oct.

Emergency holiday: 16th Nov *(B.Com., Madurai)*

[**Ans:** Average Due Date = 27th August 2004

Amount to be paid : Rs 2,300]

9. Prepare an Account Current to be rendered by B on 31st March 2004 in respect of the following transactions with A:

		Rs
Jan. 1	Bought goods from A	751
4	Paid cash to A	201
20	Purchased goods from A	580
25	Paid to A	351
Feb. 10	Purchased goods from A	490
20	Paid cash to A	1,400
Mar. 10	Bought goods from A	900
25	Paid cash to A	100

Interest @ 10% p.a. is to be taken into account. *(B.Com., MK, MS, Punjab)*

[**Ans:** Interest Rs 15

Balance Amount Rs 684]

10. Prepare an Account Current on the basis of information given below which Velu prepares on 30th June 2004. Interest is to be calculated @ 10% p.a.

The following transactions were effected between Velu and Ram:

2004		Rs
Jan. 1	Goods sold to Ram	420
Feb. 15	Received cash from Ram	150
March 2	Purchased goods from Ram	1,035
March 3	Ram accepted a Bill for one month	300
April 11	Paid to Ram	300
April 30	Sold goods to Ram (Due date 31st May)	348
May 11	Purchased goods from Ram	255
May 31	Sold goods to Ram	375
June 15	Purchased goods from Ram (Due date end of July)	435

(B.Com., Karnataka, MS)

[**Ans:** Interest Rs 13.02

Balance Amount : Rs 745.02]

11. Prepare an Account Current upto December 2003 to be rendered by A to B charging interest at 10% p.a.

2003		Rs
July 1	Opening Balance b/d (Debit)	1,500
15	Goods purchased by A from B	5,000
25	Goods sold by B to A	3,000
Aug. 6	Goods sold by A to B	8,000
22	Goods sold by A to B (Due date on 25th Aug.)	6,000

Sept. 10	Goods sold by A to B (Due on 15th Sept.)	10,000
Oct. 12	Cash paid by A to B	2,000
Nov. 15	Bill drawn by A on B for 3 months	3,000
Dec. 10	Bill accepted by A to B for 3 months	2,000

(*B.Com., Mumbai, Bharathiar*)

[**Ans:** Interest Rs 582
Balance Amount Rs 19,082]

12. Make out an Account Current to be submitted by A to B on 30th September 2004 in respect of the following transactions appearing in the books of A.

		Rs
July 1	Debit balance b/d	13,500
5	Sold goods to B	9,000
15	Received cash from B	13,500
Aug. 4	Sold goods to B	19,200
15	Received cash from B	9,000
Sept. 1	Bought goods from B	21,000
1	Paid cash to B	7,500
12	Sold goods to B	9,600
15	Paid cash to B	6,000

Interest to be taken into account at 10% p.a. calculated to the nearest rupee.

(*CAIIB*) (*B.Com., Agra, Delhi, Punjab*)

[**Ans:** Interest Rs 420
Balance Amount Rs 21,720]

13. On Ist July 2004, X owed Rs 8,000 to Y on account. During three months ended 30th September 2004, the transactions were as follows in the books of Y.

		Rs
July 10	Received two Bills for 2 months and 3 months from X (Rs 3,000 each)	6,000
Aug. 16	Paid cash to X	2,000
Aug. 25	Met a Bill for 2 months (due this day) drawn on June 22, 2004	1,500
Sept. 2	Paid cash to X	1,000
11	Received cash from X	3,000
13	X's acceptance due this day dishonoured	
18	Sold goods to X	2,000
23	Purchase goods from X	1,000

Prepare Account Current to be rendered to X on 30th September 2004 reckoning interest @ 12% p.a.

(*B.com., Madurai*)

[**Ans:** Interest Rs 279.67
Balance Amount : Rs 6,279.67]

Average Due Date

14. A purchased goods from B, the due dates are as follows:

Rs 600 due on January 1,2004
Rs 500 due on February 6, 2004
Rs 400 due on March 16, 2004

Rs 300 due on April 25, 2004

Rs 200 due on May 25, 2004

You are required to calculate the average due date. (*B.Com., Madurai*)

[Ans: Average Due Date: 26th February 2004]

15. A purchased from B, for which he accepted bills drawn by B and the bills were to be honoured after three months from the respective dates of the invoice as per the details given below.

Date of Invoice	Value of Goods
10th Jan. 2004	6,000
20th Feb. 2004	10,000
30th Mar. 2004	5,000
1st May 2004	15,000
10th Jun. 2004	12,000

A preferred to honour all the bills on 15th Oct. 2004 and interest @ 8% p.a. should be calculated with the help of the average due date. (*B.Com., Kerala, MS, MK*)

[Ans: Average Due Date: 12th July 2004
Interest Rs 996.72]

16. A trader having accepted the following several bills falling due on different dates, now desires to have these bills cancelled and to accept a new bill for the whole amount payable on the average due date:

Sl. No.	Date of Bills	Amount Rs	Usance of the Bill
1.	1st March 2004	400	2 months
2.	10th March 2004	300	3 months
3.	5th April 2004	200	2 months
4.	20th April 2004	375	1 month
5.	10th May 2004	500	2 months

You are required to find the said average due date. (*B.Com., Kerala*)

[Ans: Average Due Date: 7th June 2004]

17. A partner has withdrawn the following sum of money during the half year ending 30th June 2004:

2004	Rs
January 17	300
January 20	400
February 18	240
March 5	160
March 15	200
April 24	400
May 2	300
May 16	200
June 30	300

Interest is to be charged at 10% per annum. Find out the Average due date and calculate the interest. (*B.Com., Kerala, Madurai*)

[Ans: Average Due Date: 26th March 2004
Interest Rs 65.57]

18. A trader has accepted the following bills falling due on the dates noted against each. He now wishes to have these bills cancelled and to accept a new bill for the whole amount payable on the average due date.

	Amount of the Bills Rs	Due Date
1.	740	7th May 2004

2.	1,340	20th May 2004
3.	600	22nd May 2004
4.	1,500	23rd June 2004
5.	800	18th Aug. 2004
6.	900	10th Sept. 2004
7.	500	15th Sept. 2004

(*B.Com., Madurai, MK*)

[**Ans:** Average Due Date: 30th June 2004]

19. Iqbal owes to Mehta the following sums:

    Rs 1,000 due on 16th January 2004
    Rs 1,600 due on 20th February 2004
    Rs 1,200 due on 15th March 2004
    Rs 1,800 due on 31st March 2004

    Iqbal decides to pay all these sums together on a date which will means no loss or gain of interest to him; *i.e.*, on the average due date. Find out the average due date in this case. (*B.Com., Kerala, Madurai*)

    [**Ans:** Average Due Date: 3rd March 2004]

20. Mr. Ashok has accepted the following Bills. Find the Average Due Date:

Due Date of Bills	Amount Rs
23rd June 2004	1,500
8th July 2004	2,300
12th August 2004	3,200
6th September 2004	2,400
21st September 2004	600

(*B.Com., Kerala*)

[**Ans:** Average Due Date: 5th August 2004]

21. A partner has withdrawn the sums of money during the half year ending 30th June, 2004:

	Rs
15th Jan.	500
10th Feb.	400
12th Mar.	700
5th Apr.	800
20th May	1,000
18th June	900

Interest is to be charged at 10% per annum. Find out the average due date and calculate the interest on drawings. (*B.Com., Kerala*)

[**Ans:** Average Due Date: 13th April 2004
Interest Amount Rs 91.64]

Chapter 14

Self-Balancing Ledgers

Debtors' Ledger – Creditors' Ledger – General Ledger – Sectional Balancing – Self-Balancing – Interledgers Transfer – Multiple Ledgers – Contra Balance – Rectification of Errors – Questions – Objective Type Questions – Theoretical Questions – Practical Problems.

A small firm may keep only one ledger where all the accounts are maintained due to limited number and size of accounts. Since all the transactions are conveniently recorded in one ledger, the preparation of Trial Balance is easy apart from the easy detection of disagreement of Trial Balance, at the end of accounting period. But when the business expands, transactions become numerous. It is therefore practically impossible to maintain all accounts in one ledger. As the size of ledger increases, it is not easy to find out the desired information from the ledgers. Rectification of errors is also difficult due to its bulkiness. Preparation of final accounts may be delayed due to imbalance of Trial Balance. Ledger posting also takes a lot of time. The Trial Balance plays a vital role in the preparation of final accounts. The agreement of the books, therefore, is a must for any concern. To meet the situation, multiple ledger system is introduced by splitting the single ledger into General and Subsidiary ledgers. All the individual customers' and suppliers' also forming the bulk of overall accounts go to subsidiary ledgers and remaining accounts lie in General Ledger. Therefore, to make the task of locating errors simpler and easier, the system of self-balancing had been designed. Self-balancing is a practical system of accounting whereby a main ledger is sub-divided into more than one ledger in order to record different types of accounts at their appropriate places strictly according to their nature and whereby each such ledger is made to balance. That is, to balance each ledger individually without the help of other ledgers, is called self-balancing. Under this system each ledger is maintained in such a manner so as to contain all the materials needed for preparing a Trial Balance separately for each ledger without the help of other ledgers.

When a businessman has many customers and many suppliers, he faces difficulty of maintaining the ledgers systematically. At the same time, when the business is big, the number of Real Accounts and Impersonal Accounts do not abnormally increase, but the number of personal accounts, in proportion to the Real Accounts and Impersonal Accounts, increase too much. And with a view to facilitating the detection of errors, a system called "Self-balancing ledgers" had been evolved. Under this system, the ledgers are devised in such a way that when balances are extracted, a separate Trial Balance can be prepared from each ledger. Following are the three divisions of ledgers:

1. DEBTOR'S LEDGER

The expression 'trade debtor' signifies a credit customer to whom sale is made of goods in which a seller trades. This ledger is kept for recording the personal accounts of trade debtors only and not of any other debtors. This ledger is also known as Sales Ledger or Sold Ledger. Thus, if Mr X trades in cloth and sells it to Mr A on credit, the latter is X's trade debtor and put in sold ledger. At the same time, X sells furniture on credit in which he does not deal, A is his non-trade debtor and hence placed in the General Ledger.

2. CREDITORS' LEDGER

The expression 'trade creditor' signifies a credit supplier from whom purchase is made of goods in which a buyer deals. This ledger is kept for recording the personal accounts of trade creditors only and not of any other creditors. Thus if Mr X who trades in cloth, purchases furniture from Mr A, the latter is non-trade creditor.

3. GENERAL LEDGER

This is the main ledger which contains the rest of accounts that is, all other accounts (nominal and real accounts) except the trade debtors and trade creditors accounts. The ledger is also known as Nominal Ledger or Main Ledger or Private Ledger.

When all the three important ledgers are made self-balancing, the system is known as the self-balancing ledger system, whereas if one or two of these ledgers alone are made self-balancing, the system is known as the Sectional Balancing Ledger system. As the posting of various accounts is made in three different ledgers, it is essential to test the accuracy of each ledger by drawing a separate trial balance for each ledger. But this is not possible because none of the ledgers contains in itself all the information required for preparation of a Trial Balance. For instance, the Debtors' Ledger records only the personal accounts of the debtors, the corresponding accounts, such as credit sales, discount allowed, sales returns, cash received etc. being recorded in General Ledger. Same is the case with creditors' ledger. The following table explains the posting to various accounts.

SECTIONAL BALANCING

Self-balancing is a system of balancing all the three ledgers including the main ledger. But under sectional-balancing, only a section of the group of the ledgers is made to balance. Thus, when only one of the three different ledgers is made to balance, it may be known as sectional balancing. In fact sectional balancing is a part of the process of self-balancing. The following illustration will explain.

ILLUSTRATION 14.1

Details of the transaction of a Firm for Jan. 2004

Debtors	Credit Sales Rs	Cash received Rs	Discount allowed Rs
Ram	2,000	1,000	50
Krishna	3,000	2,000	75
Gopal	4,000	3,000	200
Total	9,000	6,000	325

The following entries are made in case of sectional balancing:

Note: The entries are to be done as and when the transactions take place. The entries in the General Ledger are made at the end of a period.

1. For credit sales, each debtor will be debited.
2. For cash received, each debtor will be credited.
3. For discount allowed, each debtor will be credited.

The various ledgers will appear as follows:

In Debtors' Ledger

Ram Account

Dr.	Rs		Cr. Rs
To Sales	2,000	By Cash	1,000
		By Discount	50
		By Balance c/d	950
	2,000		2,000
To Balance b/d	950		

Krishna Account

Dr.	Rs		Cr. Rs
To Sales	3,000	By Cash	2,000
		By Discount	75
		By Balance c/d	925
	3,000		3,000
To Balance b/d	925		

Gopal Account

Dr.	Rs		Cr. Rs
To Sales	4,000	By Cash	3,000
		By Discount	200
		By Balance c/d	800
	4,000		4,000
To Balance b/d	800		

In General Ledger

Total Debtors' Account

Dr.	Rs		Cr. Rs
To Sales	9,000	By Cash	6,000
		By Discount	325
		By Balance c/d	2,675
	9,000		9,000
To Balance b/d	2,675		

Discount Allowed Account

Dr.	Rs		Cr. Rs
To Total Debtors	325	By Balance c/d	325
To Balance b/d	325		

Cash Account

Dr.	Rs		Cr. Rs
To Total Debtors	6,000	By Balance c/d	6,000

Sales Account

Dr.	Rs		Cr. Rs
To Balance c/d	9,000	By Total Debtors	9,000
		By Balance b/d	9,000

Trial Balance of the General Ledger will appear as follows:

	Dr. Rs	Cr. Rs
Total Debtors	2,675	–
Discount Allowed	325	–
Cash	6,000	–
Sales	–	9,000
	9,000	9,000

Note: The balance shown in Total Debtors Account tallys with the total of balances as shown by the schedule of debtors. This proves the accuracy of the entries in Debtors' Ledger.

SELF-BALANCING

Self-balancing system is a system whereby separate Trial Balance can be taken out from each ledger. "General Ledger Adjustment Account" will be maintained in each of the sales and bought ledger. It is the reverse of the Total Debtors Account in Sales Ledger and Total Creditors Account in Bought Ledger. Under this system ledgers are made self-balancing by opening adjustment accounts. When goods of Rs 1,000 sold to Ram, then Ram's Account is debited with Rs 1,000 in Sales Ledger and Goods Account is credited with Rs 1,000 in General Ledger. In order to balance Sales Ledger Rs 1,000 should be credited in it, hence at the end of this ledger a General Ledger Adjustment Account is opened and Rs 1,000 are credited in it. In the same way, in all the ledgers adjustment accounts are opened.

1. At the end of Bought Ledger, a General Ledger Adjustment Account is opened, and whatever has been debited in Bought Ledger in various accounts, is credited in General Ledger Adjustment Account and whatever has been credited in Bought Ledger, is debited in General Ledger Adjustment Account.

2. At the end of Sales Ledger, General Adjustment Account is opened and all debits of Sales Ledger are recorded in the credit of General Ledger Adjustment Account.

3. At the end of General Ledger, two Adjustment accounts are opened i.e. Debtors' Ledger Adjustment Account and Creditors' Ledger Adjustment Account.

Thus:

In General Ledger:

(1) Sales Ledger Adjustment Account (same as total Debtors Account)

(2) Purchase Ledger Adjustment Account (same as total Creditors A/c)

In the Sales Ledger:

(3) General Ledger Adjustment Account (shadow of sales ledger adjustment account with the sides transposed)

In the Purchase Ledger:

(4) General Ledger Adjustment Account (shadow of purchases ledger adjustment account with the sides transposed)

To comply with the double entry principle, debit in one adjustment account is made by a corresponding credit to another adjustment account.

The relevant entries are:

1. For the items debited to customers in Debtors' Ledger:
   Debit Sold Ledger Adjustment Account (in General Ledger)
   Credit General Ledger Adjustment Account (in Sold Ledger)
2. For the items credited to customers in Debtors' Ledger:
   Debit General Ledger Adjustment Account (in Sold Ledger)
   Credit Sold Ledger Adjustment Account (in General Ledger)
3. For the items debited to suppliers in Creditors' Ledger:
   Debit Bought Ledger Adjustment Account (in General Ledger)
   Credit General Ledger Adjustment Account (in Bought Ledger)
4. For the items credited to suppliers in Crediors' Ledger:
   Debit General Ledger Adjustment Account (in Bought Ledger)
   Credit Bought Ledger Adjustment Account (in General Ledger)

The following journal entries are passed to make the Purchase Ledger self-balancing:

(1) For credit purchases, Bills Payable, dishonoured, interest and expenses charged by creditors:

General Ledger Adjustment Account (in Purchase Ledger)	Dr.
To Purchase Ledger Adjustment Account (in General Ledger)	

(2) For total cash paid to creditors, discount received and bills accepted, purchases, returns etc.

Purchase Ledger Adjustment Account (in General Ledger)	Dr.
To General Ledger Adjustment Account (Purchase Ledger)	

The following journal entries are passed to make the Sales Ledger self-balancing:

(1) For credit sales, bills receivable dishonoured, interest and expenses charged to debtors:

Sales Ledger Adjustment Account (in General Ledger)	Dr.
To General Ledger Adjustment Account (Sales Ledger)	

(2) For total of cash received from debtors, discount allowed to them bills received, sales returns and bad debts written off etc.

General Ledger Adjustment Account (in Sales Ledger)	Dr.
To Sales Ledger Adjustment Account (in General Ledger)	

Specimen of Adjustments
in the Creditors' Ledger
General Ledger Adjustment Account

Dr. Cr.

	Rs			*Rs*
To Balance b/d			By Creditors' Ledger	
To Creditors' Ledger Adjustment A/c			Adjustment A/c (in General Ledger):	
(in General Ledger):			Cash Paid	
Purchases			Discount Received	
Interest Payable			Bills Payable	
Carriage Charged			Returns Outward	
B/P Dishonoured			Allowances	
Noting Charges			Transfer	
Refund from Creditors			By Balance c/d	
Discount Disallowed				
Cheque dishonoured				

In Debtors' Ledger

General Ledger Adjustment Account

Dr.	Rs		Cr.	Rs
To Debtors' Ledger			By Balance b/d	
Adjustment A/c (in General Ledger):			By Debtors' Ledger Adjustment A/c	
Cash received			(in General Ledger):	
Discount			Sales	
Bills Receivable			Cheque dishonoured	
Allowance to Debtors			B/R dishonoured	
Returns Inward			Bills Renewed	
Bad Debts			Noting Charges	
To Bank (cheque Received)			Interest charged	
Transfer			Carriage charged	
To Balance c/d			Expenses charged	
			Refunds to Debtors	
			Discount disallowed	

In General Ledger

Creditors' Ledger Adjustment Account

Dr.	Rs		Cr.	Rs
To General Ledger Adjustment A/c			By Balance b/d	
(in General Ledger):			By General Ledger Adjustment A/c	
Cash Paid			(in Creditors' Ledger):	
Discounts			Purchases	
Bills Payable			B/R Dishonoured	
Returns Outward			Noting Charges	
Allowances			Interest Payable	
Transfer			Carriage charged	
To Balance c/d			Expenses Payable	
			Refunds to creditors	
			Discount disallowed	
			Cheque Dishonoured	

In General Ledger

Debtors' Ledger Adjustment Account

Dr.	Rs		Cr.	Rs
To Balance b/d			By General Ledger Adjustment A/c	
To General Ledger Adjustment A/c			(in Debtors' Ledger):	
(in Debtor's Ledger):				
Sales			Cash received	
Cheque dishonoured			Discount allowed	
B/R dishonoured			B/R	
Bills Renewed			Returns Inward	
Noting charges			Allowances	
Interest charged			Bad Debts	
Carriage charged			Bank (cheque received)	
Expenses charged			Transfer	
Refund to Debtors			By Balance c/d	
Discount disallowed				

SELF BALANCING VS SECTIONAL BALANCING

Self Balancing System	*Sectional Balancing System*
1. It is possible to prepare separate Trial Balance at the end of each separate ledger.	1. It is possible to prepare a Trial Balance in the General Ledger only.
2. Under this method, Debtors Ledger, Creditors Ledger and the General Ledger are separately balanced.	2. Only the General Ledger is balanced.
3. Adjustment Accounts are prepared on the basis of Double Entry principles.	3. Only the General Ledger maintains Debtors Account and Creditors Account. No adjustment accounts are necessary.

The following items will not affect the Self Balancing Ledger.

1. Any cash sale or cash purchase of goods:
2. Bills Receivbale discounted:
3. Recovery of bad debts:
4. Trade Discount:
5. Bills Receivable endorsed:
6. Bills Received honoured:
7. Any sort of provision on Debtors or Creditors etc. etc.

ILLUSTRATION 14.2

Below are given particulars from the books of a trader for the month of January.

		Rs		*Rs*
Jan. 1	Opening balance	30,000	Bills dishonoured	1,500
Jan. 31	Total Sales (Jan.)	90,000	Discount allowed to Drs.	400
	Sales Returns	500	Bad Debts	350
	Cash from debtors	40,000	Transfers from other ledger	750
	B/R	15,000		

He wants to maintain his books on self-balancing system. You are asked to journalise the above transactions and raise relevant adjustment accounts at the back of Sales Ledger and General Ledger.

SOLUTION

			Dr. *Rs*	Cr. *Rs*
Jan. 1	Sales Ledger Adjustment A/c (G.L.) To General Ledger adj. A/c (S.L.)	Dr.	30,000	30,000
Jan. 31	Sales Ledger adj. A/c (G.L.) To Gen. Ledger adj. A/c (S.L.)	Dr.	90,000	90,000
	General Ledger adj. A/c (S.L.) To Sales Ledger adj. A/c (G.L.)	Dr.	500	500
	General Ledger adj. A/c (S.L.) To Sales Ledger adj. A/c (G.L.)	Dr.	40,000	40,000
	General Ledger adj. A/c (S.L.) To Sales Ledger adj. A/c (G.L.)	Dr.	15,000	15,000
	Sales Ledger adj. A/c (G.L.) To General Led. adj. A/c (S.L.)	Dr.	1,500	1,500

General Ledger adj. A/c (S.L.) To Sales Ledger adj. A/c (G.L.)	Dr.	400	400
General Ledger adj. A/c (S.L.) To Sales Ledger adj. A/c (G.L.)	Dr.	350	350
General Ledger adj. A/c (S.L.) To Sales Ledger adj. A/c (G.L.)	Dr.	750	750

General Ledger Adjustment Account
(in Sales Ledger)

Dr. Cr.

		Rs			Rs
Jan. 1	To Sales Led. Adj. A/c as under :		Jan. 1	By Balance b/d	30,000
	Return Inwards	500	Jan 31	By Sales Led. Adj. A/c, as under:	
	Cash	40,000		Sales	90,000
	Discount	400		B/R dishonoured	1,500
	Bills Receivable	15,000			
	Bad Debts	350			
	Transfers	750			
	To Balance c/d	64,500			
		1,21,500			1,21,500
			Feb. 1	By Balance b/d	64,500

Sales Ledger Adjustment Account
(In General Ledger)

Dr. Cr.

		Rs			Rs
Jan. 1	To General Led. Adj. A/c, as under:		Jan. 1	By General Led. Adj. A/c, as under:	
	Balance b/d	30,000		Return Inward	500
Jan. 31	Sales	90,000		Cash	40,000
	B/R dishonoured	1,500	Jan. 31	Discount	400
				B/R	15,000
				Bad debts	350
				Transfer	750
				By Balance c/d	64,500
		1,21,500			1,21,500
Feb. 1	To Balance b/d	64,500	Feb. 1		

ILLUSTRATION 14.3

Prakash has three ledgers in use, viz. Debtors Ledger, Creditors Ledger and a General Ledger, which are all kept on the self-balancing system. From the following particulars, prepare (*a*) Total Debtors and Total Creditors Accounts, (*b*) Journal entries under self-balancing system and (*c*) write up the adjustment accounts as they will appear in each of these ledgers:

2004		Rs
Jan. 1	Balance of Sundry Debtors	20,350
	Balance of Sundry Creditors	15,600
Jan. 31	Credit Sales	10,400
	Cash received from Debtors	8,300
	Credit Purchases	6,900

Discount Allowed to Debtors	350
Cash paid to Creditors	7,375
Discount allowed by them	270
Bills Receivable Received	3,400
Bills Payable accepted	2,600
Returns Outwards	800
Returns Inwards	900
Bills Receivable Dishonoured	430
Bad Debts written off	600

(*B.Com., Madurai*)

SOLUTION :

(*a*)

Rough Total Debtors' Account

		Rs			*Rs*
2004			2004		
Jan. 1	To Balance b/d	20,350	Jan. 31	By Cash	8,300
Jan. 31	To Sales	10,400		By Discount Allowed	350
	To B/R Dishonoured	430		By Bills Receivable	3,400
				By Returns Inwards	900
				By Bad Debts	600
				By Balance c/d	17,630
		31,180			31,180
Feb. 1	To Balance b/d	17,630			

Rough Total Creditors' Account

		Rs			Rs
2004			2004		
Jan. 31	To Cash	7,375	Jan. 1	By Balance b/d	15,600
	To Discount Received	270		By Purchases	6,900
	To Bills Payable	2,600			
	To Returns Outwards	800			
	To Balance c/d	11,455			
		22,500			22,500
			Feb. 1	By Balance b/d	11,455

NB: The above two accounts may be treated as working or as a basis for the purpose of preparing Adjustment Accounts.

(*b*)

Journal Entries

2004				
Jan. 31	Debtors' Ledger Adjustment A/c (In General Ledger)	Dr.	10,830	
	To General Ledger Adjustment A/c (In Debtors' Ledger)			10,830
	(Being items debited to Debtors' Account Sales Rs. 10,400 + B/R dishonoured Rs. 430)			

Date	Particulars		Dr.	Rs	Rs
2004 Jan. 31	General Ledger Adjustment A/c (In Debtors' Ledger)		Dr.	13,550	
	To Debtors' Ledger Adjustment A/c (General Ledger)				13,550
	(Being items credited to Debtors' Account:				
	Cash received	Rs. 8,300			
	Discount allowed	350			
	B/R	3,400			
	Returns Inwards	900			
	Bad Debts	600)			
"	General Ledger Adjustment A/c (In Creditors' Ledger)		Dr.	6,900	
	To Creditors' Ledger Adjustment (General Ledger)				6,900
	(Being credit purchase made)				
"	Creditors' Ledger Adjustment A/c (In General Ledger)		Dr.	11,045	
	To General Ledger Adjustment A/c (In Creditors Ledger)				11,045
	(Being items debited to Creditors' A/c				
	Cash paid	Rs. 7,375			
	Discount received	270			
	B/R	2,600			
	Returns Outwards	800)			

(c) **In the General Ledger**

Debtors' Ledger Adjustment Account

Date	Particulars	Rs	Date	Particulars	Rs
2004			2004		
Jan. 1	To Balance b/d	20,350	Jan. 31	By General Ledger Adjustment Account:	
Jan. 31	To General Ledger Adjustment Account:			Cash Received	8,300
	Credit Sales	10,400		Discount Allowed	350
	Bills Receivable Dishonoured	430		Bills Receivable	3.400
				Returns Inward	900
				Bad Debts	600
				By Balance c/d	17,630
		31,180			31,180
Feb. 1	To Balance b/d	17,630			

Dr. **Creditors' Ledger Adjustment Account** Cr.

Date	Particulars	Rs	Date	Particulars	Rs
2004			2004		
Jan. 31	To General Ledger Adjustment Account:		Jan. 1	By Balance b/d	15,600
	Cash paid	7,375	Jan. 31	By General Ledger Adjustment Account:	
	Discount Received	270		Credit Purchases	6,900

	Bills Payable	2,600			
	Returns Outward	800			
	To Balance c/d	11,455			
		22,500			22,500
			Feb. 1	By Balance b/d	11,455

In the Debtors' Ledger

General Ledger Adjustment Account

Dr. Cr.

		Rs			Rs
2004			2004		
Jan. 31	To Debtors' Ledger Adjustment Account:		Jan. 1	By Balance b/d	20,350
	Cash Received	8,300	Jan. 31	By Debtors' Ledger Adjustment Account	
	Discount Allowed	350		Credit Sales	10,400
	Bills Receivable	3,400		Bills Receivable Dishonoured	430
	Returns Inward	900			
	Bad Debts	600			
	To balance c/d	17,630			
		31,180			31,180
			Feb. 1	By Balance b/d	17,630

In the Creditors' Ledger

General Ledger Adjustment Account

Dr. Cr.

		Rs			Rs
2004			2004		
Jan. 1	To Balance b/d	15,600	Jan. 31	By Creditors' Ledger Adjustment Account:	
Jan. 31	To Creditors' Ledger Adjustment Account:			Cash Paid	7,375
	Credit Purchases	6,900		Discount Received	270
				Bills Payable	2,600
				Returns Outward	800
				By Balance c/d	11,455
		22,500			22,500
Feb. 1	To Balance b/d	11,455			

Note: In the above illustration, we have prepared rough Total Debtors' Account and Total Creditors' Account. We can see that the Total Debtors Account is similar to Debtors' Ledger Adjustment Account in the General Ledger. The Total Creditors' Account is similar to Creditors' Ledger Adjustment Account in the General Ledger. To be more clear, items debited in the rough Total Debtors have been debited in the Debtors' Ledger Adjustment account and corresponding credit being given in the General Ledger Adjustment Account. The items credited in the rough total Debtors' Account have been credited in the Debtors' Ledger Adjustment Account and corresponding debit being given in the General Ledger Adjustment Account.

Similarly, items debited in the rough Total Creditors' Account have been debited in the Creditors' Ledger Adjustment Account and corresponding credit being given in the General Ledger Adjustment Account. Items credited in the rough Total Creditors' Account have been credited to Creditors' Ledger Adjustment Account and corresponding debit being given in the General Ledger Adjustment Account.

When the students become acquainted, they may dispense with the preparation of rough Total Debtors' Account and Total Creditors' Account. Here, they have been prepared only to give a clear picture of self-balancing system.

ILLUSTRATION 14.4

A keeps Debtors' Ledger, Creditors' Ledger and General Ledger. Pass necessary journal entries and open the necessary adjustment accounts from the following particulars:

		Rs
Jan. 1	Creditors' Balance	40,000
Jan. 1	Debtors' Balance	50,000
	Transactions during the month of January were as under:	Rs
	Credit Sales	20,000
	Sundry charges debited to Customers	300
	Cash received from Customers	18,000
	Discount Allowed	200
	Bills Receivable received from Debtors	10,000
	Paid cash to Creditors	25,000
	Credit Purchases	21,000
	Purchase Returns	500
	Sales Returns	200
	Allowances from Creditors	100
	Bad Debts	1,000
	Discount received from Creditors	200
	Bills Receivable dishonoured	400
	Bills Payable	3,000
	Bills Payable dishonoured	300

(*B.Com., Madurai*)

SOLUTION :

				Dr. *Rs*	Cr. *Rs*
Jan. 1	Debtors' Ledger Adjustment A/c (in General Ledger) To General Ledger Adjustment A/c (in Debtors' Ledger) (Being opening balance of Debtors)	Dr.		50,000	50,000
Jan. 31	Debtors' Ledger Adjustment A/c (in General Ledger) To General Ledger Adjustment A/c (in Debtors' Ledger) (Being Sales Rs 20,000 + B/R dishonoured Rs 400 + Sundry Charges Rs 300)	Dr.		20,700	20,700
Jan. 31	General Ledger Adjustment Account (in Debtors' Ledger) To Debtors' Ledger Adjustment A/c (in General Ledger) (Being Cash Rs 18,000 + Discount Rs 200 + Returns Rs 200 + B/R Rs 10,000 + Bad Debts Rs 1,000)	Dr.		29,400	29,400

Date	Particulars		Dr.	Cr.
Jan. 1	General Ledger Adjustment A/c (in Creditors' Ledger)	Dr.	40,000	
	To Creditors' Ledger Adjustment A/c (in General Ledger)			40,000
	(Being opening balance of Creditors)			
Jan. 31	General Ledger Adjustment Account (in Creditors' Ledger)	Dr.	21,300	
	To Creditors' Ledger Adjustment A/c (in General Ledger)			21,300
	(Being Purchase Rs 21,000 + Bills Payable dishonoured Rs 300)			
Jan. 31	Creditors Ledger Adjustment A/c (in General Ledger)	Dr.	28,800	
	To the General Ledger Adjustment A/c (in Creditors' Ledger)			28,800
	(Being Cash paid Rs 25,000 + Discount Rs 200 + B/P Rs 3,000 + Returns Rs 500 + Allowances Rs 100)			

In Debtors' Ledger

General Ledger Adjustment Account

Dr. | Cr.

Date	Particulars	Rs	Date	Particulars	Rs
Jan. 31	To Debtors Ledger Adjustment A/c:		Jan. 1	By Balance b/d	50,000
	Cash	18,000	Jan. 31	By Debtors' Ledger Adjustment A/c:	
	Discount	200		Sales	20,000
	Returns	200		B/R Dishonoured	400
	Bills Receivable	10,000		Sundry Charges	300
	Bad Debts	1,000			
	To Balance c/d	41,300			
		70,700			70,700
			Feb. 1	By Balance b/d	41,300

In Creditors' Ledger

General Ledger Adjustment Account

Dr. | Cr.

Date	Particulars	Rs	Date	Particulars	Rs
Jan. 1	To Balance b/d	40,000	Jan. 31	By Creditors' Ledger Adjustment A/c:	
Jan. 31	To Creditors' Ledger Adjustment A/c:			Cash	25,000
	Purchases	21,000		Discount	200
	B/P Dishonoured	300		Bills Payable	3,000
				Returns	500
				Allowances	100
				By Balance c/d	32,500
		61,300			61,300
Feb. 1	To Balance b/d	32,500			

In General Ledger

Debtors' Ledger Adjustment Account

Dr. Cr.

		Rs			Rs
Jan. 1	To Balance b/d	50,000	Jan. 31	By General Ledger Adjustment A/c:	
Jan. 31	To General Ledger Adjustment A/c:			Cash	18,000
	Credit Sales	20,000		Discount	200
	B/P dishonoured	400		Returns	200
	Sundry Charges	300		Bills Receivable	10,000
				Bad Debts	1,000
				By Balance c/d	41,300
		70,700			70,700
Feb. 1	To Balance b/d	41,300			

In General Ledger

Creditors' Ledger Adjustment Account

Dr. Cr.

		Rs			Rs
Jan. 1	To General Ledger Adjustment A/c:		Jan. 1	By Balance b/d	40,000
	Cash	25,000	Jan. 31	By General Ledger Adjustment A/c:	
	Discount	200		Purchases	21,000
	Bills Payable	3,000		B/P Dishonoured	300
	Returns	500			
	Allowances	100			
	To Balance c/d	32,500			
		61,300			61,300
			Feb. 1	By Balance b/d	32,500

ILLUSTRATION 14.5

On the self-balancing system, a firm maintains Sold, Bought and General Ledgers. From the following transactions, prepare the Adjustment Accounts as they would appear in each of these Ledgers:

		Rs
Jan. 1	Balance of Trade Debtors	15,000
	Balance of Trade Creditors	20,000
Jan. 31	Credit Purchases	3,000
	Credit Sales	10,800
	Paid to Creditors	9,875
	Discount Allowed by them	325
	Received cash from Debtors	7,800
	Allowed them Discount	200
	Accepted Bills Payable	1,500
	Received Bills Receivable	3,000
	Returns Inwards	875
	Returns Outwards	600
	Allowances to Debtors	275
	Allowances from Creditors	150
	Bad Debts	450
	Bills Receivable Dishonoured	375

(B. Com., Madurai, MS. Punjab)

SOLUTION :

General Ledger

Sold Ledger Adjustment Account

Dr. Cr.

		Rs			Rs
Jan. 1	To Balance b/d	15,000	Jan. 31	By General Ledger Adjustment A/c:	
Jan. 31	To General Ledger Adjustment A/c:			Cash	7,800
	Sales	10,800		Discount	200
	B/R Dishonoured	375		Bills Receivable	3,000
				Returns Inwards	875
				Allowances	275
				Bad Debts	450
				By Balance c/d	13,575
		26,175			26,175
Feb. 1	To Balance b/d	13,575			

Bought Ledger Adjustment Account

Dr. Cr

		Rs			Rs
Jan. 31	To General Ledger Adjustment A/c:		Jan. 1	By Balance b/d	20,000
			Jan. 31	By General Ledger Adjustment A/c:	
	Cash	9,875		Purchases	3,000
	Discount	325			
	Bills Payable	1,500			
	Returns Outwards	600			
	Allowances	150			
	To Balance c/d	10,550			
		23,000			23,000
			Feb. 1	By Balance b/d	10,550

Sold Ledger

General Ledger Adjustment Account

Dr. Cr.

		Rs			Rs
Jan. 31	To Sold Ledger Adjustment A/c:		Jan. 1	By Balance b/d	15,000
			Jan. 31	By Sold Ledger Adjustment A/c:	
	Cash	7,800			
	Discount	200		Sales	10,800
	Bills Receivable	3,000		Bills Receivable Dishonoured	375
	Returns Inwards	875			
	Allowances	275			
	Bad Debts	450			
	To Balance c/d	13,575			
		26,175			26,175
			Feb. 1	By Balance b/d	13,575

Bought Ledger

General Ledger Adjustment Account

Dr.		Rs			Cr. Rs
Jan. 1	To Balance b/d	20,000	Jan. 31	By Bought Ledger Adjustment A/c:	
31	To Bought Ledger Adjustment A/c:			Cash	9,875
	Purchases	3,000		Discount	325
				Bills Payable	1,500
				Returns Outwards	600
				Allowances	150
				By Balance c/d	10,550
		23,000			23,000
Feb. 1	To Balance b/d	10,550			

Advantages

1. Speedy detection of errors is possible.
2. Balancing is done quickly and thus saves time, labour and money.
3. The system helps reducing fraud.
4. Final Accounts can be prepared easily and quickly.
5. It acts as an effective internal check.
6. It is very useful when there is a large number of debtors and creditors.
7. It is easy to prepare periodical final accounts.
8. Efficient office control is possible.
9. It promotes specialisation and increases efficiency.
10. It facilitates division of work among different employees.
11. Arithmetical accuracy can be proved by drawing a Trial Balance.
12. Ledger keeping can be decentralised.

INTERLEDGERS TRANSFER

Where the same person is a customer and a supplier, his account appears in both the Debtors' Ledger and Creditors' Ledger. In normal circumstances, only one account is kept for such a person. But when the ledgers are maintained on self-balancing ledgers basis, two accounts should be operated for such a person. Then it is an appropriate case of set off. The following entries have to be passed to effect such transfer:

1. For transfer of individual balance from Debtors' Ledger to Creditors' Ledger or vice versa:

   Debit: Particular Supplier's Account (in Creditors' Ledger)

   Credit: Particular Customer's Account (in Debtors' Ledger)

2. For reduction in Total Creditors:

   Debit General Ledger Adjustment Account (in Debtors' Ledger)

   Credit Debtors' Ledger Adjustment Account (in General Ledger)

3. For reduction in Total Debtors

   Debit Creditors' Ledger Adjustment Account (in General Ledger)

   Credit General Ledger Adjustment Account (in Creditors' Ledger)

ILLUSTRATION 14.6

Debtors' List Rs 3,00,000 includes Rs 5,000 owed by P and Rs 400 by Q. Similarly, Creditors' list of Rs 2,20,000 covers Rs 7,000 owed to P and Rs 150 to Q.

The journal entries are as follows:

		Dr.	Cr.
		Rs	*Rs*
P (in Creditors' Ledger) To P (in Debtors' Ledger) (Being transfer of P from Debtors' Ledger to Creditors' Ledger)	Dr.	5,000	5,000
Q (in Creditors' Ledger) To Q (in Debtors' Ledger) (Being transfer of Q from Creditors' Ledger to Debtors' Ledger)		150	150
General Ledger Adjustment Account (in General Ledger) To Debtors' Ledger Adjustment A/c (in General Ledger) (Being reduction in total Debtors' A/c)	Dr.	5,150	5,150
Creditors' Ledger Adjustment Account (in Debtors' Ledger) To General Ledger Adjustment A/c (in Creditors' Ledger) (Being reduction in total Creditors' A/c)	Dr.	5,150	5,150

MULTIPLE LEDGERS

If the businessman deals with many customers, keeping of the accounts of all customers in one ledger becomes troublesome. Besides, when the business expands, credit customers also increase. Thus, to make the work easy, the ledgers are divided either alphabetically or sales territory or otherwise. Thus sales ledger may be divided into a number of ledgers, each ledger accommodating a given number of customers on the basis of classification.

ILLUSTRATION 14.7

Evergreen Ltd. maintains two Debtors Ledgers, A to M Debtors' Ledger and N to Z Debtors' Ledger, under the self-balancing system. The following details have been extracted from the books of the Company for the quarter ended 30th September.

		A to M	N to Z
		Rs	*Rs*
July 1	Debit Balances	50,400	30,560
	Credit Balances	1,300	750
Sep. 30	Sales	8,75,350	6,95,280
	Returns	20,200	15,430
	Cash received from Debtors	6,53,700	4,72,200
	Discount allowed	7,420	5,290
	Bills Receivable received	86,500	42,300
	Bills Receivable discounted	2,400	2,100
	Bills Receivable dishonoured		4,200
	Bad debts written off	4,300	2,230
	Credit balances	1,570	530

Miss Chowdhary in A to M Debtors' Ledger owing Rs 2,650 had her name changed to Mr Roy Chowdhary after marriage and consequently her account has been transferred to N to Z Debtors' Ledger during the period.

Prepare the necessary adjustment account. *(B.Com)*

SOLUTION :

In the General Ledger

Dr. **Debtors' Ledger Adjustment Account** Cr.

		A – M	N – Z			A – M	N – Z
		Rs	Rs			Rs	Rs
July 1	To Balance b/d	50,400	30,560	July 1	By Balance b/d	1,300	750
Sept. 30	To General Ledger			Sept.	By General Ledger		
	Adjustment A/c:			30	Adjustment Account:		
	Sales	8,75,350	6,95,280		Returns	20,200	15,430
	Bills Dishonoured		4,200		Cash	6,53,700	4,72,200
	Transfer		2,650		Discounts	7,420	5,290
	Balance c/d	1,570	530		B/R	86,500	42,300
					Bad Debts	4,300	2,230
					Transfer	2,650	–
					Balance c/d	1,51,250	1,95,020
		9,27,320	7,33,220			9,27,320	7,33,220
Oct. 1	To Balance b/d	1,51,250	1,95,020	Oct. 1	By Balance b/d	1,570	530

In A to M Debtors' Account

Dr. **General Ledger Adjustment Account**

		Rs			Rs
July 1	To Balance c/d	1,300	July 1	By Balance b/d	50,400
Sept. 30	To Debtors' Ledger Adjust-		Sept. 30	By Debtors' Ledger Adjst-	
	ment A/c:			ment A/c:	
	Returns	20,200		Sales	8,75,350
	Cash	6,53,700		By Balance c/d	1.570
	Discount	7,420			
	B/R	86,500			
	Bad Debts	4,300			
	Transfer	2,650			
	To Balance c/d	1,51,250			
		9,27,320			9,27,320
Oct. 1	To Balance b/d	1,570	Oct. 1	By Balance b/d	1,51,250

In N to Z Debtors' Account

Dr. **General Ledger Adjustment Account** Cr.

		Rs			*Rs*
July 1	To Balance c/d	750	July 1	By Balance b/d	30,560
Sept 30	To Debtors' Adjustment A/c:		Sept 30	By Debtors' Ledger Adjust-	
	Returns	15,430		ment A/c:	
	Cash	4,72,200		Sales	6,95,280
	Discount	5,290		Bills Dishonoured	4,200
	Bills Receivable	42,300		Transfer	2,650
	Bad Debts	2,230		By Balance c/d	530
	To Balance c/d	1,95,020			
		7,33,220			7,33,220
Oct. 1	To Balance b/d	530	Oct. 1	By Balance b/d	1,95,020

ILLUSTRATION 14.8

In the absence of Self-balancing System, you are asked to compile Total Debtors' and Total Creditors' Accounts from the following information:

	Dr.	Cr.
	Rs	Rs
Balances (1-10-2003)		
Debtors Ledger	35,700	500
Creditors Ledger	300	27,800

Figures for the year ended 30th Sept. 2004

Cash received from customers 1,60,400

	Rs		Rs
Discount allowed	4,500	Credit Sales	1,85,000
Bad Debts	6,000	Purchase Returns	1,400
Payment to creditors	95,000	Sales Returns	2,600
Discounts allowed by them	2,700	B/R received	7,500
Payments to customers	125	B/P granted	5,000
Credit Purchases	1,10,000	Transfer from Debtors' Ledger to Creditors to settle the accounts	4,000

SOLUTION :

Total Debtors' Account

Dr.	Rs		Cr. Rs
To Balance b/d	35,700	By Balance b/d	500
To Sales	1,85,000	By Cash	1,60,400
To Payment to Customers	125	By Discounts & Allowances	4,500
		By Bad Debtors	6,000
		By Transfer to Creditors A/c	4,000
		By Bill Receivable	7,500
		By Sales Returns	2,600
		By Balance c/d	35,325
	2,20,825		2,20,825
By Balance b/d	35,325		

Total Creditors' Account

Dr.	Rs		Cr. Rs
To Balance b/d	300	By Balance b/d	27,800
To Cash (payments)	95,000	By Purchases	1,10,000
To Discounts & Allowances	2,700		
To Purchase Returns	1,400		
To Bills Payable	5,000		
To Transfer from Debtors A/c	4,000		
To Balance c/d	29,400		
	1,37,800		1,37,800
		To Balance b/d	29,400

CONTRA BALANCE

Generally, credit customers in the Sales Ledger should show debit balances. This means the customers owe money for the goods bought by them. Similarly, creditors account in the Bought Ledger should show credit balance. Sometimes, the Debtors' Ledger may have some credit balances, indicating advances from customers, and in some cases, the debtors might have returned the goods even after making full payment. Similar is the case with creditors accounts. Where both debit and credit balances are given in Debtors' Ledger or in the Creditors' Ledger, both types of balances should be used in preparing adjustment accounts.

ILLUSTRATION 14.9

From the following transactions extracted from three ledgers, viz. Debtors' Ledgers, Creditors' Ledgers and Nominal Ledger, which are kept on sectional system of balancing, prepare the adjustment accounts as they would appear in each of these ledgers.

		Rs		Rs
July 1	Balance of Sundry Drs.	48,500	Discount received	825
	Balance of Sundry Crs.	36,900	B/P Accepted	12,000
July 31	Credit purchases	11,520	B/R Received	10,000
	Credit Sales	26,400	B/R Dishonoured	4,000
	Payments to Creditors	20,120	Goods returned from debtors	1,800
	Received from debtors	48,675	Goods returned to creditors	1,440
	Discount allowed	1,250	Bad debts	625

Solution :

In Nominal Ledger

Sales Ledger Adjustment Account

(Total Debtors' Account)

Dr. Cr.

		Rs			Rs
July 1	To Balance b/d	48,500	July 31	By Nom. Led. Adj. A/c	
31	To Nom. Led. Adj. A/c			Cash Received	48,675
	Credit Sales	26,400		Discount allowed	1,250
	B/R dishonoured	4,000		B/R received	10,000
				Returns inwards	1,800
				Bad Debts	625
				By Balance c/d	16,550
		78,900			78,900
Aug. 1	To Balance b/d	16,550			

Purchase Ledger Adjustment A/c

Dr. Cr.

		Rs			Rs
July 31	To Nom. Led. Adj. A/c		July 1	By Balance b/d	36,900
	Cash paid	20,120	31	By Nom. Led. Adj. A/c	
	Discount Received	825		Credit purchase	11,520
	B/P Accepted	12,000			
	Returns Outward	1,440			
	To Balance c/d	14,035			
		48,420			48,420
			Aug. 1	By Balance b/d	14,035

In Debtors' Ledger

Nominal Ledger Adjustment A/c

(General Ledger Adjustment Account)

Dr. Cr.

		Rs			Rs
July 31	To Drs. Led. Adj. A/c		July 1	By Balance b/d	48,500
	Cash received	48,675	31	By Drs. Led. Adj. A/c	
	Discount allowed	1,250		Credit Sales	26,400
	B/R received	10,000		B/R dishonoured	4,000
	Returns inward	1,800			
	Bad debts	625			
31	To Balance c/d	16,550			
		78,900			78,900
			Aug. 1	By Balance b/d	16,550

In Creditors' Ledger

Nominal Ledger Adjustment A/c

(General Ledger Adjustment Account)

Dr. Cr.

		Rs			Rs
July 1	To Balance b/d	36,900	July 31	By Crs. Led. Adj. A/c	
31	To Crs. Led. Adj.			Cash paid	20,120
	Credit purchases	11,520		Discount received	825
				B/P accepted	12,000
				Returns outward	1,440
				By Balance c/d	14,035
		48,420			48,420
Aug. 1	By Balance b/d	14,035			

ILLUSTRATION 14.10

Dinesh & Co. has three ledgers in use viz. (1) Debtors' Ledger (2) Creditors' Ledger and (3) Nominal Ledger, which are kept on self-balancing system. From the following particulars, prepare the adjustment accounts as they would appear in each of these ledgers.

Jan. 1	Balance of Sundry Drs.	1,60,000	Accepted B/P	15,000
Jan. 1	Balance of Sundry Crs.	1,85,000	Received B/R	30,000
Jan. 31	Credit purchases	45,000	Returns inwards	8,750
	Credit sales	98,000	Returns outwards	6,000
	Paid to creditors	98,750	Rebate allowed to debtors	2,750
	Discount allowed by them	3,250	Rebate allowed from Creditors	1,500
	Received cash from Drs.	78,000	Bad debts	4,500
	Allowed them discount	2,000	B/R dishonoured	3,750

Solution :

In Debtors' Ledger

General Ledger Adjustment A/c

Dr. Cr.

		Rs			Rs
Jan. 31	To Drs. Led. Adj. A/c		Jan. 1	By Balance b/d	1,60,000
	Cash received	78,000	Jan. 31	By Drs. Led. Adj. A/c:	
	Discount allowed	2,000		Credit Sales	98,000
	B/R received	30,000		B/R Dishonoured	3,750
	Returns inward	8,750			

		Rs			Rs
	Rebate allowed	2,750			
	Bad Debts	4,500			
Jan. 31	To Balance c/d	1,35,750			
		2,61,750			2,61,750
			Feb. 1	By Balance b/d	1,35,750

In Creditors' Ledger

Dr. **General Ledger Adjustment A/c** Cr.

		Rs			Rs
Jan. 1	To Balance b/d	1,85,000	Jan. 1	By Crs. Led. Adj. A/c:	
Jan. 31	To Crs. Led. Adj. A/c:			Cash paid	98,750
	Credit Purchase	45,000		Discount received	3,250
				B/P accepted	15,000
				Returns outward	6,000
				Rebate received	1,500
			31	By Balance c/d	1,05,500
		2,30,000			2,30,000
Feb. 1	To Balance b/d	1,05,500			

In General Ledger

Dr. **Debtors' Ledger Adjustment A/c** Cr.

		Rs			Rs
Jan. 1	To Balance b/d	1,60,000	Jan. 1	By General Led. Adj. A/c:	
31	To Gen. Led. Adj. A/c:		31	Cash received	78,000
	Sales	98,000		Discount allowed	2,000
	B/R Dishonoured	3,750		B/R Received	30,000
				Returns	8,750
				Rebate allowed	2,750
				Bad Debts	4,500
				By Balance c/d	1,35,750
		2,61,750			2,61,750
Feb. 1	To Balance b/d	1,35,750			

Dr. **Creditors' Ledger Adjustment A/c** Cr.

		Rs			Rs
Jan. 31	To General Ledger Adj. A/c:		Jan. 1	By Balance b/d	1,85,000
	Cash paid	98,750	31	By Gen. Led. Adj. A/c:	
	Discount received	3,250		Credit purchases	45,000
	B/P accepted	15,000			
	Returns outward	6,000			
	Rebate received	1,500			
	To Balance c/d	1,05,500			
		2,30,000			2,30,000
			Feb. 1	By Balance b/d	1,05,500

RECTIFICATION OF ERRORS

We have already studied the rectification of errors in Chapter 8. In sectional and self-balancing system also the same rule of rectification of errors can be applied.

In sectional balancing system, there is no double entry in Debtors and Creditors Ledger. Hence errors in these ledgers can be rectified by passing a single entry. For example, if Ramu, a debtor is wrongly debited by Rs 500 instead of credited. Thus Ramu's account is wrong. Hence it can be rectified by crediting Ramu's account with Rs 1,000.

If an error affects the total accounts, then a rectifying entry will also be passed for rectifying the total accounts. For example, goods of Rs 1,000 are returned to Balu, a creditor, was not entered in the books. The required entries in case of sectional balancing system:

(*a*) Debit Balu's Account with Rs 1,000.

(*b*) Debit Total Creditors Account with Rs 1,000.

Credit Purchase Returns Account with Rs 1,000.

When self-balancing system is introduced, then the rectification of errors is different from the above.

(1) First we must clarify whether the error affects the total of subsidiary book, or

(2) The error relates to a transfer of account from one ledger to another ledger.

If the error affects the total of subsidiary book such as sales book, purchase book, sales returns book, bills payable book, bills receivable book, cash column for receipt from sundry debtors and payments to sundry creditors, then the errors can be rectified by making the usual entry to rectify the error and also a self-balancing entry. For example, if purchase book is undercast by Rs 500, then the wrong total of the purchase book will affect:

(*a*) Purchase Account.

(*b*) Creditors' Ledger Adjustment Account in General Ledger, and

(*c*) General Ledger Adjustment Account in Creditors' Ledger.

Thus, the error can be corrected as follows:

			Rs	Rs
(*a*)	Purchase Account	Dr.	500	
	To Suspense Account			500
	(For entry made for correcting purchase account)			
(*b*)	Self-Balancing entry:			
	General Ledger Adjustment Account (in Creditors' Ledger)	Dr.	500	
	To Creditors Ledger Adjustment Account (in General Ledger)			500
	(For additional self-balancing entry passed for correcting adjustment accounts)			

If the error relates to a transfer of account from one ledger to another ledger and does not affect the total of some subsidiary book then there is no need to pass entry for correcting adjustment account. For example, Goods from Velu for Rs 1,000 is posted to Venu's account Rs 100. Then the rectifying entry will be

		Rs	Rs
Suspense Account	Dr.	900	
Venu's Account	Dr.	100	
To Velu's Account			
(For entry made for correcting the two personal accounts)			1,000

Steps to rectify the errors:

(1) Correct the error in the usual way whether it is an ordinary system or self-balancing system.

(2) If an error affects the total of some subsidiary book, then make one more journal entry to correct adjustment account. If it does not affect the total then no entry is needed.

(3) If an entry is in respect of a transfer from one ledger to another ledger which affect both the ledgers, then we must not only pass a transfer entry but also we must pass necessary self-balancing entries.

ILLUSTRATION 14.11

Write out the journal entries to correct the following errors when Self-Balancing system is in use:

1. Sales book undercast by Rs 1,500.
2. Purchase made from Mr A Rs 500 was posted Mr B account as Rs 50.
3. Goods of the value of Rs 1,000 returned by Raju were entered in Sales Day Book and posted therefrom to the credit of his account.
4. Purchase of furniture for Rs 2,000 passed through the invoice book.
5. Robert Company Limited returned goods worth Rs 5,000. This transaction was entered in the Sales Day Book and posted to the credit of Robbert Company Limited.

SOLUTION:

			Dr. Rs	Cr. Rs
1.	(*a*) Suspense Account	Dr.	1,500	
	To Sales Account			1,500
	(Being for correction of undercasting)			
	(*b*) Debtors' Ledger Adjustment Account (in General Ledger)	Dr.	1,500	
	To General Ledger Adjustment Account (In Debtors' Ledger)			1,500
	(Being additional entry passed for correcting adjustment accounts)			
2.	Suspense Account	Dr.	450	
	B Account	Dr.	50	
	To A Account			500
	(Being entry made for correcting the two personal accounts and adjustment entry is not needed)			
3.	(*a*) Sales Account	Dr.	1,000	
	Sales Returns Account	Dr.	1,000	
	To Suspense Account (in Sales Ledger)			2,000
	(Being correction entry)			
	(*b*) General Ledger Adjustment Account (in Sales Ledger)	Dr.	2,000	
	To Sales Ledger Adjustment Account (in General Ledger)			2,000
	(Being additional entry made for correcting furniture account)			
4.	(*a*) Furniture Account	Dr.	2,000	
	To Purchase Account			2,000
	(Being entry passed for correcting furniture account)			

(*b*) Suppliers Account (in Creditors Ledger) Dr.		2,000	
To Suppliers Account (in General Ledger)			2,000
(Being entry passed for closing the supplier account in Creditors' Ledger and to reopen his account in General Ledger)			
(*c*) Creditors' Ledger Adjustment Account Dr. (in General Ledger)		2,000	
To General Ledger Adjustment Account (in Creditors' Ledger)			2,000
(Being additional entry made for correcting adjustment accounts)			
5. (*a*) Sales Account. Dr.		5,000	
Sales Returns Account Dr.		5,000	
To Suspense Account			10,000
(Being entry made for correcting Sales Day Book)			
(*b*) General Ledger Adjustment Account (in Sales Ledger) Dr.		10,000	
To Sales Ledger Adjustment Account (in General Ledger)			10,000
(Being additional entry made for correcting adjustment accounts)			

QUESTIONS

Objective Type Questions.

I. *Indicate whether the following statements are "true" or "False".*

1. The Debtors Ledger contains all the personal accounts.
2. In case of transfer from one ledger to another, three entries will have to be made in the case of self-balancing system.
3. Sectional Balancing and Self-Balancing are synonymous terms.
4. The Sales Ledger Adjustment Account in the General Ledger is just the reverse of the General Ledger Adjustment Account in sales ledger.
5. Separate trial balance for each of the ledgers can be prepared under Sectional Balancing System.
6. Self-balancing system can be introduced even in small concerns where only one ledger is maintained.
7. In Sectional Balancing System, a trial balance is prepared only for the general ledger.
8. Sales ledger is also known as Debtors' Ledger.
9. Sectional Balancing is the same as self-balancing.
10. Self-balancing ledger do not follow the system of double entry.
11. Bad debts recovered appears in the sales ledger.
12. Bills endorsed to suppliers will appear in Bought Ledger.
13. Bills-Receivable dishonoured do not appear in Self-Balancing Ledger.
14. The Debtors' Ledger contains accounts of sundry debtors.
15. Provision for doubtful debts appears in the sales ledger.

(*Ans*: True: – 2, 4, 7, 8, 12, 14. False: – 1, 3, 5, 6, 9, 10, 11, 13, 15.)

II. *Fill in the blanks.*

1. Accounts relating to debtors and creditors are known as ....
2. Purchase ledger contains accounts of ....
3. An adjustment account is also known as a ....
4. For making the sales ledger self-balancing, it is necessary to open in it an account styled ....
5. Creditors ledger is also called .... ledger.
6. Debtors Ledger Adjustment Account is also termed as ....
7. General ledger adjustment are opened in .... and ....
8. In sectional balancing as well as self-balancing system, the ledger is divided into .... parts.
9. Bought ledger adjustment is opened in ....
10. Provision for doubtful debt account is opened in .... ledger.

(Ans: 1. Personal Accounts; 2. Creditors; 3. Control Account; 4. General Ledger Adjustment A/c; 5. Bought or Purchase; 6. Sales or sold Ledger Adjustment A/c; 7. Debtors Ledger; Creditors Ledger; 8. Three 9. General Ledger. 10. General

III. Select the most appropriate answer:

1. Provision for doubtful debts account is opened in the :
   (*a*) Debtors Ledger. (*b*) Creditors Ledger.
   (*c*) General Ledger.
2. General Ledger Adjustment Account is opened in :
   (*a*) Debtors Ledger. (*b*) Creditors Ledger.
   (*c*) In both Debtors and Creditors Ledgers.
3. The adjustment for B/R dishonoured will appear in:
   (*a*) Sales Ledger Adjustment A/c. (*b*) Bought Ledger Adjustment A/c.
   (*c*) None of these
4. The monthly total of purchase day book is posted to the debit side of purchase account in the :
   (*a*) Debtors Ledger. (*b*) Creditors Ledger.
   (*c*) General Ledger.
5. Bills Receivable and Bills Payable accounts are found in this ledger, under self-balancing system:
   (*a*) Debtors Ledger. (*b*) Creditors Ledger.
   (*c*) General Ledger.
6. No self balancing entry is required for:
   (*a*) Sales Return. (*b*) Bad debts recovered.
   (*c*) Purchase return.
7. Transfer from one ledger to another:
   (*a*) Decreases debtors and creditors. (*b*) Increases debtors.
   (*c*) Increases debtors and creditors.
8. The adjustment of cash sales will appear in:
   (*a*) Sales Ledger Adjustment A/c. (*b*) Bought Ledger Adjustment A/c.
   (*c*) None of the above accounts.
9. Bills receivable from X will be taken to:
   (*a*) Debtors Ledger. (*b*) General Ledger.
   (*c*) Creditors Ledger

10. Sectional balancing system ensures numerical accuracy of:
    (*a*) Debtors and Creditors Ledgers. (*b*) General Ledger only.
    (*c*) All the three ledgers.

(*Ans*: 1. (*c*); 2. (*c*); 3. (*a*); 4. (*c*); 5. (*c*); 6. (*b*); 7. (*a*); 8. (*c*); 9. (*b*); 10. (*a*).

THEORETICAL QUESTIONS

1. What are self-balancing ledgers ?
2. How do various ledgers become self-balancing ?
3. What are the advantages of self-balancing ledgers ?
4. State the objects of self-balancing. Explain briefly the procedure of self-balancing.
5. What is sectional balancing ? How does it differ from self-balancing ?

PRACTICAL PROBLEMS

1. The undermentioned particulars have been extracted from the books of Mr A. You are required to prepare the Sales Ledger Adjustment Account as on June 30, 2004:

	Rs
Balance as on January 1, 2004	55,842
Credit Sales	98,602
Cash Sales	53,250
Cash Received from Debtors	88,753
Discount Allowed	480
Bills Accepted	7,120
Returns Inwards	5,430
Bills Receivable Dishonoured	1,120
Bad Debts Written off	3,890
Amount Received against bad debts written off last year	175
Sundry Charges debited to customers	378
Transfers to bought Ledger	100

(*C.A.I.I.B.*)

[**Ans:** Sales Ledger Balance Rs 50,169]

2. Mr Tyagi has maintained his account on self-balancing system. From the following information, prepare the necessary adjustment accounts in the respective ledgers:

	Rs	
Creditors' Balance on 1st Jan.	90,200	
Creditors' Balance on 1st Jan.	5,500	(Cr.)
Credit purchases during the year	2,45,200	(Dr.)
Cash paid to Creditors during the year	1,60,000	
Bills payable accepted during the year	1,05,000	
Goods returned to Creditors	5,200	
Discount received from creditors	5,400	
Creditors' Balance on 31st Dec.	6,800	(Dr.)
Transfer from Creditors Ledger to Debtors Ledger	5,000	

(*B.Com., Bombay, Karnataka*)

[**Ans:** Purchase Ledger Adjustment A/c in General Ledger Rs 56,100
General Ledger Adjustment A/c in Purchase Ledger Rs 56,100]

3. From the following information, prepare necessary Ledger Adjustment Account in respective Ledgers of Mr George who has maintained his accounts on Self-Balancing System:

	Rs	
Debtors Balance 1st Jan.	40,000	(Dr.)
Creditors Balance —do—	5,000	(Cr.)
Cash sales to Debtors	1,50,000	
Cash received from Debtors	80,000	
Bills accepted by Debtors	50,000	
Bills dishonoured by Debtors	10,000	
Discount allowed to Debtors	2,000	
Sales Returns from Debtors	15,000	
Debtors as on 31st Dec.	3,000	(Cr.)

(*B.Com.; Madurai, Karnataka*)

[**Ans:** Debtors' Ledger Adjustment A/c in General Ledger Rs 51,000
General Ledger Adjustment A/c in Debtors' Ledger Rs 51,000]

4. The following information is given to you for April:

	Rs
Debtors on 1st April	2,00,000
Creditors on 1st April	1,00,000
Credit Sales	4,00,000
Credit purchases	1,90,000
Cash received from Debtors	2,80,000
Discount allowed	14,000
Bad Debts written off	7,000
B/R Received	15,000
Cash paid to suppliers	1,50,000
B/P issued	60,000
Cash purchases	3,000
Discount received	4,000
Cash Sales	2,000

Prepare in General Ledger:

(*a*) Sales Ledger Adjustment Account

(*b*) Bought Ledger Adjustment Account

(*CAIIB*)

[**Ans:** (*a*) Rs 2,84,000 and (*b*) Rs 76,000]

5. In a business, three ledgers are in use viz. (1) A Creditors' Ledger, (2) Debtors' Ledger and (3) a General Ledger. The following is the summary of the transactions with the debtors and creditors of the business for the month of January. Open the necessary adjustment accounts in the respective ledgers:

	Rs
Debtors Balance on 1st January	40,000
Creditors Balance 1st January	46,250
Credit Sales	24,500
Credit Purchases	11,250
Received cash from Debtors	19,500
Discount allowed to them	500
Cash paid to Creditors	24,960
Discount allowed by them	540
Received Bills Receivable	7,500
Bills Payable accepted	3,750
Returns Outwards	1,500
Returns Inwards	2,195

Allowances to Debtors	680
Allowances from Creditors	375
Bad Debts written off	1,125
Bills Receivable dishonoured	940

(*CAIIB*)

[Ans: General Ledger Adjustment A/c in Sales Ledger Rs 33,940
General Ledger Adjustment A/c in Purchase Ledger Rs 26,375
Sales Ledger Adjustment A/c in General Ledger Rs 33,940
Purchase Ledger Adjustment A/c in General Ledger Rs 26,375]

6. Assuming that the system of self-balancing has been introduced, show how the General Ledger Adjustment Account will appear in the Debtors' as well as Creditors Ledger from the following information:

Balances as on 1st April 2003:	Rs Dr.	Rs Cr.
Debtors' Ledger	35,700	500
Creditors' Ledger	300	27,800
Figures for the year ended 31st March 2004:		
Cash received from customers		1,60,400
Discounts and allowances allowed to them		4,500
Bad Debts written off		6,000
Transfer from Debtors Ledger to Creditors Ledger to settle Customers account		4,000
Payments to Creditors		95,000
Discounts and allowances allowed by them		2,700
Credit Purchases		1,10,000
Credit Sales		1,85,000
Purchase Returns		1,400
Sales Returns		2,600
B/R Received		7,500
B/P Accepted		5,000

(*B.Com., Karnataka*)

[Ans: General Ledger Adjustment A/c in Debtors' Ledger Rs 35,200
General Ledger Adjustment A/c in Creditors' Ledger Rs 29,400]

7. From the following information, prepare Sales Ledger Adjustment Account as would appear in the General Ledger:

	Rs
Sales (Ledger (Debtors)) balance on 1.1.2004	44,910
Purchase Ledger (creditors) balances on 1.1.2004	32,170
Receipts from Customers, including Rs 760 in respect of debts written off in 2000	5,46,420
Cash Sales	50,000
Credit Sales	5,81,270
Returns Outwards	4,250
Returns Inwards	8,630
Bad Debts written off	10,410
Discounts allowed by Suppliers	2,510
Increase provision for Bad Debts on 31.12.2003	1,240

Cash received from suppliers in respect of over-payment	480
Sales Ledger credit balance as on 31.12.2004	820

(*CAIIB*)

[Ans: Rs 62,300]

8. There are three self-balancing ledgers in use in a business viz. a Purchase Ledger, a Sales Ledger and a General Ledger. From the following particulars, write up the necessary adjustment accounts as they would appear in the General Ledger:

	Rs	
Debtors' Balance in General Ledger Adjustment A/c	60,500	(Cr.)
Creditors' Balance in General Ledger Adjustment Account	38,500	(Dr.)
Credit sales during the year	40,300	
Cash sales during the year	12,800	
Cash purchases during the year	16,390	
Credit purchases during the year	26,400	
Creditors paid off during the year	32,500	
Received through bank from Debtors	48,200	
Discount Allowed to the business	375	
Discount Allowed by the business	450	
Returns inwards	1,225	
Returns outwards	875	
Accepted Bills payable during the year	3,200	
Bills Receivable received	4,800	
Bills Receivable dishonoured	200	
Interest charged for dishonoured bills	15	
Trade discount during the year	975	
Bad Debts	375	
Transfer from one ledger to another	195	

Goods of the sales value of Rs 300 were returned by the customer for which fresh goods were issued. Though a credit note was issued for the return of the goods, the sales invoice was inadvertently not prepared for the issue of fresh goods.

(*B.Com., Mysore*)

[Ans: Sales Ledger Adjustment A/c (in G.L.) Rs 45,770
Purchase Ledger Adjustment A/c (in G.L.) Rs. 27,755]

Note: Trade Discount does not appear in accounting record.

9. Prepare Purchases and Sales Ledger adjustment accounts as would appear in the Nominal Ledger from the following particulars:

		Rs	
2004 Jan. 1	Balance on Purchase Ledger	174	(Dr.)
	Balance on Purchase Ledger	2,388	(Cr.)
	Balance on Sales Ledger	2,924	(Dr.)
	Balance on Sales Ledger	48	(Cr.)
2004 Dec. 31	Purchases	13,036	
	Purchase Returns	512	
	Cash paid to suppliers	11,686	
	Discount Received	336	
	Sales	17,498	
	Sales Returns	234	
	Cash received from Customers	15,248	
	Discount Allowed	564	
	Bills Payable	450	
	Bills Receivable	824	

	Rs
Transfer from Purchases Ledger to Sales Ledger	152
Purchases Ledger Balance (Dr.)	154
Sales Ledger Balance (Cr.)	84

(*B.Com., Mysore*)

[**Ans:** Purchase Ledger Adjustment Account Rs 2,268 (Cr.)
Sales Ledger Adjustment Account Rs 3,436 (Dr.)]

10. A firm has three ledgers in use viz. Debtors Ledger, Creditors Ledger and Nominal Ledger. Prepare Adjustment Accounts:

		Rs
1st Jan.	Balance of Debtors	16,000
1st Jan.	Balance of creditors	18,500
31st Jan.	Credit Purchases	4,500
	Paid to Creditors	9,875
	Received from Debtors	7,800
	Returns Inward	875
	B/P accepted	1,500
	Bad Debts	450
	Allowance to Debtors	275
	Credit Sales	9,800
	Discount Received	325
	Discount Allowed	200
	B/R Received	3,000
	Returns Outward	600
	Allowance from Creditors	150
	B/R Dishonoured	375

(*B.Com., Shivaji, Poona, Rajasthan, Bombay, Karnataka*)

[**Ans:** Sales Ledger Adjustment A/c in General Ledger Rs 14,025
Purchase Ledger Adjustment A/c in General Ledger Rs 10,550
General Ledger Adjustment A/c in Sales Ledger Rs 14,025
General Ledger Adjustment A/c in Purchase Ledger Rs 10,550]

11. From the following particulars prepare the relevant adjustment account as would appear in the General Ledger of Mr Vasu for the month of March.

Date	*Particulars*
1	Purchased from Mr X Rs 2,000.
2	Paid Rs 1,600 after adjusting the initial advance in full to Mr X.
11	Paid Rs 1,000 to Mr R towards the purchases made in Feb. in full.
13	Paid advance to Mr Y Rs 3,000.
14	Purchased goods from Mr A Rs 4,000.
25	Returned goods worth Rs 500 to Mr A.
26	Settle the balance due to A at a discount of 10%.
27	Goods purchased from Mr Y Rs 2,500 against the advance paid on 13th.
28	Received back the advance from Mr P paid on 28th Feb. Rs 2,000.
30	Purchases from B Rs 2,000.
31	Goods returned to Q Rs 750. The goods were originally purchased for cash in February.

(*CA*)

[**Ans:** Cr. Balance Rs 2,000; Dr. Balance Rs 1,250]

12. Prepare (*i*) the Creditors' Ledger Adjustment Account, and (*ii*) the Debtors' Ledger Adjustment Account, as would appear in the General Ledger of M/s Hindustan Traders for the year ending 31st Dec. 2004, from the following information:

		Rs
Opening Balances (1.1.2004)		
Creditors Ledger	Dr.	2,610
	Cr.	35,820
Debtors Ledger	Dr.	43,860
	Cr.	720
Transactions during the year		
Purchases		1,98,540
Purchases Returns		7,680
Sales		2,62,470
Sales Returns		3,510
Cash Received from Debtors		2,28,630
Discount Allowed		8,460
Cash Paid to the Creditors		1,75,290
Discount Received		4,980
Cash Refunded to the Debtors		520
Bills Receivable received		12,360
Bills Payable issued		6,750
Bills Receivable dishonoured		750
Transfer from Bought to Sales Ledger		100
Transfer from Sales to Bought Ledger		40
Closing Balances (31-12-2004)		
Creditors' Ledger	Dr.	2,310
Debtors' Ledger	Cr.	1,360

(*C.A., Inter*)

[**Ans:** Creditors' Ledger Adjustment Account Rs 2,310 (Dr.) Rs 39,220 (Cr.)
Debtors' Ledger Adjustment Account Rs 55,140 (Dr.) Rs 1,360 (Cr.)]

13. From the following particulars, prepare Sales Ledger Adjustment Account and Bought Ledger Adjustment as they would appear in the General Ledger as on 31st January 2004:

2004		Rs
Jan. 1	Balance on Bought Ledger (Dr.)	870
	Balance on Bought Ledger (Cr.)	11,940
	Balance on Sales Ledger (Dr.)	14,620
	Balance on Sales Ledger (Cr.)	240
Jan. 31	Purchase	66,180
	Purchase Returns	2,560
	Sales	87,490
	Sales Returns	1,170
	Cash received from Customers	76,210
	Discount allowed thereon	2,820
	Cash paid to suppliers	58,430
	Discount allowed thereon	1,660
	Cash paid to customers	130
	Bills Receivable	4,120
	Bills Payable	2,250
	B/R Dishonoured	250
	Bought Ledger Balance (Dr.)	770
	Sales Ledger Balance (Cr.)	420

(*B.Com., Madurai, Andhra*)

[**Ans:** Sales Ledger Adjustment A/c (in G.L.) Rs 18,350 (Dr.) Rs 420 (Cr.)
Bought Ledger Adjustment A/c (in G.L.) Rs 770 (Dr.) Rs 13,120 (Cr.)]

14. From the following particulars, prepare Debtors' Ledger Adjustment Account and Creditors' Ledger Adjustment Account in the General Ledger:

	Rs	
Opening Balance of Debtors on 1st Jan.	40,000	(Dr.)
Opening Balance of Debtors of 1st Jan.	500	(Cr.)
Opening Balance of Creditors on 1st Jan.	1,000	(Dr.)
Opening Balance of Creditors on 1st Jan.	45,000	(Cr.)
Transactions during the year:		
Credit Purchases	2,00,000	
Credit Sales	2,82,000	
Purchase Returns	8,500	
Cash Sales	1,00,000	
Cash Purchases	50,000	
Cash Received from Debtors	2,32,000	
Discount Allowed	8,000	
Cash paid to Creditors	1,60,000	
Discount Allowed by Creditors	5,000	
Bills Payable issued	7,500	
Bad Debts written off	2,000	
Bills Receivable dishonoured	2,700	
Transfer from Bought Ledger to Sales Ledger	1,300	
Bad Debts already written off, now recovered	200	
Sales Returns	3,500	
Bills Receivable received	12,000	

(*B.Com., Bangalore*)

[**Ans:** Debtors' Ledger Adjustment A/c in General Ledger Rs 65,400
Creditors' Ledger Adjustment A/c in General Ledger Rs 61,700]

15. From the following particulars as extracted from the books of Minded Ltd. who keeps account on self-balancing system, prepare General Ledger Adjustments as would appear in the Sales Ledger and the Bought Ledger:

	Rs
Debtors Balance as on 1st Jan.	45,750
Creditors balance as on 1st Jan.	54,900
Transactions for the month of January:	
Credit Purchase	20,500
Credit Sales	22,700
Returns Inwards	400
Cash received from Customers	25,500
Bad Debts written off	2,500
Sundry charges debited to Customers	345
Discount received from Creditors	670
Discount allowed to Customers	450
Cash paid to Creditors	30,700
Acceptance received from Debtors	8,500
Creditors' bills accepted	12,000
B/R returned dishonoured	1,200
B/P dishonoured	3,000
Allowances from Creditors	275

(*CAIIB*)

[**Ans:** Debtors' Ledger Adjustment A/c (in G.L.) Rs 32,645
Creditors' Ledger Adjustment A/c (in G.L.) Rs 34,155]

16. From the following particulars of the books of Soman, who maintains his ledger under Self-Balancing System, prepare necessary adjustment Accounts.

		Rs
Jan. 1	Balance on Bought Ledger (Cr.)	18,900
	Balance on Bought Ledger (Dr.)	1,250
	Balance on Sales Ledger (Dr.)	22,150
	Balance on Sales Ledger (Cr.)	800
Dec. 31	Sales	60,400
	Returns Inwards	2,400
	Cash paid to customers	700
	Purchases	37,950
	Returns Outwards	1,150
	Cash paid to suppliers	28,950
	Discount received thereon	350
	Cash collected from customers	52,150
	Discount allowed thereon	900
	Bills Receivable received	11,150
	Acceptance issued	5,200
	Bills Receivable dishonoured	300
	Bills Endorsed to suppliers	2,650
	Bad Debts written off	400
	Transfer from bought ledger to Sales Ledger	1,450
	Balance on Bought Ledger (Dr.)	650
	Balance on Sales Ledger (Cr.)	400
	Carriage Charged to Customers	100

(*B.Com., Madras*)

[**Ans:** Debtors' Ledger Adjustment A/c (in G.L.) Rs. 14,800
Creditors' Ledger Adjustment A/c (in G.L.) Rs 16,500]

Chapter 15

Consignment Accounts

Need for Consignment – Definition – Meaning – Consignment and Sales – Important Terms – Recurring Expenses – Account Sales – Del Credere – Accounting Records – Books of Consignor – Books of Consignee – Invoice Price Method – Accounting for Losses – Valuation of Stock – Memorandum Column Method – Questions – Objective Type Questions – Theoretical Questions – Practical Problems.

In these days of mass production, manufacturers and wholesalers have to push their sales by all possible ways. Thus sales are made directly or indirectly. In the case of direct sales, businessmen or manufacturers appoint salesmen and they sell the goods. As such, all sales are under the control of the businessmen or the manufacturers. On the other hand, in indirect sales, a manufacturer or a wholesaler appoints an agent on commission basis. The manufacturer despatches goods to him, who sells the goods. This system of indirect selling is known as consignment system. The accounting relation to consignment transactions are called Consignment Account.

NEED FOR CONSIGNMENT

(1) The manufacturer does not know the local condition of the market to sell his goods. Hence he appoints agents on commission basis in different places to sell his goods. As a local man, the agent will sell more goods, very easily.

(2) New goods to the market can also be sold by an agent who knows the market condition. He will take initiative to sell the goods by doing the necessary promotional work for the product.

(3) It is very expensive for the manufacturers to sell the goods directly. It is economical to send the goods on consignment to the agent for selling them.

(4) The products of the manufacturers can be sold in foreign countries by sending the goods to an agent who is in that country. It is also economical to the manufacturer.

Definition

Consignment is the despatch of goods (or transfer of goods) to an agent for the purpose of storage and sales. The person despatching the goods is known as Consignor and the agent to whom the goods is sent is called Consignee. The Consignee undertakes to sell the goods for a consideration, which is called commission.

Meaning

Consignment is an agency arrangement under which the manufacturer or the wholesaler sends his goods at his own risk to his agent in a different place for the purpose of sales on commission basis.

The person who sends the goods is known as the Consignor or the Principal. The ownership of the goods remains with the consignor. The person to whom the goods are sent for sales is known as the Consignee or the Agent. Sending of goods from consignor to consignee is known as consignment and the goods so sent are termed as goods sent on consignment. The sender is the consignor and the receiver is the consignee. Sending of goods by the consignor is outward consignment and to the consignee it is an inward consignment.

Difference between Consignment and Sales

Consignment (1)	Sales (2)
1. Consignment is a despatching (forwarding) of goods from one person to another on a commission basis.	Sales refers to the transfer of property from the seller to the buyer.
2. Legal ownership is not passed on to the agent, but is within the consignor.	Legal ownership of the goods is passed on to the buyer.
3. The relationship between the consignor and consignee is that of a principal and an agent. The reason is that the consignee sells goods on behalf of the consignor.	The relationship between the seller and the buyer is that of creditors and debtors.
4. The expenses incurred by the consignee when goods are consigned to him are met by the consignor.	Expenses after sale are met by the buyer.
5. An order is not essential for consignment.	An order is essential for sales.
6. The contract of consignment must be in writing and it is called Consignment Deed.	As soon as the offer is accepted the contract of sale is complete. The contract may be oral or in writing.
7. The chief consideration of consignment is commission.	The chief consideration of a sale is profit.
8. The risk of goods is not transferred to the consignee. It rests with the consignor.	The risk is transferred along with goods to the buyer.
9. The goods sent on consignment may be called back by the consignor.	Calling back of sold goods is impossible.
10. The consignee has to send a statement of sales, called Account Sales, to the consignor.	The buyer need not send such statement.

IMPORTANT TERMS

Proforma Invoice

When the consignor sends the goods to the consignee, he forwards a statement showing the particulars of goods such as quality, quantity, price, markings, packing etc. and this statement is called the Proforma Invoice. But in case of regular sale, an invoice is prepared and sent along with the goods. It implies that a sale has taken place.

Recurring and Non-recurring Expenses

Consignor and consignee have to incur some expenses for despatching and selling the goods. These expenses of consignment are of two types: NON-RECURRING EXPENSES and RECURRING EXPENSES.

Non-recurring Expenses

Non-recurring expenses are incurred for bringing the goods from the place of the consignor to the place of the consignee. Hence, all the expenses incurred till the goods reach the godown of the consignee are non-recurring expenses. These expenses are incurred only once on a particular consignment. It will increase the value of goods. These expenses are paid by the consignor or by the consignee on behalf of the consignor.

Non -recurring expenses of the consignor	Non-recurring expenses of the consignee
1. Packing	1. Unloading charges
2. Transport or carriage	2. Railway dues
3. Forwarding	3. Dock Dues
4. Dock dues	4. Import Duty or Customs Duty
5. Landing charges	5. Octroi
6. Freight	6. Carriage to godown/shop
7. Insurance	

The abovementioned expenses do not occur again like the recurring expenses. These expenses are met on the whole consignment. These expenses are added to the cost of the consignment so as to arrive at the cost price of goods at the point of sale. Again these are taken into consideration when the value of closing stock and abnormal losses are calculated.

Recurring Expenses

These expenses are incurred after the goods have been received at consignee's godown. These expenses are incurred quite often and of recurring in nature. These expenses occur regularly at fixed intervals. Generally these expenses are incurred after the goods have reached the place of business by consignee. They are met by the consignor or consignee. These expenses do not increase the value of goods.

Recurring expenses incurred by the consignor	Recurring expenses incurred by the consignee
1. Bank Charges	1. Godown Rent and Storage Charges
2. Expenses on Damaged goods	2. Insurance Charges
	3. Brokerage
	4. Advertising
	5. Salary to Salesmen
	6. Expenses on goods returned
	7. Expenses on goods damaged
	8. Commission on sales
	9. Establishment expenses

Advance

Sometimes, consignor may ask the consignee to pay an advance for the part of the value of goods consigned. Consignee may send the advance in the form of a draft or cheque. If the consignee is not in a position to advance money, a Bill may be drawn on consignee. Consignor discounts the Bill and gets the money. The amount of discount on the Bill may be debited to Consignment Account or debited to Discount Account. Advance given by the consignee will be deducted from the sale proceeds.

Account Sales

Periodically or when the goods consigned are sold by the consignee, the consignee will send to the consignor a statement, which is called Account Sales, showing the amount received by way of sale of goods, expenses incurred, commission charged, advance payment and balance due to the consignor and the stock still in hand. From the Account Sales, the consignor closes his entries in the books regarding the consignment for that year. He can ascertain the profit or loss resulting from the transactions. Following is the specimen of an Account sales:

Account sales differ from an invoice. Account sales are prepared and sent by a consignee to a consigner. But invoice is prepared and sent by a seller to a buyer. In the case of an invoice, the two parties are debtor and creditor. In the case of account sales, the relationship is that of a principal and an agent.

Account Sales of 90 Mixies sold by Ganesh & Company of Bhopal on account and at the risk of Messrs Devi and Sons, Delhi, by:

		Rs
Gross Proceeds:		
60 Mixies with additional Jar @ Rs 1,500		90,000
30 Mixies without additional Jar @ Rs 1,300		39,000
		1,29,000
Less: Expenses and Charges.	Rs	
Freight	3,000	
Insurance	2,000	
Warehouse Charges	2,500	
Commission @ 15%	19,350	26,850
		1,02,150
Less: Advance sent		50,000
Balance due (Cheque/Draft enclosed)		52,150

E. & O.E. Ganesh & Company, Bhopal

Stock on hand 10 Mixies

15th July 2004

Commission

Consignor pays commission to Consignee for selling his goods. Commission is generally calculated at fixed percentage of total sales as per terms laid down by the Consignor. These commissions may be simple, or ordinary, special or overriding and del credere. Ordinary commission is calculated as per terms laid down by the consignor. Generally it is calculated on the basis of total sales. Special commission is paid to give further incentive for increasing the sales. Overriding commission is paid to consignee when he overrides the specified amount of sales. The commission is also calculated on total sales.

Del Credere : The consignee is not expected to sell the goods on credit. However, the consignee has the right to sell the goods on credit, if consignor permits him to do so. Again if consignee makes credit sales and if there incurs any loss by way of bad debts then such loss should be borne by the consignor. To avoid such a loss, extra commission is given to the consignee, who is responsible for any bad debts. This extra commission is called Del Credere commission. It is given for taking risk in credit sales. In such cases, consignor receives the gross sale proceeds, whether recovered or not. This is generally calculated on total sales. Sometimes, del credere commission is restricted to credit sales only. In that case it is calculated only on credit sales.

ACCOUNTING RECORDS FOR CONSIGNMENT TRANSACTION AT COST PRICE METHOD

In the Books of Consignor:

The consignor wants to know two things which are:

(1) To ascertain profit or loss when goods on consignment sold by the consignee.

(2) To know the settlement of account by the consignee *i.e.* to know the amount due by or due to consignee.

The consignment account is opened by the consignor to know profit or loss on each consignment. Each consignment is distinguished from the other by naming it in respect to place, examples, Consignment to Madras, Consignment to Bombay etc. If there is a number of consignments in one place, then the name of the consignee is added to the consignment account, for example : Consignment to Ramu Account, Consignment to Krishna Account etc. For that, he opens a Consignment Account for each consignment. It is a revenue (Nominal) Account. It is a special Trading and Profit and Loss Account. Consignee Account is prepared to know the amount due by or due to the Consignee. It is a personal account.

Following are the set of journal entries in the books of Consignor·

(1) *When the goods are sent on consignment:*

Consignment Account Dr.
To Goods Sent on Consignment A/c
(Being the cost of goods sent on Consignment)

(2) *When expenses are incurred by the Consignor:*

Consignment Account Dr.
To Bank/Cash Account
(Being the expenses incurred on Consignment)

(3) *When advance is received from Consignee:*

Cash/Bank/Bill Receivable Account Dr.
To Consignee Account
(Being the amount of advance received from Consignee)

(4) *When the Bill is discounted by the Consignor with his banker:*

Bank Account Dr.
Discount Account Dr.
To Bills Receivable A/c
(Being the Bill is discounted)

Note: The Discount on Bills can be transferred to Profit and Loss Account or to the Consignment Account. Since it is a cost of raising finance, it can be transferred to Profit and Loss Account.

After the Consignee sends the Account Sales

(5) *When the gross sales proceeds are reported by the Consignee:*

Consignee Account Dr.
To Consignment Account
(Being the gross sales proceeds reported by the Consignee)

(6) *For expenses incurred by the Consignee:*

Consignment Account Dr.
To Consignee Account
(Being the expenses incurred by the Consignee)

(7) *For commission payable to the Consignee:*

Consignment Account Dr.
To Consignee Account
(Being the Commission due to Consignee)

(8) *For unsold stock remaining with the Consignee:*

Consignment Stock Account Dr.
Consignee Account
(Being the value of unsold stock)

(9) *For transferring the profit or loss to Profit and Loss:*

For Profit: Consignment Account Dr.
To Profit and Loss Account
(Being the profit transferred to Profit & Loss Account)

For Loss: Profit and Loss Account Dr.
To Consignment Account
(Being the loss on consignment transferred to Profit & Loss A/c)

(10) *For settlement of account by the Consignee:*

Generally the balance amount is settled by the Consignee when he sends the Account Sales:

Bank/Cash/Bill Receivable Account Dr.
To Consignee Account
(Being the amount due from Consignee is received)

(11) *When goods sent on Consignment account is closed:*

Goods sent on Consignment Account Dr.
To Trading/Purchase Account
(Being the amount of goods sent on Consignment)

Note: If it is a manufacturing concern, then the Goods sent on Consignment account is closed by transferring it to Trading Account. If it is a trading concern, then it is closed by transferring it to Purchase Account.

Valuation of Unsold Stock (at cost price)

If all the goods are not sold by the Consignee within the accounting period, then the unsold stock is brought into account by the Consignor. As usual, the unsold stock in the hands of the consignee should be valued on cost price or market price whichever is less. Here the cost means the cost at the moment when the goods reached the Consignee's godown. The cost includes by adding proportionate non-recurring expenses incurred by the consignor as well as the consignee. It is calculated as follows:

(*a*) The proportionate Cost Price and

(*b*) Proportionate direct expenses i.e. the expenses incurred by the Consignor and Consignee till the goods reached the godown of the Consignee.

Expenses incurred by the Consignee after the goods have been brought to the shop/godown are not considered. Correct profit or loss can be ascertained by the proper valuation of unsold stock which is credited to Consignment Account.

Value of unsold stock = Cost Price of Closing Stock + Proportionate non-Recurring Expenses

The Consigner usually maintains three accounts:

1. CONSIGNMENT ACCOUNT. It is a nominal account. It is in fact a Special Trading and Profit and Loss Account. The balance, in this Account, represents either profit or loss on consignment which is finally transferred to General Profit and Loss Account.

2. CONSIGNEE'S PERSONAL ACCOUNT. It is a personal account. It is mainly prepared to ascertain the amount due from the Consignee.

3. GOODS SENT ON CONSIGNMENT ACCOUNT. It is a real account. It is closed by transferring its balance to Purchase Account or sometimes credit side of Trading Account.

ILLUSTRATION 15.1

Mr. Ram Manohar of Bombay sent 100 bicycles, which cost Rs 900 each, to Gopal of Madras on consignment basis. Ram Manohar paid freight of Rs 1,200, Cartage Rs 300 and Insurance Rs 400. In Madras, Gopal has spent Rs 100 as cartage, loading and unloading Rs 50. The bicycles have been kept in a godown at a rent of Rs 100 p.m. At the end of accounting period, 20 bicycles remained unsold. The selling price of the bicycle is Rs 1,000 at Madras. What should be the value of stock unsold?

SOLUTION

Calculation of Consignment Stock

			Rs
	Cost of 20 unsold bicycles = Rs 900 × 20		18,000
	Total non-recurring expenditure for 100 bicycles:		
		Rs	
Consignor's Expenses	Freight	1,200	
	Cartage	300	
	Insurance	400	
Consignee's Expenses	Cartage	100	
	Loading & unloading for 100 bicycles	50	
		2,050	
	Therefore for 20 bicycles = $\frac{2,050}{100} \times 20$		410
			18,410

Consignee's Books

The consignee receives the goods from the Consignor. It is an inward consignment to the Consignee. An inward consignment is the receipt of goods by the Consignee from the Consignor for the purpose of sale on commission basis. Consignee is not the owner of the goods. Following are the set of journal entries recorded in the books of the Consignee:

(1) *When the goods is received:*

No entry

The Consignee is not the owner of the goods. He does not purchase the goods. Hence he does not include this in his book. The receipt of the goods is recorded in a Memorandum Book – Consignment Inward Book.

(2) *When expenses are incurred by the Consignee:*

Consignor Account Dr.
To Bank Account
(Being expenses paid on consignment)

(3) *Advance remitted to Consignor by Cash/Cheque/Bills Payable*

Consignor Account Dr.
To Cash/Bank/Bills Payable A/c
(Being advance paid to Consignor)

(4) *When Consignee sold the goods:*

(*a*) For cash sales :

Bank Account Dr.
To Consignor Account
(Being the cash sales of consignment)

(*b*) For credit sale:

Consignment Debtors Account Dr.
To Consignor Account
(Being the credit sales of consignment)

(5) *When the commission is due:*

Consignor Accounts Dr.
To Commission Account
(Being commission earned on sale of consignment)

(6) *When the Consignee collected the debt from Consignment Debtors:*

Bank Account Dr.
To Consignment Debtors A/c
(Being the Collection of consignment debts)

(7) *For bad debts if any:*

(*a*) If Del Credere Commission is not paid:

Consignor Account Dr.
To Consignment Debtors A/c
(Being bad debt incurred on sales)

(*b*) If Del Credere Commission is paid:

Bad Debts Account Dr.
To Consignment Debtors A/c
(Being bad debts incurred on consignment sales)

Note: Bad debts from Consignment debtors is transferred to Del Credere Commission Account and the balance of Del Credere Commission Account along with Commission account is transferred to his Profit and Loss Account.

(*c*) Bad debts is transferred to his Profit & Loss Account

Del Credere Commission Account Dr.
To Bad Debts Account
(Being bad debts transferred to Del Credere Commission Account)

(8) *Closing of Del Credere Commission and Commission Account:*

Commission Account Dr.
Del Credere Commission Account Dr.
To Profit and Loss Account
(Being Commission account and balance of Del Credere account is closed by transferring to Profit and Loss Account)

(9) *Settlement of Account with Consignor:*

Consignor Account Dr.
To Cash/Bank/Bill Payable A/c
(Being the amount due to Consignor is settled)

ILLUSTRATION 15.2

M/s Chand & Company of Calcutta consign goods costing Rs 25,000 to their agent Ramlal, on which they pay freight, insurance and other charges of Rs 1,500 drawing on him at 90 days Bill for Rs 20,000. They discount the Bill with a bank at a discount of Rs 150. After 3 months they receive from their agent an Account Sales informing that the entire consignment had been sold for Rs 35,000, that expenses amounting to Rs 700 have been incurred and showing as a deduction they agreed commission of 2% on the amount realised. A draft on the Bank was enclosed for the balance due.

Show the journal entries and important ledger accounts in the books of both the parties.

SOLUTION

In the books of Chand and Company

JOURNAL

			Dr.	Cr.
			Rs	Rs
	Consignment to Ramlal Account	Dr.	25,000	
	To Goods sent on consignment Account			25,000
	(Being goods sent on consignment to Ramlal)			
	Consignment to Ramlal Account	Dr.	1,500	
	To Bank Account			1,500
	(Being expenses incurred on consignment)			

Bills Receivable Account	Dr.	20,000	
To Ramlal Account			20,000
(Being bill accepted by Ramlal at 90 days)			
Bank Account	Dr.	19,850	
Discount Account	Dr.	150	
To Bills Receivable Account			20,000
(Being the bill received from Ramlal and discounted)			
Consignment to Ramlal Account	Dr.	150	
To Discount Account			150
(Being discount transferred)			
Ramlal Account	Dr.	35,000	
To Consignment Account			35,000
(Being Gross Proceeds of the consignment as per the Account Sales)			
Consignment Account	Dr.	700	
To Ramlal Account			700
(Being Expenses incurred by the consignee)			
Consignment Account	Dr.	700	
To Ramlal Account			700
(Being commission received i.e., 2% on Rs 35,000)			
Bank Account	Dr.	13,600	
To Ramlal Account			13,600
(Being the balance due from Ramlal Received)			
Consignment Account	Dr.	6,950	
To Profit and Loss Account			6,950
(Being Profit on Consignment transferred)			
Goods sent on Consignment Account	Dr.	25,000	
To Purchase Account			25,000
(Being Goods on Consignment transferred to Purchase Account)			

Note: Discounting charges on Bill may also be transferred to Finance charges account and then it may be transferred to Profit and Loss Account.

Goods sent on Consignment is closed by transferring to Purchase Account or Trading Account.

Dr. **Consignment to Ramlal Account** Cr.

	Rs		*Rs*
To Goods sent on Consignment Account	25,000	By Ramlal Account Sale proceeds	35,000
To Bank Account – Expenses	1,500		
To Discount	150		
To Ramlal Account–Expenses	700		
To Ramlal Account–Commission	700		
To Profit and Loss Account–Profit transferred	6,950		
	35,000		35,000

Goods sent on Consignment Account

Dr.	Rs	Cr.	Rs
To Purchase Account	25,000	By Consignment Account	25,000
	25,000		25,000

Ramlal Account (Consignee)

Dr.	Rs	Cr.	Rs
To Consignment Account –Sale Proceeds	35,000	By Bills Receivable Account	20,000
		By Consignment Account–Expenses	700
		By Consignment Account–Commission	700
		By Bank–Draft received	13,600
	35,000		35,000

In the books of Ramlal

JOURNAL

Particulars		Dr. Rs	Cr. Rs
Chand and Company Account To Bills Payable Account (Being bills accepted by Chand and Company)	Dr.	20,000	20,000
Bank Account To Chand and Company Account (Being goods sold on behalf of Chand and Company)	Dr.	35,000	35,000
Chand and Company Account To Bank Account (Being Expenses incurred on Consignment)	Dr.	700	700
Chand and Company Account To Commission Account (Being 2% Commission on sale proceeds)	Dr.	700	700
Chand and Company Account To Bank (Being balance amount remitted to Chand and Company)	Dr.	13,600	13,600

Chand and Company Account

Dr.	Rs	Cr.	Rs
To Bills Payable Account	20,000	By Bank Account –Sale Proceeds	35,000
To Bank Account–Expenses	700		
To Bank Account–Commission	700		
To Bank Account–Draft sent	13,600		
	35,000		35,000

ILLUSTRATION 15.3

Williams of Madras consigned 300 chests of tea at Rs 2,000 per chest to Johnson of New Delhi paying freight Rs 4,000 and other expenses Rs 2,000. Johnson sold 250 chests at Rs 2,500 per chest and 25 chest at Rs

2,200 per chest for cash. Johnson spent for freight and octroi Rs 3,000 and other expenses Rs 1,000. He remitted the amount due to Williams after deducting his commission at 5% (normal), 2½% (Overriding) and + 1/2% (del credere commission to be given on total sales). Johnson found that one customer to whom credit was allowed paid only Rs 4,800 against Rs 5,000 in full settlement. Other customers paid the amount due.

Pass journal entries in the books of both parties and prepare ledger accounts. *(B.Com., Delhi)*

SOLUTION

In the books of Williams

JOURNAL

	Particulars		Dr.	Cr.
			Rs	*Rs*
	Consignment to New Delhi Account Dr. To Goods sent on Consignment Account (Being goods sent on Consignment to Johnson)		6,00,000	6,00,000
	Consignment to New Delhi Account Dr. To Bank Account (Being expenses incurred on Consignment)		6,000	6,000
	Johnson Account Dr. To Consignment to New Delhi Account (Being sales made by Johnson– 250 chests @ Rs 2,500 and 25 chests @ Rs 2,200)		6,80,000	6,80,000
	Consignment to New Delhi Account Dr. To Johnson Account (Being expenses incurred by Johnson on freight and octroi Rs 3,000 and other expenses Rs 1,000)		4,000	4,000
	Consignment to New Delhi Account Dr. To Johnson Account (Being Commission on sale i.e. 5% normal + 2½ overriding + 1/2% del credere commission on Rs 6,80,000)		54,400	54,400
	Consignment Stock Account Dr. To Consignment to New Delhi Account (Being the value of unsold stock of consignment)		50,750	50,750
	Bank Account Dr. To Johnson Account (Being the receipt of amount due from Johnson)		6,21,600	6,21,600
	Consignment to New Delhi Account Dr. To Profit and Loss Account (Being Profit on Consignment transferred)		66,350	66,350
	Goods sent on Consignment Account Dr. To Trading Account (Being goods sent on consignment transferred to trading Account)		6,00,000	6,00,000

Consignment to Johnson Account

Dr.	Rs	Cr.	Rs
To Goods sent on Consignment Account	6,00,000	By Johnson Account –Sale Proceeds	6,80,000
To Bank Account –Expenses	6,000	By Consignment Stock Account	50,750
To Johnson Account –Expenses	4,000		
To Johnson Account –Commission	54,400		
To Profit and Loss Account –Profit transferred	66,350		
	7,30,750		7,30,750

Goods sent on Consignment Account

Dr.	Rs	Cr.	Rs
To Trading Account	6,00,000	By Consignment Account	6,00,000

Johnson (of New Delhi) Account

Dr.	Rs	Cr.	Rs
To Consignment to New Delhi Account	6,80,000	By Consignment to New Delhi Account–Expenses	4,000
		By Consignment to New Delhi Account–Commission	54,400
		By Bank Account –Draft received	6,21,600
	6,80,000		6,80,000

Note: Valuation of closing stock:

	Rs	Rs
Cost of 25 chests of Tea @ Rs 2,000		50,000
Add: Proportionate non-recurring expenses:		
Freight	4,000	
Other Expenses	2,000	
Octroi charges	3,000	
For 300 chests	9,000	
For 25 chests = $\frac{9,000}{300} \times 25$		750
		50,750

In the books of Johnson

JOURNAL

Particulars		Dr. Rs	Cr. Rs
Consignment Debtors Account	Dr.	6,25,000	
Bank Account	Dr.	55,000	
To Williams Account			6,80,000
(Being sales of 250 chests @ Rs 2,500 on credit and 25 chests @ Rs 2,200 on cash)			
Williams Account	Dr.	4,000	
To Bank Account			4,000
(Being expenses incurred on consignment)			
Williams Account	Dr.	54,400	
To Commission Account			54,400
(Being 8% commission on Sales)			
Bank Account	Dr.	6,24,800	
Bad Debts Account	Dr.	200	
To Consignment Debtors Account			6,25,000
(Being the amount received and bad debts incurred against consignment debtors)			
Williams Account	Dr.	6,21,600	
To Bank Account			6,21,600
(Being amount due to consignor paid)			
Commission Account	Dr.	200	
To Bad Debts Account			200
(Being bad debts transferred to commission account)			
Commission Account	Dr.	54,200	
To Profit and Loss Account			54,200
(Being Commission transferred to Profit and Loss Account after adjusting the bad debts)			

Dr. **Williams Account** Cr.

	Rs		Rs
To Bank–Expenses	4,000	By Consignment Debtors A/c	6,25,000
To Commission	54,400	By Bank (Sales)	55,000
To Bank (Amount due)	6,21,600		
	6,80,000		6,80,000

Invoice Price Method

The Consignor, instead of sending the goods on consignment at cost price, may send it at a price higher than the cost price. This price is known as Invoice Price or Selling Price. The difference between the cost price and the invoice price of goods is known as loading or the higher price over the cost. This is done with a view to keep the profits on consignment secret. As such, consignee could not know the actual profit made on consignment. Hence the consignor sends the Proforma invoice at a higher price than the cost price. When the consignor records the transaction in his book at invoice price, some additional entries have to be passed in order to eliminate the excess price and to arrive at the correct profit or loss on consignment.

Excess Price or Loading is to be calculated on the following items:

1. Consignment stock at the beginning
2. Goods sent on consignment
3. Goods returned by the consignee
4. Consignment stock at the end of the period

(*a*) *To remove the excess price in the opening stock:*

Consignment Stock Reserve A/c Dr.
To Consignment Account
(Being the excess value of opening stock is brought down to cost price)

(*b*) *To remove the excess price in the goods sent on consignment:*

Goods sent on Consignment Account Dr.
To Consignment Account
(Being the difference between the invoice price and cost price is adjusted)

(*c*) *To remove the excess price in goods return:*

Consignment Account Dr.
To Goods sent on Consignment A/c
(Being to bring down the value of goods to cost price)

(*d*) *To remove the excess price in closing stock:*

Consignment Account Dr.
To Consignment Stock Reserve A/c
(Being the excess value of stock is adjusted)

But these adjustments are not needed in consignee's book. Invoice price does not affect the consignee. When the stock is shown in the Balance Sheet, in Consignor's Book, the Consignment Stock Reserve is deducted.

ILLUSTRATION 15.4

Arun consigned 100 mini toy cars to Sanjoy to be sold at his risk. The cost of one mini toy car was Rs 150, but the invoice price was Rs 200. Arun paid freight Rs 600 and insurance in transit Rs 200.

Sanjoy sent a bank draft for Rs 10,000 as advance payment and later sent an Account Sales showing that 80 toy cars were sold at Rs 220 each. Expenses incurred by Sanjoy were: Carriage inward Rs 25, Octroi Rs 75, Godown rent Rs 500 and Advertisement Rs 300. Sanjoy is entitled to a commission of 5% on sales.

Journalise the above transactions in the books of Arun and Sanjoy.

SOLUTION

In the books of Arun

JOURNAL

	Particulars		*Dr.*	*Cr.*
			Rs	*Rs*
	Consignment Account Dr. To Goods sent on Consignment Account (Being 100 mini toy cars sent on consignment to Sanjoy and invoiced @ Rs 200)		20,000	20,000
	Consignment Account Dr. To Bank Account (Being expenses incurred on freight Rs 600, insurance 200)		800	800
	Bank Account Dr. To Sanjoy Account (Being bank draft received from Sanjoy as advance)		10,000	10,000

		Dr.	Cr.
Sanjoy Account To Consignment Account (Being 80 mini toy cars sold by Sanjoy @ Rs 220)	Dr.	17,600	17,600
Consignment Account To Sanjoy Account (Being expenses incurred by Sanjoy on carriage inward Rs 25, Octroi Rs 75, Godown rent Rs 500 and Advertisement Rs 300)	Dr.	900	900
Consignment Account To Sanjoy Account (Being 5% Commission to Sanjoy on Rs 17,600)	Dr.	880	880
Consignment Stock Account To Consignment Account (Being the value of unsold stock of 20 mini toy cars)	Dr.	4,180	4,180
Goods Sent on Consignment Account To Consignment Account (Being the excess of cost price @ Rs 50 i.e. Rs 200 – Rs 150 per mini toy car is removed)	Dr.	5,000	5,000
Consignment Account To Consignment Stock Reserve Account (Being the excess of cost price @ Rs 50 for 20 mini toy cars adjusted)	Dr.	1,000	1,000
Consignment Account To Profit and Loss Account (Being Profit on Consignment transferred)	Dr.	3,200	3,200
Goods sent on Consignment Account To Trading Account (Being transfer of goods sent on consignment transferred to Trading Account)	Dr.	15,000	15,000

In the books of Sanjoy

JOURNAL

		Dr.	Cr.
		Rs	Rs
Arun Account To Bank Account (Being advance payment on receipt of 100 mini toy cars)	Dr.	10,000	10,000
Arun Account To Bank Account (Being expenses incurred on carriage inward Rs 25, octroi Rs 75, godown rent Rs 500 and advertisement Rs 300)	Dr.	900	900
Bank Account To Arun Account (Being sales of 80 mini toy cars @ Rs 220)	Dr.	17,600	17,600
Arun Account To Commission Account (Being 5% Commission on sale of Rs 17,600)	Dr.	880	880

Workings:

		Rs
Valuation of Closing Stock:		
Cost of Mini Toy Cars @ Rs 200 × 20		4,000
Add: Proportionate Non-Recurring Expenses:	Rs	
Consignor:		
Freight	600	
Insurance	200	
	800	
Consignee:		
Carriage Inward	25	
Octroi	75	
	100	
For 100 mini toy cars	900	
For 20 mini toy cars	$\frac{900 \times 20}{100}$	180
		4,180

ACCOUNTING FOR LOSSES

When the consignor sends the goods, losses may arise during consignment transactions. Such losses affect consignor account and not consignee account. So consignor makes some entries to adjust the loss. The adjustment depends upon the type of losses. These losses are of two types: (1) *Normal Losses* and (2) *Abnormal Losses.*

1. Normal Losses

When goods are lost or damaged due to normally expected but unavoidable causes such as losses due to evaporation, leakage, breakage, dusting, weighment, drying, sublimation of goods etc., these losses are called Normal Losses. These types of losses cannot be avoided. Such inherent and unavoidable losses form part of the cost of goods. That is, the loss on account of normal loss is borne by good units. When calculating the cost of unsold stock, this normal loss is to be considered. The cost of unsold stock increases proportionately due to normal loss. When there is normal loss the following formula is used for calculating the consignment stock:

$$\text{Value of Closing Stock} = \frac{\text{Total cost of goods sent + Total non-recurring expenses}}{\text{Total units of goods sent} - \text{Normal loss units}} \times \text{Closing stock in units.}$$

Alternatively:

$$\text{Value of Closing Stock} = \frac{\text{Total value of goods sent}}{\text{Unit received by Consignee}} \times \text{Units in closing stock.}$$

The normal loss is not shown in the consignment account. There is no need to pass any entry in the books of account.

Normal Loss and Valuation of Unsold Stock

ILLUSTRATION 15.5

Goods consigned 500 kg @ Rs 20 per kg. Freight and Carriage paid by the consignor Rs 4,000. Consignee sold 300 kg @ Rs 35 per kg and incurred Rs 1,000 as unloading expenses, Rs 2,000 as godown rent and Rs 1,000 as selling expenses. Normal loss due to leakage is 50 kg.

Show how the loss and unsold stock will be treated in the books of the consignor.

SOLUTION

Valuation of Unsold Stock

		Rs
Cost of 500 kg @ Rs 20 per kg		10,000
Add: Non Recurring Expenses	Rs	
Freight and Carriage	4,000	
Unloading Expenses	1,000	5,000
		15,000
Actual Quantity available for sale:		
(500 kg – 50 kg normal loss)	= 450 kg	

$$\text{Value of unsold stock)} = \frac{\text{Total value of goods sent}}{\text{Units received by consignee}} \times \text{Units in closing stock} = \frac{15,000}{450} \times 150$$

$$= \text{Rs } 5,000$$

JOURNAL

			Dr.	Cr.
			Rs	*Rs*
	Consignment Stock Account Dr. To Consignment Account (Being the value of 150 kg of unsold consignment stock)		5,000	5,000

Note: No separate treatment is required for normal loss.

2. Abnormal Losses

When loss or damage of goods is caused by unnatural and unexpected reasons, then such loss is treated as abnormal loss. It is unexpected loss and beyond the control of the human beings. Loss of goods due to fire, flood, earthquake, war, theft, accidents in transit etc. are abnormal losses. Such losses occur because of bad luck, due to accident, mischief by someone or human carelessness.

Abnormal loss is calculated just like the unsold stock on consignment and credited to consignment account and debited to Abnormal or Accidental Loss Account and then transferred to General Profit and Loss Account, so as to arrive at the correct profit or loss of consignment. This is because abnormal loss has nothing to do with the particular consignment. Some businessmen take insurance policy in respect of the goods sent or received on consignment by the consignor or the consignee. Such a policy is obtained only in respect of abnormal loss which may be caused to the goods. If the insurer is liable for the loss, then the amount of claim admitted by the insurer should be debited to the insurer and balance of the loss should be debited to Profit and Loss Account.

The journal entries are:

(*a*) *When the Loss is Irrecoverable:*

Abnormal (Accidental) Loss Account Dr.
To Consignment Account
(Being the value of abnormal loss)

Profit and Loss Account Dr.
To Abnormal (Accidental) Loss A/c
(Being irrecoverable loss transferred)

(*b*) *When the Loss is insured and full amount is recoverable:*

Accidental Loss Account	Dr.
To Consignment Account	
(Being the value of abnormal loss)	
Insurance Company Account	Dr.
To Abnormal Loss Account	
(Being the loss transferred to Insurance Company)	

(*c*) *When the Loss is partly recoverable:*

Accidental Loss Account	Dr.
To Consignment Account	
(Being the value of abnormal loss)	
Insurance Co/Bank Account	Dr.
Profit & Loss Account	Dr.
To Abnormal Loss Account	
(Being loss partly recoverable and balance transferred to Profit & Loss Account)	

Valuation of Abnormal Loss and Unsold Stock

ILLUSTRATION 15.6

Goods sent on consignment 1,000 kg @ Rs 10 per kg. Expenses paid by the consignor: Freight Rs 500 and Insurance Rs 300. 200 kg were destroyed in transit due to an accident. Claim admitted by the Insurance Company was for Rs 1,500. The consignee sold 700 kg @ Rs 20 per kg and incurred the following expenses: Unloading Rs 200, Godown Rent Rs 500 and Selling Expenses Rs 300.

Pass journal entries relating to loss in transit and unsold consignment stock in the books of the consignor.

SOLUTION:

			Rs
(1)	Value of Unsold stock:		
	Cost of 1,000 kg @ Rs 10 per kg		10,000
	Add: Non Recurring Expenses prior to Loss:	Rs	
	Freight	500	
	Insurance	300	800
	Total cost of 1,000 kg		10,800
	Less: Amount relating to 200 kg, which is lost: $10,800 \times \frac{200}{1000}$		2,160
			8,640
	Add: Non-Recurring Expenses after the Loss:		200
	Cost of 800 kg		8,840
(2)	Loss in Transit:		2,160
	Less: Claim admitted		1,500
			660

(3) Cost of unsold stock: $= \frac{8,840 \times 100}{800} = \text{Rs } 1,105$

JOURNAL

	Dr.	Cr.
	Rs	Rs
Loss in Transit Account Dr.	2,160	
To Consignment Account		2,160
(Being goods lost in transit)		
Insurance Claim Account Dr.	1,500	
To Loss in Transit Account		1,500
(Being Insurance claim accepted for loss in transit)		
Profit and Loss Account Dr.	660	
To Loss in Transit Account		660
(Being excess of Abnormal Loss over admitted claim transferred)		
Consignment Stock Account Dr.	1,105	
To Consignment Account		1,105
(Being the cost of usold stock)		

Goods Lost in Transit and Valuation of Unsold Stock

ILLUSTRATION 15.7

A consignment of 10,000 kg of tea, costing Rs 50 per kg, sent on consignment on 1st February 2004 to an agent, on commission of 5% on gross sales.

The following expenses are incurred:

		Rs
(*a*)	By the Consignor:	
	Freight and Insurance	2,000
	Dock charges and Sundry Expenses	800
(*b*)	By the Consignee:	
	Godown Rent and Insurance	800
	Miscellaneous Expenses	1,400

Some packages containing 2,000 kg of tea were damaged in transit and the contents had to be destroyed on landing as having become unfit for sale. 7,000 kg of tea were sold at Rs 60 per kg and on 28th February 2004, the date of closing of accounts, the balance of the consignment remained unsold in stock.

Draw up the Consignment Outward Account and Consignee's Account in the books of the Consignor, showing the amount due from the Consignee on 28th February 2004. (*B.Com., Calcutta*)

SOLUTION

In the Books of Consignor

Consignment Account

Dr. Cr.

Date	Particulars		Rs	Date	Particulars	Rs
1.2.2004	To Goods sent on Consignment Account		5,00,000	28.2.2004	By Consignee Account–Sale Proceeds (Rs 7,000 × Rs 60)	4,20,000
	To Bank Account–Expenses:				By Profit and Loss Account Loss in Transit	1,00,560
	Freight & Insurance	2,000			By Consignment Stock Account	50.280
	Dock Charges and Miscellaneous	800	2,800			
28.2.2004	To Consignee Account:					
	Godown Rent and Insurance	800				

		Rs			Rs
	Miscellaneous Expenses 1,400				
	Commission 21,000	23,200			
	To Profit and Loss Account– Profit transferred	44,840			
		5,70,840			5,70,840

Dr. **Consignee Account** Cr.

		Rs			Rs
28.2.2004	To Consignment Outward Account–Sale Proceeds	4,20,000	28.2.2004	By Consignment Outward A/c Godown Rent and Insurance 800, Miscellaneous Expenses 1,400, Commission 21,000	23,200
				By Balance c/d	3,96,800
		4,20,000			4,20,000

Note:

Valuation of unsold stock and lost in transit:	Rs
Cost of 10,000 kg @ Rs 50	5,00,000
Add: Non-recurring Expenses:	2,800
Cost for 10,000 kg	5,02,800

$$\text{Value of unsold stock} = \frac{5,02,800 \times 1000}{10,000} = \text{Rs } 50,280$$

$$\text{Value of goods lost} = \frac{5,02,800 \times 2,000}{10,000} = \text{Rs } 1,00,560$$

MEMORANDUM COLUMN METHOD

Memorandum Column Method is a combination of Cost Price Method and Invoice Price Method. Under this method, there are two columns on each side of the Consignment Account. These two columns are used to record both cost and invoice prices of goods sent on consignment, opening stock, closing stock etc. The extra column used to record invoice price is known as Memorandum Column. Hence the method is called Memorandum Column Method. From the accounting point of view it is not important. It is provided to know and show the profits if the consignments are recorded at invoice price.

ILLUSTRATION 15.8 (Valuation of Stock and Abnormal Loss)

Mr Arun of Bombay consigned 500 toys to Ramesh. A Proforma invoice was prepared at Rs 40 per toy, the cost of which was Rs 35 per toy. Arun spent Rs 750 by way of forwarding charges including insurance premium of Rs 150. In transit 50 toys were destroyed and Ramesh received 90% of the cost price in full satisfaction of the claim with Insurance Company. Ramesh sold 400 toys at invoice price and spent Rs 300 for selling expenses. He deducted a commission at 20% on sales and paid the balance to Arun.

Prepare Consignment Account, Consignment Stock Account, Accidental Loss Account in the books of Arun under Memorandum Column Method.

SOLUTION:

In the books of Mr Arun

Consignment Account

Dr. Particulars	Invoice Price	Cost Price	Cr.	Invoice Price	Cost Price
	Rs	Rs		Rs	Rs
To Goods sent on Consignment Account	20,000	17,500	By Ramesh Account– Sale Proceeds	16,000	16,000
To Bank Account- Expenses	750	750	By Accidental Loss	2,075	1,825
To Ramesh Account– Expenses	300	300	By Consignment Stock Account	2,075	1,825
To Ramesh–Commission	3,200	3,200	By Profit and Loss Account–Loss transferred	4,100	2,100
	24,250	21,750		24,250	21,750

Consignment Stock Account

Dr.	Rs	Rs	Cr.	Rs	Rs
To Consignment Account	2,075	1,825	By Balance c/d	2,075	1,825
To Balance b/d	2,075	1,825			

Accidental Loss Account

Dr.	Rs	Rs	Cr.	Rs	Rs
To Consignment Account	2,075	1,825	By Cash Account–from Insurance Co. *i.e.* 90% of goods lost $\frac{90}{100} \times 1,750$	1,575	1,575
			By Profit & Loss A/c Loss Transferred	500	250
	2,075	1,825		2,075	1,825

Valuation of Stock and Abnormal Loss

	Invoice Price	*Cost Price*
500 toys @ Rs 40	20,000	
500 toys @ Rs 35		17,500
Add: Non-recurring Expenses	750	750
For 500 toys:	20,750	18,250
For 50 toys:	2,075	1,825

Closing stock: 50 toys

Abnormal Loss: 50 toys

MISCELLANEOUS

ILLUSTRATION 15.9

Dinesh of Bombay consigned medicines to Rao of Madras costing Rs 1,00,000. The invoice was made proforma so as to show a profit of 25% on cost. Dinesh paid freight and insurance Rs 2,000.

Rao sold part of consignment for Rs 88,000 at uniform price of 10% over invoice price and spent Rs 3,000 as warehouse charges, and Rs 1,000 as selling expenses.

Rao is entitled to a commission of 5% on sales and 20% of the net profit after charging such commission on sales. Rao paid the amount due by bank draft.

Draw up the Consignment Account and Rao's Account in the books of Dinesh. (*C.A. Inter*)

SOLUTION:

In the books of Dinesh

Dr. **Consignment Account** Cr.

	Rs		Rs
To Goods sent on Consignment Account	1,25,000	By Rao Account–Sale Proceeds	88,000
To Bank Account–Expenses	2,000	By Goods sent on Consignment Account–Excess Price	25,000
To Rao Account–Expenses	4,000	By Consignment Stock Account	45,720
To Rao Account–Commission	4,400		
To Rao Account–Share of Profit	2,864		
To Stock Reserve Account	9,000		
To Profit and Loss Account	11,456		
	1,58,720		1,58,720

Dr. **Rao Account** Cr.

	Rs		Rs
To Consignment Account–Sale Proceeds	88,000	By Consignment Account–	
		Expenses	4,000
		Commission	4,400
		Profit	2,864
		By Bank Account–Draft received	76,736
	88,000		88,000

Valuation of Stock

		Rs
Invoice value of goods		1,25,000
Less: Invoice value of goods sold : $88,000 \times \frac{100}{110}$		80,000
		45,000
Add: Proportionate Expenses		
$2,000 \times \frac{45,000}{1,25,000}$		720
		45,720
Stock Reserve :		
Invoice Price	45,000	
Less: Cost Price: $45,000 \times \frac{100}{125}$	36,000	
	9,000	

Rao's Share of Profit :

Sales	88,000
Add: Stock (Cost Price)	36,720
	1,24,720
Less: Cost of goods sent : (1,00,000 + 2,000 + 4,000 + 4,400)	1,10,400
	14,320

20% thereof = 2,864

ILLUSTRATION 15.10 (Valuation of Stock and Abnormal Loss)

Bharat Cycles of Calcutta consigned to Hind Brothers 1,000 mini cycles at Rs 300 each. Bharat Cycles paid freight Rs 20,000 and insurance in transit Rs 3,000. During the transit 100 mini cycles were totally damaged by fire. Hind Brothers took delivery of the remaining cycles and paid Rs 1,530 for octroi.

Hind Brothers sent a bank draft for Rs 1,00,000 as advance payment and later sent an Account Sales showing that 800 cycles were sold at Rs 400 each. Expenses incurred in godown rent and advertisement etc. amounted to Rs 4,000. Hind Bros. is entitled to commission of 5%. Prepare the Consignment Account, Accidental Loss Account and Hind Brothers Account in the books of Bharat Cycles of Calcutta, assuming that the claim from Insurance was settled for Rs 28,000. *(ICWA Inter)*

SOLUTION

In the books of Bharat Cycles

Consignment Account

Dr.		Rs		Cr.
		Rs		Rs
To Goods sent on Consignment Account		3,00,000	By Hind Brothers Account– Sale Proceeds	3,20,000
To Bank Account			By Accidental Loss Account	32,300
Freight	20,000		By Consignment Stock Account	32,470
Insurance	3,000	23,000		
To Hind Brothers Account				
Octroi	1,530			
Rent and Advertisement	4,000	5,530		
To Hind Brothers Account– Commission		16,000		
To Profit and Loss Account– Profit transferred		40,240		
		3,84,770		3,84,770

Accidental Loss Account

Dr.	Rs		Cr. Rs
To Consignment Account	32,300	By Insurance Company Account	28,000
		By Profit and Loss Account	4,300
	32,300		32,300

Hind Brothers Account

Dr.	Rs			Cr. Rs
To Consignment Account	3,20,000	By Consignment Account		
		Octroi	1,530	
		Godown rent and Advertisement	4,000	5,530

		By Bank Account	1,00,000
		By Consignment Account	
		Commission	16,000
		By Bank Account–Balance due	1,98,470
	3,20,000		3,20,000

Abnormal Loss

	Rs	Rs
Cost of 100 Bicycles @ Rs 300		30,000
Add: Non-Recurring Expenses		
Freight	20,000	
Insurance	3,000	
	23,000	
$\frac{1}{10}$ th of Rs 23,000 *i.e.* $\frac{100}{1000} \times 23,000$		2,300
Abnormal Loss		32,300

Valuation of Stock:	Rs
100 Bicycles @ Rs 300 each	30,000
Add: Proportionate non-recurring expenses:	
By Consignor: $23,000 \times \frac{100}{1,000}$	2,300
By Consignee: $1,530 \times \frac{100}{900}$	170
	32,470

ILLUSTRATION 15.11 (Loss in transit and goods in transit)

Jyotimal of Calcutta consigned 50 cases of cotton piecegoods costing Rs 2,000 each to Ramu of Bombay. Jyotimal paid the following expenses in connection with the consignment:

	Rs
Carriage	2,500
Freight	19,000
Loading charges	3,500

Ramu sells 30 cases at Rs 3,500 each and incurs the following expenses:

	Rs
Landing charges	3,000
Warehousing and storage	5,000
Packing and selling expenses	4,000

It is found that 2 cases have been lost in transit and 3 cases are still in transit. Ramu is entitled to a commission of 10% on gross sales. Draw up the Consignment Account in the books of Jyotimal and Jyotimal Account in the books of Ramu. (*CAIIB*)

SOLUTION

In the books of Jyotimal

Consignment to Bombay Account

Dr.		Rs	Cr.		Rs
To Goods sent on Consignment Account		1,00,000	By Ramu Account– Sale Proceeds		1,05,000
To Bank Account			By Profit and Loss Account		
Carriage	2,500		Loss is transit		5,000
Freight	19,000		By Consignment Stock Account:		
Loading Charges	3,500	25,000	In Transit	7,500	
To Ramu Account:			With Consignee	38,500	46,000
Landing	3,000				
Warehousing	5,000				
Packing	4,000	12,000			
To Ramu Account–Commission		10,500			
To Profit and Loss Account– Profit transferred		8,500			
		1,56,000			1,56,000

In the books of Ramu

Jyotimal Account

Dr.		Rs	Cr.	Rs
To Bank Account–			By Bank Account– Sale Proceeds	1,05,000
Landing	3,000			
Warehousing	5,000			
Packing	4,000	12,000		
To Bank Account–Commission		10,500		
To Balance c/d		82,500		
		1,05,000		1,05,000
			By Balance b/d	82,500

Workings:

Loss in Transit:

	Rs
Cost of 2 cases @ Rs 2,000	4,000
Add: Proportionate Expenses:	
$(2,500 + 19,000 + 3,500) \times \frac{2}{50}$	
(or $25,000 \times \frac{2}{50}$)	1,000
	5,000

Goods in Transit:

		Rs
Cost of 3 cases @ Rs 2,000	=	6,000
Add: Proportionate Expenses		
$25,000 \times \frac{3}{50}$	=	1,500
		7,500

Stock with Consignee:

Total Cases	50	
Less: Lost & in Transit	5	
	45	
Sales made	30	
	15 cases	

Value of Stock

Cost of 15 cases @ 2,000 each		30,000
Add: Proportionate Expenses:		
Consignor: $25{,}000\times\frac{15}{50}$	=	7,500
Consignee: $3{,}000\times\frac{15}{45}$	=	1,000
		38,500

ILLUSTRATION 15.12

Smith of Mysore consigned 100 machines costing Rs 50,000 to their agent Ashok at 20% above the cost, to be sold on behalf of Consignor. Consignor incurred Rs 50 for packing and other charges on each machine.

Ashok received consignment by paying Rs 500 as railway charges and spent Rs 50 for carriage to godown. He rendered an Account Sales showing that:

20 Machines realised Rs 12,000 in cash.

50 Machines sold on credit at Rs 650 each.

10 Machines taken to his own stock at Rs 610 each.

Consignee remitted the balance after deducting his commission at 5% on invoice price of goods sold and 15% on any excess price realised. Show the Consignment Account.

SOLUTION

In the books of Smith

Consignment Account

Dr. Cr.

		Rs			Rs
To Goods sent on Consignment Account		60,000	By Ashok Account:		
To Bank Account–Expenses		5,000	Cash Sales	12,000	
To Ashok Account:			Credit Sales	32,500	
Railway Charges	500		Self	6,100	50,600
Carriage to godown	50	550	By Consignment Stock Account		13,110
To Ashok Account:			By Goods sent on Consignment Account		10,000
Commission 5%	2,400				
Special Commission	390	2,790			
To Stock Reserve Account		2,000			
To Profit and Loss Account–Profit transferred		3,370			
		73,710			73,710

Workings:

Valuation of Stock

	Rs
Invoice price of machines @ Rs 600	12,000
Add: Proportionate Expenses:	

	Rs
By Consignor @ Rs 50 on each machine	1,000
By Consignee: $550 \times \frac{20}{100}$	110
	13,110

Commission

	Rs
Sale price of 80 machines by Consignee: (Rs 12,000 + 32,500 + 6,100)	50,600
Invoice price 80 machines @ Rs 600	48,000
Excess money realised	2,600
5% on Rs 48,000	2,400
15% on Rs 2,600	390
	2,790

(Normal and Abnormal Loss occur simultaneously)

ILLUSTRATION 15.13 (Valuation of stock and Abnormal loss)

Oswal Mills consigned 5,000 kg oil to Vijay Dealers. Each kilogram of oil costs Rs 8. Oswal Mills paid Rs 50 as carriage, Rs 250 as freight and Rs 200 as insurance in transit. During transit 500 kg of oil were accidentally destroyed for which the Insurance Company paid directly to the consignor Rs 2,500 in full settlement of the claim.

After three months from the date of the consignment of the goods, Vijay Dealers reported that 3,500 kg of oil was sold @ Rs 9.50 per kg and expenses being:

Godown rent Rs 500
Salesmen salary Rs 750

Vijay Dealers are entitled to a 5% commission on sales. Vijay Dealers also reported a loss of 20 kg of oil due to leakage. Prepare the necessary accounts in the books of both the parties. (*B.Com., Madurai*)

SOLUTION

In the books of Oswal Mills

Dr. **Consignment Account** Cr.

		Rs		Rs
To Goods sent on Consignment Account		40,000	By Vijay Dealers Account– Sales	33,250
To Bank Account:			By Bank Account–Insurance Claim	2,500
Carriage	50		By Profit and Loss Account– Abnormal Loss	1,550
Freight	250		By Consignment Stock Account	7,973
Insurance	200	500		
To Vijay Dealers Account:				
Godown Rent	500			
Salesmen Salary	750	1,250		
To Vijay Dealers–Commission		1,663		
To Profit and Loss Account– Profit transferred		1,860		
		45,273		45,273

Dr. Vijay Dealers Account Cr.

	Rs		Rs
To Consignment Account	33,250	By Consignment Account–Expenses	1,250
		By Consignment Account–Commission	1,663
		By Balance c/d	30,337
	33,250		33,250
To Balance b/d	30,337		

Dr. Goods sent on Consignment Account Cr.

	Rs		Rs
To Trading Account	40,000	By Consignment Account	40,000

Dr. Consignment Stock Account Cr.

	Rs		Rs
To Consignment Account	7,973	By Balance c/d	7,973
To Balance b/d	7,973		

In the books of Vijay Dealers

Dr. Oswal Mills Account Cr.

	Rs		Rs
To Bank Account–Expenses	1,250	By Cash Account–Sales	33,250
To Commission Account	1,663		
To Balance c/d	30,337		
	33,250		33,250
		To Balance b/d	30,337

Dr. Commission Account Cr.

	Rs		Rs
To Profit and Loss Account: Profit transferred	1,663	By Oswal Mills Account	1,663
	1,663		1,663

Workings:

Value of Oil Destroyed:

		Rs
500 kg @ Rs 8 per kg		4,000
Add: Expenses:		
Carriage	50	
Freight	250	
Insurance	200	
For 5,000 kg	500	
For 500 kg = $500 \times \frac{500}{5,000}$		50
		4,050

Less: Paid by Insurance Co.		2,500
		1,550

Closing stock in units:

Total Units	5,000
Less: Abnormal loss	500
	4,500
Less: Normal loss	20
	4,480
Less: Sales	3,500
	980

Value of closing stock:

	Rs
Total cost for 5,000 kg including non-recurring expenses (5,000 × 8 = 40,000 + 50 + 250 + 200)	40,500
Less: Accidental loss claimed (500 units)	4,050
Total cost of 4,500 units less normal loss	36,450

$$\text{Value} = \text{Rs } 36,450 \times \frac{980}{(4,500 - 20)} = 36,450 \times \frac{980}{4,480} = \text{Rs } 7,973$$

ILLUSTRATION 15.14 (*Abnormal Loss*)

Ramesh consigned 2,000 mt. of chemicals at a cost of Rs. 800 per mt. to Jain. Ramesh paid freight and insurance charges of Rs. 20,000. Of the above, 500 mt. of chemicals were destroyed by fire during transit. John cleared the balance of 1,500 mt. of chemicals and sold 1,000 mt. at an average price of Rs. 1,000 per mt. John incurred the following expenses : Godown rent Rs. 5,000; Insurance Rs. 3,000: clearing charges Rs. 4,500. Insurance claim received against fire Rs. 4,00,000 after admitting the salvage value of stock destroyed by fire at Rs. 10,000. John was entitled to a commission of 10% on sale proceeds. John sends the balance to Ramesh after adjusting his commission and expenses out of the sale proceeds. Prepare a consignment A/c and John's A/c in the books of Ramesh. [*C.A.*]

SOLUTION

Books of Ramesh (Consignor)

Consignment A/c

Particulars	*Rs.*	*Particulars*	*Rs.*
To Goods sent on consignment A/c (2,000 × 800)	16,00,000	By Abnormal loss A/c (1)	3,95,000
To Bank A/c (Expenses)	20,000	By John A/c (Sales)	10,00,000
To John A/c (Expenses)	12,500	By Stock on consignment (2)	4,16,500
To John A/c (Commission)	1,00,000		
To Profit & Loss A/c (Profit)	79,000		
	18,11,500		18,11,500

John A/c

Particulars	*Rs.*	*Particulars*	*Rs.*
To Consignment A/c (1,000 × 1,000)	10,00,000	By Consignment A/c (Expenses)	12,500
		By Consignment A/c (Commissino) (10,00,000 × 10%)	1,00,000
		By Bank A/c (Bal. fig.)	8,87,500
	10,00,000		10,00,000

Working Notes:

1. ***Computation of value of abnormal loss (500 mt)***

		Rs.
	Cost of 500 mt. of chemicals (500 × Rs. 800):	4,00,000
Add :	$\frac{500}{2,000} = \frac{1}{4}$ th of non-recurring expenses of consignor only.	
	Since the loss is before taking delivery by the consignee:	
	Freight & Insurance $20,000 \times \frac{1}{4}$	5,000
	Value of abnormal loss	4,05,000
Less :	Value of salvaged goods.	10,000
	Actual value of abnormal loss	3,95,000

2. *Computation of value of unsold stock:*

	No. of mt. of chemicals consigned	2,000 mt	
Less :	Destroyed by fire	500 mt	
	Received by the Consignee	1,500 mt	
Less:	Sale	1,000 mt	
	Unsold stock	500 mt	
	Cost of 500 mt. of chemicals (500 × Rs. 800)		4,00,000
Add :	$\frac{500}{2,000}$ or $\frac{1}{4}$ th of non-recurring expenses of consignor $20,000 \times \frac{1}{4}$		5,000
Add :	$\frac{500}{1,500}$ or $\frac{1}{3}$ rd of non-recurring expenses of consignee (*i.e.*, clearing charges)		
	$4,500 \times \frac{1}{3}$		1,500
	Value of unsold stock		4,06,500
Add :	Salvage value of damaged stock		10,000
	Total closing stock		4,16,500

ILLUSTRATION 15.15 (*Abnormal loss of goods*)

Messrs. Goswami Bros. were appointed agents by Sunrise Ltd. in 2000. You are given the following particulars relating to the year 2006:

	Rs.	Rs.
(i) Cost of goods despatched by the company on Consignment		7,50,000
(ii) Goods fully destroyed in transit (Original cost)		50,000
(iii) Expenses incurred by the company towards:		
Freight		2,500
Insurance		1,500
(iv) Expenses incurred by Goswami Bros:		
Landing & Clearing	1,500	
Godown rent	1,000	
Transport charges	1,000	
Advertisements	800	
Insurance	800	
(v) Advance remitted by the agent		1,50,000
(vi) Bills payable accepted	25,000	
(vii) Goods destroyed by fire (at original cost) in Agent's godown		35,000
(viii) Bad debts		3,000
(ix) Unsold stock with Agent at the close of the year (at original cost)		50,000
(x) Insurance claim recovered by the consignor towards loss in transit		48,000
(xi) Insurance claim recovered by the Agent towards loss by fire		35,000.

All sales were effected by the Agent at 25% profit on original cost. The agent is entitled to a commission of 10% on gross sales.

You are required to show the consignor's A/c (Sunrise Ltd.) as it would appear in the books of Goswami Bros. **[I.C.W.A]**

SOLUTION

Books of Goswami Bros. (Consignee)

Sunrise Ltd. A/c (Consignor)

Particulars	*Rs.*	*Particulars*	*Rs.*
To Bank A/c (Expenses)	5,100	By Bank A/c (Sales less bad debts i.e., 7,68,750 – 3,000)	7,65,750
To Commission A/c [7,68,750 × 10%]	76,875	By Bank A/c (Insurance claim recovered by the agent for loss by fire)	35,000
To Bank A/c (advance)	1,50,000		
To Bills payable A/c	25,000		
To Balance c/d (Due)	5,43,775		
	8,00,750		8,00,750

Working Notes

Calculation of Sales Made

	Rs.	Rs.
Cost of goods despatched		7,50,000
Less: Goods destroyed in transit	50,000	
Goods destroyed by fire	35,000	
Unsold stock	50,000	1,35,000
Cost of goods sold		6,15,000
Add: Profit added at 25% on cost		1,53,750
Total Sales		7,68,750

ILLUSTRATION 15.16 ***(Loss in transit and goods in transit)***

David of Coonoor consigns 2,000 cases of goods costing Rs. 100 each to Sundar of Chennai. Devid pays the following expenses:

	Rs.
Freight	6,000
Carriage	2,000
Landing charges	2,000

Sundar sells 1,400 cases at Rs. 140 per case and incurs the following expenes:

	Rs.
Clearing charges	1,700
Warehousing & Storage	3,400
Packing & Selling expenses	1,200

It is found that 100 cases have been lost in transit and 200 cases are still in transit. Sundar is entitled to a Commission of 10% on gross sales. Prepare: (*i*) Consignment A/c and (*ii*) Sundar A/c in the books of David.

(*B.Com. MS*)

SOLUTION.

Books of David (Consignor)

Consignment A/c

Particulars	*Rs.*	*Particulars*	*Rs.*
To Goods sent on Consignment A/c (2,000 × 100)	2,00,000	By Sundar A/c (Sales) (1,400 × Rs. 140)	1,96,000
To Bank A/c (Expenses)	10,000	By Abnormal loss A/c (Loss in transit)	10,500
To Sundar A/c (Expenses)	6,300		
To Sundar A/c (Commission) (1,96,000 × 10%)	19,600	By Goods-in-transit A/c	21,000
To Profit & Loss A/c (Profit) (Bal. fig.)	23,400	By Stock on Consignment A/c	31,800
	2,59,300		2,59,300

Sundar A/c

Particulars	*Rs.*	*Particulars*	*Rs.*
To Consignment A/c (Sales)	1,96,000	By Consignment A/c (Expenses)	6,300
		By Consignment A/c (Commission)	19,600
		By Balance c/d	1,70,100
	1,96,000		1,96,000
To Balance b/d	1,70,100		

Working Notes:

(1) ***Computation of value of abnormal loss (i.e., Loss in transit–100 cases)***

	Rs.
Cost of 100 cases @ Rs. 100 each	10,000
Add: $\frac{100}{2,000} : \frac{1}{20}$ th of non-recurring expenses :	

	Rs.
Consignor's expenses : $10,000 \times \frac{1}{20}$	500
Value of abnormal loss	10,500

(2) *Computation of value of Goods-in-transit (200 cases)*

	Rs.
Cost of 200 cases @ Rs. 100 each	20,000
Add : $\frac{200}{2,000} = \frac{1}{10}$ th of non-recurring expenses:	
Consignor's expenses $10,000 \times \frac{1}{10}$	1,000
Value of goods in transit	21,000

(3) *Computation of value of unsold stock on consignment*

	Cases
No. of cases sent	2,000
Less: Loss-in-transit	100
Less: Goods in transit	200
No. of cases available for sale	1,700
Less : No. of cases sold	1,400
Unsold stock	300
	Rs.
Cost of 300 cases (unsold) @ Rs. 100 each	30,000
Add: Proportionate non-recurring expenses :	
(*a*) Consignor's expenses : $\frac{10,000}{2,000} \times 300$	1,500
(*b*) Consignee's expenses : $\frac{1,700}{1,700} \times 300$	300
	31,800

ILLUSTRATION 15.17

Goods at an invoice value of Rs. 1,32,000 were consigned by Choudhury & Co. of Calcutta to their agent Gupta & Co. of Allahabad at a proforma invoice of 20% profit on cost.

Freight paid by the consigner amounted to Rs. 5,000. Gupta & Co. was allowed 5% ordinary commission and 3% del credere commission on gross sales. They were also allowed 5% of the net profits as extra commission after charging such commission. Allahabad expenses were: landing and clearing charges Rs. 1,020, godown insurance premium Rs. 2,500.

3/4th of the goods were sold at 25% profit on sales, 1/10th of the balance of goods were destroyed by fire and actual claim was settled by the insurance company.

Prepare Consignment Account, Gupta & Co. Account, Stock Destroyed Account and Consignment Stock Account in the books of Choudhury & Co. ***[C.U.B.Com. (Hons)]***

SOLUTION

In the books of Choudhury & Co.

Dr. **Consignment to Allahabad Account** Cr.

Date	*Particulars*	*Rs*	*Date*	*Particulars*	*Rs*
	To Goods Sent on Consignment A/c	1,32,000		By Goods Sent on Consignment A/c (loading)	22,000 (1)
	To Bank A/c (freight)	5,000		By Gupta & Co. A/c (sales)	1,10,000 (2)
	To Gupta & Co. A/c:			By Stock Destroyed A/c	
	Landing charges	1,020		(invoice price)	3,450.50 (3)

Date	Particulars	Rs	Date	Particulars	Rs
	Godown insurance premium	2,500		By Consignment Stock A/c	31,054.50 (3)
	Commission (8% on Rs. 1,10,000)	8,800			
	To Stock Destroyed A/c (loading)	550 (4)			
	To Gupta & Co. A/c (extra Commission)	556 (5)			
	To Stock Reserve A/c	4,950 (4)			
	To Profit & Loss on Consignment A/c	11,129			
		1,66,505			1,66,505

Dr. **Gupta & Co. Account** Cr.

Date	Particulars	Rs	Date	Particulars	Rs
	To Consignment Stock A/c	1,10,000		By Consignment to Allahabad A/c	12,320
				By Consignment to Allahabad A/c	556
				By Balance c/d	97,124
		1,10,000			1,10,000

Dr. **Stock Destroyed Account** Cr.

Date	Particulars	Rs	Date	Particulars	Rs
	To Consignment to Allahabad A/c (I.P.)	3,450.50		By Consignment to Allahabad A/c (loading)	550
	To Profit & Loss A/c	Nil		By Insurance Company A/c	2,900.50
		3450.50			3450.50

Dr. **Consignment Stock Account** Cr.

Date	Particulars	Rs	Date	Particulars	Rs
	To Consignment to Allahabad A/c	31,054.50		By Balance c/d	31,054.50

Working Notes :

1. ***Loading on Goods Sent*** Rs.

   Invoice price of goods sent 1,32,000

   Loading is 1/5th on cost or 1/6th of invoice price i.e., **Rs. 22,000**

2. ***Calculation of Sales***

   Cost price of goods sent (Rs. 1,32,000 – 22,000) 1,10,000

   Sales = Rs. 1,10,000 × 3/4 × 4/3 = **Rs. 1,10,000**

3. ***Valuation of Goods Destroyed and Closing Stock***

	Rs.
Invoice price of goods sent	1,32,000
Add : Consignor's expenses	5,000
Consignee's expenses (Non-recurring)	1,020
	1,38,020

   3/4th of the goods are sold. Therefore, balance remains 1/4th

   Goods destroyed 1/4 × 1/10 = 1/40

   Invoice price of goods destroyed = 1/40 × Rs. 1,38,020 = **Rs. 3,450.50**

   Closing stock 1/4 × 9/10 = 9/40

   Invoice price of unsold stock = 9/4 × Rs. 1,38,020 = **Rs. 31,054.50**

4. ***Calculation of Loading on Stock Destroyed and Unsold Stock***

Total loading	32,000
Loading on stock destroyed = 1/40 × Rs. 22,000	550
Loading on unsold stock = 9/40 × Rs. 22,000	4,950

5. ***Extra Commission***

Profit before special commission = Rs. 11,685. Therefore

extra commission = 5/105 × Rs. 11,685 556

ILLUSTRATION 15.18

Rahim of Bombay consigned to Raju of Madras goods to be sold at invoice price which represents 125% of cost. Raju is entitled to a commission of 10% on sales at invoice price and 25% of any excess realised over invoice price. The expenses on freight and insurance incurred by Rahim were Rs. 10,000. The account sales received by Rahim shows that Raju effected sales aggregating to Rs. 1,00,000 in respect of 75% of the consignment. His selling expenses to be reimbursed were Rs. 8,000. 10% of the consignment goods of the value of Rs. 12,500 were destroyed by fire at the Madras godown and the insurance company paid Rs. 12,000 net of salvage. Raju remitted the balance in favour of Rahim. Prepare the Consignment Account and the account of Raju in the books of Rahim along with necessary working. [C.A]

SOLUTION

In the books of Rahim

Consignment to Madras Account

Dr. Cr.

Date	Particulars	Rs	Date	Particulars	Rs
	To Goods Sent on Consignment A/c (1)	1,25,000		By Goods Sent on Consignment A/c (Loading)	25,000
	To Bank A/c (freight & insurance)	10,000		By Raju A/c (Sales)	1,00,000
	To Raju A/c (Expenses – selling)	8,000		By Abnormal Loss A/c (2)	13,500
	To Raju A/c – Commission (4)	10,938		By Stock on Consignment A/c (3)	20,250
	To Stock Reserve A/c (5)	3,750		By Profit and Loss on Consignment A/c	1,438
	To Abnormal Loss A/c (6)	2,500			
		1,60,188			1,60,188

Raju Account

Dr. Cr.

Date	Particulars	Rs	Date	Particulars	Rs
	To Consignment to Madras A/c – Sales	1,00,000		By Consignment to Madras A/c (Selling Exp.)	8,000
				By Consignment to Madras A/c (Commission)	10,938
				By Bank A/c (Final payment)	81,062
		1,00,000			1,00,000

Abnormal Loss Account

Dr. Cr.

Date	Particulars	Rs	Date	Particulars	Rs
	To Consignment to Madras A/c	13,500		By Bank A/c – claim received	12,000
	To Profit and Loss A/c	1,000		By Consignment to Madras A/c (Loading)	2,500
		14,500			14,500

Workings :

(1) 10% = Rs. 12,500

$$\therefore \quad 100\% = \text{Rs. } \frac{12,500 \times 100}{10} = \textbf{Rs. 1,25,000}$$

(2) ***Valuation of Abnormal Loss***

	Rs.
Value of stock lost by fire	12, 500
Add : Proportionate expenses up to fire (10% of Rs. 10,000)	1,000
Value of abnormal loss at invoice price	13,500

(3) ***Valuation of Stock on Consignment***

	Rs.
Invoice value of unsold stock (15% of Rs. 1,25,000)	18,750
Add : Proportionate non-recurring expenses (15% of Rs. 10,000)	1,500
	20,250

(4) ***Calculation of Commission***

	Rs.
Sale proceeds (75% of Consignment)	1,00,000
Less: Invoice value of sale proceeds (75% of Rs. 1,25,000)	93,750
Excess sale proceeds received over invoice price	6,250
Therefore, commission is:	
(1) @ 10% on sales in invoice price	9,375
(2) @ 25% on excess sale proceeds : (Rs 6,250 × 25%)	1,563
	10,938

(5) ***Calculation of Stock Reserve***

	Rs.
Total loading on goods sent	25,000
Therefore, loading on closing stock is 15% of Rs. 25,000	3,750

(6) ***Loading on Abnormal Loss***

	Rs.
Total loading on goods sent	25,000
Therefore, loading on goods lost by fire (10%)	2,500

ILLUSTRATION 15.19

The Account Sales of 1,200 transistor sets received from and sold on account of and the risk of Sri. Chopra, Calcutta.

Particulars		*Rs.*	*Rs.*
1,200 Transistor sets @ Rs. 1,200			14,40,000
Less : Expenses :	Rs.		
Unloading Expenses	3,000		
Selling Expenses	4,000		
Transport Charges	6,100		
Godown Rent	6,000		
Advertisements	2,000	21,100	
Less : Commission:			
5% Ordinary Commission	72,000		
1% Del Credere Commission	14,400	86,400	1,07,500
			13,32,500
Less : Advance sent on 10.1.2006			2,50,000
			10,82,500
Bank draft enclosed; Stock in hand (31.3.2006) — 100 sets			E.& O.E
Dated, Madras, the 26th April 2006.			S.Raman

On further information you come to know that:

(*i*) Bad Debts amounted to Rs. 2,400 against 2 sets;

(*ii*) 20% above the invoice price is the sale price which is equal to cost plus 50%;

(*iii*) Chopra incurred forwarding expenses @ Rs. 10 per set;

(*iv*) During transit 10 sets became fully damaged and Chopra recovered from insurance the full amount of the original cost.

You are required to prepare the Goods Sent on Consignment Account, Consignment Account and Loss in Transit Account in the books of Chopra. ***[I.C.W.A. (Inter)]***

SOLUTION (*See next page*)

Goods Sent on Consignment Account

Dr. Cr.

Date	*Particulars*	*Rs*	*Date*	*Particulars*	*Rs*
	To Consignment to Madras A/c	2,62,000		By Consignment to Madras A/c	13,10,000
	To Purchases A/c-transfer	10,48,000			
		13,10,000			13,10,000

Loss in Transit Account

Dr. Cr.

Date	*Particulars*	*Rs*	*Date*	*Particulars*	*Rs*
	To Consignment to Madras A/c	10,100		By Consignment to Madraws A/c (Loading)	2,000
				By Bank A/c - Insurance claim (Note 2)	8,000
				By Profit and Loss A/c	100
		10,100			10,100

Workings :

Selling price = Rs. 1,200 (100% + 50%)

Selling price = Rs. 1,200 (150%)

$$\text{Cost price} = \frac{1,200 \times 100}{150} = \textbf{Rs. 800}$$

Invoice Price = **Rs. 1,000**

Loading per set = Rs. 1,000 – Rs. 800	=	**Rs. 200**
Forwarding expenses per set is Rs. 10.		
Total sets = (1,200 + 100 + 10)	=	**1,310 sets**
Total forwarding expenses = 1,310 × Rs. 10	=	**Rs. 13,100**
Invoice price of Goods sent = 1,310 × Rs. 1,000	=	**Rs. 13,10,000**
Loss in transit (IP) = Rs. 1,000 × 10	=	Rs. 10,000
Add: Forwarding Expenses	=	100
		Rs. 10,100

ILLUSTRATION 15.20

Calcutta Ayurvedic Ltd. produces a bottle of "Draksharista" at a cost of Rs. 10. They appointed Madras Medical Stores of Madras as their agent on the terms that the agent would get commission @ 10% on invoice price of goods sold and also an extra commission at 25% on any excess amount realised over invoice price.

On 1.7.2006, Calcutta Ayurvedic Ltd. sent 50 boxes of "Draksharista", each box containing 50 bottles, at invoice price showing a profit of $33^1/_3$% on such invoice price. They spent Rs. 3,000 for freight and Rs. 2,000 for insurance. 5 boxes were completely destroyed in transit and insurance claim of Rs. 2,300 was realised from the insurance company. The agent took delivery of the remaining goods and spent Rs. 2,000 for duty and Rs.

(*Contd. on page 553*)

In the books of Mr. Chopra

Consignment to Madras Account

Dr. Cr.

Date	Particulars		Rs.	Date	Particulars		Rs.
	To Goods Sent on Consignment A/c (Note 1)		13,10,000		By Goods Sent on Consignment A/c-loading		2,62,000
	To Bank A/c – forwarding expenses		13,100		By Loss in Transit A/c		10,100
	To S.Raman A/c – expenses :	Rs.			By S.Raman A/c		14,40,000
	Unloading expenses	3,000			By Stock on Consignment A/c	Rs.	1,01,230
	Selling expenses	4,000			100 × Rs. 1,000	1,00,000	
	Transport charges	6,100			100 × Rs. 10	1,000	
	Godown rent	6,000			3,000/1,300	230	
	Advertisements	2,000	21,100			1,01,230	
	To S. Raman A/c-Commission:	Rs.					
	5% Ordinary	72,000					
	1% Del Credere	14,400	86,400				
	To Loss in Transit A/c-Loading (Rs. 200 × 10)		2,000				
	To Stock Reserve A/c (Rs. 200 × 100)		20,000				
	To Profit & Loss on Consignment a/c		3,60,730				
			18,13,330				18,13,330

1,000 for freight to carry the goods to the rented godown. He also sent a Bill of Exchange for Rs. 20,000 payable after 2 months to the consignor as advance.

At the end of the year, the agent reported that 40 boxes were sold at Rs. 18 per bottle and 1 box of goods was lost due to bad packaging. This would be treated as normal loss. The agent remitted a bank draft for the net amount after deducting his commission, advance money, godown rent Rs. 800 and selling expense Rs. 200.

On 1.1.2007, Calcutta Ayurvedic Ltd. discounted the bill of Rs. 20,000 for Rs. 19,800. On 1.3.2007, bank informed that the bill was dishonoured. Calcutta Ayurvedic Ltd. demanded the entire amount along with an additional amount of Rs. 200 as interest. The Madras agent sent a bank draft for the amount on 15.3.2007.

You are asked to show the following Ledger Accounts in the books of the consignor:

(*e*) Consignment to Madras Account;

(*a*) Madras Medical Stores Account;

(*b*) Consignment Stock Account;

(*c*) Consignment Stock Destroyed Account;

(*d*) Consignment Stock Reserve Account. ***[B.Com. (Hons.) Kolkata, M.S. Bhopal]***

SOLUTION

Madras Medical Stores Account

Dr. Date	Particulars	Rs	Date	Particulars	Cr. Rs
2006			2006		
Dec. 31	To Consignment to Madras A/c	36,000	Dec. 31	By Advance against Consignment A/c	20,000
				By Consignment to Madras A/c (exp. + comm.)	8,500
				By Bank A/c (remittance)	7,500
		36,000			36,000
2007			2007		
Mar. 1	To Bank A/c (bill dishonoured)	20,000	Mar 15	By Bank A/c (final remittance)	20,200
	To Interest Received A/c	200			
		20,200			20,200

Consignment Stock Account

Dr. Date	Particulars	Rs	Date	Particulars	Cr. Rs
2006			2006		
Dec. 31	To Consignment to Madras A/c	3,750	Dec. 31	By Balance c/d	3,750

Consignment Stock Destroyed Account

Dr. Date	Particulars	Rs	Date	Particulars	Cr. Rs
2006	To Consignment to Madras A/c (Invoice price)	4,250	2006	By Consignment to Madras A/c (loading)	1,250
				By Bank A/c (insurance claim)	2,300
				By Profit & Loss A/c (abnormal loss)	700
		4,250			4,250

Consignment Stock Reserve Account

Dr. Date	Particulars	Rs	Date	Particulars	Cr. Rs
2006			2006		
Dec. 31	To Balance c/d	1,023	Dec. 31	By Consignment to Madras A/c	1,023

(Contd. on page 555)

In the books of Calcutta Ayurvedic Limited
Consignment to Madras Account

Dr. Cr.

Date	Particulars		Rs.	Date	Particulars	Rs.
2006				2006		
July1	To Goods Sent on Consignment A/c		37,500	July 1	By Goods Sent on Consignment A/c (Loading)	12,500
	To Cash A/c:				By Consignment Stock Destroyed A/c (Note 2)	4,250
	Freight	3,000		Dec. 31	By Madras Medical Stores A/c (Sales)	36,000
	Insurance	2000	5.000		By Consignment Stock A/c (Note 4)	3,750
Dec. 31	To Madras Medical Stores A/c :					
	Duty	2,000				
	Freight	1,000				
	Godown rent	800				
	Selling	200				
	Commission (Note 1)	4,500	8.500			
	To Consignment Stock Destroyed A/c (Note 3)		1.250			
	To Consignment Stock Reserve A/c (Note 5)		1.023			
	To Profit & Loss on Consignment A/c		3.227			
			56.500			56,500

Dr. **Advance Againt Consignment Account** Cr.

Date	Particulars	Rs	Date	Particulars	Rs
2006			2006		
Dec. 31	To Madras Medical Stores A/c	20,000	July 1	By Bills Receivable A/c	20,000

Working Notes :

1. ***Calculation of Commission*** — *Rs.*

	Rs.
Sales at invoice price (40 × 50 × Rs. 15)	30,000
Ordinary commission (10% on Rs. 30,000)	3,000
Extra commission 25% of Rs. (36,000 – 30,000)	1,500
Total commission	4,500

2. ***Valuation of Abnormal Loss at Invoice Price*** — Rs.

	Rs.
Invoice price of the goods sent	37,500
Add : Expenses of the consignor	5,000
Invoice price of 50 boxes	42,500
Value of abnormal loss – 5 boxes (Rs. 42,500/50 × 5)	4,250

3. ***Loading on Abnormal Loss*** — Rs.

	Rs.
Total loading on goods sent ; Rs 12500	1250
Loading on abnormal loss 12,500/50 × 5	

4. ***Valuation of Closing Stock at Invoice Price*** — Rs.

	Rs.
Value of the goods sent at invoice price (Note 2)	42,500
Less: Value of abnormal loss at invoice price	4,250
Invoice price of 45 boxes	38,250
Add : Expenses of the consignee (non-recurring)	3,000
Total value of the goods at invoice price (44 boxes)	41,250
Value of closing stock 41,250/44 × 4	3,750

5. ***Loading on Closing Stock*** — Rs.

	Rs.
Total loading	12,500
Less : Loading on abnormal loss	1,250
	11,250
Loading on closing stock 11,250/44 × 4	1,023

QUESTIONS

Objective Type Questions

I. State whether each of the following statements is "True" or "False":

1. The consignee passes no entry in his books for unsold stock of the consignor lying with him.
2. Sales account and Account sales are synonymous terms.
3. Del Credere commission is allowed to the consignee to cover abnormal loss.
4. No entry is to be passed by the consignee when he receives the goods from the consignor.
5. Overriding commission is calculated on credit sales only.
6. The value of abnormal loss is credited to the consignment account.
7. A loss caused by theft or fire is called abnormal loss.
8. The consignee can be treated as consignor's debtor for the goods received on consignment.
9. Goods sent on consignment is a sale.
10. Losses which cannot be avoided are normal losses.

11. A proforma invoice is similar to an ordinary invoice.
12. Normal loss of goods on consignment is debited to consignment account.
13. Nomalloss is loss of goods while in the consignee's custody.
14. Abnormal loss of goods should be debited to consignment account.
15. Consignment stock is credited to consignment account.
16. The relationship between consignor and consignee is that of a principal and agent.
17. The excess of invoice price over cost represents unrealised profit.
18. Consignment profit or loss is shared by both consignor and consignee.
19. The consignee always gets del credere commission.
20. Consignment stock account appears in the consignor's Balance Sheet as an asset.

(**Ans :** *True* – 1, 4, 6, 7, 10, 11, 16, 17, 20. *False* – 2, 3, 5, 8, 9, 12, 13, 14, 15, 18, 19.)

II. Fill in the blanks:

1. The person to whom goods are sent on consignment basis is called ....
2. Despatch of goods from one person to another for the purpose of sale is known as ....
3. Extra commission paid to the consignee debtors is known as ....
4. Consignment account is a .... account.
5. Del Credere commission is calculated on ....
6. Statement containing information relating to sales, expenses etc. sent by the consignee is ....
7. Account sales is prepared by .... and is sent to ....
8. The relationship between consignor and consignee is that of .... and ....
9. Consignment stock is credited to .... account.
10. Losses which cannot be avoided are called .... losses.

(**Ans :** 1. Consignee; 2. consignment; 3. Del credere commission; 4. Nominal; 5. Total sales; 6. Account sales; 7. Consignee, consignor; 8. Principal, Agent; 9. Consignment; 10. Normal.

III. Choose the most appropriate answer:

1. Consignment account is of the nature of a :
   (*a*) Personal Account (*b*) Real Account.
   (*c*) Nominal Account.
2. Overriding commission is calculated on :
   (*a*) Total Sales. (*b*) Credit Sales.
   (*c*) Cash Sales.
3. Del credere commission is allowed to the consignee to bear :
   (*a*) Normal Loss. (*b*) Abnormal Loss.
   (*c*) Loss on account of bad debts.
4. Goods sent on consignment is a :
   (*a*) Personal Account. (*b*) Real Account.
   (*c*) Nominal Account.
5. The relationships between the consignor and consignee is one of:
   (*a*) Debtor and Creditor. (*b*) Seller and Buyer.
   (*c*) Principal and Agent.
6. The balance of consignment stock to be shown on:
   (*a*) the liability side of the Balance Sheet. (*b*) the asset side of the Balance Sheet.
   (*c*) the credit side of the Trading Account.
7. Consignee becomes a debtor of the consignor when :
   (*a*) the goods are despatched. (*b*) the goods are received.
   (*c*) the goods are sold.

8. No journal entry is required to be passed when there is:
   (*a*) Normal loss. (*b*) Abnormal loss in transit.
   (*c*) Abnormal loss in consignee's custody.
9. Account sales is a statement which shows the details about the :
   (*a*) Goods received. (*b*) Goods sold.
   (*c*) Goods lying unsold.
10. The abnormal loss on consignment is credited to:
   (*a*) Consignment Account. (*b*) Consignee Account.
   (*c*) Consignor Account.

(*Ans:* 1. (*c*); 2. (*a*); 3. (*c*); 4. (*b*); 5. (*c*); 6. (*b*); 7. (*c*); 8. (*a*); 9. (*b*); 10. (*a*)

THEORETICAL QUESTIONS

1. Define Consignment. Distinguish it from sale.
2. What is an Account Sale? How does it differ from an invoice?
3. What do you understand by the following:
   (a) Del Credere Commission
   (b) Proforma Invoice
4. Explain commission, Del Credere commission and over riding commission.
5. How will you treat the bad debt when consignee does not get Del Credere commission and when consignee gets Del Credere commission?
6. What are the adjusting entries you will pass to eliminate the excess price when the goods are invoiced at proforma invoice price on:
   (a) Opening stock of consigned goods,
   (b) Goods sent on consignment during a year,
   (c) Unsold stock of consigned goods.
7. What do you understand by Memorandum Column Method?
8. What is recurring and non-recurring expenses?

PRACTICAL PROBLEMS

1. Mr Ram of Nagercoil consigned on 10th April, 50 cases of fruit juice, costing Rs 50,000 to Fruit Stall, Trivandrum, for sale on commission of 10% on sale proceeds. Ram paid freight, packing etc. amounting to Rs 800.

   The goods arrived at Trivandrum on 11th April and the Fruit Stall paid clearing charges Rs 300; Sundry expenses Rs 200, carriage Rs 150 and godown charges Rs 10θ. On the same day, Fruit Stall paid an advance of Rs 10,000 to Ram of Nagercoil.

   The goods were sold by the Fruit Stall as under:

   10 cases @ Rs 1,300 per case
   17 cases @ Rs 1,290 per case
   8 cases @ Rs 1,150 per case
   Balance cases for Rs 20,500

   On 25th April, Fruit Stall spent an Account Sale to Ram along with a draft for the balance.

   Prepare the Account Sales, Journal entries and Ledger Accounts in the books of Ram and Fruit Stall.

   [Ans: Net amount as per Account Sales: Rs 47,417
   Profit Rs 6,617]

2. Mr Krishna of Bombay consigned goods of the value of Rs 15,000 to their agent, Mr Gopal, at Madras. Mr Krishna paid freight, insurance and other charges Rs 550 and drew a bill of exchange on Mr Gopal for Rs 13,000 at three months. The bill was discounted with the bankers at Rs 12,850. Mr Krishna received account sales of the consignment for Rs 17,290 less agent's commission Rs 710 and a bank draft for the balance.

Pass journal entries in the books of Mr Krishna and Gopal. (*B.Com., Andhra*)

[**Ans:** Profit Rs 1,590
Balance due Rs 4,290]

3. *A* consigned to *B* on 1st January 2004, 500 bales of cotton costing Rs 100 per bale. Freight charges incurred in the consignment were Rs 5,000. *A* drew a bill on *B* for Rs 50,000 payable on 30th June 2004 which *B* accepted. The bill was discounted by *A* with his bankers on 31st January, 2004 at 12% p.a.

   B rendered account to *A* on 31st March, 2004 showing sales of 300 bales for Rs 80,000 and selling expenses of Rs 5,000. *B*'s commission was 10 per cent. On this date *B* remitted to *A* the net amount due to him.

   On 31st May, 2004 *B* sold the balance stock for Rs 30,000 after incurring expenses of Rs 4,000. He remitted Rs 20,000 to *A*, the balance being treated as commission earned by him. On 30th June 2004 the bill accepted by *B* was dishonoured by him and the amount due to the bank was paid off by *A* along with incidental charges of Rs 200.

   Pass journal entries in the books of *A* (including bank transactions). (*C.A. Inter*)

   [**Ans:** Profit Rs 32,000
   Balance due Rs 50,200]

4. The Cochin Consignment Account in the books of Ranaji of Bombay showed a debit balance of Rs 1,500 representing the cost of 10 bicycles on 1st January. On March 1, Ranaji sent a further consignment to Cochin of 40 bicycles costing Rs 150 each. The freight and other charges amounted to Rs 210. On 1st June, the Cochin Agent sent an Account Sales showing that 8 bicycles from the old stock realised Rs 140 each and 25 bicycles from the second consignment realised Rs 200 each and 15 bicycles remained in stock unsold. Two bicycles from the old stock being unsaleable at Cochin were returned to Bombay, for which the Cochin Agent sent a separate debit note for Rs 30 being expenses incurred by him.

   The Cochin agent is entitled to a selling commission of 5 per cent which covers all out-of-pocket expenses in respect of the consignment. Show the necessary accounts in the books of the consignor, supposing that he closes his accounts on 30th June. (*B.Com., Punjab*)

   [**Ans:** Profit Rs 453
   Balance due Rs 5,784]

5. Mahesh Oil Company consigned 200 tins of vegetable oil (one tin contains 10 kgs of oil) to Manohar Dealer costing Rs 25 per kilogram. The consignors paid Rs 4,000 for forwarding charges and Rs 6,000 for freight. 5 tins of oil were totally damaged during transit and nothing could be realised from the Insurance Company.

   Manohar took delivery of the oil and sent an Account Sales showing that 150 tins were sold for Rs 60,000. The expenses incurred by them were customs duty and clearing charges Rs 3,580 and selling expenses Rs 1,000. They are entitled to a commission of 5% on sales.

   Manohar also reported that 10 kilograms of oil were lost due to leakage.

   Show the necessary ledger accounts in the books of Mahesh Oil Company.

   [**Ans:** Profit Rs 8,000; Amount payable by Manohar Rs 52,420;
   Abnormal loss Rs 1,500; Consignment Stock Rs 14,080]

6. Vikram Milk Foods Co. Ltd., of Vikrampur sent to Sunder Stores, Sonepuri, 5,000 kgs of baby food packed in 2,000 tins of net weight 1 kg and 6,000 packets of net weight 1/2 kg, for sale on consignment basis. The consignee commission was fixed at 5% of sale proceeds. The cost price and selling price of the product were as under:

	1 kg tin	*1/2 kg packet*
	Rs	*Rs*
Cost Price	10	6
Selling Price	15	7

   The consignment was booked on freight "To Pay" basis and freight charges came to 2% of selling value. One case containing 50 1-kg tins was lost in transit and the transport carrier admitted a claim of Rs 450.

At the end of the first half year, the following information is gathered from the "Account Sales" sent by the consignee:

(*i*) Sale proceeds

1,500 1 kg tins

4,000 1/2 kg packets

(*ii*) Store rent and insurance charges Rs 600.

Find out the value of closing stock on consignment.

Show the Consignment A/c and the Consignee's A/c in the books of Vikram Milk Food Co. Ltd., assuming that the consignees had paid the amount due from them. (*C.A. Entrance*)

[Ans: Profit Rs 7,365
Value of Unsold Stock Rs 16,915
Amount due Rs 45,935]

7. Cycles Ltd. Hyderabad sent 2,000 dynamos costing Rs 50 each for sale on consignment basis to Ramesh of Vijayawada, subject to the following terms:

   1. Normal selling price per dynamo is Rs 60.
   2. Consignees's commission to be calculated as under:

      (a) 5% commission on normal selling price;

      (b) 10% additional commission if selling price is more than the normal selling price; and

      (c) ½% Del Credere commission on total sales for guaranteeing collection of credit sales.

   Reported sales are as follows:

   Cash Sales:

   500 dynamos at Rs 60 each

   200 dynamos at Rs 75 each

   Credit Sales:

   400 dynamos at Rs 75 each

   400 dynamos at Rs 80 each

   Ascertain the commission due to consignee. (*C.A.*)

   [Ans: Commission Rs 6,735]

8. The Swastic Chemicals, Bombay, consigned 10,000 kg of chemicals to Das of Calcutta on 1st April 2004. The cost of the chemicals was Rs 2 per kg. The Swastic Chemicals paid Rs 5,000 as freight and insurance. During transit 250 kg were accidentally destroyed for which the insurer paid directly to the consignors Rs 450 in full settlement of the claim.

   Das took delivery of the consignment on the 10th April and immediately accepted a Bill drawn on him by the Swastic Chemicals for Rs 10,000 for 3 months. On 30th June Das reported that 7,500 kg were sold @ Rs 3, the expenses being: on godown rent Rs 200, on advertisement Rs 1,000 and on salesmen's salaries Rs 2,000. Das is entitled to a commission of 3% plus 1½% Del Credere.

   Das reported a loss of 100 kg due to leakage. Assuming that Das paid the amount due by Bank Draft, show the accounts in the books of Swastic Chemicals, which close the books on 30th June.

   (*B.Com., Bharathiar*)

   [Ans: Loss on Consignment Rs 656
   Stock Destroyed Rs 625
   Value of Stock: Rs 5,430.70]

Normal Loss and Abnormal Loss

9. X consigned 100 packets of cosmetics each costing Rs 300 to his agent at Bombay. He paid Rs 500 towards freight and insurance. 15 packets were destroyed on the way. Consignee took delivery of the

remaining packets and spent Rs 700 as godown rent, Rs 1,000 as clearing charges and Rs 300 as carriage outward. You are required to calculate the cost of damage and cost of stock at the end if the agent sells away 70 packets. *(C.A. Inter)*

[**Ans:** Cost of damage Rs 4,575
Cost of Stock Rs 4,751]

10. 1,000 Baby bicycles were consigned by Premier Bicycle Co., Delhi to Superior Brothers, Kanpur, a an invoice cost of Rs 150 each. Premier Bicycle Company paid freight Rs 10,000 and insurance in transit Rs 1,500. During the transit 100 bicycles were totally damaged by fire. Superior Brothers took delivery of the remaining bicycles. This loss was charged to profit and loss account.

    Superior Brothers sent a bank draft to Premier Company for Rs 50,000 as advance payment and later sent an account sales showing that 800 bicycles were sold at Rs 220 each. Expenses incurred by Superior Brothers on godown rent and advertisement etc. amounted to Rs 2,000. Superior Brothers is entitled to commission of 5%.

    Prepare Consignment Account, Superior Brothers Account and Profit and Loss Account in the books of Premier Bicycle Company, Delhi, assuming that nothing has been recovered from the insurers due to defect in the policy. *(B.Com., Punjab)*

    [**Ans:** Profit Rs 36,000
    Balance due Rs 1,15,200
    Value of Abnormal loss Rs 16,150
    Value of Unsold Stock Rs 16,150]

11. Miss Rakhi consigned 1,000 radio sets costing Rs 900 each to Miss Geeta, her agent on 1st July. Miss Rakhi incurred the following expenditure on sending the consignment:

	Rs
Carriage	650
Freight	7,000
Insurance	3,250

    Miss Geeta received the delivery of 950 radio sets. An Accounts Sale dated 30th November showed that 750 sets were sold for Rs 9,00,000 and Miss Geeta incurred Rs. 3,000 for carriage and Rs 7,500 for the customs duty at the time of taking the delivery. Miss Geeta was entitled to commission @ 6% on the sales effected by her. She incurred expenses amounting to Rs 2,500 for repairing the damaged radio sets remaining in the stock.

    Miss Rakhi lodged a claim with the insurance company which was admitted at Rs 35,000. Show the Consignment Account and Miss Geeta's Account in the books of Miss Rakhi. *(C.A. Entrance)*

    [**Ans:** Profit Rs 1,52,036
    Abnormal loss Rs 45,545
    Value of Unsold Stock Rs 1,84,391
    Balance Due Rs 8,33,000]

12. Mohan consigned 400 packets of lip-sticks, each packet containing 10 lip-sticks. Cost price of each packet was Rs 300. Mohan spent Rs 50 per packet as cartage, freight, insurance and forwarding commission. One packet was lost on the way and Mohan lodged claim with the insurance company and could get only Rs 270 as claim on average basis. Consignee took delivery of the rest of the packets and spent Rs 19,950 as other non-recurring expenses and Rs 11,250 as recurring expenses. He sold 370 packets at the rate of Rs 6.50 per lip-stick. He was entitled to 2% commission on sales plus 1% del credere commission.

    You are required to calculate the cost of stock at the end, cost of abnormal loss and profit or loss on consignment.

    [**Ans:** Profit Rs 74,035
    Value of Unsold Stock Rs 11,600
    Abnormal Loss Rs 350
    Actual Abnormal Loss Rs 80 (Rs 350 – 270)

13. On 1st April 2003, Mr Doshi of Darjeeling consigned 2,000 kg of tea costing Rs 60 per kg to Mr Naik of Nagpur. Mr Doshi incurred the following expenses:

	Rs
Freight	2,000
Insurance	400
Sundry Expenses	600

During the year ended 31st March 2004, Naik incurred the following expenses:

	Rs
Freight	600
Godown Rent	500
Carriage to Godown	1,000

On 1st Dec. 2003, Mr Naik sold 1,200 kg of tea for cash at a profit of 25% on sales. On 15th Dec. Naik returned 150 kg of tea which were of poor quality to Doshi and paid return freight and carriage of Rs 250. Out of the remaining tea 200 kg being partially damaged were valued at 30% less than cost. Naik charged his commission @ 5% and settled the accounts on 31st March 2004. Doshi closes his books every year on 31st March.

You are required to prepare the (*i*) Consignment to Nagpur Account, (*ii*) Goods sent on Consignment Account and (*ii*) Naik Account. (*ICWA*)

[**Ans:** Profit: Rs 15,150
Abnormal Loss: Rs 4,420
Value of Stock: Rs 35,880]

14. Lubrizols Ltd., of Bombay, consigned 1,000 barrels of lubricant oil costing Rs 800 per barrel to Central Oil Company, Calcutta, on 1st January 2004. Lubrizols Ltd. paid Rs 50,000 as freight and insurance. 25 barrels were destroyed on 7.1.2004 in transit. The insurance claim was settled at Rs 15,000 and was paid directly to consignors.

Central Oil Co. took delivery of the consignment on 19th January 2004, and accepted a bill drawn upon them by Lubrizols Ltd. for Rs 5,00,000 for 3 months on 31st March, 2004. Central Oil Co. reported as follows:

(*i*) 750 barrels were sold at Rs 1,200 per barrel

(*ii*) The other expenses were:

Unloading	Rs 2,500
Godown rent	Rs 10,000
Wages	Rs 50,000
Printing etc.	Rs 21,300

(*iii*) 25 barrels of oil were lost due to leakage which is considered to be a normal loss.

Central Oil Co. is entitled to a commission of 5% on all the sales effected by them. Central Oil Co. paid the amount due in respect of the consignment of 31st March itself. Show the consignment account, the account of Central Oil Co., and the loss in transit account as they will appear in the books of Lubrizols Ltd. (*I.C.W.A.*)

[**Ans:** Profit Rs 1,17,450
Abnormal Loss Rs 21,250
Value of Unsold Stock Rs 1,75,000]

When Goods are Consigned at Invoice Price

15. Nanak of Calcutta consigned 100 Prestige Toys to Rajat of Jalpaiguri, costing Rs 90 per toy, but invoiced at a price so as to show 20% profit on such invoice price. Nanak spent Rs 800 as freight and insurance. Rajat was entitled to a commission of 10% on gross sales.

Rajat sold 75 toys @ Rs 150 each and spent Rs 150 as dock dues and Rs 200 as miscellaneous expenses.

Show Consignment A/c and Consignee's A/c in the books of Consignor. *(B.Com., Bombay)*

[**Ans:** Profit Rs 2,462.50
Balance due Rs 9,775.00]

16. On 1st September, 2004, goods which cost *X* Rs 33,000 were consigned by him to his agent *Y* at a proforma price which was 20% over cost. *X* paid insurance and freight charges amounting to Rs 1,250. *Y* was allowed Rs 3,000 per annum towards establishment cost, 5% commission on gross sales and 3% del credere commission. He was also allowed 5% extra commission on the profit on such consignment sales after charging such commission. *Y* incurred an expense of Rs 255 as landing charges.

    Three-fourths of goods were sold at 33 1/3% profit on cost half of which were on credit; half of the balance of goods was damaged and a claim on insurance company was made for Rs 4,400 which was settled at a discount of 20%.

    You are required to prepare a consignment account and an abnormal loss account in the books of *X* for the year ended 31st December, 2004. *(C.A. Inter)*

    [**Ans:** Profit Rs 3,787
    Abnormal loss Rs 4,313
    Value of Unsold Stock Rs 5,138
    Commission (8%) Rs 2,145
    Extra commission Rs 189]

17. Thomas of Singapore is the agent for Mini Motors manufactured by Jaya Exports of Bombay. A motor costs Rs 300, the invoice price to Thomas of Singapore is Rs 400. Thomas is entitled to a commission of 15% of the invoice price plus 40% of the excess realised over Rs 400. He is also responsible for all expenses incurred by him but not for freight to Singapore or customs duty.

    Jaya Exports despatched 200 motors in January 2004, drawing on Thomas for Rs 40,000 for 3 months. Thomas accepted the draft. Expenses paid by Thomas were: Freight Rs 4,000, Customs Duty Rs 2,000, Storage Rs 1,000 and Insurance Rs 800.

    At the end of March 2004, Thomas reported that he has sold 150 motors at an average price of Rs 440. It was agreed then that Thomas would take over the remaining motors on his own account at landed cost plus 20%. Prepare (a) Consignment Account, (b) Thomas of Singapore Account

    (CAIIB)

    [**Ans:** Profit Rs 8,400
    Balance Due Rs 18,400]

18. Rahim of Calcutta consigned 100 cases of medicine costing Rs 1,000 per case to Karim of Kanpur on 1st January 2004. The goods were sold at 25% above the cost. Any deficiency in selling price was to be borne by Karim. Karim was however entitled to a special commission @ 15% of any surplus price realised. Karim was further entitled to an ordinary commission of 5% and Del Credere commission of 2.5% on all sales.

    Rahim incurred the following expenses:

	Rs
Packing charges	6,000
Loading charges	1,000
Lorry hire	12,000
Railway freight	21,000

    The cases were received by Karim on 15th Jan. 2004. The Account sales received from Karim on 30th June revealed the following:

    21st March 40 cases @ Rs 1,500 per case
    24th April 30 cases @ Rs 1,200 per case
    16th June, 10 cases @ Rs 1,300 per case.

5 cases of medicine were stolen by a dishonest worker. A compensation of Rs 2,000 was realised from him. Karim incurred unloading charges of Rs 2,000 and warehouse rent Rs 3,000. Karim enclosed a bank draft for the balance due.

Write up the necessary accounts in the books of Rahim. (*B.Com. Hons., Calcutta*)

[**Ans:** Loss: Rs 16,900
Balance Due Rs 96,700]

19. Manoj of Delhi sends a consignment of sewing machines to Rajesh of Saharanpur and charges proforma invoice price so as to show a profit 25% on cost. The agent received commission @ 5 per cent on all sales plus 3% del credere on credit sales made by him.

Stock of goods with the agent at the beginning of the year—40 sewing machines at proforma invoice price Rs 10,000

During the year ended 31st December, 2004, Manoj had the following transactions with Rajesh:

(*a*) Proforma invoice price of 200 sewing machines consigned to Rajesh—Rs 50,000.

(*b*) Freight and insurance on the consignment paid by Manoj—Rs 1,400.

(*c*) Advance received from Rajesh—Rs 15,000.

(*d*) Sales made by Rajesh:

(*i*) 80 sewing machines for cash—Rs 21,500.

(*ii*) 100 sewing machines on credit—Rs 28,000.

(*e*) Selling expenses made by the agent Rs 2,500 and discount allowed by him Rs 1,000.

(*f*) 30 sewing machines were damaged by the railway for which Rajesh recovered Rs 2,700. The damaged sewing machines were sold on cash by Rajesh at Rs 2,300.

(*g*) Out of machines sold on credit, Rs 2,000 was irrecoverable and considered bad by the agent.

(*h*) The agent remitted the balance due by him by a bank draft.

Show Ledger Accounts to record the above transactions in the books of Manoj.

(*B.Com., Kerala*)

[**Ans:** Profit Rs 5,705
Accidental loss Rs 6,210
Value of Unsold Stock Rs 7,710]

20. *D* in Dehradun consigns to *J* in Trichinopoly goods to the invoice value of Rs 60,000 (cost Rs 40,000), paying freight and insurance charges Rs 4,000 and draws a bill on *J* for Rs 40,000 at sixty days.

Nine-tenths of the consignment was sold by *J* for Rs 70,000 and expenses of Rs 4,000 were incurred. *J* is also entitled to a commission of 10 per cent on sales.

J sent a sight draft to *D* for the net amount held on *D*'s account.

Show by means of Journal entries how the above transactions would be recorded in the books of both *D* and *J*. (*B.Com. Hons., Calcutta*)

[**Ans:** Profit Rs 19,400
Balance due Rs 19,000]

21. Mr Achut of Bombay consigned 100 units of a commodity to Mr Rao of Delhi. The goods were invoiced at Rs 150 so as to yield a profit of 50 per cent on cost. Mr Achut incurred Rs 1,000 on freight and insurance. Mr Rao incurred Rs 500 on freight and Rs 800 on rent. Before 31st December, 2004 he sold 50 units for cash at Rs 160 per unit, 20 units for Rs 175 on credit. He retained his commission 5 per cent and 1 per cent of the del credere arrangements on all sales and remitted the balance on 31st December 2004. Mr Rao noticed that 10 units were damaged on account of bad packing and he could sell it only for Rs 80 per unit. A debtor for Rs 1,000 to whom the goods were sold by Mr Rao became insolvent and only 50 paise in a rupee was recovered. Mr Rao sent an account sales on 31st December, 2004 detailing the transactions for the quarter ended on that date and he remitted the balance due.

Make necessary ledger entries in the books of Mr Achut and Mr Rao, assuming that Mr Achut closes his books every 31st December. (*C.A. Inter*)

[**Ans:** Profit Rs 1,960
Abnormal loss Rs 398
Value of Unsold Stock Rs 4,052]

Chapter 16

Joint Venture Accounts

Introduction – Characteristics – Joint Venture and Partnership – Joint Venture and Consignment – Methods of Accounting – Consignment-cum-Joint Venture – Questions – Objective Type Questions – Theoretical Questions – Practical Problems.

Joint Venture is a business where two or more persons agree to undertake jointly a particular venture. Joint Venture is a particular partnership. Joint Venture is defined as the kind of business proposition where two or more persons jointly venture to complete a specific business undertaking on agreed conditions, to share the profits or losses arising therefrom, on a temporary partnership basis until its completion. A Joint Venture is also known as Joint Adventure or Joint Trade. It is a temporary partnership. It has no firm name. Hence it is a partnership without name. The partners or parties of a joint venture are called the Co-venturers. They agree to contribute capital to carry on a particular job. The capital may be in cash or in kind with a view to sharing profit or loss in an agreed ratio. If there is no agreement regarding the profit sharing ratio, they share the profits or losses equally, as in the partnership. As soon as the business is completed, the joint venture comes to an end.

If a trader is in need of funds or business skill or wants to spread the risk, he joins with other businessmen. Examples of such transactions are:

(*a*) Joint consignment of goods

(*b*) Construction or contract businesses

(*c*) Purchase and sale of properties and stocks of liquidated business

(*d*) Underwriting shares or debentures of joint stock companies

(*e*) Speculation in shares etc.

CHARACTERISTICS OF A JOINT VENTURE

1. Joint Venture has no firm name. Hence it is a partnership without name.
2. It is an agreement between two or more persons to share profits or losses in an agreed proportion. In the absence of agreement, they share profits or losses equally.
3. The agreement is valid only for a specific venture alone.
4. The members of the venture are known as co-venturers.
5. As soon as the task is completed, agreement of the venture comes to end.

JOINT VENTURE AND PARTNERSHIP

Joint venture is not a partnership in strict sense though we call it a temporary partnership. It differs from partnership and its salient points are outlined as follows:

Joint Venture	Partnership
1. There is no necessity for a trade name.	1. The firm has a specific trade name.
2. The parties in Joint Venture are known as co-venturers.	2. The parties in partnership are known as partners.
3. The minimum number of co-venturers is two and there is no limit for maximum.	3. Minimum number is two and maximum number is ten in case of banking business and 20 in other businesses.
4. It is temporary in nature. It is formed for special purpose and it ceases to exist on completion of a particular business.	4. It is a continuous business operation and it is not restricted to a particular operation.
5. The agreement is not registered in order to make it enforceable against the third parties.	5. It must be registered in order to make claim of partnership against the third parties.
6. Co-venturers are free to have their own independent business of the same type.	6. Partners cannot independently undertake a business of similar nature.
7. The profit is ascertained for each venture.	7. The profit is ascertained annually.
8. Co-venturers have no implied authority.	8. Partners have implied authority.
9. There is no joint and several liabilities unless there is special agreement.	9. There is joint and several liabilities on partners.
10. There is no special Act for Joint Venture.	10. There is a separate Act known as Indian Partnership Act 1932.
11. It is not necessary to maintain separate and permanent record of accounts.	11. The firm must maintain a separate set of books of account on a permanent basis.

JOINT VENTURE AND CONSIGNMENT

Joint Venture and Consignment are different methods of doing business. If co-venturers consign goods to each other or to third parties, then such transaction can be called as Joint Consignment. It is different from consignment. The differences between Joint Venture and Consignment are:

Joint Venture	Consignment
1. The parties are called co-venturers.	1. The parties are called consignor or principal and consignee or agent.
2. The relationship between the co-venturers is like that of partners.	2. The relationship between the consignor and consignee is that of principal and agent.
3. It is a temporary partnership.	3. It is not a partnership. The agent need not be a partner.
4. The profits or losses are shared equally or in agreed ratio.	4. The agent has no right to share the profits. But he receives commission.
5. All the co-venturers have equal powers to buy and sell the goods, to collect the dues etc.	5. The agent does not have any power. He has to follow the principal's orders.
6. Capital in cash or in kind is contributed by co-venturers.	6. Here capital in cash or in kind is contributed by consignor.
7. It ceases to exist when the specific business is completed by the co-venturers.	7. It is continuing for any length of time as long as the relationship between the consignor and consignee exists.
8. The business may be concerned with buying or selling or contract work or any other activities.	8. Consignments are meant for sale of goods alone.

METHODS OF ACCOUNTING

- When a separate set of books is kept
  (There are 3 accounts:
  1. Joint Bank A/c
  2. Joint Venture A/c
  3. Co-venturer's A/c)
- When a separate set of books is not kept
  - Each co-venturer maintains a complete record of all joint. venture transactions. (Complete record method) (There are 2 A/cs):
    1. Joint Venture A/c
    2. A/c of other co-venturer)
  - Each co-venturer maintains a record of only his own transactions. (Partial records) or (Memorandum joint venture method) (There are 2 A/cs):
    1. Join Venture with ... A/c
    2. Memorandum Joint Venture Account)

METHODS OF ACCOUNTING

The following are the methods generally followed where joint venture transactions take place:

(*A*) Where separate set of books is kept;

(*B*) Where no separate set of books is kept; and

(*C*) Where memorandum joint venture account is kept.

These will be discussed in detail one by one:

(A) WHERE SEPARATE SET OF BOOKS IS KEPT

This method is particularly followed where there are large transactions, that is, the venture is a large one and is continued for a comparatively long period. Accounts are prepared under double entry principle. The following three accounts are prepared under this method:

(I) Joint Venture Account

(II) Joint Bank Account

(III) Co-venturer's Account

(Venturer's Capital Account)

(I) **Joint Venture Account:** This account represents the results of the business, that is, profit or loss. It is like a Trading/Profit & Loss Account of a trading concern. This account is debited by the cost of goods, expenses, goods supplied by the venturers etc. and is credited by sale proceeds, unsold stock, stock taken by venturers etc. If credit side of this account is greater than the debit side, the difference represents profit on joint venture and vice versa in the opposite case. The profit or loss so made is transferred to co-venturer's account.

(II) **Joint Bank Account :** It is like an ordinary Cash Book or Bank Account. All incomes including the capital contribution by the ventures appear on the debit side of this account whereas all expenses of the venture appear on the credit side of this account. It is finally closed by payment to the co-venturers, leaving no balance either side.

(III) **Co-venturer's Account:** This is the capital account of the venturer relating to venture. This account is credited by the capital contributed by the venturers, goods supplied by them from their own stock, expenses made personally by them etc. whereas this account is debited for any withdrawals or any asset taken from the venture. The profit or loss so made on venture is transferred to this account in profit sharing ratio and this account is closed by cash payment from joint bank and vice versa in the opposite case.

JOURNAL ENTRIES UNDER THIS METHOD

1.	When cash contributed or invested or paid in by co-venturers	Joint Bank Account To Respective Co-venturer Account	Dr.
2.	When goods purchased for joint venture	Joint Venture Account To Joint Bank Account	Dr.
3.	When goods contributed by co-venturer	Joint Venture Account To Respective Co-venturer Account	Dr.
4.	When goods purchased on credit	Joint Venture Account To Supplier's Account	Dr.
5.	When suppliers are paid off	Suppliers' Account To Joint Bank Account	Dr.
6.	When expenses incurred	Joint Venture Account To Joint Bank Account	Dr.
7.	When expenses paid by a co-venturer	Joint Venture Account To Respective Co-venturer Account	Dr.
8.	When goods sold for cash	Joint Bank Account To Joint Venture Account	Dr.
9.	When goods sold on credit	Debtors' Account To Joint Venture Account	Dr.
10.	When cash received from debtors/Bills Receivable	Joint Bank Account To Debtors/Bills Receivable A/c	Dr.
11.	When goods taken by co-venturer	Respective Co-venturer Account To Joint Venture Account	Dr.
12.	When commission or salary payable to co-venturers	Joint Venture Account To Respective Co-venturer A/c	Dr
13.	When discount received from creditors	Creditors Account To Joint Venture Account	Dr.
14.	When discount allowed or bad debts incurred	Joint Venture Account To Debtors Account	Dr.
15.	When cash is paid to creditors/Bills Payable	Creditors/Bills Payable A/c To Joint Bank Account	Dr.
16.	Result of the joint venture: (*a*) Profit	Joint Venture Account To Each Co-venturer's Account	Dr.
	(*b*) Loss:	Each Co-venturer's Account To Joint Venture Account	Dr.

The Joint Bank Account should be now just sufficient to balance off the Co-venturers Account. That is, the Joint Bank Account is then closed by making payment to each partner of what is due to him in respect of his personal account. With the settlement of these accounts the separate books will automatically be closed off.

ILLUSTRATION 16.1

Rajeev and Ashok enter into a joint venture as dealers in land and opened a Joint Bank Account with Rs 60,000 towards which Rajeev contributed Rs 40,000. They agree to share profits and losses in proportion to their cash contribution. They purchased a plot of land measuring 5,000 square yards for Rs 50,000. It was decided to sell the land in smaller plots and a plan was got prepared at a cost of Rs 1,200. In the said plan 1/5th of the total area of the land was left over for public roads and the remaining land was divided into 8 plots of equal size. Out of 8 plots, 3 plots were sold @ Rs 15 per square yard and the remaining 5 plots were sold @ Rs 14 per square yard. Expenses incurred in connection with the plots were: Registration Expenses Rs 4,000, Stamp Duty Rs 400 and Other Expenses Rs 1,000. Allow 2% on the sale proceeds as a commission to Rajeev.

Journalise the above transactions and prepare the necessary ledger accounts. (*B.Com., Madurai*)

Journal

Date	Particulars		L.F.	Dr. Rs	Cr. Rs
	Joint Bank Account	Dr.		60,000	
	To Rajeev Account				40,000
	To Ashok Account				20,000
	(Being cash contributed by Rajeev and Ashok)				
	Joint Venture Account	Dr.		50,000	
	To Joint Bank Account				50,000
	(Being a plot of land purchased)				
	Joint Venture Account	Dr.		1,200	
	To Joint Bank Account				1,200
	(Being expenses incurred in preparation of a plan)				
	Joint Bank Account	Dr.		57,500	
	To Joint Venture Account				57,500
	(Being Sale Proceeds of: 3 plots of 500 sq. yards @ Rs 15 = 22,500 5 plots of 500 sq. yards @ Rs 14 = 35,000)				
	Joint Venture Account	Dr.		5,400	
	To Joint Bank Account				5,400
	(Being Expenses incurred: Registration Expenses 4,000 Stamp Duty 400 Other Expenses 1,000				
	Joint Venture Account	Dr.		1,150	
	To Rajeev Account				1,150
	(Being 2% commission on Rs 57,500)				
	Rajeev Account	Dr.		167	
	Ashok Account	Dr.		83	
	To Joint Venture Account				250
	(Being loss on Joint Venture transferred in the ratio of 2 : 1)				
	Rajeev Account	Dr.		40,983	
	Ashok Account	Dr.		19,917	
	To Joint Bank Account				60,900
	(Being amount paid in final settlement of Rajeev and Ashok Accounts)				

Joint Venture Account

Dr.	Rs			Cr. Rs
To Joint Bank Account	50,000	By Joint Bank Account		57,500
To Joint Bank Account–Expenses	1,200	By Loss on Joint Venture Account		
To Joint Bank Account–Expenses	5,400	Rajeev	Rs 167	
To Rajeev Account–Commission	1,150	Ashok	Rs 83	250
	57,750			57,750

Dr. **Joint Bank Account** Cr.

	Rs		Rs
To Rajeev Account	40,000	By Joint Venture Account	50,000
To Ashok Account	20,000	By Joint Venture Account	1,200
To Joint Venture Account	57,500	By Joint Venture Account	5,400
		By Rajeev Account	40,983
		By Ashok Account	19,917
	1,17,500		1,17,500

Dr. **Co-Venturers Account** Cr

	Rajeev	*Ashok*		*Rajeev*	*Ashok*
	Rs	Rs		Rs	Rs
To Joint Venture Account–Loss	167	83	By Joint Bank Account	40,000	20,000
To Joint Bank Account	40,983	19,917	By Joint Venture Account	1,150	–
	41,150	20,000		41,150	20,000

ILLUSTRATION 16.2

Das, Bose and Gupta undertake to erect a five-storied mansion for National Housing Trust Ltd. The contract price is agreed at Rs 25,00,000 to be paid in cash, Rs 22,00,000 by four equal instalments and the balance amount in 8% Debentures of the company. They agree to share equally the profit or loss.

They opened a Joint Bank Account with cash contributed as stated below :

Das Rs 3,00,000; Bose Rs 3,75,000 and Gupta Rs 2,00,000

Das arranges the preparation of building plans etc. and pays Rs 32,000 as architect's fees. Bose brings a concrete mixer and other implements valued at Rs 80,000 and Gupta brings a motor lorry valued at Rs 75,000.

They paid in cash for the following:

	Rs		Rs
Materials	12,26,800	Sundry Expenses	20,000
Wages	7,33,200	Plant	60,000

On completion of the venture concrete mixer is sold for Rs 50,000 and Plant and other implements are sold for Rs 10,000. Gupta takes back the motor lorry at Rs 40,000. Das took over the Debentures issued by the company at a valuation of Rs 2,80,000.

Show the necessary ledger accounts for the Joint Venture. (*B.Com., Calcutta*)

SOLUTION

In the books of Das, Bose and Gupta

Dr. **Joint Venture Account** Cr.

		Rs			*Rs*
To Das Account–			By Joint Bank A/c–		
Architect's Fees		32,000	Part of Contract Price		22,00,000
To Bose A/c–			By Debenture Account		3,00,000
Mixer and other Implements		80,000	By Joint Bank A/c–		
To Gupta A/c–Motor Lorry		75,000	Sale Proceeds of		
To Joint Bank A/c–			Mixer	50,000	
Materials	12,26,800		Plant	10,000	60,000
Wages	7,33,200		By Gupta A/c–		
Sundry Expenses	20,000		Motor Lorry taken back		40,000
Plant	60,000	20,40,000			
To Debenture Account		20,000			

To Profit and Loss A/c–					
Das 1/3	1,17,667				
Bose 1/3	1,17,667				
Gupta 1/3	1,17,666	3,53,000			
		26,00,000			26,00,000

Joint Bank Account

Dr.			Cr.		
		Rs			Rs
To Das A/c		3,00,000	By Joint Venture A/c–		
To Bose A/c		3,75,000	Material	12,26,800	
To Gupta A/c		2,00,000	Wages	7,33,200	
To Joint Venture A/c–			Sundry Expenses	20,000	
Part of Contract Price		22,00,000	Plant	60,000	20,40,000
To Joint Venture A/c–			By Das A/c		1,69,667
Sale Proceeds of			By Bose A/c		5,72,667
Mixer	50,000		By Gupta A/c		3,52,666
Plant	10,000	60,000			
		31,35,000			31,35,000

Co-Venturers Account

Dr.	Das	Bose	Gupta	Cr.	Das	Bose	Gupta
	Rs	Rs	Rs		Rs	Rs	Rs
To Joint Venture A/c– Debenture taken over	2,80,000			By Joint Bank A/c–	3,00,000	3,75,000	2,00,000
To Joint Venture A/c- Motor Lorry taken over			40,000	By Joint Venture A/c– Architect's Fees	32,000		
To Joint Bank A/c	1,69,667	5,72,667	3,52,666	By Joint Venture A/c– Mixer		80,000	
				By Joint Venture A/c– Motor Lorry			75,000
				By Joint Venture A/c– Share of Profit	1,17,667	1,17,667	1,17,666
	4,49,667	5,72,667	3,92,666		4,49,667	5,72,667	3,92,666

ILLUSTRATION 16.3

A and *B*, both contractors, undertook a joint venture involving the construction of a building. A Joint Bank Account was opened in which *A* contributed Rs 75,000 and *B* contributed Rs 37,500. The contract price was Rs 3,75,000. The result of joint venture was shared as to *A* 2/3 and *B* 1/3. The details of the transactions were as follows:

	Rs
Wages paid	89,000
Materials supplied by *A*	13,500
Materials supplied by *B*	12,000
Materials purchased	1,65,000
Salaries	12,000
Cartage	18,500
Architect's fee paid by *A*	10,000
Concrete mixer plant purchased	38,500

The stock of materials on the completion of the contract, valued at Rs 16,500, was taken over by *A*. Concrete mixer plant was taken over by *B* for Rs 30,000. *A* was to be paid Rs 18,000 p.a. against establishment expenses, to be charged to the Joint Venture Account. The contract lasted for 8 months.

Prepare Joint Venture Account, Joint Bank Account and Accounts of *A* and *B*. (*B.Com., Delhi*)

SOLUTION JOURNAL

Particulars		Dr. Rs	Cr. Rs
Joint Bank Account	Dr.	1,12,500	
To *A* Account			75,000
To *B* Account			37,500
(Being the amount contributed by *A* and *B*)			
Joint Venture Account	Dr.	89,000	
To Joint Bank Account			89,000
(Being wages paid)			
Joint Venture Account	Dr.	25,500	
To *A* Account			13,500
To *B* Account			12,000
(Being materials supplied by *A* and *B*)			
Joint Venture Account	Dr.	1,65,000	
To Joint Bank Account			1,65,000
(Being materials purchased)			
Joint Venture Account	Dr.	30,500	
To Joint Bank Account			30,500
(Being salaries and cartage paid)			
Joint Venture Account	Dr.	10,000	
To *A* Account			10,000
(Being architect fees paid by *A*)			
Joint Venture Account	Dr.	38,500	
To Joint Bank Account			38,500
(Being concrete mixer plant purchased)			
Joint Bank Account	Dr.	3,75,000	
To Joint Venture Account			3,75,000
(Being contract price received)			
A Account	Dr.	16,500	
To Joint Venture Account			16,500
(Being stock of materials taken over)			
B Account	Dr.	30,000	
To Joint Venture Account			30,000
(Being concrete mixer plant taken over)			
Joint Venture Account	Dr.	12,000	
To *A* Account			12,000
(Being 8 months establishment expenses paid *i.e.* Rs $18,000 \times \frac{8}{12}$)			
Joint Venture Account	Dr.	51,000	
To *A* Account			34,000
To *B* Account			17,000
(Being profit transferred to *A* and *B* in the ratio of 2/3 and 1/3)			
A Account	Dr.	1,28,000	
B Account	Dr.	36,500	
To Joint Bank Account			1,64,500
(Being the balance amount paid)			

Joint Venture Account

Dr.		Rs	Cr.	Rs
To Joint Bank A/c–Wages		89,000	By Joint Bank A/c–Contract Price	3,75,000
To *A* Account–Materials supplied		13,500	By *A* A/c–Stock of Material	16,500
To *B* Account–Materials supplied		12,000	By *B* A/c–Concrete Mixer Plant taken	30,000
To Joint Bank A/c– Materials Purchased		1,65,000		
To Joint Bank A/c– Salaries and Cartage		30,500		
To *A* A/c–Architects Fees		10,000		
To Joint Bank A/c–Concrete Mixer		38,500		
To *A* A/c–Establishment Expenses		12,000		
To Profit transferred to				
A A/c	34,000			
B A/c	17,000	51,000		
		4,21,500		4,21,500

Accounts of A and B

Dr.	A	B	Cr.	A	B
	Rs	Rs		Rs	Rs
To Joint Venture A/c–			By Joint Venture A/c–	75,000	37,500
Materials taken	16,500	–	By Joint Venture A/c–		
To Joint Venture A/c–			Materials	13,500	12,000
Concrete Mixer Plant	–	30,000	Architect's Fees	10,000	–
To Joint Bank A/c–			Establishment	12,000	–
Balance	1,28,000	36,500	By Joint Venture A/c–		
			Profit	34,000	17,000
	1,44,500	66,500		1,44,500	66,500

Joint Bank Account

Dr.	Rs	Cr.	Rs
To *A* A/c	75,000	By Joint Venture A/c–	
To *B* A/c	37,500	Wages	89,000
To Joint Venture A/c–		By Joint Venture A/c–	
Contract Price	3,75,000	Materials	1,65,000
		Salary	12,000
		Cartage	18,500
		Concrete Mixer	38,500
		By *A* A/c	1,28,000
		By *B* A/c	36,500
	4,87,500		4,87,500

ILLUSTRATION 16.4

A and *B* doing business separately as building contractor undertake jointly to construct a building for a newly started Joint Stock Company for a contract price of Rs 1,00,000 payable as to Rs 80,000 by instalments in cash and Rs 20,000 in fully paid shares of the Company. A banking Account is opened in their joint names, *A* paying Rs 25,000 and *B* Rs 15,000. They are to share profits and losses in the proportion of 2/3rd and 1/3rd respectively. Their transactions were as follows:

	Rs		Rs
Paid Wages	30,000	Materials supplied by *B*	4,000
Bought Materials	70,000	Architect's fees paid by *A*	2,000
Materials supplied by *A*	5,000		

The contract was completed and the price (cash and shares) duly received. The joint venture was closed by *A* taking up all the shares of the company at an agreed valuation of Rs 16,000 and *B* taking up the stock of materials at an agreed valuation of Rs 3,000.

Show the necessary accounts. (*B.Com, Madurai, Punjab*)

SOLUTION

Dr. **Joint Venture Account** Cr.

	Rs			Rs
To Joint Bank A/c (Material)	70,000	By Joint Bank A/c (Cash)		80,000
To Joint Bank A/c (Wages)	30,000	By Shares A/c		20,000
To *A*'s A/c (Materials)	5,000	By B (Stock taken) A/c		3,000
To *B*'s A/c (Materials)	4,000	By Loss: *A*	8,000	
To *A* A/c (Architect's fees)	2,000	*B*	4,000	12,000
To Share A/c (Loss)	4,000			
	1,15,000			1,15,000

Dr. **Joint Bank Account** Cr.

	Rs		Rs
To *A* A/c	25,000	By Jt. Venture (Materials)	70,000
To *B* A/c	15,000	By Joint Venture (Wages)	30,000
To Joint Venture A/c	80,000	By *A* (balance) A/c	8,000
		By *B* (balance) A/c	12,000
	1,20,000		1,20,000

Dr. **Share Account** Cr.

	Rs		Rs
To Joint Venture A/c	20,000	By Joint Venture (Loss) A/c	4,000
		By *A* (Share taken) A/c	16,000
	20,000		20,000

Dr. **Co-Venturers Account** Cr.

	A	*B*		*A*	*B*
	Rs	Rs		Rs	Rs
To Share A/c	16,000		By Joint Bank A/c	25,000	15,000
To Joint Venture A/c			By Joint Bank A/c		
Stock taken		3,000	Materials	5,000	4,000
To Joint Venture A/c			By Joint Venture A/c		
Loss	8,000	4,000	Architect's Fees	2,000	
To Joint Bank A/c					
Balance	8,000	12,000			
	32,000	19,000		32,000	19,000

ILLUSTRATION 16.5

Ram, Gopi and Jain jointly undertook to construct a building for P and Co., at a price of Rs 2,50,000. The price was to be paid as follows:

Rs 2,00,000 in cash, and Rs 50,000 by the issue of preference shares of the Company.

Profit was agreed to be divided equally. The partners contributed as follows: Ram–Rs 30,000; Gopi–Rs 37,500 and Jain–Rs 20,000. The amounts were deposited in a Joint Bank Account opened with the State Bank of India.

Ram got the plan prepared and paid Rs 3,500 as architect's fees. Gopi brought into the venture a concrete mixer of the value of Rs 12,000 and Jain brought a lorry of the value of Rs 26,000. They bought a plant for Rs 15,000. Materials worth Rs 1,20,000 were purchased for cash and a sum of Rs 1,05,000 was paid as wages.

On completion of the contract, Ram took over the unused materials of the value of Rs 10,000; Gopi took back the concrete mixer at a valuation of Rs 11,000; Jain took back his lorry at Rs 20,000. The plant is sold as scrap for Rs 5,000.

When the contract price was received, Ram agreed to take over the Preference Shares at Rs 40,000.

Open the Joint Venture Account, Joint Bank Account and the Accounts of Ram, Gopi and Jain.

(*B.Com., Madurai*)

SOLUTION

Dr. **Joint Venture Account** Cr.

		Rs		*Rs*
To Ram A/c– Architect's Fees		3,500	By Joint Bank A/c	2,00,000
To Gopi A/c–Mixer		12,000	By Share A/c	50,000
To Jain A/c–Lorry		26,000	By Ram A/c–Materials	10,000
To Joint Bank A/c–Plant		15,000	By Gopi A/c–Mixer	11,000
To Joint Bank A/c–Materials		1,20,000	By Jain A/c–Lorry	20,000
To Joint Bank A/c–Wages		1,05,000	By Joint Bank A/c–Scrap	5,000
To Share A/c–Loss		10,000		
To Profit and Loss A/c:				
Ram A/c	1,500			
Gopi A/c	1,500			
Jain A/c	1,500	4,500		
		2,96,000		2,96,000

Dr. **Joint Bank Account** Cr.

	Rs		*Rs*
To Ram A/c	30,000	By Joint Venture A/c	15,000
To Gopi A/c	37,500	By Joint Venture A/c	1,20,000
To Jain A/c	20,000	By Joint Venture A/c	1,05,000
To Joint Venture A/c	2,00,000	By Gopi A/c	40,000
To Joint Venture A/c	5,000	By Jain A/c	27,500
To Ram A/c	15,000		
	3,07,500		3,07,500

Dr. **Co-Venturers Account** Cr.

	Ram	Gopi	Jain		Ram	Gopi	Jain
	Rs	*Rs*	*Rs*		*Rs*	*Rs*	*Rs*
To Joint Venture A/c Materials taken	10,000			By Joint Bank A/c	30,000	37,500	20,000
To Joint Venture A/c Concrete Mixer taken		11,000		By Joint Venture A/c Architect's Fees	3,500		
To Joint Venture A/c Lorry taken			20,000	By Joint Venture A/c Concrete Mixer		12,000	
To Shares A/c	40,000			By Joint Venture A/c Lorry			26,000

To Joint Bank A/c		40,000	27,500	By Joint Venture A/c Profit	1,500		1,500
				By Joint Bank A/c	15,000	1,500	
	50,000	51,000	47,500		50,000	51,000	47,500

(B) WHERE NO SEPARATE SET OF BOOKS IS KEPT

This method is applicable where the joint venture transactions are limited and the venturers reside at two different places. Under this method each venturer will record his own transactions plus the transactions relating to other co-venturer's capital whereas the other venturer will prepare a Joint Venture Account and the capital of the others, that is, two accounts are prepared in each party's ledger. For instance, there are two venturers, namely, *A* and *B*. So, *A* will prepare a Joint Venture Account and *B*'s Capital Account in his books while *B* will also prepare a Joint Venture Account and *A*'s Capital Account in his book.

(1) **Joint Venture Account :** It should be prepared like the previous one which reveals the result of the business, that is, profit or loss which ultimately be transferred to Venturers Capital. But in this case one's own share of profit or loss should be transferred to his Profit and Loss Account but co-venturer's share of profit or loss should be transferred to his personal account.

(2) **Other Co-venturer's Account:** Since this is a personal account of the co-venturer, his account will be debited with the amount of goods purchased, expenses incurred, profit so earned etc. and is credited with the amount of sale proceeds, unsold stock taken etc. The balance of this account will go to either (*i*) the Balance Sheet, if it is so prepared, or (*ii*) the same will represent the final payment of Receipts and Payments between the venturers.

Journal Entries

	A's Books		*B's Books*	
When goods are supplied by *A*	Joint Venture A/c To Purchase A/c	Dr.	Joint Venture To *A*'s Account	Dr.
When expenses paid by *A*	Joint Venture A/c To Cash A/c	Dr.	Joint Venture A/c To *A*'s A/c	Dr.
When goods are supplied by *B*	Joint Venture A/c To *B*'s A/c	Dr.	Joint Venture A/c To Purchase A/c	Dr.
When expenses paid by *B*	Joint Venture A/c To *B*'s A/c	Dr.	Joint Venture A/c To Cash A/c	Dr.
When cash is contributed by *A*	Joint Venture A/c To Cash A/c	Dr.	Joint Venture A/c To *A*'s Account	Dr.
When cash is contributed by *B*	Joint Venture A/c To *B*'s A/c	Dr.	Joint Venture A/c To Cash A/c	Dr.
When a Bill is drawn by *A* and accepted by *B*	Bills Receivable A/c To *B*'s A/c	Dr.	*A*'s A/c To Bills Payable A/c	Dr.
When Bill is discounted by *A*	Cash A/c Joint Venture A/c (Discount amount) To Bills Receivable A/c	Dr. Dr.	Joint Venture A/c (Discount Amount) To *A*'s A/c	Dr.
When Commission allowed to *B*	Joint Venture A/c To *B*'s A/c	Dr.	Joint Venture A/c To Commission A/c	Dr.
When salary allowed to *A*	Joint Venture A/c To Salary A/c	Dr.	Joint Venture A/c To *A*'s A/c	Dr.
When goods sold by *A*	Cash A/c To Joint Venture A/c	Dr.	*A*'s A/c To Joint Venture A/c	Dr.

	A's Books		B's Books	
When credit sales are made by *A*	Sundry Debtors A/c	Dr.	*A*'s A/c	Dr.
	To Joint Venture A/c		Joint Venture A/c	
When bad debts arise:	Joint Venture A/c	Dr.	Joint Venture A/c	Dr.
(sales made by *A*)	To Sundry Debtors A/c		To *A*'s Account	
When unsold stocks taken by *A*	Purchase A/c	Dr.	*A*'s A/c	Dr.
	To Joint Venture A/c		To Joint Venture A/c	
When Joint Venture shows profit	Joint Venture A/c	Dr.	Joint Venture A/c	Dr.
	To *B*'s A/c		To *A*'s A/c	
	To Profit & Loss A/c		To Profit & Loss A/c	
When Joint Venture shows loss	Profit & Loss A/c	Dr.	Profit & Loss A/c	Dr.
	B's A/c	Dr.	*A*'s A/c	Dr.
	To Joint Venture A/c		To Joint Venture A/c	

Now, the balance in the personal account shows the amount due to or from him.

ILLUSTRATION 16.6

A and *B* were partners in a joint venture sharing profits and losses in the proportion of 60% and 40% respectively. *A* supplies goods to the value of Rs 10,000 and incurs on freight Rs 500. *B* also supplies goods to the value of Rs 8,000 and incurs Rs 400 towards freight and other incidental charges. *B* sells the entire stock of goods on behalf of the joint venture for Rs 25,000. *B* is also entitled to a commission of 5% on sales. *B* settles his account by remitting a bank draft.

Pass journal entries and ledger accounts in the books of *A* and *B*.

SOLUTION

A's Journal

	Particulars			Dr. Rs	Cr. Rs
	Joint Venture Account	Dr.		10,500	
	To Purchase Account				10,000
	To Bank Account				500
	(Being the value of goods sent to *B* and expenses incurred)				
	Joint Venture Account	Dr.		8,400	
	To *B*'s Account				8,400
	(Being the value of goods supplied and expenses incurred by *B*)				
	B's Account	Dr.		25,000	
	To Joint Venture Account				25,000
	(Being sale proceeds of goods received by *B* on behalf of joint venture)				
	Joint Venture Account	Dr.		1,250	
	To *B*'s Account				1,250
	(Being commission due to *B* at 5% on sales)				
	Joint Venture Account	Dr.		4,850	
	To *B* Account				1,940
	To Profit and Loss Account				2,910
	(Being division of profit in the agreed proportion)				
	Bank Account	Dr.		13,410	
	To *B*'s Account				13,410
	(Being receipt of balance due from *B*)				

A's Ledger

Joint Venture Account

Dr.	Rs	Cr.	Rs
To Purchase Account	10,000	By B's Account	
To Bank Account	500	(Sales Proceeds)	25,000
To *B*'s Account	8,400		
To *B*'s Account (Commission)	1,250		
To Profit:			
B's Account	1,940		
Profit & Loss A/c	2,910		
	25,000		25,000

B's Account

Dr.	Rs	Cr.	Rs
To Joint Venture	25,000	By Joint Venture A/c	8,400
(Sale Proceeds)		By Joint Venture A/c	
		(Commission)	1,250
		By Joint Venture A/c	
		(Profit)	1,940
		By Bank Account	13,410
	25,000		25,000

B's Journal

		Dr. Rs	Cr. Rs
Joint Venture Account	Dr.	10,500	
To *A* Account			10,500
(Being goods supplied and expenses met by *A*)			
Joint Venture Account	Dr.	8,400	
To Purchase Account			8,000
To Bank Account			400
(Being the value of goods supplied and expenses incurred)			
Bank Account	Dr.	25,000	
To Joint Venture A/c			25,000
(Being sale proceeds of goods in cash)			
Joint Venture Account	Dr.	1,250	
To Commission Account			1,250
(Being commission due at 5% on Rs 25,000)			
Joint Venture Account	Dr.	4,850	
To *A* Account			2,910
To Profit and Loss Account			1,940
(Being division of profit in the agreed proportion)			
A Account	Dr.	13,410	
To Bank Account			13,410
(Being remittance of balance due to *A*)			

B's Ledger

Joint Venture Account

Dr.	Rs		Cr. Rs
To *A* Account	10,500	By Bank Account	
To Purchase Account	8,000	(Sales proceeds)	25,000
To Bank Account	400		
To Commission	1,250		
To Profit:			
A Account	2,910		
Profit & Loss Account	1,940		
	25,000		25,000

A's Account

Dr.	Rs		Cr. Rs
To Bank Account	13,410	By Joint Venture Account	10,500
		By Joint Venture Account (Profit)	2,910
	13,410		13,410

ILLUSTRATION 16.7

A and *B* enter into a joint venture to sell a consignment of timber sharing profits and losses equally. *A* provides timber from stock at mutually agreed value of Rs 5,000. He pays expenses amounting to Rs 250. *B* incurs further expenses on cartage, storage, and coolie charges of Rs 650 and receives cash or sales Rs 3,000. He also takes over goods to the value of Rs 1,000 for his use in his own business. At the close, *A* takes over the balance stock in hand which is valued at Rs 1,100. Prepare joint venture account and Co-sharer's account in the books of *A*. (*B.Com., Delhi*)

SOLUTION

In the books of A

B Account

Dr.	Rs		Cr. Rs
To Joint Venture (Sales)	3,000	By Joint Venture (Exp.)	650
To Joint Venture (Goods)	1,000	By Bank (Settlement)	3,750
To Joint Venture (Loss)	400		
	4,400		4,400

Joint Venture Account

Dr.	Rs		Cr. Rs
To Purchases	5,000	By B's (Sales)	3,000
To Bank (Exp.)	250	By B's A/c (Goods)	1,000
To B's A/c (Exp.)	650	By Purchase (Goods)	1,100
		By B's A/c (Loss)	400
		By Profit & Loss (Loss)	400
	5,900		5,900

ILLUSTRATION 16.8

A and *B* agree to enter into a joint venture to buy and sell second-hand ice-cream vehicles and to share profits and losses in the ratio of 5 : 3 respectively. It was agreed that *A* would record all details of the venture in his books of account.

On 21st December, 2003, *B* purchased two vehicles and paid cash Rs 20,000 on 2nd January, 2004. He spent sums of Rs 2,480 on repairs, Rs 240 on driver's wages and Rs 360 on temporary insurance cover. He sold the vehicles a week later for Rs 28,000 subject to a 2% cash discount if paid within seven days. He paid the proceeds of sale into his bank account on 10th January, 2004.

On 31st January, 2004, *A* purchased five vehicles for Rs 50,000 of which he managed to sell three for Rs 36,000 for cash on the same day, without incurring any expenses. The fourth vehicle was sold for Rs 13,500 and on 7th February, 2004, he received a Bill Receivable to be presented for payment in three months' time.

On 31st March, 2004, the fifth vehicle was still unsold and it was agreed that *B* should take over the vehicle at a valuation of Rs 7,500.

On 31st March, 2004, the parties made a settlement between each other, *A* agreeing to take the bill receivable at a value of Rs. 13,180.

You are required to prepare Joint Venture Account and *B*'s account as they would appear in the books of *A*. (*C.A.*)

SOLUTION

In the books of A

Joint Venture Account

Dr. Cr.

Date	Particulars		Rs	Date	Particulars	Rs
2003				2004		
Dec. 21	To *B* A/c–Purchases		20,000	Jan. 9	By *B* A/c–Sales	28,000
2004				Jan. 31	By Bank– Sales	36,000
Jan. 2	To *B* A/c:			Feb. 7	By Bills Receivable A/c- Sales	13,500
	Repairs	2,480		Mar. 31	By *B* A/c–Vehicle taken over	7,500
	Driver's Wages	240				
	Insurance	360	3,080			
Jan. 10	To *B* A/c–Discount		560			
Jan. 31	To Creditors A/c–Purchases		50,000			
Mar. 31	To Bills Receivable A/c– Reduction in book value		320			
Mar. 31	To Profit transferred to Profit and Loss A/c					
	A A/c: 5/3	6,900				
	B A/c: 3/5	4,140	11,040			
			85,000			85,000

B Account

Dr. Cr.

Date	Particulars	Rs	Date	Particulars		Rs
2004			2003			
Jan. 9	To Joint Venture A/c– Sales	28,000	Dec. 21	By Joint Venture A/c– Purchases		20,000
Mar. 31	To Joint Venture A/c– Vehicle taken over	7,500	2004			
			Jan. 2	By Joint Venture A/c·		
				Repairs	2,480	
				Driver's Wages	240	
				Insurance	360	3,080

		By Joint Venture A/c– Discount	560
		By Joint Venture A/c– Share of Profit	4,140
		By Bank–Remittance	7,720
	35,500		35,500

(C) WHERE EACH CO-VENTURER MAINTAINS A RECORD OF HIS OWN TRANSACTIONS (or Partial Record Method) (or Momorandum Joint Venture Method)

Under this method each co-venturer keeps a record of Joint Venture transactions in which he is involved *i.e.* each venturer records in his own book only the transactions of joint venture which relate to him. Each party keeps his account in his own books. He will not record the transactions of other co-venturer. Hence it is a partial record. It will be clear from the following points:

1. Each Co-venturer will open one account in his book and it will be headed: Joint Venture with—(Name of other Co-Venturer) Account. This is a personal account. It is not a Nominal Account as Joint Venture, explained above. It does not disclose the profit or loss on Joint Venture. Each Co-Venturer debits the Account with the amount paid by him and credits the Account when he receives amounts.
2. In this Account, the concerned party records only his transactions. No account whatsoever is taken of the supplies made, expenses incurred etc. by the other co-venturer.

Journal entries in the books of one party, say, Mr A and the other Co-Venturer Mr B.

1. When goods are purchased by *A*

   Joint Venture with *B* Account Dr.
   To cash Account

2. When goods are sold by *A*:

   Cash Account Dr.
   To Joint Venture with B Account

3. When Commission is received by *A*

   Joint Venture with *B* Account Dr.
   To Commission Account

4. When A meets the expenses

   Joint Venture with B Account Dr.
   To Cash Account

5. When unsold stock is taken by *A*

   Purchase Account Dr.
   To Joint Venture with *B* Account

The above Account *i.e.* Joint Venture with *B* Account, is a personal account. It does not reveal profit or loss of Joint Venture. In order to ascertain profit or loss of Joint Venture we have to prepare Memorandum Joint Venture Account. In order to prepare Memorandum Joint Venture Account, one co-venturer sends another co-venturer a copy of the account kept by him. On the basis of the copy of account and his own account, Memorandum Joint Venture is prepared. In other words, Memorandum Joint Venture Account is just a combination of Joint Venture Accounts prepared by all the co-venturers. The debit side of the Joint Venture with *B* Account is put on the debit side of the Memorandum Joint Venture Account and credit side of that account is put on the credit side of the Memorandum Joint Venture Account. That is, the transactions of personal accounts of all co-venturers are entered in the Memorandum Joint Venture Account.

Memorandum Joint Venture Account is just like a trading and profit and loss Account. All the co-venturers prepare the same Memorandum Joint Venture Account. The balance amount of Memorandum Joint Account shows either profit or loss on Joint Venture. The Co-venturers share the profit or loss in the agreed ratio. For this co-venturers make the following entries:

In the books of A

If profit is there:	Joint Venture with B Account	Dr.
	To Profit and Loss Account	
If there is loss:	Profit and Loss Account	Dr.
	To Joint Venture with B Account	

Similarly, in the books of B

If profit is there:	Joint Venture with A Account	Dr.
	To Profit and Loss Account	
If there is loss:	Profit and Loss Account	Dr.
	To Joint Venture with A Account	

Remember that the balance of Joint Venture with......Account shows the amount due to the other Co-venturer or due from the other Co-venturer.

ILLUSTRATION 16.9

The illustration No. 16.6 is worked out under Method two

In the books of A

Joint Venture with B Account

Dr.	*Rs*		Cr. *Rs*
To Purchases Account	10,000	By Bank Account	13,410
To Bank Account	500		
To Profit and Loss Account	2,910		
	13,410		13,410

In the books of B

Joint Venture with A Account

Dr.	*Rs*		Cr. *Rs*
To Purchases Account	8,000	By Bank Account	25,000
To Bank Account	400	(Sale proceeds)	
To Commission A/c	1,250		
To Profit and Loss A/c	1,940		
To Bank Account	13,410		
	25,000		25,000

Memorandum Joint Venture Account

(Common to both)

Dr.		*Rs*		Cr. *Rs*
To A (Purchase and Expenses)		10,500	By B (Sale proceeds)	25,000
To B (Purchase and Expenses)		8,400		
To B (Commission)		1,250		
To Profit:				
A–60%	2,910			
B–40%	1,940	4,850		
		25,000		25,000

ILLUSTRATION 16.10

A and *B* enter into joint venture for guaranteeing the subscription at par of 1,00,000 shares of Rs 10 each of a joint stock company. They agree to share profits and losses in the ratio of 2:3. The terms with the company are 4.5% of commission in cash and 6,000 shares of the company as fully paid up.

The public took up 88,000 of the shares and the balance shares of the guaranteed issue are taken up by *A* and *B* who provide cash equally. The commission in cash is taken by partners in the ratio of 4 : 5.

The entire shareholding of the joint venture is then sold through brokers:

25% at a price of Rs 9 per share;

50% at a price of Rs 8.75 per share;

15% at a price of Rs 8.50 per share; and the remaining 10% are taken over by *A* and *B* equally at Rs 8 per share.

The sale proceeds of the shares are taken by the partners equally.

Prepare Joint Venture Memorandum Account and the separate accounts of *A* and *B* in the books of *B* and *A* respectively showing the adjustment of the final balance between *A* and *B*. Ignore interest.

(*B.Com., Calcutta*)

SOLUTION

Dr. **Memorandum Joint Venture Account** Cr.

		Rs		*Rs*
To *A* Account–Cost of Share (1)		60,000	By *A* Account–Commission (3)	20,000
To *B* Account–Cost of Share (1)		60,000	By *B* Account–Commission (3)	25,000
To Profit transferred to:			By *A* Account–Sales Proceeds (2)	71,100
A Account	32,640		By *B* Account–Sales Proceeds (2)	71,100
B Account	48,960	81,600	By *A* Account–Shares taken (4)	7,200
			By *B* Account–Shares taken (4)	7,200
		2,01,600		2,01,600

In the books of A

Dr. **Joint Venture with B Account** Cr.

	Rs		*Rs*
To Bank Account–Cost of Share (1)	60,000	By Bank Account–Commission (3)	20,000
To Profit and Loss Account	32,640	By Bank Account–Sale Proceeds (2)	71,100
To Bank Account–Final Settlement	5,660	By Shares Account–Shares taken (4)	7,200
	98,300		98,300

In the books of B

Dr. **Joint Venture with A Account** Cr.

	Rs		*Rs*
To Bank Account–Cost of Shares (1)	60,000	By Bank Account–Commission (3)	25,000
To Profit and Loss Account	48,960	By Bank Account–Sale proceeds (2)	71,100
		By Shares Account–Shares taken (4)	7,200
		By Bank Account–Final settlement	5,660
	1,08,960		1,08,960

Working Notes:

1. Purchase of Shares:

   1,00,000 – 88,000 = 12,000 shares @ Rs 10

   = Rs 1,20,000 provided by A and B equally *i.e.* Rs 60,000 each

2. Calculation of Sales:

   12,000 Shares purchased

   6,000 Shares are taken as commission

   Entire Shareholding 18,000

	Rs
25% of 18,000 = 4,500 Shares @ Rs 9.00	= 40,500
50% of 18,000 = 9,000 Shares @ Rs 8.75	= 78,750
15% of 18,000 = 2,700 Shares @ Rs 8.50	= 22,950
90%	1,42,200

   50% of Rs 1,42,200 taken by *A* = Rs 71,100

   50% of Rs 1,42,200 taken by *B* = Rs 71,100

3. Commission in Cash:

   1,00,000 Shares @ Rs 10 = Rs 10,00,000

   4½% of Rs 10,00,000 is taken by *A* and *B* in the ratio 4 : 5 *i.e.* Rs 45,000

   $$\text{For } A = 45{,}000 \times \frac{4}{9} = \text{Rs } 20{,}000$$

   $$\text{For } B = 45{,}000 \times \frac{5}{9} = \text{Rs } 25{,}000$$

4. Unsold Shares are taken equally by *A* and *B*.

   10% of 18,000 = 1,800 Shares @ Rs 8 = Rs 14,400

   A = Rs 7,200

   B = Rs 7,200

ILLUSTRATION 16.11

Mr *A* and *B* decided to work a joint venture for the sale of electric motors.

On 21st Jan., Mr *A* purchased 200 electric motors at Rs 175 each and despatched 150 motors to Mr *B* incurring Rs 1,000 as freight and insurance charges. 10 electric motors were damaged in transit. On 1st February Rs 500 were received by Mr *A* from the Insurance Company, in full settlement of his claim. On 15th March, Mr *A* sold 50 electric motors at Rs 225 each. He received Rs 15,000 from Mr *B* on 1st April.

On 25th Jan., Mr *B* took delivery of electric motors and incurred the following expenses:

	Rs
Clearing charges	170
Repairs to electric motors damaged in transit	300
Godown rent for 3 months	600

He sold the electric motors as follows:

1st Feb.:	10 damaged motors at Rs 170 each
	40 motors at Rs 200 each
15th March:	20 motors at Rs 315 each
1st April:	80 motors at Rs 250 each.

It is agreed that they are entitled to commission at 10% on the respective sales effected by them and that the profits and losses shall be shared between Mr *A* and Mr *B* in the ratio of 2 : 1.

Mr *B* remits to Mr *A* the balance amount due on 30th April.

You are required to show in the books of *A* (*i*) Joint Venture Account and (*ii*) the Memorandum of Joint Venture Account. (*CA Inter*)

SOLUTION

In the books of A

Joint Venture with B Account

Dr. Cr.

		Rs			Rs
Jan. 21	To Bank A/c–Purchase of Motors: 175 × 200	35,000	Feb. 1	By Bank A/c– Insurance Claim	500
Jan. 21	To Bank A/c– Freight and Insurance	1,000	Mar. 15	By Bank A/c– Sales: 225 × 50	11,250
Apr. 30	To Commission A/c	1,125		By Bank A/c– Remittance from B	15,000
Apr. 30	To Profit and Loss A/c– Share of Profit	3,970		By Bank A/c– Remittance from B	14,345
		41,095			41,095

Memorandum Joint Venture Account

Dr. Cr.

			Rs			Rs
					By *A* A/c:	
Jan. 21	To *A* A/c: Purchases		35,000	Feb. 1	Insurance Claim	500
Jan. 21	Freight and Insurance		1,000	Mar. 15	Sales	11,250
Apr. 30	Commission		1,125		By *B* A/c: Sales: 9,700 + 6,300 + 20,000	36,000
	To *B* A/c:					
Jan. 25	Clearing Charges		170			
Jan. 25	Repairs to Motor		300			
Jan. 25	Godown Rent		600			
Apr. 30	Commission		3,600			
Apr. 30	To Profit on Venture:					
	A 2/3	3,970				
	B 1/3	1,985	5,955			
			47,750			47,750

Workings:

In the books of B

Joint Venture with A Account

Dr. Cr.

		Rs			Rs
Jan. 25	To Bank A/c:		Feb. 1	By Bank A/c– Sales:	
	Clearing Charges	170		170 × 10 = Rs 1,700	
	Repairs to Motor	300		200 × 40 = Rs 8,000	9,700
	Godown Rent	600			
Apr. 1	To Bank A/c– Remittance to *A*	15,000	Mar. 15	By Bank A/c Sales: 315 × 20	6,300
Apr. 30	To Commission A/c	3,600	Apr. 1	By Bank A/c– Sales: 250 × 80	20,000
Apr. 30	To Profit and Loss A/c– Share of Profit	1,985			
Apr. 30	To Bank A/c– Remittance to *A*	14,345			
		36,000			36,000

N.B. The amount due from *B i.e.* Rs 14,345 is equal to the amount due to *A i.e.* Rs 14,345.

ILLUSTRATION 14.12

A and *B* enter into a joint venture as dealers in land with effect from 1st July 2005. On the same day *A* advanced Rs 90,000 and a plot of land, measuring 9,000 sq. yards, was purchased with this money. It was decided to sell the land in smaller plots and a plan was got prepared at a cost of Rs 1,000 paid by *B*. In the said plan 1/3rd of the total area of the land was left over for public roads and the remaining land was divided into 6 plots of equal size. On 1st October 2005, two of the plots were sold at Rs 30 per sq. yard, the buyer deducting Rs 1,000 per plot for stamp duty and registration expenses to be borne by the seller. The remaining plots were sold at net price of Rs 25 per sq. yard on 1st December 2005. The sale proceeds of all the plots were received by *A*. After charging interest at 6% p.a. on the investments of *A* (allowing for money received by him) and allowed 1% on the net sale proceeds of plots as commission to *B*, the net profit of the joint venture is to be shared in the proportion of 3/4th to *A* and 1/4th to *B*.

Draw up the memorandum joint venture revenue account and personal accounts in the books of *A* and *B* showing the balance payable by one to the other. Assume joint venture was completed on December 31.

(*B.Com., Delhi*)

SOLUTION

In the books of A

Joint Venture with B Account

Dr. Cr.

		Rs				Rs
2005			2005			
July 1	To Cash A/c–Advance	90,000.00	Oct. 1	By Cash A/c		
Dec. 31	To Interest A/c (1)	2,250.00		(2,000 × 30)	60,000	
Dec. 31	To Profit and Loss A/c (A)	47,812.50		Less: Expenses	2,000	58,000
Dec. 31	To Bank A/c		Dec. 1	By Cash A/c		
	–Final Settlement	18,517.50		(4,000 × 25)		1,00,000
			Dec. 1	By Interest A/c (2)		580
		1,58,580.00				1,58,580

(1) Interest receivable by *A*: 1st July to 1st Dec.: Rs $\frac{90,000 \times 6 \times 5}{100 \times 12}$ = Rs 2,250

(2) Interest payable by *A*: 1st Oct. to 1st Dec.: Rs $\frac{58,000 \times 6 \times 2}{100 \times 12}$ = Rs 580

In the books of B

Joint Venture with A Account

Dr. Cr.

		Rs			*Rs*
2005			2005		
July 1	To Cash A/c–Expenses	1,000.00	Dec. 31	By Cash A/c–	
Dec. 31	To Commission A/c			Final Settlement	18,517.50
	(1% of 1,58,000)	1,580.00			
Dec. 31	To Profit and Loss A/c–(*B*)	15,937.50			
		18,517.50			18,517.50

Memorandum Joint Venture Account

Dr. Cr.

		Rs				*Rs*
2005			2005			
July 1	To Purchases A/c-*A*	90,000	Oct. 1	By Sales A/c		
Dec. 1	To Interest A/c–*A*	2,250		2,000 × 30 =	60,000	
	To Expenses A/c–*B*	1,000		4,000 × 25 =	1,00,000	
	To Commission A/c–*B*	1,580			1,60,000	

Profits:			Less: Expenses	2,000	1,58,000
A–	47,812.50		By Interest A/c–*A*		580
B–	15,937.50	63,750			
		1,58,580			1,58,580

ILLUSTRATION 16.13

Das and Roy entered into a joint venture involving buying and selling old railway material. The profit or loss was to be shared equally. Cost of the material purchased was Rs. 42,500 which was paid by Das who drew a bill on Roy at 2 months' demand for Rs. 30,000. The bills was discounted by Das at a cost of Rs. 240.

The transactions relating to the venture were (*a*) Das paid Rs. 300 for carriage, Rs. 500 for Commission on sales and Rs. 200 travelling expenses; (*b*) Roy paid Rs. 100 travelling expenses and Rs. 150 sundry expenses; (*c*) Sales made by Das amounted to Rs 20,000 and (*d*) Sales made by Roy were Rs. 30,000.

Goods costing Rs. 1,000 and Rs. 1,500 (being unsold stock) were retained by Das and Roy respectively and these were charged to them at prices to show the same rate of gross profit as that made on the total sales (excluding these sales). Das was credited with a sum of Rs. 400 to cover the cost of warehousing and insurance. The expenses in connection with the bill were to be treated as a charge against the venture.

You are required (*a*) to show the account in the books of each party to record his own transactions and (*b*) to prepare a joint venture account. (*B.Com MS*)

SOLUTION

Dr. **Memorandum Joint Venture Account** Cr.

Particulars	*Rs*	*Particulars*	*Rs*
To Das A/c:		By Das A/c :	
Cost of Materials	42,500	Sales proceeds	20,000
Discount on B/R	240	Goods taken over (1)	1,250
Carriage	300	By Roy A/c:	
Commission	500	Sales proceeds	30,000
Travelling Expenses	200	Goods taken over (1)	1,875
Warehousing & Insurance	400		
To Roy A/c:			
Travelling expenses	100		
Sundry expenses	150		
To Profit transferred to :			
Das A/c: $8{,}735 \times \frac{1}{2} = 4{,}368$			
Roy A/c: $8{,}735 \times \frac{1}{2} = 4{,}367$	8,735		
	53,125		53,125

In the books of Roy

Joint Venture with Das A/c

Particulars	*Rs*	*Particulars*	*Rs*
To Bills Payable A/c	30,000	By Bank A/c (Sales proceeds)	30,000
To Bank A/c (Travelling exp.)	100	By Purchases A/c (1)	
To Bank A/c (Sundry exp.)	150	(Goods taken over)	1,875
To P & L A/c (Share of profit)	4,367	By Balance (due from Das) c/d	2,742
	34,617		34,617

In the books of Das

Joint Venture with Roy A/c

Particulars	*Rs*	*Particulars*	*Rs*
To Bank (Materials purchased)	42,500	By Bills Receivable A/c	30,000
To Discount on B/R A/c	240	By Bank A/c (Sales proceeds)	20,000
To Bank A/c (Carriage)	300	By Purchases A/c (1)	
To Bank A/c (Commission on sales)	500	(goods taken over)	1,250
To Bank A/c (Travelling exp.)	200		
To Bank A/c (Warehousing etc.)	400		
To P & L A/c (Share of profit)	4,368		
To Balance (due to Roy) c/d	2,742		
	51,250		51,250

Working Notes:

Computation of Gross Profit Percentage:

	Rs.
Purchases	42,500
Less : Unsold Stock (1,000 + 1,500)	2,500
Cost of goods sold	40,000
Sales (20,000 + 30,000)	50,000
Gross Profit	10,000

$$\text{Percentage of Gross profit} = \frac{10,000}{40,000} \times 100 = 25\% \text{ on Cost.}$$

(1) Computation of price at which unsold materials are taken over:

	Das *Rs.*	*Roy* *Rs*
Cost of materials	1,000	1,500
Add : Gross Profit:		
25% on Cost	250	375
	1,250	1,875

ILLUSTRATION 16.14

Ghosh and Bose enter into a joint venture for guaranteeing the subscription at par of 1,00,000 shares of Rs. 10 each of a joint stock company. They agree to share profits and losses in the ratio of 1 : 3. The terms with the company are $4\frac{1}{2}\%$ Commission in cash and 6,000 shares of the company to be allotted as fully paid up.

The public take up 94,000 of the shares and the balance shares of guaranteed issue are taken up by Ghose and Bose who provide cash equally. The commission in cash is taken by the partners in the ratio of 4 : 5.

The entire shareholding of the venture is then sold through brokers, 25% at a price of Rs. 9, 50% at a price of Rs. 8.75, 15% at a price of Rs. 8.50 and remaining 10% are taken over by Ghosh and Bose equally at Rs. 8 per share. The sale proceeds of the shares are taken by the partners equally.

Prepare a Joint Venture Memorandum A/c and the separate accounts in the books of Ghosh and Bose.

(*B.Com., Hons. Kolkata*)

SOLUTION

Dr. **Memorandum Joint Venture Account** Cr.

Particulars	Rs	Particulars	Rs
To Ghosh A/c :		By Ghosh A/c :	
Cost of Shares $6,000 \times 10 \times \frac{1}{2}$	30,000	Commission	20,000
To Bose A/c:		Sale of shares (3)	47,400
Cost of Shares $6,000 \times 10 \times \frac{1}{2}$	30,000	Unsold shares taken over (4)	4,800
To Profit transferred to :		By Bose A/c:	
Ghosh : $89,400 \times \frac{1}{4} = 22,350$		Commission	25,000
Bose: $89,400 \times \frac{3}{4} = 67,050$	89,400	Sale of shares (3)	47,400
		Unsold shares taken over (4)	4,800
	1,49,400		1,49,400

In the books of Ghosh
Joint Venture with Bose A/c

Particulars	Rs	Particulars	Rs
To Bank A/c (Contribution for unsubscribed shares : 3000 × 10)	30,000	By Bank A/c (Commission in Cash : $45,000 \times \frac{4}{9}$)	20,000
To P & L (Share of profit)	22,350	By Bank A/c (Sale of shares : $94,800 \times \frac{1}{2}$)	47,400
To Balance (due to Bose) c/d	19,850	By Shares A/c (unsold shares taken over: (600 shares × 8)]	4,800
	72,200		72,200

In the Books of Bose
Joint Venture with Ghosh A/c

Particulars	Rs	Particulars	Rs
To Bank A/c (Contribution for unsubscribed Shares)	30,000	By Bank A/c (Commission in Cash : $45,000 \times \frac{5}{9}$)	25,000
To P & L A/c (Share of Profit)	67,050	By Bank A/c (Sale of Shares : $94,800 \times \frac{1}{2}$)	47,400
		By Shares A/c (Unsold shares taken over 600 × 8)	4,800
		By Balance (due from Ghose) c/d	19,850
	97,050		97,050

Working Notes:

(i) No. of Shares to be subscribed by Co-venturers

$$= (1,00,000 - 94,000) = 6,000 \text{ shares}$$

(ii) Calculation of Commission received in Cash:

$$= 1,00,000 \times 10 \times 4\frac{1}{2}\% = \text{Rs. } 45,000$$

3. ***Calculation of Value of shares sold:***

No. of shares at the disposal of the Co-venturers:

Shares subscribed	6,000
Shares received as Commission	6,000
	12,000
	Rs.
25% of 12,000 or 3,000 shares @ Rs. 9	= 27,000
50% of 12,000 or 6,000 shares @ Rs. 8.75	= 52,500
15% of 12,000 or 1,800 shares @ Rs. 8.50	= 15,300
Total Sale Proceeds	94,800

$$\text{Ghose}: 94,800 \times \frac{1}{2} = 47,400; \ \text{Bose}: 94,800 \times \frac{1}{2} = 47,400$$

4. Calculation value of unsold shares taken over by Ghosh and Bose:

10% of 12,000 or 1,200 shares equally @ Rs. 8 per share = Rs. 9,600

$$\text{Ghosh}: 9,600 \times \frac{1}{2} = 4,800; \ \text{Bose}: 9,600 \times \frac{1}{2} = 4,800$$

Recording in One of the Party's Books

ILLUSTRATION 16.15

Anup, Rakesh and Jaipal entered into an agreement for a joint venture. Anup bought goods for Rs. 14,400 and took from his stock goods valued at 4,800. He received from Rakesh and Jaipal their shares of investment in the adventure, Rs. 6,400 each. Anup paid charges and expenses of Rs. 1,460. The gooods were sold for Rs. 24,400. Anup charged 5% commission on sales and rendered statement to Rakesh and Jaipal.

Journalise the above transactions in the books of Anup. (*B.Com. MK*)

SOLUTION

In the books of Anup

			Dr. *Rs*	Cr. *Rs*
	Cash Account	Dr.	12,800	
	To Rakesh			6,400
	To Jaipal			6,400
	(Being cash received from other co-venturers)			
	Joint Venture A/c	Dr.	14,400	
	To Cash A/c			14,400
	(Being goods purchased)			
	Joint Venture A/c	Dr.	4,800	
	To Purchase A/c			4,800
	(Goods taken from stock)			
	Joint Venture A/c	Dr.	1,460	
	To Cash A/c			1,460
	(Being charges & expenses)			

Cash Account	Dr.	24,400	
To Joint Venture A/c			24,400
(Goods sold)			
Joint Venture A/c	Dr.	1,220	
To Commission A/c			1,220
(Commission charged)			
Joint Venture A/c	Dr.	2,520	
To Rakesh			840
To Jaipal			840
To P & L A/c			840
(Being the division of profits)			
Rakesh Account	Dr.	7,240	
Jaipal Account	Dr.	7,240	
To Bank Account			14,480
(Amount paid to them)			

Joint Venture Account

Dr.	Rs		Cr. Rs
To Cash–Purchase	14,400	By Cash–Sales	24,400
To Purchase–Transfer	4,800		
To Cash–Expenses	1,460		
To Commission	1,220		
To Profit:			
Profit & Loss A/c	840		
Rakesh A/c	840		
Jaipal A/c	840		
	24,400		24,400

Rakesh Account

Dr.	Rs		Cr. Rs
To Bank A/c	7,240	By Cash	6,400
		By Joint Venture (Profit)	840
	7,240		7,240

Jaipal Account

Dr.	Rs		Cr. Rs
To Bank A/c	7,240	By Cash	6,400
		By Joint Venture (Profit)	840
	7,240		7,240

ILLUSTRATION 16.16

A and *B* entered into a Joint Venture for purchase and sale of jute. They agreed to share profits in the proportion of 2 · 1 and also to be entitled to an interest of 6% p.a. (on monthly basis) on capital invested by each of them. The following transactions took place in between themselves:

1. On June 1, *A* purchased 1,400 bales of jute @ Rs 55 per bale, the brokerage being Rs 2 per bale.

2. On July 1, *B* purchased 1,200 bales of jute @ Rs 62 per bale, the brokerage being Rs 2 per bale.
3. On August 1, *B* sold 700 bales of jute @ Rs 69 per bale, the brokerage being Re 1 per bale and took the proceeds to himself.
4. On August 15, *A* sold 1,600 bales of jute @ Rs 66 per bale, brokerage @ Re 1 per bale and took the sale proceeds to himself.

It was also agreed that each of the partners will at first sell from his own purchase and then, if required, from the stock purchased by the other one. The balance of stock was to be divided between the partners in proportion of their profit sharing ratio–the goods being valued at cost to the partner concerned.

On August 31, the partners settled their accounts. Prepare necessary accounts assuming a separate set of books is opened. (*CA Inter*)

SOLUTION

Dr. **Joint Venture Account** Cr.

			Rs				Rs
June 1	To *A* A/c:			Aug. 1	By *B* A/c:		
	Purchase 1400 @ 55	77,000			Sales	48,300	
	Add: Brokerage	2,800	79,800		Less: Brokerage	700	47,600
July	To *B* A/c:				By *A* A/c:		
	Purchase 1200 @ 62	74,400			Sales	1,05,600	
	Add: Brokerage	2,400	76,800		Less: Brokerage	1,600	1,04,000
Aug. 31	To *A* A/c				By *A* A/c		
	Interest on Capital Invested		998		Stock taken over		12,800
Aug. 31	To *B* A/c				By *B* A/c		
	Interest on Capital		530		Stock taken over		6,400
Aug. 31	To Profit transferred to:						
	A A/c (2/3)	8,448					
	B A/c (1/3)	4,224	12,672				
			1,70,800				1,70,800

Dr. **Co-Venturers Account** Cr.

		A	*B*			*A*	*B*
		Rs	*Rs*			*Rs*	*Rs*
Aug. 1	To Joint Venture A/c			June 1	By Joint Venture A/c		
	Sales less brokerage		47,600		Purchases and brokerage	79,800	
Aug. 15	To Joint Venture A/c				By Joint Venture A/c		
	Sales less brokerage	1,04,000			Purchases and brokerage		76,800
Aug. 31	To Joint Venture A/c				By Joint Venture A/c		
	Stock taken over	12,800	6,400		Interest on Capital	998	530
Aug. 31	To Bank A/c				By Joint Venture A/c		
	(A)		27,554		Profit	8,448	4,224
					By Bank A/c		
					(*B*)	27,554	
		1,16,800	81,554			1,16,800	81,554

Interest Calculation:

For *A*:

Interest for Rs 76,800 for 2½ months *i.e.* from 1st June to 15th Aug. @ 6% p.a.

$$\frac{\text{Rs } 79{,}800 \times 2\tfrac{1}{2} \times 6}{12 \times 100} = \text{Rs } 998$$

For B:

Interest for Rs 76,800 for one month *i.e.* from 1st July to 1st Aug. @ 6% p.a.

$$\frac{\text{Rs } 76{,}800 \times 1 \times 6}{12 \times 100} = \text{Rs } 384$$

Interest for Rs 29,200 (76,800 – 47,600) for one month *i.e.* 1st Aug. to 31st Aug. @ 6% p.a.

$$\frac{\text{Rs } 29{,}200 \times 1 \times 6}{12 \times 100} = \text{Rs } 146$$

Total = Rs 530

Stock taken over by *A* and *B*:

Unsold stock = 300 bales, out of B's purchase

Value of one bale = Rs 62 + Rs 2 = Rs 64

$$A \text{ takes } 2/3 \text{ of } 300 \text{ bales} = \frac{300 \times 2 \times 64}{3} = \text{Rs } 12{,}800$$

$$B \text{ takes } 1/3 \text{ of } 300 \text{ bales} = \frac{300 \times 1 \times 64}{3} = \text{Rs } 6{,}400$$

Consignment-cum-Joint Venture

Sometimes, the consignee is not satisfied simply by taking the commission as an agent of the consignor. He wants to take part in profit instead of commission. The relationship between the consignor and consignee may be changed into the relation of co-venturers. The conversion from consignment to joint venture may be made: (*i*) from a particular date with prospective effect and (*ii*) with retrospective effect.

Procedure for Prospective Conversion

(*i*) Open Consignment Account and Consignee's Account in the usual manner and ascertain the profit or loss so made which is to be transferred to Profit and Loss account up to the date of conversion. And also ascertain the Consignee's balance of account to the date of conversion.

(*ii*) Open Joint Venture Account by taking up the stock on consignment in the usual manner and ascertain the profit or loss which is to be shared between the parties.

(*iii*) Open also Consignee's account by taking up the balance and record all the transactions relating to Joint venture as we usually do.

(*iv*) Settle the Accounts.

ILLUSTRATION 16.17 (Consignment-com-Joint Venture)

Mr. Menon sent goods to Mr Gupta to be sold on consignment basis @ 5% commission. Goods costing Rs 4,00,000 were sent and Rs 40,000 expenses were incurred. Mr Gupta had to incur Rs 10,000 expenses for landing and 75% of the goods were sold out for Rs 4,80,000. Mr Gupta sent the amount due from him with the Account sale but wanted to return the balance goods as he was not agreeable to carry on as a commission agent. He was, however, persuaded to continue on joint venture basis. For one-third profit, Rs 2,00,000 worth of goods were further despatched by Mr Menon. All the goods, except Rs 20,000 which were taken over by Mr Gupta for the same amount, were sold out for Rs 5,00,000. Mr. Menon incurred Rs 20,000 expenses and expenses of Mr. Gupta amounted to Rs 17,000.

Show the necessary accounts in the books of both the parties. (*ICWA*)

SOLUTION

In the books of Menon

Consignment to Gupta Account

Dr.	Rs		Cr. Rs
To Goods sent on Consignment Account	4,00,000	By Gupta Account–Sale Proceeds	4,80,000
To Bank Account–Expenses	40,000	By Stock on consignment	
To Gupta Account–Landing Charges	10,000	(Rs 1,00,000 + Rs 12,500)	1,12,500
To Gupta Account–Commission	24,000		
To Profit on Consignment–Transferred to Profit and Loss Account	1,18,500		
	5,92,500		5,92,500

Joint Venture with Gupta Account

Dr.		Rs		Cr. Rs
To Consignment to Gupta Account		1,12,500	By Gupta Account–Sales Proceeds	5,00,000
To Goods Supplied Account		2,00,000	By Gupta Account–Goods Taken Over	20,000
To Expenses		20,000		
To Gupta Account–Expenses		17,000		
To Profit on Joint Venture Transferred to Profit and Loss Account 2/3	1,13,667			
Gupta Account 1/3	56,833	1,70,500		
		5,20,000		5,20,000

Gupta Account

Dr.	Rs			Cr. Rs
To Consignment to Gupta Account–Sale Proceeds	4,80,000	By Consignment to Gupta Account:		
		Expenses	10,000	
		Commission	24,000	34,000
		By Bank Account–Remittance		4,46,000
	4,80,000			4,80,000
To Joint Venture Account–Sale Proceeds	5,00,000	By Joint Venture Account–Expenses		17,000
To Joint Venture Account–Goods Taken Over	20,000	By Joint Venture Account –Share of Profit		56,833
		By Bank Account–Remittance		4,46,167
	5,20,000			5,20,000

In the Books of Gupta

Joint Venture with Menon Account

Dr.		Rs		Cr. Rs
To Menon Account			By Bank Account–Sales Proceeds	5,00,000
Stock on Consignment	1,12,500		By Goods Taken over	20,000
Goods Supplied	2,00,000			
Expenses	20,000	3,32,500		
To Bank Account–Expenses		17,000		
To Profit on Joint Venture				

Transferred to:					
Profit and Loss Account	56,833				
Menon Account	1,13,667	1,70,500			
		5,20,000			5,20,000

Dr. **Sri Menon Account** Cr.

		Rs			Rs
To Landing Charges		10,000	By Bank Account–Sale Proceeds		4,80,000
To Commission Account		24,000			
To Bank Account–Remittance		4,46,000			
		4,80,000			4,80,000
To Bank Account–Remittance		4,46,167	By Joint Venture Account–		
			Stock on Consignment	1,12,500	
			Goods Supplied	2,00,000	
			Expenses	20,000	
			Share of Profit	1,13,667	4,46,167
		4,46,167			4,46,167

ILLUSTRATION 16.18

Aswin of Madras and Gupta of Delhi entered into a joint venture on 1.4.2006 for the purpose of buying second-hand cars for reconditioning and selling them as airconditioned diesel cars. Aswin agreed to buy second-hand cars and recondition them and fit diesel engines. Gupta agreed to fix airconditioners and sell them at Delhi. They agreed to share the profits and losses equally and settle their accounts at the end of each year.

The following are the details of purchase, sale and expenses incurred by Aswin and Gupta during the year 1.4.2006 to 31.3.2007:

Particulars	*Aswin (Rs.)*	*Gupta (Rs.)*	*Particulars*	*Aswin (Rs)*	*Gupta (Rs)*
Cost of 10 cars	5,00,000	—	Expenses incurred :		
Reconditioning expenditure	45,000	—	Freight—local	10,000	8,000
Cost of 10 diesel engines	30,000	—	Freight—Delhi	30,000	—
Labour charges	18,000	32,000	Rent—Office	10,000	10,000
8 Airconditioners purchased	—	4,00,000	Rent—Garage	12,000	20,000
Buying commission @ 5%	25,000	—	Insurance	16,000	20,000
Selling commission @ 5%	—	60,000	Miscellaneous expenses	6,000	10,000
Sale value of 8 cars	—	12,00,000			

Gupta sent a cheque for Rs. 6,00,000 to Aswin on 1.3.2007. Of the balance of 2 cars, one car was involved in an accident on the way to garage before reconditioning and the insurance company settled the claim at Rs. 30,000 as a total loss. The old petrol engines were sold @ Rs. 500 per engine and one diesel engine was sold at Rs. 3,000 by Aswin. All of them were sold before 31.3.2007. Aswin retained the balance one car as a non-airconditioned diesel car for his personal use which was priced at the average cost.

Aswin/Gupta settled the balance due to/by them as on 31.3.2007 by sending a crossed cheque as the case may be. Prepare : (*a*) Memorandum Joint Venture Account; (*b*) Joint Venture Account with Gupta in the books of Aswin; and (*c*) Joint Venture Account with Aswin in the books of Gupta.

[(*C.A. Foundation*)]

SOLUTION

(A)

Dr. **Memorandum Joint Venture Account** Cr.

Date	Particulars	Rs	Date	Particulars	Rs
	To Aswin:			By Aswin:	
	Cost of 10 cars	5,00,000		Sale of 9 petrol engines	4,500
	Reconditioning expenditure	45,000		Sale of 1 diesel engire	3,000
	Cost of 10 diesel engines	30,000		Insurance claim received	30,000
	Labour charges	18,000		Cost of car taken over	
	Freight charges (local)	10,000		(See Note)	68,211
	Freight charges (Delhi)	30,000		By Gupta :	
	Office rent	10,000		Sale of 8 cars	12,00,000
	Garage rent	12,000			
	Commission (buying)	25,000			
	Insurance	16,000			
	Miscellaneous expenses	6,000			
	To Gupta :				
	Labour charges	32,000			
	Cost of 8 airconditioners	4,00,000			
	Freight charges (local)	8,000			
	Office rent	10,000			
	Garage rent	20,000			
	Commission (selling)	60,000			
	Insurance	20,000			
	Miscellaneous expenses	10,000			
	To Profit on Venture:				
	Aswin	21,856			
	Gupta	21,855			
		13,05,711			13,05,711

(B) **In the books of Aswin**

Dr. **Joint Venture with Gupta Account** Cr.

Date	Particulars	Rs	Date	Particulars	Rs
2007	To Bank A/c		2007	By Bank A/c–Advance	
Mar 31	Cost of 10 cars	5,00,000		from Gupta	6,00,000
	Cost of 10 diesel engines	30,000	Mar 1	By Bank A/c–Sale of 9	
	Reconditioning expenses	45,000		petrol engines	4,500
	Labour charges	18,000	Mar 31	Sale of 1 diesel engine	3,000
	Freight charges (local)	10,000		Insurance claim received	30,000
	Freight charges (Delhi)	30,000		By Motor car taken over	68,211
	Office rent	10,000		By Bank A/c–	
	Garage rent	12,000		Balance received	18,145
	Commission (buying)	25,000			
	Insurance	16,000			
	Miscellsanous expenses	6,000			
	To Profit and Loss A/c–				
	Share of Profit	21,856			
		7,23,856			7,23,856

(C) **In the books of Gupta**

Joint Venture with Aswin Account

Dr. Cr.

Date	Particulars	Rs	Date	Particulars	Rs
2007	To Bank A/c–		2007		
	Advance made to Aswin	6,00,000	Mar 31	By Bank A/c–Sale of 8 cars	12,00,000
Mar 1	To Bank A/c–Cost of				
	airconditioning	4,00,000			
	Labour charges	32,000			
	Freight charges (local)	8,000			
	Office rent	10,000			
	Garage rent	20,000			
	Commission (selling)	60,000			
	Insurance	20,000			
	Miscellaneous expenses	10,000			
	To Profit and Loss A/c–				
	Share of Profit	21,855			
	To Bank A/c–Balance paid	18,145			
		12,00,000			12,00,000

Workings :

(1)

Cost of one car (Rs. 5,00,000 ÷ 10)	Rs. 50,000
Reconditioning Expenses : Rs. 45,000 ÷ 9 =	5,000
Cost of Diesel engine	3,000
Labour charges	2,000
Freight charges	1,000
Commission	2,500
Office Rent	1,111
Garage Rent	1,333
Insurance charges	1,600
Miscellaneous expenses	667
	Rs. 68,211

(2) It is assumed that :

(*a*) Insurance is for all the cars.

(*b*) Insurance claim has been received.

(*c*) Freight were for all 10 cars.

(*d*) Delhi freight may be ignored.

QUESTIONS

Objective Type Questions.

I. State whether each of the following statements is "True" or "False":

1. Principle of 'mutual agency' is applicable in case of joint venture.
2. A Joint Venture business has an indefinite life.
3. Joint venture is the same as a particular partnership.
4. Profit or loss of a joint venture business is ascertained after the completion of the venture.
5. A 'Memorandum Joint Venture Account' does not show profit or loss on a venture.
6. The accounts of co-venturers are only personal accounts.
7. Joint bank account becomes necessary when separate set of books are maintained for each venture.
8. Joint venture account is a real account.

9. A co-venturer works on commission basis.
10. Persons agreeing to participate in a joint venture business are termed as co-venturers.

(**Ans :** 1. True; 2. False; 3. True; 4. True; 5. False; 6. True; 7. True; 8. False; 9. False; 10. True.

II. Fill in the blanks:

1. Joint Venture is a Temporary Partnership without a ....
2. Joint venture is a .... account.
3. The parties to a joint venture are generally known as ....
4. Joint venture arises as a result of an .... entered into between two or more parties.
5. Memorandum joint venture account is a .... account.
6. Capital accounts of the co-ventures are of the nature of .... account.
7. Profit or loss on joint venture is shared by the co-venture as per the ....
8. Discount received from creditors should be credited to .... account.

(**Ans.** 1. Name; 2. Nominal; 3. Co-venturers; 4. Agreement; 5. Nominal; 6. Personal; 7. Agreement; 8. Joint venture.

III. Choose the correct answer for each of the following :

1. Joint Venture Account is:
   (*a*) A Personal Account. (*b*) A Real Account.
   (*c*) A Nominal Account.
2. Memorandum Joint Venture Account is:
   (*a*) A Nominal Account. (*b*) A Real Account
   (*c*) A Personal Account.
3. Profit and Loss on Joint Venture is shared by the co-venturers:
   (*a*) Equally. (*b*) In the Capital Ratio.
   (*c*) As per the agreement.
4. When goods are purchased for the Joint Venture, the amount is debited to :
   (*a*) Purchase Account. (*b*) Joint Venture Account.
   (*c*) Venturer's Capital Account.
5. When a venturer recording the transactions brings goods to the joint venture from his own stock, the amount is credited to :
   (*a*) Joint Venture Account. (*b*) Purchase Account.
   (*c*) Capital Account.

(**Ans:** 1. (*c*); 2. (*a*); 3. (*c*); 4. (*b*); 5. (*b*)

THEORETICAL QUESTIONS

1. Define Joint Venture.
2. Distinguish Joint Venture from Partnership Firm.
3. How does a Joint Venture differ from Consignment?
4. What is Memorandum Joint Venture Account?
5. What are the different methods adopted for recording the transactions of Joint Venture?

PRACTICAL PROBLEMS

No Separate Books

1. *A* and *B* entered into a Joint Venture for the purchase and sale of an old house. They purchased one old house for an amount of Rs 30,000, each contributing Rs 15,000. *A* had to manage the disposal of the property. Since he was unable to sell the property as a whole, he decided to demolish the house and sell the property piece by piece. He sold the doors, windows and other wooden fittings to the extent of Rs 12,000. The iron materials were sold at Rs 4,000. He could secure an amount of Rs 2,300 through the sale of other miscellaneous items in the building. He spent an amount of Rs 1,400 for demolishing

the house. He also paid certain sundry expenses Rs 350 in this connection. The site of building was sold at Rs 25,000. Both the parties shared the profits to the extent of *A* 2/3 and *B* 1/3. A paid his share by cheque.

Journalise the abovementioned transactions and prepare a Joint Venture Account and *B*'s Account in A's Ledger.

[Ans: Share of Profit: *A* = Rs 7,700 and *B* = Rs 3,850
B receives Rs 18,850]

2. *C* of Calcutta entered into a joint venture with *A* of Amritsar and *M* of Mirzapur on the following arrangements:

   (*a*) *A* would purchase blankets and *M* would purchase carpets, both of whom would send the goods to *C* for sale.

   (*b*) *C* would sell the goods at the best possible price and would send the remittances to *A* and *M* in accordance with their respective dues.

   (*c*) Profits would be shared equally between the parties.

   A purchased 500 blankets at Rs 50 each and spent Rs 600 for freight etc. *M* purchased 100 carpets at Rs 350 each and spent Rs 800 for freight, etc.

   C sold all the blankets and carpets at Rs 75,000 and his expenses amounted to Rs 1,600.

   Show the Joint Venture Account and the Co-venturer's Accounts in the books of *C*. (*I.C.W.A*)

   [Ans: Profit Rs 4,000 each.
   A receives Rs 29,600 and *B* receives Rs 39,800]

3. *A* of Ahmedabad and *B* of Mumbai enter into a joint venture to consign 100 bales of *C* at Kolkata to be sold on their joint account. They agreed to share profits or losses equally.

   A sent 50 bales valued at Rs 60,000 and pays freight and expenses Rs 1,200. *B* sent 50 bales valued at Rs 55,000 and pays expenses Rs 900.

   All the bales reached Kolkata in time. However, 5 bales were found to have been tampered with during the transit. *A* recovered Rs 3,000 from the insurance company. *C* sold the remaining bales for Rs 1,35,000. He charged 3% as selling commission and deducted Rs 1,500 towards expenses.

   He remitted the balance amount to *A* by D/D on State Bank of India payable at Ahmedabad.

   Record the above transactions in the books of *A* and *B*. (*Institute of Bankers'*)

   [Ans: Share of Profit: *A* = Rs 7,675 and *B* = Rs 7,675.
   C pays *A* Rs 1,29,450]

4. *A* of Bangalore and *B* of Madras entered into a joint venture for purchase and sale of novelty goods. *A* agreed to finance the venture and *B* to undertake the sale of goods on a commission of 7% on gross sales. Both agreed to share profits and losses in the proportion of 3 : 2.

   A had incurred an expenditure of Rs 40,000 for the purchase of goods and also gave an amount of Rs 1,600 to *B* for meeting the selling expenses. *B* actually incurred an expenditure of Rs 1,200 for Carriage and Insurance. In addition, he also spent an amount of Rs 2,100 for selling the goods. He sold all the goods for Rs 47,000. Both the parties settled their accounts.

   Write up necessary Ledger Accounts in the books of both the parties for their Joint Venture.

   [Ans: Share of Profit: *A*—Rs 246, *B*—Rs 164. *B* pays to *A* Rs–41,846]

5. Mohan and Nathan enter into a Joint Venture for the purchase and sale of second-hand scooters, and to share profits and losses in the ratio of 3 : 2.

   On 15th January, Mohan bought five scooters for Rs 43,000 and on 20th January, he paid taxes and insurance Rs 1,600. On 31st January, he sold these scooters for Rs 58,000 out of which he remitted Rs 11,000 to Nathan, paying the balance into his own bank account.

   On 20th January, Nathan bought three scooters for Rs 36,000 and on 25th January, he paid taxes and inurance Rs 1,400 and repairing charges amounting to Rs 2,000. He sold one scooter on 2nd February for Rs 14,000 which he paid into his own bank account. Mohan then took over the other scooters at a valuation of Rs 26,000, and the venture was closed on 10th February.

Prepare the Memorandum Joint Venture and the Account of the Joint Venture with Nathan in the books of Mohan. *(B.Com., Calcutta)*

[Ans: Profit Rs 8,400 (Mohan)
Rs 5,600 (Nathan)]

6. *A*, *B* and *C* enter into a Joint Venture to share the profits and losses at 5 : 3 : 2. No separate set of books is maintained. Amounts contributed and received by different ventures are given below:

	A	*B*	*C*
	Rs	Rs	Rs
Cost of Materials	40,000	20,000	–
Expenses	6,000	2,000	4,000
Sale proceeds received	–	14,000	80,000
Stock taken over	–	4,000	14,000

Prepare in the books of *A* only, the following accounts:

(*i*) Joint Venture Account

(*ii*) Co-ventures Accounts *(CAIIB)*

[Ans: Profit: *A*—Rs 20,000
B—Rs 12,000
C—Rs 8,000]

7. Sakti and Sadhan agree to enter into a Joint Venture to buy and sell television sets. Profits and losses were to be shared equally.

   On May 5, 2004, Sakti purchased three television sets for Rs 3,000, Rs 3,500 and Rs 4,000 respectively. He bought a special cabinet costing Rs 750, which he fixed for one of the sets. On May 31, he sold two of the sets for Rs 4,000 each paying the proceeds in his private bank account.

   On June 15, 2004, he sold the other set for Rs 4,500 which amount he paid over to Sadhan who paid into his bank account.

   On 6th May, 2004, Sadhan purchased a TV set for Rs 3,000 having incurred expenditure of Rs 200 on repairing, sold it on 14th May, 2004, for Rs 3,800, paying the proceeds into his own bank account. This set developed mechanical trouble and on 20th May, 2004, Sadhan agreed to take the set back at a price of Rs 2,800 which he paid out of his bank account. The set was still unsold on 30 June, 2004, and it was agreed that Sadhan should take it over for his personal use at a valuation of Rs 2,600.

   Sakti incurred Rs 300 as showroom charges and Sadhan incurred Rs 225 as travelling and postage.

   You are required to prepare (a) the account of Joint Venture with Sakti as it would appear in the books of Sadhan, and (b) Memorandum Joint Venture Account showing the net profit. *(ICWA)*

[Ans: Profit Rs 563 (Sakti). Amount paid to Sakti Rs 4,112
Profit Rs 562 (Sadhan)]

8. *A* and *B* enter into a Joint Venture as dealers in land with effect from 1st July. On the same day *A* advanced Rs 90,000 and a plot of land, measuring 9,000 sq. yards, was purchased with this money.

   It was decided to sell the land in smaller plots and a plan was got prepared at the cost of Rs 1,000 paid by *B*. In the said plan 1/3rd of the total area of the land was left over for public roads and the remaining land was divided into 6 plots of equal size. On 1st October, two of the plots were sold at Rs 30 per sq. yard, the buyer deducting Rs 1,000 per plot for stamp duty and the registration expenses to be borne by the buyer. The remaining plots were sold at net price of Rs 25 per sq. yard, on 1st December. The sale proceeds of all the plots were received by *A*. After charging interest at 6% p.a. on the investments of *A* (allowing for money received by him) and allowing 1% on the net sale proceeds of plots as commission to *B*, the net profit of the joint venture is shared in the proportion of 3/4th to *A* and 1/4th to *B*.

Draw up the Memorandum Joint Venture Account and the Personal Account in the books of *A* and *B* showing the balance by one to the other. Assume that the joint venture was completed on 1st December. (*B.Com., Delhi*)

[**Ans:** Profit Rs 47,812.50 (*A*)
Rs 15,937.50 (*B*)
B pays *A* Rs 18,517.50]

9. *A* and *B* entered into joint venture to buy and sell second-hand machinery. Profit and losses were to be shared. *A*—2/3 and *B* 1/3.

   On 18th March, *A* purchased two machines for Rs 7,200 and Rs 8,400. He incurred expenditure of Rs 1,600 on repairs and on 17th April sold one of the machines for Rs 12,000 and on 24th April the other machine for Rs 11,600. He paid Rs 15,000 of the proceeds into his own bank account and paid the balance to *B*.

   On 7th May, *A* purchased further machine for Rs 14,400 which was sold on 24th May for Rs 16,000 less 5% cash discount, the proceed being handed over to *B*.

   On 25th March, *B* purchased a machine for Rs 8,000 on which he incurred expenditure of Rs 1,000 and which he sold on 12th April for Rs 10,400 which he paid into his bank Account. This machine was returned by the purchaser on 20th April and *B* paid him Rs 10,000 for it. As it was still unsold on 31st May, it was agreed that it should be taken over by *A* at a valuation of Rs 9,200.

   On 31st May, the sum required in full settlement as between *A* and *B* was paid by the party accountable.

   You are required to prepare (*a*) Joint Venture Account as it will appear in the books of *A* and (*b*) the Memorandum Account for the joint venture showing the net profit. (*B.Com., Madurai*)

   [**Ans:** Profit Rs 5,200 (*A*)
   Rs 2,600 (*B*)]

10. In March, *A* and *B* enter into a Joint Venture to buy and sell second-hand scooters. They are to share profits and losses as 2 : 1.

    On 16th March, *A* buys two scooters for Rs 4,800 and Rs 7,200 respectively and incurs an expenditure of Rs 1,800 for repairs. On 1st April, he sells one of the scooters for Rs 6,000 and on 10th April, the other scooter, for Rs 9,300. On 12th April, he buys another scooter for Rs 9,000 and sells it on 20th April for Rs 12,000. This amount was paid to *B* who sent it to his own bank account.

    On 12th March, *B* buys a scooter for Rs 6,000 and incurs an expenditure of Rs 600 on it. He sells this scooter for Rs 7,500 on 15th March but it is returned by the customer on 20th March who is allowed Rs 7,200 for it. This scooter was still unsold on 30th April and *A* agreed to take it over at a valuation of Rs 6,750. On 30th April, the amount required to settle accounts between *A* and *B* is paid by the appropriate party.

    Prepare the Joint Venture Account, as it would appear in the books of *A* and also a Memorandum Joint Venture Account showing the net profit or loss resulting from the transactions. (*B.Com., Calcutta*)

    [**Ans:** Profit Rs 3,300 (*A*)
    Rs 1,650 (*B*)
    A receives Rs 4,050]

11. Ram and Gautam entered into a joint venture to buy and sell TV sets on 1st July.

    On 1st July Ram sent a draft for Rs 10,00,000 in favour of Gautam and on 4th July, the latter purchased 200 sets at a cost of Rs 8,000. The sets were sent to Ram by lorry under freight 'to pay' for Rs 8,000 and were cleared by Ram on 15th July.

    Ram effected sales in the following manner:

Date	No. of sets	Selling Price per set	Discount on sale
		Rs	
16th July	20	12,000	10%
31st July	100	11,200	–
15th Aug.	80	10,800	5%

On 25th August, Ram settled the account by sending a draft in favour of Gautam, profits being shared equally. Gautam does not maintain any books. Show in Ram's books:

(*a*) Joint Venture with Gautam Account, and

(*b*) Memorandum Joint Venture Account. (*CA*)

[**Ans:** Profit Rs 2,74,400 each,
Ram sends Gautam Rs 8,74,400]

Separate Books

12. Dilip and Raj are doing business separately as engineering contractors. They undertake jointly to build and instal new machinery for a company for a contract price of Rs 1,34,000–Rs 84,000 payable in instalments in cash and the balance as fully paid shares in the new company. A bank account is opened in joint account, Dilip paying Rs 45,000 and Raj Rs 20,000. They are to share profits and losses in the proportion of 3/5 and 2/5 respectively. Their transactions were as follows:

	Rs
Amount advanced to suppliers for supply of materials	52,000
Value of materials supplied by suppliers	89,000
Balance amount paid to suppliers in full and final settlement	35,500
Paid Wages	36,000
Materials purchased in cash	2,500
Materials supplied by Dilip from stock	9,250
Engineering consultant fees paid	3,250
Value of stock lost by fire and not covered by insurance	3,500

The contract was completed and the price duly received.

Dilip took all the shares at the agreed value of Rs 47,000 and Raj took the balance stock of materials worth Rs 3,500 at an agreed value of Rs 2,750.

Prepare the joint venture account, showing the resultant profit or loss and the accounts of Dilip and Raj and also the Bank Account.

[**Ans:** Share of Loss: Dilip Rs 2,850. Raj Rs 1,900.
Amount paid to Dilip Rs 4,400 and Raj Rs 15,350]

13. Maran, Saran and Maravan entered into a joint venture agreeing to share profits as 6 : 3: 1 respectively. They paid into a Joint Bank Account their contribution amount as follows: Maran Rs 60,000, Saran Rs 40,000 and Maravan Rs 20,000. Purchases paid from Joint Bank Account Rs 1,00,000. Most of the goods were sold for Rs 2,50,000. Maravan took over damaged goods for Rs 1,500. Other expenses were as follows: Carriage paid by Maran Rs 5,200. Rent paid by Saran Rs 2,500 and Maravan paid for advertising Rs 2,000. Prepare the necessary ledger accounts. (*B.Com., Madurai*)

[**Ans:** Total Profit Rs 1,41,800]

14. Gopal and Ahmed undertook jointly to construct a building for a contract price of Rs 3,00,000. A joint banking account was opened by them in their joint names. Gopal paid into it Rs 1,00,000 and Ahmed Rs 50,000. Profit and loss are to be distributed in the ratio of 2 : 1. The details of transactions made are given below:

	Rs
Wages	80,000
Materials purchased	1,60,000
Materials supplied by Gopal	10,000
Materials supplied by Ahmed	8,000
Gopal paid architect's fee	4,000

After the completion of contract, the price was duly received. There was stock of unused materials which was valued at Rs 10,000, and this was taken over by Ahmed. Prepare Joint Venture A/c and Joint Bank A/c. (*CAIIB*)

[**Ans:** Total Profit Rs 48,000
Gopal receives Rs 1,46,000 and Ahmed Rs 64,000]

15. *A* and *B* enter into a joint venture to purchase and develop certain lands as Industrial Estate. For that purpose, a joint bank account was opened wherein *A* deposited Rs 60,000 and *B* deposited Rs 40,000. A piece of land measuring 18,000 sq. yards was purchased at Rs 3 per sq. yard. The following expenses were paid from the joint bank account:

	Rs
Cost of earth filling to level land	14,000
Compensation paid to a hutment dweller for vacating possession	5,000
Municipal taxes	2,000
Cost of barbed-wire fence	3,000
Architect's fees for plans	1,000
Stamp duty and Solicitor's fees	6,000
General expenses	2,000
Income from sale of timber	2,000

It was decided to sell land in smaller plots of 500 sq. yards each. One-sixth of the area was left over for public roads. 10 plots were sold at Rs 12 per sq. yard through the brokers, who were paid 2% brokerage on the sale price of land. *A* retained one plot of land for his personal use at an agreed price of Rs 5,000. The remaining plots were sold at a consolidated price of Rs 76,200 directly. *A* and *B* shared profits and/or losses of the joint venture in the proportion of the amounts invested by them. All transactions have been effected through the bank. Prepare joint venture account, joint bank account and accounts of *A* and *B* assuming that all accounts are settled. (*B.Com., Madras*)

[**Ans:** Total Profit Rs 55,000
A receives Rs 88,000 and B receives Rs 62,000]

16. Ramlal and Shamlal entered into a Joint Venture for purchase and sale of cotton. They agree to share the profits in the proportion of 2 : 1 and also to be entitled to an interest of 6% p.a. (on monthly basis) on capital invested by each of them. The following transactions took place in between themselves:

1. On 1st November Ramlal purchased 700 bales of cotton @ Rs 110 per bale, the brokerage being Rs 4 per bale.
2. On 1st December, Shamlal purchased 600 bales of cotton @ Rs 124 per bale, the brokerage being Rs 4 per bale.
3. On 1st January Shamlal sold 350 bales of cotton @ Rs 138 per bale, the brokerage being Rs 2 per bale and took the sale proceeds to himself.
4. On 15th January, Ramlal sold 800 bales of cotton @ Rs 132 per bale, the brokerage being Rs 2 per bale, and took the sale proceeds to himself.

It was also agreed that each of the partners at first sell from his own purchase and then, if required, from the stock purchased by the other one. The balance of the stock was to be divided between the partners in proportion of their profit sharing ratio, goods being valued at cost to the partners concerned.

On 31st January, the partners settled their accounts. Show the accounts of Ramlal, Shamlal and Joint Venture as would appear when maintained in a separate set of books. (*B.Com., Delhi*)

[**Ans:** Profit Rs 8,489 (Ramlal)
Rs 4,244 (Shamlal)
Shamlal receives Rs 27,574]

17. Chander and Sunder entered into a Joint Venture of one year agreeing to share profits and losses equally after allowing interest on capital at 5% p.a. Chander contributed Rs 30,000 and Sunder Rs 20,000 for which they opened a joint Bank Account. In addition, Chander invested Rs 8,000 on goods.

They purchased from Inder goods for Rs 71,500 and spent Rs 3,800 by way of freight and insurance. At the end of the year the bulk of the goods were sold for Rs 98,740. The remaining goods were taken by Chander for Rs 9,000. Selling expenses were Rs 6,940.

Prepare Joint Venture, Joint Bank Account and also Joint Venture (Investment) Account in the books of Chander and Sunder. (*B.Com., Madurai*)

[**Ans:** Profit Rs 7,300 each]

18. *A*, *B* and *C* enter into a joint venture for the construction of a multi-storied building for a joint stock company for a contract price of Rs 1,00,000.

Incidental expenses might have to be paid by the venturers but as per agreement they are entitled to be reimbursed to the extent of actual such expenditure or Rs 5,000, whichever is less. In this way A spends Rs 4,000; *B* Rs 5,000 and *C* Rs 6,000. The venturers are to share profits and losses equally but C, being a technical person, is entitled to a special commission of 10% of the profit of the venture after charging such commission.

They open a Joint Bank Account to which *A* contributes Rs 20,000, *B* Rs 15,000 and *C* Rs 15,000. *B* also gives his own plant to the venture for which he charges Rs 8,000. Materials are purchased for Rs 20,000 and wages amount to Rs 30,000.

At the end of the venture the company paid the agreed contract price (keeping Rs 10,000 as retention money) to the extent of Rs 30,000 in cash and the balance in equity shares of the company of Rs 10 at an agreed value of Rs 12 per share. The shares are subsequently sold in the market @ Rs 13 per share. Unused materials costing Rs 2,000 are taken over by *A* at Rs 1,000. The plant is taken back by *B* at an agreed value of Rs 2,000. *C* takes up the retention money of Rs 7,000.

Show necessary ledger accounts in the books of the venture. (*B.Com., Bombay*)

[**Ans:** Share of Profit: Rs 10,000 each.
A receives Rs 33,000; *B* receives Rs 36,000 and
C receives Rs 26,000]

19. Anand, Bhagavan and Gupta jointly undertake to construct a theatre building for Kala Bharathi Ltd. at a price of Rs 10,00,000 to be paid as follows:

Rs 8,00,000 in cash by instalments and

Rs 2,00,000 in Debentures of the company.

They have agreed to share the profits and losses equally and contributed Rs 1,20,000, Rs 1,50,000 and Rs 80,000 respectively. These amounts are deposited in a Joint Bank Account.

Anand has got the plans prepared by an architect and paid his fee of Rs 14,000. Bhagavan has brought into venture a concrete mixer of the value of Rs 50,000 while Gupta has bought for the venture a truck of the value of Rs 40,000 and paid the amount from his own funds.

They have purchased a plant for Rs 48,000 and materials worth Rs 4,80,000 and paid Rs 3,90,000 for wages.

On completion of the venture, Anand has taken over unused materials of the value of Rs 28,000. The concrete mixer is taken back by Bhagavan at a valuation of Rs 24,000 while Gupta has taken back the truck at Rs 16,000. The plant is sold as scrap for Rs 12,000.

On the contract price being fully received. Anand has taken over Debentures at an agreed value of Rs 1,40,000.

Show the Joint Venture Account, Joint Bank Account and the Co-venturers' Account. (*B.Com., Madurai, Madras*)

[**Ans:** Loss Rs 667 (*A*)
Rs 667 (*B*)
Rs 666 (*C*)]

Chapter **17**

Fire Insurance Claim Account

Introduction – Loss of Property and Stocks – Average Clause – Loss of Profit – Workmen's Compensation Insurance – Questions – Objective Type Questions – Theoretical Questions – Practical Problems.

The business world is dynamic and full of risks and uncertainties. During the course of running the business, the business is exposed to a number of risks – such as, fire, accident, burglary, etc. Of all these, the risk of fire is very serious. The fire accidents are not uncommon. The assets are gutted partly or wholly. This affects the normal business operations. When a fire breaks out and, in case it goes out of control, the fire destroys property and goods of the business and this causes the business a standstill, which further results in loss of profits too. Therefore, a prudent management, in order to safeguard from the loss due to fire, takes an insurance policy. A businessman can easily transfer the risk to the insurer. Insurance is a contract by which the assurer (Insurance Company), in consideration of the payment of a sum (premium), agrees to pay a specified sum to the insured on the happening of a certain event. The insurer undertakes to indemnify the assured for the loss on the happening of the event. The document specifying the terms of fire insurance is called a *fire insurance policy* and the insured sum of the items is termed the *policy amount*. Loss due to fire are of two types:

(1) Loss of property and stocks, and

(2) Loss of prospective profit in consequence of fire.

LOSS OF PROPERTY AND STOCKS

Procedure: The insured, in the event of fire accident, informs the insurer (Insurance Company) of the loss of property and stocks. The insurance contract is usually for a year and the insurer indemnifies the insured for the loss suffered. In response to the request of the insured, a technical expert is entrusted by the Insurance Company; and the technical expert, after investigation, sends his report by stating the amount payable by the Insurance Company to the insured. His report, after a careful investigation, must reveal the causes due to which the fire broke out and whether the claim is covered by the policy or not.

Claim for Loss of Stock

The values of assets, other than stock, can be ascertained at any time. The stocks, with which he deals, are not maintained daily. Moreover, stock-taking every day is not possible and is a very difficult job. In such a situation, one has to estimate the loss of value of stock on account of fire by preparing a statement or a Memorandum Trading Account. The items that are needed or available are discussed below:

STEP 1. First, try to know the value of opening stock of the year, in which the fire broke out.

STEP 2. To the above (Step 1), add the net purchases made up to the date of fire.

STEP 3. From the result of Step 2, deduct the cost of goods sold.

STEP 4. From the result of Step 3, deduct the salvaged stock; and the figure finally available is the loss of stock due to fire.

The above, put in a statement, appears like this:

	Rs
Stock in the beginning of the accounting year	–
Add: Net Purchases from the beginning of the accounting year to the date of fire	–
Less: Cost of goods sold, from the beginning of the accounting year to the date of fire	–
Value of stock on the date of fire	–
Less: Salvaged stock	–
The value of stock lost on account of outbreak of fire	===

Calculation of Cost of Goods Sold

The cost of goods can be found out in the following ways. Rather, the method of finding out the cost of goods sold depends upon the nature of questions.

(1) When sales figure has been given in the question along with the rate of Gross Profit, then deduct the Gross Profit from the sales in order to get the cost of goods sold. That is:

Sales – Gross Profit = Cost of goods sold

(2) When the rate of Gross Profit on sales is given, then the

$$\text{Gross Profit} = \frac{\text{Sales} \times \text{Rate}}{100}$$

(3) When the rate of Gross Profit on cost is given, Gross Profit is found out on the basis of sales. For instance, Gross Profit is 25% on cost, then the sales rate is 125%. Therefore, the

$$\text{Gross Profit} = \frac{\text{Sales} \times 25}{125}$$

(4) In certain cases, the rate of Gross Profit is not given in the problem. In such a situation, the percentage of Gross Profit on sales earned last year is applied to the current year. Therefore. by preparing a Trading Account of the previous year, the rate of Gross Profit is to be found out. This percentage of Gross Profit is applied to know the estimated Gross Profit in the current year, when the fire occurred.

It is important to note that when calculating the rate of Gross Profit, the abnormal circumstances of sales may be ignored. For instance, products, which were damaged, might have been sold at a low price or products were sold at higher price during over-demanded period. These situations may be ignored when calculating the Gross Profit.

It is also possible that the rate of Gross Profit may show an increased or decreased trend during the previous years – year by year. In such cases, weighted average of these rates can be found out and Gross Profit is estimated on the basis of weighted average.

Loss of stock can also be ascertained instead of Statement (mentioned above), by preparing a Memorandum Trading Account, to the date of fire. This account appears as follows:

Memorandum Trading Account

	Rs		*Rs*
To Opening Stock	–	By Sales	–
To Net Purchases	–	By Closing Stock	–
To Wages	–	(Balancing figure)	
To Gross Profit	–		

Value of stock on hand on date of fire	Rs ...
Less: Salvaged stock, if any	Rs ...
Claim to be lodged:	

ILLUSTRATION 17.1

A fire occurred in the premises on 1.1.2005 and the business books and records were saved. The following information was obtained:

	Rs
Purchases for the year ending 30.6.2004	60,000
Sales for the year ending 30.6.2004	90,000
Purchases from 1.7.2004 to 31.12.2004	35,000
Sales from 1.7.2004 to 31.12.2004	50,000
Stock on 30.6.2004	28,000
Stock on 30.6.2003	40,000

Calculate the amount of claim to be presented to the Insurance Company in respect of the loss by fire.

(B.Com., Karnataka)

SOLUTION

Determination of Gross Profit rate

Trading Account
for the year ended 30th June 2004

Dr. Cr.

	Rs		Rs
To Opening Stock	40,000	By Sales	90,000
To Purchases	60,000	By Closing Stock	28,000
To Gross Profit (20% on Sales)	18,000		
	1,18,000		1,18,000

Memorandum Trading Account
from 1.7.2004 to 31.12.2004 (1.1.2005)

Dr. Cr.

	Rs		Rs
To Opening Stock	28,000	By Sales	50,000
To Purchases	35,000	By Closing Stock (Balancing figure)	23,000
To Gross Profit (20% on Sales)	10,000		
	73,000		73,000

Hence, an amount of Rs 23,000 to be claimed from the Insurance Company.

ILLUSTRATION 17.2

A fire occurred in a small Textile Store on 15th September 2005 and considerable part of the stock was destroyed. The stock was fully insured.

The books disclosed that on Ist January 2005 the stock valued as per their business convention at a 10% above cost was shown in the books at Rs 28,567. The purchases and sales to the date of fire amounted to Rs 57,628 and Rs 93,900 respectively. The stock salvaged was agreed to be worth Rs 3,200.

During the past three years, the average Gross Profit on sales was 36%.

Prepare a statement showing the amount the Textile Stores should claim from the Insurance Company in respect of stock destroyed, assuming that the Textile Stores incurred an expense of Rs 200 to extinguish the fire.

(B.Com., Karnataka, Bombay)

SOLUTION

Memorandum Trading Account
from 1.1.2005 to 15.9.2005

Dr.		Rs		Rs Cr.
To Opening Stock	28,567		By Sales	93,900
Less: Excess:	2,597	25,970	By Closing Stock	23,502
To Purchases		57,628	(Balancing figure)	
To Gross Profit (36% on sales: given)		33,804		
		1,17,402		1,17,402

Statement of claim:

	Rs
Value of Closing stock	23,502
Less: Value of stock salvaged	3,200
	20,302
Add: Expenses incurred to extinguish the fire	200
Total Claim:	20,502

Note: Stock is valued at 10% above the cost. It is to be reduced to the true value. The excess value of 10% on given 110% is to be deducted. The excess value is:

$$\frac{28,567 \times 10}{110} = \text{Rs } 2,597$$

When the Insurance Company **admits** the claim, the following journal entries are passed in the books of the insured:

1. For the value of stock destroyed by fire	Fire Claim Account Dr. To Stock Account
2. When the amount admitted by the Insurance Company	Insurance Company Account Dr. To Fire Claims Account
3. When the money is received	Bank Account Dr. To Insurance Company Account

If there is any balance in the Fire Claims Account, it may be transferred to Profit and Loss Account. That is the amount of loss incurred but not recoverable from Insurance Company.

AVERAGE CLAUSE

In case of under-insurance, the Insurance Company applies the Average Clause. Under-insurance means insuring for lesser value of stock. This is because businessmen think that in case of fire outbreak the complete stock will not be burnt. So, they take insurance policy for partial stock, of course at a lesser premium. In order to discourage under-insurance, generally the Average Clause is inserted by the Insurance Company. If the insured value of the stock is less than the total of stock, then the Average Clause may apply, that is, the loss will be limited to that proportion of the loss as the insured value bears to the total cost. The actual amount of claim is determined by the formula:

$$\text{Claim} = \frac{\text{Loss Suffered} \times \text{Insured Value}}{\text{Total Cost}}$$

The object of such an Average Clause is to limit the liability of the Insurance Company. Both the insurer and the insured then bear the loss in proportion to the covered and uncovered sum. For instance, if Rs 1,00,000 policy is taken for Rs 1,50,000 stocks, then the under-insurance will be by Rs 50,000. Here, the insurer and insured will be the co-insurers for Rs 1,00,000 and Rs 50,000 respectively. When, in such a case, Rs 30,000 stock is lost, then the Insurance Company indemnifies only Rs 20,000 *i.e.* 30,000 × 1,00,000/1,50,000 and the balance Rs 10,000 *i.e.* Rs 30,000 × 50,000/1,50,000 is met by the insured himself. Thus, the under-insurance relieves the insurer and penalises the insured for under-insurance. Irrespective of the insertion of such Clause, the entire policy amount insured, then Insurance Company pays only the amount insured. When the loss is more than the sum insured, the insured can recover the whole amount in spite of Average Clause.

ILLUSTRATION 17.3

Malcom owns a retail stationery shop which was partly destroyed by fire on 27th June 2005. The stock was insured for Rs 13,000.

The Balance Sheet drawn on 31st December 2004 included, inter alia, the following items:

Stock	Rs 12,500
Creditors	Rs 3,500

On examination of the books of account for the subsequent period up to the date of the fire, the following particulars were obtained:

Sales	Rs 88,800
Payment to creditors for goods	Rs 75,000
Creditors as on 27th June 2005	Rs 1,800

A physical check of stock after the fire showed that items undamaged were Rs 7,000.

The normal rate of gross profit is 25% on purchases but the stock on 31st December 2004 included items of discontinued lines totalling Rs 3,800 which were all sold during next two months at cost.

You are required to compute the amount of claim to be made to the insurer. There was an average clause in the policy. *(CA Inter)*

SOLUTION

Purchases from 1.1.2005 to 27.6.2005 has not been given in this problem. It is to be found out by preparing Sundry Creditors Account, as shown below:

Dr. **Sundry Creditors Account** Cr.

	Rs		*Rs*
To Bank	75,000	By Balance b/d	3,500
To Balance c/d	1,800	By Purchases (Balancing figure)	73,300
	76,800		76,800

Dr. **Memorandum Trading Account (1.1.2005 to 27.6.2005)** Cr.

	Normal Items	*Abnormal Items*	*Total*		*Normal Items*	*Abnormal Items*	*Total*
	Rs	Rs	Rs		Rs	Rs	Rs
To Opening Stock	8,700	3,800	12,500	By Sales	85,000	3,800	88,800
To Purchases	73,300	–	73,300	By Closing Stock	14,000	–	14,000
To Gross Profit	17,000	–	17,000	(Balancing figure)			
(25% on purchases or 20% on sales)							
	99,000	3,800	1,02,800		99,000	3,800	1,02,800

	Rs
Value of stock on 27th June 2005	14,000
Less: Undamaged stocks	7,000
Cost of stock destroyed	7,000

Due to application of Average Clause the claim is restricted to : $\frac{7,000 \times 13,000}{14,000}$ = Rs 6,500

ILLUSTRATION 17.4

From the following particulars in respect of Ram Prasad, ascertain the insurance claim with regard to the loss of stock due to a fire accident on 11th May 2005:

1. The Company had the practice of valuing stock at cost less 5%.
2. The value of fire insurance taken was for Rs 2,15,000.
3. The policy was subject to average clause.
4. Stock as on 1.1.2004, Rs 2,85,000.
5. Stock as on 31.12.2004, Rs 3,80,000.
6. Purchases made during the year, Rs 5,20,000.
7. Sales for the year 2004 Rs 6,00,000.
8. Purchases from 1.1.2005 to the date of fire Rs 2,19,000.
9. Sales from 1.1.2005 to the date of fire Rs 2,70,000.
10. Value of stock salvaged Rs 30,000. *(B.Com., Madurai, MK, Bharathiar)*

SOLUTION

Determination of Gross Profit:

Trading Account

Dr. **for the year ended 31st Dec. 2004** Cr.

	Rs		Rs
To Opening Stock	3,00,000	By Sales	6,00,000
(2,85,000 × 100/95)		By Closing Stock	4,00,000
To Purchases	5,20,000	(3,80,000 × 100/95)	
To Gross Profit	1,80,000		
(Balancing figure)			
(30% of sales)			
	10,00,000		10,00,000

Memorandum Trading Account

Dr. **(up to 11th May 2005)** Cr.

	Rs		Rs
To Opening Stock	4,00,000	By Sales	2,70,000
To Purchases	2,19,000	By Closing Stock	4,30,000
To Gross Profit	81,000	(Balancing figure)	
(30% of Sales)			
	7,00,000		7,00,000

	Rs
Value of stock on 11th May 2005	4,30,000
Less: Value of stock salvaged	30,000
Cost of stock destroyed:	4,00,000

$$\text{Insurance Claim} = \text{Stock Destroyed} \times \frac{\text{Policy Amount}}{\text{Value of Stock}}$$

$$= \text{Rs } 4{,}00{,}000 \times \frac{2{,}15{,}000}{4{,}30{,}000} = 2{,}00{,}000$$

LOSS OF PROFIT

The effect of outbreak of fire on a firm not only causes the destruction of properties but also disorganises the business to a stage of dislocation. During the dislocation period, there is a loss of profit which the business would have earned during the period, had there been no accident of fire. When the business is dislocated, the profit-earning capacity is also reduced. This reduced capacity continues till the destroyed portion is restored as before. During the period, *i.e.* from the date of fire to the date of restoration, there may be no profit or very low profit. Profit reduces because of the reduced production capacity and in turn sales is affected. As long as the abnormal state continues, a businessman experiences reduction in sales, non-recovery of fixed expenses, sharp decline of earnings etc. Consequence of fire accident is thus a loss of profit which the firm would have otherwise earned. This loss of profit is not covered by ordinary fire policy insuring existing items. The loss of profit can be insured against by "Loss of Profit" or "Consequential Loss" policy. The insurer rarely admits a claim for consequential loss without admission of liability for loss of assets by fire. Therefore, Insurance Company generally insists on taking a policy for Loss of Profit on condition that the assets of the business concern are also insured.

The loss of profit policy normally covers the following items:

(1) Loss of Net Profits

(2) Standing Charges

(3) Any increased cost of working

The following are the important terms used in Loss of Profit insurance and a knowledge of the terms will be advantageous.

1. Indemnity Period

Indemnity period means the period which commences on the date of damage by fire and ends on the date when normality is restored. The indemnity period is generally stipulated in the insurance policy. This period is selected by the insured himself. The policy is taken generally for a period of one year and can be renewed annually, whereas the indemnity period commences on the day on which the accident takes place and runs up to a period of twelve or more months. It is necessary that the policy must be in force at the time of fire accident.

2. Standard Turnover

It is the turnover during the period in the twelve months immediately preceding the date of the hazard which corresponds with the indemnity period.

3. Short Sales

The term "Short Sales" refers to the loss of sales due to the dislocation of business. That is, short sale is the difference between standard turnover and actual turnover during the period of fire.

4. Standing Charges

Standing charges refer to those fixed expenses which are incurred irrespective of the reduction in turnover. Examples of standing charges are salaries to permanent staff, rent, rates, taxes, insurance premium, interest on bank overdraft, debentures etc. Only those standing charges, which are insured, can be claimed.

5. Increased Cost of Working

The insured may have to incur some additional or special expenses in order to keep the business, during the post-fire period and to avoid reduction in sales. Expenses in excess of what is essentially required may be unreasonable expenditure.

6. Rate of Gross Profit

The term "Gross Profit" has got a different meaning when it is calculated for loss of profit policy and is different from the normal rate of Gross Profit as described under "Loss of Stock". The rate of Gross Profit is calculated by taking previous year's figures.

Loss due to reduction in turnover is calculated by applying the gross profit rate to reduction in turnover. The rate of gross profit is calculated with reference to last accounting period:

$$\frac{\text{Net Profit} + \text{Insured Standing Charges}}{\text{Turnover}} \times 100$$

In case of net loss, the rate of gross profit will be determined as follows:

$$\frac{\text{Insured Standing Charges} - \text{Net Loss}}{\text{Turnover}} \times 100$$

If all the standing charges are not insured, the amount of net loss will have to be reduced as follows:

$$\frac{\text{Net Loss} \times \text{Insured Standing Charges}}{\text{All Standing Charges}}$$

Further, increased working expenses will be allowed subject to the limit which is lower of the two figures calculated as follows:

(*a*) $\frac{\text{Net Profit} + \text{Insured Standing Charges}}{\text{Net Profit} + \text{All Standing Charges}} \times \text{Increased Cost of Working}$

(*b*) Short sales avoided through increased cost of working × Rate of Gross Profit

ILLUSTRATION 17.5

Calculate from the following the amount of permissible increased working expenses:

	Rs
Net Profit	10,000
Short Sales	8,000
Rate of Gross Profit	15%
Increased Working Expenses	500
Insured Standing Charges	4,000
Uninsured Standing Charges	2,000
Short sales avoided through increased cost of working	3,000

SOLUTION

The amount of increased working expenses will be the lower of the two limits. They are:

(*a*) $\frac{\text{Net Profit} + \text{Insured Standing Charges}}{\text{Net Profit} + \text{All Standing Charges}} \times \text{Increased Cost of Working}$

$$\frac{10{,}000 + 4{,}000}{10{,}000 + 6{,}000} \times 500 = \text{Rs } 437.50$$

(*b*) Short sales avoided through increased cost of working × Rate of Gross Profit

$$\frac{3{,}000 \times 15}{100} = \text{Rs } 450$$

The increased working expenses allowed will be Rs 437.50

7. Average Clause

Average clause is applicable in respect of loss of profit insurance. If there is an increase in the turnover of business, the sum insured should also be proportionately increased. If not, it amounts to under-insurance. Under-insurance may also occur if all the standing charges are not covered by the policy.

8. Annual Turnover

It is the value of sales and services during the twelve months immediately preceding the hazard, subject to adjustment for any change in the volume of sales.

How to ascertain the amount of claim under Loss of Profit Policy?

STEP 1. Ascertain the short sale (*i.e.* excess of standard turnover over actual turnover) during the period of dislocation.

STEP 2. Find out the rate of Gross Profit.

STEP 3. Calculate the Loss of Profit by applying the rate of Gross Profit

STEP 4. Add thereto (Step 3) the net increased cost of working on account of short sales.

STEP 5. Any savings in expenses are deducted (from Step 4).

STEP 6. The result of Step 5 is the amount of gross claim.

STEP 7. Finally, the amount calculated will be adjusted, by applying average clause, if necessary.

The figure so calculated will be the amount of claim for loss of profit to be lodged with the insurance company.

ILLUSTRATION 17.6

The following are the details relating to a Company for the year ended 2004:

	Rs
Total Variable Expenses	3,50,000
Total Fixed Expenses	1,20,000
Non-operating income	60,000
Net Profit	90,000

The Company took a decision to arrange for a Loss of Profits Insurance for the year 2005. It is expected that the turnover might increase by 15% and all the fixed standing expenses will remain constant. Ascertain the extent to which the Company should finalise the amount to be insured under Loss of Profits Policy.

(*B.Com., Madurai*)

SOLUTION

(*a*) *Ascertainment of Sales*

Dr. **Trading and Profit and Loss Account for 2004** Cr.

	Rs		*Rs*
To Variable Expenses	3,50,000	By Sales (Balancing figure)	5,00,000
To Fixed Expenses	1,20,000	By Non-operating Income	60,000
To Net Profit	90,000		
	5,60,000		5,60,000

Gross Profit for 2004 = Sales – Variable Expenses
= Rs 5,00,000 – Rs 3,50,000
= Rs 1,50,000

(*b*) *Calculation of Gross Profit for 2005*

	Rs
Gross Profit for 2004	1,50,000
Add: Increase expected: 15%	22,500
	1,72,500

The Gross Profit expected in 2005, Rs. 1,72,500, should be insured under Loss of Profit Policy.

ILLUSTRATION 17.7

A fire broke out in a Company on Ist April 2005 and short sales remained for a period of six months; total sales during this period amounted to Rs 80,000, while in previous year from Ist April 2004 to 30th September 2004 were of Rs 2,00,000. Sales have increased by 10% in 2005 in the period from Ist January 2005 to Ist April 2005. Find out the short sales during this period of six months of 2005. (*B.Com., Bombay*)

SOLUTION

	Rs
Sales during six months (2004)	2,00,000
Add: Increase expected is 10%	20,000
	2,20,000
Less: Sales of this period of 2005	80,000
Short Sales	1,40,000

ILLUSTRATION 17.8

On Ist July 2005 United Furniture Ltd. took out a Profit Insurance Policy for Rs 1,50,000 with a period of indemnity of six months. Net profit of the company for the year ended 30th June 2005 was Rs 1,20,000 and the turnover for the period was Rs 4,80,000. Standing charges for that period amounted to Rs 24,000 and those were fully insured.

On 30th September 2005 a fire broke out and the normal turnover could not be restored before the end of six months. As a result, the reduction in turnover during the period of indemnity was Rs 48,000 when compared with corresponding period in the previous year. In an effort to maintain the turnover, the increased cost of working was ascertained at Rs 7,200 although there had been a saving of Rs 800 in insured standing charges over the same period. Moreover, the turnover for the twelve months ended 30th September 2005 amounted to Rs 4,90,000 indicating an increase in turnover for the 2004-05 financial year.

You are required to prepare a statement of claim against the Insurance Company. (*M.Com., Calcutta*)

SOLUTION

		Rs
1.	Rate of Gross Profit:	
	Net Profit for the last financial year	1,20,000
	Add: Insured Standing charges	24,000
	Insured Gross Profit	1,44,000
	Turnover for the last financial year	4,80,000
	Rate of Gross Profit: $\frac{1,44,000}{4,80,000} \times 100 = 30\%$	
2.	Short sales during the period of indemnity	48,000
3.	Amount of gross claim:	
	Gross Profit on short sales: 30% on Rs 48,000	14,400
	Add: Increased cost of working	7,200
		21,600
	Less: Savings in insured Standing Charges	800
		20,800

4. Net Claim after application of Average Clause:

Gross Profit on annual turnover (preceding 12 months) = 30% on Rs 4,90,000	1,47,000

Sum insured Rs 1,50,000

The sum insured is therefore adequate and the Average Clause does not apply. Consequently the entire amount of loss, *i.e.*, Rs 20,800, is payable under the policy.

ILLUSTRATION 17.9

A firm has decided to arrange for a loss of profit insurance and you are required to finalise the sum to be insured on a full insurance basis from the following figures for last financial year; it is anticipated that for the current financial year, turnover will increase by 10% and that all standing expenses will remain unchanged.

		Rs
Total Variable Expenses		21,00,000
Fixed Expenses:		
Wages and Salaries to skilled employees and salaries to administrative staff	3,00,000	
Depreciation on all Fixed assets	1,00,000	
Insurance Premiums	10,000	
Audit Fees	4,000	
Directors' Fees	4,000	
Travelling Expenses (including Motor Car Expenses)	40,000	
Postage, Cables and Telephones	3,000	
Trade subscriptions	1,000	
Rent, Rates and Taxes	30,000	4,92,000
Non-operating Income		50,000
Net Profit		4,08,000

(*CA Inter*)

SOLUTION

	Rs
Calculation of Gross Profit:	
Net Profit	4,08,000
Less: Non-operating income	50,000
	3,58,000
Add: Fixed expenses	4,92,000
Gross Profit	8,50,000

If sales increase by 10% in the current year, Gross Profit will also increase to the same extent, rate of gross profit remains the same. Therefore, the policy should be for:

	Rs
Gross Profit on the basis of last year	8,50,000
Add: 10% increase because of increase in sales by 10%	85,000
	9,35,000

Alternatively,

Memorandum Profit and Loss Account

	Rs		Rs
To Variable Expenses	21,00,000	By Sales (Balancing Figure)	29,50,000
To Fixed Expenses	4,92,000	By Non-Operating Income	50,000
To Net Profit	4,08,000		
	30,00,000		30,00,000

Sales amount is increased by 10%. Hence Gross Profit should also be increased by 10%. Therefore the policy should be:

Last year Gross Profit is Rs 8,50,000 + 10% increase *i.e.* Rs 85,000 = Rs 9,35,000

ILLUSTRATION 17.10

A Company was insured for consequential loss. A fire occurred on 31st March 2005 and as a result there was diminished turnover, as compared with the corresponding months of the preceding year, of Rs 20,000. The company was insured for a period which adequately covered the dislocation and no special factors existed.

The account for last accounting period of a year to 31st January 2005 showed a net profit of Rs 4,000 after debiting standing charges (all insured) Rs 6,000 and turnover being Rs 1,00,000. The company had taken a loss of profit policy of Rs 4,800 and the turnover for the year immediately preceding the fire was Rs 64,000. Calculate the claim on average basis. *(B.Com., Madurai)*

SOLUTION

(*a*) Rate of Gross Profit:

$$\frac{\text{Net Profit + Insured Standing Charges}}{\text{Sales}} \times 100$$

$$= \text{Rs } \frac{4,000 + 6,000}{1,00,000} \times 100 = 10\%$$

(*b*) Loss of Profit on short sales:

$$\text{Rs } 20,000 \times \frac{10}{100} = \text{Rs } 2,000$$

(*c*) Loss of profit on the sale of preceding twelve months:

$$\text{Rs } 64,000 \times \frac{10}{100} = \text{Rs } 6,400$$

(*d*) Claim for loss of profit on average basis:

$$\frac{\text{Policy}}{\text{Loss of Profit on sale of preceding 12 months}} \times \text{Loss of profit on short sale}$$

$$= \frac{4,800}{6,400} \times \text{Rs } 2,000 = \text{Rs } 1,500$$

ILLUSTRATION 17.11

On 31st December 2004, a fire damaged the premises of a firm and the business of the firm was disorganised until 31st March 2005. The firm was insured under a loss of profit policy for Rs 26,000 with a six-month period of indemnity.

The firm's accounts for the year ended 31st October 2004 showed a turnover of Rs 70,000 with a net profit of Rs 8,000. The amount of standing charges covered by the insurance and debited in that year was Rs 20,000. The turnover for the twelve months ended 31st December 2004 was Rs 78,000. The turnover during the period the business was dislocated amounted to Rs 8,000 while during the corresponding period in the preceding year it was Rs 17,000. A sum of Rs 2,000 was spent as additional expenses to mitigate the effect of the loss, there being, however, no saving in standing charges as a result of the fire.

Prepare a claim to be submitted in respect of the consequential loss policy. *(CA)*

SOLUTION

		Rs
(*a*)	Calculation of short sales:	
	Sales during 31.12.2003 to 31.3.2004	17,000
	Less: Sales during 31.12.2004 to 31.12.2005	8,000
		9,000

(*b*) Calculation of rate of gross profit:

$$\frac{\text{Net Profit + Insured Standing Charges}}{\text{Sales}} \times 100$$

$$\frac{8,000 + 20,000}{70,000} \times 100 = 40\%$$

(*c*) Calculation of loss of profit on short sales:

$$9,000 \times \frac{40}{100} = \text{Rs } 3,600$$

(*d*)	Calculation of total claim:	
	Loss of Profit	3,600
	Add: Additional Expenses	2,000
		5,600

(*e*) Claim on the average basis:

$$\frac{\text{Policy}}{\text{Loss of Profit on sale of preceding 12 months}} \times \text{Total claim}$$

$$= \frac{26,000}{40\% \text{ of Rs } 78,000} \times 5,600$$

$$= \text{Rs } 4,667$$

MISCELLANEOUS

ILLUSTRATION 17.12

The premises of a merchant caught fire on Ist November 2005 and his stock was damaged. The stock was fully insured. The merchant had made up account to 31st December each year. The following information was available:

	Rs
Stock on 31.12.2004	1,32,720
Stock on 31.12.2003	96,140
Purchases from 1.1.2005 to the date of fire	3,48,270
Purchases up to 31.12.2004	4,52,580
Sales up to 31.12.2004	5,20,000
Sales from 1.1.2005 to the date of fire	4,91,700

You are given further information:

(*a*) In May 2005, goods costing Rs 10,000 were given away for advertising purpose but no entry being made in the books.

(*b*) During 2005, a clerk had appropriated an unrecorded cash sales of Rs 4,000.

(*c*) The rate of gross profit is constant.

(*d*) The stock salvaged was agreed to be worth Rs 3,000 and the expenses incurred to extinguish the fire Rs 200.

From the above information make an estimate of stock on hand on the date of fire and prepare a statement showing the claim for loss of stock. *(B.Com., Karnataka)*

SOLUTION

Determination of rate of gross profit on sales:

Trading Account
for the year ended 31st Dec. 2004

Dr.	*Rs*		Cr. *Rs*
To Opening Stock	96,140	By Sales	5,20,000
To Purchases	4,52,580	By Stock	1,32,720
To Gross Profit (20% on sales)	1,04,000		
	6,52,720		6,52,720

Calculation of stock destroyed:

Memorandum Trading Account

Dr.		*Rs*			Cr. *Rs*
To Opening Stock		1,32,720	By Sales:	4,91,700	
To Purchases:	3,48,270		Add: Appropriation	4,[illegible]0	4,95,700
Less: Free Samples	10,000	3,38,270	By Closing stock		
To Gross Profit (20% on Sales)		99,140	(Balancing figure)		74,430
		5,70,130			5,70,130

Statement of claim:

	Rs
Stock Destroyed	74,430
Less: Salvaged Stock	3,000
	71,430
Add: Fire Expenses	200
Amount of claim	71,630

ILLUSTRATION 17.13

On 12th June 2005 a fire occurred in the premises of a paper merchant. Most of the stocks were destroyed, cost of stock salvaged being Rs 11,200. In addition, some stock was salvaged in a damaged condition and its value in that condition was agreed at Rs 10,400. From the books of account, the following particulars were available:

(*a*) The stock at the close of account on 31st December 2004 was valued at Rs 83,500.

(*b*) The purchases from 1.1.2005 to 12.6.2005 amounted to Rs 1,12,000 and sales during that period amounted to Rs 1,54,000.

On the basis of the accounts for the past three years it appears that the firm earns on an average gross profit of 25% on sales.

Stock for Rs 60,000 has been insured. Compute the amount of the claim. *(B.Com., Madurai)*

SOLUTION

Computation of loss of stock:

	Rs
Opening stock on 1.1.2005	83,500
Add: Purchase during the period	1,12,000
	1,95,500

Less: Sales during the period	1,54,000	
Less: Gross Profit at 25% on sales	38,500	1,15,500
		80,000
Less: Stock salvaged	11,200	
Value of damaged stock	10,400	21,600
		58,400

$$\text{Amount of claim: } \frac{58{,}400 \times 60{,}000}{80{,}000} = \text{Rs } 43{,}800$$

ILLUSTRATION 17.14

The premises of Fire Proof Ltd. were destroyed by fire on 30.6.2005. The following figures were ascertained:

	2002	*2003*	*2004*	*1.1.2005 to 30.6.2005*
	Rs	Rs	Rs	Rs
Opening Stock	2,000	2,200	1,180	3,402
Purchases	16,000	14,500	17,000	3,500
Sales	20,000	19,850	18,750	2,600
Carriage Inwards	500	300	500	100
Freight Outwards	600	700	300	25

In 2002, while valuing closing stock, some defective goods costing Rs 500 were valued at Rs 400. These were sold for Rs 450 in 2003.

In 2003, an item costing Rs 600 was wrongly valued at Rs 700. This was sold for Rs 550 in 2004.

In 2004, items costing Rs 1,200 were valued at Rs 1,000, 50% of these items were sold in June 2005 for Rs 600.

Subject to this, the gross profit rate is more or less uniform.

The value of salvage was Rs 800.

You are required to prepare a statement of claim in respect of loss of stock to be submitted to the Insurance Company:

(*CA Inter*)

SOLUTION

Dr. **Trading Account** Cr.

	2002	*2003*	*2004*		*2002*	*2003*	*2004*
	Rs	*Rs*	*Rs*		*Rs*	*Rs*	*Rs*
To Stock	2,000	2,200	1,180	By Sales	20,000	19,850	18,750
Less: Abnormal items		400	700	*Less*: Abnormal items		450	550
	2,000	1,800	480		20,000	19,400	18,200
To Purchases	16,000	14,500	17,000	By Closing Stock*	2,300	1,080	3,602
To Carriage-in	500	300	500				
To Gross Profit	3,800	3,880	3,822				
	22,300	20,480	21,802		22,300	20,480	21,802

* Adjusted stock

Gross Profit	19%	20%	21%
Average of three years		20%	

Memorandum Trading Account
for the period ended 30th June 2005

	Normal items	Abnormal items		Normal items	Abnormal items
	Rs	*Rs*		*Rs*	*Rs*
To Opening Stock	2,402	1,200	By Sales	2,000	600
To Purchases	3,500		By Closing Stock	4,402	600
To Carriage-in	100				
To Gross Profit (20% on sales)	400				
	6,402	1,200		6,402	1,200

Statement of claim:		Rs
Stock on the date of fire:	Normal items	4,402
	Abnormal items	600
		5,002
Less: Salvaged Stock		800
Amount of claim:		4,202

ILLUSTRATION 17.15

Messrs Central Karnatak Ltd. had fully insured their factory which was damaged by fire on 31st March 2005. The management asks you to file an insurance claim for the damages for the following particulars available from the Balance Sheet as at 30th November 2004.

Stock Rs 3,64,956; Machinery Rs 1,85,820.

Building Rs 1,38,420; Furniture Rs 8,400.

Transactions from Ist December 2004 to 31st March 2005 were:

Purchase Rs 5,88,276, Sales Rs 3,38,829 and Wages Rs 1,49,538.

Salvage recovered were:

Building Rs 6,000, Machinery Rs 9,000 and Furniture Rs 1,500.

The average profit percentage is 23 on sales.

Draw up a statement of claim. (*B.Com., Karnataka*)

SOLUTION

Memorandum Trading Account
(from 1.12.2004 to 31.3.2005)

	Rs		*Rs*
To Stock	3,64,956	By Sales	3,38,829
To Purchases	5,88,276	By Stock destroyed	8,41,872
To Wages	1,49,538		
To Gross Profit (23% on Sales)	77,931		
	11,80,701		11,80,701

Claim:			Rs
Stock destroyed			8,41,872
Building	...	(1,38,420 – 6,000)	1,32,420
Machinery	...	(1,85,820 – 9,000)	1,76,820
Furniture	...	(8,400 – 1,500)	6,900
		Total Claim:	11,58,012

ILLUSTRATION 17.16

A fire accident took place in the premises of Gouthami Ltd. on 31st August, 2005. From the following particulars, calculate the amount of claim to be lodged with the insurance company for the loss of stock:

	Rs
Stock on 1st April, 2004	36,000
Purchases in 2004-2005	1,60,000
Sales in 2004-2005	2,50,000
Stock on 31st March, 2005	44,000
Purchases from 1.4.2005 to 31.8.2005	54,000
Sales from 1.4.2005 to 31.8.2005	66,000

Stock on 1st April, 2004, was valued at 10% below cost and the stock on 31st March, 2005, was valued at 10% above the cost. Salvage value of stock after fire was Rs. 9,960. Value of insurance policy of the stock was Rs. 30,000.

(*B.Com. Andhra*)

SOLUTION

Trading Account

Dr. **for the year ended 31st Dec. 2005** Cr.

	Rs		*Rs*
To Stock, 1-4-2004		By Sales	2,50,000
$\frac{36,000 \times 100}{90}$	40,000	By Stock, 31-3-2005	
To Purchases	1,60,000	$\frac{44,000 \times 100}{110}$	40,000
To Gross Profit	90,000		
	2,90,000		2,90,000

Memorandum Trading Account

Dr. **for the period 1-4-2005 to 31-8-2005** Cr.

	Rs		*Rs*
To Stock, 1-4-2005	40,000	By Sales	66,000
To Purchases	54,000	By Stock (Balancing figure)	51,760
To Gross Profit:			
36% on sales or $\left(\frac{90,000 \times 66,000}{2,50,000}\right)$	23,760		
	1,17,760		1,17,760

	Rs
Stock on 31-8-2005	51,760
Less: Salvage	9,960
Loss of Stock	41,800

Amount of claim: $= \text{Rs. } 41,800 \times \frac{30,000}{51,760}$ = Rs. 24,227

ILLUSTRATION 17.17

A fire occurred in the premises of a merchant on 18th September, 2006, and a considerable part of the stock was destroyed. The value of the stock saved was Rs. 8,200. The books disclosed that on 1st April, 2006, the stock was valued of Rs. 66,850, purchases to the date of fire amounted to Rs. 1,85,000 and sales to Rs. 2,82,500. Goods costing Rs. 500 were taken for personal use and goods sold for Rs. 2,500 were returned to the merchant. On investigation it was found that during the past five years the average gross profit on cost was 23%.

Prepare a statement of account that the merchant has to claim from the insurance company for the stock destroyed. (*B.Com. MS.*)

SOLUTION

Memorandum Trading Account
for the period from 1-4-2006 to 18-9-2006

Dr.		*Rs*			Cr. *Rs*
To Stock, 1-4-2006		66,850	By Sales	2,82,500	
To Purchases	1,85,000		*Less* : Returns	2,500	
Less: Goods for personal use	500				2,80,000
		1,84,500	By Stock at date of fire (balancing figure)		23,708
To Gross profit (20% on cost)		52,358			
		3,03,708			3,03,708

	Rs
Loss of stock	23,708
Less : Salvage	8,200
Amount of claim	15,508
Let cost be	Rs. 100
Profit (23% on cost)	23
Sales	Rs. 123

If sales were Rs. 123 .... cost is Rs. 100

Rs. 2,80,000 .... ?

$$= \frac{100 \times 2,80,000}{123}$$

= Rs. 2,27,642

23% on cost, *i.e.*, on Rs. 2,27,642 = Rs. 52,357.66 or Rs. 52,358.

ILLUSTRATION 17.18

Determine the amount of claim to be lodged by M/s Tridev Company from the following details: The company had taken a fire insurance policy for Rs. 1,20,000 covering its stock and policy was subject to average clause.

	2004-2005	*1.10.05 to 15.3.06*
	Rs	Rs.
Sales	11,43,000	6,69,500
Purchases	7,89,500	3,94,000
Wages and salaries	1,37,400	68,900
Sales return	54,500	15,800
Purchase return	27,400	9,600
Carriage inward	27,400	9,600
Date of fire : 15-3-06		
Stock on 1-10-04	1,28,700	
Stock on 30-9-05	1,89,000	
Stock salvaged	19,310	

Stocks have always been valued at 10% below cost. (*B.Com. Bangalore*).

SOLUTION

Tridev Company

Dr. **Trading Account for the year ended 30th September, 2005** Cr.

		Rs			Rs
To Stock, 1-10-2004 $\frac{1,28,700 \times 100}{90}$		1,43,000	By Sales	11,43,000	
			Less : Returns	54,500	10,88,500
To Purchases	7,89,500		By Stock, 30-9-2005		
Less : Returns	27,400	7,62,100	$\frac{1,89,000 \times 100}{90}$		2,10,000
To Carriage inward		27,400			
Loss: Wages & salaries		1,37,400			
To Gross profit		2,28,600			
		12,98,500			12,98,500

% of gross profit on sales : $\frac{2,28,600}{10,88,500} \times 100$

$= 21\%$

Dr. **Memorandum Trading Account of Tridev Company for the period 1-10-2005 to 15-3-2006** Cr.

		Rs			Rs
To Stock, 1-10-2005		2,10,000	By Sales	6,69,500	
To Purchases	3,94,000		Less : Returns	15,800	
Less : Returns	9,600				6,53,700
		3,84,400	By Stock at date of fire		
To Carriage inward		9,600	(balancing figure)		1,56,477
To Wages & Salaries		68,900			
To Gross profit: (21% of sales)		1,37,277			
		8,10,177			8,10,177

	Rs
Loss of stock	1,56,477
Less : Salvage	19,310
Amount of claim	1,37,167

Since the average clause is applicable, the amount of claim is restricted to:

$$\text{Loss of stock} \times \frac{\text{Sum insured}}{\text{Stock at date of fire}}$$

$$1,37,167 \times \frac{1,20,000}{1,56,477} = \textbf{Rs. 1,05,191}$$

Amount of insurance claim is only Rs. 1,05,191.

WORKMEN'S COMPENSATION INSURANCE CLAIMS

Workmen's Compensation Insurance Policies are also known as Employee's Liability Insurance Policies. An employer can get a policy to cover his liability to his workmen, who sustain injuries or who contract occupational diseases during the course of their work. In case of such a policy, insurance premiums are based on total wages paid. But premiums are payable in advance before actual wages become payable. Therefore, premiums paid in advance are calculated on the previous year's wages, subject to adjustment when actual figures for current year's wages are available. After the policy period is over, premium is adjusted on the basis of the actual wages paid during the policy period. If the actual wages paid are more than what was estimated, additional premium is collected on the difference. On the contrary, if the actual wages paid are less than the estimated, a refund of premium is made.

When premium is paid, it is debited to Workmen's Compensation Insurance Suspense Account. At the end of the year, the insured will calculate the exact premium due on the basis of actual wages for the period and will debit Workmen's Compensation Insurance Account and credit Workmen's Compensation Insurance Suspense Account. The balance in Workmen's Suspense Account will be carried forward for adjustment in cash.

QUESTIONS

Objective Type Questions

I. Say whether the following statements are "True" or "False".

1. Loss of stock is the same as loss of profit since profit depends upon valuation of stock.
2. For claiming loss of profit, it is necessary to take out a separate policy.
3. Fire Insurance claim necessitates the estimation of value of stock on the date of fire.
4. The main purpose of average clause is to discourage under-insurance.
5. Under-insurance is insuring the goods for a very small amount.
6. Average clause makes the insured bear a proportion of loss by constituting him as a co-insurer.
7. Any saving in expenses is to be deducted for determining the final claim.

(Ans: 1. False; 2. True; 3. True; 4. True; 5. False; 6. True; 7. True.)

II. Fill in the blanks:

1. .... is prepared to find out loss of stock on the date of fire.
2. Fire insurance is a contract of ....
3. Fire insurance policy covers, besides loss of stock, ...
4. The average clause in a policy is to avoid .... insurance.
5. Fire insurance provides cover for ....
6. Consequential loss policy indemnifies ....
7. Loss of profit insurance policy is also known as ....
8. The difference between standard turnover and actual turnover during the indemnity period is ....
9. Cost of goods sold is calculated by deducting gross profit from ....

(Ans. 1. Memorandum Trading Account; 2. Indemnity; 3. Loss of Profit; 4. Under; 5. Loss due to fire; 6. Loss of profit; 7. Consequential Policy; 8. Short sale; 9. Sales.

III. Choose the appropriate answer from the given alternatives:

1. 'Loss of Profit' insurance covers:
   (*a*) Revenue losses. (*b*) Capital losses.
   (*c*) Both Revenue and Capital losses.
2. Consequential loss policy covers:
   (*a*) Loss of net profit. (*b*) Non-recovery of standing charges.
   (*c*) Increased cost of working. (*d*) All the three.
3. In the case of loss of stock by fire, the claim is restricted to:
   (*a*) Amount of policy. (*b*) Value of goods insured.
   (*c*) Actual loss minus salvage.
4. The average clause in a loss of profit policy protects the interest of the :
   (*a*) Insured. (*b*) Insurer.
   (*c*) Workers.
5. The average clause in a loss of stock policy discourages:
   (*a*) Over-insurance. (*b*) Under-insurance.
   (*c*) Consequential loss.

6. In case of average clause the loss is suffered by both the insurer and the insured :
   (*a*) In the ratio of risk covered. (*b*) In equal ratio.
   (*c*) Only by insurer.

(**Ans:** 1. (*a*); 2. (*d*); 3. (*c*); 4. (*b*); 5. (*b*); 6. (*a*).

THEORETICAL QUESTIONS

1. How is the loss of stock computed?
2. What do you mean by Loss of Profit Insurance? What items would normally be covered by such an insurance?
3. Explain Average Clause in insurance policy by taking imaginary illustration.
4. Write short notes on:
   (*a*) Indemnity period, (*b*) Short sales, (*c*) Standing charges,
   (*d*) Increased cost of working, and (*e*) Consequential Loss Policy.

PRACTICAL PROBLEMS

Loss of Stock

1. A fire occurred in the premises of a merchant on June 15, 2004, and a considerable part of the stock was destroyed. The value of the stock saved was Rs 4,500.

   The books disclosed that on April 1, 2004 the stock was valued at Rs 36,750; the purchases to the date of the fire amounted to Rs 1,04,940 and the sales to Rs 1,56,500. On investigation it was found that during the past five years the average gross profit on sales was 36%.

   You are required to prepare a statement showing the amount the merchant should claim from the insurance company in respect of stock destroyed by the fire. (*B.Com., Delhi*)

   [**Ans:** Claim Rs 37,030]

2. A fire occurred on 15th September, 2004, in the premises of X Company Ltd. From the following figures, calculate the amount of claim to be lodged with the insurance company for the loss of stock:

	Rs
Stock at cost on 1st January, 2003	20,000
Stock at cost on 1st January, 2004	30,000
Purchases 2003	40,000
Purchases from 1st January 2004 to 15 September 2004	88,000
Sales 2003	60,000
Sales from 1st January 2004 to 15 September 2004	1,05,000

   During the current year cost of purchases has risen by 10% above last year's level, selling prices have gone up by 5%. Salvage value of stock after fire was Rs 2,000. (*C.A. Inter*)

   [**Ans:** Claim to be lodged for Rs 64,000]

3. The whole stock of goods of Shared Ltd. was destroyed by fire on 3rd February, 2004. No Stock Register was maintained, but the following particulars were available:

	Rs
Stock at Cost on 1st January, 2003	26,580
Stock as per Balance Sheet as at 31st December, 2003	22,530
Purchases for 2003	62,310
Purchases from 1st January 2004 to 3rd February 2004	22,410
Sales for 2003	91,500

Sales from 1st January 2004 to 3rd February 2004	35,400

While valuing the stock as on 31st December, 2003, Rs 480 was written off out of the cost price of Rs 1,080 and this stock was sold in January 2004 for Rs 1,050. Except for this item, the ratio of gross profit was uniform throughout.

Value of stock salvaged was Rs 3,063. The stock was fully insured against fire.

You are required to find out the amount for which claim for loss of stock be made to the insurer.

(*B.Com., Madurai*)

[**Ans:** Rate of Gross Profit 28%
Value of Stock Rs 19,608
Calims Rs 16,545]

4. The Cheap Stores Ltd., which deals in provisions, prepares accounts annually to 31st December. The ratio of gross profit to sales is constant throughout. On 30th April 2004, the stock was partly destroyed by fire. The books and records were saved and from these the following information was obtained:

	Rs
Stock, including old stock, all at cost :	
31st December 2002	900
31st December 2003	2,200
Purchases 2003	22,510
Sales 2003	30,300
Purchases January-April 2004	8,350
Sales January-April 2004	10,400

You are required to ascertain the value of stock destroyed. (*C.A. Inter*)

[**Ans:** Stock destroyed Rs 3,270]

5. The godown of Sharad was destroyed by fire on 15 April, 2004. From the following figures, ascertain the value of goods destroyed by fire:

	Rs
Stock as on 1.1.2003	720
Purchases less Returns:	
(*i*) From 1.1.2003 to 31.12.2003	2,800
(*ii*) From 1.1.2004 to 15.4.2004	2,920
Sales less Returns:	
(*i*) From 1.1.2003 to 31.12.2003	4,000
(*ii*) From 1.1.2004 to 15.4.2004	3,200
Stock as on 31.12.2003	480
Cost price of goods salvaged	240
Cost price of the goods taken by the proprietor for personal use and not recorded in the books (from 1.1.2004 to 15.4.2004)	320

The stocks are valued at cost less 20%. (*B.Com., MS*)

[**Ans:** Amount of claim Rs 480]

6. On April 1, 2004, the stock of Sri Vyas were destroyed by fire but sufficient records were saved from which following particulars were ascertained:

	Rs
Stock at cost–January 1, 2003	73,500
Stock at cost–December 31, 2003	79,600
Purchases–year ended December 31, 2003	3,98,000

Sales–year ended December 31, 2003	4,87,000
Purchases–1.1.2004 to 30.3.2004	1,62,000
Sales–1.1.2004 to 30.3.2004	2,31,200

In valuing the stock for the Balance Sheet at December 31, 2003, Rs 2,300 had been written off certain stock which was a poor selling line, it having cost Rs 6,900. A portion of these goods was sold in March 2004 at a loss of Rs 250 on original cost of Rs 3,450. The remainder of this stock was now estimated to be worth its original cost. Subject to the above exception gross profit had remained at a uniform rate throughout the year.

The value of stock salvaged was Rs 5,800. Show the amount of the claim for loss by fire.

(*C.A. Inter*)

[**Ans:** Claim for loss of Stock Rs 52,250]

7. The premises and stock of *A* were totally destroyed by fire on 30th January 2004. From the accounts and other records that were saved, the following information is available. The stock on hand has always been valued at 10% less than cost:

	2001	*2002*	*2003*	*2004*
	Rs	Rs	Rs	Rs
Opening stock as valued	2,709	3,240	3,600	3,690
Purchases less returns	7,490	8,000	8,100	600
Sales less returns	12,000	13,200	14,000	1,200
Wages	1,740	1,900	2,090	200
Closing stock valued	3,240	3,600	3,690	–

Prepare of statement for submission to the Insurance Company in support of the claim for loss of stock.

(*B.Com., Delhi*)

[**Ans:** Claim Rs 4,036]

8. On 30th September 2004, the stock of Fred Perry was lost in a fire accident. From the available records the following information is made available to you to enable you to prepare a statement of claim on the insurers:

	Rs
Stock at cost 1.4.2003	37,500
Stock at cost on 31.3.2004	52,000
Purchases less returns for the year ended 31.3.2004	2,53,750
Sales less returns for the year ended 31.3.2004	3,15,000
Purchases less returns up to 30.9.2004	1,45,000
Sales less returns up to 30.9.2004	1,84,050

In valuing the stock on 31.3.2004, due to obsolescence 50% of the value of the stock which originally cost Rs 6,000 had been written off. In May, 2004, three-fourths of this stock had been sold at 90% of the original cost and it is now expected that the balance of the obsolete stock would also realise the same price. Except for the above, gross profit had remained uniform throughout.

Stock to the value of Rs 7,200 was salvaged. (*C.A. Inter*)

[**Ans:** Amount of claim Rs 53,150]

9. A fire occurred in the godown of Ram Seth Ltd. on 9th March 2004 destroying the entire stock. The books and records were salvaged from which the following particulars are ascertained:

	Rs
Sales for the year 2003	10,01,000
Sales for the period 1.1.2004 to 8.3.2004	3,00,000
Purchases for the year 2003	8,00,000
Purchases for the period 1.1.2004 to 8.3.2004	1,25,000

Stock on 1.1.2003	1,31,100
Stock on 31.12.2003	3,85,000

The company has been following the practice of valuing stock of goods at actual cost plus 10%. Included in the stock on 1.1.2003 were some shop-soiled goods which originally cost Rs 2,000 but were valued at Rs 1,000. These goods were sold during the year 2003 for Rs 1,000. Except for this, the rate of gross profit and the basis of valuation of stock were uniform.

You are required to ascertain the value of the stock destroyed. (*B.Com., Bombay*)

[**Ans:** Amount of claim Rs 2,50,000]

10. Fire occurred in the premises of X Ltd. on Ist of September 2004 and stock of the value of Rs 1,01,000 was salvaged and the business books and records were salvaged. The following information was obtained:

	Rs
Purchases for the year ended 31.3.2004	7,00,000
Sales for the year ended 31.3.2004	11,00,000
Purchases from 1.3.2004 to 1.9.2004	2,40,000
Sales from 1.3.2004 to 1.9.2004	3,60,000
Stock on 31st March 2003	3,00,000
Stock on 31st March 2004	3,40,000

Further information is also given that the stock on 31.3.2004 was over-valued by Rs 20,000. Calculate the amount of the claim to be presented to the Insurance Company in respect of losses. Rate of Gross Profit based on the year ended 31.3.2004.

(*B.Com., Calcutta*)

[**Ans:** Amount of claim Rs 2,33,540]

11. On Ist April 2004, the godown of Lindley was destroyed by fire. From the account books, the following particulars are gathered:

	Rs
1. Stock at cost on Ist January 2003	4,505
2. Stock as per Balance Sheet on 31.12.2003	8,520
3. Purchases during 2003	45,225
4. Purchases from 1.1.2004 to 31.3.2004	12,500
5. Sales during 2003	58,500
6. Sales from 1.1.2004 to 31.3.2004	15,250
7. Value of goods salvaged	1,050

8. Goods whose original cost was Rs 600 had been valued at Rs 250 on 31st December 2003. These were sold in March 2004 for Rs 450. Except this transaction, the rate of gross profit has remained constant.
9. On 31st March 2004 goods worth Rs 2,500 had been received by the godown keeper but had not been entered in the Purchase Account.

Calculate the value of goods damaged by fire. (*C.A. Inter*)

[**Ans:** Amount of claim Rs 11,860]

12. A fire occurred in the premises of Shri Garib Dass on Ist April 2004 and considerable part of the stock was destroyed. The stock salvaged was Rs 56,000. Shri Dass had taken a fire insurance policy for Rs 3,42,000 to cover the loss of stock by fire.

You are required to ascertain the insurance claim which Shri Garib Dass should claim from the Insurance Company for the loss of stock by fire. The following particulars are available:

	Rs
Purchases for the year 2003	18,76,000
Sales for the year 2003	23,20,000
Purchases from 1st January to 1st April 2004	3,64,000

Sales from 1st January 2004 to 1st April 2004	4,80,000
Stock on 1st January 2003	2,88,000
Stock on 31st December 2003	4,84,000
Wages paid during the year 2003	2,00,000
Wages paid during 1st January 2004 to 1st April 2004	36,000

Shri Dass had, in June 2003, consigned goods worth Rs 1,00,000 which unfortunately, however, were lost in an accident. Since there was no insurance cover taken, the loss had to be borne by him in full. Stocks at end of each year for and till the end of calendar year 2003, had been valued at cost less 10%. From 2003, however, there was a change in the valuation of closing stock which was ascertained by adding 10% to its cost. *(C.A.)*

[Ans: Amount of claim Rs 3,00,000]

13. **The premises of a Company were destroyed by fire on 15th June 2004. The records, however, were saved wherefrom the following particulars were available:**

	Rs
Stock at cost on 1.1.2003	30,000
Stock at cost on 31.12.2003	40,000
Purchases less returns for the year ended 31.12.2003	2,00,000
Sales less returns for the year ended 31.12.2003	2,50,000
Purchases less returns from 1.1.2004 to 15.6.2004	85,000
Sales less returns from 1.1.2004 to 15.6.2004	1,20,000

Rs 2,500 had been written off certain stock, which has a poor selling line, while valuing the stock for the balance sheet as at 31st December 2003. The cost of such stock was Rs 4,000. A portion of this stock was sold in March 2004 at a loss of Rs 500 on the original cost of Rs 2,000. The balance of this stock was now estimated to be worth the original cost. Excepting the above, the gross profit had remained at uniform rate throughout. The stock saved was Rs 5,000. You are required to ascertain the amount of loss of stock which was to be claimed from the Insurance Company. *(ICWA)*

[Ans: Amount of claim Rs 31,625]

14. **On 31st August 2004, the premises of a godown were destroyed by fire. The business books and records were saved and from these following particulars were available. Calculate the amount of claim to be presented to the Insurance Company in respect of loss of stock:**

	Rs
Stock at cost on 31st March 2003	88,600
Stock as per Balance Sheet on 31st March 2004	75,100
Purchases up to 31st March 2004	2,07,700
Sales up to 31st March 2004	3,05,000
Purchases from 1.4.2004 to 31.8.2004	74,700
Sales from 1.4.2004 to 31.8.2004	1,18,000

In valuing the stock on 31st March 2004, Rs 1,600 had been written off a particular line of goods which had originally cost Rs 3,600 and which was sold in May 2004 for Rs 3,500. Except as regards this transaction, the ratio of gross profit has remained unchanged throughout.

The value of stock salvaged from the burnt-out premises was Rs 10,210. *(B.Com., Madurai)*

[Ans: Amount of claim Rs 55,150]

15. **A fire occurred in the premises of a company on 1-7-2004. From the following information, calculate the claim to be made against the company:**

	Rs
Stock on 1-1-2003	63,000
Purchases for the year ending 31-12-2003	4,00,000
Sales for the year ending 31-12-2003	5,00,000
Wages for the year ending 31-12-2003	20,000

Salary for the year ending 31-12-2003	10,000
Stock on 31-12-2003	81,000
Purchases from 1-1-2004 to date of fire	2,00,000
Sales from 1-1-2004 to date of fire	3,00,000
Stock salvaged	10,000
Value of the policy	30,000

There is an average clause in the policy. It is the practice of the company to value the stock at 10% less than the cost. *(B.Com., Bangalore)*

[Ans: Amount of claim Rs 24,000]

16. On 31st May 2004, the premises and stock of a firm were totally destroyed by fire, the books of accounts, however, being saved. In order to make a claim on their fire policy they ask your advice and you are given the following information. The stock on hand has always been valued at 5% below cost:

	2001	*2002*	*2003*	*2004*
	Rs	Rs	Rs	Rs
Opening Stock valued	22,800	30,400	36,100	39,900
Purchases less returns	91,000	1,10,000	1,20,000	41,000
Sales less returns	1,40,000	1,70,000	1,86,000	75,000
Wages	28,400	31,200	34,200	12,000
Closing stock	30,400	36,100	39,900	–

Prepare a statement for submission to the Insurance Company in support of your claim for loss of stock. *(CA)*

[Ans: Amount of claim Rs 35,000]

Loss of Profit

17. From the following information, find the claims under a 'loss of profit' policy:

	Rs
Sales in 2000	1,00,000
Sales in 2001	1,20,000
Sales in 2002	1,44,000
Sales in 2003	1,72,800
Net profit in 2003	10,000
(All insured) standing charges in 2003	7,280
Date of dislocation by fire 1.1.2004	
Period of dislocation 3 months	
Sales from 1.1.2003 to 31.3.2003	43,200
Sales from 1.1.2004 to 31.3.2004	11,840
Indemnity period 9 months	
Policy value	50,000

There was no reduction in standing charges during the dislocation period, nor were there any additional costs. *(C.A. Inter)*

[Ans: Amount of claim Rs 4,000]

18. On 1st November, 2004, a severe fire broke out in the premises of Luck Company Limited. The indemnity period lasted for 4 months during which the sales of the Company were reduced to Rs 2,00,000 only. The company closes its accounts on 30th June each year. The Profit and Loss Account

for the year ended 30th June, 2004, is given below:

Profit and Loss Account

for the year ended 30th June, 2004

	Rs		*Rs*
Opening Stock	5,00,000	Sales	47,50,000
Purchases	30,00,000	Closing Stock	2,50,000
Variable Expenses	7,87,500		
Standing Charges	3,62,500		
Net Profit	3,50,000		
	50,00,000		50,00,000

The Company took a loss of profit policy for a sum of Rs 6,00,000. The sales of the company for the 12 months ending the date of fire were Rs 50,00,000 and for the 4 months from 1st November 2003 to 28th February 2004 were Rs 15,00,000.

It was noted that the sales for the first four months of the year under indemnity were 20% higher than previous year. Compute the claim for loss of profit. *(I.C.W.A.)*

[Ans: Claim for loss of profit Rs 1,92,000**]**

19. A fire occurred on 21st May, 2004, in the factory of Messrs. Bombay Steel Traders. The following particulars are obtained as regards the costs and book values of various assets affected by fire, the amounts claimed and admitted by the Yoga Kshema Insurance Company Limited:

	Book value	*Claimed*	*Admitted*
	Rs	Rs	Rs
Buildings	50,000	60,000	45,000
Plant and Machinery	70,000	75,000	60,000
Fittings	12,000	15,000	13,500
Stock damaged	28,000	30,000	17,000
Stock destroyed	45,000	50,000	40,000
Loss of Profit	–	55,000	37,000
Fire expenses	–	1,200	1,200

The buildings, plant and machinery and fittings were completely destroyed by fire and most of the stock lying in a godown adjacent to the factory was also destroyed. The damaged goods saved were sold for Rs 13,000. The claim admitted for loss of profit was Rs 9,000 in respect of the profit for the remaining portion of the year ended 30th September 2004 and Rs 28,000 for six months thereafter when a new factory was built. The actual fire expenses incurred were Rs 1,200. The insurance company paid the amount for all claims on 27th September 2004.

Make journal entries in the books of Messrs Bombay Steel Traders to record the above particulars including the cash book entries. *(B.Com., Bombay)*

[Ans: Amount of claim Rs. 2,13,700**]**

20. Bharath Ltd. met a loss of stock due to fire on 15th August 2006. From the following information, prepare a statement showing the claim to be lodged :

	Rs
Stock on 1st April 2005	38,400
Purchases during 2005-2006	1,60,000
Sales during 2005-2006	2,02,600
Closing stock on 31st March 2006	31,800
Purchases from 1.4.2006 to 15.8.2006	54,000

Sales from 1.4.2006 to 15.8.2006 61,400

An item of stock purchased in 2004-2005 at a cost of Rs. 1,000 was valued at Rs. 6,900 on 31.3.2005. Half of this stock was sold in 2005-2006 for Rs. 2,600; the remaining was valued at Rs. 2,400 on 31.3.2006. One-fourth of the original stock was sold in June 2006 for Rs. 1,400; the remaining stock was considered to be worth 60% of the original cost. Salvage was Rs. 12,000. The amount of the policy was Rs. 30,000. There is an average clause in the policy.

(*B.Com. Bharathiar*)

(**Ans:** Amount of claim Rs. 20,417)

Chapter 18

Hire Purchase and Instalment System

Introduction – Legal Provisions – Contents of Agreement – Important Terms – Distinction between Hire Purchase and Instalment Sale – Calculation of Interest – Accounting Records in the Books of Hire Purchaser – Accounting Records in the Books of Hire Vendor – Default and Respossession – Complete Repossession – Partial Repossession – Post-Sale Services – Hire Purchase Trading Account – Stock and Debtors System – Instalments – Questions – Objective Type Questions – Theoretical Questions – Practical Problems.

INTRODUCTION

Hire Purchase Trading is a system of retail business under which the seller agrees to sell the article on the condition that the buyer shall pay the purchase price by a fixed number of instalments. Here the article is not legally sold out to the buyer and hence the ownership in the goods does not pass on to the buyer. In case of cash sales, when a buyer pays down the price to the seller, the goods are immediately delivered to the buyer and the ownership is also passed along with the goods. However the credit sale is different from cash sale and Hire purchase sale. With the expansion of trade and commerce, businessmen find it easy and convenient to increase the volume of trade by making sales through credit system. Under credit system, the buyer takes the delivery of goods and is permitted to make the payment of price at a later date or as per agreement between them. The buyer pays cash on the due date or accepts a Bill drawn by the seller. Both are facilitated; the buyer gets the goods he needs and the seller gets the cash on discounting the bill. Hire Purchase System is a special system of purchase and sale. When goods are purchased on Hire Purchase System, the purchaser pays the price in instalments and these instalments may be monthly, quarterly, half-yearly, yearly or any other period. The purchaser becomes the owner only on payment of the last instalment.

Pickles defines: "Hire purchase is the system under which the property is acquired by payments made in instalments, during the period of which the title in the property remains with the Hire Vendor. The payments prior to the final are regarded as being purely in respect of hire, and the title of the property does not pass to the hire-purchaser until such final payment or some other consideration provided for in the contract has been fulfilled."

LEGAL PROVISIONS

The Hire Purchase System is regulated by the Hire Purchase Act 1972. Under Section 2(c) of the Act, "Hire Purchase Agreement means an agreement under which goods are let on hire and under which the hirer has an option to purchase them in accordance with the terms of the agreement and includes an agreement under which:

(*i*) possession of goods is delivered by the owner thereof to a person on condition that such person pay the agreed amount in periodical instalments, and

(*ii*) the property in the goods is to pass to such person on the payment of the last of such instalments, and

(*iii*) such person has a right to terminate the Agreement at any time before the property so passes."

Every Hire Purchase Agreement must be in writing and signed by all the parties thereto. (Section 3)

Contents of Hire Purchase Agreement

According to Section 4 of the Act, every hire purchase agreement shall contain the following particulars :

(*a*) The hire purchase price of the goods to which the agreement relates;

(*b*) The cash price of the goods, that is to say, the price at which the goods may be purchased by the hirer for cash;

(*c*) The date on which the agreement shall be deemed to have commenced;

(*d*) The number of instalments by which the hire purchase price is to be paid, the amount of cash of those instalments, and the date, or the mode of determining the date, upon which it is payable, and the person to whom and the place where it is payable; and

(*e*) The goods to which the agreement relates, in the manner sufficient to identify them.

IMPORTANT TERMS

Under Section 7, important terms relating to this system are as follows:

HIRE PURCHASE PRICE: It means the total sum payable by the hirer under a Hire Purchase Agreement in order to complete the purchase of, or the acquisition of property in the goods to which the agreement relates; and includes any sum so payable by the hirer under the Hire Purchase Agreement by way of a deposit or other initial payment or credited or to be credited to him under such agreement on account of any such deposit or payment, but does not include any sum payable as penalty or as compensation or damages for a breach of the Agreement.

HIRER: It means the person who obtains or has obtained possession of goods from an owner under a Hire Purchase Agreement.

HIRE: It means the sum payable periodically by the hirer under a Hire Purchase Agreement.

OWNER: It means the person who lets, or has let, delivers or has delivered possession of goods, to a hirer under Hire Purchase Agreement.

HIRE PURCHASE CHARGES: Hire purchase charges or statutory charges in respect of a cash price instalment shall be an amount calculated at the rate of 30% per annum or of a lower rate as specific under sub-section (3), at such lower rate, in accordance with the following formula:

$$SC = \frac{CI \times R \times I}{100}$$

SC: Statutory Charges

CI: The amount of cash price instalment expressed in rupees or fractions of rupees.

R: The rate

I: The time, expressed in years and fractions of years, that elapses between the date of the agreement and the date on which the hire purchase instalment corresponding to the cash price instalment is payable under the agreement.

NET HIRE PURCHASE CHARGES: It means the difference between the net hire purchase price and the net cash price of the goods comprised in the hire purchase agreement.

It is our common experience that a seller, who sells his goods on cash or on hire purchase system, quotes both the prices side by side. When one gets a product on cash basis, one has to pay lesser amount than getting the same product under hire purchase system. This is so because hire purchase system includes some element of interest on the unpaid amount for the time they remain unpaid. Since all the instalments make hire purchase price, the hire purchase price consists of *cash* and *interest.* This requires allocation of instalment money between interest (revenue) and cash price (principal or capital). These amounts *i.e.* cash price and interest varies even between equal instalments. Getting a commodity under hire purchase system and given equal instalments, the charges for the interest decreases and payment towards the principal amount increases, on every next instalment. This is so because interest is charged only on remaining (unpaid) principal amount. Thus it becomes impossible to calculate and find out the amount of cash price and interest included in each instalment.

Distinction between Hire Purchase and Instalment Sales

Hire Purchase Sale	*Instalment Sale*
1. Ownership in the goods is transferred only after the payment of the last instalment.	1. Ownership is transferred at the moment of purchase.
2. The remittance is made by the buyer through instalments.	2. Payment of price is generally made in instalments or according to agreement.
3. On default, the goods will be seized by the seller.	3. On default, the seller cannot take back the goods but recovery may be made through the court of law.
4. If the buyer sells the goods before making the last instalment, the new buyer does not get a better title than the purchaser under credit purchase.	4. If the buyer sells the goods before full payment of price, the new buyer gets better title than the hire purchaser.
5. The buyer has no right to dispose the goods.	5. The buyer has the right of disposing the goods in any manner he likes.

Calculation of Interest

Every instalment has two components – cash price and interest. Hire purchase problems require periodic computation of interest under any of the following cases.

(1) Where Cash Price, Interest Rate and Instalment are given

ILLUSTRATION 18.1

On Ist January 2003, *A* bought a television from a seller under Hire Purchase System, the cash price of which being Rs 10,450 as per the following terms:

(*a*) Rs 3,000 to be paid on signing the agreement.

(*b*) Balance to be paid in three equal instalments of Rs 3,000 at the end of each year.

(*c*) The rate of interest charged by the seller is 10% per annum.

You are required to calculate the interest paid by the buyer to the seller each year.

SOLUTION

Calculation of Interest

Date of payment	*Instalment Rs*	*Interest*		*Cash Value Rs*
1.1.2003	3,000	–		3,000.00
31.12.2003	3,000	10,450 – 3,000 = 7,450 × 10%	745.00	2,255.00
31.12.2004	3,000	7,450 – 2,255 = 5,195 × 10%	519.50	2,480.50
31.12.2005	3,000	(Balancing figure)	285.50	2,714.50
	12,000		1,550	10,450.00

Note: 1. There is no time gap between the signing of the agreement and the cash down payment of Rs 3,000 (1.1.2003). Hence no interest is calculated. The entire amount goes to reduce the cash price.

2. The interest in the last instalment is taken at the differential figure of Rs 285.50 (3,000 – 2,714.50).

(2) Where Cash Price and Instalments are given but Rate of Interest is Omitted

Where the rate of interest is not given and only the cash price and the total payments under hire purchase instalments are given, then the total interest paid is the difference between the cash price of the asset and the total amount paid as per the agreement. This interest amount is apportioned in the ratio of amount outstanding at the end of each period.

ILLUSTRATION 18.2

Mr *A* bought a machine under hire purchase agreement, the cash price of the machine being Rs 18,000. As per the terms, the buyer has to pay Rs 4,000 on signing the agreement and the balance in four instalments of Rs 4,000 each, payable at the end of each year. Calculate the interest chargeable at the end of each year.

SOLUTION

	Rs
Amount payable 4,000 + (4 × 4,000)	20,000
Cash price of the machine	18,000
Interest payable	2,000

This amount of Rs 2,000 is apportioned on the basis of ratio of amount outstading at the end of each year, as detailed below:

Year	*Amount outstanding at the end of the year* *Rs*	*Interest divided in ratio of instalment*	*Total interest divided in the ratio of instalment due* *Rs*
First year	16,000	4	2,000 × 4/10 = 800
Second year	12,000	3	2,000 × 3/10 = 600
Third year	8,000	2	2,000 × 2/10 = 400
Fourth year	4,000	1	2,000 × 1/10 = 200
			2,000

(3) Where Instalments and Rate of Interest are given but Cash Value of the Asset is Omitted

In certain problems, the cash price is not given. It is necessary that we must first find out the cash price and interest included in the instalments. The asset account is to be debited with the actual price of the asset. Under such situations, *i.e.* in the absence of cash price, the interest is calculated from the last year. It may be noted that the amount of interest goes on increasing from 3rd year to 2nd year, 2nd year to Ist year. Since the interest is included in the instalments and by knowing the rate of interest, we can find out the cash price. Thus:

Let the cash price outstanding be: Rs 100
Interest @ 10% on Rs 100 for a year: Rs 10
Instalment paid at the end of the year 110

The interest on instalment price = $\frac{10}{110}$ or $\frac{1}{11}$ as a ratio.

ILLUSTRATION 18.3

I buy a television on Hire Purchase System. The terms of payment are as follows:

Rs 2,000 to be paid on signing the agreement;
Rs 2,800 at the end of the first year;
Rs 2,600 at the end of the second year;
Rs 2,400 at the end of the third year;
Rs 2,200 at the end of the fourth year.

If interest is charged at the rate of 10% p.a., what was the cash value of the television?

No. of Instalment	*Closing Balance* *Rs*	*Amount of Instalment* *Rs*	*Total* *Rs*	*Interest* *Rs*	*Cash price at the beginning* *Rs*
4	Nil	2,200	2,200	2,200 × 10/110 = 200	2,000
3	2,000	2,400	4,400	4,400 × 10/110 = 400	4,000
2	4,000	2,600	6,600	6,600 × 10/110 = 600	6,000
1	6,000	2,800	8,800	8,800 × 10/110 = 800	8,000

Cash Price = Down payment + Rs 8,000
= Rs 2,000 + Rs 8,000 = **Rs 10,000**

(4) Calculation of Cash Price when Reference to Annuity Table, the Rate of Interest and Instalments are given

Sometimes in the problem a reference to annuity table wherein present value of the annuity for a number of years at a certain rate of interest is given. In such cases the cash price is calculated by multiplying the amount of instalment and adding the product to the initial payment.

ILLUSTRATION 18.4

A agrees to purchase a machine from a seller under Hire Purchase System by annual instalment of Rs 10,000 over a period of 5 years. The seller charges interest at 4% p.a. on yearly balance.

N.B. The present value of Re 1 p.a. for five years at 4% is Rs 4.4518. Find out the cash price of the machine.

SOLUTION

Instalment Re 1 Present value = Rs 4.4518

Instalment = Rs 10,000 Present value = Rs 4.4518 × 10,000 = Rs 44,518

Interest Calculation

	Interest		*Cash Price* *Rs*	*Instalment* *Rs*
1.	44,518 × 4/100	= 1,781	8,219	10,000
2.	44,518 – 8,219 = 36,299 × 4/100	= 1,452	8,548	10,000
3.	36,299 – 8,548 = 27,751 × 4/100	= 1,110	8,890	10,000
4.	27,751 – 8,890 = 18,861 × 4/100	= 754	9,246	10,000
5.	18,861 – 9,246 = 9,615 × 4/100	= 385	9,615	10,000
			44,518	50,000

Accounting Record in the Books of Hire Purchaser

There are two methods of making accounting record in the books of Hire Purchaser:

First Method (Capitalising Only the Portion of Cash Price Paid)

Under this method, the asset account is debited with the cash price included in each instalment. Remember, the down payment is fully towards cash price. As and when he pays the instalment, he capitalises the amount equal to the cash price of the instalment. The buyer recognises the fact that no legal title to the goods passes to him until the last instalment is paid. Here it is important to note that the hire purchaser debits the asset account with the cash price as and when he pays the instalment under gradual capitalisation method. That is, when he pays the instalment, he capitalises the amount equal to the cash price of the instalment. At the same time, he is permitted to use the asset, as he is the true owner even before the last payment. Therefore, it is appropriate to bring depreciation of the asset on its full cash price.

Journal entries : Book of hire buyer

1.	Asset Account	Dr.
	To Vendor Account	
	(Being the down payment due)	
2.	Vendor Account	Dr.
	To Bank Account	
	(Being cash down payment made)	
3.	Assets Account	Dr.
	Interest Account	Dr.
	To Vendor Account	
	(Being the instalment due)	

Note: A system of payment in which the price of goods purchased is paid in instalments is known as a Deferred Payment System.

4. Vendor Account Dr.
   To Bank Account
   (Being the instalment paid)

5. Depreciation Account Dr.
   To Asset Account
   (Being the amount of depreciation)

6. Profit & Loss Account Dr.
   To Interest Account
   To Depreciation A/c
   (Being transferring of interest and depreciation accounts)

The last four entries are repeated year after year till the last instalment is paid off.

Second Method (Capitalising the Full Cash Price)

Under this method, the hire purchaser debits the asset account at its full cash price and credits the hire vendor's account. Many hire purchasers enter into the hire purchase agreement with the intention of honouring them. The following journal entries will clarify:

Journal Entries:

1. Asset Account Dr.
   To Hire Vendor Account
   (Being record of full cash value of asset purchased on hire purchase)

2. Hire Vendor Account Dr.
   To Bank A/c
   (Being payment of cash down at the time of agreement)

3. Interest Account Dr.
   To Hire Vendor Account
   (Being the interest due)

4. Hire Vendor Account Dr.
   To Bank A/c
   (Being payment of instalment)

5. Depreciation Account Dr.
   To Asset Account
   (Being the amount of depreciation)

6. Profit & Loss Account Dr.
   To Interest Account
   To Depreciation Account
   (Being transfer of Interest and Depreciation account)

N.B. The last four entries are repeated year after year till the last instalment is paid off.

ILLUSTRATION 18.5

Mr Ramprasad purchased under hire purchase system a machine from Bombay Company on Ist January 2003, paying cash Rs 10,000 and agreeing to pay three further instalments of Rs 10,000 each on 31st December every year. The cash price of the machine is Rs 37,250 and Bombay Company charges interest at 5% p.a. Ramprasad writes off depreciation at the rate of 10% p.a. on diminishing balance method.

Journalise these transactions and open ledger accounts in the books of Ramprasad, under both the methods.

(B.Com., Madurai)

SOLUTION

Calculation of Interest

Instalment No.	Total Cash Price Rs	Instalment Rs	Interest Rs	Cash Price Paid Rs	Depreciation Rs
	37,250	10,000	–	10,000	–
Cash Down	10,000				
	27,250				
1st instalment	8,637	10,000	1,363	8,637	3,725
	18,613				
2nd instalment	9,069	10,000	931	9,069	3,353
	9,544				
3rd instalment	9,544	10,000	456*	9,544	3,017
	Nil	40,000	2,750	37,250	

* Balancing figure

First Method (*Capitalising only the portion of cash price paid*)

			Dr. Rs	Cr. Rs
2003				
Jan. 1	Machinery Account	Dr.	10,000	
	To Bombay Co. Account			10,000
	(Being purchase of machinery on Hire Purchase System)			
Jan. 1	Bombay Co Account	Dr.	10,000	
	To Bank Account			10,000
	(Being payment of cash down payment)			
Dec. 31	Machinery Account	Dr.	8,637	
	Interest Account	Dr.	1,363	
	To Bombay Co. Account			10,000
	(Being the instalment due)			
"	Bombay Co. Account	Dr.	10,000	
	To Bank Account			10,000
	(Being payment of instalment)			
"	Depreciation Account	Dr.	3,725	
	To Machinery Account			3,725
	(Being the depreciation for the year)			
"	Profit & Loss Account	Dr.	5,088	
	To Interest Account			1,363
	To Depreciation Account			3,725
	(Being transfer of Interest and Depreciation Accounts)			
2004				
Dec. 31	Machinery Account	Dr.	9,069	
	Interest Account	Dr.	931	
	To Bombay Co Account			10,000
	(Being the instalment due)			

Date	Particulars		Dr. (Rs)	Cr. (Rs)
"	Bombay Co. Account To Bank Account (Being payment of instalment)	Dr.	10,000	10,000
"	Depreciation Account To Machinery Account (Being the depreciation for the year)	Dr.	3,353	3,353
"	Profit and Loss Account To Interest Account To Depreciation Account (Being transfer of Interest and Depreciation Accounts)	Dr.	4,284	931 3,353
2005 Dec. 31	Machinery Account Interest Account To Bombay Co. Account (Being instalment due)	Dr. Dr.	9,544 456	10,000
	Bombay Co. Account To Bank Account (Being payment of instalment)	Dr.	10,000	10,000
"	Depreciation Account To Machinery Account (Being the depreciation for the year)	Dr.	3,017	3,017
"	Profit and Loss Account To Interest Account To Depreciation Account (Being transfer of Interest and Depreciation Accounts)	Dr.	3,473	456 3,017

Dr. **Machinery Account** Cr.

Date	Particulars	Rs	Date	Particulars	Rs
2003 Jan. 1	To Bombay Co. A/c	10,000	2003 Dec. 31	By Depreciation A/c	3,725
Dec. 31	To Bombay Co. A/c	8,637	"	By Balance c/d	14,912
		18,637			18,637
2004 Jan. 1	To Balance b/d	14,912	2004 Dec. 31	By Depreciation A/c	3,353
Dec. 31	To Bombay Co. A/c	9,069	"	By Balance c/d	20,628
		23,981			23,981
2005 Jan. 1	To Balance b/d	20,628	2005 Dec. 31	By Depreciation A/c	3,017
Dec. 31	To Bombay Co. A/c	9,544	"	By Balance c/d	27,155
		30,172			30,172
2006 Jan. 1	To Balance b/d	27,155			

Bombay Company Account

Dr.		Rs			Cr. Rs
2003			2003		
Jan. 1	To Bank A/c	10,000	Jan. 1	By Machinery A/c	10,000
Dec. 31	To Bank A/c	10,000	Dec. 31	By Machinery A/c	8,637
			"	By Interest A/c	1,363
		20,000			20,000
2004			2004		
Dec. 31	To Bank A/c	10,000	Dec. 31	By Machinery A/c	9,069
			"	By Interest A/c	931
		10,000			10,000
2005			2005		
Dec. 31	To Bank A/c	10,000	Dec. 31	By Machinery A/c	9,544
			"	By Interest A/c	456
		10,000			10,000

Interest Account

Dr.		Rs			Cr. Rs
2003			2003		
Dec. 31	To Bombay Co. A/c	1,363	Dec. 31	By Profit & Loss A/c	1,363
2004			2004		
Dec. 31	To Bombay Co. A/c	931	Dec. 31	By Profit & Loss A/c	931
2005			2005		
Dec. 31	To Bombay Co. A/c	456	Dec. 31	By Profit & Loss A/c	456

Depreciation Account

Dr.		Rs			Cr. Rs
2003			2003		
Dec. 31	To Machinery A/c	3,725	Dec. 31	By Profit & Loss A/c	3,725
2004			2004		
Dec. 31	To Machinery A/c	3,353	Dec. 31	By Profit & Loss A/c	3,353
2005			2005		
Dec. 31	To Machinery A/c	3,017	Dec. 31	By Profit & Loss A/c	3,017

Second Method (Capitalising the full cash price)

			Dr. Rs	Cr. Rs
2003				
Jan. 1	Machinery Account	Dr.	37,250	
	To Bombay Co. Account			37,250
	(Being purchase of machinery on Hire Purchase system)			

Date	Particulars		Dr.	Cr.
Jan. 1	Bombay Co. Account To Bank Account (Being payment of cash down payment)	Dr.	10,000	10,000
Dec. 31	Interest Account To Bombay Co. Account (Being interest credited to vendor Co.)	Dr.	1,363	1,363
"	Bombay Co. Account To Bank Account (Being payment of instalment)	Dr.	10,000	10,000
"	Depreciation Account To Machinery Account (Being the depreciation for the year)	Dr.	3,725	3,725
"	Profit & Loss Account To Interest Account To Depreciation Account (Being transfer of Interest and Depreciation Accounts)	Dr.	5,088	1,363 3,725
2004 Dec. 31	Interest Account To Bombay Co. Account (Being interest credited to vendor Co.)	Dr.	931	931
"	Bombay Co. Account To Bank Account (Being payment of instalment)	Dr.	10,000	10,000
"	Depreciation Account To Machinery Account (Being the depreciation for the year)	Dr.	3,353	3,353
"	Profit & Loss Account To Interest Account To Depreciation Account (Being transfer of Interest and Depreciation accounts)	Dr.	4,284	931 3,353
2005 Dec. 31	Interest Account To Bombay Co. Account (Being interest credited to vendor Co.)	Dr.	456	456
"	Bombay Co. Account To Bank Account (Being payment of instalment)	Dr.	10,000	10,000
"	Depreciation Account To Machinery Account (Being depreciation for the year)	Dr.	3,017	3,017
"	Profit & Loss Account To Interest Account To Depreciation Account (Being transfer of Interest and Depreciation accounts)	Dr.	3,473	456 3,017

Machinery Account

Dr.		Rs			Cr. Rs
2003			2003		
Jan. 1	To Bombay Co. A/c	37,250	Dec. 31	By Depreciation A/c	3,725
			"	By Balance c/d	33,525
		37,250			37,250
2004			2004		
Jan. 1	To Balance b/d	33,525	Dec. 31	By Depreciation A/c	3,353
			"	By Balance c/d	30,172
		33,525			33,525
2005			2005		
Jan. 1	To Balance b/d	30,172	Dec. 31	By Depreciation A/c	3,017
			"	By Balance c/d	27,155
		30,172			30,172
2006					
Jan. 1	To Balance b/d	27,155			

Bombay Company Account

Dr.		Rs			Cr. Rs.
2003			2003		
Jan. 1	To Bank A/c	10,000	Jan. 1	By Machinery A/c	37,250
Dec. 31	To Bank A/c	10,000	Dec. 31	By Interest A/c	1,363
"	To Balance c/d	18,613			
		38,613			38,613
2004			2004		
Dec. 31	To Bank A/c	10,000	Jan. 1	By Balance b/d	18,613
"	To Balance c/d	9,544	Dec. 31	By Interest	931
		19,544			19,544
2005			2005		
Dec. 31	To Bank A/c	10,000	Jan. 1	By Balance b/d	9,544
			Dec. 31	By Interest	456
		10,000			10,000

Interest Account

Dr.		Rs			Cr. Rs
2003			2003		
Dec. 31	To Bombay Co. A/c	1,363	Dec. 31	By Profit & Loss A/c	1,363
2004			2004		
Dec. 31	To Bombay Co. A/c	931	Dec. 31	By Profit & Loss A/c	931
2005			2005		
Dec. 31	To Bombay Co. A/c	456	Dec. 31	By Profit & Loss A/c	456

Depreciation Account

Dr.		Rs			Cr. Rs
2003 Dec. 31	To Machinery A/c	3,725	2003 Dec. 31	By Profit & Loss A/c	3,725
2004 Dec. 31	To Machinery A/c	3,353	2004 Dec. 31	By Profit & Loss A/c	3,353
2005 Dec. 31	To Machinery A/c	3,017	2005 Dec. 31	By Profit & Loss A/c	3,017

ILLUSTRATION 18.6

Mr Gupta purchased a machine under hire purchase agreement from Mr Pankaj. The cash price of the machine was Rs 15,500. The payment for the purchase is to be made as under:

On signing the agreement	Rs 3,000
End of the first year	Rs 5,000
End of the second year	Rs 5,000
End of the third year	Rs 5,000

Make necessary journal entries in the books of both the parties. Charge depreciation at the rate of 10% on diminishing balance method. *(CA Inter)*

SOLUTION

Journal entries in the books of Gupta

			First year Dr. Rs	First year Cr. Rs	Second year Dr. Rs	Second year Cr. Rs	Third year Dr. Rs	Third year Cr. Rs
Jan. 1	Machinery Account	Dr.	15,500					
	To Pankaj Account			15,500				
	(Being purchase of machinery on hire purchase system)							
Jan. 1	Pankaj Account	Dr.	3,000					
	To Bank Account			3,000				
	(Being remittance of cash down payment)							
Dec. 31	Interest Account	Dr.	1,250		833		417	
	To Pankaj Account			1,250		833		417
	(Being interest credited to Pankaj)							
"	Pankaj Account	Dr.	5,000		5,000		5,000	
	To Bank Account			5,000		5,000		5,000
	(Being payment of Instalment)							
Dec. 31	Depreciation Account	Dr.	1,550		1,395		1,256	
	To Machinery Account			1,550		1,395		1,256
	(Being depreciation charged to asset)							
"	Profit & Loss Account	Dr.	2,800		2,228		1,673	
	To Interest Account			1,250		833		417
	To Depreciation Account			1,550		1,395		1,256
	(Being Interest and Depreciation transferred)							

Journal entries in the books of Pankaj

			First year		Second year		Third year	
			Dr.	Cr.	Dr.	Cr.	Dr.	Cr.
			Rs	Rs	Rs	Rs	Rs	Rs
Jan. 1	Gupta Account To Hire Sales Account (Being hire purchase sales)	Dr.	15,500	15,500				
"	Bank Account To Gupta Account (Being received on down payment)	Dr.	3,000	3,000				
Dec. 31	Gupta Account To Interest Account (Being instalment credited)	Dr.	1,250	1,250	833	833	417	417
"	Bank Account To Gupta Account (Being instalment received)	Dr.	5,000	5,000	5,000	5,000	5,000	5,000
"	Interest Account To Profit & Loss Account (Being Interest transferred)	Dr.	1,250	1,250	833	833	417	417
"	Hire Sales Account To Trading Account	Dr.	15,500	15,500				

Working note:

Calculation of Interest

Total Cash Price = Rs 15,500

Total Instalment price Rs 18,000

Total Interest paid = Rs 2,500 (18,000 – 15,500)

Rs 2,500 is apportioned on the basis of the ratio of outstanding amount due at the end of each year. Thus:

Year	*Amount of outstanding at the end of the year*	*Interest is divided in the ratio*	*Interest*		
1	Rs 15,000	15 or 3	2,500 × 3/6	=	Rs 1,250
2	Rs 10,000	10 or 2	2,500 × 2/6	=	Rs 833
3	Rs 5,000	5 or 1	2,500 × 1/6	=	Rs 417*
			Total		Rs 2,500

* Balancing figure

ILLUSTRATION 18.7

On Ist January 2003, X Ltd. purchased a car from Y Ltd. on Hire Purchase System, the cash price of which was payable as Rs 12,000 down and balance in three equal annual instalments together with interest @ 10% p.a. The amount of the last instalment including interest was Rs 17,600. Depreciation was to be provided at 20% p.a. on reducing balances. At the end of 3rd year of service, the car was sold for Rs 30,000 cash.

Show Car Account and Vendor Account in the books of the buyer for three years to 31st December 2005.

(*ICWA Inter*)

SOLUTION

Car Account

Dr.		Rs			Cr. Rs
2003			2003		
Jan. 1	To Y Ltd.	60,000	Dec. 31	By Depreciation	12,000
			"	By Balance c/d	48,000
		60,000			60,000
2004			2004		
Jan. 1	To Balance b/d	48,000	Dec. 31	By Depreciation	9,600
			"	By Balance c/d	38,400
		48,000			48,000
2005			2005		
Jan. 1	To Balance b/d	38,400	Dec. 31	By Depreciation	7,680
			"	By Bank	30,000
			"	By Profit & Loss A/c	720
		38,400			38,400

Y Ltd. Account

Dr.		Rs			Cr. Rs
2003			2003		
Jan. 1	To Bank Account	12,000	Jan. 1	By Car Account	60,000
Dec. 31	To Bank Account (16,000 + 4,800)	20,800	Dec. 31	By Interest (10% on Rs 48,000)	4,800
31	To Balance c/d	32,000			
		64,800			64,800
2004			2004		
Dec. 31	To Bank (16,000 + 3,200)	19,200	Jan. 1	By Balance b/d	32,000
"	To Balance c/d	16,000	Dec. 31	By Interest (10% on Rs 32,000)	3,200
		35,200			35,200
2005			2005		
Dec. 31	To Bank	17,600	Jan. 1	By Balance b/d	16,000
			Dec. 31	By Interest (10% on Rs 16,000)	1,600
		17,600			17,600

Note: Calculation of Cash Price:

3rd Instalment is Rs 17,600 (110%)

Therefore cash price = 17,600 × 100/110 = Rs 16,000

Thus total cash price = Rs 12,000 + (Rs 16,000 × 3)

= Rs 12,000 + 48,000 = Rs 60,000

Accounting records in the books of Hire Vendor

As stated earlier, property in the goods does not pass from the Hire Vendor to the Hire Purchaser, under hire purchase system, until the payment of last instalment is paid off. But in actual practice, the Hire Vendor treats the sales as ordinary sales. Thus, the Hire Vendor makes the entries as under:

1	Hire Purchaser Account To Hire Sales (Being the entry for sales under hire purchase system)	Dr.
2.	Bank Account To Hire Purchaser A/c (Being the payment of down payment)	Dr.

At the end of the first year

3.	Hire Purchaser Account To Interest Account (Being interest due on unpaid balance)	Dr.
4.	Bank Account To Hire Purchaser A/c (Being amount of instalment received)	Dr.
5.	Interest Account To Profit & Loss A/c (Being transfer of interest)	Dr.
6.	Hire Sales Account To Trading Account (Being hire sales transferred to Trading Account)	Dr.

Note: No entry for depreciation is made in the books of the Hire Vendor. Entries 3, 4 and 5 will be repeated in all subsequent years.

ILLUSTRATION 18.8

On 1st January 2003, Gopal bought a machine from Ram & Co. on hire purchase system, the cash price of the machine being Rs 35,775, under the following terms:

(*a*) Rs 10,000 payable on signing of the agreement i.e. 1.1.2003.

(b) Remaining balance to be paid in three equal instalments of Rs 10,000 each at the end of the subsequent years.

(c) Interest to be charged at the rate of 8%.

(d) Depreciation to be provided at 10% annually.

Make necessary entries in the books of both the parties and show the ledger accounts too.

(*B.Com., Madurai*)

SOLUTION

Interest Calculation

	Rs	Interest 8% Rs	Cash Price Rs	Instalment Rs	Depreciation Rs
	35,775				
1.1.2003	10,000	–	10,000	10,000	–
	25,775				
31.12.2003	7,938	2,062	7,938	10,000	3,578
	17,837				
31.12.2004	8,573	1,427	8,573	10,000	3,220
	9,264				
31.12.2005	9,264	736	9,264	10,000	2,898
	–	4,225	35,775	40,000	

Entries in the books of Gopal

			2003		2004		2005	
			Dr.	Cr.	Dr.	Cr.	Dr.	Cr.
			Rs	Rs	Rs	Rs	Rs	Rs
Jan. 1	Machinery Account	Dr.	35,775					
	To Ram & Co. Account			35,775				
	(Being purchase of Machine on hire purchase)							
"	Ram & Co. Account	Dr.	10,000					
	To Bank Account			10,000				
	(Being cash down payment)							
Dec. 31	Interest Account	Dr.	2,062		1,427		736	
	To Ram & Co. Account			2,062		1,427		736
	(Being interest due)							
"	Ram & Co. Account	Dr.	10,000		10,000		10,000	
	To Bank Account			10,000		10,000		10,000
	(Being instalment paid)							
"	Depreciation Account	Dr.	3,578		3,220		2,898	
	To Machine Account			3,578		3,220		2,898
	(Being depreciation for the year)							
"	Profit & Loss Account	Dr.	5,640		4,647		3,634	
	To Interest Account			2,062		1,427		736
	To Depreciation Account			3,578		3,220		2,898
	(Being Interest and Depreciation Accounts transferred)							

Dr. **Machine Account** Cr.

		Rs			Rs.
2003 Jan. 1	To Ram & Co. Account	35,775	2003 Dec. 31	By Depreciation	3,578
			"	By Balance c/d	32,197
		35,775			35,775
2004 Jan. 1	To Balance b/d	32,197	2004 Dec. 31	By Depreciation	3,220
			"	By Balance c/d	28,977
		32,197			32,197
2005 Jan. 1	To Balance b/d	28,977	2005 Dec. 31	By Depreciation	2,898
			"	By Balance c/d	26,079
		28,977			28,977
2006 Jan. 1	To Balance b/d	26,079			

Ram & Co. Account

Dr.		Rs		Cr.	Rs
2003			2003		
Jan. 1	To Bank Account	10,000	Jan. 1	By Machine Account	35,775
Dec. 31	To Bank Account	10,000	Dec. 31	By Interest Account	2,062
"	To Balance c/d	17,837			
		37,837			37,837
2004			2004		
Dec. 31	To Bank Account	10,000	Jan. 1	By Balance b/d	17,837
"	To Balance c/d	9,264	Dec. 31	By Interest Account	1,427
		19,264			19,264
2005			2005		
Dec. 31	To Bank Account	10,000	Jan. 1	By Balance b/d	9,264
			Dec. 31	By Interest Account	736
		10,000			10,000

Interest Account

Dr.		Rs		Cr.	Rs
2003			2003		
Dec. 31	To Ram & Co. Account	2,062	Dec. 31	By Profit & Loss Account	2,062
2004			2004		
Dec. 31	To Ram & Co. Account	1,427	Dec. 31	By Pofit & Loss Account	1,427
2005			2005		
Dec. 31	To Ram & Co. Account	736	Dec. 31	By Profit & Loss Account	746

Depreciation Account

Dr.		Rs		Cr.	Rs
2003			2003		
Dec. 31	To Machine Account	3,578	Dec. 31	By Profit & Loss Account	3,578
2004			2004		
Dec. 31	To Machine Account	3,220	Dec. 31	By Profit & Loss Account	3,220
2005			2005		
Dec. 31	To Machine Account	2,898	Dec. 31	By Profit & Loss Account	2,898

Entries in the books of Ram & Co.

			2003		2004		2005	
			Dr.	Cr.	Dr.	Cr.	Dr.	Cr.
			Rs	Rs	Rs	Rs	Rs	Rs
Jan. 1	Gopal Account	Dr.	35,775					
	To Hire Sales Account			35,775				
	(Being sales under Hire Purchase system)							

Date	Particulars		2003 Dr.	2003 Cr.	2004 Dr.	2004 Cr.	2005 Dr.	2005 Cr.
"	Bank Account	Dr.	10,000					
	To Gopal Account			10,000				
	(Being cash down payment received)							
Dec. 31	Gopal Account	Dr.	2,062		1,427		736	
	To Interest Account			2,062		1,427		736
	(Being interest due from Gopal)							
"	Bank Account	Dr.	10,000		10,000		10,000	
	To Gopal Account			10,000		10,000		10,000
	(Being interest due from Gopal)							
"	Interest Account	Dr.	2,062		1,427		736	
	To Profit & Loss Account			2,062		1,427		736
"	Hire Sales Account	Dr.	35,775					
	To Trading Account			35,775				
	(Being Hire Sales transferred)							

Gopal Account

Dr.		Rs			Cr. Rs
2003			2003		
Jan. 1	To Hire Sales Account	35,775	Jan. 1	By Bank Account	10,000
Dec. 31	To Interest Account	2,062	Dec. 31	By Bank Account	10,000
			"	By Balance c/d	17,837
		37,837			37,837
2004			2004		
Jan. 1	To Balance b/d	17,837	Dec. 31	By Bank Account	10,000
Dec. 31	To Interest Account	1,427	"	By Balance c/d	9,264
		19,264			19,264
2005			2005		
Jan. 1	To Balance b/d	9,264	Dec. 31	By Bank Account	10,000
Dec. 31	To Interest Account	736			
		10,000			10,000

Interest Account

Dr.		Rs			Cr. Rs
2003			2003		
Dec. 31	To Profit & Loss Account	2,062	Dec. 31	By Gopal Account	2,062
2004			2004		
Dec. 31	To Profit & Loss Account	1,427	Dec. 31	By Gopal Account	1,427
2005			2005		
Dec. 31	To Profit & Loss Account	736	Dec. 31	By Gopal Account	736

DEFAULT AND REPOSSESSION

When the hire purchase customer makes default in the payment of instalment, the hire vendor has a right to repossess the goods sold under hire purchase system. The essence of a hire purchase transaction is to transfer the ownership of goods (purchased by the hire purchaser) to hire purchaser only on his paying the last instalment. On committing default in the payment of any instalment, the hire vendor reserves the right to repossess the goods and hire purchaser has to forfeit the instalment already paid. The hire vendor repossesses either all the goods hired out or only a few of them. Repossession of all the goods is known as "Complete Repossession" and repossession of a few of the goods is known as "Partial Repossession".

Complete Repossession

Hire Vendor's Book	*Hire Purchaser's Book*
1. All entries to the date of default as usual, except the entry for payment of instalment defaulted.	1. All the entries up to the date of default as usual except for the instalment due and defaulted.
2. Debit Hire Sales Return Account and credit Hire Purchaser Account with the balance left in the Hire Purchaser Account.	2. Debit Hire Seller Account (with balance in his account) and credit asset account (with the same amount).
3. Any balance left in the Hire Purchaser Account is transferred to Profit & Loss Account.	3. Any balance left in the Asset Account is closed by transferring to Profit & Loss Account.
4. Goods Returned Account is further debited with expenses incurred for repair. Then credit it with the amount of sale proceeds and close it by transferring the balance, if any, to Profit & Loss Account.	

ILLUSTRATION 18.9

Delhi Transport Ltd. purchased from Bombay Motors three trucks costing Rs 40,000 each on the Hire Purchase System. Payment was to be made Rs 30,000 down and the remainder in three equal instalments together with interest at 5%. Delhi Transport writes off depreciation @ 20% on the Diminishing balance method. It paid the instalments at the end of the first year but could not pay the next.

Give the necessary Ledger Accounts in the books of both parties for two years if the hire vendor took possession of all the three trucks. The hire vendor spent Rs 5,800 on getting the trucks thoroughly overhauled and sold them for Rs 70,000. (*B.Com., Punjab, Kerala*)

SOLUTION

In the books of Delhi Transport Ltd.

Dr. **Trucks Account** Cr.

		Rs			Rs
I Yr.	To Bombay Motors A/c	1,20,000	I Yr.	By Depreciation A/c	24,000
			"	By Balance c/d	96,000
		1,20,000			1,20,000
II Yr.	To Balance b/d	96,000	II Yr.	By Depreciation A/c	19,200
			"	By Bombay Motors A/c	63,000
			"	By Profit & Loss A/c (Balancing figure) (Loss on default)	13,800
		96,000			96,000

Bombay Motors Account

Dr.		Rs			Cr. Rs
I Yr.	To Bank Account	30,000	I Yr.	By Truck Account	1,20,000
"	To Bank Account	34,500	"	By Interest Account	4,500
"	To Balance c/d	60,000		(5% on Rs 90,000)	
		1,24,500			1,24,500
II Yr.	To Truck Account	63,000	II Yr.	By Balance b/d	60,000
			"	By Interest Account	3,000
				(5% on Rs 60,000)	
		63,000			63,000

In the books of Bombay Motors

Delhi Transport Ltd.

Dr.		Rs			Cr. Rs
I Yr.	To Hire Sales Account	1,20,000	I Yr.	By Bank Account	30,000
"	To Interest Account	4,500	"	By Bank Account	34,500
			"	By Balance c/d	60,000
		1,24,500			1,24,500
II Yr.	To Balance b/d	60,000	II Yr.	By Repossessed Stock Account	63,000
"	To Interest Account	3,000			
		63,000			63,000

Repossessed Stock Account

Dr.		Rs			Cr. Rs
II Yr.	To Delhi Transport Co.	63,000		By Bank Account	70,000
	To Bank–Repairs	5,800			
	To Profit & Loss A/c (Profit)	1,200			
		70,000			70,000

Partial Repossession

Sometimes the hire vendor may not repossess the entire goods. The vendor seizes only a part of the goods, and the valuation depends upon the agreement between the parties. All the entries are made in the books up to the date of default. Then Hire Vendor Account is debited with the agreed value of the seized goods and the Asset Account is credited with the same value. Now the Asset Account shows the value of the portion left with the buyer; of course, less depreciation. Any difference in the Asset Account represents profit or loss on default and the same is transferred to Profit and Loss Account. The Repossessed Goods Account in the books of the vendor will be prepared on the same lines as it was done in Complete Repossession.

ILLUSTRATION 18.10

Calcutta Transport Company purchased on Ist January 2004 from Bombay Motors three trucks costing Rs 40,000 each on the hire purchase system. Payment was to be made Rs 30,000 down and the remainder in three equal instalments together with interest at 5%. Calcutta Transport Co. wrote off depreciation @ 20% p.a. on Diminishing balance method. It paid the instalment due at the end of the first year but could not pay the next.

Bombay Motors agreed to leave one truck with the purchaser adjusting the value of the other two trucks against the amount due. The trucks were valued on the basis of 30% depreciation annually. Give necessary ledger accounts in the books of Calcutta Transport Co. for two years. (*B.Com., Calcutta, M.K., Madras, Agra*)

SOLUTION

Calcutta Transport Company

Truck Account

Dr.		Rs			Cr. Rs
2004			2004		
Jan. 1	To Bombay Motors	1,20,000	Dec. 31	By Depreciation	24,000
			"	By Balance c/d	96,000
		1,20,000			1,20,000
2005			2005		
Jan. 1	To Balance b/d	96,000	Dec. 31	By Depreciation	19,200
			"	By Bombay Motors	39,200*
			"	By Profit & Loss (Balance figure)	12,000
			"	By Balance c/d	25,600@
		96,000			96,000

* *Value of two trucks taken up by Bombay Motors:*

	Rs
Rs 40,000 × 2	80,000
Less: Depreciation during 2004 @ 30%	24,000
	56,000
Less: Depreciation for 2005 @ 30%	16,800
	39,200

@ *Value of truck retained:*

	Rs
Value	40,000
Less: Depreciation for 2004 @ 20%	8,000
	32,000
Less: Depreciation for 2005 @ 20%	6,400
	25,600

Bombay Motors Account

Dr.		Rs			Cr. Rs
2004			2004		
Jan. 1	To Bank Account	30,000	Jan. 1	By Truck Account	1,20,000
Dec. 31	To Bank Account	34,500	Dec. 31	By Interest (5% on Rs 90,000)	4,500
"	To Balance c/d	60,000			
		1,24,500			1,24,500
2005			2005		
Dec. 31	To Truck Account	39,200	Jan. 1	By Balance b/d	60,000
"	To Balance c/d	23,800	Dec. 31	By Interest Account (5% on Rs 60,000)	3,000
		63,000			63,000

POST-SALE SERVICES

Sometimes a dealer undertakes to perform free services and maintenance for a specified period after the transfer of goods, under hire purchase scheme. Naturally, the estimated service charges during the period are loaded in the selling price. The amount of such services should be separated from the sale price. The amount so received is credited to a separate account, called Maintenance Suspense Account. Actual services expenses are rarely same as that estimated. On rendering such maintenance and/or services, it is debited with the actual cost. An underestimation leaves the account with a debit balance and an over-estimation leaves the account with a credit balance. If there is debit balance in the Maintenance Suspense Account, it must be written off to Profit and Loss Account. And credit balance of the account may be transferred to Profit and Loss Account or carried forward to wipe off such deficiency arising in future. Further, where these transactions are uniformly spread over the year, the maintenance period should be taken to begin from the mid-year, on an average basis. For instance, if the maintenance is undertaken for two years, the coverage of financial years would be half of the current year, whole of the next year and half of third year.

Accounting treatment for goods of small value

When there are numerous transactions and goods sold are of small value, the vendor goes for alternative method of recording transactions through subsidiary books. No individual account of any hire customer is recorded on double entry. The particulars of the name of articles, selling price of article, cost of article, number of instalments, collections, outstanding balances etc. are recorded in a register. The entry for Hire Purchase Trading is recorded at cost or hire selling price. The specimen of such a Hire Purchase Register is as under:

HIRE PURCHASE REGISTER for the period ending ....

S.No.	Date of agreement	Name of customer	Name of article	Cost price	HP price	Down payment	No. of instalment	Date of payment				
								1st	2nd	3rd	4th	5th

From the register, the following information will be collected at the end of the acounting period :

(1) Cost price of the goods sold under hire purchase;

(2) Total amount of cash received from customers;

(3) Total instalments due but unpaid;

(4) Cost price of the goods lying with customers, on which instalments have not become due. The total amount of unpaid and not due instalments gives the cost price of the goods in the hands of customers and is known as "Stock out of Hire at cost price." The value of such items can be ascertained as under, if the rate of gross profit on sale is uniform.

$$(i) \text{ Value of Goods} = \frac{\text{Amount of unpaid instalments}}{\text{Amount of hire purchase price}} \times \text{Cost Price}$$

$$\text{or } (ii) \quad = \frac{\text{No. of unpaid instalments}}{\text{No. of instalments}} \times \text{Cost Price}$$

or (*iii*) = Unpaid Instalments – Gross Profit margin

Computation of Profit

The profit made by the vendor on hire purchase transactions in case of goods of small value can be calculated by any of the following methods:

(A) Debtors Method or

(B) Stock and Debtors Method

(A) Debtors Method:

The following entries will be passed in the books of the vendor:

(A) At Cost

1.	Hire Purchase Trading Account To Goods Sold on Hire Purchase Account	Dr.	For Sale of goods on hire purchase
2.	Bank Account To Hire Purchase Trading Account	Dr.	For receipt of instalments
3.	Instalment Due Account To Hire Purchase Trading Account	Dr.	For instalment due and unpaid
4.	Goods Repossessed Account To Hire Purchase Trading Account	Dr.	For goods seized due to non-payment of instalment
5.	Hire Purchase Stock Account To Hire Purchase Trading Account	Dr.	For goods lying with customers to which instalments are undue

6. Balance left in Hire Purchase Trading account represents profit or loss and is closed by transferring to General Profit and Loss Account.

(B) At Selling Price

The procedure applied is the same as "at cost price". When goods are sold at loaded price or invoice price, to find out the true profit, the following adjustment entries are made. Thus removal of loading is done at the accounting date to determine the profit from hire sales transactions:

1.	Hire Purchase Stock Reserve A/c To Hire Purchase Trading A/c	Dr.	For loading on opening stock
2.	Hire Purchase Trading Account To Hire Purchase Stock Reserve A/c	Dr.	For loading on the closing stock
3.	Goods sold on Hire Purchase A/c To Hire Purchase Trading A/c	Dr.	For the excess of hire sale price over the cost.

PROFORMA OF HIRE PURCHASE TRADING ACCOUNT (At Cost)

To H.P. Stock (Opening)	—	By Cash received from Customers	—
To Stock with Customers	—	By Hire Sales Goods Repossessed	—
To Instalments due but unpaid (opening)	—	By Stock out with Customers	—
To Goods sold on H.P.	—	By Stock at Shop (closing)	—
To Profit (Balancing figure)	—	By Loss (Balancing figure)	—

ILLUSTRATION 18.11 (Debtors Method)

Mohan sells goods on H.P. System at cost plus 60%. From the following prepare Hire Purchase Trading Account.

Jan. 1.	Goods out on H.P. System at H.P. Price	Rs. 32,000
Dec. 31.	Instalments not due and unpaid	Rs. 72,000
,,	Instalments due and unpaid	Rs. 4,000

The following transactions took place during the year:

(a)	Goods sold on H.P. Price	Rs. 1,60,000
(b)	Cash received from customers	Rs. 1,12,000
(c)	Goods received back on default valued at (instalment due Rs. 4,000)	Rs. 800

(B.Com. Madras, Bharathiar, Bharathidasan)

SOLUTION

HIRE PURCHASE TRADING ACCOUNT

for the year ended .....

Dr.	Rs		Cr. Rs
To Goods out on H.P. (Opening)	32,000	By Cash from Customers	1,12,000
To Goods sold during the year	1,60,000	By Goods Repossessed	800
		By Instalments due (Closing Debtors)	4,000
To Stock Reserve $\left(\text{Rs. } 72,000 \times \frac{60}{160}\right)$	27,000	By Stock Reserve $\left(\text{Rs. } 32,000 \times \frac{60}{160}\right)$	12,000
To Profit & Loss A/c (profit)	41,800	By Instalments not due and unpaid (Closing stock)	72,000
		By Loading on goods sold $\left(\text{Rs. } 1,60,000 \times \frac{60}{100}\right)$	60,000
	2,60,800		2,60,800

ILLUSTRATION 18.12 (Debtors Method)

From the following details of a businessman who sells goods of small value at cost plus 50%, prepare Hire Purchase Trading Account.

		Rs.
1st Jan. 2006	Stock out with the customers at HP price	9,000
	Stock at shop at cost price	18,000
	Instalments due but not received	5,000
31st Dec. 2006	Goods worth Rs. 500 repossessed (Instalments not due Rs. 2,000)	
	Cash received from customers	60,000
	Purchase made during the year	60,000
	Stock at cost at shop (excluding the goods repossessed)	20,000
	Instalments due but not received	9,000
	Stock out at HP Price with customers	30,000

(*B.Com. Pondicherry, Madras*)

SOLUTION

HIRE PURCHASE TRADING ACCOUNT

for the year ended 31st Dec. 2006

Dr.	Rs		Cr. Rs
To Stock out with customers	9,000	By Cash from Customers	60,000
To Stock at Shop	18,000	By Goods Repossessed	500
To Instalment due	5,000	By Instalments due	9,000
To Purchases	60,000	By Stock Reserve $\left(\text{Rs. } 9,000 \times \frac{50}{150}\right)$	3,000
To Stock Reserve $\left(\text{Rs. } 30,000 \times \frac{50}{150}\right)$	10,000		
To Profit & Loss A/c (Profit) (Balancing fig.)	20,500	By Stock out with Customers	30,000
		By Stock at Shop	20,000
	1,22,500		1,22,500

(B) Stock and Debtors Method

Under this method, the following ledger accounts are to be opened:

1. Hire Purchase Stock Account
2. Goods Sold on Hire Purchase Account
3. Shop Stock Account
4. Hire Purchase Adjustment Account
5. Hire Purchase Debtors Account

The following journal entries are to be passed if this method is followed :

1.	Stock at Shop Account	Dr.	When goods are purchased for hire purchase sale
	To Purchase Account		(at Cost Price)
2.	Hire Purchase Stock A/c	Dr.	When goods sold on HP (at Sale Price)
	To Goods sold on HP A/c		
3.	HP Debtors Account	Dr.	When total instalments which become
	To HP Stock Account		due (at HP Price)
4.	Cash Account	Dr.	When cash is received
	To HP Debtors Account		
5.	Goods Repossessed A/c	Dr.	(for reasliable value)
	Hire Purchase Adjustment	Dr.	(Loss)
	To HP Debtors A/c		(Instalment due and not received)
	To HP Stock A/c		(for instalment not yet due)
	To HP Ajustments A/c		(Profit on repossession)
	(When goods repossessed on default and loss is transferred to HP Adjustment A/c)		
6.	Goods sold on HP A/c	Dr.	
	To HP Adjustment A/c		(Loading)
	To Trading Account		(Cost Price)
	(For transfer of goods sold on HP)		
7.	Stock Reserve Account	Dr.	(For loading in opening stock with customers)
	To HP Adjustment A/c		
8.	HP Adjustment Account	Dr.	(For loading in closing stock with customers)
	To Stock Reserve A/c		
9.	Goods Sold on HP A/c	Dr.	(For loading in goods sold on HP)
	To HP Adjustment A/c		
10.	HP Adjustment Account	Dr.	(For transfer of profit on HP)
	To Profit & Loss A/c		

Note : In case of lose, the last entry will be reversed.

ILLUSTRATION 18.13 (Stock and Debtors Method)

X Ltd., which sells a patent product on hire purchase terms, has the following transactions for the year ending 31st December 2006. The gross profit is 25% on selling price :

		Rs.
2006	Stock out on hire purchase price	40,000
1st Jan.	Stock on hand (in the shop)	5,000
	Instalments\due (customers still paying)	3,000
Dec. 31.	Stock out on hire at HP price	46,000
	Stock in hand (in the shop)	7,000
	Instalment Due	5,000
	Cash received during the year	80,000

Prepare the necessary accounts and find out the gross profit of X Ltd. for the year ending 31st Dec. 2006.

(*ICWA*)

SOLUTION

In the books of X Ltd.

Dr. **HIRE PURCHASE DEBTORS ACCOUNT** Cr.

		Rs			Rs
2006			2006		
Jan. 1	To Balance b/d	3,000	Dec. 31	By Cash A/c	80,000
	To HP Stock A/c (Balancing fig.)	82,000		By Balance c/d	5,000
		85,000			85,000

Dr. **HIRE PURCHASE STOCK ACCOUNT** Cr.

		Rs			Rs
2006			2006		
Jan. 1	To Balance b/d	40,000	Dec. 31	By HP Debtors A/c	82,000
	To Goods sold on HP (Bal. Fig.)	88,000		By Balance c/d	46,000
		1,28,000			1,28,000

Dr. **GOODS SOLD ON HP ACCOUNT** Cr.

		Rs			Rs
2006			2006		
Dec. 31	To Shop Stock (at cost)	66,000	Dec. 31	By HP Stock A/c	88,000
	To HP Adjustment (88,000 × 25%)	22,000			
		88,000			88,000

Dr. **SHOP STOCK ACCOUNT** Cr.

		Rs			Rs
2006			2006		
Jan. 1	To Balance b/d	5,000	Dec. 31	By Goods sold on HP A/c	66,000
Dec. 31	To Purchases (Bal. fig.)	68,000		By Balance c/d	7,000
		73,000			73,000

Dr. **HIRE PURCHASE ADJUSTMENT ACCOUNT** Cr.

		Rs			Rs
2006			2006		
Dec. 31	To General P & L Account (Gross Profit) (Bal. fig.)	20,500	Jan. 1	By Balance b/d (Rs. 40,000 × 25%)	10,000
	To Balance c/d (46,000 × 25%)	11,500		By Goods Sold on HP A/c	22,000
		32,000			32,000

Alternatively:

Dr. **HIRE PURCHASE TRADING ACCOUNT** Cr.

	Rs		Rs
To Shop Stock A/c	5,000	By Cash Received	80,000
To Instalments Due A/c	3,000	By Shop Stock	7,000
To Hire Purchase Stock		By Instalments Due	5,000
at cost	30,000	By HP Stock (cost)	
(Rs. 40,000 – 10,000)		(Rs. 46,000 – 11,500)	34,500
To Purchases	68,000		
To General P & L A/c	20,500		
(Gross Profit transferred)			
	1,26,500		1,26,500

Note : Gross Profit will always be the same whether Stock Debtors Method or Simply Hire Purchase Trading Method is followed.

ILLUSTRATION 18.14

Prem sells goods at hire purchase price. Hire purchase price is made of profit at 50% on hire purchase price. Calculate profit from the information given below by preparing hire purchase trading account:

2005		Rs
Jan. 1	Instalments due in the beginning	15,000
Dec. 31	Instalments due during the year	40,000
	Cash received during the year	50,000
	Goods sold during the year	42,000
	Instalments unpaid (not due)	10,000
	Goods repossessed during the year	50
	(Amount due Rs 500)	

(*B.Com., Kerala*)

SOLUTION

Dr. **Hire Purchase Trading Account** Cr.

	Rs		Rs
To Hire Purchase Stock	8,000	By Cash	50,000
To Instalment	15,000	By Instalment Due	4,500
To Goods sold during the year	42,000	By Repossessed Stock	50
To Stock Reserve	5,000	By Instalment unpaid, not due	10,000
To Profit & Loss A/c	19,550	By Stock Reserve	4,000
		By Goods sold on Hire Purchase	21,000
	89,550		89,550

Working Note:

(1) Calculation of Instalment Due on 31.12.2005

Dr. **Instalment Due A/c** Cr.

	Rs		Rs
To Balance b/d	15,000	By Cash	50,000
To Hire Purchase Stock	40,000	By Goods Repossessed	500
		By Balance c/d	4,500
		(Balancing figure)	
	55,000		55,000

(2) Calculation of Hire Purchase Stock on 1.1.2005

Dr. **Hire Purchase Stock A/c** Cr.

	Rs		Rs
To Balance b/d (Balancing figure)	8,000	By Instalment Due A/c	40,000
To Goods sold on Hire Purchase	42,000	By Balance c/d	10,000
	50,000		50,000

ILLUSTRATION 18.15

A company supplies machines on hire purchase terms at a profit of 50% over the cost. The following are the transactions for the year ended 31st December:

		Rs
Jan. 1	Stock out on hire at cost	20,000
	Instalment due (customers still paying)	1,800
	Goods repossessed during the year (for instalments unpaid Rs 300) evaluated at	150
	Instalments realised during the year	39,000
Dec. 31	Stock out on hire at cost	16,000
	Instalments due (customers still paying)	3,000

Prepare Hire Purchase Stock Account, Hire Purchase Debtors Account and Hire Purchase Adjustment Account.

SOLUTION

Dr. **Hire Purchase Stock Account** Cr.

		Rs		Rs
To Opening Stock (20,000 + 50% of Rs 20,000)		30,000	By Hire Purchase Debtors	40,500
To Goods sold on Hire Purchase			By Balance c/d (16,000 + 50% of 16,000)	24,000
Shop stock	23,000			
H.P. Adjustment	11,500	34,500		
		64,500		64,500

Dr. **Hire Purchase Debtors Account** Cr.

	Rs		Rs
To Balance b/d	1,800	By Repossessed Stock	150
To H.P. Stock A/c (Instalment Due)	40,500	By Hire Purchase Adjustment	150
		By Cash	39,000
		By Balance c/d	3,000
	42,300		42,300

Dr. **Hire Purchase Adjustment Account** Cr.

	Rs		Rs
To Stock Reserve	8,000	By Stock Reserve	10,000
To H.P. Debtors (Loss on Repossessed Stock)	150	By Goods sold on H.P.	11,500
To Profit & Loss A/c	13,350		
	21,500		21,500

INSTALMENT

In Instalment system, there is an immediate sale, in which the price, instead of being paid in one lump sum, is spread over a period, interest being charged on unpaid balances. Under this system, the property in goods is passed on immediately to the buyer on signing the contract. The seller gives up the possession of the goods. If the buyer makes default in payment of instalment, the seller cannot repossess the goods but he can sue for the balance of debt. The distinctions between the hire purchase system and instalment system are given below:

(1) Under hire purchase system, ownership of goods is transferred to the buyer after the payment of last instalment whereas under Instalment the ownership passes to the buyer at once on delivery.

(2) Under hire purchase, it is similar to a contract of hire but later it becomes a sale, whereas under instalment system it is a sale from the very beginning.

(3) Under hire purchase, if the buyer makes default the seller has a right to take back the goods whereas under instalment the seller cannot take back the goods.

(4) Under hire purchase system, the buyer cannot sell, destroy or transfer the goods whereas under instalment buyer can do as he wishes.

(5) Hire purchaser is just like a bailee but under instalment the buyer is the owner.

Journal Entries in the books of Purchaser

1.	Asset Account Dr. Interest Suspense Account Dr. To Vendor Account (Being purchase under instalment purchase system)	
2.	Vendor Account Dr. To Bank Account (Being down payment to vendor at the time of delivery of asset)	
3.	Interest Account Dr. To Interest Suspense Account (Being interest due)	
4.	Vendor Account Dr. To Bank Account (Being payment of instalment)	
5.	Depreciation Account Dr. To Asset Account (Being charging depreciation at...)	
6.	Profit and Loss Account Dr. To Interest Account To Depreciation Account (Being transfer of Interest and Depreciation Accounts)	

Note: Entries 3, 4, 5 and 6 are repeated till the date of last instalment.

Journal Entries in the books of Vendor

1.	Buyer Account Dr. To Sales Account To Interest Suspense Account (Being sale of goods on instalment system)	
2.	Bank Account Dr. To Buyer Account (Being cash received on delivery of goods)	
3.	Interest Suspense Account Dr. To Interest Account (Being interest due)	
4.	Cash Account Dr. To Buyer Account (Being receipt of instalment)	
5.	Interest Account Dr. To Profit & Loss Account (Being transfer of interest)	
6.	Sales Account Dr. To Trading Account (Being transfer of sales to Trading Account)	

Note: Entries 3, 4 and 5 are repeated till the date of last instalment.

ILLUSTRATION 18.16

A purchased, on instalment basis, a machine from *B* on Ist January, 2003, for a sum of Rs 80,000. Rs 20,000 is to be paid on signing of the contract and rest in three instalments of Rs 20,000 each. The cash price of the machine is Rs 74,500 and interest is charged by the vendor at 5% p.a. The buyer charges depreciation at 10% p.a. on the diminishing balance.

You are required to pass necessary journal entries in the books of both the buyer and the vendor and also prepare ledger accounts. (*B.Com., Madurai*)

SOLUTION

A's Journal

			Dr. Rs	Cr. Rs
2003 Jan. 1	Machinery Account	Dr.	74,500	
	Interest Suspense Account	Dr.	5,500	
	To *B* Account			80,000
	(Being purchase of machine on instalment basis)			
"	*B* Account	Dr.	20,000	
	To Bank Account			20,000
	(Being cash down payment)			
Dec. 31	Interest Account	Dr.	2,725	
	To Interest Suspense Account			2,725
	(Being interest @ 5% for the year)			
	B Account	Dr.	20,000	
	To Bank Account			20,000
	(Being payment of instalment)			

Date	Particulars		Dr. (Rs)	Cr. (Rs)
"	Depreciation Account To Machine Account (Being depreciation @ 10% p.a.)	Dr.	7,450	 7,450
"	Profit and Loss Account To Interest Account To Depreciation Account (Being transfer of Interest and Depreciation A/cs)	Dr.	10,175	 2,725 7,450
2004 Dec. 31	Interest Account To Interest Suspense Account (Being interest @ 5% for the year)	Dr.	1,861	 1,861
"	*B* Account To Bank Account (Being payment of instalment)	Dr.	20,000	 20,000
"	Depreciation Account To Machine Account (Being depreciation @ 10% p.a.)	Dr.	6,705	 6,705
Dec. 31	Profit and Loss Account To Interest Account To Depreciation Account (Being transfer of Interest and Depreciation Accounts)	Dr.	8,566	 1,861 6,705
2005 Dec. 31	Interest Account To Interest Suspense Account (Being interest @ 5% for the year)	Dr.	914	 914
"	*B* Account To Bank Account (Being payment of instalment)	Dr.	20,000	 20,000
"	Depreciation Account To Machine Account (Being depreciation @ 10% p.a.)	Dr.	6,035	 6,035
"	Profit and Loss Account To Interest Account To Depreciation Account (Being transfer of Interest and Depreciation Accounts)	Dr.	6,949	 914 6,035

Machine Account

Dr. Cr.

Date	Particulars	Rs	Date	Particulars	Rs
2003 Jan. 1	To *B* Account	74,500	2003 Dec. 31	By Depreciation A/c	7,450
			"	By Balance c/d	67,050
		74,500			74,500

Date	Particulars	Rs	Date	Particulars	Rs
2004			2004		
Jan. 1	To Balance b/d	67,050	Dec. 31	By Depreciation A/c	6,705
			"	By Balance c/d	60,345
		67,050			67,050
2005			2005		
Jan. 1	To Balance b/d	60,345	Dec. 31	By Depreciation A/c	6,035
			"	By Balance c/d	54,310
		60,345			60,345
2006					
Jan. 1	To Balance b/d	54,310			

B Account

Dr.					Cr.
2003		Rs	2003		Rs
Jan. 1	To Bank A/c	20,000	Jan. 1	By Machine a/c	74,500
Dec. 31	To Bank A/c	20,000	"	By Interest Suspense A/c	5,500
"	To Balance c/d	40,000			
		80,000			80,000
2004			2004		
Dec. 31	To Bank A/c	20,000	Jan. 1	By Balance b/d	40,000
"	To Balance c/d	20,000			
		40,000			40,000
2005			2005		
Dec. 31	To Bank A/c	20,000	Jan. 1	By Balance b/d	20,000
		20,000			20,000

Interest Suspense Account

Dr.					Cr.
		Rs			Rs
2003			2003		
Jan. 1	To B Account	5,500	Dec. 31	By Interest Account	2,725
			"	By Balance c/d	2,775
		5,500			5,500
2004			2004		
Jan. 1	To Balance b/d	2,775	Dec. 31	By Interest Account	1,861
			"	By Balance c/d	914
		2,775			2,775
2005			2005		
Jan. 1	To Balance b/d	914	Dec. 31	By Interest Account	914
		914			914

Interest Account

Dr.					Cr.
		Rs			Rs
2003			2003		
Dec. 31	To Interest Account	2,725	Dec. 31	By Profit & Loss A/c	2,725

2004			2004		
Dec. 31	To Interest Account	1,861	Dec. 31	By Profit & Loss A/c	1,861
2005			2005		
Dec. 31	To Interest Account	914	Dec. 31	By Profit & Loss A/c	914

Depreciation Account

Dr.		Rs			Cr. Rs
2003			2003		
Dec. 31	To Machine A/c	7,450	Dec. 31	By Profit & Loss A/c	7,450
2004			2004		
Dec. 31	To Machine A/c	6,705	Dec. 31	By Profit & Loss A/c	6,705
2005			2005		
Dec. 31	To Machine A/c	6,035	Dec. 31	By Profit & Loss A/c	6,035

B's Journal

			Dr. Rs	Cr. Rs
2003				
Jan. 1	*A* Account	Dr.	80,000	
	To Sales Account			74,500
	To Interest Suspense Account			5,500
	(Being sale of goods on Instalment system)			
"	Bank Account	Dr.	20,000	
	To *A* Account			20,000
	(Being cash received on delivery)			
Dec. 31	Interest Suspense Account	Dr.	2,725	
	To Interest Account			2,725
	(Being the interest due)			
"	Bank Account	Dr.	20,000	
	To *A* Account			20,000
	(Being amount of instalment received)			
"	Interest Account	Dr.	2,725	
	To Profit and Loss Account			2,725
	(Being transfer of Interest Account)			
2004				
Dec. 31	Interest Suspense Account	Dr.	1,861	
	To Interest Account			1,861
	(Being interest due)			
"	Bank Account	Dr.	20,000	
	To *A* Account			20,000
	(Being amount of instalment received)			
"	Interest Account	Dr.	1,861	
	To Profit and Loss Account			1,861
	(Being transfer of Interest Account)			

2005				
Dec. 31	Interest Suspense Account	Dr.	914	
	To Interest Account			914
	(Being interest due)			
"	Bank Account	Dr.	20,000	
	To *A* Account			20,000
	(Being amount of instalment received)			
"	Interest Account	Dr.	914	
	To Profit and Loss Account			914
	(Being transfer of Interest Account			

B Account

Dr.		Rs		Cr.	Rs
2003			2003		
Jan. 1	To Sales Account	74,500	Jan. 1	By Bank Account	20,000
"	To Interest Suspense A/c	5,500	Dec. 31	By Bank Account	20,000
			"	By Balance c/d	40,000
		80,000			80,000
2004			2004		
Jan. 1	To Balance b/d	40,000	Dec. 31	By Bank Account	20,000
			"	By Balance c/d	20,000
		40,000			40,000
2005			2005		
Jan. 1	To Balance b/d	20,000	Dec. 31	By Bank Account	20,000

Interest Suspense Account

Dr.		Rs		Cr.	Rs
2003			2003		
Dec. 31	To Interest Account	2,725	Jan. 1	By *A* Account	5,500
"	To Balance c/d	2,775			
		5,500			5,500
2004			2004		
Dec. 31	To Interest Account	1,861	Jan. 1	By Balance b/d	2,775
"	To Balance c/d	914			
		2,775			2,775
2005			2005		
Dec. 31	To Interest Account	914	Jan. 1	By Balance b/d	914

Interest Account

Dr.		Rs		Cr.	Rs
2003			2003		
Dec. 31	To Profit & Loss A/c	2,725	Dec. 31	By Interest Suspense A/c	2,715
2004			2004		
Dec. 31	To Profit & Loss A/c	1,861	Dec. 31	By Inerest Suspense A/c	1,861
2005			2005		
Dec. 31	To Profit & Loss A/c	914	Dec. 31	By Interest Suspense A/c	914

ILLUSTRATION 18.17

On 1st January 2003, the New Colliery Company bought wagons on Instalment System. The cash price of wagons was Rs 11,175 and payment was to be made as follows:

An amount of Rs 3,000 was to be paid on signing the agreement.

The balance to be paid in three instalments of Rs 3,000 each at the end of the year.

5% interest is charged by the Wagon Company per annum.

The Company has decided to write off 10% depreciation annually on diminishing balance method.

Pass the necessary journal entries and open ledger accounts in the books of New Colliery Company and Wagon Company.

SOLUTION

Interest Calculation

Date	Rs	*Interest* Rs	*Cash Price* Rs	*Instalment* Rs	*Depreciation* Rs
	11,175				
1.1.2003	3,000	–	3,000	3,000	–
	8,175				
31.12.2003	2,591	409	2,591	3,000	1,118
	5,584				
31.12.2004	2,721	279	2,721	3,000	1,006
	2,863				
31.12.2005	2,863	137	2,863	3,000	905
	–	825	11,175	12,000	

Journal in the Books of New Colliery Company (Buyer)

			2003 Dr. Rs	2003 Cr. Rs	2004 Dr. Rs	2004 Cr. Rs	2005 Dr. Rs	2005 Cr. Rs
Jan. 1	Wagon Account	Dr.	11,175					
	Interest Suspense Account	Dr.	825					
	To Wagon Company Account			12,000				
	(Being purchase of wagons under instalment system)							
"	Wagon Company Account	Dr.	3,000					
	To Bank Account			3,000				
	(Being payment of cash on delivery)							
Dec. 31	Interest Account	Dr.	409		279		137	
	To Interest Suspense Account			409		279		137
	(Being interest becomes due)							
"	Wagon Company Account	Dr.	3,000		3,000		3,000	
	To Bank Account			3,000		3,000		3,000
	(Being payment of instalment)							
"	Depreciation Account	Dr.	1,118		1,006		905	
	To Wagon Account			1,118		1,006		905
	(Being charging of depreciation)							

Dec. 31	Profit and Loss Account Dr.	1,527		1,285		1,042	
	To Interest Account		409		279		137
	To Depreciation Account		1,118		1,006		905
	(Being transfer of Interest and Depreciation Accounts)						

Dr. **Wagon Account** Cr.

		Rs			Rs
2003			2003		
Jan. 1	To Wagon Company A/c	11,175	Dec. 31	By Depreciation A/c	1,118
			"	By Balance c/d	10,057
		11,175			11,175
2004			2004		
Jan. 1	To Balance b/d	10,057	Dec. 31	By Depreciation A/c	1,006
			"	By Balance c/d	9,051
		10,057			10,057
2005			2005		
Jan. 1	To Balance b/d	9,051	Dec. 31	By Depreciation A/c	905
			"	By Balance c/d	8,146
		9,051			9,051
2006					
Jan. 1	To Balance b/d	8,146			

Dr. **Wagon Company Account** Cr.

		Rs			Rs
2003			2003		
Jan. 1	To Bank Account	3,000	Jan. 1	By Wagon A/c	11,175
Dec. 31	To Bank Account	3,000	"	By Interest Suspense A/c	825
"	To Balance c/d	6,000			
		12,000			12,000
2004			2004		
Dec. 31	To Bank Account	3,000	Jan. 1	By Balance b/d	6,000
"	To Balance c/d	3,000			
		6,000			6,000
2005			2005		
Dec. 31	To Bank Account	3,000	Jan. 1	By Balance b/d	3,000

Dr. **Interest Suspense Account** Cr.

		Rs			Rs
2003			2003		
Jan. 1	To Wagon Company A/c	825	Dec. 31	By Interest A/c	409
			"	By Balance c/d	416
		825			825

2004			2004		
Jan. 1	To Balance b/d	416	Dec. 31	By Interest A/c	279
			"	By Balance c/d	137
		416			416
2005			2005		
Jan. 1	To Balance b/d	137	Dec. 31	By Interest A/c	137

Journal in the Books of Wagon Company (Vendor)

			2003 Dr. Rs	2003 Cr. Rs	2004 Dr. Rs	2004 Cr. Rs	2005 Dr. Rs	2005 Cr. Rs
Jan. 1	New Colliery Company A/c	Dr.	12,000					
	To Sales Account			11,175				
	To Interest Suspense A/c			825				
	(Being sale of wagons under instalment system)							
"	Bank Account	Dr.	3,000					
	To New Colliery Company			3,000				
	(Being Cash received on delivery)							
Dec. 31	Interest Suspense A/c	Dr.	409		279		137	
	To Interest Account			409		279		137
	(Being the amount of interest due)							
Dec. 31	Bank Account	Dr.	3,000		3,000		3,000	
	To New Colliery Co. A/c			3,000		3,000		3,000
	(Being the amount of instalment received)							
"	Interest Account	Dr.	409		279		137	
	To Profit and Loss A/c			409		279		137
	(Being transfer of interest)							
"	Sales Account	Dr.	11,175					
	To Trading Account			11,175				
	(Being transfer of sales)							

Dr. **New Colliery Company Account** Cr.

		Rs			Rs
2003			2003		
Jan. 1	To Sales Account	11,175	Jan. 1	By Bank Account	3,000
"	To Interest Suspense A/c	825	Dec. 31	By Bank Account	3,000
			"	By Balance c/d	6,000
		12,000			12,000
2004			2004		
Jan. 1	To Balance b/d	6,000	Dec. 31	By Bank Account	3,000
			"	By Balance c/d	3,000
		6,000			6,000
2005			2005		
Jan. 1	To Balance b/d	3,000	Dec. 31	By Bank Account	3,000

Dr. **Interest Suspense Account** Cr.

		Rs			Rs
2003			2003		
Dec. 31	To Interest Account	409	Jan. 1	By New Colliery Company	
"	To Balance c/d	416		Account	825
		825			825
2004			2004		
Dec. 31	To Interest Account	279	Jan. 1	By Balance b/d	416
"	To Balance c/d	137			
		416			416
2005			2005		
Dec. 31	To Interest Account	137	Jan. 1	By Balance c/d	137

Dr. **Sales Account** Cr.

		Rs			Rs
2003			2003		
Dec. 31	To Trading A/c	11,175	Jan. 1	By New Colliery Co.	11,175

QUESTIONS

Objective Type Questions

I. State whether each of the following statements is "True" or "False":

1. The property in goods passes to the hire purchaser as soon as the cash down payment is made.
2. The seller cannot seize the goods on failure of the purchaser to pay the price in case of instalment system.
3. The buyer has the option to return the goods in case of a hire purchase.
4. In case of hire purchase system, depreciation on asset is calculated on the cash price of the asset.
5. Under Hire Purchase System, Asset Account will be debited with the actual amount of its cash price and interest paid.
6. In case of instalment system, ownership of goods passes with payment of last instalment.
7. Down payment is compulsory in the case of hire purchase system, while it is optional in the case of instalment system.
8. If default is made under instalment system, the seller can repossess the goods.
9. Interest is calculated on the cash price at the given rate.
10. Any loss resulting on sale of repossessed goods can be recovered from hire purchaser.

(**Ans:** 1. False; 2. True; 3. True; 4. True; 5. False; 6. False; 7. False; 8. False; 9. True; 10. False.

II. Choose the most appropriate alternative in each of the following :

1. The amount of interest is credited by the buyer to :
   (*a*) Interest Account. (*b*) Asset Account.
   (*c*) Vendor Account.
2. In the books of Hire Purchaser, depreciation is charged on
   (*a*) Hire Purchase Price. (*b*) Cash Price.
   (*c*) None of the above.
3. The cost of goods sold on hire purchase is transferred to :
   (*a*) Sales Account. (*b*) Hire Purchase Trading Account.
   (*c*) Purchases Account.

4. In case of instalment system, total interest receivable by the seller is credited to :
   (*a*) Interest Suspense Account. (*b*) Interest Account.
   (*c*) Sales Account.
5. On seizure of the goods by the hire vendor, the balance in the asset account is transferred to:
   (*a*) Profit and Loss Account. (*b*) Hire Vendor's Account.
   (*c*) Goods Repossessed Account.

(**Ans:** 1. (*c*); 2. (*b*); 3. (*c*); 4. (*a*); 5. (*b*).

THEORETICAL QUESTIONS

1. What do you understand by Hire Purchase System?
2. Distinguish between hire purchase system and instalment purchase system. Discuss the accounting aspect of them.
3. What do you mean by Hire Purchase Trading Account?
4. Discuss the accounting treatment of repossessed goods on default made by the purchaser.

PRACTICAL PROBLEMS

1. *A* acquired on Ist January 2001 a machine under Hire Purchase agreement which provides for 5 half-yearly instalments of Rs 6,000 each, the first instalment being due on Ist July 2001 assuming that the applicable rates of interest is 10% p.a. Calculate the cash value of the machine. (*C.A. Final*)

[**Ans:** Cash Value Rs 25,977
Interest Rs 1,299 (1.7.2001)
Rs 1,064 (1.1.2002)
Rs 817 (1.7.2002)
Rs 558 (1.1.2003)
Rs 286 (1.7.2003)]

2. Lalchand bought a machine on Ist January 2002 on Hire Purchase basis of payment which was as follows:

	Rs
On signing the agreement	5,000
At the end of First year	6,000
At the end of Second year	3,500
At the end of Third year	2,200
	16,700

Interest included in Rs 16,700 was charged on the cash price @ 10% p.a. You are asked to ascertain the cash price of the machine and write up the necessary ledger accounts in the books of Lalchand. (*B.Com., Madurai*)

[**Ans:** Cash Value Rs 15,000
Interest Rs 1000 (First instalment)
Rs 500 (Second instalment)
Rs 200 (Third instalment)]

3. The India Motor Ltd. sells Machine on the hire purchase system. The terms of payment for the sale of a scooter are:

Rs 1,000 on delivery, Rs 1,040 at the end of the first year, Rs 960 at the end of the second year, and Rs 880 at the end of the third year, inclusive of finance charges.

Find out cash price of the Machine (*C.A. Final, Madurai*)

[**Ans:** Cash Price Rs 3,400
Interest Rs 240 (I instalment)
Rs 160 (II instalment)
Rs 80 (III instalment)]

4. Senthil purchased a motor car on Ist January 2002 from Hindustan Motors Ltd., on hire purchase basis. He agreed to pay Rs 6,900 on taking delivery of the motor car and pay three annual instalments of Rs 13,310 each. The vendors charged interest at 10% p.a. Senthil wrote off depreciation at 20% p.a. on the straight line method. Pass journal entries in the books of Senthil. (*B.Com., Madurai*)

[**Ans:** Cash Value Rs 40,000
Interest Rs 3,310 (31.12.2002)
Rs 2,310 (31.12.2003)
Rs 1,210 (31.12.2004)]

5. Textiles Ltd. purchased mini lorries on hire purchase system over a period of four years. Rs 12,000 was payable on delivery, on Ist January 2001, and the balance by annual instalments of Rs 12,000 each on 31st December in each year. Motors Ltd. who sold the lorries charged 5% p.a. interest on the yearly balances. The cash value of the lorries on delivery was Rs 54,551. Depreciation at the rate of 25% on diminishing balance was written off every year.

Show the necessary journal entries in the books of Textiles Ltd. Interest to be calculated to the nearest rupee. (*B.Com., Calcutta*)

[**Ans:** Interest Rs 2,128 (31.12.2001)
Rs 1,634 (31.12.2002)
Rs 1,116 (31.12.2003)
Rs 571 (31.12.2004)]

6. On Ist January 2002, Ram purchased a machine from a Vendor on hire purchase basis. The particulars are given below:
   1. Cash Price Rs 10,000.
   2. Rs 4,000 to be paid on signing the contract.
   3. Balance in three equal instalments of Rs 2,000 plus interest.
   4. Interest charged on outstanding balance at 5% p.a.
   5. Instalments are to be paid annually from December each year.
   6. Depreciation charged 10% p.a. on straight line method.

   Give journal entries and necessary ledger accounts in the books of purchaser.

(*B.Com., Madurai, Kerala*)

[**Ans:** Machine Account Balance Rs 7,000 (1.1.2005)
Interest Rs 300 (31.12.2002)
Rs 200 (31.12.2003)
Rs 100 (31.12.2004)]

7. On Ist January 2000 Messrs. Dubey and Company took delivery from Auto Car Limited of one motor cycle on hire purchase system, Rs 2,000 being paid on delivery and the balance in five instalments of Rs 3,000 each payable annually on 31st December. The Vendor Company charges interest at 5% per year on yearly balance. The cash down value of the motor cycle was Rs 15,000.

Show the Vendors Account, Interest Account and Motor Cycle Account in the books of Dubey and Company for the five years. Provide depreciation at the rate of 20% on the diminishing balance.

(*B.Com., Calcutta, Bombay, Delhi*)

[**Ans:** Motor Cycle Account Balance
Rs 4,915 (1.1.2005)
Interest Rs 650 (31.12.2000)
Rs 533 (31.12.2001)
Rs 409 (31.12.2002)
Rs 280 (31.12.2003)
Rs 128 (31.12.2004)

8. *X* purchases a machine on Ist January 2003 on the hire purchase system. The cash price of the machine is Rs 14,900. The terms of the agreement provided at the end of every six months for payment of Rs 4,000 over two years.

   The first payment was to be made on 30th June 2003. The rate of interest was 6% p.a. *X* writes off 10% depreciation on the reducing balance system and closed his books on the 30th June every year.

   X could not pay the instalment due on 30th June 2004 and as a result, the hire vendor took back the possession of the machine.

   Give the machine account and Vendor's Account in the books of *X* and show the loss suffered by him. (*B.Com. Pass, Delhi*)

   [**Ans:** Interest Rs 447 (June 2003)
   Rs 340 (Dec. 2003)
   Rs 231 (June 2004)
   Rs 82 (Dec. 2004)
   Loss suffered by *X* Rs 4,821 (Machine Account Closed)

9. On Ist January 2000, Ojha Company obtained wagons on hire purchase system. The price of the wagons was Rs 25,000. The payment was to be made as Rs 5,000 down and the balance by instalments of Rs 4,000 per year with interest at 4%.

   You are required to give necessary ledger accounts in the books of Ojha Company assuming depreciation to be written off at 5% annually on diminishing balance method. (*B.Com., Calcutta, Madras*)

   [**Ans:** Interest Rs 800 (31.12.2000)
   Rs 640 (31.12.2001)
   Rs 480 (31.12.2002)
   Rs 320 (31.12.2003)
   Rs 160 (31.12.2004)
   Wagon Account Balance Rs 19,344 (1.1.2005)]

10. On Ist January 2002, Sharma purchased a plant from Ahuja on Hire Purchase System. The hire purchase price was settled at Rs 60,000 payable as to Rs 15,000 on 1st Jan. 2002 and Rs 15,000 at the end of three successive years. Interest was charged at the rate of 5% p.a. The asset was to be depreciated in the books of the purchaser at 10% p.a. on reducing balance method. Given the present value of annuity of Re 1 per annum @ 5% interest is Rs 2.7232.

    Show the Vendor Account and the Plant Account in the books of purchaser. All calculations are to be made to the nearest rupee. (*ICWA*)

    [**Ans:** Plant Account Balance Rs 40,713 (1.1.2005)
    Interest Rs 2,042 (31.12.2002)
    Rs 1,365 (31.12.2003)
    Rs 715 (31.12.2004)]

11. John purchased a machine from Hindustan Company for Rs 5,60,000, payment to be made Rs 1,50,000 down and three instalments of Rs 1,50,000 each at the end of each year. John depreciates assets at 10% p.a. on written down value method.

    Because of financial difficulties, John after having paid down payment and first instalment at the end of the first year could not pay second instalment and the seller took possession of the asset.

    Prepare Machine Account and Sellers Account in the books of John. Also give Purchasers Account in the books of Hindustan Co. (*B.Com. Pass, Delhi*)

    [**Ans:** Interest Rs 20,000 (I year)
    Rs 13,333 (II year)
    Rs 6,667 (III year)
    Machine Account (Loss) Rs 1,60,267 (John's book)
    Repossessed Machine Account Rs 2,93,333 (Hindustan's book)

12. Prem Company Limited purchased a machinery on hire purchase system on 1.1.2000 from Ashok Machinery Limited and agreed to pay the price in five instalments as stated below and also agreed to pay 10% interest on unpaid balance of cash price. Prem Company Limited decided to depreciate the machinery by 10% on reducing balance method.

Ascertain cash price and prepare the machinery account for the five years in the books of Prem Company Ltd.

1st Instalment of Rs 1,500 paid on 31.12.2000
2nd Instalment of Rs 1,400 paid on 31.12.2001
3rd Instalment of Rs 1,300 paid on 31.12.2002
4th Instalment of Rs 1,200 paid on 31.12.2003
5th Instalment of Rs 1,100 paid on 31.12.2004 (*B.Com., Karnataka, Bombay*)

[**Ans:** Cash price Rs 5,000 (1.1.2000)
Interest Rs 500 (31.12.2000)
Rs 400 (31.12.2001)
Rs 300 (31.12.2002)
Rs 200 (31.12.2003)
Rs 100 (31.12.2004)
Machine Account Balance Rs 2,952 (1.1.2005)]

13. On 1st January 2000, Transport Company bought a Motor Lorry from Calcutta Motors on hire purchase, the cash price of which was Rs 52,000 and hire purchase price Rs 60,000. It was agreed to pay Rs 12,000 immediately and the balance in four yearly instalments of Rs 12,000 each. Transport Company writes off depreciation @ 20% p.a. on diminishing balance system.

Calculate the amount of interest in each instalment and prepare necessary accounts in the books of Transport Company. (*B.Com., Madurai*)

[**Ans:** Interest Rs 3,200 (I)
Rs 2,400 (II)
Rs 1,600 (III)
Rs 800 (IV)
Motor Lorry Account balance Rs 21,299 on 1.1.2004

14. On 1st July 2002, Eastern Printers purchased a printing machine on a hire purchase basis, payments to be made Rs 10,000 on the said date and the balance in three half-yearly instalments of Rs 8,200, Rs 7,440 and Rs 6,300 commencing from 31st December 2002. The Vendor charged interest at 10% p.a. Eastern Printers close their books annually on 31st December and provide depreciation at 10% p.a. on Diminishing Balance in each year.

Determine the cash price of the machine and show the necessary ledger accounts in the books of Eastern Printers. (*B.Com., Madurai*)

[**Ans:** Cash Price Rs 30,000
Interest Rs 1,000 (31.12.2002)
Rs 640 (31.7.2003)
Rs 300 (31.12.2003)

15. Ramesh Ltd. purchased a machinery on Hire Purchase System on 1st July 2001. The hire purchase price of Rs 1,50,000 is payable by bi-annual instalments of Rs 30,000 each. The seller charges interest on unpaid cash price at 6% p.a.

Calculate the cash price and prepare necessary accounts in the books of seller assuming that the payment is made on January 1 and July 1 and the accounts are closed on 31st December every year. (*B.Com., Madurai*)

[**Ans:** Cash Price Rs 1,37,391
Interest Rs 4,122 (31.12.2001)
Rs 3,345 (31.7.2002)
Rs 2,546 (31.12.2002)
Rs 1,722 (31.7.2003)
Rs 874 (31.12.2003)

16. Crompton Company purchased a machine on instalment basis from Bombay Manufacturing Company on the following terms:
   (*a*) Cash down payment at the time of signing the agreement on 1st Year beginning Rs 10,000.
   (*b*) Five annual instalments of Rs 3,300, the first to commence at the end of first year from the date of purchase.
   (*c*) Interest at 10% p.a. is charged by the seller.
   (*d*) Depreciation at 10% p.a. written down value basis is written off every year.
   (*e*) The machine is sold for Rs 13,500 on the completion of payment.

   Show the machinery account for the complete period.

   [**Ans:** Cash Price of the Machine Rs 22,509
   Machine value at the end of 5th year Rs 13,500
   Profit on sale Rs 209
   Interest Rs 1,251; 1,046, 821, 573, 300]

17. Taj Company purchased a machine on hire purchase system on 1st January 2001. The payments to be made Rs 7,500 on signing the contract and the balance in yearly instalment of Rs 7,000; Rs 6,500; Rs 6,000 and Rs 5,500 commencing from December 2001. The vendor charges interest at 10% p.a.

   The Taj Company provides depreciation @ 10% on Diminishing Balance method in each year.

   Determine the cash value and show the machinery account for the four years in the books of Taj Company.

   [**Ans:** Cash Value Rs 27,500
   Machine Account Balance Rs 18,042 (1.1.05)
   Interest Rs 2,000; Rs 1,500, Rs 1,000 and Rs 500]

18. Dobsons Limited had purchased a machine on hire purchase system from Hind Machinery Limited. The terms were that they would pay Rs 20,000 down on 1st January 2000 and 5 annual instalments of Rs 11,000 each on December 31. They charged depreciation on machinery at the rate of 15% under diminishing balance system.

   Hind Machinery Limited had charged interest at the rate of 10% per annum. Show the Machinery Account and Hind Machinery Account to record the above transactions in the books of Dobsons Ltd. till the instalments are paid off. Dobsons accounting year ended on 31st December in each year.

   (*CA Inter*)

   [**Ans:** Cash Price Rs 61,698
   Interest Rs 4,170; Rs 3,487; Rs 2,736; Rs 1,909; Rs 1,000
   Machine Account Balance Rs 27,375 (1.1.2005)]

Default and Repossession of Assets

19 Transport Ltd. purchased three buses from Arvind Motors costing Rs 75,000 each on hire purchase system. Payment was to be made, for each bus, Rs 45,000 down and the remainder in 3 equal instalments together with interest at 12%. Transport Ltd. writes off depreciation at 20% on diminishing balance. It paid the first instalment at the end of the first year but could not pay the next. Arvind Motors agreed to leave one bus with the purchaser adjusting the value of the other two buses against the amount due. The buses were valued on the basis of 30% depreciation annually. (Straight Line Method)

   Show the necessary ledger accounts in the books of Transport Ltd. for the first two years.

   (*CA Inter*)

   [**Ans:** Interest I year Rs 10,800; II year Rs 7,200
   Value of repossessed bus Rs 60,000
   Loss on surrender Rs 36,000]

20. On 1st January 2002, Madan purchased a machinery from Sadan on hire purchase system. Cash price of the machinery was Rs 60,000, Rs 15,480 to be paid on the date of purchase and five annual instalments of Rs 10,000 payable on 31st December every year. Sadan charged interest at 4% per annum, on the yearly balances. Madan failed to pay the instalment due on 31st December 2003. Thereupon Sadan took possession of the machinery and valued the same in his books after charging 20% depreciation

on diminishing balance method annually. In January 2004, he incurred Rs 2,500 as reconditioning expenses and resold the machinery for Rs 45,000. Show Madan's account and Repossessed Stock Account in the books of Sadan. (*B.Com., Madurai, Madras, Delhi*)

[Ans: Interest Rs 1,781 and Rs 1,452
Value of Repossessed Machinery Rs 38,400
Profit on Resale Rs 4,100]

21. Transport Corporation purchased a machine on hire purchase from Hindustan Machines for Rs 56,000, payments to be made Rs 15,000 down cash and three instalments of Rs 15,000 each at the end of each year. Rate of interest is charged at 15% p.a. Buyer depreciates the asset at 10% p.a. on written down value method.

Because of financial difficulties Transport Corporation after having paid the down cash and the first instalment at the end of the first year could not pay the second instalment and Hindustan Machines took possession of the machine. The seller, after spending Rs 350 on repairs of the machine, sold it for Rs 30,110.

Prepare (a) the Machine Account and the Hindustan Account in the books of Transport Corporation and (b) Transport Corporation Account and Goods on Hire Purchase Returned Account in the books of Hindustan Machines. (*B.Com., Calcutta*)

[Ans: Loss to Transport Corporation on surrender Rs 15,907
Value of Machine repossessed Rs 29,453]

22. Novel Traders purchased two machines costing Rs 1,60,000 each from Delhi Motors on 1st January 2002 on hire purchase system. The terms were:

Payment on delivery Rs 40,000 for each machine and balance in three equal instalments together with interest at 10% p.a. to be paid at the end of each year.

Novel Traders writes off 25% depreciation each on the diminishing balance method.

Novel Traders paid the instalments due on 31st Dec. 2002 and on 31st Dec. 2003 but could not pay the final instalment.

Delhi Motors repossessed one truck adjusting its value against the amount due. The repossession was done on the basis of 30% depreciation on diminishing balance method.

Write up the ledger accounts in the books of Novel Traders showing the above transactions. (*C.A., B.Com., Madras*)

[Ans: Value of machine retained Rs 67,500
Value of machine repossessed Rs 54,880]

23. Marudhu purchased 7 trucks on hire purchase on 1.7.2003. The cash purchase price of each truck was Rs 50,000. He was to pay 20% of the cash purchase price at the time of delivery and the balance in five half-yearly instalments starting from 31.12.2003 with interest at the rate of 5% per annum.

On Marudhu's failure to pay the instalment due on 30.6.2004 it was agreed that Marudhu would return 3 trucks to the vendor and remaining 4 would be retained by him. The vendor agreed to allow him (Marudhu) a credit for the amount paid against these 3 trucks less 25%.

Show the relevant accounts in the books of Marudhu assuming that his books are closed in June every year and depreciation at the rate of 20% is charged on trucks. Show also Marudhu's account in the books of vendor. (*B.Com., Madurai, Delhi, Madras*)

[Ans: Value of seized trucks Rs 40,500
Value of retained trucks Rs 1,60,000]

24. The Novel Dry Cleaners purchased from the Vendor two machines of Rs 10,500 each on hire purchase system. The payment was to be made Rs 6,000 down and the remainder in three equal instalments of Rs 5,000 each together with interest at 5% p.a. The Dry Cleaners write off depreciation at 10% p.a. on written down value. They could not pay their second instalment. After negotiations, it was agreed that vendors would leave one plant with the purchaser, adjusting the value of the other against amount due, treating the machine at 20% depreciation on diminishing balance.

Show accounts in the books of Dry Cleaners. (*B.Com., Madurai*)

[Ans: Value of seized Machine Rs 6,720
Value of Retained Machine Rs 8,505]

25. On 1st January 2003 five trucks were purchased by *A* on the Hire Purchase System. The cash price of each truck is Rs 55,000. The payment was to be made as follows:

    10% of cash price down

    25% of cash price at the end of each of the subsequent half years.

    The payment due on 31st December 2003 could not be made and hence trucks were seized by the Vendor but, after negotiations, *A* was allowed to keep three trucks on the condition that the value of the other two trucks would be adjusted against the amount due, the trucks being valued at cost less 25% depreciation. *A*'s books are closed on 30th June each year and he charges 15% depreciation on trucks on the original cost.

    The vendor spent Rs 6,000 on getting the trucks thoroughly overhauled and sold them for Rs 95,000. Show the various accounts in the books of both the parties. (*B.Com., Delhi; M.Com., Madurai*)

    [**Ans:** Loss on default to buyer Rs 11,000
    Profit to Vendor Rs 6,500]

26. On 1st January 2004, Scooter Agencies purchased from Vijay Scooter Company two scooters on Hire Purchase System, the cash price of each scooter being Rs 10,000. The Hire Purchase price of scooters was payable as under:

    15% of cash price immediately on delivery and further four half-yearly instalments of 25% of cash price on 30th June and 31st December.

    The hire purchaser could not pay the instalment due on 31st December 2004, and Vijay Scooter Company seized the scooters but on the request of the Scooter Agencies, the Company agreed to let the purchaser keep one scooter on the terms that one scooter repossessed by the Vendor by charging depreciation of 30% p.a. and adjusted the amount due from the purchaser. Scooter Agencies charge depreciation @ 20% on Original Cost of the scooters.

    Vijay Scooter Company spent Rs 800 on the captured scooter and sold it for Rs 8,000 in cash.

    Write the important accounts in the books of both the parties.

    [**Ans:** Interest Rs 1,200; Rs 900; Rs 600; Rs 300
    Profit on sale of repossessed scooter Rs 200]

27. Transport Ltd. purchased 2 trucks costing Rs 80,000 each from Auto Ltd. on 1st January 2002 on hire purchase system. The terms are:

    Payment on delivery Rs 20,000 for each truck.

    Remainder in 3 equal instalments together with interest @ 10% p.a. to be paid at the end of each year.

    Transport Ltd. write off 25% depreciation each year on diminishing balance method.

    Transport Ltd. paid the instalments due on 31st December 2002 and on 31st December 2003 but could not pay the final instalment.

    Auto Ltd. repossessed one truck adjusting its value against the amount due. The repossession was done on the basis of 30% depreciation on the diminishing balance method. The vendor spent Rs 8,560 for the repairs and overhauling of the truck and sold it for Rs 40,000.

    Write up the ledger accounts in the books of both parties. (*CA & ICWA Inter*)

    [**Ans:** Loss on default to buyer Rs 6,310
    Profit to Vendor Rs 4,000]

28. A Colliery Company acquired wagons on a hire purchase system over a term of four years on 1st January 2002. The instalments of Rs 6,000 are payable at the beginning of each year commencing from 1st January 2002. The present cash value is Rs 22,000 and the Wagon Company compute interest at the rate of 6% p.a. on unpaid balance.

    Make necessary journal entries to record these transactions in the books of purchaser under:

    (*a*) Hire Purchase System

    (*b*) Instalment System. (*B.Com., Karnataka*)

    [**Ans:** Interest: Rs 960, Rs 658, Rs 382]

Hire Purchase Trading Account

29. Clever has a hire purchase department. Goods are sold on hire purchase at 180% on cost price. From the following particulars prepare Hire Purchase Trading Account in the books of Clever.

		Rs
2004 Jan. 1	Stock in customers' hands at selling price	21,600
2004 Dec. 31	Sale of hire purchase goods at selling price	95,400
	Cash received from hire purchase customers	72,900
	Goods received back valued at (Hire purcahse instalment unpaid Rs 4,500)	1,700
	Stock at customers hand at selling price	28,800

(*ICWA*)

[Ans: Gross Profit Rs 36,400]

30. The following are the particulars from the books of Ram Chander who sells goods of small value on hire purchase system at 50% profit on cost.

Prepare Hire Purchase Trading Account for the year ending 31st December 2004:

Jan. 1	Stock with the customers	27,000
	Stock in the shop	54,000
	Instalment due	15,000
Dec. 31	Stock in the shop	61,500
	Instalment due	27,000
	Goods repossessed (Instalment due Rs 8,000) valued at Rs 1,500 which had been included in the stock at the end at Rs 1,500.	
	Cash received from customers	1,80,000
	Goods purchased during the year	1,80,000

(*B.Com. Hons., Delhi*)

[Ans: Profit Rs 60,167]

31. Ram sells goods on hire purchase basis at a profit of 50% on cost. Following particulars are given to you relating to the business during 2004 :

	Rs
Hire purchase stock (at selling price) as on 1.1.2003	9,000
Instalment due on 1.1.2004	5,000
Goods sold on hire purchase during the year (at selling price)	87,000
Cash received from hire purchase customers during the year	60,000
Goods repossessed (instalment due Rs 2,000) as valued	500
Hire Purchase stock (at selling price) as on 31.12.2004	30,000
Instalment due on 31.12.2004	9,000

Prepare Hire Purchase Trading Account showing the profit earned for 2004.

(*B.Com. (Hons.) Delhi*)

[Ans: Profit Rs 20,500]

Chapter 19

Royalty Accounts

Introduction – Rent and royalty – Minimum Rent – short-working – Recoupment of Short-working – Surplus – Abnormal fall in Output – Accounting Entries in Lessee's Books – Accounting Entries in Lesser's book – Sub-lease – Questions – Objective Type Questions – Theoretical Questions – Practical Problems.

INTRODUCTION

Royalty is a periodical payment for the use of a certain property or a right like mine, patent, copyright, to its owner. And the payment of royalty is calculated on the basis of quantity of output or sale. *Royalty is an amount which is paid as a consideration for the use of rights to the owner.* In other words, Royalty is the compensation made to the owner of an asset in exchange for the right to use the asset. The person who surrenders the right is known as Lessor. The person, who makes the payment or who uses the asset, is known as Lessee. The Royalty paid by the Lessee is received by the Lessor. When the Landlord, Patentee or an author permits another person to use the land, patent or book, the latter is called Lessee, Licensee or a publisher. The Landlord, Patentee or author are known as Lessor or Landlord.

RENT AND ROYALTY

Note that the payment for the purchase of land, patent, or copyright is a capital expenditure and recorded as fixed assets. When the payment is made for the use thereof, it is a Royalty. Accounting, relating to transactions involving the payment of royalties, is called Royalty Account. It is a Nominal Account. Royalty is an income to the owner and expense to the user.

Rent is mostly payable according to time, as per day, per week, per month or per year etc. But the payment of royalty depends on yield or production. Payment of royalty is a business expense. When the royalty payable to the Lessor is on the basis of production, it is a part of cost of production and, therefore, the Royalty Account is transferred to Trading or Manufacturing or Production Account. The Royalty payable on the basis of sales, which is a selling expenditure, is transferred to Profit and Loss Account.

ROYALTY vs. RENT

Royalty	Rent
1. The parties are known as lessor, author, patent-holder and lessee, publisher, patentee, etc.	1. The parties are known as tenant and landlord.
2. There arise a clause in the agreement to pay minimum rent.	2. No such clause is there.
3. It is payable on the basis of production, sales etc.	3. It is payable on the basis of time–weekly, monthly etc.
4. The amount is variable on the basis of production, sales etc.	4. Generally, the amount of rent is fixed with regard to time.

MINIMUM RENT

The Minimum Rent is also known as Dead Rent or Rock Rent or Flat Rent. In the agreement between the Lessor and the Lessee, there is usually a clause mentioning a minimum amount that must be paid by the Lessee to the Lessor, in any particular year, whether they derived any benefit or not, out of the right. Such a minimum amount is known as Minimum Rent. The Minimum is to avoid loss, if the amount of royalty is less than the normal one. In addition, a regular flow of income is expected by the Lessor. In certain cases, the production or the sales may be higher. But it may be remembered that the lessee is required to pay the amount of Royalty (calculated on output or sales) or the Minimum Rent (fixed in the lease agreement) whichever is higher. For instance, a mine is leased for a certain term of years at a yearly minimum rent of Rs 15,000 merging into a royalty or Rs 2 per ton. If during the first year the tonnage raised from the mine is 6,000 tons, the royalty at Rs 2 per ton would be Rs, 12,000. In this event, the Lessee would require to pay the Minimum Rent of Rs, 15,000 although the royalty rent on the output is only Rs 12,000. If, however, the tonnage in the first year reached 9,000 tons the royalty at Rs 2 per ton comes to Rs, 18,000 and the Lessee would require to pay Rs. 18,000. In other words, when the Royalty is less than Minimum Rent, the Lessee pays the minimum rent, but, when the royalty on the output exceeds the minimum rent, Royalty is payable on output or sales.

SHORTWORKING

" The excess of Minimum Rent over the actual royalty is termed as Shortworking." In other words, when the royalty is less than the Minimum Rent, the excess that the Lessee pays over and above the royalty is known as Shortworking. Shortworking is usually recoverable by the Lessee in later years when the royalty is in excess of Minimum Rent and is therefore also known as Redeemable Dead Rent. For instance, *A*, the Landlord gives his land on lease to *B* on a Minimum Rent of Rs 10,000 a year. But the actual royalty comes to Rs 8,000. The Lessee has to pay Rs, 10, 000. The deficiency of Rs 2,000 is called Shortworking.

RECOUPMENT OF SHORTWORKING

It is generally seen that in the first few years of the royalty agreement, the production or sales do not get the required momentum because of the time consumed in the preparation to start the production; thus Shortworkings arise. In order to protect the interest of the Lessee, a clause may be included in the contract that the deficiency or Shortworkings may be recouped, when there is a surplus in subsequent years. Such a provision is known as the right to recoup the Shortworkings and this right can be of two types: (1) Fixed, and (2) Floating.

An agreement may be entered into between Lessor and Leesee that the Shortworkings may be recouped in the first few years, commencing from the date of Royalty Agreement and the right is said to be *fixed* (restricted). It is presumed that only at the beginning, there may be shortworking, which should be recovered within the specified period. For instance, the Shortworkings of 2001 and 02 may be recouped till 2003, that too out of surplus and the shortworkings arising after 2003 cannot be recouped. But when the Lessor promises to compensate the shortworkings within two or three subsequent or following years, then the right is said to be floating (unrestricted). Thus, if the power to recoup shortworkings is for subsequent three years, then the shortworking of 2001 can be recouped till 2004; Shortworkings to 2002 can be recouped till 2005 and so on. When the right to recoup expires in respect of any portion of the Shortworkings, it should be written off to Profit and Loss Account.

SURPLUS

In the initial stage, the Royalty produced may be little and there may be shortworkings. But in later years, when the production increases the amount of royalty payable to Landlord will also be more than the Minimum Rent. Thus, the excess of royalty over the Minimum Rent is called *Surplus*. For instance, when the Minimum Rent is Rs 10,000 and the actual royalty earned by the Lessee is Rs 15,000, the surplus is Rs 5,000 (Royalty – Minimum Rent or Rs 15,000 – 10,000). That is, the excess of the Dead Rent is known as Surplus.

ABNORMAL FALL IN OUTPUT

In case of mines, quarries etc. an abnormal fall in the production or sales may be caused, in any year, due to strikes, accidents, lock-outs, unforeseen circumstances etc. In such a situation, Lessee finds difficult to pay the Minimum Rent. Whenever there is a stoppage due to abnormal reasons, and if the Minimum Rent is not raised, the amount of Minimum Rent is required to be adjusted as provided for in the agreement. Such agreement may have the following arrangements:

(1) A certain percentage of Minimum Rent would be reduced, say, by 25%, or

(2) The Minimum Rent shall be reduced proportionately having regard to the length of the stoppage.

(3) The actual royalties would discharge all the rental obligations of that year.

Example:

Suppose, a coalmine is leased on a Minimum Rent of Rs 24,000 a year and in a particular year, the production is affected by a strike for 2 months and the royalty produced is Rs. 17,000. Then, the royalty payable, on applying the above clause, is as follows :

(1) If the clause (1) is applied, the Minimum Rent for the year would be 75% of Rs 24,000, that is, Rs. 18,000; or

(2) If clause (2) is applied the Minimum Rent for that year would be Rs 20,000, that is,

Rs. $24{,}000 \times \frac{10}{12}$; (or)

(3) If clause (3) is applied, Lessee pays only Rs 17,000.

ACCOUNTING ENTRIES IN THE BOOKS OF LESSEE

(1) When the Royalty is less than Minimum Rent and the Minimum Rent Account is not Maintained:

(*a*) Royalties Account Dr.
(With actual amount of royalty)
Shortworkings Account Dr.
(With actual shortage)
To Landlord Account (with Minimum rent payable)
(Being the minimum rent payable to Landlord)

(*b*) Landlord Account Dr.
To Bank Account
(Being the minimum rent paid to Landlord)

(*c*) Trading/Profit & Loss Account Dr.
To Royalties Account
(Royalties account transferred to Trading/Profit & Loss Account)

(2) When the Royalty is less than Minimum Rent and the Minimum Rent Account is Maintained:

(*a*)	Minimum Rent Account	Dr.
	To Landlord Account	
	(Being minimum rent payable to Landlord)	
(*b*)	Royalties Account	Dr.
	Shortworkings Account	Dr.
	To Minimum Rent Account	
	(Being the amount or royalties earned and excess amount debited to Shortworkings Account to make up the minimum rent)	
(*c*)	Landlord Account	Dr.
	To Bank Account	
	(Being payment made to Landlord)	
(*d*)	Trading/Profit & Loss Account	Dr.
	To Royalties Account	
	(Being Royalties account transferred to Trading/Profit & Loss Account)	

(3) When Royalties are more than Minimum Rent

(*a*)	Royalties Account	Dr.
	To Landlord	
	(Being Royalties earned and payable to Landlord)	
(*b*)	Landlord Account	Dr.
	To Shortworkings Account	
	(Recoupment of shortworkings of earlier years)	
(*c*)	Landlord Account	Dr.
	To Bank Account	
	(Being payment made to Landlord)	

In the place of (*b*) and (*c*) above, the following one entry may be passed:

Landlord Account	Dr.
To Shortworkings Account	
To Bank Account	
(Being recoupment of shortworking to the extent balance paid)	

(*d*)	Trading/Profit & Loss Account	Dr.
	To Royalties Account	
	(Being transfer of Royalties A/c)	

(4) When Shortworking cannot be Recouped in Future

Profit & Loss Account	Dr.
To Shortworkings Account	
(Being transfer to irrecoverable Shortworking to Profit & Loss A/C)	

ILLUSTRATION 19.1

A company leased a colliery on Ist January 2002 at a Minimum Rent of Rs 20,000 per year, merging into a royalty of Rs. 1.50 per ton, with a power to recoup shortworkings over the first 3 years of the lease. The output of the colliery for the first four years is:

2002 9,000 tons
2003 12,000 tons
2004 16, 000 tons
2005 20,000 tons

Pass Jounral entries

SOLUTION

Analytical Table

Year	*Output*	*Royalty @ Rs 1.50 per ton*	*Minimum Rent*	*Surplus*	*Short-working*	*Shortworkings Recouped*	*Shortworkings Unrecoupted*	*Amount Payable to Landlord*
	Tons	Rs	Rs	Rs	Rs	Rs	–	Rs
2002	9,000	13,500	20,000	–	6,500	–		20,000
2003	12,000	18,000	20,000	–	2,000	–	–	20,000
2004	16,000	24,000	20,000	4,000	–	4,000	4,500	20,000
2005	20,000	30,000	20,000	10,000	–	–	–	30,000

Journal Entries in Lessee's Books

Date	Particulars		*LF*	*Rs*	*Rs*
2002 Dec. 31	Royalties Account	Dr.		13,500	
	Shortworkings Account	Dr.		6,500	
	To Landlord Account				20,000
	(Being the Minimum Rent payable to Landlord)				
	Landlord Account	Dr.		20,000	
	To Bank Account				20,000
	(Being payment made to the Landlord)				
	Profit & Loss Account	Dr.		13,500	
	To Royalties Account				13,500
	(Being the amount of Royalties transferred to Profit and Loss Account)				
2003 Dec. 31	Royalties Account	Dr.		18,000	
	Shortworkings Account	Dr.		2,000	
	To Landlord Account				20,000
	(Being the Minimum Rent payable to Landlord)				
	Landlord Account	Dr.		20,000	
	To Bank Account				20,000
	(Being payment made to the Landlord)				
	Profit & Loss Account	Dr.		18,000	
	To Royalties Account				18,000
	(Being payment made to the Landlord Profit & Loss A/c)				
2004 Dec. 31	Royalties Account	Dr.		24,000	
	To Landlord Account				24,000
	(Being Royalties earned payable)				

	Landlord Account	Dr.	24,000	
	To Shortworkings Account			4,000
	To Bank Account			20,000
	(Being recovery of shortworkings of Rs 4,000 and balance paid to Landlord)			
	Profit & Loss Account	Dr.	28,500	
	To Royalties Account			24,000
	To shortworkings Account			4, 500
	(Being Royalties A/c and unrecouped Shortworking transferred to Profit & Loss Accounts)			
2005 Dec. 31	Royalties Account	Dr.	30,000	
	To Landlord Account			30,000
	(Being Royalties earned payable to Landlord)			
	Landlord Account	Dr.	30,000	
	To Bank Account			30,000
	(Being payment made to Landlord)			
	Profit & Loss Account	Dr.	30,000	
	To Royalties Account			30,000
	(Being transfer of Royalties Account to Profit & Loss Account)			

N.B. The excess of Minimum Rent over actual Royalty is termed as Shortworkings. Here, the Lessee has a right to recover the Shortworkings over the first three years only. Therefore, in the year 2004, Lessee could recover Rs 4,000 out of the Royalty; the balance of Shortworkings Account amounting to Rs 4,500 (Rs. 6,500 + 2,000 = 8,500 – 4,000 = 4,500) written off to Profit & Loss Account, as the amount is no longer recoverable.

Alternatively,

Date			*Dr.* *Rs*	*Cr.* *Rs*
2002 Dec. 31	Minimum Rent Account	Dr.	20,000	
	To Landlord Account			20,000
	(Being Minimum Rent due)			
	Royalties Account	Dr.	13,500	
	Shortworkings Account	Dr.	6,500	
	To Minimum Rent Account			20,000
	(Being Shortworkings Account brought into accounts)			
	Landlord Account	Dr.	20,000	
	To Bank Account			20,000
	(Being amount paid to Landlord)			
	Profit & Loss Account	Dr.	13,500	
	To Royalties Account			13,500
	(Being Royalties account transferred to Profit & Loss account)			
2003 Dec.	Minimum Rent Account	Dr.	20,000	
	To Landlord Account			20,000
	(Being Minimum Rent due)			

			Dr.	Cr.
	Royalties Account	Dr.	18,000	
	Shortworkings Account	Dr.	2,000	
	To Minimum Rent Account			20,000
	(Being Shortworking Account brought intc account)			
	Landlord Account	Dr.	20,000	
	To Bank Account			20,000
	(Being the amount paid to Landlord)			
	Profit & Loss Account	Dr.	18,000	
	To Royalties Account			18,000
	(Being Royalties Account transferred to Profit & Loss Account)			

Entries for 2004 and 2005 are the same, as done. The reason is that in 2004 and 2005 the amounts of Royalties are more than the Minimum Rent. Therefore, Minimum Rent will not be opened.

ILLUSTRATION 19.2

Ram Tiles Industries Ltd. obtained a lease of land from Landlord for a period of four years from Ist January 2002, paying a minimum rent of Rs 8,000 per annum, merging in a royalty of 50 paise per ton of clay raised. The lease contains a clause to the effect that if the minimum rent paid in any year exceeds the royalty for the year, the amount of excess can be recouped by the Lessee out of the royalty payable in the following year only. Clay is raised as follows:

2002	2,000 tons
2003	10,000 tons
2004	20, 000 tons
2005	32,000 tons

Give the journal entries necessary to record these transactions in the books of the lessee, and also show the ledger accounts, including Minimum Rent Account.

SOLUTION

Royalty Payable Chart

Year	*Output*	*Royalty @ Re 0.50 per ton*	*Minimum Rent*	*Surplus*	*Short-working*	*Shortworkings*		*Amount Payable to Landlord*
						Recouped	*Unrecouped*	
	Tons	*Rs*	*Rs*	*Rs*	*Rs*	*Rs*	*Rs*	*Rs*
2002	2,000	1,000	8,000	–	7,000	–	–	8,000
2003	10,000	5,000	8,000	–	3,000	–	7,000	8,000
2004	20,000	10,000	8,000	2,000	–	2,000	1,000	8,000
2005	32,000	16,000	8,000	8,000	–	–	–	16,000

In the books of Ram Tiles Industries Ltd.

Journal Entries

Date			*LF*	*Dr.* *Rs*	*Cr.* *Rs*
2002					
Dec. 31	Minimum Rent Account	Dr.		8,000	
	To Landlord Account				8,000
	(Being the minimum rent due)				

Date	Particulars		Dr. (Rs.)	Cr. (Rs.)
	Royalties Account	Dr.	1,000	
	Shortworkings Account	Dr.	7,000	
	To Minimum Rent Account			8,000
	(Being the amount of royalties and shortworkings)			
	Landlord Account	Dr.	8,000	
	To Bank Account			8,000
	(Being the amount paid to Landlord)			
	Profit & Loss Account	Dr.	1,000	
	To Royalties Account			1,000
	(Being the Royalties transferred to Profit and Loss Account)			
2003 Dec. 31	Minimum Rent Account	Dr.	8,000	
	To Landlord Account			8,000
	(Being the minimum rent due)			
	Royalties Account	Dr.	5,000	
	Shortworkings Account	Dr.	3,000	
	To Minimum Rent Account			8,000
	(Being the amount of royalties and shortworkings)			
	Landlord Account	Dr.	8,000	
	To Bank Account			8,000
	(Being the amount paid to Landlord)			
	Profit & Loss Account	Dr.	12,000	
	To Royalties Account			5,000
	To Shortworkings Account			7,000
	(Being the amount of royalties and irrecoverable shortworkings of 2002 transferred to Profit and Loss Account)			
2004 Dec. 31	Royalties Account	Dr.	10,000	
	To Landlord Account			10,000
	(Being the royalty due)			
	Landlord Account	Dr.	10,000	
	To Shortworkings Account			2,000
	To Bank Account			8,000
	(Being the amount of shortworkings recouped and balance amount paid)			
	Profit & Loss Account	Dr.	11,000	
	To Royalties Account			10,000
	To Shortworkings Account			1,000
	(Being the amount of royalties and irrecoverable shortworkings of 2003 transferred to Profit and Loss Account)			

2005				
Dec. 31	Royalties Account Dr. To Landlord Account (Being the royalty due)		16,000	16,000
	Landlord Account Dr. To Bank Account (Being the royalty amount paid to Landlord)		16,000	16,000
	Profit & Loss Account Dr. To Royalties Account (Being the transfer of royalty to Profit and Loss Account)		16,000	16,000

Dr. **Royalties Account** Cr.

Date	Particulars	J.F.	Amount Rs	Date	Particulars	J.F.	Amount Rs
2002				2002			
Dec. 31	To Minimum Rent A/c		1,000	Dec. 31	By Profit & Loss A/c		1,000
2003				2003			
Dec. 31	To Minimum Rent A/c		5,000	Dec. 31	By Profit & Loss A/c		5,000
2004				2004			
Dec. 31	To Landlord A/c		10,000	Dec. 31	By Profit & Loss A/c		10,000
2005				2005			
Dec. 31	To Landlord A/c		16,000	Dec. 31	By Profit & Loss A/c		16,000

Dr. **Minimum Rent Account** Cr.

Date	Particulars	J.F.	Amount Rs	Date	Particulars	J.F.	Amount Rs
2002				2002			
Dec. 31	To Landlord A/c		8,000	Dec. 31	By Royalties A/c		1,000
				"	By Shortworkings A/c		7,000
			8,000				8,000
2003				Dec. 31	By Royalties A/c		5,000
Jan. 31	To Landlord A/c		8,000	"	By Shortworkings A/c		3,000
			8,000				8,000

Dr. **Landlord Account** Cr.

Date	Particulars	J.F.	Amount Rs	Date	Particulars	J.F.	Amount Rs
2002				2002			
Dec. 31	To Bank Account A/c		8,000	Dec. 31	By Minimum Rent A/c		8,000
2003				2003			
Dec. 31	To Bank Account		8,000	Dec. 31	By Minimum Rent A/c		8,000

2004				2004			
Dec. 31	To Shortworkings A/c		2,000	Dec. 31	By Royalties A/c		10,000
"	To Bank Account		8,000				
			10,000				10,000
2005				2005			
Dec. 31	To Bank A/c		16,000	Dec. 31	By Royalties A/c		16,000

Shortworkings Account Cr.

Date	Particulars	J.F.	Amount Rs	Date	Particulars	J.F.	Amount Rs
2002				2002			
Dec. 31	To Minimum Rent A/c		7,000	Dec. 31	By Balance c/d		7,000
2003				2003			
Jan. 1	To Balance b/d		7,000	Dec. 31	By Profit & Loss A/c		7,000
Dec. 31	To Minimum Rent A/c		3,000	"	By Balance c/d		3,000
			10,000				10,000
2004				2004			
Jan. 1	To Balance b/d		3,000	Dec. 31	By Landlord A/c		2,000
				"	By Profit & Loss A/c		1,000
			3,000				3,000

Changing the Minimum Rent Every Year

ILLUSTRATION 19.3

'A' owned certain patent rights. He granted a licence to 'B' to use such rights on a royalty basis. The following are the relevant particulars:

Year	*Minimum Rent*	*Royalty earned*
Rs	Rs	Rs
2001	1,750	1,500
2002	2,000	1,800
2003	2,250	1,900
2004	2,500	2,750
2005	2,500	2,600

The deficiency of any year is to be set off against excess payable within the next two years. Give journal entries and the ledger accounts in the books of '*B*'.

SOLUTION

Analytical Table

Year	*Royalty*	*Minimum Rent*	*Surplus*	*Short-working*	*Shortworkings*		*Amount Payable to Landlord*
					Recouped	*Unrecouped*	
	Rs	*Rs*	*Rs*	*Rs*	*Rs*	*Rs*	*Rs*
2001	1,500	1,750	–	250	–	–	1,750
2002	1,800	2,000	–	200	–	–	2,000
2003	1,900	2,250	–	350	–	250	2,250
2004	2,750	2,500	250	–	250	–	2,500
2005	2,600	2,500	100	–	100	200	2,500

Journal Entries in the books of B

Date			LF	Dr. Rs	Cr. Rs
2001 Dec. 31	Royalties Account	Dr.		1,500	
	Shortworkings Account	Dr.		250	
	To A's Account				1,750
	(Being the Minimum Rent payable to Landlord)				
	A's Account	Dr.		1,750	
	To Bank Account				1,750
	(Being Payment made to '*A*')				
	Profit & Loss Account	Dr.		1,500	
	To Royalties Account				1,500
	(Being transfer of Royalty Account to Profit & Loss Account)				
2002 Dec. 31	Royalties Account	Dr.		1,800	
	Shortworkings Account	Dr.		200	
	To A's Account				2,000
	(Being Minimum Rent payable to Landlord)				
	A's Account	Dr.		2,000	
	To Bank Account				2,000
	(Being payment made to '*A*')				
	Profit & Loss Account	Dr.		1,800	
	To Royalties Account				1,800
	(Being transfer of Royalty Account to Profit & Loss Account)				
2003 Dec. 31	Royalties Account	Dr.		1,900	
	Shortworkings Account	Dr.		350	
	To A's Account				2,250
	(Being Minimum Rent payable to Landlord)				
	A's Account	Dr.		2,250	
	To Bank Account				2,250
	(Being payment made to '*A*')				
	Profit & Loss Account	Dr.		2,150	
	To Royalties Account				1,900
	To Shortworkings Account				250
	(Royalties Account and irrecoverable shortworkings transferred to Profit & Loss A/c)				
2004 Dec. 31	Royalties Account	Dr.		2,750	
	To A's Account				2,750
	(Being Royalties earned and payable to Landlord)				
	A's Account	Dr.		2,750	
	To Shortworkings Account				250
	To Bank Account				2,500
	(Being shortworkings recouped and balance paid to Landlord)				

Date	Particulars		L.F.	Dr.	Cr.
	Profit and Loss Account	Dr.		2,750	
	To Royalties Account				2,750
	(Being transfer to Royalties Account to Profit & Loss Account)				
2005 Dec. 31	Royalties Account	Dr.		2,600	
	To A's Account				2,600
	(Being Royalties earned payable to Landlord)				
	A's Account	Dr.		2,600	
	To Shortworkings Account				100
	To Bank Account				2,500
	(Being shortworkings recouped and balance paid to Landlord)				
	Profit & Loss Account	Dr.		2, 800	
	To Royalties Account				2,600
	To Shortworkings Account				200
	(Royalties Account and irrecoverable Shortworkings transferred to Profit & Loss Account)				

Dr. Royalties Account Cr.

Date	Particulars	J.F.	Amount Rs	Date	Particulars	J.F.	Amount Rs
2001				2001			
Dec. 31	To A's Account		1,500	Dec. 31	By Profit & Loss A/c		1,500
2002				2002			
Dec. 31	To A's Account		1,800	Dec. 31	By Profit & Loss A/c		1,800
2003				2003			
Dec. 31	To A's Account		1,900	Dec. 31	By Profit & Loss A/c		1,900
2004				2004			
Dec. 31	To A's Account		2,750	Dec. 31	By Profit & Loss A/c		2,750
2005				2005			
Dec. 31	To A's Account		2,600	Dec. 31	By Profit & Loss A/c		2,600

Dr. Shortworkings Account Cr.

Date	Particulars	J.F.	Amount Rs	Date	Particulars	J.F.	Amount Rs
2001				2002			
Dec. 31	To A's Account		250	Dec. 31	By Balance c/d		250
2002				2003			
Jan. 1	To Balance b/d		250	Dec. 31	By Balance c/d		450
Dec. 31	To A's Account		200				
			450				450
2003				2003			
Jan. 1	To Balance b/d		450	Dec. 31	By Profit & Loss A/c		250
Dec. 31	To A's Account		350	"	By Balance c/d		550
			800				800

2004				2004			
Jan. 1	To Balance b/d		550	Dec. 31	By A's Account		250
				"	By Balance c/d		300
			550				550
2005				2005			
Jan. 1	To Balance b/d		300	Dec. 31	By A's Account		100
					By Profit & Loss Account		200
							300

A's Account

Dr. Cr.

Date	Particulars	J.F.	Amount Rs	Date	Particulars	J.F.	Amount Rs
2001				2001			
Dec. 31	To Bank A/c		1,750	Dec. 31	By Royalties A/c		1,500
					By Shortworkings A/c		250
			1,750				1,750
2002				2002			
Dec. 31	To Bank A/c		2,000	Dec. 31	By Royalties A/c		1,800
				"	By Shortworkings A/c		200
			2,000				2,000
2003				2003			
Dec. 31	To Bank A/c		2,250	Dec. 31	By Royalties A/c		1,900
				"	By Shortworkings A/c		350
			2,250				2,250
2004				2004			
Dec. 31	To Shortworkings A/c		250	Dec. 31	By Royalties A/c		2,750
	To Bank A/c		2,500				2,750
			2,750				
2005				2005			
Dec. 31	To Shortworking A/c		100	Dec. 31	By Royalties A/c		2,600
"	To Bank A/c		2,500				
			2,600				2,600

ILLUSTRATION 19.4

A Coal Company owns lease of a mine of a royalty of Rs 2 per ton of coal raised, with a Dead Rent of Rs 40,000 per annum. The agreement provides the lease with the power of recouping each year's excess of Minimum Rent over Royalties out of the royalties of the next two years. The output for the first five years was as follows:

2001	2,500 tons
2002	12,000 tons
2003	20,000 tons
2004	30,000 tons
2005	30,000 tons

Write up the Minimum Rent Account, Royalty Account, Shortworkings Account and the Landlord Account. *(B. Com. Madurai)*

SOLUTION

Analytical Table

Year	Output	Royalty @ Rs 2 per ton	Minimum Rent	Surplus	Short-workings	Shortworkings Recouped	Shortworkings Unrecouped	Amount Payable to Landlord
	Rs	Rs	Rs	Rs	Rs	Rs	Rs	Rs
2001	2,500	5,000	40,000	–	35,000	–	–	40,000
2002	12,000	24,000	40,000	–	16,000	–	–	40,000
2003	20,000	40,000	40,000	–	–	–	35,000	40,000
2004	30,000	60,000	40,000	20,000	–	16,000	–	44,000
2005	30,000	60,000	40,000	20,000	–	–	–	60,000

In the Books of the Coal Company

Dr. Royalties Account Cr.

Date	Particulars	J.F.	Amount Rs	Date	Particulars	J.F.	Amount Rs
2001				2001			
Dec. 31	To Minimum Rent A/c		5,000	Dec. 31	By Profit & Loss A/c		5,000
2002				2002			
Dec. 31	To Minimum Rent A/c		24,000	Dec. 31	By Profit & Loss A/c		24,000
2003				2003			
Dec.31	To Landlord A/c		40,000	Dec. 31	By Profit & Loss A/c		40,000
2004				2004			
Dec. 31	To Landlord A/c		60,000	Dec. 31	By Profit & Loss A/c		60,000
2005				2005			
Dec. 31	To Landlord A/c		60,000	Dec. 31	By Profit & Loss A/c		60,000

Dr. Minimum Rent Account Cr.

Date	Particulars	J.F.	Amount Rs	Date	Particulars	J.F.	Amount Rs
2001				2001			
Dec. 31	To Landlord A/c		40,000	Dec. 31	By Royalties A/c		5,000
				”	By Shortworkings A/c		35,000
			40,000				40,000
2002				2002			
Dec. 31	To Londlord A/c		40,000	Dec. 31	By Royalties A/c		24,000
				”	By Shortworkings A.c		16,000
			40,000				40,000

Dr. Landlord Account Cr.

Date	Particulars	J.F.	Amount Rs	Date	Particulars	L.F.	Amount Rs
2001				2001			
Dec. 31	To Bank Account		40,000	Dec. 31	By Minimum Rent A/c		40,000

Date	Particulars	J.F.	Amount	Date	Particulars	J.F.	Amount
2002				2002			
Dec. 31	To Bank Account		40,000	Dec. 31	By Minimum Rent A/c		40,000
2003				2003			
Dec.31	To Bank Account		40,000	Dec. 31	By Royalties A/c		40,000
2004				2004			
Dec. 31	To Shortworkings A/c		16,000	Dec. 31	By Royalties A/c		60,000
	To Bank Account		44,000				
			60,000				60,000
2005				2005			
Dec. 31	To Bank A/c		60,000	Dec. 31	By Royalties A/c		60,000

Dr. Shortworkings Account Cr.

Date	*Particulars*	*J.F.*	*Amount Rs*	*Date*	*Particulars*	*J.F.*	*Amount Rs*
2001				2001			
Dec. 31	To Minimum Rent A/c		35,000	Dec. 31	By Balance c/d		35,000
2002				2002			
Jan. 1	To Balance b/d		35,000	Dec. 31	By Balance c/d		51,000
Dec. 31	To Minimum Rent A/c		16,000				
			51,000				51,000
2003				2003			
Jan. 1	To Balance b/d		51,000	Dec. 31	By Profit & Loss A/c		35,000
				"	By Balance c/d		16,000
			51,000				51,000
2004				2004			
Jan. 1	To Balance b/d		16,000	Dec. 31	By Royalties A/c		16,000

Half-Yearly or Quartely Payment of Royalty

When royalty is payable half-yearly or quarterly, minimum rent should be calculated for half year or for quarter year in order to compare it with royalty for finding out shortworkings or surplus. Royalty is transferred to Trading or Profit & Loss Account not at the end of the quarter year or half year, but at the end of the year.

ILLUSTRATION 19.5

A Coal Company takes a lease of coal of mine for a term of 10 years from Ist January 2004 on a minimum rent of Rs 8,000 per year merging in a royatly of Re 1 per ton of coal raised payable quartely on 31st March, 30th June. 30th September and 31st December each year. Shortworkings can be recouped during the first two years of the lease. Royalty which was due on 31st December 2004 which was paid on 10 January 2005. Coal Company closes its books on 31st December each year. Coal is raised as follows:

	Ton
Up to 31.3.2004	1,500
Up to 30.6.2004	1,800
Up to 30.9.2004	2,200
Up to 31.12.2004	2,100
Up to 31.3.2005	1,600
Up to 30.6.2005	2,500
UP to 30.9.2005	2,000
Up to 31.12.2005	2,200

Prepare necessary accounts in the books of Coal Company. *(B.Com. Madurai)*

SOLUTION

Analytical Table

Year	Output	Royalty @ Re 1 per ton	Minimum Rent	Surplus	Short-workings	Shortworkings Recouped	Shortworkings Unrecouped	Amount Payable to Landlord
	Rs	Rs	Rs	Rs	Rs	Rs	Rs	Rs
2004								
March 31	1,500	1,500	2,000	–	500	–	–	2,000
June 30	1,800	1,800	2,000	–	200	–	–	2,000
Sept. 30	2,200	2,000	2,000	200	–	200	–	2,000
Dec. 31	2,100	2,100	2,000	100	–	100	–	2,000
2005								
March 31	1,600	1,600	2,000	–	400	–	–	2,000
June 30	2,500	2,500	2,000	500	–	500	–	2,000
Sept. 30	2,000	2,000	2,000	–	–	–	–	2,000
Dec. 31	2,200	2,200	2,000	200	–	200	100	2,000

Landlord Account

Dr. Cr.

Date	Particulars	J.F.	Amount Rs	Date	Particulars	J.F.	Amount Rs
2004				2004			
Mar. 31	To Bank Account		2,000	Mar. 31	By Royalty A/c		1,500
June 30	To Bank Account		2,000	Mar. 31	By Shortworkings A/c		500
Sept. 30	To Bank Account		2,000	June 30	By Royalty A/c		1,800
Sept.30	To Shortworkings		200	June 30	By Shortworkings A/c		200
Dec. 31	To Shortworkings		100	Sept. 30	By Royalty A/c		2,200
Dec. 31	To Balance c/d		2,000	Dec. 31	By Royalty A/c		2,100
			8,300				8,300
2005				2005			
Jan. 10	To Bank A/c		2,000	Jan. 1	By Balance c/d		2,000
Mar. 31	To Bank A/c		2,000	Mar. 31	By Royalty A/c		1,600
June 30	To Bank A/c		2,000	Mar. 31	By Royalty A/c		400
June 30	To Shortworkings		500	June, 30	By Royalty A/c		2,500
Sept. 30	To Bank A/c		2,000	Sept. 30	By Royalty A/c		2,000
Dec. 31	To Bank A/c		2,000	Dec. 31	By Royalty A/c		2,200
Dec. 31	To Shortworkings		200				
			10,700				10,700

Shortworkings Account

Dr. Cr.

Date	Particulars	J.F.	Amount Rs	Date	Particulars	L.F.	Amount Rs
2004				2004			
Mar. 31	To Landlord A/c		500	Sept. 30	By Landlord A/c		200
June 30	To Landlord A/c		200	Dec. 31	By Landlord A/c		100
				Dec. 31	By Balance c/d		400
			700				700

Date	Particulars	J.F.	Amount	Date	Particulars	J.F.	Amount
2005				2005			
Jan. 1	To Balance b/d		400	June 30	By Landlord A/c		500
Mar. 31	To Landlord A/c		400	Dec. 31	By Landlord A/c		200
				Dec. 31	By Profit & Loss A/c		100
			800				800

Dr. **Royalty Account** Cr.

Date	Particulars	J.F.	Amount Rs	Date	Particulars	J.F.	Amount Rs
2004				2004			
Mar. 31	To Landlord A/c		1,500	Dec. 31	By Profit & Loss A/c		7.600
June 30	To Landlord A/c		1,800				
Sept. 30	To Landlord A/c		2,200				
Dec. 31	To Landlord A/c		2,100				
			7,600				7,600
2005				2005			
Mar. 31	To Landlord A/c		1,600	Dec. 31	By Profit & Loss A/c		8,300
June 30	To Landlord A/c		2,500				
Sept. 30	To Landlord A/c		2,000				
Dec. 31	To Landlord A/c		2,200				
			8,300				8,300

Books of Lessor (Landlord)

The Lessor is entitled to receive Royalty from the Lessee. Here royalty would be an income to the Lessor. The entries would therefore be the reverse of those made in the Lessee's books. However, it may be noted that in place of Shortworkings Account, the Lessor maintains the Royalty Reserve or Royalty Suspense Account.

ACCOUNTING ENTRIES IN THE BOOKS OF LESSOR

(1) When the Royalties are less than Minimum Rent and Shortworkings are Recoverable out of future years

(*a*) Lessee's Account Dr
(with the Minimum Rent)
To Royalties Receivable Account
(with actual royalty)
To Royalties Suspense Account
(with the difference)
(Being Royalties and shortworkings due)

(*b*) Bank Account Dr.
To Lessee's Account
(Being amount of royalty received)

(*c*) Royalties Receivable Account Dr.
To Profit & Loss Account
(Royalties earned transferred)

(2) When the Royalties earned exceed the Minimum Rent and Shortworkings are recovered

(*a*) Lessee's Account Dr.
To Royalties Receivable Account
(Being the amount of royalties earned)

(*b*) Royalties Suspense Account Dr.
To Lessee's Account
(Being the recoupment of shortworkings)

(*c*) Bank Account Dr.
To Lessee's Account
(Being the amount of royalties received)

Note: In place of (*b*) and (*c*) the following combined entry may be done;
Royalties Suspense Account Dr.
Bank Account Dr.
To Lessee's Account
(Being the amount of Royalty Suspense recouped and balance received)

(*d*) Royalty Receivable Account Dr.
To Profit & Loss Account
(Being Royalty Receivable transferred to Profit & Loss Account)

If the Royalty Suspense Account shows any balance, which is no longer recoverable, it should be transferred to Profit & Loss Account:

Royalty Suspense Account Dr.
To Profit & Loss Account

ILLUSTRATION 19.6

Y company is a lessee of a mine on a royalty or Re 1 per ton of coal raised with minimum rent of Rs 8,000 per annum with power to recoup shortworkings during the first two years of the lease only. The output for the first three years is:

2003 5,000 tons
2004 9,000 tons
2005 8,000 tons

Pass the necessary journal entries in the books of landlord. *(B. Com. Maduari)*

SOLUTION

Analytical Table

Year	*Output*	*Royalty Receivable @ Re 1 per ton*	*Minimum Rent*	*Royalty Reserve*	*Royalty Reserve adjusted*	*Unrecouped Royalty*	*Actual Amount Received*
	Ton	*Rs*	*Rs*	*Rs*	*Rs*	*Rs*	*Rs*
2003	5,000	5,000	8,000	3,000	–	–	8,000
2004	9,000	9,000	8,000	–	1,000	–	8,000
2005	8,000	8,000	8,000	–	–	2,000	8,000

Journal Entries in the Books of Landlord

Year			LF	Dr. Rs	Cr. Rs
2003	Y Company Account	Dr.		8,000	
	To Royalty Receivable Account				5,000
	To Royalty Reserve Account				3,000
	(Being Minimum Rent due; the difference between Minimum Rent and Royalty Receivable transferred to Royalty Reserve)				
	Bank Account	Dr.		8,000	
	To Y Company Account				8,000
	(Being Royalty received)				
	Royalty Receivable Account	Dr.		5,000	
	To Profit & Loss Account				5,000
	(Being the amount of Royalty Receivable transferred to Profit and Loss Account)				
2004	Y Company Account	Dr.		9,000	
	To Royalty Receivable A/c				9,000
	(Being royalty earned and receivable)				
	Royalty Reserve Account	Dr.		1,000	
	Bank Account	Dr.		8,000	
	To Y Company Account				9,000
	(Royalty Reserve Account recouped by Lessee and received the balance)				
	Royalty Receivable Account	Dr.		9,000	
	Royalty Reserve Account	Dr.		2,000	
	To Profit & Loss Account				11,000
	(Being the balance of Royalty Receivable and Royalty Reserve transferred to Profit & Loss A/c)				
2005	Y Company Account	Dr.		8,000	
	To Royalty Receivable A/c				8,000
	(Being royalty receivable)				
	Bank Account	Dr.		8,000	
	To Y Company Account				8,000
	(Being cash received from Y Company)				
	Royalty Receivable Account	Dr.		8,000	
	To Profit & Loss Account				8,000
	(Being royalty receivable transferred to Profit & Loss A/c)				

ILLUSTRATION 19.7

The copyright of a book was held by B Company. C Company was allowed to publish the book on the following terms and conditions:

(*a*) Royalty payable is Rs 3 per book.

(*b*) The Minimum Royalty is fixed at Rs 9,000 p.a.

(*c*) The shortworkings can be recouped within first five years only.

The following are the details of the number of copies published by C Company.

Year	*No. of Copies*
2001	1,800
2002	2,000
2003	3,000
2004	4,300
2005	6,000

You are required to prepare Journal entries and Ledger account to record the above transactions in the books of B Company. *(B. Com. Madras)*

SOLUTION

Analytical Table

Year	Output	Royalty Receivable @ Rs 3	Minimum Rent	Royalty Reserve	Royalty Reserve Adjusted	Unrecouped Royalty Reserve	Actual Amount Received
	Nos.	Rs	Rs	Rs	Rs	Rs	Rs
2001	1,800	5,400	9,000	3,600	–	–	9,000
2002	2,000	6,000	9,000	3,000	–	–	9,000
2003	3,000	9,000	9,000	–	–	–	9,000
2004	4,300	12,900	9,000	–	3,900	–	9,000
2005	6,000	18,000	9,000	–	2,700	–	15,300

Dr. Royalties Receivable Account Cr.

Year	Particulars	J.F.	Amount Rs	Year	Particulars	J.F.	Amount Rs
2001	To Profit & Loss A/c		5,400	2001	By C Company		5,400
2002	To Profit & Loss A/C		6,000	2002	By C Company		6,000
2003	To Profit & Loss A/c		9,000	2003	By C Company		9,000
2004	To Profit & Loss A/c		12,900	2004	By C Company		12,900
2005	To Profit & Loss A/c		18,000	2005	By C Company		18,000

Dr. C Company Account Cr.

Year	Particulars	J.F.	Amount Rs	Year	Particulars	J.F.	Amount Rs
2001	To Royalty Receivable A/c		5,400	2001	By Bank Account		9,000
	To Royalty Reserve A/c		3,600				
			9,000				9,000
2002	To Royalty Receivable A/c		6,000	2002	By Bank Account		9,000
	To Royalty Reserve A/c		3,000				
			9,000				9,000
2003	To Royalty Receivable A/c		9,000	2003	By Bank Account		9,000
2004	To Royalty Receivable A/c		12,900	2004	By Royalty Reserve		3,900
					By Bank Account		9,000
			12,900				12,900
2005	To Royalty Receivable A/c		18,000	2005	By Royalty Reserve		2,700
					By Bank Account		15,300
			18,000				18,000

Dr. Royalties Reserve Account Cr.

Year	Particulars	J.F.	Amount Rs	Year	Particulars	J.F.	Amount Rs
2001	To Balance c/d		3,600	2001	By C Company		3,600
2002	To Balance c/d		6,600	2002	By Balance b/d		3,600
					By C Company		3,000
			6,600				6,600

2003	To Balance c/d		6,600	2003	By C Company b/d		6,600
2004	To C Company		3,900	2004	By Balance b/d		6,600
	To Balance c/d		2,700				
			6,600				6,600
2005	To C Company		2,700	2005	By Balance c/d		2,700

ILLUSTRATION 19.8

X Colliery Company Ltd. leased a property from a Landlord at a Royalty of Paise 50 per ton with a Minimum Rent of Rs 10,000 p.a. Each year's excess of minimum rent over royalties is recoverable out of royalties of next three years. In the event of strike if the minimum rent is not reached, the lease provided that the actual royalty earned for the year discharge all the rental obligations for that year.

The result or working was as follows:

Year	*Output in tons*
2001	15,000
2002	21,000
2003	12,000 (Strike)
2004	16,000
2005	22,000

Write up the Royalties Account, Shortworkings Account and Landlord Account for the five years.

(B. Com, Karnataka, Madurai)

SOLUTION

Analytical Payable Table

Year	*Output*	*Royalty @ Re 0.50 per ton*	*Minimum Rent*	*Short-working*	*Surplus*	*Shortworkings*		Amount Payable to Landlord
						Recouped	*Unrecouped*	
	Ton	*Rs*	*Rs*	*Rs*	*Rs*	*Rs*	*Rs*	*Rs*
2001	15,000	7,500	10,000	2,500	–	–	–	10,000
2002	21,000	10,500	10,000	–	500	500	–	10,000
2003 (Strike)	12,000	6,000	6,000	–	–	–	–	6,000
2004	16,000	8,000	10,000	2,000	–	–	2,000	10,000
2005	22,000	11,000	10,000	–	1,000	1,000	–	10,000

Dr. Royalties Account Cr.

Year	*Particulars*	*J.F.*	*Amount Rs*	*Year*	*Particulars*	*J.F.*	*Amount Rs*
2001	To Landlord A/c		7,500	2001	By Trading/ P & L		7,500
2002	To Landlord A/c		10,500	2002	By Trading/ P & L		10,500
2003	To Landlord A/c		6,000	2003	By Trading/ P & L		6,000
2004	To Landlord A/c		8,000	2004	By Trading/ P & L		8,000
2005	To Landlord A/c		11,000	2005	By Trading/ P & L		11,000

Landlord Account

Dr. Year	Particulars	J.F.	Amount Rs	Year	Particulars	J.F.	Cr. Amount Rs
2001	To Bank Account		10,000	2001	By Royalty A/c		7,500
					By Shortworkings		2,500
			10,000				10,000
2002	To Shortworkings A/c		500	2002	By Royalties A/c		10,500
	To Bank Account		10,000				
			10,500				10,500
2003	To Bank Account		6,000	2003	By Royalties A/c		6,000
2004	To Bank Account		10,000	2004	By Royalties		8,000
					By Shortworkings A/c		2,000
			10,000				10,000
2005	To Shortworkings A/c		1,000	2005	By Royalties A/c		11,000
	To Bank Account		10,000				
			11,000				11,000

Shortworkings Account

Dr. Date	Particulars	J.F.	Amount Rs	Year	Particulars	J.F.	Cr. Amount Rs
2001	To Landlord A/C		2, 500	2001	By Balance c/d		2,500
2002				2002			
Jan. 1	To Balance b/d		2,500	Dec. 31	By Landlord A/c		500
					By Balance c/d		2,000
			2,500				2,500
2003				2003			
Jan. 1	To Balance b/d		2,000	Dec. 31	By Balance c/d		2,000
2004				2004			
Jan. 1	To Balance b/d		2,000	Dec. 31	By Profit & Loss		2,000
Dec. 31	To Landlord A/c		2,000		By Balance c/d		2,000
			4,000				4,000
2005				2005			
Jan.	To Balance b/d		2,000	Dec.31	By Landlord A/c		1,000
					By Balance c/d		1,000
			2,000				2,000
2006							
Jan. 1	To Balance b/d		1,000				

ILLUSTRATION 19.9

Mr Khanna wrote a book "Advanced Accountancy" and got it published with Paul Printers on the terms that royalties will be paid at Rs 5 per copy sold, subject to a Minimum Rent of Rs, 15,000 per year, with a right to recoup the shortworkings over the first three years of the royalty agreement. The details are as under:

Year	*Number of copies printed*	*Number of copies of Closing stock*
2002	2,000	100
2003	3,000	200
2004	4,000	400
2005	5,000	500

Prepare Minimum Rent Account, Royalties Account and Khanna Accounts in the books of Paul Printers.

(B. Com., Madurai; Bangalore MS. Kerala)

SOLUTION

Number of copies sold = Opening stock + No. of copies printed – Closing stock

2002 = Nil + 2,000 – 100 = 1,900 copies sold
2003 = 100 + 3,000 – 200 = 2,900 copies sold
2004 = 200 + 4,000 – 400 = 3,800 copies sold
2005 = 400 + 5,000 – 500 = 4,900 copies sold

Analytical Table

Year	*Sales*	*Royalty*	*Minimum Rent*	*Surplus*	*Short-working*	*Shortworkings Recouped*	*Shortworkings Unrecouped*	Amount Payable to Landlord
	No.	*Rs*	*Rs*	*Rs*	*Rs*	*Rs*	*Rs*	*Rs*
2002	1,900	9,500	15,000	–	5,500	–	–	15,000
2003	2,900	14,500	15,000	–	500	–	–	15,000
2004	3,800	19,000	15,000	4,000	–	4,000	2,000	15,000
2005	4,900	24,500	15,000	9,500	–	–	–	24,500

Dr. Minimum Rent Account Cr.

Year	*Particulars*	*J.F.*	*Amount Rs*	*Year*	*Particulars*	*J.F.*	*Amount Rs*
2002	To Khanna A/c		15,000	2002	By Royalties A/c		9,500
					By Shortworkings A/c		5,500
			15,000				15,000
2003	To Khanna A/c		15,000	2003	By Royalties A/c		14,500
					By Shortworkings A/c		500
			15,000				15,000

Dr. Royalties Account Cr.

Year	Particulars	J.F.	Amount Rs	Year	Particulars	J.F.	Amount Rs
2002	To Minimum Rent A/c		9,500	2002	By Profit & Loss A/c		9,500
2003	To Minimum Rent A/c		14,500	2003	By Profit & Loss A/c		14,500
2004	To Khanna A/c		15,000	2004	By Profit & Loss A/c		19,000
	To Shortworkings A/c		4,000				
			19,000				19,000
2005	To Khanna A/c		24,500	2005	By Profit & Loss A/c		24,500

Dr. Shortworking Account Cr.

Year	Particulars	J.F.	Amount Rs	Year	Particulars	J.F.	Amount Rs
2002	To Minimum Rent A/c		5,500	2002	By Balance c/d		5,500
2003	To Balance b/d		5,500	2003	By Balance c/d		6,000
	To Minimum Rent A/c		500				
			6,000				6,000
2004	To Balance b/d		6,000	2004	By Royalty A/c		4,000
					By Profit & Loss A/c		2,000
			6,000				6,000

Dr. Khanna Account Cr.

Year	Particulars	J.F.	Amount Rs	Year	Particulars	J.F.	Amount Rs
2002	To Bank A/c		15,000	2002	By Minimum Rent A/c		15,000
2003	To Bank A/c		15,000	2003	By Minimum Rent A/c		15,000
2004	To Bank A/c		15,000	2004	By Royalty A/c		15,000
2005	To Bank A/c		24,500	2005	By Royalty A/c		24,500

ILLUSTRATION 19.10

Mr Raja owned the patent of a safety lock. He granted Dindigul Lock Company a licence for seven years to manufacture and sell locks on the following terms:

(*a*) Dindigul Lock Company to pay Raja a Royalty of Rs 5 for each lock sold with a minimum annual payment of Rs 50,000. Account to be settled annually on 31st December.

(*b*) If in any year the royalty calculated on locks sold amounted to less than Rs 50,000 Dindigul Lock Company to have the right to deduct the deficiency from the royalty payable in excess of that sum in the following two years.

The number of locks sold was as follows:

Year ended 31st December 2002	8,000
Year ended 31st December 2003	9,000
Year ended 31st December 2004	11,000
Year ended 31st December 2005	18,000

You are required to show the ledger accounts for the above transactions in the books of Dindigul Lock Company. *(B. Com., Madurai; Delhi)*

SOLUTION

Analytical Table

Year	Royalties	Minimum Rent	Short-working	Surplus	Shortworkings Recouped	Shortworkings Unrecouped	Amount payable to Landlord
	Rs	Rs	Rs	Rs	Rs	Rs	Rs
2002	40,000	50,000	10,000	–	–	–	50,000
2003	45,000	50,000	5,000	–	–	–	50,000
2004	55,000	50,000	–	5,000	5,000	5,000	50,000
2005	90,000	50,000	–	40,000	5,000	–	85,000

In the Books of Dindigul Lock Company

Royalties Account

Dr. Cr.

Year	Particulars	J.F.	Amount Rs	Year	Particulars	J.F.	Amount Rs
2002				2002			
Dec. 31	To Minimum Rent A/c		40,000	Dec. 31	By Profit & Loss A/c		40,000
2003				2003			
Dec. 31	To Minimum Rent A/c		45,000	Dec. 31	By Profit & Loss A/c		45,000
2004				2004			
Dec. 31	To Raja Account		55,000	Dec. 31	By Profit & Loss A/c		55,000
2005				2005			
Dec. 31	To Raja Account		90,000	Dec. 31	By Profit & Loss A/c		90,000

Minimum Rent Account

Dr. Cr.

Date	Particulars	J.F.	Amount Rs	Year	Particulars	J.F.	Amount Rs
2002				2002			
Dec. 31	To Raja Account		50,000	Dec. 31	By Royalties A/c		40,000
				"	By Shortworkings A/c		10,000
			50,000				50,000
2003				2003			
Decl. 31	To Raja Account		50,000	Dec. 31	By Royalties A/c		45,000
					By Shortworkings A/c		5,000
			50,000				50,000

Dr. **Shortworkings Account** Cr.

Date	Particulars	J.F.	Amount Rs	Year	Particulars	J.F.	Amount Rs
2002				2002			
Dec. 31	To Minimum Rent A/c		10,000	Dec. 31	By Balance c/d		10,000
2003				2003			
Jan. 1	To Balance b/d		10,000	Dec. 31	By Balance c/d		15,000
Dec. 31	To Minimum Rent A/c		5,000				
			15,000				15,000
2004				2004			
Jan. 1	To Balance b/d		15,000	Dec. 31	By Raja A/c		5,000
				"	By Profit & Loss A/c		5,000
				"	By Balance c/d		5,000
			15,000				15,000
2005				2005			
Jan. 1	To Balance c/d		5,000	Dec. 31	By Raja A/c		5,000

Dr. **Raja Account** Cr.

Date	Particulars	J.F.	Amount Rs	Year	Particulars	J.F.	Amount Rs
2002				2002			
Dec. 31	To Bank A/c		50,000	Dec. 31	By Minimum Rent A/c		50,000
2003				2003			
Dec. 31	To Bank A/c		50,000	Dec. 31	By Minimum Rent A/c		50,000
2004				2004			
Dec. 31	To Shortworkings A/c		5,000	Dec. 31	By Royalties A/c		55,000
"	To Bank A/c		50,000				
			55,000				55,000
2005				2005			
Dec. 1	To Shortworkings A/c		5,000	Dec. 1	By Royalties A/c		90,000
"	To Bank A/c		85,000				
			90,000				90,000

SUB-LEASE (SUB-ROYALTY)

Sometimes, there are instances that the original lease may empower the Lessee to sublet, in whole or in part thereof, to a third party. Here Lessee has a dual role to play. He is both a Landlord and a Lessee. For instance, "A" obtains a lease from "B" to work in a mine. "A" sublets a part of the land to "C".

Thus, there are three parties – Owner (Lessor) is "B", the Lessee is "A" and sub-lessee (sub-tenant) is "C". Here "A" is a tenant to "B" and is a Landlord or a Sub-lessor in relation to "C". In such case, whatever the yield is taken out by Lessee and sub-lessee is totalled up and on this total yield, Lessee has to pay Royalty to the Landlord. That is, Royalty payable by the Lessee (*i.e.* first Lessee) to the

Lessor (*i.e.* head Landlord) will be calculated on the full output *i.e.* on the total output of both the lessee and the sub-lessee. Therefore, the Lessee has to keep the following accounts:

1. Royalties Payable Account
2. Royalties Receivable Account
3. Shortworkings Recoupable Account
4. Shortworkings Allowable Account
   (Royalties Suspense/Reserve Account)
5. Landlord Account
6. Sub-Lessee Account.

The entries in the books of Sub-Lessee and Landlord will be on the lines of those of Lessee and Landlord as discussed earlier.

ILLUSTRATION 19.11

Mr Ram obtained a mining lease and from that data he sub-leases a part of the mine to Gopal. Show ledger accounts in the books of Ram from the following data:

	Lease (Ton)	Sub-Lease (Ton)
2001	1,000	1,000
2002	3,000	2,000
2003	12,000	5,000
2004	9,000	2,000 (Strike)
2005	5,000	12,000
Royalty per ton	Rs 2	Rs 3
Dead Rent p.a.	Rs. 15,000	Rs 10,000
Shortworkings recoverable	3 years	2 years

In case of strike, royalty earned will discharge all liabilities for the year only.

SOLUTION

Royalties Payable

Year	Production		Total	Royalty @ Rs 2 per ton	Minimum Rent	Short-working	Surplus	Shortworkings		Amount payable to Landlord
	Lease	Sub-lease						Recouped	Unre-couped	
	Ton	Rs	Rs	Rs	Rs	Rs	Rs	Rs	Rs	Rs
2001	1,000	1,000	2,000	4,000	15,000	11,000	–	–	–	15,000
2002	3,000	2,000	5,000	10,000	15,000	5,000	–	–	–	15,000
2003	12,000	5,000	17,000	34,000	15,000	–	19,000	16,000	–	18,000
2004	9,000	2,000	11,000	22,000	15,000	–	7,000		–	22,000
2005	5,000	12,000	17,000	34,000	15,000	–	19,000		–	34,000

Royalty Receivable

Year	Output	Royalty @ Rs 3 per ton	Minimum Rent	Surplus	Short-working	Shortworkings		Amount payable to Landlord
						Recouped	Unrecouped	
	Ton	Rs	Rs	Rs	Rs	Rs	Rs	Rs
2001	1,000	3,000	10,000	–	7,000	–	–	10,000
2002	2,000	6,000	10,000	–	4,000	–	11,000	10,000
2003	5,000	15,000	10,000	5,000		–	–	15,000
2004	2,000	6,000	6,000	–	–	–	–	6,000
2005	12,000	36,000	10,000	26,000	–	–	–	36,000

In the books of Ram

Royalty Payable Account

Dr. Cr.

Year	Particulars	J.F.	Amount Rs	Year	Particulars	J.F.	Amount Rs
2001	To Landlord A/c		4,000	2001	By Royalties Receivable A/c (1,000, × Rs 2)		2,000
					By Trading A/C (Balancing figure)		2,000
			4,000				4,000
2002	To Landlord A/c		10,000	2002	By Royalties Receivable A/c (2,000 × Rs 2)		4,000
					By Trading A/c (Balancing figure)		6,000
			10,000				10,000
2003	To Landlord A/c		34,000	2003	By Royalties Receivable A/c (5,000 × Rs 2)		10,000
					ByTrading Account (Balancing figure)		24,000
			34,000				34,000
2004	To Landlord A/c		22,000	2004	By Royalties Receivable A/c (2,000 × Rs 2)		4,000
					By Trading Account (Balancing figure)		18,000
			22,000				22,000
2005	To Landlord A/c		34,000	2005	By Royalties Receivable A/c (12,000 × Rs 2)		24,000
					By Trading Account (Balancing figure)		10,000
			34,000				34,000

Royalty Receivable Account

Dr. Cr.

Year	Particulars	J.F.	Amount Rs	Year	Particulars	J.F.	Amount Rs
2001	To Royalty Payable A/c (1,000 × Rs 2)		2,000	2001	By Gopal A/c		3,000
	To Profit & Loss A/c		1,000				
			3,000				3,000
2002	To Royalty Payable A/c (2, 000 × Rs 2)		4,000	2002	By Gopal A/c		6,000
	To Profit & Loss A/c		2,000				
			6,000				6,000
2003	To Royalty Payable A/c (5,000 × Rs 2)		10,000	2003	By Gopal A/c		15,000
	To Profit & Loss A/c		5,000				
			15,000				15,000

Year	Particulars	J.F.	Amount Rs	Year	Particulars	J.F.	Amount Rs
2004	To Royalty Payable A/c (2,000 × Rs 2)		4,000	2004	By Gopal A/c		6,000
	To Profit & Loss A/c		2,000				
			6,000				6,000
2005	To Royalty Payable A/c (12,000 × Rs 2)		24,000	2005	By Gopal A/c		36,000
	To Profit & Loss A/c		12,000				
			36,000				36,000

Dr. **Shortworkings Account** Cr.

Year	Particulars	J.F.	Amount Rs	Year	Particulars	J.F.	Amount Rs
2001	To Landlord A/c		11,000	2001	By Balance c/d		11,000
2002	To Balance b/d		11,000	2002	By Balance c/d		16,000
	To Landlord A/c		5,000				
			16,000				16,000
2003	To Balance b/d		16,000	2003	By Landlord A/c		16,000

Dr. **Royalties Suspense Account** Cr.

Year	Particulars	J.F.	Amount Rs	Year	Particulars	J.F.	Amount Rs
2001	To Balance c/d		7,000	2001	By Gopal A/c		7,000
2002	To Profit & Loss A/c		11,000	2002	By Balance b/d		7,000
					By Gopal A/c		4,000
			11,000				11,000

Dr. **Landlord Account** Cr.

Year	Particulars	J.F.	Amount Rs	Year	Particulars	J.F.	Amount Rs
2001	To Bank A/c		15,000	2001	By Royalty Payable A/c		4,000
					By Shortworkings A/c		11,000
			15,000				15,000
2002	To Bank A/c		15,000	2002	By Royalty Payable A/c		10,000
					By Shortworkings A/c		5,000
			15,000				15,000
2003	To Shortworkings A/c		16,000	2003	By Royalty Payable A/c		34,000
	To Bank A/c		18,000				
			34,000				34,000
2004	To Bank A/c		22,000	2004	By Royalty Payable A/c		22,000
2005	To Bank A/c		34,000	2005	By Royalty Payable A/c		34,000

Dr. Gopal Account Cr.

Year	Particulars	J.F.	Amount Rs	Year	Particulars	J.F.	Amount Rs
2001	To Royalty Receivable A/c		3,000	2001	By Bank A/c		10,000
	To Royalty Suspense A/c		7,000				
			10,000				10,000
2002	To Royalty Receivable A/c		6,000	2002	By Bank A/c		10,000
	To Royalty Suspense A/c		4,000				
			10,000				10,000
2003	To Royalty Receivable A/c		15,000	2003	By Bank A/c		15,000
2004	To Royalty Receivable A/c		6,000	2004	By Bank A/c		6,000
2005	To Royalty Receivable A/c		36,000	2005	By Bank A/c		36,000

ILLUSTRATION 19.12

The West Bengal Coal Co. obtained the lease, with power to sub-lease a coalmine from a Landlord for a period of 20 years from Ist January 2002. The terms of the lease were:

(*a*) Minimum Rent payable is Rs. 20,000 merging into a Royalty of Re 1 per ton of coal raised in any year.

(*b*) Shortworking is recoverable throughout the term of the lease,

(*c*) The West Bengal Coal Co. granted sub-lease of a portion of the mine on Ist Jaunary 2003 for a period of 10 years to Coal Syndicate on the following terms:

(*i*) Minimum Rent payable is Rs 12, 500 merging into a Royalty of Rs. 1.50 per ton of coal raised in any year.

(*ii*) Shortworking is recoverable during the first three years of the lease. In the first four years of the lease, the output was as follows:

	West Bangal Coal Co.	*Coal Syndicate*	*Total*
2002	7,000 tons	NIl	7,000 tons
2003	8,000 tons	5,000 tons	13,000 tons
2004	12,000 tons	8,000 tons	20,000 tons
2005	15,000 tons	10,000 tons	25,000 tons

Pass journal entries in the books of the West Bangal Coal Co. (*B. Com. Madurai; Kerala*)

SOLUTION

Analytical Table
(Royalty Payable Account)

Year	*Output (Total)*	*Royalty @ Re 1 per ton*	*Short-working*	*Surplus*	*Shortworkings Recouped*	*Shortworkings Unrecouped*	*Payable to Landlord*
	Ton	*Rs*	*Rs*	*Rs*	*Rs*	*Rs*	*Rs*
2002	7,000 + Nil = 7,000	7,000	13,000	–	–	–	20,000
2003	8,000 + 5,000 = 13,000	13,000	7,000	–	–	–	20,000
2004	12,000 + 8,000 = 20,000	20,000	–	–	–	–	20,000
2005	15,000 + 10,000 = 25,000	25,000	–	5,000	5,000	–	20,000

Analytical Table
(Royalty Receivable Account)

Year	*Output*	*Royalty @ 1.50*	*Minimum Rent*	*Short-working*	*Surplus*	*Shortworkings Recouped*	*Shortworkings Unrecouped*	*Payable to Landlord*
	Ton	Rs	Rs	Rs	Rs	Rs	Rs	Rs
2003	5,000	7,500	12,500	5,000	–	–	–	12,500
2004	8,000	12,000	12,500	500	–	–	–	12,500
2005	10,000	15,000	12,500		2,500	2,500	3,000	12,500

Journal Entries
In the books of West Bengal Coal Co.

Year			*JF*	Dr. *Rs*	Cr. *Rs*
2002	Royalties Payable Account	Dr.		7,000	
	Shortworking Recoverable A/c	Dr.		13,000	
	To Landlord Account				20,000
	(Being Royalty and shortworkings due)				
	Landlord Account	Dr.		20,000	
	To Bank Account				20,000
	(Being the entry for payment)				
	Trading Account	Dr.		7,000	
	To Royalties Payable Account				7,000
	(Being Royalties A/c transferred)				
2003	Royalties Payable Account	Dr.		13,000	
	Shortworking Recoverable A/c	Dr.		7,000	
	To Landlord Account				20,000
	(Being royalty and shortworkings due)				
	Landlord Account	Dr.		20,000	
	To Bank Account				20,000
	(Being the entry for payment)				
	Trading Account	Dr.		13,000	
	To Royalties Payable Account				13,000
	(Being Royalties A/c Transferred)				
	Coal Syndicate Account	Dr.		12,500	
	To Royalty Receivable A/c				7,500
	To Shortworkings Allowable A/c				5,000
	(Being entry for Royalties Receivable and Shortworking Allowable)				
	Bank Account	Dr.		12,500	
	To Coal Syndicate Account				12,500
	(Being the amount received from sub-lessee)				
	Royalties Receivable A/c	Dr.		7,500	
	To Trading Account				7,500
	(Being transfer of Royalties Receivable Account)				

Date	Particulars		Dr. (Rs.)	Cr. (Rs.)
2004	Royalties Payable A/c	Dr.	20,000	
	To Landlord Account			20,000
	(Being the amount due)			
	Landlord Account	Dr.	20,000	
	To Bank Account			20,000
	(Being the amount paid)			
	Trading Account	Dr.	20,000	
	To Royalties Receivable A/c			20,000
	(Royalties Receivable transferred)			
	Coal Syndicate Account	Dr.	12,500	
	To Royalties Receivable A/c			12,000
	To Shortworking Allowable A/c			500
	(Being the entry for Royalties Receivable and Shortworking Allowable A/c)			
	Bank Account	Dr.	12,500	
	To Coal Syndicate Account			12,500
	(Being Royalties Receivable transferred to Trading A/c)			
	Royalties Receivable A/c	Dr.	12,000	
	To Trading A/c			12,000
	(Being Royalties Receivable transferred to Trading A/c)			
2005	Royalties Payable A/c	Dr.	25,000	
	To Landlord Account			20,000
	To Shortwoking Recoverable A/c			5,000
	(Being the entry for the amount due and recoupment of shortworking)			
	Landlord Account	Dr.	20,000	
	To Bank Account			20,000
	(Being the payment of amount due)			
	Trading Account	Dr.	25,000	
	To Royalties Payable A/c			25,000
	(Being the entry for transfer of Royalties Payable Account)			
	Coal Syndicate Account	Dr.	15,000	
	To Royalties Receivable A/c			15,000
	(Being the entry for the amount due)			
	Shortworkings Allowable A/c	Dr	2,500	
	To Coal Syndicate A/c			2,500
	(Being the entry for recoupment of shortworking by sub-lessee)			
	Bank Account	Dr.	12,500	
	To Coal Syndicate A/c			12,500
	(Being the receipt of the amount due)			
	Shortworking Allowable A/c	Dr.	3,000	
	To Profit & Loss A/c			3,000
	(Being the irrecoverable shortworking of the sub-lessee transferred)			

QUESTIONS

Objective Type Questions

I. State whether the following statements are "True" or "False":

1. Shortworking is the excess of minimum rent over actual royalties.
2. The shortworkings account shows a credit balance in the books of the lessor.
3. Royalties Suspense Account has no relation with the amount of shortworkings exists between the lessee and sub-lessee.
4. Minimum rent is the excess of royalty over shortworking.
5. Royalty account is a real account.
6. Shortworkings should be carried forward and shown in the Balance Sheet so long as they are recoverable.
7. Royalty account is closed by transferring it to the Landlord's Account.
8. When shortworkings become irrecoverable, the same are debited to Trading Account.
9. Royalty paid on sales is debited to the Profit & Loss A/c.
10. Minimum Rent is also termed as Dead Rent.

(**Ans: True** – 1, 2, 6, 9, 10. **False** – 3, 4, 5, 7, 8.)

II. Fill in the blanks:

1. Excess of minimum rent over royalty is known as ....
2. .... may be recovered out of royalties payable in the subsequent period.
3. Shortworkings is treated as an .... for the purpose of Balance Sheet.
4. Irrecoverable short-workings of any period are transferred to .... of that period.
5. The lessee stands, in the case of a sub-lease, in the position of a .... in relation to the sub-lessee.
6. Royalty Account is a .... Account.
7. When shortworkings are recovered, debit is given to ....
8. At the time of royalty payment, the lessee debits .... A/c.
9. Minimum rent is also termed as ....
10. When the lessor receives payment, he credits .... account.

(**Ans:** 1. Shortworkings; 2. Shortworkings; 3. Asset; 4. Profit & Loss A/c; 5. Landlord; 6. Nominal; 7. Landlord A/c; 8. Landlord; 9. Dead Rent; 10. Royalty.

III. Select the most appropriate answer:

1. Royalties Account is of the nature of:
   (*a*) Nominal Account. (*b*) Real Account.
   (*c*) Personal Account.
2. In case the right to recoup short workings has expired, the balance in the short workings account is transferred to :
   (*a*) Landlord Account. (*b*) Profit & Loss Account.
   (*c*) Royalties Account.
3. Royalty payable is debited by lessee to:
   (*a*) Royalty Account. (*b*) Landlord Account.
   (*c*) Profit & Loss Account.
4. Irrecoverable shortworkings account are transferred to :
   (*a*) Trading Account. (*b*) Profit & Loss Account.
   (*c*) P & L Appropriation Account.
5. Dead Rent is also called:
   (*a*) Outstanding Rent A/c. (*b*) Pre-paid Rent A/c.
   (*c*) Minimum Rent A/c.

(**Ans :** 1. (*a*); 2. (*b*); 3. (*a*); 4. (*b*); 5. (*c*).

THEORETICAL QUESTIONS

1. What do you mean by Royalty? Point out the importance of minimum rent in royalty agreement.
2. Write short notes on the following:
   (*a*) Royalties Receivable
   (*b*) Sub-lessee
   (*c*) Right of Recoupment
   (*d*) Shortworking Suspense
   (*e*) Dead Rent

PRACTICAL PROBLEMS

1. On Ist January 2000 Hiralal, patentee of a new type of article required in Engineering concern, issued a licence to Soman for five years for manufacture and sale of the article on the following terms and conditions:
   (*a*) Royalty of Rs 5 per article manufactured.
   (*b*) Minimum Rent of Rs 5,000 p.a.
   (c) Recoupment of shortworking out of royalties in excess of minimum rent during the two years immediately following subject to a maximum of Rs 2,000 p.a.
   (*d*) Accounts were to be settled annually on 3Ist December.

   The number of articles manufactured for 5 years was as follows:

Years	*Numbers*
2000	100
2001	1,100
2002	2,600
2003	400
2004	2,200

You are required to show the Memorandum Royalty Statement only. (*ICWA*)

(**Ans:** Shortworkings Recouped: Rs. 500 (2001)
Rs. 2,000 (2002)
Rs. 2, 000 (2004)
Shortworking lapsed: Rs. 2,000 (2002)
Rs 1,000 (2004)

2. Show your understanding of each of the following journal entries in the books of Prem Chand and Sons, who are publishers of books:

(a)	Dec. 31	Royalties Account	Dr.	13,000	
		Shortworkings Account	Dr.	2,000	
		To George Account			15,000
(*b*)	Dec. 31	Royalties Account	Dr.	2,000	
		To Hanu Account			20,000
(*c*)	Dec. 31	Hanu Account	Dr.	2,000	
		To Shortworkings A/c			2,000
(*d*)	Dec. 31	George Account	Dr.	15,000	
		Hanu Account	Dr.	18,000	
		To Bank Account			33,000
(*e*)	Dec. 31	Profit and Loss Account	Dr.	11,000	
		To Shortworkings A/c			11,000

3. A Coal Company takes a lease of a mine from Ist January 2001, paying a minimum rent of Rs 10,000 p.a., merging in a royalty of Re 0.50 paise per ton of coal raised. The lease contains a provision to the effect that the Minimum rent paid in any year exceeds the royalty for the years, the amount of the

excess may be recouped by the Coal Company out of the royalty payable in the following year only. The coal is raised as follows:

2001	2,000 tons
2002	12,000 tons
2003	24,000 tons
2004	30,000 tons

Give journal entries necessary to record these transactions in the books of the Coal Company.

(B. Com. Agra)

(**Ans**: Shortworking unrecouped: Rs 9,000 (2002)
" " Rs 2,000 (2003)

4. The Bihar Coal Company Ltd. are lessee of a mine on a royalty of 50 paise per tonne of coal raised, with a dead rent of Rs 30,000 p.a., and power to recoup shortworking during the first five years of the lease. The output for the first three years was as follows:

2002	15,000 tonnes
2003	50,000 tonnes
2004	75,000 tonnes

Draw the necessary journal entries in the books of the Company giving effect to the above. You are also required to write up the Minimum Rent Account, Royalties Account, Shortworkings Account and Profit and Loss Account. *(B,Com. Madurai)*

(**Ans:** Shortworkings Recouped: Rs. 7, 500 (2004)

5. Engineers had patented a quick-boiling kettle and gave the licence to Domestic Appliance Company the right to manufacture and sell under the same licence for seven years. The stipulated terms were as follows:

(*a*) A royalty of Rs 4 to be paid on each kettle sold.

(*b*) A Minimum payment of Rs, 20, 000 p.a.

(*c*) The right to deduct in two following years any excess of the Minimum Rent over the calculated royalties in any year.

The number of kettles sold was:

Year ended 31st March 2001	4,000
Year ended 31st March 2002	4,500
Year ended 31st March 2003	5,400
Year ended 31st March 2004	6,500

Give journal entries and ledger accounts as they would appear in the books of the Domestic Appliance Company to record these transactions. *(B. Com. Bombay, Punjab, Delhi)*

(**Ans.** : Shortworkings Recouped : Rs 1,600 (2003)
" " Rs. 2, 000 (2004)
Shortworkings unrecouped : Rs. 2, 400 (2003)

6. Kasturchand, who owned a patent of a counting machine, granted licence to Kapoor Brothers to manufacture and sell such machines on the following terms:

1. The licence shall be in force for four years from Jan. 1, 2001
2. Kapoor Brothers to pay a minimum sum of Rs, 12,000 p.a. merging into a royalty of Rs 2 per machine sold, payable on 31st December each year.
3. If in any year the minimum was in excess of royalty, the same could be recovered out of the royalty in excess of the next one year only.

The number of machines sold were:

2001	4,000
2002	5,500
2003	8,750
2004	5,750

Show Royalty Account, Shortworkings Account and Kasturchand Account in the books of Kapoor Brothers. *(B. Com. Karnataka, Bombay, Delhi)*

(**Ans.** : Shortworkings Recouped: Rs. 1,000 (2003)
Shortworkings lapsed: Rs. 4,000 (2002)
Rs. 500 (2004)

7. On Ist Jaunary 2001, the Gudur Mines leased some land for a minimum rent of Rs. 3,000 for the first year, Rs. 5,000 in the second year and thereafter Rs. 10,000 per annum merging into a royalty of 50 paise per ton with power to recoup shortworkings over two years after occurring of shortworkings. The outputs were as follows:

2001	3,000 tons
2002	8,600 tons
2003	22,000 tons
2004	50,000 tons

Show how the accounts would appear in the books of the Gudur Mines.

(**Ans.** : Shortworkings Recouped Rs. 1, 000 (2003) and Rs. 700 (2004);
(Shortworkings unrecouped : Rs. 500 (2003)

8. The Bengal Mine Company obtained a mine on lease for the period of 30 years beginning from January 2001 on the following terms:

(1) To pay minimum rent of Rs 24,000 p.a.

(2) Each year's excess of minimum rent over the actual royalties *i.e.*, shortworkings can be recovered during the subsequent two years.

(3) Due to accident or strike minimum rent is to be reduced by 25% for that year.

(4) Royalty was to be calculated at 50 paise per tonne.

Production during four years from 2001 to 2004 was:

Year	*Production in tonnes*
2001	28,000
2002	36,000
2003	60,000
2004	44,000 (Strike for three months)

Open Minimum Rent Account, Royalty Account, Landlord's and Shortworkings Accounts.

(A. Com. Saurashtra)

(**Ans.** Shortworkings Recouped: Rs 6,000 (2003) and Rs 4,000 (2004)
Shortworkings Lapsed: Rs 4,000 (2003) and Rs 2,000 (2004)

9. A colliery is leased to National Coal Syndicate on a royalty of Re 1 per ton on the output. A Minimum rent of Rs. 16,000 a year and allowance for shortworkings are provided in the lease. The coal actually raised in a series of years is as follows:

I year	8,000 tons
II year	10,000 tons
III year	18,000 tons
IV year	28,000 tons
V year	14,000 tons

Draw up Royalty Account, Landlord Account, Shortworkings Account and Minimum Rent Account in the books of the National Coal Syndicate.

(**Ans**: Shortworkings Recouped: Rs. 2,000 (3rd yr.) and Rs. 12,000 (4th yr.)

10. A Collery Company took a lease of coalmine for a period of 20 years from January 1999 upon the terms of a royalty of 50 paise per ton of the output with a minimum rent of Rs 8,000 p.a. with power to recoup shortworkings over the first four years of the lease.

You are required to prepare the Royalty Account, Minimum Rent Account and Shortworkings Account in the books of the Colliery Company assuming the output for the first five years to be as follows: 6,000 tons

2000	8,000 tons
2001	16,000 tons
2002	20,000 tons
2003	18,000 tons
2004	15,000 tons

(**Ans** : Shortworkings Recouped: Rs. 2,000 (2002)
Shortworkings unrecouped Rs. 7, 000 (2002) and Rs. 500 (2004)

11. The Omega Coal Company are lessees of a mine on a royalty of Re. 1 per ton of coal raised with a Dead Rent of Rs 80,000 per annum with right to recoup shortworkings during the first five years of the lease. The output for the first five years was as under.

1st year	16,000 tons
2nd year	40,000 tons
3rd year	80,000 tons
4th year	1,00,000 tons
5th year	1,20,000 tons

Write up the Dead Rent, Royalties, Shortworking and Landlord accounts in the books of the Company.

(B. Com. Madurai, Madras)

(**Ans.** : Shortworkings Recouped: Rs. 20,000 (4th yr.) and Rs. 40, 000 (5th yr.)
Shortworkings unrecouped: Rs 44, 000 (5th yr.)]

12. Mohan owned the patent of a folding chair. On Ist Jaunary 2000, he granted Nigom a licence for 5 years to manufacture and sell the chair on the following terms:
   (*a*) Royalty of Rs 10 per chair sold.
   (*b*) Minimum Rent of Rs. 15,000 p.a.
   (*c*) Shortworkings could be recouped only within two years followings year in which the shortworkings occur subject to maximum of Rs 3,500 p.a.
   (*d*) If in any year normal sale was not attained due to strike, the minimum rent was to be regarded as having been reduced proportionately, having regard to the length of the stoppage.

Year ended 31st December 2000	900
Year ended 31st December 2001	1,300
Year ended 31st December 2002	2,000
Year ended 31st December 2003	1,100
Year ended 31st December 2004	1,400

During the year 2003 there was a stoppage due to strike lasting 4 months.

You are required to show — (*i*) Royalties Receivable Account, (*ii*) Royalties, Suspense Account and (*iii*) Nigom's Account in the books of Mohan.

(**Ans** : Shortworkings Recouped : Rs. 3,500 (2002)
" " Rs. 1, 000 (2003)
Shortworkings lapsed : Rs. 2,500 (2002)
" " Rs 1, 000 (2003)
" " Rs 1, 000 (2004)

13. Electrical Gadgets Limited holds the patent right for new type of electric heater.

On Ist January 2002, Electrical Gadgets Limited granted to Household Gadgets Limited a licence to manufacture and sell heaters. The agreement provided that Household Gadgets Limited was to pay a royalty of Rs. 2 per heater sold, subject to a minimum annual payment of Rs. 12,500 to be paid annually on 31st December. Should the royalties, calculated on the number of heaters sold, be less than Rs 12,500 in any year, the deficiency could be set off against royalties in excess of the minimum in the next year, but not afterwards.

Year	*No. of heaters*
2002	4,000
2003	7,500
2004	5,750

The payment due to Electrical Gadgets Ltd under the terms of the licence were made on 31st December every year. The Household Gadgets closes the books in December every year.

You are required to show the entries in the ledger of Household Gadgets Ltd. *(B. Com. Calcutta)*

(**Ans.** Shortworkings recouped; Rs 2, 500 (2003)
Shortworkings unrecouped : Rs. 2, 000 (2003)

14. Mr. Anu who had patented an automatic door closer granted to Doors Ltd. a licence for ten years to manufacture and sell the closer on the following terms:
    (1) Doors Ltd. to pay a royalty of Rs. 10 for every closer sold with a minimum rent of Rs. 5,000 per annum, calculations to be made annually as on 31st December and payment to be made on Ist January.
    (2) If, for any year the royalties calculated on closers sold amount to less than Rs 5,000, Doors Ltd. may set off the deficiency against royalties payable in excess of that sum in the next two years. With effect from the end of the second year the agreement was varied and a minimum annual payment of Rs 5,000 was substituted for Rs 4,000, the other terms of the agreement remaining unchanged.

    The production and closing stocks of closers for the first four years were:

	Production	*Closing Stocks*
Year ended 31st Dec. 2001	250 units	50 units
Year ended 31st Dec. 2002	450 units	100 units
Year ended 31st Dec. 2003	570 units	70 units
Year ended 31st Dec. 2004	630 units	150 units

You are required to show the ledger accounts recording the above transactions in respect of royalties in the books of the Doors Ltd. which are closed annually on 31st December.

(B. Com. Bombay, Calcutta)

(**Ans.** Sales in units : 200 (2001)
400 (2002)
600 (2003)
550 (2004)
Shortworkings Recouped : Rs 2,000 (2003)
" " Rs 1, 000 (2004)
Shortworkings lapsed : 1,000 (2003)

15. Srikant had patented a new type of pocket transistor. On Ist january 2001 he granted Parker a licence for 20 years to manufacture and sell the transistor on the following terms:
    (*a*) Parker to pay a royalty of Rs. 5 for each transistor manufactured and a further royalty of Rs 3 for each transistor sold with a minimum rent of Rs. 8,000 p.a.
    (*b*) If in any year, the royalties calculated on the transistors manufactured and sold be less than the minimum rent, Parker have the right to recoup shortworkings out of the royalties in excess of the minimum rent during the two years immediately following, subject to a maximum amount of Rs 2,000 p.a.

The number of transistors manufactured and sold for the first four years were as follows:

Year	*Manufactured*	*Sold*
2001	800	500
2002	1,000	700

2003	2,500	1,500
2004	500	2,000

All the payments were made by Parker on the due date.

Prepare (*i*) Parker's Account, (*ii*) Royalties Receivable Account, (*iii*) Shortworking Suspense Account for the first four years as they would appear in the books of Srikant. (*I.C.W.A.*)

(**Ans**: Shortworkings recouped: Rs. 2,000 (2003)
" " Rs. 500 (2004)
Shortworking lapsed : Rs. 500 (2003)
" " Rs. 400 (2004)

16. X Colliery Company leased a property from Landlord at a royalty of Re 0.50 per ton with a minimum rent of Rs 10,000 p.a. Each year's excess of minimum rent over royalty is recoverable out of royalties of next three years. In the event of strike and if the minimum rent is not reached, the lease provided that the actual royalty earned for the year discharged all the rental obligations for the years.

The result of working was as follows:

Year	*Output in tons*
2000	15,000
2001	21,000
2002	12,000
2003	16,000
2004	22,000

Write up the accounts in the books of X Colliey Company. (*B. Com., Karnataka, Madurai)*

(**Ans.** Shortworkings Recouped: Rs. 500 (2001)
" " Rs. 1, 000 (2004)
Shortworking lapsed : Rs 2,000 (2003)
" " Rs. 1,000 (2004)

17. Quarries Ltd. took a mine on lease from Landlord at a given rate or royalty with a minimum rent of Rs 40,000 per year. Each year's excess of minimum rent over royalties is recoverable out of the royalties for the next years only. In the event of a strike and the minimum rent not being realised, it was provided that the actual royalties earned for the year would be the full royalty obligation for the year.

The result of the workings was as follows:

Year	*Rs*
1st year	Nil
2nd year	12,000
3rd year	36,000
4th year	45,000
5th year	60,000

Draw up Shortworkings Account, Landlord Account, Minimum Rent Account and Royalties Account. (*B.Com., Calcutta*)

(**Ans**: Shortworkings Recouped : Rs. 5,000 (4th year)
Shortworkings lapsed : Rs. 40,000 (3rd year)
" " Rs. 23,000 (4th yr.)

18. X Coal Ltd. has taken on lease coalfields from Y on the following terms:
   (1) Lease is for 99 years.
   (2) Lease rent is to be paid @50 paise per tonne of coal raised.
   (3) Minimum Rent is Rs 30,000 p.a. The lease provided that the shortworkings, if any, can be recouped within a period of three years for which the excess payment was to be made.

(4) In case the working of the mines was affected by any strike or riot and there were no raisings, then the minimum rent payable would abate proportionately.

(5) The following were raisings for the different years.

2000	20,000 tonnes
2001	35,000 tonnes
2002	30,000 tonnes (Strike for 3 months)
2003	70,000 tonnes
2004	1,20,000 tonnes

You are required to show the Royalties Account, Shortworkings Account and Landlord Account in the books of X Coal Ltd. (*C.A. Inter*)

(**Ans.** Shortworkings recouped : Rs. 5,000 (2003)
Rs. 20,000 (2004)
Shortworkings lapsed : Rs. 15,000 (2003)

19. Dharwar Coal Co. acquired on lease a coalmine on a royalty of paise 50 per ton of coal brought on the surface with a minimum rent of Rs 56,000 a year with no right to recover shortworkings except in case of strike. 10% of the coal taken out from the mine is lost in weight in bringing the coal on the surface. The following was the production position for different years:

1st year	20,000 tons
2nd year	80,000 tons
3rd year	1,20,000 tons
4th year	1,70,000 tons
5th year	80,000 tons

In the fifth year, there was a strike. Show the Minimum Rent Account, Royalty Account and Shortworkings Account for the five years.

(*B.Com. Karnataka*)

(**Ans** : Shortworkings lasped : Rs. 47, 000 (I Yr.)
Rs. 20,000 (II Yr.)
Rs. 2,000 (III Yr.)
Shortworkings of 5th year Rs. 20,000 carried forward)

20. Magickey Limited took certain lands on lease from Manganese Estates Ltd. for a period of 15 years for mining of manganese ore with a stipulated royalty of Rs. 1.50 per ton and a minimum rent of Rs 21,000 with a clause to recoup shortworkings over three subsequent years.

The actual working results were :

Year	*Output in tons*
2000	8,000
2001	16,000
2002	13,000
2003	17,000
2004	43,800

Your are required to show the necessary ledger accounts in the books of Magickey Ltd (*I.C.W.A*)

(**Ans** : Shortworkings recouped : Rs. 3,000 (2001)
" " Rs. 4, 500 (2003)
" " Rs. 1,500 (2004)
Shortworkings lapsed : Rs. 1,500 (2003)

21. A coal company takes a lease of coal mine for a term of 8 years from 1st January 2002 on a minimum rent of Rs. 12,000 p.a. merging in a royalty of 75 paise per tonne of coal raised payable half yearly on 30th June and 31st December each year. Shortworkings can be recouped during the first three years. Royalty which was due on 31st December 2003 was paid on 2nd January 2004. Coal company closes its books on 31st December each year. Coal is raised as follows :

Half year ending on 30th June 2002	6,000 tonnes
Half year ending on 31st December 2002	8,000 tonnes
Half year ending on 30th June 2003	10,000 tonnes
Half Year ending on 31st December 2003	6,000 tonnes
Half year ending on 30th June 2004	7,000 tonnes
Half year ending on 31st December 2004	9,000 tonnes

Prepare necessary accounts in the books of coal company.

(*B.Com. Guru Nanak*)

(**Ans** : Shortworkings recouped : Rs. 1,500 (June 2003)
" " Rs. 750 (Dec. 2004)
Shortworkings lapsed : Rs. 1,500 (Dec. 2004

22. Hindustan Steel Ltd. obtained a lease from Gondwana Coal Ltd, for a coalmine on 1st January 1999 on the following terms and conditions :
    (1) Royalty at Rs, 1,000 per tonne raised.
    (2) Minimum rent Rs 12,000 p.a.
    (3) Recoupment of shortworkings on each year during three years following subject to a maximum of Rs. 2,500 p.a.
    (4) In the event of strike the minimum rent would be taken pro rata on the basis of actual working days, but in the event of lock-out, the lessee would enjoy a concession in respect of minimum rent for 50% of the period of lock-out.

    Besides the above, Hindustan Steel Ltd. have been granted cash subsidy equal to 25% of the unrecoupable shortworkings by the Central Government up to the five years of the lease.

1999	Actual royalty	Rs 7,000
2000	Actual royalty	Rs 10,200
2001	Actual royalty	Rs 16,100
2002	Actual royalty	Rs 13,600
2003	Actual royalty	Rs 10,100 (Strike 3 months)
2004	Actual royalty	Rs 9,700

(Lock-out for 4 months)

Show the ledger accounts in the books of Hindustan Steal Co.

(*B.Com. Jabalpur*)

(**Ans** : Cash subsidy : Rs. 225 (2002)
" Rs. 175 (2003).
Shortworkings recouped : Rs. 2,500 (2001)
" " Rs. 1,600 (2002)
" " Rs. 1,100 (2003)
Shortworkings lapsed : Rs. 675 (2002)
" " Rs. 525 (2003)

23. On Ist January 1999, Ramu obtained a mining lease at a royalty of 50 paise per ton with a minimum rent of Rs. 17,000 p.a. Each year's excess of minimum rent over the actual royalties was recoverable during the subsequent three years.

    The lease, however, stipulated that if in any year the normal rent was not attained due to strike or accident, the minimum rent was to be regarded as having been reduced proportionately having regard to the length of the stoppage. The output was as follows :

For the year ended 31st Dec. 1999	4,000 tons
For the year ended 31st Dec. 2000	28,000 tons
For the year ended 31st Dec. 2001	30,000 tons
For the year ended 31st Dec. 2002	46,000 tons

For the year ended 31st Dec. 2003 30,000 tons

For the year ended 31st Dec. 2004 50,000 tons

During the year 2003 there was a stoppage, due to strike, lasting three months. Give necessary accounts in the books of Ramu for each of the years.

(B.Com. Mangalore, Bhopal, Madras, Poona)

(Ans: Shortworkings recouped : Rs. 6, 000 (2002)
" " Rs. 2,250 (2003)
" " Rs. 2,000 (2004)
Shortworkings lapsed : Rs. 9,000 (2002)
" " Rs. 750 (2003)

24. The Assam Coal Company Ltd. holds a lease of coalmines for a period of 10 years commencing from Ist January 1999. According to the lease terms the company is to pay one rupee per ton as royalty with a minimum rent of Rs. 20,000 per year. Shortworkings can, however, be recovered out of the royalty in excess of the minimum rent of the next two years only. In the year of a strike, the minimum rent is to be reduced to 60%. The output for the 6 years ending 31st December 2004 has been as under:

1999	10,000 tons
2000	12,000 tons
2001	28,000 tons
2002	25,000 tons
2003	40,000 tons
2004	15,000 tons (strike)

Prepare Royalty Account, Shortworkings Account, Landlord Account in the books of Assam Coal Company Ltd. for the six years.

(B.Com. Delhi, Madras, Agra)

(Ans : Shortworkings recouped : Rs. 8,000 (2001)
" " Rs. 5,000 (2002)
Shortworkings lapsed : Rs. 2,000 (2001)
" " Rs. 3,000 (2002)

25. The Colliery Company worked under a lease which provided for the payment of royalties at 50 paise per ton with a minimum rent of Rs. 8,500 per year. Each year's excess of minimum rent over the actual royalties was recoverable during the next three years. In the event of strike the royalties actually earned is deemed to have wiped out all rental obligations. The output was as follows :

1999	2,000 tons
2000	14,000 tons
2001	19,000 tons
2002	23,000 tons
2003	15,000 tons (Strike)
2004	25,000 tons

Write up the accounts in the books of Colliery Co. and Landlord. *(B.Com., Madurai)*

(Ans : Shortworkings recouped : Rs. 1,000 (2001)
" " Rs. 3,000 (2002)
Shortworkings lapsed : Rs. 3,500 (2002)
" " Rs. 1,500 (2003)

26. Minerals Ltd. leased a property from Sarkar at a royalty of Rs. 1.50 per tonne with a minimum rent of Rs. 10,000 per annum. Each year's excess of minimum rent over royalties is recoverable out of royalties of next five years. In the event of a strike and the minimum rental not being reached, the lease provided that the actual royalties earned for the year discharge all rental obligation for the year.

The result of working of the property is given below :

Actual royalties in

	Rs.
1997	Nil
1998	3,300
1999	9,000
2000	11,100
2001	14,000
2002	15,000
2003	8,000 (Strike)
2004	15,200

Write up the Minimum Rent Account, Royalties Account and Landlord's Account in the books of the lessee for each year.

(*B.Com. Calcutta, M.Com., Bombay*)

(**Ans :** Shortworkings recouped : Rs. 1,100 (2000)
Rs. 4,000 (2001)
Rs. 5,000 (2002)
Rs. 1,000 (2004)
Shortworkings lapsed : Rs. 6,600 (2003)

27. Alok obtained on Ist January 2000 from Bobby a lease of some coal bearing land, the terms being a royalty of Rs. 0.50 a tonne of coal raised subject to a minimum rent of Rs. 2,000 per annum, with a right of recoupment of shortworkings over the first four years of the lease.

Alok granted a sub-lease of part of the land to Chandhu on a royalty of Re. 0.75 per tonne merging into a minimum rent of Rs 1,000 per annum with a right of recoupment of shortworkings during the two years following the shortworkings :

The output for the first five years is as follows :

Year	*Alok*	*Bobby*	*Total*
2000	2,200 tonnes	800 tonnes	3,000 tonnes
2001	2,320 tonnes	1,080 tonnes	3,400 tonnes
2002	2,600 tonnes	1,400 tonnes	4,000 tonnes
2003	2,800 tonnes	1,800 tonnes	4,600 tonnes
2004	3,600 tonnes	2,400 tonnes	6,000 tonnes

Give necessary ledger accounts in the books of Alok.

(*B.Com. Guru Nanak, Bombay*)

(**Ans:** Shortworkings recouped : Rs. 300 (2003)
Shortworkings lapsed : Rs. 500 (2003)
Shortworkings Suspense Allowed : Rs. 50 (2002)
Shortworkings Suspense Allowed : Rs. 190 (2003)
Shortworkings Suspense Disallowed : Rs. 350 (2002)

28. On Ist January 2002 Gadgets Limited, Patentees of a new type of electric razor, issued a licence to Domestic Utilities Limited for the manufacture and sale of the razors. Domestic Utilities Limited issued to Trimmers Limited a sub-licence for the same purpose.

The licence issued by Gadgets Limited provided for a royalty of Rs. 75,000 per annum, and the sub-licence issued by Domestic Utilities Ltd. provided for a royalty of Rs 15 per finished razor manufactured, subject to a minimum sum of Rs. 30,000 per annum. Both the licence and sub-licence provided that, should the royalties for any calendar year be less than the specified minimum, the shortworkings could be recouped out of royalties, in excess of the minimum, for either of the two immediately following calendar years.

You are given the following information :

Year	Sales by Domestic Utilities Ltd.	Sales Trimmers Ltd.	Stock held by Trimmers Ltd. on 31st December
2002	4,520 razors	1,220 razors	340 razors
2003	6,180 razors	2,790 razors	60 razors
2004	6,675 razors	1,940 razors	400 razors

All payments under both licence and sub-licence have been made annually on 31st December.

You are required to show the accounts in the books of Domestic Utilities Ltd., necessary to record these transactions for the years 2002, 2003 and 2004 closing the accounts on 31st December in each year.

(B.Com. Madras, Utkal)

(Ans: Shortworkings recouped : Rs. 14,700 (2003)

" " Rs, 1,150 (2004)

Shortworkings lapsed : Rs. 1,750 (2004)

Shortworkings Suspense Allowed : Rs. 6,600 (2003)

29. A landlord granted to the Mining Co. Ltd. a lease of minerals right over his property for a period of ten years. The rent payable was a minimum of Rs, 80,000 a year, merging in a royalty of Re 1 per ton payable annually. Shortworkings could be recouped out of subsequent excess workings over the period of the lease. The Mining Co. Ltd. granted a sub-lease to Mining Lessees Ltd. at the end of the first year. Mining Lessees were to pay a minimum rent of Rs. 44,000 merging in a royalty of Rs. 1.50 a ton annually. Shortworkings could be recouped out of subsequent excess workings in any of the three years immediately following that in which the shortworkings occurred.

The following tonnage were mined from the property:

	Mining Co. Ton	Mining Lessees Ton
1st year	40,000	–
2nd year	75,000	15,000
3rd year	60,000	18,000
4th year	65,000	20,000
5th year	70,000	35,000
6th year	49,000	35,000
7th year	46,000	40,000

Prepare Royalties Account, Shortworkings Account, Landlord Account and Mining Lessees Ltd. Account as they would appear in the books of Mining Co. Ltd.

(B.Com., Calcutta)

Royalty Payable Chart

(Ans : Shortworkings Recouped : Rs. 10,000 (2nd year)

" " Rs. 5,000 (4th year)

" " Rs. 25,000 (5th year)

" " Rs. 2,000 (6th year)

Royalty Receivable Chart

Shortworkings adjusted : Rs. 8,500 (5th year)

" " Rs. 8,500 (6th year)

" " Rs. 14,000 (7th year)

Shortworkings not returnable: Rs. 13,000 (5th Year)

" " Rs. 8,500 (6th year)

Chapter 20

Insolvency Accounts

Introduction – Act of Insolvency – Order of Adjudication – Property not available for Distribution – Fraudulent Preference – Voluntary Transfer – Reputed Ownership – Insolvency Procedure – Statement of Affairs – Balance Sheet and Statement of Affairs – Deficiency Account – Insolvency of Partnership Firm – Questions – Objective Type Questions – Theoretical Questions – Practical Problems.

A person is commonly said to be insolvent if he is unable to meet his liabilities as and when claimed. That is, when a person becomes heavily indebted due to various circumstances and it becomes impossible for him to pay his debts fully. In law, the term "insolvent" is restricted to a person whose liabilities exceed his assets and against whom the court makes an order of adjudication. Thus insolvent is a person who is not in a position to pay his liabilities in full and has been declared as an insolvent by an Insolvency court. Insolvency means the procedure by which the State takes in its possession the property of the Debtor for realisation and equitable distribution among the creditors of the insolvent. The proceedings in such cases are called Insolvency Proceedings. The terms 'Insolvency' and 'Bankruptcy' are more or less synonymous. The word 'Insolvency' is used in India and 'Bankruptcy' in England.

When a person finds it difficult to pay his liabilities in full, because of less assets, he will be harassed by his creditors. The creditors will be pressing for payment. When a person is in such a financial difficulties, the procedure is to present an insolvency petition in a court by a Creditor or the debtor himself. Petition by a Creditor can be made only if (1) the debt, singly or jointly, is at least Rs. 500 and (2) the Debtor commits an act of insolvency.

The act of insolvency is committed by a debtor in each of the following cases :

1. When a person transfers his property, wholly or partly, to a third person for the benefit of his creditors;
2. When he transfers his property with the intention to defraud or delay his creditors;
3. When he notifies his creditors that he has suspended or is about to suspend payment of his debts;
4. When he departs from or remains out of India;
5. When he departs from his dwelling house or usual place of business, or otherwise absents himself;
6. When the debtor is imprisoned in execution of a court degree for payment money;
7. When any of the property of the debtor is sold or attached for a period of not less than 21 days in execution of a degree of any court;
8. When he secludes himself so as to deprive his creditors of the means of communicating with him;
9. When the debtor petitions the court to be adjudged an insolvent;

10. When an insolvent-debtor transfers property or pays a particular creditor in preference to another creditor, more than what he could have got had the insolvent's assets been proportionately distributed amongst all the creditors, he is deemed to have shown fraudulent preference in favour of a particular creditor.

ORDER OF ADJUDICATION

When a person commits an act of insolvency, a petition may be filed either by himself or any of his creditors in a competent court for adjudication of the person as an insolvent. On such a petition, if the court is satisfied, it will pass an order of adjudication declaring the person as an insolvent. Upon such an order, the property of the insolvent vests with the Official Assignee under the Presidency Towns Insolvency Act, and, with the Official Receiver, under the Provincial Insolvency Act, for equitable distribution amongst the creditors.

PROPERTY NOT AVAILABLE FOR DISTRIBUTION

Properties held by the insolvent in his capacity as a trustee, bailee or other fiduciary capacity, are not available for distribution amongst the insolvent's creditors. Similarly, under the Presidency Towns Insolvency Act trade tools of the insolvent, wearing apparels, cooking utensils, bedding and furniture, not exceeding Rs. 300 in value, are not available for distribution. The same is true of pension, gratuity and provident fund received by an insolvent person.

FRAUDULENT PREFERENCE

When the debtor transfers his property for fraudulent preference that is fraudulent preference takes place when the debtor prefers one creditor to another and pays the preferred creditor more than what he would have received, had the assets been proportionately distributed among creditors of the debtor. Upon an order of adjudication to preferred creditor will have to return the money received by him.

VOLUNTARY TRANSFER

Voluntary transfer of property is said to take place when a person transfers it to another without consideration. If the insolvent-debtor has voluntarily transferred his property to another without consideration, during two years preceding the date of order of adjudication, the same is void under the Presidency Towns Insolvency Act. However, such transfer is voidable as against the Official Receiver in the case of Provincial Insolvency Act. As such, the same may be set aside by the court. However, transfer is not void: (*a*) when it is made in consideration of marriage, and (*b*) when it is made in favour of a purchase or encumbrance in good faith and valuable consideration.

REPUTED OWNERSHIP

The doctrine of reputed ownership is applicable to an insolvent trader, engaged in regular trade or business with goods belonging to other persons. According to this doctrine, if the insolvent carries on business with goods belonging to others but in his possession with their consent, under such circumstances as to be able to infer that he himself to be the true owner, such goods can be taken to be the property of the insolvent for the purpose of distribution amongst the creditors. The Official Assignee or the Receiver will have a right to realise the property and distribute the proceeds amongst the creditors.

This doctrine does not, however, apply to (*a*) immovable property, (*b*) goods in possession of the insolvent as repairer or carrier, and (*c*) goods in possession of the insolvent as trustee.

INSOLVENCY PROCEDURE

We discuss the whole procedure of Insolvency in the following points:

1. A petition for adjudication as insolvent may be presented either by the debtor himself or by the creditor to the appropriate Insolvency Court.

2. A creditor shall not be entitled to present insolvency petition unless the debt, singly or jointly, is at least Rs. 500 and the Debtor commits an act of insolvency (as said in the above para).

3. When the petition is admitted, the Court fixes a date for hearing the petition.

4. When the petition is admitted, Court may appoint an Interim Receiver to take immediate possession of the property of the Debtor. The appointment of the Interim Receiver is compulsory only when the petition is filed by the Debtor himself.

5. The Interim Receiver functions till the regular officer is appointed.

6. On the date of hearing the petition, the court may either dismiss the petition or pass an order of adjudication. If the court is satisfied that the petition is reasonable, it shall make an order of adjudication.

7. It is only when this order of adjudication is passed that the Debtor is said to have been declared insolvent.

8. As soon as the Debtor is thus declared insolvent, all his property vests in an Officer, appointed by the Court to conduct the insolvency proceeding. The officer is called "Official Receiver", usually a lawyer, under the Provincial Insolvency Act or "Official Assignee" under the Presidency Towns Insolvency Act.

9. When the official Assignee or Receiver takes over the property of the insolvent, it becomes his duty to sell the property with all convenient speed, at reasonable price.

10. Out of the sale proceeds, the expenses of realisation are met off and then the liabilities of the insolvent debtor are paid off to the possible extent.

11. A debtor may, at any time after the order of adjudication and within the period specified by the Court, apply to the court for an Order of Discharge.

12. The court may, if satisfied with the debtor's conduct and the report of the Official Receiver, grant or refuse an order of Discharge.

13. The court may pass either an absolute or conditional Order of Discharge. On obtaining the order of absolute Discharge, the Debtor is freed from all his liabilities and can start his life afresh. The Order of Discharge will release the insolvent from all debts and removes the disqualification imposed by the order of adjudication. He is not responsible for any debt which could not have been paid in full during his insolvency proceedings. Again, the Debtor becomes a free man and gets all the rights and privileges of an ordinary citizen of the country.

There are two legislations in India to protect the interests of Debtors. One is the Presidency Towns Insolvency Act of 1909 which is applicable to the cities of Bombay, Calcutta and Madras. And the other is the Provincial Insolvency Act of 1920 applicable to the rest of India. The objects of Insolvency Legislations are to protect the Debtor from the harassment by his creditors and secure an expeditious and equitable distribution of his assets among the creditors. Both these Insolvency Acts apply to individuals and not to Joint Stock Companies.

A person, adjudicated as an insolvent, has to make out and submit a Statement of Affairs and a Deficiency Account. The Statement of Affairs shows the insolvent's financial position at the date of the order of adjudication and the Deficiency Account explains how the deficiency appearing in the Statement of Affairs has arisen.

Statement of Affairs shows the financial position of the Debtor on a particular date. It is prepared in the prescribed form. It contains the details regarding the assets and liabilities. Assets are shown at book value and realisable value and liabilities are shown at book value as well as expected to rank values.

The Statement of Affairs is prepared in the following manner:

STATEMENTS OF AFFAIRS
(as required by the Indian Insolvency Act)

IN THE COURT OF JUSTICE
In Insolvency

To the Insolvent:

You are required to fill up carefully and accurately, this sheet and several sheets A, B, C, D, E, F, G and H, showing the state of your affairs on the day on which the order of adjudication was made against you, viz. the.....day of ......20......

Such sheets, when filled up, will constitute your Schedule and must be verified by Oath or Declaration.

Gross Liabilities	Liabilities (As stated and estimated by the Debtor)	Expected to Rank	Assets (As stated and estimated by the Debtor)	Estimated to produce
Rs.		Rs.		Rs.
	Unsecured Creditors *as—*		Property *as per List E*, viz;	
	per List A		(*a*) Cash at Bank	
—	Fully Secured Creditors		(*b*) Cash in hand	
	as per List B		(*c*) Cash deposited with solicitor	
			for cost of petition	
	Less: Estimented value		(*d*) Stock-in-trade	—
	of Securities		(*e*) Machinery	
	Surplus:		(*f*) Trade fixtures, fittings, utensils	
	Less: Amount thereof		etc.	
	carried to List C		(*g*) Furniture	
	Balance thereof to contra		(*h*) Life Policies	
—	Partly Secured Creditors		(*i*) Other properties	
	as per List C		Book Debts *as per List F*, viz.	
	Less: Estimated value of	—	Good	
	Securities		Doubtful	
			Bad	
—	Preferential Creditors *as*		Estimated to produce	—
	per List D (Creditors for		Bill of Exchange or other similar	
	Rent, Taxes, Salaries..		securities on hand *as per List G*	—
	Wages etc. payable in full			
	Deducted as per contra..		Estimated to produce	
			Surplus from securities in the hands of	—
			creditors fully secured (per contra)	
			Deduct: Creditors for preferential rent,	
			rates, taxes, wages etc. (per contra)	
			DEFICIENCY *as explained in List H*	

I/We____________________ make oath, solemnly affirm, and say, that the above statement and the several lists hereunto annexed, A, B, C, D, E, F, G and H are, to the best of my/our knowledge and belief, a full and complete statement of my/our affairs on the date of the abovementioned order of adjudication made against me/us.

Affirmed / Sworn at......this.....day of...before Commissioner

(Signature)

A number of separate lists, called List A to H, are prepared and attached to the Statement of Affairs given above. A Statement of Affairs, like a Balance Sheet, is divided into two parts. Left-hand side of the Statement of Affairs is liability and right-hand side of the Statement is assets. The explanation of each List is given below.

LIST A–Unsecured Creditors as per List A

This list includes all Creditors, who do not possess any security of the Insolvent Debtor. That is, the Creditors without security fall under this list. Some of such Creditors are:

Trade Creditors without security
Loan Creditors without security
Bank Overdraft unsecured
Bills Payable and Promissory Notes
Bills Receivable discounted likely to be dishonoured
Salary, Wages, Rent etc. over Preferential limit.

List B–Fully Secured Creditors

This list includes all the Creditors, who have a claim against the debtor and have obtained a lien, guarantee or possession of some deeds or other securities. That is, the creditors, who have sufficient securities of the insolvent Debtor to meet their claims. The value of the securities may be equal to or more than the amount of their claims. If there is any surplus of securities in the hands of fully secured creditors, such surplus will be shown on the asset side of the Statement of Affairs and will be available for distribution among the unsecured Creditors. For instance, if a loan of Rs 10,000 has been taken on a security worth Rs 15,000, this loan is fully secured. The Surplus of Rs. 5,000 (Rs. 15,000-10,000) is shown on the asset side of the Statement of Affairs.

List C–Partly Secured Creditors

There are certain Creditors, who have the security for a lesser value than the amount of their claims. That is, the Creditors of this type got only partial security for the loan advanced by them. The securities are insufficient to meet the claims. For instance, a loan of Rs 10,000 has been taken and the security for this loan is only Rs. 6,000. So, the loan is partly secured. The value of the security is not sufficient to cover their claims fully. The excess of loan over the security is shown in the outer column.

List D–Preferential Creditors

This list shows the Preferential Creditors, who are entitled to priority over other debts of the insolvent. For instance, taxes, rates, wages, salaries etc. are paid in full.

The following is the details of Preferential Creditors under the Presidency Towns Insolvency Act and Provincial Insolvency Act.

	Type of Creditors	Presidency Towns Insolvency Act (Sec. 46)	Provincial Insolvency Act (Sec.61)
1.	Amount due to Govt. or any local authority–taxes, rates etc.	Full	Full
2.	Salary	Salary of 4 months before the date of the presentation of the insolvency petitition, not exceeding Rs. 300 for each clerk	Salary, not exceeding Rs. 20 per head, in respect of services rendered during four months before the presentation of the petition.
3.	Wages	Only 4 months or Rs. 100 whichever is less.	Rs. 20 per head
4.	Rent	One month rent. No limit to the amount	Nil

The amount of the Preferential Creditors, who are paid in full, are shown in the inner column and this amount is to be deducted from the available assets.

The amount of salaries or wages or rent, in excess over the limit prescribed by the law, shall be included in the list of Unsecured Creditors under List A. All the above four lists, A to D, are shown in liability side of the Statement of Affairs.

The following are the lists shown in the asset side of the Statement of Affairs:

List E–Properties

This is a list which includes all the assets of the Insolvent, except Book Debts, Bills Receivable and assets which have not been given as security to Creditors. Here all the assets–unencumbered properties *i.e.*, free assets are shown. For instance, Cash in hand, Cash at Bank, Furniture, Machinery etc. Both book value and realisation value are shown.

List F–Book Debts

All the debtors of the insolvent are shown in this list. Good, Doubtful and Bad debts are shown separately.

List G–Bills of Exchange etc.

This list contains the information about Bills Receivable and Promissory Notes. The book value and the realisable value are shown separately.

List H–Deficiency Account

This list shows the deficiency *i.e.*, liabilities of the Debtors over realisable value of his assets. For this purpose a separate Deficiency Account is prepared. (This is explained separately.)

Now, after writing the Lists E, F and G, the surplus, as per List B, appears on the liability side, is added to the assets. From this amount, the Preferential Creditors as per List D are deducted. The balance, so arrived, is the amount of assets available for distribution among the Creditors.

Differences between Balance Sheet and Statement of Affairs

Balance Sheet	*Statement of Affairs*
1. It is prepared for the sake of proprietor and others.	1. It is prepared for the satisfaction of the Court.
2. It is prepared for all the years during which the business is carried on.	2. It is prepared at the time of Insolvency.
3. It is prepared to show the financial position of the business.	3. It is prepared to show the inability of the Debtor to pay off the liabilities.
4. It exhibits the book value of assets and liabilities.	4. It exhibits the book value as well as realisable value.
5. It shows the excess of assets over liabilities *i.e.*, Capital.	5. It shows the excess of outside liabilites over assets *i.e.*, Deficiency.
6. It includes intangible assets, both fictitious and non-fictitious	6. It excludes intangible assets, if fictitious.
7. All liabilities including preferential items are shown on liability side.	7. Preferential debts are shown as a deduction from the total assets available.
8. It is prepared at the end of the Accounting Period.	8. It is prepared on the date on which an adjudication order is passed.
9. It has no lists for the grouping of assets and liabilities.	9. It has various lists for placing assets and liabilities.
10. It does not classify Creditors among unsecured, fully secured, partly secured and preferential creditors.	10. It divides the creditors as secured, partly secured and preferential creditors.
11. It shows the book value of fixed assets, less depreciation, which may differ from its market value.	11. It shows the assets at a value for which they can be disposed of in the market.

12. It separates personal assets and liabilities from the trade assets and liabilities.	12. It integrates personal and trade assets and liabilities in case of individuals.
13. It implies balances taken from the books of Accounts.	13. Its significance is given to realisable value, as against book value.
14. It contains items like Capital, Profit, Drawings, Interest on Capital etc.	14. It excludes all such items.
15. Balance Sheet of individuals is not prepared according to any Act.	15. It is prepared according to the rules laid down in the Insolvency Act.

DEFICIENCY ACCOUNT

In addition to various lists– Lists A to List G–the Debtor has to prepare a Deficiency Account which explains as to how the deficiency shown in the Statement of Affairs has arisen. The insolvent debtor is required to account for the loss to the amount of his capital and of his Creditors. On the left-hand side of Deficiency Account appears: (1) the amount of capital, (2) increment to the Capital from the business *i.e.*, profits, interest on capital, salaries, commission etc., (3) additional contributions and (4) Realisation profits etc. On its right side appears all the losses and withdrawals by which capital is decreased. The difference between the two sides represents deficiency and this must agree with the deficiency amount as disclosed by the Statement of Affairs :

Specimen of Deficiency Account is shown below :

Deficiency Account

	Rs.		*Rs.*
Excess of assets over liabilities or Capital		Excess of liabilities over assets or losses from business	
Interest on Capital		Drawings	
Profit from business		Bad debts	
Surplus from private assets		Other losses on realisation of assets	
Profit on realisation of any assets		Loss on Bills discounted and dishonoured	
DEFICIENCY as per Statement of Affairs		Any other losses	

PRIORITY OF PAYMENTS

The Official Assignee or Receiver realises the assets and distributes the proceeds in the following order of priority :

1. Fully secured creditors, in full
2. Partly secured creditors to the extent they are secured
3. Expenses of realisation and remuneration to the receiver
4. Preferential creditors
5. Unsecured creditors, including uncovered balance of partly secured creditors.

Interest

A creditor is not allowed to claim interest after the date of insolvency. However, if all the claims have been satisfied in full, then till the date of payment, interest @ 6% is allowed.

Loan from Wife

If the wife has given the loan to her husband out of her personal property or dowry or self-earned income, then the amount of loan is included in Creditors. But if the wife's loan is out of the money given to her by her husband, then the loan is taken as the capital of Insolvent, that is, such amount is not included in the creditors list.

ILLUSTRATION 20.1

What are preferential Creditors in the following liabilities of an insolvent, Gopal, according to the Presidency Towns Insolvency Act and Provincial Insolvency Act? Also point out the unsecured creditors.

		Rs.
1.	Salaries	1,000
2.	Sales Tax	300
3.	One month wages of 10 labourers	1,200
4.	Income Tax	700
5.	Rent for 3 months	900
6.	Municipal taxes	250
7.	Salary for four clerks for two months	1,500
8.	Wages of 3 servants	900

SOLUTION

Item	*Total*	*Presidency Towns Insolvency Act*		*Provincial Insolvency Act*	
		Preferential Creditors	*Non-preferential Creditors*	*Preferential Creditors*	*Non-preferential Creditors*
	Rs.	Rs.	Rs.	Rs.	Rs.
1. Salaries	1,000	1,000		1,000	
2. Sales Tax	300	300		300	
3. Wages of 10 labourers	1,200	1,000	200	200	1,000
4. Income Tax	700	700		700	
5. Rent	900	300	600	Nil	900
6. Municipal tax	250	250		250	
7. Salary for four clerks	1,500	1,200	300	80	1,420
8. Wages of 3 servants	900	300	600	60	840
	6,750	5,050	1,700	2,590	4,160

ILLUSTRATION 20.2

On 1st April 2003, Mohan commenced business with a capital of Rs. 63,500. His profits for the years 2003-04 and 2004-05 amounted to Rs. 55,540. He suffered a loss of Rs. 25,000 in the year 2005-06. His total drawings up to 31st March 2006 were Rs. 90,000.

From the following figures, prepare a Statement of Affairs and Deficiency Account of Mohan as at 31st March 2006.

	Rs.
Cash	2,300
Stock-in-trade	10,000
Debtors – good	70,000
Debtors – doubtful	18,000
Debtors – bad	15,000
Fixtures and Fittings	5,640
Investments in shares	5,000
Unsecured Creditors (including Rs. 10,000 of his wife)	1,30,000

Secured Creditors	25,000
Value of securities held by secured creditors	35,000
Preferential claims – taxes etc.	1,900
Assume that:	
the stock-in-trade will realise	6,660
fixtures and fittings	2,820
investment in shares	the book-value
the bad and doubtful debts	6,000

(*B.Com.MS, Kerala*)

SOLUTION

Statement of Affairs of Mohan as on 31st March 2006.

Gross Liablities Rs.	*Liabilities (As stated and estimated by the Debtor)*	*Rs.*	*Expected To Rank Rs.*	*Assets (As stated and estimated by the Debtor)*	*Book Value Rs.*	*Estimated to Realise Rs.*
1,30,000	Unsecured creditors as per List A		1,30,000	Property as per List E:		
25,000	Secured creditors as per List B	25,000		Cash	2,300	2,300
	Less: Estimated value			Investment in shares	5,000	5,000
	of securities	35,000		Stock	10,000	6,660
	Surplus as per contra	10,000		Fixtures and Fittings	5,640	2,820
—	Partly secured creditors as per List C		—	Book Debts as per List F		
				Good	70,000	70,000
				Doubtful	18,000	6,000
1,900	Preferential Creditors as per List D	1,900		Bad	15,000	—
	Deducted as per contra	1,900		Surplus from Securities in the hands of creditors, fully secured		10,000
				Bills Receivable as per List G		—
						1,02,780
				Deduct preferential creditors as per contra		1,900
						1,00,880
				Deficiency as per List H.		29,120
			1,30,000			1,30,000

Deficiency Account (List H)

	Rs			Rs
Excess of Assets over Liabilities or Capital	63,500	Net Loss 2005–06		25,000
Profits for 2003-04 and 2004-05	55,540	Bad Debts (List F)		27,000
		Drawings		90,000
Deficiency as per Statement of Affairs	29,120	Loss on realisation:		
		Fix. & Fittings	2,820	
		Stock	3,340	6,160
	1,48,160			1,48,160

NB: It is assumed that Mohan's wife has lent Rs. 10,000 out of her dowry amount.

ILLUSTRATION 20.3

The assets of a merchant on 30th June 2005 as shown by his books were Rs 56,000 and his liabilities Rs 44,000. He filed his petition in the Insolvency Court and estimated his deficiency to be Rs 30,000. After making the above estimate he found that the following items were not passed through his account book:

Interest at 6% on his capital from January 2005.

A contingent liability of Rs 2,500 on Bills discounted by him for Rs 10,000.

Amount due as wages	Rs 300
Salaries	Rs 700
Rent	Rs 300
Rates and Taxes	Rs 200.

Prepare his Statement of Affairs and Deficiency Account.

(*B. Com. Sambalpur*) (*MK Poona*)

SOLUTION

Statement of Affairs as on 30th June 2005

Gross Liabilities	*Liabilities (As stated and estimated by the Debtor)*		*Expected to Rank*	*Assets (As stated and estimated by the Debtor)*	*Book Value*	*Estimated to produce*
			Rs		Rs	Rs
54,300	Unsecured Creditors as per List A		46,800	Property as per List E	56,000	14,000
Nil	Fully Secured Creditors as per List B			Book Debts as per List F		–
Nil	Partly Secured Creditors as per List C		–	Bill of Exchange and other securities as per List G		–
	Preferential Creditors as per List D					14,000
	Wages	300		Deduct Preferential Creditors as per contra		1,200
	Salaries	700				12,800
	Rate, Tax	200		Deficiency as per List H		34,000
		1,200	–			
1,200	Deducted as per contra	1,200				
			46,800			46,800

Dr. **Deficiency Account (List H)** Cr.

	Rs			Rs
Capital	12,000	Loss on Assets: (Rs 56,000-14,000)		42,000
Deficiency as per Statement of Affairs	34,000	Loss on account of unrecorded liabilities:		
		Salaries	700	
		Wages	300	
		Rate, Taxes	200	
		Rent	300	1,500
		Bill discounted and likely to be dishonoured		2,500
	46,000			46,000

Capital = Total Assets – Liabilities

= 56,000 – 44,000 = Rs 12,000

Realisation value of assets = Gross Liabilities – Estimated Deficiency

= Rs 44,000 – Rs 30,000 = Rs 14,000

List A:

	Gross liability	*Expected to Rank*
	Rs.	Rs.
Liability.	44,000	44,000
Rent	300	300
Bill discounted likely to be dishonoured	10,000	2,500
	54,300	46,800

Interest on Capital is not allowed.

ILLUSTRATION 20.4

Mr. Mohan filed a petition in Insolvency court on 30th June 2005. His books showed the following balance:

		Rs	Rs
Cash in hand		10	—
Fixtures & Fittings (estimated to produce Rs 80)		250	—
Stock (estimated to produce Rs 1,200)		1,800	
Sundry Creditors		—	2,000
Bills Payable		—	2,200
Sundry Debtors:			
Good:	Rs 1,000		
Doubtful (estimated to produce 50%)	2,000		
Bad	2,000	5,000	—
Bank Overdraft			1,200
Capital			1,660
		7,060	7,060

Liability on Bills discounted Rs 500, expected to rank Rs 100. His household furniture etc. was valued at Rs 250. He owned a house valued at Rs 750, having mortgage on it of Rs 600 at 4%. Interest paid up to the preceding 31st December.

Preferential Creditors amounted to Rs 35 (included in Sundry Creditors) and Rs 15 for Rates on the house.

Prepare a Statement of Affairs and Deficiency Account.

(*B. Com. Agra*)

SOLUTION

Statement of Affairs of Mr. Mohan as on 30th June 2005

Gross Liabilities	*Liabilities (As stated and estimated by the Debtor)*		*Expected to Rank*	*Assets (As stated and estimated by the Debtor)*	*Book Value*	*Estimated to produce*
Rs			Rs		Rs	Rs
	Unsecured creditors as per List A			Property as per List E		
	Creditors (2,000 - 35)	1,965		Cash	10	10
	Bills Payable	2,200		Stock	1,800	1,200
	Bank Overdraft	1,200		Fixtures and Fittings	250	80
				Household Furniture	–	250
5,865 [(1)]	Liability for Bills discounted	100	5,465	Book Debts as per List F		
				Good	1,000	1,000

		Rs	Rs		Rs	Rs
	Fully secured creditors as per List B			Doubtful	2,000	1,000
				Bad	2,000	–
612	Mortgage Loan	600		Surplus from securities in the hands of creditors fully secured		138
	Interest thereon	12[(2)]				3,678
		612				
	Less: Estimated value of security	750		*Less*: Preferential Creditors as per contra		50
	Surplus carried to contra	138				3,628
	Partly secured creditors as per List C			Deficiency, as per List H		1,837
	Preferential Creditors as per List D	–				
50	Rates, etc.	50				
	Deducted as per contra	50				
		–	5,465			5,465

(1) 2000 – 35 = 1,965 + 2,200 + 1,200 + 500 = Rs 5,865

(2) Interest outstanding: $600 \times \frac{4}{100} \times \frac{6}{12} =$ Rs 12

Deficiency Account (List H)

Dr. Cr.

		Rs			Rs
Excess of assets over Liabilities or Capital		1,660	Bad Debts (List F)		3,000
Surplus from estate:			Losses on realisation:		
Furniture		250	Fixtures and Fittings	170	
House (750 - 15)	735		Stock	600	770
Less: Mortgage with Interest	612	123	Loss on Bills discounted		100
Deficiency as per Statement of Affairs		1,837			
		3,870			3,870

ILLUSTRATION 20.5

Mr. Balan filed his petition on 31st December 2005 and his Statement of Affairs was composed of the following figures:

Sundry Debtors:	
Good: Rs 5,000	
Doubtful: Rs 15,250 estimated to produce Rs 10,000	
Bad: Rs 5,000	25,250
200 Shares in Textiles Ltd. (estimated to produce Rs 7,500)	12,500
Shares in X & Company (estimated to produce Rs 38,000)	42,500
Loss through betting	7,500
Creditors on open Accounts	45,000
Creditors holding first charge on X & Co. shares	20,000
Creditors holding second charge on shares of X & Co. (to the extent of Rs 15,000)	17,500
Bills Payable	2,500
Bills Receivable discounted of which Rs 1,750 is likely to be dishonoured	3,500
Creditors for Rent, Taxes etc. of which Rs 1,250 are preferential	1,500
Furniture, estimated to produce Rs 1,500	2,000
Cash on hand	60
Stock-in-trade, estimated to produce Rs 18,500	24,440

He commenced business with a capital of Rs 39,000 on 1st January 2003 and made a total profit of Rs 6,250 during the period of three years. His total drawings during the above period amount to Rs 17,500.

Prepare a Statement of Affairs and a Deficiency Account.

(B. Com. Karnataka, Madurai)
(MK. Delhi, Agra)

SOLUTION

Statement of Affairs of Balan
as on 31st Dec. 2005

Gross Liabilities	*Liabilities (As stated and estimated by the Debtor)*		*Expected to Rank*	*Assets (As stated and estimated by the Debtor)*	*Book Value*	*Estimated to realise*
Rs			Rs		Rs	Rs
	Unsecured Creditors as			Property as per List E		
	per List A			200 shares in Textiles	12,500	7,500
45,000	Creditors on open Account	45,000		Furniture	2,000	1,500
2,500	Bills Payable	2,500		Cash in hand	60	60
3,500	Lia for Bills discounted	1,750		Stock-in-trade	24,440	18,500
250	Rent etc.	250	49,500			
	Fully Secured Creditors			Book Debts as per List F		
	as per List B			Good	5,000	5,000
20,000	Creditors	20,000		Doubtful	15,250	10,000
	Less: First charge on			Bad	5,000	–
	shares of X & Co.	38,000				
		18,000		Surplus from the		
	Less: Transferred to List C	15,000		securities in the hands of		
	Surplus as per contra	3,000		fully secured creditors		3,000
	Partly Secured Creditors as per					45,560
	List C			*Less*: Preferential		
17,500	Creditors	17,500		creditors, as per contra		1,250
	Less: Value of security					44,310
	transferred from List B	15,000	2,500	Deficiency as explained in		
	Preferential Creditors			List H		7,690
	as per List D					
	Rent, Rates etc.	1,250				
	Deducted as per contra	1,250				
			52,000			52,000

Dr. **Deficiency Account (List H)** Cr.

	Rs			Rs
Capital	39,000	Drawings		17,500
Profit	6,250	Loss through betting		7,500
Deficiency as per Statement of Affairs	7,690	Loss on Realisation:		
		Shares in Textiles	5,000	
		Furniture	500	
		Stock-in-trade	5,940	
		Debtors	10,250	
		Shares in X & Co.	4,500	26,190
		Liability for Bills discounted		1,750
	52,940			52,940

ILLUSTRATION 20.6

Mr. X filed his petition on 31st March 2005. From the following information, prepare Statement of Affairs and Deficiency Account in respect of Mr.X.

	Rs
Capital on 1st April 2004	44,790
Drawings up to 31st March 2005	18,610
Losses on trading upto 31st March 2005	29,300
Preferential Creditors	2,080
Creditors	80,640
Cash at Bank	230
Cash in hand	70
Book Debts Rs 27, 370, estimated to produce	20,500
Furniture Rs 2, 480, estimated to produce	1,200
Plant and Machinery Rs 21, 250, estimated to produce	15,000
Factory Rs. 60,000, estimated to produce	55,000
(factory subject to mortgage for Rs 45,000)	
Stock, Rs 13,200 estimated to produce	8,300

Cost of winding up comes to Rs 2,820. State the amount of dividend which could be expected to be paid.

(B. Com. Karnataka)

SOLUTION

Statement of Affairs of Mr. X
as on 31st March 2005

Gross Liabilities	*Liabilities (As stated and estimated by the Debtor)*		*Expected to Rank*	*Assets (As stated and estimated by the Debtor)*	*Book Value*	*Estimated to produce*
Rs			Rs		Rs	Rs
	Unsecured creditors as per List A			Property as per List E		
				Cash in hand	70	70
80,640	Creditors		80,640	Cash at Bank	230	230
	Fully secured creditors as per List B			Furniture	2,480	1,200
				Stock	13,200	8,300
45,000	Mortgage	45,000		Plant & Machinery	21,250	15,000
	Less: Estimated value of security	55,000		Book Debt as per List F		
				Book Debts	27,370	20,500
	Surplus as per contra	10,000		Surplus from the securities in the hands of fully secured creditors		10,000
	Preferential creditors:					
2,080	Creditors payable in full	2,080				55,300
	Deducted as per contra	2,080	–	*Less*: Cost of winding		2,820
						52,480
				Less: Preferential creditors as per contra		2,080
						50,400
				Deficiency as per List H		30,240
			80,640			80,640

Dr. **Deficiency Account (List H)** **Cr.**

	Rs			Rs
Capital 1.4.2004	44,790	Drawings up to 31.3.2005		18,610
Deficiency as per Statement of Affairs	30,240	Trading Losses		29,300
		Loss on realisation:		
		Furniture	1,280	
		Stock	4,900	
		Plant	6,250	
		Debtors	6,870	
		Factory	5,000	24,300
		Cost of winding		2,820
	75,030			75.030

ILLUSTRATION 20.7

Babu Ram of Bangalore commenced business on 1st January 2001 with a Capital of Rs 1,32,000. He drew on the average Rs 12,000 a year. His profits for 3 years were Rs 28,000; he did not maintain proper accounts for the next two years. On 31st December 2005 an adjudication order was made against him. He submits the following information from which his Statement of Affairs and Deficiency Account are to be prepared:

	Rs
Sundry Creditors	80,000
Mortgage on Freehold property	16,000
Creditors secured by Life Policy estimated to be worth Rs 16,000	48,000
Landlord - 2 months' rent	800
Clerk's salary for 2 months	800
Municipal taxes owing	720
Mrs. Babu Ram's Loan	12,000
Bills Receivable, discounted and expected to rank	12,800
Freehold Property (estimated to realise Rs 80,000)	1,60,000
Machinery cost Rs 80,000, less depreciation written off Rs 24,000, estimated to realise	8,000
Second - Mortgage on Freehold Property	48,000
Book Debts, Good Rs 24,000; Doubtful Rs 8,000 estimated to realise Rs 2,400 and Bad Rs 2,000	
Fixtures and Fittings cost Rs 3,200, estimated to realise	1,400
Stock, cost Rs 32,000, estimated to realise	22.200
Cash in hand	320

(*B. Com.*)

SOLUTION

The business results of 2004 and 2005 are not given in the problem. Therefore, Trial Balance has to be prepared to find the profit or loss during 2004 and 2005.

Trial Balance as on 31st Dec. 2005

	Debit Rs	Credit Rs
Capital	–	1,32,000
Drawings (for 5 years)	60,000	–
Profits (for 3 years)	–	28,000
Sundry Creditors	–	80,000
Mortgage on Free property		16,000
Creditors secured on Life policy	–	48,000
Rent Due		800
Clerk's Salary	–	800
Municipal Taxes owing	–	720
Mrs. Babu Ram's loan	–	12,000
Freehold property	1,60,000	–
Machinery (Rs 80,000 - 24,000)	56,000	–
Second Mortgage on Freehold property	–	48,000
Book Debts (Rs. 24,000 + Rs 8,000 + Rs 2,000)	34,000	–
Fixtures and Fittings	3,200	–
Stock	32,000	–
Cash in hand	320	–
{Losses for 2004 and 2005 (Balancing Figure)}	20,800	–
	3,66,320	3,66,320

Statement of Affairs of Babu Ram as on 31st Dec. 2005

Gross Liabilities	Liabilities (As stated and estimated by the Debtor)		Expected to Rank	Assets (As stated and estimated by the Debtor)	Book Value	Estimated to produce
Rs		Rs	Rs		Rs	Rs
	Unsecured creditors			Property as per		
1,06,380	As per List A:		1,06,380[1]	List E:		
	Fully secured Creditors as per			Cash	320	320
				Stock	32,000	22,200
64,000	List B:	64,000[3]		Machinery	56,000	8,000
	Less: Estimated value of security	80,000		Fixtures & Fittings	3,200	1,400
	Surplus as per contra:	16,000		Book Debts as per List F		
	Partly Secured Creditors as per			Good	24,000	24,000
				Doubtful	8,000	2,400
48,000	List C:	48,000		Bad	2,000	–
	Less: Estimated value of Security	16,000	32,000	Surplus as per contra:		16,000
						74,320
	Preferential Creditors as per List D:	740[2]		Deducted preferential creditors as per contra:		740
	Deducted as per Contra:	740				73,580
		–		Deficiency as explained in List H		64,800
			1,38,380			1,38,380

Workings:

1. *Unsecured Creditors As Per List A:*

	Rs
Sundry Creditors	80,000
Two Months Rent	800
Clerk's Salary (Rs 800 - Rs 20)	780
Mrs. Babu Ram's Loan	12,000
Bills Receivable Discounted but expected to Rank	12,800
	1,06,380

2. *Preferential Creditors As Per List D*

Clerk's Salary	Rs 20
Municipal Taxes	Rs 720
	740

3. *Fully Secured Creditors As Per List B:*

Mortgage on Freehold Property	16,000
Second Mortgage on Freehold Property	48,000
	64,000

Deficiency Account (List H)

	Rs			Rs
Capital	1,32,000	Losses (2004 and 2005)		20,800
Profits 2001, 2002 & 2003	28,000	Bad Debts (List F)		7,600
Life Policy	16,000	Drawings		60,000
Deficiency as per Statement of Affairs	64,800	Realisation Losses:	Rs.	
		Stock	9,800	
		Freehold property	80,000	
		Machinery	48,000	
		Fixtures and fittings	1,800	
		Liability on B/R discounted	12,800	1,52,400
	2,40,800			2,40,800

ILLUSTRATION 20.8

Mr. Kuber is an insolvent. He supplies the following information as on 31st March 2005:

Trial Balance as on 31st March 2005

	Rs	Rs
Creditors (include Rs 10,000 secured against his private house property estimated to realise Rs 6,000)	–	30,000
Salary Payable to his clerk	–	800
Debtors:		
Good Rs 15,000		
Bad <u>Rs 5,000</u>	20,000	–
Income Tax Payable	–	3,200
Furniture, estimated to produce Rs 4,000	5,000	–
Stock in hand, estimated value Rs 30,000	40,000	–
Bills receivable, estimated to produce Rs 3,000	4,000	–
Drawings	15,000	–

Cash in hand	500	–
Bills Payable	–	6,000
Bank Loan, against mortgage of stock in hand	–	25,000
Loss in business trading	10,000	–
Capital	–	34,500
Loss through betting	5,000	–
	99,500	99,500

He had discounted Bills of Rs 10,000 of which bills worth Rs 3,000 are likely to be dishonoured. Prepare the Statement of Affairs and Deficiency Account assuming that Mr. Kuber resides in Madras.

(B. Com. Karnataka, Bombay)

SOLUTION

Statement of Affairs of Mr. Kuber
as on 31st March 2005

Gross Liabilities	*Liabilities (As stated and estimated by the Debtor)*		*Expected to Rank*	*Assets (As stated and estimated by the Debtor)*	*Book Value*	*Estimated to produce*
Rs			Rs		Rs	Rs
	Unsecured creditora as per List A	Rs.		Property as per List E		
				Furniture	5,000	4,000
20,000	Creditors 30,000 - 10,000	20,000	–	Cash in hand	500	500
500	Salary to clerk	500		Book Debts as per List F		
6,000	Bill payable	6,000		Good	15,000	15,000
10,000	Bill discounted likely to be dishonoured	3,000	29,500	Bad	5,000	–
	Fully Secured Creditors as per List B			Bill of exchange and other similar securities as per List G		
25,000	Bank Loan	25,000		Bills Receivable	4,000	3,000
	Less: Estimated value of securities	30,000		Surplus from securities in the hands of fully secured creditors, per contra		5,000
	Surplus as per contra	5,000				27,500
	Partly Secured Creditors as per List C					
10,000	Creditors	10,000		*Deduct* : Preferential		
	Less: Estimated value of house property	6,000	4,000	creditors, per contra		3,500
	Preferential Creditors as per List D					24,000
	Salary to Clerk	300		Deficiency as per List H		9,500
	Income Tax	3,200				
		3,500				
3,500	Deducted as per contra	3,500				
		–	33,500			33,500

Dr. **Deficiency Account (List H)** Cr.

	Rs			Rs
Capital	34,500	Trading Losses		10,000
Surplus from house property	6,000	Loss through betting		5,000
Deficiency as per Statement of Affairs	9,500	Drawings		15,000
		Loss on realisation:	Rs.	
		Bills Receivable	1,000	
		Debtors	5,000	
		Stock	10,000	
		Furniture	1,000	17,000
		Liability for Bills discounted		3,000
	50,000			50,000

ILLUSTRATION 20.9

'*A*' finding himself unable to meet his liabilities filed his petition on 31st December 2005. From the details obtained, you are asked to prepare Statement of Affairs and Deficiency Account:

	Rs
Cash on hand	50
Stock (estimated to realise 75%)	8,000
Building (due to appreciation it is likely to fetch Rs 6,000)	5,500
Furniture (estimated to bring Rs 400)	700
Debtors amounted to Rs 740 of which Rs 100 are bad and Rs 340 are good and remaining are expected to bring in Rs 200	–
Bill of Exchange	390
Scooter (mortgaged with creditors for a loan of Rs 6,700) expected to be sold for Rs 3,000	6,000
Unsecured Creditors amounted to Rs 9,030	
Creditors for Rent and Taxes are Rs 500 but only Rs 300 of this can rank as preferential.	

There are contingent liabilities on Bills discounted amounting to Rs 2,500 of which the sum of Rs 1,000 is expected to rank. Fully secured Creditors for Rs 2,000 have a charge of mortgage on the buildings.

'*A*' had a surplus of assets of Rs 5,000 on 1st January 2002. He had been withdrawing for his private expenses Rs 800 a year. It appears from his books in the first and second year that he has made a profit of Rs 2,850 and Rs 1,800 respectively and losses in the third and fourth year of Rs 2,000 and Rs 2,100 respectively, after allowing Rs 200 a year by way of interest on Capital : Surplus of Rs 200 is available from his private estate.

(*B. Com. Karnataka, Madras*)

SOLUTION

Statement of Affairs of Mr. A
as on 31st December 2005

Gross Liabilities	*Liabilities (As stated and estimated by the Debtor)*		*Expected to Rank*	*Assets (As stated and estimated by the Debtor)*	*Book Value*	*Estimated to produce*
Rs			Rs		Rs	Rs
	Unsecured creditors as			Property as per List E		
	per List A	Rs.		Cash in hand	50	50
9,030	Unsecured creditors	9,030		Stock	8,000	6,000
200	Creditors for Rent	200		Furniture	700	400
2,500	Liability for Bills			Book Debts as per List F		
	discounted	1,000	10,230	Good	340	340

	Fully Secured Creditors as per List B			Doubtful	300	200
2,000	Mortgage Loan	2,000		Bad	100	–
	Less: Estimated value of security	6,000		Bill of Exchange and other similar securities as per List G		
		4,000		Bill of Exchange	390	390
				Surplus from private estate		200
	Partly secured creditors as per List C			Surplus from the securities in the hands of fully secured creditors		4,000
6,700	Mortgage Loan	6,700				11,580
	Less: Estimated value of security	3,000	3,700	*Deducted*: Preferential Creditors as per contra		300
	Preferential creditors as per List D					11,280
300	Rent, Rates etc.	300		Deficiency as explained in List H		2,650
	Deducted as per contra	300				
			13,930			13,930

Dr. **Deficiency Account (List H)** Cr.

	Rs.	Rs		Rs.	Rs
Capital		5,000	Drawings (Rs 800 × 4)		3,200
Trading Profit	(2002) 2,850		Trading Losses	(2004) 2,000	
	(2003) 1,800	4,650		(2005) 2,100	4,100
Interest on Capital (Rs 200 × 4)		800	Loss on Realisation:		
Surplus from estate		200	Stock	2,000	
Surplus from Building (6,000 – 5,500)		500	Furniture	300	
Deficiency as per Statement of Affairs		2,650	Debtors	200	
			Scooter	3,000	5,500
			Liability for Bills discounted		1,000
		13,800			13,800

INSOLVENCY OF AN INDIVIDUAL AND OF PARTNERSHIP FIRM

In case of an insolvency of individuals, no distinction is made between private assets and business assets and private liabilities and business liabilities. But in case of insolvency of a firm, a distinction is made between the assets and liabilities of the firm and the assets and liabilities of the individuals. Private assets should first be utilised for paying off private liabilities and similarly business assets are to be utilised for paying off the liabilities of the business. If there is any surplus at one place, that can be transferred to the other, if necessity arises. But, it must be remembered that the deficiency of any partner will never be transferred to the firm. That is, if partner's private assets are less than his private liabilities, the deficiency is not made good by using the assets of the firm. In case of insolvency of the firm, separate Statement of Affairs and Deficiency Accounts are to be prepared for the firm and for each of the partners. We may come across situations, where a partner helps the firm in getting a loan by mortgaging his private property and in such cases, the Creditors will first recover the money, whatever they can, from the firm and the amount which could not be recovered from the firm is recovered from the security given by the partner.

ILLUSTRATION 20.10

'*A*' and '*B*' are in partnership and file their petition in bankruptcy. From the following particulars, prepare the Statement of Affairs and Deficiency Account of the firm as on December 31, 2005.

	Firm Rs	'A' Rs	'B' Rs
Mortgage on building	3,000	–	–
Bank Overdraft	3,000		
Sundry Creditors	12,400	1,500	2,900
Preferential Creditors	100	–	–
Capitals:			
A	3,000		
B	2,000		
Surplus	–	5,000	1,100
	23,500	6,500	4,000
Building	6,000		
Plant	6,500		
Furniture	400	1,000	1,200
Debtors	5,000		
Stocks	5,500		
Investment	–	2,500	800
Cash	100		
Capital in the firm	–	3,000	2,000
	23,500	6,500	4,000

The Bank overdraft was secured by a second mortgage on building and on B's investment. The amount expected to be realised were:

	Firm Rs	*'A' Rs*	*'B' Rs*
Buildings	4,500		
Plant	3,000		
Furniture	150	600	800
Debtors	3,100		
Stocks	3,075		
Investments	–	2,000	300

(*B.Com. Marathwada*)

SOLUTION

Statement of Affairs of 'A'
as on 31st December 2005

Gross Liabilities	*Liabilities*	*Expected to Rank*	*Assets*	*Book Value*	*Estimated to produce*
Rs		Rs		Rs	Rs
1,500	Unsecured Creditors as per List A	1,500	Property as per List E		
	Fully Secured Creditors as per List B		Furniture	1,000	600
	Partly Secured Creditors as per List C	–	Investments	2,500	2,000
	Preferential Creditors as per List D		Capital in the firm	3,000	–
	Surplus as per List H (transferred to firm)	1,100	Book Debts as per List F		–
			Bill Receivable as per List G		–
		2,600			2,600

Surplus Account of 'A'

Dr.	Rs		Cr.	Rs
Private Capital (Surplus)	5,000		Loss on Realisation:	
			Furniture	400
			Investments	500
			Capital in the firm	3,000
			Surplus as per Statement of Affairs	1,100
	5,000			5,000

Note: Capital of '*A*' in the firm is an asset for '*A*'. Rs 5,000 is a private capital (Assets - Liabilities). Surplus from private estate is transferred to the firm.

Statement of Affairs of '*B*'
as on 31st December 2005

Gross Liabilities	*Liabilities*		*Expected to Rank*	*Assets*	*Book Value*	*Estimated to produce*
Rs		Rs	Rs		Rs	Rs
2,900	Unsecured Creditors as per List A		2,900	Assets as per List E		
	Fully Secured Creditors as per List B			Furniture	1,200	800
	Partly Secured Creditors as			Capital in the firm	2,000	–
350	per List C	350	–	Book Debts as per List F		–
	Less: Estimated value of security	300	50	Bills Receivable as per List G		–
				Deficiency as per List H		2,150
			2,950			2,950

Deficiency Account of 'B'

Dr.	Rs		Cr.	Rs
Private Capital	1,100		Loss on Realisation:	
Deficiency as per Statement of Affairs	2,150		Furniture	400
			Capital in the firm	2,000
			Investments	500
			Liability on account of firm	350
	3,250			3,250

Note: The amount paid to the Bank from the firm is

As partly secured — Rs 1,500

As unsecured creditor $\frac{10,425}{13,600} \times 1,500$ — Rs. 1,150

2,650

Balance 350

3,000

The Deficiency of the private assets of '*B*' will not be transferred to firm.

Statement of Affairs of the Firm
as on 31st December 2005

Gross Liabilities	*Liabilities (As stated and estimated by the Debtor)*		*Expected to Rank*
Rs		Rs.	Rs
	Unsecured Creditors as		
12,400	per List A		12,400
	Fully Secured Creditors		
	as per List B		
3,000	Mortgage creditors	3,000	
	Less: Estimated value of Building	4,500	
		1,500	
	Less: Transferred to List C	1,500	
	Partly Secured Creditors		
	as per List C		
3,000	Bank Overdraft	3,000	
	Less: Recovery from B	300	
		2,700	
	Less: Estimated value of security (from List B)	1,500	1,200
	Preferential Creditors as		
	per List D		
100	Creditors payable in full	100	
	Deducted as per contra	100	
			13,600

Assets (As stated and estimated by the Debtor)	*Book Value*	*Estimated to produce*
	Rs	Rs
Property as per List E		
Plant	6,500	3,000
Furniture	400	150
Stock	5,500	3,100
Cash	100	100
Book Debts as per List F		
Debtors	5,000	3,075
Bills Receivable and Similar other Securities as per List G		
Surplus from A's Estate		1,100
		10,525
Deduct preferential creditors as per contra		100
		10,425
Deficiency as per List H		3,175
		13,600

Deficiency Account of the Firm

Dr.		Rs		Cr. Rs
Capital A:	3,000		Loss on Realisations:	
B:	2,000	5,000	Buildings	1,500
Further Contributions			Plant	3,500
by A:	1,100		Furniture	250
by B:	300	1,400	Stock	2,400
Deficiency as per Statement of Affairs		3,175	Debtors	1,925
		9,575		9,575

Note: In case of insolvency of a firm, it becomes essential to prepare Statement of Affairs and Deficiency/ Surplus Accounts of partners individually so that any surplus or shortage on account of private properties can be revealed. If there is a surplus, then it is used for making the payment of the firm's liabilities. If there is a deficiency, then there is no responsibility of the firm to pay them.

QUESTIONS

Objective Type Questions

I. Indicate whether the following statements are "True" or "False".

1. Rent is preferential both under Provincial Insolvency Act and Presidency Towns Insolvency Act.
2. The Statement of Affairs shows the assets and liabilities at book value only.

3. The terms bankruptcy and insolvency have synonymous meanings.
4. Under Provincial Insolvency Act rent due to the landlord is a preferential claim.
5. The Presidency Towns Insolvency Act is applicable to the whole country.
6. An insolvent is a person who has committed an act of insolvency.
7. A company may also be declared as insolvent.
8. Deficiency Account is the same as a Balance Sheet.
9. An order of discharge frees the insolvent from all his liabilities to his creditors.
10. List D in the Statement of Affairs shows fully secured creditors.

(**Ans:** True: 3, 6, 9.
False: 1, 2, 4, 5, 7, 8, 10.)

II. Fill in the blanks:

1. The unsecured creditors having a prior claim over the others are called .... creditors.
2. Bills of Exchange are shown in Statement of Affairs under List ....
3. Excess of private assets over private liabilities is shown on the .... side of the Deficiency Account.
4. Loss on Bills discounted and likely to be dishonoured is included in List ....
5. Deficiency Account is prepared to explain the .... of the deficiency.

(**Ans.** 1. Preferential; 2. G;, 3. Left hand; 4. "A", 5. Causes.)

III. Choose the most appropriate alternative in each of the following:

1. List C gives details regarding the:
   (*a*) Current Asset. (*b*) Partly Secured Creditors.
   (*c*) Fixed Assets
2. Preferential creditors are to be paid before:
   (*a*) Fully Secured Creditors. (*b*) Partly Secured Creditors.
   (*c*) Unsecured Creditors
3. List A gives details regarding the:
   (*a*) Preferential Creditors (*b*) Partly Secured Creditors.
   (*c*) Unsecured Creditors.
4. Amount of deficiency is given under:
   (*a*) List A. (*b*) List B.
   (*c*) List C. (*d*) List H
5. Amount due to Govt. or local authority is a
   (*a*) Secured Claim. (*b*) Unsecured Claim.
   (*c*) Preferential Claim.
6. Under the Provincial Insolvency Act, salary due to a clerk is preferential creditors to the extent of:
   (*a*) Rs. 20. (*b*) Rs. 100.
   (*c*) Rs. 300.
7. A Statement of Affairs shows the assets at :
   (*a*) Realisable value only. (*b*) Book value only.
   (*c*) Book value as well as Realisable value.
8. In the context of insolvency accounting, the amount of deficiency is given under:
   (*a*) List A. (*b*) List H.
   (*c*) List F.

(**Ans. 1.** (*b*), **2.** (*c*), **3.** (*c*), **4.** (*d*), **5.** (*c*), **6.** (*a*), **7.** (*c*), **8.** (*b*).)

THEORETICAL QUESTIONS

1. What do you understand by the Statement of Affairs and the Deficiency Account?
2. Differentiate between the Statement of Affairs and Balance Sheet.
3. Who are Preferential Creditors according to the Presidency Towns Insolvency Act and Provincial Insolvency Act?
4. What is Deficiency Account? How is it prepared ? *(B. Com. MK)*
5. Explain the insolvency procedure laid down by the legislation in India. *(B. Com. Bangalore)*
6. Who is an insolvent? *(B. Com. M.S.)*
7. What do you mean by the "Doctrine of Reputed Ownership"? *(B. Com. Kerala)*

PRACTICAL PROBLEMS

1. On 31st December 2004, Ram's assets and liabilities as per books amounted to Rs 60,000 and Rs 45,000 respectively. He estimated his deficiency to be Rs 20,000. He found subsequently that the following had not been taken into account:
   1. Interest on his capital of Rs 30,000 at 6% p.a. for one year.
   2. Liability on Bills discounted amounting in all comes to Rs 10,000 of which Rs 3,000 were expected to be dishonoured.
   3. Salaries Rs 1,400; Wages Rs 500 and Rent to Londload for three months Rs 150 have to be paid. Prepare his Statement of Affairs and Deficiency Account.

   (B. Com. Madurai, Karnataka)

   [**Ans:** Deficiency Amount: Rs 25,050
   Total of Statement of Affairs: Rs. 48,100
   Total of Deficiency Account: Rs 55,050

2. The capital in the business oı Mr. Harish on 31st December 2003 was Rs 700. During the year he sustained a trading loss of Rs 780, and his drawings of the business were Rs. 700. He was compelled to file his petition in the insolvency court. His assets consisted of:
   (*a*) Book debts Rs 1,000 of which Rs. 800 was considered good and the remainder estimated to produce Rs 100.
   (*b*) Stock (cost Rs 1,500) estimated to produce Rs 900.
   (*c*) Machinery (cost Rs 1,600) estimated to produce Rs. 1,100.
   (*d*) Freehold house valued at Rs 1,200 the deeds of which were lodged with the Bank as security for an overdraft on business account of Rs. 800.
   (*e*) His life policy (surrender value Rs 600) given as part security for a private loan of Rs 1,000.

   His unsecured creditors amounted to Rs 4,030, and he owed Rs 50 to his clerk, being salary for the two months ended 30th Nov. 2004.

   Prepare his Statement of Affairs and Deficiency Account. *(B.A. Delhi, Punjab)*

   [**Ans**: Deficiency Rs 1,180
   Total of Statement of Affairs: Rs 4,460
   Total of Deficiency Account: Rs. 2,680]

3. Mr. Singh's position as on 31st December 2004 was as follows:

	Rs		*Rs*
Capital (1.1.2002)	10,000	Cash	200
Trading Profit (of first two years)	6,000	Stock (estimated to realise	
Interest on Capital (of all 3 years)	1,500	Rs 5,000)	10,000
Unsecured Creditors	5,000	Machinery (estimated to realise	
Fully Secured Creditors	4,000	Rs 2,000)	8,000
Partly Secured Creditors	6,000	Shares (estimated to realise	
Preferential Creditors	15,000	Rs 2,000)	3,000

		Furniture (estimated to realise Rs 500)	2,000
		Book Debts (estimated to realise Rs 6,300)	10,300
		Trading Loss (Last year)	4,000
		Speculation Loss	5,000
		Drawings of all years	5,000
	47,500		47,500

Fully secured creditors and partly secured creditors took stock and shares respectively as security. Mr. Singh was declared insolvent on 31st December 2004. You are required to prepare his Statement of Affairs and Deficiency Account. (*B.Com., Bombay*)

[**Ans:** Deficiency: Rs 14,000
Total of Statement of Affairs: Rs 9,000
Total of Deficiency Account: Rs 31,500]

4. A and B filed their pctition under Insolvency on 31st December 2004. The books of accounts of the firm showed the following liabilities and assets:

They owed Rs 46,000 to unsecured creditors; Rs 30,000 to creditors having lien on goods and work-in-progress to the extent of Rs 10,000; Rs 24,000 to creditors who have been secured over the machinery amounting to Rs 1,20,000 and their liabilities towards ιaxes, rent and salaries amounted to Rs 2,800.

The machinery which was acquired for Rs 1,20,000 (depreciated out of Profit and Loss account by Rs 25,000), estimated to realise Rs 60,000. Goods on consignment worth Rs 20,000 were estimated to realise Rs 15,000.

Book Debts: Good Rs 12,000; Doubtful Rs 6,000 estimated to realise Rs 2,000 and Bad Rs 10,200.

Furniture and fittings worth Rs 4,000 was estimated to realise Rs 1,200.

Stock and work-in-progress Rs 30,000 estimated to realise Rs 10,000 and cash on hand Rs 840.

They commenced business on 1st January 2000 with a total capital of Rs 85,000. After charging annually Rs 5,000 for depreciation on machinery; Rs 6,000 for interest on capital, the firm has earned profits of Rs 12,000 in 2000, Rs, 6,000 in 2001 and losses of Rs 2,000, in 2002 Rs 16,000 in 2003 and Rs 16,000 in 2004. The total drawings of the partners for the five years amounted to Rs 23,760.

Draw up a Statement of Affairs and Deficiency Account from the information given above.

(*B. Com. Karnataka*)

[**Ans:** Deficiency: Rs 1,760
Total of Statement of Affairs: Rs 66,000
Total of Deficiency Account: Rs 1,34,760]

Note :There is no necessity to prepare Statement of Affairs and Deficiency Account individually as no information is available.

5. The assets of Gurumurthy of Bombay on 30th June 2004 as shown by his books were Rs 28,000 and his liabilities Rs 22,000. He filed his petition in the insolvency court and estimated his deficiency to be Rs 15,000. After making the above estimate he found the following items were not passed through his books of account:

Interest at 6% on his capital from 1st January 2004. A contingent liability of Rs 1,250 on bill discounted by him for Rs 5,000. Amounts due as wages Rs 300, Rent Rs 100 and Rates and Taxes Rs 150. Prepare insolvency account that is to be prepared as per insolvency law.

(*B. Com. Madurai*)

[**Ans:** Deficiency: Rs 16,800
Total of Statement of Affairs: Rs. 23,250
Total of Deficiency Account: Rs 22,800]

6. Roshan Lal finds himself insolvent on 31st December 2004. His position was as follows:

	Rs
Sundry Debtors - Good: Rs 5,000, Doubtful: Rs 30,000 (Estimated to produce Rs 25,000): Bad: Rs. 15,000	
1,000 shares in A Co.. Ltd. (estimated to produce Rs 15,000)	25,000
Shares in B Co. Ltd. (estimated to produce Rs 75,000)	91,500
Loss through betting	2,000
Creditors on open account	85,600
Creditors holding a second charge on the shares of B. Co.Ltd., to the extent of Rs 25,000	30,000
Creditors holding a first charge on the shares of B Co. Ltd.	40,000
Bill payable	4,000
Creditors for Rent, Rates, Taxes etc. (of which Rs 4,600 are preferential)	5,000
Furniture and Fixtures (estimated to produce Rs 3,000)	15,000
Cash in hand and at Bank	550
Stock in trade (estimated to realise Rs 30,450)	35,950
Bill Receivable (estimated to realise Rs 7,000)	9,000

Roshan Lal started with a capital of Rs 70,000 on 1st January 2002 and the business resulted in a profit of Rs 8,900 and Rs 10,000 for the first two years respectively and in a loss of Rs 5, 000 for the third year, after allowing Rs 3,500 as interest on capital each year. Withdrawals for the whole period amounted to Rs 30,000.

Prepare a Statement of Affairs and the Deficiency Account.

(*B. Com. Madurai*)

[**Ans:** Deficiency : Rs 3,600

Total of Statement of Affairs : Rs. 95,000

Total of Deficiency Account : Rs. 1,03,000]

7. A receiving order has been made against Mr. A on 15th September 2004 the particulars of his assets and liabilities are as under:

	Rs
Unsecured Creditors	14,487
Creditors fully secured (holding Life Insurance Policies valued at Rs 12,315)	10,333
Creditors partly secured (the security held is a second charge on assets pledged to fully secured creditors, the surplus available from the latter being estimated at Rs 1,020)	1,582
Preferential Creditors	37
Cash in hand	4
Life Insurance Policies, not charged, surrender value estimated	30
Stock and shares, estimated	154
Cycle used in business, estimated	249
Book debts Rs 76, of which Rs 39 are good, estimated	52

The debtor has conveyed business furniture to his wife by deed of gift dated 3rd March 2004. The value of this item is estimated at Rs 300.

The deficiency account starts from 30th June 2003 on which date the excess of liabilities over assets was Rs 3,936. The causes of failure are unsuccessful trading. Stock Exchange speculation and excessive interest on money borrowed.

Prepare the Statement of Affairs and Deficiency Account.

(*B. Com. Madras*)

[**Ans :** Deficiency : Rs 13,335

Total of Statement of Affairs : 15,049

Total of Deficiency Account : Rs 25,980]

Note : Business loss can be known by preparing a Balance Sheet.

Thus, Balance Total : Rs 26,439 and Business Loss : Rs 22,020

8. From the following information, prepare a Statement of Affairs and a Deficiency Account of Mr. Unlucky who is declared insolvent on 31st December 2004.

Total Creditors Rs 62,000 including preferential creditors Rs 1,000; Secured Creditors holding a first charge on building Rs 15,000 and another secured creditor holds a second charge on building Rs 14,000.

Building : Book value 32,000, estimated to realise Rs 25,000; Debtors Rs 18,000, Bad debts estimated at Rs 2,000. Machinery estimated to realise (60% of the book value) Rs 12,000. Stock book value Rs 6,000, estimated to realise Rs 4,000. Bank balance Rs 1,000.

He commenced his business on 1.1.2000 with initial Capital of Rs 20,000. His drawings were Rs 200 more than those of the previous year of all years. His drawings were Rs 1,800 in 2004.

The profit of business in first four years was Rs 4,200. But in the last year business incurred a loss of Rs 5,200. He paid Rs 4,000 to his creditor friend on 8.12 2004 by fraudulent preference. He gifted Rs 1,000 to his daughter on the occasion of her marriage on 9.12.2004. A discounted bill of Rs 1,200 was dishonoured on 31.12.2004

(*B. Com. Saurashtra*)

[**Ans** : Deficiency: Rs 9,200

Total of Statement of Affairs : Rs 41,200

Total of Deficiency Account : Rs 33,400]

(Drawings come to Rs 8,000)

9. Mr. Gopal files his insolvency petition on 1st January 2004. He had the following assets and liabilities (estimated to realise and expected to rank are given in brackets):

	Rs	Rs
Buildings	(35,000)	40,000
Machinery	(1,25,000)	1,55,000
Furniture	(10,000)	20,000
Stock	(3,50,000)	4,00,000
Electrical Equipment	(1,00,000)	1,00,000
Book debts:		
Good		1,50,000
Bad & Doubtful	(20,000)	50,000
Investments	(1,00,000)	1,00,000
Mortgage on Electrical Equipments		1,00,000
Loan secured by Investments		2,50,000
Loan secured by first charge on stock		50,000
Loan unsecured		5,00,000
Liability on Bills Receivable discounted	(20,000)	50,000
Preferential Creditors		20,000
Cash at Bank		500

He commenced business with a Capital of Rs 3,00,000. Profit up to 31st Dec. 2003 was Rs 2,95,500, after allowing interest on capital of Rs 30,000. He had withdrawn Rs 5,30,000.

Prepare Statement of Affairs and Deficiency Account. (*B. Com. Bangalore*)

[**Ans** : Deficiency : Rs 49,500
Total of Statement of Affairs : Rs 6,70,000
Total of Deficiency Account : Rs 6,75,000]

10. On 31st December 2004, Mr. Babu filed his petition in bankruptcy. The information you are able to obtain as to his position is as follows:

	Rs
Creditors unsecured	1,50,000
Creditors partly secured by lien on shares	80,000
Creditors fully secured by lien on stock	20,000
Liability on Bills Receivable (estimated to rank Rs 7,000)	14,000
Mortgage on Factory building	20,000
Creditors payable in full	6,000
Book Debts:	
Good	40,000
Doubtful and Bad (estimated to produce Rs 4,000)	20,000
Consignment of goods	10,000
Stock (estimated to realise Rs 80, 000)	1,20,000
Shares (cost and estimated to realise)	32,000
Cash at Bank	200
Bills of Exchange	2,800
Factory Building	22,000
Machinery (estimated to realise Rs 24,000)	30,000
Fixtures (estimated to realise Rs 3,000)	6,000
Furniture (estimated to realise Rs 6,000)	7,000

On 1st January, six years ago, he had Capital of Rs 1,00,000. Profits were made in the six year of Rs 21,200 after allowing Interest on capital Rs 20,000 and withdrawals amounted to Rs 1,27,200.

Prepare Statement of Affairs and Deficiency Account,

(*B. Com. Karnataka, Bangalore, Madurai*)

[**Ans :** Deficiency : Rs 59,000
Total of Statement of Affairs : Rs 2,05,000
Total of Deficiency Account : Rs 2,00,200]

11. Mr. Jagannath filed a petition in Bankruptcy on 31st March 2004 when his balance sheet was as under :

Liabilities	*Rs.*	*Assets*	*Rs.*
Sundry Creditors	60,000	Cash in hand	600
Bank Overdraft	20,000	Land and Buildings	38,000
Bills Payable	10,000	Plant and Machinery	12,000
Income Tax Payable	600	Sundry Debtors	15,000
		Bills Receivable	4,000
		Drawings Account	21,000
	90,600		90,600

From the information given below, prepare Statement of Affairs and Deficiency Account:

(*a*) Bank overdraft has a first charge on land and buildings and sundry creditors have a second charge up to Rs 7,000.

(*b*) Sundry creditors include Rs 6,000 due to his wife, which amount belonged to her father.

(*c*) Mr. Jagannath gave furniture of Rs 2,000 as a gift to his brother on 1.1.2004. He recorded the said transaction in his books of accounts as under:

Drawings Account	Dr.	2,000	
To Furniture Account			2,000

(*d*) A decree has been passed for Rs 1,800 against him for which no liability has been created in his book value.

(*e*) Assets (including furniture) are estimated to realise 50% of the value.

(*f*) Mr. Jagannath's capital at commencement of business was Rs 15,000, his trade losses were Rs 6,000, loss in speculation was Rs 10,000 and his withdrawals were Rs 20,000 resulting in his net debit balance of the drawings account Rs 21,000 as shown in the Balance Sheet.

(*B. Com. Poona*)

[**Ans** : Deficiency : Rs 56,300
Total of Statement of Affairs : Rs 72,800
Total of Deficiency Account : Rs 71,300]

12. Mr. Bhagyawan filed his insolvency petition on 31st December 2004 and his Statement of Affairs was composed of the following :

		Dr.	*Cr.*	*Estimated to realise or rank*
		Rs	Rs	Rs
Buildings		70,000		60,000
Machinery		3,00,000		2,40,000
Electric Machinery		2,20,000		2,20,000
Furniture		60,000		30,000
Stock-in-trade		13,00,000		9,00,000
Book Debts:				
Good		4,00,000		4,00,000
Doubtful		1,00,000		40,000
Bad		1,00,000		
Investments		3,20,000		3,20,000
Mortgage on Electric machinery			2,00,000	2,00,000
Loan partly secured on Investments			8,00,000	8,00,000
Loan fully secured by Lien on Stock			2,000	2,000
Loan Unsecured			15,00,000	15,00,000
Liability on Bills discounted worth Rs 1,40,000				70,000
Preferential Creditors			60,000	60,000
Bill of Exchange		28,000		28,000
Cash with Bank		2,000		2,000
Capital (1.1.2000)	10,00,000			
Add : Profit	4,10,000			
Add: Interest	2,00,000			
	16,10,000			
Less : Drawings	12,72,000		3,38,000	
		29,00,000	29,00,000	

(*B. Com. Poona*)

[**Ans** : Deficiency : Rs 3,92,000
Total of Statement of Affairs : Rs 20,50,000
Total of Deficiency Account : 20,02,000]

13. Prepare a Statement of Affairs and Deficiency Account of Mr. Babulal who filed his petition on 31st December 2004. The books showed that he owed Rs 40,100 of which creditors amounting to Rs 6,500 held stock of the estimated value of Rs 7,200, other amounting to Rs 29,000 held stock of the estimated value of Rs 15,300 and a mortgage on the property at Calcutta at Rs 13,000: the Landlord being a preferential creditor for Rs 100.

Bills had been discounted amounting to Rs 3,500, in respect of which it was estimated that the firm would be liable for Rs 500.

The assets consisted of the following:

Book Debts: Good Rs 1,500; Doubtful Rs 600 estimated to produce Rs 400 and Bad Rs 700.

Furniture and fittings Rs 300, estimated to produce Rs 150, Cash Rs 50. Bills receivable Rs 350 ; Stock Rs 1,600, estimated to produce Rs 1,200.

The firm commenced business on 1st January 2000 with a capital of Rs 25,000. After charging Rs 1,000 a year for interest on capital and Rs 1,300 a year for salary (which were credited to Capital Account and not withdrawn), he had profit in the first year of Rs 2,700, but in the following four years losses were Rs 2,000; Rs 3,700; Rs 4,000 and Rs 6,500 respectively. He drew out of cash at the rate of Rs 1,200 a year. The property at Calcutta cost Rs 22,000 and stock mortgaged was subjected to a discount of 25%.

(*B. Com., Karnataka*)

[**Ans** : Deficiency : Rs 1,450

Total of Statement of Affairs : Rs 5,700

Total of Deficiency Account : Rs 40,650]

14. Laxmipati filed his insolvency petition on 1st April 2004. The following information was available:

	Rs
Buildings (estimated to produce Rs 60,000)	70,000
Machinery (estimated to produce Rs 2,40,000)	3,00,000
Motor Car (estimated to produce Rs 10,000)	20,000
Furniture & Fixtures (realise value Rs 30,000)	60,000
Stock-in-trade (estimated to realise Rs 10,00,000)	12,00,000
Book debts :	
Good	4,00,000
Doubtful to realise Rs 1,40,000	2,00,000
Investments (estimated to produce Rs 3,50,000)	3,20,000
Mortgage on Machinery	2,00,000
Loan and Overdrafts secured by Investments	7,00,000
Liability on Bills discounted (estimated to rank Rs 70,000)	1,40,000
Creditors payable in full	62,000
Bill Receivable (estimated to realise Rs 20,000)	28,000
Cash on hand	200
Cash at Bank	1,800
Loans unsecured	15,00,000

Laxmipati started his business with a capital of Rs 8,00,000 and he has made a profit of Rs 3,38,000 to the date of his application, after allowing interest on capital to the extent of Rs 1,00,000. His personal expenses and withdrawals amounted to Rs 11,00,000

Prepare the Statement of Affairs and Deficiency Account

(*B Com. Karnataka*)

[**Ans** : Deficiency : Rs 2,80,000

Total of Statement of Affairs : Rs 19,20,000

Total of Deficiency Account : Rs. 15,48,000]

15. Mr. Himan was adjudged insolvent on 1st January 2004. From the following information as to his position, prepare his Statement of Affairs as on that date and Deficiency Account for the three years ended on that date:

	Rs
Sundry Debtors	
Good : Rs 20,000	
Bad and Doubtful: Rs 81,000	
estimated to realise Rs 40,000	1,01,000
Shares in Platinum Ltd. (estimated to produce Rs 1,82,000)	2,20,000
Creditors on open account	1,90,000
Creditors holding a first charge on the investment	80,000
Creditors holding a second charge on the investment to the extent of Rs 60,000	70,000
Bills Receivable discounted (out of which Rs 7,000 are executed to rank)	12,000
Creditors for Rent, Taxes etc. (preferential Rs 3,000)	6,000
Furniture (estimated to realise Rs 6,000)	8,000
Cash in hand	240
Stock (estimated to realise Rs 60,000)	71,760
Bills Receivable (estimated to realise Rs 14,000)	26,000
Loses on Stock Exchange	30,000

Mr. Himan started the business on 1st January 2001 with a Capital of Rs 1,00,000. In first two years, there was a profit of Rs 55,000 and in the third year, there was a loss of Rs 10,000. He had been allowed interest at 6% p.a. on his original capital for each of the three years. Withdrawals for the whole period amounted to Rs 52,000. Out of his withdrawals he had purchased jewellery for his wife at a price of Rs 6,000. His wife had offered this jewellery towards paying the debts of her husband. The jewellery is expected to realise Rs 8,000.

(*B. Com. Poona*)

[**Ans** : Deficiency : Rs. 22,760
Total of Statement of Affairs : Rs 2,10,000
Total of Deficiency Account : Rs 2,03,760]

16. *A* filed his petition on 31st December 2004 and his Statement of Affairs was composed of the following figures:

	Rs
Creditors for goods	75,000
Bills Payable	5,000
Creditors secured by lien on Shares	40,000
Creditors secured by lien on stock	15,000
Liability on Bills discounted, estimated to rank Rs 3,000	7,000
Mortgage on Mill	10,000
Creditors Payable in full	3,000
Book Debts :	
Good:	20,000
Doubtful and Bad, estimated to produce Rs 2,000	10,000
Consignments considered good	5,000
Shares, estimated to realise Rs 16,000	15,000

Stock, estimated to realise Rs 40,000	60,000
Cash at Bank	100
Bill of Exchange	1,400
Mill, estimated to realise Rs 11,000	20,000
Machinery, estimated to realise Rs 12,000	15,000
Fixtures, estimated to realise Rs 4,500	9,800

On 1st January, six years ago, he had a capital of Rs 50,000. Profits were made in the six years totalling Rs 45,500 in the first four years and losses were incurred totalling Rs 25,000 in the last two years after allowing Rs 2,500 p.a. interest on capital. Withdrawals amounted to Rs 77,200.

Prepare his Statement of Affairs and Deficiency Account.

(*B. Com. Madurai*)

[**Ans** : Deficiency : Rs. 34,000
Total of Statement of Affairs : Rs 83,000
Total of Deficiency Account : Rs 1,44,500]

17. A firm of Kane and Rane file their petition in bankruptcy and you are asked to draw up a Statement of Affairs and Deficiency Account as on 31st December 2004 from the following information:

Sundry assets on 31st December 2004 amounted to Rs 1,22,184 (estimated to realise Rs 94,600) as against Rs 1,20,000 on 1.1.2000. The sundry creditors on 31st December 2004 amounted to Rs 1,07,270 as against Rs 92,686 on 1.1.2000.

The Capital Accounts (excluding the current accounts) on 31st Dec. 2000 showed a credit of Rs 20,000.

The partners drawings amounted to Rs 2,800 p.a. (Rs 1,600 for Kane and Rs 1,200 for Rane).

Trading result after charging Rs 1,000 p.a. interest on capitals and Rs 400 p.a. Rane's salary were:

2000 Profit	Rs 2,600
2001 Profit	Rs 800
2002 Loss	Rs 3,200
2003 Profit	Rs 400
2004 Loss	Rs 6,000

On 1st January 2000, Rane had introduced further cash of Rs 4,000 duly credited to his capital account.

(*B. Com., Bombay*)

[**Ans:** Deficiency : Rs. 12,670
Total of Statement of Affairs : Rs 1,07,270
Total of Deficiency Account : Rs. 50,784]

Chapter 21

Voyage Account, Investment Account, Etc.

Voyage Account – Investment Account– Package or Containers Account – Questions – Objective Type Questions – Theoretical Questions – Practical Problems.

Voyage Account

The method of accounting followed by shipping companies is known as voyage accounting. Shipping companies prepare their accounts periodically and also prepare the results of each voyage separately. Shipping companies carry goods from one place to another. Some companies carry passengers also in addition to goods from one place to another place. In order to ascertain the result of operating a ship's voyage, Voyage Account is prepared. The Voyage Account is a revenue account. It is important to note that there is no difference in the manner of preparing accounts period-wise and voyage-wise. All expenses connected with the voyage, such as port charges, wages and salaries of the crew, captain and other staff, transhipment, agency fees, provisions, loading and unloading charges, bunker and harbour wages, freight and insurance, insurance of the ship on a time policy according to duration of voyage, depreciation arising as a result of the journey, address commission paid to brokers for freight for the ship, commission to captain on net profit etc. are debited to concerned Voyage Account. All incomes such as freight on cargo carried, passage money, primage etc. are credited. Following are some of the items of income and expenditure peculiar to Voyage Accounts.

Voyage Account is debited usually with the following items:

1. **Bunker Cost.** This is the expenditure incurred on fuel oil, diesel, coal and fresh water used during the voyage. Now-a-days oil and diesel are used in place of coal. The bin or storing place of coal is referred to as bunker. Hence the name bunker costs.

2. **Port Charges.** Port is used by the shipping companies for loading and unloading of goods and parking of ships, hence the charges paid for these purposes are known as port charges.

3. **Depreciation.** Depreciation of the ship for the period of voyage is calculated and charged to the Voyage Account.

4. **Insurance.** Insurance premium of cargo must be entirely debited to the concerned Voyage Account whereas the insurance charges of the ship are charged proportionately to each voyage on the basis of time of voyage.

5. **Address Commission and Brokerage.** This is payable to the brokers and agents who help the shipping company in procurement of cargo, *i.e.*, freight or business. This is calculated at a certain per cent of the freight earned including the primage or surcharge and debited to Voyage Account. Address commission is payable to the Charterer whereas brokerage is payable to the agent of the charterer.

6. **Stevedoring Charges.** The expenses which are incurred in loading of goods on the ships and unloading of goods from the ships are known as stevedoring charges.

7. **Port Charges.** These are the charges paid to port authorities for allowing the ship to use the port either for loading or unloading the cargo.

8. Salaries and wages of the crew, captain and other staff.
9. Harbour charges
10. Manager's commission, if any.

Voyage Account is credited usually with the following items:

1. *Freight*: The amount which is charged by the shipping companies for taking goods or cargo from one place to another is called freight. It is an income.

2. *Primage*: It is additional freight just like surcharge on freight originally collected for the captain of the ship, now-a-days it is treated as income of the shipping company.

3. *Passage Money*: Fare collected from the passengers travelled in addition to the fare collected for merchandise.

4. Closing stocks of stores, provisions, coal, fuel etc.

Generally, voyage profit represents the excess of voyage incomes earned over the expenses incurred for this purpose. But if, however, the voyage is in progress, the incomes and expenses relating to the unfinished voyage are carried forward to the next year. Excess of credit side of Voyage Account over its debit side is profit on the voyage. Excess of debit side of Voyage Account over its credit side is loss on the voyage. This profit or loss is transferred to General Profit and Loss Account of the shipping company.

ILLUSTRATION 21.1

India Shipping Company of Bombay had a ship by name Bharat, whose written down value as on 1st July 2005 was Rs. 24 lakhs. The ship was insured for Rs. 30 lakhs at 1% for voyage policy of hull. The ship made a trip to Sydney and returned to Madras during the period Ist July 2005 to 30th Sept. 2005. The particulars relating to the voyage are given below:

1. Expenses incurred:

	Rs
Salaries of the crew	25,000
Fuel	55,000
Port dues	30,000
Stores expenses	32,000
Shares of overhead for the ship	16,000

2. Stevedoring at the rate of Rs. 3 per tonne.
3. Depreciation was charged on the written down value of the ship at the rate of 10% p.a.
4. The freight was insurerd at 1%.
5. The particulars of the freight consisted of the following:
   (*a*) Leather goods 1,100 tonnes at the rate of Rs. 120 per tonne.
   (*b*) Cotton 500 tonnes at the rate of Rs. 150 per tonne.
   (*c*) Sugar 1,700 tonnes at the rate of Rs. 100 per tonne.
6. In addition to primage @ 10%, the brokerage payable was @ 5%.

Prepare Voyage Account for the three months. (*M. Com.*)

SOLUTION

India Shipping Company
Voyage Account
from 1st July 2005 to 30th Sept. 2005

	Rs.		*Rs.*
To Salaries of the crew	25,000	By Freight:	
To Fuel	55,000	Leather goods: 1,100 × Rs. 120	1,32,000
To Port Dues	30,000	Cotton 500 × Rs. 150	75,000
To stores expenses	32,000	Sugar 1,700 × Rs. 100	1,70,000

To Shares of Overhead	16,000	By Primage 10% on Rs. 3,77,000	37,700
To Stevedoring @ Rs. 3 per 3,300 Tonnes	9,900		
To Insurance of Hull at 1%	30,000		
To Insurance for freight at 1% on Rs. 3,77,000	3,770		
To Depreciation @ 10% on Rs. 24,00,000 for 3 months	60,000		
To Brokerage at 5% on Rs. 4,14,700	20,735		
To Profit	1,32,295		
	4,14,700		4,14,700

ILLUSTRATION 21.2

MV Indian Express is regularly employed on cargo trade between India and East Africa. She set on her voyage on 1st July 2005 and arrived at her destination on 14th August 2005. You are required to prepare a Voyage Account bearing in mind the following particulars:

(*i*) The vessel was purchased in 1998 for Rs. 100 lakhs and at the time of purchase it had 16 years of working life left: Depreciation on ship is charged on straight line method.

(*ii*) Standing cost per day excluding recovery of depreciation is Rs. 22,000.

(*iii*) The vessel consumes daily 14 tonnes of fuel oil, 2 tonnes of diesel and 15 tonnes of fresh water. The cost of these are Rs. 1,000; Rs. 1,350 and Rs. 20 per tonne respectively.

(*iv*) The vessel carried the under mentioned cargo:
4,000 tonnes on which freight of Rs. 375 per tonne was charged and 3,500 tonnes on which the rate of freight was Rs. 190 per tonne. Both the rates are to be enhanced by a surcharge of 20% over the basic rates.

(*v*) Freight brokers were due a brokerage of 2.5%.

(*vi*) Port charges at the loading and discharging ports were Rs. 40,000 and Rs. 85,000 respectively.

(*C.A*)

SOLUTION

MV Indian Express
Voyage Account
from 1st July 2005 to 14th Aug. 2005

	Rs			*Rs*
To Standing Charges Rs. 22,000 × 45 days	9,90,000	By Freight:		
To Bunker Cost:		4000 × Rs. 375:	15,00,000	
Fuel: 14 × 45 × Rs. 1,000	6,30,000	3500 × Rs. 190:	6,65,000	
Diesel: 2 × 45 × Rs. 1,350	1,21,500		21,65,000	
Fresh Water: 15 × 45 × Rs. 20	13,500	*Add*: Surcharge at 20%	4,33,000	25,98,000
To Depreciation: $1,00,00,000 \times \frac{1}{16} \times \frac{45}{365}$	77,055			
To Brokerage 2.5% on Rs. 25,98,000	64,950			
To Port Charges	1,25,000			
To Profit on Voyage	5,75,995			
	25,98,000			25,98,000

ILLUSTRATION 21.3

Hind Shipping Limited owns tramp steamer by name Jalabharati which was chartered on voyage on 1st March 2005 on the following terms:

(*i*) Bombay to Basra with general cargo at Rs. 500 per tonne. The charter stipulates for an address commission to the charterer at 2% of the freight payable on raising the bill of loading together with a brokerage of 5% to the charterer's agent, one-third of which is repayable to the ship.

(*ii*) Basra to Dubai with fertilisers at Rs. 240 per tonne. Address commission of 2% of freight is payable to charterers and a brokerage of 1% is payable to agents on signing the charter.

The vessel is insured with Lloyds on an annual premium of Rs. 6,60,000. The master of the vessel is entitled to 1% of the net profits of each voyage after charging such commission.

Further details are:

Repairs and Renewals: at Bomaby Rs. 40,000
at Basra Rs. 18,000

Stores, Supplies and Provisions: at Bombay Rs. 1,40,000
at Basra Rs. 1,60,000
at Dubai Rs. 90,000 out of which Rs. 40,000 was in stock at the conclusion of voyage

Consumption of Bunkers: Fuel oil 6 tonnes a day, diesel 2 tonnes a day and fresh water 25 tonnes a day while the vessel is in port and fuel oil 15 tonnes a day, diesel 2 tonnes a day and fresh water 25 tonnes a day while sailing. Fuel oil, diesel and fresh water Rs. 1,200; Rs. 2,500 and Rs. 50 per tonne respectively.

Stevedoring Charges: At Bombay Rs. 20 per tonne, at Basra Rs. 15 per tonne for loading and Rs. 20 per tonne for discharging; and at Dubai Rs. 12 per tonne for loading/discharging.

Captain's Expenses: at Basra Rs. 16,000
at Dubai Rs. 20,000

Port Charges: at Bombay Rs. 60,000
at Basra Rs. 70,000
at Dubai Rs. 54,000

The vessel loaded the following cargo:

At Bombay – general cargo – 8,000 tonnes, out of which 6,000 tonnes were to be discharged at Basra and the rest at Dubai. The freight from Bombay to Dubai was fixed at Rs. 600 per tonne.

At Basra – fertiliser – for discharge at Dubai – 6,000 tonnes.

The vessel completed the voyage on 30th April 2005. Number of sailing days as per ship's log came to 16.

Prepare Voyage Account bearing in mind that the company has to provide towards special survey repairs of the vessel Rs. 24 lakhs every year.

SOLUTION

Jalabharati
Voyage Account
From Bombay to Basra and Basra to Dubai
Commenced on 1st March 2005 and Completed on 30th April 2005

	Rs.		*Rs.*
To Port Charges[1]	1,84,000	By Freight[8]	56,40,000
To Stevedoring Charges[2]	4,66,000	By Brokerage Refund	50,000
To Caplain's Expenses	36,000	(1/3 of Rs 1,50,000)	
To Stores, Supplies and Provisions	3,90,000	By Stock of Stores, Supplies and	40,000
To Repairs and Renewals	58,000	Provisions	
(Rs. 40,000 + 18,000)			
To Provision for special[3] survey repairs	4,00,000		

To Consumption of Bunkers[4]	9,93,250		
To Insurance Rs. 6,60,000 × 2/12	1,10,000		
To Address Commission[5]	88,800		
To Brokerage[6]	1,64,400		
To Commission to Master[7]	28,114		
To Profit on Voyage	28,11,436		
	57,30,000		57,30,000

1. Rs. 70,000 + Rs. 60,000 + Rs. 54,000 = Rs. 1,84,000

2.

	Rs.
Loading at Bombay: 8,000 tonnes × Rs. 20	1,60,000
Unloading at Basra 6,000 tonnes × Rs. 20	1,20,000
Loading at Basra 6,000 tonnes × Rs. 15	90,000
Unloading at Dubai 8,000 tonnes × Rs. 12	96,000
	4,66,000

3. Rs. 24,00,000 × $\frac{2}{12}$: Rs. 4,00,000

4. Consumption of Bunkers:

	Rs.
On Sailing Day: Fuel Oil: 15 tonnes × Rs. 1,200 =	18,000
Diesel: 2 tonnes × Rs. 2,500	5,000
Fresh water 25 tonnes × Rs. 50	1,250
For one day	24,250
For 16 days: Rs. 24,250 × 16	3,88,000
During Stay Days	Rs.
Fuel Oil: 6 tonnes × Rs. 1,200	7,200
Diesel: 2 tonnes × Rs. 2,500	5,000
Fresh water 25 tonnes × Rs. 50	1,250
For one day	13,450
For 4 days: 13,450 × 45	6,05,250

Total: Rs., 3,88,000 + Rs. 6,05,250 = Rs. 9,93,250

5.

2% on Rs. 30,00,000	60,000
2% on Rs. 14,40,000	28,800
	88,800

6.

5% on Rs. 30,00,000	1,50,000
1% on Rs. 14,40,000	14,400
	1,64,400

7. Rs. 28,39,550 × 10 — 28,114

8.

6000 × Rs. 500 (Bombay to Basra)	30,00,000
2000 × Rs. 600 (Bombay to Dubai)	12,00,000
6000 × Rs. 240 (Basra to Dubai)	14,40,000
	56,40,000

VOYAGE IN PROGRESS

At the end of the year, a voyage may be in progress (incomplete voyage). In that case, the expenses incurred on the unfinished voyage should be carried forward. If any freight or passage money has been received, it should also be carried forward. This will be clear from the following illustration.

ILLUSTRATION: 21.4

Jal Tarang commenced a voyage on 1st October from Mumbai to Chennai. The details of complete voyage, that is, Mumbai to Chennai and back to Mumbai, were as follows:

	Rs.
Coal Consumption	70,000
Port Charges	14,000
Depreciation	40,000
Sundry Expenses	4,000
Wages	8,000
Freight	4,00,000
Stores Consumed	30,000
Salaries	48,000
Insurance (Ship)	40,000
Insurance (Freight)	16,000

Primage and address commission are 10% and 5% repsectively. Freight relating to the return journey amounted to Rs. 1,20,000 only. The accounts are closed on 31st December. The ship was on her half way back to Mumbai on the date of closing the accounts.

Prpeare Voyage Account up to 31st December.

(B. Com.MK)

SOLUTION

JAL TARANG
Voyage Account
from 1st October to 31st December

		Rs.		Rs.
To Coal Consumed		70,000	By Freight	4,00,000
To Port Charges		14,000	By Primage	
To Depreciation		40,000	(10% of Rs. 4,00,000)	40,000
To Sundry Expenses		4,000	By Voyage in Progress:*	1,38,400
To Wages		8,000		
To Stores Consumed		30,000		
To Salaries		48,000		
To Insurance (Ship)		40,000		
To Insurance (Freight)		16,000		
To Address Commission				
(Rs. 4,40,000 × 5%)		22,000		
To Provision for				
Incomplete Voyage:				
Freight	Rs. 1,20,000			
Add: 10% Primage	12,000	1,32,000		
To Net Profit		1,54,400		
		5,78,400		5,78,400

	Rs.
* Coal Consumed	70,000
Port Charges	14,000
Depreciation	40,000
Sundry Expenses	4,000
Wages	8,000
Stores Consumed	30,000
Salaries	48,000
Insurance of ship	40,000
	2,54,000
Half of Rs. 2,54,000	1,27,000
Add: Rs.38,000 × 1,20,000 / 4,00,000	11,400
	1,38,400

INVESTMENT ACCOUNTS

A business concern must necessarily invest its funds in various assets like land and buildings, furniture and fixtures, plant and machinery, inventories and other assets to enable it to operate its business successfully. The business activities decide the type of assets to be acquired by the business concern and the assets are meant for use in the process of creating goods or services. Assets which are not used directly in production or trading operations but occupy only auxiliary relationship to the main business are considered as investments. The term 'Investment' refers to funds invested in various securities consisting of Government and semi-Government Loans, Shares and Debentures of Companies, etc. Investors, who have surplus funds or savings, generally like to invest their money to earn interest or dividend over a period or/and to make profit by sale. Employment of funds with specific objective of earning income or profit is known as investment. The funds invested represent investments.

Types of Investment

When an investment carries a fixed rate of interest or dividend, it is known as Fixed Interest Investment. At fixed rates, interest or dividend are calculated on their face value and discharged periodically. The object of these investments is not to make profit by selling them. On the other hand, Variable Yield Investment or Floating Investments are made with the sole object of making profit by selling them when prices are favourable. On these securities, one may get interest or dividend.

Interest and dividend

All the investments are expected to yield some income to the investors in the form of a fixed rate of interest or a certain percentage of dividend on their face value at regular intervals. The yield on shares of Joint Stock Companies, Corporations etc. is termed as 'dividends', whereas a fixed return provided by Government, local authorities, corporations and companies on their securities such as bonds, loans, debentures, certificates etc. is 'interest'.

Purchase and sale of investments

Investments are bought and sold like any other commodity in the stock market through brokers, agents, banks etc. The buying and selling prices of these investments are normally governed by forces such as rate of interest, demand and supply, state of money market, political conditions etc. When dealing with stock exchange securities, certain terms used frequently should be understood:

1. *Face Value*: Face value is the nominal value of the security concerned. It is the value declared on the face of the security document, Interest/Dividend is paid on the face value of the security.

2. *Market Value*: The securities are freely sold and purchased in the market. The rate at which a security is currently being sold or purchased is its market value.

3. *At Par Price*: When investments are purchased or sold at face value, this purchase or sale is called at par, as to purchase a share of Rs. 1,000 at Rs. 1,000. That is, market value is the same as the face value.

4. *At Discount Price*: When investments are purchased or sold at less than face value, this purchase or sale is called at discount. That is, market value is less than the face value, the security is said to be sold or purchased at discount. For instance, purchase of a share of Rs. 100 at Rs. 95. This is a purchase at discount.

5. *At Premium Price*: When investments are purchased or sold at above face value, it is known as purchase or sale at premium. That is, market value is more than the face value. For instance, purchase of a security of Rs. 1,000 is made at Rs. 1,100. This is a purchase at premium.

6. *Cum Interest (or Dividend) Quotation*: Accrual of interest on fixed investments is a continuous process but payment of interest is made periodically, say, once in six months on fixed dates. Purchase and sale of investments may take place on any day of the year, not necessarily on the date on which interest is paid. This situation creates a problem regarding the person to whom interest should be paid when investments are sold or purchased before the due date of payment of interest. In the absence of any agreement the holder of the investment (generally purchaser) is entitled to receive interest or dividend. For instance, the interest on an investment is paid every six months on April 1 and October 1. If the investment is sold on December 1, the next instalment of interest falls due on April 1. In this case, the seller has held the investment for two months, that is, October and November, and he is entitled to receive interest for this period. The company will not pay interest for two months to the seller and four months to the purchaser. Interest will be paid for all the six months to the person whose name appears in the register of members. When the right to receive interest or dividend passes from seller to buyer, the transaction is termed "Cum interest" or "Cum-dividend" sale or Purchase.

As said, in the case of fixed interest-bearing securities other than preference shares of companies, however, interest automatically becomes payable after the expiry of the specified period. But, the purchase and sale transactions pertaining to investment may not coincide with the date of payment of dividend or interest. Further, in the case of registered securities, interest is paid to the person whose name is inscribed in the register meant for the purpose, and in the case of bearer securities to the bearer of the same. In the case of shares, however, dividend is paid to the person whose name appears in the register of members. It is, therefore, necessary at the time of purchase, whether the buyer should get the benefit of interest or dividend or the seller. This depends upon the price quoted. If the price quoted is cum-dividend or interest, it means that the quoted price of security on which dividend is declared or interest has become payable includes the right to receive dividend or interest.

Thus, the right to receive interest or dividend from the issue of security passes from the seller to the buyer, and the transaction is known as "Cum-Interest or" Cum-Dividend" purchased or sale. In other words when the accrued interest or dividend from the last interest or dividend date up to the date of transactions is included in the quoted price, the capital cost of investment purchased or sold is ascertaind by deducting the accrued interest – dividend from the quoted prices. And the difference between the quoted price and the actual cost may be represented as Cum-Interest or Cum-Dividend.

7. *Ex-Interest or Ex-Dividend Quotation*: When the seller retains the right to receive the interest or dividend; the transaction is called "Ex-Interest" or "Ex-Dividend" purchase or sale. In other words, when the price quoted is exclusive of accrued interest/dividend, the price so quoted is treated as the capital cost of investment, that is, the buyer has to pay accrued interest due from the last interest date to the date of transaction to the seller along with the cost price of investment.

8. *Brokerage and Other Expenses*: Generally, investment transactions are made through brokers. They charge a certain small commission against their services which is known as 'Brokerage'. The stamp duty at the prescribed rates is also to be paid in executing the transaction. Since the brokerage

and stamp duty are capital in nature, these are to be added with the cost price of the investments, that is, brokerage will be added at the time of purchasing the securities and the same will be deducted from the sale price of the investment at the time of sale. As a result, only the net price is to be recorded in the capital column of the Investment Account.

Accounting entries in case of cum-interest purchase:

When Securities are purchased at Cum-interest:		
Investment Account	Dr.	(Cost of Securities bought)
Interest Account	Dr.	(Amount towards interest)
To Bank Account	Cr.	(Total amount paid)

(**Note:** Interest is for the period from the last declaration date up to the date of purchase.)

When interest is received on due date:

Bank Account	Dr.	(Cash received)
To Interest Account (Entire amount of interest)		

Balance of interest account is transferred to Profit and Loss Account

Accounting entries in case of cum-interest sale:

When securities are sold at Cum-interest:

Bank Account	Dr.	(Total amount)
To Investment Account (Cost of securities sold)		
To Interest Account (Claim of accrued Interest)		

Interest account is closed by transferring it to Profit and Loss A/c.

Note: When it is not mentioned in the question that purchase or sale is cum-interest or ex-interest, *then it is always presumed that it is cum-interest.*

ILLUSTRATION 21.5

On Ist February 2005, Abraham purchased from Manohar 25 7% Debentures of Rs. 100 each at Rs 140 each cum-interest. Interest is payable on these debentures on 30th June and 31st December each year. Pass the necessary entries in the books of purchaser and seller.

SOLUTION

Books of Abraham (Purchaser)

			Rs	*Rs*
2005				
Feb. 1	7% Debentures Account	Dr.	3,485.40	
	Interest Account	Dr.	14.60[1]	
	To Bank Account			3,500.00[2]
	(Being purchaser of 25, 7% Debentures at Rs. 140 cum-interest)			
June 30	Bank Account	Dr.	87.50	
	To Interest Account			87.50
	(Being receipt of interest for six months)			
Dec. 31	Bank Account	Dr.	87.50	
	To Interest Account			87.50
	(Being receipt of interest for six months)			
Dec. 31	Interest Account	Dr.	160.40	
	To Profit and Loss Account			160.40[3]
	(Being transfer of interest)			

1. Interest for one month (1.1. 2005 to 1.2.2005)

$$\frac{2500 \times 7 \times 1}{100 \times 12} = \text{Rs. } 14.58 \text{ or Rs. } 14.60$$

2. 25 × Rs. 140 = Rs. 3,500.
3. Rs. 87.50 + Rs. 87.50 = Rs. 175 – Rs. 14.60 = 160.40

In the Books of Manohar (Seller)

			Rs	Rs
2005				
Feb. 1	Bank Account	Dr.	3,500.00	
	To Debenture Account			3,485.40
	To Interest Account			14.60
	(Being sales of 25.7% debentures at Rs. 140 cum-interest)			
Dec. 31	Interest Account	Dr.	14,60	
	To Profit and Loss A/c			14.60
	(Being transfer of interest)			

Note: Interest is always calculated on the face value of investment but not on its purchase price or sale price.

Accounting entries in case of ex-interest purchase.

When Securities are purchased at ex-interest:

Investment Account	Dr.	(Cost-Ex-interest price)
Interest Account	Dr.	(Accrued interest acquired)
To Bank Account	Cr.	(Ex-interest price-Accrued interest)

When Interest is received:

Bank Account	Dr.	(Cash received)
To Interest Account	Cr.	(Entire amount of interest)

Then close the Interest Account by transferring it to Profit and Loss A/c.

Accounting entries in case of ex-interest sale:

When securities are sold at Ex-interest:

Bank Account	Dr.	(Ex-interest price + accrued interest)
To Investment Account	Cr.	
To Interest Account	Cr.	(Entire amount of interest)

Balance of interest account is transferred to Profit and Loss Account.

ILLUSTRATION 21.6

On 1st December 2005, a purchaser purchased 200 6% Debentures of Rs. 100 each @ Rs. 104 ex-interest per debenture. He paid 1/2% brokerage in this connection. Interest is payable on 30th June and 31st December each year. Pass entries in the books of purchaser.

SOLUTION

Books of Purchaser

			Rs.	Rs.
2005				
Dec. 1	6% Debentures Account	Dr.	20,900	
	Interest Account	Dr.	500	
	To Bank Account			21,400
	(Being purchase of 6% Debentures at Rs. 104 per debenture Ex-interest)			

Dec. 31	Bank Account Dr. To Interest Account (Being receipt of interest)		600	600
Dec. 31.	Interest Account Dr. To Prófit and Loss A/c (Being transfer of interest)		100	100

ILLUSTRATION 21.6

Mr. A buys 12% Debentures of the nominal value of Rs. 20,000 at Rs. 96 cum-interest on 31st March 2006. Interest is payable half yearly on 30th June and 31st Dec. Calculate the total purchase price and show its allocation to capital and revenue. ***(M. Com. Madras)***

SOLUTION

	Rs.
Purchase price of 200 debentures @ Rs. 96 cum-interest	19,200
Less: Interest for the expired period of 3 months $\frac{(20,000 \times 12 \times 3)}{100 \quad 12}$	600
	Rs. 18,600

Capital amount : Rs. 18,600

Revenue amount Rs. 600

ILLUSTRATION 21.7

On 31st January, Mr. A purchased for cash trom B – 6% Debentures of Rs. 100 at Rs. 110.50 cum-interest. ınterst payable on 1st June and 1st December each year.

How wiıı you record the transaction in the books of A and B if each party has to pay a bank commission of 25 paise per Rs. 100 on nominal value

(B.Com. Delhi)

SOLUTION:

Books of A

Date	*Particulars*	*LF*	*Dr. (Rs.)*	*Cr. (Rs.)*
31st Jan.	Investment Account Dr. Interest Account Dr. To Bank Account (Purchase of investment at Rs. 110.50 cum-interest plus commission)		439 4	443

	Price of 4 debentures : Rs. 110.50 × 4	=	Rs. 442
Add:	Bank Commission @ 25 paise per Rs. 100	=	1
			443
Less:	Accrued interest for 2 months at 6%		4
	Value of investment		439

Books of B

Date	*Particulars*	*LF*	*Dr. Rs.*	*Dr. Rs.*
31st Jan.	Bank Account Dr. To Investment A/c To Interest A/c (Sale of investment at Rs. 110.50: cum-interest less commission paid)		441	437 4

			Rs.
	Sales amount Rs. 110.50 × 4	=	442
Less:	Bank commission @ 25 paise per Rs. 100		Rs. 1
			441
Less:	Accrued interest for 2 months at 6%		4
			437

ILLUSTRATION 21.8

On 1-1-2006, Sri Devi purchased 500 Equity shares of Rs. 100 each in Reliance Ltd. @ Rs. 120 each from a broker who charged 2%. She incurred 50 paise per Rs. 100 as cost of share transfer stamps. On 30-11-2006 bonus was declared in the ratio of 1 : 2. Before and after the record date of bonus shares, the shares were quoted at Rs. 175 per share and Rs. 90 per share. On 31-12-2006 Sri Devi sold bonus shares to a broker who charged 2%. Show the Investment Account in the books of Sri Devi who held the shares as current assets. *(C.A. Inter)*

SOLUTION

In the Books of Sri Devi

Investment Account–Equity shares of Reliance Ltd.

for the year ending 31st December, 2006

Dr | **Cr**

	Nominal Rs	*Income* Rs	*Cost* Rs		*Nominal* Rs	*Income* Rs	*Cost* Rs
1-1-2006				31-12-2006			
To Bank A/c	50,000		61,500	By Bank A/c	25,000		22,050
30-11-2006				,, Balance c/d	50,000		41,000
To Bonus shares	25,000		–				
31-12-2006							
To P & L A/c	–		1,550				
	75,000	–	63,050		75,000	–	63,050

Cost of equity shares purchased on 1-1-2006:

	Rs. 120 × 500	=	Rs. 60,000
Plus :	2% of Rs. 60,000	=	Rs. 1,200
Plus:	$\frac{\text{Rs } 60{,}000}{\text{Rs. } 100} \times 0.50$	=	Rs. 300
			61,500

Sale proceeds of equity shares sold on 31-12-2006

250 × Rs. 90 – 2% of Rs. 22,500 = Rs. 22,050

Profit on sale of bonus shares on 31-12-2006:

Sale proceeds – Average cost

$$= \text{Rs. } 22{,}050 - \frac{(\text{Rs. } 61{,}500 \times 25{,}000)}{75{,}000} = \text{Rs. } 22{,}050 - \text{Rs. } 20{,}500 = \text{Rs. } 1{,}550$$

Value of equity shares on 31-12-2006

$$\text{Cost} = \frac{61{,}500 \times 50{,}000}{75{,}000} = \text{Rs. } 41{,}000$$

Market value = 500 × Rs. 90 = Rs. 45,000

Market value being higher than cost, shares have been valued at cost or market value whichever is lower, i.e., at cost, Rs. 41,000

ILLUSTRATION 21.9.

A purchased on 1st March, Rs. 24,000 5% Bharat Debentures Stock at 90 cum-interest, interest being payable on 31st March and 30th September each year. Stamp and expenses on purchase amounted to

Rs. 20 and brokerage at 2% was charged on cost. Interest for the half-year was received on the due date. On 1st September, Rs. 10,000 of the stock was sold at 92 ex-interest less brokerage at 2%. On 30th September, Rs. 8,000 stock was purchased at 91 ex-interest plus brokerage at 2% and charges 10. On 1st December, Rs. 6,000 stock was sold at 95 cum-interest less brokerage 2%. The market price of stock on 31st December was 88-1/2%. Show the Investment Account for the year ended 31st December making all calculations in months. *(C.A. Inter)*

SOLUTION

In the Books of A

5% BHARAT DEBENTURE STOCK ACCOUNT

(Interest payable on 31st March & 30th Sept.)

	Nominal Value	*Income*	*Cost*		*Nominal Value*	*Income*	*Cost*
	Rs	Rs	Rs		Rs	Rs	Rs
1-3- To Bank A/c — Purchase @ 90 cum-interest plus Rs. 432 and stamp Rs. 20	24,000	500	21,552	31-3 By Bank A/c — Interest		600	
				" Bank A/c — @ 92 ex-interest less brokerage Rs. 184	10,000	208	9,016
30-9- Purchase @ 91 ex-interest plus brokerage Rs. 146	8,000	200	7,426	" Bank A/c — Interest		550	
				Interest @ 94 cum-interest less brokerage Rs. 113	6,000	50	5,477
				" Accrued interest for 3 months on Rs. 16,000		300	
31-12- To P & L A/c — Interest & profit on sale		908	4	" Balance c/d	16,000		14,489
	32,000	1,608	28,982		32,000	1,708	28,982

Value of investment at the end of the year on the basis of average cost:

Total cost Rs. 32,000, investment Rs. 21,552 + Rs. 7,426 = Rs. 28,978

$$28{,}978 \times \frac{16{,}000}{32{,}000} = \text{Rs. } 14{,}489$$

The quotation cum-interest not only covers the cost but also includes the interest accrued up to the date of purchase; when interest becomes due, it would be the right of the buyer to claim that.

The quotation Ex-interest only includes the cost of the investments and the buyer is liable to pay additional amount as interest accrued up to the date of purchase of investment.

DISTINCTION BETWEEN CUM-INTEREST AND EX-INTEREST

Cum-interest	Ex-interest
(A) In case of cum-interest, nothing is payable in addition for accrued interest.	(A) In case of ex-interest, interest is payable in addition to the price quoted.
(B) Cum-interest means including interest.	(B) Ex-interest means excluding interest.
(C) In case of cum-interest, purchase price is more than the real price, *i.e.* capital portion of the security	(C) In case of ex-interest, purchase price quoted is the real price.

ILLUSTRATION 21.10

On Ist November, Ram sold 80.9% Debentures of Rs. 100 at Rs. 120 Ex-interest per Debenture. He paid 1/2 % brokerage on this sale. Interest is payable on 30th June and 31st December each year.

Pass entries in the books of Ram.

SOLUTION

Books of Ram

			Rs.	Rs.
Nov. 1	Bank Account	Dr.	9,800[1]	
	To 9% Debentures A/c			9,560[2]
	To Interest A/c			240[3]
	(Being purchase of 9% Debentures at Rs. 120 Ex-interest)			
Dec. 31.	Interest Account	Dr.	240	
	To Profit & Loss A/c			240
	(Being transfer of interest)			

80 × Rs. 120 = Rs. 9,600

Less: 1/2% of 80 × Rs. 100 = Rs. 40

Rs. 9,560[2]

Rs. 9,560 + Rs. 240 = Rs. 9,800[1]

$80 \times \text{Rs. } 100 = \text{Rs. } 8{,}000 \times 9\% \times \frac{4}{12} = \text{Rs. } 240$[3]

INVESTMENT LEDGER

Where an investor makes investments in several securities, it is but natural for him to keep separate account of each such investment. In that case he maintains a separate ledger or register known as Investment Ledger wherein he opens a separate account for each investment.

INVESTMENT ACCOUNT

Each investment account is generally maintained in columnar form. It is provided with three columns on either side for recording:

1. Nominal or Face Value of securities.
2. Income *i.e.,* interest or dividend earned, received, acquired or surrendered.
3. Principal or Capital or True Value of the investments.

The account is headed with the name of the security with further details such as dates of payment of dividend or interest, rate of interest etc. The face value of securities bought and sold is entered in NOMINAL column; the real cost and real sale proceeds in PRINCIPAL column and accrued interest and interest received in INTEREST column. The investment Account is a real account.

The difference between the capital cost of securities and the consideration received towards capital at the time of sale reveals the profit or loss on sale of investment. The profit or loss may be ascertained either for each individual sale or may be ascertained for all selling transactions at the end of the year as a whole. And if the entire investment are sold, the difference between the two Principal columns represents profit or loss as the case may be. But if a part of investments is sold, the balance of investments on hand should be ascertained first. Therefore, the balance is either valued at cost if the investment is treated as fixed asset, or the balance is valued at cost or market price, whichever is less, if the investment is treated as current asset. Naturally, the value of investments at hand is entered on the credit side of the investment account in Principal column and the difference represents the profit or loss on sale of investment. The profit or loss on such sale is transferred to Profit and Loss Account if the investment is treated as a current asset or the profit or loss on such sale is treated separately in the investment as fixed asset.

The balance of Investment Account is ascertained at the end of the accounting period. The balance of Nominal column reveals the face value of the investment in hand and after recording the closing balance in investment in Principal column, the profit or loss is to be ascertained, which has been indicated above. And the difference between the two Interest/Income columns represents income/interest from the Investment Account which is ultimately transferred to Profit and Loss Account.

BONUS SHARES

If both shares are received, entry is made in the debit side of Investment Account in Nominal column only and nothing is to be recorded in Principal column. The bonus shares do not involve any payment by the investor.

RIGHT SHARES

The shareholders have the right to avail the Right himself or he can refer to third party. The face value of such right shares is recorded in the Nominal column and the amount so paid in this regard is to be entered in the Principal column. But in the case of sale, the amount so received against the sale or Right will be entered on the credit side of Investment Account in Principal column.

ILLUSTRATION 21.11

Mr. A held on Ist January 2005 Rs, 1,00,000 of 3.5% Government Loan at Rs. 95,000. Three months' interest had accrued.

On 31st May he had purchased further Rs. 40,000 of the loan at Rs. 96 (net) cum-interest.

On 31st July Rs. 30,000 of the loan was sold at Rs. 94 (net) ex-interest.

On 30th November Rs. 20,000 of the loans was sold at Rs. 96 (net) cum-interest.

Interest on the loans was paid each year on 31st March and 30th September and was collected on 4th April and 5th October.

The price of the loan on 31st December was Rs. 96.

Draw up the Loans Account. Ignore income tax and paise. (*CAIIB*)

SOLUTION

3.5% Government Loans Account

Date	Particulars	Nominal Rs.	Interest Rs.	Principal Rs.	Date	Particulars	Nominal Rs.	Interest Rs.	Principal Rs
2005					2005				
Jan. 1	To Balance b/d	1,00,000	–	95,000	April 4	By Bank (Interest)	–	1,750[2]	–
Jan. 1	To Accrued	–	875[1]	–					
May 31	To Bank	40,000	233[3]	38,167[4]	July 31	By Bank (Sales)	30,000	350[5]	28,200[6]
					July 31	By Profit & Loss	–	–	300[7]

Date	Particulars	Nominal	Interest	Principal	Date	Particulars	Nominal	Interest	Principal
Nov. 30	To Profit & Loss A/c (19,083–19,000)	–	–	83	Oct. 5	By Bank (Collection of Interest)	–	2,450[8]	–
Dec. 31	To Profit & Loss A/c	–	4,347	–	Nov. 30	By Bank (Sale)	20,000	117	19,083[9]
					Dec. 31	By Interest Accrued	–	788	–
					Dec. 31	By Balance c/d	90,000		85,667[11]
		1,40,000	5,455	1,33,250			1,40,000	5,455	1,33,250
Jan. 1	To Balance b/d	90,000	–	85,667					
Jan. 1	To Accrued Interest	–	788						

Working:

1. Rs. 1,00,000 × 3.5% × $\frac{3}{12}$ = Rs. 875
2. Rs. 1,00,000 × 3.5% × $\frac{6}{12}$ = Rs. 1,750
3. Rs. 40,000 × 3.5% × $\frac{2}{12}$ = Rs. 233
4. Rs. 38,400 – Rs. 233 = Rs. 38,167
5. Rs. 30,000 × 3.5% × $\frac{4}{12}$ = Rs. 350
6. Rs. $\frac{30,000 \times 94}{100}$ = Rs. 28,200
7. Rs. 30,000 × $\frac{95}{100}$ = Rs. 28,500 (Cost)
   Less: Rs. 28,200
   Loss = 300
8. Interest: Rs. 1,40,000 × 3.5% × $\frac{6}{12}$ = Rs. 2,450
9. Amount received: Rs. 20,000 × $\frac{96}{100}$ = Rs. 19,200
   2 months' interest thereof Rs. 117
   20,000 × 3.5% × $\frac{2}{12}$ 19,083
10. Rs. 90,000 × 3.5% × $\frac{3}{12}$ = Rs. 788
11. Rs. 50,000 comprising Opening loan Rs. 47,500
    Rs. 40,000 purchased at Rs. 38,167
    85,667

ILLUSTRATION 21.12

Jaipur Investment Ltd. hold 1,000 15% Debentures of Rs. 100 each in Udaipur Industries Ltd. as on 1st April 2004, at a cost Rs. 1,05,000. Interest is payable on 30th June and 31st December every year. On 1st May 2004, 500 Debentures are purchased cum-interest at Rs. 53,500. On Ist November 2004, 600 Debentures are sold ex-interest at Rs. 57,300. On 30th November 2004, 400 Debentures are purchased ex-interest at Rs. 38,400. On 31st December 2004, 400 Debentures are purchased ex-interest at Rs. 38,400. On 31st December 2004, 400 Debentures are sold cum-interest for Rs. 55,000.

Prepare Investment Account valuing holdings on 31st March 2005 at cost, applying F.I.F.O. method.

(*CA*)

(*Table see next page*)

ILLUSTRATION 21.13

On 1st January 2004, X Ltd. had 10,000 Equity Shares of Rs. 10 each in Alpha Ltd. purchased for Rs. 1,25,000. The Company unlike Investment Companies does not make any apportionment of dividends (received or receivable) in between capital and revenue.

On 15th May 2004, Alpha Ltd. made a bonus issue of one fully paid share for two held. In addition, on the same day Right Shares were issued at 3 for 5 held on that date at a premium of Rs. 3, Rs. 7 to be paid on application and the balance in one call after a month. These shares are not to rank for dividend for the year ending 30th June 2004. 2,000 Right shares were taken up by X Ltd. and balance right being sold at Rs 2 each on 25th May 2004.

On 15th Oct. 2004, the company declared a dividend of 20% for the year ending 30th June 2004.

Make out the Investment Account in the books of X Ltd.

Ignore income tax. (*CA.B. Com. (Hons) Calcutta*)

SOLUTION (*See page no. 773*)

PACKAGES OR CONTAINERS ACCOUNT

Every businessman wants to maximise his profits. For this, he wants to increase his sales. Various facilities are provided to the customers. Packages or containers play an important role in increasing sales. Goods are very often packed into bottles, boxes, bags, cans, drums, etc. for the purpose of preserving, transporting and marketing. These packing materials, which are called packages, containers or empties, are durable as well, as reusable. The goods are packed by the suppliers for safe delivery at the destination of the customers and also with the object of putting the goods in a saleable condition. Packages or containers may either be manufactured by the concern itself or bought from outside. In either the case, they involve expenditure which must be recovered from the sale price of the articles packed. Therefore, there is the need for accounting of packages or containers.

The accounting procedure for containers largely depends upon the way in which they are handled. This could be broadly classified into these categories:

1. Containers Non-returnable:
   (*a*) When a separate charge is not made
   (*b*) When a separate charge is made
2. Containers Returnable:
   (*a*) When separate charge is not made
   (*b*) When separate charge is made

These have been explained below :

1. *Containers Non-Returnable* – When a separate charge is not made:

Some packages are such which cannot be returned by the customers. For instance, tooth paste, scent, oil etc. Their remaining with the products is essential. In certain cases, some cases or packages, if returned, cannot be used again. Since packages are essential for the products, cost of the packages

SOLUTION 21.12

Investment (15% Debentures) Account

Date	Particulars	Nominal Rs	Interest Rs	Principal Rs	Date	Particulars	Nominal Rs	Interest Rs	Principal Rs
2004					2004				
April 1	To Balance b/d	1,00,000		1,05,000	June 30	By Bank (Interest) (Rs 1,50,000 × 15% × 6/12)	–	11,250	–
April 1	To Accrued Interest (Rs 1,00,000 × 15% × 3/12)	–	3,750	–	Nov. 1	By Bank (Ex-interest) (60,000 × 15% × 4/12)	60,000	3,000	57,300
May 1	To Bank	50,000	2,500	51,000	Dec. 31	By Bank (cum-Interest) (40,000 × 15% × 6/12)	40,000	3,000	52,000
Nov. 30	To Bank (Ex-interest) (40,000 × 15% × 5/12)	40,000	2,500	38,400	Dec. 31	By Bank (Interest) (Rs 90,000 × 15% × 6/12)	–	6,750	–
2005					2005				
March 31	To Profit & Loss A/c	–	18,625	4,300	March 31	By Balance c/d	90,000	–	89,400
					March 31	By Accrued Interest	–	3,375	–
		1,90,000	27,375	1,98,700			1,90,000	27,375	1,98,700
2005									
April	To Balance b/d	90,000	3,375	89,400					

SOLUTION (21.13)

In The Books of X Ltd.
Investment Account

Date	Particulars	Nominal Rs	Interest Rs	Principal Rs	Date	Particulars	Nominal Rs	Interest Rs	Principal Rs
2004					2004				
Jan. 1	To Balance b/d	1,00,000	–	1,25,000	May 25	By Bank (4,000 Right shares sold @ Rs 2 per share)	–	–	8,000
May 15	To Bonus Shares (10,000/2 × Rs 10)	50,000	–	–	Oct. 15	By Bank (Dividend at 20% on 10,000 shares	–	20,000	–
May 15	To Bank (Share application money for 2,000 shares)	20,000	–	14,000	Dec. 31	By Balance c/d	1,70,000	–	1,43,000
June 15	To Bank (Call Money)	–	–	12,000					
Dec. 31	To Profit & Loss A/c (Balancing figure)	–	20,000	–	Dec. 31				
		1,70,000	20,000	1,51,000			1,70,000	20,000	1,51,000
2005									
Jan. 1	To Balance b/d	1,70,000		1,43,000					

Total Rights : $10,000 \times \frac{3}{5} = 6,000$ – Right exercised (2000) = 4,000 Right Sold

will be included in the selling price of the commodity. Under such circumstances, containers or packages stock account is opened. This Packages or Containers Stock Account is debited with the Opening Stock and Purchases and Credit with the Closing Stock. The difference between the two sides shows the cost of containers consumed. The consumption of packages or containers be transferred to Trading Account, if the expense is considered as part of the cost of the goods sold or transferred to Profit and Loss Account if treated as Selling Expenses.

ILLUSTRATION 21.14

A scent manufacturing company had a stock of 10,000 bottles valued at Rs. 25,000 on Ist Jan. During the year, the company purchased 50,000 bottles @ Rs. 2.50 per bottle. At the close of the year 7,000 bottles were in the stock. Write the Containers Stock Account.

SOLUTION

Dr. **Containers Stock Account** Cr.

		No.	Rs.			No.	Rs.
Jan. 1	To Balance b/d	10,000	25,000	Dec. 31	By Trading Account (Balancing figure)	53,000	1,32,500
	To Cash Account	50,000	1,25,000		By Balance c/d	7,000	17,500
		60,000	1,50,000			60,000	1,50,000

2. *Containers Non-Returnable*—When a separate charge is made:

If cost of packages is not included in sale price, the cost is charged from customers separately in addition to the price of the goods sold. In this case, Package Account is opened. This Account is debited with opening stock of containers and purchases. It is credited with the amount charged to customers and closing stock. The amount charged to customers is generally higher than the cost price. Therefore, the difference represents profit which the firm makes on account of sale of packages. This profit is transferred to Profit and Loss Account.

ILLUSTRATION 21.15

From the following information, prepare Containers Account:

1. Opening Stock of containers Rs. 8,000
2. Purchased during the year Rs. 72,000
3. Amount charged to customers Rs. 83,000
4. Closing stock on Dec. 31 Rs. 15,000

SOLUTION

Dr. **Containers Account (Special Trading Account)** Cr.

	Rs.		Rs.
To Balance b/d (Opening stock of containers in hand)	8,000	By Customers A/c (Containers sent to customers)	83,000
To Cash (Purchase of containers)	72,000	By Balance c/d (Closing stock of containers)	15,000
To Profit and Loss A/c (Balancing figure)	18,000		
	98,000		98,000

3. *Containers Returnable* – When separate charge is not made:

In this case no separate charge is made for the packages or containers. Since packages or containers are returnable, it is necessary to have a separate account for the packages or containers held by the customers. Hence opening stock and closing stock of packages or containers is divided into two – one for the packages or containers kept in hand and the other in the hands of the customers. In this case, the cost of containers is merged with the selling price of the goods and accounted for along with the goods sold. That is, the customers are not charged out separately. However, they are expected to return the containers within a given period. Normally, the following journal entries are passed:

1.	When containers are purchased	Containers Stock Account To Cash/Bank Account	Dr.
2.	When goods are sold in containers	Customers Account To Sales Account	Dr.
3.	When containers are returned treated Sales Returns but valued at depreciated value	Sales Returns Account To Customers Account	Dr.
4.	When contaicrs are repaired at additional expenditure	Containers Stock Account To Cash Account	Dr.
5.	When containers are lost or destroyed	Profit and Loss Account To Containers Stock Account	Dr.
6.	When adjusting entries are made for stock of containers	Closing Stock of Containers A/c To Packages on Hand A/c (Cost) To Packages with Customers A/c (Cost)	Dr.

ILLUSTRATION 21.16

Goods are delivered by a manufacturing concern in drums which are valued in books at Rs. 20 per item, but charged out to customers at Rs. 40 each. Customers are, however, credited with Rs. 30 for each drum if returned within two months in good condition.

Otherwise drums are not returnable, for which they are treated as sold. From the following information, draw up Drums Stock Account in the books of the manufacturing concern:

	No. of Drums
Stock in hand as on 1.1.2005	5,000
Stock with customers as on 1.1. 2005 (All returnable)	10,500
Purchased at Rs. 25 each during the year	8,200
Sent to Customers (new 5,000)	16,500
Returned by Customers	12,630
Destroyed in an accident	80
Sold as scrap for Rs. 1,500	250
Repairs charges Rs. 100	

Out of the total number of drums lying with customers as on 31st Dec. 2005, 6,000 were not returnable.

(*B. Com Calcutta*)

(*Please see page 777*)

4. *Containers Returnable* – When separate charge is made:

Under this method, returnable containers are considered to be the special items for trading account. As such, their cost is not included in the sale price of the goods sold in such containers. The price of the containers is charged separately to customers. Generally the price charged to customers is above cost price and hence a profit is made on this account. The price at which they are charged when sent to customers is known as the "charging out price". The amount credited to a customer on the return of packages is called "returnable price". The trader makes a profit on containers sent out regardless of whether they are returned or not. There are two methods of accounting to deal with returnable packages and when customers are charged out separately.

Method I

Under this method, two accounts are prepared – (*a*) Packages Stock Account and (*b*) Packages Trading Account. The former is a real account and the purpose is to have a control over the quantity of packages. Thus it does not disclose any profit or loss. The packages trading account is a nominal account and the purpose is to ascertain the profit or loss arising on the issue of packages.

(*a*) PACKAGES STOCK ACCOUNT:

It is debited with the following items:

(*i*) Opening stock of containers in shop: at cost

(*ii*) Opening stock of containers with customers: at cost

(*iii*) Purchase of containers at purchase price

It is credited with the following items:

(*i*) Containers destroyed, lost, stolen etc. at cost price

(*ii*) Containers scrapped at cost price

(*iii*) Depreciation on containers

(*iv*) Stock of containers in hand and with customers at cost

(*b*) CONTAINERS TRADING ACCOUNT

It is debited with the following items:

(*i*) Cost of containers scrapped

(*ii*) Cost of containers retained

(*iii*) Cost of maintenance

(*iv*) Depreciation, if any

It is credited with the following items:

(*i*) Sale of retained containes at returnable price;

(*ii*) Rental or hire charges of containers issued to customers;

(*iii*) Rental on stock returned;

(*iv*) Cash realised from sale of scrap.

The difference between the two sides is either profit or loss.

Method II

Under this method, the following two accounts are prepared: (*i*) Packages or Containers Stock Account and (*ii*) Packages Suspense or Reserve or Provision Account. The former account discloses profit or loss on packages and the latter is meant for recording the movement of packages from the trader to customers and vice versa.

(*a*) PACKAGES STOCK ACCOUNT:

It is debited with the following items:

(*i*) Opening stock at hand at cost price;

(*ii*) Opening stock with customers at cost price;

(*iii*) Purchase of containers at purchase price;

(*iv*) Cost of maintenance, repairs etc.

(*v*) Provision in respect of containers sent to customers at return price.

It is credited with the followings items:

(*i*) Cost of containers destroyed (abnormal loss)

SOLUTION (21.16)

Drum Stock Account

Date	Particulars	Quantity Rs	Rate Rs	Amount Rs	Date	Particulars	Quantity Rs	Rate Rs	Auount Rs
2005					2005				
Jan. 1	To Balance b/d				Dec. 31	By Drums Sold	6,000	40	2,40,000
	In Hand	5,000	20	1,00,000	"	By Bank A/c	250	20	1,500
	With Customers	10,500	20	2,10,000	"	By Profit and Loss A/c	80		5,100*
Dec. 31	To Purchases A/c	8,200	25	2,05,000	"	By Balance c/d:			
Dec. 31	To Repairs	–	–	100		In Hand (New)	3,200	25	80,000
Dec. 31	To Profit and Loss A/c	–	–	94,900		In Hand (Old)	5,800	20	1,16,000
	(Profit on sale)					With Customers	8,370	20	1,67,400
		23,700		6,10,000			23,700		6,10,000
2006									
Jan. 1	To Balance b/d								
	In Hand (Old)	5,800	20	1,16,000					
	In Hand (New)	3,200	25	80,000					
	With Customers	8,370	20	1,67,400					

Workings:

1. Drums with Customers

Drums with customers on 1st Jan.		10,500
Add: Sold to them		16,500
		27,000
Less: Returned by them	12,630	
Drums retained or sold	6,000	18,630
		8,370

2. Drums in Hand

Drums in Hand (Opening)		5,000
Drums with Customers (Opening)		10,500
Purchases		8,200
		23,700
Less: Sold	6,000	
Destroyed	80	
Scrap	250	
With Customers	8,370	14,700
		9,000

(New – 3,200

(Old – 5,800

* 250 + 80 = 330 drums × Rs. 20 = 6,600 – Scrap value Rs. 5,100 loss transferred to Profit and Loss account

(*ii*) Sale proceeds of containers scrapped at actual price

(*iii*) Containers sent to customers at charged price.

(*iv*) Containers retained by customers at returnable price.

(*v*) Closing stock on hand at cost (or valuation)

(*vi*) Closing stock with customers at cost

The difference between the two sides is either profit or loss.

(*b*) CONTAINERS SUSPENSE ACCOUNT:

It is debited with the following: items:

(*i*) Containers returned by customers at return price;

(*ii*) Containers retained by customers at return price;

(*iii*) Provision necessary at return price for those containers which are in the hands of customers.

It is credited with the following items:

(*i*) Balance of containers in the hands of customers at return price (beginning provision)

(*ii*) Containers sent to customers at return price

The two sides of the account must tally.

ILLUSTRATION 21.17

New Chemical Company sells its products in returnable drums. Customers are billed at Rs. 5 for each drum at the time of sale and credited with Rs. 4 if the drums are returned in two months. In case drums are returned in damaged condition, credit is given only for Rs. 2. The following figures are available for the year ended on 31st March 2005:

	Numbers	*Rs.*
Returnable stock with customers on Ist April 2004	20,000	40,000
Stock on hand as on 1st April 2004	5,000	10,000
Drums purchased during the year	15,000	45,000
Drums sent out during the year	50,000	
Returnable drums with customers as on 31st March 2005	10,000	
Drums returned in damaged condition during the year	5,000	
Drums not returned at the scheduled time during the year	20,000	

All stock is to be valued at cost. Damaged drums are to be valued at 50% of cost. During the year Rs. 1,00,000 was received from Debtors on account of drums.

SOLUTION

1. DRUMS RETURNED:

Opening stock with customers	20,000
Sent out during the year	50,000
	70,000
Less: Retained by customers	20,000
	50,000
Less: Returnable drums with Customers	10,000
	40,000

2. DRUMS IN HAND:

Opening stock on 1.4. 2004	5,000
Purchase during the year	15,000
Returned by customers	40,000
	60,000
Less: Sent to customers	50,000
(Good: 5,000 + Damaged: 5,000)	10,000

Dr. **Drums Stock Account** Cr.

	No.	*Rs.*		*No.*	*Rs.*
To Balance b/d:			By Customers A/c		
On hand @ Rs. 2	5,000	10,000	(50,000 sent @ Rs.5)	–	2,50,000
With customers @ Rs. 2	20,000	40,000	By Drums Suspense A/c		
To Purchase @ Rs. 3	15,000	45,000	(Drums retained @ Rs. 4)	20,000	80,000
To Drums Suspense			By Customers A/c (Rentals		
(Provision on Drums			of 5,000 damaged drums		
sent: 5,000 × Rs. 4)	–	2,00,000	@ Rs. 2)		10,000
To Profit & Loss (Profit)	–	95,000	By Balance c/d:		
			On hand 5,000 (Old)		
			@ Re.1	5,000	5,000
			On hand (New) @ Rs. 3	5,000	15,000
			With Customers (New)		
			@ Rs. 3	10,000	30,000
	40,000	3,90,000		40,000	3,90,000

Dr. **Drums Suspense Account** Cr.

	No.	*Rs.*		*No.*	*Rs.*
To Customers A/c			By Balance b/d		
(Drums returned @ Rs. 4)	40,000	1,60,000	(Reserve on opening		
To Drums Trading			stock with customers		
(Retained @ Rs. 4			@ Rs. 4)	20,000	80,000
provision)	20,000	80,000	By Drums Trading A/c		
To Balance c/d			(Provision @ Rs. 4 on	50,000	2,00,000
(Reserve on closing stock			sent)		
with customers @ Rs. 4)	10,000	40,000			
	70,000	2,80,000		70,000	2,80,000

ILLUSTRATION 21.18

Bombay Chemicals Limited supply their products in returnable containers. A container is invoiced to the customer at Rs. 50 but if it is returned within two months, a credit of Rs. 45 is given to the customer. A container costs Rs. 40 to the company and its life is estimated at 5 years at the end of which the scrap value is likely to be Rs. 5.

The following particulars are supplied to you:

	Numbers
Containers with customers (1-1-2006)	20,000
Containers in stock (1-1-2006)	4,000
Containers sent to customers during the year 2006	80,000
Containers returned by customers	85,000
Containers returnable	12,000
Containers purchased during the year	5,000
Containers condemned during the year useful life being over	1,000

Amount realised by sale of condemned contianers Rs. 6,000

Depreciation is to be provided on straight line method.

Prepare Containers Stock Account and Containers Suspense Account for the year and ascertain the profits or losses earned or incurred in the year assuming a separate account for provision for depreciation is maintained

(C.A. Inter)

SOLUTION

Dr **CONTAINERS STOCK ACCOUNT** *Cr*

Particulars	*Number*	*Rate* Rs	*Amount* Rs	*Particulars*	*Number*	*Rate* Rs	*Amount* Rs
To Balance b/d				By Customers' A/c —			
In hand	4,000	40	1,60,000	" Containers sent to			
With customers	20,000	40	8,00,000	Customers at chargeable			
" Purchases	5,000	40	2,00,000	Price (hire charges or rental)		50	40,00,000
" Containers Suspense A/c–				" Containers Suspense A/c–			
Provision for 80,000				Containers retained at			
containers sent out at							
return price		45	36,00,000	return price	3,000	45	1,35,000
" Profit and Loss A/c			4,16,000	" Bank A/c — Sale of			
				condemned containers	1,000	–	6,000
				" Provision for Depreciation A/c – Depreciation			
				on condemned containers			
				(1,000 × 35)	–	–	35,000
				" Balance c/d			
				in hand	13,000	40	5,20,000
				With customers	12,000	40	4,80,000
	29,000		51,76,000		29,000		51,76,000

PROFIT AND LOSS ACCOUNT

Particulars	*Rs.*	*Particulats*	*Rs.*
To Provision for Depreciation A/c		By Containers Stock A/c	4,16,000
Depreciation on 25,000 containers			
at Rs. 40 – Rs. 5 = Rs. 35 ÷ 5 = Rs. 7	1,75,000		
" Net profit	2,41,000		
	4,16,000		4,16,000

CONTAINERS SUSPENSE ACCOUNT

Particulars	*Number*	*Rate* Rs	*Amount* Rs	*Particulars*	*Number*	*Rate* Rs	*Amount* Rs
To Customers' A/c –				By Balance b/d – Provision			
Containers returned	85,000	45	38,25,000	for opening stock with			
" Containers Stock A/c–				customers	20,000	45	9,00,000
Containers retained	3,000	45	1,35,000	" Containers Stock A/c—			
" Baalance c/d—Provision				Provision for containers			
for closing stock				sent out	80,000	45	36,00,000
with customers	12,000	45	5,40,000				
	1,00,000		45,00,000		1,00,000		45,00,000

Alternative method:

CONTAINERS STOCK ACCOUNT

Particulars	Number	Rate Rs	Amount Rs	Particulars	Number	Rate Rs	Amount Rs
To Opening Stock				By Containers Suspence A/c–			
In hand	4,000	40	1,60,000	Containers retained or sold	3,000	45	1,35,000
With customers	20,000	40	8,00,000	" Containers Suspense A/c–			
" Purchases	5,000	40	2,00,000	Hire charges on 80,000			
" Provision for deprecia-				containers @ Rs. 5	–	–	4,00,000
tion — 25,000 containers				" Bank A/c—Sale of scrap			
at close @ Rs. 7	–	–	1,75,000	condemned containers	1,000	–	6,000
To Profit and Loss A/c—				By Provision for Depreciation			
Profit on containers				on 1,000 condemned			
issued	–	–	2,41,000	containers @ Rs. 35	–	–	35,000
				" Balance c/d—Stock at end			
				In hand	13,000	40	5,20,000
				With customers	12,000		4,80,000
	29,000		15,76,000		29,000		15,76,000

CONTAINERS SUSPENSE ACCOUNT

Particulars	Number	Rate Rs	Amount Rs	Particulars	Number	Rate Rs	Amount Rs
To Customers' A/c—				By Balance b/d—Provision			
Containers returned	85,000	45	38,25,000	for opening stock			
" Containers Stock A/c–				with customers	20,000	45	9,00,000
Containers retained	3,000	45	1,35,000	" Customers' A/c—			
" Containers Stock A/c–				Provision for containers			
Hire charges	–	–	4,00,000	sent out	80,000	50	40,00,000
" Balance c/d—Provision							
for closing stock	12,000	45	5,40,000				
with customers							
	1,00,000		49,00,000		1,00,000		49,00,000

QUESTIONS

Objective Type Questions.

I. State whether the following statements are "True" or "False".

1. Cum-Interest quotation means the quoted price including interest also.
2. Investment in land is a short-term investment.
3. Government Bonds usually fetch regular income.
4. Investment has its market value apart from the face value.
5. Investment is a fixed asset.
6. Cum-dividend means absence of right to receive dividends.
7. Stevedoring is the payment for loading and unloading.
8. The maximum commission payable to the underwriters is to be calculated on the issue price of the security.

9. A sub-underwriter gets his commission from the company whose shares have been underwritten.
10. Containers Reserve Account discloses the profit or loss on containers received and issued by the firm.

(Ans: True: 1, 3, 4, 7, 8,
False: 2, 5, 6, 9, 10

II. Fill in the blanks:

1. A price which includes the interest for the period for which the seller held the securities is termed as.......... .
2. The extra amount charged by a shipping company as a percentage of freight is termed as ....
3. A person, who undertakes the full responsibility for getting subscription for the shares or debentures issued by a company is called ....
4. Voyage Account is a .... account
5. Voyage Account is prepared to ascertain .... from each voyage.
6. Investment Account is a .... account.
7. Cum-interest means .... interest.
8. Brokerage is .... to the cost of investment in the books of purchaser of investment.
9. Ex-interest means .... interest.
10 Stevedoring is the payment for .... and ....

(Ans.1. Cum-interest price; 2. Primage; 3. Underwriter; 4. Nominal; 5. Profit or Loss; 6. Real; 7. Including; 8. Added; 9. Excluding; 10. Loading Unloading

III. Choose the most appropriate answer:

1. Brokerage is calculated on the:
   (*a*) Market value of securities.
   (*b*) Nominal value of securities.
   (*c*) None of the above.
2. When a firm makes investment in Government. Bonds, it is:
   (*a*) An asset
   (*b*) A liability
   (*c*) A revenue expenditure
3. When FIFO system is used for closing stock valuation, the closing stock contains:
   (*a*) Latest price
   (*b*) Earliest price
   (*c*) Neither of them
4. The price to be credited to customers for returning containers is:
   (a) Always lower than the issue price
   (b) Higher than the issue price.
   (c) Same price or lower than issue price.
5. Voyage Account is prepared:
   (a) Annually
   (b) Quarterly
   (c) For each voyage

(Ans: 1 (a): 2. (a): 3. (a): 4. (c): 5. (c)

THEORETICAL QUESTIONS

1. Distinguish between "Ex-interest" and "Cum-interest" quotations of securities. (*B. Com. MS*)
2. Discuss the method of accounting for packages and containers.
3. How are containers not returnable treated in accounts?
4. Write a note on Investment Accounts.
5. What is Voyage Account?

PRACTICAL PROBLEMS

Voyage Account

1. The Odyssey undertook a voyage from Athens to Calcutta on 1st January 2004 and reaching on 31st March 2004. The cargo consisted of 900 tonnes of foodgrains and 100 tonnes of engineering goods. The freight charges were Rs. 150 per tonne for foodgrains and Rs. 100 per tonne for engineering goods. In addition, primage was 10%. Brokerage was payable at 5%. The expenses were:

	Athens	*Calcutta*
	Rs.	Rs.
Coal and Diesel	20,000	–
Port Charges	9,000	2,000
Harbour wages	3,000	1,000
Loading charges	2,000	–
Other expenses:		
Stores	10,000	
Discharging Expenses	2,000	
Postage	1,000	
Salaries of Crew	10,000	

The ship was insured for Rs. 10,00,000 at 1% for voyage policy of Hull. The freight was insured @ 1/2%. Depreciation is charged on the written down value of the ship at 5% p.a. The value of ship as on Ist January 2004 was Rs. 8,00,000.

[Ans. Profit Rs. 70,727]

2. A Bombay Company acquired a new ship Jalapriya at a cost of Rs. 30,00,000. The ship was ready for service on 1st April. An insurane policy at 2% was taken out on the ship. Freight was insured at a premium of Rs. 10,000 p.a. During the three months the ship had made 2 complete voyages, one to London and back and half to London. The ship carried the following freight.

To London	6,000 tonnes at Rs. 20 per tonne
From London	7,000 tonnes at Rs. 18 per tonne
Unfinished voyages	7,500 tonnes at Rs. 18 per tonne.

5 % commission was paid to agents in addition to 1% address commission. The expenses incurred were as follows:

	Rs.
Salaries and wages of crew	60,000
Fuel	30,000
Port Dues Bombay Rs. 6,000	
London Rs. 4,000	10,000
Stevedoring at Rs. 2 per tonne	41,000
Share of overhead for the ship for the period	25,000
Sundry expenses Rs.	6,000

Prepare Voyage Account of the period of 3 months ending 30th June. (*B. Com*)

[Ans. Profit Rs. 85,940]

3. SS Jaihind commenced a 2004 voyage on 1st October 2004 from Bombay to London and back. The voyage was completed on 30th November 2004. It carried a consignment of tea on its outward journey and of machinery on its return journey. The ship was insured and annual premium was Rs. 1,20,000.

Prepare Voyage Account from the following:

	Rs.
Freight earned (Outward)	5,00,000
Freight earned (inward)	3,50,000
Port Dues	25,000
Bunker	1,50,000
Wages and salaries	2,50,000
Stores	84,000
Sundry Expenses	25,000
Passage money received	50,000
Lighterage charges	33,000
Depreciation annual	4,80,000

Address commission 5% on outward and 4% on inward frieght.

Primage is 5% on freight

The manager is entitled 5% commission on the profit earned after charging such commission.

Stores and coal on hand were valued Rs. 15,000 on 30th Nov. 2004. (*M. Com*)

[Ans. Profit Rs. 2,37,667]

4. SS Kanishka sailed from Calcutta port on 1st Feb. 2004 and arrived at Madras port on 31st March 2004 via Visagappatinam port on voyage No. 403. The following goods were loaded.

1,000 M.T. and 200 M.T. at Calcutta port for Madras port and Visagappatinam port respectively. Another 500 M.T. were loaded at Visagappatinam for Madras. The freight charges were:

Calcutta port to Madras port Rs. 600 M.T.

Calcutta port to Visagappatinam port Rs. 500 per M.T.

Visagappatinam port to Madras port Rs. 400 per M.T.

The freight is subject to 10% primage, 5% address commission and 2.5% brokerage. The freight was insured at 1/2%. Hull was insured for the voyage at 1%. Depreciation was provided at 3% p.a. The cost of the ship was Rs. 1 crore. The following were the expenses incurred at different ports:

	Rs. Calcutta	Rs. Visagappatinam	Rs. Madras
Port Charges	36,000	20,000	20,000
Coal	1,00,000	30,000	—
Captain's contingencies	7,000	2,000	10,000
Harbour wages	10,000	20,000	15,000

Stores purchased for the voyage amounted to Rs. 50,000. Opening stock of stores was Rs. 40,000 and closing stock was estimated at Rs. 30,000. Stock of coal at close was estimated at Rs. 30,000 as against stock of Rs. 10,000 at the beginning. The ship will not come back to Calcutta port in the near future as part of the voyage programme. Salaries and wages amounted to Rs. 80,000 p.m. Prepare Voyage No. 403 Account. (*CA Inter*)

[Ans. Profit Rs. 2,90,800]

Investment Account

5. On 1st April 2004, XY & Company held 9% Debentures in B Ltd. of the face value of Rs. 10,000 at a cost of Rs. 8,000. Market value on that date was Rs. 9,000. Interest is payable on 31st Dec. every year. On 1st December 2004, Debentures of nominal value of Rs. 6,000 were purchased for Rs. 5,000 ex-interest and on 31st December 2004, Debentures of nominal value of Rs. 2,000 were sold cum-interest for Rs. 1,900. On 1st Jan. 2005, Debentures of nominal value of Rs. 6,000 were brought at Rs. 5,800. The market value of the Debentures on 31st March 2005 was at Rs. 90.

   Make out 9% Debentures Account in the books of XY & Company showing Profit and Loss on sale of investment. Stocks on 31st March each year valued at lower of cost or market price. *(CA)*

   [Ans. Profit Rs. 1,170]
   Closing Balance Rs. 20,000 (Rs. 17,200)

6. Mr. Investor furnishes the following details relating to his holding in 6% Government Bonds:

   Opening balance Face Value Rs. 60,000 – Cost Rs. 59,000.

   1.3.2004—100 units purchased ex-interest at Rs. 98.

   1.7.2004—Sold 200 ex-interest out of the original holdings at Rs. 100.

   1.10.2004—Purchased 50 units at Rs. 98 cum-interest.

   1.11.2004—Sold 200 units ex-interest at Rs. 99 out of the original holdings.

   Interest dates are 30th September and 31st March. Mr. Investor closes his books every 31st December. Show the Investment Account as it would appear in his books. *(CA)*

   [Ans: Profit Rs. 3,375
   Closing Balance Rs. 35,000 (Rs. 34,366)

7. Calcutta Investment hold 400 12% Debentures of Rs. 100 each in Acma Ltd. as on Ist April 2004 at a cost of Rs. 50,000. Interest is payable on 30th June and 31st December each year. On Ist June 2004 200 Debentures are purchased cum-interest at Rs. 21,400.

   On 1st November 2004, 300 debentures are sold ex-interest at Rs. 28,650.

   On 30th November 2004, 200 Debentures are purchased ex-interest at Rs. 19,200.

   On 31st December 2004, 300 Debentures are sold cum-interest for Rs. 32,250.

   Prepare Investment Account valuing closing stock as on 31st March 2005 at (applying FIFO method) or market price whichever is lower. The Debentures were quoted at par on 31st March 2005. *(CA)*

   [Ans. Loss on Sale: Rs. 11,300; Profit Rs. 5,200
   Closing Investment: Rs. 20,000 (Rs. 19,200)

8. Investors Ltd. held on 1st Jan. 2004 Rs. 60,000 of 12% Government securities (Tax free) of Rs. 100 each at Rs. 56,500. On Ist June 2004 the Company purchased a further of Rs. 40,000 of the security at 96 1/2 cum-interest, brokerage being 1/2%.

   On 31st July 2004, Rs. 50,000 of security was sold at 94 1/2 ex-interest, brokerage being 1/2%. On Ist December 2004, Rs. 20,000 of the security was again sold at 96.

   Interest on the security was paid each year on 31st March and 30th Sept. and was credited by the bank on 3rd April and 4th Oct. respectively. The price of the security on 31st Dec. 2004 was 96. Investors Ltd. closes its books on 31st December each year.

   Draw up the Investment Account in the books of Investors Ltd. *(ICWA)*

   [Ans. Profit Rs. 7,300
   Balance Rs. 30,000 (28,350)

Packages and Containers Account

9. A firm sells its goods in containers bought at Rs. 10 each. Customers are charged at Rs. 12 per container and are allowed Rs. 8 for each container returned within a given period. For stock purpose at account closing time the containers are valued at Rs. 7 each.

From the following information, draw up Containers Stock Account and Containers Reserve Account:

Number of containers in hand on 1st Jan.	4,500
Number of containers with customers (all returnable) on 1st Jan.	3,600
Number of containers with customers (all returnable) on 31st December	2,900
Purchases during the year	6,000
Sent to customers during the year	10,000
Returned by customers during the year	6,800

(B. Com. Calcutta)

[Ans: Profit Rs. 19,500**]**

10. A factory delivers goods to its customers in drums, charging them out at Rs. 12 each. Customers are credited with Rs. 8 if returned within a month.

From the following information prepare drums stock account and drums trading account:

	Drums
Stock in hand on 1st Jan. 2004 (valued at Rs. 6 each)	1,000
Drums with customers on 1st Jan. 2004 (still returnable)	2,100
Purchases at Rs. 7 each	1,500
Drums sent out to customers	3,200
Drums returned by customers	2,300
Drums sold as scrap for Rs. 100	30
Drums sold as scrap for Rs. 100	50

On 31st December 2004, 1,900 drums were with customers who could return them.

(B. Com. Poona)

[Ans: Profit Rs. 14,620**]**

11. X Ltd. supplied goods to customers in packages, which are priced at 20 paise in the account books. The company charges them at 40 paise each but credits the customers at 35 paise each when packages are returned within a specified period. On 1st January 2004, there were 2,000 packages in stock and 4,000 packages in the hands of the customers. The company made a fresh purchase at 25 paise each for 5,000 packages during the year up to 31st December 2004 and sent out to customers 7,000 packages. 7,400 packages were returned to the company, 250 packages were sold as scrap for Rs. 25. At the end of the year 2,600 packages were in the hands of the customers to be returned. Show the ledger accounts to record the above transactions. *(CA Inter)*

[Ans. Profit Rs. 475**]**

12. A company sells linseed oil in steel drums. An empty drum costs Rs. 50 but is charged out to customers at Rs. 60 on condition that their account would be credited at Rs. 40 for every drum in good condition returned within three months of issue.

You are asked to write up the necessary ledger accounts for the year ended 31st March 2004 from the particulars given below:

Stocks on 1st April 2003	2,000 drums
Stock with customers on 1st April 2003 (within 3 months of the issue)	14,000 drums

Transactions during the year:	
Purchases	20,000 drums
Issued to customers	40,000 drums
Returned by customers	35,000 drums
Sold as scrap for Rs. 5,000	1,000 drums
Stock with customers on 31st March 2004 (within 3 months of the issue)	18,000 drums

Opening stock in hand and with customers are valued at Rs. 30 per drum.

(B. Com. Hons. Calcutta)

[Ans. Profit Rs. 3,85,000]

13. Bombay Chemical Ltd. supply their products in returnable containers. A container is invoiced to the customers at Rs. 40 but if it is returned within two months, a credit of Rs. 35 is given to the customer. A container costs Rs. 35 to the company and its life is estimated at 6 years at the end of which scrap value is likely to be Rs. 5. The following particulars are supplied to you:

	Nos.
Containers with customers (1.1.2004)	10,000
Containers in stock (1.1.2004)	14,000
Containers sent to customers during 2004	60,000
Containers returned by customers	63,000
Containers returnable	6,000
Containers purchased during the year	1,000
Containers condemned during the year, useful life being over	1,500
Amount realised by sale of condemned containers	Rs. 8,000

Depreciation is to be provided on straight line basis.

Prepare the Containers Trading Account for the year and ascertain the profits or losses earned or incurred in the year. *[C.A. Inter]*

[Ans. Profit Rs. 1,88,000]

14. X sells his goods in boxes which he charged out to customers at Rs. 6 each. Customers are allowed a credit of Rs. 4 per box returned within 60 days of sale.

While closing his accounts for the year ended 30th September 2003, X valued the stock of boxes in his factory and returnable boxes in the hands of customers invoiced within 60 days of the close of accounting year, at Rs. 2 per box. The number of such boxes was 10,000 and 25,000 respectively.

For the year ended 30th September 2004 the following transactions took place:

50,000 boxes were purchased at Rs. 2,50 per box.

80,000 boxes charged to customers.

75,000 boxes were returned by customers.

2,500 boxes out of those returned were scrapped and sold for Rs. 1,500.

1,000 boxes were damaged by rain and discarded.

At the close of the year, 15,000 boxes were with customers.

Cash received on account of rentals and sales from customers was Rs. 2,50,000.

Record the above transactions in the books of X and draw Memorandum Debtors Account, Boxes Stock Account, Boxces Trading Account and Boxes Debtors Account. *(CA Inter)*

[Ans. Profit Rs. 1,84,500]

15. On 1st January 2004, a trader had a stock of packages valued at a cost of Rs. 30,000; out of these, packages costing Rs. 6,000 were in the hands of customers. When packages are sent out to customers they are charged 33 1/3% above the cost price. When packages are returned, credit for full charged value is given. During 2004 packages costing Rs. 1,20,000 have been despatched to customers and they have been given credit for Rs. 1,56,000 on account of returns. Packages costing Rs. 2,400 have been retained by the customers. At the end of the year, the stock of packgages in the hands of the trader, besides those in the hands of the customers, are valued Rs. 27,000.

You are required to prepare the necessary ledger accounts in the books of the trader.

(B. Com. Hons. Calcutta)

[Ans. Profit Rs. 800]

Chapter 22

Departmental Accounts

Accounting Procedure – Allocation of Common Expenses – Inter-Departmental Transfers – Questions – Objective Type Questions – Theoretical Questions – Practical Problems

Departmental Accounts are accounts relating to the several departments or sections of a business, drawn up with a view to ascertaining their individual performances. A business may have a number of departments, each dealing in a different type of goods. For instance, Departmental Store is an example of large scale trading by a retail trader. In order to carry on the business more efficiently, a businessman divides his store into many sections, each section is called a Department. In order to ascertain the profit or loss made by each department, it is desirable to prepare separate Trading and Profit and Loss Account for each department. The preparation of such Trading and Profit and Loss Account separately for each department enables to compare the results of trading activities; in brief:

1. It enables to compare the performance of one department with that of another and to measure the progress of the department itself by comparing year-wise performance.
2. It enables to measure the profitability of each department. In the absence of departmental accounting, if there is a loss, the businessman thinks that the whole business is at loss. Thus he may stop the business and may start a new business, because he is unable to understand the performance of each department. But, by preparing departmental accounts separately, the contribution of profit made by each department can be known. Thus a good profit-making department can be developed and the department which gives small margin of profit or no profit can be closed down. It is also possible to check the profit of a department, not to be eaten away by the department which makes no profit.
3. It helps in formulating new policies and to adopt new and latest techniques in the departments, thereby further profitability of the department can be expected.
4. Departmental Managers of the profit-making department can be encouraged by adopting a method of commission on the basis of departmental profit. This step will further boost the profit-making department.

ACCOUNTING PROCEDURE

There are two methods of keeping departmental accounts:

1. Independent Basis

In this method, accounts of each department are maintained separately. Each department prepares Trading and Profit and Loss Account. Finally, the profit or loss of each department is transferred to the (General) Profit and Loss Account for all the departments. The independent departmental book-keeping is an expensive one.

2. Columnar Basis

In this method, there is a single set of books. All accounts of all the departments are maintained together, but in a columnar or tabular form. In order to enable the preparation of departmental trading and profit and loss accounts, various subsidiary books, such as purchases, sales, returns books, are prepared in a columnar form and this shows the record, in detail, for each department. The following is the speciinen of a purchase book and a sales book:

Departmental Purchase Book

Date	Particulars	L.F.	Total	Dept. 1	Dept. 2	Dept. 3

Departmental Sales Book

Date	Particulars	L.F.	Total	Dept. 1	Dept. 2	Dept. 3

The same pattern of rulings may be followed in case of other subsidiary books.

Departmental Trading and Profit and Loss Account

When the books and accounts are maintained on a columnar basis, Trading and Profit and Loss Account can also be prepared on columnar basis. There arises no difficulty in finding out gross profit and net profit for each department separately. From the analytical ledger accounts and subsidiary books, department-wise figures are readily available. If an item of expense is definitely identified with a particular department, it can be termed as *direct* expenses with reference to the department. For instance, salary of Manager and salesman of a particular department, special advertising, separately metered electricity etc. are *direct* expenses and exclusively meant for and identified with particular departments. Apart from this, there are some expenses termed as *indirect* expenses. Certain types of expenses are not readily identifiable departmentally and the benefit of such type of expenses goes to all departments. And such types of expenses, called joint expenses, are incurred for the business as a whole. For instance, rent, depreciation, selling expenses, welfare expenses, advertising etc. Allocation of such expenses among the various departments becomes indispensable on an equitable basis at the date of account. The important point in such cases is to fix the basis on which the different revenue items are to be split up. It is neither possible nor desirable to sub-divide all items on equal basis

ALLOCATION OF COMMON EXPENSES

Normally, all direct expenses are charged to the respective departments. In case of indirect or general expenses, proper allocation among the departments must be made in order to ascertain the profit and loss made by each department. Each department is charged with proper share of the various business expenses. If the basis for such allocation is not specially mentioned, then the following procedure may be followed.

Indirect Expenses	*Basis of Allocation*
1. Expenses on Purchases, for instance, Carriage, Freight, Duty, Octroi, etc.	In the ratio of departmental Net Purchases. (But ignore inter-departmental purchases)
2. Expenses on Selling, for instance, Selling Commission, Bad Debts, Discount Allowed, Advertisements, Carriage out etc.	In the ratio of Net Sales of various departments. (Ignore inter-departmental sales)

3. Expenses on Land and Building, for instance, Rent, Rates, Depreciation, Repairs.	On the basis of space occupied by each department.
4. Expenses on Machinery, for instance, Depreciation, Repairs etc.	On the basis of value of machineries of each department.
5. Expenses on Electricity, for instance, Lighting, Heating etc.	On the basis of Meter reading or points or space occupied by each department.
6. Expenses on Insurance	On the basis of Stock value or/and cost of machineries or actual premiums.
7. Expenses on Welfare, Canteen, Recreation etc.	On the basis of number of employees of each department.
8. Expenses on workmen's compensation.	On the basis of wages of each department.
9. Salary of Factory Manager.	On the basis of time devoted by him for each department.
10. Non-departmental expenses	When allocation of some expenses is impossible, they can be charged to General Profit and Loss Account.

Some expenses cannot be apportioned and no basis of apportionment is practicable. For instance, interest on Loan, Income Tax, Salary to General Manager, Share Transfer expenses, Bank charges, Audit fees etc. Here these expenses can safely be transferred to General Profit and Loss Account. Similarly, income of general nature such as Interest on Calls-in-arrears, Interest on Investment, fees on share transfer etc. credited to General Profit and Loss Account. The Departmental Trading Account shows the Gross Profit or Loss and Departmental Profit and Loss Account shows the Net Profit or Loss earned or suffered by each department.

ILLUSTRATION 22.1

The proprietor of a large retail store wished to ascertain approximately the net profit of the X, Y and Z departments separately for the three months ended 31st March 2006. It is found impracticable actually to take stock on that date, but an adequate system of departmental accounting is in use, and the normal rates of gross profit for the three departments concerned are respectively 40%, 30% and 20% on turnover before charging the direct expenses. The indirect expenses are charged in proportion to departmental turnover.

The following are the figures for the departments:

	X Rs.	Y Rs.	Z Rs.
Opening stock (1-1-2006)	10,000	14,000	7,000
Purchases	12,000	13,500	9,700
Sales	20,000	18,000	16,000
Direct expenses	2,000	1,500	700

The total indirect expenses for the period (including those relating to other departments) were Rs. 5,400 on the total turnover of Rs. 1,08,000.

Prepare a statement showing the approximate net profit, making a stock reserve of 10% for each department on the estimated value on 31-3-2006

SOLUTION

Departmental Trading & Profit & Loss A/c for three months ended 31st March 2006

	X	Y	Z		X	Y	Z
	Rs.	Rs.	Rs.		Rs.	Rs.	Rs.
To Opening stock	10,000	14,000	7,000	By Sales	20,000	18,000	16,000
To Purchases	12,000	13,500	9,700	By Closing			
To Gross profit c/d	8,000	5,400	3,200	stock (bal. fig)	10,000	14,900	3,900
	30,000	32,900	19,900		30,000	32,900	19,900
To Direct expenses	2,000	1,500	700	By Gross profit	8,000	5,400	3,200
To Indirect expenses	1,000	900	800				
To Stock reserve @ 10%	1,000	1,490	390				
To Net profit (bal. fig)	4,000	1,510	1,310				
	8,000	5,400	3,200		8,000	5,400	3,200

Note (1) Indirect expenses applicable to the three departments.

$\frac{54,000}{1,08,000} \times 5,400 = \text{Rs. } 2,700$ to be apportioned in the ratio of 10 : 9 : 8 (Rs. 1,000 ; 900 : 800)

(2) Direct expenses are not shown in Trading A/c because rates of gross profit given are before charging the direct expenses.

ILLUSTRATION 22.2

From the following particulars you are required to prepare Trading and Profit and Loss Accounts for the year ended 31st December 2005, showing the gross and net profits of each department. Apportion the general expenses of the business on the basis of turnover. Also prepare the Balance Sheet.

Trial Balance (31-12-2005)

		Rs	Rs
Capital			65,000
Plant *less* Depreciation		15,000	–
Stock (1.1.2005)	Dept. A	25,000	–
	Dept. B	19,000	–
Purchases	Dept. A	46,480	–
	Dept. B	22,050	–
Wages	Dept. A	11,600	–
	Dept. B	5,360	–
Departmental charges	Dept. A	7,530	–
	Dept. B	3,230	–
Returns out	Dept. A	–	1,160
	Dept. B	–	700
Sales	Dept. A	–	80,000
	Dept. B	–	40,000
Rent, Rates etc.		3,750	–
Salaries and Commission		9,450	–
Advertising		3,750	–
Discount & Interest		2,040	–
Sundry Expenses		1,530	–
Depreciation		750	–
Sundry Debtors		12,530	–
Sundry Creditors		–	6,570
Cash at Bank		4,380	–
		1,93,430	1,93,430

Stock in hand Dec. 31, 2005 Dept. A Rs 30,000 and B Rs 20,500.

Total sales are Rs 1,20,000 *i.e.*, Dept. A Rs 80,000 and B Rs 40,000. Proportion of general or indirect expenses chargeable to A 2/3 and B 1/3. (*B.Com., Madurai, MS, Bharathiar*)

SOLUTION

Trading and Profit and Loss Account

Dr. **for the year ended 31st Dec. 2005** Cr.

	Dept. A	Dept. B	Total		Dept. A	Dept. B	Total
	Rs	Rs	Rs		Rs	Rs	Rs
To Stock: Opening	25,000	19,000	44,000	By Sales	80,000	40,000	1,20,000
To Purchase (net)	45,320	21,350	66,670	By Stock: Closing	30,000	20,500	50,500
To Wages	11,600	5,360	16,960				
To Dept. Expenses	7,530	3,230	10,760				
To Gross Profit	20,550	11,560	32,110				
	1,10,000	60,500	1,70,500		1,10,000	60,500	1,70,500
To Rent, Rates	2,500	1,250	3,750	By Gross Profit	20,550	11,560	32,110
To Salaries & Commission	6,300	3,150	9,450				
To Advertising	2,500	1,250	3,750				
To Dis. & Interest	1,360	680	2,040				
To Sundry Expenses	1,020	510	1,530				
To Depreciation	500	250	750				
To Net profit	6,370	4,470	10,840				
	20,550	11,560	32,110		20,550	11,560	32,110

Balance Sheet as on 31st December 2005

Liabilities		Rs	*Assets*		Rs
Sundry Creditors		6,570	Cash at Bank		4,380
Capital	65,000		Sundry Debtors		12,530
Add: Profit	10,840	75,840	Stock:		
			Dept. A.	30,000	
			Dept. B.	20,500	50,500
			Plant	15,750	
			Less: Depre.	750	15,000
		82,410			82,410

ILLUSTRATION 22.3

The following purchases were made by a business house having three Departments:

Department A – 1,000 units
Department B – 2,000 units } at a total cost of Rs 1,00,000
Department C – 2,400 units

Stocks on 1st January were:

Department A – 120 units
Department B – 80 units
Department C – 152 units

The Sales were:

Department A – 1,020 units @ Rs 20 each
Department B – 1,920 units @ Rs 22.50 each

Department C – 2,496 units @ Rs 25 each

The rate of Gross Profit is the same in each case. Prepare Departmental Trading Account.

(*B.Com., Madurai*)

(*M.Com., M.S. University*)

SOLUTION

Departmental Trading Account

Dr. for the year ended... Cr.

	Dept. A	*Dept. B*	*Dept. C*		*Dept. A*	*Dept. B*	*Dept. C*
	Rs	Rs	Rs		Rs	Rs	Rs
To Stock	1,920	1,440	3,040	By Sales	20,400	43,200	62,400
To Purchases	16,000	36,000	48,000	By Stock	1,600	2,880	1,120
To Gross Profit c/d	4,080	8,640	12,480				
	22,000	46,080	63,520		22,000	46,080	63,520

Workings:

Closing Stock (in units)

	Dept. A	*Dept. B*	*Dept. C*
	Units	Units	Units
Opening Stock	120	80	152
Add: Purchases	1,000	2,000	2,400
	1,120	2,080	2,552
Less: Sales	1,020	1,920	2,496
Closing Stock	100	160	56

We know that the total purchase price of the following units:

Department A – 1,000 units
Department B – 2,000 units Cost comes to Rs 1,00,000
Department C – 2,400 units

If the purchased units would have been sold at a given rate, then the total selling price of the above (complete) units:

Department A – 1,000 units @ Rs 20	=	Rs 20,000
Department B – 2,000 units @ Rs 22.50	=	Rs 45,000
Department C – 2,400 units @ Rs 25	=	Rs 60,000
		1,25,000

Thus, the total profit is 25% of cost price or 20% of selling price.

Rate of Gross Profit is the same in each case. So, we can find out the cost price:

	Selling Price	*Profit*	*Cost Price*
	Rs	*Rs*	*Rs*
Department A 20% of	20.00	4.00	16.00
Department B 20% of	22.50	4.50	18.00
Department C 20% of	25.00	5.00	20.00

Proof:

Department A – 1,000 units @ Rs 16	=	16,000
Department B – 2,000 units @ Rs 18	=	36,000
Department C – 2,400 units @ Rs 20	=	48,000
		1,00,000

INTER-DEPARTMENTAL TRANSFERS

Goods are often supplied from one Department to another – Inter-Departmental transfer. Such transfer must be credited to Supplying Department and debited to Receiving Department. If the transfers are made at cost price, then it can be treated as mere transfer. No further adjustment is needed.

However, if the transfer of goods are made at selling price, then a profit is earned by the supplying department of the same organisation. When the goods, transferred from one department to another, still remain unsold with the transferee department, at the end of the accounting period, there arises a necessity to eliminate the unrealised profit on such stock on hand. This is because, so much of issuing department's profit (notional) remain unrealised from the viewpoint of the firm as a whole. The reserve will be equal to the profit included in respect of unsold goods at the end of closing. The entry is:

General Profit and Loss Account Dr.
To Stock Reserve

In certain cases, the transferee department may have some stock in the beginning of the accounting period, against which stock reserve was already created in the previous year, will also be transferred to General Profit and Loss Account by means of Journal entry:

Stock Reserve Account Dr.
To General Profit and Loss Account

Alternatively, a single journal entry can be passed for the unrealised profit on the basis of the difference between unrealised profit included in opening and closing stock.

ILLUSTRATION 22.4

A firm has two departments — Piecegoods and Readymade dresses. All goods purchased by the Readymade department from Piecegoods department are charged at the usual selling price. From the following particulars prepare departmental trading and profit and loss accounts for the year ended Dec. 31, 2005.

	Piecegoods	Readymade
	Rs	Rs
Stock 1.1.2005	1,00,000	25,000
Purchases	10,00,000	7,500
Sales	11,00,000	2,25,000
Transfer to Readymade	1,50,000	
Expenses:		
Manufacturing		30,000
Selling	10,000	3,000
Stock on 31.12.2005	1,00,000	30,000

The stocks in the Readymade department be considered as consisting of 75% cloth supplied from Piecegoods dept. and 25% expenses and cloths from outside. The Piecegoods department earned gross profit in 2004 at the same rate as in 2005. General expenses of the business as a whole in 2005 amounted to Rs 45,000

(B.Com., Madurai)

SOLUTION

Departmental Trading and Profit and Loss Account
for the year ended 31st Dec. 2005

Dr. Cr.

	Piece-goods	*Ready-made*	*Total*		*Piece-goods*	*Ready made*	*Total*
	Rs	*Rs*	*Rs*		*Rs*	*Rs*	*Rs*
Stock Opening	1,00,000	25,000	1,25,000	Sales	11,00,000	2,25,000	13,25,000
Purchases	10,00,000	7,500	10,07,500	Transfer to			
Transfer from Piece-				Readymade	1,50,000	–	1,50,000
goods	–	1,50,000	1,50,000	Stock: Closing	1,00,000	30,000	1,30,000

Manufacturing Expenses	–	30,000	30,000				
Gross Profit c/d	2,50,000	42,500	2,92,500				
	13,50,000	2,55,000	16,05,000		13,50,000	2,55,000	16,05,000
Selling Expenses	10,000	3,000	13,000	Gross Profit b/d	2,50,000	42,500	2,92,500
Net Profit	2,40,000	39,500	2,79,500				
	2,50,000	42,500	2,92,500		2,50,000	42,500	2,92,500

Rate of Gross Profit on Sale (Piecegoods) $= \dfrac{\text{Gross Profit} \times 100}{(\text{Sales} + \text{Transfer})}$

$= \dfrac{25{,}000 \times 100}{(12{,}50{,}000)} = 20\%$

75% of Rs 30,000 (closing) is from Piecegoods= Rs 22,500

Therefore unrealised profit $= \dfrac{22{,}500 \times 20}{100} =$ Rs 4,500

Less: Existing Provision on Opening Stock:

(Piecegoods) $= \dfrac{25{,}000 \times 75}{100} \times \dfrac{20}{100} =$ Rs 3,750

750*

General Profit and Loss Account
for the year ended 31st Dec. 2005

Dr. Cr.

	Rs		*Rs*
To General Expenses	45,000	By Profit from Piecegoods	2,40,000
To Provision for unrealised Profit	750*	By Profit from Readymade	39,500
To Net Profit	2,33,750		
	2,79,500		2,79,500

ILLUSTRATION 22.5

From the following balances extracted from the books of a firm, prepare Departmental Trading and General Profit and Loss Account for the year ended 31st December 2005 and a Balance Sheet as on that date after adjusting the unrealised departmental profits, if any.

		Rs			*Rs*
Land and Buildings		12,500	Capital		30,000
Furniture		2,500	Sales:	Dept. A	2,00,000
Opening Stock:	Dept. A	3,000		Dept. B	3,20,000
	Dept. B	4,000	Creditors		10,000
Purchases:	Dept. A	1,00,000			
	Dept. B	1,50,000			
General Expenses		1,40,000			
Debtors		20,000			
Drawings		28,000			
Cash at Bank		1,00,000			
		5,60,000			5,60,000

Additional information:

1. Closing stock of Dept. A – Rs 13,000 including goods from Dept. B Rs 4,000 at cost to Dept. A.
2. Closing stock of Dept. B – Rs 26,000 including goods from Dept. A Rs 9,000 at cost to Dept. B.
3. Sales Dept. A includes transfer of goods to Dept. B of the value of Rs 20,000 and sales of Dept. B includes transfer of goods to Dept. A of the value of Rs 30,000, both at market price to transferor departments.
4. Opening stock of Dept. A and Dept. B includes goods to the value of Rs 1,000 and Rs 1,500 taken from Dept. B and Dept. A respectively at cost price to transferor departments.
5. Depreciate land and buildings by 5% and furniture by 10% p.a. *(CA Inter)*

(B.Com., Madurai, Madras)

SOLUTION

Departmental Trading Account
for the year ended 31st December 2005

Dr. Cr.

	Dept. A	*Dept. B*	*Total*		*Dept. A*	*Dept. B*	*Total*
	Rs	Rs	Rs		Rs	Rs	Rs
To Opening Stock	3,000	4,000	7,000	By Sales	1,80,000	2,90,000	4,70,000
To Purchases	70,000	1,30,000	2,00,000	By Transfers	20,000	30,000	50,000
To Transfers	30,000	20,000	50,000	By Closing Stock	13,000	26,000	39,000
To Gross Profit	1,10,000	1,92,000	3,02,000				
	2,13,000	3,46,000	5,59,000		2,13,000	3,46,000	5,59,000

General Profit and Loss Account
for the year ended 31st Dec. 2005

Dr. Cr.

		Rs		*Rs.*
To General Expenses		1,40,000	By Gross Profit:	
To Depreciation:			Dept. A	1,10,000
Land & Building	625		Dept. B	1,92,000
Furniture	250	875		
To Provision for unrealised Profit:				
Dept. A	2,400			
Dept. B	4,950	7,350		
To Net Profit		1,53,775		
		3,02,000		3,02,000

Workings:

Calculation of provision for unrealised profit on stock:

$$\text{Dept. A: Rate of Gross Profit} = \frac{1,10,000}{2,00,000} \times 100 = 55\%$$

$$\text{Dept. B: Rate of Gross Profit} = \frac{1,92,000}{3,20,000} \times 100 = 60\%$$

Provision required on closing stock:

Dept. A: 60% of Rs 4,000 = Rs 2,400

Dept. B: 55% of Rs 9,000 = Rs 4,950

N.B. There is no need for any adjustment for opening stock which includes inter-departmental transfers. This is because goods have been valued at cost to the transferor department and not to transferee departments.

Balance Sheet as on 31st December 2005

Liabilities		*Rs*	*Assets*		*Rs*
Capital:	Rs 30,000		Fixed Assets:		
Add: Profit	1,53,775		Land and Buildings	12,500	
	1,83,775		*Less*: Depreciation	625	11,875
Less: Drawings	28,000	1,55,775	Furniture	2,500	
Sundry Creditors		10,000	*Less*: Depreciation	250	2,250
			Stock: Dept. A:	13,000	
			Dept. B:	26,000	
				39,000	
			Less: Provision for unrealised profit	7,350	31,650
			Sundry Debtors		20,000
			Cash at Bank		1,00,000
		1,65,775			1,65,775

ILLUSTRATION 22.6

A company has two departments viz. Piecegoods and Tailoring. All goods purchased by the Tailoring Department from Piecegoods Department are sold at normal market prices, same as prices charged to outside customers. From the following particulars prepare Departmental Trading and Profit and Loss Account and a Balance Sheet as on 31st March 2005

	Piecegoods Dept.	Tailoring Dept.
	Rs	Rs
Opening Stock	20,000	Nil
Purchases	2,20,000	10,000
Goods from Piecegoods dept.	–	60,000
Wages	600	6,400
Salaries (Departmental)	4,800	1,200
Closing Stock (at cost to the Dept.)	38,600	14,000
Sales	2,43,000	1,36,000
Printing and Stationery	1,000	600
Machinery	–	12,000

Further information:

	Rs
Advertisement	10,000
Salaries (General)	18,000
Capital	1,20,000
Debtors	54,000
Creditors	7,000
Drawings	1,00,000
Cash at Bank	41,000
Cash in Hand	6,400

Depreciate Machinery by 10%. The general unallocated expenses are to be apportioned in the ratio of Piecegoods – 3 and Tailoring – 2. *(CA Inter)*

SOLUTION

Departmental Trading and Profit and Loss Account

Dr. **for the year ended 31st March 2005** Cr.

	Piecegoods Dept.	*Tailoring Dept.*	*Total*		*Piecegoods Dept.*	*Tailoring Dept.*	*Total*
	Rs	*Rs*	*Rs*		*Rs*	*Rs*	*Rs*
To Opening Stock	20,000	–	20,000	By Sales	2,43,000	1,36,000	3,79,000
To Purchases	2,20,000	10,000	2,30,000	By Goods to Tailoring	60,000	–	60,000
To Goods from Piecegoods	–	60,000	60,000	By Closing Stock	38,600	14,000	52,600
To Wages	600	6,400	7,000				
To Gross Profit	1,01,000	73,600	1,74,600				
	3,41,600	1,50,000	4,91,600		3,41,600	1,50,000	4,91,600
To Salaries (Departmental)	4,800	1,200	6,000	By Gross Profit	1,01,000	73,600	1,74,600
To Salaries (General) (3 : 2)	10,800	7,200	18,000				
To Printing & Stationery	1,000	600	1,600				
To Advertisement (3 : 2)	6,000	4,000	10,000				
To Depreciation	–	1,200	1,200				
To Net Profit	78,400	59,400	1,37,800				
	1,01,000	73,600	1,74,600		1,01,000	73,600	1,74,600
To Provision for unrealised profit			4,000	By Net Profit: Piecegoods	78,400		
To Net Profit transferred to capital			1,33,800	Tailoring	59,400		1,37,800
			1,37,800				1,37,800

Note: The rate of Gross Profit of Piecegoods Department is calculated as follows:

$$\frac{\text{Gross Profit} \times 100}{\text{Sales to Outsiders} + \text{Sales to Tailoring Dept.}}$$

$$= \frac{\text{Rs } 1,01,000 \times 100}{\text{Rs } 2,43,000 + 60,000} = 33\ 1/3\%$$

Calculation of Provision for Unrealised Profit

The composition of the Closing Stock of Tailoring Department is not given. The Tailoring Department possesses stock of Rs 14,000. There is no doubt that the stock consists of goods from Piecegoods and Outside. It can be assumed that the stock consist of both types of goods *i.e.* from Piecegoods and Outside, in the ratio of their purchases. Therefore, the value of goods of Piecegoods Department included in the closing stock of Tailoring Department can be calculated as under:

$$\frac{\text{Value of Purchases from Piece goods Dept.}}{\text{Value of Total Purchases}} \times \text{Total Closing Stock of Tailoring Dept.}$$

$$= \frac{\text{Rs } 60,000}{\text{Rs } 70,000} \times 14,000 = \text{Rs } 12,000$$

So, unrealised profit thereof = 33 1/3% of Rs 12,000 = Rs 4,000

Balance Sheet as on 31st March 2005

Liabilities		*Rs*	*Assets*		*Rs*
Capital:	1,20,000		Machinery	12,000	
Add: Profit	1,33,800		*Less*: Depreciation	1,200	10,800
	2,53,800		Closing Stock		
Less: Drawings	1,00,000	1,53,800	Piecegoods	38,600	
			Tailoring	14,000	
Creditors		7,000		52,600	
			Less: Provision for unrealised Profit	4,000	48,600
			Sundry Debtors		54,000
			Cash at Bank		41,000
			Cash in hand		6,400
		1,60,800			1,60,800

ILLUSTRATION 22.7

Following is the Trial Balance of Mr. Rajan as on 31st December 2006

		Dr. *Rs.*	*Cr.* *Rs.*
Capital A/c		–	40,000
Drawings A/c		1,500	–
Opening Stock	Dept. A	8,500	–
	Dept. B	5,700	–
	Dept. C	1,200	–
Purchases	Dept. A	22,000	–
	Dept. B	17,000	–
	Dept. C	8,000	–
Sales	Dept. A	–	54,000
	Dept. B	–	33,000
	Dept. C	–	21,000
Sales Returns	Dept. A	4,000	–
	Dept. B	3,000	–
	Dept. C	1,000	–
Freight and Carriage	Dept. A	1,400	–
	Dept. B	800	–
	Dept. C	200	–
Wages	Dept. A	800	–
	Dept. B	550	–
	Dept. C	150	–
Furniture & fixtures		4,600	–
Plant and Machinery		20,000	–
Bills Receivable		4,200	–
Bills payable		–	8,000
Motor vehicles		40,000	–
Sundry Debtors		8,000	–
Sundry Creditors		–	7,000
Salaries		4,500	–
Power and Water		1,200	–
Telephone charges		2,100	–

Bad debts	750	–
Rent and Taxes	6,000	–
Insurance	1,500	–
Printing and Stationery	2,000	–
Advertising	3,500	–
Bank overdraft	–	12,000
Cash in hand	850	–
	1,75,000	1,75,000

Prepare Departmental Trading and Profit and Loss A/c and the Balance Sheet taking into account the following adjustments:

a) Outstanding Wages Dept. B = Rs. 150
Dept. C = Rs. 50

b) Salaries payable = Rs. 500

c) Depreciate plant & machinery and motor vehicles @ 10%

d) Create a Reserve of 5% for bad and doubtful debts.

e) Each Department shall share the expenses in proportion to their sales.

f) Closing stock: Dept A = Rs. 3,500
Dept. B = Rs. 2,000
Dept. C = Rs. 1,500

(B.Com. Madras, MS)

SOLUTION

Departmental Trading A/c of Mr. Rajan for the year ending 31st December 2006

	A	B	C		A	B	C
	Rs.	Rs.	Rs.		Rs.	Rs.	Rs.
To Opening stock	8,500	5,700	1,200	By Sales	54,000	33,000	21,000
To Purchases	22,000	17,000	8,000	*Less:* Sales Returns	4,000	3,000	1,000
To Freight & Carriage	1,400	800	200	Net Sales	50,000	30,000	20,000
To Wages *Add*: Wages due	800	700	200	By Closing stock	3,500	2,000	1,500
To Power & water [sales ratio-5:3:2]	600	360	240				
To Gross profit c/d	20,200	7,440	11,660				
	53,500	32,000	21,500		53,500	32,000	21,500

Departmental Profit & Loss of Mr. Rajan for the year ending 31st December 2006

	A	B	C		A	B	C
	Rs.	Rs.	Rs.		Rs.	Rs.	Rs.
To Salaries (5,000) (including due)	2,500	1,500	1,000	By Gross profit	20,200	7,440	11,660
To Telephone charges	1,050	630	420				
To Bad debts	375	225	150				
To Rent & taxes	3,000	1,800	1,200				
To Insurance	750	450	300				
To Printing & stationery	1,000	600	400				
To Advertising	1,750	1,050	700				
To Depreciation							
On Plant & Machinery	1,000	600	400				
On Motor vehicles	2,000	1,200	800				
To Provision for Debtors	200	120	80				
To Net profit	6,575		6,210	By Net loss	–	735	
	20,200	8,175	11,660		20,200	8,175	11,660

Note: All expenses are divided in Sales Ratio, as per instruction given.
Sales Ratio = A – Rs. 50,000, B – Rs. 30,000 C – Rs. 20,000 or 5 : 3 : 2

Balance Sheet of Mr. Rajan as on 31st December 2006

Liabilities			*Rs.*	*Assets*		*Rs.*
Capital	40,000			Fixture & Furniture		4,600
Less: Drawings	1,500	38,500		Plant & Machinery	20,000	
Add: Net profit (6,575 + 6,210)		12,785		*Less:* 10% Depreciation	2,000	18,000
		51,285		Motor vehicle	40,000	
Less: Net loss (Dept. B)		735	50,550	*Less:* 10% Depreciation	4,000	36,000
Salary due			500	Bills receivable		4,200
Outstanding wages				Sundry Debtors	8,000	
Dept. B	150			*Less:* 5% provision	400	7,600
Dept. C	50		200	Cash in hand		850
Bills payable			8,000	Stock:		
Sundry creditors			7,000	Dept. A	3,500	
Bank overdraft			12,000	Dept. B	2,000	
				Dept. C	1,500	7,000
			78,250			78,250

ILLUSTRATION 22.8

From the undermentioned information and instructions, prepare Departmental Trading and Profit and Loss Account in columnar form of the three Departments of the Outfitters Ltd.

	Tailoring	Ladies Wear	Outfitting
	Rs	Rs	Rs
Stock on 1st January 2005	41,280	33,975	93,721
Stock on 31st December 2005	32,840	13,828	81,626
Purchases	2,10,342	75,296	1,39,109
Purchase Returns	14,382	5,629	1,823
Sales for the year	4,00,173	1,54,085	3,62,189
Sales Returns	Nil	3,259	11,217
Wages	72,823	30,084	24,613

Goods were transferred as follows (all at cost):

Tailoring to Ladies wear Rs 389 and Outfitting Rs 6,679; Ladies wear to Tailoring Rs 5,315; Outfitting to Tailoring Rs 4,271 and to Ladies Wear Rs 5,801.

Apportion equally: Stationery Rs 921; Postage Rs 663; General charges Rs 39,627. Insurance Rs 1,785 and Depreciation Rs 5,460.

Allocate the following further expenditure as you think best and append notes stating the basis selected for each item.

Establishment Rs 63,395; Bad Debts Rs 19,823; Advertising Rs 7,293 and Income Tax Rs 11,028.

Rent and taxes Rs 45,437 is to be split up in proportion to space occupied *i.e.* Tailoring 4; Ladies Wear 2; Outfitting 3 and others 2.

Approximate apportionment is all that is necessary: charge any odd balance to Outfitting Department.

(*CA*)

SOLUTION

Departmental Trading and Profit and Loss Account
for the year ended 31st December 2005

Dr.	Tailoring	Ladies Wear	Outfitting		Tailoring	Ladies Wear	Outfitting Cr.
	Rs	Rs	Rs		Rs	Rs	Rs
To Opening Stock	41,280	33,975	93,721	By Sales	4,00,173	1,54,085	3,62,189
To Purchases	2,10,342	75,296	1,39,109	By Transfer to Ladies Wear	389	–	5,801
To Transfer from Tailoring	–	389	6,679	By Transfer to Outfitting	6,679	–	–
To Transfer from Ladies Wear	5,315	–	–	By Transfer to Tailoring	–	–	4,271
To Transfer from Outfitting	4,271	5,801	–			5,315	
	2,61,208	1,15,461	2,39,509		4,07,241	1,59,400	3,72,261
Less: Returns	14,382	5,629	1,823	Less: Returns	–	3,259	11,217
	2,46,826	1,09,832	2,37,686		4,07,241	1,56,141	3,61,044
To Wages	72,823	30,084	24,613	By Closing Stock	32,840	43,828	81,626
To Gross Profit	1,20,432	60,053	1,80,371				
	4,40,081	1,99,969	4,42,670		4,40,081	1,99,969	4,42,670
To Stationery	307	307	307	By Gross Profit b/d	1,20,432	60,053	1,80,371
To Postage	221	221	221				
To General Charges	13,209	13,209	13,209				
To Insurance	595	595	595				
To Depreciation	1,820	1,820	1,820				
To Establishment (Sales Ratio)	28,176	10,565	24,654				
To Bad Debts (Sales Ratio)	8,810	3,304	7,709				
To Advertising (Sales Ratio)	3,242	1,216	2,835				
To Rent and Taxes (given Ratio 4 : 2 : 3)	16,523	8,261	12,392				
To Rent and Taxes– other space: equality	2,754	2,754	2,753				
To Income tax	2,804	1,122	7,102				
To Net Profit	41,971	16,679	1,06,774				
	1,20,432	60,053	1,80,371		1,20,432	60,053	1,80,371

Sales Ratio: 4,00,173 : 1,50,826 : 3,50,972 or 400 : 150 : 350 : or 8 : 3 : 7

Rent and Taxes of other space divided equally.

Income Tax has been divided on the ratio of profit before tax: that is Rs 44,776 : 17,802 : 1,13,874 or 45 : 18 : 11.

QUESTIONS

Objective Type Questions

I. State whether each of the following statements are "True" or "False":

1. Management expenses are charged to General Profit and Loss Account.
2. Depreciation on plant is divided equally over the different departments.
3. Stock Reserve for unrealised profit is charged to General Profit and Loss Account.
4. When goods are transferred from one department to the other, debit is given to the Receiving Department.
5. Items of expenses, which can be identified with a particular department, are charged to that department.

[Ans : 1. True: 2. False : 3. True: 4. True: 5. True.]

II. Fill in the blanks:

1. Rent and rates are apportioned on the basis of .... occupied by each department.
2. Depreciation on plant is divided on the basis of ......
3. Departmental accounts are prepared to know the .... or .... of each department.
4. Building expenses should be divided among the departments on the basis of .... by each department.
5. When goods are transferred from one department to the other, debit is given to .... department.

[Ans. 1. Floor Area; 2. Plant Value; 3. Profit. Loss; 4. Space Occupied; 5. Receiving.]

III. Choose the appropriate answer from the given alternative:

1. Non-Departmental items of expenses are charged to :
 (*a*) Departments on the basis of sales.
 (*b*) General Profit & Loss Account.
 (*c*) Departments, based on fixed assets employed.

2. Repairs to machinery is apportioned over the departments on the basis of:
 (*a*) Number of machines in each department.
 (*b*) Value of machinery.
 (*c*) Floor area of each machine.

3. What is the amount of gross profit on a sale of Rs. 1 lakh, if the rate of gross profit is 25% of cost:
 (*a*) Rs. 25,000
 (*b*) Rs. 20,000
 (*c*) Rs. 33,333

4. Selling expenses should be divided among the departments on the basis of:
 (*a*) Purchase
 (*b*) Space occupied
 (*c*) Sales

5. Rent and rates paid are apportioned among the departments on the basis of:
 (*a*) Sales
 (*b*) Space occupied
 (*c*) Purchase

Ans: 1. (b): 2. (b); 3. (b); 4. (c); 5. (b);

THEORETICAL QUESTIONS

1. What are the bases for the allocation of common expenses to different departments of an organisation? (*B.Com., Madurai*)
2. What are departmental accounts? Explain their advantages. (*B.Com., MK*)

3. Explain the procedure for the preparation of departmental accounts. *(B.Com., Bangalore)*
4. How are transfers from one department to another treated in departmental accounts? *(B.Com., Calicut)*

PRACTICAL PROBLEMS

1. From the following, prepare Departmental Trading and Profit and Loss Account for the year ended 31st December 2004

	Departments A	Departments B
	Rs	Rs
Stock (January)	40,000	–
Purchase from Outside	2,00,000	20,000
Wages	10,000	1,000
Transfer of goods from Department A	–	50,000
Stock (December) at cost to the Department	30,000	10,000
Sales to Outsiders	2,00,000	71,000

B's entire stock represents goods from Department A which transfers them at 25% above its cost. Administrative and selling expenses amount to Rs 15,000, which are to be allocated between departments A and B in the ratio of 4 : 1 respectively.

(B.Com., Madras, Madurai, Bombay, Calicut, Agra)

[Ans: Gross Profit (Dept. A) Rs 30,000
Gross Profit (Dept. B) Rs 10,000
Net Profit (Dept. A) Rs 18,000
Net Profit (Dept. B) Rs 7,000
Total Net Profit Rs 23,000]

2. The firm B.K. Industries have two Departments—Cloth and Tailoring. Tailoring Department gets all its requirements of cloth from the Cloth Department at the usual selling price. From the following particulars, prepare Departmental Trading and Profit and Loss Account for the year ended 31st March 2004:

	Cloth Dept.	Tailoring Dept.
	Rs	Rs
Stock on 1.4.2003	60,000	8,000
Purchases	3,40,000	5,000
Sales	4,00,000	80,000
Transfer of cloth to Tailoring Department	50,000	–
Manufacturing Expenses	–	12,000
Selling Expenses	5,000	2,000
Stock on 31.3.2004	1,00,000	15,000

The Stock in Tailoring Department may be assumed to consist 80% cloth and 20% other expenses. General Expenses of the business for the year comes to Rs 23,000. In 2002-03 the Cloth Department earned a gross profit of 30% on sales. *(B.Com., Madurai, Calcutta, Madras)*

[Ans:	Cloth	Tailoring
Gross Profit	Rs 1,50,000	Rs 20,000
Net Profit	Rs 1,45,000	Rs 18,000

Total Net Profit Rs 1,37,920]

3. The following balances were extracted from the books of Vijay Shanker. You are required to prepare departmental trading account and profit and loss account for the year ended 31st December, 2004, after adjusting the unrealised department profits if any.

	Dept. A	Dept. B
	Rs	Rs
Opening Stock	50,000	40,000
Purchases	6,50,000	9,10,000
Sales	10,00,000	15,00,000

General expenses incurred for both the departments were Rs 1,25,000 and you are also supplied with the following information: (*a*) Closing stock of Department A Rs 1,00,000 including goods from Department B for Rs 20,000 at cost to Department A. (*b*) Closing stock of Department B Rs 2,00,000 including goods from Department A for Rs 30,000 at cost to Department B. (*c*) Opening stock of Department A and Department B include goods of the value of Rs 10,000 and Rs 15,000 taken from Department B and Department A respectively at cost to transferee departments. (*d*) The gross profit is uniform from year to year. (*Company Secretaries*)

[Ans:	Dept. A	Dept. B
Gross Profit	Rs 4,00,000	Rs 7,50,000
Net Profit	Rs 3,50,000	Rs 6,75,000
Stock Reserve	Rs 5,000	Rs 6,000

Total Net Profit Rs 10,14,000]

4. X Ltd. has two departments A and B. From the following particulars prepare the consolidated Trading Account and Departmental Trading Accounts for the year endng 31st December, 2004:

	A	B
	Rs	Rs
Opening Stock (at cost)	20,000	12,000
Purchases	92,000	68,000
Sales	1,40,000	1,12,000
Wages	12,000	8,000
Carriage	2,000	2,000
Closing Stock:		
(*i*) Purchased goods	4,500	6,000
(*ii*) Finished goods	24,000	14,000
Purchased goods transferred:		
by B to A	10,000	
by A to B		8,000
Finished goods transferred:		
by A to B	35,000	
by B to A		40,000
Return of finished goods:		
by A to B	10,000	
by B to A		7,000

You are informed that purchased goods have been transferred mutually at their respective departmental purchase cost and finished goods at departmental market price and that 25% of the finished stock (closing) at each department represented finished goods received from the other departments. (*C.A. Inter*)

[Ans:	Dept. A	Dept. B
Gross Profit	Rs 42,500	Rs 42,000
Net Profit	Rs 41,625	Rs 40,200
Stock Reserve	Rs 875	Rs 1,800]

5. A firm had two departments, Timber and Furniture. Furniture was made by the firm itself out of timber supplied by the Timber Department at its usual selling price. From the following figures, prepare Departmental Trading and Profit and Loss Accounts for the year 2004:

	Timber Rs	Furniture Rs
Opening Stock (1-1-2004)	3,00,000	50,000
Purchases	20,00,000	15,000
Sales	22,00,000	4,50,000
Transfer to Furniture Department	3,00,000	–
Expenses–Manufacturing	–	60,000
–Selling	20,000	6,000
Stock–31.12.2004	2,00,000	60,000

The stocks in the Furniture Department may be considered as consisting of 75 per cent of timber and 25 per cent other expenses. Timber Department earned gross profit at the rate of 20 per cent in 2003. General expenses of the business as a whole came to Rs 1,10,000. *(B.Com., Bharatidasan)*

[Ans:	Timber	Furniture
Gross Profit	Rs 4,00,000	Rs 85,000
Net Profit	Rs 3,80,000	Rs 79,000

Additional Provision Required Rs 1,575]

6. Mr. Gopa Kumar of Bombay purchased goods for his three departments as under:

Department			
Department	A:	400 pieces	at a total cost of Rs 4,300
	B:	1,600 pieces	
	C:	1,000 pieces	

Sales for three departments were:

Department	A:	200 pieces at Rs 15 per piece
	B:	1,800 pieces at Rs 20 per piece
	C:	1,200 pieces at Rs 5 per piece

Other information about stock at the beginning was:

Department	A:	200 pieces
	B:	500 pieces
	C:	300 pieces

Mr. Gopa Kumar informs you that the rate of gross profit is the same for all departments.

Prepare Department Trading Account. *(B.Com. MS, Mysore; M.Com., Bombay)*

[Ans: Gross Profit:
Dept. A Rs 2,700
Dept. B Rs 32,400
Dept. C Rs 5,400]

7. The Directors of Departmental Stores Ltd. wish to ascertain approximately, the net profits of the A, B and C departments separately for the quarter ended March 2004. It is found impracticable actually to take stock on the date but adequate system of department account is in use and the normal rates of gross profit for the departments concerned are 40%, 30% and 20% on turnover, respectively. Indirect expenses are charged in proportion to departmental turnover.

Following are the figures for each department:

	A	B	C
Stock on 1.1.2004	30,000	35,000	15,000
Purchase to 31.3.2004	35,000	37,500	23,500
Sales to 31.3.2004	60,000	50,000	30,000

Direct Expenses	10,100	7,250	3,550

Total indirect expenses for the period (including those relating to other departments) were Rs 21,000 on total sales of Rs 4,20,000.

Prepare a statement showing gross profit and net profit after making reserve for stock at 10% in respect of each department.

(*B.Com., Madurai*)

[Ans:	Dept. A	Dept. B	Dept. C
Gross Profit	Rs 24,000	Rs 15,000	Rs 6,000
Net Profit	Rs 17,090	Rs 8,025	Rs 2,695]

8. The Trading and Profit and Loss Account of a Company for the six months ended 31st March 2004 is presented to you in the following form:

	Rs		*Rs*
To Purchases:		By Sales:	
Television (A)	1,40,700	Televisions (A)	1,50,000
Radio (B)	90,600	Radios (B)	1,00,000
Spare parts for servicing (C)	64,400	Receipts from Servicing and Repairs (C)	25,000
To Salaries and Wages	48,000	By Stock on 31.3.2004	
To Rent	10,800	Televisions (A)	60,100
To Sundry Expenses	11,000	Radios (B)	20,300
To Profit	34,500	Spare parts for Servicing (C)	44,600
	4,00,000		4,00,000

Prepare Departmental Accounts for each of three departments A, B and C mentioned above after taking into consideration the following information:

1. Televisions and radios are sold at the showroom. Servicing and repairs are carried out at the workshop.
2. Salaries and wages comprise as follows:

   Showroom 3/4

   Workshop 1/4

   It was decided to allocate the showroom salaries and wages in the ratio 1 : 2 between the Departments A and B.
3. The workshop rent is Rs 1,000 p.m. The rent of the showroom is to be divided equally between the Departments A and B.
4. Sundry Expenses are to be allocated on the basis of the turnover of each department.

(*B.Com., Bombay Delhi*)

[Ans:	Dept. A	Dept. B	Dept. C
Gross Profit	Rs 69,400	Rs 29,700	Rs 5,200
Net Profit	Rs 49,000	–	–
Net Loss	–	Rs 700	Rs 13,800]

9. From the following Trial Balance, prepare Departmental Trading and Profit and Loss Accounts for the year ended 31st December, 2004, and Balance Sheet as at that date

		Dr. Rs	Cr. Rs
Stock at 1.1.2004	A Dept.	5,400	–
	B Dept.	4,900	–
Purchases	A Dept.	9,800	–
	B Dept.	7,350	–
Sales	A Dept.	–	16,900

		Dr.	Cr.
	B Dept.	–	13,520
Wages	A Dept.	1,340	–
	B Dept.	240	–
Rent		1,870	–
Salaries		1,320	–
Lighting and Heating		420	–
Discount allowed		441	–
Discount received		–	133
Advertising		738	–
Carriage Inward		469	–
Furniture and Fittings		600	–
Plant and Machinery		4,200	–
Sundry Debtors		1,820	–
Sundry Creditors		–	3,737
Capital		–	9,530
Drawings		900	–
Cash in Hand		32	–
Cash at Bank		1,980	–
		43,820	43,820

The following information is also provided:

(*a*) Rent, Lighting and Heating, Salaries and Depreciation are to be apportioned to A and B Depts. as 2 : 1.

(*b*) Other expenses and income are to be apportioned to A and B Depts. on suitable basis.

(*c*) The following adjustments are to be made:

Rent pre-paid Rs 370, Lighting and Heating outstanding Rs 180, and depreciation on Furniture and Fittings and Plant & Machinery 10% p.a.

(*d*) The Stock at 31st December, 2004: A Dept. Rs 2,748, B Dept. Rs 2,401. (*I.C.W.A.*)

[**Ans:**	A Dept.	B Dept.
Gross Profit	Rs 2,840	Rs 3,230
Net Profit	–	Rs 1,463
Net Loss	Rs 339	–

Balance Sheet Total Rs 13,671]

10. Tailors Ltd. have two departments, Cloth and Outfitting. The latter department gets all its requirements of cloth from the Cloth Department at the usual selling price. On 31st December, 2004 the following was the Trial Balance:

		Dr. Rs	Cr. Rs
Share Capital		–	2,00,000
Stock: Cloth Department		80,000	–
Outfitting Department (cloth at cost to the company)		4,500	–
Purchases:	Cloth	11,00,000	–
	Outfitting	10,000	–
Sales:	Cloth	–	12,50,000
	Outfitting	–	1,50,000

Transfer of Cloth to Outfitting Department (Selling Price)	50,000	50,000
Directors' Fees and Remuneration	30,000	–
Wages and Salaries Cloth	20,000	–
—do— Outfitting	40,000	–
Rent & Rates (3/4 to Cloth)	8,000	–
Lighting (—do—)	2,000	–
Departmental Depreciation (Outfitting)	5,000	–
Depreciation (Cloth)	1,000	–
Office Salaries	16,000	–
Furniture and Fittings	20,000	–
Office Expenses	3,000	–
Equipment	50,000	–
Carriage inwards (on cloth)	66,000	–
Investments	1,00,000	–
Income from Investments	–	9,500
Cash at Bank	54,000	
	16,59,500	16,59,500

Closing stock of cloth on hand in the Cloth Department was Rs 96,000 and that in Outfitting amounted to Rs 7,500 (at cost to the respective departments). It is desired to ascertain profit or loss on strict accountancy principles. Trading conditions and accounting methods in 2004 were the same as in 2003.

(*B.Com., Madurai*)

[**Ans:** Cloth Out fitting
Gross Profit Rs 1,30,000 Rs 52,500
Net Profit Rs 1,21,500 Rs 45,000
General Net Profit Rs 1,26,750
Balance Sheet Total Rs 3,26,750]

11. From the following balances appearing in the books of Rama Rao prepare Departmental Trading and Profit & Loss A/c for the year ended 31-12-2004 and Balance Sheet as at that date:

Particulars	A Dept. Rs	B Dept. Rs	Total Rs
Opening Stock	1,70,000	14,500	31,500
Purchases	35,400	30,200	65,600
Sales	60,800	51,250	1,12,050
Wages	8,200	2,700	10,900
Rent, Rates, Taxes, Insurance			9,390
Sundry Expenses			3,600
Salaries			3,000
Lighting and Heating			2,100
Discounts Allowed			2,220
Discounts Received			650
Advertising			3,680
Carriage Inwards			2,340
Furniture & Fittings			3,000
Plant & Machinery			21,000

Sundry Debtors	6,060
Sundry Creditors	18,600
Rama Rao's Capital	47,660
Rama Rao's Drawings	4,500
Cash at Bank	9,900
Cash in Hand	170

The following information is also provided:

(1) Internal transfer of goods from A Dept. to B Dept. Rs 420

(2) The items Rent, Rates, Taxes and Insurance, Sundry Expenses, Lighting and Heating, Salaries and Carriage Inwards to be apportioned 2 : 1.

(3) Advertisement to be apportioned equally.

(4) Discounts allowed and received are apportioned on the basis of Department Sales and Purchases (excluding transfers).

(5) Depreciation at 10% p.a. on furniture and fittings and on Plant and Machinery to be charged 3/4 to A Dept. and 1/4 to B Dept.

(6) Services rendered by B Dept. to A Dept. included in Wages Rs 500.

(7) Closing Stock A Dept. Rs 16,740, B Dept. Rs 12,050.

(8) There are no additions or sales of Plant or furniture. (*B.Com., Madras*)

[Ans:	A Dept.	B Dept.
Gross Profit	Rs 15,300	Rs 15,200
Net Profit	–	Rs 6,014
Net Loss	Rs 1,254	–

Balance Sheet Total Rs 66,520]

12. A businessman wishes to ascertain the separate net profits of two departments X and Y for the six months ended 30th June, 2004. It is not practicable to take stock on that date. However, the rates of gross profits (calculated without reference to direct expenses) are determined at 40 per cent and 30 per cent on sales at the two departments respectively. There are in all six departments. Indirect expenses are to be charged in proportion to departmental sales except as to one-third, which is to be divided equally. The following figures are extracted from the books for the period ending 30th June, 2004

	X Rs	Y Rs
Stock, 1st January, 2004	30,000	28,000
Sales	1,40,000	1,20,000
Purchases	90,000	72,000
Direct Expenses	18,300	28,400

Indirect Expenses of all six departments were Rs 36,000. The sales of other departments were Rs 1,40,000. Prepare Columnar Trading and Profit and Loss Account for the period ending 30th June, 2004, making a stock reserve for each department at 7 per cent on estimated value of stock at 30th June, 2004. (*B.Com., Madurai*)

[Ans:	X	Y
Gross Profit	Rs 56,000	Rs 36,000
Net Profit	Rs 24,780	–
Net Loss	–	Rs 2,720]

13. Complex Limited has three departments A, B and C. The following information is provided:

	A Rs	B Rs	C Rs
Opening Stock	3,000	4,000	6,000
Direct materials	8,000	12,000	–
Wages	5,000	10,000	–
Closing Stock	4,000	14,000	8,000
Sales	–	–	34,000

Stocks of each department are valued at cost to the department concerned. Stocks of A department are transferred to B at a margin of 50% above departmental cost. Stock of B department are transerred to C department at a margin of 10% above departmental cost.

Other expenses were:

	Rs
Salaries	2,000
Printing and Stationery	1,000
Rent	6,000
Interest paid	4,000
Depreciation	3,000

Allocate expenses in the ratio of departmental gross profits. Opening figures of reserves for unrealised profits and departmental stocks were:

	Rs
Department B	1,000
Department C	2,000

Prepare Departmental Trading and Profit and Loss Account. (*C.A. Inter*)

[**Ans:**	Dept. A	Dept. B	Dept. C
Gross Profit	Rs 6,000	Rs 3,000	Rs 3,000
Net Loss	Rs 2,000	Rs 1,000	Rs 1,000]

14. The following Trial Balance for the year ended 31st March, 2004, was extracted from the books of Shri Bikram Singh:

	Dr. Rs	Cr. Rs
Capital on 1-4-2003	–	50,000
Drawings Account	10,000	–
Stock on 1-4-2003		
Radio	45,000	–
Watches	21,000	–
Sales:		
Radio	–	2,94,000
Watches	–	1,46,000
Purchases:		
Radio	2,25,000	–
Watches	1,15,000	–
Salaries	12,600	–
Publicity Expenses	8,900	–
Rent, Rates and Taxes	3,200	–
Commission	10,600	–
Miscellaneous Expenses	5,000	–
Furniture and Fixtures	12,400	–
Sundry Debtors	16,800	–
4% Govt. of India Loan	10,000	–
Sundry Creditors	–	8,800
Interest	–	400
Provision for Bad and Doubtful Debts	–	800
Cash Balance	4,500	–
	5,00,000	5,00,000

Prepare the Departmental Trading and Profit and Loss Account for the year ended 31st March, 2004 after taking into account the following:

(*i*) The stock as on 31st March, 2004, was: Radio Rs 30,000; Watches Rs 24,000.

(*ii*) An amount of Rs 1,200 out of Sundry Debtors has to be written off as bad and the provision of doubtful debts has to be increased thereafter to 10 per cent of the debts outstanding.

(*iii*) The following expenses are outstanding as on 31st March, 2004:
Publicity Rs 1,300; Salaries Rs 1,200; Commission Rs 1,700

(*iv*) Provide 10 per cent depreciation on Furniture and Fixtures.

(*v*) Revenue Items to be allocated in the ratio of 2 : 1 as between Radios and Watches.
Ignore fractions of a Rupee in calculations. (*M.Com., Bombay*)

[**Ans:**	Radio	Watch
Gross Profit	Rs 54,000	Rs 34,000
Net Profit	Rs 22,467	Rs 18,233]

Chapter 23

Branch Accounts

Introduction – Objects of Branch Account – Types of Branches – Dependent Branch – Accounting Systems – Independent Branch – Characteristics of Independent Branch – Inter-Branch Transactions – In-transit items – Incorporation of Trial Balance in HO Books – Foreign Branch – Questions – Objective Type Questions – Theoretical Questions – Practical Problems.

INTRODUCTION

A branch is different from a department. First, a branch is situated in other locality while a department is located in the same building where Head Office is located. Secondly, through a branch sales can be increased while department can increase the efficiency of business. Thirdly, accounting records are kept at one place under departmental system while accounting records are kept at branch, though they are also kept at Head Office.

A producer or manufacturer, who produces goods on a large scale, likes to sell them in different places and for this purpose, he has to open branches in different places. When various divisions of the business are located in different places, in the same city or different cities, they are called branches. The producers set up their own branches in various places on the basis of demand for the goods they manufacture. The main place of business is the Head Office and its subsidiary units are known as branches.

OBJECTS OF BRANCH ACCOUNTS

A business firm establishes branches for the purpose of marketing the products or services. The parent firm is always interested to know the trading results of its branches. For this purpose, branch accounts are kept. The main purpose of Branch Accounts are as follows, in brief:

1. Branch Account helps to know the profit or loss of each branch.
2. It enables the Head Office to know the financial position of each branch.
3. It shows the requirements of goods or cash for each branch.
4. Branch Account is the basis and helps the Head Office to control the activities of Branch.
5. Suggestions and improvements are based on the Branch Accounts, which is a diagnostic measure.

TYPES OF BRANCHES

Branches can be broadly divided into three categories:

1. Dependent Branch
2. Independent Branch
3. Foreign Branch

1. DEPENDENT BRANCH

The branches depend solely on the Head Office for all their requirements *i.e.* for goods and expenses. These Branches operate as distribution departments for which goods are supplied by the Head Office to be sold on its behalf.

Main Features of Dependent Branch

1. Branch does not maintain its own set of books. The Head Office maintains record of all transactions relating to Branch.
2. Cash received on account of cash sales and from Debtors is daily remitted to Head Office or deposited with a local Bank, in the account of Head Office.
3. Generally, branch makes sales on cash basis; in certain cases credit sales may be made with authorisation from Head Office.
4. Branch receives goods from Head Office but outside purchases by Branch is not allowed.
5. Branch receives such goods at cost price or invoice price.
6. All expenses of Branch are directly paid by the Head Office through cheques.
7. Branch may be provided with small amount of cash in order to meet petty expenses—cartage, repairs, coolie etc. The Branch Manager keeps the accounts in Petty Cash Book or on impress system.

However, the Branch may maintain a Debtors' Register and Stock Register. Debtors' Register enables the Branch Manager to find out the amount due from customers on account of credit sales. Stock Register provides information relating to movement of goods from Head Office to Branch and *vice-versa*.

ACCOUNTING SYSTEM

The dependent Branch is required to send returns daily, weekly or monthly, as is instructed by Head Office, relating to the transactions taken place in Branch. Head Office on the basis of returns maintains accounts in their books in order to know the profit or loss of each branch for a particular period. The accounts of the dependent Branch are maintained by the Head Office in any one of the following ways:

1. Debtors System
2. Stock and Debtors System
3. Final Account System
4. Wholesale Branch System

1. Debtors System

Under this system the Head Office opens one Branch Account to record various transactions with the Branch. Branch Account is maintained in the form of a Debtor Account. In the books of the Head Office, Branch Account is debited with the goods supplied and all expenses met by Head Office and credited with all remittances and returns, similar to Customers Account. Therefore, the system can be called Debtors System or One Account System. The excess of the credit over its debit represents a profit or *vice-versa*, and is transferred to General Profit and Loss Account of Head Office. Branch Account is prepared in the books of Head Office and is a Nominal Account.

From the accounting point of view, the following are the further classifications:

(*a*) Branches receive goods from Head Office at cost price and are authorised to sell them for cash only.

(*b*) Branches receive goods from Head Office at cost price and are authorised to sell them for cash as well as on credit.

(*c*) Branches receive goods from Head Office at cost plus certain percentage.

(A) Branches receive goods from Head Office at Cost Price and are authorised to sell them for cash only

The following journal entries are passed in the books of the Head Office for recording different Branch transactions:

Transaction	Journal Entry	
1. Goods supplied to Branch	Branch Account	Dr.
	To Goods sent to Branch Account	
2. Goods returned by Branch	Goods Sent to Branch Account	Dr.
	To Branch Account	
3. Sales of goods for cash by the Branch	There is no journal entry in the books of Head Office. This transaction does not relate to the Head Office.	
4. Remittance of cash by Branch	Bank Account	Dr.
	To Branch Account	
5. Cash sent to Branch by the Head Office for expenses	Branch Account	Dr.
	To Bank Account	
6. Unsold stock lying with Branch	Closing Stock Account	Dr.
	To Branch Account	
7. Closing balance of Petty Cash	Branch Petty Cash Account	Dr.
	To Branch Account	
8. For Profit or Loss of the Branch		
(*a*) If Profit	Branch Account	Dr.
	To General Profit and Loss Account	
(*b*) If Loss:	General Profit and Loss Account	Dr.
	To Branch Account	

The above journal entries are posted in the Branch Account. The Branch Account appears as follows:

Branch Account

Dr. **(In the books of the Head Office)** Cr.

	Rs		*Rs*
To Stock (Opening Balance)		By Bank (Cash received)	
To Petty Cash (Opening Balance)		By Goods sent to Branch (Returns)	
To Goods sent to Branch		By Balance c/d:	
To Bank Account:		Closing Stock	
Salary		Petty Cash	
Rent		By Loss (if any) transferred to	
Petty Expenses		General Profit and Loss A/c	
To Profit, transferred to General Profit and Loss Account			

A simple Branch Account in the books of the Head Office appears as given above. The following entries may also be considered when there is opening balance and closing balance of stocks, furniture, Outstanding expenses, Pre-paid expenses etc.

Transaction	Journal Entry	
9. Closing balances of furniture, pre-paid expenses etc.	Branch Furniture Account	Dr.
	Branch Prepaid Expense A/c	Dr.
	To Branch Account	

10. Closing liabilities of Branch Account	Branch Account Dr. To Branch Liabilities A/c

Note: Closing balance of the Branch Account will be opening balance in the following year. S.No. 9 and 10 entries may be reversed.

11. To transfer the balance in Goods Sent to Branch Account	Goods Sent to Branch Account Dr. To Trading Account

ILLUSTRATION 23.1

Mr. Ram of Cochin has opened a Branch at Madras which sells goods for cash only. The following are the transactions between Branch Office and the Head Office for the year ended 31st December 2005:

	Rs
Opening Stock at 1st January 2005	2,00,000
Goods supplied to Branch	5,00,000
Cash sent to Branch for Rent	2,000
–do– for other expenses	1,000
Cash received from Branch during 2005	6,00,000
Closing Stock on 31st December 2005	1,50,000
Petty Cash balance on 31st December 2005	100

From the above, pass journal entries and prepare Madras Branch Account.

SOLUTION

In the books of the Head Office

			Dr. *Rs*	Cr. *Rs*
2005 Dec. 31	Madras Branch Account To Goods sent to Madras Branch A/c (Being goods supplied to Madras Branch)	Dr.	5,00,000	5,00,000
"	Madras Branch Account To Bank Account (Being cash sent to Madras Branch to meet Rent Rs 2,000 and other expenses Rs 1,000)	Dr.	3,000	3,000
"	Bank Account To Madras Branch Account (Being cash received from Branch)	Dr.	6,00,000	6,00,000
"	Stock at Madras Branch Account Petty Cash at Madras Branch Account To Madras Branch Account (Being entry for closing stock and Petty cash at the Branch)	Dr. Dr.	1,50,000 100	1,50,100
"	Madras Branch Account To General Profit and Loss A/c (Being net profit transferred)	Dr.	47,100	47,100

Dr. **Madras Branch Account** Cr.

			Rs			Rs
2005				2005		
Jan. 1	To Balance b/d:			Dec. 31	By Bank Account	6,00,000
	Opening Stock		2,00,000	Dec. 31	By Balance c/d:	
	To Goods sent to Madras				Stock	1,50,000
	Branch Account		5,00,000		Petty Cash	100
	To Bank Account:					
	Rent	2,000				
	Expense	1,000	3,000			
Dec. 31	To Net Profit transferred to					
	General Profit & Loss A/c		47,100			
			7,50,100			7,50,100

ILLUSTRATION 23.2

From the following particulars, prepare Branch Account showing the profit or loss of the branch:

	Rs
Opening stock at the Branch	30,000
Goods sent to Branch	90,000
Sales (Cash)	1,20,000
Expenses:	
Salaries	10,000
Other expenses	4,000

Closing stock could not be ascertained, but it is known that the Branch generally sells at cost plus 20%. The Branch Manager is entitled to a commission of 5% on the profit before charging such commission.

(CA Entrance)

(B.Com., MK, Mysore, Calicut)

SOLUTION

In the Books of Head Office

Branch Account

			Rs			Rs
?	To Balance b/d					
	–Stock		30,000	?	By Bank – Sales	1,20,000
	To Goods sent to Branch		90,000		By Balance c/d	20,000 (1)
	To Bank:				–Stock	
	Salaries	10,000				
	Other Expenses	4,000	14,000			
	To Manager's Commission		300 (2)			
	To General Profit & Loss		5,700			
	Account					
			1,40,000			1,40,000

Workings:

(1) Closing Stock:

Opening Stock	Rs 30,000
Add: Goods sent to Branch	90,000
	Rs 1,20,000

Less: Cost of sales (Rs 1,20,000 × $\frac{100}{120}$)	1,00,000
	20,000

(2) Manager's Commission:

Before charging commission, profit = Rs 6,000 (Rs 1,40,000 – 1,34,000)

Commission Payable = 5% of Rs 6,000 = Rs 300

(B) Branches receive goods from Head Office at Cost Price and are authorised to sell them for cash as well as on credit

All the journal entries we have studied under (*A*) above are equally applicable to this method also. Here the Branch is permitted to sell the goods on credit in addition to cash sales. Branch has to keep records relating to credit sales. When credit sales are allowed, the following additional journal entries are to be done in the books:

12. Credit Sales effected at the Branch	No entry in the books of Head Office	
13. Cash received from Debtors by the Branch	No entry in the books of Head Office	
14. Cash received from Debtors by the Branch and remitted to Head Office	Bank Account To Branch Account	Dr.
15. Discount allowed by the Branch to Sundry Debtors	No entry in the books of Head Office	
16. Bad Debts incurred by the Branch	No entry in the books of Head Office	
17. Goods returned by Branch Debtors to Branch	No entry in the books of Head Office	
18. For closing Debtors of the Branch Debtors	Branch Debtors Account To Branch	Dr.

ILLUSTRATION 23.3

M/s Mahaveer Company invoiced goods to their Branches at cost. From the following details relating to a Branch, prepare Branch Account for 2005 and calculate profit.

	Rs		Rs
Debtors on 31st Dec.	2,000	Discounts to customers	40
Goods sent to Branch during 2005	7,000	Stock on 1st Jan.	2,000
Goods returned by Branch	800	Stock on 31st Dec.	1,600
Goods returned by customers to Branch	150	Bad Debts	70
Cash Sales	4,300	Rent paid by Head Office	
Credit Sales	6,000	(1.1.2005 to 31.1.2006)	1,300
Cash remitted to Head Office	11,300	Insurance (1.4.2005 to 31.3.2006)	1,800
		Salaries and wages	2,800

(*B.Com., Madurai, Andhra*)

In the books of Mahaveer Company

Dr. **Branch Account** Cr.

2005		*Rs*	2005		*Rs*
Jan. 1	To Balance b/d:		Dec. 31	By Bank Account:	
	Stock	2,000		Cash Sales	4,300
	Debtors	3,260		Collected from Branch	
"	To Goods sent to Branch			Debtors	7,000
	Account	7,000	"	By Goods Sent to	

"	To Bank Account:			Branch Account	800
	Rent	1,300	"	By Balance c/d:	
	Insurance	1,800		Stock	2,000
	Salary and Wages	2,800		Debtors	1,600
				Rent prepaid	100
				Insurance prepaid	450
			"	By Loss, transferred to General Profit and Loss Account	1,910
		18,160			18,160

Note:

(*a*) Discounts, Bad Debts, Returns etc. will not appear in Branch Account.

(*b*) Rent is for 13 months. Therefore, Rs 100 is prepaid.

(*c*) Insurance is from April 2005 to March 2006. Thus Rs 450 is prepaid.

Workings:

1. The amount of cash collected from Debtors:

	Rs
Total Amount remitted to Head Office	11,300
Less: Cash from cash sales	4,300
The amount collected from Debtors	7,000

2. To find out Opening Balance, if any, Branch Debtors Account has to be prepared.

Branch Debtors Account

Dr.	*Rs*		*Rs* Cr.
To Balance b/d (Balancing figure)	3,260	By Discounts	40
To Credit Sales	6,000	By Bad Debts	70
		By Returns	150
		By Cash	7,000
		By Balance c/d	2,000
	9,260		9,260

ILLUSTRATION 23.4

A trading firm has a retail branch, which is supplied with goods from the Head Office and which keeps its sales ledger and remits all cash received daily to the Head Office, the branch expenses being paid by the Head Office by weekly cheques.

From the following particulars draw up the Branch Account as they would appear in the Head Office books for the six months ended on 31st December:

	Rs
Six months' credit sales	2,485
Cash Sales	1,460
Returns Inward	30
Cash received Ledger Accounts	2,387
Debtors on 1st July	1,345
Stock on 1st July	840
Stock on 31st December	1,280
Goods received from Head Office	2,276

Bad Debts at the Branch	65
Wages and other expenses	415
Rent, Rates and Taxes	402

(*B.Com., Manomoniam, MK; Mysore*)

SOLUTION

In the Books of Head Office

Branch Account

			Rs				Rs
July 1	To Balance b/d:			Dec. 31	By Bank:		
	Stock	840			Cash Sales		1,460
	Debtors	1,345	2,185		Cash on Ledger A/c		2,387
Dec. 31	To Goods Sent to Branch		2,276	"	By Balance c/d:		
					Stock	1,280	
	To Bank:				Debtors	1,348*	2,628
	Wages	415					
	Rent, Rates etc.	402	817				
	To General Profit and Loss A/c		1,197				
			6,475				6,475

Workings:

***Branch Debtors Account**

		Rs			Rs
July 1	To Balance b/d	1,345	Dec. 31	By Cash	2,387
Dec. 31	To Sales	2,485	"	By Bad Debts	65
			"	By Returns	30
			"	By Balance c/d	1,348
		3,830			3,830

Alternative Method

Trading and Profit and Loss Account for the year ended....

	Rs			Rs
To Stock	840	By Sales: Cash	1, 460	
To Goods sent to Branch	2,276	Credit	2,485	
To Wages	415		3,945	
To Gross Profit	1,664	*Less:* Returns	30	
				3,915
		By Closing Stock		1,280
	5,195			5,195
To Bad Debts	65	By Gross Profit		1,664
To Rent, Rates	402			
To General Profit & Loss Account	1,197			
	1,664			1,664

SOME IMPORTANT ASPECTS

While preparing Branch Accounts, special care should be taken with respect to the following items (points worth noting);

(1) Credit Sales, Bad Debts, Discount Allowed, Sales Returns

Credit sales, Bad debts, Discount allowed, Returns from Debtors to branch are not direct transactions from the Head office and as such they are not recorded in the Branch Account. However, these items will be taken into consideration while ascertaining the amount of Closing or Opening Balance of Debtors or Cash Received from Debtors, in the Memorandum Branch Debtors Account. In short, the above items are not shown in the Branch Account, however; the net effect of these items is automatically given effect in the Branch Account, by showing Opening Debtors, Closing Debtors and Cash Received from Debtors.

(2) Loss of Stock, Surplus of Stock

Shortage or surplus of stock at the Branch due to normal or abnormal reasons are not shown in the Branch Account.

(3) Depreciation of Fixed Assets

Depreciation of Branch fixed assets is not shown in the Branch Account. However, the opening balance of the fixed assets and closing balance of the fixed assets (of course deducting depreciation) are shown in the Branch Account. It is important to note that when opening balance and closing balance of fixed assets are entered in the Branch Account, automatically the effect of depreciation is there.

(4) Goods in Transit

Goods - in - transit is the difference between goods sent by Head Office and received by the Branch. Such goods will be shown either on both sides of the Branch Account or will be ignored altogether while preparing the Branch Account.

(5) Expenses Incurred by Branch

Expenses actually paid by Branch are not shown in the Branch Account. But the amount remitted by Head Office to Branch for meeting expenses is debited in Branch Account. If actual amount spent by Branch is less, the cash balance is shown as a part of closing balance, in the credit side of the Branch Account. This will be clear from the following example:

Example : If Opening Balance of Branch cash is Rs. 100; cash remitted by Head Office to Branch is Rs. 600 and the closing Balance of cash with Branch is Rs. 50; actual amount spent is Rs. 650 (Rs. 100 + Rs. 600 – 50), these items appear in Branch Account, as under:

Branch Account

	Rs		*Rs*
To Opening Balance of Cash	100	By Closing Balance of	
To Cash (remitted)	600	cash	50

(6) Purchase of Fixed Asset by Branch

When the Branch has purchased any fixed asset for cash, the remittance from the Branch to Head Office is to be reduced by the amount and fixed asset should be shown on credit side of Branch Account, as closing balance. If the Branch has purchased fixed asset on credit basis, the liability arising from such purchases should be shown on the debit side of Branch Account as closing balance of liability.

(7) Sale of Fixed Asset

When the Branch has sold fixed asset for cash, the proceeds is remitted to Head office. The asset will reduce in value to be shown on the credit side of the Branch Account. If the Branch has sold fixed asset on credit basis, the amount due is shown as debtors at the Branch at the close of the accounting period. Loss or profit arising from such sale of fixed asset will not be shown in the Branch Account as this is automatically adjusted through the above adjustments.

(8) In case Opening or Closing balance of Branch Debtors are not given, Memorandum Branch Debtors Account has to be prepared to find out missing figure. This account is prepared on the same pattern on which Total Debtors Account is prepared under Şingle Entry System. Similarly, if opening or closing balance of Branch stock is missing, then Memorandum Branch Stock Account has to be prepared.

ILLUSTRATION 23. 5

The Bombay General Stores invoices goods to their various branches at cost, and the branches sell the goods not only for cash but on credit also. Expenses of branches are paid by the Head Office. From the following particulars relating to the Calcutta Branch, prepare the neccesary account in the Head Office books:

		Rs
Stock at branch on 1 - 4 - 2006		8,000
Debtors at branch on 1-4 - 2006		4,000
Petty cash at branch on 1 - 4 - 2006		500
Furniture at branch on 1 - 4 - 2006		6,000
Goods sent to branch during 2006 -2007		22,000
Goods returned by branch		800
Cheques sent to branch during 2006-2007	Rs.	
For salaries	2,000	
For Rent	1,000	
For Petty cash	300	
		3,300
Cash remitted by branch during 2006-2007:		
Cash sales	10,000	
Cash received from debtors	9,000	
Credit sales during 2006-2007		19,000
Goods returned by debtors during 2006-2007		25,000
Discount allowed to Debtors		400
Bad debts		500
Stock at branch on 31-3-2007		100
Petty cash at branch on 31-3-2007		10,000
Write off depreciation on furniture @10%		200

SOLUTION

In the Books of the Bombay General Stores

Dr CALCUTTA BRANCH ACCOUNT *Cr*

Particulars	*Rs*	*Particulars*		*Rs*
To Balance b/d 1 - 4 - 2006		By Goods sent to branch A/c		800
Stock	8,000	" Bank:		
Debtors	4,000	Cash sales	10,000	
Petty cash	500	Cash received from debtors	9,000	
Furniture	6,000			19,000
" Goods sent to branch A/c	22,000	" Balance c/d 31-3-2007:		
" Bank:		Stock		10,000
Salaries	2,000	Debtors		19,000
Rent	1,000	Petty cash		200
Petty cash	300	Furniture		5,400
" General Profit and Loss A/c	10,600			
	54,400			54,400

Dr **Memorandum Branch Debtors Account** Cr

Particulars	Rs	Particulars	Rs
To Balance b/d 1-4-2006	4,000	By Cash	9,000
" Credit sales	25,000	" Discount	500
		" Returns	400
		" Bad debts	100
		" Balance c/d	19,000
	29,000		29,000

Note: Closing Balance of debtors not given in the problem has to be found out by preparing memorandum debtors account. Closing balance of furniture is after deducting depreciation. Branch profit can also be found out by preparing a trading and profit and loss account in the usual way by ignoring the opening and closing balances except stock, and showing all expenses and losses in the profit and loss account.

Alternatively: Trading and Profit and Loss Account of the Calcutta Branch for the year ended 31st March 2007

Dr. Cr

Particulars		Rs	Particulars		Rs
To Stock, 1 - 4 - 2006		8,000	By Sales:		
" Goods sent to			Cash	10,000	
Calcutta Branch A/c	22,000		Credit	25,000	
Less: Returns	800			35,000	
		21,200	*Less* : Returns	400	
" Gross Profit c/d		15,400			34,600
			" Stock, 31-3-2007		10,000
		44,600			44,600
To Salaries		2,000	By Gross Profit b/d		15,400
" Rent		1,000			
" Petty Cash Expense					
(Rs. 500 + Rs. 300 – Rs. 200)		600			
" Discount		500			
" Bad Debts		100			
" Depreciation		600			
" Net Profit		10,600			
		15,400			15,400

ILLUSTRATION 23. 6

The Bombay Trading Company invoiced goods to its branch at Delhi at cost. The Head Office paid all the branch expenses from its bank, except petty cash expenses which were met by the branch. All the cash collected by the branch was banked on the same day to the credit of the Head Office account. The following is a summary of the transactions of the branch during the year ended March 31, 2006.

	Rs.		Rs.
Stock, April 1, 2005	7,000	Bad debts	600
Debtors, April 1, 2005	12,600	Goods returned by customers	500
Petty cash, April 1, 2005	200	Salaries and wages	6,200
Goods sent to branch	26,000	Rent and Rates	1,200
Goods returned by branch	1,000	Sundry expenses	800
Cash sales	17,500	Cash received on ledger accounts	28,500
Credit sales	28,400	Stock, March 31, 2006	6,500
Allowances to customers	200	Debtors, March 31, 2006	9,800
Discount to customers	1,400	Petty cash, March 31, 2006	100

From the above particulars, prepare the Delhi Branch Account in the Head Office Books.

SOLUTION

(A) In the Books of the Bombay Trading Company

Dr DELHI BRANCH ACCOUNT Cr

Particulars		Rs	Particulars		Rs
To Balance b/d 1 - 4 - 2005:			By Bank:		
Stock		7,000	Cssh Sales	17,500	
Debtors		12,600	Cash received on ledger accounts	28,500	
Petty cash		200			46,000
" Goods sent to Branch A/c		26,000	" Returns to Head Office		1,000
" Bank:			" Balance on 31-3-2006:		
Salaries and Wages	6,200		Stock		6,500
Rent and Rates	1,200		Debtors		9,800
Sundry expenses	800				
		8,200	Petty cash		100
" General Profit & Loss A/c		9,400			
		63,400			63,400

Dr MEMORANDUM BRANCH DEBTORS' ACCOUNT Cr

Particulars	Rs	Particulars	Rs
To Balance b/d 1- 4- 2005	12,600	By Returns	500
" Credit sales	28,400	" Cssh	28,500
		" Discount	1,400
		" Allowances	200
		" Bad debts	600
		Balance c/d 31-3-2006	9,800
	41,000		41,000

Note: The branch account, as prepared above, is a nominal account showing profit or loss made by the branch. If it is desired to prepare a trading and profit and loss account for ascertaining profit or loss, the accompanying branch account will only be a personal account showing the total of closing balances as the difference between the two sides.

Alternatively: In the Books of the Bombay Trading Company

(B) TRADING AND PROFIT AND LOSS ACCOUNT OF THE DELHI BRANCH

Dr for the year ended 31st March, 2006 Cr

Particulars		Rs	Particulars			Rs
To Stock 1-4-2005		7,000	By Sales:			
" Goods sent to branch	26,000		Cash sales		17,500	
Less: Returns	1,000		Credit sales	28,400		
		25,000	*Less:* Returns	500	27,900	
" Gross Profit c/d		19,900				45,400
			" Stock 31-3-2006			6,500
		51,900				51,900
To Salaries and Wages		6,200	By Gross Profit b/d			19,900
" Rent and Rates		1,200				
" Sundry expenses		800				
" Petty cash expenses		100				
" Allowances		200				
" Discount		1,400				
" Bad debts		600				
" Net profit		9,400				
		19,900				19,900

POINTS WORTH NOTING

(A) If percentage (%) of *profit on COST* is given,
COST PRICE should be taken as Rs. 100.
For example: Profit (Loading) is 25% on Cost Price

Invoice Price (Sale Price)	Profit Rs.	Cost Price Rs.
125	25	100
1/5th	25	1/4th

1/5th of Invoice Price (Sale Price) = 1/4th of Cost Price
(or) 20% of Invoice Price (Sale Price) = 25% of Cost Price

(B) If percentage (%) of *Profit on Invoice price (Sale Price)* is given, Invoice Price (Sale Price) should be taken as Rs. 100.

For example, Profit (Loading) is 25% on Invoice Price (Sale Price)

Cost Price Rs.	Profit Rs.	Invoice (Sale) Price Rs.
75	25	100
1/3rd	25	1/4th

1/3rd of Cost Price = 1/4th of Invoice (Sale) Price (or) $33^1/_3$% of Cost price = 25% of Invoice (Sale) Price

(C) Branches receive goods from Head Office at Cost plus Certain Percentage

Under the above two methods -- (A) and (B) – the Head Office sends the goods at cost price. In certain cases, while sending the goods to Branches, the Head Office invoices the goods at cost plus certain percentage *i.e.* at selling price or market price or loaded price. The main purpose of sending the goods at invoice price is that the Head Office does not want to reveal the real profit to the management of the Branch. Here, the Opening stock, Goods sent to Branch, Goods returned by Branch and Closing stock will appear at invoice price only. To find out the real profit, adjustment entries are to be made to remove the excess price or the difference between the invoice price and the cost price. The accounting entries are given below:

1 To adjust the difference in the Opening stock at Branch	Stock Reserve Account Dr. To Branch Account
2. To adjust the difference in goods supplied to Branch	Goods Sent to Branch Account Dr. To Branch Account
3. To adjust the difference in the goods returned by Branch	Branch Account Dr. To Goods Sent to Branch Account
4. To adjust the difference in the Closing stock	Branch Account Dr. To Stock Reserve Account

Note: When we prepare Branch Account through Single Column Method the above adjustment entries are needed.

Alternatively, Branch Account can be prepared through Double Column Method and if so, an adjustment entry is needed. This we prove by solving a problem under both the methods. (Illustration 23.10)

ILLUSTRATION 23.7

The Head Office of a company invoices to its Coimbatore Branch at cost plus 20%. The Coimbatore Branch also purchases independently from local parties goods for which payments are made by the Head Office. All the cash collected by the Branch is banked on the same day to the credit of the Head Office and all expenses are directly paid by the Head Office except for a petty cash account maintained by the Branch for which periodical transfers are made by the Head Office. From the following particulars show the Branch Account as maintained by the Head Office reflecting the Branch profit for the year ended 31st December 2005.

	Rs
Imprest Cash:	
On 1st July 2005	2,000
On 31st December 2005	1,850
Sundry Debtors on 1st July 2005	25,000
Stock on 1st July 2005:	
From HO at invoice price	24,000
Directly purchased by Branch	16,000
Cash Sales	45,000
Credit Sales	1,30,000
Direct purchases	45,000
Returns from customers	3,000
Goods sent to Branch at invoice price	60,000
Transfer from HO for petty expenses	2,500
Bad debts	1,000
Discount to customers	2,000
Cash received from customers	1,25,000
Branch Expenses	3,000
Stock: (31.12.2005)	
From HO at invoice price	18,000
Directly purchased by Branch	12,000

(*M.Com., Madurai, Bangalore, Calicut, Bharathiar*)

In the Books of H.O.

Branch Account

2005			Rs	2005			Rs
July 1	To Balance b/d:			Dec. 31	By Bank:		
	Stock: H.O.	24,000			Cash Sales	45,000	
	Local	16,000	40,000		From Debtors	1,25,000	
	Debtors		25,000			1,70,000	
	Petty Cash		2,000		*Less*: Petty		
Dec. 31	To Goods sent		60,000		Cash	150	1,69,850
"	To Bank A/c: Expenses		3,000	"	By Goods sent to		
"	To Petty Cash		2,500		Branch (Load)		10,000
"	To Direct Purchases		45,000	"	By Branch Stock		
	To Branch Stock Reserve		3,000		Reserve (Load)		4,000
"	To General P & L A/c		59,350	"	By Balance c/d:		
					Stock (HO)	18,000	
					Stock (Local)	12,000	30,000
					Debtors		24,000
					Petty Cash		
					(1,850 + 150)		2,000
			2,39,850				2,39,850

Note : Petty cash is maintained under imprest system. Therefore, the Branch has to deduct Rs 150 from the cash to be remitted to H.O., so that petty cash balance at the end to be Rs 2,000.

Memorandm Debtors Account

	Rs		Rs
To Balance b/d	25,000	By Cash	1,25,000
To Sales	1,30,000	By Sales Returns	3,000
		By Bad Debts	1,000
		By Discounts Allowed	2,000
		By Balance c/d (Bal. fig.)	24,000
	1,55,000		1,55,000

2. Stock and Debtors System

Under the Debtors System, the profit or loss can be found out by preparing a Branch Account in the books of Head Office. The Branch Account has been treated as a customer, a personal account in an impersonal name. This type of accounting treatment works well in small Branches. When authorised to make credit sales also, the Debtors System proves inadequate. Details of credit sales remains unaccounted in this system. To overcome this, Stock and Debtors System has been devised.

Under Stock and Debtors System, the Head Office maintains several accounts relating to each Branch. The following are the accounts to record the branch transactions:

(A) When Goods are Supplied at Cost

1. *Branch Stock Account* (Real Account): This account is a record of transactions relating to goods and discloses the gross profit or loss of a branch. Head Office can have effective control over the Branch stock.

2. *Branch Debtors Account* (Personal Account): This account is maintained to keep the transactions relating to Branch Debtors.

3. *Branch Expense Account* (Nominal Account): This account discloses all branch expenses and losses incurred by the Branch.

4. *Branch Profit and Loss Account* (Nominal Account): This account incorporates the gross profit from Branch Stock Account and expenses from Branch Expense Account. Its balance represents the net results.

5. *Goods Sent to Branch Account* is prepared to know the goods supplied to and returns received from the Branch.

6. *Branch Cash Account* reveals all the cash transactions with Branch.

(B) When Goods are Supplied at Invoice Price

1. *Branch Stock Account:* This account is maintained to record the transactions of goods at invoice price. This account will not disclose profit or loss, but discloses shortage, surplus or closing stock of goods.

2. *Branch Adjustment Account:* This account is kept for finding out gross profit made at the Branch. All loadings in the goods sent to the Branch, Opening Balance, Closing Balance, Returns from the Branch, apart from shortages and surpluses etc., are recorded in this account.

3. *Branch Debtors Account,*

4. *Branch Expense Account,*

5. *Goods Sent to Branch Account,* and

6. *Branch Profit and Loss Account* are explained above.

ILLUSTRATION 23.8 (Missing value of credit sales)

From the following information, ascertain sales to the customers of the Branch on credit and prepare the Branch Account in the books of Head Office for the year ended 31st December 2005. All expenses are paid by the Head Office.

	Rs
Stock on 31.12.2005	90,000
Stock 1.1.2005	60,000
Debtors on 1.1.2005	40,000
Debtors on 31.12.2005	60,000
Cash sales remitted to Head Office	1,50,000
Cash collected from Debtors and remitted to Head Office	1,60,000
Goods invoiced to Branch	3,60,000
Rent	3,000
Salary	6,000
Goods returned to Head Office	6,000
Petty Cash on 1.1.2005	100
Petty Cash on 31.12.2005	50
Sale of Gunny bags	200

(Goods are invoiced by Head Office at 20% above the cost)

(B.Com., Karnataka, Mysore)

SOLUTION

In the books of Head Office

Branch Account

Dr.		Rs			Rs. Cr.
To Balance b/d:			By Cash A/c		
Stock	60,000		Cash Sales	1,50,000	
Debtors	40,000		Cash Collected	1,60,000	
Petty Cash	100	1,00,100	Sales of Bags	200	3,10,200
To Goods Sent to Branch A/c		3,60,000	By Stock Reserve A/c		10,000
To Bank A/c:			By Goods Sent to Branch A/c		
Rent	3,000		Returns		6,000
Salary	6,000	9,000	By Goods Sent to Branch A/c		
			Loading in Goods Sent		60,000
To Stock Reserve A/c		15,000	By Balance c/d:		
To Goods Sent to Branch A/c		1,000	Stock	90,000	
To General Profit and Loss A/c		51,150	Debtors	60,000	
			Petty Cash	50	1,50,050
		5,36,250			5,36,250

Debtors Account

Dr.	Rs		Rs Cr.
To Balance b/d	40,000	By Cash A/c	1,60,000
To Sales–Credit (Balancing figure)	1,80,000	By Balance c/d	60,000
	2,20,000		2,20,000

ILLUSTRATION 23.9 (Imprest system of Petty Cash and Assets Purchased by Branch)

Mr. Govind had a Branch at Agra. Goods are supplied by Head Office to Branch at cost plus 25%. All the

Branch expenses are paid by Head Office, except petty expenses, which are to be paid out of petty cash balance of Rs 200 kept on Imprest System.

	Rs
Stock on 1.1.2005	5,000
Debtors on 1.1.2005	3,000
Petty Cash on 1.1.2005	200
Furniture on 1.1.2005	6,000
Goods invoiced to Branch	20,000
Returns from Debtors	1,000
Allowances to Customers	100
Bad Debts written off	50
Cash Sales	3,000
Credit Sales	15,000
Expenses at Branch:	
Salary	1,000
Rent (for 9 months)	900
Petty expenses paid by Branch Manager	120
Furniture purchased by Branch Manager (1.10.2005)	3,000
Cash paid to Head Office	16,000
Stock on 31.12.2005	3,000
Cash collected from Debtors	16,000

Write off 10% depreciation on Furniture. *(B.Com., Madurai, Bangalore)*

SOLUTION

In the books of Govind

Agra Branch Account for the year ended 31st Dec. 2005

Dr.		Rs			Rs Cr.
To Balance c/d:			By Cash Account		16,000
Stock	5,000		By Goods sent to Branch:		
Debtors	3,000		(Loading)		4,000
Petty Cash	200		(20,000 × 25/125)		
Furniture	6,000	14,200	By Stock Reserve		
To Goods Sent to Branch		20,000	(Opening Stock)		1,000
To Bank Account:			(5,000 × 25/125)		
Salary	1,000		By Bank c/d:		
Rent	900	1,900	Stock	3,000	
To Bank (Petty Cash)		120	Debtors	850	
To Stock Reserve			Petty Cash	200	
(Closing Stock)		600	Furniture	8,325	12,375
(3,000 × 25/125)			By General Profit and Loss		
To Rent Outstanding		300	Account		3,745
		37,120			37,120

ILLUSTRATION 23.10

Mr. Ganesh had a Branch at Agra and charges all goods sent to the Branch at cost plus 33 1/3%. It is arranged that all cash received by the Branch is to be paid daily to the Head Office Account in the Bank and necessary advice sent to the Head Office. The Branch is to effect very little credit sales. From the following particulars, prepare the Branch Account for 2005 under Single Column Method and Double Column Method.

	Rs
Stock on 1st January 2005	12,000
Goods sent to Branch	80,000
Debtors on 1st Jan. 2005	1,500
Cash sent to Head Office	1,24,000
Rent, Rates and Taxes	3,200
Salaries and wages	4,800
Debtors on 31st Dec. 2005	1,600
Stock on 31st Dec. 2005	14,800

SOLUTION

(*A*) *Single Column Method*

In the books of Head Office

Branch Account

Dr. Cr.

			Rs.			Rs.
2005				2005		
Jan. 1	To Balance b/d:			Dec. 31	By Bank Account	1,24,000
	Stock	12,000			By Branch Stock	14,800
	Debtors	1,500	13,500		By Branch Debtors	1,600
	To Goods sent to Branch		80,000		By Difference in value of opening stock	3,000@
	To Bank Account:				By Goods Sent to Branch A/c	20,000&
	Rent etc.	3,200				
	Salaries etc.	4,800	8,000			
	To Difference in value of Stock A/c		3,700*			
	To Net Profit, transferred to General Profit and Loss A/c		58,200			
			1,63,400			1,63,400

Note: The values of Opening Balance, Goods sent to Branch and Closing Stock are given under Invoice Price *i.e.,*

$$100 + 33\ 1/3\% = 133\ 1/3\%$$

Therefore, the excess price included:

$$\text{in Opening Stock} = \frac{12{,}000 \times 33\ 1/3\%}{133\ 1/3\%} = \text{Rs } 3{,}000^{@}$$

$$\text{in Goods sent to Branch} = \frac{80{,}000 \times 33\ 1/3\%}{133\ 1/3\%} = \text{Rs } 20{,}000^{\&}$$

$$\text{in Closing Stock} = \frac{14{,}800 \times 33\ 1/3\%}{133\ 1/3\%} = \text{Rs } 3{,}700^{*}$$

(B) Double Column Method:

In the books of Head Office

Branch Account

Dr.		Cost Price Rs	Invoice Price Rs		Cost Price Rs	Invoice Price Rs Cr.
To Balance b/d:				By Bank Account	1,24,000	1,24,000
Opening Stock		9,000	12,000	By Branch Stock A/c	11,100	14,800
Debtors		1,500	1,500	By Branch Debtors A/c	1,600	1,600
To Goods Sent to Branch Account		60,000	80,000	By Difference in value of opening stock	–	3,000
To Bank Account:				By Goods Supplied to Branch A/c	–	20,000
Rent etc.	3,200					
Salaries etc.	4,800	8,000	8,000			
To Difference in value of closing stock		–	3,700			
To Net Profit, transferred to General Profit & Loss A/c		58,200	58,200			
		1,36,700	1,63,400		1,36,700	1,63,400

The following points may be remembered while you prepare the Branch Account:

1. No entry is made for credit sales at the Branch in the books of Head Office. Head Office makes entry only for the cash received on account of remittance from the cash sales along with cash received from Branch Debtors.

2. Petty expenses, paid by the Branch Manager out of petty cash, are not shown in the Branch Account. Branch Account is debited with the opening balance of cash and further sum sent by Head Office to Branch. At the closing time, Branch Account is credited with the closing balance of Petty Cash. Thus, the petty expenses are automatically charged to Branch Account.

3. Head Office makes no entry for the discount allowed, Bad Debts written off, Returns made by Branch Debtors etc. But these are considered while preparing Branch Debtors Account.

4. Depreciation of Branch fixed assets is not shown in the Branch Account. However, the Branch Account is debited with the value of the fixed assets in the beginning of the accounting period and credited with the value of fixed assets at the end of the accounting period. Thus the difference *i.e.*, depreciation is automatically charged.

5. Fixed assets may be sold by Branch at a profit or loss, for which no entry is made in the Branch Account. The sale proceeds of such fixed assets are remitted to Head Office. Similarly when purchase of asset is made, remittance is reduced to that extent. When sale of asset takes place remittance increases and the value of asset decreases; when purchase of asset takes place remittance decreases and the value of asset increases. The Branch Account is recorded with the closing figure *i.e.*, Opening Balance + Purchase – Sale Proceeds of asset.

6. In case Opening or Closing balance of Branch Debtors are not given, Memorandum Branch Debtors Account has to be prepared to find out missing figure. This account is prepared on the same pattern on which Total Debtors Account is prepared under Single Entry System. Similarly, if opening or closing balance of Branch stock is missing, then Memorandum Branch Stock Account has to be prepared.

Journal entries under Stock and Debtor System

1. Goods supplied to Branch	Branch Stock Account To Goods Supplied to Branch A/c	Dr.
2. Cash Sales made at Branch	Branch Cash Account To Branch Stock Account	Dr.
3. Credit sales made at Branch	Branch Debtors Account To Branch Stock Account	Dr.
4. Goods returned to Head Office by Branch	Goods Sent to Branch Account To Branch Stock Account	Dr.
5. Goods damaged/destroyed etc.	Defective Goods Account To Branch Stock Account	Dr.
6. Cash received from Branch Debtors	Branch Cash Account To Branch Debtors Account	Dr.
7. Goods returned by Branch Debtors	Branch Stock Account To Branch Debtors Account	Dr.
8. Branch expenses	Branch Expenses Account To Bank/Cash Account	Dr.
9. On transferring Branch Expenses	Branch Adjustment Account To Branch Expenses Account	Dr.
10. Disposing of damaged goods (S.No. 5)	Branch Adjustment Account (Loading in such goods) Branch Profit & Loss Account (Cost price of such goods) To Damaged Goods Account	Dr. Dr.
11. Purchase of asset for Branch	Branch Asset Account To Cash Account	Dr.
12. Depreciation on Branch Assets	Branch Profit and Loss Account To Branch Asset Account	Dr.

ILLUSTRATION 23.11 (Stock and Debtors System)

Corkwood Industries, Mumbai, has a Branch at Mangalore to which office goods are invoiced at cost plus 25%. The Branch makes sales both for cash and on credit. Branch expenses are paid direct from Head Office and the Branch has to remit all cash received into the Head Office Bank Account at Mangalore.

From the following details, relating to calendar year 2005, prepare the accounts in the Head Office ledger and ascertain Branch profits. Branch does not maintain any books of account, but sends weekly returns to Head Office.

	Rs
Goods received from Head Office at invoice price	60,000
Returns to Head Office at invoice price	1,200
Stock at Mangalore Branch on 1st Jan. 2005	6,000
Sales in the year for cash	20,000
Sales in the year against credit	36,000
Sundry Debtors at Mangalore on Jan. 2005	7,200
Cash received from Debtors	32,000
Discounts allowed to Debtors	600
Bad Debts in the year	400
Sales returns at Mangalore Branch	800

Rent, Rates and Taxes at Branch	1,800
Salaries, Wages and Bonus at Branch	6,000
Office Expenses	600
Stock at Branch on 31st December 2005	12,000

(*CA Inter*)
(*B.Com., Osmania*)

SOLUTION

In the books of Corkwood Industries, Mumbai

Mangalore Branch Stock Account

Dr.	Rs		Cr. Rs
To Balance b/d	6,000	By Bank A/c	
To Goods Sent to Branch A/c	60,000	Cash Sales	20,000
To Branch Debtors A/c		By Branch Debtors A/c	
Returns	800	Credit Sales	36,000
To Branch Profit and Loss A/c		By Goods Sent to Branch A/c	
Surplus	2,400	Returns	1,200
		By Balance c/d	
		Closing stock	12,000
	69,200		69,200

Mangalore Branch Debtors Account

Dr.	Rs			Cr. Rs
To Balance b/d	7,200	By Bank A/c		32,000
To Branch Stock A/c		By Branch Profit and Loss A/c		
Sales	36,000	Discount	600	
		Bad Debts	400	1,000
		By Branch Stock A/c		
		Returns		800
		By Balance c/d		9,400
	43,200			43,200

Mangalore Branch Adjustment Account

Dr.	Rs		Cr. Rs
To Goods Sent to Branch A/c		By Balance b/d	
Load on Returns to Head Office	240	Load on Opening Stock	1,200
To Branch Profit and Loss A/c	10,560	By Goods Sent to Branch A/c	
To Branch c/d		Load on Goods Sent	12,000
Load on Closing Stock	2,400		
	13,200		13,200

Mangalore Branch Expenses Account

Dr.		Rs		Cr. Rs
To Bank A/c:			By Profit and Loss A/c	8,400
Rent, Rates etc.	1,800			
Salaries etc.	6,000			
Office Expenses	600	8,400		
		8,400		8,400

Mangalore Branch Profit and Loss Account

Dr.		Rs		Cr. Rs
To Branch Expenses A/c		8,400	By Branch Adjustment A/c	10,560
To Branch Debtors A/c			By Branch Stock A/c	2,400
Discount	600			
Bad Debts	400	1,000		
To General Profit and Loss A/c		3,560		
		12,960		12,960

Goods Sent to Mangalore Branch Account

Dr.	Rs		Cr. Rs
To Branch Adjustment A/c	12,000	By Mangalore Branch Stock A/c	60,000
To Branch Stock A/c	1,200	By Branch Adjustment A/c	240
To Purchases A/c	47,040		
	60,240		60,240

Note: Branch Stock Account discloses shortage or surplus after entering the closing stock at selling price on the credit side. Stock is taken at actual count. If the debit side is more, shortage occurs; and if credit side is more it is surplus. Shortage is entered on the credit side while surplus is entered on the debit side. In this illustration, it is surplus and is transferred to Branch Profit and Loss Account.

ILLUSTRATION 23.12 (Stock and Debtors System)

The Bright Trading Company Ltd. invoices goods to its Delhi Branch at cost plus 25%. Both cash and credit sales are effected by the Branch. Branch expenses are paid direct from Head Office, all cash received by the Branch being remitted to the Head Office. The following are the details of the transactions for the six months ended on 30th September 2005:

	Rs
Goods received from Head Office at Invoice price	20,000
Returns to Head Office at Invoice price	500
Stock at Invoice price on 1.4.2005	5,000
Credit Sales for the half year	11,000
Debtors on 1.4.2005	3,800
Bad Debts written off	300
Rent, Rates etc.	240
Salaries and Wages	800
Sundry Expenses	120
Sundry Debtors on 30.9.2005	2,540
Stock at invoice price on 30.9.2005	4,000
Returns from customers	200
Discounts allowed to customers	160
Cash received on ledger accounts	11,600
Cash Sales for the half year	10,800

Record the above transactions in the Head Office books and close the accounts concerned at 30th September 2005. (*C.A.*)

(*B.Com., Delhi, Agra*)

SOLUTION

In the books of Bright Trading Co. Ltd.

Branch Stock Account

Dr.		Rs			Cr. Rs
2005			2005		
April 1	To Balance b/d	5,000	Sept. 30	By Goods Sent to Branch A/c	500
Sept. 30	To Goods Sent to Branch A/c	20,000	Sept. 30	By Branch Debtors A/c	11,000
Sept. 30	To Branch Debtors A/c	200	Sept. 30	Branch Cash A/c	10,800
Sept. 30	To Branch Adjustment A/c (Apparent Profit)	1,100	Sept. 30	By Balance c/d	4,000
		26,300			26,300
Oct. 1	To Balance b/d	4,000			

Goods Sent to Branch Account

Dr.		Rs			Cr. Rs.
2005			2005		
Sept. 30	To Branch Stock A/c	500	Sept. 30	By Branch Stock A/c	20,000
Sept. 30	To Branch Adjustment A/c (Rs 19,500 × 25/125)	3,900			
Sept. 30	To Head Office Purchase A/c	15,600			
		20,000			20,000

Branch Debtors Account

Dr.		Rs			Cr. Rs
2005			2005		
Apr. 1	To Balance b/d	3,800	Sept. 30	By Branch Cash A/c	11,600
Sept. 30	To Branch Stock A/c	11,000	Sept. 30	By Branch Expense A/c (Discount)	160
			Sept. 30	By Branch Expense A/c (Bad Debts)	300
			Sept. 30	By Branch Stock A/c (Returns)	200
			Sept. 30	By Balance c/d	2,540
		14,800			14,800
Oct. 1	To Balance b/d	2,540			

Branch Expense Account

Dr.			Rs			Cr. Rs
2005				2005		
Sept. 30	To Branch Debtors A/c		160	Sept. 30	By Branch Adjustment A/c	1,620
Sept. 30	To Branch Debtors A/c		300			
Sept. 30	To Head Office Cash A/c					
	Rent, Rates etc.	240				
	Salaries and Wages	800				
	Sundry Expenses	120	1,160			
			1,620			1,620

Dr. **Branch Cash Account** Cr.

		Rs			Rs
2005			2005		
Sept. 30	To Branch Stock A/c	10,800	Sept. 30	By Head Office Cash A/c	22,400
Sept. 30	To Branch Debtors A/c	11,600			
		22,400			22,400

Dr. **Branch Adjustment Account** Cr.

		Rs			Rs
2005			2005		
Sept. 30	To Stock Reserve A/c (20% of Rs 4,000)	800	Apr. 1	By Stock Reserve A/c (20% of Rs 5,000)	1,000
Sept. 30	To Gross Profit c/d	5,200	Sept. 30	By Goods Sent to Branch A/c	3,900
				By Branch Stock A/c	1,100
		6,000			6,000
Sept. 30	To Branch Expense A/c	1,620	Sept. 30	By Gross Profit b/d	5,200
Sept. 30	To General Profit and Loss A/c (Net Profit)	3,580			
		5,200			5,200

Dr. **Stock Reserve Account** Cr.

		Rs			Rs
2005			2005		
Sept. 30	To Branch Adjustment A/c	1,000	Apr. 1	By Balance b/d	1,000
Sept. 30	To Balance c/d	800	Sept. 30	By Branch Adjustment A/c	800
		1,800			1,800
			Oct. 1	By Balance b/d	800

ILLUSTRATION 23.13

A Head Office in Kolkata supplies goods to its branch at Chennai at cost. The branch sells the goods for cash and on credit and remits the proceeds of the Head Office promptly, the branch expenses being met by the Head Office by cheque. The following are the transactions relating to the branch for the year ended 31st December 2005 :

	Rs
Branch Stock (1.1.2005)	6,000
Branch debtors (1.1.2005)	8,000
Goods sent to Branch during the year	45,000
Cash sales by the Branch during the year	22,000
Credit sales by the Branch during the year	52,000
Returns from customers during the year	2,000
Collections from Debtors during the year	42,000
Discount allowed during the year	2,000
Bad Debts written off during the year	1,000

Cheques sent by Head Office towards Branch Expenses:

Salaries	5,000	
Rent	2,500	
Petty expenses	500	8,000
Stock at Branch (31.12.2005)		9,000

Prepare necessary accounts in the H.O. books under synthetic method. *(B.Com., Bangalore, Poona)*

SOLUTION

In the books of Head Office

Chennai Branch Account

Dr.			Rs				Rs Cr.
2005				2005			
Jan. 1	To Balance b/d			Dec. 31	By Bank A/c		
	Stock	6,000			Remittance Received		
	Debtors	8,000	14,000		Cash Sales	22,000	
Dec. 31	To Goods Sent to Branch A/c		45,000		Collection from		
Dec. 31	To Bank A/c–Expenses:				Debtors	42,000	64,000
	Salaries	5,000		Dec. 31	By Balance c/d		
	Rent	2,500			Stock	9,000	
	Petty Expenses	500	8,000		Debtors	13,000	22,000
Dec. 31	To Profit and Loss A/c						
	Branch Profit Transferred		19,000				
			86,000				86,000

Goods Sent to Branch Account

Dr.		Rs			Rs Cr.
2005			2005		
Dec. 31	To Trading Account	45,000	Dec. 31	By Chennai Branch A/c	45,000

Working Note:

Closing Debtors have not been given in this problem. It can be ascertained by preparing a Memorandum Branch Debtors Account.

Memorandum Branch Debtors Account

Dr.	Rs		Rs. Cr.
To Balance b/d	8,000	By Bank – Collections	42,000
To Credit Sales	52,000	By Discount Allowed	2,000
		By Returns Inward	2,000
		By Bad Debts	1,000
		By Balance c/d (Balancing figure)	13,000
	60,000		60,000

ILLUSTRATION 23.14

Illustration No. 23.13 is solved under Stock and Debtors System:

SOLUTION:

In the books of Head Office

Branch Stock Account

Dr.		Rs			Rs. Cr.
2005			2005		
Jan. 1	To Balance b/d	6,000	Dec. 31	By Bank A/c	
Dec. 31	To Goods sent to			Cash Sales	22,000

		Rs			Rs
	Branch A/c	45,000		By Branch Debtors A/c	
Dec. 31	To Branch Debtors			Credit Sales	52,000
	Customers Returns	2,000		By Balance c/d	9,000
Dec. 31	To Branch Profit and Loss A/c				
	Gross Profit transferred	30,000			
		83,000			83,000

Dr. **Branch Debtors Account** Cr.

		Rs			Rs
2005			2005		
Jan. 1	To Balance b/d	8,000	Dec. 31	By Bank A/c	
Dec. 3	To Branch Stock A/c			Collection	42,000
	Credit Sales	52,000	Dec. 31	By Branch Stock A/c	
				Customers Returns	2,000
			Dec. 31	By Branch Expenses and Charges A/c	
				Discount Allowed 2,000	
				Bad Debts 1,000	3,000
				By Balance c/d	13,000
		60,000			60,000

Dr. **Goods Sent to Branch Account** Cr.

		Rs			Rs
2005			2005		
Dec. 31	To Trading A/c		Dec. 31	By Branch Stock A/c	45,000
	Transfer	45,000			

Dr. **Branch Expenses and Charges Account** Cr.

			Rs			Rs
2005				2005		
Dec. 31	To Bank A/c			Dec. 31	By Branch Profit and Loss A/c	
	Salaries	5,000			Transfer	11,000
	Rent	2,500				
	Petty Expenses	500	8,000			
Dec. 31	By Branch Debtors A/c					
	Discount Allowed	2,000				
	Bad Debts	1,000	3,000			
			11,000			11,000

Dr. **Branch Profit and Loss Account** Cr.

		Rs			Rs
2005			2005		
Dec. 31	To Branch Expenses and Charges A/c	11,000	Dec. 31	By Branch Stock A/c	
Dec. 31	To General Profit and Loss A/c			Gross Profit	30,000
	Branch Profit transferred	19,000			
		30,000			30,000

ILLUSTRATION 23.15

Mumbai Soap Mills Ltd. has two branches at Kolkata and Chennai. Goods are invoiced to branches at cost plus 50%. Branches remit all cash received to the Head Office and all expenses are met by Head Office. From the following particulars, prepare the necessary account on Stock and Debtors System to show the profit earned at the Branches:

	Kolkata Rs	*Chennai* Rs
Stock on 1.1.2005 (Invoice price)	9,300	15,600
Debtors on 1.1.2005	6,800	8,700
Goods invoiced to Branches (Cost Price)	34,000	36,000
Sales at Branches:		
Cash	25,010	35,000
Credit	31,000	30,100
Cash collected from Debtors	30,400	29,800
Goods returned by Debtors	1,200	1,500
Goods returned by Branch to H.O.	1,500	–
Goods transferred from Chennai to Kolkata	2,100	2,100
Surplus in Stock	–	300
Shortage in Stock	450	–
Discount allowed to Customers	200	350
Expenses at Branches	5,400	6,700

(*M.Com., Madurai*)

SOLUTION

Dr. **Branch Stock Account** Cr.

	Kolkata Rs	*Chennai* Rs		*Kolkata* Rs	*Chennai* Rs
To balance b/d	9,300	15,600	By Cash Sales A/c	25,010	35,000
To Goods Sent to Branch A/c	51,000	54,000	By Branch Debtors A/c	31,000	30,100
To Branch Debtors A/c (Returns)	1,200	1,500	By Goods Sent to Branch A/c (Returns)	1,500	–
To Goods Sent to Branch A/c (from Chennai)	2,100	–	By Goods Sent to Branch A/c (From Kolkata)	–	2,100
To Branch Adjustment A/c (Loading on Surplus)	–	100	By Branch Adjustment A/c (Loading on shortage)	150	–
To Branch P & L A/c (Cost of surplus)	–	200	By Branch P & L A/c	300	–
			By Balance c/d	5,640	4,200
	63,600	71,400		63,600	71,400

Dr. **Branch Debtors Account** Cr.

	Kolkata Rs	*Chennai* Rs		*Kolkata* Rs	*Chennai* Rs
To Balance b/d	6,800	8,700	By Cash	30,400	29,800
To Branch Stock	31,000	30,100	By Branch Stock A/c (Returns)	1,200	1,500
			By Branch Expenses A/c (Discount)	200	350
			By Balance c/d	6,000	7,150
	37,800	38,800		37,800	38,800

Branch Expenses Account

Dr.	Kolkata	Chennai		Kolkata	Chennai Cr.
	Rs	Rs		Rs	Rs
To Branch Debtors	200	350	By Branch Profit and Loss A/c	5,600	7,050
To Cash A/c	5,400	6,700			
	5,600	7,050		5,600	7,050

Branch Adjustment Account

Dr.	Kolkata	Chennai		Kolkata	Chennai Cr.
	Rs	Rs		Rs	Rs
To Branch Stock A/c	1,880	1,400	By Stock Reserve	3,100	5,200
To Branch Stock A/c (Loading on Shortage)	150	–	By Goods Sent to Branch	17,200	17,300
To Branch P & L A/c (Gross Profit)	18,270	21,200	By Branch Stock A/c (Loading on Surplus)	–	100
	20,300	22,600		20,300	22,600

Loading on goods sent to Branches

Kolkata			*Chennai*		
	Goods sent From Chennai	Rs 51,000 Rs 2,100		Goods sent *Less*: Transfer	Rs 54,000 Rs 2,100
		53,100			51,900
	Less: Returns	1,500			
		51,600			
1/3 thereof	Rs 17,200			1/3rd thereof	Rs 17,300

Branch Profit and Loss Account

	Kolkata	Chennai		Kolkata	Chennai
	Rs	Rs		Rs	Rs
To Branch Expenses A/c	5,600	7,050	By Branch Adjustment A/c (Gross profit)	18,270	21,200
To Branch Stock A/c (Cost of shortage)	300	–	By Branch Stock A/c (Cost of surplus)	–	200
To Net Profit	12,370	14,350			
	18,270	21,400		18,270	21,400

Goods Sent to Branch Account

	Kolkata	Chennai		Kolkata	Chennai
	Rs	Rs		Rs	Rs
To Branch Stock A/c (Returns)	1,500	–	By Branch Stock A/c	51,000	54,000
To Branch Adjustment A/c	17,200	17,300	By Branch Stock A/c	2,100	
To Branch Stock A/c	–	2,100			
To Purchases A/c (Transfer)	34,400	34,600			
	53,100	54,000		53,100	54,000

3. Final Account System (Branch Trading and Profit and Loss Account)

The profit or loss of a dependent Branch can also be known by preparing a Memorandum Branch Trading and Profit and Loss Account. This Account is usually prepared in cost price. Besides the final accounts, Branch Account is also to be prepared. This Branch Account is different from the Branch Account prepared under the Debtors System. The Branch Account, appearing under Debtors System, is a nominal account. But the Branch Account, appearing under Final Account System, is a personal Account. Generally the Branch Account, under this system, will have debit balance.

ILLUSTRATION 23.16

A Kolkata trading firm has a branch at Patna to which the goods are charged out at cost plus 25%. Branch keeps its own Sales ledger and remits daily all cash received to the Head Office. All expenses are paid from the Head Office. The transactions for the branch for the year 2005 are given below:

	Rs
Stock on 1-1-2005	55,000
Sundry Debtors on 1-1-2005	550
Petty cash balance on 1-1-2005	450
Cash Sales	13,250
Collections on Ledger Accounts	1,05,000
Goods returned to Head Office	1,500
Bad Debts	1,500
Allowances to Customers	1,250
Returns Inwards	2,500
Cheques sent to Branch	
For Rent	2,500
For Wages	1,500
For Salary and other Expenses	4,500
Stock on 31.12.2005	60,000
Sundry Debtors on 31-12-2005	15,000
Petty cash on 31.12.2005 (including sundry income of Rs 50 not remitted)	500

Prepare (*a*) the Branch Account and (*b*) Branch Trading and Profit and Loss Account for the year 2005 in the Head Office books. *(B.Com., Hons., Calcutta)*

(B.Com., Madurai, Bharathidasan)

SOLUTION

(a) In the books of Kolkata Head Office

Dr. **Patna Branch Account** Cr.

			Rs				Rs
2005				2005			
Jan. 1	To Balance b/d			Jan. 1	By Stock Reserve A/c		
	Stock	55,000			Load on Opening Stock		
	Debtors	550			(25/100 × 55,000)		11,000
	Petty Cash	450	56,000	Dec. 31	By Bank A/c–Remittance		
Dec. 31	To Goods Sent to				Received:		
	Branch A/c		1,00,000		Cash Sales	13,250	
Dec. 31	To Bank A/c Remittance				Collection from		
	for				Debtors	1,05,000	1,18,250
	Rent	2,500		Dec. 31	By Goods Sent to		
	Wages	1,500			Branch A/c		

Date	Particulars		Rs	Date	Particulars		Rs
	Salary and other				Returns from Branch		1,500
	Expenses	4,500	8,500	Dec. 31	By Goods Sent to		
Dec. 31	To Goods Sent to				Branch A/c		
	Branch A/c				Load on Goods Sent		
	Load on Return				(25/100 × 1,00,000)		20,000
	(25/100 × 1500)		300	Dec. 31	By Balance c/d		
Dec. 31	To Stock Reserve A/c				Stock	60,000	
	Load on Closing Stock				Debtors	15,000	
	(25/100 × 60,000)		12,000		Petty Cash	500	75,500
Dec. 31	To Profit and Loss A/c						
	Branch Profit Transferred		49,450				
			2,26,250				2,26,250

(b) Patna Branch Trading and Profit and Loss Account

Dr. **for the year ended 31st December 2005 (cost price)** Cr.

Particulars		Rs	Particulars		Rs.
To Opening Stock		44,000	By Sales–Cash	13,250	
To Goods Sent to Branch	80,000		Credit	1,24,700	
Less: Returns	1,200	78,800		1,37,950	
To Gross Profit c/d		60,650	*Less*: Returns	2,500	1,35,450
			By Closing Stock		48,000
		1,83,450			1,83,450
To Rent		2,500	By Gross Profit b/d		60,650
To Wages		1,500	By Miscellaneous Income		50
To Salary and other Expenses		4,500			
To Bad Debts		1,500			
To Allowances to Customers		1,250			
To Net Profit		49,450			
		60,700			60,700

Dr. **Memorandum Branch Debtors Account** Cr.

Particulars	Rs	Particulars	Rs
To Balance b/d	550	By Bank A/c–Collection	1,05,000
To Credit Sales A/c (Balancing figure)	1,24,700	By Bad Debts A/c	1,500
		By Allowances A/c	1,250
		By Returns Inwards A/c	2,500
		By Balance c/d	15,000
	1,25,250		1,25,250

ILLUSTRATION 23.17

The Bengal Trading Corporation invoices goods to its Cuttack Branch at cost which sells on credit as well as for cash. Cash received by the Branch is remitted to the H.O. Branch expenses are paid direct from the H.O. except petty expenses which are met by the Branch and for which periodical transfers are made from the H.O.

You are asked to prepare the Cuttack Branch Account and Branch Trading and Profit & Loss Account in the Head Office books from following the particulars:

	Rs
Opening Stock at Branch	6,000
Opening Petty Cash at Branch	250
Opening Debtors at Branch	15,200
Goods from Head Office	38,270
Goods returned by Customers	360
Total Sales	53,540
Cash Sales	15,320
Goods returned by customers	450
Allowances to customers	200
Discount allowed to customers	1,530
Bad Debts	370
Rent and Rates	1,200
Salaries and Wages	3,500
Petty expenses by the Branch	1,350
Closing Stock at Branch	7,560
Pilferage of goods at Branch	780
Closing Debtors at Branch	15,400
Closing Petty Cash at Branch	210

(*B.Com., Madurai, Punjab, Poona*)

SOLUTION

In the books of Bengal Trading Corporation

Cuttack Branch Account

Dr.		*Rs*			Cr. *Rs*
To Balance b/d			By Bank A/c–Remittance Received		
Stock	6,000		Cash sales	15,320	
Debtors	15,200		Collection from Debtors	35,560	50,880
Petty Cash	250	21,450	By Goods Sent to Branch A/c		
To Goods Sent to Branch A/c		38,270	Returns from Branch:	450	
To Bank A/c–Remittance for:			Stock	7,560	
Rent and Rates	1,200		Debtors	15,400	
Salaries and Wages	3,500		Petty Cash	210	23,620
Petty Expenses	1,310	6,010			
To Profit and Loss A/c					
Branch Profit Transferred		8,770			
		74,500			74,500

Alternatively

Cuttack Branch Trading and Profit and Loss Account

for the year ended...

Dr.		*Rs*			Cr. *Rs*
To Opening Stock		6,000	By Sales	53,540	
To Goods Sent to Branch	38,270		*Less*: Returns	360	53,180
Less: Returns	450	37,820	By Pilferage of Goods		780
To Gross Profit c/d		17,700	By Closing Stock		7,560
		61,520			61,520

To Rent and Rates	1,200	By Gross Profit b/d	17,700
To Salaries and Wages	3,500		
To Petty Expenses	1,350		
To Pilferage of Goods	780		
To Allowances to Customers	200		
To Discount Allowed	1,530		
To Bad Debts	370		
To Net Profit	8,770		
	17,700		17,700

Dr. **Memorandum Branch Debtors Account** Cr.

	Rs		Rs
To Balance b/d	15,200	By Returns Inward A/c	360
To Credit Sales A/c		By Allowances A/c	200
(Rs 53,540 – 15,320)	38,220	By Discount Allowed A/c	1,530
		By Bad Debts A/c	370
		By Bank A/c	
		Collection (Balancing figure)	35,560
		By Balance c/d	15,400
	53,420		53,420

Dr. **Memorandum Branch Petty Cash Account** Cr.

	Rs		Rs
To Balance b/d	250	By Petty Expenses A/c	1,350
To Bank A/c		By Balance b/d	210
Remittance (Balancing figure)	1,310		
	1,560		1,560

4. Wholesale System

There are many producers, now-a-days, who have their own retail shop (Branch). It deals in both retail and wholesale transactions. The profit rates earned by Branches differ between the retail sale and wholesale. Here, it is necessary to account the additional profit made by a Branch through retail trading over the wholesale trading. Wholesale price is always less than retail price. For instance, the cost of a product is Rs 100, the wholesale price is Rs 140 and the retail price is Rs 160. If the Branch sells the product, the profit will be Rs 60; but the real profit earned by the Branch is Rs 20 (Rs 160 – 140), which is the contribution of Branch. The profit of Rs 40 (Rs 140 – Rs 100) would have been made by the Head Office by selling on wholesale basis to others. Under this situation, to find out the real profit earned by a Branch, the Head Office charges the Branch with wholesale price. This facilitates the Head Office to know the retail profit earned by a Branch. In other words, the difference between the wholesale price and selling price is the pure profit on retailing.

The Head Office sends the goods to Branch at wholesale price and in case all the goods have been sold, there is no problem. If not, the unsold goods lying with the Branch will be at invoice price and in such case adjustment for the unrealised profit of the Head Office Trading Account must be made through Branch Stock Reserve Account in order to find out true profit of the concern as a whole.

ILLUSTRATION 23.18

Ascertain the profit that you consider as having been earned by the Delhi Branch of Jaipur Industries Ltd. from the following:

	Rs
Stock on 1st January 2005 (invoice price)	20,000
Goods sent to Branch during 2005 (at invoice price)	1,10,000
Expense at Branch during the year	6,000
Sales during the year	1,20,000

Goods are invoiced to the Branch at cost plus 25%; the sale price is cost plus 50%. Also ascertain the Stock Reserve that must be maintained in respect of unrealised profit. (*B.Com., Madras*)

SOLUTION

Jaipur Industries Ltd.

Trading and Profit and Loss Account of Delhi Branch

for the year ended 31st Dec. 2005

Dr.	*Rs*		Cr. *Rs*
To Opening Stock	20,000	By Sales	1,20,000
To Goods from Head Office	1,10,000	By Closing Stock*	30,000
To Gross Profit	20,000		
	1,50,000		1,50,000
To Expenses	6,000	By Gross Profit	20,000
To Net Profit transferred to General Profit and Loss	14,000		
	20,000		20,000

* Closing stock at Delhi Branch:

	Rs	
Opening Stock	20,000	
Goods from Head Office	1,10,000	1,30,000
Less: Cost of goods sold: (1,20,000 × 125/150)		1,00,000
Closing stock (invoice price)		30,000

Stock Reserve in respect of closing stock Rs 30,000 = 30,000 × 25/125 = Rs 6,000

ILLUSTRATION 23.19 (Wholesale Branch)

A Head Office sends goods to its Branch at 20% less than the list price. Goods are sold to consumers at cost plus 100%. From the following ascertain the profit made at the Head Office and the Branch on wholesale basis:

	Head Office Rs	Branch Rs
Purchases	2,00,000	–
Goods sent to Branch (Invoice price)	80,000	–
Sales	1,70,000	80,000

(*B.Com., Delhi*)

SOLUTION

Trading and Profit and Loss Account

for the year ended.....

Dr.	*Head Office Rs*	*Branch Office Rs*		*Head Office Rs*	Cr. *Branch Office Rs*
To Purchases	2,00,000	–	By Goods sent to Branch	80,000	
To Goods from H.O.	–	80,000	By Sales	1,70,000	80,000

To Gross Profit	1,15,000	16,000	By Closing Stock	65,000	16,000
	3,15,000	96,000		3,15,000	96,000
To Stock Reserve	6,000	–	By Gross Profit	1,15,000	16,000
To Net Profit Transferred to Head Office		16,000			
To Net Profit	1,09,000				
	1,15,000	16,000		1,15,000	16,000

Cost Price = 100%

Invoice price = 160% (20% less than List price)

List Price = 200% (100% + 100%)

Stock at Head Office:

			Rs
Purchases			2,00,000
Less: Goods sent to Branch			
(Rs 80,000 × 100/160)	=	50,000	
Less: Sales to Customers			
(Rs 1,70,000 × 100/120)	=	85,000	1,35,000
Stock at Head Office			65,000

Stock at Branch:

Goods sent to Branch	80,000
Less: Invoice price of goods sold	64,000
(80,000 × 160/200)	
Stock at Branch	1,6000

Stock Reserve = 16,000 × 60/160 = Rs 6,000

2. INDEPENDENT BRANCH

Independent Branch, like the Head Office, keeps all its records separately and independently on Double Entry System. Dependent Branches are those with little power and depend on Head Office for their supplies and expenses and is like a Minor Son. Independent Branches are those which make purchases from outside, get goods from Head Office, supply goods to Head Office and fix the selling price by itself. Thus an independent Branch enjoys a good amount of freedom like an American Son.

Characteristics of an Independent Branch

1. Independent Branch keeps a complete set of books. Such Branch gets goods from Head Office and from outside parties. It has its own Bank Account. Thus, the Branch keeps full system of accounting.
2. It prepares its own Trial Balance, Trading and Profit and Loss Account and Balance Sheet. Copies of these statements are sent to Head Office for incorporating in the Head Office Books.
3. The books contain an Account called "Head Office Account" or "Head Office Current Account" which is credited with everything received from the Head Office and debited with everything sent to Head Office. That is, all transactions relating to Head Office are recorded in this Account. The Head Office Current Account is thus a Proprietorship Account (*i.e.* Capital Account). Inspite of the independent status, the Branch cannot function without resources, and the resources, specially at the initial stage, are provided by the Head Office. Thus, the investments made by the Head Office seen from the Head Office Account is a

Personal Account in nature.

Similarly, the Head Office in its books opens an Account "Branch Current" Account, which is also a running account between the Branch and the Head Office and incorporates all the transactions between Branch and the Head Office. A special feature is that the Head Office Current Account in the books of Branch and Branch Current Account in the books of Head Office are maintained on a reciprocal basis.

The balance of these Accounts on any date will be equal to the difference between the assets and liabilities at the Branch on that date. The Branch Current Account in the Head Office books and Head Office Current Account in the Branch books show the same but opposite balance on a particular date.

4. There may be inter-branch transactions. That is, goods transferred by one Branch to another Branch of the same Head Office. Such entries have been explained later.
5. On receipt of the accounts and statements by the Head Office, the Head Office reconciles the balances, which is shown in Head Office Account in the Branch books with the Branch Account in Head Office books. Differences are reconciled. This is dealt with separately.

Accounting Entries, in the books of Branch, for Normal Transactions

1. Purchases made at Branch	Purchase Account To Cash/Creditors Account	Dr.
2. Sales effected at Branch	Cash/Debtors Account To Sales Account	Dr.
3. Payment of expenses at Branch	Expenses Account To Cash Account	Dr.
4. Any income received by the Branch	Cash/Bank Account To Concerned Income Account	Dr.

Accounting Entries for Transactions between Branch and Head Office

	Branch Book		*Head Office Book*	
1. Goods supplied to Branch by Head Office	Goods Supplied by Head Office A/c To Head Office A/c	Dr.	Branch Account To Goods Supplied to Branch Account	Dr.
2. Cash received from Head Office	Cash Account To Head Office A/c	Dr.	Branch Account To Bank Account	Dr.
3. Goods returned to Head Office by Branch	Head Office A/c To Goods Supplied by Head Office A/c	Dr.	Goods Supplied to Branch A/c To Branch Account	Dr.
4. Cash sent to Head Office by Branch	Head Office Account To Cash Account	Dr.	Bank Account To Branch Account	Dr.
5. When asset purchased by Branch and the Asset Account is kept by Head Office	Head Office Account To Cash Account	Dr.	Branch Asset Account To Branch Account	Dr.
6. Depreciation for the above	Depreciation A/c To Head Office A/c	Dr.	Branch Account To Branch Asset A/c	Dr.
7. Head Office expenses chargeable to Branch	Expense Account To Head Office A/c	Dr.	Branch Account To Profit & Loss A/c	Dr.

Inter-Branch Transactions

When a Head Office has several Branches, transactions may take place among themselves and such transactions are known as inter-branch transactions. No branch need carry an account with any other Branch. Inter-branch transactions are treated as the transactions with the Head Office. The entries are:

In the books of Sending Branch	Head Office Account To Goods Supplied Account	Dr.
In the books of Receiving Branch	Goods Received Account To Head Office Account	Dr.
In the books of Head Office	Receiving Branch Account To Sending Branch Account	Dr.

ILLUSTRATION 23.20

A Head Office has three Branches in three places–A, B and C. They are independent Branches. But they are under the control of Head Office. They buy and sell goods at cost price from one another, under intimation to the Head Office. The following table shows the transactions amongst the Branches:

Buying Branches	*Sending Branches*		
	A	B	C
	Rs	Rs	Rs
A	–	10,000	9,000
B	8,000	–	16,000
C	12,000	13,000	–

Show the journal entries in the books of Branches as well as in the books of Head Office to record the above transactions. *(B.Com., Rohtak)*

SOLUTION

A Branch Journal

				Dr	Cr.
				Rs	Rs
For Buying	Goods Received from Head Office A/c	Dr.		19,000	
	To Head Office Current Account				19,000
	(Being goods received from B Branch Rs 10,000 and from C Branch Rs 9,000)				
For Selling	Head Office Current Account	Dr.		20,000	
	To Goods Supplied to Head Office A/c				20,000
	(Being goods supplied to B Branch Rs 8,000 and to C Branch Rs 12,000)				

B Branch Journal

				Rs	Rs
For Buying	Goods Received from Head Office A/c	Dr.		24,000	
	To Head Office Current Account				24,000
	(Being goods received from A Branch Rs 8,000 and C Branch Rs 16,000)				
For Selling	Head Office Current Account	Dr.		23,000	
	To Goods Supplied to Head Office A/c				23,000
	(Being goods supplied to A Branch Rs 10,000 and to C Branch Rs 13,000)				

C Branch Journal

			Rs	Rs
For Buying	Goods Received from Head Office A/c	Dr.	25,000	
	To Head Office Current Account			25,000
	(Being goods received from A Branch Rs 12,000 and B Branch Rs 13,000)			
For Selling	Head Office Current Account	Dr.	25,000	
	To Goods Supplied to Head Office A/c			25,000
	(Being goods supplied to A Branch Rs 9,000 and to B Branch Rs 16,000)			

Head Office Journal

			Rs	Rs
	B Branch Current Account	Dr.	8,000	
	C Branch Current Account	Dr.	12,000	
	To A Branch Current Account			20,000
	(Being goods supplied by A Branch to B Branch Rs 8,000 and C Branch Rs 12,000)			
	A Branch Current Account	Dr.	10,000	
	C Branch Current Account	Dr.	13,000	
	To B Branch Current Account			23,000
	(Being goods supplied by B Branch to A Branch Rs 10,000 and C Branch Rs 13,000)			
	A Branch Current Account	Dr.	9,000	
	B Branch Current Account	Dr.	16,000	
	To C Branch Current Account			25,000
	(Being goods supplied by C Branch to A Branch Rs 9,000 and B Branch Rs 16,000)			

In-transit Items

Ordinarily, the balance shown by Branch Current Account in Head Office books is equal to the balance shown by Head Office Current Account in Branch books. The balances on these Current Accounts should be same, but in opposite sides, in both the set of books. The difference arises under the following circumstances:

1. When a Branch sends goods or cash to the Head Office, an entry is made by the Branch in the Head Office Account. But the same is recorded in the Head Office books only on receipt of goods or cash. For instance, the goods or cash sent by the Branch just before the closing of the accounting year may not reach the Head Office in the same accounting year. Therefore, in the books of the Head Office, Branch Account is not credited but at the same time in the books of Branch, Head Office Account is debited. Thus difference between the two books arises.
2. Similarly, Head Office may send cash or goods to Branch. On sending them, the Branch Current Account is debited in the books of Head Office. The corresponding entry is not passed in the Branch books, if the items are not received by them.

In this way, goods or cash sent by Head Office to Branch or Branch to Head Office and have not been received by the recipient, are known as *in-transit.*

1. When goods or cash sent by the Branch are in transit, the following entries are to be passed:

(a) Goods-in-transit	Goods-in-transit Account Dr. To Head Office Account
(b) Cash-in-transit	Cash-in-transit Account Dr. To Head Office Account

2. When goods or cash sent by Head Office are in transit, the following entries are to be passed:

(a) Goods-in-transit	Goods-in-transit Account Dr. To Branch Account
(b) Cash-in-transit	Cash-in-transit Account Dr. To Branch Account

The above said entries remain in the books for a short period or till the arrival of cash in transit or goods. When the in-transit goods or cash is received by the recipient, the entries made should be reversed and thus Transit Account is closed.

ILLUSTRATION 23.21

A Company at Chennai has two branches at Mysore and Bangalore. The Head Office and Branches close their books of Account on 31st December. The following adjustments have not yet been given effect to and therefore you are required to give the adjusting entry for the following:

(a) Remittance of Rs 4,500 made by Mysore to Head Office on 30th December received by the Head Office on 5th January.

(b) Goods valued at Rs 2,000 despatched by Bangalore Branch on 27th December under instructions from Head Office and received by Mysore Branch on 30th December.

(c) Depreciation amounting to Rs 1,100 on Mysore Branch assets, the accounts of such assets being maintained by Head Office.

(d) Goods worth Rs 9,000 despatched by the Head Office to Mysore Branch on 30th December received by that Branch on 7th January.

Show the entries in the books of the Head Office. (*B.Com., Bangalore, Calicut, Osmania, M.K.*) (*C.S.*)

SOLUTION

In the books of the Head Office

Journal Entries

	Particulars		Dr. Rs	Cr. Rs
	Cash-in-transit Account	Dr.	4,500	
	To Mysore Branch Account			4,500
	(Being remittance by Head Office still in transit)			
	Mysore Branch Account	Dr.	2,000	
	To Bangalore Branch Account			2,000
	(Being goods sent by Bangalore Branch to Mysore Branch under instruction from Head Office)			
	Mysore Branch Account	Dr.	1,100	
	To Mysore Branch Asset Account			1,100
	(Being depreciation of fixed assets when such assets being maintained at Head Office books)			
	Goods-in-transit Account	Dr.	9,000	
	To Mysore Branch Account			9,000
	(Being goods sent to Mysore Branch still in transit)			

ILLUSTRATION 23.22

A Head Office at Mangalore had branches at Puttur and Udupi. Give entries in the Head Office Books to rectify or adjust the following, assuming the books are closed on 31st March, 2006.

(1) Expenses, Rs. 4,800, to be charged to the Udupi Branch for work done on its behalf by the Head Office.

(2) Puttur Branch paid Rs. 3,600 as salary to a visiting Head Office official. The Branch has debited the amount to Salaries account.

(3) Depreciation at 10% p.a. is to be charged on Furniture at Puttur costing Rs. 10,000, the account of which is in the Head office.

(4) Goods costing Rs. 2,400 purchased by the Head Office from D'Souza Brothers, but payment made by Puttur Branch.

(5) A remittance of Rs. 3,750 made by Udupi Branch to Head Office on 28th March, 2006, was received by the latter on 1st April, 2006. *(B.Com, Mangalore)*

SOLUTION

In the books of the Mangalore Head Office
Journal Entries

S. No.	*Particulars*		*L.F.*	*Debit* Rs	*Credit* Rs
(1)	Udupi Branch A/c	Dr.		4,800	
	To Bank A/c				4,800
	(For expenses incurred by the H.O. on behalf of Udupi Branch)				
(2)	Salary A/c	Dr.		3,600	
	To Puttur Branch A/c				3,600
	(For salary paid by the Puttur Branch to a Head Office official) The Branch will pass the rectifying entry debiting the H.O. and crediting salary.				
(3)	Puttur Branch A/c	Dr.		1,000	
	To Puttur Branch Furniture A/c				1,000
	(For depreciation of branch furniture when Furniture A/c is in the Head Office books)				
(4)	Purchases A/c	Dr.		2,400	
	To Puttur Branch A/c				2,400
	(For purchases made by H.O. and payment for the same by Puttur Branch)				
(5)	No entry in the H.O. books				
	OR				
	Cash in Transit A/c	Dr.		3,750	
	To Udupi Branch A/c				3,750
	(For cash remitted by the Udupi branch but not received by the financial closing)				

ILLUSTRATION 23.23

A Head Office at Mumbai has Branch at Kolkata. The Company closes its account on 31st March each year. What adjustment entries are required to be passed in the books of both the Head Office and the Kolkata branch in regard to the following?

(*i*) A remittance of Rs. 5,000 by the Kolkata Branch on 22nd March is received by the HO on 5th April.

(*ii*) Goods worth Rs. 10,000 sent by HO on 20th March reach the Branch on 6th April.

(*iii*) Depreciation at 10% p.a. is to be provided on machinery at Kolkata costing Rs. 70,000, the account of which is in the books of HO.

(*iv*) The Kolkata Branch paid Rs. 100 dividend to a local shareholder on behalf of the HO.

(*v*) The Kolkata Branch received an amount of Rs.50 towards calls in arrears on shares from a local/ share-holder on behalf of HO. (*B.Com. Bangalore*)

SOLUTION

In the books of the Mumbai Head Office

Journal Entries

S. No.	*Particulars*		*L.F.*	*Debit* Rs	*Credit* Rs
(*i*)	No entry OR Remittance in Transit A/c To Kolkata Branch Account (Cash remitted by the Branch but not received by the H.O. on 31st March)	Dr.		5,000	5,000
(*ii*)	Goods-in-Transit A/c To Kolkata Branch Account (For goods sent to Branch, but received by the Branch after the date of financial closing)	Dr.		10,000	10,000
(*iii*)	Kolkata Branch Account To Kolkata Branch Machinery A/c (For depreciation of branch machinery when Machinery A/c is in the H.O. books)	Dr.		7,000	7,000
(*iv*)	Dividend A/c To Kolkata Branch A/c (For dividend paid by the branch on behalf of the H.O.)	Dr.		100	100
(*v*)	Kolkata Branch Account To Calls-in-arrear (For calls-in-arrear received by the branch on behalf of the H.O.)	Dr.		50	50

In the books of the Kolkata Branch

S. No.	Particulars		L.F.	Debit Rs	Credit Rs
(i)	Remittance in Transit A/c To Mumbai Office Account (For remittance to H.O. received by it after the date of financial closing)	Dr.		5,000	5,000
(ii)	No entry OR Goods in Transit A/c To Mumbai Office A/c (For goods sent by the H.O. but not received within the date of financial closing)	Dr.		10,000	10,000
(iii)	Depreciation A/c To Mumbai Office A/c (For depreciation of machinery, the account of which is in H.O. books)	Dr.		7,000	7,000
(iv)	Mumbai Office Account To Bank A/c (For payment of dividend on behalf of the H.O.)	Dr.		100	100
(v)	Bank A/c To Mumbai Office Account (For receiving call money on behalf of the H.O.)	Dr.		50	50

Incorporation of Branch Trial Balance in Head Office Books

When the Branches are dependent, the accounting for such Branches is done at Head Office itself and therefore the incorporation of Branch results is relatively simple. The profit is transferred from Branch Account, under Debtors System or Branch Adjustment Account, under Stock Debtors System, to General Profit and Loss Account. Independent Branch, which has its own accounting system, prepares a Trial Balance and sends a copy of it to the Head Office. After the receipt of Trial Balance from Branch, Head Office passes incorporating entries in order to prepare Branch Trading and Profit and Loss Account and a combined Balance Sheet. With the help of Branch Trial Balance, Head Office records in its books regarding Branch; this process is known as Incorporation of Branch Trial Balance. There are two ways:

(A) Incorporation of all the Items in Trial Balance

The items are divided into two parts:

(*a*) Items relating to Trading and Profit and Loss Account

(*b*) Items relating to Balance Sheet.

(*a*) **Items Relating to Trading and Profit and Loss Account**

1.	Branch Trading Account To Branch Account (Being incorporation of Opening Stock, purchases, goods from Head Office, carriage etc. from Branch Trial Balance)	Dr.	
2.	Branch Account To Branch Trading Account (Being incorporation of Sales less returns, Closing Stock etc. from Branch Trial Balance)	Dr.	
3. (*a*)	Branch Trading Account To Branch Profit & Loss Account (Being transfer of gross profit)	Dr.	
(*b*)	Branch Profit and Loss Account To Branch Trading Account (Being transfer of gross loss)	Dr.	
4.	Branch Profit and Loss Account To Branch Account (Being incorporation of Salaries, Rent, and similar items)	Dr.	
5.	Branch Account To Branch Profit and Loss Account (Being incorporation of Branch incomes)	Dr.	
6. (a)	Branch Profit and Loss Account To General Profit and Loss Account (Being transfer of Net Profit)	Dr.	
(*b*)	General Profit and Loss Account To Branch Profit and Loss Account (Being transfer of Net Loss)	Dr.	

By passing the above six journal entries, the Head Office prepares the Branch Trading and Profit and Loss Account. If the Head Office desires to close the Branch book by incorporating the assets and liabilities of the Branch, the following two more entries should be passed:

(*b*) **Items Relating to Balance Sheet**

7.	Branch Cash Account	Dr.	
	Branch Furniture Account	Dr.	
	Branch Stock Account	Dr.	
	Branch Asset Account	Dr.	
	To Branch Account		
	(Being incorporation of various assets from Branch Trial Balance)		
8.	Branch Account	Dr.	
	To Branch Liabilities Account		
	(Being incorporation of various liabilities from Branch Trial Balance)		

After passing all these eight entries, total of debit side of Branch Account will be equal to total of credit side Branch Account and thus the Branch Account in Head Office books will be automatically balanced. That is, if the branch assets and liabilities are incorporated, the Branch Account in Head Office books prepared after adjustments and incorporating will leave no balance.

If the Branch assets and liabilities are not incorporated, the Branch Account in Head Office books prepared in the above manner will leave a closing balance equal to net assets (Assets less liabilities) as on the closing date.

ILLUSTRATION 23.24

The following is the Trial Balance of a Bellary Branch as at 30th September 2005:

	Dr. Rs	Cr. Rs
Head Offie Account	3,240	–
Stock on 1-10-2004	6,000	–
Purchases	16,800	–
Goods received from Head Office	9,000	–
Sales	–	37,000
Goods supplied to Head Office	–	6,000
Salaries	1,600	–
Debtors and Creditors	3,700	1,850
Rent	860	–
Office Expenses	470	–
Cash and Bank balance	1,820	–
Furniture	1,360	–
	44,850	44,850

Stock on hand was valued at Rs 2,700. The Branch Account in the Head Office books on 30th September 2005 stood at Rs 460 debit. On 27th September, the Head Office forwarded goods to the value of Rs 2,500 to the Branch where they were received on 4th October 2005. Similarly, a cash remittance of Rs 1,200 by the Branch on 28th September was received by Head Office on 2nd October 2005.

You are to give the journal entries necessary to incorporate the above in the Head Office books showing the result of Trading at Branch and Branch appearing finally in the Head Office books.

(*B.Com., Karnataka, Madurai, Agra*)

SOLUTION

In the books of the Head Office

Date	Particulars		Dr. Rs	Cr. Rs
30.9.2005	Bellary Branch Trading Account	Dr.	31,800	
	To Bellary Branch Account			31,800
	(Being Opening Stock, purchases and goods from Head Office incorporated)			
	Bellary Branch Account	Dr.	45,700	
	To Bellary Branch Trading Account			45,700
	(Being sales, goods to Head Office and closing stock incorporated)			
	Bellary Branch Trading Account	Dr.	13,900	
	To Bellary Profit and Loss Account			13,900
	(Being Branch Gross Profit transferred to Branch Profit and Loss Account)			
	Bellary Branch Profit and Loss Account	Dr.	2,930	
	To Bellary Branch Account			2,930
	(Being Branch salaries, rent and office expenses incorporated)			
	Bellary Branch Profit and Loss Account	Dr.	10,970	
	To General Profit and Loss Account			10,970
	(Being Net Profit transferred to General Profit and Loss Account)			
	Bellary Branch Account	Dr.	1,850	
	To Bellary Branch Creditors Account			1,850
	(Being Branch Creditors incorporated)			
	Goods-in-transit Account	Dr.	2,500	
	To Bellary Branch Account			2,500
	(Being goods sent to Branch are in transit)			
	Branch Cash & Bank Account	Dr.	1,820	
	Branch Debtors Account	Dr.	3,700	
	Branch Furniture Account	Dr.	1,360	
	Branch Closing Stock Account	Dr.	2,700	
	Cash-in-transit Account	Dr.	1,200	
	To Bellary Branch Account			10,780
	(Being various assets incorporated)			

In the books of Head Office

Bellary Branch Trading Account

for the year ended 30th Sept. 2005

Dr. Cr.

		Rs			Rs
To Bellary Branch Account			By Bellary Branch A/c		
Opening Stock	6,000		Sales	37,000	
Purchases	16,800		Goods to H.O.	6,000	
Goods from H.O.	9,000	31,800	Closing Stock	2,700	45,700
To Bellary Gross Profit		13,900			
		45,700			45,700

Bellary Branch Profit and Loss Account
for the year ended 30th Sept. 2005

Dr.		Rs			Cr. Rs
To Bellary Branch A/c			By Bellary Branch A/c		
Salaries	1,600		Gross Profit		13,900
Rent	860				
Office Expenses	470	2,930			
To General Profit & Loss A/c		10,970			
		13,900			13,900

Bellary Branch Current Account

Dr.		Rs			Cr. Rs
To Balance b/d		460	By Bellary Branch Trading Account		
To Bellary Branch Trading Account			Opening Stock	6,000	
Sales	37,000		Purchases	16,800	
Goods to H.O.	6,000		Goods to H.O.	9,000	31,800
Closing Stock	2,700	45,700	By Bellary Branch P & L		2,930
To Branch Creditors		1,850	By Goods-in-transit A/c		2,500
			By Bellary Branch Assets A/c		
			Debtors	3,700	
			Cash & Bank	1,820	
			Furniture	1,360	
			Closing Stock	2,700	
			Cash in transit	1,200	10,780
		48,010			48,010

ILLUSTRATION 23.25

You are required to prepare the Trading and Profit and Loss account and consolidated Balance Sheet of Eve Ltd. in Calcutta and its Branch at Delhi. Give journal entries for inorporation of Delhi Branch Accounts in the Head Office and the Branch Account in Head Office books after incorporating therein the assets and liabilities.

The Trial Balance as on 31st December 2005 is as follows:

	H.O. Dr.	Branch Dr.	H.O. Cr.	Branch Cr.
	Rs	Rs	Rs	Rs
Manufacturing Expenses	30,000	10,000		
Salaries	30,000	10,000		
Wages	1,00,000	40,000		
Cash in hand	10,000	2,000		
Purchases	1,50,000	80,000		
Capital			2,00,000	
Goods received from H.O.		15,000		
Rent	8,000	4,000		
General Expenses	20,000	5,000		
Sales			4,50,000	1,50,000
Goods sent to Branch			15,000	
Purchases Returns			5,000	1,000
Opening Stock	50,000	30,000		
Discount earned			2,000	1,000
Machinery H.O.	1,50,000			

Machinery Branch	50,000			
Furniture–H.O.	7,000			
Furniture–Branch	3,000			
Debtors	40,000	15,000		
Creditors			30,000	5,000
H.O. Account				54,000
Branch Account	54,000			
	7,02,000	2,11,000	7,02,000	2,11,000

Closing stock at Head Office was Rs 40,000 and at Branch Rs 30,000. Depreciation is to be provided on Machinery @ 20 per cent and Furniture @ 15 per cent. Rent outstanding is Rs 500 (for Branch).

(*I.C.W.A. Inter*)

Head Office books

Journal

Date	Particulars			Dr. Rs	Cr. Rs
2005 Dec. 31	Delhi Branch Account		Dr.	10,450	
	To Delhi Branch Machinery Account				10,000
	To Delhi Branch Furniture Account				450
	(Being depreciation on Branch assets charged to Branch)				
	Delhi Branch Trading Account		Dr.	1,74,000	
	To Delhi Branch Account				1,74,000
	(Being incorporation of the following items:)				
	Stock	Rs 30,000			
	Net Purchases	79,000			
	Wages	40,000			
	Manufacturing Wages	10,000			
	Goods from H.O.	15,000			
		1,74,000			
	Delhi Branch Account		Dr.	1,80,000	
	To Delhi Branch Trading Account				1,80,000
	(Being incorporation of Branch Sales and Closing Stock)				
	Delhi Branch Trading Account		Dr.	6,000	
	To Delhi Branch Profit & Loss Account				6,000
	(Being the transfer of Gross Profit)				
	Delhi Branch Profit & Loss Account		Dr.	29,950	
	To Delhi Branch Account				29,950
	(Being incorporation of the following items)				
	Rent Rs 4,000 + 500	4,500			
	Salaries	10,000			
	General Expenses	5,000			
	Depreciation	10,450			
	Delhi Branch Account		Dr.	1,000	
	To Delhi Branch Profit & Loss A/c				1,000
	(Being incorporation of discount earned)				

General Profit and Loss Account	Dr.	22,950	
To Branch Profit & Loss Account			22,950
(Being the loss transferred to Profit and Loss Account of the Head Office)			
Branch Debtors Account	Dr.	15,000	
Branch Cash Account	Dr.	2,000	
Branch Stock Account	Dr.	30,000	
To Delhi Branch Account			47,000
(Being the transfer of various assets at Branch to Head Office books)			
Delhi Branch Account	Dr.	5,500	
To Branch Creditors Account			5,000
To Branch Expenses Outstanding Account			500
(Being the transfer of liabilities at Branch to Head Office books)			

Dr. **Delhi Branch Account** Cr.

	Rs		Rs
To Balance b/d	54,000	By Delhi Trading Account–Opening Stock, purchases etc.	1,74,000
To Branch Assets–Depreciation	10,450	By Delhi Profit and Loss Account–Expenses	29,950
To Delhi Trading Account–Sales and Stock	1,80,000	By Sundry Assets	47,000
To Delhi Profit and Loss Account–Discount	1,000		
To Sundry Liabilities A/c	5,500		
	2,50,950		2,50,950

Trading and Profit and Loss Account of Eve Ltd.
for the year ended 31st Dec. 2005

Dr. Cr.

	Head Office	*Delhi Branch*		*Head Office*	*Delhi Branch*
	Rs	Rs		Rs	Rs
To Opening Stock	50,000	30,000	By Goods sent to Branch	15,000	–
To Purchases: *Less* Returns	1,45,000	79,000	By Sales	4,50,000	1,50,000
To Goods from H.O.	–	15,000	By Closing Stock	40,000	30,000
To Wages	1,00,000	40,000			
To Manufacturing Wages	30,000	10,000			
To Gross Profit	1,80,000	6,000			
	5,05,000	1,80,000		5,05,000	1,80,000
To Rent + O/s	8,000	4,500	By Gross Profit	1,80,000	6,000
To Salaries	30,000	10,000	By Discount	2,000	1,000
To General Expenses	20,000	5,000	By Net Loss	–	22,950
To Depreciation:					
Machinery	30,000	10,000			
Furniture	1,050	450			
To Net Profit	92,950	–			
	1,82,000	29,950		1,82,000	29,950

Balance Sheet of Eve Limited
as on 31st December 2005

Liabilities		*Rs*	*Assets*		*Rs*
Share Capital		2,00,000	Fixed Assets:		
Profit & Loss:			Machinery: H.O.	1,50,000	
Head Office	92,950		Machinery Branch	50,000	
Less: Loss of Branch	22,950	70,000		2,00,000	
Sundry Creditors:			*Less*: Depreciation	40,000	1,60,000
Head Office	30,000		Furniture:		
Branch	5,000	35,000	H.O.	7,000	
Rent Outstanding		500	Branch	3,000	
				10,000	
			Less: Depreciation	1,500	8,500
			Current Assets:		
			Stock: Head Office	40,000	
			Branch	30,000	70,000
			Debtors: H.O.	40,000	
			Branch	15,000	55,000
			Cash: Head Office	10,000	
			Branch	2,000	12,000
		3,05,500			3,05,500

(B) Incorporation of Net Profit/Loss, Liabilities and Assets of Branch

Instead of transferring all the items, the Branch may prepare a Trading and Profit and Loss Account and only the Net Profit or Loss may be transferred to Head Office with or without assets and liabilities.

If the assets and liabilities are transferred, the Head Office will leave no balance. If, however, the assets and liabilities are not transferred, there will remain a balance in Head Office Account equal to net assets. At the time of preparing consolidated Balance Sheet, however, this account is substituted by Branch assets and liabilities. The entries are:

1. To transfer the assets	Branch Assets Account To Branch Account	Dr.
2. To transfer the liabilities	Branch Account To Branch Liabilities Account	Dr.
3. To transfer the profit Reverse entry for loss	Branch Account To General Profit & Loss Account	Dr.

ILLUSTRATION 23.26

The Agra Branch of the National Industry Ltd. sent the following Trial Balance to the Head Office on 31.12.2005:

	Dr. Rs	Cr. Rs
Sundry Creditors	–	8,600
Sundry Debtors	12,000	–
Cash on hand	6.250	–
Furniture	1,900	–

Stock on 1.1.2005	2,250	
Purchases	66,450	
Sales		1,12,500
Goods from Head Office	34,000	
Goods returned to Head Office		2,250
Wages and Salaries	5,500	
Trade Expenses	5,250	
Head Office Account		10,250
	1,33,600	1,33,600

The stock on hand on 31.12.2005 was Rs 5,200. Close the books of the Branch and prepare a Trading and Profit and Loss Account in the books of the Branch. Also prepare the Head Office Account.

(*B.Com., Madurai, Delhi, Madras*)

SOLUTION

In the books of Agra Branch
Trading and Profit and Loss Account
Dr. **for the year ended 31st December 2005** Cr.

	Rs		Rs
To Stock A/c 1-1-2005	2,250	By Goods Returned to Head Office	2,250
To Goods received from Head Office	34,000	By Sales	1,12,500
To Purchases	66,450	By Stock 31-12-2005	5,200
To Gross Profit c/d	17,250		
	1,19,950		1,19,950
To Wages and Salaries	5,500	By Gross Profit b/d	17,250
To Trade Expenses	5,250		
To Head Office A/c–Net Profit	6,500		
	17,250		17,250

Only the net profit is transferred to Head Office Account by debiting Profit and Loss Account and crediting Head Office Account, *i.e.*,

			Rs	*Rs*
	Profit and Loss Account	Dr.	6,500	
	To National Industries Ltd			6,500
	(Being transfer of profit to Head Office)			

In such case, Head Office and Balance Sheet appear as follows:

Dr. **The National Industries Ltd. Account** Cr.

	Rs		Rs
To Balance c/d	16,750	By Balance b/d	10,250
		By Profit and Loss A/c	6,500
	16,750		16,750

Balance Sheet
as on 31st December 2005

Liabilities	*Rs*	*Assets*	*Rs*
Sundry Creditors	8,600	Cash on Hand	6,250
Head office Account	16,750	Sundry Debtors	12,000
		Stock	5,200
		Furniture and Fixtures	1,900
	25,350		25,350

Alternatively, when branch assets and liabilities are transferred, Head Office Account shows no balance. In such case, the entries in the branch books are as follows:

			Dr. Rs	Cr. Rs
	The National Industries Ltd. A/c	Dr.	1,13,450	
	To Opening Stock A/c			2,250
	To Goods received from Head Office A/c			34,000
	To Purchase A/c			66,450
	To Wages and Salaries A/c			5,500
	To Trade Expenses A/c			5,250
	(Being transfer of revenue items to Head Office)			
	Returns to Head Office A/c	Dr.	2,250	
	Sales A/c	Dr.	1,12,500	
	Closing Stock A/c	Dr.	5,200	
	To National Industries Ltd. A/c			1,19,950
	(Being transfer of revenue items to Head Office)			
	To National Industries Ltd. A/c	Dr.	25,350	
	To Cash on Hand A/c			6,250
	To Sundry Debtors A/c			12,000
	To Closing Stock A/c			5,200
	To Furnitre and Fixtures A/c			1,900
	(Being transfer of assets to Head Office)			
	Sundry Creditors A/c	Dr.	8,600	
	To National Industries Ltd. A/c			8,600
	(Being transfer of Creditors to Head Office)			

Dr. **The National Industries Ltd.** Cr.

	Rs		Rs
To Sundries A/c–Revenue Items Debit Balances	1,13,450	By Balance b/d	10,250
To Sundries A/c–Assets	25,350	By Sundries A/c–Revenue Items Credit Balance	1,19,950
		By Sundries A/c–Liabilities	8,600
	1,38,800		1,38,800

Instead of transferring all the revenue items to the Head Office to close each account as is done above, the net effect of the revenue items may be transferred by passing a single entry for profit.

		Dr.	Cr.
		Rs	Rs
Profit and Loss A/c	Dr.	6,500	
To National Industries Ltd. A/c			6,500
(Being transfer of net profit to Head Office)			
The National Industries Ltd. A/c	Dr.	25,350	
To Cash in Hand			6,250
To Sundry Debtors A/c			12,000
To Stock A/c			5,200
To Furniture and Fixtures A/c			1,900
(Being transfer of assets to Head Office)			
Sundry Creditors A/c	Dr.	8,600	
To National Industries Ltd. A/c			8,600
(Being transfer of Branch Creditors to Head Office)			

Dr. **The National Industries Ltd.** Cr.

	Rs		Rs
To Cash A/c	6,250	By Balance b/d	10,250
To Sundry Debtors A/c	12,000	By Profit and Loss A/c	6,500
To Stock A/c	5,200	By Sundry Creditors A/c	8,600
To Furniture and Fixtures A/c	1,900		
	25,350		25,350

ILLUSTRATION 23.27

X Ltd., whose Head Office is in Kolkata, has a Branch at Chennai which obtains supplies partly from HO at cost and partly from other local suppliers. The Branch keeps a separate set of books. On 31st December 2005, the following balances were extracted:

	Kolkata		*Chennai*	
	Dr.	*Cr.*	*Dr.*	*Cr.*
	Rs	Rs	Rs	Rs
Share Capital	–	1,00,000	–	–
Fixed Assets	88,000	–	30,000	–
Opening Stock at cost	15,000	–	7,000	–
Profit and Loss A/c (1.1.2005)	–	15,000	–	–
Debtors and Creditors	18,000	6,000	5,000	3,000
Bank	17,000	–	4,000	–
Purchases and Sales	3,00,000	3,20,000	20,000	82,000
Sundry Expenses	12,000	–	9,000	–
Goods from HO to Branch	–	35,000	30,000	–
Current Accounts	26,000	–	–	20,000
	4,76,000	4,76,000	1,05,000	1,05,000

The difference between the balances of the Head Office and Branch Current Accounts is due to (*i*) Goods-in-transit, and (*ii*) Cash-in-transit as at the date of Trial Balance. Depreciation is to be charged @ 10% p.a. Stock on 31st December 2005 were Head Office Rs 25,000 and Branch Rs 12,000.

You are asked to prepare a combined Trading and Profit and Loss Account for the year ended 31s December 2005 and a Balance Sheet as on that date. (*M.Com., Madras, Madurai, Bangalore*)

SOLUTION

Balance Sheet
as on 31st December 2005

Liabilities		*Rs*	*Assets*		*Rs*
Share Capital		1,00,000	Fixed Assets:		
Profit & Loss A/c:			H.O.	88,000	
Balance (1.1.2005)	15,000		Branch	30,000	
Profit (During 2005)	69,200	84,200		1,18,000	
Current Liabilities:			*Less*: Depreciation		
Creditors:			(Rs 8,800 + Rs 3,000)	11,800	1,06,200
H.O.	6,000		Current Assets:		
Branch	3,000	9,000	Stocks:		
			H.O.	25,000	
			Branch	12,000	37,000
			Stock-in-Transit		5,000
			Debtors:		
			H.O.	18,000	
			Branch	5,000	23,000
			Bank:		
			H.O.	17,000	
			Branch	4,000	21,000
			Cash-in-Transit		1,000
		1,93,200			1,93,200

Note:

Goods-in-Transit and Cash-in-Transit:

	Rs
Difference between the two Current Accounts (Rs 26,000 – Rs 20,000)	6,000
Less: Goods-in-Transit (Rs 35,000 – Rs 30,000)	5,000
Balance, being Cash-in-Transit	1,000

3. FOREIGN BRANCH

In modern times the market for a commodity does not remain confined to a particular country but extends to other countries as well. In order to sell goods abroad branches have to be opened in that country; such branches are known as Foreign Branches. A Foreign Branch is nothing but an independent Branch located in a foreign country. One of the important distinctions between an independent Branch located in home country and one located in foreign country is that the latter maintains its books of accounts in the currency of the foreign country from where it is operating its business. When the Head Office receives the Trial Balance, the main problem is to convert it in the currency of the Head Office, because so long as the Trial Balance is not converted it cannot be incorporated in the Head Office books. The question, therefore, arises as to how the conversion is to be done where some fluctuation in the rates of exchange is obvious in the open market. The fluctuations may be grouped into three categories:

1. Stable currency where there is practically no fluctuation in exchange rates.
2. Moderate fluctuation where the rate of exchange fluctuates within moderate limits.
3. Wide fluctuation where the fluctuation goes beyond certain limit.

IN THE BOOKS OF HEAD OFFICE
Trading and Profit and Loss Account
for the year ended 31st Dec. 2005

	H.O.	*Branch*	*Total*		*H.O.*	*Branch*	*Total*
	Rs	Rs	Rs		Rs	Rs	Rs
To Opening Stock	15,000	7,000	22,000	By Sales	3,20,000	82,000	4,02,000
To Purchases	3,00,000	20,000	3,20,000	By Goods sent to Branch	30,000	–	30,000
To Goods from H.O.	–	30,000	30,000	By Closing Stock	25,000	12,000	37,000
To Gross Profit	65,000	37,000	1,02,000	By Stock-in-Transit	5,000	–	5,000
	3,80,000	94,000	4,74,000		3,80,000	94,000	4,74,000
To Sundry Expenses	12,000	9,000	21,000	By Gross Profit	65,000	37,000	1,02,000
To Depreciation	8,800	3,000	11,800				
To Net Profit	44,200	25,000	69,200				
	65,000	37,000	1,02,000		65,000	37,000	1,02,000

1. Stable currency where there is practically no fluctuation in exchange rates

When the rate of foreign exchange between the two countries is fairly stable, the figures contained in the foreign Branch Trial Balance are converted at a fixed rate *i.e.* official rate with the exception of (*a*) Remittances from Branch which are converted at the actual rates at which the remittances are made and (*b*) Head Office Account which is not converted but is taken at the figure at which the Branch Account appears on the date in the Head Office books. The converted Branch Trial Balance would show a small difference in the Head Office books. This is put on the shorter side against an account designated as "Difference in Exchange" which will be closed by transfer to the Branch Profit and Loss Account.

2. In case of moderately fluctuating exchange rate

The following rules should be followed:

Items	*Rate of conversion*
1. Fixed Assets	The rate prevailing when purchased
2. Fixed Liabilities	The rate prevailing when incurred
3. Current Assets Current Liabilities	At the rate on the accounting date, called closing rate
4. Opening Stock Closing Stock	The rates ruling on the respective dates
5. Goods from Head Office Remittance to and from Head Office Account	Actual rate *i.e.* actual figures appearing in the respective reciprocal accounts of the head office.
6. Depreciation	The rate applicable to the related fixed asset
7. Provision for Bad Debts	The rate applicable to the Debtors
8. Trading account and Profit and Loss account items	At an average rate. Average is equal to opening rate plus closing rate divided by 2.

A difference is often bound to arise as a result of conversion of Branch Trial Balance in home currency. This is called "Difference in Exchange". It may mean a profit or loss. If there is a profit, the same may be carried forward against future loss on exchange. If loss is there, it may be adjusted against the past profit on exchange, carried forward. If not, it may be transferred to Profit and Loss Account.

3. Wide fluctuation where the fluctuation goes beyond certain limit

When the rate of exchange fluctuates very frequently between two countries and the market rate or actual rate varies considerably from the standard or official rate, the rate of exchange is said to be widely fluctuating. In each set of books the actual receipts or payments should be entered and these should be converted at an artificial fixed rate. The difference will be transferred to Exchange Reserve Account.

ILLUSTRATION 23.28

On 31st December, 2005, the following balances appeared in the books of the Kolkata Branch of an English firm having its head office in London:

	Dr.	Cr.
	Rs	Rs
Stock on 1-1-2005	12,600	—
Purchases and Sales	75,000	1,12,500
Debtors and Creditors	39,000	26,000
Bills of Exchange	10,400	9,100
Wages and Salaries	4,800	—
Rent, Rates and Taxes	3,600	—

Sundry Charges	1,500	–
Furniture and Fixtures	4,910	–
Bank Balance	28,990	–
London Office	–	33,200
	1,80800	1,80,800

Stock on 31.12.2005 was Rs 32,500. Kolkata Branch A/c in the books of London Office showed a debit balance of £ 2,580 on 31.12.2005. Furniture and Fixtures were acquired from a remittance from London of £ 350 which exactly covered the cost of such fixtures, etc.

The rates of exchange may be taken at:

Date	*Rate*
31-12-2004	Rs 14 per £
31-12-2005	Rs 13 per £

The average rate for the year 2005 may be taken at Rs 12 per ₤.

Prepare the Trading and Profit and Loss Account and Balance Sheet relating to Kolkata Branch in the London books. (*C.A.*)

In London H.O. books

Converted Trial Balance

	Branch Currency		*Rate*	*H.O. Currency*	
	Dr. Rs	Cr. Rs		Dr. £	Cr. £
Stock on 1.1.2005	12,600	–	14	900	–
Purchases and Sales	75,000	1,12,500	12	6,250	9,375
Debtors and Creditors	39,000	26,000	13	3,000	2,000
Bills of Exchange	10,400	9,100	13	800	700
Wages and Salaries	4,800	–	12	400	–
Rent, Rates and Taxes	3,600	–	12	300	–
Sundry Charges	1,500	–	12	125	–
Furniture and Fixtures	4,910	–	actual	350	–
Bank Balance	28,990	–	13	2,230	–
London Office		33,200	actual	–	2,580
Difference in Exchange (loss)	–			300	–
	1,80,800	1,80,800		14,655	14,655
Closing Stock		32,500	13	2,500	

Kolkata Branch Trading and Profit & Loss Account
for the year ended 31st December, 2005

Dr.	£		Cr. £
To Opening Stock	900	By Sales	9,375
To Purchases	6,250	By Closing Stock	2,500
To Gross Profit c/d	4,725		
	11,875		11,875
To Wages and Salaries	400	By Gross Profit b/d	4,725
To Rent, Rates and Taxes	300		
To Sundry Charges	125		
To Difference in Exchange	300		
To Net Profit	3,600		
	4,725		4,725

Kolkata Branch Balance Sheet
as at 31st December, 2005

Liabilities		£	*Assets*	£
Head Office A/c	2,580		Furniture & Fixtures	350
Add: Net Profit	3,600	6,180	Closing Stock	2,500
Creditors		2,000	Sundry Debtors	3,000
Bills Payable		700	Bills Receivable	800
			Bank	2,230
		8,880		8,880

ILLUSTRATION 23.29

From the following details, prepare a Branch Trading and Profit & Loss and a Branch A/c in the Head Office books of a business with Head Office in India and Branch in New York.

Trial Balance as on 30-6-2005

Particulars	*H.O.*	*Branch*	*Particulars*	*H.O.*	*Branch*
	Rs	$	Rs		$
H.O. Current A/c	–	5,000	Branch Current A/c	24,890	–
Purchases	1,25,000	–	Goods to Branch	36,300	–
Goods from H.O.	–	7,400	Head Office (1-7-2004)	–	6,000
Goods from Branch	485	–	Sales	50,000	9,300
Branch A/c (1-7-2004)	29,100	–	Creditors	25,000	–
Opening Stock	10,000	500	Capital A/c	52,410	–
Debtors	15,000	1,000	Goods to H.O.	–	100
Salaries	3,000	400			
Rent and Taxes	2,000	300			
Furniture (1-7-2004)	3,000	500			
Cash on hand	1,015	300			
	1,88,600	15,400		1,88,600	15,400

You are given the following information:

(1) The rate of exchange on 1.7.2004 was $ 1 = Rs 4.80 and rate of exchange on 30.6.2005 was $ 1 = Rs 4.90. The average rate was $ 1 = Rs 4.85.

(2) The closing stock at the branch is $ 220.

(3) Goods to branch are invoiced at 10% over cost to H.O.

(4) Depreciate Branch furniture at 10%. (*C.A.*)

SOLUTION

In H.O. books

Converted Trial Balance of New York Branch

	Branch Currency		*Rate*	*H.O. Currency*	
	Dr.	*Cr.*		*Dr.*	*Cr.*
	£	£		Rs	Rs
H.O. Current A/c	5,000	–	actual	24,890	–
Goods from H.O.	7,400	–	actual	36,300	–
Opening Stock	500	–	4.80	2,400	–
Debtors	1,000	–	4.90	4,900	–
Salaries	400	–	4.85	1,940	–
Rent & Taxes	300	–	4.85	1,455	–

Furniture	500	–	4.85	2,425	–
Cash on hand	300	–	4.90	1,470	–
H.O. A/c	–	6,000	actual	–	29,100
Sales	–	9,300	4.85	–	45,105
Goods to H.O.	–	100	actual	–	485
Difference in Exchange (profit)	–	–	–	–	1,090
	15,400	15,400		75,780	75,780
Closing Stock	220		4,90	1,078	

Note: Branch 'Furniture' has been converted at the average rate in the absence of information regarding the rate of exchange on the date of acquisition of furniture.

New York Branch Trading and Profit & Loss Account

for the year ended 30th June, 2005

Dr.		Rs		Cr. Rs
To Opening Stock (100/110 × 2,400)		2,182	By Sales	45,105
To Goods from H.O.			By Closing Stock	
(100/110 × 36,300)	33,000		(100/110 × 1,078)	980
Less: Returns (100/110 × 485)	441	32,559		
To Gross Profit c/d		11,344		
		46,085		46,085
To Salaries		1,940	By Gross Profit b/d	11,344
To Rent & Taxes		1,455		
To Depreciation on Furniture 10% on Rs 2,425		243		
To Net Profit		7,706		
		11,344		11,344

New York Branch Account

Dr.	Rs			Cr. Rs
1-7-2004		30-6-2005		
To Balance b/d 30-6-91	29,100	By Branch Current A/c transfer		24,890
To General P/L A/c		By Branch Stock Adjustment A/c		
Branch net profit	7,706	transfer		3,376
To Difference in Exchange A/c		By Branch Assets	Rs	
Profit on exchange	1,090	Debtors	4,900	
		Furniture		
		(2,425 – 243)	2,182	
		Cash	1,470	
		Stock	1,078	9,630
	37,896			37,896

Branch Stock Adjustment Account

	Rs		Rs
To Goods from Branch (Load on goods returned)	44	By Balance b/d (Load on opening stock)	218
To Branch A/c–transfer (Balancing figure)	3,376	By Goods to Branch (Load on goods sent)	3,300
To Balance c/d (Load on Closing Stock)	98		
	3,518		3,518

QUESTIONS

Objective Type Questions

I. State whether each of the following statements is "True" or "False":

1. A branch is an establishment carrying on the same business as that of the Head Office.
2. A dependent branch has to maintain full set of account books.
3. From the accounting point of view, branches are distinguished as dependent and independent branches.
4. The branch account of a dependent branch prepared in Head Office books is a nominal account showing profit or loss of the branch.
5. Branch Stock Account is always prepared at cost price under Stock and Debtor System.
6. The difference between the Goods Sent Account appearing in Head Office Trial Balance and the Branch Trial Balance is termed as "Goods-in-transit".
7. Branch Stock Account reveals the shortage or surplus of stock at branch under Stock and Debtor System.
8. Branch Account under Debtor System is a Nominal Account.
9. Remittances from Branch are shown on the liability side of the Balance Sheet.
10. "Goods Sent to Branch" Account appears on the credit side of the Head Office Trial Balance.

[**Ans.** True – 1, 3, 4, 6, 7, 8, 10. False – 2, 5, 9.]

II. Fill in the blanks:

1. A Branch, which does not maintain its own set of books, is called .... Branch.
2. Cash sent by Branch but not received by the Head Office is known as ....
3. A Head Office invoices goods to its Branch at Rs. 25. The cost of the goods is Rs. 20. Loading is ....%.
4. Branch Stock Account opened in the Head Office Books shows stock............
5. A Branch, which maintains its own set of book, is called .... Branch.

[**Ans :** 1.Dependent; 2.Cash-in-transit; 3. 25. 4. Discrepancy ; 5. Independent.]

III. Choose the correct answer:

1. Goods supplied by Head Office to its Branch may be charged at:
   (*a*) Cost Price
   (*b*) Selling Price
   (*c*) None of these.

2. Stock Reserve in relation to opening stock appears:
   (*a*) On the debit side of Branch Account.
   (*b*) On the credit side of Branch Account.
   (*c*) None of the above.

3. When Head Office purchases branch asset, and the asset account is to be kept at the Branch, the Head Office
   (*a*) Debits Branch Asset Account.
   (*b*) Debits Branch Current Account.
   (*c*) Credits Branch Current Account.

4. Goods sent to Branch at cost + 25%. The loading on the invoice price is :
   (*a*) 16%
   (*b*) 20%
   (*c*) 25%
   (*d*) 125%

5. If goods are returned by a customer to Branch, the entry to be passed in the books of Head Office is:

(a) Branch Stock A/c Dr to Returns Inward A/c

(b) Branch Stock A/c Dr to Branch Debtors A/c.

(c) Branch Debtors A/c Dr. to Branch Stock A/c.

6. In case of manufacturing concerns, the balance in "Goods sent to Branch A/c" will be transferred to :

(a) Purchase Account.

(b) Sales Account.

(c) Trading Account.

(d) Branch Account.

7. Under Debtor System, Branch Account is a :

(a) Personal Account.

(b) Real Account

(c) Nominal Account.

8. Object of Branch Accounting is to know :

(a) Profit & Loss of Head Office.

(b) Profit/Loss of each Branch.

(c) None of the above.

9. Cash remitted by Branch, not received by the Head Office, is debited by the Head Office to :

(a) Cash-in-transit Account.

(b) Branch Account.

(c) Cash Account.

10. Under Foreign Branch, revenue items should be converted at :

(a) Opening rate of exchange.

(b) Closing rate of exchange.

(c) Average rate of exchange.

(**Ans** :1. (c); 2. (b); 3. (a); 4. (b) ; 5. (b) 6. (c); 7. (c); 8. (b); 9. (a); 10. (c).

THEORETICAL QUESTIONS

1. What are the main classes of Branch Accounts? Explain briefly. *(B.Com., MS)*
2. Describe the accounting procedure involved in a department Branch. *(B.Com., Chennai)*
3. What do you understand by inter-branch transactions? *(B.Com., MK)*
4. Write a short note on Stock and Debtors system.
5. Explain the Dependent and Independent Branch. *(B.Com., MS)*
6. What are cash-in-transit and goods-in-transit? *(B.Com., Agra)*
7. State the reasons for the difference between the balances of Branch Account in the Head Office books and the Head Office Account in the Branch books. How would you reconcile the balances of the two accounts? *(B.Com., Kerala)*

PRACTICAL PROBLEMS

Debtors System

1. RAM Company Ltd., Bangalore, has a Branch at Jaipur to which goods are invoiced at cost plus 30%. The following are the transactions between the Head Office and the Branch for the year ending 31.12.2004:

	Rs
Stock at the Branch on 1-1-2004	13,000
Sundry Debtors on 1.1.2004	25,000
Petty Cash on 1.1.2004	125

Goods sent to Branch	65,000
Total sales effected during the year	1,10,000
Cash sales	85,000
Cash received from Branch Debtors	42,000
Expenses incurred by the Branch for the year	11,500
Branch stock on 31.12.2004	52,000
Petty Cash on 31.12.2004	65

Prepare the necessary journal entries for these transactions and also show how the Branch Account will appear in the books of the Head Office. (*B.Com., Madurai, Bangalore*)

[Ans: Profit Rs 78,440**]**

2. A head office in Mumbai has a branch in Ahmedabad to which goods are invoiced by the head office at cost price plus 25%. All cash received by the branch is daily remitted to the head office. All expenses are paid from Mumbai. From the following particulars show how the branch account will appear in head office books (entries to be made at invoice price):

	Rs	Rs
Stock on 1st July, 2004 (at invoice price)		12,500
Debtors on 1st July, 2004		12,000
Goods invoiced from Mumbai		40,000
Remittances to Mumbai:		
Cash sales	16,000	
Cash received from debtors	29,000	45,000
Goods returned to Head Office		2,400
Cheques received from Mumbai:		
Wages and Salaries	11,000	
Rent, rates, etc.	3,000	
Sundry expenses	510	14,510
Stock on 31st December, 2004 (Invoice Price)		15,000
Debtors on 31st December, 2004		22,500

(*B.Com., Madras, Punjab*)

[Ans: Profit Rs 13,410**]**

3. The Mumbai Head Office sent goods to Chennai Branch at 25% profit over costs. From the following details, prepare the Branch Account in the Head Office books and ascertain the net profit at the Branch.

	Rs
Opening stock of goods at Branch at invoice price	20,000
Goods sent to Branch at invoice price	90,000
Loss of goods in transit at invoice price	6,000
Pilferage at branch at cost to Branch	1,200
Closing stock at Branch at its cost	16,000
Sales at Branch	1,05,000
Salaries and wages at Branch	6,000
Other expenses at Branch	3,000

Chennai Branch received Rs 4,000 from the Insurance Company in settlement of the claim for the loss of goods in transit. (*M.Com., Madurai, Andhra, Calicut, Agra*)

[Ans: Profit Rs 24,800**]**

4. A head office in Mumbai sends goods to its branch at Chennai marked 20 per cent above cost. From the following particulars show how the branch account will appear in the Head Office books. Also

give the journal entries necessary for the Head Office to adjust the branch account for arriving at the profit or loss made by the branch.

		Rs			Rs
Stock on 1.7.2003 at the branch		1,800	Cheques sent to branch:		
Debtors on 1-7-2003 at the branch		3,000	Salary	900	
Petty cash in hand at the branch		30	Rent & Taxes	150	
Goods supplied to the branch		30,000	Petty cash	110	1,160
Remittances from the branch:			Stock at branch on		
Cash sales	6,000		30-6-2004		3,000
Money received			Debtors at branch on		
from debtors	21,000	27,000	30-6-2004		4,800
			Petty cash at branch on		
			30-6-2004		20

(Company Secretaries)

[Ans: Profit Rs 3,630]

5. A Company of Delhi has a branch at Chennai. Goods are sent by the Head Office at invoice price which is at the profit of 20% on cost price. All expenses of the branch are paid by the Head Office. From the following particulars, prepare branch account in the Head Office books: (*a*) When goods are shown at cost price, and (*b*) When goods are shown at invoice price.

	Rs
Opening Balance:	
Stock at invoice price	11,000
Debtors	1,700
Petty Cash	100
Goods sent to Branch at invoice price	20,000
Expenses made by Head Office:	
Rent	600
Wages	200
Salary	900
Remittances made to Head Office:	
Cash Sales	2,650
Cash collected from Debtors	21,000
Goods returned by Branch at invoice price	400
Balances at the end:	
Stock at invoice price	13,000
Debtors at the end	2,000
Petty Cash	25

(B.Com. (Pass), Delhi, MK, Mysore, Madras)

[Ans: Profit Rs 8,095]

6. Novelties Ltd., with its Head Office in Kolkata, invoiced goods to its branch at Mumbai, at 20% less than the catalogue price which is cost plus 50%, with instructions that cash sales were to be made at invoice price and credit sales at catalogue price less discount at 15% on prompt payment.

From the following particulars available from the Branch, prepare the Branch Trading and Profit and Loss Account for the year ended 31st March 2004 (showing adjustments) in the Head Office books so as to show the actual profit or loss of the Branch for the year:

	Rs
Stock on 1st April 2003 (Invoice Price)	12,000
Debtors on 1st April 2003	10,000
Goods received from H.O. (Invoice Price)	1,32,000

Sales (Cash)	46,000
Sales (Credit)	1,00,000
Cash realised from Debtors	85,635
Discount allowed to Debtors	13,365
Expenses at the Branch	6,000
Remittance to Head Office	1,20,000
Debtors on 31st March 2004	11,000
Cash in hand on 31st March 2004	5,635
Stock on 31st March 2004 (Invoice Price)	15,000

It was further reported that a part of the stock at the Branch was lost by fire (not covered by Insurance) during the year whose value is to be ascertained and a provision should be made for discount to be allowed to Debtors as on 31st March 2004 on the basis of the year's trend of prompt payment.

(*CA Inter*) (*B.Com., Madras, MK*)

[**Ans:** Loss of stock by fire Rs 2,500 (Cost Price)
Provision for discount on debtors Rs 1,337
Profit Rs 17,798]

7. The Mumbai Stores invoices goods to their various branches at cost, and the branches sell the goods not only for cash but on credit also. Expenses of branches are paid by the Head Office. From the following particulars relating to Chennai Branch, prepare Branch Account in the books of Head Office:

		Rs
Stock at Branch on 1st Jan.		8,000
Debtors at Branch on 1st Jan.		4,000
Petty cash at Branch on 1st Jan.		500
Furniture at Branch on 1st Jan.		6,000
Goods sent to branch during the year		22,000
Goods returned to Branch		800
Cheques sent to Branch during the year:	Rs	
For salaries	2,000	
For Rent	1,000	
For Petty Cash	300	3,300
Cash remitted by Branch during the year:		
Cash sales	10,000	
Cash from Debtors	9,000	19,000
Credit sales during the year		25,000
Goods returned by Debtors during the year		400
Discount allowed to Debtors		500
Bad Debts		100
Stock at Branch on 31st Dec.		10,000
Petty Cash at Branch on 31st Dec.		200
Write off depreciation on Furniture @ 10%.		

(*B.Com., Madurai, Andhra, Punjab*)

[**Ans:** Closing: Debtors Rs 19,000
Profit Rs 10,600]

8. Relax Ltd. has a Branch in New Delhi and the transactions of the Branch for the year ended 31st December were:

	Rs	
Stock of goods at Branch 1st Jan.	9,200	(Invoice Price)

Goods sent to Branch	68,400	(-do-)
Salaries and Wages	3,720	
Gross Cash sales by Branch	68,550	
Rates, Taxes and Insurance	880	
Rent	1,450	
Sundry Expenses	390	
Stock of goods on 31st Dec.	8,950	(Invoice Price)

The Branch sales are exclusively cash and the goods sent to Branch have been invoiced at $33^1/_3$% on cost. You are required to prepare the Branch Account, assuming that all cash sales proceeds are remitted to Head Office and all expenses of the Branches are separated from Head Office.

(ICWA) (B.Com., MK, Bangalore, Bharathidasan)

[Ans: Profit Rs 10,622]

9. Head Office of a Company invoices goods to its Shillong Branch at cost plus 20%. The Shillong Branch also purchases independently from local parties goods for which payments are made by the Head Office. All cash collected by the Branch is banked on the same day to the credit of the Head Office and all expenses are directly paid by the Head Office except for a Petty Cash Account maintained by the Branch for which periodical transfers are made from the Head Office.

   From the following particulars, show Branch Account as maintained in the Head Office books reflecting the Branch profit for the year ended 31st December.

	Rs
Imprest Cash: On 1st Jan.	2,000
On 31st Dec.	1,850
Sundry Debtors on 1st Jan.	25,000
Stock on 1st Jan.	
H.O. Goods at Invoice Price	24,000
Direct purchases by Branch	16,000
Cash Sales	45,000
Credit Sales	1,30,000
Direct Purchases	45,000
Returns from Customers	3,000
Goods sent to Branch from H.O. (Invoice Price)	60,000
Transfer from H.O. for petty expenses	2,500
Bad Debts	1,000
Discounts to customers	2,000
Cash Received from Customers	1,25,000
Branch Expenses	30,000
Stock on 31st Dec. Directly purchased	12,000
From Head Office	18,000

(CA Inter, Mysore, Punjab)

[Ans: Closing: Debtors Rs 24,000
Profit Rs 32,350]

10. A head office invoices goods to its branch at 20% less than the list price. Customers are charged for goods sold to them at cost plus 100%. From the particulars given below prepare accounts for the year 2004 to show the profit made by the Head Office and the Branch.

In case of branch on the wholesale basis.

	Head Office	Branch
	Rs	Rs
Opening stock at cost (Invoice Price in case of branch)	40,000	16,000

Purchases	4,00,000	–
Goods sent to branch (Invoice Price)	96,000	–
Sales	6,00,000	80,000
Expenses	86,000	4,000

(*B.Com., Punjab, Mysore, MK, Andhra*)

[**Ans:** Gross Profit (H.O.) Rs 3,36,000
Gross Profit (Branch) Rs 16,000
Net Profit (H.O.) Rs 2,38,000
Net Profit (Branch) Rs 12,000
Closing Stock (H.O.) Rs 80,000
Closing Stock (Branch) Rs 48,000]

Stock and Debtors

11. Messrs Liberty Traders, Madurai, have opened a branch at Trichy on 1.7.2003. The goods were sent by the Head Office to the branch and invoiced at selling price of the branch which was 125% of the cost price of the Head Office.

The following are the particulars relating to the transactions of Trichy branch:

		Rs
Goods sent to branch (at cost to Head Office)		2,80,800
Sales: Cash		1,25,000
Credit		1,75,000
Cash collected from debtors		1,56,000
Discount allowed		4,000
Wages	3,000	
Freight	11,000	
Other expenses including godown rent	6,000	20,000
Spoiled cloth in bales written off at invoice price		500
Stock on June 30, 2004, at invoice price		55,500

Ascertain the gross profit and net profit for the Trichy Branch for the year ended June 30, 2004, after preparing Branch Stock Account and Branch Debtors Account.

(*B.Com., Madras, Andhra, Jabalpur*)

[**Ans:** Gross profit Rs 59,000
Net profit Rs 34,600
Stock Surplus Rs 5,000]

12. B.K. Ltd. opened a new Branch at Baroda on 1st Jan. where goods are sent by H.O. at 25% above cost. All expenses of Branch are met from Branch cash and the balance remitted to H.O. Branch sells goods both for cash and on credit. From the following particulars, prepare the necessary accounts in the books of H.O. and ascertain the profit or loss made by the branch for the year ended 31st December assuming that the Branch does not maintain double entry books of accounts:

	Rs
Cost of goods sent to Branch	1,00,000
Goods received by Branch till 31st Dec. (Invoice Price)	90,000
Normal loss during transit (at invoice price)	5,000
Debtors on 31st Dec.	10,000
Cash at Branch on 31st Dec.	4,000
Cash remitted to H.O.	90,000

H.O. remitted cash to Branch	5,000
Expenses paid by H.O.	10,000
Credit Sales	95,000
Bad Debts and Allowances to customers	1,000
Closing Stock at Invoice Price	20,000

(*B.Com., Bangalore, Maharashtra*)

[Ans: Profit Rs 39,000**]**

13. B.K. Ltd. operates a retail Branch at Ranchi. All purchases are made by the Head Office in Kolkata, goods for the Branch being delivered to it direct and charges out at selling price which is cost price plus 50%. All cash received by the Branch is remitted to Kolkata. Branch expenses are paid by the Branch out of an imprest amount which is reimbursed by Kolkata monthly.

The Branch keeps a Sales Ledger and certain essential subsidiary books, but otherwise all branch transactions are recorded in the books of Kolkata office.

On 1st Jan., Stock-in-trade at the Branch, at selling price, amounted to Rs 48,660 and Debtors to Rs 6,440.

During the year ended 31st Dec. the following transactions took place at the Branch:

	Rs
Goods received by the Branch at selling price	1,21,800
Cash Sales	64,150
Credit Sales	51,250
Goods returned to Kolkata at selling price	1,560
Reduction in selling price authorised by H.O.	970
Cash received from Debtors	42,660
Debtors written off as irrecoverable	650
Cash discount allowed	1,120

A consignment of goods despatched to the Branch in Dec. at a selling price of Rs 1,200 was not received by the Branch until 31st December and had not been included in its stock figure. The expenses relating to the Branch for the year ended 31st December amounted to Rs 17,290. On 31st December physical stock at the Branch, at selling price, amounted to Rs 52,200.

You are required to write up the Branch Stock Account, the Branch Adjustment Account including Branch Profit and Loss Account in Kolkata books for the year ended 31st December.

(*B.Com. (Hons.) Calcutta, Madras*)

[Ans: Profit Rs 18,570**]**

14. Goods are invoiced in the first year to a new Branch at Rs 2,400 being cost price plus 20% on cost. The sales by the Branch are:

(*i*) Cash Rs 210

(*ii*) Credit Rs 1,800

The stock on hand at loaded price is Rs 390, and bad debts written off are Rs 200 and discounts allowed to Debtors Rs 50; Rs 1,300 is received from Debtors and all proceeds are remitted to Head Office intact.

In the second year, goods costing Rs 1,440 are sent to the Branch while total sales are Rs 1,980 (Rs 100 cash sales). The stock on hand at loaded price is Rs 108. Discount allowed to Debtors is Rs 100. Rs 50 cash received has not yet been remitted by the Branch. Closing Debtors Rs 130. There is discrepancy between the balance in the Branch Stock Account and the actual value (at selling price) of the stock in hand, the Branch Stock Account recording Rs 30 in excess.

Show ledger accounts in the Head Office books for (*a*) Branch Stock Account, (*b*) Goods Sent to Branch Account and (*c*) Branch Debtors Account. (*M.Com., Calcutta*)

[Ans: Profit Rs 335 (1st year)

Profit Rs 330 (2nd year)

15. Electronic Ltd. has a Branch at Chennai. All purchases are made by the Head Office in Bangalore and goods for the Branch are delivered direct and charged out at selling price being cost plus 50%. All cash is received by the branch out of an imprest account which is reimbursed by the Chennai office, monthly. The Branch keeps a sales ledger and the necessary subsidiary books; otherwise all Branch transactions are recorded in the books of the Head office. In April 2003, stock at the Branch at selling price amounted to Rs 39,750, and Debtors Rs 5,820. During the year ended March 31, 2004, the following transactions took place at the Branch:

	Rs
Authorised reduction in selling price	1,050
Discount allowed to Debtors	1,160
Cash received from Debtors	38,260
Cash Sales	43,400
Credit sales less returns	40,420
Debtors written off	430
Goods received by Branch at selling price	1,02,900
Goods returned to Head Office at selling price	1,680

A consignment of goods despatched to the Branch in March 2004, with a selling price of Rs 1,540, was not received by the Branch until 10th April, 2004, has not been included in its figures.

On 31st March 2004, stock at the Branch at selling price was Rs 53,600.

You are required to write up the Branch Stock Account and the Branch Debtors Account in the Head Office books. (*M.Com., Madurai, Madras, Calcutta*)

[**Ans:** Gross Profit Rs 28,290
Net Profit Rs 23,983]

Independent Branch

16. A Mumbai merchant has a Branch in Chennai. The Ledger Balances of the Branch for the year ended 31.3.2004 were as follows:

	Rs
Interest received	2,500
Purchases	9,000
Sales	30,000
Goods from Head Office	14,000
Creditors	1,200
Sundry Expenses	400
Bank (Dr.)	3,300
H.O. Current Account	22,000
Machinery	10,000
Stock (1.4.2003)	15,000
Debtors	4,000
Closing Stock	7,000

You get the following information from the Head Office:

(1) The Head Office sent goods to Branch Rs 1,000 on 30.3.2004 which the Branch received on 3.4.2004.

(2) Branch Furniture Account stood in Head Office books at Rs 800.

(3) Branch Current Account in Head Office books had a balance of Rs 23,000.

Prepare Trading, Profit & Loss A/c and Balance Sheet in Branch books after depreciating furniture by 5% and machinery by 10%.

Also give the Branch Current Account in H.O. books after posting incorporating entries to that account. (*B.Com., Calcutta, Kerala, Bhopal*)

[**Ans:** Gross Loss Rs 1,000
Net Profit Rs 60
Balance Sheet Total Rs 23,300
Branch A/c (in H.O. books) Rs 24,300]

17. Universal Ltd. had its Head Office in Kolkata and a Branch in Mumbai which keeps its own books. Summarised Trial Balances at 31st December 2004 are given below. The Mumbai profit for 2004 has not been incorporated in the Head Office books.

KOLKATA	Dr. Rs	Cr. Rs
Capital	–	1,00,000
Fixed Assets	1,40,000	–
Current Assets and Liabilities	88,000	49,000
Profit and Loss Account:		
Balance 1st January, 2004	–	67,000
Kolkata Profit for 2004	–	54,000
Mumbai Branch Account, 1st January, 2004	66,400	–
Remittances from Branch	–	30,000
Goods sent to Branch (at cost)	5,600	–
	3,00,000	3,00,000

MUMBAI	Dr. Rs	Cr. Rs
Fixed Assets	36,500	–
Current Assets and Liabilities	31,800	17,300
Head Office Account, 1st January, 2004	–	66,400
Remittances to Head Office	32,000	–
Goods from Head Office	–	5,150
Profit & Loss Account, 2004	–	11,450
	1,00,300	1,00,300

The Branch remitted Rs 2,000 cash to Head Office on 30th December 2004 and Head Office sent goods to the Branch of Rs 450 (at cost) on the same day.

Write up the Branch Account in Head Office ledger, the Head Office Account in Branch ledger. You are also required to prepare a summarised Balance Sheet for the entire business. (*B.Com., Calcutta*)

[**Ans:** Branch Profit Rs 11,450
Balance Sheet Total Rs 2,98,750]

18. A firm whose Head Office is in Mumbai has a Branch at Agra. The Branch keeps its own books and the following was the trial balance of these books as on 31st December 2004 :

Agra Branch Trial Balance

	Rs	Rs
Cash in hand	200	–
Bank Balance	7,000	–

Stock (at cost) on 1st January 2004	41,000	–
Debtors	35,000	–
Creditors	–	12,000
Remittance to Head Office	60,000	–
Head Office Current Account	–	1,15,200
Shop Fittings	3,000	–
Motor Van	4,000	–
Purchases by Branch	80,000	–
Goods from H.O.	36,000	–
Sales	–	1,83,000
Sales Returns	12,000	–
Rent	5,000	–
Salaries	15,000	–
Motor Expenses	2,400	–
Trade Expenses	9,600	–
	3,10,200	3,10,200

The Branch stock on 31st December, 2004, amounted at cost to Rs 32,000. Depreciation is to be provided at the rate of 5% per annum on Shop Fittings and 20% per annum on Motor Vans.

Rs 2,000 of Head Office Salaries are to be charged to the Branch Account for supervision.

The Branch Manager is entitled to a commission of 1% of the net sales of the Branch.

Goods which cost Rs 5,000 had been forwarded by the Head Office to the Branch on 31st December, 2004. The transaction had been entered in the Head Office books but no record had been made in the Branch Books nor had the goods been taken into stock.

You are required (*a*) to incorporate these transactions in the Head Office books showing the Branch A/c and Branch Trading and Profit & Loss A/c in the Head Office Ledger as on 31st December, 2004, and (*b*) to prepare the Branch Balance Sheet as on that date.

(*B.Com., Bombay*)

[**Ans:** Gross profit Rs 46,000
Net profit Rs 9,340
Branch Balance Sheet Total Rs 80,250]

19. A Kolkata Head Office passes one entry at the end of each month to adjust the position arising out of inter-branch transactions during the month. From the following inter-branch transactions in April, 2004, make the entry in the books of Kolkata Head Office:

(*a*) Delhi Branch:
- (*i*) Received goods from Nagpur Branch Rs 9,000 and Ahmedabad Branch Rs 6,000.
- (*ii*) Sent goods to Ahmedabad Branch Rs 15,000 and Nagpur Branch Rs 12,000.
- (*iii*) Received bills Receivable from Ahmedabad Branch Rs 9,000.
- (*iv*) Sent acceptances to Nagpur Branch Rs 6,000 and Ahmedabad Branch Rs 3,000.

(*b*) Kanpur Branch [apart from (*a*) above)]
- (*i*) Received goods from Nagpur Branch Rs 15,000 and Delhi Branch Rs 6,000.
- (*ii*) Cash sent to Nagpur Branch Rs 3,000 and Delhi Branch Rs 6,000.

(*c*) Nagpur branch [apart from (*a*) and (*b*) above]
- (*i*) Sent goods to Ahmedabad Branch Rs 9,000.
- (*ii*) Received Bills Receivable from Ahmedabad Branch Rs 9,000.
- (*iii*) Received cash from Ahmedabad Rs 5,000. (*I.C.W.A. Inter*)

[**Ans:** Kanpur Branch Account Dr. Rs 12,000

Nagpur Branch Account Dr. Rs 2,000
To Delhi Branch Account Rs 12,000
To Ahmedabad Branch Account Rs 2,000]

20. Raj and Company of Chennai has two branches, one at Mysore and the other at Bangalore. The Head Office and branches close their accounts on 31st December. The following adjustments have not yet been given effect to and therefore you are required to give the adjusting entry for the following:
   (*a*) Remittance of Rs 4,500 made by Mysore Branch to Head Office on 30th December received by the Head Office on 5th of Jan.
   (*b*) Goods valued at Rs 2,200 despatched by Bangalore Branch on 27th December under instructions from Head Office and received by Mysore Branch on 30th December.
   (*c*) Depreciation amounting to Rs 1,100 on Mysore Branch assets, the accounts of such assets being maintained by the H.O.
   (*d*) Goods worth Rs 9,000 despatched by the Head Office to Mysore Branch on 30th December received by that Branch on 7th Jan.

   Show the entries in the books of the Head Office. (*B.Com., Bangalore*)

21. A Head Office at Mumbai has Branch at Kolkata. The Company closes its accounts on 31st December each year. What adjustment entries are required to be passed in the books of both the Head Office and the Kolkata Branch for the following:
   (*a*) A remittance of Rs 5,000 by the Kolkata Branch on 22nd December is received by the Head Office on 5th of Jan.
   (*b*) Goods worth Rs 10,000 sent by H.O. on 20th December reach the Branch on 6th Jan.
   (*c*) Depreciation at 10% p.a. is to be provided on machinery at Kolkata costing Rs 70,000, the account of which is in the Head Office books.
   (*d*) The Kolkata Branch paid Rs 100 dividend to a local share-holder on behalf of the Head Office.
   (*e*) The Kolkata Branch received an amount of Rs 50 towards call-in-arrears on shares from a local shareholder on behalf of the Head Office.

   Show the entries in the books of the Head Office. (*B.Com., Bangalore*)

22. A Chennai Office has an independent Branch at Ahmedabad. From the following particulars, give journal entries to close the books of the Branch and prepare the Head Office Account in the books of the Branch.

Trial Balance as on 31st December 2004

	Dr. Rs	Cr. Rs
Stock on 1st Jan. 2004	8,200	–
Purchases	12,800	–
Wages	6,550	–
Manufacturing Expenses	3,440	–
Rent	1,700	–
Salaries	5,500	–
Debtors and Creditors	4,000	2,700
Sales	–	34,950
Discount	–	150
Returns to Creditors	–	300
General Expenses	2,200	–
Goods received from H.O.	7,200	–
Cash at Bank	750	–
Chennai Office Account	–	14,000
	52,100	52,100

Adjustments:

(*a*) Closing stock at Branch Rs 14,350.

(*b*) Branch fixed assets maintained in the Head Office books are:

Machinery, Rs 25,000 and Furniture Rs 1,000
Depreciation is to be charged at 10% p.a. on
Machinery and 15% on Furniture.

(*c*) Rent due Rs 150.

(*d*) A remittance of Rs 4,000 made by the Branch on 28th Dec. 2004 was received by the Head Office on 5th Jan. 2005.

Prepare :

(*i*) Journal entries to incorporate the Branch Trial Balance in Head Office books.

(*ii*) Head Office Account in the books of Branch.

(*iii*) Entries to close the books of the Branch.

(*iv*) Branch Account in the books of the Branch. (*M.Com., Madurai*)

[Ans: Gross Profit Rs 11,450
Net Loss Rs 400]

23. A limited company with its Head Office at Delhi has a Branch Office in Kanpur, which obtains supplies partly from Head Office at cost and partly from outside suppliers. The branch keeps a separate set of books. On 30th June 2004, the following trial balances were extracted:

	Head Office		Branch Office	
	Dr. Rs	Cr. Rs	Dr. Rs	Cr. Rs
Share capital	–	30,000	–	–
Fixed assets	16,000	–	8,000	–
P. & L. A/cs on 1st July, 1989	–	4,000	–	–
Opening stock at cost	14,000	–	1,900	–
Debtors and creditors	17,000	10,000	1,500	2,050
Cash	3,000	–	1,000	–
Purchases and sales	1,20,000	1,40,000	6,750	22,500
Sundry expenses	15,000	–	2,250	–
Goods from Head Office	–	12,000	11,500	–
Current account	11,000	–	–	8,350
	1,96,000	1,96,000	32,900	32,900

Fixed assets are to be depreciated at 10%: Stock on 30th June: Head Office Rs 10,000 and Branch Rs 2,100.

Prepare the company's Profit and Loss Account for the year ended 30th June, 2004, and its Balance Sheet on the same date. (*B.Com., Madras*)

[Ans: Gross profit (H.O.) Rs 28,000
Gross profit (Branch) Rs 4,450
Net profit (H.O.) Rs 11,400
Net profit (Branch) Rs 1,400
Balance Sheet Total Rs 58,850]

Chapter 24

Accounts of non-profit Organisation

Introduction – Final Accounts of Non–trading Concerns – Receipts and Payments Account – Features – Income and Expenditure Account – Features – Distinction between the two – Treatment of Special items – Some Important Adjustments – Types of Problems – Distinction between Income and Expenditure Account and Profit and Loss Account – Account of Professional Men – Question-objective type questions – Theoretical Questions – Practical Problems.

INTRODUCTION

Non-trading institutions are created for promotion of Arts, Culture, Games and Sports, Fine Arts, Hospitals etc. Examples of such institutions are Schools, Colleges, Libraries, Athletic Clubs, Societies, Associations etc. These non-trade institutions do not prepare Trading and Profit and Loss Account because it is not their objective to earn profit. These types of associations, consisting of persons, are formed with a view to render services to its members in particular, and to the society in general. Non-trading concerns are of two types: (*a*) Concerns without profit motive, such as Educational Institutions, Sports Clubs, Missionary Organisations, Trade Unions etc. which offer valuable services to the members and to the society; (*b*) Concerns with profit motive, for example, professions such as Medical Practitioners, Legal Practitioners, Chartered Accountants etc.

In the previous chapter we have dealt with trading institutions which deal in purchasing and selling of goods and to earn profit as their objective. The non-trading institutions deal in services. Majority of the transactions are in cash and credit transactions are nearly nil or a few in number. The non-trading concerns usually receive their incomes by way of donations from the general public, subscriptions from members and grants from Governments. Their income is spent in achieving the objects for which they are started. To avoid misappropriation of money, it is essential to maintain proper books. They may have to compare their current expenses with current incomes in order to find out whether or not the expenses are being met out of the incomes. Thus, book keeping records consist of Cash Book, Journal, Ledger etc. through double entry system, and periodically they prepare a Trial Balance from their books. The non-trading organisations have to prepare the financial statements at the end of the year. These statements have nothing special and are similar to financial statements which we have discussed in earlier chapters.

FINAL ACCOUNTS OF NON-TRADING CONCERN

The Final Accounts of non-trading concerns consists of:

1. Receipts and Payments Account
2. Income and Expenditure Account, and
3. Balance Sheet.

1. Receipts and Payments Account

It is a Real Account. It is a consolidated summary of Cash Book. It is prepared at the end of the accounting period. All cash receipts are recorded on the debit side and all cash payments are recorded on the credit side. Cash Book consisting of entries of receipts and payments in a chronological order while the Receipts and payments is a summary of total cash receipts and cash payments. It starts with opening balance of Cash and Bank and ends with closing balance of Cash and Bank. It does not take into account outstanding amounts of receipts and payments. Receipts and Payments may be of Capital or Revenue nature; they may relate to the current or previous year or subsequent year; so long as they are actually received or paid, they must appear in this account.

Features of Receipts and Payment Account, in brief:

1. It starts with opening balance and ends with closing balance
2. It is the summary of cash and bank transactions.
3. Actual cash transactions are entered.
4. It includes capital as well as revenue items.
5. It follows cash system of accounting
6. It shows cash position and excludes all non-cash items.
7. It is a real account.
8. It does not take any income/expense outstanding at the beginning or at the end.

2. Income and Expenditure Account

It is a Nominal Account. It is in the form of Profit and Loss Account. It is concerned with only revenue items—expenses and incomes. It records all losses and expenses on its debit side and all incomes and gains on its credit side. Of the incomes and expenses of revenue nature, only the portion pertaining to the current year is shown in the Income and Expenditure Account i.e. amount relating to the previous year or future year are excluded. Again, the incomes and expenses of current year, whether received or not, must be shown. In other words, incomes and expenses have to be adjusted for both out-standing and pre-payments. All non-cash items, Depreciation, Bad Debts, Provision for Doubtful Debts etc. are taken into account. The difference between the debit side and the credit side is either surplus or deficit for the year concerned and the difference will be transferred to the Capital Fund (also called General Fund or Accumulated Fund) appearing in Balance Sheet.

Features of Income and Expenditure Account, in brief:

1. It is prepared in lieu of Profit and Loss Account.
2. It is a nominal account.
3. It is based on mercantile system of accounting.
4. There is no opening balance.
5. It ends with Surplus or Deficit.
6. It excludes all capital income and capital expenses.
7. It includes only revenue items.
8. It records all expenses whether paid or not, and all incomes whether received or not.

Distinction between Receipts and Payments Account and Income and Expenditure Account

Receipts and Payment Account	*Income and Expenditure Account*
1. It is a Real Account	1. It is a Nominal Account
2. It starts with opening balance.	2. It does not start with opening balance.
3. It ends with closing balance either cash	3. It ends with a surplus (excess of income over

in hand or at bank.	expenditure) or deficit (excess of expenditure over incomes)
4. It is similar to Cash Book.	4. It is similar to Profit and Loss Account.
5. Receipts are shown on the debit side and payments are shown on the credit side.	5. Expenses or losses are shown on the debit side and incomes and gains are shown on the credit side.
6. It contains both Capital and Revenue items.	6. It contains only Revenue items.
7. It includes receipts and payments whether they relate to any period past, previous and subsequent.	7. It includes only revenue items of the current year only.
8. No adjustments are made for outstanding or prepaid incomes and expenses	8. It takes into account the outstanding expenses and incomes.
9. Generally, it is not followed by Balance Sheet.	9. It is followed by Balance Sheet.
10. This is based on Cash system of accounting.	10. This is based on mercantile system.

3. Balance Sheet

Balance Sheet in case of non-trading concern is prepared in the usual manner and consists of all liabilities and assets on the date on which it is prepared. The excess of assets over liabilities is termed Capital Fund or General Fund. Again, The Capital Fund are accumulated with Capital Receipts, Receipts that are capitalised and further increased by surplus or decreased by deficit, during the year. At the inception of a non-trading concern, there will be no formal Capital Fund and in such case, the Surplus, if any, earned during the year constitute the Capital Fund at the end of the year.

TREATMENT OF SPECIAL ITEMS

Subscriptions from members are collected periodically. These are regular revenue incomes and credited to Income and Expenditure Account. These are the major source of income for the non-trading concern. However, special subscriptions, if collected are kept separately from the General Fund for the specific purpose. There are certain items which are peculiar to non-trading concerns and they need special treatment and are:

1. Donations

Charitable institution may receive donations from time to time. If the amount is small and if such collections are frequent, then they may be treated as an income. Donations may also be of two types—General Donations and Specific Donations. Any donations received, not for a specific purpose, are treated as General Donations. The General Donations of comparatively small amount may be taken to Income and Expenditure Account. General Donations of comparatively huge amount, which are of non-recurring nature, may be added to the Capital Fund. The nature and size of the organisation decide about the amount of donation being small or big. In case of donations received for any specific purpose then it is termed Specific Donations. Such amount cannot be used for any other purpose, except the purpose of donor. Therefore, such amount may be shown in Balance Sheet (liability side). All the Donations debited to Receipts and Payments Account and these amount may be credited to Income and Expenditure Account or Liability side of the Balance Sheet, if it is for a specific purpose.

2. Legacy

It is like donation. It is the amount given to a non-trading concern as per the will of deceased person. It is taken to the Receipts and Payments Account as Capital Receipts. These are not income but may appear in Balance Sheet. These types of receipts are of non-recurring nature.

3. Life Members Fee

Non-trading concerns usually collect subscriptions every month from their ordinary members. There are another category of members called "Life Members", from whom the subscriptions are collected as a lump sum. Such subscription is called life subscription and are capital receipts. This can also be kept in a separate account and an amount equal to annual subscription can be transferred to subcrtiption account. The balance in such account, on the death of the member must be transferred to Capital Fund.

4. Entrance Fee (Admission Fee)

These are the fees collected from every member at the time of his admission into membership. It is paid only once by the new entrants on becoming a member of a society or a club. Generally, there may be bye-laws as regards the accounting treatment of such amount. In the absence of any bye-laws, it is taken as an item for income. Against treating it as an income, there are arguments favouring it as a capital receipt as the members pay such fees only once and therefore treat it as a capital receipt. In the absence of any instruction, it may be treated as an income and is credited to Income and Expenditure Account.

5. Sale of Old Sports Materials and Old Newspapers

The amount received on account of sale of old sports materials and old newspapers are recurring incomes to a concern and therefore, treated them as revenue incomes. The purchase of balls, nets, etc. are revenue expenditure.

6. Purchase of Equipment

The price paid for acquiring any equipment is a Capital Expenditure.

7. Honorarium Paid

It is a payment of remuneration to a person who is not an employee of the organisation. Such as any special performance is done, by an outsider, at the organisation, then the payment is honorarium and is taken to Income and Expenditure Account as it is a revenue expenditure.

8. Subscription

It is a primary source of income of a non-profit organisation. It is usually collected every month from all the ordinary members. Subscription is the amount paid by the members to keep their membership alive. The subscription amounts are treated as revenue receipts. Subscription received from members is credited to Income and Expenditure Account on accrual basis i.e. total amount receivable from all the members as subscription should be considered as income for the year.

9. Special Fund

If there is any specific fund, such as Prize Distribution Fund, the expenses or incomes relating to the fund may be adjusted to the fund itself (on the liability side of the Balance Sheet). Such expenses or incomes may not be taken to Income and Expenditure Account.

10. Sale of Old Assets

If any asset is sold, the amount is debited to Receipts and Payments Accounts. It is not taken to Income and Expenditure Account. The profit or loss made on sale of old asset is recorded in Income and Expenditure Account.

SOME IMPORTANT ADJUSTMENTS

(A) ***Subscription:*** Subscription received from members is treated as revenue income. In income and Expenditure Account, subscription for current year will be shown. If total subscription received as per Receipts and Payments Account during the year is given, adjustments will be made for outstanding subscription in the beginning and at the end of the year; and advance subscription in the beginning and at the end of the year.

(B) ***Expenses:*** Total expenses paid during the year are shown in Receipts and Payments Account. These expenses may include outstanding of previous year and advance for next year. Similarly, some account may still be outstanding. Therefore, to calculate correct figure of expenses to be shown in Income and Expenditure Account, adjustments will have to be made.

(C) ***Consumable Items:*** If institution consumes certain items such as medicines by hospital or sports items by clubs, relevant figures for Receipts and Payments Account and Income and Expenditure Account will be calculated. The value of goods consumed is shown in Income and Expenditure Account and the amount paid to creditors is shown in Receipts and Payments Account.

ILLUSTRATION 24.1

Calculate the amount to be posted to Income and Expenditure Account for the year ended 2004:

Receipts and Payments Account show that subscriptions received Rs 9,000. This account of subscriptions includes Rs 800 outstanding in the previous year and Rs 1,000 for the next year. Rs 2,000 is still outstanding for current year.

SOLUTION

Income and Expenditure Account
for the year ended Dec. 2004

Dr. Cr.

			Rs	*Rs*
	By Subscription received		9,000	
	Add: Outstanding for the current year:		2,000	
			11,000	
	Less: Outstanding for previous year:	800		
	Less: Received for next year:	1,000	1,800	9,200

ILLUSTRATION 24.2

In 2004, the subscriptions received were Rs 17,500 which include Rs 400 for 2003 and Rs 600 for 2005. At the end of 2004 subscriptions outstanding were Rs 500. The subscriptions due but not received at the end of the previous year *i.e.*, 2003 were Rs 600.

What amount should be credited to Income and Expenditure Account as subscriptions.

SOLUTION

Income and Expenditure Account
for the year ended 31st Dec. 2004

		Rs	*Rs*
	By Subscription (2004)	17,500	
	Less: Subscriptions received for 2003	400	
		17,100	
	Less: Subscriptions received for 2005	600	
		16,500	
	Add: Subscriptions outstanding for 2004	500	
			17,000

ILLUSTRATION 24.3

During the year 2004, the expenses actually paid were Rs 3,250. Find out the actual expenses chargeable to Income and Expenditure Account for the year ended 2004, if prepaid and outstanding are as follows:

Prepaid Expenses on 31.12.2003	Rs 300
Prepaid Expenses on 31.12.2004	Rs 400
Outstanding Expenses on 31.12.2003	Rs 450
Outstanding Expense on 31.12.2004	Rs 500

SOLUTION

Income and Expenditure Account
for the year ended 31st Dec., 2004

	Rs	*Rs*	
To Expenses Paid	3,250		
Add: Prepaid expeses in 2003	300		
Add: Outstanding expenses in 2004	500		
	4,050		
Less: Prepaid Expenses in 2004	400		
	3,650		
Less: Expenses Outstanding in 2003	450		
		3,200	

ILLUSTRATION 24.4

1. Subscriptions received as per Receipts and Payment Accounts during the year 2004 — Rs 15,960
2. Subscriptions received in advance for 2005, during 2004 — Rs. 1,500
3. Subscriptions outstanding on Dec. 2003 — Rs 750
4. Subscriptions received in advance *i.e.* for 2004, during 2003 — Rs 710
5. Subscriptions outstanding on 31st Dec. 2004 — Rs 500

SOLUTION

		Rs
Subscriptions as per Receipts and Payment Account		15,960
Add: Subscriptions received in 2003 for 2004		710
Add: Subscriptions outstanding on 31st Dec. 2004		500
	Rs	17,170
Less: Subscription received during 2004 for the year 2005	1,500	
Less: Subscriptions outstanding for 2003	750	2,250
Subscriptions to be credited to Income and Expenditure Account during 2004		14,920

ILLUSTRATION 24.5

Calculate the amount of stationery to be debited to Income and Expenditure Account during 2004:

1. Amount paid for stationery during the year 2004, as per Receipts and Payments Account — Rs 1,750
2. Stock of stationery on 1.1.2004 — Rs 150
3. Paid advance for stationery on 31.12.2004 — Rs 200
4. Paid advance for stationery during Dec. 2003 but received stationery during the year 2004 — Rs 250
5. Creditors for stationery on 1.1.2004 — Rs 370
6. Stock of stationery on 31.12.2004 — Rs 415
7. Creditors for stationery on 31.12.2004 — Rs 300

SOLUTIONS

	Rs	*Rs*
Amount paid for stationery as per Receipts and Payment Account		1,750
Add: Stock of stationery on 1.1.2004		150
Add: Paid advance during Dec. 2003 and received during 2004		250
Add: Creditors for stationery on 31.12.2004 (Stationery has been		

received but the payment is outstanding)		300
		2,450
Less: Paid advance for stationery 31.12.2004 (payment has been made but stationery not received)	200	
Less: Creditors for stationery 1.1.2004 (Stationery has been received during 2003 but the payment is made in 2004)	370	
Less: Stock of stationery on 31.12.2004 (Not consumed)	415	985
Amount of stationery to be debited to Income and Expenditure Account		1,465

ILLUSTRATION 24.6

Calculate the amount to be shown in Receipts and Payments Account for the year ended 31st Dec. 2004

1. Income and Expenditure Account shows a sum of Rs 7,500 against subscription during 2004.
2. Subscriptions outstanding at Dec. 2003—Rs 600.
3. Subscriptions received in advance in Dec. 2003—Rs 450
4. Subscriptions received in advance in Dec. 2004—Rs 270
5. Subscriptions outstanding at Dec. 2004—Rs 750

SOLUTION

Receipts and Payment Account

Dr. **for the year ended 31st December 2004** Cr.

	Rs	*Rs*	
To subscriptions as per Income and Expenditure Account	7,500		
Add: Subscriptions outstanding for 2003	600		
Add: Subscriptions received for 2005	270		
	8,370		
Less: Subscriptions received in 2003	450		
	7,920		
Less: Subscriptions outstanding in 2004	750		
		7,170	

ILLUSTRATION 24.7

From the following, find out the amount of subscriptions to be credited to Income and Expenditure Account for the year 2006.

Subscriptions received in 2006 – Rs. 48,000 which include Rs. 4,000 for 2005 and Rs. 8,000 for 2007.

Subscriptions due but not received at the end of the year 2006 were Rs. 20,000.

Subscriptions received in 2005 in advance for 2006 were Rs. 12,000

(*B. Com. Kerala*)

SOLUTION:

Computations of subscriptions for 2006

	Rs
Subscriptions received during the year	48,000
Less: Received for previous year (2005)	4,000
	44,000

Less: Received for the next year (2007)	8,000
	36,000
Add: Outstanding subscriptions for 2006	20,000
	56,000
Add: Received in advance in 2005 for 2006	12,000
Subscriptions to be credited to Income and Expenditure Account for 2006	68,000

TYPES OF ACCOUNTING PROBLEMS

1. Preparation of Income and Expenditure Account and Balance Sheet from a given Receipts and Payment Account with additional information.
2. Preparation of Opening Balance Sheet and Closing Balance Sheet from a given Receipt and Payment Account and Income and Expenditure Account.
3. Preparation of Receipt and Payment account from a given income and Expenditure Account and other information given.
4. Income and Expenditure Account and Balance Sheet from a given Trial Balance with additional information.

1. *Preparation of Income and Expenditure Account and Balance Sheet from a given Receipts and Payment Account with additional information.*

The Income and Expenditure Account is simply another name for the Profit and Loss Account drawn up for a non-profit organisation. In this account, all losses and expenses relating to the period are debited and all gains and incomes relating to the same period are credited. It must be remembered that only the revenue items relating to the period are dealt within this Account. In examinations, sometimes, Receipts and Payments Account is given and the students are required to prepare Income and Expenditure Account and in such situation, the following steps are to be followed:

1. Do not take the opening balance and closing balance of Cash in hand and at Bank.
2. Do not take Capital Receipts and Capital Expenditure.
3. Pick up only the revenue receipts and revenue payments and exclude the portions relating to previous and subsequent years.
4. Add the portions of incomes and expenses prepaid in the previous year on account of current year.
5. Add also the portions of incomes and expenses of the current year due but remaining unpaid.
6. Provide for depreciation, Reserve for doubtful debts etc. as needed in the problems.
7. Surplus or Deficit will be transferred to Capital Fund.

ILLUSTRATION 24.8

The Calcutta Cricket Club gives you the following information:

Dr. **Income and Expenditure Account for 2004** Cr.

	Rs			*Rs*
To Remuneration to Coach	4,500	By Donation and Subscriptions		25,500
To Wages	5,000	By Bar Room: Receipts:	3,000	
To Rent	2,500	Payments:	2,500	500
To Printing and Stationery	2,600	By Interest on Saving A/c		500
To Repairs	4,500	By Proceeds of Club:		
To Honorarium to Secretary	6,000	Night:	8,800	
To Depreciation on Equipment	4,700	Expenses:	4,000	4,800
To Surplus	1,500			
	31,300			31,300

Balance Sheet as on 31st Dec. 2004

31.12.2003	Liabilities		31.12.2004	31.12.2003	Assets	31.12.2004
Rs			Rs	Rs		Rs
	Expenses Unpaid:			1,000	Cas in hand	500
1,000	Printing and Stationery		800	3,000	Cash at Bank	1,000
	Wages		2,000	20,300	Savings Bank	21,100
4,000	Honorarium to Secretary		6,000	1,500	Subscriptions Outstanding	1,000
800	Subscriptions received in Advance		300	8,000	Equipment	17,500
28,000	Capital Fund	28,000				
	Entrance Fees	2,500				
	Surplus	1,500	32,000			
33,800			41,100	33,800		41,100

Prepare the Receipts and Payments Account of the Club for 2004. (*M.Com., Kolkata*)

Solution :-

In the Books of Kolkata Cricket Club
Receipts and Payments Accounts
For the year ended 31st Dec. 2004

Dr. Cr.

	Rs		Rs
To Balance b/d:		By Remuneration to Coach	4,500
Cash in hand	1,000	By Wages[(4)]	3,000
Cash at Bank:		By Rent	2,500
Current Account	3,000	By Printing and Stationery[(2)]	2,800
Savings Account	20,300	By Repairs	4,500
To Donations and Subscriptions[(1)]	25,500	By Honorarium to Secretary[(3)]	4,000
To Bar Room Receipts	3,000	By Bar Room Expenses	2,500
To Interest on Savings A/c	500	By Night Club Expenses	4,000
To Proceeds of Night Club	8,800	By Equipment[(5)]	14,200
To Entrance Fees	2,500	By Balance c/d:	
		Cash	500
		Cash at Bank:	
		Current Account	1,000
		Savings Account	21,100
	64,600		64,600

Workings:

		Rs.
1.	*Donations and Subscriptions received in 2004*	
	As per Income and Expenditure Account:	*25,500*
	Add: Outstanding on 31st Dec. 2003	*1,500*
		27,000
	Add: Received in advance for 2005	*300*
		27,300
	Less: Outstanding on 31st Dec. 2004	*1,000*
		26,300
	Less: Received in advance during 2003	*800*
		25,500

2.	*Printing and Stationery paid in 2004*	
	As per Income and Expenditure	*Rs 2,600*
	Less: Outstanding on 31st Dec. 2004	*800*
		1,800
	Add: Outstanding on 31st Dec. 2003	*1,000*
		2,800
3.	*Honorarium to Secretary paid in 2004*	
	As per Income and Expenditure	*Rs 6,000*
	Add: Outstanding on 31st Dec. 2003	*4,000*
		10,000
	Less: Outstanding on 31st Dec. 2004	*6,000*
		4,000
4.	*Wages paid in 2004*	
	As per Income and Expenditure	*Rs 5,000*
	Less: Outstanding on 31st Dec. 2004	*2,000*
		3,000
5.	*Purchase of Equipment in 2004*	
	Equipment on 31st Dec. 2004	*17,500*
	Add: Depreciation charged	*4,700*
		22,200
	Less: Opening Balance	*8,000*
		14,200

ILLUSTRATION 24.9

Calicut Sports Association extracts the following Receipts and Payments Account for the year ended 31st December 2004. From the particulars given, prepare Income and Expenditure Account for the year ended 31st December 2004.

Receipts and Payments Account
for the year ended 31st Dec. 2004

Dr. Cr.

	Rs		*Rs*
To Balance b/d	1,125	By Newspapers	750
To Subscriptions	2,900	By Rent	250
To Tournament Fund	750	By Salaries	1,800
To Life Membership	1,000	By Office Expenses	1,200
To Enterance Fees	100	By Sports Equipments	1,150
To Donations for Building	1,500	By Tournament Expenses	450
To Sales of Newspapers	50	By Balance c/d	1,825
	7,425		7,425

Subscriptions outstanding on 31st December 2003 Rs 450 and on 31st December 2004 Rs 400. Subscriptions received includes Rs 100 on account of the year 2005.

Sports equipment was valued on 31st December 2003 at Rs 550 and on 31st December 2004 at Rs 1,090.

Office expenses include Rs 150 for 2003 whereas Rs 200 is still payable on this account for 2004

Tournament Fund is treated as Capital Receipt. (*B.Com., Calicut*)

SOLUTION

Income and Expenditure Account
for the year ended 31st December 2004

Dr. Cr.

Expenditure		Rs	Income		Rs
To Newspaper		750	By Subscriptions:	2,900	
To Rent		250	Less: for 2003	450	
To Salaries		1,800		2,450	
To Office Expenses	1,200		Add: Outstanding (2004)	400	
Less: Paid for 2003	150			2,850	
	1,050		Less: Received for 2005	100	2,750
Add: Outstanding for 2004	200	1,250	By Entrance Fees		100
			By Sale of Newspaper		50
To Depreciation on Equipment:		610	By Excess Expenditure over Income		1,760
		4,660			4,660

Note: Life members' fee is capitalised. Tournament Expenses are shown separately.

ILLUSTRATION 24.10

The following is the Receipts and Payments Account of the Bombay Club for the year ending 31st December 2006.

Receipts	Rs.	Rs.	Payments	Rs.	Rs.
To Balance b/d		600	By Rent		10,400
To Entrance fees		1,100	By Stationary Expenses etc.		6,136
To Subscriptions:			By Wages		10,660
2005	400		By Billiards table		7,800
2006	33,800		By Repairs & Renewals		1,612
2007	600		By Interest		3,000
		34,800	By Balance c/d		4,792
To Lockers Rent		1,000			
To Special subscriptions for Governor's party		6,900			
		44,400			44,400

Lockers rent Rs. 120 refers to 2005 and Rs. 180 is still owing; Rent Rs. 2,600 pertaining to 2005 and Rs. 2,600 is still owing; stationery expenses etc. Rs. 624 related to 2005; Still owing Rs. 728; Subscription unpaid for 2006 Rs. 1,736; Special subscriptions for Governor's party outstanding Rs. 1,100.

The club owned sports materials of the value Rs. 32,000 on 1-1-2006. This was valued at Rs. 27,000 on 31-12-2006. The Club took a loan of Rs. 40,000 in 2005.

Prepare the Income and Expenditure A/c for 2006 and Balance sheet as at 31st December 2006.

(B.Com. Madurai M.S.)

SOLUTION:

Income & Expenditure Account of Bombay Club for the year ending 31st December 2006

Expenditure	Rs.	Rs.	Income	Rs.	Rs.
To Rent paid	10,400		By Entrance ffes		1,100
Less: Unpaid for 2005	2,600		By Subscriptions		
			received for 2006	33,800	
	7,800		*Add*: Outstanding	1,736	

	Rs	Rs		Rs	Rs
Add: Unpaid for 2006	2,600				35,536
		10,400	By Lockers Rents received	1,000	
To Stationery			*Less:* Accrued for 2005	120	
Expenses paid	6,136				
Less: Unpaid for 2005	624				
	5,512			880	
Add: Unpaid for 2006	728		*Add:* Accrued for 2006	180	
		6,240			
To Wages		10,660			1,060
To Reparis & Renewals		1,612			
To Interest		3,000			
To Depreciation on sports materials (32,000–27,000)		5,000			
To Surplus – Excess of Income over expenditure (Bal fig)		784			
		37,696			37,696

Note: Special subscriptions for governor's party is treated as a 'Special purpose collection' and is shown in Balance sheet till that purpose is served.

Balance sheet of the Bombay Club as on 31st December 2006.

Liabilities	*Rs*	*Rs*	*Assets*	*Rs*	*Rs*
Expenses unpaid:			Cash Balance		4,792
Rent	2,600		Sports materials		27,000
Stationery	728		Bolliards table		7,800
		3,328	Subscription outstanding		1,736
Special subscription			Special subscription due		1,100
for Governor's party			Lockers Rent outstanding		180
received	6,900		Deficiency on 1-1-2006	10,104	
Add: Outstanding	1,100		*Less:* Surplus		
		8,000	for 2006	784	
Loan		40,000			9,320
Subscription received in advance		600			
		51,928			51,928

Note: Special subscriptions due is an adjustment which has Double effect in Balance sheet itself

Working Note:

Computation of Capital Fund:

The club has a deficiency (instead of Capital fund). This is ascertained by preparing balance sheet as on 31st December 2005

Bombay Club

Balance sheet as on 31st December 2005

Liabilities	*Rs*	*Rs*	*Assets*	*Rs*	*Rs*
Rent Outstanding		2,600	Subscriptions due		400
Stationery etc. Outstanding Loan		624	Cash		600
Loan		40,000	Sports materials		32,000
			Lockers Rents due		120
			Deficiency (Bal fig)		10,104
		43,224			43,224

ILLUSTRATION 24.11

Prepare Income and Expenditure Account and Balance Sheet from the following Receipts and Payments Account and Balance Sheet as on 31st December 2004:

Receipts and Payments Account
for the year ending 31st Dec. 2004

Dr.	Rs	Rs		Cr. Rs
To Balance b/d		10,000	Expenses for 2003	1,200
To Subscriptions:			2004	2,000
2003	200		By Land	4,000
2004	2,100		By Interest	400
2005	100	2,400	By Miscellaneous Expenses	2,000
To Entrance Fees		800	By Balance c/d	8,300
To Lockers Rent		700		
To Miscellaneous Income		4,000		
		17,900		17,900

Balance Sheet as on 31st December 2003

Liabilities	Rs	*Assets*	Rs
Capital Fund	33,620	Building	30,000
Subscription Received in advance	600	Outstanding Subscriptions	380
Outstanding Expenses	1,400	Outstanding Locker Rent	240
Loan	5,000	Cash	10,000
	40,620		40,620

(B.Com., Delhi, Madurai)

SOLUTION

Income and Expenditure Account
for the year ended 31st December 2004

Dr. *Expenditure*	Rs	*Income*	Rs	Cr. Rs
To Expenses	2,000	By Subscription	2,100	
To Interest	400	Add: Received in Advance in 2003	600	2,700
To Miscellaneous Expenses	2,000	By Entrance Fees		800
To Excess of Income over		By Lockers Rent	700	
Expenditure	3,560	Less: Received for 2003	240	460
		By Miscellaneous Income		4,000
	7,960			7,960

Balance Sheet as on 31st December 2004

Liabilities		Rs	*Assets*	Rs
Outstanding Expenses for 2003			Cash	8,300
(Rs. 1400 – 1200)		200	Outstanding Subscription for 2003	
Subscription Received in Advance			(Rs 380 – 200)	180
for 2005		100	Land	4,000
Capital Fund	33,620		Building	30,.000
Add: Excess of Income	3,560	37,180		
Loan		5,000		
		42,480		42,480

ILLUSTRATION 24.12

Following is the Receipts and Payments Account of Delhi Club for the year ended 31st December 2004

Dr.					Cr.
Receipts		*Rs*	*Payments*		*Rs*
To Balance b/d	Cash	2,000	By Secretary Remuneration		5,000
	Bank	10,000	By Salary to Staff		5,000
To Subscriptions:			By Canteen Expenses		12,000
2003		5,000	By Newspapers and Magazines		1,000
2004		200	By Construction of Buildings		15,000
2005		100	By Balance c/d:	Cash	800
To Interest from 5% Govt. Security				Bank	2,000
(Purchased in the past) at 1% discount		2,000			
To Sale of old Furniture		1,000			
To Sale of old Newspapers		500			
To Canteen collections		10,000			
To Donation for Building Fund		10,000			
		40,800			40,800

With the additional information given below, prepare the Income and Expenditure Account for the year ended 31st December 2004 and the Balance Sheet as on that date.

		As on 31st Dec. 2003 Rs	As on 31st Dec. 2004 Rs
(*a*)	Subscription Receivable	1,000	?
(*b*)	Subscription received in advance	200	100
(*c*)	Salary to Staff O/S	2,000	1,000
(*d*)	Canteen expenses prepaid	1,000	500
(*e*)	Furniture etc.	10,000	?
(*f*)	Construction expenses O/S		2,000
(*g*)	Subscription due for the year 2004 Rs 5,500		
(*h*)	The book value of furniture sold in December was Rs 3,000		
(*i*)	Charge depreciation on furniture at 10% on the closing net balance.		

(*CA Inter*)

SOLUTION

Delhi Club
Income and Expenditure Account
for the year ended 31st December 2004

Dr.					Cr.
Expenditure	*Rs*	*Rs*	*Income*	*Rs*	*Rs*
To Salary to Staff	5,000		By Subscription	5,000	
Less: Outstanding for 2003	2,000		Add: Subscription due for 2004	5,500	
	3,000		Add: Subscription Received in		
Add: Outstanding for 2004	1,000	4,000	advance for 2004	200	10,700
			By Interest on Government		
To Secretary Remuneration		5,000	Securities		2,000
To Newspapers and Magazines		1,000	By Sale of Newspaper		500
To Loss on sale of old Furniture			By Excess of Expenditure over		
Book Value	3,000		Income transferred to Capital Fund		2,000
Less: Depreciation	300				
	2,700				
Less: Sale	1,000	1,700			

	Rs	Rs		Rs
To Loss on Canteen:				
Canteen Expenses	12,000			
Add: Prepaid for 2003	1,000			
	13,000			
Less: Canteen Collection	10,000			
	3,000			
Less : Prepaid for 2005	500	2,500		
To Depreciation on Furniture		1,000		
		15,200		15,200

Balance Sheet
as on 31st December 2004

Liabilities	*Rs*	*Rs*	*Assets*		*Rs*	*Rs*
Subscription in Advance		100	Cash in Hand			800
Outstanding Expenses:			Cash at Bank			2,000
Salary to Staff		1,000	Subscription in arrear:			
Construction Expenses		2,000	for 2004		5,500	
Capital Fund	61,400		for 2003	1,000		
Add: Donation for Building Fund	10,000		Less: Received in 2004	200	800	6,300
	71,400		Canteen Expenses Prepaid			500
Less: Excess of Expenditure over Income	2,000	69,400	5% Government Securities (face value)		40,000	
			Less 1% Discount		400	39,600
			Furniture		10,000	
			Less: Depreciation		1,000	
					9,000	
			Less: Furniture sold (depreciated value)		2,700	6,300
			Buildings		15,000	
			Add: Construction Expenses Outstanding		2,000	17,000
		72,500				72,500

Workings:

Balance Sheet
as on 31st December 2003

Liabilities	*Rs*	*Assets*	*Rs*
Subscription in Advance	200	Cash in Hand	2,000
Outstanding Salary to Staff	2,000	Cash at Bank	10,000
Capital Fund (Balancing Figure)	61,400	Subscription in Arrear	1,000
		Canteen Expenses Prepaid	1,000
		Investments in Government Securities $\left(\frac{100}{5} \times 2000 \times \frac{99}{100}\right)$	39,600
		Furniture	10,000
	63,600		63,600

ILLUSTRATION 24.13

From the following information relating to Cricket Club, prepare Income and Expenditure Account for the year ended 31st March 2004, Balance Sheet as at 31st March 2004 and Balance Sheet as at 31 March 2003:

Dr. Cr.

Receipts	*Rs*	*Payments*	*Rs*
To Memebers Subscriptions	50,000	By Upkeep of Field and Pavilion	20,000
To Members' Admission Fees	3,000	By Expenses for Tournament	7,000
To Sale of Old Balls, Bats etc.	500	By Rate & Insurance	2,000
To Hire of ground	3,000	By Telephones	500
To Subscription for V.J. Tournament	10,000	By Printing and Stationery	1,000
To Cash drawn from Bank	40,000	By General Expenses	500
To Donations	1,00,000	By Honorarium to Secretary	1,700
		By Grass Seeds	300
		By Bats, Balls etc.	7,000
		By Cash deposited into Bank	1,66,500
	2,06,500		2,06,500

Assets as on 1st April 2003:

	Rs
Cash at Bank	30,000
Stock of Balls Bats etc.	15,000
Printing and Stationery	2,000
Subscription due	5,000
Liabilities	Nil

Donations received and surplus on account of V.J. Tournament should be kept in Reserve for a permanent Pavilion. Subscriptions due at 31st March 2004 were Rs 7,500. Write off 50% of Bats, Balls Account and 25% of Printing and Stationery Account. *(CAIIB)*

(B. Com. MK)

SOLUTION

Cricket Club
Balance Sheet as on 31st March 2004

Liabilities			*Rs*	*Assets*		*Rs*
Capital fund		52,000		Cash at Bank:		
Add: Excess of Income		22,250	74,250	Opening Balance	30,000	
				Deposit into Bank	1,66,500	
Reserve for Pavilion:					1,96,500	
Donations		1,00,000		Less: Withdrawn	40,000	1,56,500
Subscription for V.J.				Subscription Outstanding		7,500
Tournament	10,000			Stock of Printing and Stationery	3,000	
Less: Expenditure	7,000	3,000	1,03,000	Less: Depreciation	750	2,250
				Stock of Bats, Balls etc.	22,000	
				Less: Depreciation	11,000	11,000
			1,77,250			1,77,250

Workings:

Cricket Club
Balance Sheet as on 31st March 2003

Liabilities	*Rs*	*Assets*	*Rs*
Capital Fund		Cash at Bank	30,000
(Balancing Figure)	52,000	Stock of Bats, Balls etc.	15,000
		Printing and Stationery	2,000
		Subscriptions Due	5,000
	52,000		52,000

Cricket Club
Income and Expenditure Account
for the year ended 31st March 2004

Dr. Cr.

Expenditure		*Rs*	*Income*		*Rs*
To Upkeep of Field and Pavilion		20,000	By Member's Subscriptions	50,000	
To Rates and Insurance		2,000	Less: Previous year		
To Telephones		500	Subscription	5,000	
To General Expenses		500		45,000	
To Honorarium to Secretary		1,700	Add: Subscription		
To Grass Seeds		300	Outstanding for 2004	7,500	52,500
To Printing and Stationery :					
Opening Stock	2,000		By Admission Fees		3,000
Add: Purchased	1,000		By Sale of Old Balls, Bats etc.		500
	3,000		By Hire of Ground		3,000
Depreciation @ 25% for Rs 3,000		750			
To Depreciation on Bats					
Balls etc., @ 50%					
Opening Stock	15,000				
Add: Purchases	7,000				
	22,000	11,000			
To Excess of Income over					
Expenditure		22,250			
		59,000			59,000

ILLUSTRATION 24.14

Following are the assets and liabilities of library on 31st December 2003

	Rs			*Rs*
Outstanding creditors for Expenses	650	Cash		3,200
Capital Fund:		Furniture		4,850
Excess of income over expenditure	44,350	Debtors: Outstanding:		
		Subscriptions	750	
		Amount to be received for		
		the use of lecture hall	350	1,100
		Library Books		16,850
		Investments		5,000
		Buildings		14,000
	45,000			45,000

Dr. **Cash book (for the year 2004)** Cr.

	Rs		Rs
Balance b/d	3,200	Salaries	2,400
Entrance Fees	2,600	Municipal Taxes	700
Subscriptions	8,500	Insurance on Buildings	500
Receipts from sale of old furniture	600	Increase in the books of Library	1,250
Receipts from sale of old newspapers	60	Payment to last year's creditors	650
Rent of Library Hall	1,040	Repairs	250
Proceeds from lectures and entertainment	3,000	Electric fittings	4,500
		Printing and Stationery	400
		Postal Charges	50
		Sundry Expenses	150
		Balance c/d	8,150
	19,000		19,000

It was found out at the end of the year that amounts to be received for subscriptions were Rs 1,100 and for use of library hall were Rs 375, prepaid insurance on building was Rs 175 and outstanding sundry expenses were Rs 800. Provide for depreciation 2½% on building and write off 5% on investments and 10% on the opening amount of library books. Whole of the entrance fee is to be treated as revenue income. Prepare Income and Expenditure Account and Balance Sheet for the year ending at 31st December 2004. *[B.Com (Hons.) Kolkata]*

SOLUTION

Income and Expenditure Account

Dr. **for the year ended 31st December 2004** Cr.

Expenditure		*Rs*	*Income*		*Rs*
To Salaries		2,400	By Entrance Fees		2,600
To Municipal Taxes		700	By Subscription	8,500	
To Insurance on Building	500		Add: Outstanding	1,100	
Less: Prepaid Insurance	175	325		9,600	
To Repairs		250	Less: Outstanding in 2003	750	8,850
To Printing and Stationery		400			
To Postal Charges		50	By Rent of Library Hall	1,040	
To Sundry Expenses	150		Add: Received in use of		
Add: Outstanding	800	950	Library Hall	375	
To Depreciation:				1,415	
Building	350		Less: Previous years Amount		
Library Books	1,685		to be received	350	1,065
Investments	250	2,285	By Sale of Old Newspapers		60
To Excess of Income over			By Proceeds from Lectures		
Exenditure		8,215	and Entertainments		3,000
		15,575			15,575

Balance Sheet

as on 31st December 2004

Liabilities		*Rs*	*Assets*		*Rs*
Outstanding Sundry Expenses		800	Cash		8,150
Capital Fund			Debtors		
Excess of Income over			Subscription Outstanding	1,100	
Expenditure on 31-12-2003	44,350		For use of Library Hall	375	1,475

Add: Excess of Income over			Investments	5,000	
Expenditure on 31-12-2004	8,215	52,565	Less: Depreciation	250	4,750
			Library Books	16,850	
			Less: Depreciation	1,685	
				15,165	
			Add: Purchase	1,250	16,415
			Furniture	4,850	
			Less: Sold	600	4,250
			Electric Fittings		4,500
			Prepaid Insurance		175
			Building	14,000	
			Less: Depreciation	350	13,650
		53,365			53,365

2. *Opening Balance sheet and Closing Balance Sheet from a given Receipts and Payments Account and Income and Expenditure Account.*

Follow the following steps:

(A) ***Opening Balance Sheet:***

(1) Consider Opening Cash and Bank balances from Receipts and Payments Account and write them in the asset side of the Balance Sheet.

(2) Consider other adjustments from income and Expenditure Account either income or expenses and put them in asset side or liability side of the Balance sheet.

(3) The difference between the asset side and liability side will reflect the capital Fund, as balancing figure.

(B) ***Closing Balance Sheet:***

(1) Take all the assets from Opening Balance Sheet, after due effect of depreciation (from Income and Expenditure A/c) additions (from Receipts and Payment A/c) and sold (from Receipts and Payments A/c), the net figure will be written in the asset side of the Balance Sheet.

(2) Take the Capital Fund from Opening Balance Sheet and add surplus or deduct deficit; and all other liabilities (from Income and Expenditure A/c) go to liability side of the Balance sheet.

(3) Closing cash and Bank Balances (from Receipt and Payment A/c) will be written on asset side.

(4) Compare each item from Income and Expenditure with Receipts and Payments Account and write suitably to closing Balance Sheet.

ILLUSTRATION 24.15

The following particulars related to Sports Clubs of Delhi Income and Expenditure Account for the year ended 31st December 2004.

Dr. Cr.

	Ps		*Rs*
To Salaries	6,000	By Admission Fees	15,000
To Printing and Stationery	2,500	By Subscription	25,000
To Advertising	1,000	By Rent Receivable	4,800
To Insurance Charges	900		
To Electric Charges	500		
To Depreciation on Sport equipments	12,000		
To Excess of Income over Expenditure	21,900		
	44,800		44,800

Receipts and Payment Account
for the year ended 31st Dec. 2004

Dr.		Rs	Cr.	Rs
To Balance b/d		5,000	By Salary (including advance)	7,500
To Admission Fee:			By Printing and Stationery	2,500
2003	2,500		By Advertising	1,000
2004	13,500	16,000	By Insurance charges (Partly for next year)	1,200
To Subsciptions:			By Electricity	500
2003	1,000		By Purchase of fixed assets	20,000
2004	23,000		By Balance c/d	17,900
2005	2,000	26,000		
To Rent		3,600		
		50,600		50,600

On 1st January 2004, the club had the following assets:

	Rs
Land and Buildings	60,000
Sports Equipments	30,000
Funiture	4,500

Prepare Opening and Closing Balance Sheets.

SOLUTION

Sports Club of Delhi
Balance Sheet
as on 1st January 2004

Liabilities	*Rs*	*Assets*	*Rs*
Capital Fund (Balancing Figure)	1,03,000	Cash at Bank	5,000
		Subscription Outstanding	1,000
		Admission Fees Outstanding	2,500
		Sports Equipment	30,000
		Furniture	4,500
		Land and Building	60,000
	1,03,000		1,03,000

Sports Club of Delhi
Balance Sheet as on 31st December 2004

Liabilities		*Rs*	*Assets*		*Rs*
Subscription Received in Advance		2,000	Cash at Bank		17,900
Capital Fund:	1,03,000		Subscription Outstanding		2,000
Add: Excess of Income	21,900	1,24,900	Admission Fees Outstanding		1,500
			Salary Advance		1,500
			Rent Outstanding		1,200
			Prepaid Insurance		300
			Sports Equipment	30,000	
			Less: Depreciation	12,000	18,000
			Furniture		4,500
			Fixed Assets		20,000
			Land and Building		60,000
		1,26,900			1,26,900

ILLUSTRATION 24.16

Receipts and Payments A/c and Income and Expenditure A/c of Asiatic Public Library for the year ended 31st Dec 2005 were as follows:

Receipts and Payments A/c

Receipts		*Rs.*	*Payments*	*Rs.*
To Balance b/d		700	By Books Purchased	33,000
To Subscriptions :			By Printing & Stationary	1,500
2004	4,000		By Salaries for 2005	8,000
2005	30,000		By Salaries for 2004	2,000
2006	2,000		By Telephone charges	1,500
		36,000	By Miscellaneous expenses	3,000
To Interest (including Rs. 200 for 2004)		4,000	By Balance c/d	200
To Donations for specific fund		5,000		
To Rent:				
2005	2,500			
2006	1,000			
		3,500		
		49,200		49,200

Income & Expenditure A/c

Expenditure		*Rs.*	*Income*	*Rs.*
To Salaries		12,000	By Interest	3,800
To Printing & Stationary		1,500	By Subscription	35,000
To Telephone charges		1,500	By Rent	2,500
To Mis. Expenditure		3,000		
To Depreciation on :				
Books	5,000			
Buildings	5,000			
Furniture	1,000			
		11,000		
To Excess of Income over Expenditure		12,300		
		41,300		41,300

On enquiry you find that the Library has the following other assets on 1st January 2005

	Rs.
Buildings	2,00,000
Furniture	10,000
Books	17,000
Investments	38,000

You are asked to prepare Balance sheets of the Library as on 31st December 2004 and 2005

[C.A.I.I.B. B.Com. Punjab, Bhopal, MK]

SOLUTION

Asiatic Public Library
Balance sheet as at 31st December 2004

Liabilities	*Rs.*	*Assets*	*Rs.*
Outstanding Salaries	2,000	Cash	700
Capital Fund (Bal. Fig)	2,67,900	Investments	38,000

			Outstanding Subscriptions		4,000
			Outstanding interest		200
			Furniture		10,000
			Books		17,000
			Buildings		2,00,000
		2,69,900			2,69,900

Balance Sheet as at 31st December 2005

Liabilities		*Rs.*	*Assets*		*Rs.*
Capital fund	2,67,900		Cash		200
Add: Surplus	12,300		Investments		38,000
		2,80,200	Outstanding Subscriptions		5,000
Subscriptions received in advance		2,000	(35,000-30,000)		
Rent received in advance		1,000	Books	17,000	
Salaries outstanding		4,000	*Add:* Additions	33,000	
(12,000-8,000)					
Donations (Specific Fund)		5,000		50,000	
			Less: Depreciation	5,000	
					45,000
			Furniture	10,000	
			Less: Depreciation	1,000	
					9,000
			Building	2,00,000	
			Less : Depreciation	5,000	
					1,95,000
		2,92,200			2,92,200

ILLUSTRATION 24.17.

The following are the items of receipts and payments of the All India Sports Club summarised from the books of accounts maintained by the Secretary:

Receipts		*Rs.*	*Payments*	*Rs.*
Opening balance 1-4-2005		4,200	Manager's salary	1,000
Entrance fees:			Printing & Stationery	2,600
2004-05	1,000		Advertising	1,200
2005-06	10,000		Fire insurance	1,800
		11,000	Investments	20,000
			Closing balance 31-3-2006	7,600
Subscriptions:				
2004-05	600			
2005-06	15,000			
2006-07	400			
Interest on Investments		16,000		
		3,000		
		34,200		34,200

Income and Expenditure Account
for the year ending 31st March, 2006.

Expenditure		*Rs.*	*Income*	*Rs.*
Manager's salary		1,500	Entrance fees	10,500
Printing & Stationery	2,000		Subscriptions	15,600
Add: O/s	400		Interest on Investments	4,000
		2,400		
Advertising		1,600		
Audit fees		500		
Fire Insurance		1,000		
Depreciation		4,940		
Excess of income over expenditure		18,160		
		30,100		30,100

You are required to prepare the Balance Sheets of the Club as on 1-4-2005 and 31-3-2006. The book values of the assets on 1-4-2005 were as under.

Building Rs.44,000; Furniture Rs. 4,000, Cricket equipment Rs. 25,000

The depreciation rate on Buildings 5%, on Cricket Equipment 10% and on Furniture 6%.

(B.Com. Pass, Delhi, B.Com. Andhr. Bangalore)

SOLUTION

All India Sports Club
Balance Sheet as on 1st April, 2005

	Rs.		*Rs.*
Outstanding Printing and Stationery	600	Cash balance	4,200
Capital Fund (balancing figure)	78,200	Cricket Equipment	25,000
		Furniture	4,000
		Buildings	44,000
		Outstanding Entrance fees	1,000
		Outstanding Subscriptions	600
	78,800		78,800

Balance Sheet
as on 31st March, 2006

		Rs.			*Rs.*
Capital Fund	78,200		Cash balance		7,600
Excess Income	18,160		Cricket Equipment	25,000	
		96,360	*Less:* Depreciation at 10%	2,500	
Subscriptions received in advance		400			22,500
Outstanding Printing and Stationery		400	Furniture	4,000	
Outstanding Advertising		400	*Less*: Depreciation at 6%	240	
Audit fee outstanding		500			3,760
Outstanding salary		500	Buildings	44,000	
			Less: Depreciation at 5%	2,200	41,800
			Outstanding Entrance fees		500
			Outstanding subscriptions		600
			Prepaid insurance		800
			Investments		20,000
			Interest on Investments due		1,000
		98,560			98,560

ILLUSTRATION 24. 18.

The following is the Receipts and Payments Account and Income and Expenditure Account of the Club for the year ending 31st March, 2006

Receipts	*Rs*	*Payments*	*Rs*
To Balance b/d	4,000	By salaries	6,000
" Endowment	2,000	" Advertisement	1,200
" Subscription	10,200	" Provisions purchased	6,800
" Entrance fees	800	" Printing and stationery	700
" Donation for books	1,300	" Bank	1,000
" Entertainment	4,000	" Sports material	2,800
" Printing and stationery	750	" Creditors (2004-05)	1,300
" Sale of Furniture (book value Rs. 800)	700	" Investments 4%	
		(at Rs. 96 – purchased on 1-10-2004)	1,920
		Balance c/d	1,280
	23,000		23,000

Income and Expenditure Account for the year ending 31st March, 2006

Expenditure	*Rs*	*Income*	*Rs*
To Loss on sale of Furniture	100	By subscriptions	10,000
" Salaries	6,700	" Entrace fees	400
" Advertisement	1,000	" Interest on Investments at 4% on Rs. 2,000	80
" Audit Fees	300	" Entertainment	4,000
" Provisions	6,000	" Excess of Expenditure over Income	2,370
" Printing and stationery	750		
" Sports Materials (Written off)	2,000		
	16,850		16,850

Prepare Balance sheets as on 31st March 2005 and 31st March , 2006 *(C.A.I.I.B)*

SOLUTION

The Club

Balance Sheet as on 31st March, 2005

	Rs		*Rs*
Creditors	1,300	Cash balance	4,000
O/s creditors for investments purchased	1,920	Investment purchased	1,920
Capital Fund (Balancing figures)	3,500	Furniture	800
	6,720		6,720

Balance sheet as on 31st March, 2006

		Rs			*Rs*
Endowment		2,000	Cash		1,280
Entrance fees		400	Bank		1,000
Donation for books		1,300	Investments		1,920
Subscriptions in advance		200	Sports materials	2,800	
Outstanding salaries		700	Less: Written off	2,000	
Outstanding audit fees		300			800
Outstanding printing		50	Provisions on hand		800
Capital Fund	3,500		Interest on Investments accrued		80
Less: Excess of Expenditure	2,370	1,130	Prepaid advertisement		200
		6,080			6,080

ILLUSTRATION 24.19

From the following information relating Delhi Sports Club, prepare the Balance sheet as on 1-4-2005 and on 31-3-2006:

(*i*) Assets on 1-4-2005 are : Club grounds and pavilion Rs. 50,000; Sports Equipment Rs. 30,000; Furniture Rs. 7,000; subscription in arrears on that date Rs. 1,000 and Creditors for stationery Rs. 1,000

(*ii*) **Receipts and Payments Account for the year ending on 31st March 2006**

Receipts		*Rs*	*Payments*	*Rs*
To Balance b/d		5,000	By printing & Stationery	3,000
" Subscription:			" Salaries	11,000
	2004-05	900	" Advertising	2,000
	2005-06	18,000	" Fire Insurance	1,500
	2006-07	500	" Furniture	2,000
" Sale of old newspapers		300	" Investment	18,000
" Rent received		2,200	" Balance c/d	1,400
" Entrance fees		12,000		
		38,900		38,900

(*iii*) **Income and Expenditure Account for the year ending on 31st March, 2006**

Expenditure	*Rs*	*Income*	*Rs*
To salaries	12,000	By subscription	19,000
" Printing & Stationery	2,800	" Entrance fees	12,000
" Audit fees	500	" Rent received	2,400
" Advertising	2,000	" Sale of old newspapers	300
" Fire insurance	1,200		
" Depreciation on: Sports Equipment	6,000		
Furniture	800		
" Excess of Income over Expenditure	8,400		
	33,700		33,700

(*B.Com Hons. Delhi*)

SOLUTION

Delhi Sports Club

Balance sheet as at 31st March 2005

	Rs		*Rs*
Creditors for stationery	1,000	Cash	5,000
Capital Fund (Balancing figure)	92,000	Club grounds & pavilion	50,000
		Sports Equipment	30,000
		Furniture	7,000
		Subscription in arrear	1,000
	93,000		93,000

Delhi Sports Club

Balance Sheet as at 31st March, 2006

		Rs.			*Rs.*
Capital Fund	92,000		Cash		1,400
Add: Excess Income	8,400		Club grounds	50,000	
		1,00,400	*Less:* Depreciation	—	
Subscriptions in advance		500			50,000

Liabilities	Rs	Assets	Rs	Rs
Salaries outstanding	1,000	Sports Equpment	30,000	
Audit fees outstanding	500	*Less:* Depreciation	6,000	
Creditors for stationery	800			24,000
		Furniture	7,000	
		Additions	2,000	
			9,000	
		Less: Depreciation	800	
				8,200
		Outstanding Subscriptions		
		2004-05	100	
		2005-06	1,000	
				1,100
		Outstanding Rent		200
		Prepaid insurance		300
		Investments		18,000
	1,03,200			1,03,200

ILLUSTRATION 24.20

The account set out below has been submitted to you for audit. If you do not approve of it, criticise and amend it. Also prepare the Balance Sheet of the Club.

Calcutta Checkers Society
Income and Expenditure Account
31st December 2004

Dr. Cr.

Expenditure		*Rs*	*Income*	*Rs*
To Entrance Fees (21 @ Rs 10)		210	By Salaries & Wages	675
To Fees for Life Membership (5 @ Rs 52)		260	By Secretary's Salary	350
To Annual subscription	1,565		By Rent, Rates etc.,	1,265
Annual subscription paid			By Printing & Postage	37
in advance	65	1,630	By Repairs to Premises	124
To Interest on G.P. Notes		70	By Interest on Bank Loan	57
To Sundry Receipts		60	By Balance c/d	960
To Balance from last years		1,238		
		3,468		3,468

Treasurer's Note. The subscriptions in arrears amount to Rs 120. Sundry Tradesmen's bills Rs 42 were outstanding on 31st December, but have since been paid. The secretary's salary although sanctioned by resolution of the committee, has not yet been paid. The 3½% G.P. Notes of the face value of Rs 2,000 were purchased at Rs 90. The lease of the club premises cost Rs 2,124. The balance of the Bank Loan now outstanding is Rs 1,000 secured by mortgage in the leasehold premises. (*B.Com., Madurai*)

SOLUTION

Calcutta Checkers Society
Income and Expenditure Account
for the year ended 31st December 2004

Dr. Cr.

Expenditure	*Rs*	*Income*		*Rs*
To Salaries and Wages	675	By Entrance Fees		210
To Secretary's Salary Outstanding	350	By Annual Subscription	1,630	
To Rent and Rates etc.	1,265	Less: Received in Advance	65	1,565
To Printing and Postage	37	By Interest on G.P. Notes		70

	Rs		Rs
To Repairs to Premises	124	By Sundry Receipts	60
To Interest on Bank Loan	57	By Excess of Expenditure over Income	645
To Sundry Expenses Outstanding	42		
	2,550		2,550

Calcutta Checkers Society
Balance Sheet as on 31st December 2004

Liabilities		*Rs*	*Assets*	*Rs*
Subscription Received in Advance		65	Cash in Hand	1,190
Outstanding Secretary's Salary		350	G.P. Notes	1,800
Outstanding Sundry Expenses		42	Outstanding Subscriptions	120
Fees for Life Membership		260	Lease Hold Club Premises	2,124
Bank Loan		1,000		
Capital Fund	4,162			
Less: Excess of Expenditure				
over Income	645	3,517		
		5,234		5,234

Workings:

Calcutta Checkers Society
Receipts and Payments Account
for the year ended 31st December, 2004

Dr. Cr.

Receipts	*Rs*	*Payments*	*Rs*
To Balance b/d	1,238	By Salaries and Wages	675
To Entrance Fees	210	By Rent, Rates etc.	1,265
To Fees for Life Membership	260	By Printing and Postage	37
To Subscription Received		By Repairs to Premises	124
(Rs 1565 – 120 + 65)	1,510	By Interest on Bank Loan	57
To Interest on G.P. Notes	70	By Balance c/d	1,190
To Sundry Receipts	60		
	3,348		3,348

Calcutta Checkers Society
Balance Sheet
as on 31st December 2003

Liabilities	*Rs*	*Assets*	*Rs*
Bank Loan	1,000	Cash in Hand	1,238
Capital Fund (Balancing figure)	4,162	G.P. Notes	1,800
		Lease Hold Club Premises	2,124
	5,162		5,162

3. *Preparation of Receipts and Payments Account from a given Income and Expenditure Account and other information.*

Sometimes, Income and Expenditure is given and students are required to prepare Receipts and Payments Account and in such a situation, the following procedure may be followed:

1. All expenditure, whether Capital or Revenue, irrespective of the periods, are shown on the Payment side.
2. All receipts, whether Capital or Revenue, irrespective of the periods, are shown on Receipt side.
3. Pick up opening balance and closing balance to the account.
4. Eliminate all adjustments made while preparing Income and Expenditure Account.
5. Purchase of assets may be calculated and shown on the payment side. For this compare the values of the assets at the beginning and closing of the period.

ILLUSTRATION 24.21

The following is the Receipts and Payments Accounts of Appollo Club in respect of the year 31st March 2004:

Receipts and Payments Account
for the year ended 31st March 2004

Dr. Cr.

		Rs			Rs
1.4.2003	To Balance b/d:		31.3.2004	By Salaries	3,000
	Cash in hand	2,000		By Stationery	1,000
31.3.2004	To Subscriptions:			By Rates and Taxes	300
	2002-03 Rs 3,000			By Telephone Charges	1,500
	2003-04 Rs 4,000			By 8% Securities at par	5,000
	2004-05 Rs 1,000	8,000		By Sundry Expenses	200
"	To Profit on Sports	3,000		By Balance c/d	
"	To Interest on 8% Securities	1,000		(Cash in hand)	3,000
		14,000			14,000

The following additional facts are ascertained:

1. There are 500 members, each paying an annual subscription of Rs 10, Rs 3,500 being in arrears for 2002-03 at the beginning of 2003-04. During 2002-03, subscriptions were paid in advance by 30 members for 2003-04.
2. Stock of stationery at 31st March 2003 was Rs 400 and at March 2004 Rs 500.
3. At 31st March 2004, the Rates and Taxes were prepaid to the following 31st January, the yearly charge being Rs 300.
4. A quarter's charge for telephone is outstanding, the amount accrued being Rs 300. The charges for each quarter is same both for 2002-03 and 2003-04.
5. Sundry expenses accruing at 31st March 2003 were Rs 50 and at 31st March 2004 Rs 60.
6. At 31st March 2003, building stood in the books at Rs 30,000 and it is required to write off depreciation at 10% p.a.
7. Value of 8% securities at 31st March 2003 was Rs 15,000 which was purchased at that date at par, additional securities worth Rs 5,000 are purchased on 31st March 2004.

You are required to prepare:

(*a*) An Income and Expenditure Account for the year ended 31st March 2004.
(*b*) A Balance Sheet as at that date.

SOLUTION

Income and Expenditure Account
for the year ended 31st March 2004

Expenditure		*Rs*	*Income*		*Rs*
To Salaries		3,000	By Subscriptions (500 × Rs 10)		5,000
To Stationery	1,000		or (Rs 4000 + 300 + 700)		
Add: Opening Stock	400		By Profit on Sports		3,000
	1,400		By Interest on 8%		
Less: Closing Stock	500	900	Securities	1,000	

To Rates and Taxes	300		Add: Outsanding	200	1,200
Add: Pre-paid (2002-03)	250				
	550				
Less: Pre-paid (2004-05)	250	300			
To Telephone Charges	1,500				
Less: Outstanding (2002-03)	600				
	900				
Add: Outstanding (2003-04)	300	1,200			
To Sundry Expenses	200				
Less: Paid for 2002-03	50				
	150				
Add: Outstanding (2003-04)	60	210			
To Depreciation on Buildings		3,000			
To Excess of Income over Expenditure		590			
		9,200			9,200

Balance Sheet
as on 31st March 2004

Liabilities		*Rs*	*Assets*		*Rs*
Subscription Received in Advance		1,000	Cash in Hand		3,000
Outstanding Telephone Charges		300	Outstanding Subscription for 2003-04		700
Outstanding Sundry Expenses		60	Outstanding Subscription for 2002-03		500
Capital Fund	50,200		Stock of Stationery		500
Add: Excess of Income			Prepaid Rates and Taxes (300 × 10/12)		250
over Expenditure	590	50,790	Outstanding Interest on Investments		200
			Investments		20,000
			Building	30,000	
			Less: Depreciation	3,000	27,000
		52,150			52,150

Workings:

Balance Sheet
as on 31st March 2003

Liabilities	*Rs*	*Assets*	*Rs*
Subscription Received in Advance	300	Cash in Hand	2,000
Outstanding Sundry Expenses	50	Outstanding Subscription	3,500
Outstanding Telephone Charges	600	Stock of Stationery	400
Capital Fund (Balancing Figure)	50,200	Prepaid Rates and Taxes	250
		Investments	15,000
		Building	30,000
	51,150		51,150

4. *Preparation of Income and Expenditure Account and Balance Sheet from a given Trial Balance with additional information.*

Steps:

(1) All the current year's revenue incomes are to be credited in the Income and Expenditure Account.

(2) All the current year's revenue expenditures are to be debited in the Income and Expenditure Account.

(3) If the credit side is greater than the debit side, there will be 'Surplus' or 'Excess' of income over expenditure, and vice-versa in the opposite case.

(4) The surplus or deficit so made is to be added or deducted against the capital fund.

(5) All the capital incomes or Capital expenditures are to be shown in the Balance Sheet.

ILLUSTRATION 24.22

From the following Trial Balance and accompanying notes for adjustments, prepare Income and Expenditure Account for the year ended 31st December 2004 and the Balance Sheet as on that date of a Club:

	Dr.	Cr.
	Rs	*Rs*
Club Buildings	37,400	—
Library Books	2,280	—
Furniture and Fixtures	3,520	—
Glass, Cutlery etc. (1st Jan. 2004)	2,000	—
Glass, Cutlery puchased during the year	1,000	—
Printing and Stationery	225	—
Rent Received	—	10,370
Annual Subscription	—	12,150
Entertainment cost	345	—
Billiard Room Receipts	—	3,845
Billiard Board	10,400	—
Billiard Room Expenses	2,135	—
Canteen Profit	—	1,200
Subscription arrears, on 1st Jan. 2004	1,125	—
Honorarium	1,500	—
Sales of tickets for Annual Dinner	—	1,600
Annual Dinner Expenses	1,875	—
Salaries to Staff	2,700	—
Donations	—	8,500
Audit Fees	600	—
Repairing, Clearing etc.	350	—
Newspapers and Magazines	180	95
Interest on Bank Deposit	—	25
Bank Charges	20	—
Entrance Fees	—	225
Election Expenses	2,995	—
Stock of canteen provision on 31st December 2004	300	—
Sundry Creditors	—	3,135
Cash in Hand	1,400	—
Cash at Bank	1,735	—
General Fund	—	32,940
	74,085	74,085

Notes for adjustments:

(*a*) Out of the total subscriptions, Rs 1,125 represented arrears collected and Rs 760 paid in advance.

(*b*) An amount of Rs 500 was outstanding on account of rent.

(*c*) Unpaid salary amounts to Rs 200.

(*d*) Entrance fees to be capitalised.

(*e*) Out of the donation, Rs 3,600 represented donation towards election expenses and of the balance, half the amount shall be capitalised.

(*f*) Depreciation to be provided as under:

Library Books at 10%

Furniture and Fixtures at 15%

Club Buildings at 5%

Glass, Cutlery etc. Rs 1,700 (*CAIIB*)

SOLUTION

Income and Expenditure Account
for the year ended 31st December 2004

Dr. Cr.

Expenditure		Rs	*Income*		Rs
To Printing and Stationery		225	By Rent Received	10,370	
To Entertainment Cost		345	Add: Outstanding	500	10,870
To Billiard Room Expenses		2,135	By Annual Subscription	12,150	
To Honorarium		1,500	Less: For 2003	1,125	
To Annual Dinner Expenses		1,875		11,025	
To Salaries	2,700		Less: for 2005	760	10,265
Add: Outstanding	200	2,900	By Billiard Room Receipts		3,845
To Audit Fees		600	By Canteen Profit		1,200
To Repairs and Cleaning Charges		350	By Sale of tickets for Annual		
To Newspapers and Magazines		180	Dinner		1,600
To Bank Charges		20	By Donations	8,500	
To Depreciation:			Less: for Election Expenses	3,600	
Library Books	228			4,900	
Furniture and Fixtures	528		Less: Capitalised	2,450	2,450
Club Buildings	1,870		By Newspapers and Magazines		95
Glass, Cutlery etc.	1,700	4,326	By Interest on Bank Deposits		25
To Excess of Income over					
Expenditure		15,894			
		30,350			30,350

Balance Sheet
as on 31st December 2004

Liabilities		Rs	*Assets*		Rs
Subscription Received in Advance		760	Cash in Hand		1,400
Outstanding Salary		200	Cash at Bank		1,735
Sundry Creditors		3,135	Stock of Canteen Provision		300
Donation	3,600		Rent Outstanding		500
Less: Election Expenses	2,995	605	Library Books	2,280	
Capital Fund:			Less: Depreciation	228	2,052
Entrance Fees	225		Glass, Cutlery etc.		
General Fund	32,940		on 1st Jan. 2004	2,000	
Add: Donation Capitalised	2,450		Add: Purchased	1,000	
	35,615			3,000	
Add: Excess of Income	15,894	51,509	Less: Depreciation	1,700	1,300
			Furniture and Fixtures	3,520	
			Less: Depreciation	528	2,992
			Billiard Board		10,400
			Club Building	37,400	
			Less: Depreciation	1,870	35,530
		56,209			56,209

DISTINCTION BETWEEN INCOME AND EXPENDITURE ACCOUNT AND PROFIT AND LOSS ACCOUNT

The Income and Expenditure Account of a Non-trading concern is similar to profit and Loss Account of a Trading concern. However, the following differences may be noted:

1. Income and Expenditure Account is prepared by a Non-trading concern while Profit and Loss Account is prepared by a trading concern.
2. Income and Expenditure shows Surplus or Deficit while Profit and Loss Account shows Net Profit or Net Loss.
3. Income and Expenditure Account does not start with Gross Profit or Gross Loss while Profit and Loss Account starts with Gross Profit or Gross Loss.
4. The Surplus (or Deficit) shown in the Income and Expenditure is added (or deducted) to/from Capital Fund and is not distributed among the owners: whereas the Net Profit shown in the Profit and Loss Account is distributed among the owners.

ACCOUNTS OF PROFESSIONAL MEN

Professional men like Doctors, Lawyers, Architects etc. prefer to keep their accounts on what is called a Cash Receipt basis. They record their transactions on complete double entry system and prepare Trial Balance. They record their cash transactions in Receipts and Payments Account. A revenue Account called Receipts and Expenditure is prepared by professional people. And this Account is partly based on Cash System and partly on Accrual System. That is while preparing the Receipts and Expenditure Account, Cash System is followed for recording incomes but mercantile system is followed for recording expenditure. Again, all outstanding expenses are taken into account but ignore outstanding incomes which have not been received. While preparing the Receipts and Expenditure Account, credit is taken for the outstanding incomes but at the same time a provision is created for an amount equal to the outstanding income by debiting the Receipts and Expenditure Account. This reduces the fees earned to a "Cash Received Basis". Here, the debtors for outstanding fees are of a very uncertain nature. Besides this, the professional people do not approach the court for recovery of such outstanding incomes. Thus, they do not treat the outstanding incomes as earned until received in cash.

ILLUSTRATION 24.23

Mr Premlal who is a doctor commenced practice on 1st January 2004 with a cash of Rs 1,00,000. At the end of the year the following details of his receipts and payments are available:

Receipts and Payments Account
for the year ended 31st Dec. 2004

Dr. Cr.

	Rs		*Rs*
To Cash Introduced	1,00,000	By Furniture	10,000
To Fees Received	50,000	By Equipments	25,000
To Receipts from Dispensing	1,20,000	By Drugs	24,000
To Miscellaneous Receipts	1,000	By Assistant's Salary	10,000
		By Rent	12,000
		By Stationery	500
		By Electricity	1,000
		By Journals	900
		By Drawings	36,000
		By Cash at Bank	1,50,000
		By Cash in Hand	1,600
	2,71,000		2,71,000

Other information

1. Fees Rs 5,000 are still to be received.
2. Salary to assistant unpaid Rs 750.
3. Creditors for drugs purchased Rs 10,000.
4. Stock of drugs still in hand Rs 5,000.
5. Depreciate furniture and equipment by 10% p.a.

Prepare Receipts and Expenditure Account and Balance Sheet as on 31st December 2004.

SOLUTION

Receipts and Expenditure Account
Dr. **for the year ended 31st December 2004** Cr.

		Rs			Rs
To Drugs Consumed:			By Fees Received	50,000	
Paid	24,000		Add: Outstanding	5,000	55,000
Add: Outstanding	10,000		By Receipts from Dispensing		1,20,000
	34,000		By Miscellaneous Receipts		1,000
Less: Stock	5,000	29,000			
To Salary	10,000				
Add: Outstanding	750	10,750			
To Rent		12,000			
To Stationery		500			
To Electricity		1,000			
To Journals		900			
To Provision for Fees earned, but not received		5,000			
To Depreciation on Furniture		1,000			
To Depreciation on Equipments		2,500			
To Surplus		1,13,350			
		1,76,000			1,76,000

Balance Sheet as on 31st Dec. 2004

Liability		*Rs*	*Assets*		*Rs*
Outstanding Salary		750	Cash in Hand		1,600
Outstanding Creditors		10,000	Cash at Bank		1,50,000
Capital:	1,00,000		Fees Accrued	5,000	
Add: Surplus	1,13,350		Less: Provision	5,000	
	2,13,350		Drugs Stock		5,000
Less: Drawings	36,000	1,77,350	Furniture	10,000	
			Less: Depreciation	1,000	9,000
			Equipment	25,000	
			Less: Depreciation	2,500	22,500
		1,88,100			1,88,100

MISCELLANEOUS

ILLUSTRATION 24.24

	Rs
Subscription income for 2005-2006 as per Income and Expenditure Account	82,000

Advance subscription received in 2004-05	4,000
Subscriptions outstanding at the end of 2005-06 (including Rs. 1,000 for 2004-05)	9,500
Advance subscriptions received for 2006-07	2,000
Subscriptions written off during 2005-06	500
Subscriptions receivable on 1.4.2005	5,000
Subscriptions collected (2005-06) by the Secretary but not deposited	1,000

Prepare a Statement showing subscriptions received in 2005-2006 as per Receipts and Payments Account

(ICWA Inter)

SOLUTION:

		Rs.
Subscriptions income for 2005-2006 as per Income and Expenditure Account		82,000
Add: subscription receivable on 1.4.2005 collected	5,000	
Less: Outstanding at the end 2005 - 2006	1,000	
	4,000	
Less: Subscription written off	500	3,500
		85,500
Add: Advance Subscription received for 2006-2007		2,000
		87,500
Less: Advance subscription received in 2004-2005		4,000
		83,500
Less: Subscription outstanding at the end of 2005-2006, minus Rs. 1,000 relating to 2004-2005		8,500
		75,000
Less: Subscription for 2005-2006 collected by the Secretary but not deposited		1,000
Subscription received in 2005-2006 as per Receipts and Payments Account.		74,000

ILLUSTRATION: 24. 25

Calculate the amount of stationery to be posted to Income and Expenditure Account for the year 2006:

	Rs
Stock of stationery on 1st January 2006	300
Creditors for stationery on 1st January 2006	200
Advance paid for stationery on 31st Dec. 2005	20
Amount paid for stationery in 2006	1,080
Stock of stationery on 31st December 2006	50
Creditors for stationery on 31st December 2006	130
Advance paid for stationery on 31st December 2006	30.

(B. Com. MS)

SOLUTION:

	Rs
Stock of Stationery on 1st January 2006	300
Add: Amount paid for stationery in 2006	1,080
	1,380
Less: Payment made to creditors 1.1.2006	200
	1,180
Add: Advance paid on 31st December 2005	20
	1,200
Add: Creditors for stationery on 31.12.2006	130
	1,330
Less: Advance for stationery on31st Dec. 2006	30
	1,300
Less: Stock of stationery on 31st Dec. 2006	50
Amount of stationery to be posted to Income and Expenditure Account	1,250

ILLUSTRATION 24.26

GAMA Sports Club gives you the following Receipts and Payments Account for the year ended 31st march 2006

RECEIPTS AND PAYMENTS A/C

Receipts	*Rs.*	*Payments*	*Rs.*
To Balance b/d	4,820	By Salaries	12,000
To Subscriptions	28,600	By Rent & Electricity	7,220
To Miscellaneous income	700	By Library books	1,000
To Interest on fixed deposit	2,000	By Magazines of newspapers	2,172
		By Sundry Expenses	10,278
		By Sports equipments	1,000
		By Balance c/d	2,450
	36,120		36,120

Figures of Other assets & liabilities:

	31-3-2005 Rs	31-3-2006 Rs
Outstanding salaries	710	170
Outstanding rent & electricity	864	973
Outstanding for magazines and newspapers	226	340
Fixed deposit (10%) with bank	20,000	20,000
Interest accrued thereon	500	500
Subscriptions receivable	1,263	1,575
Prepaid expenses	417	620
Furniture	9,600	–
Sports equipments	7,200	–
Library books	5,000	–

The closing values of furniture and sports equipments are to be determined after charging depreciation at 10% and 20% p.a. respectively inclusive of additions, if any during the year. The library books are revalued at the end of every year and the value at the end of 31st March 2006 was Rs. 5,250

Required

(i) Balance sheet as at 31st March 2005

(ii) Income & Expenditure A/c for the year ended on 31st March 2006

(iii) Balance sheet as at 31st March 2006

[C.A.]

SOLUTION:

(i)

GAMA Sports Club

Balance sheet as on 31st March 2005

Liabilities	*Rs*	*Assets*	*Rs*
Outstanding Salaries	710	Furniture	9,600
Outstanding Rent & Electricity	864	Library Books	5,000
Creditors for magazines & Newspapers	226	Sports Equipment	7,200
Capital Fund (Bal.fig)	47,000	Fixed Deposit (10%)	20,000
		Cash in hand & at bank	4,820
		Prepaid Expenses	417
		Subscriptions due	1,263
		Accrued interest	500
	48,800		48,800

(II)

Income and Expenditure A/c of GAMA Sports club for the year ending 31st March 2006

Expenditure	*Rs.*	*Rs.*	*Income*	*Rs.*	*Rs.*
To Salaries	12,000		By Subscriptions	28,600	
Less: Outstanding (2005)	710		*Less:* Unpaid in 2005	1,263	
	11,290			27,337	
Add: Outstanding (2006)	170				
		11,460	*Add:* Unpaid in 2006	1,575	
To Rent & Electricity	7,220				28,912
Less: Outstanding (2005)	864				
			By Interest on FD	2,000	
	6,356		*Add:* Closing accrued	500	
Add: Outstanding (2006)	973				
		7,329		2,500	
To Magazine & Newspapers	2,172		*Less:* Opening accrued	500	
					2,000
Less: Outstanding (2005)	226		By Miscellaneous Income		700
	1,946		By Deficit–Excess of		
Add: Outstanding (2006)	340		Expenditure over		
		2,286	income		2,888
The Sundry Expenses	10,278				
Add: Prepaid (2005)	417				
	10,695				
Less: Prepaid (2006)	620				
		10,075			
To Depreciation on :					
Sports equipment (7,200 + 1,000) × 20%	1,640				
Furniture at 10%	960				
Library books (5,000 + 1,000 – 5,250)	750	3,350			
		34,500			34,500

(III) **Balance sheet of GAMA Sports Club as on 31st March 2006**

Expenditure	*Rs.*	*Rs.*	*Income*	*Rs.*	*Rs.*
Capital fund	47,000		Furniture	9,600	
Less Deficit	2,888		*Less:* Depreciation	960	
		44,112			8,640
Outstanding Expenses			Sports Equipment	7,200	
Salaries		170	*Add* : Addition	1,000	
Rent & Electricity		973			
Magazines & Newspapers		340		8,200	
			Less: Depreciation	1,640	
					6,560
			Library Books	5,000	
			Add: Addition	1,000	
				6,000	
			Less: Depreciation	750	
					5,250
			Fixed Deposit (10%)		20,000
			Accrued Interest on F.D.		500
			Cash in hand and Bank		2,450
			Subscription due		1,575
			Prepaid Expenses		620
		45,595			45,595

ILLUSTRATION 24.27

The Jubilee Club, Salem had the following assets and liabilities as on 1st January 2006.

	Rs.
Cash in hand	2,000
Subscriptions Receivable	200
Furniture	1,000
Sports materials	600
Investments	2,500
Buildings	5,000
Outstanding creditors for supplies	300
Capital fund	11,000

During 2006, the club did the following business.

Subscriptions received (including arrears) Rs. 3,000; Subscription due Rs. 300; paid the outstanding creditors for supplies; Subscriptions to newspapers Rs. 500; Sports materials purchased Rs. 1,000; Sale of old newspapers Rs. 50; Meeting expenses Rs. 450, Lighting charges Rs. 400; Salaries of establishment Rs. 1,000; Stock of Sports materials at the end Rs. 500; Interest received on investments Rs. 75 (outstanding Rs. 25); Borrowings Rs. 2,000; Purchased furniture Rs. 400 (end of the year); expenditure on annual function Rs. 375; Donations received Rs. 1,800 (half to be capitalised). Provide depreciation at 5% on Furniture and buildings.

Prepare Receipts and Payments A/c and Income & Expenditure A/c for the year ended 31-12-2006 and a Balance sheet as on that date.

SOLUTION:

Receipts & Payments A/c, for the year ended 31st December 2006

Receipts	*Rs*	*Payments*	*Rs*
To Cash in hand (On 1-1-2006)	2,000	By O/s Creditors for supplies	300
To Subscriptions	3,000	By Subscriptions to Newspapers	500
To Sale of Old Newspapers	50	By Sports materials purchased	1,000
To Interest on investments	75	By Meeting expenses	450
To Borrowings	2,000	By Lighting expenses	400
To Donations	1,800	By salaries of Establishment	1,000
		By Furniture purchased	400
		By Annual function expenses	375
		By Cash in hand (on 31-12-2006)	4,500
	8,925		8,925

Income and Expenditure A/c for the year ended 31st December 2006

Expenditure		*Rs.*	*Income*		*Rs.*
To Salaries		1,000	By Subscriptions	3,000	
To Subscriptions to Newspapers		500	*Less:* For previous year	200	
To Sports materials:					
Opening Stock	600			2,800	
Add: Purchased	1,000		*Add*: Due for 2006	300	
					3,100
	1,600		By sale of old newspapers		50
Less: Closing Stock	500		By Interest on		
		1,100	investments	75	
To Meeting Expenses		450	*Add:* Outstanding	25	
To Lighting Charges		400			100
To Annual function Expenses		375	By Donations (1,800 × 50%)		900
To Depreciation on :					
Furniture	50				
Buildings	250				
		300			
To Surplus - Excess of Income over expenditure		25			
		4,150			4,150

Balance Sheet as on 31st December 2006

Liabilities		*Rs*	*Assets*		*Rs*
Capital Fund	11,000		Cash in hand		4,500
Add: Donations			Subscription Receivable		300
(Rs. 1,800 × 50%)	900				
Surplus	25	11,925	Furniture	1,000	
Borrowings		2,000	*Less:* Depreciation	50	
				950	
			Add: Addition	400	1,350
			Investments		2,500
			Outstanding Interest		
			Investments		25

		Stock of sports		
		Materials		500
		Buildings	5,000	
		Less: Depreciation	250	4,750
	13,925			13,925

QUESTIONS

Objective Type Questions

I. Indicate whether the following statements are "True" or "False".

1. The Income and Expenditure Account serves the same purpose as that of Profit & Loss Account of a trading concern.
2. The Receipts and Payments Account shows excess of income over expenditure.
3. The primary object of a non-profit organisation is to render service to its members.
4. The main source of income of a non-trading concern is sales revenue.
5. Receipts and Payments Account is a nominal account.
6. Receipts and Payments Account starts with opening balance.
7. Amount received from life membership is totally credited to Income and Expenditure Account.
8. Proceeds from the sale of old newspapers treated as other incomes.
9. Subscriptions received in advance is an income.
10. Legacies are generally capitalised and taken to Balance Sheet.

[**Ans:** True: – 1, 3, 6, 8, 10
False: – 2, 4, 5, 7, 9.

II. Fill in the blanks

1. Receipts and Payments Account is a summary of .... receipts and ..... payments.
2. Receipts and Payments Accounts need not be accompanied by .....
3. Expenditure which results in the acquisition of permanent asset is .... expenditure.
4. The profit in non-profit concern is called ....
5. Excess of expenditure over income is .... from Capital Fund.

[**Ans:** 1. Cash: Cash; 2. Balance Sheet; 3. Capital; 4. Surplus; 5. Deducted]

III. Choose the appropriate answer.

1. Income and Expenditure Account reveals:
   (a) Cash in hand
   (b) Capital Account
   (c) Surplus or Deficiency
2. Receipts and Payments Account is:
   (a) Personal Account
   (b) Real Account
   (c) Nominal Account
3. Income and Expenditure Account records transactions of:
   (a) Revenue nature only
   (b) Capital nature only
   (c) Both capital and Revenue nature.
4. Subscriptions received in advance is
   (a) An Income
   (b) An asset
   (c) A liability

5. Receipts and Payments Account shows:
   (a) Income and Expenditure
   (b) Cash Receipts and Payments.
   (c) Assets and Liabilities
6. Non–trading institutions prepare:
   (a) Profit & Loss Account
   (b) Manufacturing Account
   (c) Income and Expenditure Account
7. Donations received for a special purpose will be taken to the:
   (a) Liability side of the Balance Sheet
   (b) Asset side of the Balance Sheet
   (c) Income and Expenditure Account
8. Legacies are generally:
   (a) Treated as income
   (b) Capitalised and taken to Balance Sheet
   (c) Treated as expenditure
9. Credite side balance in Income & Expenditure A/c indicates:
   (a) Excess of expenditure over income
   (b) Excess of cash receipts and payments
   (c) Excess of income over expenditure
10. A profit on sale of furniture of a club will be taken to:
   (a) Income and Expenditure A/c
   (b) Cash Account
   (c) Receipts and Payments Account

(**Ans:** 1. (c); 2. (b); 3. (a); 4. (c); 5. (b): 6. (c); 7. (a); 8. (b); 9. (c): 10. (a).

THEORETICAL QUESTIONS

1. State the difference between Receipts and Payments Account and Income and Expenditure Account.
2. What is Receipts and Payments Account?
3. What are the procedures to be adopted for the preparation of the Income and Expenditure Account from a given Receipts and Payments Account.
4. What are the essential features of Receipts and Payments Account?

PRACTICAL PROBLEMS

1. How would you show the following items relating to subscriptions in Incomes and Expenditure Account for the year ending 31st December 2004 and the Balance Sheet as at 31st December 2003 and 31st December 2004.

	Rs
Subscriptions received during 2004	7,170
Subscriptions outstanding at the end of 2003	600
Subscriptions received in advance on 3st December 2003	450
Subscriptions received in advance on 31st December 2004	270
Subscriptions outstanding on 31st December 2004 (including Rs 250 for 2003)	750

[**Ans:** Subscription to be credited to Rs 7,500]

2. The following particulars relate to the Cosmopolitan Club for the year ended 31.12.2004 and you are required to prepare therefrom an Income and Expenditure account for the year and a Balance Sheet as on 31.12.2004

Dr. **Summary of Cash Book** Cr.

		Rs		Rs
Balance from last year		2,350	Salaries	1,200
Entrance Fees		300	Electricity	120
Subscriptions:	Rs		Newspapers and journals	525
2003	50		Fixed deposits	2,500
2004	3,500		Utensils	200
2005	75	3,625	Payment to creditors	1,000
Profits from refreshments		100	Balance carried forward to next year	1,150
Locker rents		200		
Sundry income		120		
		6,695		6,695

The assets and liabilities on 1st January, 2004 were: Utensils Rs 800; Furniture Rs 2,500; Consumable stores Rs 350; Creditors Rs 1,200.

On 31.12.2004 value of consumable stores was Rs 700; creditors amounted to Rs 550; the subscriptions outstanding were Rs 75; and the interest accrued on fixed deposit was Rs 25.

(*B.Com., Madras*)

[**Ans:** Surplus Rs 2,475
Beginning Capital Fund Rs 4,850
Balance Sheet Total Rs 7,950.]

3.The following particulars relate to Madura Club for the year ended 31st December, 2004.

Receipts and Payments Account
for the year ended 31-12-2004

Dr. Cr.

Receipts	*Rs*		*Payments*	*Rs*
To Balance b/d		600	By Salaries	1,245
To Subscriptions			By Stationery	240
Arrears	24		By Rates and Taxes	360
Current	1,266		By Telephone	60
Advance	48	1,338	By Investments	750
To Profit from Canteen		900	By Advertisements	105
To Miscellaneous		45	By Postage	100
To Sale of old newspapers		112	By Sundries	350
To Dividends		485	By Balance c/d	270
		3,480		3,480

You are required to prepare an income and expenditure account and balance sheet after making the following adjustments:

(1) There are 450 members each paying annual subscription of Rs 3: Rs 27 being in arrears for 2003 at the beginning of this year.

(2) Stock of stationery on 31st December 2003 was Rs 30; on 31st December, 2004 Rs 54.

(3) Cost of buildings is Rs 6,000. Depreciate at the rate of 5 per cent. (*B.Com., Madras*)

[**Ans:** Surplus: Rs 156.
Beginning Capital Fund Rs 6,657.
Balance Sheet Total 6,861.]

4. The following is the Receipts and Payments Account of the Manian Sports Club for the year ending December 31, 2004:

Dr Cr.

Receipts		Rs	Payments	Rs
To Balance on 1.1.2004		2,500	By Wages	500
To Subscriptions:			By Furniture (purchased on 1.10.2004)	1,500
2003	250		By Sports expenses	1,250
2004	7,500		By Sundry expenses	7,600
2005	500	8,250	By Balance c/d	7,000
To Life Members' Fees		6,000		
To Sale of Scrap		100		
To Interest on Sports Fund Investments		1,000		
		17,850		17,850

The Club has 1,600 members each paying an annual subscription of Rs 5. Subscriptions of Rs 225 are still in arrears for 2003

On 1.1.2003 the Club's assets and liabilities included furniture of Rs 1,000, sports fund Rs 15,000, sports fund investment Rs 15,000. The investment was at 10%. Provide depreciation on furniture at 20%.

Prepare Income and Expenditure A/c for the year ended December 31st, 2004, and Balance Sheet as on that date. *(B.Com., Madurai)*

[**Ans:** Deficit Rs 25.
Beginning Capital Fund Rs 3,975.
Balance Sheet Total Rs 25,450.]

5. Following is the summary of receipts and payments of Janata Nursing Society for the year ended 31st December 2004.

Dr. Cr.

Receipts	Rs	Payments	Rs
To Balance at Bank on 1-1-2004		By Salaries	7,150
To Deposit on Building Fund A/c	19,000	By Medicines	2,100
To Current A/c	1,260	By Rent and Rates	900
To Members' Subscriptions	12,900	By Electricity	600
To Fees from non-members	1,200	By Telephone, etc.	400
To Grant from Local Authority	2,500	By General Expenses	1,700
To Donations for Building Fund	5,000	By Car Expenses	350
To Interest on Deposit on Building Fund A/c	1,140	By Cost of a secondhand car	3,860
		Balance at Bank on 31-12-2004:	
		Deposit on Building Fund A/c	25,140
		Current A/c	800
	43,000		43,000

The following information is also available:

(*a*) In 2002, the society purchased a plot of freehold land costing Rs 8,000.

(*b*) Fees from non-members include Rs 50 as fees received in advance for 2005.

(*c*) Rent of Rs 50 for January 2005 was paid on 15th Dec., 2004.

(*d*) Salaries of Rs 650 for December 2004 were not paid until 5th January 2005.

(*e*) Members' subscriptions include Rs 200 as subscriptions due in 2003.

Taking the above information into account, prepare the Income and Expenditure Account of the Society for the year ended 31.12.2004 and the Balance Sheet as at that date. *(B.Com., Mangalore)*

[**Ans:** Surplus Rs 2,550
Beginning Capital Fund Rs 9,460
Balance Sheet Total Rs 37,850]

6. Given below is the Receipts and Payments accounts of a club.

Receipts and Payments Accounts
for the year ended 31st December 2004

Dr. Cr.

Receipts		*Rs*	*Payments*	*Rs*
Balance: Cash	60		Salary of Secretary	3,600
Bank	3,000	3,060	Honorarium	450
Subscription (including sub.			Wages	2,400
for 2003 Rs 150)		9,000	Charities	2,000
Sale of old furniture			Printing & Stationery	300
(on 1st January 2004)		750	Postage	100
Sale of old newspapers		50	Rent & Taxes	1,200
Legacies		3,000	Upkeep of Land	500
Interest on Investments			Sports Materials	2,500
(cost of investment Rs 20,000)		1,200	Balance	14,850
Endowment fund Receipts		10,000		
Proceeds of concerts		800		
Advertisement in Year Book		40		
		27,900		27,900

Current assets and liabilities as on 31st December 2003 and 31st December 2004 are as follows:

	31-12-2003	31-12-2004
Subscription in arrears	200	450
Subscription in advance	300	600
Furniture	2,000	1,080

Depreciation was 10% p.a. on the furniture left after selling a part of it. It was decided that half of the legacies may be capitalised. Prepare Income and Expenditure Account for the year ending 31st December 2004 and Balance Sheet as on that date. You are also required to show calculations for the loss on sale of furniture. (*B.Com., Madurai*)

[**Ans:** Deficit Rs 630
Beginning Capital Fund Rs 24,960
Balance Sheet Total Rs 36,430
Loss on sale of furniture Rs 50]

7. The following so-called 'Balance Sheet' is submitted to you by the Secretary of the Mis-Town Bank Employees Club of which you are the President. You find that the moneys of the Club were not kept separate by the Secretary, but presumably mixed up with his own private cash. Prepare accounts—Receipts and Payments A/c, Income and Expenditure A/c for the year ended 31st December, 2004 and a Balance Sheet as on 1st January, 2004 and as on 31st December, 2004 from the following information:

Balance Sheet for the year 2004

Receipts	*Rs*	*Expenditure*	*Rs*
Opening Balance	750	Rent and Taxes	2,040
Arrears of Subscription	110	Salary	250
Subscription (Current Year)	1,640	Cost of Charity Show	150
Charity Show Tickets sold	210	Club-Day Collection Expenses	100
Club-Day Collections	140	Owing for Charity Show Tickets	50
Refreshments Sold	2,350	Owing for Donations to Building Fund	70
Receipts from Games	170	Refreshments bought	1,700

Donations for 'Building Fund'	190	Stock of Refreshments	150
		Subscriptions Owing	80
		Cost of Furniture	350
		Closing Balance	620
	5,560		5,560

(*C.A.I.I.B.*)

[**Ans:** Surplus Rs 550
Cash Balance Rs 970
Beginning Capital Fund Rs 860
Balance Sheet Total Rs 1,670]

8. From the following particulars, which relate to a Musical Society, prepare an Income and Expenditure Account and a Balance Sheet as at 31st December 2004.

Balance Sheet as at 31st December 2003

Liabilities	*Rs*	*Assets*	*Rs*
Outstanding Rent	425	Cash at Bank	3,000
Capital Fund:		Govt. Securities	10,000
Excess of Income over expenditure	15,575	Accrued Interest	125
		Outstanding Subscription	400
		Library Books	1,000
		Furniture and Fittings	1,475
	16,000		16,000

The transactions for the year were:

Receipt: Subscription Rs 2,500; Proceeds received from Entertainment and Lectures Rs 1,000; Interest on Securities Rs 475; Entrance fees received Rs 500; Sale proceeds of old chairs Rs 75 (Book Value Rs 100).

Payment: Rent Rs 600; Printing Rs 150; Advertising Rs 200; Sundries Rs 55; Govt. Securities Rs 2,500; Furniture Rs 400; Library books Rs 300; Cost of Entertainment Rs 750.

The following were outstanding as on 31st December 2004. Printing Rs 75; Rent Rs 100; Interest on Securities Rs 150; and Subscription Rs 325. (*C.A.I.I.B*)

[**Ans:** Surplus Rs 2,895
Cash in hand Rs 2,595
Balance Sheet Total Rs 18,645]

9. From the following particulars relating to Rama Krishna Mission Charitable Hospital, prepare Income and Expenditure Account for the year ended 31st December 2004 and Balance Sheet as at that date.

Receipts & Payments Account
for the year ended 31st December 2004

Dr. Cr.

Receipts	*Rs*	*Payments*	*Rs*
To Cash in Hand (1-1-2004)	7,130	By Medicines	30,590
To Subscriptions	47,996	By Doctor's Honorarium	9,000
To Donation	14,500	By Salaries	27,000
To Sale of Old Equipment (Cost Rs 200)	100	By Newspapers	400
		By Petty Expenses	461
To Interest on Investment (at 7% for full year)	7,000	By Equipments	15,000
		By Expenses on Charity Show	750
To Proceeds from charity show	10,250	By Cash in Hand	3,775
To Sale of Newspaper	100		
	87,076		87,076

Additional information:

	On 1-1-2004	On 31-12-2004
	Rs	Rs
1. Subscriptions due	240	280
2. Subscriptions received in advance	64	100
3. Stock of Medicines	8,810	9,740
4. Estimated value of Equipment	21,200	31,600
5. Building (Cost less Depreciation)	40,000	38,000
6. Salaries Outstanding	100	200
7. Prepaid Salaries	—	300

(*B.Com., Madurai*)

[**Ans:** Surplus Rs 6,179
Beginning Capital Fund Rs 1,77,216
Balance Sheet Total Rs 1,83,695]

10. The following is the summary of cash transactions of Gymkhana Club for the year ended 31st December, 2004:

Dr. Cr.

Receipts	*Rs*	*Payments*	*Rs*
To Opening Balance	2,000	By Rent	6,000
To Membership Subscription	50,000 (1)	By Advertisement	2,600 (3)
To Subscription for Dinner	10,000	By Furniture	8,000
To Donation for Flood Relief	5,000	By Flood Relief Expenses	6,000
To Legacy	1,500	By Salary	7,200 (4)
To Sale of Furniture	4,000 (2)	By Expenses for Dinner	11,000
To Miscellaneous Income	1,000	By Misc. Expenses	2,000
		By Investment	25,000
		By Upkeep of Ground	4,000
		By Closing Balance	1,700
	73,500		73,500

Further Information:

(1) Of the membership subscription, Rs 3,000 relates to 2003 and Rs 6,000 is outstanding for 2004.

(2) Sale of furniture represents old furniture of Rs 5,000 sold out of the balance of Rs 40,000 as on 31.12.2003.

	As on 31-12-2003	As on 31-12-2004
	Rs	Rs
(3) Advertisement bills unpaid	500	700
(4) Salary Outstanding	1,000	1,500
(5) Accrued Income on Investments	Nil	1,200
(6) Depreciation to be charged on closing balance of furniture @ 10%		

You are required to prepare the Income and Expenditure Account for the year ended 31st December, 2004 and to draw up a Balance Sheet as on that date. (*C.A. Inter*)

[**Ans:** Surplus Rs 26,900
Beginning Capital Fund Rs 43,500
Balance Sheet Total Rs 72,600]

11. The following particulars relate to the Nonesuch Sports Club:

Income and Expenditure Account

Dr. **for the year ended December 31, 2004** Cr.

	Rs		Rs
To Salaries	1,500	By Entrance Fees	10,500
To Printing and Stationery	2,200	By Subscriptions	15,600
To Advertising	1,600	By Rent	4,000
To Audit Fees	500		
To Fire Insurance	1,000		
To Depreciation on Sports Equipments	9,000		
To Excess of Income over Expenditure	14,300		
	30,100		30,100

Receipts and Payments Account

for the year ended December 31, 2004

	Rs		Rs
To Balance b/d	4,200	By Salaries	1,000
To Entrance fees	10,500	By Printing and Stationery	2,600
To Subscriptions:		By Advertisement	1,600
2003	600	By Fire Insurance	1,200
2004	15,000	By Investments	20,000
2005	400	By Balance c/d	7,800
To Rent Received	3,500		
	34,200		34,200

The assets on 1st January 2004 included club grounds and pavilion Rs 44,000; Sports Equipment Rs 25,000 and furniture and fixtures Rs 4,000. Subscriptions in arrears on that date were Rs 800.

Prepare the Balance Sheet as at December 31st, 2004. (*Madurai University*)

[**Ans:** Beginning Capital Fund Rs 77,600
Balance Sheet Total Rs 93,300]

12. Given below is Income and Expenditure Account and the Receipts and Payments Accounts of Bombay Sports Club for the year ended 31st December 2004:

Income and Expenditure Account

Dr. **for the year ended 31st December, 2004** Cr.

	Rs		Rs
To Salaries	8,600	By Entrance Fees	12,000
To Printing and Stationery	2,400	By Subscriptions	18,800
To Advertising	1,200	By Rents	5,000
To Audit fees	800		
To Fire Insurance	1,000		
To Miscellaneous Expenses	4,900		
To Depreciation on Sports Equipments	3,000		
To Excess of income over expenditure	13,900		
	35,800		35,800

Receipts and Payments Account
for the year ended 31st December, 2004

Dr.			Cr.	
		Rs		*Rs*
To Balance b/d		5,900	By Salaries	8,200
To Entrance Fees		12,000	By Printing and Stationery	3,000
To Subscriptions:	Rs		By Advertising	1,200
2003	950		By Fire Insurance	1,200
2004	18,200		By Investments	15,000
2005	700	19,850	By Sports Equipment	5,000
To Rent Received		4,500	By Miscellaneous Expenses	4,700
			By Balance c/d	3,950
		42,250		42,250

The assets on 1st January 2004 included Club Ground and Pavilion Rs 48,000, Sports Equipments Rs 25,000 and Furniture and Fixtures Rs 6,000. On that date subscriptions in arrears were Rs 1,300 and subscription paid in advance were Rs 200, and creditors for Stationery were Rs 600.

You are required to prepare the Balance Sheet as at 31st December, 2004. *(C.A. Inter)*

[Ans: Beginning Capital Fund Rs 85,400
Balance Sheet Total Rs 1,01,400]

13. The following is the receipts and payments statement of the Madras Sports Club for the year ended 31st December 2004.

Dr.		Cr.	
	Rs		*Rs*
To Balance (January 2004)	2,400	By Secretary's Salary	3,600
To Entrance Fees	500 (*a*)	By Upkeep of grounds	2,100 (*c*)
To Subscriptions	8,700	By Wages of groundmen	2,400 (*d*)
To Proceeds of Concerts	1,500	By Ground Rent	150
To Interest on Investment	500 (*b*)	By Printing & Postage	200
		By Sundry Repairs	175
		By Balance (31-12-2004)	4,975
	13,600		13,600

(*a*) This item includes subscription outstanding brought over from previous year Rs 500.
(*b*) This amount includes Rs 100 in respect of interest accrued in preceding period.
(*c*) This item includes Rs 300 applicable to the previous year.
(*d*) This item includes Rs 150 applicable to the previous year.

Other ledger balances at the commencement of the financial period were: Capital fund Rs 40,100; Income and expenditure account credit balance brought forward Rs 8,900; Club premises and grounds (as per valuation) Rs 30,000; Investments Rs 10,000; Sports materials Rs 2,450, Furniture and fixtures Rs 4,000.

From the above particulars, prepare a balance sheet at the commencement of period, and income and expenditure account for the period and a balance sheet as at the close of the period.

Entrance fees are to be capitalised. The outstanding liabilities on 31st December 2004 were: Wages Rs 200 and printing Rs 100. Interest accrued and outstanding on investments was Rs 120. Depreciation club premises by 2%, furniture by 5% and Sports equipment by 30%. *(B.Com., Madras)*

[Ans: Surplus Rs 210
Balance Sheet Total Rs 50,010]

14. Prepare the receipts and payments account of the sports club for the year ended 31st December 2004 and also compile its Balance Sheet as on 31st Dec., 2003 from the following information furnished at (*a*), (*b*) and (*c*):

(*a*) Balance Sheet as on 31st December 2004

	Rs			*Rs*
Subscription received in advance	900	Cash in Hand		1,000
Outstanding salary	2,000	Cash at Bank		3,000
Capital Fund	20,400	Sports Equipment	15,500	
		Less Depreciation	500	15,00
		Subscription arrears		4,000
		Prepaid Insurance		300
	23,300			23,300

(*b*) Income and Expenditure Account
for the year ended 31st December 2004

Dr. Cr.

Expenditure		*Rs*	*Income*	*Rs*
To Salaries		11,000	By Subscriptions	42,000
To Periodicals		800	By Profit in sale of sports equipments	
To Entertainment Expenses		9,000	(book value is Rs 1,000)	400
To Printing & Stationery		1,000		
To Tournament Expenses & Prizes		3,000		
To Audit Fees		900		
To Insurance		1,000		
To Depreciation		500		
To Restaurant Loss				
Expenses	42,000			
Less collection	30,000	12,000		
To Surplus being the excess of income over expenditure		3,200		
		42,400		42,400

(c) Further particulars available as on 31st December 2003 are:

Subscriptions received in advance	Rs	1,500
Subscriptions Due	Rs	2,600
Cash in hand	Rs	700
Sports Equipment	Rs	11,000

(*B.Com., Madurai*)

[Ans: Beginning Capital Fund Rs 12,800
Receipts and Payments Account Total Rs 76,500]

15. From the following data, prepare an Income and Expenditure Account for the year ended 31st December, 2004, and a statement of affairs as at date of the Mayura Hospital:

Receipts and Payments Account
for the year ended 31st December 2004

Dr. Cr.

		Rs		*Rs*
To Balances:			By Salaries: (Rs 3,600 for 2003)	15,600
Cash	400		By Hospital Equipment	8,500
Bank	2,600	3,000	By Furniture purchased	3,000
To Subscriptions:			By Additions to Building	25,000

For 2003	2,550	By Printing & Stationery		1,200
For 2004	12,250	By Diet Expenses		7,800
For 2005	1,200	By Rent and Rates (Rs 150 for 2005)		1,000
To Government Grant:		By Electricity and Water charges		1,200
For Building	40,000	By Office Expenses		1,000
For Maintenance	10,000	By Investments		10,000
To Fees from Sundry Patients	2,400	By Balance:		
To Donations (not to be capitalised)	4,000	Cash	700	
To Net collections from benefit shows	3,000	Bank	3,400	4,100
	78,400			78,400

Additional information: Rs.

Value of building under construction as on 31-12-2004	70,000
Value of hospital equipment on 31-12-2004	25,500
Building fund as on 1-1-2004	40,000
Subscription in arrears as on 31-12-2003	3,250

Investments in 8% Government Securities were made on 1st July 2004 (*C.A. Inter*)

[**Ans:** Surplus Rs 8,000
Beginning Capital Fund Rs 24,650
Balance Sheet Total Rs 1,13,850]

16. The following is the Receipts and Payments Account of the Delhi Literary Society for the year ended 31st March, 2004:

Dr. Cr.

	Rs		*Rs*
To Cash at Bank	12,500	By Salaries	2,500
To Subscriptions	52,500	By Printing and Stationery	1,250
To Annual Day Receipts	26,800	By Annual Day Expenses	1,500
To Mushaira Receipts	22,500	By Mushaira Expenses	10,000
To Dividends on Shares	2,500	By Telephone Charges	2,500
		By Sundry Expenses	2,000
		By Shares Purchased	75,000
		By Postage and Telegrams	2,200
		By Building Maintenance	6,340
		By Cash at Bank	13,510
	1,16,800		1,16,800

The following further information is furnished:

(1) The value of the Building owned by the Society stood at Rs 50,000 as at 1st April, 2003. Depreciation at 5 per cent has to be provided.

(2) There were 200 members paying subscriptions at the rate of Rs 250 per annum each.

(3) As on 1st April 2003 no subscriptions had been received in advance but subscriptions were outstanding to the extent of Rs 1,000 as at 31st March 2003 and on 31st March, 2004 subscription outstanding were Rs 1,500.

(4) Postage Stamp worth Rs 250 were with the Secretary at the beginning of the year and the stamps at the end of the value of Rs 150.

(5) The investment in shares at the beginning of the year was to extent of Rs 5,000.

(6) An amount of Rs 250 in respect of the Annual Day Receipts was yet to be received.

(7) The rent of the theatre (amounting Rs 2,500) where the mushaira (poetic symposium) was held is still to be paid.

(8) Hire of telephone to the extent of Rs 300 is paid in advance.

You are required to prepare the Income and Expenditure Account for the year ended 31st March 2004 and the Balance Sheet as at that date. (*C.A. Inter*)

[**Ans:** Surplus Rs 68,960
Beginning Capital Fund Rs 68,750
Balance Sheet Total Rs 1,43,210]

17. The following is the Receipts and Payments Accounts of Madras Junior Club for the year ended 31st December, 2004.

Dr. Cr.

Receipts		*Rs*	*Payments*	*Rs*
To Balance at Bank on 1-1-2004		1,020	By Salaries	4,160
To Entrance Fees		1,000	By Rent	1,860
To Subscriptions:	Rs		By Electricity	1,280
2003	250		By Postage and Stationery	330
2004	3,050		By Insurance Premium	180
2005	350	3,650	By General Expenses	460
To Sale of Investments		7,500	By Part payment on account of new furniture	4,500
To Loan taken from Krishnaswamy on 1-7-2004 at 10% interest p.a.		2,000	By Balance at Bank	2,400
		15,170		15,170

(1) The following information is also available:

	31-12-2003	31-12-2004
Rent due	180	360
Electricity	640	200
Subscriptions due	250	400
Insurance Paid in Advance	50	70

(2) The cost of the investments sold was Rs 5,000. The surplus is to be treated as income.

(3) Furniture was valued at Rs 3,000 on 31.12.2003. On 30th June 2004 the Club purchased additional new furniture at a cost of Rs 5,200. Depreciation at the rate of 10% is to be provided on all furniture.

(4) The entrance fees are not to be capitalised.

Prepare an income and expenditure account for the year ended 31st December, 2004 and a balance sheet as on that date. (*B.Com., Madras*)

[**Ans:** Deficit Rs 1,700
Beginning Capital Fund Rs 8,500
Balance Sheet Total Rs 10,510]

18. Mr Prim and Mr Proper are in partnership as proprietors of a Boarding School, sharing profits Mr Prim 3/5ths and Mr Proper 2/5ths. The trial balance extracted from their books as on 31st March, 2004 which coincided with the end of the last term of the year, was as follows:

Debits	*Amount*	*Credits*	*Amount*
	Rs		*Rs*
Furniture and Fittings at cost	3,920	Capital Account:	
Stocks at 1st April 2003		Mr Prim	10,500
Food	560	Mr Proper	8,400
Fuel	280	Reserve for depreciation on furniture and fittings	2,520
Purchases:			
Food	18,760	Fees and Extras	61,880

Fuel	2,520	
Salaries, wages and medical attention	16,800	
Repairs	1,680	
Laundry	5,040	
Stationery	1,260	
Drawings:		
Mr Prim	6,650	
Mr Proper	4,200	
Cash at Bank	21,630	
	83,300	83,300

You are given the following additional information:

(1) On 31st March, 2004 stocks of food and fuel were Rs 840 and Rs 210 respectively.

(2) On 31st March, 2004 amounts owing for food and laundry were Rs 630 and Rs 420 respectively.

(3) Fees, other than extras are payable in advance and accounts are sent out at the beginning of each term. Each account includes extras for the previous term. At 31st March, 2004 all amounts due had been received with the exception of Rs 588 (not yet accounted, of which Rs 238 was bad). The extras for the last term, not yet billed, were Rs 2,100.

(4) No interest is to be credited on capital accounts.

(5) Mr Prim, who owns the premises, is to be credited with Rs 2,800 for the use of the premises.

(6) Repairs include Rs 280 for the purchase of a steel cupboard, which is to be capitalised under furniture and fittings.

(7) Depreciation on furniture and fittings is to be provided at the rate of 5% per annum on cost at the end of the year.

(8) Mr Sweet the Senior Master is entitled to 5% of the net profits after charging such commission.

Prepare the revenue account for the year ended 31st March, 2004 and the balance sheet as on that date. *(B.Com., Madras)*

[Ans: Profit Prim Rs 8,400 and Proper Rs 5,600
Balance Sheet Total Rs 26,600]

19. The following particulars related to Fast Sports Club Income and Expenditure Account for the year ended 31st December 2004:

	Rs		*Rs*
To Salaries	6,000	By Admission Fees	15,000
To Printing and Stationery	2,500	By Subscriptions	25,000
To Advertising	1,000	By Rent Receivable	4,800
To Insurance Charges	900		
To Electricity Charges	500		
To Depreciation on Sports Equipments	12,000		
To Excess of Income over Expenditure	21,900		
	44,800		44,800

Receipts and Payments Account
for the year ended 31st December 2004

		Rs		*Rs*
To Balance b/d		5,000	By Salaries (Including Advance)	7,500
To Admission Fees:			By Printing and Stationery	2,500
2003	2,500		By Advertising	1,000
2004	13,500	16,000	By Insurance Charges (partly for	

To Subscriptions:			next year)	1,200
2003	1,000		By Electricity	500
2004	23,000		By Purchase of Fixed Assets	20,000
2005	2,000	26,000	By Balance c/d	17,900
To Rent		3,600		
		50,600		50,600

On 1st January 2004, the Club had the following assets:

Land and Buildings	Rs 60,000
Sports and Equipment	Rs 30,000
Furniture	Rs 4,500

Prepare Opening and Closing Balance Sheets. (*C.A. Entrance*)

[**Ans:** Capital Fund (1.1.2004) Rs 1,03,000
B/s Total (1.1.2004) Rs 1,03,000
B/s Total (31.12.2004) Rs 1,26,900]

20. From the following accounts taken from the books of S.S. Hospital for the year ending 31st December, 2004 you are required to prepare its opening, i.e., at 1st January, 2004 and its closing, i.e., as at 31st December, 2004, balance sheets:

Receipts and Payments Account

Dr.	*Rs*		Cr. *Rs*
To Balance:		By Payments:	
Cash	600	Furniture purchased	1,000
Bank	7,000	Instruments purchased	2,000
Govt. Securities	1,80,000	Surgery and dispensary	1,500
To Receipts:		Diet Expenses	2,500
Subscriptions	30,000	Rent and Taxes	2,400
Donations	6,000	Insurance	500
Interest	10,000	Office Expenses	1,200
Miscellaneous	500	Salaries	24,000
		Miscellaneous Expenses	200
		By Closing Balances:	
		Cash	1,800
		Bank	17,000
		Govt. Securities	1,80,000
	2,34,100		2,34,100

Income and Expenditure Account
for the year ending 31st December 2004

Dr.		*Rs*			Cr. *Rs*
To Salaries:			By Subscription:		
Paid	24,000		Receipts	30,000	
Less: For 2003	1,500		Less: For 2003	10,000	
	22,500			20,000	
Add: Outstanding	1,000	23,500	Add: Outstanding	8,000	28,000
To Diet Expenses		2,500	By Donations		6,000
To Surgery and Dispensary			By Interest:		

Expenses		1,500	Received	10,000	
To Rent and Taxes:			Less: For 2003	2,500	
Paid	2,400			7,500	
Less: For 2003	200		Add: Outstanding	2,500	10,000
	2,200		By Miscellaneous Receipts		500
Add: Outstanding	250	2,450			
To Insurance	500				
Less: Prepaid	100	400			
To Office Expenses		1,200			
To Miscellaneous Expenses		200			
To Depreciation:					
Building @ 2½%		5,000			
Furniture @ 10%		400			
Instruments @ 20%		1,200			
To Surplus		6,150			
		44,500			44,500

Depreciation on all assets has been worked out for the full year. Value of building is exclusive of the cost of land of the hospital amounting to Rs 50,000. Govt. securities of the face value of Rs 2,00,000 (cost Rs 1,80,000) Represent investment of the endowment fund of the hospital.

(*Institute of Company Secretaries*)

[Ans: Beginning Capital Fund: Rs 2,75,400
Beginning Balance Sheet Total Rs 4,57,100
Closing Balance Sheet Total Rs 4,62,800]

21. "Citizens Club" was registered in a city and the Accountant prepared the following Receipts and Payments Account for the year ended October 31st, 2004 and showed a deficit of Rs 14,520.

Dr. Cr.

Receipts	*Rs*	*Payments*	*Rs*
To Subscription	62,130	By Premises	30,000
To Fair Receipts	7,200	By Honorarium to Secretary	12,000
To Variety Show Receipts (net)	12,810	By Rent	2,400
To Interest	690	By Rates and Taxes	3,780
To Bar Collection	22,350	By Printing and Stationery	1,410
To Cash Spent More	1,000	By Sundry Expenses	5,350
To Deficit	14,520	By Wages	2,520
		By Fair Expenses	7,170
		By Bar Purchases-Payments	17,310
		By Repairs	960
		By New Car (Less proceeds of old car Rs 9,000)	37,800
	1,20,700		1,20,700

The following additional information could be obtained.

	1-11-2003	31-10-2004
	Rs	Rs
Cash in Hand	450	—
Bank Balance as per Pass Book	24,690	10,440
Cheques issued not presented for Sundry Expenses	270	90
Subscriptions due	3,600	2,940
Premises at cost	87,000	1,17,000

Accumulated Depreciation on Premises	56,400	—
Car at cost	36,570	46,800
Accumulated Depreciation on Car	30,870	—
Bar Stock	2,130	2,610
Creditors for Bar Purchases	1,770	1,290

Cash overspent represent honorarium to Secretary not withdrawn due to cash deficit. His annual honorarium is Rs 12,000. Depreciation on premises and car is to be provided at 5 per cent and 20 per cent on written down value.

You are required to prepare the correct Receipts and Payment Account, Income and Expenditure Account and Balance Sheet as at October 31,2004. (*ICWA Inter*)

[**Ans:** Balance Cash in hand Rs 10,350; Surplus Rs 43,490;
Beginning Capital Fund Rs 65,130; Balance Sheet Total Rs 1,10,910]

22. The following Summary of the Cash Book has been prepared by the Treasurer of a Club:

Receipts and Payments
for the year ended 31st March 2004

	Rs		*Rs*
To Balance b/d	4,740	By Wages–Outdoor staff	13,380
To Subscriptions	29,720	By Restaurant Purchase	50,400
To Entrance Fees	3,200	By Rent–18 months to July 2004	7,500
To Restaurant Receipts	56,800	By Rates	2,200
To Games Competition Receipts	13,640	By Secretary's salary	3,120
		By Lighting	7,700
		By Competition Prizes	4,000
		By Printing and Postage etc.	6,000
		By Placed in Fixed Deposit	8,000
		By Balance c/d	5,800
	1,08,180		1,08,100

On 1st April 2003, the Club's assets were:
Furniture Rs 48,000
Restaurant Stock Rs 2,600
Stock of Prizes Rs 800
Rs 5,200 was owing for supplies to the restaurant.
On 31st March 2004, the Restaurant stock were Rs 3,000 the prizes in hand were Rs 500
While the Club owed Rs 5,600 for restaurant supplies.
It was also found that subscriptions unpaid at 31st March 2004 amounted to Rs 1,000 and that of the figure of Rs 29,720 shown in the Cash book included Rs 700 in respect of previous year and Rs 400 paid in advance for the following year.
Prepare an account showing the Profit and Loss made on the Restaurant and a General Income and Expenditure Account for the year ended 31st March 2004, together with a Balance Sheet as at that date, after writing 10% off the Furniture. (*M.Com., Calcutta*)

[**Ans:** Surplus: Rs 3,160
Capital Fund Rs 50,390 (1.4.2003)
B/S Total Rs 62,750 (31.3.2004)

23. From the following Trial Balance of a Club taken out on the 31st March 2004, prepare and Expenditure Account for the year and a Balance Sheet as on that date:

	Rs	Rs
Rent for the year	5,000	–
Rates, Taxes and Insurance for the year	4,360	–
Loan @ 5%	–	3,000
Sundry Creditors	–	10,220
Entrance Fees	–	3,500
Cash at Bank	300	–
Cash in hand	20	–
Secretary's Remuneration	1,500	–
Sundry Debtors	1,180	–
Subscriptions received in Advance	–	1,600
Furniture and Fixtures	12,000	–
Steward's and Servent's wages	6,000	–
Club House	10,000	–
Improvement to Club House	6,840	–
Printing, Stationery and Newspapers	1,450	–
Law charges	180	–
Annual Subscriptions	–	21,370
Card and Billiard Room Receipts	–	1,230
Washing of Liveries and Sundries	1,070	–
Wines, Cards and Cigars sold	–	4,300
Repairs to House and Furniture	4,090	–
Conversation Expenses	950	–
Wines, Cards and Cigars purchased	3,410	–
Stock of Cigars (1st April 2003)	150	–
Interest on Loan	60	–
Excess of Income over Expenditure brought forward from last year–	–	12,950
	58,560	58,560

Rs 1,200 are to be written off the Furniture and Fixtures and Rs 1,000 off the Club House. There was no stocks at the end of the year. *(CA)*

[Ans: Surplus Rs 370
B/S Total Rs 28,140]

24. Following is the Income and Expenditure of the United Club for the year ended on 30th June 2004.

Income and Expenditure Account
for the year ended 30th June 2004

	Rs		Rs
To Salaries	15,750	By Subscriptions	45,000
To Stationery	1,250	By Donations	7,500
To Postage	800	By Sale of Furniture (Profit)	1,000
To Sundry Expenses	4,700	By Government Grant	4,000
To Repairs and Maintenance	3,600	By Interest on Fixed Deposit	800
To Sports Expenditure	1,800		
To Swimming Pool Expenditure and Maintenance	2,000		
To Affiliation Fee	500		
To Electricity	3,250		
To Billiard Room Expenses	1,250		
To Periodicals	1,200		

To Audit Fees	250		
To Depreciation on:			
Sports Equipment	1,000		
Buildings	2,500		
Furniture	450		
To Surplus	18,000		
	58,300		58,300

The above Account is prepared after considering the information mentioned below:

	As on 1-7-2003	As on 30-6-2004
	Rs	Rs
1. Buildings	1,00,000	97,500
2. Sports Ground	1,00,000	1,00,000
3. Sports Equipments	6,000	9,000
4. Furniture	5,000	–
5. Fixed Deposit in Bank	8,000	8,000
6. Bank Account (Savings Deposit)	–	25,000
7. Subscriptions Outstanding	5,000	2,000
8. Subscriptions received in advance	3,000	1,000
9. Stock of Stationery	250	500
10. Audit Fees Outstanding	200	250
11. Salaries Outstanding	500	1,000
12. Affiliation Fee paid in advance	–	250

Cash in hand on 1.7.2003 was Rs 1,250; new Furniture, by disposing the old, for Rs 9,000 has been purchased on credit but not entered in books. Depreciation has been charged on this Furniture @ 5%.

You are required to prepare:

(1) Receipts and Payments Account for the year ended on 30.6.2004

(2) Balance Sheet as at 30.6.2004. *(ICWA)*

[**Ans:** Cash Balance on 30.6.2004 Rs 250
Capital Fund on 30.6.2003 Rs 2,21,800
B/S Total on 30.6.2004 Rs 2,51,050]

25. From the following particulars for the year 2004 prepare Receipts and Payments Accounts, Income and Expenditure Account and Balance Sheet of Everactive Club.

	Rs
Cash and Bank Balance	14,320
Member Entrance Fees received	2,20,000
Subscription received	88,000
Hall hire charges received	69,000
Receipts from Canteen Sales	3,14,650
Purchases of Provisions for Canteen	3,13,860
Buildings repairs, paintings etc.	28,750
Ground Maintenance	45,000
Donations for Club Annexe Building Fund	1,00,000
Advance to Building Contractor for construction of Club Annexe	11,000
Payments for Bats and Balls etc.	12,000

Lighting and other facilities for members	27,000
Payments to New Furniture Mart	86,000

As per by-laws of the Club, 50% of the Entrance Fees is to be capitalised. The Capital Fund and Building Fund for Club Annexe at the beginning of the year were Rs 3,67,000 and Rs 25,000 respectively. Depreciate Building by 5% and Furniture by 30%. Other information:

	31-12-2003	31-12-2004
	Rs	Rs
Sundry Creditors:		
For Bats and Balls	1,820	—
For Furniture	23,000	17,000
Subscriptions due from Members	8,500	13,500
Buildings (Written Down Value)	2,75,000	—
Furniture (Written Down Value)	1,10,000	—
Bats and Balls (Revalued)	9,000	12,000

(*CAIIB*)

[**Ans:** Closing Cash Rs 2,82,360
Surplus Rs 1,32,110
Capital Fund on 31.12.2003 Rs 3,67,000
B/S Total on 31.12.2004 Rs 7,51,110]

26. The following is the copy of the accounts prepared by the Secretary of a Trade Union. Prepare therefrom an Income and Expenditure Account and a Balance Sheet.

Balance Sheet as at 31st December 2004

	Rs		*Rs*
Cash in Secretary's hand	25	General Expenses	2,400
Property on 1st Jan. 2004	4,537	Affiliation Fees	3,000
Cash at Bank on 1.1.2004	6,775	Administration charges	600
Contribution and Fees:		Printing and Stationery	720
Branch 1	5,200	Remitted to Branch 2	120
Branch 2	2,500	Legal charges for purchase of property	900
Dividends received	289	Purchase of Govt. Securities	3,800
Rentals received	1,700	Property on 31.12.2004	9,857
Bank Overdraft 31.12.2004	385	Cash in Secretary's hand on 31.12.2004	14
	21,411		21,411

The following funds in the hands of Branch secretaries have not been included in the above.

	Branch 1	Branch 2
	Rs	Rs
1.1.2004	120	90
31.12.2004	96	150

(*M.Com. Madurai*)

[**Ans:** Surplus Rs 2,885
Capital Fund on 1.1.2004 Rs 11,547
B/S Total on 31.12.2004 Rs 14,817]

Chapter 25

Contract Account

Introduction – Features – Types – Accounting Procedure – Work Certified – Work Uncertified – Treatment of Profits – Escalation Clause – Cost Plus Contract – Work - in - progress – Accounting Standard – Questions – Objective Type Questions – Theoretical Questions – Practical Problems

INTRODUCTION

A contract account is prepared by a Contractor. A contract, by and large, involves an agreement between parties who undertake jobs, such as construction of a dam or a building or a ship; laying down railway lines or roads etc. Generally a contract is a big job requiring considerable length of time to complete and the work may be undertaken outside the factory. The person who agrees to perform the work is called a Contractor. The person who gives the contract or for whom the work is done is called the Contractee. The sum of money agreed upon to be paid by the Contractee is known as Contract Price. The agreement between the Contractor and the Contractee to complete a job is called a Contract. A contract account is prepared to find out the cost of the contract and to know the profit or loss made on the contract. On the basis of the contract, other similar contracts can be undertaken.

According to the Accounting Standard – 7 (AS – 7) issued by the Institute of Chartered Accountants of India, a construction contract" is a contract for the construction of an asset or of a combination of assets which together constitute a single project. Examples of activity covered by such contracts include the construction of bridges, dams, ships, buildings and complex pieces of equipment."

A Contractor has to maintain a separate account known as Contract Account for each job and this facilitates to know the profit earned or loss incurred. It is akin to factory job costing, but varies only in size; and the contract continues for a longer time. A contractor undertakes a small number of big contracts at a time. For example, builders, civil engineering firms, constructional and mechanical engineering firms etc., adopt this method of costing.

FEATURES

1. The execution of a contract job may extend to a period which may be greater than one accounting year and two or three contracts may be undertaken by one contractor at the same time.
2. When big contract work is undertaken, there arise problems of cost control on materials, labour, stores etc. and losses, pilferage, damage or loss to plants or tools etc.
3. As most of the items of expenses can be directly identified with a contract, though indirect, are treated as direct expenses.

TYPES OF CONTRACTS

Basically, there are two types of construction work

(a) Fixed price contracts and (b) Cost Plus Contracts.

(A) Fixed Price Contracts

Contracts which are agreed to be executed for a fixed price are known as Fixed Price Contracts. Any loss due to increase in price of materials, labour etc., will have to be born by the contractor. The contract price, once fixed, cannot be changed.

(B) Cost Plus Contract

Certain contracts are such that their cost cannot be estimated in advance. Under this circumstance, the contractor is assured of the actual cost to which a margin of profit is added. The profit is in the form of a fixed amount or of a percentage on actual cost. The total cost incurred by the contractor is subject to scrutiny by the contractee, who possesses the right.

Cost plus contract is advantageous to both the contractor and the contractee. Neither of them stand to lose. The contract receives a reasonable profit and the contractee is ensured of a reasonable price. This type of contract is undertaken for the production of special articles, not usually manufactured; e.g., in case of urgent repairs of ships, vehicles, power-house and construction during war time etc.

Escalation Clause

It is a clause in the agreement of a contract, which provides to compensate the contractor to accommodate the price variance in the cost of materials or labour, because of the market fluctuations. This clause is included in the case of long period contracts. It safeguards the contractor and the contractee against unfavourably (rise or fall) changes in prices of materials and labour.

ACCOUNTING PROCEDURE

A contract ledger is kept in which a separate account is opened for each contract undertaken. It is usual to give each contract a distingui ..ng number. A contract account is debited with all direct and indirect expenditure incurred in relation to the contract. It is credited with the amount of contract price on completion of the contract. The balance represents profit or loss made on the contract and is transferred to Profit and Loss Account. The treatment of important expenses dealt with is as follows:

(a) Material

(*a*) Materials needed for a contract may be obtained either from direct purchase or from the store. When the materials are purchased from outside for the use of a contract, the total cost is directly debited to the related contract. If the materials are received through Material Requisitions from store, the cost of the material will be debited to the related contract. Each Material Requisition contains the contract number. Alternatively, material cost of a job can be known from the Material Abstract, prepared on the basis of Material Requisition and debited to the contract directly, in summary, either weekly or monthly.

There may be two types of wastages - normal and abnormal. In the case of normal wastages, the issue rate of materials is inflated in order to recover the normal wastages and the total cost of materials at the inflated rate is debited to the contract. The abnormal wastage is to be transferred to profit and loss account. Any type of theft or destruction of materials is lost which is transferred to profit and loss account.

Surplus materials lying at the site are credited to the contract account with the cost, whether the surplus is returned to the store or transferred to another job. Sometimes, the customer himself supplies certain materials for the contract; and the same should be entered into a separate book of accounts and not debited to the contract.

At the time of closing accounts, materials, if any, in hand are credited to the contract account.

(b) Labour

The contracts are carried out at the site of the construction i.e., away from the contractor's premises. Therefore, there arises a problem of control. The labour employed on contracts is treated as direct labour, and the labour cost is debited to the contract. When there are a number of contracts, a pay-roll is prepared for each contract. The total amount of each contract is to be debited to the respective contracts. The salaries of supervisory staff, supervising two or more contracts, are apportioned on equitable basis. Wages accrued will also be debited to the contract account.

(c) Overhead

Generally apportioning overhead expenses do not arise, because most of the expenses such as lighting, power, maintenance of plant, architect fees, hire charges of special plant etc., are entirely charged to the contracts. However, costs common to more than one contract such as Head Office expenses should be apportioned and charged to each contract with respective share on some suitable basis; for example, labour-hour rate.

(d) Plant

The cost of the plant used for the contract is charged. Special types of plants are brought to the site for use, such as cement concrete mixer, crane, tractor, floor polishing machine etc. A clear record may be kept and properly accounted. There are two methods of charging the contract for using the machines.

(1) Contract is debited with the full value of the plant. When a new plant or old plant is issued to a contract, the cost of the plant or book value of the old plant is debited to the contract. The plant is revalued at the end of the year and credited to the contract with revalued (depreciated) value. This method is good when the plant is put under regular use for the contract for a longer period. In certain cases, the plant gets completely worn out before completion of the work. The depreciated value of the plant is carried forward as the opening balance at the commencement of the next accounting year.

(2) Alternatively, the depreciation calculated on the basis of hourly or daily rate, is debited to the contract. In such case, the value of the plant is not debited to contract. For this, an 'Upkeep Account' is to be maintained. The cost of running expenses of the plant, repairs, maintenance, oil etc., is debited, a hire rate is fixed with the help of this account and the contract is charged accordingly.

When a portion of the plant is returned to the store, the contract is credited with the depreciated value of that part. If the plant is sold, the full value is debited to the contract and credit must also be given to the contract. When the plant is lost or destroyed, it will be transferred to profit and loss account.

(e) Sub - contracts

Sometimes, the contractor gives a portion of work to sub-contractor. For instance, the work of painting, special flooring etc., may be given to another contractor. The cost of the sub-contract is directly charged to the main contract.

(f) Extra Work

It is possible that the contractor may be given additional work or the original contract may be altered by the contractee. In such cases, the work is additional and will be subjected to a separate charge. If the amount is small, the contract is debited or if the amount is large, a separate account is to be opened. In both the cases, the cost of extra work is added to the cost of the original contract.

WORK CERTIFIED

A contractor undertakes to execute the contract on the basis of the price agreed upon, and this price is known as the contract price. The contract price is payable by the contractee either in a lump sum on the completion of the contract or in instalments on the basis of the work done. In the case of small contracts, the payment is made after the completion of the work. The contract account is credited and the balancing figure is transferred to profit and loss account. In the case of large contracts, a good amount of working capital is needed and the contractor may not wait till the completion of the contract. In such cases, there may be a provision for payment of contract price in instalments on the basis of work progress certificate issued by the architect or surveyor or engineer as the work done so far. The amount of the work certified is credited to the contract account and debited to the contractee's account. Generally, it is seen that the full amount for the work certified is not paid by the contractee but a certain percentage is retained. This retained sum is known as retention money. This is done in order to protect the contractee, in case faulty work appears or faulty work is not rectified or a penalty is to be imposed on the contractor for undue delay. The retention money may be from 10% to 20%. On receipt of the certificate, any one of the following methods is followed:

(A)	Contractee's A/c	Dr.	For value of work certified
	To Contract Account		
	Bank Account	Dr.	
	To Contractee's Account		When cash is received

NB: The balance in Contractee's Account (Retention Money) is shown in Balance Sheet (Asset side)

(B)	Work-in-progress Account	Dr.	
	To Contract Account		For value of work certified
	Bank Account	Dr.	
	To Contractee's Account		When cash is received

NB: The work-in-progress Account will be shown in Balance Sheet after deducting the amount received from Contractees.

The second method is popular and widely followed. And this method is adopted in the illustrations.

WORK UNCERTIFIED

If the progress of a work is unsatisfactory, not reaching the stipulated stage, though certain work is completed, such work does not qualify for a certificate by the architect. This work is known as work done but uncertified. It is valued at cost.

Profits on Incomplete Contracts

Big contracts take several years for completion. The exact amount of profit can be ascertained only after the completion of the contract. Incomplete contracts are known as work-in-progress and are valued at cost. Generally profits should not be anticipated. As such, no profit should be transferred to profit and loss account in respect of incomplete contracts. If it is so, there may be wide fluctuations in the profit and loss account and may invite serious repercussions. For example, profit and loss account in respect of incomplete contracts will show a loss not withstanding the fact that the year was a good year of profits. Secondly, trading result will differ from year to year and will be uncomparable. Thirdly, high rate of income tax will have to be paid, if the profit is ascertained after the completion of the contract. Therefore, on account of these drawbacks, it is desirable that the entire profit are not shown in one year, because the profit are not earned in a year. Hence, the profits on incomplete contracts are anticipated carefully.

TREATMENT OF PROFITS

1. If the contract is recently started and the work completed is one-fourth or less than one - fourth of the total work, no profit should be transferred to profit and loss account.

2. If the contract has reasonably advanced and if the architect of the contractee certifies that the work completed is more than one-fourth, but less than half of the work, one-third of the notional profits is normally credited to the profit and loss account. This is further reduced by the ratio cash received to work certified *i.e.*,

$$\text{Notional profit} \times \frac{1}{3} \times \frac{\text{Cash received}}{\text{Work certified}} = \text{Profit to be credited.}$$

3. If more than half or the contract is nearing completion, then two-thirds of the notional profit may be credited on the basis of cash received to profit and loss account, i.e.,

$$\text{Notional profit} \times \frac{2}{3} \times \frac{\text{Cash received}}{\text{Work certified}} = \text{Profit to be credited.}$$

In the second case 2/3 of the profit and in the third case 1/3 of the profit are left over to meet future contingencies such as penalties, increase in costs or losses if any.

Work-in-Progress

Incomplete contracts are referred to as work-in-progress includes the value of work certified and the cost of work uncertified. When less than 1/3 of the work is complete, the net expenditure incurred upto date is taken to be the value of work-in-progress. Net expenditure means gross expenditure MINUS value of material, plant in hand at the end of the year.

When contract is well progressed of nearing completion, the work-in-progress is valued either way for Balance Sheet purpose:

First Method

Value of work certified	
Add: Uncertified Work	–
Total	–
Less: Profit carried forward, and Cash Received	–
WIP for B/S Purpose	–

Second Method

Net Expenditure incurred	–
Add: Profit taken credit for	–
Total	–
Less: Cash Received	–
WIP for B/S purpose	–

Proof (*illustration No. 25. 1*)

First Method

		Rs.
Value of Work Certified		Rs. 6,00,000
Add: Uncertified work		–
Total		6,00,000
Less: Profit Carry		
Forward	12,507	
Cash Received	4,80,000	4,92,507
WIP for B/s Purpose		1,07,493

Second Method

	Rs.
Net Expenditure incurred: (Rs. 6,25,200 – Rs. 52,000)	5,73,200
Add: Profit taken credit for	14,293
Total	5,87,493
Less: Cash Received	4,80,000
WIP for B/S purpose:	1,07,493

ILLUSTRATION 25.1

The following was the expenditure on a contract for Rs 12,00,000 commenced in January.

	Rs
Materials	2,40,000
Wages	3,28,000
Plant	40,000
Overheads	17,200

Cash received on account of the contract on 31st December was Rs 4,80,0(being 80% of the work certified. The value of materials in hand was Rs 20,000. The plant had undergone 20% depreciation. Prepare contract account.

(B Com. Calicut)

SOLUTION

Dr. Contract Account Cr

for the year ended 31st Dec.

	Rs		Rs.
To Materials	2,40,000	By Work certified	6,00,000*
To Wages	3,28,000	By Materials in hand	20,000
To Plant	40,000	By Plant in hand	32,000
To Overheads	17,200		
To Notional Profit	26,800		
	6,52,000		6,52,000
To Profit & Loss (26800 × 2/3 × 80/100)	14,293	By Notional Profit	26,800
To Balance c/d	12,507		
	26,800		26,800

* Work Certified:

If 80% = Rs 4,80,000

$$100\% = \frac{4,80,000 \times 100}{80} = \text{Rs } 6,00,000$$

ILLUSTRATION 25.2

Show how you deal with plant in Contract Account with the following information:

Plant issued to Contract on 1st March costing Rs. 1,00,000. Plant costing Rs 5,000 was transferred to 'A' Contract on 30th August. Plant costing Rs 4,000 was stolen and another costing Rs 3,000 was destroyed by fire. The plant was insured against fire to the full value. Plant costing Rs 5,000 was sold for Rs 4,000. Plant at the end of December was valued by charging depreciation @ 10% p.a. on 31st December and transferred to 'B' Contract Account.

SOLUTION

Contract Account/Plant Account

Dr.		Rs				Cr. Rs
March 1	To Plant (Store)	1,00,000	Aug. 30	By Contract 'A' A/c	5,000	
				Less: Depreciation	250	4,750
				By Profit & Loss A/c (Plant Stolen)		4,000
				By Insurance Co. (Plant destroyed)		3,000
				By Cash (Plant sold)		4,000
				By Profit & Loss (Loss: 5,000 - 4,000)		1,000
			Dec. 31	By Balance c/d (transferred to 'B' Contract)	83,000	
				Less: Depreciation	6,917	76,083

ILLUSTRATION 25.3

A firm of builders, carrying out large contracts kept in a contract ledger separate accounts for each contract. The following particulars relate to a certain contract carried out during the year ended 30th June.

	Rs
Work certified by Architects	1,43,000
Cash received from the contractee	1,30,000
Materials sent to site	64,500
Labour engaged on site	54,800
Plant installed at site	11,300
Value of plant at 30th June (closing)	8,200
Cost of work not yet certified	3,400
Establishment charges	3,250
Direct expenditure	2,400
Wages accrued due	1,800
Materials, closing balance	1,400
Materials returned to store	400
Direct expenses accrued due	200
Contract price	2,00,000

You are required to prepare an account, showing the profit on the contract to 30th June.

(B. Com. Andhra, Jabalpur, Delhi)

SOLUTION

Contract Account
for the year ended 30th June.

Dr.	Rs			Cr. Rs
To Materials	64,500	By Work-in-Progress		
To Labour	54,800	Work Certified:	1,43,000	
To Wages Outstanding	1,800	Work uncertified	3,400	1,46,400
To Plant	11,300	By Materials Returned		400
To Establishment	3,250	By Plant on hand		8,200
To Direct Expenditure	2,400	By Material on hand		1,400
Add: Outstanding	200			

	Rs		Rs
To Notional Profit	18,150		
	1,56,400		1,56,400
To Profit & Loss	11,000	By Notional Profit	18,150
(18150 × 2/3 × 130,000/143000			
To Balance c/d	7,150		
	18,150		18,150

ILLUSTRATION 25.4

On 1st January A undertook a contract for Rs 5,00,000. He incurred the following expenses during the year.

	Rs
Materials issued from stores	50,000
Materials purchased for the contract	45,000
Plant installed at cost	35,000
Wages paid	1,00,000
Wages accrued due on 31st Dec.	40,000
Direct expenses paid	10,000
Direct expenses accrued due on 31st Dec.	2,500
Establishment	6,500

Of the plant and materials charged to the contract, the plant which cost Rs 2,000 and the materials costing Rs 1,500 were lost. Some of the materials costing Rs 2,000 were sold for Rs 2,500. On 31st December, the plant which cost Rs 500 was returned to the stores, and a part of the plant which cost Rs 200 was damaged, rendering itself useless

The work certified was Rs 2,40,000 and 80% of the same was received in cash. The cost of work done, but uncertified was Rs 1,000. Charge 10% p.a. depreciation on plant and prepare the Contract Account for the year ended 31st December, by transferring to the profit and loss account the portion of the profit, if any which you think is reasonable? Show also the particulars relating to the contract in the balance sheet of the contractor as on 31st December. *(B. Com. Bangalore, Poona, Agra)*

SOLUTION

Dr. **Contract Account** **Cr.**

for the year ended 31st December

	Rs			Rs
To Materials (stores)	50,000	By Work certified		2,40,000
To Materials (purchase)	45,000	By Work uncertified		1,000
To Wages	1,00,000	By P& L A/c :	Plant lost	2,000
To Direct expenses	10,000		Materials lost	1,500
To Plant	35,000	By Sale of materials		2,500
To Establishment	6,500	By Plant returned, less depreciation		450
To Wages accrued	40,000	By Plant damaged		200
To Direct expenses O/s	2,500	By Plant on hand		29,070
To Profit & Loss (Materials)	500	By Profit & Loss A/c		12,780
	2,89,500			2,89,500

Balance Sheet as on 31st December

	Rs			Rs
Wages O/s	40,000	Plant at cost	35,000	
Direct expenses O/s	2,500	Less: Loss & Damage	2,200	
			32,800	
		Less: Returned	500	
			32,300	

		Less: Depreciation	3,230	29,070
		Work-in-Progress	2,41,000	
		Less: Cash	1,92,000	49,000
		Profit & Loss		
		Loss	12,780	
		Loss on plant & materials	3,500	
		Damage	200	
			16,480	
		Less: Profit on materials	500	15,980

ILLUSTRATION 24.5

A contract secured to supply and erect machinery for a sum of Rs 1,50,000. Progress payments were to be made from time to time equal to 90% of the certified value of the work performed. He commenced the work on 1st January 2005 and incurred the following expenses during the year:

	Rs
Plant and Tools	14,000
Machinery and Stores	40,000
Sundry Expenses	6,000
Establishment Charges	8,000
Wages	30,000

Plant costing Rs 4,000 was unsuited for the work was sold at a profit of Rs 1,000.

The value of plant and tools on 31st December 2005 was Rs 8,000 and the value of machinery and stores then on hand was Rs 6,000.

By 31st December 2005, he had received payments amounting to Rs 87,750, being 90% of the certified value of the work done upto 31st December 2005.

Prepare Contract Account for the year ending 31st Dec.2005.

SOLUTION

Dr. **Contract Account** **Cr.**

for the year ended 31st December 2005

	Rs		Rs
To Plant and Tools	14,000	By Plant (sold)	4,000*
To Machinery and Stores	40,000	By Plant at site	8,000
To Wages	30,000	By Machinery and Stores on hand	6,000
To Sundry Expenses	6,000	By Work-in-progress:	
To Establishment Charges	8,000	Work Certified: $(87,750 \times \frac{100}{90})$	97,500
To Notional Profit c/d	17,500		
	1,15,500		1,15,500
To General Profit & Loss Account $(17,500 \times 2/3 \times \frac{90}{100})$	10,500	By Notional Profit b/d	17,500
To Balance c/d	7,000		
	17,500		17,500

*The plant has sold at a profit of Rs 1,000 which will be credited to the General Profit and Loss Account directly. Therefore, only Rs 4,000, has been credited in the Contract Account.

ILLUSTRATION 25.6

Messrs Anand Associates commenced the work on a particular contract on 1st April 2005. They close their books of account for the year on 31st December each year. The following information is available from their costing records on 31st Dec. 2005.

Materials sent to site	Rs	43,000
Foreman's salary	Rs	12,620

Wages paid Rs 1,00,220

A machine costing Rs 30,000 remained in use on site for 1/5th of the year. Its working was estimated at 5 years and scrap value at Rs 2,000. A supervision is paid Rs 2, 000 per month and he had devoted one- half of his time on the contract.

All other expenses were Rs 14,000. The materials on site were Rs 2,500. The contract price was Rs 4,00,000. On 31st December 2005, 2/3 rds of the contract was completed; however, the architect gave a certificate only for Rs 2,00,000, on which 80% was paid. Prepare the Contract Account.

(*M. Com. Kerala, Agra, Andhra*)

SOLUTION

Dr. **Contract Account** **Cr.**

for the year ended 31st December 2005

	Rs			Rs
To Materials	43,000	By Work in Progress		
To Wages	1,00,220	Work Certified	2,00,000	
To Foreman's Salary	12,620	Work Uncertified	44,365*	2,44,365
To Supervisor Salary	9,000	By Materials at Site		2,500
To Depreciation				
(30,000 – 2,000)/5 years × 1/5)	1,120			
To Other Expenses	14,000			
To Balance c/d	66,905			
	2,46,865			2,46,865
To Profit & Loss A/c	35,683	By Balance b/d		66,905
(66,905 × 2/3 ×80/100)				
To Balance c/d	31,222			
	66,905			66,905

* Work Uncertified:

Net expenditure = Gross expenditure–Value of materials on hand

Rs 1,77,460 = 1,79,960 - 2500

Rs 1,77,460 represent the cost of two-thirds of the work.

Therefore full cost of the contract

=1,77,460 X 3/2 = 2,66,190

Therefore half of full cost

=2,66,190/2 = Rs 1,33,095

Therefore the difference of 2/3 and 1/2 of contract price

=1,,77,460 - 1,33,095 = Rs 44,365 (work not certified)

ILLUSTRATION 25.7

M/s Raju and Mohan Contractors Ltd. were engaged on one contract during the year. The contract price was Rs 4,00,000. The Trial Balance extracted from their books as on 31st December 2005 stood as follows:

	Dr.	*Cr.*
	Rs	*Rs*
Share Capital	–	80,000
Sundry Creditors	–	8,000
Land and Buildings	34,000	–
Bank	9000	–
Contract Account:	-	
Materials	75,000	–
Plant	20,000	

Wages	1,05,000	–
Expenses	5,000	–
Cash received (80% of work certified)	–	1,60,000
	2,48,000	2,48,000

Of the plant and Material charged to the contract, Plant costing Rs 3,000 and Materials costing Rs 2,400 was destroyed in an accident.

On 31st December 2005, Plant which cost Rs 4,000 was returned to the Store, the value of Materials on site was Rs 3,000 and the cost of work done but not certified was Rs 2,000.
Charge 10% depreciation on Plant. Prepare Contract Account and Balance Sheet as on 31st December 2005.

(B. Com. Mysore, MK, Calcutta)

SOLUTION

Contract Account
for the year ended 31st Dec. 2005

Dr.	Rs			Cr. Rs
To Materials	75,000	By Profit and Loss A/c		
To Plant	20,000	Plant Destroyed	3,000	
To Wages	1,05,000	Materials Destroyed	2,400	5,400
To Expenses	5,000	By Plant Returned	4,000	
To Notional Profit	20,700	Less: Depreciation	400	3,600
		By Plant at Site	13,000	
		Less: Depreciation	1,300	11,700
		By Materials at Site		3,000
		By Work-in-progress		
		Work Certified	2,00,000	
		Work Uncertified	2,000	2,02,000
	2,25,700			2,25,700
To Profit & Loss A/c	11,040	By Notional Profit		20,700
(20,700 × 2/3 × 80/100)				
To Balance c/d	9,660			
	20,700			20,700

Balance Sheet as on 31st December 2005

Dr.	Rs	Rs		Rs	Cr. Rs
Share Capital		80,000	Land and Buildings		34,000
Profit & Loss A/c			Plant in Store		3,600
Profit:	11,040		Plant at site	13,000	
Less: Plant and			Less: Depreciation	1,300	11,700
Materials			Materials at site		3,000
Destroyed:	5,400	5,640	Bank		9,000
Sundry Creditors		8,000	Work-in-progress		
			Work Certified	2,00,000	
			Work uncertified	2,000	
				2,02,000	
			Less: Reserve	9,660	
				1,92,340	
			Less: Cash received	1,60,000	32,340
		93,640			93,640

ILLUSTRATION 25.8

The following information relates to building contract for Rs 10,00,000 and for which 80% of the value of work-in-progress as certified by the architect is being paid by the contractee.

	I Year Rs	II Year Rs	III Year Rs
Materials issued	1,20,000	1,45,000	84,000
Direct wages	1,10,000	1,55,000	1,10,000
Direct expenses	5,000	17,000	6,000
Indirect expenses	2,000	2,600	500
Work certified	2,35,000	7,50,000	10,00,000
Uncertified work	2,800	8,000	–
Plant issued	14,000	Nil	
Materials on site (closing)	2,000	5,000	8,000

The value of the plant at the end of I, II and III year was Rs 11,200, Rs 7,000, Rs 3,000 respectively. Prepare contract account for these three years, taking into account such profit as you think proper in incomplete contract.

(B. Com. Delhi)

SOLUTION

Dr. Contract Account Cr.

	Rs		Rs
I Year: To Materials	1,20,000	By Work-in-Progress :	
To Wages	1,10,000	Work Certified	2,35,000
To Direct Expenses	5,000	Work uncertified	2,800
To Indirect Expenses	2,000	By Plant at site	11,200
To Plant	14,000	By Materials at site	2,000
	2,51,000		2,51,000
II Year: To Work-in-Progress	2,37,800	By Work-in-Progress	
To Plant	11,200	Work Certified	7,50,000
To Materials at site	2,000	Work Uncertified	8,000
To Materials	1,45,000	By Materials at site	5,000
To Direct Wages	1,55,000	By Plant at site	7,000
To Direct Expenses	17,000		
To Indirect Expenses	2,600		
To Profit			
(1,99,400 × 2/3 × 80/100)	1,06,347		
To Reserve	93,053		
	7,70,000		7,70,000
III Year: To Work-in-progress		By Contractee A/c	10,00,000
(Rs 7,58,000 - 93,053)	6,64,947	By Plant at site	3,000
To Materials at site	5,000	By Materials at site	8,000
To Plant	7,000		
To Materials	84,000		
To Direct Wages	1,10,000		
To Direct Expenses	6,000		
To Indirect Expenses	500		
To Profit and Loss	1,33,553		
	10,11,000		10,11,000

ILLUSTRATION 25.9

The following information relates to two contracts of X Ltd., in 2005.

	Contract A	Contract B
	Rs	Rs
Materials sent to site	1,70,698	1,46,534
Labour	1,48,750	1,37,046
Plant	30,000	25,000
Direct expenses	6,334	5,718
Establishment charges	8,252	7,704
Materials returned to store	1,098	1,264
Work certified	3,90,000	2,90,000
Work uncertified	9,000	6,000
Materials at site (31.12.2005)	3,766	3,472
Wages accrued (31.12.2005)	4,800	4,200
Direct expenses accrued (31.12.2005)	480	360
Value of plant (31.12.2005)	22,000	19,000

The contract price was Rs 5,00,000 for A and Rs 4,00,000 for B. The cash received from the contractee was 80% of the value of work certified.

Prepare the Contract Accounts and Contractee's Account. *(B.Com., Kerala, Mysore, Calicut)*

SOLUTION

Dr. Contract "A" Account Cr.

		Rs				Rs
2005	To Materials	1,70,698	2005	By Materials Returned		1,098
	To Labour	1,48,750		By Work-in-Progress		
	To Plant	30,000		Certified	3,90,000	
	To Direct Expenses	6,334		Uncertified	9,000	3,99,000
	To Establishment Charges	8,252		By Materials at site		3,766
	To Wages Accrued	4,800		By Plant at site		22,000
	To Expenses Accrued	480				
	To Balance c/d	56,550				
		4,25,864				4,25,864
2005	To Profit & Loss A/c		2005	By Balance b/d		56,550
	(56,550 × 2/3 × 80%)	30,160				
	To Balance c/d	29,390				
		56,550				56,550

Dr. Contractee's Account Cr.

	Rs			Rs
To Balance c/d	3,12,000	2005	By Cash	3,12,000
		2006 Jan. 1	By Balance b/d	3,12,000

Dr. Contract "B" Account Cr.

		Rs				Rs
2005	To Materials	1,46,534	2005	By Materials Returned		1,264
	To Labour	1,37,046		By Work-in-Progress		
	To Plant	25,000		Certified	2,90,000	
	To Direct Expenses	5,718		Uncertified	6,000	2,96,000
	To Establishment Charges	7,704		By Materials in hand		3,472

	To Wages Accrued	4,200		By Plant	19,000
	To Direct Expenses O/s	360		By Profit and Loss A/c	6,826
		3,26,562			3,26,562

Dr. Contractee's Account Cr.

2005	To Balance c/d	2,32,000	2005	By Cash	2,32,000
			Jan. 1 2006	By Balance b/d	2,32,000

ILLUSTRATION 25.10

A company of contractors began to trade on 1st Jan. 2005. During 2005 the company was engaged on only one contract of which the contract price was Rs 5,00,000.

Of the plant and materials charged to contract, plant costing Rs 5,000 and material costing Rs 4,000 were lost in an accident. On 31st Dec. 2005, plant costing Rs 5,000 was returned to the stores. Cost of work uncertified, but finished Rs 2,000 and materials costing Rs 4,000 were in hand on site.

Charge 10% depreciation on plant and compile Contract Account and Balance Sheet from the following:

	Dr	Cr. Rs
Share capital	–	1,20,000
Creditors	–	10,000
Cash received (80% of work certified)	–	2,00,000
Land and Buildings	43,000	–
Bank balance	25,000	–
Charged to contract:		
Materials	90,000	–
Plant	25,000	
Wages	1,40,000	
Expenses	7,000	–
	3,30,000	3,30,000

(*B. Com., Delhi, Madras, Andhra, Poona*)

SOLUTION

Dr. Contract Account for the year ended 31st Dec. 2005 Cr.

	Rs			Rs	
To Materials	90,000	By Profit and Loss:			
To Wages	1,40,000	Plant lost		5,000	
To Plant	25,000	Material lost		4,000	9,000
To Expenses	7,000				
To Notional Profit	21,000	Plant returned		5,000	
		Less: Depreciation		500	4,500
		By Materials in hand			4,000
		By Plant		25,000	
		Less: lost	5,000		
		returned	5,000	10,000	
				15,000	
		Less: Depreciation		1,500	13,500
		By Work-in-Progress			
		Certified (200000 × 100/80)			2,50,000
		Work uncertified			2,000
	2,83,000				2,83,000
To Profit & Loss A/c (21,000 × 2/3 × 80/100)	11,200	By Notional Profit			21,000
To Balance c/d	9,800				
	21,000				21,000

Balance Sheet as on 31st December 2005

Dr.		Rs		Rs	Rs Cr.
Share Capital		1,20,000	Land and Buildings		43,000
Profit & Loss	11,200		Plant at stores	4,500	
Less: Loss	9,000	2,200	Plant at site	13,500	18,000
Creditors		10,000	Materials at site		4,000
			Work-in-progress		
			Certified Work	2,50,000	
			Uncertified Work	2,000	
				2,52,000	
			Less: Cash received	2,00,000	
				52,000	
			Less: Reserve	9,800	42,200
			Bank		25,000
		1,32,200			1,32,200

ILLUSTRATION 25.11

The following is the Trial Balance of Premier Company, engaged on the execution of Contract No. 747 for the year ended 31st December 2005

	Rs	Rs
Contractee's A/c	–	3,00,000
Buildings	1,60,000	–
Creditors	–	72,000
Bank	35,000	–
Capital	–	5,00,000
Materials	2,00,000	–
Wages	1,80,000	–
Expenses	47,000	–
Plant	2,50,000	–
	8,72,000	8,72,000

The work on Contract No. 747 was commenced on 1st January 2005. Materials costing Rs 1,70,000 were sent to the site of the contract, but those of Rs 6,000 were destroyed in an accident. Wages of Rs 1,80,000 were paid during the year. Plant costing Rs 50,000 was used on the contract throughout the year. Plant costing Rs 2,00,000 was used from 1st January to 30th September and was then returned to the Stores. Materials to the cost of Rs. 4,000 was at site on 31st December 2005.

The contract was for Rs 6,00,000 and the contractee paid Rs. 300,000. Work certified was 80% of the total contract at the end of 2005. Uncertified work is estimated at Rs 15,000 on 31st December 2005. Expenses are charged to the contract at 25% of wages. Plant is to be depreciated at 10% for the entire year.

Prepare Contract No. 747 Account for the year ended on 31st December 2005 and make out the Balance Sheet as on 31st Dec. 2005. *(B. Com., Delhi)*

SOLUTION

Contract Account
for the year ended on 31st December 2005

Dr.	Rs			Rs Cr.
To Materials	1,70,000	By Profit & Loss A/c		6,000
To Wages	1,80,000	(Loss of Materials)		
To Expenses	45,000	By Work-in-Progress:		
(25% of Rs 1,80,000)		Certified Work	4,80,000	
To Depreciation		Uncertified Work	15,000	4,95,000

	Rs		Rs
(Rs 5,000 + Rs 15,000)	20,000	By Materials at site	4,000
To Notional Profit	90,000		
	5,05,000		5,05,000
To Profit & Loss A/c		By Notional Profit	90,000
(90,000 × 2/3 × 3,00,000/4,80,000	37,500		
To Balance c/d	52,500		
	90,000		90,000

Balance Sheet as on 31st December 2005

Liabilities		Rs	*Assets*		Rs
Capital		5,00,000	Buildings		1,60,000
Profit & Loss	37,500		Plant at site & Store		
Less : Loss of materials	6,000		(Rs 2,50,000 – 25,000)		2,25,000
	31,500		Materials in Store and site		34,000
Less: Expenses unabsorbed					
(47,000 – 45,000)	2,000		Work-in-Progress		
	29,500		Certified	4,80,000	
Less: Depreciation	5,000	24,500	Uncertified	15,000	
Creditors		72,000		4,95,000	
			Less: Profit Reserved	52,500	
				4,42,500	
			Less: Cash Received	3,00,000	1,42,500
			Bank		35,000
		5,96,500			5,96,500

ACCOUNTING STANDARD 7 (REVISED)

Construction Contracts[1]

Accounting standard 7 (Revised): Construction Contracts, issued by the Council of the Institute of Chartered Accountants of India, comes into effect in respect of all contracts entered into during accounting period commencing on or after 1 – 4 – 2003 and is mandatory in nature from that date. 'Accordingly, Accounting Standard (AS) – 7 for Construction Contracts', issued by the Institute in December 1983, is not applicable in respect of such contracts. Early application of this Standard is however, encouraged.

The basic features of AS – 7 are being summarised below.

I. Objective

The objective of this Standard is to prescribe the accounting treatment of revenue and costs associated with construction contracts.

II. Scope

This Standard should be applied in accounting for construction contracts in the financial statements of contractors.

III. Definitions

The following terms are used in this Standard with the meaning specified.:

(1) A Construction Contract is a contract specifically negotiated for the construction of an asset or a combination of assets that are closely interrelated or interdependent in terms of their design, technology and function or their ultimate purpose or use.

(2) A Fixed Price Contract is a construction contract in which the contractor agrees to a fixed contract price, or a fixed rate per unit of output, which in some cases is subject to cost escalation clauses.

(3) A Cost Plus Contract is a construction contract in which the contract is reimbursed for allowable or otherwise defined costs, plus percentage of these costs of a fixed fee.

IV. Combining and Segmenting Construction Contracts

(1) When a contract covers a number of assets, the construction of each asset should be treated as a separate construction contract when:

(a) separate proposals have been submitted for each asset;

(b) each asset has been subject to separate negotiation and the contractor and customer have been able to accept or reject that part of the contract relating to each asset; and

(c) the costs and revenues of each asset can be identified.

(2) A group of contracts, whether with a single customer or with several customers, should be treated as a single construction contract when;

(a) the group of contracts is negotiated as a single package:

(b) the contracts are so closely interrelated that they are, in effect, part of a single project with an overall profit margin; and

(c) the contracts are performed concurrently or in a continuous sequence

(3) A contract may provide for the construction of an additional asset at the option of the customer or may be amended to include the construction of an additional asset. The construction of the additional asset should be treated as a separate construction contract when:

(a) the asset differs significantly in design, technology or function from the asset or assets covered by the original contract; or

(b) the price of the asset is negotiated without regard to the original contract price

V. Contract Revenue

Contract revenue should comprise:

(a) the initial amount of revenue agreed in the contract; and

(b) variations in contract work, claims and incentive payments:

(i) to the extent that it is probable that they will result in revenue; and

(ii) they are capable of being reliably measured.

VI. Contract Costs

Contract costs should comprise:

(a) Costs that relate directly to the specific contract;

(b) Costs that are attributable to contract activity in general and can be allocated to the contract; and

(c) Such other costs as are specifically chargeable to the customer under the terms of the contract

VII. Recognition of Contract Revenue and Expenses

(1) When the outcome of a construction contract can be estimated reliably, contract revenue and contract costs associated with the construction contract should be recognised as revenue and expenses respectively by reference to the stage of completion of the contract activity at the reporting date. An expected loss on the construction contract should be recognised as an expense immediately in accordance with paragraph VIII (1).

(2) In the case of a fixed price contract, the outcome of a construction contract can be estimated reliably when all the following conditions are satisfied:

(a) total contract revenue can be measured reliably;

(b) it is probable that the economic benefits associated with the contract will flow to the enterprise.

(c) both the contract costs to complete the contract and the stage of contract completion at the reporting date can be measured reliably; and

(d) the contract costs attributable to the contract can be clearly identified and measured reliably so that actual contract costs incurred can be compared with prior estimates.

(3) In the case of a cost plus contract, the outcome of a construction contract can be estimated reliably when all the following conditions are satisfied;

(a) it is probable that the economic benefits associated with the contract will flow to the enterprise; and

(b) the contract costs attributable to the contract, whether or not specifically reimbursable, can be clearly identified and measured reliably.

(4) Under the percentage of completion method, contract revenue is recognised as revenue in the statement of profit and loss in the accounting periods in which the work is performed. Contract costs are usually recognised as an expense in the statement of profit and loss in the accounting periods in which the work to which they relate is performed. However, any expected excess of total contract costs over total contract revenue for the contract is recognised as an expense immediately in accordance with paragraph VIII (1).

(5) A contractor may have incurred contract costs that relate to future activity on the contract. Such contract costs are recognised as an asset provided it is probable that they will be recovered. Such costs represent an amount due from the customer and are often classified as contract work-in-progress.

(6) The stage of completion of a contract may be determined in a variety of ways. The enterprise uses the method that measures reliably the work performed. Depending on the nature of the contract, the methods may include:

(a) the proportion that contract costs incurred for work performed upto the reporting date bear to the estimated total contract costs; or

(b) surveys of work performed; or

(c) completion of a physical proportion of the contract work

Progress payments and advances received from customer may not necessarily reflect the work performed.

(7) When the outcome of a construction contract cannot be estimated reliably:

(a) revenue should be recognised only to the extent of contract costs incurred of which recovery is probable; and

(b) contract costs should be recognised as an expense in the period in which they are incurred

An expected loss on the construction contract should be recognised as an expense immediately in accordance with paragraph VIII (1).

(8) When the uncertainties that prevented the outcome of the contract being estimated reliable no longer exist, revenue and expenses associated with the construction contract should be recognised in accordance with paragraph VII (1) rather than in accordance with paragraph VII (7).

VIII. Recognition of Expected Losses

(1) When it is probable that total contract costs will exceed total contract revenue, the expected loss should be recognised as an expense immediately.

(2) The amount of such a loss in determined irrespective of:

(a) Whether or not work has commenced on the contract;

(b) the stage of completion of contract activity; or

(c) the amount of profits expected to arise on other contracts which are not treated as a single construction contract is accordance with paragraph IV (2).

IX. Disclosure

(1) An enterprise should disclose:

(a) the amount of contract revenue recognised as revenue in the period;

(b) the methods used to determine the contract revenue recognised in the period; and

(c) the methods used to determine the stage of completion of contracts in progress.

(2) An enterprise should disclose the following for contracts in progress at the reporting date:

(a) the aggregate amount of costs incurred and recognised profits (less recognised losses) upto the reporting date;

(b) the amount of advances received; and

(c) the amount of retentions

(3) Retentions are amounts of progress billings which are not paid until the satisfaction of conditions specified in the contract for the payment of such amounts or until defects have been rectified. Progress billings are amounts billed for work performed on a contract whether or not they have been paid by the customer. Advances are amounts received by the contractor before the related work is performed.

(4) An enterprise should present:

(a) the gross amount due for customers for contract work as an asset; and

(b) the gross amount due to customers for contract work as a liability.

QUESTIONS

Objective Type Questions

I. State whether the following statements are "True" or "False".

1. When the contract work is completed, the contract price is debited to the Contractee Account.
2. In a Cost Plus Contract, the contractor runs risks of incurring loss.
3. Amount received from the sale of surplus materials is credited to the Contract Account.
4. Retention money is that portion of work certified which is not paid till the contract is completed.
5. Most of the items of costs are direct in Contract Account.
6. Work-in-progress includes both work certified and work uncertified.
7. Escalation clause is inserted in the contracts for the benefit of the contractee.
8. A contract is a big job while a job is a small contract.
9. The contract price is held over till after completion of the contract
10. Only hire of plant or its depreciation is charged to contract account

[Ans: True: 1, 3, 4, 5, 6, 8, 10 False: 2, 7, 9]

II. Fill in the blanks

1. In Contract Accounts, the unit is a ....
2. In .... contracts, the contractor will get cost plus a stipulated profit
3. The loss incurred on an incomplete contract is transferred to ...... Account.
4. When the contract is completed, but less than 25%, so the total expenditure is transferred to .... Account.
5. Work certified is always valued at .....
6. Entrusting a portion of the contract work by the contractor to another contractor is known as ....
7. Work-in-progress is shown as an ..... in the Balance Sheet.
8. Value of work done and approved by the architect is known as .....

{**Ans:** 1. Contractor; 2. Cost Plus; 3. Profit & Loss; 4. Work-in-progress; 5. Cost; 6. Sub-contracting; 7. Asset; 8 Work certified

III. Indicate the correct alternative in each of the following cases:

1. Most of expenses are direct in:

(a) Output Costing

(b) Contract Costing

(c) Operating Costing

2. When amount of profit transferred to Profit & Loss Account, when the completed work is less than 25 % of the total work:
   (a) 25% of the Notional Profit
   (b) 1/3 of the Notional Profit
   (c) 2/3 of the Notional Profit
   (d) No Profit
3. In contract costing, Contract Account is prepared by the:
   (a) Contractee
   (b) Contractor
   (c) Both of them jointly
4. In Contract Account, the amount of work-in-progress consists of:
   (a) Cost of work not completed
   (b) Work completed but not certified
   (c) Work certified and cost of work uncertified
5. Profit on an incomplete contract is called notional profit because:
   (a) Real profit will be known when work completed
   (b) It is imaginary profit
   (c) Approximated profit
6. Cash received on contract is credited to:
   (a) Work-in-progress Account
   (b) Contract Account
   (c) Contractee Account
7. The degree of work completion is determined by comparing the work certified with:
   (a) Work-in-progress
   (b) Contract Price
   (c) Cash received on contract
8. Contract price is not fixed in case of:
   (a) Cost plus contracts
   (b) Escalation Clause
   (c) None of the above
9. When 50% of the contract work is completed, the amount of profit to be taken to Profit & Loss Account is usually:
   (a) The actual Profit earned
   (b) 50% of Notional Profit
   (c) Two-third of Notional Profit × Cash received Ratio
10. When the job is big and spread over a long period of time, the method of costing used is:
   (a) Job Costing;
   (b) Multiple Costing;
   (c) Contract Costing

[Ans: 1. (b); 2. (d); 3. (b); 4. (c); 5. (a); 6. (c); 7. (b); 8. (a); 9. (c); 10. (c)**]**

THEORETICAL QUESTIONS

1. Explain the treatment of expenses in Contract Cost Account. (*B. Com. Calicut*)
2. Explain
   (*a*) Retention Money
   (*b*) Cost Plus Contract.
   (*c*) Escalation Clause (*B Com. MS,*

3. What are the method of computing profit on incomplete contract?

(B. Com. Madurai, Kerala)

4. Is it necessary to calculate profit on incomplete contracts?

   If yes, under what circumstances would you recommend calculation of profit on such contracts?

   (B. Com. Kerala)

5. What is a cost plus contract? Discuss this from the point of view of (*a*) the manufacturer and (*b*) the contractee.
6. What do you mean by work uncertified and incomplete contract?

   Explain how the profits are determined in the case of incompleted contracts.
7. How do you deal with the following:
   (*a*) Plant at work sight
   (*b*) Materials at site
   (*c*) Amount received from the contracts
   (*d*) Work-in-progress
8. Describe the two method of charging a Contract Cost Account for use of plant. State which method is preferable and why?

   (B. Com. MK)

PRACTICAL PROBLEMS

1. Thekedar accepted a contract for the construction of a building for Rs 10,00,000 the contractee agreeing to pay 90% of work certified as complete by the architect. During the first year the amounts spent were:

	Rs
Materials	1,20,000
Labour	1,50,000
Marchinery	30,000
Other expenses	90,000

At the end of the year, the machinery was considered to be worth Rs 20,000 and the materials at the site were of the value of Rs 5,000. Work certified during the year totalled Rs 4,00,000. In addition, the work-in-progress, but not certified at the end of the year cost Rs 15,000.

Prepare contract A/c in the books of Thekedar. Also show various figures of profit that can be transferred reasonably to profit and loss account. *(B. Com. Delhi)*

(Ans: Profit: Rs 15,000)

2. The following was the expenditure on a contract for Rs 6,00,000 commenced in 1st April 2004.

	Rs
Materials	1,20,000
Wages	1,64,400
Plant	20,000
Business Charges	8,600

Cash received amounted to Rs 2,40,000 being 80% of work certified. The value of materials on hand at the close was Rs 10,000. Prepare contract account for 2004 showing the profit to be credited to Profit and Loss Account. Plant is to be depreciated at 10%.

(B. Com. Madurai)

(Ans: Profit: Rs.8000)

3. A firm of Builders, carrying out large contracts, kept in a ledger, separate account for each contract. On June 30th, 2004, the following were shown as being the expenditure in connection with contract No. 555.

	Rs
Materials purchased	1,16,126
Materials issued from store	19,570
Plant which has been used on other contracts	25,046
Additional Plant	7,220
Wages	1,47,268
Direct Expenses	4,052
Proportionate Establishment charges	17,440

The contract which had commenced on 1st February 2004 was for Rs 6,00,000 and the amount certified by the Architect, after deduction of 20% retention money, was Rs 2,41,600, the work being certified on 30th June 2004. The materials on site were Rs 19,716. A contract plant ledger was also kept in which depreciation was dealt with monthly; the amount debited in respect of Contract No 555 to 30th June 2004 was Rs 2,260.

Prepare the Contract Account showing the profit on the contract.

(B. Com. Madurai)

(**Ans** : profit: Rs 8,000)

4. The following are the particulars relating to a contract which was begun on 1st January 2004.

	Rs		
Contract Price	5,00,000	Overheads	8,240
Machinery	30,000	Materials Returned	1,600
Materials	1,70,600	Materials from other contract	1,000
Wages	1,48,750	Materials transferred to other contracts	4,000
Direct Expenses	6,330		
Wages Outstanding	5,380	Materials on hand on Dec. 2004	3,700
Uncertified work	9,000	Materials on hand on Dec. 2004	22,000
Value of work certified	3,90,000	Cash Received	3,51,000

Prepare the Contract Account for the year 2004 showing the amount of profit that may be taken to the credit of Profit and Loss Account of the year.

(B. Com. Madurai)

(**Ans** : Profit: Rs 36,000)

5. The following balance were extracted from the books of a building contractor at 31st March 2004

	Rs
Materials issued to site	62,720
Wages paid	73,455
Wages outstanding on 31st March 2004	720
Plant issued to site	6,000
Direct charges paid	2,515
Direct charges outstanding on 31st March 2004	210
Establishment charges	5,650
Stock of materials of site on 31.3.2004	1,200
Value of certified work on 31.3.2004	1,65,000
Cost of work not yet certified	3,500
Cash received on contract	1,41,075

The work was commenced on 1st April 2003 and the contract price agreed at Rs 2,45,000. Prepare Contract Account for the year, providing for depreciation of plant at 25%. Calculate the profit or loss on the contract to date and make such provision in the Contract Account as you consider desirable. Set out also the Contractor's Balance Sheet so far as it relates to the contract.

(*B. Com. Rohtak*)

(**Ans** : Profit: Rs. 13,070)

6. S.V. Construction Limited have obtained a contract for construction of a bridge. The value of the contract is Rs 12,00,000 and the work commenced on 1st October 2003. The following details are shown in their books for the year ended on 30th September 2004.

	Rs
Plant purchases	60,000
Wages Paid	3,40,000
Materials issued to site	3,36,000
Direct Expenses	8,000
General Overheads	32,000
Wages accrued as on 30.9.2004	2,800
Materials at site as on 30.9.2004	4,000
Direct Expenses accrued as on 30.9.2004	1,200
Work not yet certified at cost	14,000
Cash received, being 80% of work certified	6,00,000

Life of the Plant purchased is five years and scrap value is nil. Prepare the Contract Account for the year ended on 30th September 2004 and show the amount of profit which you consider might be fairly taken on the contract and how you have calculated it. (*CA*)

(**Ans:** Profit: Rs 19,200)

7. A file of builders, carrying on large contracts, kept in a Contract Ledger separate accounts for each contract. On 30th June 2004, the following was shown as being the expenditure in connection with a contract.

	Rs
Materials purchased	58,063
Materials from stores	9,785
Plant which had been used on other contracts	12,523
Additional plant purchased	3,610
Wages	73,634
Direct expenses	2,026
Proportion of establishment charges	8,720

The contract which had commenced on 1st February 2004 was for Rs 3,00,000 and the amount of Rs 1,20,800, after deducting 20% received against the work certification, upto 30th June 2004.

The materials on the site at the date were valued at Rs 9,858. A contract plant ledger was also kept in which depreciation was dealt with monthly, the amount debited in respect of the plant, on the contract to 30th June 2004 was Rs 1,130.

You are required to prepare an account showing the profit on the contract to 30th June 2004

(*B. Com. Andhra*)

(**Ans:** Profit: Rs 4,000)

8. Kurian Construction Company undertook the construction of a bridge. The value of contract was Rs 75,00,000, subject to retention of 20% until one year after certified completion of the contract and the final approval of contracts engineer. The following are the details as shown in the books on 30th September 2004.

Labour on site	24,30,000
Materials directly bought at site	19,20,000
Materials from store	4,97,200
Hire and use of plant-plant upkeep	72,600
Direct expenses	1,38,000

Overheads charged to contract	2,22,600
Materials on hand (30.9.2004)	37,800
Wages accrued (30.9.2004)	9,600
Work not yet certified cost	99,000
Work certified	66,00,000
Cash Received on account	52,80,000
Materials lost in fire accident	10,000

Prepare (a) Contract account (b) Contractee's account. Show how the items relating to contract appear in the Balance Sheet.

(*B. Com., Osmania*)

(**Ans**: Profit: Rs 7,76,960)

9. The following particulars relate to a contract undertaken by Ajit Engineers:

	Rs
Materials sent to site	85,349
Labour engaged on site	74,375
Plant installed at site	15,000
Direct expenditure	3,167
Establishment charges	4,126
Materials returned to stores	549
Work Certified	1,95,000
Cost of work not certified	4,500
Materials in hand at the end of year	1,883
Wages accrued at the end of year	2,400
Direct expenses accrued at the end of year	240
Value of Plant at the end of year	11,000
The contract price has been agreed at	2,50,000
Cash received from contract	1,80,000

You are required to prepare the Contract account showing profit, Contractee's account and show suitable entries in the Balance Sheet of the Contractor.

(*B. Com. Hons., Delhi*)

(**Ans:** Profit: Rs. 17,400)

10. A firm of building contractors began to trade on 1.4.2003. The following was the expenditure on the contract for Rs 3,00,000.

Materials issued to contract	Rs. 51,000
Plant issued for contract	Rs. 15,000
Wages incurred	Rs. 81,000
Other expenses incurred	Rs. 5,000

Cash received on account to 31.3.2004 amounted to Rs. 1,28,000 being 80% of the work certified. Of the plant and materials charged to the contract, plant which cost Rs 3,000 and materials which cost Rs 2,500 were lost. On 31.3.2004 plant which cost Rs. 2,000 was returned to stores, the cost of work done but uncertified was Rs. 1,000 and materials costing Rs. 2,300 were in hand on site.

Charge 15% depreciation on plant and take to the Profit and Loss Account 2/3 of the profit received. Prepare a Contract Account and Balance Sheet from the above particulars.

(*B. Com. Andhra*)

(**Ans:** Profit: Rs. 14,400)

11. Two contract that commenced on 1st January and 1st July 2004 respectively, were undertaken by a contractor and his accounts on 31st December 2004 showed the following position.

	Contract I	Contract II
	Rs	Rs
Contract price	4,00,000	2,70,000
Expenditure		
Materials	72,000	58,000
Wages paid	1,10,000	1,12,400
General charges	4,000	2,800
Plant installed	20,000	16,000
Materials on hand	4,000	4,000
Wages accrued	4,000	4,000
Work certified	2,00,000	1,60,000
Work done but not certified (at cost)	6,000	8,000
Cash received in respect thereof	1,50,000	1,20,000

The plants were installed on the date of commencement of each contract depreciation thereon is to be taken at 10% per annum.

Prepare the Contract's Account in the tabular form and ascertain the profit or loss to be taken to profit and loss account.

(*B. Com. Kerala*)

(**Ans:** Profit: Rs 9,000 (contract I)

Loss : Rs 6000 (contract I)

12. The following is the summary of the entries in a contract Ledger as on the 31st December 2004 in respect of contract No 51.

	Rs
Materials bought directly	35,000
Materials from stores	7,000
Wages	18,000
Direct expenses	7,000
Establishment charges	8,000
Plant	34,200
Scrap sold	1,820

Further information is as follows:

(1) The amount that accrued on 31st December 2004 were wages Rs 900 and direct expenses Rs 1,200.

(2) The cost of the work uncertified included materials Rs 2,600, wages Rs 1,000 and expenses Rs 1,500.

(3) Rs 2,000 worth of plant was sold for Rs 3,000 and Rs 3,000 worth of material were destroyed by the fire.

(4) Rs 5,000 worth of plant was sold for Rs 3,000 and materials costing Rs 5,000 were sold for Rs 6,000.

(5) Depreciation till 31st December 2004 on plant was Rs 10,000.

(6) Materials at site was valued at Rs 5,000.

(7) Cash received from the contractee was Rs 60,000 being 80% of the work certified.

(8) Contract price was Rs 1,00,000.

Show the Contract account and work in progress account. Show the same in the Balance Sheet.

(*B. Com. Mysore*)

(**Ans:** Profit: Rs. 4,170)

13. The Construction Limited is engaged in two contracts– A and B during the year. The following particulars are obtained at the end of the year, 31st December:

	Contract A	Contract B
	Rs	Rs
Date of Commencement	April I	April I
Contract Price	6,00,000	5,00,000
Materials Issued	1,60,000	60,000
Materials Returned	4,000	2,000
Materials on hand (Dec. 31st)	22,000	8,000
Direct Labour	1,50,000	42,000
Direct Expenses	66,000	35,000
Establishment Expenses	25,000	7,000
Plant installed at cost	80,000	70,000
Value of Plant on closing	65,000	64,000
Cost of work uncertified	23,000	10,000
Value of work certified	4,20,000	1,35,000
Cash from Contractee	3,78,000	1,25,000
Architect Fees	2,000	1,000

During the period materials amounting to Rs 9,000 have been transferred from, Contract A to Contract B. You are required to show:

(*a*) Contract Account,

(*b*) Contractee Account,

(*c*) Extract in Balance Sheet as on 31st December clearly showing the calculation of work-in-progress.

(*B. Com. Poona*)

(**Ans:** Profit: Rs. 36,000 (A)
Loss: Rs. 5,000 (B)

14. The following information relates to a building contract for Rs 10,00,000

	2003	2004
	Rs	Rs
Materials issued	3,00,000	84,000
Direct Wages	2,30,000	1,05,000
Direct Expenses	22,000	10,000
Indirect Expenses	6,000	1,400
Work Certified	7,50,000	10,00,000
Materials at site	5,000	7,000
Work Uncertified	8,000	–
Plant issued	14,000	2,000
Cash Received from Contractee	6,00,000	10,00,000

The value of the plant at the end of 2003 and 2004 were Rs 7,000 and Rs 5,000 respectively. Prepare (i) Contract Account, and (ii) Contractee Account for two years -- 2003 and 2004 taking into consideration such profit for transfer to the Profit and Loss Account as think proper.

(*B. Com. Hons. Delhi*)

(**Ans:** Profit Rs. 1,05,600 (2003)
Profit Rs 1,32,000 (2004)

15. Mr. Bhagavandas undertook a contract for Rs 15,00,000 on arrangement that 80% of the value of the work done as certified by the Architect of the Contractee, to be paid immediately and that the remaining 20% be retained until the contract was completed.

In 2002 the amount expended were:

Materials	Rs 1,80,000
Carriage	6,000
Wages	1,70,000
Sundry Expenses	3,000
Cartage	1,000

The work certified was for Rs. 3,75,000 and 80% of this was paid as agreed.

In 2003 the amount expended were:

Materials	Rs 2,20,000
Carriage	23,000
Sundry Expenses	4,000
Wages	2,30,000
Cartage	2,000

3/4 of the contract was certified as done by 31st December and 80% of this was received accordingly. The value of work uncertified was ascertained Rs 20,000.

In 2004 the amount expended were:

Materials	Rs 1,26,000
Cartage	6,000
Wages	1,70,000
Sundry Expenses	3,000

And on 30th June 2004 the whole contract was completed.

Prepare Contract Account, Contractee Account and Balance as would appear each of these years in the books of the Contractor assuming the balance due to him was received on completion of the contract.

(*B. Com. Punjab, Bombay*)

(**Ans:** Profit: Rs. 1,90,933)

16. The following Trial Balance was extracted on 31st December 2004 from the book of Swastik Company Limited Contractors:

	Rs	Rs
Share Capital: Shares of Rs 10 each	–	3,51,800
Profit and Loss Account (June. 2004)	–	25,000
Provision for Depreciation on Machinery	–	63,000
Cash Received on Contract No.7	–	12,80,000
Creditors	–	81,200
Land and Building at cost	74,000	–
Machinery at cost	52,000	–
Bank	45,000	–
Contract No. 7 :		
Materials	6,00,000	–
Direct Labour	8,30,000	–
Expenses	40,000	–
Machinery on site (cost)	1,60,000	–
	18,01,000	18,01,000

The contract No 7 was begun on 1st January 2004. The Contract price is Rs 24,00,000 and the customer has so far Rs 12,80,000 being 80% of the work certified.

The cost of the work done since certification is estimated at Rs 16,000.

On 31st December 2004 after the above Trial Balance was extracted, Machinery costing Rs 32,000 was returned to store and materials then on site were valued at Rs 27,000.

Provision is to be made for direct labour due Rs 6,000 and for depreciation of all machinery at 12.5% on cost.

You are required to prepare:

(a) The Contract Account,

(b) A statement of profit; if any, to be properly credited to Profit and Loss Account for 2004.

(*c*) The Balance Sheet of Swastik Company Limited as on 31st December 2004.

(*M. Com. Jabalpur*)

(**Ans:** Profit Rs. 78,400

Balance Sheet Total: Rs 5,42,400

17. The Manufacturers Limited began to trade on 1st January 2004. During 2004 , the company was engaged on only one contract, the price of which was Rs 1,50,000.

Of the plant and materials charged to the contract, the plant which cost Rs. 1,500 and materials which cost Rs. 1,200 were lost. On 31st December 2004, the plant which cost Rs. 1,500 was returned to the stores, and materials cost Rs. 1,200 were on site. The cost of work done but uncertified was Rs 600

Charge 10% depreciation on plant and prepare the Contract Account, the Work-in-progress Account and the Balance Sheet as on 31st December 2004 from the following Trial Balance:

	Rs	Rs
Share Cpital	–	36,000
Creditors	–	3,000
Cash Received on contract (80% of certified work)	–	60,000
Land and Buildings	12,900	–
Bank Balance	7,500	–
Charged to Contract:		
Materials	27,000	–
Plant	7,500	–
Wages	42,000	–
Expenses	2,100	–
	99,000	99,000

(*B.Com., Bangalore*)

(**Ans:** Profit Rs. 3,360

Balance Sheet Total Rs. 39,660

Chapter 26

Farm Accounting

Introduction – Farm Accounting – Non-popularity – Features – Objectives - Accounting for Farms - Profitability of Crops - Books of Accounts - Cost and Revenue - Treatment of Specific Items -Apportionment bases for Common Costs - Final Accounts Questions - Objective Type Questions - Theoretical Questions - Practical Problems

INTRODUCTION

In recent years, commercial farming has been assuming great importance. Agricultural activity is a predominant activity in India. Farming activities now comprises not only of growing crops but also include animal husbandry, poultry farming, sericulture (silk werm breeding), pisciculture (rearing fish, floriculture (growing flowers) etc. Thus, farming, these days, is basically mixed farming. In advanced countries like the UK and the USA, commercial farming is being done on a large scale and hence farm accounting has also become popular and developed. However, in our country, farm accounting is of recent origin. A standard form of accounts for recording, farming transactions has yet to develop.

FARM ACCOUNTING

Farm accounting or accounting for agricultural farms is the application of accounting practices to agricultural operations. In recent years, commercial farming has been engaging the attention of many and as a result a number of farmers are coming up. Corporate entities are entering into the farming business in a big way. Therefore, the Institute of Cost and Works Accountant of India issued a booklet, explaining how the farm books should be kept and how the profit or loss arising from the farming operations should be ascertained. The farm accounting is a technique of using accounting data for cost and profit ascertainment of each farming activity and decision making with regard to the most profitable line of activity.

NON-POPULARITY OF FARM ACCOUNTING

Farm accounting, particularly of agricultural operations, is not popular in India because of the following reasons.

1. Farming sector in India is by and large, unorganised and dominated by small-scale operation of the household. Level of education of the farmers is also low.
2. Even big farmers are not aware of accounting techniques which can prove useful for managerial decisions.
3. Agricultural Income Tax does not insist on maintenance of proper books of accounts.
4. An average farmer cannot afford the additional expenses, by employing someone to maintain the accounts.
5. The collection of statistical data is done in a conventional manner.

FEATURES OF FARM ACCOUNTING

Farming is similar to any other business, occupation etc. However, it has some special or peculiar features. These peculiar features deserve special attention while designing farm accounting or accounting practices. These features of farm transactions are given below:

1. ***Dominance of Barter Transactions:*** The transactions relating to agriculture are not controlled by money alone but, even today, many transactions are settled with the help of barter system. Many settlements are not measured in terms of money. For example, a field worker is settled by agricultural produces. For proper accounting, the money value is essential.
2. ***Family Type Business:*** The farm business is family type. It is confined to the family. The farmer keeps a single bank account for business and for his private purposes. The family head, being the owner of farm, combines his personal transactions with those relating to his farm, without distinguishing between the two transactions.
3. ***Diverse Activities:*** Farming activities are not confined to raising crops alone. Besides raising crops, the farmers engage themselves in other farming activities like, poultry, dairying, pig production, rearing fish, growing-flowers *etc*. Farmers may adopt mixed farming. For proper accounting, it is necessary to find out profit or loss for each activity. It is more important that finished output of one activity may become the raw-materials for another farming activity.
4. ***Family Labour:*** The farmer and his family members may work on the farm without receiving any specified wages.
5. ***Domestic Consumption:*** A part of the production from farming may be consumed by the farmer and his family. The surplus is sold. The output, when consumed by the family, is not accounted for.
6. ***Valuation of Inventory:*** The valuation of inventory is the most difficult task in case of farm accounting. Farm inventories such as standing crops, cattle, poultry *etc*. are the most difficult to be valued in the absence of their market price.
7. ***Uncertainties:*** Agricultural operations on a farm are subject to natural calamities such as pests, diseases, floods, weather conditions etc. and variations in Government policies, market price of inputs, like, fertilizers, seeds, chemicals *etc*.
8. ***Use of Self-generated Assets:*** In many cases, the assets which are used in farming are maintained by farm household. As such, it is very difficult to ascertain their proper valuation and depreciation on them. In this case, of course, the assets are valued on the basis of selling price.

OBJECTIVES OF FARM ACCOUNTING

Agricultural sector in India is most unorganised and it is mostly based on small-scale operation of the household. Even big farmers are not fully aware of the technique of using accounting data and its utility for managing farms efficiently. However, efforts should be made to make farm accounting popular so that advantages of farm accounting may be obtained by Indian farmers. A suitably designed accounting system can render the following advantages.

1. It is easy to ascertain the financial position of the farming operations at any time.
2. Providing acceptable accounting records which can form the basis for securing finance from Banks and other financial institutions.
3. Crop-wise performance can be known. Thus profitable and unprofitable activities can be segregated and corrective action can be taken so as to reduce the cost and improve performance.

4. Comprehensive information on yield, revenue, input and cost of the farm is available.
5. Management will be enabled to have better control over farming activities.
6. Useful information for claiming compensation from Government or insurance companies in case of loss suffered due to natural calamities.
7. Reliable and useful information for assessment of agricultural income tax.
8. Providing useful accounting data for decision-making. For example: (a) Owning or hiring of assets for ploughing, irrigation *etc.*, (b) selection of crop mix, (c) Disinvestment decision, (d) Choice of Crop-diversification etc.

ACCOUNTING FOR FARMS

Transactions, relating to farming activities may be categorised into four – Cash, credit, exchange and notional. The cash and credit transactions are recorded in normal manner as any other business transaction. The exchange transactions, in the nature of barter, for example, exchange of animal labour for human labour, exchange of seeds for output, *etc.* are normally recorded at opportunity cost – the price in the open market.

Notional transactions are those that take place between the members of the owner's family and the farm, viewing the farm as an independent entity notionally. Some examples of such transactions are: use of household capital, use of land owned by the farm household, labour provided by members of the family, consumption of output by the family *etc.*

PROFITABILITY OF CROPS

The performance of each crop shall be found out separately. The direct cost clearly identifiable with a crop, shall be charged accordingly. The common cost should be suitably allocated on some accepted basis, For instance, depreciation or repairs can be divided on the basis of estimation of usage by different crops. Interest on fixed loan can be divided on the basis of length of crop season *etc.*

BOOKS OF ACCOUNTS

The basic document needed is farm diary, where transactions are recorded in chronological order.

(1) *Cash book*: As the business is carried on by families, it may not have time and resources for an elaborate system. The business is mostly carried on cash basis and therefore, by providing analytical columns in the cash book, both on receipts and payments side, the accounting can be made very simple. Analytical column cash book will help the farmer to do away with other subsidiary books and also the ledger and yet, he will obtain all the information, he needs to prepare the final accounts.

(2) *Debtors and Creditors Register*, to keep credit transactions.

(3) *Stock Register*, which shows input and output of goods, sale, wastage and balance of stock.

(4) *Fixed Assets Register*, contains details of cost of assets, depreciation and balance of assets.

(5) *Loan Register*, contains record of loans, details of interest *etc.*

(6) Register for Notional Transactions for making a record of transactions between farm and farm household.

(7) *Cost Analysis register*, for keeping records of each farming activity, in order to know the profit of each activity.

COST AND REVENUE

Expenses and incomes associated with farming activities, other than agricultural activities are given below:

(A) POULTRY FARM

Expenses or Costs:

1. Costs of chicken, feed;
2. Stocks like hay, packing boxes, fuel ;
3. Maintenance cost of sheds;
4. Medicines;
5. Salaries and wages.

Revenue:

1. Sale of eggs, chickens, broiler, hens;
2. Sale of poultry excretions as manures.

(B) DAIRY FARMS

Expenses or costs:

1. Cattle feed and hay;
2. Cost of cultivation of feed crop, if any;
3. Insecticides;
3. Salaries and wages;
5. Cost of maintaining milk processing facilities.

Revenue:

1. Sale of milk;
2. Sale of milk products;
3. Sale of calves;
4. Sale of dairy cattle;
5. Sale of slaughtered cattle.

(C) FISHERIES

1. Cost of seed;
2. Cost of water;
3. Cost of fish feed;
4. Maintenance costs of tanks;
5. Catching expenses;
6. Depreciation of nets and other assets;
7. Salaries and wages.

Revenue:

1. Sale of fish.

TREATMENT OF SPECIFIC ITEMS

1. ***Land Development Expenses:*** A business may purchase land for cultivation. A lot of money may have to be spent by the business on cleaning, levelling the land, providing drainage, irrigation facilities *etc.* before the land can be used for cultivation. All these expenses are termed as " Land Development Expenses", and should preferable be added to the cost of land.
2. ***Drawings:*** A farmer or his family may consume a part of farm production. It is recorded as:

Drawings Account	Dr.
To Crop or Milk or Poultry or Fish Account.	

3. Similarly, when farm products are consumed by farm workers it is recorded as:

   Wages Account Dr.

   To Crop or Milk or Poultry or Fish Account

APPORTIONMENT BASIS FOR COMMON COSTS

Seed, fertilizer, manure, pesticides, direct wages (Notional and Actual), land rent (Notional and actual) *etc.* can be identified crop-wise. But other costs like irrigation, services of agricultural machinery, implements or animal power depreciation, interest on capital *etc.* cannot be classified simply by nomenclature. Common costs of the agricultural farms are to be suitably apportioned among the crops for which such costs were incurred. Many a time, common costs have been incurred for crop enterprises as well as livestock enterprises. Common costs should be apportioned among the crop enterprises on the basis of usage, wherever use of assets can be quantified. In other cases, length of crop season can be used. The following list, not exhaustive, are given below:

Cost Element	Apportionment Base
Maintenance of farm shed and depreciation	Length of crop season
Maintenance of draught animal and depreciation	Animal base
Maintenance of agricultural machinery implements and depreciation	Machine hours
Interest on working capital	(Ratio) working capital investment for various crops
Interest on fixed capital	Length of crop season

PREPARATION OF FINAL ACCOUNTS

Farm final accounts can be prepared according to any of the following two methods:

1. Single Entry Method:
2. Double Entry Method.

1. Single Entry Method:

This method does not require maintenance of an elaborate system of accounting to ascertain the profit or loss and financial position of the business. The method requires the preparation of two statement of affairs - one at the beginning of the accounting period and the other at the end of the accounting period. The excess of assets over liabilities is the net-worth of the business. The profit or loss made by the business during a period can be ascertained by comparing the net-worth of the business on two dates, after making suitable adjustments for drawings, introduction of additional capital *etc.* (For more details, refer Single Entry System of Accounting).

2. Double Entry Method:

Accounting information contained in the accounting records may be presented in the form of an account for each type of product, for example, Wheat Account, Rice Account etc. Each Account is to be debited with opening stock, and the relevant expenses incurred, and credited with the sale proceeds and the closing stock. The difference between the two sides of each account shows profit or loss. The profit or loss of each such account is transferred to General Profit and Loss Account, to which common expenses of all the activities of the farm are charged so as to arrive at net profit or loss, to be transferred to Capital Account. Finally, Balance Sheet is prepared.

NB: Land is usually not depreciated because its monetary value tends to increase with the passage of time.

ILLUSTRATION 26.1

From the data given below, prepare a 'Cattle Account':

	Rs
Opening stock of livestock	1,50,000
Closing stock of livestock	2,50,000
Opening stock of Cattle feed	8,000
Closing stock of cattle feed	6,000
Purchase of cattle during the year	4,00,000
Sale of cattle during the year	6,00,000
Sale of carcasses	2,000
Purchase of cattle feed	25,000
Wages for rearing cattle	8,000

Crop worth Rs. 10,000 grown in the farm was used for feeding cattle. Out of calves born, four died and their carcasses realised Rs. 100 *(B.Com., Mysore)*

SOLUTION

Cattle Account

	Amount		Amount
To Opening Stock:		By Sale of cattle	6,00,000
Livestock	1,50,000	" Sale of carcasses :	
Cattle feed	8,000	of cattle	2,000
" Purchase of cattle	4,00,000	of calves	100
" Purchase of cattle feed	25,000	" Closing stock:	
" Crop Account – Crop grown		Livestock	2,50,000
used for feeding cattle	10,000	Cattle feed	6,000
" Wages – Cattle rearing	8,000		
" Profit transferred to			
General P & L A/c	2,57,100		
	8,58,100		8,58,100

(B.Com. MS)

ILLUSTRATION 26.2

From the following information, prepare 'Crop Account':

	Rs
Opening stock:	
Fertilizer	15,000
Seeds	10,000
Wheat	50,000
Purchases:	
Seeds	6,000
Fertilizer	9,000
Wages:	
Paid in cash	68,000
Paid in kind by giving wheat	46,000
Sale of wheat	3,54,000
Wheat consumed by the proprietor	16,000
Depreciation on machinery	20,000

Closing stock:

Wheat	40,000
Seeds	7,000
Fertilizer	8,000

(B.Com., Mysore, Delhi)

SOLUTION

Crop Account

	Rs.		Rs.
To Opening stock:		By Sale of wheat	3,54,000
Wheat	50,000	" Wages in kind (Contra)	46,000
Seeds	10,000	" Drawings – Consumption by	
Fertilizer	15,000	proprietor	16,000
" Purchases:		" Closing stock:	
Seeds	6,000	Wheat	40,000
Fertilizer	9,000	Seeds	7,000
" Depreciation	20,000	Fertilizer	8,000
To wages:			
In cash	68,000		
In kind	46,000		
To Profit, transferred to General P & L A/c	2,47,000		
	4,71,000		4,71,000

ILLUSTRATION 26. 3

From the following information prepare crop account to find out the profit made by the crop section.

	Rs	Rs
Opening stock	2,600	
Grain	600	
Fertilizers	400	3,600
Purchases		
Seeds	400	
Fertilizers	600	1,000
Wages paid in cash		3,500
Wages paid in kind by giving grain		2,500
Sale of grain		25,400
Grain consumed by the proprietor		600
Grain consumed on the livestock section		2,400
Depreciation on farm machinery		1,000
Repairs and maintenance of farm machinery		2,000
Closing stocks		
Grain	2,000	
Seeds	400	
Fertilizers	600	3,000

(B.Com Bhopal)

SOLUTION:

Crop Account

		Rs			Rs
To Opening stock			By sale of grain		25,400
Grain	2,600		By Grain consumed by the proprietor (Drawings)		600
Seeds	600				
Fertilizers	400	3,600	By Grain consumed by Live stock section		2,400
To Purchases					
Seeds	400		By Wages in kind (contra)		2,500
Fertilizers	600	1,000	By Closing stock		
To Wages			Grain	2,000	
in cash	3,500		Seeds	400	
in kind	2,500	6,000	Fertilizers	600	3,000
To Depreciation		1,000			
To Repairs and maintenance		2,000			
To Profit and Loss Account		20,300			
		33,900			33,900

ILLUSTRATION 26.4

From the following information given by Kiran, prepare Farm Accounts for the year ended 31st March 2005:

	Workers	*Proprietor*
	Rs	Rs
Milk	1,750	1,500
Poultry	1,200	600
Crops	2,400	1,250

	Stock as on 1-4-2004	*Stock as on 31-3-2005*
	Rs	*Rs*
Crops	3,900	4,100
Seeds	1,800	2,250
Cattle	71,000	1,02,000
Growing crops	3,000	3,900
Cattle feed	10,000	7,500
Poultry	9,000	12,000
Fertilizers	3,800	3,900
Poultry feed	1,100	2,300

	Rs
Purchases during the year	
Seeds	1,250
Cattle	40,000
Poultry	15,000
Fertilizers	4,000
Cattle feed	14,000
Poultry feed	3,000
Sales during the year:	
Cattle	37,500
Eggs	15,000
Crops	22,500
Poultry	13,000
Milk	11,000

(*B. Com., Kuvempu*)

SOLUTION

Farm Accounts

(Crop. dairy and Poultry Divisions)

	Crops	*Dairy*	*Poultry*		*Crop*	*Dairy*	*Poultry*
To Opening Stock:	Rs.	Rs.	Rs.	By Sales:	Rs.	Rs.	Rs.
Crops	3,900	—	—	Crops	22,500	—	—
Seeds	1,800	—	—	Cattle	—	37,500	—
Growing	—	—	—	Milk	—	11,000	—
crops	3,000	—	—	Poultry	—	—	13,000
Fertilizers	3,800	—	—	Eggs	—	—	15,000
Cattle	—	71,000	—	" Wages	2,400	1,750	1,200
Cattle feed	—	10,000	—	" Drawings	1,250	1,500	600
Poultry	—	—	9,000	" Closing stock:	—	—	—
Poultry feed	—	—	1,100	Crops	4,100	—	—
" Purchases:	—	—	—	Seeds	2,250	—	—
Seeds	1,250	—	—	Growing crops	3,900	—	—
Fertilizers	4,000	—	—	Fertilizers	3,900	—	—
Cattle	—	40,000	—	Cattle	—	1,02,000	—
Cattle feed	—	14,000	—	Cattle feed	—	7,500	—
Poultry	—	—	15,000	Poultry	—	—	12,000
Poultry feed	—	—	3,000	Poultry feed	—	—	2,300
" Gross profit	22,550	26,250	16,000				
	40,300	1,61,250	44,100		40,300	1,61,250	44,100

ILLUSTRATION 26.5

From the following trial balance of Ram Singh prepare trading and profit and loss Account for the year ending 31st December 2006 and a balance sheet as on that date.

		Rs		Rs
Opening stock			Sales	
Paddy	500		Paddy	3,000
Potatoes	800		Potatoes	2,000
Cattle	1,000		Sugarcane	3,000
Sheep	700	3,000	Cattle	10,000
Purchases			Milk etc.	2,000
Cattle	8,000		Sheep	3,000
Sheep	1,000		Loan from Land Development bank	8,700
Seeds	500		Capital balance	20,000
Manures	1,000		Creditors for supplies	2,000
Cattle feed	1,000	11,500		
Crop expenses				
Labour	400			
Other expenses	300	700		
Livestock expenses				
Veterinary and medicines	500			
Labour	200			
Dairy expenses	300	1,000		
Expenses of machinery				
Repairs	300			
Diesel and oil	500			

Particulars		Rs	Rs
Electricity	200	1,000	
General overheads			
Rent and Rates	1,000		
Insurance	200		
Wages for permanent labour	800		
Bank interest	500	2,500	
Farm machinery		10,000	
Cash in hand		1,000	
Cash at bank		3,000	
Land		20,000	
		53,700	53,700

Additional information

(1) Closing stock

	Rs
Paddy	1,000
Potatoes	600
Cattle	1,500
Sheep	1,000

(2) 50 % of rent and rates may be taken as the share of Mr. Ram Singh for his residence.

(3) Mr. Ram Singh has consumed the following out of farm output

	Rs
Milk *etc.*	200
Potatoes	100
Paddy	700

(4) Provide 10% depreciation on machinery

(*M Com. Kolkata*)

SOLUTION:

TRADING ACCOUNT

For the year ending 31-12-2006

		Rs			Rs
To Opening stock			By Sale of crops		
Paddy	500		Paddy	3,000	
Potatoes	800		Potatoes	2,000	
Cattle	1,000		Sugarcane	3,000	8,000
Sheep	700	3,000	By Produce consumed by Ram singh		1,000
To Purchases			By Sale of livestock		
Cattle	8,000		Cattle	10,000	
Sheep	1,000	9,000	Milk	2,000	
To Crop expenses			Sheep	3,000	15,000
Seed	500		By Closing stock		
Manure	1,000		Paddy	1,000	
Labour	400		Potatoes	600	
Other expenses	300	2,200	Cattle	1,500	
To Livestock expenses			Sheep	1,000	4,100
Feed	1,000				
Veterinary	500				
Labour	200				
Diary expenses	300	2,000			
To Gross Profit		11,900			
		28,100			28,100

Profit and Loss Account
for the year ending 31.12.2006

		Rs		Rs
To General overheads			By Gross Profit	11,900
Rent and rates	1,000			
Less Ram Singh's share				
for his residence	500	500		
Insurance		200		
Wages for permanent labour		800		
Bank interest		500		
To Expenses of machinery				
Repairs	300			
Diesel and oil	500			
Electricity	200			
Depreciation	1,000	2,000		
To Net Profit		7,900		
		11,900		11,900

BALANCE SHEET
as on 31. 12. 2006

		Rs			Rs
Creditors for Supplies		2,000	Cash in hand		1,000
Loan from Land			Cash at bank		3,000
development Bank		8,700	Inventory		
Capital	20,000		Paddy	1,000	
Add Net Profit	7,900		Potatoes	600	
	27,900		Cattle	1,500	
Less: Drawings	1,500	26,400	Sheep	1,000	4,100
			Farm machinery	10,000	
			Less Depreciation	1,000	9,000
			Land		20,000
		37,100			37,100

ILLUSTRATION 26.6

The following particulars relate to Birjala Farm:

(a) Trial Balance as at 31st March, 2006:

	Rs	Rs
Capital		8,00,000
Stocks, 1st April, 2005		
Cattle	2,00,000	
Poultry	70,000	
Fertilizers	20,000	
Cattle food	30,000	
Poultry food	2,000	
Seeds	5,000	
Crops	10,000	
Growing crops	8,000	

	Dr.	Cr.
Purchases:		
Cattle	80,000	—
Poultry	38,000	—
Cattle food	30,000	—
Poultry food	7,000	—
Fertilizers	10,000	—
Sales:		
Cattle	—	70,000
Poultry	—	1,60,000
Crops	—	2,19,000
Milk	—	1,18,000
Butter	—	3,000
Eggs	—	28,000
Land and Buildings	6,00,000	—
Agricultural Equipments	2,00,000	—
Debtors and Creditors	30,000	20,000
Cash and Bank	5,000	—
Wages and Salaries	1,10,000	—
Crop insurance	10,000	—
Bank Loan	—	1,00,000
Interest on loan	12,000	—
Miscellaneous expenses	15,000	—
Drawings	26,000	—
	15,18,000	15,18,000

(b) Consumption of certain items by workers and proprietor:

	Workers Rs	*Proprietor* Rs
Poultry	10,500	4,000
Eggs	1,000	500
Butter	–	2,000
Milk	2,500	3,500

(c) Depreciation on agricultural equipment is to be provided at 12%.

(d) Salaries, miscellaneous expenses and interest expenses are to be apportioned as:

Cattle division	20%
Poultry division	30%
Crop division	50%

(e) Closing stocks, 31st March, 2006:

	Rs.
Cattle	2,80,000
Poultry	1,20,000
Fertilisers	10,000
Cattle food	6,000
Poultry food	4,000
Seeds	7,000
Crops	20,000
Growing crops	12,000

You are required to prepare the final accounts of Birjala Farm. *(I.C.W.A. Final)*

SOLUTION:

Profit And Loss Account of Birjala Farm
for the year ended 31st March, 2006

Particulars	*Cattle*	*Poultry*	*Crop*	*Particulars*	*Cattle*	*Poultry*	*Crop*
	Rs.	*Rs.*	*Rs.*		*Rs.*	*Rs.*	*Rs.*
To Stocks 1-4-2005	2,00,000	70,000	18,000	By Sales	70,000	1,60,000	2,19,000
" Stocks				" Consumption by workers	2,500	11,500	
Fertilizers			20,000	" Consumption by proprietor	5,500	4,500	
Cattle food	30,000			" Sale of milk	1,18,000		
Poultry food		2,000		" Sale of butter	3000		
Seeds			5,000	" Sale of eggs		28,000	
" Purchases	80,000	38,000		" Stocks, 31-3-2006	2,80,000	1,20,000	32,000
Cattle food	30,000			" Stocks			
Poultry food		7,000		Fertilizers			10,000
Fertilizers			10,000	Cattle food	6,000		
" Wages & Salaries	24,800	37,200	62,000	Poultry food		4,000	
" Misc. expenses	3,000	4,500	7,500	Seeds			7,000
" Interest	2,400	3,600	6,000		10,000		
" Depreciation			24,000				
" Crop insurance			10,000				
" Net profit	1,14,800	1,65,700	1,05,500				
	4,85,000	32,8000	2,68,000		4,85,000	3,28,000	2,68,000

Balance Sheet as on 31st March, 2006

		Rs.			Rs.
Capital	8,00,000		Land and Buildings		6,00,000
Add: Net profit			Agricultural Equipment	2,00,000	
Cattle	1,14,800		*Less:* Depreciation	24,000	
Poultry	1,65,700				1,76,000
Crops	1,05,500		Stocks:		
	11,86,000		Cattle		2,80,000
Less Drawings	26,000		Poultry		1,20,000
	11,60,000		Crops		20,000
Drawings in kind	10,000		Growing crops		12,000
		11,50,000	Fertilizers		10,000
Bank Loan		1,00,000	Cattle food		6,000
Creditors		20,000	Poultry food		4,000
			Seeds		7,000
			Debtors		30,000
			Cash at Bank		5,000
		12,70,000			12,70,000

QUESTIONS

Objective type questions

I. State whether the following statements are "True" or "False".

1. There is no need to provide depreciation on land.
2. The produce consumed by the proprietor and laborers is to be ignored.

3. Inventory valuation is the most difficult aspect of farm accounting.
4. No depreciation need be provided on farm machinery, equipment *etc.*
5. Common expenses should be distributed to different farming activities in an equitable manner.

[Ans: True – 1, 3, 5, False – 2, 4.]

II. Fill in the blanks.

1. Book-keeping in farm accounting, can be simplified by employing the .... Cash Book.
2. Direct costs which vary with farm output are debited to ....
3. Fixed costs which do not vary directly with production are debited to......
4. The entry for farm output consumed by the proprietor is .... Dr. To .....
5. Output used by owner's family should be treated as ......

[Ans: 1. Analytical; 2. Trading Account; 3. Profit & Loss A/c; 4. Drawings Account, Crop Account; Drawings.]

III. Choose the correct alternative:

1. The Cash Book usually maintained by the farmer is:
   (*a*) Petty Cash Book
   (*b*) Two column Cash Book
   (*c*) Analytical Cash Book
2. Crops are valued at:
   (*a*) Market Price
   (*b*) Cost Price
   (*c*) Economic Value
   (*d*) Capitalised Value
3. Grain consumed by livestock will figure:
   (*a*) In the livestock account
   (*b*) In the crop account
   (*c*) Both in the livestock and crop Account
4. Livestock purchase will figure in
   (*a*) The Balance Sheet
   (*b*) The Trading Account
   (*c*) The Profit & Loss Account
5. Livestock in the case of mixed farming is
   (*a*) A fixed Asset
   (*b*) A current asset
   (*c*) A wasting asset
   (*d*) A tangible asset
6. Final accounts of a farmer can be prepared under
   (*a*) Single Entry Method
   (*b*) Double Entry Method
   (*c*) Both Single and Double Entry Methods
7. Output used by owner's family, should be treated
   (*a*) As Income
   (*b*) As expenditure
   (*c*) As Drawings
8. Losses due to natural calamities should be treated
   (*a*) As normal loss.
   (*b*) As business loss
   (*c*) As abnormal loss

9. The work done by family members of the farmer should be treated
   (*a*) As free work
   (*b*) As labour, like any other workers
   (*c*) Neither of the above
10. Closing Stock should be valued at
   (a) Cost Price
   (b) Market Price
   (c) Cost price or Market price whichever is lower

[Ans: 1. (c); 2. (a); 3. (c); 4. (b); 5. (b); 6. (c); 7. (c); 8. (c); 9. (b); 10. (c)]

THEORETICAL QUESTIONS

1. What are the reasons of slow growth of farm accounting?
2. How does accounting for the farm help the management?
3. What are the objectives of farm accounting?
4. Discuss briefly the peculiar characteristics of farm transactions.
5. Mention the special features of farm accounting.

Problem 1. From the following information prepare Cattle Account to ascertain the profit made by he cattle division

	No.	Value Rs.
Opening stock of livestock	100	2,00,000
Closing stock of livestock	118	2,42.000
Opening stock of Cattle food		4,000
Closing stock of Cattle food		5,000
Purchases of cattle during the year	180	3,70,000
Sale of cattle during the year	175	4,38,000
Sale of carcasses	5	1,000
Purchases of cattle food		40,000
Wages for rearing cattle		10,000

Crop worth Rs. 11,000 grown in the farm was used for feeding the cattle. Out of the calves born 4 died and their carcasses realised Rs. 100

[Ans. Profit Rs. 51,000] (*B.Com Mumbai*)

Problem 2. Find the following details make up the Cattle Account in the books of Feeders' Ranch

	No.	Value Rs.
Cattle (Opening Value of Livestock)	100	3,00,000
Cattle Food (Opening stock)	–	30,000
Purchases of cattle Food	–	1,35,000
Purchases of Cattle (during the year)	200	5,85,000
Sale (total) of Slaughtered Cattle	150	5,62,500
Sale of carcasses	40	1,80,000
Cattle (Closing value of Livestock)	5	750
Cattle (Closing value of Livestock)	115	5,85,000
Cattle food (Closing stock)		37,500

Out of calves born during the year 4 died and the carcasses of the calves did not realise anything.

Crop worth Rs. 22,500 grown in the farm was used for feeding, Rs. 15,000 is estimated to be wages for rearing *etc.* Slaughter house expenses amounted to Rs. 22,500

Charge depreciation Rs. 7,500 and insurance Rs. 3,750 (*I.C.W.A. Final*)

(**Ans:** Profit Rs. 2,44,500)

Problem 3. From the following information, prepare "Crop Account" to find out the profit made by the crop section of the farm.

	Rs.	Rs.
Opening stock:		
Grain	2,600	
Seeds	600	
Fertilizers	400	
		3,600
Purchases:		
Seeds	400	
Fertilizers	600	
		1,000
Wages paid in cash		3,500
Wages paid in kind by giving grain		2,500
Sale of grain		25,400
Grain consumed by the proprietor		600
Grain consumed by the livestock section		2,400
Depreciation on farm machinery		1,000
Repairs and maintenance of farm machinery		2,000
Closing Stock:		
Grain	2,000	
Seeds	400	
Fertilizers	600	
		3,000

[**Ans:** Profit Rs. 20,300)

(*B.Com.Hons. Kolkata*)

4. From the information given below, prepare a "Crop Account" to ascertain gross margin made by this division of the farm.

	Rs.
Opening Stocks:	
Grain	3,000
Seeds and Fertilizers	2,000
Purchases:	
Seeds	500
Fertilizers	1,500
Sale of grain	15,000
Grain distributed as wages	2,000
Wages paid in cash	3,000
Grain consumed by the proprietor	2,000
Grain consumed by the livestock section	1,500
Repairs and maintenance of farm machinery	1,200
Depreciation on farm machinery	300
Crop insurance	500
Closing stock:	
Grain	6,000
Seeds and fertilizers	3,000

(**Ans:** Profit Rs. 15,500)

(*B.Com.Hons. Kolkata*)

5. Mr Gopal has a five acres farmland. He grows rice on four acres. The balance area has mango trees. Other particulars about his activities, during 2005-2006 are:

	Amount Rs
Opening Stock	30,000
Rice saplings purchased	50,000
Water charges	12,000
Sprinkler system	60,000
Pump	30,000
Fertilizer purchases	90,000
Insecticide spraying charges	9,000
Wooden boxes purchased during the year	6,000
Jute bags purchased during the year	48,000
Agriculture labour wages	60,000
Orchard labour wages	24,000
Threshing machine	10,000
Dead trees sold	5,000
Salary to Manger	6,000

During the year, he obtained 90,000 mangoes from his trees, which he disposed off at Rs. 10 per dozen. All the boxes were used for packing.

He also obtained 100 quintals rice per acre, half of which fetched him Rs. 7 per kilo and the rest Rs. 5 per kilo. One - tenth quantity of the bags purchased, remained unutilised. Fertilizers, worth Rs. 20,000 remained in stock at the end of the year. Depreciation is to be provided at 10 per cent. Rural development authority of his region monitors his performance and he needs to provide productwise Profit and Loss Account to them. He apportions common expenses in proportion of the area under each product. Insecticide is required to be sprayed once in every three years on mango trees to keep them free from harmful insects.

Prepare productwise Profit & Loss Accounts. [*ICWA* (*Final*)]

(**Ans:** Loss (Rice) Rs. 15,800: Profit (Mango) Rs. 21,600

Note: 1) Consumption of items such as fertilizers is worked out from opening stock, purchase and closing stock figures.

2. Apportionment of Common Expenses = 4 : 1.
3. Expenditure on Insecticide, deferred basis: $9,000 \times \frac{1}{3}$ = Rs. 3,000
4. Jute bags and use of thresher is only for Rice cultivation and hence no charge for Mango
5. Wooden Boxes, Insecticide spraying are only for Mango and hence no charge for Rice.

6. Khetribari Farm presents the following trial balance for the year ended 31.3.2006:

	Rs		*Rs*
Agricultural equipment	18,00,000	Land	25,00,000
Capital	45,00,000	Cash at Bank	90,000
Receivables	6,40,000	Loan from Bank	10,00,000
Opening stock of crop	5,00,000	Opening stock of fertilizer	2,20,000
Opening stock of livestock	4,00,000	Sale of livestock	11,00,000
Purchase of livestock	2,30,000	Farm worker's wages	1,60,000
Farm electricity	30,000	Farm Manager Salary	1,20,000
Livestock feed purchase	4,70,000	Sale of crops	22,50,000
Payables	90,000	Administrative expenses	40,000
Interest	1,20,000	Crop insurance	40,000
Farm House	6,80,000	Purchase of fertilizer	6,00,000
Crop processing expenses	3,00,000		

Depreciation is to be charged on agricultural equipment @ 10% and on farm house @ 5%. The former is to be borne fully by the crop account, while the latter is to be equally shared by the crop account and the livestock account.

Livestock account is to bear 25% of all manpower cost. During the year, crop worth Rs. 50,000 grown on the farm was used as food for livestock.

The closing stock of crop, fertilizer and feed amounts to Rs. 2,00,000, Rs. 2,40,000, Rs. 3,20,000 and Rs. 20,000 respectively. Loan is used for crops and livestock in the ratio of 2 : 1.

On the basis of the forgoing information, prepare the Crop and livestock account, the profit and loss Account and the Balance Sheet.

[ICWA]

[Ans: Profit (Crop) Rs. 5,63,000
Profit (livestock) Rs. 1,63,000
Net Profit Rs. 6,86,000
Balance Sheet Total Rs. 62,76,000**]**

7. From the trial balance and additional information of Meenakshi Farm Limited, Madurai, you are required to prepare the final accounts, for the year ending 31st December 2006.

Trial Balance as on 31.12.2006

Debit Balances	Rs	*Credit balances*		Rs
Stock as on 1.1.2006		Issued, subscribed and called		
Crops and fertilizers	5,000	up capital 20,000 equity		
Cattle	3,000	Shares of Rs. 10 each		2,00,000
Sheep	2,000	Mortgage loans from Land		
Purchases		Development Bank		40,000
Seeds and fertilizers	1,000	Crop loans from State Bank		
Cattle	2,000	of India		10,000
Sheep	1,000	Profit and Loss Account		
Cattle feed	1,000	balance as on 1.1.2006		10,000
Crop expenses	3,000	Sundry creditors		
Livestock expenses	2,000	Inputs	5,000	
Maintenance of farm machinery	1,000	Expenses	2000	
Mortgage interest	3,000			7,000
Bank interest	1,000	Depreciation Reserve		
Cash on hand	5,000	on farm machinery		13,000
Cash at bank	15,000	Sales		
Sundry debtors	15,000	Cattle	15,000	
Farm machinery	25,000	Sheep	10,000	
manager's salary	5,000	Milk etc.	5,000	
Salary of other staff	3,000			30,000
Directors' fees	1,000	Paddy	10,000	
Auditor's fees	1,000	Fruits	10,000	
Land and buildings	2,40,000	Vegetables	5,000	
				25,000
	3,35,000			3,35,000

Additional information:

(1) Provide 10% depreciation on farm machinery.

(2) Rs. 1,500 worth of farm produce was consumed by the livestock.

(3) Salaries of manager and other staff are to be apportioned as follow: 60% crops, 40% livestock.

(4) Stocks as on 31.12.2006:

Cattle	5,000
Sheep	3,000
Cattle-feed	2,000
Seeds	2,000
Crops and fertilizers	6,000

[**Ans:** Profit Rs. 45,500
Balance sheet Total : Rs. 3,02,500) *B.Com (Hons). Kolkata*

8. The following particulars relate to Birjala Farm:

(*a*) Trial Balance as at 31st March, 2006:

	Rs	Rs
Capital		8,00,000
Stock (1st April, 2005)		
Cattle	2,00,000	—
Poultry	70,000	—
Fertilisers	20,000	—
Cattle food	30,000	—
Poultry food	2,000	—
Seeds	5,000	—
Crops	10,000	—
Growing crops	8,000	—
Purchases	—	
Cattle	80,000	—
Poultry	38,000	—
Cattle food	30,000	—
Poultry food	7,000	—
Fertilizers	10,000	—
Sales		
Cattle	—	70,000
Poultry	—	1,60,000
Crops	—	2,19,000
Milk	—	1,18,000
Butter	—	3,000
Eggs	—	28,000
Land and buildings	6,00,000	—
Agricultureal equipments	2,00,000	—
Debtors and creditors	30,000	20,000
Cash and Bank	5,000	—
Wages and salaries	1,10,000	—
Crop insurance	10,000	—
Bank loan	—	1,00,000
Interest on loan	12,000	—
Miscellaneous expenses	15,000	—
Drawings	26,000	—
	15,18,000	15,18,000

(*b*) Consumption of certain items by workers and proprietor:

	Workers Rs.	Proprietor Rs.
Poultry	10,500	4,000
Eggs	1,000	500
Butter	–	2,000

Milk	2,500	3,500

(c) Depreciation on agricultural equipment is to be provided at 12%

(d) Salaries, miscellaneous and interest expenses are to be apportioned as:

Cattle division	20%
Poultry division	30%
Crop division	50%

(e) Closing stocks (31st March 2006):

	Rs
Cattle	2,80,000
Poultry	1,20,000
Fertilizers	10,000
Cattle food	6,000
Poultry food	4,000
Seeds	7,000
Crops	20,000
Growing crops	12,000

You are required to prepare final accounts of Birjala Farm. *[ICWA]*

(**Ans:** Net profit (cattle) Rs. 1,14,800
Net Profit (poultry) Rs. 1,65,700
Net Profit (Crops)Rs. 1,05,500
Balance sheet Rs. 12,70,000)

9. Ramnaresh Ram is engaged in commercial farming activity. The following Trial Balance of his farm is drawn as on 31st March, 2004:

Particulars	Debit Rs.	Credit Rs.
Land & Buildings	12,00,000	
Capital		10,50,000
Stock 1st April, 2003		
Crops	20,000	
Fertilizers	5,000	
Cattle	15,000	
Sheep	10,000	
Purchases		
Seeds	5,000	
Cattle	10,000	
Sheep	5,000	
Cattle Feed	5,000	
Sales		
Cattle		75,000
Sheep		50,000
Milk		25,000
Vegetables		75,000
Paddy		50,000
Bank Loan from Rural Development Bank (RDB)		2,50,000
Cash	20,000	
Bank	80,000	
Sundry Debtors	75,000	
Bank Interest	20,000	
Farm Machinery	1,25,000	

	Dr.	Cr.
Salaries:		
Manager	15,000	—
Staff	35,000	—
Expenses:		
Crops	15,000	—
Livestock	10,000	—
Machinery Repairs	5,000	—
Sundry Creditors	—	35,000
Co-operative Loan	—	65,000
	16,75,000	16,75,000

Other relevant particulars:

(*a*) Closing Stock (31st March, 2004)

	Rs.
Cattle	25,000
Sheet	15,000
Cattle Feed	10,000
Seeds	10,000
Crops	8,000
Fertilizers	22,000

(*b*) Depreciation is to be provided at 10% on farm machinery

(*c*) Farm produce consumed by the livestock Rs. 7,500

(*d*) Salaries are to be apportioned as :

60% crops

40% livestock

(*e*) Interest accrued on co-operative loan Rs. 4,000

(*f*) Personal consumption:

	Rs.
Milk	3,000
Vegetables	2,000
Paddy	8,000

(*g*) No depreciation is to be charged on land and buildings.

From the above information, prepare the final accounts of Ramnaresh Ram for the year 31st March, 2004.

(*I.C.W.A. Inter*)

(Ans. Net Profit Rs. 1,86,500

Balance Sheet rs. 15,77,500)

Chapter 27

Government Accounting

Introduction – Government Accounting – Commercial Accounting and Government Accounting – The Principles of Government Accounting – Classification of Government Accounting – Audit and Accounts Department – The Comtroller and Auditor-General of India – Compilation of Accounts – Finance Accounts – Combined Finance and Revenue Accounts – Theoretical Questions

Government Accounting is of special significance in our country because of the fact that the Government has the largest volume of monetary transactions. Maintenance of detailed government account is necessary to provide information for different kinds of revenues and expenses.

PRINCIPLES AND METHODS OF GOVERNMENT ACCOUNTING

The activities of good government in any country are determined by the needs of the country. Since the main branches of its activities are known, it becomes necessary to decide what expenditure will be necessary during any year in carrying out these activities and how to raise sufficient money to meet that expenditure. The same is done by preparing a budget which is duly passed by the Parliament or a State Legislature.

The classification of transactions in government accounts is determined, firstly, by the administrative classification of the activities and, secondly, by the classification of the nature of the transactions. The accounting is therefore, more elaborate than the commercial accounts. Since, the immediate objective of government accounting is not to ascertain the gain or loss on transactions of the government as a whole in carrying out its activities, the method of budgeting and accounting under the service heads is not designed to bring out the relation in which government stands to its material assets in use, its liabilities are discharged at more or less at a distant date. The usual accounting methods that are followed in a commercial firm is found to be unsuitable and unnecessary in the case of government accounting. In its budget for a year, a government is interested to forecast with the greatest possible accuracy what is expected to be received or paid during the year, and whether the former, together with the balance of the past year, is sufficient to cover the latter. Similarly, in the compiled accounts for the year, it is concerned to see to what extent the forecast has been justified by the facts, and whether it has a surplus or a deficit balance as a result of the year's transactions.

In short, on the basis of the budgets and accounts, government accounts are designed to enable the government to determine how little money it needs which are taken out from the tax payers in order to maintain its necessary activities at the proper standard of efficiency.

The most of the government accounts is kept under Single Entry System. There is, however, a portion of the accounts which is prepared under Double Entry System, the main purpose of which is to bring out the balance of accounts with regard to which the Government acts as banker or remitter or borrower or lender. Such balances are worked out by single entry basis which can accurately be ascertained by double entry principles.

Government Accounting *

Government Accounting, on the other hand, refers to the Governments (both States and Central). That is, the objectives of this accounting is the financial administration of the activities of the Government to promote maximisation of welfare in the form of various services.

Thus, the principles of Commercial Accounting and Government Accounting differ in certain essential / basic points. The difference is due to the fact that, while primary function of a concern / firms is trade or manufacturer and thereby to make profit, that of a Government is to govern a country and to administer the several departments of its activities to promote welfare among the people in the best possible way.

The differences between Commercial Accounting and the Government Accounting are enumerated below:

(a) Methods of Accounting

In commercial accounting, *accrual basis* of accounting is followed in order to find out the result of the operation by preparing Profit and Loss Account and to ascertain the financial position at the end of the year by preparing Balance Sheet. But, in Government Accounting, *cash basis* of accounting is usually followed since a Government /State has to decide upon its range of activities at first and then to ascertain its various sources (*viz*. borrowing, taxation etc.). In short, a Government has to ensure its sources of finance and then its applications.

(b) System of Accounting

In commercial accounting, *Double Entry System* of book keeping is followed for its practical purposes. That is, a Profit and Loss Account is prepared (by taking up all the revenue incomes and revenue expenses) and a Balance Sheet (by taking up the result of the concern along with the personal and real accounts). But in Government Accounting, *Single Entry System* of accounting is usually followed. The following two statements are generally prepared, *viz*.:

(*i*) Government Account– It exhibits the net result of the incomes and expenditure including capital expenditures; and

(*ii*) Statement of Balancing Account– It reveals only the balance, *i.e.*, whether the Government has to receive money or is liable to pay to others.

(c) Classification of heads of Accounting

We know, in commercial accounting, accounts are broadly classified into: (a) Personal Account (b) Nominal and (c) Real Account. These are classified accounting to Double Entry principles. However, in Government accounting, the classifications are quite different. They are classified as under :

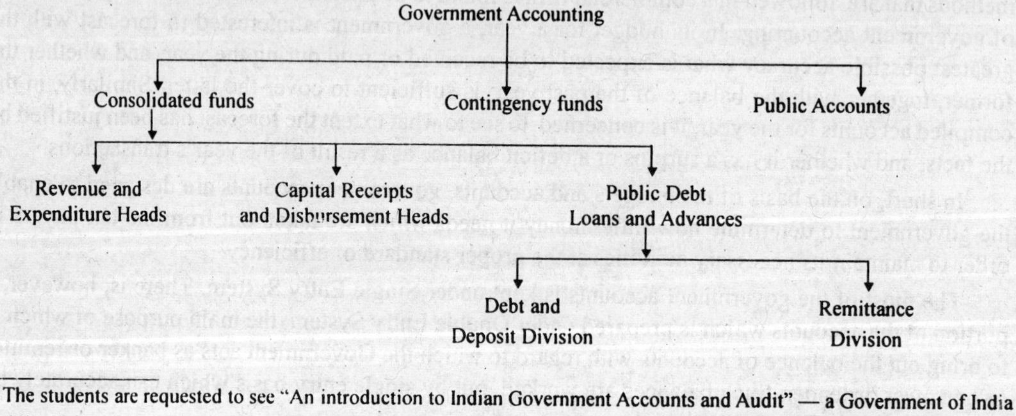

* The students are requested to see "An introduction to Indian Government Accounts and Audit" — a Government of India publication.

(d) Maintenance of Records

In commercial accounting, a separate set of books – known as costing books– is maintained in order to find out the cost of production and sales to fix up the selling price after adding certain percentage of profit and also to see the proper utilisation of resources.

But, in Government Accounting, a Budget is to be prepared (which is duly passed by the Parliament or State Legislature) by making an estimate of expenditure to be incurred and the sources of funds to be raised to meet the said expenditures. For this purpose, different charts and diagrams are to be prepared in order to make a proper comparison of expenditure and incomes of the past years.

The principles of Government Accounting may be summarised as under:

(a) System of Accounting

It has already been explained that the Government usually follows the Single Entry System of Accounting. But, in some cases, (*viz.*, Loans and Borrowings) the system of Double Entry has been followed. Because, in order to ascertain this arithmetical accuracy by preparing a Trial Balance and to determine the balance of the account as well, Double Entry System has to be taken into consideration.

(b) Commercial Enterprises under Public Sector

In public sector enterprises, however, Double Entry System has been followed under mercantile basis like commercial accounting. Because, for ascertaining the results of the undertaking, the Profit and Loss Account and the Balance Sheet are to be prepared. But, in some cases, however, various management techniques, Cash Flow Analysis, Funds Flow Analysis, Ratio Analysis *etc.* and some charts and diagrams with the help of statistical data, are taken into consideration.

(c) Classification of Incomes and Expenditures

According to the requirements of the Government, it is necessary to classify the incomes and expenditures of the services under various heads and sub-heads. For example, revenue of the Central, Budget are classified into:

(*i*) Tax Revenue and (*ii*) Non–Tax Revenue

Tax-Revenue again sub–divided into:

(*i*) Taxes on incomes and expenditures;
(*ii*) Taxes on property and capital transactions;
(*iii*) Taxes on commodities and services, *etc.*

Similarly, Non–Tax Revenue is again sub–divided into:

(*i*) Interest Receipts;
(*ii*) Dividend and Profits;
(*iii*) Others.

At the same time, expenditure in the form of different services are also classified under various heads and sub–heads, as under:

(*i*) General Services,
(*ii*) Social Services,
(*iii*) Economic Services and
(*iv*) Grant-in-aid and contribution.

Now, general services is again sub–divided into:

(*i*) administrative services;
(*ii*) defence services;
(*iii*) servicing of debts;
(*iv*) fiscal services etc.

The classification of Receipts and Expenditure are discussed in details in a subsequent paragraph.

(d) Consolidated Transactions

In Government accounting, although the transactions are recorded primarily under various heads of accounts, later they are consolidated in order to show the combined result for the period concerned.

Classification of Government Accounting in India

According to the Indian Constitution, the following three funds or accounts have been provided for:

(*a*) Consolidated Funds;

(*b*) Contingency Funds; and

(*c*) Public Accounts.

(a) Consolidated Funds

The Union Government and each State Government may have a separate fund which is known as Consolidated Fund of India or, 'Consolidated Fund of ...... State'. The fund includes:

(*i*) All revenues received by the Government of India;

(*ii*) All loans raised by the Government of India by issue of treasury bills;

(*iii*) Money obtained by means of 'Ways and Means' of advances;

(*iv*) All money received in repayment of loans previously made out of the consolidated fund.

Consolidated Fund may be sub–divided into:

(*i*) Revenue and Expenditures;

(*ii*) Capital receipts and disbursement; and

(*iii*) Debts, Loans and Advances.

Part I – Consolidated Fund

(*i*) Revenue and Expenditures

	Rs.		*Rs.*
A. Taxes, Duties and other Principal Heads of Revenue.		A. Collection of Taxes, Duties and other Principal Revenues —	
(iv) Taxes on Income other than corporation taxes and Estate Duty		(4) Taxes on Income other than Corporation Taxes and Estate Duty	
(v) Estate Duty etc.		(7) Land Revenue etc.	
C. Irrigation		C. irrigation	
E. Debt Services		E. Debt Services	
F. Administrative Services etc.		F. Administrative Services etc.	
Total — Revenue Receipts		Total Expenditure on Revenue Account	
Revenue Surplus			
Revenue Deficit			

(ii) Capital Receipts and Disbursements

	Rs.		Rs.
		Payment of Compensators etc.	
		Irrigation	
		Agricultural Improvements etc.	
(Public Debts)		Total—Capital Expenditures	

(iii) Debts, Loans and Advances

	Rs.		Rs.
Permanent Debt		Permanent Debt	
Loans from Central Govt. etc.		Loans from Central Govt. etc.	
Total Consolidated Fund		Total — Consolidated Fund	

(b) Contingency Fund

The Central Government and each State Government may have a separate Contingency Fund, *viz.*, 'The Contingency Fund of India' or 'The Contingency Fund of .....State' which is in the nature of an imprest. The fund is at the disposal of President or Governor to enable advances to be made by him out of such fund for meeting unforeseen expenditures pending authorisation of such expenditure by Parliament or the State Legislature, under appropriations made by Law. Each such fund is financed from time to time by such sums as may be determined by the Act of the appropriate legislature establishing the fund.

Part II–Contingency Fund

	Rs.		Rs.
Contingency Fund		Contingency Fund	
Total		Total	

(c) Public Accounts

The Central Government or the State Government may also have separate Public Accounts, *viz.*, 'The Public Account of India' or 'The Public Account of ... State', where all other public moneys received by or on behalf of Central /State Government are credited and disbursements are made from such fund according to the prescribed rules. The Public Accounts have two main sections, *viz.*, (*i*) Debit (other than those included in the Consolidated Fund), and (*ii*) Deposits and Remittances.

Part III–Public Accounts
Debt (other than those mentioned in Part I) and Deposit

	Rs.		Rs.
Unfounded Debts		Unfounded Debts	
Deposits and Advances etc.		Deposits and Advances etc.	
		Total	
Remittance–		Remittance—	
Total-Public Accounts		Total-Public Accounts	
Total Receipts		Total-Disbursement	
Opening Cash Balance		Closing Cash Balance	
Grand Total		Grand Total	

Note: The first section comprises receipts and payments for which Government incurs a liability to repay moneys received with payment of the former and recoveries of the latter whereas the second section comprises all adjustments, *e.g.* remittance of cash between treasuries.

AUDIT AND ACCOUNTS DEPARTMENT

This department is composed of all establishments who are engaged to prepare the accounts and audit for the same, both for Central and State Government, headed by the Comptroller and Auditor-General of India. This department is responsible to keep accounts and audit of transactions relating to

Public Works, Civil and Forest Departments. In order to perform the duties, civil audit offices are opened in the various States of India under the Auditor and Accountant General.

Similarly, this department also takes the responsibility of the accounts of Railways (with the help of Director of Railway Audit). For this purpose, chief auditors are appointed for various Railway zones. At the same time, it is the duty of this department to audit the Defence Accounts through Director of Audit, Defence Service. Thus, this department performs very significant duties relating to accounts and audit.

THE COMPTROLLER AND AUDITOR - GENERAL OF INDIA

The office of the Auditor-General was recognised for the first time statutorily with the introduction of the constitutional reforms of 1919 and in audit matters, he was made by statute independent of the Govt. of India. He was also recognised as the administrative head of the Indian Audit Department under the Constitution of India. Under the provision of the Govt. of India Act, 1935, as well as under the adaptations of the said Act made as a result of the Indian Independence Act, 1947, the independence of the Auditor-General was fully secured. In short, he shall be the impartial head of the audit and accounts system of India. In order to discharge his duty properly, his office should be independent, so as to discharge his duties without fear or favour.

The Indian Constitution has recognised the Comptroller and Auditor General as a high, independent statutory authority. It is his duty to see, on behalf of the legislatures, that the expenses voted by them are not exceeded and that the money expended was legally available for and applicable to the purpose for which it is meant. The Constitution also safeguards the independence and freedom of the Comptroller and Auditor-General in a variety of ways for the purpose of securing the highest standard of financial integrity of the administration and watching the interest of tax payers and also for the purpose of legislative control over the entire executive Government and its officers. Article 148 of the Constitution provides that the Comptroller and Auditor-General shall be appointed by the President under his hand and seal and shall only be removed from office in like manner and on grounds as a Judge of the Supreme Court.

Conditions of Service

His salary and conditions of services shall be statutory and shall not be liable to variation during his term of office. Under this power, Parliament has enacted the Comptroller and Auditor-General (Condition of the Service) Act, 1971, (replacing the earlier Act of 1935) which has been amended in 1976, and provides as follows:

(*i*) "The term of office of the Comptroller and Auditor-General shall be 6 years from the date on which he assumes office. But -

- (*a*) He shall vacate office on attaining the age of 65 years, if earlier than the expiry of the 6-year term;
- (*b*) He may, at any time, resign his office, by writing under his hand, addressed to the President of India;
- (*c*) He may be removed by impeachment.

(*ii*) His salary shall be equal to that of a Judge of the Supreme Court.

(*iii*) On retirement, he shall be eligible to an annual pension of Rs. 15,000.

(*iv*) In other matters, his conditions of service shall be determined by the Rules applicable to a member of the I. A. S., holding the rank of a Secretary to the Govt. of India.

(*v*) He shall be disqualified for any further Government 'office' after retirement - so that he shall have no inducement to please the executive of the Union or the State.

(*vi*) The salaries etc. of the Auditor-General and his staff and the administrative expenses of his office shall be charged upon the revenue of India and shall, thus, be non-votable (Art. 148)."

Therefore, the position of the Comptroller and Auditor-General shall be similar to that of a judge of a Supreme Court.

Powers and Duties

As per Articles 149, 150 and 151, the Comptroller and Auditor-General has two distinct functions, *viz.*; (*i*) Compilation of Accounts and (*ii*) Conduct of Audit. The duties and powers of the Comptroller and Auditor-General in relation to accounts of the Union (including Union Territories) with legislatures and State Government are laid down in Article 150 of the Constitution, Sections 10 to 24 of 'The Comptroller and Auditor-General's Act, 1971'. Article 150 of the Constitution empowers the Comptroller and Auditor-General, with the approval of the President, to present the forms in which the accounts of the Union (including Union Territories) with legislatures and of the States are to be kept. He is statutorily responsible for keeping of the accounts of the Union and of the State, other than the accounts relating to Defence and Railways and also the accounts relating to the transactions in the U. K. But he is relieved of the responsibility for keeping initial accounts kept in treasuries and department offices including Accounts of Stores and Stocks, Trading, Manufacturing and Profit & Loss Accounts that may be required to be kept in any particular office or department. But this does not impair his authority to prescribe the form where accounts are to be rendered at his office.

Under Section 11 of The Comptroller and Auditor-General's Act, 1971, as amended in 1976, the Comptroller and Auditor-General has to prepare in each year comprehensive accounts of receipts and expenditures of each Government, classifying the transactions under respective heads and to submit them to the Government concerned. These accounts are known as *Finance Accounts.* Besides, the Comptroller and Auditor-General has also to submit annually to each government in respect of accounts kept by him, known as *Appropriation Accounts, i.e.* accounts relating to expenditures during a financial year for the several items specified in the schedules to Appropriation Acts passed in accordance with the provisions of Articles 114 and 204 of the Constitution.

Under Article 18 of the Account Code, the Comptroller and Auditor-General has also to prepare annually in such form as he, with the concurrence of the President, may determine and to submit to the President a General financial Statement incorporating a summary of the accounts of the Union and of all the States and Union Territories with legislature for the preceding financial year and particulars of their balances, outstanding liabilities and containing such other information regarding their financial position as the President may direct them to be included in the Statement. This General Financial Statement is known as the *Combined Finance and Revenue Accounts* of the Central, State and Union Territories.

Under the provisions of Section 12 of the said Act, 'it is also his duty, so far as the accounts for the compilation of which he is responsible, enable him to do so, to give to the Union Government and to the government of every State and Union Territory with legislature such information as they may from time to time require and such assistance in the preparation of their annual financial statements as they may ask for.

Similarly, Section 18 of The Comptroller and Auditor-General's Act, 1971, empowers the Comptroller and Auditor-General to inspect any office of accounts which is under the control of the Central Government or of State or of a Union Territory with legislature including treasuries and such offices responsible for keeping of initial or subsidiary accounts. Such a provision is necessary in order to ensure the correctness and accuracy of the initial and subsidiary accounts kept in treasuries and departmental offices.

With Regard to Audit

The primary duties and powers of the Comptroller and Auditor-General with regard to audit of Government Accounts as derived from Sections 13 to 17 of The Comptroller and Auditor-General's Act, 1971 are as follows:

(1) It is the duty of the Comptroller and Auditor-General—

(*i*) to audit all expenditures from the Consolidated Fund of India and of each State and of each Union Territory having legislative assembly and to ascertain whether money shown in the accounts as having been disbursed were legally available for and applicable to the service or purpose to which they have been applied or charged and whether the expenditure conforms to the authority which governs it;

(ii) to audit all transactions of the Union and of the State/Union 'territories with' legislatives relating to contingency fund and Public Accounts;

(iii) to audit all trading, manufacturing and Profit & Loss accounts and Balance Sheets kept by order of the President or of the Governor of the State or of the administrator of Union Territory:

— and in each case, to report on the expenditure, transactions or accounts so audited by him,

(2) It is the duty of the Comptroller and Auditor-General—

(i) to audit and report on the receipts of any department of the Union or of a State or Union Territory;

(ii) to audit and report on the accounts of stores and stock kept in any office or department of the Union or of a State/Union Territory.

Besides the duties and functions which the Comptroller and Auditor-General exercises in relation to the accounts of the Union, the States, Union Territories with legislature and of certain other authorities and bodies under specific provision of law, he has also to undertake the audit of the accounts of certain authorities or bodies, *e.g.*, the Municipal funds, by consent on such terms regarding recovery of cost *etc.* as have been settled between him and the Government concerned.

Other prescribed duties

The duties and functions relating to the keeping and auditing of and reporting upon the accounts of the Union, of the States and of the Union Territories with legislature, the Comptroller and Auditor-General may be entrusted with duties and functions in relation to accounts of any other authority or body as may be permitted by or under any law made by Parliament-Art. 149.

The expression "any other authority or body" does not include private, commercial and quasi-commercial undertakings in which the Government of India may be participating.

Under Art. 279 (1) of the Indian Constitution, the Comptroller and Auditor-General is also to ascertain and certify the net proceeds of any tax or duty or of' any part of such tax or duty, in or attributable to any area.

Powers of Comptroller and Auditor-General under the Initial and Subsidiary Accounts rules

The initial and subsidiary accounts rules relieve the Comptroller and Auditor-General from the responsibility of maintaining accounts of a specified class or character without derogating from his power to prescribe the form in which such accounts shall be rendered to him and in which the initial accounts from which the accounts so rendered are compiled or on which they are based shall be kept. The provisions are noted below:

(i) Initial accounts required to be kept in treasuries;

(ii) Initial and subsidiary accounts which may be required to be kept in any office or department of the Federation or, as the case may be, of any State;

(iii) Accounts of stores and stocks which may be required to be kept in any office or department of the Federation or, of a State by order of the Governor-General or Governor of a State:

(iv) As per Article 150 of the Indian Constitution, the Comptroller and Auditor-General is empowered with the approval of the President, to prescribe the form of initial accounts from which the accounts rendered to the Indian Audit and Accounts Department are compiled or on which those accounts are based.

(v) According to Paragraph 11 (2) of the Audit and Accounts Order, 1936, the forms of accounts including Appropriation Accounts, relating to Defence, Railways or any other Department or service whose accounts are not maintained by the Comptroller and Auditor-General, may be determined by the departmental accounting authorities.

Compilation of Accounts

The monthly accounts received from the treasuries and the civil departmental officers are compiled by Civil Accountant-Generals into consolidated monthly accounts of States, Union Territories and of the Union Government (Civil). The transactions of the Union Government (Civil) taking place throughout India are consolidated from month to month by the Accountant-General, Central Revenues, to whom other Accounts Offices furnish the monthly accounts of union transactions taking place in their accounts circles. The transactions of the Posts and Telegraphs, Railway and Defence services taking place throughout India are similarly consolidated monthly by the Director-General, Posts and Telegraphs, the Railway Board and the Comptroller-General of Defence, Accounts, respectively, from the figures furnished by their subordinate officers.

Each Civil Accounts Officer works out progressive figures during the year of the Union, State and Union Territory accounts of his circle. A progressive account is furnished by him to the State/ Union Territory Government; A copy of the statement of Central transactions, incorporating all corrections, is to be furnished to the Comptroller and Auditor-General also. Similarly, the Accountant-Generals, Post and Telegraphs, Railways and Defence Services compile the annual accounts of their respective departments and submit the same to the Comptroller and Auditor-General.

The annual Finance Accounts, together with the Appropriation Accounts, are submitted by the Comptroller and Auditor-General of India to President (Governor of the State)/ Administrator of the Union Territory at the end or each year for the purpose of presenting to the Parliament/State Legislature/legislature of the Union Territory as the case may be. Besides, the Comptroller and Auditor-General consolidates the various Finance Accounts and Returns received from Accounts Officers including the Chief Accounts Officer to the High Commissioner of India in London into one account for the whole country for submission to the President. This account is known as *'Combined Finance and Revenue Accounts'* of the Central Government, State Government and Union Territories of India.

The Finance Accounts and the Combined Finance and Revenue Accounts of the Union and State Governments

Finance Accounts

It has already been stated earlier that the Comptroller and Auditor-General is to prepare a comprehensive accounts of receipts and expenditure of each State Government every year to be classified under respective heads and submit the same to the appropriate Government. These accounts are known as *Finance Accounts.* When the accounts are closed at the end of the year, the Finance Accounts of each State Government is prepared by the respective Accountant-General which is submitted to the Comptroller and Auditor-General for approval. The same is transmitted to the Governor of the State before the respective legislature. The Finance Accounts of the Union Government are compiled by the Accountant-General, Central Revenue which is submitted to the Comptroller and Auditor-General for approval. The same is submitted to the President before the Parliament.

The Finance Accounts reveal the records of receipts and outgoings of the Government for the year along with the financial results disclosed by the Revenue and Capital Accounts, the accounts of the public Debts and the assets and liabilities of the Government concerned.

The Finance Accounts are prepared in the following two parts:

Part I Summarised Statement

Part II Detailed Accounts and other Statements.

Statement Part I informs the following (in a summarised form)

(*i*) Transactions for the year relating to Consolidated Fund, Contingency Fund and the Public Accounts.

(*ii*) (*a*) Capital outlay outside the Revenue Account and progressive Capital expenditure to the end of the year.

(*b*) Revenue expenditure temporarily capitalised.

(*iii*) Financial results of irrigation and electricity schemes.

(*iv*) Debt position of Government including expenditure incurred on the service of debt.

(*v*) Loans and advances by Government.

(vi) Guarantees given by Government.

(*vii*) Cash balances and investment of Cash Balances.

(viii) Summary of balances under Consolidated Fund, Contingency Fund and Public Accounts.

Statement Part II contains the following

(*i*) Accounts of revenue and expenditure during the year by minor heads of accounts.

(*ii*) Particulars of capital expenditure outside the Revenue Account during and to the end of the year.

(*iii*) Particulars of investment of the Government in the shares of Statutory Corporations, Government Companies, Joint Stock Companies, Co-operative Banks and Societies, *etc*.

(*iv*) Information regarding capital and other expenditure to the end of the year and the principal sources from which the funds were provided for the expenditure.

(*v*) Accounts showing receipts, disbursements and balances under heads of accounts relating to its remittances and contingency fund, and

(*vi*) Detailed statement of debt and other interest-bearing obligations of Government.

(*vii*) Detailed statement of loans and advances, made by Government.

(*viii*) Particulars of earmarked balances relating to Reserve Fund, *etc*.

(*ix*) Statistical information with regard to revenue and expenditure under different heads expressed as a percentage of total revenue/total expenditure, and distribution between charged and voted expenditure.

Combined Finance and Revenue Account

The Comptroller and Auditor-General is to submit annually a *General Financial Statement* to the President which will incorporate a summary of the accounts of the Central Government and of all the States including Union Territories for the preceding financial year. It also includes the particulars of balances and outstanding liabilities and other necessary information as the President may direct. This general financial statement is known as the *Combined Finance and Revenue Accounts of the Central and the State Governments of India.* These accounts which are designed to present the accounts of all the Governments in India on a common and comparable basis comprise—(i) the General Accounts and (ii) the Subsidiary Accounts.

The General Accounts include :

(*i*) Summary of Receipts and Disbursements of the Central, Union Territories and State Governments by Sectional Head of Accounts.

(*ii*) Accounts of Revenues of the Central, Union Territory and State Governments by major heads.

(*iii*) Accounts of Expenditure met from Revenue of the Central, Union Territory and State Governments by major heads.

(*iv*) Account of capital receipts and disbursements and of transactions relating to the contingency funds and Public Accounts of the Central, Union Territory and State Governments, generally by major heads.

The Subsidiary Accounts, on the other hand, give the details, generally by minor heads of the figures shown in the General Accounts. They also exhibit the balances at the beginning and at the end of the year under the head Debt, Deposits etc. The distribution of expenditure between *charged* and *voted* is also shown at the end of each relevant subsidiary accounts.

The Combined Finance and Revenue Accounts are prepared mainly from the following accounts and the same is submitted to the President in February each year.

1. Finance Accounts of the State Governments received from the Accountant-General and Finance Accounts of Central Government compiled by the Comptroller-General of Accounts.

2. Accounts of P & T Dept. received from P & T Board.
3. Railway Capital and Revenue Accounts received from Ministry of Railways (Railways Board).
4. Accounts of Defence Services, received from the Comptroller-General of Defence Accounts.
5. Accounts of Sterling transactions of Central Government finally brought to account in England, received from the Chief Accounting Officer of the High Commissioner for India in London.
6. Subsidiary Returns.

THEORETICAL QUESTIONS

1. Distinguish between Commercial Accounting and Govt. Accounting.
2. Discuss the principles and methods of Commercial Accounting and Govt. Accounting.
3. Discuss the general structures of the Financial Administration of India.
4. Define: Supplementary Grant, Public Accounts Committee; Initial Account, Compitation of Accounts. Discuss the various classifications of Govt. Accounting in India.
5. Discuss the power, duties, conditions of services of Comptroller and Auditor General of India.

Chapter 28

Sale or Return Transactions

Transactions are very few – Transactions are Frequent – Transactions are numerous – Questions – Objective Type Questions – Theoretical Questions – Practical Problems

Businessman provides many facilities to his customers with a view to increase his sales. One of the facilities is that goods are delivered to the customers with the option to retain or return the same within a specified short period. When a businessman sends goods with such an option it is generally called "Sale or Return". When a businessman sends goods under " Sale or Return" basis to a customer, it cannot be treated as sales. Delivery of goods on approval basis implies a change of possession only and not a transfer of ownership unless the specified period expires without return or the customer earlier informs of his approval. Till the expiry of period or approval from customers, transactions are not sale *i.e.* ownership vests with the businessman. Businessman earn profits only on absolute sale. Therefore, there is a need of a special accounting treatment. The accounting method of goods sent on Sale or Approval basis is based upon the frequency of sales; and they are:

1. Transactions are very few.
2. Transactions are frequent.
3. Transactions are numerous.

1. Transactions are very Few

When transactions are very few in number, no special accounting treatment is needed. And in such a case, the goods sent on approval basis can be treated as sales. The relevant entries are:

(*a*) On sending the goods on approval	Customers Account To Sales Account	Dr.
(*b*) On approval	No entry. Because on sending the goods, it has been treated as sales.	
(*c*) On return	Sales Account To Customers Account	Dr.
(*d*) When approval is pending	Sales Account To Customers Account	Dr.

The goods not approved or not rejected need some adjustment at the end of the accounting year. They are included in the stock either at cost price or market price whichever is less.

ILLUSTRATION 28.1

In preparing the final account of a company it is found that the amount of sundry debtors Rs 2,00,000 includes Rs 40,000 worth of goods sent out on approval and debited to customers' accounts, in respect of which the time for returning the goods has not yet expired. These goods have been invoiced at 33 1/3% above the cost.

Show the journal entries in respect of goods sent on approval basis.

SOLUTION

Journal Entries

			Dr. Rs	Cr. Rs
1 At the time of sending the goods	Customers Account	Dr.	40,000	
	To Sales Account			40,000
2. Closing of financial year the approval is pending. Therefore the adjustment	Sale Account	Dr.	40,000	
	To Customers Account			40,000
3. The goods lying with customers on approval basis included in stock at cost price Rs. 40,000 × 3/4	Stock with Customers A/c	Dr.	30,000	
	To Trading Account			30,000

ILLUSTRATION 28.2

A Departmental Store has credited certain items of Sales on Approval aggregating Rs 15,000 to Sales Account. Of these, goods to the value of Rs 4,000 have been returned and taken into stock at cost Rs 2,000 though the record of return was omitted in the accounts. And in respect of another parcel of Rs 3,000 (cost being Rs 1,500) the period of approval did not expire on the closing date.

Show the adjustment and correcting entries in the books of Departmental Store.

SOLUTION

Journal Entries

			Dr. Rs	Cr. Rs
	Sales Account	Dr.	4,000	
	To Customers Account			4,000
	(Being return of goods by customers sent out on approval basis and included in sales)			
	Sales Account	Dr.	3,000	
	To Sale or Return Account			3,000
	(Being goods sent out on approval basis included in sale but not yet approved)			
	Stock on Sale or Return Account	Dr.	1,500	
	To Trading Account			1,500
	(Being cost of goods lying with customers, included in stock)			

2. Transactions are Frequent

When there are frequent transactions, but not many, they are entered in a separate Register, which has four columns, as shown below:

Credit 'Sales on Approval' Register

Deliveries						*Returns*			*Sales*			*Balance (on accounting date)*	
Date	Party's Name	Quantity	Rate	Amount	Approval Period	Date	Quantity	Amount	Date	Quantity	Amount	Date	Amount
(1)						(2)			(3)			(4)	
No entry in Financial book						No entry in Finance book			To be recorded as sales			To be treated as stock	

1. Column one is filled up with details of goods sent on approval basis to customer, at the time of dispatch.

2. Column two is filled up with the details of goods not approved by the customers. All returns by the customers are shown.

3. Column three is filled up, when the goods sent on approval basis is approved by the customers. On the basis of this column, customers are debited and sales account is credited.

4. At the close of the accounting period, the goods about which approval has not been given or the stipulated time has not been expired are recorded. The total of this column is the value of stock lying with customers. It is taken to stock at cost price or market price whichever is less.

3. Transactions are Numerous

When Sale or Return transactions are quite good in number, it is advisable to maintain a separate set of books for the purpose. Mainly three books are kept: (1) Goods Sent on Sale or Return Day Book, (2) Sales or Returns Ledger, and (3) Sales and Return Day Book.

When goods are sent on Sale or Return basis, record is made in the Sales or Returns Day Book. At the end of the period, the total should be posted to the credit of Sale or Returns Total Account while individual items should be debited to the individual customers account. When goods are approved or rejected by the customers, record is made immediately in Sales and Returns book.

The journal entries:

1.	When goods are sent on approval	Customers Personal Account To Sales on Approval Account	Dr.
2.	When goods are approved	Customers Personal Account To Sale Account	Dr.
3.	When goods are not approved	Sale on Approval Account To Customers Personal Account	Dr.
4.	At the close of accounting period (balance of sale on approval account)	Stock with Customers Account To Trading Account	Dr.

ILLUSTRATION 28.3

M/s Bajaj Electronics supplied goods on Sale or Return basis, the particulars of which are as under:

2005		Rs	2005	
March 10	Roy & Co	3,700	March 14	Returned
15	Sen & Co.	5,200	March 27	Retained
20	Mitter & Co.	2,400	March 27	Goods worth Rs 1,000 returned
27	Sen & Co.	3,500		No intimation till 31-3-2005
28	Mitter & Co.	1,800		- do -

Books of Bajaj Electronics are closed on 31st March every year.

Exhibit the entries as they would appear in the books of Bajaj Electronics *viz.* the Goods Sent on Sale or Return Day Book, Goods on Sale or Return Sold and Returned Day Book. Also show how the Goods on Sale or Return Total Account would appear.

SOLUTION

Bajaj Electronics

Goods sent on Sale or Return Day Book

Date	*Particulars*	*Sales or Return L.F.*	*Amount*
2005			Rs
March 10	Roy & Co.		3,700
15	Sen & Co.		5,200
20	Mitter & Co.		2,400
27	Sen & Co.		3,500
28	Mitter & Co.		1,800
			16,600

Goods on Sale or Return : Sold and Returned Book

Date	*Details*	*Sale or Return L.F.*	*Sale L.F.*	*Goods sold Rs*	*Goods Returned Rs*
2005					
March 14	Roy & Co.			–	3,700
17	Sen & Co.			5,200	–
25	Mitter & Co.			1,400	1,000
				6,600	4,700

Dr. **Goods on Sale or Return Total Account** Cr.

		Rs			Rs
2005			2005		
Mar. 31	To Sundries (Sales)	6,600	Mar.31	By Sundries: Goods sent on sale or return	16,600
	To sundries (Returns)	4,700			
	To Balance c/d	5,300			
		16,600			16,600
			April 1	By Balance b/d	5,300

QUESTIONS

Objective Type Questions

I. Indicative whether the following statements are "True" or "False".

1. Sale or return is a sale transaction entered in the sales book.
2. A transaction of sale or return is not the same as actual sale.
3. A sale or return transaction involves transfer of property in the goods sent.
4. Sale or return transaction is the same as a consignment Account transaction.
5. Goods sent on approval are not included in the closing stock of the vendor till the date of acceptance by the person to whom goods are sent.
6. If the number of transactions are very few, a sale or return transaction may be treated as actual sales.
7. When goods sent on sale or return are not frequent, the transaction may be recorded as actual sale.

[**Ans:** True – 2, 6, 7. False – 1, 3, 4, 5.]

II. Fill in the blanks

1. A sale or return transaction involves transfer of ...... goods.
2. Where the number of transactions are limited, a sale or return transaction may be treated as ......
3. There are ...... recognised methods of accounting for sale or return transactions.

[Ans. 1. Possession; 2. Actual Sale; 3. three]

III. Choose the correct alternative to complete each of the following:

1. Stock is valued at:
   (a) Cost Price.
   (b) Cost Price or Market Price, whichever is less.
   (c) Market Price.
2. When goods are sent to a customer on approval basis, the following journal entry is passed:
   (a) Customer Account Dr. To Sales account.
   (b) Sale of Return A/c Dr. To Customer Account.
   (c) Stock A/c Dr. To Customer's A/c.
3. When goods are sold on sale or return basis, it is a mere transfer of possession of goods:
   (a) True
   (b) False
   (c) None of the above

[Ans. 1. (b); 2. (a); 3. (a)]

Theoretical Questions:

1. What is sale or return? explain its salient features.
2. Explain the methods of recording the transactions of goods sold on 'sale or return' basis.

PRACTICAL PROBLEMS

1. Messrs Condensed Book Publishers sent consignment of their publications to the following customers on sale return basis in the first week of April, 2004.

		Rs
(*a*)	Mr. Menon, Madras	500
(*b*)	Mr. Narain, Madras	200
(*c*)	Mr. Ramesh, Bombay	300
(*d*)	Mr. Govind, Bombay	1,000
(*e*)	Mr. Ghosh, Calcutta	450
(*f*)	Mr. Poddar, Calcutta	250

The letter to the customers mentioned that if the books were not approved by them, they should be returned within one month, failing which they would be treated as sold. By the end of that month, the customers from Madras had retained the books, while those from Calcutta had returned them in time. Mr. Govind of Bombay had accepted one of the consignments of Rs 700 but returned the others and the time of approval had not yet expired for Mr. Ramesh. Show the entries in the sale or return day book and the accounts of the Bombay parties in the personal ledger. (*C.A.*)

2. X sends goods on approval basis as follows:-

Date	*Customers Name*	*Sale Price of Goods Sent Rs*	*Good Accepted Rs*	*Good Returned Rs*
2004				
January 8	A	3,500	3,000	500
January 10	B	2,800	2,800	–

January 15	C	3,680	–	3,680
January 22	D	1,260	1,000	260
January 28	E	2,000	–	–
January 30	F	1,000	–	–

Show how these transactions will be dealt with when books are kept on double entry system. Date of approval has not expired in all the cases.

3. **A trader has credited certain items of sales 'on approval' aggregating Rs 10,000 to the sales account. Of these, goods to the value of Rs 3,000 have been returned and taken into stock at cost of Rs 1,500 though the record of return was omitted in the accounts; and in respect of another parcel of Rs 1,000 (sale price being cost + 100%), the period of approval did not expire on the closing date. Show adjustment and correcting entries in the books of the trader.** *(C.A. Inter)*

4. **Automobiles Ltd. sent out machines on 'Sale or Return', They maintained a separate set of books for this type of business. During the month of April, they sent out machines on 'Sale or Return' as follows:**

April 2	**Y and Co.**	**Rs 10,000**	**April 7 Returned**
April 16	**X and Co.**	**Rs 15,000**	**April 20 Returned**
April 20	**Y and Co**	**Rs 16,000**	**April 25 Returned**
April 28	**Y and Co.**	**Rs 20,000**	**No intimation received yet.**

Show the Day Book. *(ICWA)*

5. **A Trader sends goods to his customers on sale or return basis. The following transactions took place during the year 2004.**

		Rs
July 10	**Sent goods to customers on sale or return (basis at cost plus 25%)**	**40,000**
15	**Goods returned by customers**	**10,000**
Aug. 4	**Received sales information from customer for goods valued at**	**20,000**
Dec. 31	**Goods with customers neither sold nor returned**	**10,000**

Assuming that the Trader records the transactions on ordinary sales basis and that the date of final accounts was December 31st, Show the entries. *(B. Com. Calcutta)*

Chapter 29

Partnership Accounts-General

Kinds of Partners – Duties of Partners – Rights of Partners – Partnership Deed – Non-Registration – Effect of Registration – Advantages of Registration – Accounts of Firm – Profit and Loss Appropriation Account – Important Calculations – Adjustments of Distributable Profits – Guarantee of Profits to a Partner – Final Accounts – Questions – Objective Type Questions – Theoretical Questions – Practical Problems.

We have studied the methods of keeping the books relating to one person. A sole trader is a person who owns and carries on business exclusively on his own account and risk. His organisation is the simplest one. When the business expands, there arises the need for more capital, better organisation, more abilities, sounder decisions etc. Thus, we can have many instances of businesses in which several persons are interested. Partnership is a very common type of business organisation, where two or more persons join together to carry on the business and to share the resultant profit in the agreed proportions.

The law relating to partnership is contained in the Indian Partnership Act, 1932. The Act came into force with effect from 1st October 1932. Prior to enactment of the aforesaid Act partnership business used to be governed by the Indian Contract Act, 1872. The need for a separate Act for regulating partnership was felt because the provisions of the Indian Contract Act relating to Partnership Law were not exhaustive. Since partnership comes into existence as a result of an agreement between parties, the provisions of the Indian Contract Act except when they are inconsistent with the express provision of the Partnership Act continue to apply to partnership firms (Sec.3). According to Section 4 of the Indian Partnership Act 1932 defines, "Partnership is the relation between persons who have agreed to share the profit and losses of a business carried on by all or any of them acting for all." A Partnership is similar to a single proprietorship except that in a single proprietorship one person is the owner while in the partnership two or more persons share the ownership. Each member of partnership is known as a partner. The number of partners is restricted to 10 in case of banking business and 20 in case of any other type of business. Persons, constituting the partnership, are individually known as *PARTNERS* and collectively known as *FIRM*. The name under which their business is carried on is called the *FIRM'S NAME*.

KINDS OF PARTNERS

There may be different kinds of partners in a partnership firm and the most important are as follows:

1. *ACTIVE PARTNER:* Partners actively engaged in the conduct of the business are known as active or actual or ostensible partners.
2. *DORMANT or SLEEPING PARTNER:* A partner who does not take active part in the conduct of the business of the partnership firm is known as Dormant or Sleeping Partner.
3. *NOMINAL PARTNER:* The nominal partner is one who lends his name to the partnership firm without any real interest in terms of investing money in the firm or sharing the profits.

4. *PARTNER IN PROFIT ONLY:* A person who does not want to take risk of loss may agree to become a partner for profits only.
5. *SUB-PARTNER:* When a partner agrees to share his share of profit in a partnership firm with an outsider, such an outsider is called a sub-partner.
6. *PARTNER BY ESTOPPEL OR HOLDING OUT:* This kind of partner is not a real partner of the firm but "by words spoken or written, or by conduct, represents himself, or knowingly permits himself to be represented, to be a partner in a firm."

Essentials of Partnership are :

1.	*Agreement*	:	A partnership is created by agreement - express or implied - between the partners.
2.	*Business*	:	It is created in order to run a lawful business.
3.	*Persons*	:	There must be at least two persons: maximum is twenty, but in case of banking business, the maximum is ten.
4.	*Profit Sharing*	:	The business is pursued to earn profits for distribution among its partners, as a right. Sharing losses by one or two partners may be exempted.
5.	*Mutual and implied agency*	:	Mutual and implied agency is the very essence of partnership. Every partner is both an agent and principal of the other partners.

DUTIES OF PARTNERS

The duties of a partner towards the firm are as follows :

1. Every partner must diligently carry on the business of the firm for the greatest common advantage. There is no remuneration unless otherwise agreed upon.
2. Every partner must be just and faithful to the other partners.
3. A partner is bound to keep and render true, proper and correct accounts of the partnership and must allow other partners to inspect and copy the accounts of the partnership.
4. A partner must indemnify the firm for any loss caused by his wilful neglect or fraud in the conduct of the business.
5. A partner must not carry on a business in competition with the business of the firm. If he does so, he must hand over the profits of that business to the partnership.
6. A partner cannot assign or transfer his partnership interest to any other person so as to make him a partner in the business.
7. Every partner is liable, jointly with all the other partners and also severally, for all acts of the firm done while he is a partner.
8. Each partner is liable to contribute for the firm's losses equally, in the absence of any contract to the contrary.
9. The property of the firm is the property of all the partners and each partner should use them exclusively for the purposes of the firm.
10. Every partner is bound to act within the scope of the authority. In case, if he exceeds his authority, he is liable, unless such act is ratified by other partners.

RIGHTS OF PARTNERS

1. Every partner has a right to take part in the conduct of the business of the firm.
2. Every partner has a right to be consulted and heard before any matter is decided.
3. Every partner has a right of free access to all records, books and accounts of the business and also the right to examine and copy them.
4. A partner is entitled to share equally for the losses sustained by the firm, with other partners.

5. In the absence of agreement to the contrary a partner is not entitled to interest on capital.
6. Every partner has a right to receive interest @ 6% p.a. on the sum contributed over and above the sum agreed to be invested as capital.
7. Every partner has a right to be indemnified by the firm for all acts done by the partners in the course of the partnership business, for all payments made by him in respect of partnership debts or liabilities and for expenses and disbursement made in an emergency for protecting the firm from loss.
8. A partner has a right to see that the partnership property is used exclusively for the purposes of the firm.
9. A partner has a right to prevent the introduction of new partners into the firm, without his consent.
10. A partner has right to prevent any fundamental changes in the business of the firm without his consent.
11. A partner has the right to continue in the business and not to be expelled from it.
12. A partner has the right to retire according to agreement or with the consent of all the other partners.
13. A partner has the right to receive either interest at 6% p.a. or the profits earned with his capital left in the business, on retirement as he chooses. The legal heirs of a deceased partner have a similar right.

PARTNERSHIP DEED

Partnership may be created by an oral agreement or an agreement in writing. It is not necessary that the agreement should be in writing. But it is better that the various terms thereof must be reduced in writing, so as to avoid future disputes. The document, in writing, containing the important terms of the partnership as agreed to by the partners between themselves is called the PARTNERSHIP DEED. It is stamped according to the provisions of the Stamp Act. Since, the partnership accounts are regulated by the Partnership Deed, it is usual to include the following therein:

1. The name of the firm and names and addresses of the partners, who compose it.
2. The nature of the partnership business.
3. The commencement and duration of the business.
4. The amount of capital to be contributed by each partner and the system of maintaining the capital - Fixed or Fluctuating.
5. The disposal of profits, particularly the ratio in which profits or losses are to be shared.
6. The amount and timings of partners withdrawals.
7. Rate of Interst, if any, to be applied on capitals, loans, drawings etc.
8. Salaries, commission etc if any, payable to partners.
9. Variations, if any, in usual rights and duties of partners.
10. Method of computation and treatement of goodwill on the variation of profit sharing ratio, admission, retirement, death etc.
11. The procedure by which a partner's account is settled, in case of retirement or death and the method of payment of dues to him.
12. The settlement of accounts on the dissolution of firms and the manner in which the accounts will be settled.
13. The situation under which the partnership will be stand dissolved.
14. Keeping of accounts, their inspection audit etc.

In the absence of any agreement, that is, when there is no agreement between the partners, the Partnership Act, 1932 will be applicable to settle the accounts of the firm. The Act provides that:

1. Partners are entitled to share equally in the profits earned and contribute equally to losses sustained by the firm.
2. A partner is not entitled to receive any remuneration for taking part in the conduct of the business.
3. Interest neither be allowed on partners capital nor charged on drawings. If agreed for interest on capital, it must be allowed only out of profits of the firm.
4. If any partner has made any advance or loan besides his capital for the purpose of business, he is entitled to claim interest thereon at 6% p.a.
5. Every partner has to take interest in the management of the firm.

NON–REGISTRATION

When the partnership deed is prepared, the firm should be registered. Although registration of firm is not compulsory, a non-registered firm is subjected to certain disabilities, for example, (a) the firm cannot enforce its claims against any third party for recovering a debt, exceeding Rs. 100. (b) A partner cannot sue for enforcing his rights against any of his co-partners or against the firm.

Thus, the necessity for registration arises due to the fact that it safeguards the legitimate rights and obligations of the partners concerned when dispute or disagreement arises. But it should be remembered that Non-registration does not preclude a third party to sue the firm or its partners and as such, the partners may sue for the:

(a) Dissolution of the firm;

(b) Accounts after dissolution;

(c) Realisation of assets after dissolution

The registration can be effected at any time, even at the time of the suit or even after suit has been filed by the firm, which may be withdrawn and filed again after dissolution.

EFFECT OF REGISTRATION

It is an obligation of a registered firm to supply the following information to the registrar in relation to:

(a) The alteration in the firm name and principal place of business;

(b) The opening and closing of branches;

(c) The change in constitution;

(d) The withdrawal of a minor as a partner.

ADVANTAGES OF REGISTRATION

The following advantages may be stated if the firm is registered:

(a) Registration of firm will enable a firm to enforce its claim against third parties in a court of law.

(b) It will enable a partner to enforce his claim either against his co-partners or against third parties.

(c) It also safeguards third parties against fraud or misrepresentation done by a partner of a firm.

(d) Registration enables an incoming partner to empower himself for dues against his fellow partners without relying on their faith.

Rules applicable where there is no agreement among partners.

1. No partner is entitled to earn interest on capital.
2. No partner is entitled to receive salary from the firm.
3. No interest on drawings is to be charged.
4. Interest on partner's loan is to be charged @ 6% p.a.
5. Profit and losses should be divided equally.

ACCOUNTS OF PARTNERSHIP FIRM

Capital Accounts of Partners

A partnership organisation maintains accounts of its transactions in the same manner as a Sole Tradership. Since partnership has two or more partners, separate capital account for each partner has to be maintained. Usually every partner contributes something in cash or in kind to provide funds for the running of a business. The amount of contribution is mutually settled and need not necessarily be equal. The sum of the contributions represents the capital of the firm. The partnership deed usually mentions the method of maintaining capital accounts of partners. There are two methods by which capital accounts are maintained *i.e*, *FIXED CAPITAL* and *FLUCTUATING CAPITAL.*

Fixed Capital

When the partners agree to keep their capital at their original figures, year after year, they are said to have fixed capitals. They continue to appear at their original figures unless contribution is made by way of additional capital or refund is allowed of the surplus capital, if any. Under the fixed capital, separate *CURRENT ACCOUNT* of each partner is opened. This current account will be credited at the end of every year with his (*a*) share of profits, (*b*) Interest on capital and (*c*) salary or any other remuneration; and debited with his (*a*) Drawings (*b*) Interest on Drawings and (*c*) Share of loss, if any. The current account may show credit and debit balance at the end of the year. If they show CREDIT balances, they appear on the liability side of the Balance Sheet of the firm alongwith Fixed Capitals. If the Current Accounts show DEBIT balances, they appear on the asset side of the Balance Sheet. A Debit Balance of the Current account implies that the concerned member has overdrawn his Current account and owes that amount to the firm. A Credit balance of the Current account represents the amount which a partner is entitled to draw but has not actually drawn. In some cases, interest is allowed on the credit balance and charged to the debit balance; if so entries are passed through respective partners Current accounts.

Fluctuating Capital

Fluctuating Capital is one which changes from year to year. There is only one account for each partner in case óf fluctuating capital system. All entries relating to introduction of fresh capital, interest on capital, salary, commission, share of profit etc. are credited to the capital account and similarly capital account is debited with drawings, interest on drawing, losses etc. All entries for all items are passed through his capital accounts; as such, the amounts of his capital at the end of the year will be different from what it was at the beginning of theyear. The balance of the capital goes on fluctuating year after year and is known as *FLUCTUATING CAPITAL.* In the absence of the contract to the contrary, capital accounts are fluctuating. Partner's drawings are, however, recorded in his Drawings Account which will be closed at the end of the year, by transferring to the capital accounts.

Loan Account

Where advance is made by a partner, credit is given to him by opening his separate Loan Account and not through his capital account. In the absence of agreement to the contrary, the Partnership Act provides that interest at 6% p.a. shall be allowed on such loan, irrespective of profits. Interst on such advance or loan should be credited to Loan Account or Current Account.

Unless the Partnership Deed expressly lays down that the partners Capital Accounts shall be kept fixed, they are treated as fluctuating.

ILLUSTRATION 29.1

A and B started a business on 1st January 2005, contributing Rs. 50,000 by A and Rs. 40,000 by B. On 30th June, 2005 B made a further contribution of Rs. 10,000 towards his capital. Drawings during the year come to Rs. 4,000 by A and Rs. 5,000 by B. 6% interest is to be charged on capitals and no interest is to be charged on drawings. B is to be allowed a salary of Rs. 500 p.m. The profit for the year comes to Rs. 32,000 before charging salary and interest on capitals. Show the Profit and Loss Appropriation Account and the partners capital accounts under Fixed capital method and Fluctuating Capital Method.

SOLUTION

Profit and Loss Appropriation Account
for the year ended 31st December 2005

		Rs.		Rs.
To Interest on Capital :			By Net Profit	32,000
A: 6% on Rs. 50,000 for one year	3,000			
B: 6% on Rs. 40,000 for one year	2,400			
6% on Rs. 10,000 for 6 months	300	5,700		
To Salary A/c		6,000		
To Net Profit :				
A	10,150			
B	10,150	20,300		
		32,000		32,000

When the Capitals are fixed :

Dr. **Capital Accounts** Cr.

		A	B			A	B
2005		Rs.	Rs.	2005		Rs.	Rs.
Dec. 31	To balance c/d	50,000	50,000	Jan.	By Cash	50,000	40,000
				June 30	By Cash	-	10,000
		50,000	50,000			50,000	50,000
				2006			
				Jan.1	By Balance b/d	50,000	50,000

Dr. **Current Accounts** Cr.

		A	B			A	B
2005		Rs.	Rs.	2005		Rs.	Rs.
Dec. 31	To Drawings	4,000	5,000	Jan.	By Interest	3,000	2,700
	To Balance c/d	9,150	13,850		By Salary	-	6,000
				June 30	By Net Profit	10,150	10,150
		13,150	18,850			13,150	18,850
				2006			
				Jan.1	By Balance b/d	9,150	13,850

When the Capital are Fluctuating

Dr. **Capital Accounts** Cr.

		A	B			A	B
2005		Rs.	Rs.	2005		Rs.	Rs.
	To Drawings	4,000	5,000	Jan. 1	By Cash	50,000	40,000
				June 30	By Cash	-	10,000
Dec. 31	To Balance c/d	59,150	63,850	Dec. 31	By Interest	3,000	2,700
				Dec. 31	By Salary	-	6,000
					By Net Profit	10,150	10,150
		63,150	68,850			63,150	68,850
				2006			
				Jan. 1	By Balance b/d	59,150	63,850

Interest on Capital

Interest on Capital is usually allowed by an agreement between the partners. The Partnership Act is silent on this point that is, no interest on capital is allowed. Interest on capital is generally allowed on capitals so that the partner who contributes more than the proportionate capitals is properly compensated. If partners contribute equal amounts of capital and share profits equally, no need arises for any interest to be allowed on capital. Where capital contributions are equal but the profit sharing ratios are unequal, a partner, with a lower share of profit, stands to loss. Besides, where capitals are unequal but profit sharing ratios are equal, a partner with large capital contribution is affected financially. Interest on capital tends to balance capital account equitably, without allowing any partner to enjoy an unfair advantage over the others. Interest on capital is a loss or expense to the firm and thus debited to Interest on capital account and finally transferred to Profit and Loss Appropriation Account. And it is an income or gain to the partners and their Capital Account or Current Account is credited with the amount of interest.

Drawings

The Partnership Deed may allow partners to withdraw money or goods from the business to meet their private requirements. The amount of withdrawals at each interval need not be equal. To avoid congestion entries in Capital or Current Account, in respect of withdrawals, a separate Drawing Account is opened for each partner. The amount drawn at each time is debited therein. At the closing date, the Drawings Account is closed by transferring it to Capital Account, if Capital Account is fluctuating, or to Current Account, if the Capital Account is fixed. But the Current Account is not transferred to Capital Account.

Interest on Drawings

Interest on Drawings also depends upon the Partnership Deed. There are many cases, where Capitals bear interest but Drawings are not Chargeable with interest. Generally, Partnership Deed stipulates the maximum amount that each partner is permitted to withdraw, without paying interest. If any partner exceeds the limit, he has to pay interest on Drawings. Where the withdrawals of the partners are unequal, partners accounts are equitably adjusted through the mechanism of interest on drawings. To the firm it is an income and therefore the Capital or Current Accounts of the partners are debited and Interest on Drawing Account is credited. Interest on Drawings is a loss to the partners. To make calculation of the interest on Drawings, three things must be present - the interest rate, the amount and the period. (See the illustrations.)

Partner's Salary

Sometimes, a partner may fully devote his time to the working of the business. It is similar to allowing interest on capital to a partner, who contributes larger amount towards capital. When the partners decide to honour the service of a partner, an additional benefit in the name of salary is allowed. The Salary Account is debited and the capital or Current Account is credited with the amount of salary.

Commission to Partners

Under the partnership law all partners are supposed to devote their time to the affairs of the firm but in practice many partners may not devote any time and some of the partners may have to carry on the entire work of the firm. Thus, a percentage of profit is paid to a partner for the special work or service done. This commission may be payable before charging such commission or after charging such commission. (see the illustrations.)

PROFIT AND LOSS APPROPRIATION ACCOUNT

The Profit and Losses of the partnership are divisible equally or in any other manner agreed upon by the partners. In case of partnership accounting, it is usual that adjustments relating to Interest on Capital, Interest on Drawings, Salary, Commission, Share of profits etc. to be made through the Profit and Loss Appropriation Account. The Profit disclosed by Profit and Loss Account, is transferred to Profit and Loss Appropriation Account and the adjustment entries relating to partners are made through this account. Then, the remaining profit is transferred to Capital Account or Current Account on the basis of Profit sharing ratio.

Adjusting Journal Entries

(1)	For Interest on Capital	Interest on Capital Account To Partners' Capital/Current Account	Dr.
(2)	For Interest on Drawings	Partners Capital/Current Account To Interest on Drawings Account	Dr.
(3)	For Partners Salary/Commission etc.	Partners' Salary/Commission Account To Partners' Capital/Current Account	Dr.
(4)	For Interest on Partners' Loan Account	Interest on Loan Account To Partners' Loan Account	Dr.
(5)	For Adjusting Net Profit	Profit & Loss Appropriation Account To Partners' Capital/Current A/c	Dr.
(6)	For Adjusting Net Loss	Partners Capital/Current Account To Profit & Loss Appropriation A/c	Dr.

IMPORTANT CALCULATIONS

Calculation of Interest on Drawings

(1) Product Method

If interest on Drawings is to be charged then it is always with reference to time. As said earlier, it is essential to know the amount of drawings, the period and the rate of interest for the calculation of interest. When drawings are made frequently then interest on Drawings can be easily calculated with the help of product method. Find out the number of months from the date of drawings to the date of closing of the financial year, of each drawings, multiply the amount of drawings with these respective months, and then find total of the products. Then calculate the interest at the prescribed rate.

$$\text{Interest on Drawings} = \frac{\text{Total of Products} \times \text{Rate of Interest}}{100} \times \frac{1}{12}$$

Illustration 29.2

A and B are partners sharing profits in the ratio of 1:1. A draws Rs.300 regularly at the beginning of every month during the year 2005. B draws Rs.1,000 on 1.4.2005, Rs. 600 on 1.7.2005, Rs. 800 on 1.10.2005 and Rs.400 on 1.12.2005. Calculate interest on their drawings at 6% p.a.

SOLUTION

Following the Product method, interest on Drawings of A

Date of drawings	Amount withdrawn Rs.	Period for which interest is due	Product Rs.
1.1.2005	300	12 Months	3,600
1.2.2005	300	11 Months	3,300
1.3.2005	300	10 Months	3,000
1.4.2005	300	9 Months	2,700
1.5.2005	300	8 Months	2,400
1.6.2005	300	7 Months	2,100
1.7.2005	300	6 Months	1,800
1.8.2005	300	5 Months	1,500
1.9.2005	300	4 Months	1,200
1.10.2005	300	3 Months	900
1.11.2005	300	2 Months	600
1.12.2005	300	1 Month	300
		The sum of Products	23,400

Interest for One Month @ 6% p.a.

$$\frac{23,400 \times 6 \times 1}{100 \times 12} = \text{Rs. } 117$$

Note: When the amount withdrawn is same every time and is drawn at regular intervals, a still easier method is :

Take the period at the average of the periods applicable to the first and the last instalments. In this illustration, the period of first installment is 12 months and that of the last instalments is one month.

$$\text{Average is} = \frac{12+1}{2} = 6\tfrac{1}{2} \text{ months}$$

Then calculate interest at given rate for 6 1/2 months on the total amount withdrawn during the year. In this case A withdraws Rs. 3,600 during the year.

Interest on his Drawings, as per this formula :

$$\text{Rs. } 3,600 \times \frac{6}{100} \times \frac{6\frac{1}{2}}{12} = \textbf{Rs 117}$$

Under Average Due Date Method :

Interest for $\frac{23,400}{3,600}$ months @ 6% p.a. on Rs. 3,600

$$\text{That is } \frac{23,400}{3,600} \times \frac{6}{100} \times \frac{3,600}{12} = \textbf{Rs 117}$$

Note: If drawings are made in the beginning of each month, interest can be calculated on the whole of the amount for 6 1/2 months.

If drawings are made at the end of each month, the period is 5 1/2 months for the total amount.

If drawings are made at the middle of each month, the period is 6 months for the total amount.

Interest on Drawings of B is :

Date of Drawings	Amount Drawn Rs.	Period for which interest is due	Product
1.4.2005	1,000	9 Months	9,000
1.7.2005	600	6 Months	3,600
1.10.2005	800	3 Months	2,400
1.12.2005	400	1 Month	400
	Total of Products		15,400

Interest for one month @ 6% p.a. = 15,400 × 6/100 × 1/12 = Rs. 77

ILLUSTRATION 29.3

A and B started a business in a partnership from 1st January, 2005, without any Partnership Agreement, with a Capital of Rs. 20,000, to which A contributes Rs.15,000 and B contributes Rs.5,000. In the Middle of the year, A further introduces Rs.3,000 to the partnership, as a loan without any agreement as to interset. The profit for the year ended December 2005 comes to Rs. 12,000. During the whole year, B was fully engaged in the business. There arises a dispute between A and B. Both of tnem put forward their claims as follows

A demands :

(*i*) Interest @ 10% on his capital and loan.

(*ii*) Division of profits on the basis of contribution of Capital.

B demands :

(*i*) Since he is fully engagaed in the firm, he needs a salary of Rs. 500 p.m.

(*ii*) Divisible profits should be divided equally

(*iii*) Interest should be allowed on capital and loan at 5% p.a.

SOLUTION

Dr. **Profit And Loss Appropriation Account** Cr.

		Rs.		*Rs.*
To Interest on A's Loan of Rs.3,000 for half year at 6% p.a.		90	By Net Profit	12,000
To Net Profit transferred to Capital Accounts				
A –	5,955			
B –	5,955	11,910		
		12,000		12,000

Note: In the absence of agreement between the partners, the Partnership Act 1932 will apply. Accordingly,

1. No interest is provided on partners Capital in the absence of Partnership Deed.
2. Partners are entitled to interest @ 6% p.a. on loans advanced to the firm apart from the capital contribution.
3. A partner is not allowed to receive any remuneration/salary.
4. Partners are entitled to share equally in the profits of the business, and must contribute equally to losses sustained by the firm.

ILLUSTRATION 29.4

A and B are partners in a firm sharing profits and losses in the ratio of 4 : 1. On 1st April 2004, the Capital of the partners: A – Rs 50,000 and B – Rs 40,000. The Profit and Loss Account of the firm for the year ended 31st March 2005 showed a net profit of Rs 1,75,000.

You are required to give the Profit and Loss Appropriation Account of the firm after taking into consideration the following:

(*i*) Interest on Capital at 5% p.a.

(*ii*) Interest on B's Loan Account of Rs 50,000 for the whole year.

(*iii*) Interest on drawings of partners at 6% p.a.
Drawings of A – Rs 15,000; B – Rs 10,000.

(*iv*) Transfer 10% of the distributable profit, before distribution, to the Reserve Fund of the firm.

(*B.Com., Kolkata, Madurai*)

SOLUTION

Profit and Loss Appropriation Account
for the year ended 31st March 2005

Dr.		Rs			Rs Cr.
To Interest on Capital:			By Profit & Loss Account		1,75,000
A –	2,500		By Interest on Drawings:		
B –	2,000	4,500	A–	450	
To Interest on B's Loan		3,000	B –	300	750
To Reserve Fund 10%		16,825			
To Share of Profit:					
A –	1,21,140	1,51,425			
B –	30,285				
		1,75,750			1,75,750

Note: In the absence of any agreement to the contrary interest on partners' loan is at 6% p.a.

Actual date of drawings is not given in the problem. Therefore, interest thereon has been calculated for the average period, that is 6 months

Reserve Fund: (Rs 1,75,000 + 750) – (4,500 + 3,000) = 1,68,250 and 10% thereof is Rs 16,825.

ILLUSTRATION 29.5

A, B andC are partners in a firm with Capitals of Rs. 40,000; Rs. 24,000 and Rs. 20,000 respectively on 1.1.2005. The Partnership Deed contains the following clauses :

1. Interest on Capital @ 5% p.a.
2. Interest on Drawings @ Rs. 4% p.a.
3. A to get a salary @ Rs. 400 per month
4. B and C to get 10% commission each on the net profit.
5. Profit and Losses to be shared :
   (*i*) upto Rs.4,500 in the ratio of 4:3:2
   (*ii*) Above Rs.4,500 equally.

The net profit of the firm for the year ended 31st December 2005 amounts to Rs.20,500 and the Drawings of the partners are : A Rs.2,400; B Rs.1,600 and C Rs. 1,000.

Prepare Profit and Loss Appropriation Account and Capital Accounts of the partners assuming (*i*) Capitals are fixed and (*ii*) Capitals are fluctuating. (*B.Com, Madurai, Agra, Delhi, Poona*)

SOLUTION

Profit and Loss Appropriation Account
for the year ended 31st Dec. 2005

Dr.	Rs.	Rs.		Rs.	Rs. Cr.
To Interest on Capitals :			By Profit & Loss A/c		20,500
A–	2,000		By Interest on Drawings		
B –	1,200		(Average Period)		
C –	1,000	4,200	A –	48	
To Salary to A		4,800	B –	32	
To Commission to B –	2,050		C –	20	100
C –	2,050	4,100			

Particulars	Rs.	Rs.	Particulars	Rs.
To Share of Profit :				
First Rs. 4,500				
A = 4,500 × 4/9	= 2,000			
B = 4,500 × 3/9	= 1,500			
C = 4,500 × 2/9	= 1,000			
Next Rs. 3,000	A = 1,000			
	B = 1,000			
	C = 1,000	7,500		
		20,600		20,600

(*i*) **When Capitals are fixed :**

Dr. **Capital Account** Cr.

		A	B	C			A	B	C
2005		Rs.	Rs.	Rs.	2005		Rs.	Rs.	Rs.
Dec. 31	To Balance c/d	40,000	24,000	20,000	Jan. 1	By Balance b/d.	40,000	24,000	20,000
		40,000	24,000	20,000			40,000	24,000	20,000
					2006				
					Jan. 1	By Balance b/d	40,000	24,000	20,000

Dr. **Current Accounts** Cr.

		A	B	C			A	B	C
2005		Rs.	Rs.	Rs.	2005		Rs.	Rs.	Rs.
Dec.31	To Drawings	2,400	1,600	1,000	Dec.31	By Interest on			
"	To Interest on					Capital	2,000	1,200	1,000
	Drawings	48	32	20	"	By Salary	4,800	–	–
"	To Balance c/d	7,352	4,118	4,030	"	By Commission	–	2,050	2,050
						By Profit			
						First Rs 4,500	2,000	1,500	1,000
						Next Rs 3,000	1,000	1,000	1,000
		9,800	5,750	5,050			9,800	5,750	5,050
					2006				
					Jan. 1	By Balance b/d	7,352	4,118	4,030

(*ii*) **When Capitals are Fluctuating:**

Dr. **Capital Account** Cr.

		A	B	C			A	B	C
2005		Rs.	Rs.	Rs.	2005		Rs.	Rs.	Rs.
Dec. 31	To Drawings	2,400	1,600	1,000	Jan. 1	By Balance b/d.	40,000	24,000	20,000
"	To Interest on	48	32	20	Dec. 31	By Interest on			
	Drawing					Capitals	2,000	1,200	1,000
"	To Balance c/d	47,352	28,118	24,030					
					"	By Salary	4,800	–	–
					"	By Commission	–	2,050	2,050

					"	By Profit			
						First 4,500	2,000	1,500	1,000
						Next 3,000	1,000	1,000	1,000
		49,800	29,750	25,050			49,800	29,750	25,050
					2006				
					Jan. 1	By Balance c/d	47,352	28,118	24,030

Note: When the capitals are fixed, all amounts due to the partners, such as interest on Capital, Salary, Commission, Share of profit etc. are credited to the Current Account. Similarly, Drawings and interest thereon are debited thereto.

When the capitals are fluctuating, all the debits and credits as shown in (*ii*) are made in the Capital Accounts.

ILLUSTRATION 29.6

A, B and C are partners sharing profits and losses in the proportion of 4:3:2. During the year 2005, their Fixed Capitals and Drawings (including salaries) were as follows :

Partners	Capital (fixed)	Drawings including salaries
	Rs.	Rs.
A	2,40,000	24,000
B	1,60,000	18,000
C	1,00,000	15,000

Each partner is entitled to a salary of Rs.1,000 per month and interest @ 5% p.a. on the capital. At the middle of the year, A made an advance of Rs. 1,00,000 to the firm bearing interest at 6% p.a.

The net profit for the year stood at Rs. 1,09,000 before charging interest on Capitals and Loan but after charging partners salaries.

Prepare the Partner's Current Account. *(B.Com., Madurai, Colcutta)*

Dr. **Profit and Loss Appropriation Account** Cr.

	Rs.	*Rs.*		*Rs.*
To interest on Capitals :			By Profit & Loss A/c	
A –	12,000		Net Profit	1,09,000
B –	8,000			
C –	5,000	25,000		
To Interest on A's Loan		3,000		
To Share of Profit :				
A = 4/9 =	36,000			
B = 3/9 =	27,000			
C = 2/9 =	18,000	81,000		
		1,09,000		1,09,000

Dr. **Partner's Current Accounts** Cr.

	A	*B*	*C*		*A*	*B*	*C*
	Rs.	Rs.	Rs.		Rs.	Rs.	Rs.
To Drawings A/c	24,000	18,000	15,000	By Salary A/c	12,000	12,000	12,000
To Balance c/d	39,000	29,000	20,000	By Interest on Capital A/c	12,000	8,000	5,000
				By Interest on Loan A/c	3,000	–	–
				By Share of Profit	36,000	27,000	18,000
	63,000	47,000	35,000		63,000	47,000	35,000
				By Balance b/d	39,000	29,000	20,000

ILLUSTRATION 29.7

Show how the following items appear in the Capital Accounts of the partners, Nikhil and Udith when their Capitals are fluctuating :

	Nikhil Rs.	Udith Rs.
Capitals as on 1st Jan. 2005	8,00,000	7,00,000
Drawings during the year	1,60,000	1,40,000
Interest at 5% on drawings	4,000	2,000
Interest on capital at 6%	48,000	42,000
Share of profit for 2005	84,000	66,000
Salary	72,000	Nil

(B.Com., Bharathidasan, Madras, Madurai)

SOLUTION :

Partner's Capital Account

		Nikhil	Udith			Nikhil	Udith
2005		Rs.	Rs.	2005		Rs.	Rs.
Dec.31	To Drawings	1,60,000	1,40,000	Dec.31	By Balance b/d	8,00,000	7,00,000
	To Interest on Drawings	4,000	2,000		By Interest on Capital	48,000	42,000
	To Balance c/d	8,40,000	6,66,000		By Salary	72,000	–
					By Profit	84,000	66,000
		10,04,000	8,08,000			10,04,000	8,08,000
				2006 Jan. 1	By Balance b/d	8,40,000	6,66,000

ADJUSTMENTS OF DISTRIBUTABLE PROFITS

When the accounts have been closed, sometimes, adjustments are to be made in respect of (*i*) Omissions and errors in records (*ii*) Changes in the interest rate, (*iii*) Making Changes in accounting system or (*iv*) Changes in Sharing of Profits etc. from retrospective effect. The following illustration clarifies the method.

ILLUSTRATION 29.8

A, B, C and D are partners sharing profits and losses in the ratio of 4 : 3: 3 : 2 and their respective capitals on 31st December 2005 were Rs. 3,000; Rs. 4,500; Rs. 6,000 and Rs. 4,500. After closing and finalising the accounts it was found that interest on Capital @ 6% p.a. was omitted. Instead of altering the signed accounts it was decided to pass *single adjusting entry* on 1st January 2006 crediting or debiting the respective partner's accounts.

Show the journal entry. *(B.Com., Madurai, Bombay)*

SOLUTION

The interest on capital is calculated on opening balance of capital accounts. The question states closing balance. The profit credited to capitals have not been given. So, we assume that the capitals of partners are fixed.

The interest on capitals comes to Rs.1,080 (A-Rs.180, B-Rs.270; C-Rs.360; D-Rs.270) which is distributed to the partners in the profit sharing ratio, which should have been in the capital ratio, that is interest on capital. Now Rs.1,080 should be written back by debiting the partners account in the profit sharing ratio and then distribute the same to partners account in the capital ratio.

Statement Showing the Adjustment

Partners	*Profit to be written back*	*Interest to be distributed*	*Adjustment*
A	– 360 $(\frac{4}{12})$	+ 180	-180
B	– 270 $(\frac{3}{12})$	+ 270	Nil
C	– 270 $(\frac{3}{12})$	+ 360	+ 90
D	– 180 $(\frac{2}{12})$	+ 270	+ 90
	1,080	1,080	

Adjusting Journal Entry

			Rs.	*Rs.*
2006 Jan. 1	A's Current Account	Dr.	180	
	To C's current account			90
	To D's Current Account			90
	(Being interest on capital omitted, now adjusted)			

ILLUSTRATION 29.9

After including the profits for the year ended 31st December and dealing with drawings, the Capital Accounts of A, B and C stood at Rs.40,000; Rs. 30,000 and Rs. 20,000 respectively.

Subsequently, the following omissions were noticed and it was decided to bring them into account :

(*i*) Interest on Capital @ 5% p.a.

(*ii*) Interest on Drawings A Rs. 250; B Rs. 190 and C Rs. 130.

(*iii*) Commission to the manager at 5% on the net profit after charging such commission.

The profit for the year in arriving at the above figures of capital amounted to Rs.60,000 and their drawings had been A Rs.10,000; B Rs.7,500; C Rs.4,500. They shared profits and losses as to A one half, B one third and C one sixth.

Give the adjusted Capital accounts of the partners with entries necessary for such adjustments.

(B.Com., Andhra, MK, Calcutta, Agra)

SOLUTION

JOURNAL

			Rs	*Rs*
Dec. 31	A's Capital Account	Dr.	1,645	
	B's Capital Account	Dr.	912	
	C's Capital Account	Dr.	203	
	To Outstanding Commission			2,760
	(Being the omissions brought into account)			

Adjusted Capital :

	A Rs.	*B* Rs.	*C* Rs.
Closing capital, that is before the adjustment	40,000	30,000	20,000
Less : Omissions brought into account	1,645	912	203
	38,355	29,088	19,797

Opening Capital :

	A	*B*	*C*
	Rs.	*Rs.*	*Rs.*
Capital (closing)	40,000	30,000	20,000
Add : Drawings	10,000	7,500	4,500
	50,000	37,500	24,500
Less: Profit credited (Rs.60,000 in the ratio of 3 : 2 : 1)	30,000	20,000	10,000
Opeining Capital	20,000	17,500	14,500
Interest on Capital @ 5% p.a.	1,000	875	725

Commission to Manager :

	Rs.
Profit after adjustment :	
Before adjustment	60,000
Less : Interest on Capital (Rs. 1,000 + 875 + 725)	2,600
	57,400
Add: Interest on Drawings (250 + 190 + 130)	570
	57,970

$$\text{Rs. } 57{,}970 \times \frac{5}{105} = 2{,}760$$

Statement Relating to Adjustment

	Manager		A		B		C		Firm	
	Dr.	Cr.	Dr.	Cr.	Dr.	Cr.	Dr.	Cr.	Dr.	Cr.
	Rs.	Rs.	Rs.	Rs.	Rs.	Rs.	Rs.	Rs.	Rs.	Rs.
Interest on Capitals	–	–	–	1,000	–	875	–	725	2,600	–
Interest on Drawings	–	–	250	–	190	–	130	–	–	570
Manager's Commission	–	2,760	–	–	–	–	–	–	2,760	–
The loss of the Firm is distributed among partners $(\frac{1}{2}:\frac{1}{3}:\frac{1}{6})$	–	–	2,395	–	1,597	–	798	–	–	4,790
Balance (Profit & Loss)	2,760			1,645	–	912	–	203		
	2,760	2,760	2,645	2,645	1,787	1,787	928	928	5,360	5,360

ILLUSTRATION 29.10

X,Y and Z started a business in partnership on 1st Jan.2005 and their accounts prepared for the year 2005 showed a profit of Rs.50,400. This was credited in agreed proportion of 3 : 2 : 1 to partners Capital Accounts, which then have credit balances of X Rs. 75,200; Y Rs, 55,800 and Z Rs. 30,400.

After closing the books it was realised that the Partnership Deed required interest in Capital and Drawings to be provided at 5% p.a. Drawings for the year had been Rs.20,000 by X, Rs.16,000 by Y, and Rs.8,000 by Z, on which Rs.480, Rs.380 and Rs.240 should have been charged for interest.

Show by journal entries how you would adjust the accounts concerned in accordance with the Partnership Deed. Give Capital accounts of the partners. *(C.A. Inter)*

SOLUTION

Workings: When interest on capital is to be allowed as per the agreement then interest on capital must be calculated with reference to time and it must be calculated on CAPITAL AT THE BEGINNING. Here the capital accounts are fluctuating. Let us find out the Opening Capital :

Opening Capital :

	X	Y	Z
	Rs.	Rs.	Rs.
Capital as on 31.12.2005	75,200	55,800	30,400
Add: the Drawings of 2005	20,000	16,000	8,000
	95,200	71,800	38,400
Less: Share of Profit credited to Capital Accounts (Rs.50,400 in 3:2:1 ratio)	25,200	16,800	8,400
Capital as on 1.1.2005	70,000	55,000	30,000

Net Divisible Profit : On the basis of Partnership Deed:

			Rs.
Profit before the Adjustment:			50,400
Add: Interest on Drawings :	X	Rs.480	
	Y	Rs. 380	
	Z	Rs. 240	1,100
			51,500
Less: Interest on Capitals :			
X @ 5% on Rs.70,000 =		3,500	
Y @ 5% on Rs. 55,000 =		2,750	
Z @ 5% on Rs. 30,000 =		1,500	7,750
			43,750
Credited to	X 3/6	21,875	
	Y 2/6	14,583	
	Z 1/6	7,292	43,750

Capital Accounts (Revised)

Dr. Cr.

		X	Y	Z			X	Y	Z
2005		Rs.	Rs.	Rs.	2005		Rs.	Rs.	Rs.
31 Dec.	To Drawings A/c	20,000	16,000	8,000	Jan.1	By Balance b/d	70,000	55,000	30,000
	To Interest on Drawings A/c	480	380	240		By Interest on Capital A/c	3,500	2,750	1,500
	To Balance c/d	74,895	55,953	30,552		By Profit and Loss Appropriation A/c	21,875	14,583	7,292
		95,375	72,333	38,792			95,375	72,333	38,792
					2006 Jan. 1	By Balance b/d	74,895	55,953	30,552

Now we make a comparison between the Revised Capital Accounts and the Capital Accounts given in the Problems :

Comparison of Capitals

X			*Y*			*Z*		
Before Adjustment	After Adjustment	Differ-ence	Before Adjustment	After Adjustment	Differ-ence	Before Adjustment	After Adjustment	Differ-ence
Rs.	Rs.	Rs.	Rs.	Rs.	Rs.	Rs.	Rs.	Rs.
75,200	74,895	305	55,800	55,953	153	30,400	30,552	152

The required answer :

Journal

			Rs.	Rs.
2006 Jan. 1	X Account	Dr.	305	
	To Y Account			153
	To Z Account			152
	(Being excess credit given to X is adjusted now)			

Now the adjusted Capital Accounts :

Dr. **Partners Capital Accounts (Adjusted)** Cr.

		X	Y	Z			X	Y	Z
2005		Rs.	Rs.	Rs.	2005		Rs.	Rs.	Rs.
Dec.31	To Y Capital A/c	153			Dec.31	By Balance b/d	75,200	55,800	30,400
"	To Z Capital A/c	152				By X Capital A/c		153	152
"	To Balance c/d	74,895	55,953	30,552					
		75,200	55,953	30,552			75,200	55,953	30,552
					2006 Jan. 1	By Balance b/d	74,895	55,953	30,552

ILLUSTRATION 29.11

The Capital accounts of A and B stood at Rs.40,000 and Rs.30,000 respectively after the necessary adjustments in respect of the drawings and the net profit for the year ended 31st Dec. It was subsequently ascertained that 5% interest p.a. on capital and drawing were not taken into account in arriving at the net profits. The drawings of the partners had been :

A Rs. 1,200 drawn at the end of each quarter and

B Rs. 1,800 drawn at the end of each half year.

The profits for the year as adjusted amounted to Rs.20,000. The partners share profits in proportion of A 3/5 and B 2/5. You are required to pass journal entries and to show the adjusted Capital Accounts of the partners. *(ICWA Inter)*

SOLUTION

Journal Entries

			Dr.	Cr.
31st Dec.			Rs.	Rs.
	A's capital account	Dr.	90	
	B's Capital Account	Dr.	45	
	To Profit & Loss Adjustment A/c			135
	(Being interest on drawings @5% p.a. charged to partners Capital Accounts)			

Profit & Loss Adjustment A/c	Dr.	2,920	
To A's Capital Account			1,640
To B's Captal Account			1,280
(Being interest on Capitals @5% p.a. allowed to partners)			
A's Capital Account	Dr.	1,671	
B's Capital Account	Dr.	1,114	
To Profit and Loss Adjustment A/c			2,785
(Being loss on Adjustments debited to partner's Capital Account)			

Dr. **Capital Accounts** Cr.

	A	*B*		*A*	*B*
	Rs.	Rs.		Rs.	Rs.
To Profit & Loss Adj. A/c	90	45	By Balance b/d.	40,000	30,000
To Profit & Loss Adj. A/c	1,671	1,114	By Profit & Loss Adj. A/c	1,640	1,280
To Balance c/d	39,879	30,121			
	41,640	31,280		41,640	31,280
			By Balance b/d	39,879	30,121

Calculation of Interest on Capital:

	A	B
	Rs.	Rs.
Capital (31st Dec.)	40,000	30,000
Add: Drawings	4,800	3,600
	44,800	33,600
Less: Profit already credited	12,000	8,000
Capital (1st Jan.)	32,800	25,600
Interest thereon @ 5%	1,640	1,280

Calculation of Interest on Drawings :

Partner A

	Amount Rs.	Period	Product Rs.
31st March	1,200	9 Months	10,800
30th June	1,200	6 Months	7,200
30th Sept.	1,200	3 Months	3,600
31st Dec.	1,200	0	0
			21,600

$$\text{Interest : } 21,600 \times \frac{5}{100} \times \frac{1}{12} = \text{Rs } 90$$

Partner B

	Amount Rs.	Period	Product Rs.
30th June	1,800	6 Months	10,800
31st Dec.	1,800	0	0
			10,800

$$\text{Interest : } 10{,}800\ \frac{5}{100}\times\frac{1}{12} = \text{Rs } 45$$

ILLUSTRATION 29.12

On 31st December 2005 after the close of the Accounts, the Capital Accounts of A, B and C stood in the books of the firm at Rs.40,000; Rs.30,000; and Rs.20,000 respectively. It was subsequently discovered that interest at 5% p.a. on partners Capitals at the beginning of the year and interest on drawings of partners were left out of considerations. The interest on drawings amounted to A Rs. 250; B Rs. 180; C Rs.100. The profit for the year in arriving at the above figures of capitals amounted to Rs.60,000 and partners drawings had been A Rs.10,000; B Rs.7,500 and C Rs.4,500. The partners shared profit and losses as A one half, B one-third and C one sixth respectively.

You are required to give the necessary journal entry to rectify the above omissions.

(B.Com. Madurai, Agra, Madras)

SOLUTION

Statement of Opening Capitals

	A Rs.	*B* Rs.	*C* Rs.
Capital (31st Dec.)	40,000	30,000	20,000
Add: Drawings	10,000	7,500	4,500
	50,000	37,500	24,500
Less: Profit already credited	30,000	20,000	10,000
Capital (1st Jan.)	20,000	17,500	14,500

Adjustment of Capitals

Items	*A* Dr. Rs.	*A* Cr. Rs.	*B* Dr. Rs.	*B* Cr. Rs.	*C* Dr. Rs.	*C* Cr. Rs.	*Firm* Dr. Rs.	*Firm* Cr. Rs.
Interest on Capitals	–	1,000	–	875	–	725	2,600	–
Interest on Drawings	250	–	180	–	100	–	–	530
Distribution of Loss	1,035	–	690	–	345	–	–	2,070
	1,285	1,000	870	875	445	725	2,600	2,600
Credit/Debit to be given	285			5		280		

Journal Entry

			Rs.	*Rs.*
Dec.31	A's Capital Account	Dr.	285	
	To B's Capital Account			5
	To C's Capital Account			280
	(Being the net adjustment made in the Capital Accounts)			

ILLUSTRATION: 29.13

A, B, C and D are equal partners. On 1st January 2006, their Capital Accounts stood as follows:

		Rs
A	–	8,000
B	–	12,000
C	–	20,000
D	–	40,000

After the accounts for the year 2006 have been prepared, it is found that interest on capitals at 5% p.a. as agreed upon, has not been credited to the Partners Capital Accounts before distribution of profits. Instead of altering the signed Balance Sheet, it is decided to make an adjusting entry at the beginning of the next year.

Give the adjusting journal entry

(B.Com. Orissa)

SOLUTION

Journal Entries

2007			*Rs*	*Rs*
Jan. 1	A's Current Account	Dr	600	
	B's Current Account	Dr	400	
	To D's Current Account			1,000
	(Being interest on capital omitted, now adjusted)			

Workings:

Partners	*Profits to be Written back*	*Interest to be charged*	*Adjustment*
	Rs	Rs	Rs
A	– 1,000 (1/4)	+ 400	– 600
B	– 1,000 (1/4)	+ 600	– 400
C	– 1,000 (1/4)	+1,000	–
D	– 1,000 (1/4)	+ 2,000	+ 1,000
	4,000	4,000	

NB: Interest on capital was not charged, therefore, the profit was increased, in 2006, by the total amount of interest, which was Rs. 4,000 and credited to partner's current account equally, that is, profit sharing ratio. So, Rs. 4,000 should be written back.

ILLUSTRATION 29.14

A and B are partners and on 31st December 2004, the Capital of the partnership was Rs.2,10,000 of which Rs.1,40,000 stood at the credit of A and Rs.70,000 at the credit of B. Profit and Loss were to be divided as to 2/3 and 1/3 respectively.

On 31st December 2005, the following information was given to you as to the position of affairs :

(*a*) The total combined capital was Rs.2,46,500.

(*b*) B had drawn Rs.3,000.

(*c*) B had to be credited with Rs.5,000 as special salary earned during the year 2005, as agreed by the partners.

(*d*) The partners were to be credited with 5% interest on capital. You are required to prepare a statement showing how the capital of Rs.2,46,500 is divided between A and B. *(B.Com., Madurai)*

SOLUTION

Statement of Profit or Loss for the year 2005

	Rs.
Combined Capital as on 31st Dec.2005	2,46,500
Add: Drawings during the year	3,000
	2,49,500
Less: Combined Capital as on 31st Dec.2004 (Rs. 1,40,000 + 70,000)	2,10,000
Profit during the year	39,500

Profit and Loss Appropriation Account

	Rs.	Rs.		Rs.
To Salary to B		5,000	By Profit	39,500
To Interest on Capitals:				
A	7,000			
B	3,500	10,500		
To Profit transferred to Capitals				
A 2/3	16,000			
B 1/3	8,000	24,000		
		39,500		39,500

Capital Accounts

	A	B		A	B
	Rs.	Rs.		Rs.	Rs.
To Drawings	-	3,000	By Balance b/d	1,40,000	70,000
To Balance c/d	1,63,000	83,500	By Salary	-	5,000
			By Interest on Capital	7,000	3,500
			By Profit	16,000	8,000
	1,63,000	86,500		1,63,000	86,500
			By Balance b/d	1,63,000	83,500

Total Capital = Rs. 2,46,500

GUARANTEE OF PROFITS TO A PARTNER

Many a time a partner's share of profits is guaranteed by one of the existing partners or all the existing partners. A minimum amount of profit is guaranteed to a new partner even if there is no profit or his share of profit falls short of the guaranteed minimum amount.

Calculate the amount due to the new partner as per the profit sharing ratio. If this amount is more than the amount guaranteed, no further adjustment is needed. When there is no deficiency to be borne by the other partners, i.e, the new partner gets more than the guaranteed amount, then the total profit will simply be divided in the profit sharing ratio. When there is deficiency to be borne by the existing partners, then the deficiency or the difference must be debited to the existing partners in the ratio in which they have agreed to make the deficieny good.

ILLUSTRATION 29.15

Weakheart and Longhead are in partnership sharing profits and losses in the ratio of 3 : 2. They decided to admit Coramin, their manager as a partner with effect from 1st April 2004, giving one-fourth share of profits.

Coramin, while a manager, was in receipt of salary of Rs 13,500 p.a. and a commission of 10% of the net profit after charging such salary and commission.

In terms of the partnership deed, any excess amount which Coramin will be entitled to receive as a partner over the amount which would have been due to him if he continued to be the manager, would have to be personally borne by Weakheart out of his share of profit. Profit for the year ended 31st March 2005 amounted to Rs 1,12,500.

You are required to show the Profit and Loss Appropriation Account for the year ended 31st March 2005.

(*C.A. Inter*)

SOLUTION

Profit and Loss Appropriation Account

Dr.	Rs	Rs		Cr. Rs
To Share of Profit			By Profit & Loss A/c	
Weakheart	48,375		Net Profit	1,12,500
Longheart	36,000			
Coramin	28,125	1,12,500		
		1,12,500		1,12,500

Workings:

Coramin's share as a partner: 1/4th of Rs 1,12,500		28,125
Less: His share as a Manager		
Salary	13,500	
Commission		
$\frac{10}{110} \times (1{,}12{,}500 - 13{,}500)$	9,000	22,500
Difference chargeable to Weakheart		5,625

	Rs	Rs
Profit for the year	1,12,500	
Less; Coramin's share	22,500	
	90,000	
Weakheart's share = 3/5 of Rs 90,000		54,000
Less: Coramin's share to be borne		5,625
		48,375
Longhearts share = 2/5 of Rs 90,000		36,000

ILLUSTRATION 29.16

X, Y and Z are in partnership sharing profits and losses in the ratio of 3 : 2 : 1. Z's share is, however, guaranteed by X and Y at a fixed minimum of Rs 8,000. The net profit for the year ended 31st Dec. 2005 was Rs 36,000. Show the Profit and Loss Appropriation Account indicating the amount due finally to each partner.

(*B.Com., Madurai, Kolkata*)

SOLUTION

Profit and Loss Appropriation Account
for the year ended 31st Dec. 2005

Dr.		Rs		Cr. Rs
To Share of Profit:			By Profit & Loss A/c	36,000
X: 3/6 × 36,000	18,000			
Less: Adjustment for guarantee:				
3/5 of Rs 2,000	1,200	16,800		

Y: 2/6 × 36,000	12,000			
Less: Adjustment for guarantee:				
2/5 of Rs 2,000	800	11,200		
Z: 1/6 × 36,000	6,000			
Add: Adjustment for guarantee (X and Y)	2,000	8,000		
		36,000		36,000

Alternatively:

Profit and Loss Appropriation Account
for the year ended 31st Dec. 2005

Dr. Cr.

	Rs		Rs
To Share of Profit		By Profit & Loss A/c	36,000
Z: Guaranteed minimum	8,000		
X: 3/5 of Rs 28,000	16,800		
Y: 2/5 of Rs 28,000	11,200		
	36,000		36,000

Workings:

1/6th of the profits *i.e.* Rs 36,000 comes to Rs 6,000. The minimum guaranteed amount is Rs 8,000. The deficiency is shared by X and Y (3 : 2).

FINAL ACCOUNTS

Final Accounts i.e, Trading Account, Profit and Loss Account and Balance Sheet are prepared in the same manner as in the case of Sole Proprietorship. Some firms divide the Profit and Loss Account into parts - the first part is Profit and Loss Account and the second Part is Profit and Loss Appropriation Account. The Final Account may consist of Trading Account, Profit and Loss Account, Profit and Loss Appropriation Account and Balance Sheet. The net profit is transferred to the Profit and Loss Appropriation Account. This is an extension of usual Profit and Loss Account for the purpose of adjusting transactions relating to Partnership Deed.. These transactions are not mixed with the general trading transactions. The Final Profit, then is transferred to Capital Account, in case of Fluctuating Capital System or to Current Account, in case of Fixed Capital System.

ILLUSTRATION : 29.17

A and B are partners sharing profits and losses in the proportion of three -fifths and two-fifths respectively. The undermentioned balances were extracted from their books on 31st December 2005

	Rs.
A's Capital Account	65,000
A's Drawing Account	4,000
B's Capital Account	40,000
B's Drawing Account	3,000
Goodwill	40,000
Sales	1,60,000
Sundry Creditors	14,500
Returns Outward	2,500
Bills Payable	8,900
Office Furniture	5,000
Purchases	85,000

Sundry Debtors	40,500
Returns Inward	1,500
Rent	3,750
Postage and Telegrams	500
Advertising	9,000
Stock on 1st Jan. 2005	11,500
Stock on 31st Dec. 2005	12,500
Cash in hand	16,000
Wages	14,000
Telephone Charges	500
Salaries	12,250
Printing and Stationery	740
Commission Paid	5,000
Travelling Expenses	2,000
Carriage Inward	5,800
Motor Vans	20,860
Plant and Machinery	10,000

Take into account the following adjustments :

1. Write off Rs. 250 from office furniture
   10% on Plant and Machinery
   20% on Motor Vans
2. Create a Reserve of 5% on Sundry Debtors for Bad Debts.
3. Write off one-fifth of the Advertising Expenses.
4. Partners are entitled to interest on Capitals @5% p.a.
5. B is entitled to salary of Rs.1,800 p.a.

Prepare :

(*a*) Trial Balance.

(*b*) Trading and Profit and Loss Account for the year ended on 31st Dec. 2005.

(*c*) Balance as at that date. *(CAIIB)*

SOLUTION:

Trial Balance of A and B
as on 31st Dec. 2005

Ledger Balances	Dr. Rs.	Cr. Rs.
A's Capital Account	-	65,000
A's Drawing Account	4,000	-
B's Capital Account	-	40,000
B's Drawing Account	3,000	-
Goodwill	40,000	-
Sales	-	1,60,000
Sundry Creditors	-	14,500
Returns Outward	-	2,500
Bills Payable	-	8,900
Office Furniture	5,000	-
Purchases	85,000	-
Sundry Debtors	40,500	-
Returns Inward	1,500	-

Rent	3,750	-
Postage and Telegrams	500	-
Advertising	9,000	-
Stock on 1st Jan. 2005	11,500	-
Cash in hand	16,000	-
Wages	14,000	-
Telephone Charges	500	-
Salaries	12,250	-
Printing and Stationery	740	-
Commission Paid	5,000	-
Travelling Expenses	2,000	-
Carriage Inward	5,800	-
Motor Vans	20,860	-
Plant and Machinery	10,000	-
	2,90,900	2,90,900

Trading and Profit and Loss Account
for the year ended 31st December, 2005

Dr.		Rs.			Cr. Rs.
To Stock on Jan.2005		11,500	By Sales	1,60,000	
To Purchases	85,000		Less: Returns	1,500	1,58,500
Less: Returns	2,500	82,500	By Stock on 31st Dec 2005		12,500
To Wages		14,000			
To Carriage Inward		5,800			
To Gross Profit c/d		57,200			
		1,71,000			1,71,000
To Salaries		12,250			
To Rent		3,750	By Gross Profit c/d		57,200
To Postage and Telegrams		500			
To Advertisement (1/5th of 9,000)		1,800			
To Telephone		500			
To Printing & Stationery		740			
To Commission		5,000			
To Travelling Expenses		2,000			
To Bad Debts Provision		2,025			
To Depreciation					
Furniture		250			
Plant and Machinery		1,000			
Motor Vans		4,172			
To Net Profit		23,213			
		57,200			57,200

Profit and Loss Appropriation Account

Dr.	Rs	Rs		Cr. Rs
To Salary to B		1,800	By Profit & Loss A/c	23,213
To Interest on Capitals :				
A	3,250			
B	2,000	5,250		

To Share of Profit to :				
A	9,698			
B	6,465	16,163		
		23,213		23,213

Balance Sheet of A and B
as on 31st December 2005

Dr.	Rs	Rs		Rs	Rs. Cr.
Creditors		14,500	Cash		16,000
Bills Payable		8,900	Sundry Debtors:	40,500	
Capital Accounts :			Less: Provision	2,025	38,475
A	65,000		Stock		12,500
Add: Interest	3,250		Furniture:	5,000	
Add: Net Profit	9,698		Less : Depreciation	250	4,750
	77,948		Motor Vans	20,860	
Less: Drawings	4,000	73,948	Less : Depreciation	4,172	16,688
			Plant and Machinery	10,000	
B:	40,000		Less : Depreciation	1,000	9,000
Add: Interest	2,000		Goodwill		40,000
Add: Salary	1,800		Advertising		7,200
Add: Net Profit	6,465				
	50,265				
Less: Drawings	3,000	47,265			
		1,44,613			1,44,613

ILLUSTRATION: 29.18

From the following Trial Balance of a firm of *A* and *B*, as at 31st March 2006, prepare the final accounts:

	Dr. Rs.	Cr. Rs.
A's Capital	–	80,000
B's Capital	–	1,00,000
Stock 1–4 2005 Raw Materials	2,500	
Finished goods	6,500	–
Purchases	64,500	–
Sales	–	1,19,000
Sales Returns	2,000	–
Wages	16,000	–
Manufacturing expenses	12,000	
Salaries	8,000	–
Insurance	1,500	–
Postage	100	–
Advertisement	1,000	–
Bad debts	300	–
Bills Payable	–	12,000
Discount	–	500
Land and Buildings	90,000	–

Plant and Machinery	70,000	–
Furniture	1, 000	–
Sundry Debtors	25,400	–
Sundry Creditors	–	42,000
A's Drawings	1,800	–
B's Drawings	1,400	–
Cash in hand	500	–
Cash at Bank	49,000	–
	3,53,500	3,53,500

Adjustments to be made :

(1) Stock on 31 st March 2006: Raw Materials Rs. 4, 000, Finished Goods Rs. 12,000

(2) Provide depreciation on Land and Building @ 5%, Furniture @ 10% and Plant and Machinery @ 5%.

(3) Outstanding Salaries Rs. 1,500, Wages Rs, 2,100.

(4) Insurance is paid for 15 month up to June 2006.

(5) Write off bad debts Rs. 400.

(6) Reserve for doubtful debts at 5% on Debtors.

(7) Goods withdrawn by *A* for personal use Rs. 2,000.

(8) *A* and *B* are equal partners. *(B. Com. Osmania)*

SOLUTION.

Manufacturing Account of *A* and *B*
for the year ended 31st March 2006

Dr. *Cr.*

		Rs.		Rs.
To Stock, 1–4–2005.			By Stock, 31–3–2006.	
Raw Materials		2,500	Raw Materials	4,000
" Purchases	64,500		" Cost of production	91,100
Lss: Drawing	2,000	62, 500		
" Wages	16,000			
Add: Outstanding	2,100	18,100		
" Manufacturing expenses		12,000		
		95,100		95,100

Trading and profit and loss account of A and B
for the year ended 31st March 2006.

		Rs.		Rs.	
To Stock 1–4–2005			By Sales	1,19,000	
Finished Goods		6,500	*Less*: Returns	2,000	
" Cost of production		91,100			1,17,000
" Gross Profit		31,400	" Stock, 31–3–2006.		
			" Finished Goods		12,000
		1,29,000			1,29,000
To Salaries	8,000		By Gross Profit b/d		31,400
Add: O/s	1,500	9,500	" Discount		500
" Insurance	1,500				
Less: Prepaid	300				
		1,200			
" Postage		100			
" Advertisement		1, 000			

" Bad Debts	300			
Add : Further				
Bad debts	400			
		700		
" Provision for Doubtful debts		1,250		
" Depreciaton:				
Land & Buildings 5%		4,500		
Furniture 10%		100		
Plant & Machinery 5%		3,500		
" Net profit A : Rs 5,025				
B : Rs 5,025		10,050		
		31,900		31,900

Balance Sheet of A and B as at 31st March 2006.

		Rs.			*Rs*
Sundry Creditors		42,000	Cash in hand		500
Bills Payable		12,000	Cash at Bank		49,000
Outstanding liabilities:			Sundry Debtors	25,400	
Wages	2,100		*Less*: Bad Debts	400	
Salaries	1,500	3,600		25,000	
Capital Accounts:			*Less*: Provision		
A	80,000		for Doubtful Debts	1,250	23,750
Less: Drawing					
Cash & Goods	3,800		Stocks:		
			Raw Material	4,000	
	76,200		Finished Goods	12,000	
Add: Profit	5,025				16,000
		81,225	Prepaid Insurance		300
B	1,00,000		Furniture	1,000	
Less: Drawing	1,400		*Less*: Depreciation	100	900
	98,600		Plant and Machinery	70,000	
Add: Profit	5,025	1,03,625	*Less*: Depreciation	3,500	66,500
			Land and Buildings	90,000	
			Less: Depreciation	4,500	85,500
		2,42,450			2,42,450

QUESTIONS

Objective Type Questions

I. State whether each of the following statements are "true" or "False".

1. Partners are mutual agents for each other.
2. Current Accounts are maintained in case of Fluctuating Capital System.
3. Every partner has a right to be consulted in all matters affecting the business of partnership.
4. A partnership firm enjoys a separate legal personality apart from its partners.
5. In the absence of any contract to the contrary, partners are required to share profits and losses equally.
6. The relation between partners is governed by agreement.
7. Interest on capital is a profit to the firm

8. A working partner is entitled to salary from his firm.
9. The basic financial statements of a partnership are the same as those of a sole trader.
10. Partner's current accounts are the same as the firm's current account with a bank.
11. Partners are bound to share profits and losses equally.
12. When one of the partners does most of the work, he is entitled to a salary from the firm.
13. Interest on capital is chargeable to a firm to the extent of available profits only.
14. The document embodying the partnership agreement is known as the partnership deed.
15. The maximum number of partners for a non-banking partnership concern is twenty.

(Ans: True – 1, 3, 5, 6, 9, 13, 14, 15.
False – 2, 4, 7, 8, 10, 11, 12.

II. Fill in the blanks:

1. Articles of partnership is the same as....
2. In a partnership, capital accounts may be maintained either under.... or ... systems.
3. Current account of the partners is prepared when the capitals are....
4. Partner's salary is an ... profits
5. Partnership.... determines the terms among the partners.

(Ans: 1. Partership Deed; 2. Fixed, Fluctuating; 3. Fixed; 4. Appropriate from: 5. Dead.)

III. Select the best choice to complete each statement given below:

1. Any amount payable to a partner (except rent) should be treated as:
   (a) An appropriate
   (b) An expense
   (c) None of these
2. Under Fixed Capital Method, drawings of each partner is debited in his:
   (a) Capital Account
   (b) Current Account
   (c) Profit & Loss Account
3. When a partner draws a fixed sum at the beginning of each month, interest on drawings, at an agreed rate, will be equal to interest of:
   (a) 6.5 Months
   (b) 5.5 Months
   (c) 6 Months
4. An ordinary partnership firm can have:
   (a) Not more than 20 partners
   (b) Not more than 50 partners
   (c) Note more than 3 partners
5. In the absence of any provisions in the partnership agreement, partners loan to the firm can carry:
   (a) Interest at 9% p.a.
   (b) Interest at 12% p.a.
   (c) Interest at 6% p.a.
6. Commission paid to partners is debited to:
   (a) Profit & Loss Account
   (b) Trading Account
   (c) Profit & Loss Appropriate A/c
7. The interest on partners' capital accounts is to be credited to:
   (a) Partners' Capital Account
   (b) Interest Account
   (c) Profit & Loss Account

8. Capital contribution by the partners should be:
   (a) Equal;
   (b) As per the profit-sharing ratio
   (c) None of these

(**Ans:** 1. (a); 2. (b); 3. (a); 4. (a); 5. (c); 6. (c).; 7. (a); 8. (c)

THEORETICAL QUESTIONS

1. Define Partnership.
2. Explain Fixed and Fluctuating Capital Accounts.
3. What is the meaning of partnership deed?
4. In the absence of Partnership Deed, how are the mutual relations of partners governed?

PRACTICAL PROBLEMS

1. Vijay and Bhargav are partners sharing profits and losses equally with capitals of Rs.30,000 and Rs.20,000 respectively. Their drawings during the year are as follows :

Vijay's Drawing on 31.3.2004	Rs. 500
30.4.2004	600
1.7.2004	450
1.12.2004	1,400

Bhargav drew Rs. 300 at the end of the each month. The deed provides interest on capitals and drawings @6%. Calculate interest on Capitals and Drawings. (*Karnataka*)

[**Ans:**	Vijay	Bhargav
Interest on Capital Rs	1,800	1,200
Interest on Drawings Rs	67	99]

2. Mr X is the partner in a firm. He withdraws Rs. 200 at the end of each month. His capital in the firm is Rs.8,000. He gave a loan of Rs. 4,000 to the firm on 1st July, 2004. Rate of Interest on capital, drawings and loan is 10% p.a. Books are closed on 31st december each year. Calculate the amount of Interest.

[**Ans:** Interest on Drawings : 110
Interest on Capitals : 800
Interest on Loan : 200]

3. X is the partner of a firm. He withdraws Rs. 200 on the first day of each month. The rate of interest on drawings is 8% p.a. and the books are closed on 31st Dec. Calculate the amount of Interest on drawings.

[**Ans:** Interest Rs. 104]

4. A and B commenced business in partnership on 1st Jan. 2004 The partnership was oral and no specific terms were agreed upon. A and B contributed Rs. 40,000 and Rs. 10,000 respectively as their capitals. In addition A also advanced Rs. 20,000 as a loan to the firm on 1st July 2004.

On 1st April 2004 A met with a serious accident and could not attend to the business of the firm for 3 months.

The profits for the year ended 31st dec. 2004 ammounted to Rs. 56,600 Disputes have arisen between the partners to the exact way of sharing the profits.

A Claims :

(*i*) Interest on his capital as well as a Loan Account at 10% per annum as his captial contribution is larger as compared to that of B.

(*ii*) That the Net Profit of the firm should be shared in the ratio of capital contribution of each partner.

B Claims :

(*i*) That net profits should be shared equally.

(*ii*) That he should be allowed salary of Rs.1,000 per month during the period of A's illness.

(*iii*) Interest on Capital and Loan Accounts should be allowed at 6% p.a. only.

You are requested to allocate the profits correctly giving your reasons in support of the allocation you may prefer in the matter. *(B.Com., Bombay)*

[Ans: Share of profit Rs. 25,000 each.]

5. X, having a capital of Rs 60,000, takes Y and Z into partnership on January 1, 2004 on the following terms:

Y to bring in Rs 20,000 as capital; interest on capital to be allowed at 5%; Y to receive a salary of Rs 6,000 annually.

Z is guaranteed by X that his minimum share of profit shall be Rs 6,000 per annum; and profits are to be shared as X one-half, Y one-third and Z one-sixth.

In the first year of partnership the business shows a profit of Rs 4,000 before charging Y's salary or interest on capital. They had drawn during the year X Rs 10,000; Y Rs 8,000 (including salary) Z Rs 6,000.

Show the position of partners' accounts on December 31, 2004 after adjustment. No interest on drawings is to be allowed.

What did each partner gain or lose for the year? *(B.Com., Andhra)*

[Ans: Share of Loss to X : Rs 1,500
Y : Rs 1,000
Z : Rs 500
Capital (after adjustments)
X – Rs 42,000
Y – Rs 18,000
Z – Nil

6. The summarised Capital Accounts of the Partners of a firm are as under:

		Kamal	Kumar	Keerti			Kamal	Kumar	Keerti
		Rs	Rs	Rs			Rs	Rs	Rs
2004					2004				
Dec. 31	To Drawings	12,000	12,000	12,000	Jan. 1	By Balance b/d	20,000	30,000	40,000
Dec. 31	To Balance c/d	23,000	33,000	43,000	Dec. 31	By Profit	15,000	15,000	15,000
		35,000	45,000	55,000			35,000	45,000	55,000

On Ist January 2005, it is agreed that the following would be effective retrospectively from Ist January 2004:

(i) Kamal shall be entitled to a salary of Rs 750 p.m.

(ii) Interest shall allowed on partner's capital at 5% on opening balance.

(iii) Keerti's share of profit exclusive of intererst on his capital shall not fall below Rs 15,000, the deficit, if any, being contributed by Kamal out of his share.

(iv) Profit shall be shared in proportion to opening balance in capital account.

You are required to show the entries in the capital accounts Ist January 2005 to give effect to the above arrangement. *(C.A.)*

[Ans: Debit Kumar with Rs 3,000
Credit Kamal with Rs 1,000
Credit Keerti with Rs 2,000]

7. Three Chartered Accountants Das, Roy and Sen form a partnership, profits being divisible in the ratio 3:2:1 subject to the following :

(i) Sen's Share of profit is guaranteed to be not less than Rs. 15,000 per annum.

(ii) Roy gives guarantee to the effect that gross fees earned by him for the firm shall be equal to his average gross fee of the proceeding five years when he was carrying on profession along (which average works out at Rs.25,000).

The profit for the first year of the partnership is Rs. 75,000 The gross fees earned by Roy for the firm are Rs.16,000.

You are required to show the distribution of profit. *(C.A. Inter)*

[**Ans:** share of profit : Rs. 41,400 (Das)
27,600 (Roy)
15,000 (Sen)]

8. X, Y, Z Company is a partnership concern, having three partners X, Y and Z. Their capital accounts stood at Rs.30,000, Rs.15,000 and Rs. 15,000 respectively on 1st January 2004.

Deed of partnership provided that :

(*a*) Z should be allowed a remuneration of Rs. 30,000 p.a.

(*b*) Interest at 5% p.a. has to be allowed on capital.

(*c*) Balance Profit/Loss is to be divided in the proportion of 2 : 2: 1

Ignoring the above terms, the profits of Rs.18,000 for the year ended 31st Dec.2004 was divided equally.

You are now required to pass the Journal entry to rectify the error.

[**Ans:** Debit Y Account with 450
Credit X Account with 300
Credit Z Account with 150]

9. The capital accounts of Madhu, Manoj and Manak showed a balance of Rs. 35,000; Rs.27,500; Rs.20,000 after the necessary adjustments in respect of drawings and net profit of Rs.22,500 in the ratio 2:2:1 for the year ended 31st March 2004. After closing the books, it was found out that 5% interst on capital and drawings had been omitted. The drawings of the partners had been Rs. 7,500; Rs.5000 and Rs.3,000 respectively, the interest being thereon Rs. 270, Rs. 200 and Rs. 160 respectively.

Give necessary journal entries for these adjustments and prepare adjusted Capital Account of the partners.

[**Ans:** Debit Manoj Capital Account with Rs.283
Credit Madhu Capital Account with Rs. 147
Credit Manak Capital Account with rs. 136
Capital Accounts after the adjustments Rs. 35,147 (Madhu);
Rs. 27,217 (Manoj);
Rs. 20,136 (Manak)

10. The net profit of a firm for the year ended 30th June, 2004 was Rs 15,000 which has been duly distributed among its three partners Ram, Shyam and Gopal in their agreed proportions of 2 : 2 : 1 respectively. On 5th July, 2004 it was discovered that the undermentioned transactions were not passed through the books of accounts of the firm for the year ended 30th June, 2004 which stood duly closed on that date:

(*a*) Commission due to Ram for a special transaction of Rs 1,700.

(*b*) Interest on capital at 5 per cent per annum.

(*c*) Interest on drawings: Ram Rs 165, Shyam Rs 125 and Gopal Rs 100.

In addition to these, the rent of Ram's house amounting to Rs 200 paid by the firm had been charged in the Profit and Loss Account.

The capital accounts of the partners are fixed and on the close of business on 30th June, 2004 were: Ram Rs 40,000, Shyam Rs 25,000 and Gopal Rs 15,000.

You are required to give one journal entry to rectify the above omission. (*B.Com., Madurai*)

[Ans: Debit Shyam Current Account with Rs 919
Debit Gopal Current Account with Rs 372
Credit Ram Current Account with Rs 1,291]

11. Gold, Silver and Copper entered into partnership on Ist January 2004 sharing profits and losses in the ratio of 2 : 2 : 1. Gold, however, personally guaranteed that Copper's share of profits, after charging interest on capital @ 5% p.a., would not be less than Rs 8,000 in any year. The Capitals were A Rs 50,000, B Rs 30,000 and C Rs 20,000. The profit for the year ended 31st December 2004 amounted to Rs 35,000

Show the profit and loss appropriation Account.

[Ans: Share of profit: Rs 10,000 (Gold)
Rs 12,000 (Silver)
Rs 8,000 (Copper)

12. Arjun and Bheem are partners in a firm sharing profits and losses as Arjun 3/4ths and Bheem 1/4th. The Profit & Loss Account of the firm for the year ended 31st March, 2004 shows a net profit of Rs 75,000. You are required to prepare the Profit & Loss Appropriation Account by taking into consideration the under-mentioned information:

(*i*) The partners' Capital Accounts–Arjun Rs 40,000, Bheem Rs 30,000. Interest on Capital was to be calculated at 5% p.a. (*ii*) The Current Accounts of partners–Arjun Rs 15,000 (Cr.), Bheem Rs 10,000 (Cr.), (*iii*) Partners' Drawings amounted to Arjun, Rs 10,000 and Bheem Rs 7,500. Interest on Drawings was to be charged at 10% p.a. at an average of 6 months. (*iv*) Partners' salaries– Arjun Rs 6,000 and Bheem Rs 4,500. (*v*) Arjun's Loan Account Rs 25,000 (The loan was contracted two years back).

(*B.Com., Calcutta*)

[Ans: Divisible Profit : Rs 60,375
Share of Arjun : Rs 45,281
Share of Bheem : Rs 15,094]

13. From the following particulars prepare the Capital and Current Accounts of the partners. Also prepare the Profit and Loss Appropriation Account of the partnership firm:

	Particulars	*A*	*B*	*C*
1.	Profit Sharing Ratio	1	2	3
2.	Capital as on 1.1.2004	30,000	40,000	50,000
3.	Current Accounts on 1.1.2004	Dr. 5,000	Cr. 8,000	Cr. 2,000
4.	Additional Capital brought on 1.9.2004	3,000	–	5,000
5.	Loan Account on 1.7.2004	–	10,000	–
6.	Partner's Drawings at the end of every month	300	400	500
7.	Salary for Partners every month	200	600	–
8.	Interest on Drawings and Capital @ 6% p.a.			
9.	Interest on Loan @ 9% p.a.			
10.	Profit for the year before charging interest on Capital, Drawings and Loan Rs 16,000			

(*B.Com., Madurai*)

	A	B	C
	Rs	Rs	Rs
Share of Profit	1,431	2,862	4,293
Capitals (31.12.2004)	33,000	40,000	55,000
Current A/c (31.12.2004)	3,008 (Dr.)	15,980 (Cr.)	3,228 (Cr.)]

14. A,B and C are partners sharing profits and losses in proportion to their capitals at the beginning of the year. They are entitled to draw Rs.6,000 Rs.5,000 and Rs. 4,000 out of their anticipated shares of

profit. Any drawings in excess of these amounts are to be regarded as advances taken from the firm and are subject to interest at an rate of 5 % p.a.

The capitals of the partners at the beginning of the year were A Rs. 80,000; B Rs. 60,000 and C Rs. 40,000. The credit balances of their current accounts were A Rs.2,304; B Rs.3,728; and C Rs.1,152. Their drawings during the year were A Rs. 10,000; B 12,000 and C 5,000. The profits for the year were Rs.3 0,096 before making any adjustment for interset as above.

Draw up the Capital and current accounts of the partners. *(CAIIB)*

[Ans: Current account balances :

A: Rs. 5,760

B: Rs. 1,580

C: Rs. 2,940]

15. On 1st January 2004, A and B enter into partnership contributing Rs 20,000 and Rs 15,000 respectively, and sharing profits and losses in the ratio of 3 : 2. B is allowed a salary of Rs 4,000 per year. Interest on capitals is to be charged at 5% per annum and 5% interest is to be charged on drawings. During the year A withdrew Rs 3,000 and B Rs 6,000, interest on drawings being Rs 70 and Rs 50 respectively. Profit in 2004 before the above noted adjustments amounted to Rs 10,580. Show how the profit is to be distributed. Also show the capital accounts of A and B under Fixed Capital Method and Fluctuating Capital Method. *(B.Com., Karnataka)*

[Ans: Under Fixed Capital Method:

A's Current Account: Rs 890 (Cr.)

B's Current Account: Rs 690 (Cr.)

Under Fluctuating Capital Method:

A's Capital Account Rs 20,890

B's Capital Account: Rs 15,690]

16. On 1st January, 2004 Sunil and Kapil commenced business as partners with an initial capital of Rs 20,000 and Rs 30,000 in their respective accounts. The partnership deed provides that:

1. Profit and loss shall be shared in the ratio of 2 : 3 as between Sunil and Kapil.
2. Partners shall be entitled to interest on capital at the commencement of each year at 6% p.a.
3. Interest on drawings shall be charged 8% p.a.

During the year ended 31st December, 2004 the firm made a profit of Rs 19,280 before adjustment of interest on capital and drawings. The partners withdraw during the year Rs 3,000 each at the end of every quarter commencing from 31.3.2004.

You are required to open Profit & Loss Appropriation Account and show the entries for interest on capital and drawings and distribution of profits. And also prepare Capital Accounts.

(B.Com., Madurai)

[Ans: Share of profit to Sunil Rs 6,800

and to Kapil Rs 10,200

Capital Account balances: Rs 15,640 (Sunil)

Rs 29,640 (Kapil)]

17. Hari and Mohan were in partnership sharing profits in proportion of 3 : 2. On 1st January 2004, their capitals were Rs 30,000 and Rs 20,000 respectively. Interest was agreed to be allowed on capital and charged on drawings at 10% p.a. Mohan is to be allowed an annual salary of Rs 4,800 which had not been withdrawn. During the year 2004 Hari withdrew Rs 200 p.m. and Mohan Rs 400 p.m. on the first day of every month in anticipation of profits. The profits for the year, prior to calculation of interest on capital and drawings but after charging Mohan's salary amounted to Rs 22,500. A provision of manager's commission at 5% on net profit (after charging such commission) is to be made.

Show the allocation of profits and prepare the partners' Current Accounts, if the capitals are fixed.

(B.Com., Madurai)

[Ans: Share of Profit to Hari : Rs 10,223

Mohan : Rs 6,815

Current Account Balances : Rs 10,693 (Hari)
Rs 8,555 (Mohan)]

18. A, B and C are partners in a firm, sharing profits and losses in the ratio 2 : 1 : 1. It is agreed that interest on capital will be allowed at 5 per cent per annum and interest on Drawings will be charged at 4 per cent per annum. (No interest will be charged or allowed on Current Accounts).
The following are the particulars of the Capital, Current and Drawings Accounts of the partners:

	A	B	C
	Rs	Rs	Rs
Capital A/c (1.1.2004)	75,000	40,000	30,000
Current A/c (1.1.2004)	10,000	5,000	5,000 (Dr.)
Drawings	15,000	10,000	10,000
Interest on Drawings (2004)	500	190	350

The draft accounts for 2004 showed a net profit of Rs 60,000 before taking into account interest on Capital and Drawings and subject to the following adjustments:
(*a*) Life Insurance Premium of A amounting to Rs 1,000 paid by the firm on 1.10.2004 has been charged to Miscellaneous Expenditure Account
(*b*) Repairs to machinery amounting to Rs 10,000 has been debited to Plant Account and depreciation thereon charged @ 20 per cent.
(*c*) Travelling expenses of Rs 3,000 of B for a pleasure trip to U.K. paid by the firm on 30.6.2004 has been debited to Travelling Expenses A/c.
Prepare the Profit and Loss Appropriation Account for the year ended 31st December 2004 and Current Accounts of the partners for the year. (*C.A. Inter*)

[**Ans:** Share of Profit : Rs 24,930 (A)
Rs 12,465 (B)
Rs 12,465 (C)
Current Account Balances:
Rs 22,170 (Cr.) : (A)
Rs 6,215 (Cr.) : (B)
Rs 1,385 (Dr.) : (C)

19. Genius, Talent and Intellect are in partnership and on 1st April 2003, their respective capitals were Rs 80,000, Rs 55,600 and Rs 31,800. Talent and Intellect are entitled to draw salary of Rs 5,000 and Rs 4,000 per annum respectively, before division of profits. Interest is allowed on capital at 10% p.a. and is not charged on drawings. Of the net profit, first Rs 20,000 is divided in the ratio of 40 : 35 ; 25 among Genius, Talent and Intellect respectively. Balance profit is shared equally.
The profit for the year ended 31st March 2004, after charging partners' salaries, but before charging interest on capital, was Rs 46,340 and the partners had drawn Rs 15,000 each for personal expenses.
Prepare Profit & Loss Appropriation Account and Partners' Capital Account for the year ended 31st March 2004. (*B.Com., Calcutta*)

[**Ans:** Share of Profit : Rs 11,200 (Genius)
Rs 10,200 (Talent)
Rs 8,200 (Intellect)
Capital Account Balances:
Genius – Rs 84,200
Talent – Rs 61,360
Intellect Rs 32,180]

20. From the following details, prepare Manufacturing Trading and profit and Loss Account, and Profit and Loss Appropriation account for the year ending 31st March, 2004 and a balance sheet as on 31st March 2004

	Dr. Rs.	Cr. Rs.
Opening Stock :		
Raw Materials	60,000	--
Work in Progress	5,000	--
Finished Goods	20,000	--
Purchases :		
Raw Materials	2,10,000	--
Finished Goods	10,000	--
Cash	2,000	--
Factory Rent	12,000	--
Office Rent, Rates and Taxes	3,000	--
Factory Salary	18,000	--
Office Salary	12,000	--
Debtors and Creditors	78,000	56,000
Sales	--	3,30,000
Selling expenses	8,000	--
Interest on loan paid	4,000	--
Discount allowed	3,000	--
Discount received	--	1,100
Capital :		
A	--	68,000
B	--	30,000
Partnership Salary drawn :		
A	6,000	--
B	3,000	--
Loan	--	50,000
Wages	30,000	--
Interest on partners Capital drawn:		
A	500	--
B	600	--
Machinery	45,000	--
Furniture	5,000	--
	5,35,100	5,35,100

(1) Provide 10% depreciation on Machiner and Furniture.

(2) Loan Carries 10% interest and the amount is brought forward from earlier year.

(3) Provide 6% interest on partners capital

(4) Closiong Stock

	Rs.
Raw Materials	50,000
Work in Progress	10,000
Finisehd goods	35,000

(5) Salary outstanding on 31 March, 2004

Factory	2,000
Office	1,000

(6) A and B share profits and losses as 3 : 2 after charging a salary @ Rs. 500 and Rs. 250 per month to A and B respectively.

(7) Outstanding factory rent is Rs. 1,000. (*CAIIB*)

[**Ans :** Cost of production : Rs. 2,82,500
Gross Profit : Rs 52,500
Net Profit : Rs 21,100

Divisible profit : Rs 6,220
Share of Profit : Rs 3,732 (to A)
Share of Profit : Rs 2,488 (to B)
Balance sheet total : Rs 2,20,000]

21. Black and White are partners sharing profits and losses in proportion to their capitals. At the close of their financial year on 31st December 2004, the following balances stood to the credit of the partners:

Capital Accounts: Black Rs 20,000 and White Rs 5,000
Current Accounts: Black Rs 1,060 and White Rs 2,800

The partnership deed Provides:

(*a*) That White shall be credited with a salary of Rs 1,000 p.a. for managing the business.

(*b*) That white shall be entitled to 10% of the net profit after charging his salary, and interest on capital, Current Accounts and Drawings.

(*c*) Interest at 5% p.a. to be allowed on Capital and Current Accounts.

The partners drawings were:
Black Rs 10,000
White Rs 330 and which the following amounts of interest are to be charged:
Black Rs 330 and White Rs 80.

In addition to the above, the following balances were extracted from the books of the firm as on 31st December 2004:

	Rs		*Rs*
Freehold Premises	15,000	Machinery Ist Jan. 2004	13,280
Sundry Creditors	24,150	Machinery addition in 2004	1,560
Advertising	4,339	Cycles	900
Office salaries	2,189	Factory Expenses paid	
Sundry Debtors	16,020	in advance	70
Office Expenses	622	Cash at Bank	2,841
Insurance	364	Cash in hand	31
Delivery Expenses	2,203	Mortgage on Freehold	
Stock on 31st Dec. 2004	21,069	Premises at 6% p.a.	10,000
Provision for Bad Debts		Office Furniture	300
Ist Jan. 2004	600	Patents	4,000
Trading Account (Cr. Balance)	34,628	Mortgage Interest	450

You are required to prepare Profit and Loss Account for the year ended 31st December 2004 and a Balance Sheet as on that date.

When preparing the above the following matters are to be taken into consideration regarding which no entries had been made in the books.

(*a*) Depreciation to be provided as follows:
Plant (Old) 10% p.a.
Plant (addition) 25%
Office Furniture 10% p.a.
Patnets 10% p.a.

(*b*) Cycles were valued at Rs 800.

(*c*) The provision for bad debts to be made upto 5% on debtors.

(*d*) Interest on mortgage has been paid to 30th Sept. 2004

(*e*) The following amounts are to be carried forward to next year:
Insurance Rs 62: Advertising Rs 878.

(*f*) Office salaries Rs 69 were owing at 31st Dec. 2004. (*CAIIB*)

[**Ans:** Net profit Rs 22,733 (Profit & Loss Account)
Divisible profit Rs 18,630 (P & L Appropriation Account)
Share of profit to Black : Rs 14,904
Share of Profit to White: Rs 3,726
Balance Sheet Total : Rs 72,962]

Chapter 30

Partnership Accounts–Admission

Adjustment in the Profit and Loss Sharing Ratio – Adjustment for Revaluation of Assets and Liabilities – Adjustment for Goodwill – Adjustment of Undistributed Profits or Losses – Adjustment of Rearrangement of Capitals – Questions – Objective Type Questions – Theoretical Questions – Practical Problems

A new partner can be admitted only with unanimous consent of all existing partners. Quite often a partnership firm decides to admit a new partner because it may need more capital or special skill etc. Any change in relations of the partners will result in the reconstitution of the partnership firm. Reconstitution of partnership occurs when any change is made in relation to partners. Therefore, a firm is said to be reconstituted when there is an admission, retirement, death or insolvency of partners or when a partnership firm gets amalgamated with other firms. When additional capital or managerial ability or technical know-how is needed in the course of expansion, it is quite usual to take a new partner or partners into the partnership firm. Expansion of business is possible either through external borrowings or investing more capital. The possible and convenient way of getting additional capital is by admitting a new partner. When a new partner is admitted, he is not liable for the liabilities of the firm incurred before his admission. When such an admission takes place, the incoming partner becomes entitled to share the Profit/Loss that would arise in the firm, from the date of his admission. It is possible that there may be secret profits because of unrevealed profits, undervaluation of assets, or omission of some assets or over-statement of liabilities etc. or losses in reverse cases. On the admission of a partner the various assets and liabilities are revalued since the existing partners are entitled to any profit that has arisen till the date of admission. Similarly, they are also responsible for all the losses that may have occurred. It is not only proper from the point of view of the new partner but also from the point of view of existing partners that the Balance Sheet just after admission should be true and correct.

There are certain accounting procedures that have to be followed by a partnership firm when a new partner is admitted and they are:

I. Adjustment in the Partnership Profit and Loss Sharing Ratio.
II. Adjustment for Revaluation of Assets and Liabilities.
III. Adjustment for Goodwill.
IV. Adjustment regarding Undistributed or Accumulated Profits and Losses.
V. Adjustment of Capitals.

I. ADJUSTMENT IN THE PROFIT AND LOSS SHARING RATIO

When a new partner is admitted, he should be given a portion of the profit of the firm. As the incoming partner is entitled to get a profit share, the profit share of all or some of the old partners will be reduced. The profit shares of all the old partners will be reduced, if all of them make a sacrifice. What the old partners sacrifice, is in favour of the new partner. Thus, PROFIT SHARING RATIO should necessarily be changed when a new partner is admitted. The ratio at which the profits should be divided among the old partners and the new partners is called the NEW PROFIT SHARING RATIO. After the admission of a new partner into the firm, NEW PROFIT SHARING RATIO should be found out, without which the profit cannot be divided among partners, including the new partner. The following cases may arise while calculating the new Profit and Loss sharing ratio:

(1) When the share of the new partner is given, then it should assume that the remaining profit should be shared by the old partners in their old profit sharing ratio.

(2) When the share of the new partner is purchased out of the share of profit of one of the old partners, then the old partner forgoes a portion of the profit, which goes to the new partner.

(3) The old partners may sacrifice their share of profits for the new partner in their existing profit sharing ratio.

(4) New partner's share of profit is out of the profit of all partners in the equal ratio.

In all the cases, profit and loss sharing ratio is completely changed. All the types of cases are discussed below.

ILLUSTRATION 30.1

A and B are partners in a business sharing profits and losses in the ratio of 3 : 2. They admit C into the firm. Find out the new profit and loss sharing ratio in the following cases:

(*a*) When C is given 1/6th share in profit.

(*b*) When C is given 1/6th share in profits out of A's share.

(*c*) When C is given 1/6th share in profits from A and B in the ratio of 1 : 1.

(*d*) When C is given 1/6th share of profits from A and B in their profit and loss sharing ratio.

SOLUTION:

(*a*) Let the total share of profit be 1.

The newcomer C is given 1/6th share in the profit

Balance of share in Profit = 1 – 1/6 = 5/6.

5/6th share of profit is shared by A and B in 3 : 2 ratio

Therefore A's new share of profit = 5/6 × 3/5 = 3/6

B's new share of profit = $\frac{5}{6} \times \frac{2}{5} = \frac{2}{6}$

New profit sharing among A, B and C = 3/6 : 2/6 : 1/6

(or) **3 : 2 : 1**

(*b*) Let the total share of profit be 1.

C's share of profit $= \frac{1}{6}$

C's share of profit is borne by A. So, A's new profit sharing proportion $= \frac{3}{5} - \frac{1}{6} = \frac{18-5}{30} = \frac{13}{30}$

B's profit sharing ratio remains the same.

New profit sharing ratio among A, B, C $= \frac{13}{30} : \frac{2}{5} : \frac{1}{6} = \frac{13}{30} : \frac{12}{30} : \frac{5}{30}$

(or) **13 : 12 : 5**

(*c*) Let the total share of profit be 1.

C's share of profit = 1/6 or 10/60

A and B sacrifice equally i.e. 1/6 ÷ 2 = 1/6 × 1/2 = 1/12

So, A's new share of profit = $\frac{3}{5} - \frac{1}{12} = \frac{36-5}{60} = \frac{31}{60}$

B's new share of profit = $\frac{2}{5} - \frac{1}{12} = \frac{24-5}{60} = \frac{19}{60}$

Therefore, new profit sharing = **31 : 19 : 10**

(*d*) Let the total profit share be 1.

C gets 1/6th share in the profit and is sacrificed by A and B in 3 : 2 ratio:

∴ A has to sacrifice 3/5 of 1/6 = 3/30

B has to sacrifice 2/5 of 1/6 = 2/30

A's new profit sharing proportion = 3/5 – 3/30 = $\frac{18-3}{30}$ = 15/30

B's new profit sharing proportion = 2/5 – 2/30 = $\frac{12-2}{30}$ = 10/30

C will get 1/6 $\left(\frac{5}{30}\right)$

New profit sharing proportion = 15 : 10 : 5

(or) **3 : 2 : 1**

(*a*) and (*d*) give equal answers. That is, when C is given 1/6th share of the profit and nothing else mentioned in the problem. It means the existing partners forgoing shares in the ratio of their old profit and loss sharing ratio. In other words, the remaining profit *i.e.* 5/6th share is shared by old partners in their old profit sharing ratio *i.e.* 3 : 2. That is,

A's share = 5/6 × 3/5 = 3/6

B's share = 5/6 × 2/5 = 2/6

ILLUSTRATION 30.2

A and B are partners sharing profits and losses in the ratio of 5 : 3. They admit C as a partner. C requires his share *i.e.* 4/20 from A and 2/20 from B. Find out the new profit sharing ratio and sacrificing ratio.

(*B.Com., Madras*)

SOLUTION:

A's old ratio = $\frac{5}{8}$

A sacrifices to C = $\frac{4}{20}$

A's new share = $\frac{5}{8} - \frac{4}{20} = \frac{50-16}{80} = \frac{34}{80}$

B's old ratio = $\frac{3}{8}$

B sacrifices to C = $\frac{2}{20}$

B's new share = $\frac{3}{8} - \frac{2}{20} = \frac{30-8}{80} = \frac{22}{80}$

C's share = $\frac{4}{20} + \frac{2}{20} = \frac{6}{20}$ or $\frac{24}{80}$

New ratio of A, B and C = 34 : 22 : 24 or **17 : 11 : 12**

Sacrificing ratio = **2 : 1** (Already given)

ILLUSTRATION 30.3

A and B are partners sharing profit and loss in the ratio of 7 : 5. They take C into the partnership. C is given 1/6th share which he acquires 1/24 from A and 1/8 from B. Calculate the future profit sharing ratio and also sacrificing ratio.

(*B. Com. Delhi*)
MS.MK. Madras

SOLUTION:

Computation of profit sharing ratio:–

Old Ratio – Sacrificing Ratio - New Ratio (or) OR – SR = NR

$$A - \frac{7}{12} - \frac{1}{24} = \frac{14-1}{24} = \mathbf{\frac{13}{24}}$$

$$B - \frac{5}{12} - \frac{3}{24} = \frac{10-3}{24} = \mathbf{\frac{7}{24}}$$

$$C - \frac{1}{24} + \frac{1}{8} = \frac{1+3}{24} = \mathbf{\frac{4}{24}}$$

Future profit sharing ratio of A, B and C = **13 : 7 : 4**

Sacrificing Ratio (given) = **1:3**

ILLUSTRATION 30.4

A and B are in partnership sharing profits and losses in the ratio of 4 : 1. They have taken C into the partnership for 1/3 share of the profits. A and B, between themselves, agree to share future profits and losses equally. Calculate (a) future profit sharing ratio and (b) sacrificing ratio

(*B. Com. Andhra*)

SOLUTION:

(a) C is given $\frac{1}{3}$ rd share of profit

Balance available share = $1 - \frac{1}{3} = \frac{2}{3}$

$\frac{2}{3}$ is shared by A and B equally, *i.e.* $\frac{1}{3}$ each

So new profit sharing of A, B and C = **1 : 1 : 1**

(b) Sacrificing Ratio

$$A = \frac{4}{5} - \frac{1}{3} = \frac{12-5}{15} = \frac{7}{5} \text{(Sacrifices)}$$

$$B = \frac{1}{5} - \frac{1}{3} = \frac{3-5}{15} = \frac{-2}{15} \text{(Gains)}$$

$$C - \frac{1}{3}\text{(given)} = \frac{5}{15}\text{(gains)(New Ratio)}$$

A alone sacrifices $\frac{7}{15}$, of which B takes $\frac{2}{15}$ and C takes $\frac{5}{15}$

ILLUSTRATION 30.5

A and B are partners sharing profits and losses in the ratio 3 : 2. On Jan. 1, 2007, they agreed to admit Kamal as a partner on the following conditions:

(a) that he brings in Rs. 45,000

(b) that he further brings Rs. 10,000 as premium for goodwill, to be retained in the business

New Profit sharing ratio will be 4 : 3 : 2.

Show the journal entries

(B.Com. MK)

SOLUTION:

JOURNAL ENTRIES

			Rs	Rs
2007 Jan 1.	Bank Account To Kamal's Capital Account To A's Capital Account To B's Capital Account (Being capital introduced by kamal and premium credited to A and B, in Sacrificing Ratio)	Dr	55,000	 45,000 7,000 3,000

OR – NR = SR

$$A = \frac{3}{5} - \frac{4}{9} = \frac{27-20}{45} = \frac{7}{45} \text{ (Sacrifice)}$$

$$B = \frac{2}{5} - \frac{3}{9} = \frac{18-15}{45} = \frac{3}{45} \text{ (Sacrifice)}$$

$$C = \frac{7}{45} + \frac{3}{45} = \frac{10}{45} \text{ or } \frac{2}{9} \text{ (New Ratio)}$$

ILLUSTRATION 30.6

A, B and C are partners sharing profits equally. On 31st December 2006, their capitals were as follows:

A – Rs. 15,000

B – Rs. 10,000

C – Rs. 5,000

On 1st January 2007, they admit D as an equal partner, and he agreed to bring Rs. 4,000 as capital and Rs. 3,000 for goodwill. Each of the partners was to leave one half of his share of goodwill in the business and withdraw the other half.

Show the journal entries

(B. Com. Calicut)

SOLUTION

JOURNAL ENTRIES

			Rs	*Rs*
2007 Jan.1	Bank Acccount To D's Capital Account To Goodwill Account (Being capital and goodwill brought in)	Dr	7,000	 4,000 3,000

	Goodwill Account	Dr	3,000	
	To A's Capital Account			1,000
	To B's Capital Account			1,000
	To C's Capital Account			1,000
	(Being goodwill credited to A, B and C in Sacrificing Ratio)			
	A's Capital Account	Dr	500	
	B's Capital Account	Dr	500	
	C's Capital Account	Dr	500	
	To Bank Account			1,500
	(Being half of premium drawn by the partners)			

ILLUSTRATION 30.7

A and B were in partnership, sharing profits and losses in the ratio of 3 : 2. They took C into partnership for one-fifth share. But C was unable to pay any amount for goodwill although a goodwill account was raised in the books for Rs. 25,000 and which was written off accordingly.

Show the journal entries (*B. Com. Punjab*)

SOLUTION

JOURNAL ENTRIES

	Goodwill Account	Dr	25,000	
	To A's Capital Account			15,000
	To B's Capital Account			10,000
	(Being goodwill raised at its full value)			
	A's Capital Account	Dr	12,000	
	B's Capital Account	Dr	8,000	
	C's Capital Account	Dr	5,000	
	To Goodwill Account			25,000
	(Being goodwill written off)			
(OR)	C's Capital Account	Dr	5,000	
	To A's Capital Account			3,000
	To B's Capital Account			2,000
	(Being net adjustment for goodwill)			

ILLUSTRATION 30.8

P, Q and R, sharing profits and losses equally, have capitals of Rs. 20,000, Rs. 15,000 and Rs. 10,000 respectively. For the year 2006, interest was credited to them at 6% instead of 5%. Give adjusting journal entry

SOLUTION

JOURNAL ENTRIES

2007				
Jan. 1	P's Capital Account	Dr	50	
	To R's Capital Account			50
	(Excess charge of interest, now rectified)			

Workings:

	P	Q	R	Total
Interest already credited at 6%	1,200	900	600	2,700
Interest that should have been credited at 5%	1,000	750	500	2,250
Partners were over-credited thus, the net effect of increasing the profit for the firm	200	150	100	450
The increased profit is divided equally; Rs. 450	150	150	150	450
Net effect	(–)50	–	(+)50	–

ILLUSTRATION 30.9

A and B are partners in a business sharing profits in the ratio of 5 : 3. They decide to admit C into the firm giving him 1/6th share. Calculate the new profit sharing and sacrificing ratio of the partners.

(*B. Com. MS, MK*)

SOLUTION

Let the total profit of the new firm $= 1.$

Share given to C $= \frac{1}{6}$

Remainder $= 1 - \frac{1}{6} = \frac{5}{6}$

A's new share $= \frac{5}{6} \times \frac{5}{8} = \frac{25}{48}$

B's new share $= \frac{5}{6} \times \frac{3}{8} = \frac{15}{48}$

C's share $= \frac{1}{6} \text{ or } \frac{8}{48}$

New profit sharing of A, B and C $=$ **25: 15 : 8**

Sacrificing Ratio = Old Ratio – New Ratio

$$A = \frac{5}{8} - \frac{25}{48} = \frac{30-25}{48} = \frac{5}{48}$$

$$B = \frac{3}{8} - \frac{15}{48} = \frac{18-15}{48} \quad \frac{3}{48}$$

∴ Sacrificing Ratio of A and B = **5 : 3**

ILLUSTRATION 30.10

A and B are partners sharing profits in the ratio of 3 : 2. They admit C into partnership, C paying a premium of Rs 1,000 for 1/4 share of profit. No goodwill account appears in the books. They withdraw the amount of goodwill. Journalise.

(*B.Com., Madras, MK*)

SOLUTION

JOURNAL ENTRIES

			Rs	*Rs*
	Cash Account	Dr.	1,000	
	To Goodwill Account			1,000
	(Cash brought by C for goodwill)			
	Goodwill Account	Dr.	1,000	
	To A's Capital Account			600
	To B's Capital Account			400
	(Goodwill credited in sacrificing ratio)			
	A's Capital Account	Dr.	600	
	B's Capital Account	Dr.	400	
	To Cash Account			1,000
	(Cash withdrawn by old partners)			

ILLUSTRATION 30.11

A and B are partners sharing profits in the ratio of 3 : 2 with capitals of Rs 12,000 and Rs 5,400 respectively. C is admitted as a new partner for 1/3 share of profits with a capital of Rs 7,500. Adjust the capitals of them in the new profit sharing ratio.

Give necessary journal entries. (*B.Com., Bharathidasan, Manonmanian*)

SOLUTION

New profit sharing ratio of A, B and C = **6 : 4 : 5**

Total Capital of the firm, on the basis of C's Capital

$$= \text{Rs } 7{,}500 \times \frac{3}{1} = \text{Rs } \mathbf{22{,}500}$$

$$\therefore \text{ A's Capital should be } \left(\text{Rs } 22{,}500 \times \frac{6}{15}\right) = \text{Rs } \mathbf{9{,}000}$$

$$\therefore \text{ B's Capital should be } \left(\text{Rs } 22{,}500 \times \frac{4}{15}\right) = \text{Rs } \mathbf{6{,}000}$$

Excess Capital of A = Rs 12,000 – Rs 9,000 = Rs **3,000**

Deficit Capital of B = Rs 6,000 – Rs 5,400 = Rs **600**

JOURNAL ENTRIES

			Rs	*Rs*
	A's Capital Account To A's Current Account (Excess Capital transferred to Current A/c)	Dr.	3,000	3,000
	B's Current Account To B's Capital Account (Deficit in Capital account adjusted)	Dr.	600	600

Capital Accounts

	A	*B*	*C*		*A*	*B*	*C*
	Rs	*Rs*	*Rs*		*Rs*	*Rs*	*Rs*
To Current A/c	3,000	–	–	By Balance b/d	12,000	5,400	–
To Balance c/d	9,000	6,000	7,500	By Cash A/c	–	–	7,500
				By Current A/c	–	600	–
	12,000	6,000	7,500		12,000	6,000	7,500
				By Balance b/d	9,000	6,000	7,500

ILLUSTRATION 30.12

A, B and C are partners sharing profits and losses in the ratio of 3 : 2 : 1. They admit D and gave him a quarter share of profit. This share was contributed by all of them in the ratio of 2 : 3 : 1. Find out new profit sharing ratio of all. (*B.Com . Calicut*)

SOLUTION

Sacrificing ratios of the old partners are given in the problem. If it is calculated, one will get the same ratio. It is shown below:

D's share = 1/4 which is contributed by A, B and C in 2 : 3 : 1 ratio.

$$\text{A's sacrifice} = \frac{1}{4} \times \frac{2}{6} = \frac{2}{24}$$

B's sacrifice = $\frac{1}{4} \times \frac{3}{6} = \frac{3}{24}$

C's sacrifice = $\frac{1}{4} \times \frac{1}{6} = \frac{1}{24}$

Thus, the sacrificing ratio = 2 : 3 : 1 (as given)

The new profit sharing ratio is calculated by deducting the sacrifice ratios from their respective old profit sharing ratio, thus.

New ratio = Old Ratio – Sacrifice Ratio

A's New Ratio = $\frac{3}{6} - \frac{2}{24} = \frac{12-2}{24} = \frac{10}{24}$

B's New Ratio = $\frac{2}{6} - \frac{3}{24} = \frac{8-3}{24} = \frac{5}{24}$

C's New Ratio = $\frac{1}{6} - \frac{1}{24} = \frac{4-1}{24} = \frac{3}{24}$

D gets $\frac{1}{4}$ share of profit *i.e.*, $\frac{2}{24} + \frac{3}{24} + \frac{1}{24}$ or $\frac{6}{24}$ or $\frac{1}{6}$

Net Profit

Ratio of A, B, C and D = 10 : 5 : 3 : 6.

ILLUSTRATION 30.13

A and B are partners sharing profits and losses in the ratio of 2 : 1. They admit C for 1/4th share. Later, i.e., after C's admission, they admit D for 1/5th share.

Calculate new profit sharing ratio.

SOLUTION:

New profit and loss sharing ratio, after C's admission:

C : $\frac{1}{4}$

A : $\frac{3}{4} \times \frac{2}{3} = \frac{2}{4}$

B : $\frac{3}{4} \times \frac{1}{3} = \frac{1}{4}$

New profit and loss sharing ratio of A, B and C = 2 : 1 : 1

New profit and loss sharing ratio, after D's admission:

D : $\frac{1}{5}$

A = $\frac{4}{5} \times \frac{2}{4} = \frac{2}{5}$

B = $\frac{4}{5} \times \frac{1}{4} = \frac{1}{5}$

C = $\frac{4}{5} \times \frac{1}{4} = \frac{1}{5}$

New profit and loss sharing ratio of A, B, C and D = 2 : 1 : 1 : 1.

ILLUSTRATION 30.14

Ravi and Murali are partners sharing profits and losses as 7 : 5. Vidya is admitted as a partner on the condition that Vidya should bring in Rs 20,000 as capital and pay Rs 15,000 as premium for Goodwill. The future profit sharing ratio amongst the partners is 9 : 6 : 5. Give journal entries. (*B.Com., Madurai*)

SOLUTION

Goodwill is credited to old partners' capital accounts on the basis of sacrificing ratio.

Sacrificing Ratio = Old Ratio – New Ratio

	Old Proportion	New Proportion	Sacrificing
Ravi	$\frac{7}{12}$	$\frac{9}{20}$	$\frac{8}{60}\left(\frac{35-27}{60}=\frac{8}{60}\right)$
Murali	$\frac{5}{12}$	$\frac{6}{20}$	$\frac{7}{60}\left(\frac{25-18}{60}=\frac{7}{60}\right)$
Vidya	–	$\frac{5}{20}$	
Total	1	1	–

JOURNAL ENTRIES

			Rs	Rs
	Cash Account	Dr.	35,000	
	To Vidya Capital A/c			35,000
	(Being cash brought by Vidya)			
	Vidya Capital Account	Dr.	15,000	
	To Ravi Capital Account			8,000
	To Murali Capital Account			7,000
	(Being goodwill credited to old partners' capital account in Sacrificing Ratio 8 : 7)			

Ratio and Proportion

If the profit earned by a firm is taken as one unit, share of each partner in such unit is called Ratio or Proportion. Ratio is expressed by integers *i.e.* in whole number. Proportion is expressed in terms of fractions. For instance, A and B are equal partners; their profit sharing ratio is 1 : 1 or their profit sharing proportion is 1/2 and 1/2. Further example, A, B and C are partners; their profit sharing ratio is 2 : 2 : 1 or their profit sharing proportion is 2/5, 2/5 and 1/5.

II. ADJUSTMENT FOR REVALUATION OF ASSETS AND LIABILITIES

When a new partner is admitted, the existing assets and liabilities are to be revalued. To avoid any undue gain or loss to the incoming partner, the existing partners sometimes revalue the assets and liabilities. The revaluation can be done in two ways:

(1) When assets and liabilities are revalued, the revised values are shown in the books of accounts.

(2) When the assets and liabilities are revalued, revised values are not to be shown in the books of accounts.

(1) When Assets and Liabilities Revalued and the Revised Values are shown in the books of Accounts

When a new partner takes admission in a firm, it is desirable for him as well as the existing partners to verify the correctness as to the values of assets and liabilities in order to satisfy themselves. It is also proper from the point of view of both. There may be depreciations (decrease) or appreciations (increase) in the values of assets and liabilities. For this purpose, the assets and liabilities are valued and the decrease and increase are brought into a separate account known as PROFIT AND LOSS ADJUSTMENT ACCOUNT (also known as REVALUATION ACCOUNT) which is a nominal account. Any profit or loss that arises out of revaluation account should be credited or debited to the old partners' capital account in their old profit sharing ratio. Following are the journal entries on revaluation. It can be written in three groups. They are:

(*a*) *For Profit Items:*

For any increase in the value of assets	Assets Account To Revaluation Account	Dr.
For any decrease in the value of liabilities	Liabilities Account To Revaluation Account	Dr.

(*b*) *For Loss Items:*

For any decrease in the value of assets	Revaluation Account To Assets Account	Dr.
For any increase in the value of liabilities	Revaluation Account To Liabilities Account	Dr.

(*c*) *For Transferring the Profit or Loss on Revaluation Account:*

For Profit on Revaluation Account	Revaluation Account To Old Partners' Capital Account	Dr.
For any Loss on Revaluation Account	Old Partners' Capital Account To Revaluation Account	Dr.

ILLUSTRATION 30.15

X and Y were in partnership sharing profits and losses in the ratio of 3 : 1. On 31st December 2005, their Balance Sheet stood as under:

Balance Sheet of X and Y
as on 31st December 2005

	Rs		*Rs*
Sundry Creditors	37,500	Cash at Bank	22,500
Capitals:		Bills Receivable	3,000
X	40,000	Sundry Debtors	16,000
Y	10,000	Stock	20,000
		Furniture	1,000
		Buildings	25,000
	87,500		87,500

On that date they admit Z as a new partner on the following terms:

(*a*) To create a goodwill in the firm for Rs 20,000.

(*b*) Stock and Furniture to be depreciated by 10%.

(*c*) Buildings to be appreciated by 20%.

(*d*) Reserve for doubtful debts to be created to the extent of 5% on Debtors.

(*e*) Z pays Rs 10,000 as his share of Capital.

Pass journal entries to give effect to these arrangements, and show the Revaluation Account, Capital Accounts and the Balance Sheet of the new firm. (*B.Com., MK*)

SOLUTION:

Journal Entries

Date	Particulars		Dr. Rs	Cr. Rs
2005 Dec. 31	Revaluation A/c	Dr.	2,900	
	To Stock A/c			2,000
	To Furniture A/c			100
	To Reserve for Bad Debts A/c			800
	(Being Stock and furniture depreciated and a provision for Bad Debts created)			
	Building Account	Dr.	5,000	
	To Revaluation A/c			5,000
	(Being the Building appreciated)			
	Revaluation A/c	Dr.	2,100	
	To X Capital A/c			1,575
	To Y Capital A/c			525
	(Being profit on Profit and Loss Adjustment account transferred to old partners' capital)			
	Goodwill Account	Dr.	20,000	
	To X Capital Account			15,000
	To Y Capital Account			5,000
	(Being goodwill raised and credited to old partners' capital accounts)			
	Bank Account	Dr.	10,000	
	To Z Capital Account			10,000
	(Being capital contributed by Z)			

Dr. **Revaluation Account** Cr.

	Rs		Rs
To Stock A/c	2,000	By Building A/c	5,000
To Furniture A/c	100		
To Reserve for Bad Debts	800		
To Capitals : X (profit)	1,575		
Y (profit)	525		
	5,000		5,000

Dr. **Capital Accounts** Cr.

	X	Y	Z		X	Y	Z
	Rs	Rs	Rs		Rs	Rs	Rs
To Balance c/d	56,575	15,525	10,000	By Balance b/d	40,000	10,000	–
				By Revaluation A/c	1,575	525	–
				By Goodwill	15,000	5,000	–
				By Cash	–	–	10,000
	56,575	15,525	10,000		56,575	15,525	10,000
				By Balance b/d	56,575	15,525	10,000

Balance Sheet of New Firm
as on 31st December 2005

Liabilities		*Rs*	*Assets*		*Rs*
Sundry Creditors		37,500	Cash		32,500
Capital Account	X: 56,575		Bills Receivable		3,000
	Y: 15,525		Sundry Debtors	16,000	
	Z: 10,000	82,100	*Less*: Provision	800	15,200
			Stock		18,000
			Furniture		900
			Building		30,000
			Goodwill		20,000
		1,19,600			1,19,600

ILLUSTRATION 30.16

The following was the Balance Sheet of A, B and C sharing Profit and Losses in the proportion of 6/14, 5/14 and 3/14 respectively:

		Rs		Rs
Creditors		18,900	Land & Buildings	50,400
Bills Payable		6,300	Furniture	7,350
Reserve		7,000	Stock	29,400
Capitals:			Debtors	26,460
A	39,900		Cash at Bank	8,890
B	33,600			
C	16,800	90,300		
		1,22,500		1,22,500

They agreed to take 'D' into partnership and give him 1/8 share of the profits on the following terms:

(*a*) That *D* brings in Rs 10,000 as his capital.

(*b*) That Furniture be written down by Rs. 920 and Stock be depreciated by 10%.

(*c*) That provision of Rs. 1,320 be made for outstanding repair bills.

(*d*) That the value of Land and Buildings be written up to Rs. 65,100

(*e*) That the value of goodwill be fixed at Rs. 8,820

(*f*) That the capital of A, B and C be adjusted on the basis of D's capital by opening Current Accounts.

Give the necessary journal entries and also the Balance Sheet of the firm as newly constituted.

(*B.Com. Bharathiar)*

SOLUTION:

A, B AND C'S JOURNAL

Date	*Particulars*		*Debit* *Rs.*	*Credit* *Rs.*
	Reserve A/c	Dr.	7,000	
	To A's Capital A/c			3,000
	" B's Capital A/c			2,500
	" C's Capital A/c			1,500
	(For dividing reserve amongst old partners in their original ratios)			
	Revaluation A/c	Dr.	5,180	
	To Furniture			920
	" Provision for Outstanding Repair Bills			1,320
	" Provision for Stock			2,940
	(For writing down assets and creating provisions)			

Land and Buildings A/c	Dr.	14,700	
To Revaluation A/c			14,700
(For appreciation in the value of land and buildings)			
Revaluation A/c	Dr.	9,520	
To A's Capital A/c			4,080
" B's Capital A/c			3,400
" C's Capital A/c			2,040
(For dividing profit on revaluation)			
Bank A/c	Dr.	10,000	
To D's Capital A/c			10,000
(For D's contribution towards capital)			
Goodwill A/c	Dr.	8,820	
To A's Capital A/c			3,780
" B's Capital A/c			3,150
" C's Capital A/c			1,890
(For adjusting goodwill to old partners' capital accounts)			
A's Capital A/c	Dr.	20,760	
B's Capital A/c	Dr.	17,650	
C's Capital A/c	Dr.	7,230	
To A's Current A/c			20,760
To B's Current A/c			17,650
To C's Current A/c			7,230
(For transferring excess of capital over profit proportions to respective current accounts)			

BALANCE SHEET OF A, B, C AND D as at ....

		Rs.			Rs.
Creditors		18,900	Land and Buildings		65,100
Bills Payable		6,300	Furniture		6,430
Outstanding Repair Bill		1,320	Stock	29,400	
Capital Accounts:			*Less:* Provision	2,940	26,460
A	30,000		Debtors		26,460
B	25,000		Cash at Bank		18,890
C	15,000		Goodwill		8,820
D	10,000	80,000			
Current Accounts:					
A	20,760				
B	17,650				
C	7,230	45,640			
		1,52,160			1,52,160

Computation of new ratios:

D's share is 1/8. Hence the balance, 1 – 1/8 = 7/8 to be shared by A, B and C

A would get 6/14 of 7/8 = 42/112

B would get 5/14 of 7/8 = 35/112

C would get 3/14 of 7/8 = 21/112

D would get 1/8 or = 14/112

Dividing both numerator and denominator by 7, the new ratios would be

A : 42/112 or 6/16

B: 35/112 or 5/16

C : 21/112 or 3/16

D: 14/112 or 2/16

If D brings in Rs. 10,000 for 1/8 share, the total capital of the firm should be 10,000 × 8 = Rs. 80,000.

A's 6/16 share of the total capital	$= \dfrac{80,000 \times 5}{16}$	= Rs. 30,000
B's 5/16th share of total capital		= 25,000
C's 3/16th share of total capital		= 15,000

A's present capital after all the adjustments	Rs. 50,760
A's capital for 6/16th share	30,000
Excess transferred to his Current Account	20,760
Similarly, B's capital after adjustments	Rs. 42,650
B's capital for 5/16th share	25,000
Excess transferred to B's Current Account	17,650
Similarly, C's capital after adjustments	22,230
C's capital for 3/16th share	15,000
Excess transferred to C's Current Account	7,230

2. When the Assets and Liabilities Revalued but Not to be Shown in the books of Accounts

Sometimes the existing partners and the new partner decide that the revaluation of assets and liabilities should not be shown in the books of the new firm. In such a circumstance, all journal entries passed through Revaluation Account are reversed. For instance, if earlier, the Revaluation Account is debited and the Building Account is credited, the reverse entry is that Building Account is debited and the Revaluation Account is credited. That is, there is another Revaluation Account for the purpose of restoring the assets and liabilities at their original values. As said earlier that what is done, is reversed by passing reversal entries. Thus, two Revaluation Accounts are prepared, one to revalue the assets and liabilities and the other to restore them at original values. The combination of two such accounts is known as MEMORANDUM REVALUATION ACCOUNT. In the first section, the Revaluation Account is debited or credited with the difference in the book figures in respect of all changes in the assets and liabilities; and is balanced and the balance is transferred to the old partners' capital account in their Old Profit Sharing Ratio. By this, the first section of the Memorandum Revaluation Account is closed. In the second section, reversal entries (of the changes made in the first section) are recorded. That is, the effect of the first section of Memorandum Revaluation is nullified by the second revaluation, making the final result zero. Hence the Memorandum Revaluation Account.

It is important to note:

1. The profit or loss of the first section is transferred to the old partners' capital account in the *old profit and loss sharing ratio.*
2. The profit or loss of the second section is transferred to all the partners' capital account, including the new partner, in the *new profit and loss sharing ratio.*
3. If the first section shows a gain, then the second section shows a loss and vice versa.
4. When Balance Sheet is drawn, all assets and liabilities appear at the original values.
5. There will be certain changes in the Capital Accounts of all the partners due to such Memorandum Revaluation Account.

ILLUSTRATION 30.17

The following was the Balance Sheet of A and B who were sharing profit two-thirds and one-third, on 31st December 2005.

	Rs		*Rs*
Creditors	65,900	Cash at Bank	1,200
Capitals :		Sundry Debtors	9,700
A	30,000	Stock	20,000

B	20,000	Plant and Machinery	35,000
		Buildings	50,000
	1,15,900		1,15,900

They agreed to admit C into partnership on the following terms:

(1) C was to be given one-third share in profit and was to bring Rs 15,000 as capital.
(2) That the value of Stock and Plant and Machinery were to be reduced by 10%.
(3) That a provision of 5% was to be created for doubtful debts.
(4) That the Building Account was to be appreciated by Rs 9,500.
(5) Investments worth Rs 400 (not mentioned in the Balance Sheet) were taken into account.
(6) That the value of liabilities and assets other than cash are not to be altered.

Prepare Memorandum Revaluation Account, Capital Accounts and the Balance Sheet of the newly reconstituted firm. *(B.Com., Madurai, Delhi, Poona)*

Dr. **Memorandum Revaluation Account** Cr.

		Rs			*Rs*
To Stock		2,000	By Building		9,500
To Plant		3,500	By Investment		400
To Provision for Doubtful Debts		485			
To Profit transferred to Capital Accounts:					
A 2/3	2,610				
B 1/3	1,305	3,915			
		9,900			9,900
To Reversal of credit entries of first revaluation (Rs. 9500 + Rs. 400)		9,900	By Reversal of debit entries of first revaluation (Rs. 2000 + 3500 + 485)		5,985
			By Loss transferred to Capital Accounts:		
			A 4/9	1,740	
			B 2/9	870	
			C 3/9	1,305	3,915
		9,900			9,900

Dr. **Capital Accounts** Cr.

	A	*B*	*C*		*A*	*B*	*C*
	Rs	Rs	Rs		Rs	Rs	Rs
To Loss on Revaluation A/c	1,740	870	1,305	By Balance b/d	30,000	20,000	–
To Balance c/d	30,870	20,435	13,695	By Profit on Revaluation A/c	2,610	1,305	–
				By Cash A/c			15,000
	32,610	21,305	15,000		32,610	21,305	15,000
				By Balance b/d	30,870	20,435	13,695

Balance Sheet as on 31st December 2005

Liabilities	*Rs*	*Assets*	*Rs*
Creditors	65,900	Cash	16,200
Capital Accounts:		Sundry Debtors	9,700

A	30,870		Stock	20,000
B	20,435	65,000	Plant	35,000
C	13,695		Buildings	50,000
		1,30,900		1,30,900

III. ADJUSTMENT FOR GOODWILL

Goodwill Defined. In a comprehensive sense "Goodwill" may be defined as an attribute of a business which enables a concern to earn super-profits in excess of normal return. That is, super-profits mean additional profits over normal profits. The concept of goodwill can be understood on the basis of its operational significance. Goodwill is what goodwill does. It brings in more customers to a firm, without much persuasion. Goodwill arises mainly on account of (1) Good reputation of the owners, (2) Established popularity of products, (3) Effectiveness of Advertising, (4) Favourable Locality, (5) Monopoly and (6) Non-availability of similar products etc. There can be goodwill only for established business. Goodwill is reputation with which a business attracts more customers, more sales, in turn earning more profits. So, it is treated as an asset. Goodwill is like any other property of the firm, came into existence gradually and is not tangible. Despite this difference, it is a valuable asset for a successful firm. Sometimes, a firm may be able to get more for its goodwill than for the tangible assets. Therefore, it is not proper to treat goodwill as fictitious one. No doubt, it is intangible i.e. cannot be seen or felt or touched, but it is valuable in case of profitable concerns. It is an intangible asset arising out of the super earning capacity of a firm. Without the reasonable probability of the earning of future super profit, no present value in the form of goodwill can exist. In case a firm is not going and is not successful, there will be no value attached to goodwill; if any value appears, then it will be not only intangible but also fictitious. Goodwill arises only if a firm earns extra profits, which is called super profits. There are two points : (1) When one buys a business, he will be able to get profits in future only and is not concerned with the past profits at all. (2) Goodwill is paid for the ability to earn super profits and not for ordinary profits. Goodwill is the value of reputation of a firm in respect of profits expected in future over and above the normal profits. The value of goodwill depends upon such factors as favourable location of business, nature of the business, managerial efficiency, reputation of the firm, special attraction offered to customers, pleasing service, superior quality of its product, etc. The excess over the normal profit, called the superprofit, is the tangible evidence of goodwill.

"Goodwill is nothing more than the probability that the old customers will resort to the old place."

"Goodwill is the value of the reputation which the business builds due to its efficient service to its customers and quality of its products."

Need for Valuing Goodwill

The original partners have taken pain to bring the business into a well-established business. In the beginning stage, they undertake risk by investing their money in new business. A firm may become a well established one and attract customers and this leads to super profit-earning capacity. It is because of past endeavours. When a new partner is admitted, the existing partners have to sacrifice a portion of the profit for the new partner. The newcomer invests his capital in a business, where there is no risk. For enjoying the right to participate in the future profits of the firm, the new partner has to compensate the existing partners, who sacrifice a portion of their share of profit. Therefore, the newcomer has to pay something extra to the old partners, in addition to the capital, to compensate them. This extra payment is made for goodwill, that exists in the business. Thus goodwill may be considered as a compensation paid by the newcomer to the old partners for their past efforts and the risk of capital that they took and for their agreeing to sacrifice a share of future profits. Therefore, valuation of goodwill is necessary at the time of admission.

Indications for the Existence of Goodwill

There are a number of contributing factors responsible for the existence of goodwill. The following are some of the deciding factors in favour of the existence of goodwill:

1. In a manufacturing firm, the quality, standardisation, and price of a product etc. are important factors.
2. In a distribution firm, the terms and conditions of the credit facility etc. are important.
3. In bank services, the safety of money deposited, liberal policy of lending, prompt services etc. are indicators of goodwill.
4. In hotels, the taste and quality of the food, cleanliness and courteous service etc. are indicators of goodwill.
5. In a firm of Doctors, the diagnostic ability, surgical dexterity are evidence for goodwill.
6. In a firm of Chartered Accountants, the sharp insight is an indication of goodwill.
7. In a provision store, the courtesy shown to the customers, supply of good quality items at reasonable price etc. are the proof of existence of goodwill.

Because of all these special attractions, a firm may attract many customers, in turn more sales, in turn more profits, in turn establish the existence of goodwill. The goodwill is a silent super-salesman and an attractive force by which customers become invitees without persuasion.

Methods of Valuing Goodwill

The usual methods of computing the value of goodwill are:

(1) Average Profit Method

The average profit method of computation of goodwill is a simple but unscientific device. The value of goodwill is calculated on the basis of the average profit for the past few years and the average is multiplied by the agreed number of years during which it is anticipated. For instance, a firm had earned profit during the last four years as follows :

2002	Rs 20,000
2003	Rs 15,000
2004	Rs 17,000
2005	Rs 18,000

Suppose the goodwill of a partnership is agreed to be valued at two years purchase of the average profits of last four years, then the goodwill is calculated as follows:

Total of 4 years profit = 70,000

Annual Average profit = 70,000/4 = Rs 17,500

The value of goodwill Rs 17,500 × 2 = Rs 35,000

(2) Super Profit Method

Under this method, goodwill is considered to be equal to a certain number of year's purchase of the super profit of the business concerned. Super profit is taken as a basis for calculating goodwill. Super profit is the difference (*i.e.* excess) between the average annual earning (Actual) and the normal return of capital invested in similar business. In other words, excess of average profit over normal yield is known as SUPER PROFIT. This super profit is multiplied by number of years (as mentioned in Partnership Deed) so as to get the amount of goodwill. For instance, if average annual profit of a business is Rs 40,000 on capital invested Rs 3,00,000 and the normal earning capacity of similar business is 8%. Then the super profit is calculated as follows:

Average Profit = Rs 40,000

Normal Annual Return = 8% of Rs 3,00,000 = Rs 24,000

Super Profit = 40,000 – 24,000 = Rs 16,000

If goodwill is agreed to be valued at 3 years' purchase of the super profit, then the goodwill is Rs 16,000 × 3 = Rs 48,000.

(3) Capitalisation Method

The average profit is capitalised on the basis of normal rate of return and then excess of this capitalised amount over the net assets of the firm is goodwill.

$$\text{Goodwill} = \left(\frac{\text{Average Profit} \times 100}{\text{Percentage of normal returns}}\right) - \text{Net Assets}$$

ILLUSTRATION 30.18

The average profit of a firm is Rs 9,000. The firm's capital is Rs 60,000 and the normal return on business is expected at 10%. Find out goodwill by capitalisation method.

SOLUTION

$$\text{Goodwill} = \frac{\text{Average Profit} \times 100}{\text{Percentage of normal returns}} - \text{Net Assets}$$

$$= \left(\frac{9{,}000 \times 100}{10}\right) - \text{Rs } 60{,}000$$

$$= \text{Rs } 90{,}000 - \text{Rs } 60{,}000$$

$$= \text{Rs } 30{,}000$$

Alternatively:

Super profit = Rs 9,000 – 6,000 = Rs **3,000**

Normal Return = 10%

Capitalised value = 3,000/10% = 3,000 × 100/10 = Rs **30,000**

ILLUSTRATION 30.19

Calculate the value of goodwill in the following cases:

(*a*) The goodwill of a firm is estimated at three years purchase of the average profits of the preceding four years. The profits were :

2002 Rs 8,000; 2003 Rs 10,000; 2004 Rs 16,000 and 2005 Rs 14,000

(*b*) In a firm, the total capital invested is Rs 1,00,000 and the normal rate of interest is 10%. The remuneration for the services of partners is estimated at Rs 6,000. The average profit for the last 5 years is Rs 20,000. Goodwill is to be estimated at three years purchase of the super profits.

(*c*) A firm earned a net profit of Rs 15,000 with a capital of Rs 1,00,000. The normal rate of return in similar industry is 10%. Use the method of capitalisation of super profits.

SOLUTION

(*a*) Average profits of the last four years $= \dfrac{8{,}000 + 10{,}000 + 16{,}000 + 14{,}000}{4}$

$= \dfrac{48{,}000}{4} = 12{,}000$

Three years of purchase of average profit = 12,000 × 3 = Rs 36,000

Therefore, value of goodwill = Rs 36,000

(*b*) Average profit	= Rs 20,000
Less: Normal return	
@ 10% on Rs 1,00,000	10,000
	10,000

Less: Salary estimated:	6,000
	4,000

Value of goodwill on the basis of three years purchase of super profits = Rs 4,000 × 3 = Rs **12,000**

(*c*) The required amount of capital to earn a

profit of Rs 15,000 @ 10% = Rs $\frac{15,000 \times 100}{10}$ = Rs 1,50,000

Less: Capital employed in the business 1,00,000

50,000

Thus capitalised value of goodwill = Rs **50,000**

Alternatively:

Actual profits	15,000
Less: Normal profit on capital employed at 10%	10,000
	5,000

The capitalised value of super profits at 10% return = $5,000 \times \frac{100}{10}$ = Rs **50,000**

The question of goodwill arises in partnership in the following cases:

1. Change in profit sharing ratio.
2. On the admission of a new partner.
3. On the retirement or death of a partner.
4. On amalgamation of firms.
5. On dissolution of firms.
6. On sale of a firm, etc.

1. Change in the Profit Sharing Ratio

If the existing partners decide to make a change in the existing profit sharing ratio, the future profit sharing will be different from the existing ratio. By making changes in the profit sharing ratio, some partner will lose his share of the profit in future and some partner will gain. The partner, who gains in the new ratio, will have to compensate the losing partner. In other words, one partner makes a purchase of a share of profits from one partner, who was enjoying it previously. For instance, A and B are partners sharing profits in the ratio of 2 : 1. They mutually agreed to make changes in the profit sharing ratio as 1 : 1, then A is forgoing or selling to B 1/6th share of profits. Because the mutual profit sharing ratio changes, now A gets 3/6 (2/3 – 1/6) and B gets 3/6 (1/3 + 1/6). That is, 1/6th share of profit is gained by B and to that extent A is losing. If the profit is Rs 60,000, according to old profit sharing ratio, A gets Rs 40,000 and B gets Rs 20,000. After the change of profit sharing ratio, A and B get equal share *i.e.* each gets Rs 30,000. Thus, now A loses Rs 10,000, which is a gain to B. Therefore, B will pay to A an amount equal to 1/6th of the total value of goodwill. If the total value of goodwill is Rs 18,000, B must pay to A 1/6th of Rs 18,000 *i.e.* Rs 3,000.

ILLUSTRATION 30.20

A and B are trading in partnership sharing profits and losses in the ratio of 3 : 1. As from 1st January 2005, it was decided to change the profit sharing ratio to 3 : 2. Goodwill will be valued at two years' purchase of the average of three years' profits. The profits for 2002 Rs 15,000; 2003 Rs 20,000 and 2004 Rs 25,000. Pass the necessary journal entry to give effect to the arrangement.

SOLUTION

		Rs
Total profit	2002	15,000
	2003	20,000
	2004	25,000
		60,000

$$\text{Average profit} = \frac{\text{Rs } 60{,}000}{3} = \text{Rs } 20{,}000$$

Goodwill at two years' purchase = Rs 20,000 × 2 = Rs 40,000

	Old Ratio	New Ratio
A	3/4	3/5
B	1/4	2/5

A loses = 3/4 – 3/5 = 15 – 12/20 = 3/20

B gains = 2/5 – 1/4 = 8 – 5/20 = 3/20

$$\text{Compensation (goodwill) payable by B} = 40{,}000 \times \frac{3}{20} = \mathbf{6{,}000}$$

Journal Entry

			Rs	*Rs*
2005				
Jan. 1	B's Capital A/c	Dr.	6,000	
	To A's Capital A/c			6,000

Goodwill – Accounting Treatment

Once the value of goodwill is arrived at, the next step is to account it, in the books of the firm. The various possibilities of accounting treatment, in brief, are:

1. Premium Method

This is a method, where a new partner is asked to bring in *cash* against goodwill which is adjusted in the old partners' capital accounts. They are of three types:

(*a*) The amount of goodwill, brought in by the incoming partners, is paid to the old partners, as it is a private transaction. Hence no journal entry.

(*b*) This method is adopted when a new partner is required to bring in cash towards the goodwill – equal to his share of goodwill. This amount is adjusted to the old partners' capital accounts in the sacrificing ratio. The amount may be retained in the firm as an additional working capital.

(*c*) The premium brought in by the incoming partner is credited to old partners, in the sacrificing ratio, but the amount is withdrawn by the old partners.

2. Revaluation Method

Sometimes, the old partners allow the newcomer to become a partner in the business, without paying anything for goodwill. But the goodwill is worked out, valued and is adjusted to the old partners' capital accounts in the old profit sharing ratio.

3. Memorandum Revaluation Method

Here also the newcomer, who becomes a partner, does not bring any amount as goodwill. The goodwill is first raised by crediting the old partners' capital accounts in the old profit sharing ratio and after the admission, the goodwill is written off among all the partners, including the new partner, in the new profit sharing ratio.

The various methods of treating goodwill in the books of the firm at the time of admission of a new partner are:

(1) When Goodwill is Brought in Cash and not Recorded in the Books

The goodwill amount brought in by the newcomer is not shown in the books of account. Many occasions are there where the amount of goodwill is not brought into the firm but the old partners are paid by the new partners as if it is an outside transaction. This system is not scientific as it avoids income tax and leads to black money. This is not a healthy practice in the business. Since the matter is settled out of the firm privately, no journal entry is necessary.

(2) When the Goodwill is Received in Cash and Retained in the Business

The amount of goodwill brought in by the incoming partner is taken to the books of account. The existing partners apportion the goodwill among themselves in the sacrificing ratio. The amount is retained in the business as additional working capital. The following entries are made:

When the amount is brought in by the incoming partner as Capital and Goodwill	Bank Account To Incoming Partner's Capital A/c	Dr.
When the Goodwill is credited to the existing partners' Capital Account.	Incoming Partner's Capital A/c To Existing Partners' Capital A/c	Dr.

If the sacrificing ratio is not known, then the amount of goodwill is credited to the existing partners' Capital Accounts in the old profit sharing ratio. This is because the ratio of their sacrificing coincides with their old profit sharing ratio.

(3) When the Amount of Goodwill is Received by the Firm and is Withdrawn by the Old Partners

The amount of goodwill brought in by the incoming partner is credited to the existing partners with their respective share of goodwill and they may withdraw the amount fully or partially. In the previous method, the cash is retained in the business as an additional capital, but under this method, the existing partners withdraw either full or partially the amount of goodwill. Thus, in addition to the above entries in (2) above, the following entry is needed to record the withdrawals of the amount by the existing partners:

When cash is withdrawn by the old partners	Old Partners' Capital Account To Bank Account	Dr.	

(4) When the Goodwill is raised at its Full Value

Very often, the incoming partner is not in a position to bring anything in cash for goodwill. Under this circumstance it becomes desirable to bring the goodwill at its full value by debiting the goodwill and crediting the old partners' Capital Account in their old profit sharing ratio. This allows full credit to all the old partners for their interest in the overall goodwill. Goodwill Account then appears as an asset in the firm's Balance Sheet. It is not necessary that it should be allowed to stand there for an indefinite period. After crediting the goodwill to the old partners, their capital accounts increase and thus the firm's status as regards the earning capacity descends from super earning to the normal earning one. At this stage any share in partnership firm that is assigned to the incoming partner refers to the normal profit as against super profit. Therefore, the newcomer cannot be asked for any extra payment because none gains or sacrifices super profit. When the purpose is fulfilled the goodwill is written back to partners of newly constituted firm in the new profit sharing ratio.

The journal entries are:

When goodwill is raised in the books at full value	Goodwill Account To Old Partners' Capital A/c (Old ratio)	Dr.

The raised goodwill is written off	All Partners' Capital Account To Goodwill Account (Goodwill written off including new partner in the new profit sharing ratio)	Dr.

(5) When Goodwill is already appearing in the Books

If the goodwill appearing in the books coincides with its present value, no entry whatsoever is required at the time of admission of a partner. If the goodwill appears in the books at a value lower than the value at present, then the difference between the present value and the value appearing in the books may be credited to the old partners' capital account in the old profit sharing ratio by debiting the goodwill account. If the value of goodwill appearing in the books is higher, then the difference *i.e.* the excess value, is debited to the old partners' capital account in their old profit sharing ratio and credit is given to goodwill account.

ILLUSTRATION 30.21

A and B are partners sharing profits in the ratio 2 : 1. They admit C as a partner for 1/4th share. His share of goodwill is Rs 9,000. Give journal entries in the following cases:

(1) When the amount of goodwill is paid privately.
(2) When the goodwill is received in cash and retained in the business.
(3) When the goodwill is received in cash and withdrawn by old partners.
(4) When goodwill is raised at full value and then written back.
(5) When the goodwill is already shown in the books at Rs 27,000.
(6) When the goodwill is already shown in the books at Rs 42,000.

SOLUTION

Journal Entries

			Dr. *Rs*	Cr. *Rs*
(1)	NO ENTRY			
(2)	Cash Account	Dr.	9,000	
	To A Capital Account			6,000
	To B Capital Account			3,000
	(Being the goodwill amount credited to old partners' Capital Account: sacrificing ratio 2 : 1)			
(3)	Cash Account	Dr.	9,000	
	To A Capital Account			6,000
	To B Capital Account			3,000
	(Being the goodwill amount credited to old partners' Capital Account 2 : 1)			
	A Capital Account	Dr.	6,000	
	B Capital Account	Dr.	3,000	
	To Cash Account			9,000
	(Being the amount of goodwili withdrawn by partners)			
(4)	Goodwill Account	Dr.	36,000	
	To A Capital Account			24,000
	To B Capital Account			12,000
	(Being goodwill raised at full value and credited to partners' Capital Account in profit sharing ratio)			

	A Capital Account	Dr.	18,000	
	B Capital Account	Dr.	9,000	
	C Capital Account	Dr.	9,000	
	To Goodwill Account			36,000
	(Being goodwill written back in new profit sharing ratio)			
(5)	Goodwill Account	Dr.	9,000	
	To A Account			6,000
	To B Account			3,000
	(Being goodwill debited with the difference *i.e.* 36,000 – 27,000 = 9,000)			
(6)	A Capital Account	Dr.	4,000	
	B Capital Account	Dr.	2,000	
	To Goodwill Account			6,000
	(Being the excess value of goodwill written back: Rs 42,000 – 36,000 = 6,000)			

Note: A (share of profit) = 1 – 1/4 = 3/4 × 2/3 = 2/4
B (share of profit) = 3/4 × 1/3 = 1/4
C (share of profit) = 1/4

Thus, profit sharing ratio = 2/4 : 1/4 : 1/4 or 2 : 1 : 1

IV. ADJUSTMENT OF UNDISTRIBUTED PROFITS OR LOSSES

To expand the business in the future, the partnership firm reserves some profits as General Reserve or undistributed profits. These accumulated profits appear in the liabilities side of the Balance Sheet. These undistributed profits belong to old partners. Therefore, these undistributed profits are transferred to the old partners' account in their old profit sharing ratio before the admission of a new partner.

In the same manner, it is possible that undistributed losses, if any, may appear in the assets side of the Balance Sheet. These undistributed losses are also transferred to Partners' Capital/Current Account in the old profit sharing ratio.

After these adjustments, the general reserve or undistributed losses do not appear in the Balance Sheet.

Journal Entries:

For Profit/General Reserve:

Profit and Loss Account	Dr.
General Reserve Account	Dr.
To Old Partners' Capital/Current A/c	

For Losses:

Old Partners' Capital/Current Account	Dr.
To Profit and Loss Account	

ILLUSTRATION 30.22

The Balance Sheet of A and B as on 31st December 2005 is set out below. They share profits and losses in the ratio of 2 : 1.

Liabilities	*Rs*	*Assets*	*Rs*
A's Capital	40,000	Freehold Property	20,000
B's Capital	30,000	Furniture	6,000

General Reserve	24,000	Stock	12,000
Creditors	16,000	Debtors	60,000
		Cash	6,000
		Profit & Loss A/c	6,000
	1,10,000		1,10,000

They admit C into the firm subject to the following terms and conditions:

(*a*) C will bring in Rs 21,000, of which Rs 9,000 will be treated as premium for Goodwill to be retained in the business.

(*b*) He will be entitled to 1/4th share of the profits of the firm.

(*c*) 50% of the General Reserve is to remain as a Reserve for Bad and Doubtful Debts.

(*d*) Depreciation is to be provided on furniture @ 5%.

(*e*) Stock is to be revalued at Rs 10,500.

Show the journal entries giving effect to the aforesaid arrangement and prepare the opening Balance Sheet of the new partnership. (*B.Com., Calcutta*)

Journal Entries

			Dr.	Cr.
			Rs	*Rs*
2005				
Dec. 31	General Reserve Account	Dr.	24,000	
	To Reserve for Bad and Doubtful Debts Account			12,000
	To A Capital Account			8,000
	To B Capital Account			4,000
	(Being 50% of General Reserve retained as Reserve for Bad and Doubtful Debts and the balance credited to Old Partners' Capital Account)			
	Profit and Loss Adjustment Account	Dr.	1,800	
	To Furniture Account			300
	To Stock Account			1,500
	(Being Stock and Furniture depreciated)			
	A Capital Account	Dr.	1,200	
	B Capital Account	Dr.	600	
	To Profit and Loss Adjustment Account			1,800
	(Being loss on Profit and Loss Adjustment Account transferred to Old Partners' Capital Account)			
	A Capital Account	Dr.	4,000	
	B Capital Account	Dr.	2,000	
	To Profit and Loss Account			6,000
	(Being accumulated loss debited to Old Partners' Capital Account)			
	Cash Account	Dr.	9,000	
	To A Capital Account			6,000
	To B Capital Account			3,000
	(Being premium for Goodwill brought in by C, credied to Old Partners' Capital Account)			
	Cash Account	Dr.	12,000	
	To C Capital Account			12,000
	(Being Capital contributed by C)			

Note: As the profit sharing ratio of A and B remains the same after C's admission, sacrifice ratio is the old ratio.

On the admission of the new partner, any undistributed profit or loss is required to be transferred to the Capital Accounts of the old partners in their old profit sharing ratio.

Balance Sheet
as on 31st December 2005

Liabilities		*Rs*	*Assets*		*Rs*
Creditors	Rs	16,000		Rs	
Capital Accounts:			Cash	6,000	
A	48,800		*Add*: Goodwill	9,000	
B	34,400		*Add*: Capital	12,000	27,000
C	12,000	95,200	Debtors	60,000	
			Less: Provision	12,000	48,000
			Stock	12,000	
			Less: Depreciation	1,500	10,500
			Furniture	6,000	
			Less: Depreciation	300	5,700
			Freehold Property		20,000
		1,11,200			1,11,200

Dr. **Capital Accounts** Cr.

	A	*B*	*C*		*A*	*B*	*C*
	Rs	Rs	Rs		Rs	Rs	Rs
To Profit and Loss A/c	4,000	2,000		By Balance b/d	40,000	30,000	
To Profit and Loss Adjustment Account	1,200	600		By General Reserve	8,000	4,000	
				By Goodwill	6,000	3,000	
To Balance c/d	48,800	34,400	12,000	By Cash	–	–	12,000
	54,000	37,000	12,000		54,000	37,000	12,000
				By Balance b/d	48,800	34,400	12,000

V. ADJUSTMENT OF REARRANGEMENT OF CAPITALS

At the time of admission of a new partner, sometimes capital rearrangements may be made on the basis of partners' decision. This capital rearrangement means the contribution of partners towards capitals are rearranged on the basis of new profit sharing ratio. For this purpose, the Capital Accounts of the old partners must first be adjusted with Goodwill, Revaluation Account, past profits if any. Then the Capitals of all partners are rearranged in any of the following ways:

(*a*) Calculation of amount of Capital is made on the basis of New Partners' Capital contribution.

(*b*) Calculation of amount of Capital is made on the basis of Old Partners' Capital Account.

(*c*) The Capital Accounts of all partners are re-adjusted on the basis of New Profit Sharing Ratio.

ILLUSTRATION 30.23

X and Y are partners in a firm sharing profits and losses. X–75% and Y–25%. Their Balance Sheet as on 31st December 2005 is given below:

Liabilities	*Rs*	*Assets*	*Rs*
Sundry Creditors	40,000	Cash	20,000
Profit and Loss	10,000	Sundry Debtors	15,000
Capital Accounts:		Stock	35,000

X	30,000		Furniture	5,000
Y	20,000	50,000	Land and Buildings	25,000
		1,00,000		1,00,000

Z was admitted as a new partner on the following terms:

(*i*) The value of the stock was to be increased to Rs 40,000 and that of Land and Buildings to be reduced by 25%. Furniture was to be depreciated by 10%. Reserve of 5% was to be raised against Sundry Debtors.

(*ii*) Z was to pay Rs 15,000 to the existing partners as premium for Goodwill for 20% of the future profits of the firm. He was also to bring in capital equal to 1/5th of the combined adjusted capitals of X and Y.

You are required to journalise the entries in the books of the firm and give the opening Balance Sheet of the new firm on completion of the transactions. (*B.Com., Calcutta, MK, Poona, Delhi*)

Journal Entries

			Dr.	Cr.
			Rs	*Rs*
2005				
Dec. 31	Profit and Loss Account	Dr.	10,000	
	To X Capital Account			7,500
	To Y Capital Account			2,500
	(Being the profit credited to Old Partners' Capital Account)			
	Stock Account	Dr.	5,000	
	To Profit and Loss Adjustment Account			5,000
	(Being increase in the value of stock)			
	Profit and Loss Adjustment Account	Dr.	7,500	
	To Land and Building Account			6,250
	To Furniture Account			500
	To Provision for Bad Debts Account			750
	(Being Land and Building and Furniture depreciated and a provision for Bad Debts created)			
	X Capital Account	Dr.	1,875	
	Y Capital Account	Dr.	625	
	To Profit and Loss Adjustment Account			2,500
	(Being loss on Profit and Loss Adjustment Account transferred to Old Partners' Capitals)			
	Cash Account	Dr.	15,000	
	To X Capital Account			11,250
	To Y Capital Account			3,750
	(Being Goodwill brought in by Z and credited to Old Partners in their sacrifice ratio of 3 : 1)			
	Cash Account	Dr.	18,125	
	To Z Capital Account			18,125
	(Being Capital contributed by Z)			

Dr. **Capital Accounts** Cr.

	X	Y	Z		X	Y	Z
	Rs	Rs	Rs		Rs	Rs	Rs
To Profit and Loss Adjustment Account	1,875	625		By Balance b/d	30,000	20,000	–
To Balance c/d	46,875	25,625	18,125	By Profit and Loss Account	7,500	2,500	
				By Cash Account	11,250	3,750	
				By Cash Account	–	–	18,125
	48,750	26,250	18,125		48,750	26,250	18,125
				By Balance b/d	46,875	25,625	18,125

Balance Sheet
as on 31st December 2005

Liabilities		*Rs*	*Assets*		*Rs*
Sundry Creditors		40,000	Cash	20,000	
Capital Accounts:			*Add*: Goodwill	15,000	
A	46,875		*Add*: Capital	18,125	53,125
B	25,625				
C	18,125	90,625	Sundry Debtors	15,000	
			Less: Provision	750	14,250
			Stock		40,000
			Furniture	5,000	
			Less: Depreciation	500	4,500
			Land and Building	25,000	
			Less: Depreciation	6,250	18,750
		1,30,625			1,30,625

* Adjusted Capital:

X – Rs 48,750 – Rs 1,875 = Rs 46,875

Y – Rs 26,250 – Rs 625 = Rs 25,625

Rs 72,500

For $\frac{4}{5}$th profit, the required capital = Rs 72,500

For $\frac{1}{5}$th share of profit, the required capital = Rs 72,500 × $\frac{5}{4} \times \frac{1}{5}$

= Rs 18,125

ILLUSTRATION 30.24

A and B are partners in a firm sharing profits and losses in the ratio of 3 : 2. On 31st March 2005 their Balance Sheet stands as follows:

Liabilities	*Rs*	*Assets*	*Rs*
Capital Accounts:		Leasehold Property	12,000
A	20,000	Fixture and Fittings	2,000
B	10,000	Stock	16,500
Reserve	7,800	Debtors	6,000
Sundry Creditors	5,000	Cash	3,800
		Profit and Loss A/c	2,500
	42,800		42,800

On the same date they admit C as a partner and the new profit sharing becomes 6 : 4 : 3. C is to bring required premium *i.e.*, Rs 2,400 and proportionate capital. The Capitals of A and B as between themselves are also to be adjusted in profit sharing ratio.

Pass journal entries, show the capital accounts of the partners and draw Balance Sheet of the new firm.

(*B. Com Kerala*)

Journal Entries

			Dr.	Cr.
			Rs	*Rs*
2005				
March 31	Reserve Account	Dr.	7,800	
	To A Capital Account			4,680
	To B Capital Account			3,120
	(Being Reserve account credited to Capital Accounts of A and B in the ratio of 3 : 2)			
	A Capital Account	Dr.	1,500	
	B Capital Account	Dr.	1,000	
	To Profit and Loss Account			2,500
	(Being accumulated loss debited to Capital Accounts of A and B in the ratio of 3 : 2)			
	Cash Account	Dr.	13,710	
	To C Capital Account			13,710
	(Being cash brought in by C on his admission as a partner)			
	C Capital Account	Dr.	2,400	
	To A Capital Account			1,440
	To B Capital Account			960
	(Being the amount of premium brought in by C credited to A and B's Capital Accounts in sacrificing ratio *i.e.* 3 : 2)			
	Cash Account	Dr.	2,000	
	To B Capital Account			2,000
	(Being cash brought in by B to make up his capital Rs 15,080)			
	A Capital Account	Dr.	2,000	
	To Cash Account			2,000
	(Being excess cash paid back to A)			

Capital Accounts

Dr. Cr.

		A	B	C			A	B	C
		Rs	Rs	Rs			Rs	Rs	Rs
2005					2005				
Mar. 31	To Profit & Loss A/c	1,500	1,000	–	Mar. 31	By Balance b/d	20,000	10,000	–
	To A and B Capitals (Goodwill)			2,400		By Reserve	4,680	3,120	–
	To Cash	2,000				By Cash	–	–	13,710
	Balance c/d	22,620	15,080	11,310		By C Capital (Goodwill)	1,440	960	–
						By Cash	–	2,000	–
		26,120	16,080	13,710			26,120	16,080	13,710
					April 1	By Balance b/d	22,620	15,080	11,310

Balance Sheet of New Firm
as on 1st April 2005

Liabilities		*Rs*	*Assets*	*Rs*
Capital Accounts			Leasehold property	12,000
A	22,620		Fixtures and Fittings	2,000
B	15,080		Stock	16,500
C	11,310	49,010	Debtors	6,000
Sundry Creditors		5,000	Cash	17,510
		54,010		54,010

Note: Premium brought in by C = Rs 10,400 × 3/13 = Rs 2,400

The amount of premium is distributed between A and B in sacrificing ratio *i.e.* 3 : 2.

The combined Capitals of A and B = Rs 30,000 + 7,800 – 2,500 + 2,400 = Rs 37,700

To adjust the Capitals of A and B, their profit sharing ratio will be

A = Rs 37,700 × 6/10 = Rs 22,620

B = Rs 37,700 × 4/10 = Rs 15,080

Thus, the excess amount paid to A = Rs 2,000 (Rs 24,620 – 22,620)

The deficit amount of B = Rs 2,000 (Rs 15,080 – 13,080)

C's contribution towards capital = Rs 37,700 × $\frac{13}{10} \times \frac{3}{13}$ = Rs 11,310

ILLUSTRATION 30.25

A and B are partners, sharing profits and losses in the ratio of 3 : 1. Their Balance Sheet at 31st December 2005 was as follows:

Liabilities	*Rs*	*Assets*	*Rs*
Creditors	37,500	Cash at Bank	22,500
General Reserve	4,000	Bills Receivable	3,000
Capitals:		Debtors	16,000
A	30,000	Stock	20,000
B	16,000	Furniture	1,000
		Buildings	25,000
	87,500		87,500

On 1st January 2006, they admit C on the following terms:

(1) That C pays Rs 10,000 as his capital for a fifth share in the future profits.

(2) That goodwill account be raised in the books at a value of Rs 20,000.

(3) That stock and furniture be reduced by 10% and a provision of 5% be made for doubtful debts.

(4) That the value of Buildings be appreciated by 20%.

(5) That the Capital Accounts of all the partners be readjusted on the basis of their profit sharing arrangements and for this purpose Current Accounts are to be opened.

Set out journal entries, prepare the Revaluation Account, Capital Accounts and show the opening Balance Sheet of the firm as on 1st January 2006. (*B. Com Madurai*)

Journal Entries

			Dr. *Rs*	Cr. *Rs*
2006				
Jan. 1	Revaluation Account	Dr.	2,900	
	To Stock Account			2,000
	To Furniture Account			100

Particulars		Dr. (Rs)	Cr. (Rs)
To Provision for Doubtful Debts			800
(Being stock and Furniture depreciated and Provision for Doubtful Debts created)			
Building Account	Dr.	5,000	
To Revaluation Account			5,000
(Being the increase in the value of Building)			
Revaluation Account	Dr.	2,100	
To A Capital Account			1,575
To B Capital Account			525
(Being the profit transferred to Old Partners' Capital Account)			
General Reserve Account	Dr.	4,000	
To A Capital Account			3,000
To B Capital Account			1,000
(Being the General Reserve divided between the old partners 3 : 1)			
Goodwill Account	Dr.	20,000	
To A Capital Account			15,000
To B Capital Account			5,000
(Being the value of Goodwill raised)			
Bank Account	Dr.	10,000	
To C Capital Account			10,000
(Being the Capital contribution of C)			
A Capital Account	Dr.	19,575	
B Capital Account	Dr.	12,525	
To A Current Account			19,575
To B Current Account			12,525
(Being the transfer of the excess of capitals over profit sharing ratio to respective Current Accounts)			

Revaluation Account

Dr.	Rs		Cr. Rs
To Stock	2,000	By Buildings	5,000
To Furniture	100		
To Provision for Doubtful Debts	800		
To A Capital Account	1,575		
To B Capital Account	525		
	5,000		5,000

Capital Accounts

Dr.	A Rs	B Rs	C Rs	Cr.	A Rs	B Rs	C Rs
To Current Account	19,575	12,525		By Balance b/d	30,000	16,000	
To Balance b/d	30,000	10,000	10,000	By Revaluation Account	1,575	525	
				By General Reserve	3,000	1,000	
				By Goodwill	15,000	5,000	
				By Bank			10,000
	49,575	22,525	10,000		49,575	22,525	10,000
				By Balance b/d	30,000	10,000	10,000

Balance Sheet of A, B and C
as on 1st January 2006

Liabilities		*Rs*	*Assets*		*Rs*
Creditors		37,500	Cash at Bank (Rs 22,500 + Rs 10,000)		32,500
Current Accounts:			Bills Receivable	Rs	3,000
A		19,575	Debtors	16,000	
B		12,525	*Less*: Provision	800	15,200
Capital Accounts:	Rs		Stock		18,000
A	30,000		Furniture		900
B	10,000		Buildings	(25,000 + 5,000)	30,000
C	10,000	50,000	Goodwill		20,000
		1,19,600			1,19,600

Note: C pays Rs 10,000 as his capital for a fifth share and on this basis, the capitals of A and B are adjusted.

ILLUSTRATION 30.26

Seed and Stalk were partners carrying on a business of fruit-gardening and sharing profits and losses in the ratio of 3 : 2. On 30th June 2005 their Balance Sheet was as follows:

Liabilities	*Rs*	*Assets*	*Rs*
Capitals: Seed	30,000	Land	40,000
Stalk	25,000	Fruit Trees	20,000
Reserve	10,000	Stock	11,000
Creditors	16,000	Sundry Debtors	8,000
		Cash	2,000
	81,000		81,000

On the abovementioned date, Flower was admitted into the partnership on the following terms:

(1) Flower was to pay Rs 20,000 as capital and Rs 10,000 as goodwill for a one-fourth share in profits.

(2) Land was to be revalued at Rs 45,000 and Fruit Trees at Rs 25,000. Stock was to be written down by Rs 2,000. Creditors included Rs 500 no longer payable and this sum was to be written back.

(3) Capitals of all partners were to be in the profit sharing ratio, and for this purpose Current Accounts were to be opened.

Give journal entries to record matters arising out of Flower's admission and Balance Sheet of the firm as newly constituted. (*B.Com., Delhi, Agra, MK, Kerala*)

Journal Entries

			Dr.	Cr.
			Rs	*Rs*
2005				
June 30	Reserve Account	Dr.	10,000	
	To Seed Capital Account			6,000
	To Stalk Capital Account			4,000
	(Being Reserve transferred to Old Partners' Capital Account in the profit sharing ratio i.e. 3 : 2)			
	Land Account	Dr.	5,000	
	Fruit Trees Account	Dr.	5,000	
	Creditors Account	Dr.	500	
	To Revaluation Account			10.500
	(Being changes in the value of assets and liabilities)			

Particulars		Dr. (Rs)	Cr. (Rs)
Revaluation Account	Dr.	2,000	
To Stock Account			2,000
(Being the value of stock depreciated)			
Revaluation Account	Dr.	8,500	
To Seed Capital Account			5,100
To Stalk Capital Account			3,400
(Being the profit on revaluation transferred to Old Partners' Capital Account *i.e.* 3 : 2)			
Cash Account	Dr.	30,000	
To Flower Capital Account			30,000
(Being cash brought in by Flower)			
Flower Capital Account	Dr.	10,000	
To Seed Capital Account			6,000
To Stalk Capital Account			4,000
(Being Goodwill credited to Old Partners' Capital Account in sacrificing ratio i.e. 3 : 2)			
Seed Capital Account	Dr.	11,100	
To Seed Current Account			11,100
(Being the transfer of excess amount)			
Stalk Capital Account	Dr.	12,400	
To Stalk Current Account			12,400
(Being the transfer of excess amount)			

Capital Accounts

	Seed	*Stalk*	*Flower*		*Seed*	*Stalk*	*Flower*
	Rs	Rs	Rs		Rs	Rs	Rs
To Seed and Stalk	–	–	10,000	By Balance b/d	30,000	25,000	–
To Current Account	11,100	12,400	–	By Cash	–	–	30,000
To Balance c/d	36,000	24,000	20,000	By Flower Capital	6,000	4,000	–
				By Revaluation	5,100	3,400	–
				By Reserve	6,000	4,000	–
	47,100	36,400	30,000		47,100	36,400	30,000
				By Balance b/d	36,000	24,000	20,000

Balance Sheet
as on 30th June 2005

Liabilities		Rs	*Assets*		Rs
Sundry Creditors		15,500	Cash		32,000
Current Account			Sundry Debtors		8,000
Seed	11,100		Stock	11,000	
Stalk	12,400	23,500	*Less*: Depreciation	2,000	9,000
Capital Accounts			Fruit Trees	20,000	
Seed	36,000		*Add*: Increasing value	5,000	25,000
Stalk	24,000		Land	40,000	
Flower	20,000	80,000	*Add*: Appreciation	5,000	45,000
		1,19,000			1,19,000

Note:

(1) Calculation of New Profit Sharing Ratio

Flower's share of profit	= 1/4
Remaining profit	= 1 – 1/4 = 3/4
Seed's share of profit	= 3/4 × 3/5 = 9/20
Stalk's share of profit	= 3/4 × 2/5 = 6/20
Flower's share of profit	= 1/4 or 5/20

New Profit Sharing Ratio : 9 : 6 : 5

(2) Sacrificing Ratio

	Old Share	New Share	
Seed	3/5	9/20	= 12 – 9/20 = 3/20
Stalk	2/5	6/20	= 8 – 6/20 = 2/20

Sacrificing Ratio 3 : 2

Goodwill is credited to partners on sacrificing ratio.

(3) Calculation of amount to be transferred to or from current accounts.

	Balance as per Capital Accounts	Capital in profit sharing ratio	Amount to be adjusted
Seed	47,100	36,000	+ 11,100
Stalk	36,400	24,000	+ 12,400
Flower	20,000	20,000	Nil

ILLUSTRATION 30.27

The following is the Balance Sheet of A, B and C sharing profits and losses in the proportion of 6/14, 5/14 and 3/14 respectively:

	Rs		Rs
Creditors	18,900	Cash	1,890
Bills Payable	6,300	Debtors	26,460
General Reserve	10,500	Stock	29,400
A's Capital	35,400	Furniture	7,350
B's Capital	29,850	Land and Buildings	45,150
C's Capital	14,550	Goodwill	5,250
	1,15,000		1,15,500

They agreed to take D into partnership and give him 1/8th share of profits and losses on the following terms:

(1) That furniture be depreciated by Rs 920.

(2) That stock be depreciated by 10%.

(3) That a provision of Rs 1,320 be made for outstanding repairs bills.

(4) That the value of land and buildings having appreciated be brought up to Rs 59,850.

(5) That the value of goodwill be brought up to Rs 14,070.

(6) That D should then bring in Rs 14,700 as his capital.

(7) That after making the above adjustments the capital accounts of the old partners be adjusted on the basis of the proportion of D's Capital to their shares in the business, *i.e.*, actual cash to be paid off or brought in by the old partners as the case may be.

Pass the necessary journal entries and prepare the Capital Accounts and Balance Sheet of the new firm.

(*M.Com., Bombay, Calcutta, Jabalpur, Poona, Bharathiar*)

SOLUTION

Journal Entries

Particulars		Dr. Rs	Cr. Rs
General Reserve Account	Dr.	10,500	
To A Capital Account			4,500
To B Capital Account			3,750
To C Capital Account			2,250
(Being general Reserve transferred)			
Goodwill Account	Dr.	8,820	
To A Capital Account			3,780
To B Capital Account			3,150
To C Capital Account			1,890
(Being goodwill transferred)			
Revaluation Account	Dr.	5,180	
To Furniture Account			920
To Stock Account			2,940
To Provision for Repairs Account			1,320
(Being the depreciated value transferred)			
Building Account	Dr.	14,700	
To Revaluation Account			14,700
(Being the appreciation of Building transferred)			
Revaluation Account	Dr.	9,520	
To A Capital Account			4,080
To B Capital Account			3,400
To C Capital Account			2,040
(Being transfer of profit)			
Cash Account	Dr.	14,700	
To D Capital Account			14,700
(Being Capital brought by D)			
A Capital Account	Dr.	3,660	
B Capital Account	Dr.	3,400	
To Cash Account			7,060
(Being excess cash paid off)			
Cash Account	Dr.	1,320	
To C Capital Account			1,320
(Being deficit cash brought in)			

Capital Accounts

	A	B	C	D		A	B	C	D
	Rs	Rs	Rs	Rs		Rs	Rs	Rs	Rs
To Cash	3,660	3,400	–	–	By Balance b/d	35,400	29,850	14,550	–
To Balance c/d	44,100	36,750	22,050	14,700	By General Reserve	4,500	3,750	2,250	–
					By Goodwill	3,780	3,150	1,890	–
					By Revaluation	4,080	3,400	2,040	–
					By Cash	–	–	1,320	
					By Bank	–	–	–	14,700
	47,760	40,150	22,050	14,700		47,760	40,150	22,050	14,700
					By Balance b/d	44,100	36,750	22,050	14,700

Dr. **Cash Account** Cr.

	Rs		Rs
To Balance b/d	1,890	By A	3,660
To D	14,700	By B	3,400
To C	1,320	By Balance c/d	10,850
	17,910		17,910
To Balance b/d	10,850		

Balance Sheet

As on ....

Liabilities		Rs	*Assets*	Rs
Capitals:	Rs		Goodwill	14,070
A	44,100		Land and Building	59,850
B	36,750		Furniture	6,430
C	22,050		Stock	26,460
D	14,700	1,17,600	Debtors	26,460
Provision for Repairs		1,320	Cash	10,850
Bills Payable		6,300		
Creditors		18,900		
		1,44,120		1,44,120

Calculation of Ratios:

D's Share of profit = $\frac{1}{8}$

Balance available = $1 - \frac{1}{8} = \frac{7}{8}$

A's Share = $\frac{7}{8} \times \frac{6}{14} = \frac{6}{16}$

B's Share = $\frac{7}{8} \times \frac{5}{14} = \frac{5}{16}$

C's Share = $\frac{7}{8} \times \frac{3}{14} = \frac{3}{16}$

New Ratio = 6 : 5 : 3 : 2

Calculation of proportionate capital

For $\frac{1}{8}$th share of profit D brings Rs 14,700

∴ The total amount of capital should be = Rs 14,700 × $\frac{8}{1}$ = Rs 1,17,600

A's share of capital = Rs 1,17,600 × $\frac{6}{16}$ = Rs 44,100

B's share of capital = Rs 1,17,600 × $\frac{5}{16}$ = Rs 36,750

C's share of capital = Rs 1,17,600 × $\frac{3}{16}$ = Rs 22,050

Excess Cash paid to A = Rs 47,760 – Rs 44,100 = Rs 3,660
Excess Cash paid to B = Rs 40,150 – Rs 36,750 = Rs 3,400
Deficit cash brought in by C = Rs 22,050 – Rs 20,730 = Rs 1,320

QUESTIONS

Objective Type Questions

I. State whether each of the following statements is "True" or "False":

1. In case the newly admitted partner pays cash for his share of goodwill, it will be credited to the old partners in their sacrificing ratio.
2. All accumulated profits and reserves are to be transferred to the Profit and Loss Adjustment Account on admission of a new partner.
3. Revaluation Account and Profit and Loss Adjustment Account are same.
4. Memorandum Revaluation Account is prepared when the revised values of assets and liabilities are not to be shown in the books of account
5. At the time of admission of a new partner, undrawn profits, if any, should be shared by the old partners in their sacrificing ratio.
6. The amount that the new partner brings in for goodwill is known as premium for goodwill.
7. Revaluation Account is a real account.
8. Goodwill is a fictitious asset.
9. The incoming partner has to pay for his capital only in the form of cash.
10. Goodwill is a fixed asset intangible in nature.
11. The need for valuation of goodwill arises when there is a change in the profit sharing ratios.
12. Memorandum Revaluation Account is the same as Revaluation Account
13. New profit sharing ratios and sacrificing ratios are one and the same.
14. It is necessary to bring unrecorded asset or liabilities into books of account at the time of admission of a partner.
15. Valuation of goodwill becomes necessary when a partner is admitted into the firm:.

(**Ans:** True – 1, 3, 4, 6, 10, 11, 14, 15.
False – 2, 5, 7, 8, 9, 12, 13..

II Fill in the blanks:

1. The incoming partner has to bring in capital contribution and his share of ....
2. Where partners agree not to alter the book value of assets and liabilities, they open a ....
3. Premium paid by a new partner must be shared by the old partners in their............
4. Profit on revaluation is to be credited to old partners in their............
5. Accumulated losses are transferred to the Capital Accounts of the old partners in............
6. Old profit sharing ratio minus the new profit ratio is equal to............
7. Revaluation Account is a .... Account.
8. A and B share profits and losses in the ratio of 3 : 2. C is admitted as a partner and is given one-fifth share. So, the sacrifice ratio............

(**Ans:** 1. Goodwill; 2. Memorandum Revaluation Account; 3. Sacrifice Ratio; 4. Old Ratio; 5. Old profit sharing ratio; 6. Sacrifice or gain; 7. Nominal; 8. 3 : 2.

III. Choose the correct answer for each of the following:

1. Goodwill is:
   (*a*) A tangible asset
   (*b*) An intangible asset

(*c*) A fictitious asset

2. The profit or loss on revaluation of assets at the time of admission is transferred to the partners in the:
   (*a*) Capital ratio
   (*b*) New profit sharing ratio
   (*c*) Old profit sharing ratio
   (*d*) Sacrificing ratio
3. When a goodwill account is raised, credit is given to old partners in:
   (*a*) Old profit sharing ratio
   (*b*) New profit sharing ratio
   (*c*) Sacrificing ratio
4. The premium paid by the new partner is shared by the old partners in:
   (*a*) Capital ratio
   (*b*) Profit sharing ratio
   (*c*) Gaining ratio
   (*d*) Sacrificing ratio
5. Any amount to be written off after admission of a partner is transferred to the capital accounts of the partners in:
   (*a*) Old Ratio
   (*b*) New Ratio
   (*c*) Capital Ratio
6. Old profit sharing ratio minus new profit sharing ratio is equal to:
   (*a*) Sacrificing Ratio
   (*b*) Gaining Ratio
   (*c*) Capital Ratio
7. On admission of a new partner, decrease in value of asset is debited to:
   (*a*) Trading Account
   (*b*) Balance Sheet
   (*c*) Profit & Loss Adjustment Account
8. The need for valuation of goodwill arises when:
   (*a*) a partner transfers his interest to a third party.
   (*b*) a partner becomes a lunatic.
   (*c*) there is a change in the profit sharing proportions
9. On the admission of a partner, if the goodwill is raised at full value, it should be debited to:
   (*a*) Cash Account
   (*b*) Old Partners' Capital Account
   (*c*) Goodwill Account
10. A and B are partners sharing profits in the ratio of 3 : 2. C is admitted paying a premium of Rs. 2,000 for 1/4th share of profit, B will get:
   (a) Rs. 800
   (b) Rs. 500
   (c) Rs. 1,200

(Ans: 1. (b); 2; (c); 3. (a); 4. (d); 5. (b); 6. (a); 7. (c); 8. (c); 9. (c); 10. (a).

THEORETICAL QUESTIONS

1. What are the adjustments carried out at the time of admission of a partner?
2. What is a Revaluation Account? How does it differ from Realisation Account?
3. What do you mean by Profit sharing ratio?

4. How is the new Profit sharing ratio calculated after admission of a partner?
5. What is goodwill?
6. Explain the various methods of calculation of goodwill.
7. Define goodwill. Mention the factors affecting goodwill.
8. How is goodwill brought in cash by the new partner treated in the books?
9. What is sacrifice ratio? What is it used for?

PRACTICAL PROBLEMS

1. A, B and C were partners sharing profits and losses in the ratio of 3 : 2 : 5. They admitted D and gave him 1/4 share. This share was contributed by them in the ratio of 1 : 1 : 3. Find out the new profit-loss sharing ratio of all the partners. (*B.Com., MS*)

   [Ans: New Ratio 5 : 3 : 7 : 5]

2. A and B were partners sharing profits and losses in the ratio of 3 : 2. They admitted C as a partner. A contributed 3/4 of his share and B contributed 1/4 of his share to C. Find out the sacrifice ratio of the old partners and also the new profit-loss sharing ratio of all the partners. (*B.Com., MS*)

   [Ans: Sacrificing Ratio of A and B 9 : 2, New Ratio of A, B and C 3 : 6 : 11]

3. A and B were partners sharing profits and losses in the ratio of 5 : 3. They admitted C and gave him 1/5 share. Find out the sacrifice ratio of the old partners and also the new profit-loss sharing ratio of all the partners. (*B.Com., Madras*)

   [Ans: Sacrificing Ratio of A and B 5 : 3
   New Ratio of A, B and C 5 : 3 : 2]

4. A and B were partners in a firm sharing profits in the ratio of 3 : 2. They admit C into partnership and the new ratio for sharing profits will be 4 : 3 : 2. You are required to calculate the sacrificing ratio. (*B.Com., Madurai*)

   [Ans: 7 : 3]

5. A, B and C are partners in a firm, sharing profits and losses in the ratio of 4 : 3 : 2. D is admitted into the firm. What will be the profit and loss sharing ratio:
   (*a*) if D's share in the profit and loss is 1/5,
   (*b*) if D's share in the profit and loss is 1/3,
   (*c*) if D's share in the profit and loss is 1/8,
   (*d*) if D's share in the profit and loss is 1/10,
   (*e*) if D's share in the profit and loss is 1/5, which he takes 1/10 from A and 1/10th from B?

   [Ans: (*a*) 16 : 12 : 8 : 9
   (*b*) 8 : 6 : 4 : 9
   (*c*) 28 : 21 : 14 : 9
   (*d*) 4 : 3 : 2 : 1
   (*e*) 31 : 21 : 20 : 18]

6. Calculate the new profit and loss sharing of the partners in the following cases:
   (*a*) A and B are partners sharing profits and losses in the ratio of 3 : 2. They admit C giving 1/4th share in the profits.
   (*b*) A and B sharing profits and losses in the ratio of 3 : 2, admit C giving him 1/4th share, which C buys 1/6th share from A and 1/12 from B.
   (*c*) A and B are partners sharing profits and losses in the ratio of 3 : 2. They admit C into firm and A surrenders 1/5 of his own share and B surrenders 1/2 of his own share in favour of C.
   (*d*) A and B are partners sharing profits in the ratio of 3 : 2. They admit C giving him 1/4 share and decide to divide the remaining profit in the ratio of 7 : 3.
   (*e*) A and B are partners sharing profits in the ratio of 6 : 4. They admit C for a sixth share.

   [Ans: (*a*) 9 : 6 : 5

(*b*) 26 : 19 : 15

(*c*) 12 : 5 : 8

(*d*) 21 : 9 : 10

(*e*) 3 : 2 : 1

7. Calculate new profit and loss sharing ratio in the following cases:
   (*a*) A and B are partners sharing profits and losses in the ratio of 2 : 1. They admit C for 1/4th share in the profits.
   (*b*) A and B are partners sharing profits and losses in the ratio of 3 : 2. They admit C for 1/5th share in the profits.
   (*c*) A and B are partners sharing profits and losses in the ratio of 4 : 5. They admit C into the firm to whom they give 1/4th share of profits.
   (*d*) A and B are partners sharing profits and losses in the ratio of 8 : 7. They admit C for 1/3 share of profits.
   (*e*) A and B are parthers sharing profits and losses in the ratio of 1 : 2. They admit C for 1/4th share in the profits.

[**Ans:** (*a*) 2 : 1 : 1

(*b*) 12 : 8 : 5

(*c*) 4 : 5 : 3

(*d*) 16 : 14 : 15

(*e*) 1 : 2 : 1.

8. A and B were partners sharing profits and losses in the ratio of 3 : 2. C was admitted as a partner with the following conditions:
   1. The share of goodwill of C was decided as Rs 9,000 which he was not able to pay in cash.
   2. C was allotted 3/8 share in the profits and losses for which he had to bring an amount of Rs 25,000 as capital.
   3. It was agreed to write off the goodwill raised in the books.
   4. The profit-loss sharing ratio between A and B in the new firm was decided as 2 : 3.

   Pass necessary journal entries for the above adjustments in the partnership firm.

[**Ans:** New Ratio of A, B and C : 2 : 3 : 3

Debit A's Capital (2/8) Rs 2,250

Debit B's Capital (3/8) Rs 3,375

Debit C's Capital (3/8) Rs 3,375

Credit Goodwill A/c: Rs 9,000]

9. C and D are equal partners in a firm. On 1st January 2004 their capitals are Rs 13,000 and Rs 11,000. They made E as a partner for 1/4th share of the firm. This new partner brought his capital on the basis of the combined capitals of the old partners. Pass necessary journal entries in the books of the firm and also adjust Old Partners' Capital Account according to new ratio.

[**Ans:** E brings in Capital Rs 8,000

C withdraws excess amount of Rs 1,000

D brings in Rs 1,000]

10. X and Y are partners in a firm sharing profits and losses as X 75% and Y 25%. Their capital accounts as on 1st Jan. 2004 were Rs 50,000 and Rs 40,000 respectively. They admit Z as a partner for 1/5th share of future profits of the firm. Z introduces Rs 40,000, of which Rs 20,000 was to be considered as premium for goodwill.

    You are asked to record the above transactions in the books of the firm and show also the future profit sharing ratio. (*B.Com., Calcutta*)

[**Ans:** New Ratio : 3 : 1 : 1

Sacrificing Ratio: 3 : 1

Credit X Account with Rs 15,000 and Y Account with Rs 5,000]

11. X and Y are in partnership sharing profits and losses as 3 : 2. They admit Z into the firm, Z paying a premium of Rs 36,000 for 1/6th share of profits. As between themselves, X and Y agree to share future profits and losses equally. Draft journal entry showing the appropriation of premium money.

(ICWA) (B.Com., Kerala)

[**Ans:** New Ratio : 5 : 5 : 2]

12. Give journal entries to record the following arrangements in the books of the firm:
   (*i*) A and B are partners sharing profits and losses equally. They admit C with a 1/4 share of profit on the condition that he will bring in Rs 12,000 as capital and Rs 2,000 as goodwill. No Goodwill Account appears in the books.
   (*ii*) A and B are partners sharing profits in the ratio of 4 : 3. C enters paying a premium of Rs 4,000 for his share of profits in the firm. All the partners decide to share future profits equally. No Goodwill Account appears in the books.
   (*iii*) A and B are partners sharing profits in the ratio of 5 : 4. C is admitted into partnership paying a premium of Rs 6,000. Goodwill appears in the books at Rs 10,000. All the partners decide to share future profits in the ratio of 4 : 3 : 3.
   (*iv*) A and B are partners sharing profits in the ratio of 3 : 2. They admit C for 3/10 share of profit in the new firm of which he takes 2/3 from A and 1/3 from B. Goodwill Account appears in the books at Rs 8,000. C could not bring his share of goodwill in cash. However, the Goodwill Account was raised to Rs 13,000.
   (*v*) A, B and C are partners sharing profits in the ratio of 4 : 4 : 2. The goodwill of the firm does not appear in the books but it is valued at Rs 12,000. It is now agreed that the partners will share profits equally and that no Goodwill Account is to remain in the books.

[**Ans:** (*i*) Sacrificing Ratio : 1 : 1
(*ii*) Sacrificing Ratio: 5 : 2
(*iii*) Sacrificing Ratio: 14 : 13
(*iv*) Sacrificing Ratio: 2 : 1
(*v*) Raise goodwill of Rs 12,000, crediting Partners Capital Account in the ratio of 4 : 4 : 2.
Then write it off in 1 : 1 : 1]

13. Brick, Sand and Cement were partners in a firm sharing profits and losses in the ratio 3 : 2 : 1 respectively. Following is their Balance Sheet as on 31st December 2004:

Liabilities		*Rs*	*Assets*	*Rs*
Capital Accounts:			Land & Buildings	50,000
Brick	30,000		Furniture	15,000
Sand	20,000		Stock	20,000
Cement	10,000	60,000	Sundry Debtors	7,500
Reserve		29,800	Bills Receivable	5,000
Sundry Creditors		6,200	Cash and Bank	2,500
Bills Payable		4,000		
		1,00,000		1,00,000

Lime is to be admitted as a partner with effect from 1st Jan. 2005, on the following terms:
   (*a*) Lime will bring Rs 15,000 as capital and Rs 12,000 as premium for goodwill. Half of the goodwill will be withdrawn by partners.
   (*b*) Lime will be entitled to 1/6th share in the profits of the firm.
   (*c*) The assets will be revalued as follows:

	Rs.
Land and Buildings	56,000
Furniture	12,000
Stock	16,000

Debtors 7,000

(*d*) The claim for a creditor for Rs 2,300 is paid at Rs 2,000

(*e*) Half of the Reserve is to be withdrawn by the partners.

Record the journal entries in the books of the firm Capital Account and show the opening Balance Sheet of the firm. (*B.Com., Calcutta*)

[Ans: Balance Sheet Total: Rs 1,02,600]

14. X and Y share profits in the ratio of 3 : 1. On 1st March, 2004, their Balance Sheet stood as under:

Liabilities		*Rs*	*Assets*		*Rs*
Creditors		25,500	Cash in hand		500
General Reserve		8,000	Cash at Bank		3,000
Profit and Loss Account		4,000	Bills Receivable		2,000
Capital Accounts:			Debtors	34,000	
X	60,000		*Less*: Provision	2,000	32,000
Y	32,000	92,000	Stock		40,000
			Fixtures		2,000
			Land and Buildings		50,000
		1,29,500			1,29,500

From April 1, 2004, Z was admitted into partnership on the following terms:

(*a*) That Z pays Rs 30,000 as his capital for one-fifth share in future profits of the firm.

(*b*) That Stock and Fixtures be reduced by 10% and provision for bad debts be maintained at 5%.

(*c*) That the value of Land and Buildings having appreciated raised to Rs 60,000.

(*d*) That the share of Z in the firm's goodwill be valued at Rs 4,000, but that Z will not be required to bring cash for goodwill.

(*e*) That the capitals of the partners be in their profit sharing ratio, the necessary amounts being paid in or withdrawn.

Pass journal entries and prepare the balance sheet following the admission of Z in the firm. Also give working notes in detail. (*B.Com., Calcutta*)

[Ans:	X	Y	Z
	Rs	Rs	Rs
Revaluation gain	4,575	1,525	
Capital Accounts	90,000	30,000	30,000

Balance Sheet Total Rs 1,75,500]

15. The Balance Sheet of Mathur and Manzur carrying on business in partnership and sharing profits in proportions of two-thirds and one-third stood on June 30, 2004, as follows:

	Rs		*Rs*
Mathur's Capital	1,02,900	Cash in hand	4,500
Manzur's Capital	73,500	Stock	54,000
Creditors	23,600	Debtors	36,000
Bills Payable	500	Furniture	6,000
		Plant & Machinery	1,00,000
	2,00,500		2,00,500

On July 1, 2004, they agreed to take Mathews into partnership giving him one-fifth share of profit on the following terms: (*a*) The Goodwill of the firm is to be valued at two years' purchase of profits calculated on the average of the last three years' profits amounting to Rs 40,000, Rs 30,000 and Rs 44,075, (*b*) Mathews brings his share of goodwill in cash which is retained in the business, (*c*) Mathews also brings in capital in proportion to his profit sharing arrangements.

Show the calculations of (*a*) Goodwill, (*b*) New profit sharing ratio, and (*c*) Mathews' share of capital. Also draft the necessary journal entries to give effect to the above arrangements, and prepare the opening Balance Sheet of the new firm.

[**Ans:** Goodwill Rs 76,050
New Profit & Loss sharing ratio 8 : 4 : 3
Mathews' Capital Rs 47,903
Balance Sheet Total Rs 2,63,613]

16. P, Q and R were in partnership sharing profits and losses in the ratio 6 : 3 : 1. They decided to take S into partnership with effect from 1st April 2003, on the following terms and conditions:

(1) S is to bring his proportionate share of goodwill in Cash. Goodwill is not to be brought into the books but necessary adjustments are to be made in the Old Partners' Capital Accounts.

(2) Goodwill to be valued at 60% of the average annual profits of the previous three of four years whichever is higher.

(3) The average profits for the purpose of goodwill for the past years were:

Year ended 31st March	2000	Rs 48,000
	2001	Rs 30,300
	2002	Rs 31,200
	2003	Rs 42,500

(4) The new profit sharing ratio between P, Q, R and S will be 3 : 3 : 3 : 1.

(5) S should bring in Rs 20,000 as capital.

(6) The new partner is to receive an annual salary of Rs 12,000 in addition to his share of profit. R personally guaranteed that the aggregate of salary and share of profit of the new partner shall not be less than Rs 25,000 per annum.

Draft accounts for the year ended 31st March 2004 showed a profit of Rs 1,32,000 before taking into account the salary of S.

Show the journal entries, including cash at the time of admission of the new partner and also the distribution of the net profit for the year ended 31st March 2004 between the partners. (*C.A.*)

[**Ans:** Profits P : Rs 36,240
Q : Rs 36,240
R : Rs 35,320
S : Rs 13,000]

17. The following is the Balance Sheet of Sethi and Sobti who share profits and losses 3/5th and 2/5th respectively:

		Rs			*Rs*
Sundry Creditors		1,500	Land & Building		3,500
Reserve Fund		1,000	Plant		4,500
Capital Accounts:			Stock		3,500
Sethi	8,000		Book Debts	2,500	
Sobti	3,500	11,500	*Less*: Provision	500	2,000
			Cash at Bank		500
		14,000			14,000

They agreed to admit Mahajan into partnership giving him a fifth share on the following terms:

(*a*) The value of Land and Building to be increased to Rs 5,000.

(*b*) The value of Stock to be increased by Rs 2,200 and plant to be depreciated by 10 per cent.

(*c*) Goodwill to be valued at Rs 2,000.

(*d*) Provision for Doubtful Debts to be increased by Rs 750.

(*e*) Mahajan to bring in capital to the extent of 1/5th of the total of the new firm after adjustment.

Show Ledger entries recording these adjustments and prepare the Balance Sheet of the new firm, assuming Mahajan to have brought in the requisite cash. Also show the calculation for capital to be introduced by Mahajan. *(B.Com., Madurai)*

[**Ans:** Revaluation Profit : Rs 2,500 (Sethi: Rs 1,500 and Sobti: Rs 1,000)
Mahajan's Capital: Rs 4,250
Balance Sheet Total: Rs 22,750]

18. Rajesh and Himanshu are partners sharing profits in the ratio of 3 : 2. Akhilesh is admitted and the new profit sharing ratio is 2 : 2 : 1. Akhilesh brings in cash Rs 40,000 for capital and Rs 10,000 for goodwill for his share of profit. The balance sheet of Rajesh and Himanshu is as follows:

Liabilities	*Rs*	*Assets*	*Rs*
Capital Accounts:		Goodwill	15,000
Rajesh	32,500	Plant & Machinery	35,000
Himanshu	32,500	Furniture	4,000
Creditors	10,200	Stock	16,000
Reserve Fund	10,000	Debtors	10,000
		Cash	5,200
	85,200		85,200

Partners decided that goodwill account should appear in the new firm's books at Rs 25,000. Give journal entries and prepare balance sheet of the new firm. *(B.Com., Madras)*

[**Ans:** Balance Sheet Total: Rs 1,45,200]

19. Set out below is the Balance Sheet of Biren and Niren who share profits and losses as 60% to Biren and 40% to Niren.

Liabilities		*Rs*	*Assets*	*Rs*
Creditors		40,000	Cash at Bank	2,000
Capital Accounts			Debtors	25,000
Biren	40,000		Stock	40,000
Niren	30,000	70,000	Plant	43,000
		1,10,000		1,10,000

The partners admit Dhiren into the firm on the following terms:

(*i*) Dhiren will pay Rs 20,000 as his capital for 40% of the future profits of the firm. (*ii*) The firm's assets are to be revalued before his admission: Stock was to be reduced to Rs 35,000 and Plant was to be depreciated by 10%. A reserve of 2½% is to be raised against Debtors. (*iii*) As the new partner is unable to pay anything for the goodwill premium, a Goodwill Account is to be raised in the books for Rs 30,000.

(*a*) You are required to give the Journal entries, the Profit and Loss Adjustment Account and the opening Balance Sheet of the new firm.

(*b*) In what ratio will the partners share future profits of the firm? *(B.Com., Calcutta)*

[**Ans:** Revaluation Loss: Rs 9,925 (Debit: Rs 5,955 to Biren and
Debit: Rs 3,970 to Niren)
Balance Sheet Total: Rs 1,50,075
Profit Sharing Ratio: 9 : 6 : 10]

20. A, B and C are partners in a firm of accountants who maintain on the cash basis sharing profits and losses in the ratio of 2 : 3 : 1. Their Balance Sheet as on 31st March, 2004, on which date D is admitted as a partner, is as follows:

Liabilities	*Rs*	*Assets*	*Rs*
B's Capital	35,000	Furniture	10,000
C's Capital	22,000	Motor Car	20,000
		Cash at Bank	18,000
		A's Capital	9,000
	57,000		57,000

D is given 1/4th share in the profits and losses in the firm and the profit and loss sharing ratio as between the other partners remains as before. The following adjustments are to be made prior to D's admission:

(*a*) The Motor Car is taken over by B at a value of Rs 25,000.

(*b*) The furniture is revalued at Rs 18,000.

(*c*) Goodwill account is raised in the books at Rs 50,000. It is agreed among A, B and C that C is interested in goodwill only up to a value of Rs 30,000.

(*d*) Fees billed but not realised Rs 11,000 are brought into account.

(*e*) Expenses incurred but not paid Rs 3,000 are provided for.

D brings in Rs 20,000 in cash as his capital contribution. He is also to be credited with Rs 20,000 for having agreed to amalgamate his separate practice as Chartered Accountant with this firm.

Prepare Revaluation Account, Capital Accounts and the Balance Sheet of the firm after D's admission.

(*C.A. Inter*)

[**Ans:** Revaluation Gain: Rs 21,000

(Rs 7,000 to A, Rs 10,500 to B and Rs 3,500 to C)

Capital Accounts:

A : Rs 16,000

B : Rs 47,500

C : Rs 30,500

D : Rs 40,000

Balance Sheet Total : Rs 1,37,000]

21. Marigold and Rose were in partnership sharing profits and losses as to two-thirds and one-third. As from 1st October, 2003, they agreed to take Jasmine as a new partner. The new partner will have one-sixth share, the old partners agreeing to share equally as between them in the new firm. Jasmine brings in Rs 50,000 as Capital and Rs 4,000 as his share of goodwill to be retained in the firm.

The following is the Balance Sheet of the old firm as on 30th September 2003.

Liabilities	*Rs*	*Assets*	*Rs*
Capital Accounts:		Cash	7,000
Marigold	62,500	Stock	50,000
Rose	37,500	Debtors	30,000
Creditors	50,000	Plant	25,000
		Investments	38,000
	1,50,000		1,50,000

The following revaluation is agreed upon:

Stock Rs 55,000; Plant Rs 20,000; Investments Rs 35,000.

Debtors: Subject to reserve for bad debts of 5%.

It is further agreed that Marigold alone is to be charged with any loss arising from the above. The profit for the year ended 30th September 2004 was Rs 1,20,000 and the drawings of the partners were: Marigold Rs 40,000; Rose Rs 40,000; Jasmine Rs 10,000.

You are required to journalise the opening adjustments and draw up the Balance Sheet as on 30th September 2004 making such assumptions as may be necessary. (*C.A. Inter*)

[**Ans:** Revaluation Loss: Rs 4,500
Balance Sheet Total: Rs 2,29,500]

22. A, B and C were partners sharing profits and losses in the ratio of 3 : 2 : 1. On 1st January, 2004, they admitted D into partnership on the following terms:
D to have one-sixth share which he purchased entirely from A, paying A Rs 40,000 for that share of goodwill (through the books of the firm). Of this amount A was to withdraw Rs 30,000 and D to bring in proportionate capital. It was further agreed that investments should be reduced to their market value *viz.*, Rs 18,000 and that plant should be reduced to Rs 29,000. A sum of Rs 3,000 included in creditors was to be written back as there was no liability to pay the amount.
The Balance Sheet on 31st December, 2003, was as follows:

Liabilities	*Rs*	*Assets*	*Rs*
Creditors	1,05,000	Cash at Bank	40,000
Capital Accounts:		Debtors	60,000
A	60,000	Stock	50,000
B	40,000	Investments at cost	30,000
C	20,000	Furniture and Fittings	10,000
		Plant	35,000
	2,25,000		2,25,000

The profits for 2004 were Rs 60,000 and the drawings were Rs 15,000 for A and B each and Rs 7,500 for C and D each.
Journalise the entries to be made on D's admission, and give the Capital Accounts and Balance Sheet on 31st December, 2004. (*B.Com., Delhi*)

[**Ans:** Capital Accounts: A : Rs 67,500
B : Rs 40,000
C : Rs 20,000
D : Rs 25,500
Balance Sheet Total : Rs 2,55,000]

23. Sun and Moon are two partners in a firm sharing profits and losses in the ratio of 3 : 2. Their Balance Sheet as at 30th June 2004, is as follows:

Liabilities		*Rs*	*Assets*		*Rs*
Sundry Creditors		14,000	Cash in hand		40,000
Bank Overdraft		6,000	Sundry Debtors:	22,000	
Reserve		10,000	*Less*: Reserve	2,000	20,000
Capital Accounts:			Furniture		10,000
Sun	25,000		Stock		30,000
Moon	45,000	70,000			
		1,00,000			1,00,000

Star is to be taken as a third partner with effect from 1st July 2004 on the following terms:

(*a*) The new profit sharing ratio of Sun, Moon and Star shall be 5 : 3 : 2.
(*b*) Reserve for bad debts is to be created at 10% out of Reserve.
(*c*) Goodwill is to be created in the books for Rs 40,000, 50% of which will be withdrawn by partners.
(*d*) Book value of goodwill is to be written off after admission.
(*e*) Star is to pay off the Bank Overdraft and to bring such an amount in cash so as to make his capital one-sixth of total capital of the new firm after above adjustments.

You are asked to journalise the entries in the books of the firm and also show the resultant Balance Sheet of the new firm. (*ICWA*)

[Ans: Balance Sheet Total: Rs 95,360]

24. Abhay and Vinay were partners sharing profits in the ratio of 4 : 3. On 1st July 2004 Chinmay was admitted into partnership on the following conditions:

Chinmay to have 1/4th share, of which 3/4 was purchased from Abhay and 1/4th from Vinay paying them Rs 10,000 for his share of goodwill. Of this amount half of the cash was withdrawn by the partners and Chinmay to bring in proportionate capital. It was further agreed that furniture should be reduced to Rs 5,000 and machinery should be increased to Rs 30,000. A sum of Rs 4,000 included in creditors was to be written back as there was no liability to pay the amount. The contingent liability for bills discounted is also expected to be Rs 3,000. The Balance Sheet as on 30th June, 2004, was as given below:

Liabilities		*Rs*	*Assets*	*Rs*
Creditors		65,000	Cash at Bank	16,000
Bills Payable		20,000	Book debts	50,000
Building Fund		14,000	Stock	40,000
Capital Accounts:			Furniture	7,000
Abhay	47,000		Motor Car	20,000
Vinay	50,000	97,000	Machinery	25,000
			Building	38,000
		1,96,000		1,96,000

You are required to prepare Revaluation Account, Partners' Capital Accounts and the Balance Sheet as on 1st July, 2004. (*ICWA*)

[Ans: Revaluation Gain: Rs 4,000 (Abhay: Rs 2,286 + Vinay: Rs 1,714)
Capital Accounts: Abhay : Rs 61,036
Vinay : Rs 58,964
Chinmay : Rs 40,000
Balance Sheet Total : Rs 2,44,000]

25. Madan and Krishna are partners in a business. Their balance sheet as on 31st December, 2004, stood as under:

Liabilities		*Rs*	*Assets*	*Rs*
Creditors for expenses		10,000	Cash in hand	4,000
Sundry creditors		30,000	Cash at bank	56,000
Bank overdraft		20,000	Debtors	30,000
Bills Payable		30,000	Furniture	12,000
Reserves		18,000	Machinery	24,000
Capital Accounts:			Buildings	57,000
Madan	45,000			
Krishna	30,000	75,000		
		1,83,000		1,83,000

They decided to admit Ram on the following terms: (*i*) That machinery, buildings and furniture be depreciated at 5%. (*ii*) That a reserve at 5% created for doubtful debts. (*iii*) That a goodwill account for Rs 30,000 be opened in the books of the firm. (*iv*) That Ram brings Rs 45,000 as capital and he will receive 1/4th share in future profits. (*v*) That the Capital Accounts of all partners be adjusted in proportion to their profit sharing ratio.

Prepare revaluation account, capital accounts of the partners, bank account and the initial balance sheet of the firm. Show new profit sharing. (*B.Com., Maharashtra*)

[**Ans:** Revaluation Loss Rs 6,150 (Madan : Rs 3,075 + Krishna : Rs 3,075)
Capital Accounts: Madan : Rs 67,500
Krishna: Rs 67,500
Ram: Rs 45,000
Madan brought in cash: Rs 1,575
Krishna brought in cash: Rs 16,575
Balance Sheet Total: Rs 2,70,000
New Profit Sharing Ratio : 3 : 3 : 2]

26. Pataudi and Sobers are equal partners and on 31st Dec. 2004 their Balance Sheet stood as follows:

Liabilities	*Rs*	*Assets*	*Rs*
Reserve for Doubtful Debts	4,000	Stock-in-Trade	45,000
Reserve Fund	5,000	Sundry Debtors	81,000
Capital Accounts:		Fixtures & Fittings	3,000
Pataudi	50,000	Cash in hand	500
Sobers	30,000	Investments	4,500
Sundry Creditors	47,900	Bank Balance	2,900
	1,36,900		1,36,900

Mr. Manjrekar was taken in partnership as from 1st Jan. 2005 and it as agreed between Pataudi and Sobers to make the following adjustments:

(*a*) To write off Bad Debts amounting to Rs 5,500.

(*b*) To write 25 per cent off fixtures and fittings.

(*c*) To depreciate stock-in-trade by Rs 3,750.

(*d*) To write off loss of Rs 500 on investments.

(*e*) To create a Goodwill Account of Rs 10,000.

Mr Manjrekar then introduces Rs 35,000 as his third share of capital to which it has been agreed that the capitals of the other two partners shall be adjusted. Pass necessary journal entries to carry out these transactions and prepare the Balance Sheet of the firm immediately after Mr Manjrekar's admission as a partner. (*I.C.W.A.*)

[**Ans:** Balance Sheet Total: Rs 1,70,150]

27. Deepak, Harish and Farokh were equal partners in a firm by name "Enterprises" and the following Balance Sheet as at 1st July 2004 was produced by them:

		Rs	
Fixed Assets:			
Goodwill		1,19,000	
Building		1,95,000	
Furniture		24,000	
			3,38,000
Working Capital:			
Stock	1,14,000		
Debtors	1,08,000		
Cash	6,000		
		2,28,000	
Less: Creditors	33,000		
Bills Payable	60,000		
		93,000	1,35,000
		Total Assets	4,73,000

Represented by:		
Capital Accounts:		
Deepak	2,17,000	
Harish	1,66,000	
Farokh	90,000	4,73,000

On 1st July 2004, they agreed to take Ram as an equal partner on the following terms:

(*a*) Ram should bring in Rs 1,50,000 as his capital and Goodwill. His share of goodwill was evaluated at Rs 50,000.

(*b*) The goodwill account is to be written off before admission.

(*c*) Provision for loss on Stock and Provision for Debtors was to be made at 10% and 5% respectively.

(*d*) The value of Building was to be taken at Rs 2,70,000.

(*e*) The total capital of the new firm was fixed at Rs 4,00,000 and the partners' accounts be in their profit sharing ratio, any excess is to be transferred to Current Account or deficit to be introduced in cash.

You are required to prepare the Profit and Loss Adjustment Account, Balance Sheet of the new firm and the partners' Capital Account. (*ICWA*)

[Ans: Balance Sheet Total : Rs 6,68,800]

28. On 1st Jan. 2004, A and B, who were trading in partnership, sharing 7/12th and 5/12th respectively, take in C, giving him 1/6th share, over and above his capital. C brings in Rs 96,000 as his goodwill for the 1/6th shares which he has acquired 1/24th from A and 1/8th from B. The cash brought in by C as his capital as well as for his share in goodwill is credited in one separate account in his personal name. On 31st Dec. 2004, their Trial Balance stood as follows:

	Rs		*Rs*
Machinery	6,00,000	A's Capital	3,36,000
Furniture	40,000	B's Capital	2,40,000
Stock	1,20,000	C's Account (Personal)	2,24,000
Debtors	2,00,000	Creditors	48,000
A's Drawings	32,000	Current Year Profit	2,32,000
B's Drawings	52,000		
C's Drawings	8,000		
Cash in hand	28,000		
	10,80,000		10,80,000

Interest on Drawings is to be ignored but interest on capital is to be allowed at 5% p.a. after the necessary adjustment therein as regards the goodwill in cash brought in by C.

Prepare the Balance Sheet of the firm as on 31st Dec. 2004, showing full details in the Capital Accounts of all partners. (*GDA*)

[Ans: Capital Accounts:
A : Rs 4,50,000
B : Rs 3,31,600
C : Rs 1,58,400
Balance Sheet Total : Rs 9,88,000]

29. Balance Sheet as on 31st Dec. 2004 of Ramesh, Kumar and Papu who were sharing profits and losses in the ratio of 2 : 3 : 5 is as follows:

Liabilities	*Rs*	*Assets*	*Rs*
Capitals:		Cash	18,000
Ramesh	36,000	Bills Receivable	24,000
Kumar	44,000	Furniture	28,000
Papu	52,000	Stock	44,000
Creditors	64,000	Debtors	42,000
Bills Payable	32,000	Investments	32,000
Profit & Loss A/c	14,000	Machinery	34,000
		Goodwill	20,000
	2,42,000		2,42,000

They admit Shilpa into partnership on the following terms:

1. Furniture, Investments and Machinery to be reduced by 15%.
2. The value of stock to be taken at Rs 48,000.
3. Goodwill to be valued at Rs 26,000.
4. Shilpa to bring Rs 32,000 towards capital for 1/6 share and old partners to adjust their capitals accordingly.
5. Outstanding rent amounted to Rs 1,800.
6. Prepaid salaries Rs 800.
7. Adjustments of capitals to be made by cash.

Prepare Revaluation A/c, capital accounts of the old partners, cash account and the balance sheet of the new firm. (*B.Com., Karnataka*)

[**Ans:** Total Revaluation Loss: Rs 11,100
(Rs 2,220 to Ramesh; Rs 3,330 to Kumar and Rs 5,550 to Papu)
Capital Accounts: Ramesh: Rs 32,000
Kumar: Rs 48,000
Papu: Rs 80,000
Shilpa: Rs 32,000
Balance Sheet Total : Rs 2,89,800]

30. A, B and C are partners in a firm sharing profits and losses in the ratio of 3 : 2 : 1. Their Balance Sheet on 1st January 2004 was as follows:

Liabilities		*Amount* Rs	*Assets*	*Amount* Rs
Creditors		8,800	Cash in hand	600
General Reserve		7,200	Stock in trade	15,400
Capital Accounts:			Debtors	11,100
A	18,000		Bills Receivable	5,700
B	15,000		Investments	2,950
C	11,000	44,000	Land and Building	26,000
Current Accounts:			B's Current Account	250
A	780			
C	1,220	2,000		
		62,000		62,000

On the above date, D was admitted into partnership on the following conditions:

1. D should bring Rs 5,000 as his capital.
2. Goodwill was valued at Rs 15,000.
3. A, B, C and D will share profits in the ratio of 4 : 3 : 2 : 1 respectively.

4. The value of stock reduced by Rs 2,000 and a provision for doubtful debts be made @ 10% on debtors.
5. Land and Building be appreciated by 25%.
6. A liability of Rs 1,290 be created against bills discounted.
7. The Capital Accounts of the partners be readjusted on the basis of their profit sharing ratio through current accounts.

Prepare Revaluation Account, Partners' Capital and Current Accounts and the Balance Sheet of the new firm, assuming that the new firm does not show the goodwill in the books.

(B.Com., Kerala, Madurai, Punjab)

[**Ans:** Capital Accounts:
A : Rs 20,000
B : Rs 15,000
C : Rs 10,000
D : Rs 5,000
Revaluation gain : Rs 2,100 (A : Rs 1,050; B : Rs 700
and C : Rs 350)
Balance Sheet Total : Rs 71,640]

31. Messrs Dalal, Banerji and Malick is a firm sharing profits and losses in the ratio of 2 : 2 : 1. Their Balance Sheet as on 31st March, 2004 is as follows:

Liabilities		*Rs*	*Assets*	*Rs*
Sundry Creditors		12,850	Land and Buildings	25,000
Outstanding liabilities		1,500	Furniture	6,500
General Reserve		6,500	Stock of goods	11,750
Capital Accounts:			Sundry debtors	5,500
Mr Dalal	12,000		Cash on hand	140
Mr Banerji	12,000		Cash at Bank	960
Mr Malick	5,000	29,000		
		49,850		49,850

The partners have agreed to take Mr Mistri as a partner with effect from 1st April, 2004, on the following terms:

(1) Mr Mistri shall bring Rs 5,000 towards his capital.
(2) The value of stock should be increased by Rs 2,500.
(3) Reserve for bad and doubtful debts should be provided at 10% of the debtors.
(4) The furniture should be depreciated by 10%.
(5) The value of land and buildings should be enhanced by 20%.
(6) The value of the goodwill be fixed at Rs 15,000.
(7) General Reserve will be transferred to the Partners' Capital Accounts.
(8) The new profit sharing ratio shall be:

Mr Dalal	5/15
Mr Banerji	5/15
Mr Malick	3/15
Mr Mistri	2/15

(9) The Goodwill account shall be written back to the partners' accounts in accordance with the new profit sharing proportion.
(10) The outstanding liabilities include Rs 1,000 due to Mr Sen which has been paid by Mr Dalal. Necessary entries were not made in the books.

Prepare (*i*) Revaluation Account, (*ii*) the Capital Accounts of the Partners, and (*iii*) the Balance Sheet of the firm as newly constituted (journal entries are not required). (*C.A. Inter*)

[**Ans:** Revaluation Gain: Rs 6,300
(Rs 2,520 to A; Rs 2,520 to B and Rs 1,260 to C)
Capital Accounts:
A : Rs 19,120
B : Rs 18,120
C : Rs 7,560
D : Rs 3,000
Balance Sheet Total : Rs 61,150]

32. A and B are partners in a firm sharing profits and losses in ratio 7 : 3. Their Balance Sheet as at 31st March 2004 is as follows:

Liabilities		*Rs*	*Assets*		*Rs*
Sundry Creditors		40,000	Cash in hand		36,000
Bank Overdraft		20,000	Sundry Debtors:	46,500	
Reserve		10,000	*Less*: Provision for Bad Debts	2,000	44,000
Capital Accounts:			Furniture		30,000
A	50,000		Stock		50,000
B	40,000	90,000			
		1,60,000			1,60,000

On 1st April 2004, C joins the firm as a third partner for 1/4th share of the profits on the following terms:

(*a*) Goodwill is valued at Rs 40,000 and C is to bring necessary amount in cash as premium for goodwill.

(*b*) 20% of the Reserve is to remain as a provision against bad and doubtful debts.

(*c*) Stock is to be reduced by 40% and Furniture is to be reduced to 40%.

(*d*) A is to pay off the Bank Overdraft.

(*e*) C is to introduce Rs 30,000 as his share of capital to which other partners' capital shall have to be adjusted.

Show the necessary journal entries to carry out the above transactions and prepare an amended Balance Sheet of the firm immediately after C has become a partner. (*ICWA*)

[**Ans:** Balance Sheet Total : Rs 1,60,000
Profit Sharing Ratio : 21 : 9 : 10]

Chapter 31

Partnership Accounts: Retirement or Death of a Partner

Introduction — Various Adjustments on Retirement – Amount Due to Outgoing Partner – Admission and Retirement – Death of a Partner – Amount Due to Deceased Partner – Joint Life Policy – Questions – Objective Type Questions – Theoretical Questions – Practical Problems.

INTRODUCTION

The retirement of a partner extinguishes his interest in the Partnership firm and this leads to dissolution of the firm or reconstitution of the Partnership. A partner, who goes out of a firm, is called retiring partner or outgoing partner. Causes for the retirement may be that a retiring partner may be too old or he may have better opportunity in a different line or he may dislike the co-partners' attitude or any other reasons. The following are the ways in which a partner can retire:

1. With the consent of all the other partners,
2. In accordance with an express agreement among the partners,
3. By giving a written notice of intention to retire to all the other partners where partnership is at will.

VARIOUS ADJUSTMENTS ON RETIREMENT

When a partner retires his share in the properties of the firm has to be ascertained and paid off. Certain adjustments have to be made in order to ascertain the amount he is to get from the firm. These adjustments are very similar to those which we saw in connection with admission of a partner. When a partner retires from the business, it becomes necessary to prepare the accounts so as to ascertain the amount payable to him. When a partner retires, the following adjustments must be made:

1. Adjustment of accumulated reserves and undistributed profit and losses.
2. Revaluation of assets and liabilities.
3. Adjustment for goodwill of the firm.
4. Calculation of new profit and loss sharing ratio.
5. Calculation of the amount due to retiring partner and the mode of payment.

We shall discuss these points.

1. Adjustment of Accumulated Reserves and Undistributed Profits and Losses

Any reserves or undistributed profits appearing on the liability side of the Balance Sheet, at the time of retirement, are past profits, which are created to strengthen the financial position of the firm. The retiring partner has a right over such profits. Therefore, it is necessary to divide the accumulated reserve or undistributed profit among all the partners in their old profit or loss sharing ratio. When the distribution is over, they do not appear in the Balance Sheet.

The journal entries are:

General Reserve Account	Dr.	
Profit and Loss Account	Dr.	
To All Partners Capital Account		
(Being transfer of General Reserve and profit in the old profit sharing ratio)		

Alternatively, instead of transferring the entire reserve or profit, only the share of the Retiring Partner may be transferred to the Retiring Partner's Capital Account. The balance in the reserve or profit account continues to appear on the liability side, at reduced amount.

General Reserve Account	Dr.	
Profit and Loss Account	Dr.	
To Retiring Partner's Capital Account		
(Being the share of accumulated profits transferred to Retiring Partner Capital Account)		

In case the firm has incurred any losses in the past and the losses were not adjusted so far to the capital accounts, then such losses, which is found in the asset side of balance sheet, be transferred to the Retiring Partner's Capital Account, to the extent of his share. By doing so, the losses continue to appear on asset side of the Balance Sheet, at a reduced amount.

2. Revaluation of Assets and Liabilities

Revaluation of assets and liabilities is equally necessary at the time of retirement of a partner, as at admission. The revaluation is done on the same principles as in case of admission. Even if the Partnership Deed is silent, it is better to revalue assets and liabilities. If it is agreed to revalue the assets and liabilities on the retirement of a partner, Profit and Loss Adjustment Account or Revaluation Account is prepared. The profit or loss arising out of this account is transferred to all partners including retiring partner in OLD RATIO. Therefore, the assets and liabilities will then appear in the books at the revised values. If the continuing partners decide to maintain the assets and liabilities at their original value, then a MEMORANDUM REVALUATION ACCOUNT is prepared by passing reversal entry and the profit or loss of this account is transferred to continuing partners capital account in their NEW PROFIT SHARING RATIO.

ILLUSTRATION 31.1

A and B are partners in a business sharing profits and losses as A 3/5ths and B 2/5ths. Their Balance Sheet as on 1st January 2005 is given below:

Liabilities			*Rs*	*Assets*	*Rs*
Capitals:	A	20,000		Machinery	19,500
	B	15,000	35,000	Stock	16,000
Reserve			15,000	Debtors	15,000
Sundry Creditors			7,500	Cash at Bank	6,000
				Cash in hand	1,000
			57,500		57,500

B decides to retire from the business owing to illness and A takes it over and the following revaluation are made:

(*a*) Goodwill of the firm is valued at Rs 15,000.

(*b*) Depreciate Machinery by 7.5% and Stock by 15%.

(*c*) A Bad Debts provision is raised against Debtors at 5% and a Discount Reserve against Creditors at 2.5%.

Journalise the above transaction in the books of the firm, prepare ledger accounts and the Balance Sheet of A.

(*B.Com., Delhi, MK*)

SOLUTION

Journal Entries

	Particulars		Dr. Rs	Cr. Rs
	Goodwill Account	Dr.	15,000	
	To A's Capital Account			9,000
	To B's Capital Account			6,000
	(Being goodwill raised and credited to Partners Capital Account in profit sharing ratio)			
	Revaluation Account	Dr.	4,613	
	To Machinery Account			1,463
	To Stock Account			2,400
	To Bad Debts Provision			750
	(Being value reduced on assets on retirement)			
	Provision for Discount on Creditors A/c	Dr.	188	
	To Revaluation Account			188
	(Being provision for discount on creditors created)			
	A's Capital Account	Dr.	2,655	
	B's Capital Account	Dr.	1,770	
	To Revaluation Account			4,425
	(Being loss on revaluation of assets transferred to Capital Account in profit sharing ratio)			
	Reserve Account	Dr.	15,000	
	To A's Capital Account			9,000
	To B's Capital Account			6,000
	(Being reserve credited to Capital Accounts in profit sharing ratio)			
	B's Capital Account	Dr.	25,300	
	To B's Loan Account			25,300
	(Being B's Capital Account transferred to his loan account)			

Revaluation Account

Dr.	Rs			Cr. Rs
To Machinery Account	1,463	By Provision for Discount on Creditors		188
To Stock Account	2,400	By Loss: Transferred to Capital A/c A:	2,655	
To Bad Debts Provision	750	B:	1,770	4,425
	4,613			4,613

Capital Accounts

Dr.	A Rs	B Rs	Cr.	A Rs	B Rs
To Revaluation A/c	2,655	1,770	By Balance b/d	20,000	15,000
To B's Loan A/c		25,230	By Goodwill	9,000	6,000
To Balance c/d	35,345		By Reserve	9,000	6,000
	38,000	27,000		38,000	27,000

Balance Sheet of A
as on 1st January 2005

Liabilities		*Rs*	*Assets*		*Rs*
Sundry Creditors	7,500		Goodwill		15,000
Less: Provision	188	7,312	Cash in hand		1,000
B's Loan Account		25,230	Cash in Bank		6,000
A's Capital Account		35,345	Debtors	15,000	
			Less: Provision	750	14,250
			Stock	16,000	
			Less: Depreciation	2,400	13,600
			Machinery	19,500	
			Less: Depreciation	1,463	18,037
		67,887			67,887

ILLUSTRATION 31.2

A, B and C were partners, sharing profits in the proportions of one-half, one-third and one-sixth respectively. The firm's Balance Sheet as on 31st March 2005 stood as under:

Liabilities		*Rs*	*Assets*		*Rs*
Sundry Creditors		19,000	Cash		2,500
Bills Payable		5,000	Debtors	16,000	
Reserve Fund		12,000	*Less*: Provision	500	15,500
Capitals: A	40,000		Stock		25,000
B	30,000		Motor Vans		8,000
C	25,000	95,000	Plant and Machinery		35,000
			Factory Buildings		45,000
		1,31,000			1,31,000

B retires on that date subject to the following adjustments:

(1) The goodwill of the firm to be valued at Rs 18,000.

(2) Plant to be depreciated by 10% and Motor vans by 15%.

(3) Stock to be appreciated by 20% and Buildings by 10%.

(4) Provision for doubtful Debts to be increased by Rs 1,950.

(5) Liability for workmen's compensation to the extent of Rs 450 is to be brought into account.

It was agreed that A and C will share profits in future in the ratio of A–3/5th and C–2/5th.

Pass journal entries, prepare Memorandum Revaluation Account, Capital Accounts and Balance Sheet when the assets and liabilities are to continue to appear at their original figures. (*B.Com., Madurai*)

SOLUTION

Journal Entries

			Dr. *Rs*	Cr. *Rs*
	Goodwill Account	Dr.	18,000	
	To A's Capital Account			9,000
	To B's Capital Account			6,000
	To C's Capital Account			3,000
	(Being goodwill raised in the books)			
	A's Capital Account	Dr.	1,200	
	C's Capital Account	Dr.	2,800	

Particulars		Dr.	Cr.
To B's Capital Account (Being B's share of reserve credited to his account and debited to capital accounts of A and C in gaining ratio: *i.e.* 3 : 7)			4,000
A's Capital Account	Dr.	10,800	
C's Capital Account	Dr.	7,200	
To Goodwill Account (Being Goodwill written off in the new ratio)			18,000
Memorandum Revaluation Account	Dr.	2,400	
To A's Capital Account			1,200
To B's Capital Account			800
To C's Capital Account (Being profit on revaluation transferred to all partners' capital accounts in old ratio)			400
A's Capital Account	Dr.	1,440	
C's Capital Account	Dr.	960	
To Memorandum Revaluation Account (Being profit on revaluation account written back to continuing partners' capital account in new profit sharing ratio)			2,400
B's Capital Account	Dr.	40,800	
To B's Loan Account (Being balance due to B transferred to his Loan Account)			40,800

Memorandum Revaluation Account

Dr.		*Rs*			Cr. *Rs*
To Decrease in value of	Rs		By Increase in value of	Rs	
Plant	3,500		Stock	5,000	
Motor Van	1,200		Buildings	4,500	9,500
Debtors	1,950	6,650			
To Increase in value of:					
Workmen's Compensation		450			
To Profit Transferred to Capital Accounts:					
A: 3/6	1,200				
B: 2/6	800				
C: 1/6	400	2,400			
		9,500			9,500
To Reversal of entries on credit side		9,500	By Reversal of entries on debit side		7,100
			By Loss transferred to Capital Accounts:		
			A – 3/5	1,440	
			B – 2/5	960	2,400
		9,500			9,500

Balance Sheet of A and C

Liabilities		*Rs*	*Assets*		*Rs*
Sundry Creditors		19,000	Cash	Rs	2,500
Bills Payable		5,000	Debtors:	16,000	
Reserve Fund		12,000	*Less*: Provision	500	15,500
B's Loan Account		40,800	Stock		25,000
Capital Accounts:	Rs		Motor Vans		8,000
A:	36,760		Plant and Machinery		35,000
B:	17,440	54,200	Factory Buildings		45,000
		1,31,000			1,31,000

Capital Accounts

Dr.	*A*	*B*	*C*		*A*	*B*	*C* Cr.
	Rs	*Rs*	*Rs*		*Rs*	*Rs*	*Rs*
To B's Capital Accounts	1,200	–	2,800	By Balance b/d	40,000	30,000	25,000
To Goodwill	10,800	–	7,200	By Capital Accounts of A and C	–	4,000	–
To Memorandum Revaluation A/c	1,440	–	960	By Goodwill	9,000	6,000	3,000
To B's Loan A/c	–	40,800	–	By Memorandum Revaluation A/c	1,200	800	400
To Balance c/d	36,760	–	17,440				
	50,200	40,800	28,400		50,200	40,800	28,400
				By Balance b/d	36,760	–	17,440

3. Adjustment of Goodwill

The valuation of goodwill may be done according to the provisions of the Partnership Deed and in the same manner as in case of admission by any one of the following methods:

A. *When Goodwill does not appear in the books:*

(*i*) When goodwill is raised at its full value	Goodwill Account Dr. To All Partners' Capital A/c (Being goodwill raised at its full value and credited to all partners' capital account in old profit sharing ratio)	It appears in Balance Sheet
(*ii*) When goodwill is raised and written off.	Goodwill Account Dr. To All Partners' Capital A/c (Being goodwill raised at its full value and credited to all partners' capital account in old profit sharing ratio) Continuing Partners Capital A/c Dr. To Goodwill Account (Being goodwill written off in new profit sharing ratio)	It does not appear in Balance Sheet
(*iii*) When goodwill raised only to the extent of retiring partners' share.	Goodwill Account Dr. To Retiring Partners' Capital Account (Being goodwill raised to the extent of outgoing partners' share)	

	Continuing Partners' Capital A/c Dr. To Goodwill Account (Being goodwill written off in gaining ratio)	It does not appear in Balance Sheet
(*iv*) When goodwill is given to outgoing partner, without raising or recording it in the books	Continuing Partners' Capital A/c Dr. To Outgoing Partners Capital Account (Being outgoing partner's share of goodwill is credited to him and debited to continuing partners' capital accounts in gaining ratio)	It does not appear in Balance Sheet

B. *When goodwill already appears in the books*

(*i*) If goodwill appears at correct value	No Entry	
(*ii*) If goodwill appears at less value than the actual/present value	Goodwill Account Dr. To All Partners' Capital A/c * (Being goodwill raised in full value: only the difference (Old profit sharing ratio)	It appears in Balance Sheet
(*iii*) If goodwill appears at higher value than the actual value	All Partners' Capital Account Dr. To Goodwill Account (Being the excess value of goodwill written off by debiting all partners' capital accounts in old ratio)	It appears in Balance Sheet

ILLUSTRATION 31.3

A, B and C were partners in a firm with capitals of Rs 10,000, Rs 8,000 and Rs 6,000 respectively and sharing profits and losses in the ratio of 3 : 2 : 1. On 31st December 2005, B retires. For the purpose of retirement, the goodwill of the firm was valued at Rs 18,000.

Pass necessary journal entries under the following circumstances and also find out the amount payable to B:

(*a*) Total goodwill raised and maintained in the books.
(*b*) Total goodwill raised but written off later.
(*c*) Only B's share of goodwill is raised and maintained in the Books.
(*d*) Only B's share of goodwill is raised but later on written off.
(*e*) B is given his share of goodwill without raising Goodwill Account.

SOLUTION

Journal Entries

			Dr.	Cr.
			Rs	Rs
(*a*)	Goodwill Account Dr.		18,000	
	To A's Capital Account			9,000
	To B's Capital Account			6,000
	To C's Capital Account			3,000
	(Being goodwill raised in the books at full value at the time of B's retirement)			
(*b*)	Goodwill Account Dr.		18,000	
	To A's Capital Account			9,000
	To B's Capital Account			6,000
	To C's Capital Account			3,000
	(Being goodwill raised in the books at full value at the time of B's retirement)			

	A's Capital Account	Dr.	13,500	
	C's Capital Account	Dr.	4,500	
	To Goodwill Account			18,000
	(Being goodwill written off in the New Ratio *i.e.* 3 : 1)			
(*c*)	Goodwill Account	Dr.	6,000	
	To B's Capital Account			6,000
	(Being only B's share of goodwill raised in the books)			
(*d*)	Goodwill Account	Dr.	6,000	
	To B's Capital Account			6,000
	(Being only B's share of goodwill raised in the books)			
	A's Capital Account	Dr.	4,500	
	C's Capital Account	Dr.	1,500	
	To Goodwill Account			6,000
	(Being B's share of goodwill raised is now written off in beneft ratio : *i.e.* 3 : 1)			
(*e*)	A's Capital Account	Dr.	4,500	
	C's Capital Account	Dr.	1,500	
	To B's Capital Account			6,000
	(Being B's share of goodwill raised is adjusted to continuing partners' capital account in benefit ratio, *i.e.* 3 : 1, without raising goodwill account)			

ILLUSTRATION 31.4

(*a*) A, B and C are equal partners. Goodwill appears in the books at Rs 10,000. C retires and goodwill is revalued at Rs 15,000. Now A and B decide to share future profits and losses in the ratio of 3 : 2.

(*b*) X, Y and Z are partners sharing profits in the ratio of 4 : 3 : 3. Goodwill does not appear in the books. Z retires from the firm and his share of goodwill is estimated to be Rs 6,000, which was purchased by X and Y in equal proportion. X and Y decide not to open Goodwill Account.

(*c*) Ram, Mohan and Moni were partners sharing profits in the ratio of 2 : 2 : 1. On 1st January 2005, their goodwill was valued at Rs 30,000 and there is no Goodwill Account appearing in the books. Mohan retired. No goodwill is to appear in the books.

Pass journal entries.

SOLUTION

Joursnal Entries

			Dr. *Rs*	Cr. *Rs*
(*a*)	Goodwill Account	Dr.	5,000	
	To A's Capital Account			1,667
	To B's Capital Account			1,667
	To C's Capital Account			1,666
	(Being goodwill account is raised and benefit credited to partners capital account in their profit sharing ratio)			

If it is desired to write off the Goodwill:

			Rs	Rs
	A's Capital Account	Dr.	9,000	
	B's Capital Account	Dr.	6,000	
	To Goodwill Account			15,000
	(Being goodwill written off in the New Profit sharing ratio)			
(b)	X's Capital Account	Dr.	3,000	
	Y's Capital Account	Dr.	3,000	
	To Z's Capital Account			6,000
	(Being Z's share of goodwill credited to him and debited to X and Y in their gaining ratio: *i.e.* 1 : 1)			
(c)	Ram's Capital Account:	Dr.	8,000	
	Moni's Capital Account	Dr.	4,000	
	To Mohan's Capital Account			12,000
	(Being Mohan's share of goodwill credited to him and debited to continuing partners' capital account, in benefit ratio)			

4. Calculation of New Profit and Loss Sharing Ratio

When a partner of a firm retires, it is for the continuing partners to agree amongst themselves as to in what ratio, they shall share the profit and loss of the firm in future. The ratio so agreed upon is called NEW PROFIT SHARING RATIO. In the absence of any agreement between the partners, the continuing partners will continue to share the profit or loss in between themselves in the same ratio in which they were sharing before retirement. For instance, A, B and C were partners sharing profits in the ratio of 3 : 2 : 1 and if C retires, nothing is given about the new profit sharing ratio, then the profit sharing ratio of the continuing partners would be 3 : 2. Ratio of their gain will also be 3 : 2 which was their old profit sharing ratio.

Sometimes, the continuing partners may agree to have a new profit sharing ratio, by making changes in the existing profit sharing ratio and sometimes, the remaining partners may agree to purchase the share of the retired partner in a different ratio. This is explained below:

Calculation of Benefit Ratio and New Ratio

	AMONG CONTINUING PARTNERS	
	New Ratio	*Benefit Ratio*
When New Ratio is given	As given in the question	New Ratio – Old Ratio
When New Ratio is not given	Old Ratio among themselves	Old Ratio among themselves
When Benefit Ratio is given	Old Ratio + Benefit Ratio	As given in the problem

Sacrificing Ratio Vs. Gaining Ratio

Sacrificing Ratio	Gaining Ratio
1. The term is used generally in case of admission of a partner.	1. The term is used generally in case of retirement or death of a partner.
2. It is the ratio in which the existing partners lose a share of profit on admission of a partner.	2. It is the ratio in which the continuing partners gain on retirement or death of a partner.
3. OR – NR = SR	3. NR – OR = GR

4. The purpose is to determine the amount of compensation to be given to old partners.	4. The purpose is to determine the amount of compensation to be given to the retirement partner by the continuing partners.

ILLUSTRATION 31.5

X, Y and Z were partners sharing profits in the ratio of 2 : 2 : 1. Z retires and his share was taken up by X and Y in the ratio of 3:2. Calculate new profit sharing ratio and gaining ratio of X and Y. (*B. Com. MK, Kerala*)

SOLUTIONS

Z's share = $\frac{1}{5}$

Z's share is taken up by X and Y in 3:2 ratio.

Thus X takes up = $\frac{1}{5}\times\frac{3}{5}=\frac{3}{25}$

Y takes up = $\frac{1}{5}\times\frac{2}{5}=\frac{2}{25}$

X's new ratio = $\frac{2}{5}+\frac{3}{25}=\frac{10+3}{25}=\frac{13}{25}$

Y's new ratio = $\frac{2}{5}+\frac{2}{25}=\frac{10+2}{25}=\frac{12}{25}$

New Ratio of X and Y = **13:12**

Gaining Ratio = New Ratio – Old Ratio

$X=\frac{13}{25}-\frac{2}{5}=\frac{13-10}{25}=\frac{3}{25}$

$Y=\frac{12}{25}-\frac{2}{5}=\frac{12-10}{25}=\frac{2}{25}$

∴ Gaining Ratio of X and Y = **3 : 2**

ILLUSTRATION 31.6

A, B and C are in partnership sharing profit or losses in the ratio of 5 : 3 : 2. Find the new ratio and gaining ratio in the following cases:

(*a*) A retires, B and C continue.

(*b*) B retires, A and C continue.

(*c*) C retires, A and B continue

SOLUTION

In the absence of any agreement between the partners as regards the new profit sharing ratio, the continuing partners will continue to share the profit or loss in between themselves, in the same ratio in which they were sharing profits before retirement of partner.

Situations	*Continuing Partners*	*P/L Ratio*	*Gaining Ratio*
A retires	B and C	3 : 2	3 : 2
B retires	A and C	5 : 2	5 : 2
C retires	A and B	5 : 3	5 : 3

In other words, retiring partner's share of profit is shared by remaining partners in their old profit sharing ratio. For example, take the case of (a) above.

(*a*) B's share of profit = 3/10 + (5/10 × 3/5) = 3/10 + 3/10 = **6/10**

C's share of profit = 2/10 + (5/10 × 2/5) = 2/10 + 2/10 = **4/10**

(Or) Ratio is 6 : 4 or **3 : 2**

Gaining Ratio = **3 : 2**

Similarly, it can be proved with case (*b*) and (*c*).

ILLUSTRATION 31.7

X, Y and Z are partners, sharing profit and losses in the ratio of 2 : 3 : 1. X retires and his share is purchased by Y and Z in the ratio of 3 : 2. What is new profit sharing ratio?

SOLUTION

Old profit sharing ratio of X, Y and Z = 2 : 3 : 1

Y and Z purchased X's share *i.e.* 2/6 in the ratio of 3 : 2.

	Old Ratio	*Gaining Ratio*	*New Ratio*
Y	3/6	2/6 × 3/5 = 1/5 or 3/15	3/6 + 1/5 = 7/10
Z	1/6	2/6 × 2/5 = 2/15	1/6 + 2/15 = 9/30 (or) 3/10

New Profit Sharing ratio of Y and Z is 7/10 and 3/10 or 7 : 3

Gaining Ratio of Y and Z = 3 : 2 (given)

(That is the ratio at which they purchased X's share.)

ILLUSTRATION 31.8

A, B and C are partners in a business, sharing profit and losses in the ratio of 2 : 2 : 1. A retires by selling his share in the business for a sum of Rs 6,000 which is paid by A and B as to Rs 4,800 and Rs 1,200 respectively. Find out the new profit sharing ratio of B and C.

SOLUTION

B and C purchased A's share in the ratio of 4800 : 1200 (or) 4 : 1

B's future share in profits or losses = 2/5 + (2/5 × 4/5) = 2/5 + 8/25 = **18/25**

C's future share in profit or losses = 1/5 + (2/5 × 1/5) = 1/5 + 2/15 = **7/25**

∴ The new profit or loss sharing ratio of B and C = 18/25 : 7/25 or **18 : 7**.

5. Calculation of Amount Due to Outgoing Partner

To find out the amount payable to retiring partner, the following items are considered:

1. Balance to his Capital Account, as per last Balance Sheet.
2. Proportionate profit on revaluation.
3. Share of goodwill.
4. Interest on capital up to the date of retirement.
5. Salary, if any, payable to him.
6. Share of past profit or loss of the firm.
7. Share of profit till his date of retirement.
8. Share of proceeds of Joint Life Policy

Any withdrawals and interest due thereon should be deducted from the amount payable to the outgoing partner. The firm is obliged to make payment to the retiring partners of the firm due to him at the time of retirement. The total amount so calculated will be transferred to retiring partner's loan account by debiting the retiring partner's capital account. If he is paid in full immediately after retirement, the account is settled. Sometimes, the agreement may be to settle the share of the retiring partner by paying him a fixed annual sum (annuity).

ILLUSTRATION 31.9

The Balance Sheet of A, B and C who are sharing profits and losses in the proportion of one-half, one-third and one-sixth, respectively, was as follows on 30th June 2002:

Liabilities			*Rs*	*Assets*	*Rs*
Bills Payable			6,400	Cash in Hand	150
Sundry Creditors			12,500	Cash at Bank	25,500
Capitals:	A	40,000		Bills Receivable	5,400
	B	25,000		Book Debts	17,800
	C	20,000	85,000	Stock	22,300

Profit and Loss	4,500	Furniture	3,500
		Plant and Machinery	9,750
		Buildings	24,000
	1,08,400		1,08,400

A retires from the business on 1st July 2002 and his share in the firm is to be ascertained on a revaluation of the assets as follows:

Stock at Rs 20,000
Furniture Rs 3,000
Plant and Machinery Rs 9,000
Buildings at Rs 20,000
Rs 850 to be provided for Doubtful Debts
The goodwill of the firm is agreed to be valued at Rs 6,000

A is to be paid Rs 11,050 in cash on retirement and the balance in three equal yearly instalments together with interest at 5% p.a.

Show the necessary accounts required to give effect to the above, the Balance Sheet of the continuing partners and the Account of A till it is finally closed. *(B.Com., Madras, Madurai)*

SOLUTION

Dr. **Revaluation Account** Cr.

	Rs			*Rs*
To Stock Account	2,300	By Loss Transferred to Capital		
To Furniture Account	500	Account:	Rs	
To Plant and Machinery Account	750	A:	4,200	
To Buildings Account	4,000	B:	2,800	
To Bad Debts Provision Account	850	C:	1,400	8,400
	8,400			8,400

Dr. **Goodwill Account** Cr.

	Rs		*Rs*
To A's Capital Account	3,000	By Balance c/d	6,000
To B's Capital Account	2,000		
To C's Capital Account	1,000		
	6,000		6,000

Balance Sheet of B and C

Liabilities		*Rs*	*Assets*		*Rs*
Bills Payable		6,400	Cash in Hand		150
Sundry Creditors		12,500	Cash at Bank		25,500
A's Loan Account		41,050	Bills Receivable	Rs	5,400
Capital Accounts:	Rs		Book Debts:	17,800	
B:	25,700		*Less*: Reserve	850	16.950
C:	20,350	46,050	Stock		20,000
			Furniture		3,000
			Plant and Machinery		9,000
			Buildings		20,000
			Goodwill		6,000
		1,06,000			1,06,000

Dr. **A's Loan Account** Cr.

		Rs			Rs
2002			2002		
July 1	To Bank Account	11,050	July 1	By A's Capital A/c	41,050
2003			2003		
June 30	To Balance c/d	31,500	June 30	By Interest A/c	1,500
		42,550			42,550
2003			2003		
July 1	To Bank Account	11,500	July 1	By Balance b/d	31,500
2004			2004		
June 30	To Balance c/d	21,000	June 30	By Interest	1,000
		32,500			32,500
2004			2004		
July 1	To Bank Account	11,000	June 30	By Balance b/d	21,000
2005			2005		
June 30	To Balance c/d	10,500	June 30	By Interest	500
		21,500			21,500
2005			2005		
July 1	To Bank Account	10,500	June 30	By Balance b/d	10,500
		10,500			10,500

Dr. **Capital Accounts** Cr.

	A	B	C		A	B	C
	Rs	*Rs*	*Rs*		*Rs*	*Rs*	*Rs*
To Revaluation A/c Loss	4200	2800	1400	By Balance b/d	40,000	25,000	20,000
				By Profit & Loss A/c	2,250	1,500	750
To Loan Account	41,050			By Goodwill Account	3,000	2,000	1,000
To Balance c/d		25,700	20,350				
	45,250	28,500	21,750		45,250	28,500	21,750
				By Balance b/d	–	25,700	20,350

ILLUSTRATION 31.10

On 31st March 2006, the Balance Sheet of M/s Ram, Hari and Mohan sharing profits and losses in the ratio of 2 : 3 : 2 stood as follows:

	Rs.		*Rs.*
Capital Accounts		Land and Buildings	10,00,000
Ram	10,00,000	Machinery	17,00,000
Hari	15,00,000	Stock	5,00,000
Mohan	10,00,000	Sundry Debtors	6,00,000
Sundry Creditors	5,00,000	Cash and Bank balances	2,00,000
	40,00,000		40,00,000

On 31st March, 2006, Hari desired to retire from the firm and the remaining partners decided to carry on the same business. It was agreed to revalue the assets and liabilities on that date on the following basis:

1. Land and Buildings be appreciated by 30%.

2. Machinery be depreciated by 20%
3. Closing stock to be valued at Rs. 4,50,000
4. Provision for bad debts be made at 5%
5. Old credit balances of sundry creditors Rs. 50,000 be written back.
6. Joint Life Policy of the partners surrendered and cash obtained Rs. 3,50,000
7. Goodwill of the entire firm be revalued at Rs. 6,30,000 and Hari's share of the goodwill be adjusted in the accounts of Ram and Mohan who share the future profits and losses in the ratio of 3: 2. No goodwill account be raised.
8. The total capital of the firm is to be the same as before retirement. Individual capital be in their profit sharing ratio.
9. Amount due to Hari is to be settled on the following basis:

   50% on retirement and the balance 50% within one year.

Prepare revaluation account, capital accounts of partners, cash account and balance sheet as on 1-4-2006 of M/s Ram and Mohan.

SOLUTION

Dr. **Revaluation account** *Cr.*

	Rs.		*Rs.*
To Machinery Account	3,40,000	By Land and Buildings A/c	3,00,000
" Stock A/c	50,000	" Sundry Creditors A/c	50,000
" Provision for bad debts	30,000	" Partners' Capital A/c:	
		Ram	20,000
		Hari	30,000
		Mohan	20,000
	4,20,000		4,20,000

Dr. **Bank Account** *Cr.*

	Rs.		*Rs.*
To Balance b/d	2,00,000	By Hari's Capital A/c	9,45,000
" Ram's Capital A/c	12,18,000	" Balance c/d	12,15,000
" Mohan's Capital A/c	3,92,000		
" Joint Life Policy A/c	3,50,000		
	21,60,000		21,60,000
To Balance c/d	12,15,000		

Dr. **Ram** *Cr.*

	Rs.		*Rs.*
To Revaluation A/c	20,000	By Balance b/d	10,00,000
" Hari's A/c (Goodwill)[1]	1,98,000	" Joint Life Policy A/c	1,00,000
" Balance c/d	21,00,000	" Bank A/c — Cash brought in	12,18,000
	23,18,000		23,18,000
		By Balance b/d	21,00,000

Hari

Dr.	Rs.		Cr. Rs.
To Revaluation A/c	30,000	By Balance b/d	15,00,000
" Bank A/c	9,45,000	" Joint Life Policy A/c	1,50,000
" Hari's Loan A/c	9,45,000	" Ram's Capital A/c	1,98,000
		" Mohan's Capital A/c	72,000
	19,20,000		19,20,000

Mohan

Dr.	Rs.		Cr. Rs.
To Revaluation A/c	20,000	By Balance b/d	10,00,000
" Hari's Capital A/c (Goodwill)	72,000	" Joint Life Policy A/c	1,00,000
" Balance c/d	14,00,000	" Bank A/c — Cash brought in	3,92,000
	14,92,000		14,92,000
		By Balance b/d	14,00,000

BALANCE SHEET OF M/S RAM AND MOHAN

as at 1st April 2006

	Rs.			Rs.
Hari's Loan Account	9,45,000	Bank		12,15,000
Sundry Creditors	4,50,000	Stock		4,50,000
Capital Accounts		Debtors	6,00,000	
Ram	21,00,000	*Less*: Provision	30,000	
Mohan	14,00,000			5,70,000
		Land and Buildings		13,00,000
		Machinery		13,60,000
	48,95,000			48,95,000

1. Rs. 6,30,000 $\times \frac{3}{7}$ = Rs. 2,70,000 $\times \frac{11}{15}$ = Rs. 1,98,000

Rs. 2,70,000 $\times \frac{4}{15}$ = Rs. 72,000

ILLUSTRATION 30.11

A, *B* and *C* were in partnership sharing profits in the proportions of 5 : 4 : 3. Their Balance Sheet on 31st March, 2006, was as under:

	Rs.		Rs.
Capital Accounts:		Goodwill	40,000
A	1,35,930	Fixtures	8,200
B	95,120	Stock	1,57,300
C	61,170	Sundry Debtors	93,500
Sundry Creditors	41,690	Cash	34,910
	3,33,910		3,33,910

A had been suffering from ill-health and gave notice that he wished to retire. An agreement was, therefore, entered into as on 31st March, 2006, the terms of which were as follows:

(*i*) The Profit and Loss Account for the year ended 31st March, 2006, which showed a net profit of Rs. 48,000 was to be reopened . *B* was to be credited with Rs. 4,000 as bonus, in consideration of the extra work which had developed upon him during the year. The profit sharing ratio was to be revised as from 1st April 2005 to 3 : 4 : 4.

(ii) Goodwill was to be valued at two years' purchase of the average profits of the preceding five years. The Fixtures were to be valued by an independent valuer. A provision of 2% was to be made for doubtful debts and the remaining assets were to be taken at their book values.

The valuations arising out of the above agreement were Goodwill Rs. 56,800 and Fixtures Rs. 10,980.

B and *C* agreed, as between themselves, to continue the business, sharing profits in the ratio of 3:2 and decided to eliminate goodwill from the Balance Sheet, to retain the Fixtures on the books at the revised value and to increase the provision for doubtful debts to 6%.

You are required to submit the journal entries necessary to give effect to the above arrangements and to draw up the capital account of the partners after carrying out all adjusting entries as stated above. (*C.A.*)

SOLUTION

Journal Entries

Date	*Particulars*		*L.F.*	*Debit* Rs.	*Credit* Rs.
	A's Capital A/c	Dr.		20,000	
	B's Capital A/c	Dr.		16,000	
	C's Capital A/c	Dr.		12,000	
	To Profit and Loss Adjustment A/c				48,000
	(Being the entry for writing back profit already divided)				
	Profit and Loss Adjustment A/c	Dr.		4,000	
	To *B*'s Capital A/c				4,000
	(Being the entry for crediting B with bonus)				
	Profit and Loss Adjustment A/c	Dr.		44,000	
	To *A*'s Capital A/c				12,000
	To *B*'s Capital A/c				16,000
	To *C*'s Capital A/c				16,000
	(Being the entry for dividing the balance of profit to the revised ratio of 3 : 4 : 4)				
	Goodwill A/c	Dr.		16,800	
	Fixtures A/c	Dr.		2,780	
	To Provision for Bad Debts A/c				1,870
	To *A*/s Capital A/c				4,830
	To *B*'s Capital A/c				6,440
	To *C*'s Capital A/c				6,440
	(Being the entry for revaluing goodwill and fixtures and crediting capitals with the appreciated value)				
	A's Capital A/c	Dr.		1,32,760	
	To *A*'s Loan A/c				1,32,760
	(Being the entry for transferring the amount due to *A* to his Loan Account)				

B's Capital A/c	Dr.	36.324	
C's Capital A/c	Dr.	24,216	
To Goodwill A/c			56,800
To Provision for Bad Debts A/c			3,740
(Being the entry for writing off goodwill and making provision for bad debts)			

Dr. **A's CAPITAL ACCOUNT** *Cr.*

	Rs.		*Rs.*
To P&L Adjustment A/c	20,000	By Balance b/d	1,35,930
" A's Loan A/c	1,32,760	" P & L Adjustment A/c	12,000
		" Goodwill and Fixtures	4,830
	1,52,760		1,52,760

Dr. **B's CAPITAL ACCOUNT** *Cr.*

	Rs.		*Rs.*
To P&L Adjustment A/c	16,000	By Balance b/d	95,120
" Goodwill and Provision	36,324	" P & L Adjustment A/c	4,000
" Balance c/d	69,236	" P & L Adjustment A/c	16,000
		" Goodwill and Fixtures	6,440
	1,21,560		1,21,560

Dr. **C's CAPITAL ACCOUNT** *Cr.*

	Rs.		*Rs.*
To P&L Adjustment A/c	12,000	By Balance b/d	61,170
" Goodwill and Provision	24,216	" P & L Adjustment A/c	16,000
" Balance c/d	47,394	" Goodwill and Fixtures	6,440
	83,610		83,610

Adjustment of Capitals to be Proportionate to the Profit Sharing Ratio

On the retirement of a partner, sometimes the continuing partners wish to keep the Capital Accounts to be proportionate to new profit sharing ratio. This implies determination of overall capital after making all adjustments. Then find out the total amount of capital and the amount of each partner's share, on the basis of profit sharing ratio. Then continuing partners will meet their deficiency, if any, by introducing cash into the firm of the surplus, if any, may be withdrawn or transferred to Current Accounts, if the Capital Accounts are fixed.

ILLUSTRATION 30.12

The Balance Sheet of A, B and C who were sharing profits in the ratio of 3 : 2 : 1 respectively stood as follows on 31st December 2005:

Liabilities		*Rs*	*Assets*		*Rs*
Sundry Creditors		10,000	Land and Buildings		30,000
Capitals: A	30,000		Plant and Machinery		10,000
B	18,000		Stock		8,000
C	12,000	60,000	Sundry Debtors	6,000	

		Less: Provision	500	5,500
		Investments		6,500
		Cash at Bank		10,000
	70,000			70,000

B having given notice to retire from the firm, the following adjustments in the books of the firm were agreed upon:

(*a*) That investment be reduced to 90%.

(*b*) That land and building be appreciated by 10%.

(*c*) That the stock be appreciated by Rs 1,250.

(*d*) That the goodwill of the firm be fixed at Rs 12,000 and B's share of the same be adjusted through the Capital Accounts of A and B.

(*e*) That the entire capital of the newly constituted firm be fixed at Rs 60,000 and be readjusted between A and B in their profit sharing ratio *i.e.* 3 : 1, by bringing in or paying out cash.

From the above particulars, prepare Revaluation Account, Partners' Capital Accounts and the Balance Sheet of the new firm showing B's balance as loan. (*B.Com., Madurai, Madras*)

SOLUTION

Dr. **Revaluation Account** Cr.

		Rs		*Rs*
To Investments		650	By Land and Buildings	3,000
To Capital Accounts	Rs		By Stock	1,250
A:	1,800			
B:	1,200			
C:	600	3,600		
		4,250		4,250

Balance Sheet of A and C
as on 1st January 2006

Liabilities		*Rs*	*Assets*		*Rs*
Sundry Creditors		10,000	Land and Building		33,000
B's Loan A/c	Rs	23,200	Plant and Machinery		10,000
Capitals: A:	45,000		Stock		9,250
C:	15,000	60,000	Sundry Debtors	6,000	
			Less: Provision	500	5,500
			Investments		5,850
			Cash at Bank		29,600
		93,200			93,200

Note: The Capital of the firm is fixed at Rs 60,000. Therefore, A's Capital should be Rs 45,000 and C's Rs 15,000.

The amount to be brought by them:

	Rs		Rs
A:	45,000	C:	15,000
Less: Existing Capital		*Less*: Existing Capital	
(31,800 – 3,000)	28,800	(12,600 – 1,000)	11,600
	16,200		3,400

Thus A brings in Rs 16,200 and C brings in Rs 3,400.

Dr. **Capital Accounts** Cr.

		A	B	C			A	B	C
		Rs	Rs	Rs			Rs	Rs	Rs
2005					2005				
Dec. 31	To B's Capital A/c (Goodwill)	3,000	–	1,000	Dec. 31	By Balance b/d	30,000	18,000	12,000
"	To B's Loan A/c		23,200		"	By Revaluation A/c	1,800	1,200	600
"	To Balance c/d	45,000	–	15,000	"	By A's Capital (Goodwill)	–	3,000	
					"	By C's Capital (Goodwill)	–	1,000	
					"	By Cash	16,200	–	3,400
		48,000	23,200	16,000			48,000	23,200	16,000
					2006				
					Jan. 1	By Balance b/d	45,000	–	15,000

ADMISSION AND RETIREMENT

When a partner retires from a firm, there arise the need for finance. The retiring partner is to be paid off. If cash is paid, then the working capital is affected. Therefore, when a partner retires from the firm, the continuing partners feel the urgency of admitting an outsider as a partner to their firm. The retiring partner can easily be paid off with the amount contributed by the incoming partner. But the simultaneous retirement and admission do not introduce any new principles of accounting. The principles studied under admission and retirement are combined–the combination of the two sets of transactions.

ILLUSTRATION 31.13 (Retirement-cum-admission)

A and B were working in partnership sharing profits equally. On 31st December 2004, A decided to retire and in his place, it was decided that C would be admitted as partner from 1st January 2005 and his share in the profits will be one-third.

Balance Sheet of the firm as on 31st December 2004 was as follows:

		Rs		Rs
Sundry Creditors		29,400	Goodwill	30,000
Capitals:	Rs		Land and Buildings	80,100
A:	1,08,600		Furniture	18,600
B:	96,000	2,04,600	Motor Car	24,000
			Sundry Debtors	48,300
			Cash at Bank	33,000
		2,34,000		2,34,000

It was further decided as follows:

1. The goodwill should be raised to Rs 40,000.
2. The motor car would be taken over by A at its book value.
3. The value of land and buildings would be increased by Rs 16,560.
4. B and C would introduce sufficient capital to pay off A to leave thereafter a sum of Rs 14,700 as working capital in a manner that the capitals of the new partners will be proportional to their profit sharing ratio.
5. The new partners decide to show the goodwill as an asset.

The partners introduced the capital on 10th January 2005. Show the accounts of the partners and Bank Account with necessary Journal entries. Also prepare the Balance Sheet of the new firm.

(B.Com., Mangalore, Chennai, Utkal)

SOLUTION

Journal Entries

Date	Particulars		Dr. Rs	Cr. Rs
2004 Dec. 31	Goodwill Account	Dr.	10,000	
	To A's Capital Account			5,000
	To B's Capital Account			5,000
	(Being goodwill raised by Rs 10,000 and credited to partners' capital account)			
"	Land and Buildings Account	Dr.	16,560	
	To Revaluation Account			16,560
	(Being value increased)			
"	Revaluation Account	Dr.	16,560	
	To A's Capital Account			8,280
	To B's Capital Account			8,280
	(Profit on revaluation transferred to partners' capital account)			
2005 Jan. 10	Bank Account	Dr.	79,580	
	To B's Capital Account			16,627
	To C's Capital Account			62,953
	(Being cash brought by B and C to make the capitals in proportion to profit sharing ratio)			
	A's Capital Account	Dr.	1,21,880	
	To Motor Car Account			24,000
	To Bank Account			97,880
	(Being account settled on retirement of A)			

Bank Account

Dr. Cr.

	Rs		Rs
To Balance b/d	33,000	By A's Capital Account	97,880
To B's Capital A/c	16,627	By Balance c/d	14,700
To C's Capital A/c	62,953		
	1,12,580		1,12,580
To Balance b/d	14,700		

Balance Sheet of B and C as on 1st January 2005

Liabilities		*Rs*	*Assets*	*Rs*
Sundry Creditors	Rs	29,400	Goodwill	40,000
Capitals: B	1,25,907		Land & Buildings	96,660
C:	62,953	1,88,860	Furniture	18,600
			Sundry Debtors	48,300
			Cash at Bank	14,700
		2,18,260		2,18,260

Capitals of B and C is ascertained as follows:

	Rs	(as above)
Total of Assets	2,18,260	
Less: Creditors	29,400	
Total capital of firm:	1,88,860	

	Rs
B's capital = 2/3 of Rs 1,88,860	1,25,907
Less: Capitai in the firm after adjustment (96,000 + 13,280)	1,09,280
Cash to be brought in :	16,627
C's share: 1/3 of Rs 1,88,860	Rs. 62,953

Capital Accounts

Dr.		*A*	*B*	*C*			*A*	*B*	*C* Cr.
		Rs	Rs	Rs			Rs	Rs	Rs
2004					2004				
Dec. 31	To Motor Car	24,000	—	—	Dec. 31	By Balance b/d	1,08,600	96,000	–
"	To Bank	97,880	—	—	"	By Goodwill A/c	5,000	5,000	
2005					"	By Revaluation A/c	8,280	8,280	–
Jan. 10	To Balance c/d	—	1,25,907	62,953	2005 Jan. 10	By Bank		16,627	62,953
		1,21,880	1,25,907	62,953			1,21,880	1,25,907	62,953
					2005 Jan. 11	By Balance b/d		1,25,907	62,953

ILLUSTRATION 31.14 (Retirement-cum-admission)

A, B and C are in partnership sharing profits and losses in the ratio of 2 : 2 : 1. On 31st December 2005, the firm's Balance Sheet stands as follows:

Liabilities		*Rs*	*Assets*	*Rs*
Capitals:			Sundry Assets	55,000
A:	30,000		Bank	15,000
B:	20,000			
C:	10,000	60,000		
Sundry Creditors		10,000		
		70,000		70,000

On that date, C decides to retire. The value of goodwill to be Rs 15,000 and sundry assets are taken to have increased in value by Rs 25,000.

On C's retirement, D is admitted as a partner. He pays no premium for goodwill but brings in Rs 15,000 as capital. Profits and losses are to be shared in the ratio of 4 : 3 : 3.

Show Capital Accounts and draw up two Balance Sheets, one after C's retirement and the other after D's admission. The goodwill account is to be wiped off from the books and restore the sundry assets at its original value after D's admission. *(B.Com., Bombay)*

SOLUTION

Memorandum Revaluation Account

		Rs			Rs
To Capital Accounts:			Sundry Assets		25,000
A:	10,000				
B:	10,000				
C:	5,000	25,000			
		25,000			25,000
To Reversal of items		25,000	By Capital Accounts		
			A:	10,000	
			B:	7,500	
			C:	7,500	25,000
		25,000			25,000

Capital Accounts

	A	B	C		A	B	C
	Rs	Rs	Rs		Rs	Rs	Rs
To C's Loan A/c	–	–	18,000	By Balance b/d	30,000	20,000	10,000
To Balance c/d	46,000	36,000	–	By Revaluation A/c	10,000	10,000	5,000
				By Goodwill A/c	6,000	6,000	3,000
	46,000	36,000	18,000		46,000	36,000	18,000
				By Balance b/d	46,000	36,000	–

Balance Sheet as on 31st Dec. 2005 (after C's retirement)

Liabilities		Rs	*Assets*	Rs
Capital Accounts:			Sundry Assets (Rs 55,000 + 25,000)	80,000
A:	46,000		Goodwill A/c	15,000
B:	36,000	82,000	Bank A/c	15,000
C's Loan Account		18,000		
Sundry Creditors		10,000		
		1,10,000		1,10,000

Capital Accounts

	A	B	D		A	B	D
	Rs	Rs	Rs		Rs	Rs	Rs
To Memorandum Revaluation A/c	10,000	7,500	7,500	By Balance	46,000	36,000	–
To Goodwill	6,000	4,500	4,500	By Bank	–	–	15,000
To Balance c/d	30,000	24,000	3,000				
	46,000	36,000	15,000		46,000	36,000	15,000
				By Balance b/d	30,000	24,000	3,000

Balance Sheet as on 31st Dec. 2005 (after D's admission)

Liabilities		*Rs*	*Assets*	*Rs*
Capital Accounts:			Sundry Assets (80,000 – 25,000)	55,000
A:	30,000		Bank: Rs 15,000 + 15,000	30,000
B:	24,000			
D:	3,000	57,000		
C's Loan A/c		18,000		
Sundry Creditors		10,000		
		85,000		85,000

ILLUSTRATION 31.15 (Retirement-cum-admission)

The following is the Balance Sheet of Raman and Deshpande as at 30th June 2005 on which date Raman retired and his son Pritam joined that firm from 1st July 2005 with one-fourth share in the profits of the business:

Liabilities		*Rs*	*Assets*	*Rs*
Creditors		10,000	Goodwill	12,000
Capitals: Raman	50,000		Plant	40,000
Deshpande	31,000	81,000	Investments	14,000
			Debtors	15,000
			Cash at Bank	10,000
		91,000		91,000

The following adjustments and arrangements have been agreed upon for the purposes of retirement and admission of partners:

(*i*) Goodwill to be written up to Rs 30,000 and Plant to Rs 50,000.

(*ii*) Sufficient money to be introduced so as to leave Rs 11,000 cash after payment of amount due to Raman.

(*iii*) Deshpande and Pritam to provide such fund as would make their capitals proportionate to their share of profit.

Show the journal entries to record the above transactions assuming that Deshpande and Pritam have paid in cash due on 2nd July 2005 and the amount due to Raman was paid on the same day. (*C.A., Inter*)

(*B. Com. MS*)

SOLUTION

Journal Entries

		Dr. *Rs*	Cr. *Rs*
2005			
July 1	Goodwill Account Dr.	18,000	
	To Raman's Capital A/c		9,000
	To Deshpande's Capital A/c		9,000
	(Being goodwill written up)		
	Plant Account Dr.	10,000	
	To Revaluation Account		10,000
	(Being increase in value)		
	Revaluation Account Dr.	10,000	
	To Raman's Account		5,000
	To Deshpande's Account		5,000
	(Being profit on Revaluation transferred to Capital A/c)		

Bank Account Dr.		65,000	
To Deshpande's Capital A/c			37,500
To Pritam's Capital A/c			27,500
(Being amount brought by partners to make their capital in proportion to profit sharing ratio)			
Raman's Capital Account Dr.		64,000	
To Bank Account			64,000
(Being payment of amount due to retired partner)			

Dr. **Capital Accounts** Cr.

	Raman	Deshpande	Pritam		Raman	Deshpande	Pritam
	Rs	Rs	Rs		Rs	Rs	Rs
To Cash	64,000	—	—	Balance b/d	50,000	31,000	—
To Balance c/d	—	82,500	27,500	Goodwill	9,000	9,000	—
				Revaluation	5,000	5,000	—
				Cash		37,500	27,500
	64,000	82,500	27,500		64,000	82,500	27,500
				By Balance b/d		82,500	27,500

Balance Sheet of Deshpande and Pritam

as on 1st July 2005

Liabilities			*Rs*	*Assets*	*Rs*
Creditors		Rs	10,000	Goodwill	30,000
Capitals:	Deshpande	82,500		Plant	50,000
	Pritam	27,500	1,10,000	Investments	14,000
				Debtors	15,000
				Cash at Bank	11,000
				(Rs 10,000 (+) 65,000 75,000 (−) 64,000 11,000)	
			1,20,000		1,20,000

Workings:

Total capital after admission of Pritam:

	Rs
Total assets other than cash (Rs 30,000 + 50,000 + 14,000 + 15,000)	1,09,000
Cash	11,000
	1,20,000
Less: Creditors	10,000
Total Capital of the new firm required after admission of Pritam	1,10,000

	Deshpande (3/4)	Pritam (1/4)
Total Capital Rs 1,10,000	82,500	27,500
Less: Amount in credit	45,000	
Cash to be brought:	37,500	27,500

ILLUSTRATION 31.16

X, Y and Z were in partnership sharing profits and losses in the ratio of 8 : 7 : 5. Their Balance Sheet as on 30th September 2005 was as follows:

Liabilities	*Rs*	*Assets*		*Rs*
Capital Accounts:		Leasehold premises at cost		15,000
X	20,400	Plant at cost		16,000
Y	11,600	Stock		8,400
Z	7,200	Debtors	6,800	
Loan – Y	6,000	*Less*: Provision for B/D	1,200	5,600
Provision for Depreciation on Plant	5,600	Bank		13,400
Creditors	7,600			
	58,400			58,400

Y retired on 30th September 2005 and X and Y continued in partnership sharing profits and losses in the ratio of 3 : 2. It was agreed that Rs 16,000 of the balance remaining to him including his earlier loan should remain as loan to the firm and balance amount will be paid to him on 1st October 2005.

The following adjustments were agreed upon:

(1) The lease was acquired on 1st October 2003 for 15 years. This was to be written off over the period of lease. Depreciation not provided from the beginning.

(2) The plant was to be revalued at Rs 11,600.

(3) The provision for bad debts was to be increased by Rs 240.

(4) Creditors for expenses amounting to Rs 1,000 had been omitted from the books.

(5) Rs 800 were to be written off the stock in respect of obsolete items included therein.

(6) Provision of Rs 240 was to be made for professional charges in connection with the revaluation.

The partnership agreement provided that on the retirement of a partner goodwill was to be valued at an amount equal to the average profit of the three years expiring on the date of retirement and that in arriving at the profit, a notional amount of Rs 16,000 should be charged for partner's salaries and that for the purpose of valuing goodwill, revaluation of the plant and the professional charges should not be regarded as affecting the profits.

The profits for the years ended on 30th Sept. 2003, 2004 and 2005 were Rs 28,800; Rs 33,600 and Rs 37,640, as shown by the draft accounts, respectively.

No Accounts for goodwill was to be maintained in the books, adjusting entries of transaction between the partners being made in their Capital Accounts. (*C.A. England*)

SOLUTION

Dr. **Revaluation Account** Cr.

	Rs			*Rs*
To Leasehold Premises[1]	2,000	By Provision for Depreciations[2]		1,200
To Bad Debts Provision	240	By Capital Accounts		
To Expenses Outstanding	1,000	X: (8/20)	1,232	
To Stock	800	Y: (7/20)	1,078	
To Provision for professional charges	240	Z: (5/20)	770	3,080
	4,280			4,280

Capital Accounts

Dr.	X	Y	Z		X	Y	Z Cr.
	Rs	Rs	Rs		Rs	Rs	Rs
To Revaluation (Loss)	1,232	1,078	770	By Balance b/d	20,400	11,600	7,200
To Y's Capital (Goodwill)[3]	3,200		2,400	By X Account[3] (Goodwill)	–	3,200	–
To Cash–		6,122		By Z Account (Goodwill)	–	2,400	–
To Y's Loan	–	10,000	–				
To Balance c/d	15,968	–	4,030				
	20,400	17,200	7,200		20,400	17,200	7,200
				By Balance b/d	15,968	–	4,030

Balance Sheet as on 30th Sept. 2005

		Rs			Rs
Capital Accounts:			Leasehold premises	15,000	
X:	15,968		*Less*: Depreciation	2,000	13,000
Z:	4,030	19,998	Plant		16,000
Y's Loan: (Rs 6,000 + 10,000		16,000	Debtors	6,800	
Provision for Depreciation on plant (Rs 5,600 – 1,200)		4,400	*Less*: Provision B/d	1,440	5,360
Outstanding Expenses		1,000	Bank (Rs 13,400 – 6,122)		7,278
Outstanding professional charges		240	Stock (Rs. 8,400 – 800)		7,600
Creditors		7,600			
		49,238			49,238

Notes:

(1) The lease was taken for 15 years. So, yearly depreciation per year comes to Rs 1,000. For 2 years, depreciation is Rs 2,000.

(2) Existing provision for depreciation is Rs 5,600. Now it is required only Rs 4,400 (Rs 16,000 – 11,600). Therefore the excess provision of Rs 1,200.

(3) Adjusted Profits:

		Oct. 2002 to Sept. 2003	Oct. 2003 to Sept. 2004	Oct. 2004 Sept. 2005
		Rs	Rs	Rs
Given Net profits		28,800	33,600	37,640
Less: Partner's salary		16,000	16,000	16,000
		12,800	17,600	21,640
		–	1,000	1,000
Less: Depreciation (lease)		12,800	16,600	20,640
Less: Provision B/D	Rs 240			
O/S Expenses	Rs 1,000			
Stock: Written off	800	–	–	2,040
		12,800	16,600	18,600

$$\text{Value of Goodwill} = \frac{\text{Rs } 12{,}800 + \text{Rs } 16{,}600 + \text{Rs } 18{,}600}{3} = \text{Rs } 16{,}000$$

	X	Y	Z
	Rs	Rs	Rs
Goodwill (8 : 7 : 5)	6,400 (Cr.)	5,600 (Cr.)	4,000 (Cr.)
Goodwill (3 : 2)	9,600 (Dr.)	–	6,400 (Dr.)
Net Effect	3,200 (Dr.)	5,600 (Cr.)	2,400 (Dr.)

DEATH OF A PARTNER

The problems arising on the death of a partner are similar to those arising on retirement. Retirement can be anticipated and planned. Thus the date of retirement coincides with the date of closing of the firm's books of accounts. The death may occur at any time during the course of trading period. In the event of death of a partner, the Legal Representatives of the Deceased Partner will be entitled to receive from the firm the amount due on account of the following:

1. Capital Account of the deceased partner as per the last Balance Sheet of the firm.
2. Interest on capital, if any, to the date of death of the partner.
3. Share in the goodwill of the firm.
4. Share in the revaluation of assets and liabilities.
5. Share in the accumulated reserves.
6. Share in the undistributed profits.
7. Share in the profit of the firm from the last Balance Sheet to the date of his death.
8. Share in the Joint Life Policy.
9. Salary, if any, due to him till the date of his death.

Further the amount due to the deceased partner as reduced by (*a*) Drawings, (*b*) Interest on Drawings and (*c*) Undistributed losses, if any, should be transferred to the loan account in the name of his Executor's Account. Then the amount may be paid immediately or by instalments. If payment is made by instalments, it will carry interest @ 6% p.a.

ILLUSTRATION 31.17

A and *B* were carrying on a business in partnership sharing profits and losses in the ratio of 3 : 2 respectively. They closed their books of account on 31st December, 2005. Their Balance Sheet was as follows:

	Rs		*Rs*
Capital Accounts		Furniture	20,000
A:	90,000	Stock	1,00,000
B:	60,000	Debtors	50,000
Reserve	30,000	Cash	30,000
Creditors	20,000		
	2,00,000		2,00,000

B died on 1st May, 2006. Partnership Deed provided that in the event of death of a partner his heirs would be entitled to be paid out:

(*a*) Capital to his credit at the date of death.

(*b*) His share of reserve at the date of the last balance sheet.

(*c*) His share of profits at the date of his death based on the average profits of the last three accounting years.

(*d*) By way of goodwill his share of total profits for the preceding three accounting years.

The profits for the three preceding accounting years were:

2003 Rs. 41,800, 2004 Rs. 39,200, and 2005 Rs. 45,000

Prepare B's capital account transferring the amount due to B's heirs loan account. Clearly show your calculations. (*I.B.B.M. Bangalore*)

SOLUTION

Dr. **B's CAPITAL ACCOUNT** *Cr.*

	Rs		Rs
To Heirs of *B* (deceased) Loan Account	1,34,000	By Balance b/d	60,000
		" Reserve	18,000
		" Profit & Loss Account 2/5 of Rs. 42,000 for 4 months	5,600
		" Goodwill, 2/.5 of Rs. 1,26,000	50,400
	1,34,000		1,34,000

ILLUSTRATION 31.18

Ram, Rahim and Robert carry on business sharing the profits in the ratio of 1/2 : 1/3 : 1/6 respectively. Capitals as on 31-3-2006 are Ram Rs. 20,000, Rahim Rs. 15,000 and Robert Rs. 10,000. On 30-6-2006 Robert died and his executors claim the following as per Partnership Deed:

(*i*) The joint and several life policies against which premiums are charged to the Profit and Loss Account are valued at 40% of the sum assured. The policies of the partners are: Ram Rs. 10,000, Rahim Rs. 7,500 and Robert Rs. 17,000.

(*ii*) Allow interest on capital at 6% p.a.

(*iii*) Calculate Robert's share of profits till the date of death on the basis of average profits of the preceding 3 years.

(*iv*) Calculate the goodwill of the firm at 2 years' purchase of the average profits of the preceding 5 years. The annual profit or loss figures of preceding five years were:

2001-2002	Rs. 12,000
2002-2003	Rs. 9,000
2003-2004	Rs. 6,000 (Loss)
2004-2005	Rs. 18,000
2005-2006	Rs. 9,000

Prepare an account for presentation to the executors of Robert. Drawing till the date of death of Robert was Rs. 5,000 (*B. Com., Mangalore*)

SOLUTION

(*i*) *Life policy:*

Robert's policy Rs. 17,000

His share of the same : 1/6 of 17,000 – Rs. 2,833

Ram and Rahim's policies : Rs. 17,500

Surrender value 40% of 17,500 = Rs. 7,000

Robert's share : 1/6 of Rs. 7,000 – Rs. 1,667

Total of Robert's share : Rs. 2,833 + Rs. 1,667 = Rs. 4,500

(*ii*) *Interest:* @ 6% p.a. on Rs. 10,000 for 3 months :

$$\frac{10{,}000 \times 6 \times 3}{100 \times 12} = \text{Rs. } 150$$

(*iii*) *Profit:*

Profits for three preceding years:

2003-2004	Rs. 6,000 (Loss)
2004-2005	Rs. 18,000
2005-2006	Rs. 9,000
Total	Rs. 21,000

Average Profit = 21,000 ÷ 3 = Rs. 7,000

Robert's share (for 3 months) = $\frac{7,000 \times 3}{12}$ = Rs. 1,750

1/6th of Rs. 1,750 = **Rs. 300**

(*iv*) Goodwill:

Average profits of preceding 5 years:

2001-2002	Rs. 12,000	
2002-2003	Rs. 9,000	
2003-2004	Rs. 6,000	(Loss)
2004-2005	Rs. 18,000	
2005-2006	Rs. 9,000	
Total	Rs. 42,000	

Average Profit = 42,000 ÷ 5 = Rs. 8,400

Two years' average profit = Rs. 16,800

Robert's share of goodwill = 1/6th of Rs. 16,800 = Rs. 2,800.

Dr. **Robert's Capital Account** *Cr.*

	Rs		*Rs*
To Drawings	5,000	By Balance b/d	10,000
Robert's Executor's A/c—Transfer	12,750	" Life Policy A/c	2,833
		" Ram's Capital A/c	1,000
		" Rahim's Capital A/c 3 : 2	667
		Rs. $\frac{1,667 \times 3}{5}$ = Rs. 1,000.20 or Rs.1,000	
		Rs. $\frac{1667 \times 2}{5}$ = Rs. 666.80 or Rs. 667	
		" Interest on capital	150
		" Profit Suspense A/c	300
		" Goodwill	2,800
	17,750		17,750

Dr. **Robert's Executor's Account** *Cr.*

	Rs		*Rs*
30-6-2006		30-6-2006	
To Balance c/d	12,750	By Robert's Capital A/c	12,750
	12,750		12,750
		By Balance b/d	12,750

ILLUSTRATION 31.19

Sundar, Raman and Sekhar share profits in 3 : 2 : 2 ratio. Sekhar died on 1st July 2006. The Balance Sheet on 31-3-2006 was:

	Rs		*Rs*
Capital:		Goodwill	9,450
Sundar	15,000	Assets	20,000
Raman	10,000	Investments	2,500

Sekhar	10,000	Stock of goods	5,000
General Reserve	2,600	Debtors	5,000
Reserve for Bad Debts	400	Cash and Bank	2,500
Creditors	6,450		
	44,450		44,450

The following arrangements were agreed upon :

(*a*) Assets be valued at Rs. 29,000; Investments at Rs. 2,350; Stock Rs. 4,700

(*b*) Goodwill be valued at two years' purchase of the average profits of the past five years.

(*c*) Sekhar's profit to the date of death be calculated on the basis of the average profits of the past three years.

(*d*) The profits of the last five years were:

2001-2002 Rs. 5,750
2002-2003 Rs. 7,000
2003-2004 Rs. 4,500
2004-2005 Rs. 4,000
2005-2006 Rs. 5,000

Prepare continuing partners' capital accounts and Sekhar's account and show the new Balance Sheet.

(*B.Com., Bharathidasan*)

SOLUTION

Dr. **Revaluation Account** *Cr.*

	Rs		*Rs*
To Investments	150	By Assets A/c	9,000
" Stock	300		
" Sundar's Capital A/c	3,664		
" Raman's Capital A/c	2,443		
" Sekhar's Capital A/c	2,443		
	9,000		9,000

Goodwill : Profit of the past five years:

2001-2002	Rs. 5,750
2002-2003	7,000
2003-2004	4,500
2004-2005	4,000
2005-2006	5,000
Total	Rs. 26,250

Average profit : $\frac{\text{Rs } 26{,}250}{5} = \text{Rs } 5250$

Two years' purchase of the average = 5,250 × 2 =	10,500
Less: Recorded goodwill	9,450
Increased value of goodwill	Rs. 1,050

Sundar gets 3/7 of Rs. 1,050 = Rs. 450, Raman and Sekhar 2/7 of Rs. 1,050 *i.e.* Rs. 300 each.

Profit : Average profits of the past three years

2003-2004	4,500
2004-2005	4,000
2005-2006	5,000
Total	13,500
	3

Average = Rs. 4,500 (for 1 year)

For 3 months, *i.e.*, date of Sekhar's death = 4,500 × 3/12 = Rs. 1,125

Sekhar's share : 2/7 of Rs. 1,125 = Rs. 322

Sundar's Capital Account

Dr.	Rs		Cr. Rs
To Balance c/d	20,228	By Balance b/d	15,000
		" Revaluation A/c	3,664
		" General Reserve	1,114
		" Goodwill	450
	20,228		20,228
		By Balance b/d	20,228

Raman's Capital Account

Dr.	Rs		Cr. Rs
To Balance c/d	13,486	By Balance b/d	10,000
		" Revaluation A/c	2,443
		" General Reserve A/c	743
		" Goodwill A/c	300
	13,486		13,486
		By Balance b/d	13,486

Sekhar's Capital Account

Dr.	Rs		Cr. Rs
To Sekhar's Executor's A/c	13,808	By Balance b/d	10,000
		" Revaluation A/c	2,443
		" General Reserve A/c	743
		" Goodwill A/c	300
		" Profit Suspense A/c	322
	13,486		13,808

Balance Sheet of Sundar and Raman *as at 1-7-2006*

Dr.	Rs			Cr. Rs
Capital Accounts :		Goodwill		10,500
Sundar	20,228	Assets		29,000
Raman	13,486	Investments		2,350
Sekhar's Executor's A/c	13,808	Stock		4,700
Creditors	6,450	Debtors	5,000	
		Less: Provision	400	4,600
		Cash at Bank		2,500
		Profit Suspense A/c		322
	53,972			53,972

ILLUSTRATION 31.20

The following is the Balance Sheet of A, B and C on 31st December 2004:

Liabilities			*Rs*	*Assets*	*Rs*
Sundry Creditors			4,500	Cash in hand	300
Reserve Fund			4,800	Cash at Bank	7,500
Capital Accounts:		Rs			
	A	15,000		Sundry Debtors	9,000
	B	7,500		Furniture	12,000
	C	7,500	30,000	Tools	1,500
			39,300		39,300

C died on 31st March 2005. Under the terms of the Partnership Deed, the Executors of a deceased Partner were entitled to:

(*a*) Amount standing to the credit of the Partner's Capital Account.

(*b*) Interest on Capital @ 5% p.a.

(*c*) Share of goodwill on the basis of twice the average of the past three years' profits.

(*d*) Share of profits from the closing of the last financial year to the death on the basis of last year's profits.

Profits for 2002 Rs 9,000; for 2003 Rs 12,000 and for 2004 Rs 10,500. Profits were shared in the ratio of capitals.

Pass the necessary journal entries and find out the amount payable to the heir of C. (*B.Com., Madurai*)

SOLUTION

Journal Entries

		Dr.	Cr.
		Rs	*Rs*
Interest on Capital Account	Dr.	93.75	
To C's Capital Account			93.75
(Being interest on Capital @ 5% for 3 months)			
Goodwill Account	Dr.	5,250.00	
To C's Capital Account			5,250.00
(Being share of goodwill credited)			
Profit & Loss Appropriation	Dr.	656.25	
To C's Capital Account			656.25
(Being profit for 3 months)			
Reserve Fund Account	Dr.	1,200.00	
To C's Capital Account			1,200.00
(Being C's share of reserve fund)			

Dr. **C's Capital Account** Cr.

	Rs		*Rs*
To Executor's Account	14,700	By Balance b/d	7,500.00
		By Interest on Capital	93.75
		By Goodwill Account	5,250.00
		By Profit & Loss A/c	656.25
		By Reserve Fund Account	1,200.00
	14,700		14,700.00

Goodwill = 9,000 + 12,000 + 10,500 × 2/3 = Rs **21,000**

C's Share = 21,000 × 1/4 = Rs **5,250**

Profit = Rs 10,500 × 1/4 × 3/12 = Rs **656.25**

ILLUSTRATION 31.21

It was provided under the Partnership Deed among A, B and C that in the event of the death of a partner, the survivors would have to purchase his share in the firm on the following terms:

(*a*) Deceased's share of goodwill to be taken at three years' purchase of his share of profits on average of previous four years.

(*b*) Total amount due to his representatives to be paid by survivors in four equal and half yearly instalments commencing at 6 months after the date of death with 5% interest on outstanding dues.

They shared profits and losses in the proportion of 9 : 4 : 3 and accounts were drawn up each year at 30th June. A died on 31st December 2003 and their capital Accounts on that date were :

A	Rs 10,800
B	Rs 6,400
C	Rs 3,600

A's Current Account on 31st December 2003 after crediting his share of profit to that date, however, showed a debit of Rs 960.

Firm's profit for the year ended 30th June 2000 Rs 35,200; 30th June 2001 Rs 28,160; 30th June 2002 Rs 24,080 and 30th June 2003 Rs 8,704.

Show the relevant ledger accounts in the books of the firm recording half-yearly payments to A's estate by surviving partners. (*B.Com., Calcutta*)

SOLUTION

Dr. **A's Capital Account** Cr.

		Rs			Rs
2003			2003		
Dec. 31	To Current A/c	960	Dec. 31	By Balance b/d	10,800
"	To Executors of A's Account	50,400	"	By Goodwill A/c	40,560
		51,360			51,360

Dr. **Executors of A's Account** Cr.

		Rs			Rs
2004			2003		
June 30	To Bank A/c	13,860	Dec. 31	By A's Capital A/c	50,400
	(Rs 12,600 + 1,260)		2004		
"	To Balance c/d	37,800	June 30	By Interest A/c	1,260
		51,660			51,660
2004			2004		
Dec. 31	To Bank A/c	13,545	July 1	By Balance b/d	37,800
	(Rs 12,600 + 945)		2004		
"	To Balance c/d	25,200	Dec. 31	By Interest	945
		38,745			38,745
2005			2005		
June 30	To Bank A/c	13,230	Jan. 1	By Balance b/d	25,200
	(Rs 12,600 + 630)		June 30	By Interest	630
"	To Balance c/d	12,600			
		25,830			25,830
2005			2005		
Dec. 31	To Bank A/c	12,915	July 1	By Balance b/d	12,600
			Dec. 31	By Interest	315
		12,915			12,915

Workings:

$$\text{Goodwill} = \frac{\text{Rs } 35,200 + 28,160 + 24,080 + 8,704}{4} \times 3/4 = \text{Rs } 72,108$$

A's share thereof = Rs 72,108 × 9/16 = Rs **40,560**

JOINT LIFE POLICY

When a partner dies, the continuing partners are to make payment to the Executors of the deceased partner. They may desire to settle it without disturbing the working capital. The relationship among the partners is based on mutual trust, faith and confidence and as such there is a mutual belief among themselves. But the relationship with the Executor of deceased partner is entirely a new one and there exists no relation. Thus, the entire amount may be payable to the Executor in one lump sum. If so, the working capital of the firm will be depleted and the business will be affected. In such a similar position, precautionary measures are to be taken to safeguard the firm from the financial breakdowns. The step to overcome this is to take a Joint Life Policy on the partners, by paying a small amount known as premium and in the event of death of any one of the partners the amount of the policy is payable. The firm gets the full amount of the policy either on its maturity or on the death of a partner, whichever is earlier. Thus the deceased partner's account can be settled with the policy amount, without disturbing the business activities.

The Policy may be on individual life or may be on the lives of all the partners–Joint Life Policy. The accounts relating to the Joint Life Policy can be maintained in any one of the following methods:

Method I

When premium is paid on the Joint Life Policy, it is treated as an expense and is debited to the Profit and Loss Appropriation Account. On happening of death or maturity or surrender, the amount received from the Insurance Company is treated as an income and is credited in the partners' capital accounts in their profit sharing ratio. There is no Joint Life Policy Account separately maintained.

The journal entries are:

1.	Premium on Policy Account To Bank Account (Being the premium paid)	Dr.
2.	Profit & Loss Appropriation Account To Premium on Policy Account (Being premium amount transferred to Profit & Loss Appropriation A/c)	Dr.
3.	Bank Account To Joint Life Policy Account (Being the policy amount received from Insurance Company)	Dr.
4.	Joint Life Policy Account To Partner's Capital Account (Being the amount credited to partners' capital accounts in profit sharing ratio)	Dr.

Method II

Here, the surrender value of the policy is taken into account. The premium paid is treated as an asset and is debited to Policy Account. At the end of the year, the amount of premium in excess of the surrender value is treated as a loss and is debited to the Profit and Loss Account. The surrender value is shown on the asset side of the Balance Sheet every year at its computed value. On the death or maturity, the excess amount received from the Insurance Company over the accumulated surrender value is credited to the partner's capital accounts in profit sharing ratio. The journal entries are:

Joint Life Policy Account To Bank Account (Being payment of premium)	Dr.
Profit and Loss Account To Joint Life Policy Account (Being excess of surrender value transferred)	Dr.
Cash Account To Joint Life Policy Account (Being amount received from Insurance Company)	Dr.
Joint Life Policy Account To All Partners Capital Account (Being distribution of amount among partners' capital accounts in profit sharing ratio)	Dr.

Method III

Here, a Joint Life Policy and also a Joint Life Policy Reserve or Fund Account are maintained at surrender value. The Policy Account will then appear at its surrender value on the asset side of the Balance Sheet and Policy Reserve Account will appear on the liability side of the Balance Sheet. The excess of the amount of policy received over the surrender value of the policy is treated as a profit and credited to partners' capital accounts in profit sharing ratio. This method is similar to that of Depreciation Fund method

The journal entries are:

1.	Joint Life Policy Account To Bank Account (Being premium paid)	Dr.
2.	Profit & Loss Appropriation A/c To Joint Life Policy Reserve A/c (Being appropriation of a reserve equal to premium paid out of profits)	Dr.
3.	Joint Life Policy Reserve A/c To Joint Life Policy A/c (Being the excess of surrender value written off to Joint Life Policy Reserve Account)	Dr.
4.	Bank Account To Joint Life Policy Account (Being amount received from Insurance Company)	Dr.
5.	Joint Life Policy Reserve A/c To Joint Life Policy A/c (Being balance of Joint Lire Policy Reserve account is transferred)	Dr.
6.	Joint Life Policy A/c To All Partners' Capital Account (Being the amount distributed among the partners' capital accounts)	Dr.

ILLUSTRATION 31.22

A and B sharing profits and losses in the ratio of 5 : 3 took out a Joint Life Policy for Rs 40,000 in January 2002 for 20 years paying an annual premium of Rs 2,200. The surrender values were:

2002 Rs Nil; 2003 Rs 500; 2004 Rs 1,200 and 2005 Rs 2,050;

B died on April 20 2005 and the claim was received on 25th May. Show the necessary accounts in all the methods. *(B.Com., Madurai)*

SOLUTION

First Method

Dr. **Premium on Joint Life Policy Account** Cr.

		Rs			Rs
2002			2002		
Jan. 1	To Bank Account	2,200	Dec. 31	By Profit & Loss A/c	2,200
2003			2003		
Jan. 1	To Bank Account	2,200	Dec. 31	By Profit & Loss A/c	2,200
2004			2004		
Jan. 1	To Bank Account	2,200	Dec. 31	By Profit & Loss A/c	2,200
2005			2005		
Jan. 1	To Bank Account	2,200	Dec. 31	By Profit & Loss A/c	2,200

Dr. **Joint Life Policy Account** Cr.

		Rs			Rs
2005			2005		
May 25	To Profit:		May 25	By Bank Account	40,000
	A:	25,000			
	B:	15,000			
		40,000			40,000

Second Method

Dr. **Joint Life Policy Account** Cr.

		Rs			Rs
2002			2002		
Jan. 1	To Bank Account	2,200	Dec. 31	By Profit & Loss A/c	2,200
2003			2003		
Jan. 1	To Bank Account	2,200	Dec. 31	By Profit & Loss A/c	1,700
			"	By Balance c/d	500
		2,200			2,200
2004			2004		
Jan. 1	To Balance b/d	500	Dec. 31	By Profit & Loss A/c	1,500
"	To Bank Account	2,200	"	By Balance c/d	1,200
		2,700			2,700
2005			2005		
Jan. 1	To Balance b/d	1,200	May 25	By Bank Account	40,000
"	To Bank Account	2,200			
May 25	To A's Capital Account	22,875			
"	To B's Capital Account	13,725			
		40,000			40,000

Third Method

Joint Life Policy Account

Dr.		Rs		Cr.	Rs
2002			2002		
Jan. 1	To Bank Account	2,200	Dec. 31	By Joint Life Policy Reserve Account	2,200
2003			2003		
Jan. 1	To Bank Account	2,200	Dec. 31	By Joint Life Policy Reserve Account	1,700
			"	By Balance c/d	500
		2,200			2,200
2004			2004		
Jan. 1	To Balance b/d	500	Dec. 31	By Joint Life Policy Reserve Account	1,500
"	To Bank Account	2,200	"	By Balance c/d	1,200
		2,700			2,700
2005			2005		
Jan. 1	To Balance b/d	1,200	Dec. 31	By Bank Account	40,000
"	To Bank Account	2,200	"	By Joint Life Policy Reserve Account	3,400
"	To Profit to:				
	A's Capital A/c	25,000			
	B's Capital A/c	15,000			
		43,400			43,400

Joint Life Policy Reserve Account

Dr.		Rs		Cr.	Rs
2002			2002		
Dec. 31	To Joint Life Policy A/c	2,200	Dec. 31	By Profit & Loss A/c	2,200
2003			2003		
Dec. 31	To Joint Life Policy A/c	1,700	Dec. 31	By Profit & Loss A/c	2,200
"	To Balance c/d	500			
		2,200			2,200
2004			2004		
Dec. 31	To Joint Life Policy A/c	1,500	Jan. 1	By Balance b/d	500
"	To Balance c/d	1,200	Dec. 31	By Profit & Loss A/c	2,200
		2,700			2,700
2005			2005		
May 25	To Joint Life Policy A/c	3,400	Jan. 1	By Balance b/d	1,200
			May 25	By Profit & Loss A/c	2,200
		3,400			3,400

Note: In the case of policies on the lives of individual partners, the deceased partner has also a right to share the amount of surrender value, which the other partners' policies acquired at the time of death.

QUESTIONS

Objective Type Questions

I. Indicate whether each statement below is "True" or "False":

1. A firm can take a joint life policy on the lives of all the partners.
2. The profit or loss on revaluation of assets and liabilities is transferred to continuing partners in the new ratio.
3. At the time of retirement, undrawn profits or retained earnings should be distributed among all partners in the old profit sharing ratio.
4. Joint life policy is taken by the partners in order to provide working capital for the firm.
5. The retiring partner is entitled to an agreed rate of interest for the unpaid balance from the firm.
6. When a retiring partner is paid his share of goodwill, the same is adjusted to the capitals of continuing partners in the sacrificing ratio.
7. Joint life policy reserve is in the nature of accumulated profits.
8. The firm is dissolved on death of a partner.
9. Whether recorded or unrecorded, goodwill has to be valued when a partner retires or dies.
10. Joint life policy appears as an asset at the full value of the policy amount.
11. Deceased partner's share in the firm's goodwill is written back to the surviving partners in the gaining ratio.
12. Premium paid on joint life policy is always charged to firm's profits.
13. The amount due to retiring partner, if not paid, is transferred to his loan account.
14. A dormant partner has to give a public notice of his retirement.
15. The retiring partner may claim a share in the profits of the firm even after his retirement, if his accounts are not settled.

(**Ans:** True: 1, 3, 5, 7, 9, 11, 13, 15,
False: 2, 4, 6, 8, 10, 12, 14.

II. Fill in the blanks:

1. Revaluation Account is a .... Account.
2. Goodwill is an .... asset.
3. In the event of death of a partner, the accumulated profits and losses are shared by the partners in their .... profit sharing ratio.
4. Joint life policy is an .... Account.
5. At the time of retirement, retained earnings should be distributed amongst all the partners in the .... profit sharing ratio.

(**Ans:** 1. Nominal; 2. Intangible; 3. Old; 4. Asset; 5. Old.

III. Select the correct answer for each of the following:

1. General Reserves appearing in the Balance Sheet at the time of retirement or death of a partner, is divided amongst the partners in :
   (*a*) Original Ratios
   (*b*) New Ratios
   (*c*) Sacrificing Ratios
   (*d*) Gaining Ratios.
2. P, Q and R are sharing profits equally. P retires. The goodwill is appearing in the books at Rs. 3,000. It is valued at Rs. 6,000. P will be credited with:
   (*a*) Rs.2,000
   (*b*) Rs. 1,000
   (*c*) Rs. 3,000

3. A, B and C are partners sharing profits in the ratio of 2 : 2 : 1 . C retired. The new profit sharing ratio between A and B will be:
   (a) 2 : 1
   (b) 3 : 2
   (c) 1 : 1.
4. In case of retirement of a partner, goodwill at its full value is credited to the account or accounts of:
   (*a*) Only Retiring Partner.
   (*b*) All Partners.
   (*c*) Only remaining partners.
5. In the case of retirement of a partner profit on revaluation is credited to the capital accounts of the partners:
   (*a*) Equally
   (*b*) In proportion to their capitals.
   (*c*) In their profit sharing ratio.
6. The amount of General Reserve is transferred to Partners' Capital accounts in:
   (*a*) Old profit sharing ratio.
   (*b*) Capital Ratio
   (*c*) New profit sharing ratio.
7. Joint life policy account is:
   (*a*) A Personal Account.
   (*b*) A Nominal Account
   (*c*) A Real Account
8. Joint life policy amount after the maturity of the policy should be transferred to the capital accounts of the partners in:
   (*a*) New profit sharing ratio.
   (*b*) Old Ratio
   (*c*) Capital Ratio
9. On retirement of a partner, profit on the adjustment in the value of assets should be credited to the capital accounts of:
   (*a*) All partners in the old profit sharing ratio.
   (*b*) Continuing partners in their new profit sharing ratio.
   (*c*) The remaining partners in their old profit sharing ratio.
10. The Partnership Act provides interest on the accounts left by the retiring or deceased partner at:
   (*a*) New Ratio.
   (*b*) Old Ratio.
   (*c*) Capital Ratio.

(Ans.: 1. (a); 2. (b); 3. (c); 4. (b); 5. (c); 6. (a); 7. (c); 8. (b); 9. (a); 10. (a)

THEORETICAL QUESTIONS

1. Show the procedure to be followed in settling the accounts of a retiring partner.
2. What is meant by Joint Life Policy ? Why is it taken in a partnership firm?
3. What are the different methods of treating premium paid on Joint Life Policies?
4. Why should a Joint Life Policy be taken in partnership?

PRACTICAL PROBLEMS

Retirement of Partner

1. A, B and C are three partners sharing profits in the ratio of 4 : 3 : 2. B retires and goodwill of the firm

is valued at Rs 10,800. No goodwill appears in the books of the firm. A and C decide to share the profits in the future in the ratio of 5 : 3 and that no goodwill account will be raised in the books of the firm. Find out gaining ratio. Pass entries *(B.Com., (Pass) Delhi)*

[Ans: 13 : 11]

2. A, B and C are partners sharing profits and losses in the ratio of 4 : 3 : 1. B retires selling his share of profit to A and C for Rs 8,100; Rs 3,600 being paid by A and Rs 4,500 paid by C. The profit for the year after B's retirement was Rs 10,500.

   You are required (*i*) to give necessary journal entry to record the above said sale of B's share to A and B; and (*ii*) to calculate the new profit sharing ratio and distribute the profit between A and C.

   (B.Com., Bombay)

   [Ans: New Ratio 2 : 1]

3. Ram, Shyam and Rahim are partners sharing profits in the ratio of 4 : 3 : 2. Shyam retires and the goodwill is valued at Rs 21,600. No goodwill appears as yet in the books of the firm. Assuming that Ram and Rahim share profits in the future in the ratio of 5 : 3. Pass entries for goodwill separately under the following conditions:
   (*a*) When goodwill account is raised.
   (*b*) When goodwill account is raised and written off.
   (*c*) When only Shyam's share of goodwill account is raised and then written off. *(CA Entrance)*

   [Ans: (*a*) Raise goodwill by crediting all partners' capital account in 4 : 3 : 2 ratios.
   (*b*) Raise goodwill by crediting all partners' capital account in 4 : 3 : 2 and then write off by debiting Ram and Rahim's capital accounts in 5 : 3 ratio.
   (*c*) Credit Shyam's capital account with Rs 7,200 and corresponding debit of Rs 3,900 to Ram's account and Rs 3,300 to Rahim's account. (13 : 11)

4. A, B and C were partners sharing profits and losses in the ratio of 2 : 2 : 1. On 1st July 2004, their goodwill was valued at Rs 30,000, there being no account for it in the books. On this date, B retired. Pass journal entries to record the goodwill if:
   (*a*) It is allowed to remain in the books;
   (*b*) It is not allowed to remain in the books;
   (*c*) Only B's share is recorded; and
   (*d*) No account is raised for goodwill. *(B.Com., Delhi)*

   [Ans: Gaining Ratio: 2 : 1]

5. Calculate the new profit sharing ratio in the following cases:
   (*a*) A, B and C share profits in the ratio of 5 : 4 : 3. Find the new profit sharing ratio:
   (1) A retires
   (2) B retires
   (3) C retires
   (*b*) A, B and C profits in the ratio of 1/2, 1/5 and 3/10. Find the new profit sharing ratio:
   (1) A retires
   (2) B retires
   (3) C retires
   (*c*) A, B and C share are partners sharing profits in the ratio of 1/4, 2/5 and 7/20. C retires and his share is taken by A and B in the ratio of 1 : 2.

   [Ans: (*a*) (1) 4 : 3
   (2) 5 : 3
   (3) 5 : 4
   (*b*) (1) 2 : 3
   (2) 5 : 3
   (3) 5 : 2
   (*c*) 11 : 19]

6. Journalise the following:

(*a*) A, B and C are in partnership sharing profits in the ratio of 5 : 3 : 2. A retires and the goodwill of the firm on the date of his retirement is valued at Rs 25,000. B and C decided to continue the business and write off the goodwill so created.

(*b*) A, B and C are equal partners. Goodwill appears in the books at Rs 10,000. C retires and goodwill is revalued at Rs 16,000. Now A and B decide to share future profits and losses in the ratio of 3 : 2.

(*c*) A, B and C are partners sharing profits in the ratio of 4 : 3 : 3. Goodwill does not appear in the books. C retires from the firm and his share of goodwill is estimated to be Rs 6,000, which was purchased by A and B in equal proportion. A and B decide not to open goodwill account.

(*B.Com., Kerala*)

[**Ans:** (*a*) Write off Goodwill in 3 : 2 ratio
(*b*) Create Goodwill Rs 6,000 and credit all partners' account.
(*c*) Gaining Ratio : Equal]

7. P, Q and R were partners sharing profits and losses in the ratio of P 5/10, Q 3/10, R 2/10. They had taken out a joint life policy of the face value of Rs 20,000. On 31st December, 2004, its surrender value was Rs 4,000. On this date the balance sheet of the firm stood as under:

Liabilities		*Rs*	*Assets*	*Rs*
Sundry creditors		5,300	Fixed assets	25,000
Expenses outstanding		700	Stock	11,000
Reserve		3,000	Book debts	9,000
Capitals:			Cash at Bank	2,000
P	20,000			
Q	10,000			
R	8,000	38,000		
		47,000		47,000

On this date Q decided to retire and for the purpose: (i) Goodwill was valued at Rs 15,000, (ii) Fixed Assets were valued at Rs 30,000; and (iii) Stock was considered as worth Rs 10,000.

Q was to be paid through cash brought in by P and R in such a way as to make their capitals proportionate to their new profit sharing ratio which was to be P 3/5 and R 2/5. Goodwill was to be passed through books without raising a goodwill account; the joint life policy was also not to appear in the balance sheet.

Record these matters in the journal of the firm and prepare the resultant balance sheet.

(*B.Com., Delhi*)

[**Ans:** Revaluation profit Rs 4,000 (Rs 2,000 - P
Rs 1,200 - Q
Rs 800 - R)
Balance Sheet Total: Rs 51,000]

8. A, B and C are carrying on business in partnership sharing profits and losses in the ratio of 3 : 2 : 1 respectively. On 31st December, 2004, Balance Sheet of the firm stood as follows:

Liabilities		*Rs*	*Assets*	*Rs*
Sundry Creditors		13,590	Cash	5,900
Capital Accounts:			Debtors	8,000
A	15,000		Stock	11,690
B	10,000		Buildings	23,000
C	10,000	35,000		
		48,590		48,590

B retired on the abovementioned date on the following terms:

(*i*) Buildings be appreciated by Rs 7,000.

(*ii*) Provision for bad debts be made @ 5% on Debtors.

(*iii*) Goodwill of the firm be valued at Rs 9,000 and adjustment in this respect be made without raising Goodwill Account.

(*iv*) Rs 5,000 be paid to B immediately and the balance due to him be treated as a loan carrying interest @ 6% per annum.

Pass journal entries to record the abovementioned transactions and show the Balance Sheet of the firm as it would appear immediately after B's retirement. (*B.Com., Delhi*)

[**Ans:** Revaluation Profit: Rs 6,600 (Rs 3,300 - A
Rs 2,200 - B
Rs 1,100 - C)
Balance Sheet Total Rs 50,190]

9. X, Y and Z were partners in a glassware business and shared profits in the ratio 1/2 : 1/3 : 1/6 respectively. On January 1, 2004, their Balance Sheet stood as follows:

	Rs		*Rs*
Sundry Creditors	3,000	Goodwill	10,000
Capital Accounts:		Sundry Assets	12,000
X	14,000	Cash at Bank	11,000
Y	10,000		
Z	6,000		
	33,000		33,000

Immediately after the preparation of the above Balance Sheet, the followings changes took place:

(1) Z retires from the business, and his share valued at Rs 8,000 was taken over by X and Y who paid the former according to their profit sharing proportions, from their personal resources.

(2) S was then introduced in the business as a 1/6 partner on condition that a further sum of Rs 6,000 was allowed to be credited to X and Y in their respective proportions and that he contributed such a sum as would make his capital equal to 1/4 of the total capital of X and Y after the above adjustments.

Show the Capital Accounts of all the partners and the Balance Sheet on S's admission.

(*M.Com., Madurai*)

[**Ans:** Capitals:
X : – Rs 22,400
Y : – Rs 15,600
S : – Rs 9,500
Balance Sheet Total : Rs 50,500]

10. A, B and C are partners in a firm sharing profits and losses as A 1/2, B 1/6 and C 1/3 respectively. The Balance Sheet on 31st December, 2004, was as follows:

Liabilities		*Rs*	*Assets*		*Rs*
Bills Payable		10,000	Freehold Premises		50,000
Sundry Creditors		20,500	Plant and Machinery		25,000
Reserve		12,000	Furniture and Fixtures		2,500
Capital Accounts:			Stock in trade		22,500
A	25,000		Sundry Debtors	20,000	
B	20,000		*Less*: Reserve for Bad		
C	35,000	80,000	Debts	1,000	19,000
			Cash		3,500
		2,22,500			2,22,500

C retires from the business and the partners agree to the following revaluations.

Freehold Premises and Stock are to be appreciated by 20% and 15% respectively.

Plant and Machinery and Furnitures and Fixtures are to be depreciated by 10% and 7 1/2% respectively.

Bad Debts Reserve is to be increased to Rs 1,500.

A Goodwill Account is to be raised at Rs 20,000.

Give effect to the above arrangement and show the Partners' Capital Accounts, and also the Balance Sheet of A and B as at 1st January, 2005, assuming they write back the Goodwill Account.

(B.Com., Andhra)

[Ans: Revaluation Gain : Rs 10,187 (A : 5,094
B : 1,698
C : 3,395)
Balance Sheet Total : Rs 1,32,687]

11. A, B and C were partners entitled to 1/2, 1/3 and 1/6 share of profits respectively. A summary of their Balance Sheet as on 31.12.2004 was as follows:

		Rs		*Rs*
Sundry Creditors		15,000	Goodwill	50,000
Capitals:			Block Account	60,000
A	70,000		Cash	55,000
B	50,000			
C	30,000	1,50,000		
		1,65,000		1,65,000

The following steps were taken on 1 January 2005:

(1) C retires and his interest in firm was valued at Rs 40,000. It was purchased by A and B from their private resources in their profit sharing proportion.

(2) The existing goodwill is written off.

(3) D was admitted and became entitled to 1/6 share of profits on the condition that A and B should be credited proportionately for Goodwill amounting to Rs 30,000. He should bring in capital equal to 1/5 of the combined capital of A and B after adjustments.

Prepare partners' capital accounts and show the opening Balance Sheet of the reconstituted firm as on 1.1.2005.

(B.Com., Punjab)

[Ans: Capital Accounts: A : Rs 76,000
B : Rs 54,000
D : Rs 26,000
Balance Sheet Total : Rs 1,71,000]

12. Anil, Bimal and Charu are partners sharing profits and losses in the ratio 3 : 2 : 1. Balance Sheet of Anil, Bimal and Charu as on December 31, 2004 was as follows:

		Rs		*Rs*
Capital Accounts			Goodwill	10,000
Anil	65,000		Sundry debtors	61,400
Bimal	38,000		Sundry assets	1,48,000
Charu	28,000	1,31,000		
General reserve		38,400		
Sundry creditors		50,000		
		2,19,400		2,19,400

Charu desires to retire from the firm on January 1, 2005. In terms of the agreement, goodwill is to be revalued at Rs 50,000, sundry debtors at Rs 41,400, and other sundry assets at Rs 1,50,000. The amount payable to the retired partner is for the present to be treated as a loan with 5% interest. On the same day, *i.e.* on January 1, 2005, Dinen is admitted as a partner on payment of Rs 32,000. Profits and losses are henceforth to be shared in the ratio of 4 : 3 : 2 between Anil, Bimal and Dinen. No alteration is made in the book value of assets (other than cash brought in by Dinen and the General Reserve).

Draw up the final Balance Sheet as on January 1, 2005, on the above basis, after the admission of Dinen. (*B.Com., Madurai*)

[Ans: Capital Accounts:
Anil : Rs 85,422
Bimal : Rs 50,800
Dinen : Rs 27,111
Charu's Loan Account : Rs 38,067
Balance Sheet Total : Rs 2,51,400]

13. The balance sheet of Xavier, Yusuf and Zaman, who were sharing profits in the ratio of 4 : 3 : 2 respectively, stood as follows on 31st December, 2004:

Liabilities		*Rs*	*Assets*		*Rs*
Sundry Creditors		4,140	Cash at bank		3,300
Capital Accounts:			Sundry debtors	3,045	
Xavier	12,000		*Less*: Provision	105	2,940
Yusuf	9,000		Stock		4,800
Zaman	6,000	27,000	Plant and Machinery		5,100
			Land and building		15,000
		31,140			31,140

Yusuf having given notice to retire from the firm, the following adjustments in the books of the firm were agreed upon :

(*a*) That land and building be appreciated by 10 per cent. (*b*) The provision for bad debts is no longer necessary. (*c*) That the stock be appreciated by 20 per cent. (*d*) That adjustment be made in the accounts to rectify a mistake previously made whereby Yusuf was credited in excess by Rs 810 while Xavier and Zaman were debited in excess by Rs 420 and Rs 390 respectively. (e) That the goodwill of the firm be fixed at Rs 5,400 and Yusuf's share of the same be adjusted to that of Xavier and Zaman who are going to share in future profits in the ratio of 2 : 1. (f) That the entire capital of the firm, as newly constituted, will be re-adjusted by bringing in or paying of cash so that the future capital of Xavier and Zaman be in the ratio of 2 : 1.

Pass journal entries and prepare the balance sheet of the new firm showing Yusuf's balance as loan. (*I.C.W.A. Inter*)

[Ans: Revaluation Profit : Rs 2,565 (Rs - 1,140 : Xavier
Rs 855 : Yusuf
Rs 570 : Zaman
Yusuf Loan Account : Rs 10,845
Balance Sheet Total : Rs 33,705]

14. P and Q were working in partnership sharing profits and losses equally. On 31.12.2004 P decided to retire; in his place, his son R was admitted as partner from 1 January, 2005, with 1/3rd share in profit as partner from 1st January, 2005.

The balance sheet of the firm as on 31.12.2004 was as follows:

Liabilities		*Rs*	*Assets*	*Rs*
Sundry Creditors		14,700	Goodwill	15,000
Capital:			Land & Buildings	40,050
P	54,000		Motor Car	12,000

Q	48,300	1,02,300	Furniture	9,300
			Sundry Debtors	24,150
			Cash at Bank	16,500
		1,17,000		1,17,000

It was decided as follows:

(*a*) The goodwill should be raised to Rs 20,000. (*b*) The motor car would be taken over by P at its book value. (*c*) The value of Land and Buildings would be increased by Rs 8,280. (*d*) Q and R would introduce sufficient capital to pay off P and to leave thereafter a sum of Rs 7,350 as Bank Balance, in a manner to make their capitals in proportion to their share of profits. (*e*) The capital payable by R was to be gifted to him by his father. (*f*) The new partners decided not to show goodwill as an asset.

The above arrangements were duly complied with. Show the Partners' Capital accounts and the Bank account. (*ICWA Inter*)

[Ans: Capital Accounts : Q : Rs 49,620
R : Rs 24,810
Cash paid to P : Rs 17,163
Q brings in Cash : Rs 8,013
Bank Balance : Rs 7,350]

15. Firm ABC consisted of three partners A, B and C, sharing profits and losses in the ratio of 5 : 3 : 2. The partner A died on February 20, 2004. The Profit and Loss Account for the period up to the date of death and the Balance Sheet as on that date were prepared.

Balance Sheet
as on February 20, 2004

Liabilities		*Rs*	*Assets*	*Rs*
Capital Accounts:			Goodwill	6,000
A	12,000		Machinery	35,000
B	16,000		Furniture	6,000
C	12,000	40,000	Stock	9,000
Loan from A		5,000	Debtors	15,000
General Reserve		7,000	Bank	3,000
Creditors		22,000		
		74,000		74,000

In addition to the assets shown above, the firm had three Life Policies in the name of each partner, at an insured value of Rs 20,000 each, the premium of which were charged to the Profit and Loss Account.

According to the partnership deed, on the death of a partner, the assets and liabilities are to be revalued by a valuer. The revalued figures were:

(1) Goodwill Rs 21,000; machinery Rs 45,000; debtors are subject to a provision for doubtful debts at 10% and furniture at Rs 7,000.

(2) Provision for taxation to be created for Rs 1,500.

(3) Death claim for policy in the name of A will be realised in full and the surrender values of the other two policies were Rs 7,500 each.

The business will be continued by B and C henceforth, sharing profits and losses equally. The net balance due to A is transferred to a Loan Account, which will be paid off later.

Show the Capital Account, Revaluation Account and the new Balance Sheet of the firm. (*I.C.W.A.*)

[Ans: Revaluation Profit : Rs 8,000 (Rs 4,000 to A
Rs 2,400 to B
Rs 1,600 to C

Capital Accounts: B : Rs 28,000
C : Rs 17,500
Balance Sheet Total : Rs 1,18,500]

16. ABC and Company is a partnership firm and their Balance Sheet as on 30th June 2004 is as follows:

Liabilities		*Rs*	*Assets*	*Rs*
Capital Accounts:			Goodwill	30,000
A:	50,000		Fixed Assets	75,000
B:	30,000		Current Assets	35,000
C:	20,000	1,00,000	Cash	24,000
Creditors		64,000		
		1,64,000		1,64,000

B retires on the above date and D is admitted as a new partner from 1st July 2004. The following adjustments were agreed upon :

(1) Fixed assets to be valued at Rs 70,000. Current Assets at Rs 45,000 and Goodwill is upvalued by Rs 15,000.

(2) After admission of new partner, the goodwill account is to be completely wiped out from the books.

(3) ABC share profits and losses in ratio of their Capitals. In the new firm, A, C and D shall share profits and losses in the ratio of 2 : 2 : 1 and their capital accounts should be adjusted accordingly.

(4) B is paid 50% of the amount due to him and the balance remains as a loan to the firm.

(5) D brings in cash Rs 40,000 as his capital. A and C will bring in cash or be paid cash after adjustment of their capital as mentioned in item 3 above.

Prepare Profit and Loss Adjustment Account, Capital Accounts, Cash Account and the Balance Sheet of the new firm. *(CAIIB)*

[**Ans:** Revaluation Profit : Rs 5,000 (Rs 2,500 to A
Rs 1,500 to B
Rs 1,000 to C
Capital Accounts: A : Rs 62,000
C : Rs 62,000
D : Rs 31,000
Cash Account Balance : Rs 1,22,000
Balance Sheet Total : Rs 2,37,000]

17. On 31st December 2004 the Balance Sheet of M/s A, B and C, sharing profits and losses in proportion to their capitals stood as follows:

Liabilities		*Rs*	*Assets*		*Rs*
Creditors		1,08,000	Cash at Bank		80,000
Capital Accounts:			Debtors	1,00,000	
A	4,50,000		*Less*: Reserve	2,000	98,000
B	3,00,000		Stock		90,000
C	1,50,000	9,00,000	Machinery		2,40,000
			Land and Building		5,00,000
		10,08,000			10,08,000

On that date, B wants to retire from the firm and the remaining partners decide to carry on the firm. The following re-adjustments of assets and liabilities have been agreed upon before the ascertainment of the amount payable to B:

(*i*) that out of the amount of insurance premium which was debited annually entirely to Profit and Loss A/c, Rs 10,000 be carried forward for unexpired insurance on 31.12.2004;

(*ii*) that the land and building be appreciated by 10%;
(*iii*) that the Reserve for doubtful debts be brought up to 5% on debtors;
(*iv*) that machinery be depreciated by 5%;
(*v*) that a provision for Rs 15,000 be made in respect of an outstanding bill for repairs;
(*vi*) that the goodwill of the entire firm be fixed at Rs 1,80,000 and B's share of the same adjusted in the accounts of A and C who share future profits in the proportions of 3/4 and 1/4 respectively (no goodwill account being raised); and
(*vii*) that B be paid Rs 50,000 in cash and the balance be transferred to his loan account.

Prepare Revaluation A/c, Capital A/cs of the partners and the Balance Sheet of the firm of A and C.

(*C.A. Inter*)

[**Ans:** Revaluation Profit : Rs 30,000 (A : Rs 15,000
B : Rs 10,000
C : Rs 5,000)
Capital Accounts : A : Rs 4,20,000
C : Rs 1,40,000
Balance Sheet Total : Rs 10,03,000

18. On 31st March 2004, the Balance Sheet of M/s Ram, Rahul and Rohit, sharing profit and losses in proportion to their capital, stood as follows:

	Rs		*Rs*
Capital Accounts		Land & Building	2,00,000
Ram	3,00,000	Machinery	2,00,000
Rahul	2,00,000	Closing Stock	1,00,000
Rohit	1,00,000	Sundry Debtors	2,00,000
Creditors	2,00,000	Cash at Bank	1,00,000
	8,00,000		8,00,000

On 31st March 2004, Ram desired to retire from the firm and the remaining partners decided to carry on. It was agreed to revalue the assets and liabilities on that date on the following basis:

(1) Land & Building be appreciated by 30%.
(2) Machinery be depreciated by 20%.
(3) Closing stock to be valued at Rs 80,000.
(4) Provision for Bad Debts be made at 5%.
(5) Old credit balance of sundry creditors Rs 10,000 written back.
(6) Joint Life Policy surrendered and cash obtained Rs 60,000.
(7) Goodwill of the firm be valued at Rs 1,80,000 and Ram's share of goodwill be adjusted in the accounts of Rahul and Rohit who share the future profits equally. No goodwill account being raised.
(8) The total capital of the firm is to be the same before retirement. Individual capital be in their profit sharing ratio.
(9) Amount due to Ram is to be settled on the following basis:
50% on retirement and the balance 50% within one year.

Prepare Revaluation Account, Capital Accounts, Cash Account and Balance Sheet as on 1st April 2004.

(*CA*)

[**Ans:** Revaluation Profit : Rs 60,000 (Rs 30,000 to Ram
Rs 20,000 to Rahul
Rs 10,000 to Rohit)
Capital Accounts : Rahul : Rs 3,00,000
Rohit : Rs 3,00,000

Cash Balance : Rs 3,10,000

Balance Sheet Total : Rs 10,00,000]

19. For some years X has been carrying on proprietorship business with a capital of Rs 77,500 and his accounts are closed annually to 31st March.

On 1st April, 2001, Y joined him as a partner with 1/3 interest in the profit and goodwill. Y introduced a sum of Rs 40,000 on account of capital and it was agreed that X be credited with goodwill of Rs 22,500.

The deed of partnership provided *inter alia*:

(*a*) Capital and Current Accounts be kept separately.

(*b*) Drawings be – X Rs 3,000 per month and Y – Rs 2,000 per month including salary as mentioned below.

(*c*) Y be allowed salary on capital at 5% p.a.

(*d*) Interest be allowed on capital at 5% p.a.

On the death of a partner, executors be entitled to :

(*a*) Balance of Capital and Current Accounts;

(*b*) Interest on Capital and Salary up to the date of death;

(*c*) Accruing share of profit to be based on the profits for the completed year immediately preceding the date of death;

(*d*) Share of goodwill, the value of which is to be calculated at two years' purchase of the average profits, after charging interest on Capital and partner's salary, for 3 completed years immediately preceding the date of death.

Profits before charging interest on capital and partners' salaries were as given hereunder:

Year ending 31st March 2002	Rs 67,000
Year ending 31st March 2003	Rs 70,000
Year ending 31st March 2004	Rs 77,000

On 30th September 2003, Y introduced additional capital Rs 16,000.

Y died on 30th June 2004. It was ascertained that up to 31st March 2004, he had drawn the amount as mentioned in (*b*) above and from 1st April 2004 to the date of death his drawing had been Rs 5,500.

Prepare:

(*i*) Profit and Loss Appropriation Account for each of the three years ending 31st March 2002, 2003 and 2004.

(*ii*) Y's capital and Current accounts to show respective balances on 31st March 2004.

(*iii*) Detailed computation of the amount due to the Executor of the deceased as on 30th June 2004.

(*CA Inter*)

[**Ans:** Y's Executor Account: Rs 99,867]

20. The following is the Balance Sheet of A, B and C who were sharing profits in the ratio of 2 : 2 : 1 on 31.12.2004:

Liabilities		*Rs*	*Assets*	*Rs*
Creditors		12,000	Plant and Machinery	49,000
5% Mortgage Loan		16,600	Furniture	4,800
Capital Accounts:			Stock in trade	22,800
A	33,600		Sundry Debtors	21,600
B	25,200		Cash in hand	1,200
C	12,000	70,800		
		99,400		99,400

On 1.1.2005, C retired from the business and claimed his share in the secret reserve/profit arising out of the following:

(1) During the year 2004, purchase of machinery at a cost of Rs 5,000 was charged to purchase account, the installation charge of Rs 300 to erect the machinery being charged to machinery repairs account.

(2) Rs 1,200 received from Mr X towards rent of property sub-let was credited to his personal account instead of to rent account, so as to reduce his debit balance from Rs 1,600 to Rs 400 debit.

(3) Interest on Mortgage loan was paid in advance up to 31.12.2005 and the whole amount was charged to Interest A/c in 2004.

After rectifying the above errors, it was mutually decided as under:

(*a*) The Goodwill of the firm be valued at three times the average profits of the last three years. Such profits should be the correct profits and not the book profits. The book profits for the last three years were:

2002 Rs 13,830, 2003 Rs 32,000, 2004 Rs 12,020.

(*b*) Machinery be depreciated by 10% and the provision for bad and doubtful debts be made at 5% on debtors.

(*c*) There is a liability for Rs 483 for bills discounted.

(*d*) Goodwill should appear in the books to the extent of the retiring partner's share therein.

(*e*) C should be paid half his dues in cash which shall be brought in by A and B in their profit-sharing proportions and the other half shall be left in the business as C's loan.

Show ledger accounts and Balance Sheet of A and B. (*B.Com., Mangalore*)

[Ans: Balance Sheet Total: Rs 1,13,196]

21. P, Q and R are partners in a business sharing profits 3/4, 1/8 and 1/8 respectively, and their Balance Sheet as on 31st December 2004 was as follows:

Liabilities		*Rs*	*Assets*	*Rs*
Sundry Creditors		40,000	Plant and Machinery	60,000
General Reserve		5,000	Patents	10,000
Capital A/cs:			Sundry Debtors	35,000
P	50,000		Stock	20,000
Q	30,000		Cash	25,000
R	25,000	1,05,000		
		1,50,000		1,50,000

R retires on 31st December 2004 on the following terms:

(1) Goodwill is to be valued at three years' purchase of the last four years. The profits were as follows:

	Rs		Rs
2001	50,000	2003	40,000
2002	60,000	2004	50,000

(2) Goodwill account is not to appear in the books after R's retirement.

(3) Plant and Machinery was valued at Rs 50,000, Patents at Rs 15,300 and Stock at Rs 18,000.

(4) A provision of 5% on Debtors was necessary.

(5) On 30th June 2004, a shed was constructed at a cost of Rs 10,000. This sum was charged to Profit and Loss Account. This asset is now to be brought in the books, after allowing 5% per annum depreciation on the original cost. (This adjustment should be ignored for the purpose of valuation of goodwill to be provided as per Term 1.)

(6) Q was to acquire the whole of the share of profit of R.

(7) The total capital of the firm was to be Rs 80,000 and capitals of P and Q were to be in their profit-sharing ratio, necessary adjustments to be made in cash.

(8) R is to leave Rs 30,000 in the business as loan at 12%. The remaining amount is to be paid to him immediately.

You are required to prepare:

(1) Revaluation A/c.

(2) Partners' Capital A/cs showing all the adjustments.

(3) Balance Sheet of the firm after R's retirement.

(4) Give full working for Goodwill A/c and Cash A/c. (*CAIIB*)

[Ans: Revaluation Profit Rs 1,300 (P : 976
Q : 162
R : 162)
Capital Accounts : P : Rs 60,000
Q : Rs 20,000
Cash to be brought in by P : Rs 5,274
Q : Rs 7,963
R's Share of Goodwill : Rs 18,750
Balance Sheet Total : Rs 1,50,000]

22. The firm of Bobby and Company consisted of three partners X, Y and Z who shared profits and losses in the ratio of 5 : 3 : 2 respectively. The following was their balance sheet as on 31st December 2004:

Liabilities	*Rs*	*Assets*		*Rs*
Trade Creditors	60,000	Goodwill		1,00,000
Bills Payable	75,000	Furniture		15,000
X's Loan	10,000	Stock		1,67,000
Capitals:		Debtors		3,00,000
X	2,40,000	*Less*: Reserve for		
Y	1,75,000	bad debts	6,000	2,94,000
Z	1,25,000	Investments		50,000
		Bank		59,000
	6,85,000			6,85,000

Mr X retired as from that date on the following terms:

(*a*) His capital account is to be credited with Rs 50,000 for his share of goodwill.

(*b*) Furniture and Stock is to be depreciated by 10 per cent.

(*c*) The provision for Bad Debts is to be increased to 3%.

(*d*) Investments are to be appreciated by 4 per cent.

(*e*) Mr X's capital and loan accounts were paid off on the first day of January 2005.

The partners after the retirement of Mr X agreed to eliminate goodwill from the books, to share profits and losses equally and to equalise their contributions to the partnership capital accounts. Necessary funds to be brought in by Y and Z to pay off X and thereafter to keep a bank balance of Rs 10,000.

You are required to prepare:

(1) Revaluation A/c.

(2) Partners' Capital A/c.

(3) Balance Sheet after Mr X's retirement.

(4) Working for amount brought in by Y and Z. (*CAIIB*)

[Ans: Revaluation Loss : Rs 19,200 (X – Rs 9,600
Y – Rs 5,760
Z – Rs 3,840)
Capital Accounts : Y : Rs 1,90,900
Z : Rs 1,90,900
Balance Sheet Total : Rs 5,16,800

23. Compass, Cone and Circle are in partnership sharing profits and losses in the ratio of 3 : 2 : 1.

BALANCE SHEET as on 31st March 2004

Liabilities		*Rs*	*Assets*		*Rs*
Capital Accounts			Machinery	50,000	
Compass	40,000		*Less*: Provision for		
Cone	60,000		depreciation	8,000	42,000
Circle	20,000	1,20,000	Furniture		1,000
Reserve		30,000	Debtors	80,000	
Sundry Creditors		60,000	*Less*: Provision for		
			doubtful debts	3,000	77,000
			Stock		50,000
			Cash at Bank		40,000
		2,10,000			2,10,000

On 31st March 2004, Cone retired and Compass and Circle continued in partnership, sharing profits and losses in the ratio of 3 : 2. It was agreed that the following adjustments were to be made in the Balance Sheet as on 31st March 2004:

(1) The machinery was to be revalued at Rs 45,000.
(2) The stock was to be reduced by 2%.
(3) The furniture was to be reduced to Rs 600.
(4) The provision for doubtful debts would be Rs 4,000.
(5) A provision of Rs 300 was to be made for outstanding expenses.

The partnership agreement provided that on the retirement of a partner, goodwill was to be valued at Rs 24,000 and Cone's share of the same was to be adjusted into the accounts of Compass and Circle. The profits up to the date of retirement was estimated at Rs 18,000.

Cone was to be paid off in full. Compass and Circle were to bring such an amount in cash so as to make their capitals in proportion to the new profit sharing ratio, subject to the condition that a cash balance of Rs 20,000 was to be maintained as working capital.

Pass the necessary journal entries to give effect to the above arrangement and prepare the partners capital accounts as on 31st March 2004. (*CA*)

[**Ans:** Capital Accounts:
Compass : Rs 66,180
Circle : Rs 44,120
Cash paid to Cone : Rs 84,100]

24. On 31st December 2004, the Balance Sheet of A, B and C who were sharing profits and losses in proportion to their capitals stood as follows:

		Rs			*Rs*
Creditors		10,800	Cash at Bank		8,000
Capital Accounts:			Debtors	10,000	
A	45,000		*Less*: Reserve	200	9,800
B	30,000		Stock		9,000
C	15,000	90,000	Machinery		24,000
			Land and Buildings		50,000
		1,00,800			1,00,800

B retires and the following re-adjustments of the assets and liabilities have been agreed upon before the ascertainment of the amount payable to B:

(*i*) That out of the amount of insurance which was debited entirely to Profit and Loss Account, Rs 1,000 be carried forward as unexpired insurance.

(*ii*) That the land and building be appreciated by 10%.

(*iii*) That the Reserve for doubtful debts be brought up to 5% of debtors.

(*iv*) That machinery be depreciated by 5%.

(*v*) That a provision of Rs 1,500 be made in respect of an outstanding bill for repairs.

(*vi*) That the goodwill of the entire firm be fixed at Rs 18,000 and B's share of the same be adjusted into the accounts of A and C who are going to share future profits in the proportion of 3/4 and 1/4 respectively (no goodwill account being raised).

(*vii*) That the entire capital of the firm as newly constituted be fixed at Rs 60,000 between A and C in the proportion of 3/4 and 1/4 after passing entries in their accounts for adjustments *i.e.* actual cash to be paid off or to be brought in by the continuing partners as the case may be.

(*viii*) That B be paid Rs 5,000 in cash and the balance be transferred to his loan account.

Prepare the capital accounts of the partners and the Balance Sheet of the firm of A and C.

(*B.Com., Delhi*)

[Ans: Revaluation Profit Rs 3,000 (A : Rs 1,500
B : Rs 1,000
C – Rs 500)
Capitals : A – Rs 45,000
C – Rs 15,000
B's Loan Account Rs 32,000
Balance Sheet Total : Rs 1,04,300]

25. Brown and Smith are partners. The Partnership Deed provides *inter alia*:

(*i*) That the accounts be balanced on 31st December each year. (*ii*) That the profits be divided as follows: Brown one-half. Smith one-third, and carried to a Reserve Account one-sixth. (*iii*) That in the event of death of a partner, his Executors will be entitled to be paid out: (*a*) The capital to his credit at date of death; (*b*) His proportion of Reserve at date of the last Balance Sheet; (*c*) His proportion of profits to death based on the average profits of the last three completed years; (*d*) By way of Goodwill his proportion of total profits for the preceding three years.

On 31st December, 2004, the Ledger Balances were:

	Rs	Rs
Brown's Capital	—	90,000
Smith's Capital	—	60,000
Reserve	—	30,000
Bill's Receivable	20,000	—
Investments	50,000	—
Cash	1,40,000	—
Creditors	—	30,000
	2,10,000	2,10,000

The profits for the three years were : 2002 – Rs 42,000; 2003 – Rs 39,000; 2004 – Rs 45,000.

Smith died on 1st May 2005. Show the workings of Smith's :

(*i*) Share of Reserve; (*ii*) Share of profits; (*iii*) Share of Goodwill and draw up Smith's Executor's Account as would appear in the firm's ledger transferring the amount to his Loan Account.

(*B.Com., Delhi*)

[Ans: Capital : Rs 60,000
Share of Reserve : Rs 12,000
Share of Profit : Rs 5,600
Share of Goodwill : Rs 50,400
Amount Payable : 1,28,000]

26. A, B and C were in partnership sharing profits equally. C died on 31st March, 2005. The Balance Sheet of the firm as at 31st December 2004 was as under:

Liabilities		*Rs*	*Assets*	*Rs*
Sundry		15,600	Cash in hand & at Bank	4,000
General Reserve		6,000	Debtors	18,000
Investment Fluctuation Fund		2,100	Stocks	28,000
Reserve for Doubtful Debts		1,800	Investments (at cost)	8,000
Capital:			Freehold property	30,000
A	30,000		Goodwill	13,500
B	25,000			
C	21,000	76,700		
		1,01,500		1,01,500

On the date of death it was found that: (1) Freehold property was worth Rs 57,000; (2) Debtors were all good; (3) Stocks were valued at Rs 25,000; (4) Investments were valued at Rs 7,500 and were taken over by A at that value; (5) A liability for workmen's compensation for Rs 3,000 was to be provided for; (6) Goodwill was to be valued at one year's purchase of average profits of last 5 years; (7) C's share of profit up to the date of death was to be calculated on the basis of last year's profit.

The profits of the last 5 years were as under:

2000 Rs 11,500; 2001 Rs 12,500; 2002 Rs 8,000;

2003 Rs 10,000; 2004 Rs 12,000.

Prepare : (*i*) Revaluation Account, (*ii*) Capital Account of C and (*iii*) Balance Sheet of the remaining partners. (*CAIIB*)

[Ans: Revaluation Profit : Rs 24,400 (A – Rs 8,133
B – Rs 8,133
C – Rs 8,134)
Payable to C's Executor : Rs 31,234
Balance Sheet Total : Rs 1,15,800]

27. The following is the Balance Sheet of the firm of ABC as on 31.12.2003. Their profit sharing ratio is 3 : 2 : 1.

Capital and Liabilities		*Rs*	*Assets*	*Rs*
Capital Accounts			Fixed Assets	40,000
A		16,000	Sundry Debtors	32,000
B		12,000	Insurance Policy on Joint	
C		10,000	Life of partners	6,000
Current Accounts:			Stock	24,000
A		4,000	Bank	9,000
B		3,000	Cash	3,000
C		1,000		
Reserve		18,000		
Profit and Loss A/c:				
Opening balance	6,000			
Profit for the year	14,000	20,000		
Creditors		20,000		
Bank O/D		10,000		
		1,14,000		1,14,000

B died on 31.3.2004. His account has to be settled and paid. For the year 2004 proportionate profit of 2003 is to be taken into account. For 2003, a bad debt of Rs 2,000 has to be adjusted. Goodwill has to be calculated 3 times of the four years' average profits. A policy is taken on the joint life of partners for Rs 35,000 and the annual premium of Rs 2,000 has to be paid on February 1, every year. The profits for 2008 - Rs 12,000; 2009 - Rs. 20,000; 2010 - Rs. 16,000 and 2011 - Rs. 12,000. Goodwill accoun: need not be kept in the accounts. Calculate the amount payable to B's heirs. Show the necessar; ledger accounts of all partners and other detailed calculations. *(C.A. Entrance)*

[**Ans:** Amount payable to B's Executor : Rs 52,000]

28. A, B and C are partners sharing profits and losses in the ratio of 5 : 3 : 2.

Balance Sheet of A, B, C prior to A's Death

	Rs		*Rs*
Capital Accounts:		Goodwill	1,00,000
A	2,00,000	Machinery	1,00,000
B	1,50,000	Debtors	3,00,000
C	1,00,000	Stock	2,00,000
Reserve	50,000	Cash at Bank	50,000
Creditors	2,50,000		
	7,50,000		7,50,000

A died. Profit up to the date of death is estimated at Rs 90,000 without considering any depreciation. One Joint Life Policy of Rs 1,50,000 (without profit) was taken in the last year. Premium of 10,000 was written off to the Profit and Loss Account. Each of the current assets (except Csh and Bank) is estimated to have gone up by 20%. Creditors have increased by Rs 20,000. Goodwill is to be calculated at 2 years' purchase of average profit of three years. The profit of the preceding 3 years was Rs 1,80,000; Rs 2,00,000 and Rs 2,20,000.

Dues to the deceased partner's representatives were to be settled on receipt of the insurance claim to the extent possible. The balance carrying 10% interest from the date of death was to be paid after one year. Machinery was valued at Rs 80,000. Prepare necessary accounts and a Balance Sheet immediately after A's death. *(I.C.W.A.)*

[**Ans:** Revaluation Profit : Rs 60,000 (A – Rs 30,000
B – Rs 18,000
C – Rs 12,000)
Capital Accounts : A : Rs 3,18,000
C : Rs 2,12,000
A's Executor Account : Rs 5,25,000
Balance Sheet Total : Rs 13,25,000]

29. X, Y and Z were partners in a business sharing profits 3/4, 1/8 and 1/8 respectively and their Balance Sheet as on 31st December 2004 was as follows:

Liabilities		*Rs*	*Assets*	*Rs*
Creditors		25,000	Plant	50,000
Capital Accounts:			Debtors	35,000
X	50,000		Stock	20,000
Y	30,000		Bank	25,000
Z	25,000	1,05,000		
		1,30,000		1,30,000

Z died on 30th September 2004 and the partnership deed provided the following:

(*a*) The deceased partner will be entitled to his share of profit up to the date of death, calculated on the previous year's profit.

(*b*) He will be entitled to his share of goodwill of the firm, calculated on the basis of 3 years' purchase of the average profits of the last four years. The net profits for the last four years were:

2000 – Rs 80,000
2001 – Rs 60,000
2002 – Rs 40,000
2003 – Rs 20,000

His drawings amounted to Rs 1,800 up to the date of death. Interest on capital was to be allowed and on drawings to be charged at 5% (in case of drawings on the total amount) p.a.

Ascertain the amount payable to the legal representatives of the deceased partner.

(*B.Com., Bangalore*)

[Ans: Z's Executor A/c Rs. 44,695]

30. X, Y and Z carried on business in partnership, profits being divisible to X – 1/2, to Y – 1/3 and to Z – 1/6.

The Balance Sheet on 31st December 2003 showed their capitals to be X Rs. 20,000, Y Rs. 15,000 and Z Rs. 10,000. On 31st March, 2004, X died; and you are instructed to prepare an account for presentation to his executors having regard to the following facts:

(*a*) The firm had insured the partners' lives severally, X for Rs. 10,000; Y for Rs. 7,500 and Z for Rs. 5,000. The premiums have been charged to Profit and Loss Account and the surrender value of 31st March, 2004, amounted in each case to one-half of the sum assured.

(*b*) Capital carried interest @6% p.a.

(*c*) X's drawings from Ist January, 2004 to the date of his death amounted to Rs. 3,500

(*d*) X's share of profits for the portion of the current financial year for which he lived was to be taken at the sum calculated on the average of the last three completed years and goodwill was to be raised on the basis of two years' purchase of the average profit of those three years.

The annual profits were Rs. 7,500, Rs. 8,000 and Rs.9,000 respectively.

Pass the necessary journal entries and show the account of the executor of X.

(*CA Inter*)

(Ans: X's Executor A/c Rs. 34,113)

Chapter 32

Partnership Accounts: Amalgamation and Sale of Firm

Introduction – Reasons for Amalgamation – Closing of Books of Amalgamating Firms – Sale of Firm – Questions – Objective Type Questions – Theoretical Questions – Practical Problems

INTRODUCTION

When a firm admits a new partner with a view to secure additional capital or better business skill, it is known as admission of partner in an existing firm. In the same manner, two or more independent firms, engaged in identical business activities, may combine their activities into a New Firm and this combination or consolidation is known as Amalgamation of Firms. Thus, two or more firms are said to amalgamate when they join together, pool their resources and run the business into a composite form, as a new firm – as a single integrated unit.

REASONS FOR AMALGAMATION

The major objectives of amalgamation are:

(*a*) To achieve internal and external economies of production in order to maximise profits.
(*b*) To gain monopoly in the particular trade.
(*c*) To avoid cut-throat competition.
(*d*) To achieve large operations.
(*e*) To achieve efficient work by combination of men with different qualities.
(*f*) To reduce unnecessary expenses on advertising.
(*g*) To become a big business unit by increasing capitals.
(*h*) To achieve mass production at minimum cost.

The amalgamation may be in any one of the following forms:

1. Amalgamation of two sole trading concerns and formation of Partnership.
2. Amalgamation of one sole trader with another Partnership (similar to admission).
3. Amalgamation of one partnership with another partnership.

As a result of combination, the merging units lose their independence and the proprietors or partners of such merging units become the partners of an altogether new unit.

Amalgamation involves the closing down of two or more separate units and opening of a new firm. The assets and liabilities of the amalgamating firms are to be revalued to ascertain the true capital brought into the new firm by each partner. Generally, the following problems come up while existing firms are merged into a new firm.

1. REVALUATION OF ASSETS AND LIABILITIES

1. In certain cases, the new firm takes over the complete or partial assets and liabilities of the amalgamating firms either at book value or at revised value. If revaluation is agreed upon, the amalgamating firms have to prepare Revaluation Account. The surplus or deficit of such

account is transferred to the Partners' Capital Account (in profit sharing ratio) of the amalgamating firms.

(*a*) Assets or Liabilities Account Dr
To Revaluation Account
(For increase in value of assets or decrease in value of liabilities)

(*b*) Revaluation Account Dr
To Assets or Liabilities Account
(For decrease in value of assets or increase in value of liabilities)

(*c*) Revaluation Account Dr
To Partners' Capital Account
(To transfer revaluation profit to partners' capital account, in profit sharing ratio)

NB: In case of loss, the above entry will be reversed)

2. ASSETS AND LIABILITIES, NOT TAKEN OVER BY THE NEW FIRM

The assets and liabilities (of the amalgamating firm) which are not taken over by the amalgamated firm (New Firm) is transferred to the Partners' Capital Accounts in CAPITAL RATIO and not in profit sharing ratio. It is also possible for the partners of merging firms to sell the assets, by realising in cash and to pay the liabilities, instead of transferring them to the Capital Accounts.

(*a*) Partners' Capital Account Dr
To Assets Account
(Assets taken over by partners)

(*b*) Liabilities Account Dr
To Partners' Capital Account
(Liabilities taken over by partners)

Note: The assets or liabilities not taken over by the new firm will be sold away or paid off. Any profit or loss on such transaction will be transferred to capital account in profit sharing ratio. However, if assets or liabilities are not disposed off, they will be transferred to Capital Accounts in the ratio of Capitals.

3. ACCUMULATED PROFITS AND LOSSES

The accumulated profit or loss, if any, in the amalgamating firms should be transferred to the Partners' Capital Accounts in profit sharing ratio.

Profit & Loss Account Dr
Reserve Account Dr
To Partners' Capital Account
(To distribute the undistributed past profits)

4. GOODWILL OF THE FIRM

Goodwill, if valued, should be raised in the books of existing firms and credited to Partners' Capital Account in their old profit sharing ratios.

Goodwill Account Dr
To Partners' Capital Account
(When raising goodwill)

5. TRANSFER OF ASSETS AND LIABILITIES TO NEW FIRM

New Firm's Account* Dr
Sundry Liabilities Account Dr
To Assets Account
*Balancing figure
(Assets and liabilities are taken at revised values for the purpose of transferring)

6. FINAL CLOSING OF CAPITAL ACCOUNTS

Partners' Capital Account Dr
To New Firm's Account
(The Partners' Capital Accounts, as finally ascertained, are closed by debiting them and crediting with the New Firm's Account)

By the above steps, the books of the old firm are closed.

Opening Entries in the New Firm

Various Assets Account Dr.

To Various Liabilities Account

To Capital Accounts of Partners

Recording readjustment of capital, if any, partners may be asked to bring cash as additional Capital or may be allowed to withdraw a part of the existing Capital.

(a) Cash Account Dr
To Partners' Capital Account
(Bringing cash to the new firm)

NB: In case of withdrawal of cash, the above entry will be reversed.

ILLUSTRATION 32.1

Mr. Singh and Khan have each been carrying on business as General Merchants. They decide to amalgamate and, henceforth, trade under the name of Singh and Khan on the following terms:

1. Each partner shall have a fixed capital of Rs. 10,000.
2. Singh's stock is to be brought in at Rs. 3,200 and Khan's at Rs. 2,700.
3. Provisions for Bad Debts are to be increased to 6% on debtors.
4. Khan's furniture is not to be taken over while Singh's furniture is to be taken at Rs. 450.
5. Singh is to pay the loan from his son before amalgamation.
6. Any deficiency on the net assets brought in is to be paid into the firm's bankers while any excess is to be withdrawn.

Singh's Balance Sheet as on 31st December 2005

Liabilities	*Rs.*	*Assets*		*Rs.*
Creditors	1,200	Furniture and Fixtures		350
Loan from his son	600	Machinery		5,000
Capital	10,635	Stock-in-trade		3,400
		Debtors	2,750	
		Less: Provision	120	2,630
		Cash at Bank		1,055
	12,435			12,435

Khan's Balance Sheet on 31st December 2005

Liabilities	*Rs.*	*Assets*		*Rs.*
Creditors	2,100	Furniture and Fixtures		200
Capital	10,100	Machinery		5,500
		Stock-in-trade		2,800
		Debtors:	3,025	
		Less: Provision	125	2,900
		Cash at Bank		800
	12,200			12,200

The above were the Balance Sheets. Give journal entries necessary to adjust each trader's books prior to amalgamation and the opening entries in the new firm and Balance Sheet. *(B. Com Madurai)*

SOLUTION

Journal Entries (Singh)

			Dr.	Cr.
2005			Rs	Rs
Dec. 31	Revaluation Account	Dr	245	
	To Stock-in-trade Account			200
	To Provision for Bad Debts			45
	(Being reduction in stock value and creation of provision @ 6% on Rs. 2,750 *i.e.* Rs. 165–120 = Rs. 45)			
	Furniture & Fixture Account	Dr.	100	
	To Revaluation Account			100
	(Being increase in value of furniture)			
	Singh's Capital Account	Dr.	145	
	To Revaluation Account			145
	(Being loss on revaluation transferred to Capital Account)			
	Son's Loan Account	Dr.	600	
	To Bank Account			600
	(Being loan repaid)			
	New Firm's Account	Dr.	10,490	
	Creditors Account	Dr.	1,200	
	Provision for Bad Debts Account	Dr.	165	
	To Furniture & Fixtures A/c			450
	To Machinery Account			5,000
	To Stock Account			3,200
	To Debtors Account			2,750
	To Cash at Bank Account			455
	(Being transfer of assets and liabilities to new firm)			
	Singh's Capital Account	Dr.	10,490	
	To New Firm's Account			10,490
	(Being transfer of capital to the new firm)			

Balance Sheet of Singh, with Revised Values, at the time of Amalgamation (31st Dec. 2005)

Liabilities	*Rs.*	*Assets*		*Rs.*
Creditors	1,200	Furniture and Fixtures		450
Capital	10,490	Machinery		5,000
		Stock		3,200
		Debtors:	2,750	
		Less: Provision	165	2,585
		Cash at Bank		455
	11,690			11,690

Journal Entry (Khan)

			Dr.	Cr.
			Rs	*Rs*
2005 Dec. 31	Revaluation Account	Dr.	157	
	To Stock-in-trade Account			100
	To Provision for Bad Debts Account			57
	(Being reduction in stock value and creation of provision @ 6% on Rs. 3,025 *i.e.* Rs. 182 – 125 = Rs. 57)			
	Khan's Capital Account	Dr.	200	
	To Furniture & Fixture A/c			200
	(Being furniture and fixtures transferred to Capital Account)			
	Khan's Capital Account	Dr.	157	
	To Revaluation Account			157
	(Being loss on revaluation transferred to capital account)			
	New Firm's Account	Dr.	9,743	
	Creditors Account	Dr.	2,100	
	Provision Account	Dr.	182	
	To Machinery Account			5,500
	To Stock Account			2,700
	To Debtors Account			3,025
	To Bank Account			800
	(Being assets and liabilities transferred to new firm)			
	Khan's Capital Account	Dr.	9,743	
	To New Firm's Account			9,743
	(Being capital transferred to the new firm)			

Balance Sheet of Khan, with Revised Values, at the time of Amalgamation 31st Dec. 2005

Liabilities	*Rs.*	*Assets*		*Rs.*
Creditors	2,100	Machinery		5,500
Capital	9,743	Stock		2,700
		Debtors:	3,025	
		Less: Provision	182	2,843
		Cash at Bank		800
	11,843			11,843

Journal Entry (Singh and Khan)

Date	Particulars		Dr. Rs	Cr. Rs
2005 Dec. 31	Furniture Account	Dr.	450	
	Machinery Account	Dr.	5,000	
	Stock Account	Dr.	3,200	
	Debtors Account	Dr.	2,750	
	Cash at Bank Account	Dr.	455	
	To Creditors Account			1,200
	To Provision Account			165
	To Singh's Capital Account			10,490
	(Being assets and liabilities taken over)			
	Machinery Account	Dr.	5,500	
	Stock Account	Dr.	2,700	
	Debtors Account	Dr.	3,025	
	Cash at Bank Account	Dr.	800	
	To Creditors Account			2,100
	To Provision (Doubtful Debts) Account			182
	To Khan's Capital Account			9,743
	(Being assets and liabilities taken over)			
	Singh's Capital Account	Dr.	490	
	To Cash Account			490
	(Being excess capital adjusted)			
	Cash Account	Dr.	257	
	To Khan's Capital Account			257
	(Being cash brought by Khan)			

Balance Sheet of Singh and Khan
as on 1st January 2006

Liabilities		*Rs.*	*Assets*		*Rs.*
Sundry Creditors		3,300	Furniture and Fixtures A/c		450
Capital: Singh	10,000		Machinery		10,500
Khan	10,000	20,000	Stock		5,900
			Debtors :	5,775	
			Less: Provision	347	5,428
			Cash		1,022
		23,300			23,300

Workings:

Dr. **Cash Account** Cr.

	Rs		Rs.
To Singh	455	By Singh Capital Account	490
To Khan	800	(Rs 10,490 – 10,000)	
To Khan's Capital		By Balance c/d	1,022
(Rs. 10,000 – 9,743)	257		
	1,512		1,512

Rough Balance Sheet after Amalgamation

Liabilities	*Singh*	*Khan*	*Singh & Khan*	*Assets*		*Singh*	*Khan*	*Singh & Khan*
	Rs.	*Rs.*	*Rs.*			*Rs.*	*Rs.*	*Rs.*
Creditors	1,200	2,100	3,300	Furniture		450	–	450
Capital	10,490	9,743		Machinery		5,000	5,500	10,500
Capital, after amalgamation			20,000*	Stock		3,200	2,700	5,900
				Debtors	2,750			
				Less: Provision	165	2,585		
				Debtors	3,025			
				Less: Provision	182		2,843	5,428
				Cash		455	800	
				Cash after Amalgamation				1,022[1]
	11,690	11,843	23,300			11,690	11,843	23,300

ILLUSTRATION 32.2

Following were the Balance Sheets as at 31st December 2005 of two firms M/s A and B and M/s C and D

Liabilities	*A & B*	*C & D*	*Assets*	*A & B*	*C & D*
	Rs.	Rs		Rs.	Rs
Creditors	3,000	25,000	Stock	50,000	75,000
Bills Payable	6,000	–	Debtors	30,000	45,000
Bank Overdraft	–	10,300	Premises	20,000	–
Capitals: A	50,000		Plant and Machinery	5,000	20,000
B	50,000		Bank	1,500	–
C		52,500	Furniture	500	300
D		52,500	Defence Bonds	2,000	–
	1,09,000	1,40,300		1,09,000	1,40,300

The two firms decided to amalgamate their business as from Ist January 2006. For this purpose it was agreed that the premises and Plant and Machinery belonging to A and B should be taken over by the new firm at Rs. 25,000 and Rs. 10,000 respectively.

C and D were to be credited with Rs. 5,000 for the value of certain patent rights they possessed, which became the property of the partnership and which were not included in their Balance Sheet.

All the other assets were taken over at the values stated in the respective Balance Sheets except the Defence Bonds belonging to A and B, which were not taken over. Both firms undertook to discharge their own liabilities and it was agreed that A and B should introduce cash to make their capitals equal to that of C and D.

Pass necessary journal entries in the books of the old firms and the Opening Entries in the books of the New Firm, M/s A, B, C and D.

Also prepare the Balance Sheet of the new Firm.

---

* Rs. 10,490 – Rs. 490 = Rs. 10,000

Rs. 9,743 + Rs. 257 = Rs. 10,000

20,000

[1] Rs. 455 + Rs.800 + Rs. 257 = Rs. 1,512 – Rs. 490 = Rs. 1,022.

Journal Entries in the books of A and B

Date	Particulars		Dr. Rs	Cr. Rs
2005 Dec. 31	Plant and Machinery Account	Dr.	5,000	
	Premises Account	Dr.	5,000	
	To Revaluation Account			10,000
	(Being appreciation in the value of Plant and Machinery and Premises)			
	Revaluation Account	Dr.	10,000	
	To A's Capital Account			5,000
	To B's Capital Account			5,000
	(Being division of profit on revaluation between A and B)			
	Credits Account	Dr.	3,000	
	Bills Payable Account	Dr.	6,000	
	To A's Capital Account			4,500
	To B's Capital Account			4,500
	(Being transfer of liabilities not taken over by the New Firm, to the Capital Accounts of A and B)			
	A's Capital Account	Dr.	1,000	
	B's Capital Account	Dr.	1,000	
	To Defence Bonds Account			2,000
	(Being transfer of asset not taken over by the New Firm, to the Capital Account of A and B)			
	M/s A, B, C and D Account	Dr.	1,17,000	
	To Bank Account			1,500
	To Stock Account			50,000
	To Debtors Account			30,000
	To Premises Account			25,000
	To Plant and Machinery Account			10,000
	To Furniture Account			500
	(Being various assets taken over by the New Firm)			
	A's Capital Account	Dr.	58,500	
	B's Capital Account	Dr.	58,500	
	To M/s A, B, C and D (New Firm)			1,17,000
	(Being transfer of Capital Accounts to the New Firm)			

Journal Entries in the books of C and D

Date	Particulars		Dr. Rs	Cr. Rs
2005 Dec. 31	Patent Right Account	Dr.	5,000	
	To Revaluation Account			5,000
	(Being patent rights brought into Accounts)			
	Revaluation Account	Dr.	5,000	
	To C's Capital Account			2,500
	To D's Capital Account			2,500
	(Being distribution of profit on revaluation between C and D)			

Date	Particulars		Dr.	Cr.
	Creditors Account	Dr.	25,000	
	Bank Overdraft Account	Dr.	10,300	
	To C's Capital Account			17,650
	To D's Capital Account			17,650
	(Being transfer of liabilities, not taken over, to the Capital Accounts of C and D)			
	M/s A, B, C and D Account	Dr.	1,45,300	
	To Stock Account			75,000
	To Debtors Account			45,000
	To Plant and Machinery Account			20,000
	To Patent Account			5,000
	To Furniture Account			300
	(Being various assets taken over by the New Firm)			
	C's Capital Account	Dr.	72,650	
	D's Capital Account	Dr.	72,650	
	To M/s A, B, C and D (New firm)			1,45,300

Journal Entries in the books of A, B, C and D

Date	Particulars		Dr. Rs	Cr. Rs
2005 Dec. 31.	Bank Account	Dr.	1,500	
	Stock Account	Dr.	50,000	
	Debtors Account	Dr.	30,000	
	Premises Account	Dr.	25,000	
	Plant and Machinery Account	Dr.	10,000	
	Furniture Account	Dr.	500	
	To A's Capital Account			58,500
	To B's Capital Account			58,500
	(Being taking over the assets of A and B)			
	Stock Account	Dr.	75,000	
	Debtors Account	Dr.	45,000	
	Plant and Machinery Account	Dr.	20,000	
	Patents Account	Dr.	5,000	
	Furniture Account	Dr.	300	
	To C's Capital Account			72,650
	To D's Capital Account			72,650
	(Being taking over the assets of C and D)			
	Bank Account	Dr.	28,300	
	To A's Capital Account			14,150*
	To B's Capital Account			14,150*
	(Being cash brought by A and B to make their capitals equal to C and D)			

* Rs. 72,650 – 58,500 = 14,150 each

Balance Sheet of A, B, C and D
as on 1st January 2006

Liabilities	*Rs.*	*Rs.*	*Assets*	*Rs.*
Capitals: A	72,650		Cash at Bank	29,800
B	72,650		Sundry Debtors Account	75,000
C	72,650		Stock Account	1,25,000

D	72,650	2,90,600	Patent Rights Account	5,000
			Furniture Account	800
			Plant and Machinery A/c	30,000
			Premises Account	25,000
		2,90,600		2,90,600

ILLUSTRATION 32.3

A, B and C carried on a manufacturing business in partnership sharing profits and losses in 2/5, 2/5 and 1/5 respectively. They agreed to amalgamate as on 31st December 2005 with D, who carried on a similar business. The summarised balance sheets of the firms on that date are as follows:

	ABC	D			ABC	D
	Rs.	Rs.			Rs.	Rs.
Capital Accounts:			Premises		6,000	—
A	8,000		Plant		3,600	2,400
B	6,000		Stock		6,000	2,500
C	4,000		Debtors	7,400		
D	—	3,000	*Less*: Provision	400	7,000	3,600
Creditors	9,000	2,000	Bank		4,400	—
Bank Overdraft		3500				
	27,000	8,500			27,000	8,500

It was agreed:

(*a*) A was to be retired on 31st December 2005 and the balance due to him being left with the new firm as a loan.

(*b*) Profits to be shared among B, C and D in the ratio of 1/2, 1/4 and 1/4 respectively.

(*c*) The value of goodwill were agreed at Rs. 10,000 for ABC firm and Rs. 4,000 for D firm.

(*d*) The new firm was to take over all the assets and discharge all the liabilities of the two businesses, but certain assets were to be revalued as under:

	ABC Firm	D Firm
	Rs.	Rs.
Premises	8,000	—
Plant	3,200	2,900
Debtors	6,800	3,160

(*e*) The capital of the new firm was to be Rs. 10,000 and was to be contributed by the partners in their profit-sharing ratios, any surplus or deficit being transferred to Current Accounts.

(*f*) No account for goodwill was to be maintained in the books, adjusting entries for transactions between the partners being made in the Partners' Capital Accounts.

You are required to give:

(*a*) Journal entries in the books of the old firms and the new firm, and

(*b*) Balance Sheet of the new firm.

SOLUTION

Journal Entries in the books of ABC Firm

			Dr.	Cr.
2005			*Rs.*	*Rs.*
Dec. 31.	Goodwill Account	Dr.	10,000	
	To A's Capital Account			4,000
	To B's Capital Account			4,000
	To C's Capital Account			2,000
	(Being goodwill raised credited to Partner's Capital Account)			

Particulars		Dr. Rs.	Cr. Rs.
Premises Account	Dr.	2,000	
To Revaluation Account			2,000
(Being value of premises increased)			
Revaluation Account	Dr.	600	
To Plant Account			400
To Provision for Bad Debts A/c			200
(Being decrease in value of plant and increase in provision)			
Revaluation Account	Dr.	1,400	
To A's Capital Account			560
To B's Capital Account			560
To C's Capital Account			280
(Being profit on revaluation transferred to Capital Accounts)			
A's Capital Account	Dr.	12,560	
To A's Loan Account			12,560
(Being the Capital Account transferred to Loan Account : Rs. 8,000 + Rs 4,000 + Rs 560 = Rs. 12,560)			
New Firm Account	Dr.	39,000	
To Goodwill Account			10,000
To Premises Account			8,000
To Plant Account			3,200
To Stock Account			6,000
To Debtors Account			7,400
To Bank Account			4,400
(Being transfer of various assets to the New Firm)			
Provision for Doubtful Debts A/c	Dr.	600	
Trade Creditors Account	Dr.	9,000	
A's Loan Account	Dr.	12,560	
To New Firm Account			22,160
(Being transfer of various liabilities to New Firm)			
B's Capital Account	Dr.	10,560	
C's Capital Account	Dr.	6,280	
To New Firm Account			16,840
(Being transfer of Capitals)			

Journal Entries in the books of D Firm

Date	Particulars		Dr. Rs.	Cr. Rs.
2005 Dec. 31.	Goodwill Account	Dr.	4,000	
	To D's Capital Account			4,000
	(Being raised goodwill)			
	Plant Account	Dr.	500	
	To Revaluation Account			500
	(Being increase in value of plant)			

	Particulars		Dr.	Cr.
	Revaluation Account	Dr.	440	
	To Provision for Bad Debts A/c			440
	(Being provision created)			
	Revaluation Account	Dr.	60	
	To D's Capital Account			60
	(Being profit on revaluation transferred to Capital Account)			
	New Firm Account	Dr.	13,000	
	To Goodwill Account			4,000
	To Plant Account			2,900
	To Debtors Account			3,600
	To Stock Account			2,500
	(Being transfer of various assets)			
	Bank Overdraft Account	Dr.	3,500	
	Trade Creditors Account	Dr.	2,000	
	Provision for Bad Debts Account	Dr.	440	
	To New Firm Account			5,940
	(Being transfer of various liabilities)			
	D's Capital Account	Dr.	7,060	
	To New Firm Account			7,060
	(Being transfer of Capital)			

Journal Entries in the books of New Firm

			Dr.	Cr.
2005			*Rs.*	*Rs.*
Dec. 31	Goodwill Account	Dr.	10,000	
	Premises Account	Dr.	8,000	
	Plant Account	Dr.	3,200	
	Stock Account	Dr.	6,000	
	Debtors Account	Dr.	7,400	
	Bank Account	Dr.	4,400	
	To Provision for Bad & Doubtful Debts A/c			600
	To Trade Creditors A/c			9,000
	To A's Loan Account			12,560
	To B's Capital Account			10,560
	To C's Capital Account			6,280
	(Being assets and liabilities of ABC firm brought into account)			
	Goodwill Account	Dr.	4,000	
	Plant Account	Dr.	2,900	
	Debtors Account	Dr.	3,600	
	Stock Account	Dr.	2,500	
	To Bank Overdraft Account			3,500
	To Trade Creditors Account			2,000
	To Provision for Doubtful Debts Account			440
	To D's Capital Account			7,060
	(Being assets and liabilities of D's firm brought into account)			
	B/s Capital Account	Dr.	7,000	
	C's Capital Account	Dr.	3,500	
	D's Capital Account	Dr.	3,500	
	To Goodwill Account			14,000
	(Being goodwill written off in new profit sharing ratio)			
	Bank Overdraft Account	Dr.	3,500	
	To Bank Account			3,500
	(Being discharge of bank overdraft)			

B's Current Account To B's Capital Account (Being deficiency in Capital Account Adjusted)	Dr.	1,440	1,440
C's Capital Account To C's Current Account (Being excess money transferred to Current Account)	Dr.	280	280
D's Capital Account To D's Current Account (Being excess money transferred to Current Account)	Dr.	1,060	1,060

Dr. **Capital Accounts** Cr.

	B	*C*	*D*		*B*	*C*	*D*
	Rs.	Rs.	Rs.		Rs.	Rs.	Rs.
Goodwill Account	7,000	3,500	3,500	Balance b/d	10,560	6,280	7,060
Current Account	—	280	1,060	Current A/c	1,440	—	—
Balance c/d	5,000	2,500	2,500				
	12,000	6,280	7,060		12,000	6,280	7,060
				Balance b/d	5,000	2,500	2,500

Balance Sheet of B, C and D
as on 1st January 2006

Liabilities		*Rs.*	*Assets*		*Rs.*
Capitals			Premises		8,000
B	5,000		Plant (Rs. 3,200 + 2,900)		6,100
C	2,500		Stock (Rs. 6,000 + 2,500)		8,500
D	2,500	10,000	Debtors: (7,400 + 3,600)	11,000	
Current Accounts:			*Less*: Provision	1,040	9,960
C	280		Bank (Rs. 4,400 – 3,500)		900
D	1,060	1,340	B's Current Account		1,440
A's Loan Account		12,560			
Trade Creditors		11,000			
		34,900			34,900

ILLUSTRATION 32.4

Two firms P & Q and R & S agreed to amalgamate their business. Their position as on 31st December 2005 were as follows:

Balance Sheet of P and Q
as on 31st December 2005

Liabilities	*Rs.*	*Assets*	*Rs.*
Creditors	1,04,000	Cash at Bank	1,56,000
Capitals:		Debtors	1,30,000
P:	1,82,000	Stock-in-trade	42,000
Q:	1,30,000	Buildings	78,000
		Furniture	10,000
	4,16,000		4,16,000

Balance Sheet of R and S
as on 31st December 2005

Liabilities	*Rs.*	*Assets*	*Rs.*
Creditors	52,000	Cash at Bank	65,000
Capitals:		Debtors	1,04,000
R:	91,000	Stock-in-trade	26,000
S:	65,000	Furniture	13,000
	2,08,000		2.,08,000

Creditors and debtors were not taken over by the new firm PQRS. Office Buildings were retained by P and Q but the new firm agreed to pay a monthly rent of Rs 400. The cash required for working of the new firm was estimated at Rs. 1,30,000 to be provided by the partners in their new profit sharing proportions as under:

P – 3/10; Q – 3/10; R – 2/10; S – 2/10

1. Give journal entries in the books of P & Q and R & S.
2. Give the opening Balance Sheet of PQRS. (*B.Com., Madurai, Madras, Bangalore, Agra*)

SOLUTION

Journal Entries in the books of P and Q

			Dr.	Cr.
2005			*Rs*	*Rs*
Dec. 31	Creditors Account	Dr.	1,04,000	
	To Bank Account			1,04,000
	(Being payment to creditors, not taken over by the new firm)			
	P Capital Account	Dr.	1,21,333	
	Q Capital Account	Dr.	86,667	
	To Debtors Account			1,30,000
	To Building Account			78,000
	(Being assets not taken over, are transferred to Capital Accounts in Capital Ratio *i.e.* 1.82.000 : 1.30.000 or 7:5)			
	PQRS Account	Dr.	1,04,000	
	To Stock-in-trade Account			42,000
	To Furniture Account			10,000
	To Cash Account			52,000
	(Rs. 1,56,000 – Rs. 1,04,000)			
	(Being assets transferred to new firm)			
	P Capital Account	Dr.	60.667	
	Q Capital Account	Dr.	43,333	
	To PQRS Account			1,04,000
	(Being revised capitals transferred)			

Journal in the books of R and S

			Dr.	Cr.
2005			*Rs*	*Rs*
Dec. 31	Creditors Account	Dr.	52,000	
	To Bank Account			52,000
	(Being payment to creditors, not taken over by the new firm)			

	R Capital Account	Dr.	60,667	
	S Capital Account	Dr.	43,333	
	To Debtors Account			1,04,000
	(Being debtors, not taken over by the new firm, transferred to capital accounts in the ratio: 91 : 65 or 7 : 5)			
	PQRS Account (Rs. 1,56,000 – Rs.1,04,000)	Dr.	52,000	
	To Stock-in-trade Account			26,000
	To Furniture Account			13,000
	To Bank Account (Rs. 65,000 – Rs. 52,000)			13,000
	(Being assets transferred to new firm)			
	R Capital Account	Dr.	30,333	
	S Capital Account	Dr.	21,667	
	To PQRS Account			52,000
	(Being revised capitals transferred)			

Journal Entries in the books of PQRS

			Rs	Rs
2005				
Dec. 31	Stock-in-trade Account	Dr.	42,000	
	Furniture Account	Dr.	10,000	
	Bank Account	Dr.	52,000	
	To P Capital Account			60,667
	To Q Capital Account			43,333
	(Being assets taken over from P and Q firm)			
	Stock-in-trade Account	Dr.	26,000	
	Furniture Account	Dr.	13,000	
	Bank Account	Dr.	13,000	
	To R Capital Account			30,334
	To S Capital Account			21,666
	(Being assets taken over from R and S firm)			
	Bank Account	Dr.	65,000	
	To P Capital Account			19,500
	To Q Capital Account			19,500
	To R Capital Account			13,000
	To S Capital Account			13,000
	(Being contribution of further cash in 3 : 3 : 2 : 2 ratio)			

Balance Sheet of PQRS
as on 31st December 2005

Liabilities	*Rs.*	*Assets*	*Rs.*
Capital Accounts:			
P :	80,167	Bank	1,30,000
Q :	62,833	Stock-in-trade	68,000
R :	43,334	Furniture	23,000
S :	34,666		
	2,21,000		2,21,000

ILLUSTRATION 32.5 (One Partnership firm and one sole proprietor)

B and S are in partnership sharing profits and losses equally and T is trading alone in the same line. On 1.10.2006, they decided to amalgamate the two businesses and to form a new firm M/s. BST & Co., wherein B, S and T would be partners sharing profits and losses equally. Their Balance Sheets on that date are as under:

Capital & Liabilities	*B & S*	*T*	*Property & Assets*	*B & S*	*T*
	Rs.	Rs		Rs.	Rs.
Capitals:			Land & Buildings	5,000	6,000
B	8,000	–	Machinery	3,500	4,000
S	6,000	–	Furniture	1,500	1,750
T	–	10,000	Investments	3,500	–
Creditors	7,500	5,000	Stock	4,000	5,000
Loan	–	5,000	Debtors	3,000	5,250
Outstanding Expenses	1,000	1,500	Cash and Bank	2,000	500
	22,500	21,500		22,500	21,500

For the purpose of amalgamation, assets and liabilities are revalued as follows:

	B & S	*T*
Land & Buildings	5,000	5,000
Machinery	3,500	4,000
Furniture	1,250	1,250
Debtors	2,750	3,500
Stock	4,000	4,000
Outstanding Expenses	2,000	1,750

In addition to the above, it is decided –

(*i*) that the new firm will not take over investments of B & S and the loan of T.

(*ii*) that the Goodwill of B & S and T is valued at Rs. 5,000 and Rs, 2,500 respectively in the first instance, but for the purpose of the Balance Sheet of new firm, the combined Goodwill will be valued at Rs. 6,000.

(*iii*) That the reconstructed capital of partners should be Rs. 7,500 each, any excess or deficit to be paid off or brought in cash.

You are required to show:

(*a*) The journal entries to close the books of B and S.

(*b*) The journal entries to close the books of T,

(*c*) The journal entries to open the books of BST & Co., and

(*d*) The Balance Sheet of the new firm.

(*B. Com. Madras*)
(*Modified*)

SOLUTION

Books of B & S
Journal Entries

Date	*Particulars*	*L.F.*	'Dr' *Rs.*	'Cr' *(Rs.*
	Revaluation A/c Dr.		1,500	
	To Furniture A/c			250
	" Debtors A/c			250
	" Outstanding Expenses A/c			1,000
	(Being decrease in the value of different assets and increase in the value of liabilities)			

Particulars		L.F.	Dr. (Rs.)	Cr. (Rs.)
B's Capital A/c	Dr.		1,750	
S's Capital A/c	Dr.		1,750	
To Investments A/c				3,500
(Being investments not taken over by the new firm adjusted through Capitals)				
Goodwill A/c	Dr.		5,000	
To B's Capital A/c				2,500
" S's Capital A/c				2,500
(Being Goodwill raised and distributed in profit sharing ratio)				
Creditors A/c	Dr.		7,500	
Outstanding Expenses A/c	Dr.		2,000	
M/s BST & Co. A/c (Balancing figure)	Dr.		14,000	
To Goodwill A/c				5,000
" Land & Building A/c				5,000
" Machinery A/c				3,500
" Furniture A/c				1,250
" Debtors A/c (net)				2,750
" Stock A/c				4,000
" Cash & Bank A/c				2,000
(Being transfer of different assets & liabilities to the new firm)				
B's Capital A/c	Dr.		750	
S's Capital A/c	Dr.		750	
To Revaluation A/c				1,500
(Being loss on revaluation transferred)				
B's Capital A/c	Dr.		8,000	
S's Capital A/c	Dr.		6,000	
To M/s BST & Co. A/c				14,000
(Being transfer of capital to the new firm)				

CAPITAL ACCOUNTS

Dr. *Cr.*

	B (Rs.)	S (Rs.)		B (Rs.)	S (Rs.)
To Investments A/c.	1,750	1,750	By Bal.b/d	8,000	6,000
" Revaluation A/c	750	750	" Goodwill	2,500	2,500
" Bal. c/d	8,000	6,000			
	10,500	8,500		10,500	8,500

Books of T
Journal Entries

Date	Particulars		L.F.	'Dr.' (Rs.)	'Cr' (Rs.)
	Revaluation A/c	Dr.		3,500	
	To Land & Building A/c				1,000
	" Furniture A/c				500
	" Stock A/c				1,000
	" Debtors A/c				750
	" Outstanding Expenses A/c				250
	(Being values of different assets decreased & liability increased)				

Particulars		L.F.	Dr. Rs.	Cr. Rs.
T's Capital A/c	Dr.		3,500	
To Revaluation A/c				3,500
(Being loss on revaluation transferred)				
T's Loan A/c	Dr.		5,000	
To T's Capital A/c				5,000
(Being discharge of loan not taken over by the new firm)				
Goodwill A/c	Dr.		2,500	
To T's Capital A/c				2,500
(Being goodwill raised as per terms)				
Outstanding Expenses A/c	Dr.		1,750	
Creditors A/c	Dr.		5,000	
M/s B S T & Co. A/c (Balancing figure)	Dr.		14,000	
To Goodwill A/c				2,500
To Land & Building A/c				5,000
" Machinery A/c				4,000
" Furniture A/c				1,250
" Stock A/c				4,000
" Debtors A/c				3,500
" Cash & Bank A/c				500
(Being various assets & liabilities transferred to the new firm)				
T's Capital A/c	Dr.		14,000	
To B S T & Co. A/c				14,000
(Being transfer of Capital to the new firm)				

Books of M/s BST & Co.

Journal Entries

Date	Particulars		L.F.	'Dr.' Rs.	'Cr' Rs.
	Goodwill A/c	Dr.		2,500	
	Land & Building A/c	Dr.		5,000	
	Machinery A/c	Dr.		4,000	
	Furniture A/c	Dr.		1,250	
	Stock A/c	Dr.		4,000	
	Debtors A/c	Dr.		3,500	
	Cash & Bank A/c	Dr.		500	
	To Creditors A/c				5,000
	To Outstanding Expenses A/c				1,750
	To T's Capital A/c				14,000
	(Being various assets & liabilities transferred to the new firm)				
	Goodwill A/c	Dr.		5,000	
	Land & Building A/c	Dr.		5,000	
	Machinery A/c	Dr.		3,500	
	Furniture A/c	Dr.		1,250	
	Stock A/c	Dr.		4,000	
	Debtors A/c	Dr.		2,750	
	Cash & Bank A/c	Dr.		2,000	
	To Sundry Creditors A/c				7,500

" Outstanding Expenses A/c			2,000
" B's Capital A/c			8,000
" S's Capital A/c			6,000
(Being transfer of different assets & liabilities to the new firm)			
B's Capital A/c Dr.		500	
S's Capital A/c Dr.		500	
T's Capital A/c Dr.		500	
To Goodwill A/c			1,500
(Being goodwill written off (2,500 + 5,000 – 6,000)			
Bank A/c Dr.		2,000	
To S's Capital A/c			2,000
(Being amount brought in as per terms)			
T's Capital A/c Dr.		6,000	
To Bank A/c			6,000
(Being amount paid off as per terms)			

Capital Accounts

Dr. Cr.

	B	*S*	*T*		*B*	*S*	*T*
	Rs.	*Rs.*	*Rs.*		*Rs.*	*Rs.*	*Rs.*
To Goodwill	500	500	500	By Bal. b/d	8,000	6,000	14,000
" Bank	—	—	6,000	" Cash/Bank	—	2,000	—
" Bal. c/d	7,500	7,500	7,500				
	8,000	8,000	14,000		8,000	8,000	14,000

M/S BST & CO.
Balance Sheet
as at 1st October 2006

Liabilities		*Rs.*	*Assets*	*Rs.*
Capital A/c			Goodwill	6,000
B	7,500		(7,500 – 1,500)	
S	7,500		Land & Building	10,000
T	7,500	22,500	Machinery	7,500
Creditors		12,500	Furniture	2,500
Outstanding expenses		3,750	Stock	8,000
Bank Overdraft		1,500	Debtors	6,250
		40,250		40,250

NB: Cash available = Rs. 2,000 + Rs. 500 + Rs. 2,000 = Rs. 4,500. Payment made to T is Rs. 6,000. So, it is assumed that the new firm arranged an overdraft of Rs. 1,500 from Bank. This overdraft is shown in the Balance Sheet.

ILLUSTRATION 32.6

The respective Balance Sheets of A & B and C & D on the date of amalgamation are as follows:

Balance Sheet of A & B
31st March 2006

Liabilities		*Rs.*	*Assets*	*Rs.*
Sundry Creditors		21,500	Cash at Bank	3,000
Capitals–			Sundry Debtors	20,000
A	25,000		Stock	30,000
B	15,000	40,000	Investment	8,000
			Office fixtures	500
		61,500		61,500

Balance Sheet of C & D
31st March 2006

Liabilities		*Rs.*	*Assets*		*Rs.*
Sundry Creditors		21,000	Cash at Bank		1,000
Reserve Fund		11,500	Book debts	25,000	
Capitals:			*Less:* Reserve	500	24,500
C	19,000		Stock		20,000
D	11,000	30,000	Trade fixture		1,000
			Leasehold Premises		12,000
			Goodwill		4,000
		62,500			62,500

It was agreed that the Balance Sheet of A & B should be adjusted as follows before amalgamation :

(*a*) That Rs. 400 be reserved for doubtful debts.

(*b*) That the stock & furniture be depreciated by 10%.

(*c*) That Investments be taken over at Rs. 10,000.

(*d*) That Rs. 300 be reserved for discount on creditors.

The following adjustments were agreed upon in C &D Balance Sheet —

(*a*) That Book debts, Stock & Trade fixtures be taken over at book figures.

(*b*) That the leasehold premises and Goodwill be valued at Rs. 18,000 and Rs. 6,000 respectively.

The Capitals of A, B C & D in the new firm were fixed at Rs. 25,000, Rs. 15,000, Rs. 30,000 and Rs 20,000 respectively.

Pass Journal entries in the books of:

(*a*) A and B

(*b*) C and D

(*c*) A, B, C and D, the new firm, and

(*d*) Prepare Balance Sheet of amalgamated firm.

(*CA Inter*)

SOLUTION

BOOKS OF A & B

Journal Entries

Date	Particulars		L.F.	'Dr.' Rs.	'Cr' Rs.
	Revaluation A/c	Dr.		3,450	
	To Provision for doubtful debts A/c				400
	" Stock A/c				3,000
	" Fixtures A/c				50
	(Being the following revaluations made on assets)				
	Investment A/c	Dr.		2,000	
	Provision for discount on creditors A/c	Dr.		300	
	To Revaluation A/c				2,300
	(Being revaluations made on assets and liabilities)				
	A's Capital A/c	Dr.		575	
	B's Capital A/c	Dr.		575	
	To Revaluation A/c				1,150
	(Being loss on revaluations transferred)				
	Sundry Creditors A/c	Dr.		21,500	
	M/s A, B. C & D (New Firm) A/c (Balancing figure)	Dr.		38,850	
	Provision for doubtful debt A/c	Dr.		400	
	To Cash at Bank A/c				3,000
	" Sundry Debtors A/c				20,000
	" Stock A/c				27,000
	" Investments A/c				10,000
	" Office Furniture A/c				450
	" Provision for discount on Sundry Creditors A/c				300
	(Being transfer of different assets & liabilities to the New Firm)				
	A's Capital A/c (Rs. 25,000 – Rs. 575 = Rs. 24,425)	Dr.		24,425	
	B's Capital A/c (Rs. 15,000 – Rs. 575 = Rs. 14,425)	Dr.		14,425	
	To M/s A, B, C & D A/c				38,850
	(Being transfer to A and B's Capital to the new firm)				

Books of C & D

Journal Entries

Date	Particulars		L.F.	Dr. Rs.	Cr. Rs.
	Leasehold Premises A/c	Dr.		6,000	
	To Revaluation A/c				6,000
	(Being value of Leasehold Premises increased by Rs. 6,000)				
	Goodwill A/c	Dr.		2,000	
	To C's Capital A/c				1,000
	" D's Capital A/c				1,000
	(Being Goodwill further raised by Rs.2,000)				
	Revaluation A/c	Dr.		6,000	
	To C's Capital A/c				3,000
	" D's Capital A/c				3,000
	(Being profit on revaluation transferred)				

Particulars		L.F.	Dr. Rs.	Cr. Rs.
Reserve Fund A/c	Dr.		11,500	
To C's Capital A/c				5,750
" D's Capital A/c				5,750
(Being Reserve Fund distributed equally)				
Sundry Creditors A/c	Dr.		21,000	
Provision for doubtful debt A/c	Dr.		500	
M/s. A, B, C &D (New Firm) A/c (Balancing figure)	Dr.		49,500	
To Cash at Bank A/c				1,000
" Book debts A/c				25,000
" Stock A/c				20,000
" Trade Fixture A/c				1,000
" Goodwill A/c				6,000
" Leasehold Premises A/c				18,000
(Being various assets & liabilities transferred to New Firm A/c)				
C's Capital A/c	Dr.		28,750[1]	
D's Capital A/c	Dr.		20,750[2]	
To M/s A, B, C & D A/c				49,500
(Being Capital of C & D transferred to the new firm)				

	A	*B*
Capitals	Rs. 19,000	Rs. 11,000
Add: Goodwill	1,000	1,000
Add: Revaluation Profit	3,000	3,000
Add: Reserve Fund	5,750	5,750
	[1]28,750	[2]20,750

Determination of Capital in the new firm

	A	*B*	C	D
Capital transferred to the new firm	24,425	14,425	28,750	20,750
Capital should be in the new firm	25,000	15,000	30,000	20,000
(–) Short/excess (+)	(–) 575	(–) 575	(–) 1,250	(+) 750

BOOKS OF M/S A, B, C & D

Journal Entries

Date	*Particulars*		*L.F.*	Dr. *Rs.*	Cr. *Rs.*
	Cash at Bank A/c	Dr.		3,000	
	Sundry Debtors A/c	Dr.		20,000	
	Stock A/c	Dr.		27,000	
	Investment A/c	Dr.		10,000	
	Office Furniture A/c	Dr.		450	
	Provision for discount on Creditors A/c	Dr.		300	
	To Sundry Creditors A/c				21,500
	" Provision for doubtful debt A/c				400
	" A's Capital A/c				24,425
	" B's Capital A/c				14,425
	(Being various assets & liabilities of A & B taken over by the new firm)				

	Cash at Bank A/c	Dr.	1,000	
	Book debts A/c	Dr.	25,000	
	Stock A/c	Dr.	20,000	
	Trade Fixtures A/c	Dr.	1,000	
	Goodwill A/c	Dr.	6,000	
	Leasehold Premises A/c	Dr.	18,000	
	To Sundry Creditors A/c			21,000
	" Provision for doubtful debt A/c			500
	" C/s Capital A/c			28,750
	" D's Capital A/c			20,750
	(Being transfer of various assets & liabilities of C & D to the new firm)			
	Cash/Bank A/c	Dr.	2,400	
	To A's Capital A/c			575
	" B's Capital A/c			575
	" C's Capital A/c			1,250
	(Being shortfall of Capital brought in by the Partners as per agreement)			
	D's Capital A/c	Dr.	750	
	To Bank A/c			750
	(Being the excess amount of Capital refunded as per agreement)			

M/S. A, B, C & D
Balance Sheet
as at 1.4.99

Liabilities		*Rs.*	*Assets*		*Rs.*
Sundry Creditors					
(21,000 + 21,500)	42,500		Goodwill (4,000 + 2,000)		6,000
Less: Provision for discount	300	42,200	Leasehold Premises		18,000
Capitals			Fixture & Furniture		1,450
A	25,000		(1,000 + 450)		
B	15,000		Investment		10,000
C	30,000		Stock (27,000 + 20,000)		47,000
D	20,000	90,000	Sundry Debtors		
			(20,000 + 25,000)	45,000	
			Less: Provision		
			(400 + 500)	900	44,100
			Cash at Bank		5,650
			(3,000) + 1,000 + 2,400 – 750)		
		1,32,200			1,32,200

SALE OF FIRM

A partnership firm may be converted into a limited company or the business may be sold to an existing company. Conversion of firm into a company takes the advantage of the principle of limited liability. In both cases, *i.e.* either selling or conversion, the firm is dissolved and its books are closed. When a business is sold, the seller and the purchaser may agree as to the amount of sale price, termed as Purchase consideration. The Purchase Price paid by the purchasing company (Vendee) to the selling company (Vendor) is called purchase consideration. The procedure for closing the books of the firm is the same as we have already seen (earlier chapter) when the firm is dissolved.

1.	Transfer assets to Realisation Account. If the Company takes over cash, it will also be transferred.	Debit: Credit:	Realisation Account Various Assets Account
2.	Transfer liabilities to Realisation Account	Debit: Credit:	Liabilities Account Realisation Account
3.	When the Purchase Price is receivable from the Purchasing Company.	Debit: Credit:	Purchasing Company Account Realisation Account
4.	When selling company receives selling price in shares or Debentures or cash	Debit: Debit: Debit: Credit:	Cash Account Share Account Debenture Account Purchasing Company Account
5.	If any asset, not taken over by the firm, realised by the selling firm	Debit: Credit:	Cash Account Realisation Account
	If any asset is taken over by the partners,	Debit: Credit:	Partners' Account Realisation Account
6.	If any liability, not taken over by the company, are paid by the selling company	Debit: Credit:	Realisation Account Cash Account
	If any liability taken over by the partner	Debit: Credit:	Realisation Account Partners' Capital Account
7.	When expenses on realisation is paid	Debit: Credit:	Realisation Account Cash Account
8.	If there is any reserve/Past Profits/Past losses etc. it may be transferred to Partners' Capital Account	*For Profit* : Debit: Credit:	 Reserve Account Partners' Capital Account
		For Loss : Debit: Credit:	 Partner's Capital Account Loss Account
9.	Profit/Loss on realisation should be transferred to Capital Account in profit sharing ratio.	*For Profit* : Debit: Credit:	 Realisation Account Partners' Capital Account
		For Loss : Debit: Credit:	 Partners' Capital Account Realisation A/c
10.	Current Account, if any, in the books is transferred to Capital Account	Debit: Credit:	Capital Account Current Account
11.	Pay off the Partner's Loan Account, if any	Debit: Credit:	Partner's Loan Account Cash Account

12. Final settlement will be made, by paying off balances in the Capital Account, which would coincide with the available Cash or Shares or Debenture. In the absence of any agreement, distribution of final settlement is made in the ratio of their final claim, after realisation.

Partners' Capital Account Dr.
To Shares Account
To Debentures Account
To Cash Account

Thus the books of partnership firm are finally closed.

Those assets and liabilities, which have not been taken over by the purchasing company, can be disposed off by the firm. That is, such assets or liabilities need not be transferred to Realisation Account. But only the balance left in the asset or liability account, being gain or loss, is transferred to Realisation Account.

JOURNAL ENTRIES IN THE BOOKS OF PURCHASING COMPANY

1. **For the purchase consideration:**

Business Purchase Account Dr
    To Vendor Firm Account

2. **For taking over of assets and liabilities:**

Sundry Assets Account Dr
    To Sundry Liabilities Account
    To Business Purchase Account

(**NB:** The revalued figures of assets and liabilities are taken into account. If purchase price is more than the net value of assets taken over, the difference will be debited to Goodwill Account. On the other hand, if the purchase price is less than the net value of assets taken over, the difference is credited to Capital Reserve Account.

3. **For settlement of Purchase Price:**

Vendor Firm Account Dr
    To Share Capital Account
    To Debenture Account
    To Bank Account

ILLUSTRATION 32.7

Black, White and Green are in partnership. Their profit-sharing ratio is 1/2, 1/3 and 1/6 respectively. They decide to convert their firm into a Private Limited Company as BWG Private Limited on 31st March 2005. Their Balance Sheet as at that date was as follows:

Liabilities	*Rs.*	*Assets*		*Rs.*
Creditors	8,000	Land and Buildings		11,400
Capitals: Black	17,400	Stock		10,000
Green	8,000	Debtors	10,000	
White	6,000	*Less*: Provision	1,000	9,000
		Cash		6,000
		Profit & Loss		3,000
	39,400			39,400

BWG Private Ltd was incorporated on 31st March 2005 with an authorised capital of Rs. 50,000 (500 shares of Rs. 100 each) for the purpose of purchasing and continuing the partnership business of Black, Green and White. Rs. 32,900 was the purchase price, which was paid by allotment of 180 shares (fully paid) in BWG Private Ltd and the balance in cash. The company then issued the remaining shares to Brown and Blue in equal proportion, who paid for them in full. Pass the journal entries necessary to close the books.

(*B. Com. Marathwada, Madurai*)

SOLUTION

Journal Entries in the books of Black, White and Green

Date	Particulars		Dr. Rs.	Cr. Rs.
2005 March 31	Realisation Account	Dr.	37,400	
	To Bank Account			11,400
	To Stock Account			10,000
	To Debtors Account			10,000
	To Cash Account			6,000
	(Being transfer of assets to Realisation Account)			
	Creditors Account	Dr.	8,000	
	Provision for Doubtful Debts A/c		1,000	
	To Realisation Account			9,000
	(Being transfer of liabilities to Realisation Account)			
	BWG Private Ltd Account	Dr.	32,900	
	To Realisation Account			32,900
	(Being purchase consideration recorded)			
	Realisation Account	Dr.	4,500	
	To Black Account			2,250
	To White Account			1,500
	To Green Account			750
	(Being profit on Realisation account is credited to Partners' Capital A/c)			
	Black Capital Account	Dr.	1,500	
	White Capital Account	Dr.	1,000	
	Green Capital Account	Dr.	500	
	To Profit & Loss A/c			3,000
	(Being loss transferred to Capital Accounts)			
	Shares in BWG Private Ltd. Account	Dr.	18,000	
	Cash Account	Dr.	14,900	
	To BWG Private Ltd account			32,900
	(Being purchase consideration received)			
	Black Capital Account	Dr.	9,000	
	White Capital Account	Dr.	6,000	
	Green Capital Account	Dr.	3,000	
	To Share in BWG Pvt. Ltd.			18,000
	(Being distribution of shares among partners)			
	Black Capital Account	Dr.	9,150	
	White Capital Account	Dr.	2,500	
	Green Capital Account	Dr.	3,250	
	To Cash Account			14,900
	(Being distribution of cash among partners)			

Dr. **Capital Account** Cr.

	Black	White	Green		Black	White	Green
	Rs.	Rs.	Rs.		Rs.	Rs.	Rs.
Profit & Loss	1,500	1,000	500	Balance b/d	17,400	8,000	6,000
Shares in BWG	9,000	6,000	3,000	Profit on	2,250	1,500	750
Cash (Balancing figure)	9,150	2,500	3,250	Realisation			
	19,650	9,500	6,750		19,650	9,500	6,750

ILLUSTRATION 32.8

A and B are in partnership sharing profits and losses as to two-thirds and one-third respectively. Their Balance Sheet on 31st December 2005 on which date they have agreed to convert their business into a private limited company is as follows:

Liabilities		*Rs.*	*Assets*	*Rs.*
Sundry Creditors		30,000	Cash	7,000
Mortgage on Freehold premises		10,000	Sundry Debtors	26,000
Capitals: A	20,000		Stock	16,000
B	10,000	30,000	Plant and Machinery	5,000
			Freehold premises	16,000
		70,000		70,000

The Company takes over all the assets and liabilities with the exception of the mortgage on freehold premises, the purchase price being Rs. 60,000 payable as to Rs. 12,000 in cash, Rs 24,000 in Debentures and the balance in equity shares of the company.

Close the books of the firm after the above transactions have been carried out including the payment of mortgage. The partners agree to share the debentures and shares in proportions of their capitals.

(*B.Com., Andhra, Madurai, Ms, Kerala*)

SOLUTION

Dr. **Realisation Account** Cr.

	Rs.		*Rs.*
Cash	7,000	Sundry Creditors	30,000
Sundry Debtors	26,000	Private Ltd. Company	60,000
Stock	16,000	(Purchase consideration)	
Plant and Machinery	5,000		
Freehold Premises	16,000		
Profit transferred to Capitals:			
A	13,333		
B	6,667		
	90,000		90,000

Dr. **Mortgage on Freehold Premises** Cr.

	Rs.		*Rs.*
To Cash	10,000	By Balance b/d	10,000

Private Limited Company

Dr.	Rs.		Cr. Rs.
To Realisation A/c	60,000	By Cash	12,000
		By Debentures	24,000
		By Shares (Balancing figures)	24,000
	60,000		60,000

Capital Accounts

Dr.	A	B		A	B
	Rs.	Rs.		Rs.	Rs.
To Shares (in Capital ratio)	16,000	8,000	By Balance b/d	20,000	10,000
To Debentures (in Capital ratio)	16,000	8,000	By realisation (Profit)	13,333	6,667
To Cash (Balancing figure)	1,333	667			
	33,333	16,667		33,333	16,667

Cash Accounts

Dr.	Rs.		Cr. Rs.
To Balance b/d	7,000	By Realisation Account (transferred)	7,000
To Private Ltd. Co.	12,000	By Mortgage on Freehold Premises	10,000
		By A's Capital Account	1,333
		By B's Capital Account	667
	19,000		19,000

ILLUSTRATION 32.9

Sangita, Debjani and Barnali are partners in a firm, sharing profits and losses in the ratio 3 : 2 : 1, respectively. The Balance Sheet of the firm as on 31st December, 2006, in given below:

Liabilities		Rs.	*Assets*	Rs.
Sundry Creditors		30,000	Plant & Equipment	60,000
Capital Account:			Debtors	50,000
Sangita	60,000		Bills Receivable	8,000
Debjani	40,000		Stock	25,000
Barnali	20,000	1,20,000	Cash at Bank	5,000
			Cash in hand	2,000
		1,50,000		1,50,000

The partners agree to sell the business to a limited company which was incorporated with 65,000 shares of Rs. 10 each. The purchasing company agrees to take over the assets and liabilities and discharge the purchase consideration by the issue of 8,250 shares of Rs. 10 each and cash Rs. 56,000. The cost of dissolution Rs. 2,500 is paid by the firm and balance amount of cash is distributed among the partners.

You are asked to prepare Journal entries and necessary ledger Accounts in the books of the firm and opening Journal entries in the Books of Ltd. Co. *(B.Com. Hons. Kolkata)*

Solution

Calculation of Purchase Consideration

	Rs.	Form
8,250 shares @ Rs. 10 each	82,500	Cash
Cash	56,000	Cash
	1,38,500	

SOLUTION:

Books of the Firm
Journal Entries

Date	Particulars		L.F.	Dr. Rs.	Cr. Rs.
	Realisation A/c	Dr.		1,50,000	
	To Plant & Equipment A/c				60,000
	" Debtors A/c				50,000
	" Bills Receivable A/c				8,000
	" Stock A/c				25,000
	" Cash at Bank A/c				5,000
	" Cash in hand A/c				2,000
	(Being transfer of different assets to realization A/c)				
	Sundry Creditors A/c	Dr.		30,000	
	To Realization A/c				30,000
	(Being transfer of sundry creditors to realization A/c)				
	Co. Ltd. A/c	Dr.		1,38,500	
	To Realization A/c				1,38,500
	(Being Purchase Consideration due transferred to realization A/c)				
	Equity Shares in ..... Co. Ltd. A/c	Dr.		82,500	
	Cash A/c	Dr.		56,000	
	To ..... Co. Ltd.A/c				1,38,500
	(Being Purchase Consideration received)				
	Realization A/c	Dr.		2,500	
	To Cash A/c				2,500
	(Being Cost of dissolution paid)				
	Realisation A/c	Dr.		16,000	
	To Sangita Capital A/c				8,000
	" Debjani Capital A/c				5,333
	" Barnali's Capital A/c				2,667
	(Being profit on realization transferred)				
	Sangita's Capital A/c (Rs. 41,250 + Rs. 26,750	Dr.		68,000	
	Debjani's Capital A/c (Rs. 27,500 + Rs. 17,833	Dr.		45,333	
	Barnali's Capital A/c (Rs. 13,750 + Rs. 8,917)	Dr.		22,667	
	To Equity Shares in Limited Co. A/c				82,500
	To Cash A/c				53,500
	(Being distribution of shares & cash to the partners)				

Realization Account

Dr.		Rs.		Dr. Rs.
To Plant & Equipment A/c		60,000	By Sundry Creditors A/c	30,000
" Debtors A/c		50,000	" Limited Co. A/c –	
" Bills Receivable A/c		8,000	Purchase Consideration	1,38,500
" Stock A/c		25,000		
" Cash at Bank A/c		5,000		
" Cash in Hand A/c		2,000		
" Cash A/c-Cost of dissolution		2,500		
" Capital A/cs				
Sangita	8,000			
Debjani	5,333			
Barnali	2,667	16,000		
		1,68,500		1,68,500

Capital Account

Dr.	Sangita	Debjani	Barnali	Cr.	Sangita	Debjani	Barnali
	Rs.	Rs.	Rs.		Rs.	Rs.	Rs.
To Equity Shares in Limited Co. A/c	41,250	27,500	13,750	By Bal.b/d	60,000	40,000	20,000
" CashA/c (56,000–2,500)	26,750	17,833	8,917	Realization A/c-profit	8,000	5,333	2,667
	68,000	45,333	22,667		68,000	45,333	22,667

NB: Distribution of shares in profit sharing ratio. Balancing figure is the basis for cash payment.

Journal entries in the Books of Limited Co.

Particulars		Rs.	Rs.
Goodwill (Balancing figure)	Dr.	18,500	
Plant & Equipment A/c	Dr.	60,000	
Debtors A/c	Dr.	50,000	
Bills Receivable A/c	Dr.	8,000	
Stock A/c	Dr.	25,000	
Cash at bank A/c	Dr.	5,000	
Cash in hand A/c	Dr.	2,000	
To Sundry Creditors			30,000
" Liquidator of M/s Sangita, Debjani & Barnali (Amount of Purchase consideration)			1,38,500
(Being various assets & liabilities taken over and the difference is paid for Goodwill)			
Liquidator of M/s Sangita, Debjani & Barnali A/c	Dr.	1,38,500	
To Eq. Share Capital A/c			82,500
" Cash A/c			56,000
(Being discharge of Purchase consideration by Payment of Shares & Cash)			

ILLUSTRATION 32. 10

A, B, and C were partners in business, sharing profits and losses in the ratio of 2 : 1 : 1. Their Balance Sheet as at 31-3-2005 is as follows .

Balance Sheet As at 31st March 2005

(Figures in Rs. '000)

Liabilities		*Rs.*	*Assets*		*Rs.*
Fixed Capital :			Fixed Assets		300
A	200		Investments		50
B	100		Current Assets :		
C	100		Stock	100	
Current Accounts :		400	Debtors	60	
A	40		Cash & Bank	150	
B	20				310
		60			
Unsecured Loans		200			
		660			660

On 1-4-2005, it is agreed among the partners that BC (P) Ltd., a newly formed company with B and C having each taken up 100 shares of Rs. 10 each, will take over the firm as a going concern including goodwill but excluding cash & bank balances. The following points are also agreed upon :

(*a*) The Goodwill will be valued at 3 years' purchase of super profit.

(*b*) The actual profit for the purpose of goodwill valuation will be Rs. 1,00,000.

(*c*) Normal rate of return will be 15% on fixed capital.

(*d*) All other assets and liabilities will be taken over at book values.

(*e*) The purchase consideration will be payable partly in shares of Rs. 10 each and partly is cash. Payment in cash being to meet the requirement to discharge A, who has agreed to retire.

(*f*) B and C are to acquire equal interest in the new company.

(*g*) Expenses of liquidation Rs. 40,000 .

You are required to prepare the necessary Ledger Accounts. *(C. A. B.Com. MS Inter)*

SOLUTION

REALISATION ACCOUNT

	Rs.			Rs.
To Fixed Assets	3,00,000	By Unsecured Loans		2,00,000
To Investments	50,000	By BC (P) Ltd.		4, 30,000
To Stock	1,00,000	By Loss on Realisation		
To Debtors	60,000	transferred to :		
			Rs.	
To Goodwill	1,20,000	A's Capital A/c	20,000	
To Bank (Expenses)	40,000	B's Capital A/c	10,000	
		C's Capital A/c	10,000	
				40,000
	6,70,000			6,70,000

Calculation of Goodwill

Actual profit for the purpose of goodwill valuation --------- 1,00,000 -----------

Less : Normal profit @ 15% on fixed capital of Rs. 4,00,000 --------- 60,000

(Fixed capital : A Rs.2,00,000

B Rs. 1,00,000

C Rs. 1,00,000 Rs. 4,00,000)

Super Profit	40,000
Goodwill at 3 years' Purchase : Rs. 40,000 × 3 ----------	1,20,000

Calculation of Purchase Consideration

	Rs.
Fixed Assets	3,00,000
Investments	50,000
Stock	1,00,000
Debtors	60,000
Goodwill	1,20,000
Value of Assets taken over	6,30,000
Less : Unsecured Loan	2,00,000
Purchase Consideration	4,30,000

PARTNERS' CAPITAL ACCOUNTS

	A	B	C		A	B	C
	Rs.	Rs.	Rs.		Rs.	Rs.	Rs.
To Realisation A/c (Loss)	20,000	10,000	10,000	By Balance b/d	2,00,000	1,00,000	1,00,000
To Shares in BC (P) Ltd.	—	1,30,000	1,30,000	By Current A/cs (Transfer)	40,000	20,000	—
				By Goodwill	60,000	30,000	30,000
To C's Capital A/c (Capital Adjustment)	—	10,000	—	By B's Capital A/c (Capital Adjustment)	—	—	10,000
To Bank	2,80,000	—	—				
	3,00,0000	1,50,000	1,40,000		3,00,000	1,50,00	1,40,000

BC (P) LTD.

	Rs.		Rs.
To Realisation A/c (Purchase Consideration)	4,30,000	By Bank	1,70,000
		By Shares in BC (P) Ltd. (Bal. figure) (26,000 shares of Rs. 10 each)	2,60,000
	4,30,000		4,30,000

BANK ACCOUNT

	Rs.		Rs.
To Balance b/d	1,50,000	By Realisation A/c (Expenses)	40,000
To BC (P) Ltd. (Bal. figure)	1,70,000	By A's Capital A/c	2,80,000
	3,20,000		3,20,000

SHARES IN BC (P) LTD.

	Rs.		Rs.
To BC (P) Ltd.	2,60,000	By B's Capital A/c	1,30,000
		By C's Capital A/c	1,30,000
	2,60,000		2,60,000

ILLUSTRATION 32.11

A, B and C were partners in a business and shared profits in the proportion of 1/2, 1/3, 1/6 respectively.

Balance Sheet of A, B and C as on 31st December 2005

Liabilities		*Rs.*	*Assets*	*Rs.*
Creditors		3,000	Goodwill	10,000
Capital Accounts:			Sundry Assets	12,000
A	14,000		Cash at Bank	11,000
B	10,000			
C	6,000	30,000		
		33,000		33,000

On January 1, 2006, the following changes took place:

1. C retired from the business and his share, valued at Rs. 8,000, was taken over by A and B who paid the former in their profit sharing proportions, from their personal resources.
2. S was then introduced into the business as a partner with 1/6 share on the condition that a further sum of Rs. 6,000 was allowed to be credited to A and B in their respective proportions, and that S contributed such a sum as would make his capital equal to 1/4 of the total capital of A and B after all the above adjustments.
3. The new firm was converted into a limited company which took over the whole of the assets (except cash) for a consideration of Rs. 34,000 payable in fully paid shares of Rs. 10 each.

The Bank balance of the firm was utilised in payment to creditors and the partners. You are required to show the Capital Accounts of all the partners, giving effect to the above transactions.

(*B. Com, Madurai, Kerala, Mysore*)

SOLUTION

Dr. **Capital Accounts of A, B and C** Cr.

	A	*B*	*C*		*A*	*B*	*C*
	Rs.	Rs.	Rs.		Rs.	Rs.	Rs.
A's Capital A/c	–	–	4,800	Balance b/d	14,000	10,000	6,000
B's Capital A/c	–	–	3,200	Goodwill	–	–	2,000
Balance c/d	18,800	13,200	–	C's Capital A/c	4,800	3,200	–
	18,800	13,200	8,000		18,800	13,200	8,000
				Balance b/d	18,800	13,200	

Note: When C's share is valued at Rs. 8,000 and his capital account shows a credit balance of Rs. 6,000, the difference *i.e.* Rs. 2,000 is by way of goodwill.

The amount due to C is paid by A and B in their profit sharing ratio. Thus A brings Rs. 4,800 and B brings Rs. 3,200 and these are credited to their capital accounts.

Dr. **Capital Accounts of A, B and S** Cr.

	A	*B*	*S*		*A*	*B*	*S*
	Rs.	Rs.	Rs.		Rs.	Rs.	Rs.
Balance c/d	22,400	15,600	9,500	Balance b/d	18,800	13,200	–
				Goodwill	3,600	2,400	–
				Cash	–	–	9,500
	22,400	15,600	9,500		22,400	15,600	9,500
				Balance b/d	22,400	15,600	9,500

Note: The S's contribution is 1/4 of total capital of A and B.

1/4 of (Rs. 22,400 15,600) = 1/4 of Rs. 38,000 = Rs. 9,500

Realisation Account

Dr.				Cr.
		Rs		*Rs*
To Assets		12,000	By Limited Company	34,000
To Goodwill (10,000 + 2,000 + 6,000)		18,000	(Purchase Consideration)	
To Profit: A	1,800			
B	1,200			
C	1,000	4,000		
		34,000		34,000

Note: Profit sharing ratio is 9 : 6 : 5.

Capital Accounts of A, B and S

Dr.	*A*	*B*	*S*		*A*	*B*	*S* Cr.
	Rs	Rs	Rs		Rs	Rs	Rs
Shares in New Co.	15,980	11,090	6,930	Balance b/d	22,400	15,600	9,500
Cash				Realisation A/c	1,800	1,200	1,000
(Balancing figure)	8,220	5,710	3,570				
	24,200	16,800	10,500		24,200	16,800	10,500

Note: The shares have been distributed among the partners in their final claim *i.e.* 24,200 : 16,800 : 10,500 or 242 : 168 : 105 and balance is settled by giving cash.

Cash Account

Dr.			Cr.
	Rs.	*Rs.*	
To Balance b/d	11,000	By Creditors	3,000
To S's Capital A/c	9,500	By A's Capital	8,220
		By B's Capital	5,710
		By S's Capital	3,570
	20,500		20,500

QUESTIONS

Objective Type Questions

I. State whether the following statements are "True" or "False":

1. General reserve at the time of amalgamation of firms will be transferred to New Firm's Account.
2. The purchase consideration at the time of sale of a firm to a company will be transferred to Realisation Account.
3. The assets taken over by the new firm are debited to the New Firm's account.
4. Assets not taken over by the purchasing company is sold in the market and cash received is debited to Realisation A/c.
5. The liabilities taken over are credited by the new firm in its books at old values.
6. Realisation accounts are prepared to close the books of amalgamated firms.
7. Revaluation Account is opened in each firm's books for revaluation of assets and liabilities when amalgamation of firms takes place.
8. In the case of sale of a firm to a company, the profit or loss on sale is ascertained through a Revaluation Account.
9. Shares and Debentures received from the purchasing company are distributed amongst partners in the ratio of their final amount due in the absence of an agreement.

10. At the time of sale of a firm to a company, the excess of purchase consideration over the net worth of business is called goodwill.

(**Ans:** True: 2, 3, 7, 9, 10.
False: 1, 4, 5, 6, 8.

II. Fill in the blanks:

1. Two firms joining together to form a new firm is called ....
2. General reserve at the time of amalgamation of firms will be transferred to Partners .... Accounts
3. When a firm sells business as a going concern, cash balance is transferred to .... Account.
4. Goodwill Account appearing in the books on the dissolution date is closed by transferring it to .... side of the .... account.
5. Unrecorded liability paid at the time of dissolution is debited to .... Account.

(**Ans:** Amalgamation; 2. Capital; 3. Realisation 4. Debit, Realisation; 5. Realisation

III. Choose the correct answer for each of the following from the given alternatives:

1. The assets, liabilities and capital accounts of the amalgamating firms are closed by opening:
   (*a*) Realisation Account
   (*b*) Evaluation Account
   (*c*) New Firm's Account
2. At the time of amalgamation, liabilities not taken over by the new firm will be transferred to:
   (*a*) Capital Accounts of partners
   (*b*) New Firm's Account
   (*c*) Realisation Account
3. In the case of a sale to a company, the profit or loss on sale is ascertained through:
   (*a*) Revaluation Account
   (*b*) Realisation Account
   (*c*) Memorandum Revaluation Account
4. Assets not taken over by the new firm at the time of amalgamation are transferred to:
   (*a*) New Firm's Account
   (*b*) Revaluation Account
   (*c*) Realisation Account
   (*d*) Partners' Capital Account
5. Reserves and profits shown in the Balance Sheets of the amalgamating firms should be transferred to:
   (*a*) New Firm's Account
   (*b*) Capital Accounts
   (*c*) Realisation Account
6. Realisation Account is:
   (*a*) Personal Account
   (*b*) Real Account
   (*c*) Nominal Account
7. In the event of amalgamation of partnership firms, the goodwill of each business is credited to the partners account of the respective firms in their:
   (*a*) Old profit sharing ratio
   (*b*) New profit sharing ratio
   (*c*) Capital ratio

(**Ans:** 1. (c); 2. (a); 3. (b); 4. (d); 5. (b); 6. (c); 7. (a)

THEORETICAL QUESTIONS

1. What do you understand by Amalgamation?
2. What are the reasons for Amalgamation?

PRACTICAL PROBLEMS

1. A and B are sole traders dealing in textile retail selling. They agreed to form a partnership firm on the basis of their respective Balance Sheets given below:

Balance Sheet of A as on December 31, 2004

Liabilities	*Rs.*	*Assets*	*Rs.*
Sundry Creditors	6,000	Cash in hand	500
Bills Payable	2,000	Land and Building	30,000
Bank Overdraft	8,000	Furniture	11,500
Capital	58,000	Stock-in-trade	17,000
		Sundry Debtors	11,000
		Bills Receivable	4,000
	74,000		74,000

Balance Sheet of B as on December 31, 2004

Liabilities	*Rs.*	*Assets*	*Rs.*
Sundry Creditors	8,000	Cash in hand	400
Bills Payable	5,000	Cash at Bank	2,600
General Reserve	1,000	Stock-in-trade	15,000
Capital	19,000	Furniture and Fixtures	3,000
		Sundry Debtors	12,000
	33,000		33,000

They agree to merge the assets and liabilities of their business at book value. It is also decided to share profits and losses in the ratio of 3 :1.

Pass necessary journal entries to close the books of A and B and also prepare the Balance Sheet of the newly constituted partnership firm.

[**Ans:** Balance Sheet Total Rs. 1,07,000]

2. Two partnership firms, carrying on similar business under the names of Black and Company and White and Company, decide to amalgamate into Grey and Company with effect from Ist April 2004. The respective Balance Sheets as on 31st March 2004 are given below:

Balance Sheet of Black and Company as on 31st March 2004

Liabilities	*Rs.*	*Assets*	*Rs.*
B's Capital	19,000	Plant and Machinery	10,000
Sundry Creditors	10,000	Stock in trade	20,000
Bank Overdraft	15,000	Sundry Debtors	10,000
		A's Capital	4,000
	44,000		44,000

A and B share profits and losses in the proportion of 1 : 2.

Balance Sheet of White and Company
as on 31st March 2004

Liabilities	*Rs.*	*Assets*	*Rs.*
X's Capital Account	10,000	Goodwill	10,000
Y's Capital Account	2,000	Stock in trade	5,000
Sundry Creditors	28,000	Sundry Debtors	10,000
		Cash in hand	6,000
		Cash at Bank	9,000
	40,000		40,000

X and Y share profits and losses equally.

The following further information is given:

1. All fixed assets are to be devalued by 20%.
2. All stock in trade is to be appreciated by 50%.
3. Black and Company owe Rs. 5,000 to White and Company as on 31st March 2004. This debt is settled at Rs. 2,000.
4. Goodwill is to be ignored for the purpose of amalgamation.
5. The fixed Capital Accounts in the new firm are to be:
   A—Rs. 2,000
   B—Rs. 3,000
   X—Rs. 1,000
   Y—Rs. 4,000
6. B takes over the bank overdraft of Black and Company and gifts to A the amount of money to be brought in by A to make up his capital contribution.
7. X is paid off in cash from White and Company and Y brings in sufficient cash to make up his required capital contribution.

Pass journal entries to close the books of both the firms as on 31st March 2004.

(CA., M., Com. Madurai)

3. A and B are the partners in a firm sharing profits and losses in the ratio of 2 : 3. X and Y are the partners in another firm sharing equally. The Balance Sheets as on 30th June 2004 were as under:

Liabilities	*AB*	*XY*	*Assets*	*AB*	*XY*
	Rs.	Rs.		Rs.	Rs.
Capital A/cs:			Goodwill	5,000	5,000
A	30,000		Machinery	24,000	—
B	40,000		Furniture	1,000	1,000
X		24,000	Stock	20,000	24,000
Y		22,000	Debtors	22,000	20,000
Reserves	10,000	—	Cash and Bank Balance	13,000	2,000
Loan	3,000	2,000			
Creditors	2,000	4,000			
	85,000	52,000		85,000	52,000

They decided to amalgamate and form a new firm. The following terms were agreed upon:

1. The new firm is to take over all assets and liabilities of both the firms with the exception of the loan of M/s AB, which is to be paid by that firm out of its bank account.
2. A provision for bad debts is to be created on Debtors at 5%.
3. Goodwill of both the firms is to be valued at one year's purchase of the average profits of the last years, which were as follows:

	AB	XY
Year ended June 30, 2004	8,000	6,000
Year ended June 30, 2003	7,000	7,000
Year ended June 30, 2002	9,000	5,000
Year ended June 30, 2001	8,400	7,000

4. Machinery of M/s AB was depreciated by Rs. 4,000 and furniture of both the firms was over depreciated by Rs. 200 each.

You are required to close the books of both the firms and prepare the Balance Sheet of the new firm.

[**Ans.** Realisation loss of (AB) Rs. 2,200 (A—Rs. 880 and B—Rs. 1,320)
Realisation gain of (XY) 50 (Rs. 25 each)
Capital Accounts A— Rs. 33,120, B—Rs. 44,680
X—Rs. 24,025, Y—Rs. 22,025
Balance Sheet Total Rs. 1,31,850]

4. The Balance Sheet of Messrs A and B and Messrs C and D as on 31st July 2004 were as follows:

Balance Sheet

	A & B	*C & D*		*A & B*	*C & D*
	Rs.	Rs.		Rs.	Rs.
Capital			Land & Workshop	10,000	12,000
A	10,000		Machinery & Tools	7,000	8,000
B	10,000		Furniture & Fixtures	3,000	3,500
C		15,000	Sundry Debtors	6,000	8,500
D		15,000	Stock	8,000	10,000
Creditors	15,000	10,000	Cash & Bank	3,000	1,000
O/s Expenses	2,000	3,000			
	37,000	43,000		37,000	43,000

The two firms decided to amalgamate and form into ABCD & Company with effect from 1st August 2004. Partners would share profits and losses equally between themselves as they were doing prior to amalgamation and they agreed to the following revaluation of assets and liabilities:

	A & B	*C & D*
	Rs.	Rs.
Land and Workshop	10,000	10,000
Machinery and Tools	7,000	8,000
Furniture and Fixtures	2,500	2,500
Sundry Debtors	5,500	7,000
Stock	8,000	8,000
Outstanding expenses	2,000	3,500

In addition to the above, it was decided:

(*i*) That the goodwill of A & B and C & D was valued at Rs. 10,000 and Rs. 5,000 respectively in the first instance but for the purposes of Balance Sheet of the new firm, the combined goodwill would be valued at Rs. 12,000; and

(*ii*) That the reconstructed capitals of partners should be Rs. 14,000 each, partners introducing cash, if necessary. You are required to prepare:

(*a*) The Revaluation accounts of Messrs A & B and Messrs C & D and their capital accounts prior to and after amalgamation.

(*b*) Opening Balance Sheet of the New firm assuming that all the arrangements have been duly carried out. (*CAIIB*)

[**Ans.** Balance Sheet Total Rs. 86,500]

5. Following were the Balance Sheets as on 31st December 2004 of two firms, M/s A and B and M/s C and D:

Balance Sheet

	A & B	*C & D*		*A & B*	*C & D*
	Rs.	Rs.		Rs.	Rs.
Creditors	20,000	10,000	Bank	15,000	8,000
Bills Payable	5,000	—	Investments	10,000	8,000
Bank Overdraft	2,000	10,000	Debtors	9,000	8,000
A's Loan	6,000	—	Furniture	12,000	6,000
Reserve	10,000	4,000	Premises	30,000	—
Capitals:			Building	—	50,000
A	35,000		Machinery	15,000	—
B	22,000		Goodwill	9,000	—
C		36,000			
D		20,000			
	1,00,000	80,000		1,00,000	80,000

The two firms decided to amalgamate their businesses on 1st January 2005. For this purpose, it was decided that the new firm shall not take furniture of both the firms. The new firm agrees to take over the investments of both the firms at 10% less, and Land and Buildings at Rs. 80,000, Premises at Rs. 45,000 and Machinery at Rs. 9,000.

Further, the new firm agrees to take over only trade liabilities of both the firms and to pay Rs. 20,000 to each firm for Goodwill.

The capital of the new firm was agreed at Rs. 1,60,000 to be divided among the partners equally.

Note. Any assets not taken over by the new firm is to be shared equally by the partners as per the agreement.

You are required to pass journal entries in the books of the two firms M/s A & B and M/s C & D and prepare Balance Sheet of the new firm. (*B.Com. Bangalore*)

[Ans. Balance Sheet Total Rs. 2,31,700**]**

6. A and B carry on independent business in Provisions and their positions as at 30th September 2004 are reflected in the Balance Sheet given below:

	A	*B*
	Rs.	Rs.
Stock	1,70,000	98,000
Sundry Debtors	89,000	37,000
Cash at Bank	13,000	7,500
Cash in hand	987	234
Furniture and Fixtures	2,750	1,766
Investment	513	—
	2,76,250	1,44,500
	Rs.	Rs.
Represented by:		
Sundry Creditors for:		
Purchase	1,10,000	47,000
Expenses	750	2,000
Bills Payable (not for purchases)	12,500	—
Capital Account	1,53,000	95,500
	2,76,250	1,44,500

Both of them want to form a partnership firm from Ist October 2004 on the following understanding:

(*a*) The capital of the partnership would be Rs. 3,00,000 which would be contributed by them in the ratio of 2 : 1.

(*b*) The assets of the individual business would be evaluated by C and the firm will take them over and the value would be adjusted against the contribution due by A and B.

(*c*) C gave his valuation report as follows:

Business of A: Stock to be written down by 15%. A portion of sundry debtors amounting to Rs. 9,000 estimated unrealisable not to be assumed by the firm.

Furniture and fixture to be valued at Rs. 2,000 and investments to be taken at market value of Rs. 1,000.

Assets of B: Stocks to be written up by 10%.

Sundry Debtors to be admitted at 85% of their value.

Rest of the assets to be assumed at their book value.

(*d*) The firm is not to assume any creditors other than the dues on account of purchase made.

Prepare the opening Balance Sheet of the firm. (*C.A.*)

[Ans. Balance Sheet Total: Rs. 4,58,750]

7. Amit and Asit were in partnership sharing profits and losses: Amit two-thirds; Asit one-third. The summarised partnership Balance Sheet as on March 31, 2004, was as follows:

Liabilities		*Rs.*	*Assets*		*Rs.*
Fixed Capital A/cs			Fixed Assets		70,000
Amit	50,000		Current Assets		
Asit	40,000	90,000	Stock	35,000	
Current Accounts			Debtors	65,000	
Amit	20,000		Balance at Bank	15,000	1,15,000
Less: Asit	10,000	10,000			
Loan—Asit		30,000			
Creditors		55,000			
		1,85,000			1,85,000

The fixed assets included two motor-cars having book values of Rs. 8,000 and Rs. 6,000 respectively. The partners desiring to retire from business accepted the offer of Western India Limited to acquire the stock and fixed assets, other than the motor-cars, at an agreed purchase price of Rs. 1,60,000. The purchase consideration was to be satisfied by a cash payment of Rs. 56,000, the allotment by the company to the partners of 400 5% preference shares of Rs. 100 each and the balance by the allotment by the company to the partners of 900 equity shares of Rs. 100 each.

The debtors realised Rs. 61,000 and the creditors were settled for Rs. 51,000.

The partners agreed that the following should be the basis of distribution on dissolution of the partnership:

1. Amit to take over one car at a valuation of Rs. 12,000 and Asit the other at Rs. 8,000.
2. Asit to be allotted preference shares to the value of this loan, the remainder to be allotted to Amit.
3. The equity shares to be allotted in proportion of fixed capitals.
4. Both the preference and equity shares to be valued at Rs. 80 per share.
5. The balance to be settled in cash.

You are required to prepare:

(*a*) The Realisation Account,

(*b*) The Bank Account; and

(*c*) The Partners' Capital Accounts showing the final settlement between them.

(*C.A. Inter*)

[Ans. Realisation Profit Rs. 75,000;

Cash payment to Amit Rs. 66,000 and Asit Rs. 15,000])

8. A, B and C carrying on business in partnership, profit and loss sharing ratio being 1/2, 1/3 and 1/6 respectively, decide to form a private limited company, ABC Company (Private) Limited, with an authorised capital of Rs. 1,20,000 divided into 90,000 equity shares of Re. 1 each and 30,000, 6% preference shares, of Re. 1 each. The company is incorporated on 31st March 2004 and takes over the business, goodwill and some of the assets of the firm as on 31.3-2004, on which date the Balance Sheet of the firm is as given hereunder:

	Rs.		Rs.
Creditors	5,600	Cash at Bank	17,200
A's Loan	8,000	Debtors	10,400
Current Accounts:		Current Account: B	4,200
A	5,850	Stock in Trade	36,000
C	4,150	Furniture and Fixtures	1,200
Capital Accounts:		Scooters	3,600
A	30,000	Machinery	13,000
B	20,000		
C	12,000		
	85,600		85,600

A, who retires, is presented with a scooter, book value being Rs. 1,200. The company takes over the remaining scooter for Rs. 2,000. A takes over all the debtors and agrees to pay off creditors. He also received certain furniture for which he is charged Rs. 300. The company agrees to discharge A's loan by issuing to him 6,000 preference shares of Re. 1 each fully paid and the balance in cash. C is the owner of the premises from where the business of the firm is carried on. C agrees to sell the above premises to the company for Rs. 20,000 in consideration whereof he agrees to receive 20,000 preference shares of Re. 1 each fully paid.

The company takes over the remaining furniture at Rs 600, stock at Rs 33,200, Cash at Bank and machinery at book value. The goodwill is valued at Rs 8,000 for the purpose of taking over.

The purchase consideration is to be discharged by the issue to the partner at par Rs 60,000 equity shares of Re. 1 each in proportion to final balance of their combined Capital and Current Account and the balance is to be paid in cash.

Preliminary expenses amounting to Rs 800 are paid by the company.

Prepare (*i*) Realisation Account, (*ii*) Combined Capital and Current Account of partners, (*iii*) Opening Balance Sheet of the limited company. (*C.A. Inter*)

[Ans: Realisation profit Rs 4,500
Balance Sheet Total Rs 86,000]

9. A, B and C are partners sharing profits and losses in the ratio of 2 : 2 : 1. They decided to dissolve the partnership but C continues the business by firm's name by taking over the goodwill of the firm at Rs 20,000. Their Balance Sheet as on 31st Dec. 2004 is given below:

Liabilities	*Rs.*	*Assets*	*Rs.*
Sundry Creditors	14,300	Goodwill	6,000
Capital Accounts:		Machinery	16,000
A:	38,000	Furniture	10,000
B:	35,000	Investments	14,600
C:	20,000	Sundry Debtors	28,800
		Stock	25,600
		Cash and Bank	6,300
	1,07,300		1,07,300

It is, however, agreed that:

1. A takes over investments for Rs. 12,000.
2. B takes over the furniture for Rs. 11,500.
3. All other assets and liabilities are taken over by C, subject to the following revaluations:
   (*a*) Stock at Rs. 22,000
   (*b*) Machinery at Rs. 17,400
4. Sundry Debtors are taken at book value but A and B leave Rs. 1,000 each with the firm as guarantee to cover the possible losses.
5. C brings in cash to pay off the partners.

Write up the ledger accounts to close the books of the firm and show the Balance Sheet of C.

(*M. Com,, Kolkata, Chennais*)

[**Ans.** Realisation Profit: Rs. 10,700
Balance Sheet Total: Rs. 88,200]

10. A and B, sharing profits and losses equally, decided to convert their business into a limited company on 31st December, 2004, when the Balance Sheet was as under:

Liabilities		*Rs.*	*Assets*	*Rs.*
Creditors		24,000	Debtors	30,000
Loan		20,000	Bills Receivable	5,000
Bank Overdraft		8,000	Stock	18,000
Reserve Fund		3,000	Patents	4,000
Capitals:			Machinery	8,000
A:	20,000		Land and Buildings	30,000
B:	20,000	40,000		
		95,000		95,000

The goodwill of he firm was to be valued at two years' purchase of the average profits of the previous three years. The Loan Creditors have agreed to accept 7 1/2% Preference Shares in settlement of their claim. Land and buildings and Machinery were to be revalued at Rs. 50,000 and Rs. 12,000 respectively. The vendors were to be allotted Equity Shares of the value of Rs. 1,05,000. The work results of the firm showed that they had made profits of Rs. 15,000 in 2002, Rs. 18,000 in 2003 and Rs. 21,000 in 2004 after transferring Rs. 1,000 to Reserve Fund each year. You are required to show the Realisation Account and Capital Accounts in the books of the firm, and the Opening Balance Sheet of the Company assuming that all the transactions are duly completed. (*B.Com. Agra, Jabalpur*)

[**Ans.** Realisation profit 24,000 (A — Rs. 12,000 and B— Rs. 12,000)
Balance Sheet total Rs. 1,57,000]

11. S and V, sharing profits and losses equally, decided to convert their business into a limited company on 31st December, 2004, when their balance sheet stood as follows:

Liabilities		*Rs.*	*Assets*	*Rs.*
Sundary creditors		48,000	Sundry debtors	60,000
Loan creditors		40,000	Bills receivable	10,000
Bank overdraft		16,000	Stock-in-trade	36,000
Reserve fund		6,000	Patents	8,000
Capital Accounts:			Plant and Machinery	16,000
S	40,000		Land and building	60,000
V	40,000	80,000		
		1,90,000		1,90,000

(*a*) The goodwill of the firm was to be valued at two years' purchase of the profits of the previous three years.

(*b*) The loan creditor was agreed to accept 7 1/2% redeemable preference shares in settlement of his claim.

(*c*) Land and buildings and plant and machinery were to be valued at Rs. 1,00,000 and Rs. 24,000 respectively.

(*d*) The vendors were to be allotted equity shares of the value of Rs. 2,10,000.

(*e*) The past working results of the firm showed that they had made profits of Rs. 30,000 in 2002, Rs. 36,000 in 2003 and Rs. 42,000 in 2004 after setting aside Rs. 2,000 to reserve fund each year.

You are required to show realisation account and capital account in the books of the firm assuming that all the transactions are duly completed.

[**Ans.** Realisation profit Rs. 1,24,000 (A: Rs. 62,000 and B : Rs. 62,000)
Purchase Consideration Rs. 2,10,000]

12. X Limited was formulated to take over the business of M/s. X and Y who are carrying on business in a partnership. The balance sheet of the firm as on 31st December 2004 was:

Liabilities	*Rs.*	*Assets*	*Rs.*
Sundry creditors	65,000	Plant & Machinery	2,60,000
Bills Payable	22,000	Land & Buildings	69,000
Profit & Loss A/c	43,000	Stock	1,30,000
Partner's Capital:		Investment	52,000
X	2,00,000	Sundry Debtors	1,38,000
Y	3,19,000		
	6,49,000		6,49,000

The company took over all the assets and liabilities except the investments at their book value and the purchase consideration of Rs. 5,50,000 was satisfied by issue of Rs. 2,00,000 7% Debentures of X Company Limited and the balance in fully paid shares of Rs. 100 each in X Ltd. The investments were taken over by Y at book value. The shares in X Ltd. have been taken over by the partners in the ratio of 3 : 2 and the final settlement being made in form of debentures.

(*a*) Pass the entries to close the books of the firm.

(*b*) Pass the entries in the books of X Ltd. and draft its Balance Sheet.

(*B.Com., Karnataka MK, Bangalore*)

[**Ans.** Balance Sheet total Rs. 6,37,000]

13. Santosh and Prakash were in partnership sharing profits and losses in the ratio of 3 : 1. Following is the Balance Sheet of the firm as on 31st Dec. 2004.

Balance Sheet as at 31st Dec. 2004

Liabilities		*Rs.*	*Assets*	*Rs.*
Capital Account			Fixed Assets	31,500
Santosh	36,000		Stock	16,800
Prakash	12,000	48,000	Debtors	29,400
Current Account			Cash at Bank	5,580
Santosh	6,300			
Prakash	3,000	9,300		
Loan from Prakash		4,500		
Creditors		21,480		
		83,280		83,280

Prashant Ltd. agred to take over stock and fixed assets excluding the value of motor car Rs. 6,150, for a consideration of Rs. 72,000 which is to be satisfied—

(*i*) By the payment of cash Rs. 24,000,

(*ii*) Allotment of 240 preference shares of Rs. 100 each valued at Rs. 75 per share, and

(*iii*) The balance by allotment of 2,400 Equity shares of the face value of Rs. 10 each.

The debtors realised Rs. 28,800 and the creditors were satisfied for Rs. 21,000. The following were agreed upon between partners:

(*i*) Equity shares be allotted in the capital ratio.

(*ii*) Santosh to take over the motor car at an agreed value of Rs. 6,300.

(*iii*) The preference share to be allotted to Prakash to the value of loan amount and the remaining preference shares be allotted to partners equally.

(*iv*) The balance remaining be paid in cash.

You are required to show :

(*a*) Realisation Account

(*b*) Partners' Capital Accounts

(*c*) Bank Account

(*d*) Statement showing distribution of shares. (*B. Com., Karnataka, Madurai*)

[**Ans.** : Revaluation profit Rs. 29,880

(Santosh Rs. 22,410 and Prakash Rs. 7,470

Purchase Consideration:—	Rs.
Cash	24,000
Preference shares (240 × 75)	18,000
Equity shares (@ Rs. 12.50)	30,000
	72,000

Final Settlement:	*Santosh*	*Prakash*
	Rs.	Rs.
Preference shares (18,000–4,500)	6,750	6,750
Equity shares	22,500	7,500
Bank	29,160	8,220]

14. Ajit, Ajay and Askashya were carrying on partnership business and sharing profits and losses in the ratio of 1 : 2: 3. On March 31, 2004, their balance sheet was as under:

Balance Sheet

as on 31st March 2004

Liabilities		*Rs.*	*Assets*	*Rs.*
Partners' Capitals:			Building	20,000
Ajit	10,000		Machinery	30,000
Ajay	20,000		Motor Car	5,000
Akshaya	30,000	60,000	Debtors	20,000
Ajay's loan (carrying Interest 8% p.a.)		20,000	Stock	15,000
Creditors		15,000	Cash	9,000
Bills Payable		5,000	Investments	1,000
		1,00,000		1,00,000

On the above date a private limited company was incorporated to take over the above business on the following terms and conditions:

1. All assets (except cash and investments) and all liabilities (except Ajay's loan) to be taken over by the company for which all assets are valued at par except building which is considered worth Rs. 27,000 and stock worth Rs. 14,000. Further, goodwill is valued at Rs. 30,000.
2. Ajay's loan to be partly liquidated by his taking over the firm's cash and investments at par. For the balance he is given 8% debentures received from the company in part discharge of purchase consideration.
3. The balance of the purchase consideration is received in the form of equity shares of the company which are to be appropriately distributed amongst the partners.

Show journal entries and ledger accounts to close the books of the firm. *(B. Com., Bombay)*

[**Ans.** Realisation profit Rs. 36,000
Purchase consideration Rs. 1,06,000]

15. A, B and C, sharing profits and losses equally, decided to convert their business into a limited company as on 31st December 2004 when their balance sheet stood as follows:

Liabilities	*Amount*	*Assets*	*Amount*
	Rs		Rs
Sundry Creditors	40,000	Sundry Debtors	40,000
Bank Overdraft	20,000	Bills Receivable	16,000
General Reserve	12,000	Stock in Trade	25,000
Loan from X	6,000	Plant	6,000
Capitals		Furniture	14,000
A	20,000	Patents	8,000
B	10,000	Goodwill	11,000
C	12,000		
	1,20,000		1,20,000

(*i*) The goodwill of the firm was valued at two years' purchase of the average profits of the last three years: the profits being Rs. 12,000 and Rs. 16,000 respectively.

(*ii*) The plant and furniture was valued at Rs. 8,000 and Rs. 16,000 respectively.

(*iii*) The debtors were taken at 5% less.

(*iv*) The firm was allotted 1,000 10% preference shares of Rs. 20 each, 3,000 equity shares of Rs. 10 each and the balance was paid in cash.

(*v*) Expenses of realisation were Rs. 2,000.

(*vi*) A, B and C agreed to take preference shares in the ratio of 4 : 3 : 3 and equity shares in the ratio of 5 : 3 : 2.

Prepare the necessary accounts to close the books of the firm.

[**Ans:** Purchase Consideration Rs. 65,000

	A	B	C
	Rs.	Rs.	Rs.
Realisation Profit:	3,000	3,000	3,000
Final Settlement:			
Preference Shares	8,000	6,000	6,000
Equity Shares	15,000	9,000	6,000
Cash	4,000	2,000	7,000]

16. A, B and C are equal partners of ABC and Company. The Balance Sheet of the firm as on 31st December 2004 stood as follows:

Liabilities	Rs.	Assets	Rs.
A's Capital Account	5,00,000	Land	5,00,000
B's Capital Account	10,00,000	Pland and Machinery	20,00,000
Loan from Banks	50,00,000	Buildings	7,00,000
Creditors	10,00,000	Stock	30,00,000
		Debtors	10,00,000
		C's Capital Account	3,00,000
	75,00,000		75,00,000

On that date, it is decided to convert the partnership into a Limited Company on the following terms:

(*a*) Land to be valued at Rs. 15,00,000.

(*b*) Plant and Machinery to be valued at Rs. 25,00,000.

(*c*) Depreciation amounting to Rs. 2,00,000 to be written off on buildings.

(*d*) A provision of 10% of book value to be made for obsolete stocks.

(*e*) A reserve for doubtful debts to be made at 10% of the debtors.

(*f*) A discount of 6% would be earned on creditors when paid out.

(*g*) The new company will issue 12,000 equity shares of Rs. 100 each credited as fully paid up, such share capital being valued at Rs. 15,00,000 and the balance payable is to be discharged by issue of 8% Debenture certificates of Rs. 1,000 each.

Show the necessary ledger account to close the books of ABC and Company and show the opening Balance Sheet of the new company. You may assume that (*i*) all partners are solvent and have sufficient cash resources as may be necessary for purposes of settling accounts, and (*ii*) shares and cash divided equally among the partners. (*B. Com. Bombay*)

[**Ans.** Purchase Consideration Rs. 21,60,000

Realisation Profit Rs. 9,60,000

Final Settlement:	A	B	C
	Rs.	Rs.	Rs.
Shares	5,00,000	5,00,000	5,00,000
Debentures	80,000	5,80,000	—
Cash	2,40,000	2,40,000	2,40,000

(C brings in Rs. 7,20,000)]

Chapter 33

Dissolution of Partnership Firm

Introduction – Dissolution – Settlement of Accounts – Firm's Debt and Personal Debts – Dissolution Accounts – Insolvency of a Partner – Garner Vs. Murray Decision – Fixed and Fluctuating Capitals – When all Partners are Insolvent – Piece-Meal Distribution – Basis of Distribution – Surplus Capital Method – Maximum Possible Loss Method – Questions – Objective Type Questions – Theoretical Questions – Practical Problems

INTRODUCTION

The dissolution of partnership among all the partners of a firm is called the Dissolution of the Firm (Sec. 39 of the Partnership Act, 1932). Dissolution of Partnership involves a change in the relation of partnership business, if the remaining partners resolve to continue the concern. In such cases there will be a new partnership but the firm will continue in a reconstituted form.

DISSOLUTION

Dissolution of firm means complete breakdown of the relation of partnership among all the partners. When all the partners resolve to dissolve the partnership, the dissolution of firm occurs, *i.e.* the firm is wound up. If the business comes to an end, it is said that the firm has been dissolved. Dissolution of firm means the closing down of the business. Firm's dissolution implies partnership dissolution but not vice versa. That is dissolution of partnership does not mean dissolution of firm, but the dissolution of firm will be dissolved on any one of the following ways:

(A) Dissolution by Agreement (Sec. 40)

A firm may be dissolved at any time with the consent of all partners. For instance, when a firm does not expect good prospects in the future, a firm can be dissolved by mutual consent of all partners.

(B) Compulsory Dissolution (Sec. 41)

A firm is compulsorily dissolved by operation of law when all the partners except one become insolvent or when all the partners become insolvent or when business becomes illegal or when the number of partners exceed twenty in case of ordinary business or ten in case of banking.

(C) Dissolution on the Happening of Certain Contingencies (Sec. 42)

A firm is dissolved, in the absence of contrary, in the event of any of the following circumstances:

(*i*) The expiry of the term for which it was formed.

(*ii*) The completion of the venture for which the partnership was constituted.

(*iii*) The death of a partner.

(*iv*) The adjudication of a partner as an insolvent.

(D) Dissolution by Notice of Partnership at Will (Sec. 43)

Where a partnership is at will, the firm may be dissolved by any partner giving notice in writing to all the other partners of his intention to dissolve the firm.

(E) Dissolution by the Court (Sec. 44)

The court is empowered to order the dissolution of a firm consequent on a suit by a partner in the following cases:

(i) When a partner becomes insane or unsound of mind.

(*ii*) When a partner becomes permanently incapable of performing his duties, be it mental or physical.

(*iii*) When a partner is proved guilty of misconduct which is likely to affect adversely the business of the firm.

(*iv*) When a partner conduct himself in such a way that it is not possible for the other partners to carry on partnership with him.

(*v*) When a partner transfers his interest or share to third party.

(*vi*) When the business cannot be carried out except at a loss. (It must be remembered that the object of partnership is to earn profits and if that object is not fulfilled, the firm can be dissolved).

(*vii*) When it appears to be just and equitable. For instance, continued quarrelling, deadlock in the management, refusal to attend matters of business, absence of cooperation etc. among the partners. (The court has wide discretionary powers).

Liability for Acts done after Dissolution (Sec. 45)

When a firm is dissolved a public notice must be given of the dissolution. If it is not done, the partners continue to be liable as such to third parties for any act done by any of them after the dissolution, and in such a case, the act of a partner done after dissolution is deemed to be an act done before the dissolution.

SETTLEMENT OF ACCOUNTS (Sec. 48)

As soon as a firm is dissolved, it ceases to transact normal business. The mode of settlement of accounts between partners after the dissolution of a firm is determined by the partnership agreement. In the absence of any specific agreement as to the mode of settlement of accounts after the dissolution of the firm, the Partnership Act laid down the following provisions (Sec. 48) for settlement of accounts.

(*a*) Losses, including deficiencies of capital, shall be paid first out of profit, next out of capital, and lastly, if necessary, by the partners individually in their profit-sharing ratio.

(*b*) The assets of the firm including any sums contributed by the partners to make up deficiencies of capital, shall be applied in the following manner and order:

(*i*) In paying the debts of the firm to third parties.

(*ii*) In paying each partner rateably what is due to him from the firm for advances.

(*iii*) In paying to each partner rateably what is due to him on account of capital, and

(*iv*) The surplus, if any, will be divided among the partners in their profit sharing ratio.

FIRM'S DEBT AND PERSONAL DEBTS

Where debts are owing both the firm and the partners individually, the rule under section 49 is (*i*) to apply the firm's assets first in paying off the firm's debts and out of the surplus left, if any, each partner's share thereof is applied in meeting his personal debts, and (*ii*) to apply the private property of each partner first in paying off his personal debts and the residue, if any, is applied to pay off the firm's debts.

DISSOLUTION ACCOUNTS

When a business is discontinued, the firm is said to be dissolved. As a result, all the accounts be closed. It is, therefore, necessary to open Realisation Account, Cash or Bank Account and Partners Capital Accounts.

(*i*) REALISATION Accounts is opened for all transactions relating to realisation of assets and payment of liabilities. That is, on dissolution, it is essential to make sale of assets of the firm, realise cash and paying off the liabilities. Realisation of assets and settlement of liabilities are centred round the Realisation Account. It is a nominal Account. The transactions – realisation and settlement – are over, the difference, being gain or loss will be transferred to Capital Accounts.

(*ii*) CASH/BANK Account is opened to record all cash transactions. When the purpose is over the Cash Account shows a balance, which is equal to the amounts due to partners.

(*iii*) CAPITAL Accounts are opened to make all entries connected with the partners' accounts. Current Accounts, if any, are transferred to Capital Accounts. Finally the Capital Accounts are closed by receiving or paying cash.

The following steps are taken to close the books of accounts:

1.	Transfer all the assets of the firm at their book value excepts cash, Bank and Losses.	Realisation Account To Individual Assets Accounts (Being transfer of various assets at their books value to Realisation Account)	Dr.

Note : (*a*) Cash Account and Bank Accounts are not transferred to Realisation Account as they are already in liquid form.

(*b*) Similarly Sundry Debtors Account and Provision for Doubtful Debts Accounts are two separate Accounts. The Sundry Debtors amount, i.e., gross amount to be transferred.

(*c*) Losses, debit balance of Profit and Loss Account are not transferred to Realisation Account.

2.	Transfer to losses of debit balance of Profit and Loss Account.	Partner's Capital/ Current Account To Profit & Loss Account (Being transfer to accumulated losses)	Dr.
3.	Transfer all outside Liabilities.	Various Liabilities Account To Realisation Account (Being transfer of various liabilities such as Creditors, Bills payable, Bank Overdraft O/S expenses etc. to Realisation Accounts)	Dr.
4.	Transfer Past Profits or Reserve Fund.	Profit & Loss Account Reserve Fund Account To Partner's Capital/ Current Account (Being transfer of past profits and Reserve Fund to Partners' Capital/Current Account)	Dr. Dr.
5.	When assets are sold or may be taken over by any partner.	(*a*) Cash Account To Realisation Account (Being assets sold for cash) (*b*) Partners' Capital Account To Realisation Accounts (Being assets taken over by partners)	Dr. Dr.
6.	When outside liabilities are paid off.	Realisation Account To Cash/ Bank Account (Being payment of liabilities to third parties)	Dr.

Transaction	Journal Entry
7. When outside liabilities are discharged by a partner	Realisation Accounts Dr. To Partner's Account (Being liabilities taken over at an agreed valuation by the partner)
8. (*a*) When expense are paid on realisation by the firm.	Realisation Account Dr. To Cash/Bank Account (Being expense on realisation paid)
(*b*) When it is paid by a partner.	Realisation Account Dr. To Partner's Capital Account (Being expenses paid on realisation by the partners)
9. When the purpose of the Realisation Account is over, it is closed to find out profit or loss on realisation of assets and discharging the liabilities.	
(*a*) If it shows profit	Realisation Account Dr. To Partners' Capital Account (Being profit on realisation accounts is transferred to Capital Accounts of partners in profit sharing ratio)
(*b*) If it shows loss	Partners' Capital Accounts Dr. To Realisation Account (Being loss incurred on realisation is transferred to Partner's Capital Account in profit sharing ratio)
10. When Partner's loan is paid off.	Partners' Loan Account Dr. To Cash/Bank Account (Being partner's loan repaid)
11. Now transfer Current Accounts, if any. (*a*) If it shows credit balance	Partner's Current Account Dr. To Partners' Capital Account (Being transfer of current accounts)
(*b*) If it shows a debit balance.	Partner's Capital Account Dr. To Partners' Current Account (Being transfer of current accounts)
12. When Capital Account of any partner shows a debit balance (after the adjustment or Realisation Account), then he must clear off his debt.	Cash/ Bank Account Dr. To Concerned Partner's Capital A/c (Being the deficiency in Capital account brought by the partner)
13. If there are unrecorded or undisclosed assets and liabilities, they may be dealt with as follows:	
(*a*) When unrecorded assets are realised (it is a gain).	Cash/ Bank Account Dr. To Realisation Account (Being realisation or unrecorded assets)
(*b*) When unrecorded liabilities are paid off (it is a loss).	Realisation Account Dr. To Cash/Bank Account (Being payment of unrecorded liabilities)
14. When closing Capital Accounts.	Partners' Capital Account Dr. To Cash/ Bank Account (Being final payment paid to partners what is due to each partner).

To sum up, when all the assets are realised and the liabilities are paid off, the balance of cash or Bank must be equal to the amount due finally to the partners' capital account, after transferring the current account, if any. Sometimes, the capital account shows a debit balance, representing the amount due to the firm by the concerned partner. The principle of unlimited liability is applied, that is, the partner, whose capital account shows a debit balance, should bring the amount to clear off the debit balance in his capital account. Then the cash in hand plus the amount so received, is applied in paying off all the partners whose accounts show credit balances. *Thus, all the accounts of assets, liabilities, partners' capital, cash, etc are closed.*

The above method of preparation of Realisation Account is called Total Method. Alternatively, there is another method, known as Balance Method to prepare the Realisation Account. Under the Balance Method, the assets appearing in the Balance sheet are not transferred to Realisation Account at their book value. But, only the difference between the Book Value of Assets and the amount realised by their sale is transferred to Realisation. The sales proceeds are not taken through Realisation Account. The liabilities too are not transferred to Realisation Account but only the difference between the book value and payments paid is transferred to Realisation Accounts.

For instance, consider the following:

(*i*) When assets realised in cash	Cash Account To Assets Account (Being proceeds against the sale of assets)	Dr.
(*a*) If there is a loss on realisation of the assets.	Realisation Account To Assets Account (Being loss on sale transferred to Realisation Account)	Dr.
(*b*) If there is a gain on realisation of the assets.	Assets Account To Realisation Account (Being gain on sale transferred to Realisation Account)	Dr.

Note: Return of Premium on Premature Dissolution

Where a partner has paid a premium on entering into partnership for a fixed term, and the firm is dissolved before the expiration on the term otherwise than by the death of a partner, he shall be entitled to repayment of the premium or of such part thereof as may be reasonable unless the dissolution is mainly due to his own misconduct, or the dissolution is in pursuance of an agreement containing no provision for the return of the premium or any part of it.

(*ii*) When liabilities are paid off	Liabilities Account To Cash/ Bank Account (Being Liabilities are paid off)	Dr.
(*a*) If there is loss.	Realisation Account To Liabilities\Account (Being loss on settlement is transferred to Realisation Accounts)	Dr.
(*b*) If there is a gain.	Liabilities Account To Realisation Account (Being gain on settlement is transferred to Realisation Account)	Dr.

(iii) When Cash received against sale of unrecorded assets (it is gain).	Cash/Bank Account To Realisation Account (Being sale of unrecorded assets)	Dr.
(iv) When cash paid against unrecorded liabilities (it is loss).	Realisation Account To Cash/Bank Account (Being payment to unrecorded liabilities)	Dr.

ILLUSTRATION 33.1

The following is the Balance Sheet of a firm as on 31st December 2005.

Liabilities		*Rs.*	*Assets*	*Rs.*
Sundry Creditors		8,000	Cash in hand	500
Bills Payable		2,000	Sundry Debtors	2,000
Bank Overdraft		1,500	Machinery	6,000
Capital Accounts			Stock	2,000
Ram:	10,000		Factory Premises	15,000
Shyam:	6,000	16,000	Profit & Loss Account	2,000
		27,500		27,500

The firm was dissolved on 31st December 2005. The assets were realised as follows:

Debtors Rs. 1,500; Machinery Rs, 3,000; Stock Rs, 1,200 and Factory Premises Rs, 10,000.

Bank overdraft and Bills Payable were paid in full. Creditors were settled in Rs 7,800. Realisation expenses amounted to Rs 200.

Pass journal entries and prepare ledger accounts to close the books of the firm assuming that the profit sharing ratio between Ram and Shyam is 3 : 2. *(B. Com., Madurai, Bombay, MS, Agra, Mysore,)*

SOLUTION

Journals Entries

			Dr.	Cr.
2005			*Rs*	*Rs*
Dec. 31	Realisation Account	Dr	25,000	
	To Sundry Debtors Account			2,000
	To Machinery Account			6,000
	To Stock Account			2,000
	To Factory Premises Account			15,000
	(Being various assets transferred to Realisation A/c)			
	Sundry Creditors Account	Dr.	8,000	
	Bills Payable Account	Dr.	2,000	
	Bank Overdraft Account	Dr.	1,500	
	To Realisation Account			11,500
	(Being various liabilities transferred to Realisation Account)			
	Cash Account	Dr.	15,700	
	To Realisation Account			15,700
	(Being amount realised on Debtors Rs, 1,500; Machinery Rs, 3,000. Stock Rs, 1,200 and Factory premises Rs, 10,000)			
	Realisation Account	Dr.	11,300	
	To Cash Account			11,300
	(Being Settlement, Creditors Rs, 7,800 and Bills Payable Rs 2,000 and Overdraft Rs, 1,500)			

Particulars		Dr. (Rs)	Cr. (Rs)
Realisation Account	Dr.	200	
To Cash Account			200
(Being expenses paid)			
Ram's Capital Account	Dr.	5,580	
Shyam's Capital Account	Dr.	3,720	
To Realisation Account			9,300
(Being realisation loss transferred to Capital Account)			
Ram's Capital Account	Dr.	1,200	
Shyam's Capital Account	Dr.	800	
To Profit & Loss Account			2,000
(Being loss transferred to Capital Account)			
Ram's Capital Account	Dr.	3,220	
Shyam's Capital Account	Dr.	1,480	
To Cash Account			4,700
(Being final settlement of partners account)			

Cash Account

Dr.			Cr.		
2005		Rs	2005		Rs
Dec. 31	To Balance b/d	500	Dec. 31	By Realisation Account	11,300
"	To Realisation A/c	15,700		(Payment of Liabilities)	
	(sale of assets)			By Realisation Account	200
				(Expenses paid)	
				By Ram's Capital Account	3,220
				(Final settlement)	
				By Shyam's Capital Account	1,480
				(Final settlement)	
		16,200			16,200

Realisation Accounts

Dr.			Cr.			
2005		Rs	2005			Rs
Dec. 31	To Sundry Debtors A/c	2,000	Dec. 31	By Sundry Creditors A/c		8,000
"	To Machinery A/c	6,000	"	By Bills Payable A/c		2,000
"	To Stock A/c	2,000	"	By Bank Overdraft A/c		1,500
"	To Factory Premises A/c	15,000	"	By Cash A/c (Assets realised)		15,700
"	To Cash A/c	11,300		Ram:	5,580	
	(Payment of liabilities)			Shyam:	3,720	9,300
"	To Cash A/c (Expenses paid)	200				
		36,500				36,500

Capital Accounts

Dr.		Ram	Shyam	Cr.		Ram	Shyam
2005		Rs	Rs	2005		Rs	Rs
Dec. 31	To Realisation A/c (Loss)	5,580	3,720	Dec. 31	By Balance b/d	10,000	6,000
"	To Profit and Loss A/c (Loss)	1,200	800				
"	To Cash A/c	3,220	1,480				
		10,000	6,000			10,000	6,000

ILLUSTRATION 33.2

A, B and C sharing profits in the ratio of 3 : 2 : 1, agreed upon dissolution of firm. A was appointed to realise the assets and pay off the liabilities for which he was entitled to a lump-sum amount of Rs 1,000. The Balance Sheet of the firm on 31st December 2005 was as under.

Liabilities		*Rs*	*Assets*		*Rs*
Capitals : A	50,000		Machinery		40,500
B:	20,000	70,000	Stock		7,500
Creditors		18,500	Investments		20,000
Investment Fluctuation Fund		6,000	Debtors	9,300	
			Less: Provision	600	8,700
			C's Capital A/c		11,500
			Cash		6,300
		94,500			94,500

The investments are taken over by A for Rs 18,000. B takes over all the stocks at Rs, 7,000 and debtors amounted to Rs 5,000 at Rs 4,500. Machinery is sold for Rs 55,000. The remaining debtors realise 50% of the book value.

Prepare necessary ledger account on completion of the dissolution of the firm. *(B. Com., Madurai)*

SOLUTION

Dr. **Realisation Account** Cr.

			Rs			*Rs*
2005				2005		
Dec. 31	To Machinery Account		40,500	Dec. 3	By Creditors A/c	18,500
"	To Stock Account		7,500	"	By Investment Fluctuation Fund A/c	6,000
"	To Investment Account		20,000	"	By Provision for Bad Debts A/c	600
"	To Debtors Account		9,300	"	By A's Capital Account	18,000
"	To A's Capital A/c (Expenses)		1,000	"	(Investment taken over)	
"	To Cash A/C (Creditors paid)		18,500	"	By B's Capital Account (Stock and part of Debtors taken over)	11,500
"	To Capital A/c (gain)			"	By Cash A/c (Machinery sold)	55,000
	A:	7,475		"	By Cash A/c (50% or remaining Debtors realised)	2,150
	B:	4,983				
	C:	2,492	14,950			
			1,11,750			1,11,750

Dr. **Partner's Account** Cr.

		A	B	C			A	B	C
		Rs	Rs	Rs			Rs	R	Rs
2005					2005				
Dec. 31	To Balance b/d	–	–	11,500	Dec. 31	By Balance c/d	50,000	20,000	–
"	To Realisation A/c (Assets take over)	18,000	11,500	–	"	By Realisation A/c (Expenses)	1,000	–	–
"	payment	40,475	13,483		"	By Realisation A/c (Gain)	7,475	4,983	2,492
					"	By Cash			9,008
		58,475	24,983	11,500			58,475	24, 983	11,500

Dr. **Cash Account** Cr.

		Rs			Rs
2005			2005		
Dec. 31	To Balance b/d	6,300	Dec. 31	By Realisation (Paid to Creditors)	18,500
"	To Realisation A/c (Machinery sold)	55,000	"	By A's Capital A/c	40,475
	To Realisation A/c (Debtors realised)	2,150	"	By B's Capital A/c	13,483
"	To C's Capital A/c	9,008			
		72,458			72,458

ILLUSTRATION 33.3

Chopra, Shah and Patel were carrying on business as manufacturers of sports goods. The profit-sharing ratio was 3 : 2 : 1 respectively. Their Balance Sheet on 30th June 2005 was as under.

Liabilities		Rs	*Assets*		Rs
Sundry Creditors		1,50,000	Plant and Machinery		1,60,000
Mrs. Chopra's Loan		1,30,000	Stock		1,50,000
Repairs and Renewals Reserve		12,000	Sundry Debtors	2,00,000	
Capital Accounts:			Less: Provision	10,000	1,90,000
Chopra	1,00,000		Prepaid Insurance		4,000
Shah	1,50,000		Investments		30,000
Patel	20,000	2,70,000	Cash		28,000
		5, 62, 000			5,62,000

On this date the firm was dissolved. The assets realised as under:

Plant and Machinery	Rs 1,00,000
Stock	Rs 1, 20,000
Sundry Debtors	Rs 1,60,000

The investments were taken over by Chopra at a value of Rs 20,000. He also agreed to pay Mrs Chopra's loan. During the course of realisation it was found that a bill for Rs 50,000 previously discounted by the firm was dishonored and had to be paid.

Expenses of realisation come to Rs 8,000.

Prepare Realisation Account, Partners' Capital Account and Cash Account. *(CAIIB)*

SOLUTION : *(B.Com Periyar, Utkal)*

Dr. **Realisation Account** Cr.

		Rs				Rs
2005						
June 30	To Plant and Machinery	1,60,000	June 30	By Sundry Creditors		1,50,000
"	To Stock	1,50,000	"	By Mrs. Chopra's Loan		1,30,000
"	To Sundry Debtors	2,00,000	"	By Repair & Renewals Reserve		12,000
"	To Prepaid Insurance	4,000		By Provision for Bad Debts		10,000
June 30	To Investments	30,000	June 30	By Cash Account (Assets Realised):		
"	To Chopra's Capital A/c (Mrs. Chopra's Loan)	1,30,000		Plant	1,00,000	
"	To Cash A/c: Dishonored Bill	50,000		Stock	1,20,000	
"	To Cash A/c (Sundry Creditors)	1,50,000		Debtors	1,60,000	3,80,000

"	To Cash Ac		"	By Chopra's Capital A/c	
"	To Cash A/c			(Investments)	20,000
	(Expenses)	8,000	"	By Capital Accounts (Loss)	
				Chopra: 90,000	
				Shah: 60,000	
				Patel : 30,000	1,80,000
		8,82,000			8,82,000

Dr. **Cash Account** Cr.

		Rs			Rs
2005			2005		
June 30	To Balance b/d	28,000	June 30	By Realisation A/c	
"	To Realisation A/c	3,80,000		(Dishonoured Bill)	50,000
"	To Patel's Capital A/c	10,000	"	By Realisation A/c	
				(Sundry Creditors)	1,50,000
			"	By Realisation A/c	
				(Expenses)	8,000
			"	By Chopra's Capital A/c	1,20,000
			"	By Shah's Capital A/c	90,000
		4,18,000			4,18,000

Dr. **Partner's Account** Cr.

		Chopra	Shaha	Patel			Chopra	Shah	Patel
		Rs	Rs	Rs			Rs	R	Rs
2005					2005				
June 30	To Realisation A/c				June 30	By Balance b/d	1,00,000	1,50,000	20,000
	(Investment)	20,000	–	–	"	By Realisation			
"	To Realisation A/c					(Mrs. Chopra's Loan)	1,30,000		–
	(Loss)	90,000	60,000	30,000	"	By Cash	–	–	10,000
"	To Cash A/c								
	(Final payment)	1,20,000	90,000	–					
		2,30,000	1,50,000	30,000			2,30,000	1,50,000	30,000

ILLUSTRATION 33.4

X, Y and Z sharing profits and losses in the proportion of 3 : 2 : 1 decided to dissolve partnership on 31st December 2005 on which date their Balance Sheet was as under.

Liabilities		*Rs*	*Assets*		*Rs*
Capital Accounts:			Goodwill		20,000
X	30,000		Leasehold Buildings		12,500
Y	10,000		Machinery		30,520
Z	10,000	50,000	Stock-up-trade		7,556
Bank Loan		11,500	Investments		6,330
Leasehold Redemption Fund		6,000	Joint Life Policy		12,000
Life Policy Fund		12,000	Sundry Debtors	5,800	
Sundry Creditors		16,206	Less: Provision	500	5,300
			Cash at Bank		1,500
		95,706			95,706

The Joint Life Policy is surrendered for Rs 10,000. The investments are taken over by Y for Rs. 8,000 and X agreed to discharge the Bank Loan. The remaining assets are sold for Rs 86,706. The expenses on realisation amount to Rs. 850.

Show the necessary ledger accounts including the final settlement of the partner's accounts.

(CAIIB) (B. Com., Bharathiar, Madras, Punjab)

SOLUTION

Dr. **Realisation Account** Cr.

			Rs			Rs
2005				2005		
Dec. 31	To Goodwill Account		20,000	Dec. 31	By Bad Debts Provision A/c	500
"	To Leasehold Buildings A/c		12,500	"	By Bank Loan A/c	11,500
"	To Machinery Account		30, 520	"	By Leasehold Redemption Fund A/c	6,000
"	To Stock-in-trade A/c		7,556			
"	To Investments A/c		6,330	"	By Life Policy Fund A/c	12,000
"	To Joint Life Policy A/c		12,000	"	By Sundry Creditors A/c	16,206
"	To Sundry Debtors A/c		5,800	"	By Bank A/c (Life Policy)	10,000
"	To X's Capital A/c (Bank Loan)		11,500	"	By Bank A/c (Assets realised)	86,706
"	To Bank A/c (Sundry Creditors)		16,206	"	By Y's Capital A/c (Investments)	8,000
"	To Bank A/c (Expenses)		850			
"	To Capital Accounts: (Profits)					
	X	13,825				
	Y	9,217				
	Z	4,608	27,650			
			1,50,912			1,50,912

Dr. **Bank Account** Cr.

		Rs			Rs
2005			2005		
Dec. 31	To Balance b/d	1,500	Dec. 31	By Realisation A/c (Creditors)	16,206
"	To Realisation A/c (Life Policy)	10.000	"	By Realisation A/c (Expenses)	850
"	Th Realisation A/c (Assets realised)	86,706	"	By X's Capital A/c	55,325
			"	By Y's Capital A/c	11,217
			"	By Z's Capital A/c	14,608
		98,206			98,206

Dr. **Partner's Capital Account** Cr.

		X	Y	Z			X	Y	Z
		Rs	Rs	Rs			Rs	R	Rs
2005					2005				
Dec. 31	To Realisation A/c (Investment take over)	–	8,000	–	Dec. 31	By Balance b/d	30,000	10,000	10,000
					"	By Realisation A/c (Bank Loan)	11,500	–	–
"	To Bank Account (Final Settlement)	55,325	11,217	14,608	"	By Realisation A/c (Profit)	13,825	9,217	4,608
		55,325	19,217	14,608			55,325	19,217	14,608

ILLUSTRATION 33.5

The following is the Balance Sheet of Sudhir and Ramesh as on 31st December 2005:

Liabilities		*Rs*	*Assets*		*Rs*
Sundry Creditors		76,000	Cash at Bank		23,000
Loan from Sudhir's wife		20,000	Stock-in-trade		12,000
Loan from Remesh		30,000	Sundry Debtors	40,000	
Reserve Fund		10,000	Less : Provision	2,000	38,000
Capital Account:			Furniture		8,000
Sudhir:	20,000		Plant		56,000
Ramesh	16,000	36,000	Investment		20,000
			Profit & Loss Account		15,000
		1,72,000			1,72,000

The firm was dissolved on 31st December 2005 following was the result:

(*i*) Sudhir took over investment at an agreed value of Rs, 16,000 and agreed to pay off the Loan to Sudhir's wife.

(*ii*) The assets realised as under:

		Rs
(*a*)	Stock	10,000
(*b*)	Debtors	37,000
(*c*)	Furniture	9,000
(*d*)	Plant	50,000
	Expenses were	2,200

(*iii*) The Sundry Creditors were paid off less 2.5% discount.

Sudhir and Ramesh share profits and losses in the ratio of 3:2.

Show Realisation Account, Partners' Capital Account and Cash Account.

Prepare Realisation Account, Partners' Capital Account and Cash Account. *(CAIIB)*

(M. Com., Calcutta, Mysore, Allahabad)

SOLUTION

Dr. **Realisation Account** Cr.

		Rs				*Rs*
2005			2005			
Dec. 31	To Stock-in-trade A/c	12,000	Dec. 31	By Sundry Creditors A/c		76,000
"	To sundry Debtors A/c	40,000	"	By Loan from Sudhir's Wife A/c		20,000
"	To Furniture A/c	8,000	"	By Bad Debt Reserve A/c		2,000
"	To Plant A/c	56,000	"	By Sudhir's Capital A/c		
"	To Investment A/c	20,000		(Investments)		16,000
"	To Sudhir's Capital A/c (Mrs. Sudhir's Loan)	20,000	"	By Bank A/c (Assets realised		1,06,000
				Stock	10,000	
"	To Bank A/c (Creditors)	74,100		Debtors	37,000	
"	To Bank A/c (Expenses)	2,200		Furniture	9,000	
				Plant	50,000)	
			"	By Capital Accounts: Loss)		
				Sudhir:	7,380	
				Ramesh:	4,920	12,300
		2,32,300				2,32,300

Ramesh Loan Account

Dr.					Cr.
2005			2005		
Dec. 31	To Bank Account	30,000	Dec. 31	BY balance b/d	30,000

Bank Account

Dr.		Rs		Cr.	Rs
2005			2005		
Dec. 31	To Balance b/d	23,000	Dec. 31	By Realisation A/c (Creditors)	74,100
"	To Realisation A/c (Assets realised)	1,06,000	"	By Ramesh Loan A/c	30,000
			"	By Realisation A/c (Expenses)	2,200
			"	By Sudhir's Capital A/c	13,620
			"	By Ramesh's Capital A/c	9,080
		1,29,000			1,29,000

Capital Account

Dr.		Sudhir	Ramesh		Cr.	Sudhir	Ramesh
		Rs	Rs			Rs	Rs
2005				2005			
Dec. 31	To Profit & Loss A/c	9,000	6,000	Dec. 31	By Balance b/d	20,000	16,000
"	To Realisation A/c (Investment taken over)	16,000	–	"	By Reserve Fund A/c	6,000	4,000
"	To Realisation A/c (Loss on realisation)	7,380	4,920	"	By Realisation A/c (Mrs. Sudhir's Loan)	20,000	–
"	To Bank A/c (Final settlement)	13,620	9,080				
		46,000	20,000			46,000	20,000

ILLUSTRATION 33.6

A, B and C were sharing profits in the ratio of 3 : 2 : 1.

They agreed to dissolve the partnership since the business was running under continuous loss. On that date their Balance Sheet stood as under:

BALANCE Sheet as on 31st Dec. 2005

Liabilities		*Rs*	*Assets*		*Rs*
Creditors		18,500	Machinery		40,500
Joint Life Policy Fund		14,000	Stock		7,550
Investment Fluctuation Fund		6,000	Investments		20,830
Mrs. A's Loan		10,000	Joint Life Policy		14,000
Capital Accounts:			Debtors	9,300	
A	40,000		Less : Provision	600	8,700
B	20,000	60,000	Cash at Bank		5,420
			C's Capital Account		11,500
		1,08,500			1,08,500

The life policy was surrendered for Rs, 12,000. The investment was taken over by A for Rs, 17,500. A agreed to discharge his wife's loan. B took over all the stock for Rs, 7,000. Debtors worth Rs, 5,000 were also taken over by A at Rs, 4,000. Machinery was sold for Rs, 55,000. The remaining debtors realised 50% of the book value. The expenses of realisation amounted to Rs 600. It was found that investment worth Rs 3,000 was not recorded in the books. The same was taken over by one of the creditors at this value.

Prepare the necessary ledger accounts and close the books of the firm.

(B.Com., Bangalore, Madurai; CA)

SOLUTION

Dr. **Realisation Account** Cr.

		Rs			Rs
2005			2005		
Dec. 31	To Machinery A/c	40,500	Dec. 31	By Creditors A/c	18,500
"	To Stock A/c	7,550	"	By Joint Life Policy Fund A/c	
14,000					
"	To Investments A/c	20,830	"	By Investment Fluctuation Fund A/c	6,000
"	To Joint Life Policy A/c	14,000	"	By Mrs. A's Loan A/c	10,000
"	To Debtors A/c	9,300	"	By Bad Debts Reserve A/c	600
"	To Bank A/c (Expenses)	600	"	By A's Capital A/c (Investment)	17,500
"	To Bank A/c (Creditors Rs 18,500 less Investment Rs 3,000)	15,500	"	By B's Capital A/c (Stock : Rs 7,000 and Debtors Rs 4,000	11,000
"	To A's Capital A/c (Wife's loan)	10,000	"	By Bank A/c (Assets realised: Machinery 55,000; Life Policy 12,000; Debtors 2,150)	69,150
"	To Capital Accounts: (Profit) A 14,235; B 9,490; C 4,745	28,470			
		1,46,750			1,46,750

Dr. **Bank Account** Cr.

		Rs			Rs
2005			2005		
Dec. 31	To Balance b/d	5,420	Dec. 31	By Realisation A/c (Expenses)	600
"	To Realisation A/c (Assets realised)	69,150	"	By Realisation A/c (Creditors)	15,500
"	To C's Capital A/c	6,755	"	By A's Capital A/c	46,735
			"	By B's Capital A/c	18,490
		81,325			81,325

Dr. **Capital Account** Cr.

		A	B	C			A	B	C
		Rs	Rs	Rs			Rs	R	Rs
2005					2005				
Dec. 31	To Balance b/d	–	–	11,500	Dec. 31	By Balance b/d	40,000	20,000	–
"	To Realisation A/c (Investment take over)	17,500	–	–	"	By Realisation A/c (Wife's Loan)	10,000	–	–
"	To Realisation A/c (Stock 7,000 Debtors 4,000	–	11,000		"	By Realisation A/c (Profit)	14,235	9,490	4,745
"	To Bank A/c (Final Settlement)	46,735	18,490	–	"	By Bank A/c	–	–	6,755
		64,235	29,490	11,500			64,235	29,490	11,500

ILLUSTRATION 33.7

Ramesh and Suresh are equal partners. They decide to dissolve the partnership on 31st December 2005 when their Balance Sheet was as follow:

Balance Sheet as on 31st December 2005

Liabilities		*Rs*	*Assets*	*Rs*
Creditors		1,200	Premises	30,000
Capital Account:			Plant	9,600
Ramesh	24,000		Debtors	2,880
Suresh	24,000	48,000	Stock	3,480
			Cash at Bank	3,240
		49,200		49,200

Ramesh is to take over the business and pay Rs 6,000 for goodwill, which had not been previously valued. He is also to take over the premises and stock at book values and plant at Rs. 9,000.

During the period up to 30th April 2006, they collect Rs 2,400 from the firm's debtors and pay and liabilities, getting Rs 120 for cash discount. He also pays for the cost of dissolution agreement amounting to Rs 240.

You are required to prepare the Realisation Account, Cash Account and Partners' Capital Accounts, showing the amount Ramesh pays to Suresh assuming the settlement was made on 30th April, 2006.

(B. Com., Punjab, Shivaji, Poona)

SOLUTION

Dr. **Realisation Account** Cr.

			Rs				Rs
2005				2005			
Dec. 31	To Premises A/c		30,000	Dec. 31	By Creditors A/c		1,200
"	To Plant A/c		9,600		By Ramesh's Capital: A/c		
"	To Debtors A/c		2,880		Goodwill	6,000	
"	To Stock A/c		3,480		Premises	30,000	
"	Cash at Bank A/c		3,240		Plant	9,000	
					Stock	3,480	
					Cash	3,240	51,720
2006				2006			
April 30	To Ramesh Capital A/c: (Creditors paid)		1,080	April 30	By Ramesh Capital A/c: (Debtors Collected)		2,400
"	To Ramesh Capital A/c: (Expenses)		240				
"	To Profit transferred to Capitals A/c :						
	Ramesh	2,400					
	Suresh	2,400	4,800				
			55,320				55,320

Dr. **Ramesh's Capital Account** Cr.

		Rs			Rs
2005			2005		
Dec. 31	To Realisation A/c (Assets take over)	51,720	Dec. 31	By Balance b/d	24,000
2006			2006		
April 30	To Realisation A/c (Debtors amount)	2,400	April 30	By Realisation A/c (Creditors paid)	1,080

			"	By Realisation A/c (Expenses)	240
			"	By Realisation A/c (Profit)	2,400
			"	By Cash A/c	26,400
		54,120			54,120

Dr. **Cash Account** Cr.

2006			2006		
April 30	To Ramesh's Capital	26,400	April 30	By Suresh's Capital	26,400

Dr. **Suresh's Capital Account** Cr.

		Rs			Rs
			2005		
			Dec. 31	By Balance b/d	24,000
2006			2006		
April 30	To Cash Account	26,400	April 30	By Realisation A/c (Profit)	2,400
		26,400			26,400

ILLUSTRATION 33.8

A, B and C carrying on business sharing profits and losses equally agreed to dissolve the partnership on 31st December 2005.

Balance Sheet of A, B and C on 31st December 2005

Liabilities		*Rs*	*Assets*	*Rs*
Capital Accounts:			Land and Buildings	50,000
A	40,000		Plant and Machinery	40,000
B	10,000		Furniture	10,000
C	50,000	1,00,000	Stock	35,000
Loan from X		30,000	Sundry Debtors	25,000
Sundry Creditors		45,000	Cash in hand	15,000
		1,75,000		1,75,000

X agreed to take the entire stock in full settlement of his loan. Sundry Debtors were realised at Rs 20,000 and Creditors were settled at Rs 34,000.

It was decided that A and B would take over the following assets at the following sums:

	Rs
Land and Building	60,000
Plant and Machinery	30,000
Furniture	6,000

A and B decided to form a partnership sharing profits and losses in the ratio of 3 : 1. It was agreed that the firm would require a total capital of Rs 1,00,000 which A and B would bring their capitals being in proportion to their profit sharing ratio.

Draw up the relevant accounts to close the books of A, B and C and prepare the opening Balance Sheet of A and B. *(ICWA)*

SOLUTION

Realisation Account

Dr.		Rs			Cr. Rs
2005			2005		
Dec. 31	To Land and Buildings A/c	50,000	Dec. 31	By Sundry Creditors A/c	45,000
"	To Plant and Machinery A/c	40,000	"	By Loan from X A/c	30,000
"	To Furniture A/c	10,000	"	By A & B Account	96,000
"	To Stock A/c	35,000		(assets taken over)	
"	To Sundry Debtors A/c	25,000	"	By Cash A/c (Debtors)	20,000
"	To Cash A/c	34,000	"	By Capital A/cs:	
				A 1,000	
				B 1,000	
				C 1,000	3,000
		1,94,000			1,94,000

Note: No further payment to X is required. The stock is taken in full satisfaction of the loan. So it does not appear in Realisation Account.

Capital Account

Dr.	A	B	C	Cr.	A	B	C
	Rs	Rs	Rs		Rs	R	Rs
To Realisation A/c (Loss)	1,000	1,000	1,000	By Balance b/d	40,000	10,000	50,000
To Cash A/c (settlement)			49,000	By Cash	36,000	16,000	–
To A & B's A/c	75,000	25,000	–				
	76,000	26,000	50,000		76,000	26,000	50,000

A and B Account

Dr.		Rs			Cr. Rs
2005			2005		
Dec. 31	To Realisation A/c	96,000	Dec. 31	By A's Capital A/c	75,000
	(Assets taken over)		"	By B's Capital A/c	25,000
"	To Cash A/c	4,000			
		1,00,000			1,00,000

Cash Account

Dr.		Rs			Cr. Rs
2005			2005		
Dec. 31	To Balance b/d	15,000	Dec. 31	By Realisation A/c	34,000
"	To Realisation A/c			(Creditors)	
	(Sundry Debtors)	20,000	"	By C's Capitral A/c	49,000
"	To A's Capital A/c	36,000		(Settlement)	
"	To B's Capital A/c	16,000	"	By A and B Firm A/c	4,000
		87,000			87,000

Balance Sheet of A and B as on 1st January 2006

Liabilities	*Rs*	*Assets*	*Rs*
A's Capital Account	75,000	Cash in hand	4,000
B's Capital Account	25,000	Furniture	6,000
		Plant and Machinery	30,000
		Land and Buildings	60,000
	1,00,000		1,00,000

ILLUSTRATION 33.9

Kalyan, Meena and Somu are three partners in a firm sharing profits and losses in the ratio of 5 : 4 : 3. On 31st March 2005, they decided to dissolve the firm when there state of affairs was as follow:

Liabilities		*Rs*	*Assets*	*Rs*
Sundry Creditors		10,860	Cash and Bank	710
Capital Accounts:			Investments	12,400
Kalyan	20,000		Debtors	7,950
Meena	9,000		Stock	9,240
Somu	73,030	1,02,030	Machinery	12,000
			Buildings	20,500
			Leaseholds	37,300
			Goodwill	12,790
		1,12,890		1,12,890

Kalyan agreed to take over the buildings at Rs 32,000 and Meena took over goodwill, stock and debtors at book values, leasholds, at Rs 29,250 and machinery at Rs 5,780. Meena also agreed to clear the creditors. Somu took the investments at the agreed value of Rs 11,500.

Pass necessary journal entires and show the Realisation Account, Partner's Capital Accounts and Bank Account. *(B. Com. Madurai)*

SOLUTION

Journal Entries

			Dr.	Cr.
2005			Rs	Rs
March 31	Realisation A/c	Dr.	1,12,180	
	To Investments A/c			12,400
	To Debtors A/c			7,950
	To Stock A/c			9,240
	To Machinery A/c			12,000
	To Buildings A/c			20,500
	To Leaseholds A/c			37,300
	To Goodwill A/c			12,790
	(Being the Assets transferred to the Realisation A/c at their books values)			
"	Sundry Creditors A/c	Dr.	10,860	
	To Realisation A/c			10,860
	(Being the liability transferred to Realisation A/c)			
"	Kalyan Capital A/c	Dr.	32,000	
	To Realisation A/c			32,000
	(Being the building taken over by Kalyan)			

Date	Particulars		L.F.	Dr. Rs	Cr. Rs
"	Meena Capital A/c	Dr.		65,010	
	To Realisation A/c				65,010
	(Being the various assets taken over by Meena i.e. Goodwill Rs 12,790, Stock Rs 9,240, Debtors Rs 7, 950, Leasehold Rs 29,250, Machinery Rs 5,780)				
"	Realisation A/c	Dr		10,860	
	To Meena Capital A/c				10,860
	(Being payment made to creditors by Meena)				
"	Somu Capital A/c	Dr		11,500	
	To Realisation A/c				11,500
	(Being the Investment taken over by Somu)				
"	Kalyan Capital A/c	Dr.		1,529	
	Meena Capital A/c	Dr.		1,223	
	Somu Capital A/c	Dr.		918	
	To Realisation A/c				3,670
	(Being Realisation Loss transferred to Partners' Capital A/c in the profit sharing ratio)				
"	Bank A/c	Dr.		59,902	
	To Kalyan Capital A/c				13,529
	To Meena Capital A/c				46,373
	(Being the amount brought by Kalyan and Meena)				
"	Somu capital A/c	Dr.		60,612	
	To Bank A/c				60,612
	(Being the amount paid to Somu and final settlement)				

Dr. **Realisation Account** Cr.

		Rs				Rs
2005			2005			
March 31	To Investments A/c	12,400	March 31	By Sundry Creditors A/c		10,860
"	To Debtors A/c	7,950	"	By Kalyan's Capital A/c		
"	To Stock A/c	9,240		(Buildings)		32,000
"	To Machinery A/c	12,000	"	By Meena's Capital A/c :		65,010
"	To Buildings A/c	20,500		(Goodwill	12,790	
"	To Leasehold A/c	37,300		Stock	9,240	
"	To Goodwill A/c	12,790		Debtors	7,950	
"	To Meena's Capital A/c	10,860		Leasehold	29,250	
	(Creditors)			Machinery	5,780	
			"	By Somu's Capital A/c		
				(Investments)		11,500
			"	By Capital Accounts: (Loss)		
				Kalyan	1,529	
				Meena	1,223	
				Somu	918	3,670
		1,23,040				1,23,040

Bank Account

Dr.		Rs			Cr. Rs
2005			2005		
March 31	To Balance b/d	710	March 31	By Somu's Capital (Final settlement)	60,612
"	To Kalyan's Capital (Cash brought)	13,529			
"	To Meena's Capital (Cash brought)	46,373			
		60,612			60,612

Capital Account

Dr.		Kalyan	Meena	Somu			Kalyan	Meena	Somu Cr.
		Rs	Rs	Rs			Rs	R	Rs
2005					2005				
Mar. 31	To Realisation A/c	32,000	65,010	11,500	Mar. 31	By Balance b/d	20,000	9,000	73,030
"	To Realisation A/c	1,529	1,223	918	"	By Realisation A/c	–	10,860	–
"	To Bank A/c	–	–	60,612	"	By Bank A/c	13,529	46,373	–
		33,529	66,233	73,030			33,529	66,233	73,030

ILLUSTRATION 33.10

The following was the Balance Sheet of A and B as on 31st December 2005:

Liabilities	*Rs*	*Assets*		*Rs*
Sundry Creditors	38,000	Cash at Bank		11,500
Mrs A's Loan	10,000	Stock-in-trade		6,000
B's Loan	15,000	Debtors	20,000	
Reserve Fund	5,000	Less: Provision	1,000	19,000
Capitals : A	10,000	Fixtures and Fittings		4,000
B	8,000	Plant and Machinery		28,000
		Investments		10,000
		Profit & Loss A/c		7,500
	86,000			86,000

The firm was dissolved on 31st December 2005 and the following was the result:

(1) A took over the investment at an agreed value of Rs 8,000. He also agreed to pay off the loan to Mrs. A.

(2) The assets realised as follows:

Stock Rs 5,000

Debtors Rs 18,500

Fixtures and Fittings Rs 4,500

Plant and Machinery Rs 25,000

(3) The expenses were Rs 1,100

(4) The sundry creditors were paid off less 2.5% discount.

A and B shared profits and losses in the ratio of 3 : 2. Journalise the entries to be made on dissolution and prepare the ledger accounts. *(B. Com., Periyar, Madras, MK, Agra Manonmaniam, Jabalpur)*

SOLUTION

Journal Entries

Particulars		Dr. Rs	Cr. Rs
Realisation Accounts	Dr.	68,000	
To Sundry, Assets Accounts			68,000
(Transfer of various assets)			
Creditors Accounts	Dr.	38,000	
Provision Account	Dr.	1,000	
To Realisation Account			39,000
(Transfer of creditors and Provision A/c)			
A's Capital Account	Dr.	8,000	
To Realisation Account			8,000
(Investments taken over by A)			
Bank Account	Dr.	53,000	
To Realisation Account			53,000
(Various assets sold: Rs, 5,000+18,500+4,500 + 25,000)			
Realisation Account	Dr.	37,050	
To Bank Account			37,050
(Creditors paid off at 2.5% discount)			
Realisation account	Dr.	1,100	
To Bank Account			1,100
(Payment of expenses on dissolution)			
A's Capital Account	Dr.	3,690	
B's Capital Account	Dr.	2,460	
To Realisation Account			6,150
(Loss on realisation transferred)			
Mrs. A's Loan Account	Dr.	10,000	
To A's Capital Account			10,000
(Loan transferred)			
B's Loan Account	Dr.	15,000	
To Bank Account			15,000
(Loan paid off)			
Reserve Fund Account	Dr.	5,000	
To A's Capital Account			3,000
To B's Capital Account			2,000
(Reserve Fund closed)			
A's Capital Account	Dr.	4,500	
B's Capital Account	Dr.	3,000	
To Profit and Loss Account			7,500
(Past Loss transferred)			
A's Capital Account	Dr.	6,810	
B's Capital Account	Dr.	4,540	
To Bank Account			11,350
(Final settlement of capital account)			

Dr. **Realisation Account** Cr.

	Rs			Rs
To Sundry Assets Account	68,000	By Creditors A/c		38,000
(Rs 6,000 + 20,000 + 4, 000 +		By Provision A/c (Doubtful debt)		1,000
28,000 + 10.000)		By A's Capital A/c (Investment)		8,000
To Bank A/c (Creditors)	37,050	By Bank A/c		53,000
To Bank A/c (Exports)	1,100	(Rs 5,000 + 18,5000 +		
		45000 + 25000)		
		By Capital A/c (Loss)		
		A:	3,690	
		B:	2,460	6,150
	1,06,150			1,06,150

Dr. **Capital Account** Cr.

	A	B		A	B
	Rs	Rs		Rs	Rs
To Profit & Loss A/c	4,500	3,000	By Balance b/d	10,000	8,000
To Realisation A/c	8,000	–	By Mrs A's Loan A/c	10,000	–
(Investment)			By Reserve Fund A/c	3,000	2,000
To Realisation A/c (Loss)	3,690	2,460			
To Bank A/c	6,810	4,540			
(Final Settlement)					
	23,000	10,000		23,000	10,000

Dr. **Bank Account** Cr.

	Rs		Rs
To Balance b/d	11,500	By B's Loan A/c	15,000
To Realisation A/c	53,000	By Realisation A/c	37,050
(Assets sold A/c)		(Creditors, paid off)	
		By Realisation A/c (Expenses)	1,100
		By A's Capital A/c	6,810
		By B's Capital A/c	4,540
	64,500		64,500

INSOLVENCY OF A PARTNER

The Capital Account of a partner may show a debit balance because of excess drawals or losses on account of realisation or some other reasons. Such a debit balance is called Capital Deficiency. If the Capital Account of a partner shows a debit balance as a result or various entries passed on account of dissolution of the firm, it is expected that he will pay the money from his estate. If this is done, the other partners will be able to get in full what is due to them. If the partner is solvent, he will have to make good such capital deficiency by bringing cash. But if the partner is unable, he may not be able to pay off even his own private liabilities. In some cases, after paying the private liabilities, a small sum which is lesser than the amount due to the firm, may be given by the partner, whose capital account shows a debit balance. When a partner is insolvent, then such a capital deficiency will be a loss to other solvent partners. For example, if there are two partners in a firm and if one of them is insolvent, then the capital deficiency will be borne by the other partner, who is solvent. But, when there are more than 2 partners, there arise problems as to the ratio in which the capital deficiency be borne by the remaining partners. In such a case, the deficiency shown by the insolvent partner's capital account should be divided among the solvent partners in the ratio which has already been agreed upon by them for the purpose. Prior to the decision in the leading case of Garner vs. Murray, this loss was borne by the solvent partners in the profit sharing ratio just like trading losses. No distinction was observed between trading loss and capital loss. The rule was laid down by Justice Joyce, in November 1903, in Garner vs, Murray.

Garner vs. Murray Decision

Garner, Murray and Wilkins were partners, in a firm, sharimg profits and losses equally. Their capitals were not equal. There was no partnership deed. The firm dissolved on 30th June 1900. The positon was as follows, after dissolution:

Balance Sheet as on 30th June 1900

	£		£
Garner Capital Account	2,500	Cash	1,916
Murray Capital Account	314	Wilkin's Capital	263
		Loss on Realisation	635
	2,814		2,814

Mr. Wilkins became insolvent and could not pay anything against the capital deficiency. When the loss on realisation is distributed, Garner Capital account would be reduced of £2,288 (£ 2,500 – 212), Murray's capital would be reduced to £ 102 (314–212) and Wilkins' capital deficiency would be increased to £ 474 (£ 263 + 211). Such a loss which is due to capital deficiency, prior to Garner vs. Murray decision, was to be borne by the solvent partners in profit sharing ratio. But, here, Murray had raised an objection and claimed that the loss is a capital loss and not a business loss. Therefore, such loss due to capital deficiency of a partner to be borne in capital ratio and not in profit sharing ratio. Murray got the decision in his favour. In Garner vs. Murray, a historic decision was given by Justice Joyce, upholding the contention of Murray i.e. capital deficiency of insolvent partner is a capital loss and is to be shared by the solvent partners, in capital ratio, just before dissolution.

Main Points of Garner vs. Murray Decision

1. Loss due to insolvency is a capital loss.
2. Such loss, due to insolvency, is to be shared by solvent partners in their capital ratio just before dissolution.
3. All solvent partners should bring in their share or realisation loss in cash.
4. If a partner's capital account shows a debit balance, he need not share the capital loss of the insolvent partner.

Application of Garner vs. Murray rule in India

The rule of Garner vs. Murray is applicable in India only if.

(*a*) There is no agreement to the contrary.

(*b*) The capitals of partners are not in profit sharing ratio.

(*c*) There must be capital deficiency in a partner's capital account.

If there is a provision in the partnership deed as to the ratio in which losses or gains including losses arising from capital deficiency of a partner shall be borne, then the solvent partners will bear the insolvent partner's deficiency in that ratio. In the absence of any such agreement, the adjustments shall be made according to the decision in Garner vs. Murray case. The amount left unsatisfied or unpaid by the insolvent partner has to be transferred to the capital accounts of the other partners in the ratio of their capitals just before the dissolution. As regards the cash to be brought in by the solvent partners, it is only a notional entry, actually no cash is brought. In India specially, there does not seem to be any need for the solvent partners bringing in cash equal to their share of the loss or realisation. But the main point decided in Garner vs. Murray that the loss is to be borne by the solvent partners in the ratio of their capitals just before the commencement of dissolution stands.

FIXED AND FLUCTUATING CAPITALS

If partners' Capitals are fixed, all adjustments regarding undistributed profits, interest on capitals, and drawings etc. are made in their respective Current Account. The following steps may be followed after the completion of Realisation Account, when dealing with the capital deficiency of insolvent partner:

1. Transfer any undistributed profits or losses, reserve etc. to the Current Account of the partners in profit sharing ratio.
2. Transfer the loss of Realisation to the Partners' Current Account in their profit sharing ratio.
3. The insolvent partner's Current Account should then be transferred to his Capital Account in order to find out the total amount due from him.
4. The insolvent partner's total capital deficiency should be distributed among the solvent partners' Capital Account in the ratio of their FIXED CAPITALS and should be debited to their respective Current Accounts.
5. The solvent partners' Current Account should then be closed by transfer to their respective Capital Account. Then they are paid what is due to them from the firm.

Again, Fixed Capitals without any adjustments are taken as the last agreed Capital, to determine the ratio for the division of the capital deficiency among the solvent partners.

If partners' Capitals are fluctuating, then, their Capital Accounts undergo adjustments for drawings, undistributed profits or losses etc. to arrive at the ratio of the solvent partners' last agreed capitals. In brief, the following steps may be followed:

1. Transfer any undistributed profits or losses, reserves etc. to the Capital Accounts of the partners in profit sharing ratio.
2. Transfer the loss on realisation to the Partners' Capital Account in profit sharing ratio.
3. If the decision laid down in the case of Garner vs. Murray is followed, the solvent partners should be asked to contribute further cash to make up their share of loss on realisation.
4. The insolvent partner's total capital deficiency should then be distributed among the solvent partners in the ratio of their capitals. The loss on realisation debited to the Capital accounts in neutralised by the corresponding credit for cash brought in by them. Then partners are paid what is due to them for the firm.

ILLUSTRATION 33.11

A, B and C were in Partnership sharing profits and losses in the ratio 8 : 5 : 3 respectively. The Capital Accounts were fixed under the partnership agreement, and as the result of continuous losses, the firm resolved to dissolve the partnership. The Balance Sheet of the firm was as follow:

Balance Sheet as on 31St December 5005

		Rs			*Rs*
Capital Accounts:	A	10,000	Current Accounts:	A	4,390
	B	4,000		B	3,466
	C	2,000		C	3,040
Sudnry Creditors A/c		5,906	Plant A/c		2,100
Bank Loan A/c		11,000	Stock A/c		12,118
			Sundry Debtors A/c		7,144
			Cash A/c		648
		32,906			32,906

The firms' assets were realised as follows:

Plant	1,200
Stock	10,460
Debtors	7,110

C was adjudicated as insolvent and could contribute nothing towards his deficiency in the firm. You required to close the books of the firm in accordance with decision in Garner vs. Murray.

SOLUTION

Dr. **Realisation Account** Cr.

		Rs				Rs
2005			2005			
Dec. 31	To plant A/c	2,100	Dec. 31	By Sundry Creditors A/c		5,906
"	To Stock A/c	12,118	"	By Bank Loan A/c		11,000
"	To Sundry Debtors A/c	7,144	"	By Cash (Assets realised 1,200 + 10, 460 + 7, 110)		18,770
"	To Cash A/c (Payment to Creditors)	5,906	"	By Current Accounts: (Loss)		
"	To Cash A/c (Payment of Loan)	11,000		A	1,296	
				B	810	
				C	486	2,592
		38,268				38,268

Dr. **Cash Account** Cr.

		Rs			Rs
2005			2005		
Dec. 31	To Balance b/d	648	Dec. 31	By Realisation A/c (Payment to creditors)	5,906
"	To Realisation A/c (Assets realised)	18,770	"	By Realisation A/c (Bank Loan Cleared)	11,000
"	To A's Current A/c	1,296	"	By A's Capital A/c (Final Payment)	4,520
"	To B's Current A/c	810	"	By B's Capital A/c (Final Payment)	98
		21,524			21,524

Dr. **Capital Account** Cr.

		A	B	C			A	B	C
		Rs	Rs	Rs			Rs	R	Rs
2005					2005				
Dec. 31	To C's Current A/c	—	—	3,526	Dec. 31	By Balance b/d	10,000	4,000	2,000
"	To Current A/c	5,480	3,902	—	"	By A's Capital A/c (10/14)	—	—	1,090
"	To Cash A/c (Final (settlement)	4,520	98	—	"	By B's Capital A/c (4/14)	—	—	436
		10,000	4,000	3,526			10,000	4,000	3,526

Note: When separate Current Accounts are maintained, Fixed Capital System is followed. Therefore, the deficiency of the insolvent partner C is borne by A and B in the ratio of their Fixed Capital i.e. 10:4.

Dr. **Current Account** Cr.

		A	B	C			A	B	C
		Rs	Rs	Rs	2005		Rs	R	Rs
2005									
Dec. 31	To Balance b/d	4,390	3,466	2,040	Dec. 31	By C's Capital A/c	–	–	3,526
"	To Realisation A/c (Loss	1,296	810	486	"	By Cash A/c (Loss brought in)	1,296	810	–
"	To C's Capital A/c (Deficiency met) in 10 : 4 ratio)	1,090	436		"	By Capital A/c (Transfer)	5,480	3,902	–
		6,776	4,712	3526			6,776	4,712	3526

ILLUSTRATION 33.12

A, B and C were partners sharing profits and losses in the ratio of 3 : 2: 1. On 31st December their Balance Sheet was as follows:

Liabilities		*Rs*	*Assets*		*Rs*
Sundry Creditors		30,000	Cash at Bank		9,500
Bills Payable		5,000	Stock		15,500
A's Loan A/c		6,000	Sundry Debtors		32,000
Reserve Fund		12,000	Furniture		5,000
Profit and Loss A/c		6,000	Plant		21,000
Capital Account:			Drawing Account:		
A	20,000		A	4,000	
B	15,000	35,000	B	1,000	5,000
			C's Capital Account		6,000
		94,000			94,000

The assets reaslied as follows:

	Rs
Stock	12,200
Sundry Debtors	30,100
Furniture	4,200

Plant is taken over by A at Rs 18,000. A contingent liability for Bill Receivable discounted materialised to the extent of Rs 600. Realisation expenses amounted to Rs 600. C is insolvent but his estate pays Rs 1,900. Prepare necessary accounts to close the books assumes that the capitals are fluctuating.

(B.Com., Madurai, Madras, Allahabad, Mysore)

SOLUTION

Realisation Account

		Rs				Rs
2005			2005			
Dec. 31	To Stock A/c	15,500	Dec. 31	By Sundry Creditors A/c		30,000
"	To Sundry Debtors A/c	32,000	"	By Bills Payable A/c		5,000
"	To Furniture A/c	5,000	"	By Bank A/c (Assets realised: (12,200 + 30,100 + 4,200)		46,500
"	To Plant A/c	21,000				
"	To Contingent Liability A/c (Bills Discounted)	600	"	By A's Capital A/c (Plant taken over)		18,000
"	To Bank A/c (Payment to Creditors)	30,000	"	By Capital Accounts:		
"	To Bank A/c (Bills Payable)	5,000		A (3/6):	5,100	
"	To Bank A/c (Expenses)	600		B (2/6):	3,400	
				C (1/6):	1,700	10,200
		1,09,700				1,09,700

Bank Account

Dr.		Rs			Cr. Rs
2005			2005		
Dec. 31	To Balance b/d	9,500	Dec. 31	By Realisation A/c (Contingent Liability)	600
"	To Realisation A/c (Assets realised)	46,500	"	By Realisation A/c (Payment to Creditors)	30,000
"	To C's Capital A/c	1,900	"	By Realisation A/c (Bills Payable)	5,000
"	To A's Capital A/c	5,100	"	By Realisation A/c (Expenses)	600
"	To B's Capital A/c	3,400	"	By A's Loan A/c	6,000
			"	By A's Capital A/c (Final settlement)	5,444
			"	By B's Capital A/c (Final settlement)	18,756
		66,400			66,400

Capital Accounts

Dr.		A	B	C			A	B	Cr. C
2005		Rs	Rs	Rs	2005		Rs	Rs	Rs
Dec. 31	To Balance b/d	–	–	6,000	Dec. 31	By Balance b/d	20,000	15,000	–
"	To Drawings A/c	4,000	1,000	–	"	By Reserve Fund A/c	6,000	4,000	2,000
"	To Realisation A/c (Plant taken over)	18,000	–	–	"	By Profit & Loss A/c	3,000	2,000	1,000
	To Realisation (Loss)	5,100	3,400	1,700		By Bank A/c (Realisation loss brought in)	5,100	3,400	–
	To C's Capital A/c (Deficiency)	1,556	1,244	–		By Bank A/c	–	–	1,900
	To Bank A/c (Final settlement)	5,444	18,756	–		By A's Capital A/c (5/9 of C's deficiency)	–	–	1,556
						By B's Capital A/c (4/9 of C's deficiency)	–	–	1,244
		34,100	24,400	7,700			34,100	24,400	7,700

Workings:

Deficiency of C is met by A and B in the following ratios, before the date of dissolution.

	A Rs	B Rs
Balance as per Balance Sheet	20,000	15,000
Plus: Reserve Fund	6,000	4,000
Plus: Profit and Loss	3,000	2,000
	29,000	21,000
Less: Drawings	4,000	1,000
	25,000	20,000

The ratio is 25,000 : 20,000 or 5 : 4

The deficiency of C comes to Rs 2,800 which is met by A and B in the ratio of 5 : 4 : Rs 1,556, Rs 1,244.

ILLUSTRATION 33.13

Ajay, Vijay, Ram and Shyam are partners in a firm sharing profits and losses in the ratio 4 : 1 : 2 : 3. The following is their Balance Sheet as on 31st March, 2005:

Liabilities		*Rs*	*Assets*		*Rs*
Sundry Creditors		3,00,000	Sundry Debtors	3,50,000	
Capital A/cs:	Rs		*Less*: Doubtful Debts	50,000	
Ajay	7,00,000				3,00,000
Shyam	3,00,000		Cash in hand		1,40,000
		10,00,000	Stocks		2,00,000
			Other Assets		3,10,000
			Capital A/cs:		
			Vijay		2,00,000
			Ram		1,50,000
		13,00,000			13,00,000

On 31st March, 2005 the firm is dissolved and the following points are agreed upon:

Ajay is to take over sundry debtors at 80% of book value

Shyam is to take over the stocks at 95% of the value and

Ram is to discharge sundry creditors

Other assets realise Rs.3,00,000 and the expenses of realisation come to Rs. 30,000

Vijay is found insolvent and Rs. 21,900 is realised from his estate.

Prepare Realisation Account and Capital Accounts of the partners. Show also the Cash A/c. The loss arising out of capital deficiency may be distributed following the decision in Garner vs. Murray *(C.A. Inter)*

SOLUTION

REALISATION ACCOUNT

	Rs.			*Rs*
To Sundry Debtors A/c	3,50,000	By Sundry Creditors A/c		3,00,000
To stock A/c	2,00,000	By Provision for Doubtful Debts A/c		50,000
To Other Assets A/c	3,10,000	By Ajay's Capital A/c (Debtors)		
To Ram's Capital A/c:		(80% of Rs. 3,50,000)		2,80,000
(Creditors)	3,00,000	By Shyam's Capital A/c (Stock)		
To Cash A/c (Expenses of Realisation)	30,000	(95% of Rs. 2,00,000)		1,90,000
		By Cash A/c (other assets)		3,00,000
		By Loss transferred to		
		Capital A/cs:	Rs	
		Ajay	28,000	
		Vijay	7,000	
		Ram	14,000	
		Shyam	21,000	
				70,000
	11,90,000			11,90,000

Capital Account

	Ajay Rs.	Vijay Rs.	Ram Rs.	Shyam Rs.		Ajay Rs.	Vijay Rs.	Ram Rs.	Shyam Rs.
To Balance b/f		2,00,000	1,50,000	–	By Balance b/f	7,00,000	–	–	3,00,000
To Realisation A/c (Debtors)	2,80,000				By Realisation A/c (Creditors)	–	–	3,00,000	
To Realisation A/c (Stock)	–	–	–	1,90,000	By Balance c/d	–	2,07,000		–
To Realisation A/c (Loss)	28,000	7,000	14,000	21,000					
To Balance c/d	3,92,000	–	1,36,000	89,000					
	7,00,000	2,07,000	3,00,000	3,00,000		7,00,000	2,07,000	3,00,000	3,00,000
To Balance b/d	–	2,07,000	–	–	By Balance b/d	3,92,000	–	1,36,000	89,000
To Vijay's A/c	1,29,570	–	–	55,530	By Cash A/c	–	21,900	–	–
To Cash A/c	2,62,430	–	1,36,000	33,470	By Ajay A/c	–	1,29,570	–	–
					By Shyam A/c	–	55,530	–	–
	3,92,000	2,07,000	1,36,000	89,000		3,92,000	2,07,000	1,36,000	89,000

Cash Account

	Rs.			Rs
To Balance b/f	1,40,000	By Realisation A/c (Expenses)		30,000
To Realisation A/c	3,00,000	By Capital A/cs:	Rs.	
To Vijay's Capital A/c	21,900	Ajay	2,62,430	
		Ram	1,36,000	
		Shyam	33,470	4,31,900
	4,61,900			4,61,900

Note: Vijay's deficiency will be borne by Ajay and Shyam in the ratio of 7 : 3 i.e. opening Capitals of Rs. 7,00,000 and Rs. 3,00,000. Ram will not bear any portion of the loss since at the time of dissolution he had a debit balance in his capital account.

1. 2,07,000 (–)
   21,900

   $1,85,100 \times \frac{7}{10}$ = Rs. 1,29,570

   $1,85,100 \times \frac{3}{10}$ - Rs. 55,530
2. Sundry Creditors have been directly transferred to Ram's Capital Account instead of transferring it through Realisation Account.

ILLUSTRATION 33.14 (Insolvency of more than one partner)

P, Q and R are partners sharing profits and losses as 5 : 3 : 2. The business is dissolved on 31st December 2005 when the Balance Sheet stands as below:

Liabilities		Rs	*Assets*	Rs
Capital Accounts:			Machinery	50,000
P	10,000		Motor Bike	10,000
Q	40,000		Stock	60,000
R	20,000	70,000	Debtors	45,000
Creditors		1,00,000	Cash at Bank	5,000
		1,70,000		1,70,000

Machinery and stock are sold for Rs 25,000 and Rs 18,000 respectively. Motor Bike is taken by Q for Rs 12,000. Debtors realise Rs 20,000.

According to Partnership deed, the deficiency of any partner in Capital Account is to be met by other partners in profit-loss sharing ratio.

P is insolvent and R can bring in Rs 5,000 only.

Prepare the accounts in the books of the firm. (*B.Com., Calcutta, Madurai, Jiwaji*)

SOLUTION

Realisation Account

Dr.		Rs			Cr. Rs
2005			2005		
Dec. 31	To Machinery A/c	50,000	Dec. 31	By Bank A/c : Assets realised (25,000 + 18,000 + 20,000)	63,000
"	To Motor Bike A/c	10,000	"	By Q's Capital A/c (Motor Bike)	12,000
"	To Stock A/c	60,000	"	By Capital Accounts: (Loss)	
"	To Debtors A/c	45,000		P 45,000	
				Q 27,000	
				R 18,000	90,000
		1,65,000			1,65,000

Bank Account

Dr.		Rs			Cr. Rs
2005			2005		
Dec. 31	To Balance b/d	5,000	Dec. 31	By Creditors A/c	1,00,000
"	To Realisation A/c (assets realised)	63,000			
"	To R's Capital A/c	5,000			
"	To Q's Capital A/c	27,000			
		1,00,000			1,00,000

Creditors Account

2005			2005		
Dec. 31	To Bank A/c	1,00,000	Dec. 31	By Balance b/d	1,00,000

Capital Accounts

Dr.		P Rs	Q Rs	R Rs			P Rs	Q Rs	Cr. R Rs
2005					2005				
Dec. 31	To Realisation A/c (Bike taken over)	–	12,000	–	Dec. 31	By Balance b/d	10,000	40,000	20,000
"	To Realisation A/c (loss)	45,000	27,000	18,000	"	By Capital A/c of Q and R (Deficiency)	35,000	–	–
"	To Capital A/c of P (Deficiency in 3 : 2)	–	21,000	14,000	"	By Bank A/c	–	–	5,000
"	To Capital A/c of R (Deficiency	–	7,000	–	"	By Capital A/c of Q (Deficiency)	–	–	7,000
					"	By Bank A/c	–	27,000	–
		45,000	67,000	32,000			45,000	67,000	32,000

Note: P is an insolvent and nothing can be contributed. Thus, P's deficiency of Rs 35,000 has been debited to Q and R in the ratio of 3 : 2. Again, R could give only Rs 5,000 and this results in deficiency of Rs 7,000. This amount has again been debited to Q's Account.

WHEN ALL PARTNERS ARE INSOLVENT

When the liabilities of a firm cannot be paid in full, then all the partners are said to be insolvent. If the partners of a firm are insolvent, obviously, creditors will have to bear the loss arising due to such event. That is, Creditors cannot be paid in full. The firm's liabilities would be more than the firm's assets and private assets of the partners, when all the partners of a firm become insolvent. The steps are:

1. Realisation Account is prepared in the same manner described above. The external liabilities and their payments are not recorded in it. Only assets should be transferred to the Realisation Account. Realisation loss is transferred to Capital Account.
2. The cash available in the firm and received from private estate of the partners is paid to Creditors, after meeting the realisation expenses, if any. The unpaid balance will be transferred to Deficiency Account.
3. Balance of Capital Accounts of all partners should be transferred to Deficiency Account. Thus the books will be closed.

ILLUSTRATION 33.15 (Insolvency of all the partners)

A and B were in equal partnership. Their Balance Sheet stood as under on 31st December 2005 when the firm was dissolved:

Liabilities	*Rs*	*Assets*	*Rs*
Creditors	3,200	Machinery	1,200
A's Capital	400	Furniture	300
		Debtors	500
		Stock	400
		Cash	180
		B's Drawings	1,020
	3,600		3,600

The assets realised as under:

	Rs		Rs
Machinery	600	Debtors	400
Furniture	100	Stock	300

The expenses of realisation amounted to Rs 140. A's private estate is not sufficient even to pay his private debts, whereas in B's private estate there is a surplus of Rs 140 only.

Give necessary accounts to close the books of the firm. (*B.Com., Calcutta*)

SOLUTION

Dr. **Realisation Account** Cr.

		Rs				Rs
2005			2005			
Dec. 31	To Machinery A/c	1,200	Dec. 31	By Cash A/c – Assets realised:		
"	To Furniture A/c	300		(600 + 400 + 100 + 300)		1,400
"	To Debtors A/c	500	"	By Capital Account Loss		
"	To Stock A/c	400		A	570	
"	To Cash A/c – Expenses	140		B	570	1,140
		2,540				2,540

Sundry Creditors

Dr.		Rs			Cr. Rs
2005			2005		
Dec. 31	To Cash A/c	1,580	Dec. 31	By Balance b/d	3,200
"	To Deficiency A/c (Transfer)	1,620			
		3,200			3,200

Deficiency Account

Dr.		Rs			Cr. Rs
2005			2005		
Dec. 31	To A's Capital A/c	170	Dec. 31	By Sundry Creditors A/c	1,620
"	To B's Capital A/c	1,450			
		1,620			1,620

Cash Account

Dr.		Rs			Cr. Rs
2005			2005		
Dec. 31	To Balance b/d A/c	180	Dec. 31	By Realisation A/c – Expenses	140
"	To Realisation A/c (Assets realised)	1,400	"	By Sundry Creditors A/c	1,580
"	To B's Capital A/c	140			
		1,720			1,720

Capital Accounts

Dr.		A	B			A	Cr. B
2005		Rs	Rs	2005		Rs	Rs
Dec. 31	To Balance b/d	–	1,020	Dec. 31	By Balance b/d	400	–
"	To Realisation A/c (Loss)	570	570	"	By Cash A/c	–	140
				"	By Deficiency A/c (Transfer)	170	1,450
		570	1,590			570	1,590

Note: Since all the partners are insolvent, the creditors cannot receive in full. Partners' capital deficiencies will therefore be borne by them. Cash in hand together with amount realised on sale of assets and surplus from private estate of B has been applied in making the payment to the creditors after meeting the realisation expenses. The balance of Creditors Account has been transferred to Deficiency Account. The balance of capital accounts have also been transferred to Deficiency Account to close the books.

Illustration: 33.16 (All Partners are insolvent)

The Balance Sheet of A, B and C, who are sharing profits and losses in the ratio of 2 : 2 : 1, was as follows on 31st March, 2005, the date of dissolution:

BALANCE SHEET OF A, B AND C

as on March 31,2005

Liabilities	*Rs*	*Assets*	*Rs*
Sundry Creditors	1,20,000	Cash	1,000
Bank Loan (with a charge on stock)	50,000	Stock	60,000
Capitals:		Other Assets	1,09,000
A	30,000	Goodwill	30,000

B	20,000	Capital:	
		C	20,000
	2,20,000		2,20,000

Stock realised Rs. 52,000 and other assets were sold for Rs. 90,000

Expenses of realisation amounted to Rs. 3,000

Assuming that all the partners are insolvent, prepare the necessary ledger accounts to close the books of the firm *(B.Com. MS. MK)*

SOLUTION

Realisation Account

	Rs	Rs		Rs	Rs
To Sundry Assets A/c :			By Cash (Other Assets)		90,000
Stock	60,000		By Cash A/c (Stock)		52,000
Other Assets	1,09,000		By Loss to Capital A/c		
Goodwill	30,000		A	24,000	
		1,99,000	B	24,000	
To Cash A/c (Realisation Expenses)		3,000	C	12,000	
					60,000
		2,02,000			2,02,000

Cash Accounts

Rs	Rs		Rs
To Balance b/d	1,000	By Realisation A/c (Expenses)	3,000
"Realisation A/c (Other Assets)	90,000	" Bank Loan A/c	50,000
"Realisation A/c (Stock)	52,000	" Sundry Creditors A/c	90,000
	1,43,000		1,43,000

Sundry Creditors Account

	Rs		Rs
To Cash A/c	90,000	By Balance b/d	1,20,000
"Deficiency A/c	30,000		
	1,20,000		1,20,000

Capital Accounts

	A Rs	B Rs	C Rs		A Rs	B Rs	C Rs
To balance b/d	—	—	20,000	By Balance b/d	30,000	20,000	—
"Realisation A/c	24,000	24,000	12,000	"Deficiency A/c	—	4,000	32,000
"Deficiency A/c	6,000	—	—				
	30,000	24,000	32,000		30,000	24,000	32,000

Deficiency Account

	Rs		Rs
To B's Capital A/c	4,000	By Sundry Creditors A/c	30,000
To C's Capital A/c	32,000	By A's Capital Account	6,000
	36,000		36,000

PIECE-MEAL DISTRIBUTION

It has so far been presumed that the assets are disposed of on the same day of dissolution and liabilities are also simultaneously discharged. But in actual practice, the sale of assets realise gradually unless the business is sold to a buyer (vendee). The dissolution process takes some time during which period assets are gradually realised. This is because assets are sold piece by piece and the realisation of assets will be slow and gradual. Similarly the liabilities are paid gradually depending upon amount realised from the sale of assets. Therefore, the final results are known only when all assets are completely realised and all liabilities are completely discharged.

On realisation of assets, the cash realised is distributed in the following order:

1. Payment of realisation expenses.
2. Payment to outside liabilities i.e. Creditors, Overdraft, Bills Payable, Outstanding expenses etc.
3. Payment of Partner's loans and advances.
4. Payment of Partners' balance in Capital Accounts.

After making payments to outside liabilities and partner's loan, the capitals of the partners are returned. Unless the profit or loss on realisation is known, the amount payable to partners cannot be ascertained. If it is so, it means that the partners should not be paid till the realisation is complete. This creates a problem. This is because the profit or loss on account of realisation is to be credited or debited to Partners' Capital Account. It is also necessary to see that all partners have been paid and the unpaid balance of each partner being a loss must be in the ratio of profit and loss sharing ratio. It is, therefore, necessary to find out a method by which the partners are paid, as and when cash is received, without waiting till the realisation of all assets and at the same time to ensure that no partner is paid in excess and amounts left unpaid are in profit and loss sharing ratios.

Basis of Distribution

When a firm decides to make distribution of cash as and when received, there arise a problem of determination of basis i.e. ratio in which the available cash is to be distributed, keeping share of loss to each partner in profit and loss sharing ratio. The capital contribution or balance in the Capital Account of the Partners may not be in their profit and loss sharing ratio. The ultimate realisation loss cannot be ascertained when the distribution of cash is made on the interim basis. In such case, when the Capital is not in profit and loss sharing ratio, whichever ratio is followed, the loss shared by the partners will not be in profit and loss sharing ratio. See Illustration 33.17.

ILLUSTRATION 33.17

A and B, are partners with Capital of Rs 5,000 and Rs 15,000 and share the profit and loss in the ratio of 2/3 and 1/3 respectively. The firm wound up and after paying off Creditors, the firm collected Rs 3,000 as first instalment and Rs 4,500 as second instalment and distributed the amount on the basis of profit and loss sharing ratio, then the distribution as follows:

	A	B
	Rs	Rs
Final Claims:	5,000	15,000

	A	B
First instalment of Rs 3,000 distributed in profit and loss sharing ratio: i.e. 2 : 1	2,000	1,000
Balance:	3,000	14,000
Second instalment of Rs 4,500 distributed in profit and loss sharing ratio: 2 : 1	3,000	1,500
Balance (being loss)	Nil	12,500

Here the loss is not in profit and loss sharing ratio. But the loss goes to B alone. The loss that they should bear should also be in 2 : 1 ratio. Therefore, this method is not suitable.

Suppose the distribution is made on the basis of the Capitals, then the distribution is as follows:

	A Rs	B Rs
Final Claims	5,000	15,000
First instalment of Rs 3,000 distributed in Capital ratio that is, 5 : 15 (or 1 : 3)	1,000	2,000
Balance:	4,000	13,000
Second instalment of Rs 4,500 distributed in Capital ratio that is, 5 : 15	1,125	3,375
Balance (being loss)	2,875	9,625

Here, the loss is not in profit and loss sharing ratio. But the loss suffered by A and B in the ratio of 23 : 77 (2,875 : 9,625) whereas the profit and loss sharing is 2 : 1. Therefore, this method is also not suitable.

Out of the available cash (as mentioned above), distribution of cash may be done in the following manner:

1. *First, outside liabilities* are to be paid
2. *Secondly, Partners Loans* or Advances are to be paid
3. *Thirdly and lastly, Partners' Capital* are to be paid

Now the question arises how the available cash to be distributed to the partners. The balance in the Capital Accounts of Partners may not be in profit sharing ratio. It is necessary to see that after making payments to partners, the unpaid balance of each partners, being a loss must be in Profit Sharing Ratio.

Therefore, if the Capitals of the Partners are not in profit sharing ratio, then in order to make the Partners' Loss on realisation in their profit and loss sharing ratio and to make equitable distribution of cash, on piece-meal basis, without affecting the interest of Partners, either of the following two methods can be adopted:

1. *Surplus capital Method (Proportionate Capital Method)*

(or) 2. *Maximum Possible Loss*

I. Surplus Capital Method (Proportionate Capital Method)

When the Capitals of the Partners are not in proportion to their profit and loss ratio, the partner who has contributed more than his proportionate share of capital is paid first, in priority to the other partners. For this purpose, the Surplus Capitals are to be found out on the basis of profit and loss sharing ratio. Thus, the initial payments are made in such a way that the capitals of all the partners are adjusted to their profit and loss sharing ratio. When this is done, the capitals will be in proportion to the profit and loss sharing ratio. The steps are detailed below:

1. Divide undistributed profit, if any, among the Partners, in profit and loss sharing ratio.
2. Pay off realisation expenses or make a provision for it.
3. Pay off outside liabilities. If the amount is insufficient, then apportion the amount in the ratio of their claims.
4. After paying off the outside liabilities, pay off Partners' Loans when more than two partners are there and available cash is insufficient, then apportion the amount in the ratio of their claims.
5. Now partners' capitals are to be refunded. Find out the amount payable to Partners whose capitals are relatively in excess of their profit and loss sharing ratios. When the excess amounts have been paid off, the ratio of remaining balances in the Capital Account and profit and loss sharing ratio are one and the same.

To find out the excess capital, the following steps are needed:

(*a*) Partners' actual capitals are divided with their respective ratio figures.

(*b*) Take the relatively lowest capital as the base and find out notionally adjusted capital.

(*c*) Find out the excess of capital by comparing actual capital and notional capitals.

(*d*) Repeat these above steps till the number thereof reduced to one partner.

(*e*) Then, start paying off from the last ultimate excess first, then preceding excess till all the excesses are paid off.

(*f*) The balance i.e. the unpaid capitals (or losses) will be in profit and loss sharing ratio. Generally the unpaid balance would be loss on realisation.

II. Maximum Possible Loss

Under this method, it is assumed that at every stage of realisation of assets, think that the remaining unrealised assets are worthless. Therefore, at every stage loss can be ascertained and this loss is distributed among the partners in profit and loss sharing ratio. The balance in the capital accounts and the cash available will be equal and the cash is paid. The steps are:

1. Pay off Creditors first and then partners' loan account if any, out of the realised amounts.
2. Now the capitals are there to be paid. Whenever any cash is received, find out the difference between the available cash and the balance in the capital accounts. This difference is maximum loss.
3. The Maximum Loss is distributed to Capital Accounts in profit and loss sharing ratio, that is from the Capital Account, the share of losses are deducted.
4. Now distribute the available cash among the partners according to their Capital Accounts as adjusted above. Here the cash available equals the sum of the partners' adjusted credit balance.
5. If any partners' capital shows a debit balance, write it off according to Garner vs. Murray ruling.

As and when further realisations are made and cash is to be distributed, the above procedure is to be followed, in all subsequent payments among the partners.

ILLUSTRATION 33.18

A, B and C are partners sharing profits and losses as 5 : 3 : 2. The following is their Balance Sheet as at December 31st 2004, when they dissolve the business:

Liabilities		*Rs*	*Assets*	*Rs*
Creditors		40,000	Premises	40,000
A's Loan A/c		10,000	Plant	30,000
Capital Accounts:			Stock	30,000
A	Rs 50,000		Debtors	60,000
B	Rs 15,000			
C	Rs 45,000	1,10,000		
		1,60,000		1,60,000

It was agreed to repay the amount due to the partners as and when the assets were realised, viz.

1st February 2005	Rs 30,000
1st April 2005	73,000
1st June 2005	47,000

Prepare the statement showing how the distribution should be made and write up the Cash Account and Partners' Capital Accounts. *(B.Com., Madurai; Punjab; Agra; MK)*

SOLUTION

We solve the problem in both the methods i.e. ***Surplus Capital Method and Maximum Possible Loss Method:***

(*a*) Surplus Capital Method

When the capitals of the partners are not in proportion to their profit and loss ratio, the partner who has contributed more than his proportionate share of capital is paid first, in priority to the other partners. After paying off the outside liabilities and Partner's Loan, the capitals are refunded to partners whose capitals are relatively in excess of their Profit and Loss sharing ratio. In this problem, the capitals are not in their profit sharing ratio. Therefore, the capitals of the partners which are in excess of the profit sharing ratios would be reduced by payment from time to time until the capitals of all the partners are brought on a level with their profit sharing ratio. To find out the surplus capital, we have to prepare a statement showing the cash distribution.

Statement showing surplus capital on the basis of profit sharing ratio

	A	B	C
1. Profit and Loss Ratio	5	3	2
2. Capitals as per Balance Sheet	Rs 50,000	Rs 15,000	Rs 45,000
3. Capitals are divided in Profit and Loss sharing ratio: Capital per unit of profit share (Step 2 divide by Step 1)	10,000	5,000	22,500
4. Proportionate Capitals or National Capitals, taking B's capital as the basis i.e. per unit of profit-share (Least figure is taken)	25,000 (5,000 × 5)	15,000 (5,000 × 3)	10,000 (5,000 × 2)
5. Surplus Capital (Step 2 minus Step 4)	25,000	–	35,000
6. Proportionate Capitals as between A and C, taking A's Capital as the basis i.e. Rs 5,000 per share of profit.	25,000 (5,000 × 5)		10,000 (5,000 × 2)
7. Final Surplus			25,000

Note: Priority of Cash distribution:

1. First pay off Creditors Rs 40,000 and A's Loan Rs 10,000
2. Next make refund of Capitals:

   (*a*) Pay Rs 25,000 to C (Ultimate Surplus)

(*b*) Pay Rs 25,000 to A and Rs 10,000 to C (Surplus)

(*c*) Then, cash is distributed to A, B and C in profit sharing ratio.

Statement showing Distribution of Cash

			Creditors	A's Loan	A	B	C
			Rs	Rs	Rs	Rs	Rs
2004							
Dec. 31	Balance as per Balance Sheet		40,000	10,000	50,000	15,000	45,000
2005							
Feb. 1	Realisation:	30,000					
	Paid to Creditors	30,000	30,000				
	Balance		10,000	10,000	50,000	15,000	45,000
2005							
April 1	Realisation	73,000					
	Paid to Creditors and Partner's Loan	20,000	10,000	10,000			
	Balance	53,000	–	–	50,000	15,000	45,000
	Paid to C	25,000			–	–	25,000
	Balance	28,000			50,000	15,000	20,000
	Paid to A and C in 5 : 2 ratio	28,000			20,000	–	8,000
	Balance	–			30,000	15,000	12,000
2005							
June 1	Realisation	47,000					
	Paid to A and C (Balance of surplus)	7,000			5,000		2,000
	Balance	40,000			25,000	15,000	10,000
	Paid to A, B and C in 5 : 3 : 2	40,000			20,000	12,000	8,000
	Balance, being loss				5,000	3,000	2,000

Dr. **Capital Accounts** Cr.

		A	B	C			A	B	C
		Rs	Rs	Rs			Rs	Rs	Rs
2005					2005				
April 1	To Cash A/c	–	–	25,000	Dec. 31	By Balance b/d	50,000	15,000	5,000
"	To Cash A/c	20,000	–	8,000					
June 1	To Cash A/c	5,000	–	2,000					
"	To Realisation A/c (loss)	5,000	3,000	2,000					
"	To Cash A/c	20,000	12,000	8,000					
		50,000	15,000	45,000			50,000	15,000	45,000

Cash Account

Dr. Cr.

		Rs			Rs
2005			2005		
Feb. 1	To Realisation A/c	30,000	Feb. 1	By Creditors A/c	30,000
April 1	To Realisation A/c	73,000	April 1	By Creditors A/c	10,000
June 1	To Realisation A/c	47,000	"	By A's Loan A/c	10,000
			"	By C's Capital A/c	25,000
			"	By A's Capital A/c	20,000
			"	By C's Capital A/c	8,000
			June 1	By A's Capital A/c	5,000
			"	By C's Capital A/c	2,000
			"	By A's Capital A/c	20,000
			"	By B's Capital A/c	12,000
			"	By C's Capital A/c	8,000
		1,50,000			1,50,000

(*b*) Maximum Possible Loss

It is assumed that at every stage of realisation of assets, the remaining unrealised assets are worthless. Therefore, at every stage, the loss can be ascertained and this loss is distributed among the partners in Profit and Loss sharing ratio. Then the balance in the capital accounts and the cash available will be equal and cash is paid.

ILLUSTRATION 33.19 (Illustration No. 33.18)

Statement showing Distribution of Cash

			Creditors	A's Loan	A	B	C
			Rs	Rs	Rs	Rs	Rs
2004							
Dec. 31	Balance as per Balance Sheet		40,000	10,000	50,000	15,000	45,000
2005							
Feb. 1	Realisation:	30,000					
	Paid to Creditors	30,000	30,000				
	Balance	–	10,000	10,000	50,000	15,000	45,000
2005							
April 1	Realisation	73,000					
	Paid to Creditors and Loan	20,000	10,000	10,000			
	Balance	53,000	–	–	50,000	15,000	45,000
	Cash available is only Rs 53,000, so the maximum loss is Rs 57,000 i.e. A	50,000					
	B	15,000					
	C	45,000					
		1,10,000					
	Less:	53,000					

Date	Particulars	Rs		A	B	C
	Rs 57,000 is allocated to A, B and C in profit sharing ratio	57,000		28,500	17,100	11,400
	Balance at Credit			21,500	–2,100	33,600
	B's deficiency allocated to A and C in their capital ratio i.e. 50 : 45			–1,105	+2,100	–995
	Balance i.e. distribution of Rs 53,000 (Now the credit balance shown in the Capital Accounts have been paid: the amount at credit is equal to the cash available)			20,395		32,605
	Balance being unpaid amount			29,605	15,000	12,395
2005 June 1	Realisation A/c Maximum Loss is Rs 10,000 i.e. 29,605 + 15,000 + 12,395 – 47,000 = 10,000, which is allocated in profit sharing ratio	47,000		5,000	3,000	2,000
	Balance at Credit and Cash paid Rs 47,000			24,605	12,000	10,395
	Balance, being loss			5,000	3,000	2,000

Cash Account

Dr.					Cr.
Date	Particulars	Rs	Date	Particulars	Rs
2005			2005		
Feb. 1	To Realisation A/c	30,000	Feb. 1	By Creditors A/c	30,000
April 1	To Realisation A/c	73,000	April 1	By Creditors A/c	10,000
June 1	To Realisation A/c	47,000	"	By A's Loan A/c	10,000
			"	By A's Capital A/c	20,395
			"	By C's Capital A/c	32,605
			June 1	By A's Capital A/c	24,605
			"	By B's Capital A/c	12,000
			"	By C's Capital A/c	10,395
		1,50,000			1,50,000

Capital Accounts

Dr.									Cr.
		A	B	C			A	B	C
		Rs	Rs	Rs			Rs	Rs	Rs
2005					2005				
April 1	To Cash A/c	20,395	–	32,605	Dec. 31	By Balance b/d	50,000	15,000	45,000

Date	Particulars	A	B	C	Date	Particulars	A	B	C
June 1	To Realisation A/c (loss)	5,000	3,000	2,000					
"	To Cash A/c	24,605	12,000	10,395					
		50,000	15,000	45,000			50,000	15,000	45,000

ILLUSTRATION 33.20 (Surplus Capital Method)

A, B and C trade in partnership sharing profits and losses in the ratio of 3 : 2 : 1.

They decide to dissolve the firm with effect from 1st January 2005 when the firm's Balance Sheet stood as follows:

Liabilities		*Rs*	*Assets*	*Rs*
Capitals: A	54,000		Land and Buildings	80,000
B	40,000		Furniture and Fittings	12,000
C	25,000	1,19,000	Plant and Machinery	30,000
General Reserve		6,000	Stock-in-trade	18,000
Sundry Creditors		90,000	Sundry Debtors	60,000
Bank Overdraft		30,000	Investments	35,000
			Cash and Bank Balance	10,000
		2,45,000		2,45,000

The assets are being realised gradually. After meeting the expenses of realisation, the first instalment of realisation including cash and bank balance fetches Rs 75,000; the second Rs 32,000, the third Rs 60,000 and the fourth Rs 63,000.

If distribution amongst partners is to be made after each instalment of realisation, as far as possible, prepare a statement showing the distribution to partners at each instalment although the final results were not yet known.

(*B.Com., Calcutta; Madurai*)

SOLUTION

Statement showing Surplus Capital on the basis of Profit Sharing Ratio

	A Rs	B Rs	C Rs
1. Profit and Loss Ratio	3	2	1
2. Capitals as per Balance Sheet Add: General Reserve (3 : 2 : 1)	54,000 3,000	40,000 2,000	25,000 1,000
3. Final Capitals	57,000	42,000	26,000
4. Capitals are divided with Profit and Loss Sharing ratio: capital per unit of profit share.	19,000 (57,000 ÷ 3)	21,000 (42,000 ÷ 2)	26,000 (26,000 ÷ 1)
5. Proportionate capitals or Notional Capitals, taking A's Capital as the basis i.e. per unit of profit-share. (Least figure is taken)	57,000 (19,000 × 3)	38,000 (19,000 × 2)	19,000 (19,000 × 1)
6. Surplus Capital (3 – 5)	–	4,000	7,000
7. Proportionate capitals as between B and C, taking B as the basis i.e. Rs 2,000 per share of profit	–	4,000 (2,000 × 2)	2,000 (2,000 × 1)
8. Final Surplus	–	–	5,000

Statement showing Distribution of Cash

			Creditors	Bank Overdraft	Capitals A	B	C
		Rs	Rs	Rs	Rs	Rs	Rs
2005							
Jan. 1	Amount due:		90,000	30,000	57,000	42,000	26,000
	I Realisation A/c :	75,000					
	Paid to Creditors and Bank in 9 : 3 ratios.	75,000	56,250	18,750			
	Balance Due		33,750	11,250	57,000	42,000	26,000
	II Realisation A/c	32,000					
	Paid to Creditors and Bank in 9 : 3	32,000	24,000	8,000			
	Balance Due		9,750	3,250	57,000	42,000	26,000
	III Realisation A/c	60,000					
	Paid to Creditors and Bank	13,000	9,750	3,250			
	Balance	47,000					
	Paid to C Final Surplus	5,000					5,000
	Balance	42,000					
	Paid to B and C Surplus	6,000				4,000	2,000
	Balance	36,000					
	Paid to A, B and C in 3 : 2 : 1	36,000			18,000	12,000	6,000
	Balance Due				39,000	26,000	13,000
	IV Realisation A/c	63,000					
	Paid to A, B and C in 3 : 2 : 1	63,000			31,500	21,000	10,500
	Unpaid Balance (Loss)				7,500	5,000	2,500

Priority of distribution

1. First day off to the Creditors and Bank Overdraft, totalling Rs 1,20,000.
2. Then surplus of Rs 5,000 to C.
3. Then surplus of Rs 4,000 to B and Rs 2,000 to C.
4. Then available amount is distributed in profit sharing ratios.
5. Ultimately, the final unpaid balance is losses to partners and as in profit and loss sharing ratios.

ILLUSTRATION 33.21

A, B and C were in partnership sharing profits and losses in the proportion of 1/2, 1/3 and 1/6 respectively. The Partnership firm was dissolved on 30th September 2005 when the position was as given below:

Liabilities		*Rs*	*Assets*	*Rs*
Sundry Creditors		3,15,000	Cash in hand and at Bank	42,000
Capital Accounts:			Stock-in-trade	1,68,000
A	2,10,000		Sundry Debtors	4,41,000
B	1,05,000			
C	21,000	3,36,000		
		6,51,000		6,51,000

The Partners desired that the net realisation should be distributed according to rules at the end of each month. The realisations and expenes were as under:

	Expenses	Stock & Debtors
	Rs	Rs
31.10.2005	10,500	1,26,000
30.11.2005	8,400	1,89,000
31.12.2005	7,350	1,05,000
31.1.2006	5,250	1,15,000
28.2.2006	5,250	53,250

Set out the Cash Account and Capital Accounts showing monthly distribution of cash realised.

(*B.Com., Calcutta*)

SOLUTION

Net Realisation

31.20.2005 : Rs 1,26,000	–	10,500	=	1,15,500
30.11.2005 : Rs 1,89,000	–	8,400	=	1,80,600
31.12.2005 : Rs 1,05,000	–	7,350	=	97,650
31.1.2006 : Rs 1,15,000	–	5,250	=	1,09,750
31.2.2006 : Rs 53,250	–	5,250	=	48,000

Statement showing Distribution of Cash (Maximum Loss Method)

			Creditors	Capitals		
				A	B	C
			Rs	Rs	Rs	Rs
2005						
Sept. 30	Balance as per Balance Sheet		3,15,000	2,10,000	1,05,000	21,000
	Cash in hand	42,000				
	Paid to Creditors	42,000	42,000			
	Balance Due		2,73,000	2,10,000	1,05,000	21,000
Nov. 30	Net Realisation:	1,15,500				
	Paid to Creditors	1,15,500	1,15,500			
	Balance Due		1,57,500	2,10,000	1,05,000	21,000
Nov. 30	Realisation:	1,80,600				
	Paid to Creditors	1,57,500	1,57,500			
	Surplus	23,100				
	Maximum Possible Loss:					
	Net Capital claims:	3,36,000				
	Less: Cash available	23,100				
	Divided in the ratio of 3 : 2 : 1	3,12,900		1,56,450	1,04,300	52,150
	C's Deficiency allocated to A and B			53,550	700	–31,150
	in the Capital ratio i.e. 2 : 1					
				–20,767	10,383	+31,150
				32,783	–9,683	–
	B's Deficiency allocated to A			–9,683	+ 9,683	
	Cash paid			23,100		
Dec. 31	Balance Due			1,86,900	1,05,000	21,000
	Net Realisation	97,650				

	Maximum possible Loss (1,86,900 + 1,05,000 + 21,000 – 97,650) 2,15,250 allocated in 3 : 2 : 1	2,15,250	1,07,625	71,750	35,875
			79,275	33,250	–14,875
	C's Deficiency allocated to A and B in 2 : 1		–9,917	–4,958	+14,875
	Cash paid		69,358	28,292	–
2006					
Jan. 31	Balance Due		1,17,542	76,708	21,000
	Net Realisation	1,09,750			
	Maximum Possible Loss (2,15,250 – 1,09,750)	1,05,500	52,750	35,167	17,583
	Cash paid		64,792	41,541	3,417
Feb. 28	Balance Due		52,750	35,167	17,583
	Net Realisation	48,000			
	Maximum Possible Loss (1,05,500 – 57,500)	57,500	28,750	19,167	9,583
	Cash paid		24,000	16,000	8,000
	Thus loss on realisation		28,750	19,167	9,583

Dr. **Cash Account** Cr.

Date	Particulars	Rs	Date	Particulars	Rs
2005			2005		
Sept. 30	To Balance b/d	42,000	Sept. 30	By Sundry Creditors	42,000
Oct. 31	To Realisation A/c	1,26,000	Oct. 31	By Expenses A/c	10,500
			"	By Sundry Creditors	1,15,500
		1,26,000			1,26,000
Nov. 30	To Realisation A/c	1,89,000	Nov. 30	By Expenses A/c	8,400
			"	By Sundry Creditors	1,57,500
			"	By A's Capital A/c	23,100
		1,89,000			1,89,000
Dec. 31	To Realisation A/c	1,05,000	Dec. 31	By Expenses A/c	7,350
			"	By A's Capital A/c	69,358
			"	By B's Capital A/c	28,292
		1,05,000			1,05,000
2006			2006		
Jan. 31	To Realisation A/c	1,15,000	Jan. 31	By Expenses A/c	5,250
			"	By A's Capital A/c	64,792
			"	By B's Capital A/c	41,541
			"	By C's Capital A/c	3,417
		1,15,000			1,15,000
Feb. 28	To Realisation A/c	53,250	Feb. 28	By Expenses A/c	5,250
			"	By A's Capital A/c	24,000
			"	By B's Capital A/c	16,000
			"	By C's Capital A/c	8,000
		53,250			53,250

Capital Accounts

Dr.		A	B	C			A	B	C Cr.
		Rs	Rs	Rs			Rs	Rs	Rs
2005					2005				
Nov. 30	To Cash A/c	23,100	–	–	Sept.	By Balance b/d	2,10,000	1,05,000	21,000
Dec. 31	To Cash A/c	69,358	28,292	–					
2006									
Jan. 31	To Cash A/c	64,792	41,541	3,417					
Feb. 28	To Realisation A/c	28,750	19,167	9,583					
"	To Cash A/c	24,000	16,000	8,000					
		2,10,000	1,05,000	21,000			2,10,000	1,05,000	21,000

ILLUSTRATION 33.22

A, B and C are in partnership sharing Profits and losses in the ratio of 3 : 2 : 1. They decided to dissolve the business on 31.12.2006 on which date their Balance Sheet was as follows:

Liabilities			*Rs*	*Assets*	*Rs*
Capital Accounts:	A	38,700		Land and Buildings	30,810
	B	10,680		Motor Car	5,160
	C	11,100	60,480	Investments	1,080
Loan Account:	C		3,000	Stock	19,530
Creditors			10,320	Debtors	11,280
				Cash	5,940
			73,800		73,800

The assets were realised piece-meal as follows and it was agreed that cash should be distributed as and when realised.

15.1.2007 — Rs. 10,380;

20.2.2007 — Rs. 27,900;

23.3.2007 — Rs. 3,600;

15.4.2007 — C took over the investments at Rs. 1,260;

27.4.2007 — Rs. 19,200

Dissolution expenses were originally provided for an estimated amount of Rs. 2,700 but actual amount spent on 29.3.2007 was Rs. 1,920. The creditors were settled for Rs. 10,080

You are required to prepare a statement showing distribution of cash amongst the partners.

(*I.C.W.A.* (*inter*)

SOLUTION:

STATEMENT SHOWING SURPLUS CAPITAL (BASIS: PROFIT SHARING RATIO)

	A	*B*	*C*
1. Profit sharing Ratio	3	2	1
	Rs	Rs	Rs
2. Capital as per Balance sheet	38,700	10,680	11,100
3. Step 2 divided by step 1	12,900	5,340	11,100
4. Proportionate capital, taking B's capital as the basis	16,020	10,680	5,340
5. Step 2 minus step 4	22,680	–	5,760
6. Proportionate capital, taking C's capital as the basis	17,280	–	5,760
7. Final surplus (Step 5 minus step 6)	5,400	–	

Statement Showing Priority of Distribution

First, Rs. 10,080 to be paid to the creditors (adjusting discount) after providing Rs. 2,700 for dissolution expenses.

Next, Rs. 3,000 to be paid to C for loan.

Next, Rs. 5,400 to be paid to A for Absolute Surplus.

Next, Rs. 23,040 to be paid to A and C in the ratio of 3 : 1. (Rs. 17,280: Rs. 5,760)

Balance to be paid to A, B and C in the ratio of 3 : 2 : 1.

Statement Showing Distribution of Proceeds of Realisation

	Amount available	*Creditors Rs*	*Loan C*	*Capitals A*	*B*	*C*
Amount Due		10,320	3,000	38,700	10,680	11,100
Cash in hand	5,940					
Less :Provision for dissolution expenses	2,700					
	3,240					
Less : Paid to the Creditors	3,240	3,240				
Balance Due		7,080	3,000	38,700	10,680	11,100
Realisation of 15.1.2007	10,380					
Less : Paid to the Creditors	6,840	6,840	—	—	—	
	3,540	240	—	—	—	
Less : Paid to C (Loan)	3,000	—	3,000			
Adjusted for discount received	—	240				
	540					
Less : Paid to A (Absolute Surplus)	540			540		
Balance Due				38,160	10,680	11,100
Realisation of 20.2.2007	27,900					
Less : Paid to A (Absolute Surplus)	4,860			4,860	—	—
Less : Paid to A and C (3 : 1)	23,040			17,280	—	5,760
Balance Due				16,020	10,680	5,340
Realisation of 23.3.2007	3,600					
Less : Paid to A, B and C (3 : 2 : 1)	3,600			1,800	1,200	600
Balance Due				14,220	9,480	4,740
Surplus of dissolution expensses : Rs (2,700 – 1, 920)	780					
Less : Paid to A, B and C (3 : 2 : 1)	780			390	260	130
Balance Due				13,830	9,220	4,610
Investments taken over by C (Note 1)			—		—	1,260
Realisation of 27.4.2007	19,200					
Less : Paid to A and B (Note 1)	6,300			3,780	2,520	—
	12,900					
Less : Paid to A, B and C (3 : 2 : 1)	12,900			6,450	4,300	2,150
Balance left unpaid (Being loss on realisation)				3,600	2,400	1,200

Working Note :

(1) Techinically, C will be allowed to take over investments only after the realisation of 27th April.

(2) Out of realisation of 27.4.2007 Rs 3,780 (1,260 × 3) to be paid to A and Rs 2,520 (1,260 × 2) to B to adjust the value of investments taken over by C. The balance is to be distributed among A, B and C in the raio of 3 : 2 : 1.

ILLUSTRATION 33.23

A, B and C carrying on business in the partnership decided to dissolve it on and from 30th September 2007. The following was their Balance sheet on that date:

Liabilities	*Rs*	*Assets*	*Rs*
Creditors	20,000	Fixed Assets	50,000
A's Capital	40,000	Current Assets	42,000
B's Capital	10,000	Bank	10,000
C's Capital	20,000		
General Reserve	12,000		
	1,02,000		1,02,000

As per the arrangement with the bank, the partners were entitled to withdraw an amount of Rs. 5,000 only at present and the balance amount of Rs. 5,000 could be withdrawn after 1st December, 2007. It was actually withdrawn on 20th December, 2007.

It was decided that after keeping aside an amount of Rs. 2,000 for estimated realization expenses the available cash should be distributed between the partners immediately.

Actual realization expenses amounted to Rs. 1,550 only. Prepare a statement showing the distribution of cash between the partners applying the "Surplus capital method".

The following were the realisations:

	Fixed Assets	**Current Assets**
	Rs.	**Rs.**
31.10.2007	10,000	19,000 = Rs. 29,000
25.11. 2007	26,000	20,000 = Rs. 46,000
20.12.2007	10,000	9,000 = Rs. 19,000

SOLUTION.

CALCULATION OF ABSOLUTE SURPLUS CAPITAL

	A	*B*	*C*
1. Profit sharing ratio	1	1	1
Capitals	Rs	Rs	Rs
	40,000	10,000	20,000
General Reserve	4,000	4,000	4,000
2. Adjusted Capitals	44,000	14,000	24,000
3. Proportionate capitals taking B's capitals taking B's capital as the basis	14,000	14,000	14,000
4. Surplus (Step 2 – Step 3)	30,000		10,000
5. Proportionate capital, taking C's capital as the basis	10,000		10,000
6. Final surplus	20,000		

Statement showing priority of Distribution

First, Rs. 2,000 should be kept for realisation expenses

Next, Rs. 20,000 to be paid to the creditors

Next, Rs. 20,000 to be paid to A (absolute Surplus Capital)

Next, (Rs. 10,000 + Rs. 10,000) = Rs. 20,000 to be paid to A & C equally

Balance to be paid to A, B & C equally

STATEMENT SHOWING DISTRIBUTION OF PROCEEDS OF REALISATION

	Amount available	*Creditors Rs*	*Capital A*	*B*	*C*
Amount due including gerneral reserve)		20,000	44,000	14,000	24,000
Cash withdrawn from Bank	5,000				
Less : Provision for realisation expenses	2,000				
	3,000				

Less : Paid to the creditors	3,000	3,000			
Balance due		17,000	44,000	14,000	24,000
Realisation of Octorber 2007	29,000				
Less : Paid to the creditors	17,000	17,000			
	12,000				
Less : Paid to a (Absolute Surplus)	12,000	—	12,000		
Balance due			32,000	14,000	24,000
Realisation of November 2007	46,000				
Less : Paid to A (Absolute Surplus)	8,000		8,000		
	38,000				
Less : Paid to A & C (1:1)	20,000		10,000	—	10,000
	18,000				
Less : Paid to A, B & C (1 : 1: 1)	18,000		6,000	6,000	6,000
Balance due			8,000	8,000	8,000
Realisation of december 2007	19,000				
Withdrawn from Bank	5,000				
Excess provision of realisation expenses (Rs 2,000 – 1,550)	450				
	24,450				
Less : Paid to A, B & C	24,450		8,150	8,150	8,150
Excess payment (Being profit on realisation)			150	150	150

QUESTIONS

Objective Type Questions

I. State whether the following statements are "True" or "False"

1. Dissolution of partnership is different from dissolution of firm
2. When a firm is dissolved, a Revaluation Account is opened
3. In the case of insolvency of all partners, it is necessary to open a Deficiency Account
4. Alternation of partnership relation is known as dissolution of firm.
5. Monetary consideration for the acquistion of business is known as purchase consideration
6. Realisation is a real account
7. Dissolution of a firm may be brought about by an order of Court
8. Loss on realisation is transferred to partners' capital account in their capital ratio
9. Any amount realised from the sale of an unrecorded asset is credited to the Realisation Account
10. In case of insolvency of a partner, his deficiency is borne by the solvent partners in their profit sharing ratio
11. Dissolution of the firm means the dissolution of the partnership between all the partners of the firm.
12. Partner's loan is transferred to the Realisation Account
13. The liability of the partners is joint and several
14. Advance to a partner is transferred to Realisation Account
15. Goodwill is realised like any other asset
16. Loss on realisation is transferred to the Capital Accounts of partners in the ratio of their capitals.
17. Investment Fluctuation Reserve transferred to the Realisation Account
18. A secured creditor always stands in a stronger position than an unsecured creditor
19. Firm's assets are first used for payment of firm's debts.
20. If any partner has a debit balance in his capital account, than he is required to bring in cash to clear it off.

(**Ans:** 1, 3, 5, 7, 9, 11, 13, 15, 17, 18, 19, 20.
False: 2, 4, 6, 8, 10, 12, 14, 16.

II. Fill in the blanks

1. The expenses of realisation are debited to .... Account.
2. When the firm is dissolved, Reserve Fund is transferred to .... in their profit sharing ratio
3. Unrecorded liability paid at the time of dissolution is to be debited to .... Account
4. Goodwill account appearing in the books on the dissolution date is closed by transferring it to .... side of the ..... account
5. After making the payment to third parties, the ..... due to partner is paid
6. If a partner takes over any liability, which is not recorded, the amount is to be credited to ....
7. Goodwill, on dissolution, is transferred to .... Account
8. Bank overdraft is transferred to ... Account
9. On dissolution, cash balance in hand is transferred to ..... A/c
10. Provision for doubtful debts at the time of dissolution of firm is transferred to ..... Account

(**Ans:** 1. Realisation; 2. Partners' Account; 3. Realisation; 4. Debit, Realisation; 5. Loan 6. Partners' Capital A/c; 7. Realisation; 8. Realisation; 9. Cash; 10. Realisation.)

III. Choose the correct answer to the following:

1. Unrecorded liability when paid on dissolution of a firm is debited to:
   (*a*) Realisation Account
   (*b*) Partners' Capital Account
   (*c*) Liability Account
2. In the absence of any contract to contrary, capital profit on dissolution of partnership firm is credited to partners account:
   (*a*) In Capital Ratio
   (*b*) In Profit sharing Ratio
   (*c*) Equally
3. In the event of dissolution of a partnership firm, the provision for doubtful debts is transferred to:
   (*a*) Partners' Capital Account
   (*b*) Sundry Debtors Account
   (*c*) Realisation Account
4. When realisation expenses are to be borne by a partner, the same are debited to:
   (*a*) Partners Capital Account
   (*b*) Cash Account
   (*c*) Profit & Loss Account
   (*d*) Realisation Account
5. Purchase consideration received in the form of shares is distributed among the partners in:
   (*a*) Profit sharing
   (*b*) Ratio of Fixed Capital
   (*c*) Ratio of final claim
   (*d*) Capital Ratio
6. An unrecorded liability when paid on dissolution of a firm is debited to:
   (*a*) Realisation Account
   (*b*) Partners Capital Account
   (*c*) Liability Account
7. General Reserve appearing at the time of dissolution of a firm is transferred to:
   (*a*) Realisation Account
   (*b*) Capital Accounts
   (*c*) Cash Account
8. The expenses of realisation are debited to:
   (*a*) Realisation Account

(b) Cash Account
(c) Capital Account

9. At the time of dissolution, all the assets of the firm are transferred to the realisation account at:
(a) Market value
(b) Book value
(c) Asset value

10. Upon dissolution of a firm, liability taken over by a partner is to be:
(a) Debited to the partners' Capital Account
(b) Credited to Realisation Account
(c) Credited to the partners' capital Account

(**Ans:** 1. (a); 2. (b); 3. (c); 4. (d); 5. (c); 6. (a); 7. (b); 8. (a); 9. (b); 10. (c).

THEORETICAL QUESTIONS

1. Define dissolution of a firm.
2. Who is an insolvent?
3. Explain with illustration Garner vs. Murray Case.
4. How does Realisation Account differ from Revaluation Account?
5. Distinguish between dissolution of firm and dissolution of partnership.
6. What is meant by piecemeal distribution of cash?
7. What is maximum loss method?
8. State the order in which payments are made on dissolution of a partnership firm due to insolvency of a partner.

PRACTICAL PROBLEMS

Dissolution

1. Varma and Sharma were running business in partnership sharing profits and losses in the ratio of 5 : 3. Firm was dissolved on 30th September 2004 when firm's position stood as below:

Liabilities		*Rs*	*Assets*		*Rs*
Reserve Fund		7,500	Cash at Bank		2,500
Outstanding liabilities			Machiner		4,200
Salary	500		B/R		1,600
Rent	900	1,400	Stock		3,200
Capital A/c			Debtors	3,500	
Varma	3,700		Less R.D.D.	600	2,900
Sharma	1,800	5,500	Joint Life Policy		
Joint Life Policy Reserve		4,000	(at surrender value)		4,000
		18,400			18,400

Machinery and stock realised 80% of book value whereas Rs 3,080 is collected from customers. Creditors for salary were agreed to accept Rs 390. But rent is paid in full. Goodwill of the firm realised Rs 2,500. Joint Life Policy is surrendered. Expenses of realisation Rs 200 paid by Varma. Mr Varma is allowed commission of 10 per cent on all assets realised except Goodwill. Show ledger accounts.

(*B.Com., Madurai*)

[**Ans:** Profit on Realisation: Rs 2,610; Rs 1,631 to Varma and Rs 979 to Sharma. Varma gets Rs 11,119 and Sharma gets Rs 5,591]

2. A and B were in partnership sharing profits in the ratio of 3 : 1. They agreed to dissolve the firm. The assets, other than cash of Rs 2,000 of the firm realised were worth Rs 1,10,000. The liabilities and other particulars on that date of the firm were as follows:

	Rs	
Creditors Account	40,000	
A's Capital Account	1,00,000	
B's Capital Account	10,000	(Dr.)
Profit and Loss A/c	8,000	(Dr.)
Realisation Expenses	1,000	

Creditors were settled in full settlement at Rs 38,000.

Prepare the Realisation Account, Cash Account and Capital Account. (*B.Com., Madurai*)

[Ans: Loss on Realisation: Rs 9,000 or Rs 6,750 to A and Rs 2,250 to B. B brings in Rs 14,250 and A gets Rs 87,250]

3. Anwar, Balan and Charles were partners sharing profits and losses in the ratio of 5/10 : 3/10 : 2/10. The partnership was dissolved on December 31st 2004.

Balance Sheet of Anwar, Balan & Charles as on December 31st 2004

Liabilities	*Rs*	*Assets*	*Rs*
Sundry Creditors	20,000	Cash in hand	10,000
Capital Accounts:		Furniture	5,000
Anwar	50,000	Stock	15,000
Balan	30,000	Sundry Debtors	30,000
Charles	20,000	Plant and Machinery	60,000
	1,20,000		1,20,000

Charles had joined the firm on January 1, 1997, paying a premium of Rs 20,000 on the understanding that the partnership would continue for 10 years. Due to Balan's ill health, the dissolution became necessary. Before Charles' admission, the partners were sharing profits and losses in the ratio of Anwar 3/5 and Balan 2/5.

Furniture and stock were realised for Rs 4,500 and Rs 13,500 respectively. The debtors were taken over by Anwar at Rs 28,500 expecting bad debts of Rs 1,500. Plant and machinery was sold for Rs 55,000. Sundry creditors have accepted Rs 19,000 in full satisfaction. Close the books of the firm.

(*B.Com., Bombay; MS*)

[Ans: Realisation Loss: Anwar Rs 3,750; Balan Rs 2,250 and Charles Rs 1,500. Final settlement to Anwar Rs 15,750, Balan Rs 25,750 and Charles Rs 22,500. Unexpired portion of goodwill is Rs 4,000 debited to Anwar and Balan in 1 : 1 ratio.]

4. Following was the balance sheet of M/s. Fat and Thin as on 31st December 2004:

Liabilities	*Rs*	*Assets*		*Rs*
Fat's Capital	26,000	Cash at Bank		5,000
Thin's Capital	10,000	Stock		20,000
Reserve Fund	8,000	Furniture		2,000
Fat's Loan	5,000	Plant and Machinery		10,000
Bills Payable	1,000	Investment		5,000
Outstanding Expenses	500	Building		15,000
Sundry Creditors	14,500	Debtors	8,800	
		Less: Provision	800	8,000
	65,000			65,000

The firm was dissolved on 31st December 2004.

(1) Fat took over Investment at Rs 4,000.

(2) Thin agreed to take over furniture at Rs 1,500 and agreed to meet the Bills payable privately.

(3) Other assets realised as follows:

Stock Rs 19,500. Debtors Rs 8,500. Plant & Mach. Rs 11,000. Building Rs 10,000.

(4) The Sundry creditors were settled at a discount of Rs 250.

(5) Dissolution proceedings required Rs 500 duly spent.

(6) Fat and Thin shared profits and losses in the proportion of 3 : 2.

Prepare necessary ledger accounts. (*B.Com., Shivaji; Agra*)

[**Ans:** Loss on Realisation Rs 5,750 or Rs 3,450 to Fat and Rs 2,300 to Thin. Fat gets Rs 23,350 and Thin gets Rs 10,400]

5. The Balance Sheet of A, B and C sharing profit and losses as 3 : 2 : 1 respectively as follows on 31st March 2004.

		Rs		*Rs*
Creditors		50,400	Cash at Bank	3,700
Reserve Fund		10,000	Stock	20,100
Profit and Loss A/c		12,000	Debtors	62,600
Capital Accounts:			Investments	16,000
A	30,000		Furniture	6,500
B	20,00		Buildings	23,500
C	10,000	60,000		
		1,32,400		1,32,400

The firm was dissolved on that date. For the purpose of dissolution the investments were valued at Rs 18,000 and stock at Rs 17,500, A agreed to take over the investments and B to take over the stock and C to take over the furniture at book value. Debtors and buildings realised Rs 57,000 and Rs 25,000 respectively. Expenses of realisation amounted to Rs 450. In addition one bill for Rs 500 under discount was dishonoured an had to be taken up by the firm.

Give journal entries for the above. (*I.B.Com., Bangalore, Madras, Kerala*)

[**Ans:** Loss on Realisation: Rs 5,650 i.e., Rs 2,825 to A; Rs 1,883 to B and Rs 942 to C. Final settlement: A gets Rs 20,175, B gets Rs 7,950 and C gets Rs 6,225]

6. A, B and C were carrying on business as manufacturers of sports goods. The profit sharing ratio was 3 : 2 : 1 respectively. Their Balance Sheet on 30th June 2004 was as under:

Liabilities	*Rs*	*Assets*		*Rs*
Sundry Creditors	1,50,000	Plant and Machinery		1,60,000
Mrs A's Loan	1,30,000	Stck		1,50,000
Reserve for Repairs	1,000	Sundry Debtors:	2,00,000	
Capital Accounts:		Less: Provision for B/D	10,000	1,90,000
A;	1,00,000	Prepaid Insurance		4,000
B:	1,50,000	Investments		30,000
C:	20,000	Cash		28,000
	5,62,000			5,62,000

On this date the firm was dissolved. The assets realised as under:

Plant and Machinery	Rs 1,00,000
Stock	Rs 1,20,000
Sundry Debtors	Rs 1,60,000

The investments were taken over by A at a value of Rs 20,000. He also agreed to pay Mrs A's Loan. During the course of realisation it was found that a bill for Rs 50,000 previously discounted by the firm was dishonoured and had to be paid. Expenses came to Rs 8,000.

Prepare:

(*i*) Realisation Account,

(*ii*) Partners' Capital Account,

(*iii*) Cash Account. (*CAIIB*)

[**Ans:** Loss on Realisation: Rs 1,92,000: Rs 96,000 to A: Rs 64,000 to B; Rs 32,000 to C. Final settlement: C brings in Rs 10,000. Paid to A Rs 1,20,000 and Rs 90,000 to B]

7. P, Q and R carrying on business as merchants and sharing profits and losses in the ratio of 2 : 2 : 1, dissolved their firm as on December 31st, 2004 on which date their Balance Sheet was as follows:

Liabilities		Rs	*Assets*		Rs
Sundry Creditors		20,300	Cash at Bank		4,500
Reserve Fund		10,000	Stock		16,000
Joint Life Policy Reserve		8,000	Debtors	10,000	
Capital Accounts:			Less: Provision	500	9,500
P	15,000		Joint Life Policy		11,000
Q	15,000		Premises		30,300
R	3,000	33,000			
		71,300			71,300

Note: There is a bill for Rs 1,000 under discount. The bill was received from Z.

The assets except Cash at Bank and Joint Life Policy, were sold to a company which paid Rs 65,000 in cash. The Joint Life Policy was surrendered and Rs 11,300 were received. Z proved nsolvent and dividend of 50% was received from his estate. Sundry creditors were paid Rs 19,500 in full settlement. The expenses amounted to Rs 3,000.

Prepare the Realisation Account, Cash Account and Partners' Accounts.

(*B.Com., Madurai; Punjab; MS*)

[**Ans:** Profit on Realisation: Rs 14,800 i.e., Rs 5,920 to P; Rs 5,920 to Q and Rs 2,960 to R. Final settlement: P gets Rs 24,920; Q gets Rs 24,920 and R gets Rs 7,960]

8. The Crescent Company Limited was formed to acquire the business of A and B who share profits 2/3 and 1/3 respectively.

The Balance Sheet of A and B was as under on December 31, 2004:

Liabilities		Rs	*Assets*	Rs
Bills Payable		7,200	Land and Buildings	40,000
Sundry Creditors		21,600	Machinery	20,000
Mrs A's Loan		3,200	Stock	24,000
Capitals:			Debtors	23,200
A	64,000		Bills Receivable	6,400
B	40,000	1,04,000	Investments	4,800
			Cash at Bank	9,600
			Goodwill	8,000
		1,36,000		1,36,000

It was agreed by the company to take over the assets at book value with the exception of Land and Buildings and Stock which are taken over at Rs 45,000 and Rs 20,000 respectively. The investments are retained by the firm and sold by them for Rs 4,000. They also discharge the loan of Mrs A. The company takes over the remaining liabilities. The value of goodwill is fixed at Rs 28,800.

The Purchase consideration is discharged as follows: 10,000 ordinary shares of Rs 10 each and the balance in cash. Close the books of the firm. (*B.Com., Madurai*)

[**Ans:** Profit on Realisation: Rs 21,000 i.e.,
Rs 14,000 to A and Rs 7,000 to B.

Final Settlements:	A Rs	B Rs
Shares	62,400	37,600
Cash	15,600	9,400
	78,000	47,000

9. Read, Write and Add give you the following Balance Sheet as on December 31, 2004:

Liabilities		*Rs*	*Assets*		*Rs*
Read's Loan		15,000	Plant and Machinery at cost		30,000
Capital Accounts:			Fixtures & Fittings		2,000
Read	30,000		Stock		10,400
Write	10,000		Debtors	18,400	
Add	2,000	42,000	Less: Provision	400	18,000
Sundry Creditors		17,800	Joint Life Policy		15,000
Loan on hypothecation of Stock		6,200	Patents & Trade Marks		10,000
Joint Life Policy Reserve		12,400	Cash at Bank		8,000
		93,400			93,400

The partners shared profit and losses in the ratio of Read 4/9, Write 2/9; and Add 1/3. The firm was dissolved on December 31, 2004 and you are given the following information:

(*a*) Add had taken a loan from insurers for Rs 5,000 on the security of the Joint Life Policy. The Policy was surrendered and Insurer paid a sum of Rs 10,200 after deducting Rs 5,000 for Add's loan and Rs 300 interest thereon.

(*b*) One of the creditors took some of the patents whose book value was Rs 6,000 at a valuation of Rs 4,500. The balance to that creditor was paid in cash.

(*c*) The firm had previously purchased some shares in a joint stock company and had written them off on finding them useless. The shares were now found to be worth Rs 3,000 and the loan creditor agreed to accept the shares at this value.

(*d*) The remaining assets realised the following amounts:

	Rs
Plant and Machinery	17,000
Fixtures and Fittings	1,000
Stock	9,000
Debtors	16,500
Patents – 50% of their book value	

(*e*) The liabilities were paid and a total discount of Rs 500 was allowed by the creditors.

(*f*) The expenses of Realisation amounted to Rs 2,300.

Prepare the Realisation Account, Bank Account and Partners' Capital Accounts.

(*B.Com., Madurai*)

[**Ans:** Loss on Realisation: Rs 6,300 i.e., Read Rs 2,800;
Write Rs 1,400 and Add Rs 2,100.
Final Settlement: Add brings in Rs 5,400;
Read gets Rs 27,200 and Write gets Rs 8,600]

10. A and B, who make up their accounts annually to 31st December were in Partnership sharing profits and losses in the ratio of 2 : 1. No interest was charged on drawings or credited to capital.

The following was the summary of the balances as on 31st December, 2004.

	Rs		Rs
Fixtures and Fittings	22,000	Partners Capital A/c	
Leasehold Premises	50,000	A	31,000
Stock (opening)	7,600	B	10,000
Debtors	1,800	Loan from A at 8% p.a.	20,000
Purchases	48,000	Creditors	6,400
General Expenses	16,000	Sales	1,04,000
Partners' Drawings		Depreciation on Motor Vehicle	
A	6,000	as on 1-1-1992	3,600
B	4,800	Bank Overdraft	26,200
Motor Vehicle at cost	9,000		
Wages	36,000		
	2,01,200		2,01,200

For the purpose of closing of accounts on 31.1.2004, closing stock was valued at Rs 6,200 and furniture and fittings at Rs 18,000. Provision for depreciation on motor vehicle is to be made at 20% p.a. calculated on cost and for accrued general expenses Rs 1,200. In addition one year's interest is to be provided on A's Loan.

The partnership was dissolved on 1.1.2005, it being agreed that:

(*i*) A should take over stock for Rs 6,000.

(*ii*) B should take over motor vehicle at Rs 2,700 and part of the fittings and fixtures for Rs 7,500.

(*iii*) Interest on A's loan should cease with effect from 1.1.2005.

During January, 2005 the following transactions took place:

(*a*) Leasehold Premises were sold, realising a net amount of Rs 60,000.

(*b*) Rs 1,600 was collected from debtors and the balance was taken over by A.

(*c*) A portion of the fittings and fixtures were auctioned and realised Rs 10,000. It was also agreed that the balance of fixtures and fittings should be taken over by B for Rs 500.

(*d*) Creditors and accrued general expenses were paid in full.

(*e*) Realisation expenses amounted to Rs 1,400.

(*f*) All amounts receivable and payable by A and B were settled.

Prepare:

(1) Profit and Loss Account for the year ended 31st December, 2004.

(2) Realisation Account.

(3) Cash Account for January, 2005.

(4) Partners' Accounts showing the final settlement of dissolution. (*I.C.W.A.*)

[**Ans:** Trading net loss to A Rs 4,000 and B Rs 2,000.
Realisation profit to A Rs 5,000 and B Rs 2,500
Final settlement: B brings cash Rs 5,000. Payment to A Rs 19,800]

11. A, B and C are partners of a firm, sharing profits and losses equally.

Balance Sheet of A, B, C as on September 30, 2004

Liabilities		*Rs*	*Assets*	*Rs*
Capital Accounts:			Plant and Machinery	23,760
A	20,000		Furniture and Fittings	4,240
B	25,000		Sundry Debtors	14,165
C	12,500	57,500	Joint Life Policy	2,105
Current Accounts:			Bill receivable	8,610
A	18,600		Stock in trade	29,940
C	7,200	25,800	B's Current A/c	12,400
Sundry Creditors		17,720	Cash at Bank and on Hand	4,200
Bills Payable		8,400		
		1,09,420		1,09,420

The value of the Joint Life Policy shown in the Balance Sheet represents the surrender value of the policy taken by the firm for 30,000 to enable the settlement of accounts with a partners' estate in case of a partner's death during the continuance of the firm.

A died on October 1, 2004. The remaining partners could not arrive at any understanding with the legal representatives of A, with the result that it was decided that firm would be dissolved, subject to the following adjustments:

(1) The sum assured was realised from the Insurance Company.

(2) Plant and machinery realised only 70% of the book value.

(3) Furniture and fittings were taken over by C at a market value of Rs 2,500.

(4) Bills receivable and sundry debtors had to be discounted by 4%.

(5) Stock in trade comprised of: (*a*) Easily marketable items 70% of the total inventory which realised its full value. (*b*) Obsolete items – 10% of the total inventory which had to be discarded. (*c*) The rest of the items which realised 50% of their book value.

(6) A liability for Rs 1,500 which had not been recorded in the firm's books had to be settled by the firm before its dissolution.

Draw up accounts showing intersettlement among the partners. (*C.A.*)

[Ans: Realisation Profit: A – Rs 210; B – Rs 209; and C – Rs 209. Paid to A's executor Rs 38,810; Paid to B – Rs 12,809; Paid to C – Rs 17,410]

12. The following is the Trial Balance of the firm of P, Q and R on 31st March 2004:

	Rs	Rs
Freehold Property (Bombay)	4,50,000	–
Leasehold Property (Calcutta)	1,50,000	–
Leasehold Property (Madras)	1,20,000	–
Investments	60,000	–
Office Furniture	10,000	–
Stock (Bombay)	1,80,000	–
Stock (Calcutta)	1,60,000	–
Stock (Madras)	1,40,000	–
Sundry Debtors	1,25,000	–
Sundry Creditors		1,85,000
Capitals: P		5,00,000
Q		4,50,000
R		3,00,000
Cash at Bank	40,000	–
	14,35,000	14,35,000

The partners agreed to dissolve the firm on the above date on the following terms:

(*a*) Freehold Propert was sold and realised Rs 5,00,000;
Investments realised Rs 75,000
Debtors Rs 1,15,000
Office Furniture Rs 6,000

(*b*) P retired from the business altogether.

(*c*) Q took over the Calcutta business and the assets in connection therewith at the book values, the goodwill thereof being valued at Rs 1,00,000.

(*d*) R took over Madras business and the corresponding assets at book values, the goodwill for the purpose being valued at Rs 50,000.

(e) Expenses of realisation amounted to Rs 12,000.

(f) Bombay stock was taken over by Q and R equally at book values.

(g) P, Q and R shared profits in proportions of 3/5, 1/5 and 1/5 respectively.

(h) There was an unrecorded liability of Rs 8,000 which was paid off.

Prepare:

(i) Realisation Account,

(ii) Partners' Capital Accounts,

(iii) Bank Account

Close the books of the firm, assuming that each partner finally settles his account with the firm.

(*CAIIB*)

[**Ans:** Profit on Realisation: Rs 1,81,000 i.e., Rs 1,08,600 to P; Rs 36,200 to Q and Rs 36,200 to R. Final settlement: Q brings in Rs 13,800 R brings in Rs 63,800 and P gets Rs 6,08,600]

13. The following is the Trial Balance of the firm Ishwar, Isaac and Ibrahim as on December 31, 2004:

Trial Balance

Debit Balances	*Rs*	*Credit Balances*	*Rs*
Freehold property (Madras)	22,500	Sundry Creditors	9,250
Leasehold property (Madurai)	7,500	Ishwar's Capital A/c	25,000
Leasehold property (Mayuram)	6,000	Isaac's Capital A/c	22,500
Investments	3,000	Ibrahim's Capital A/c	15,000
Office Furniture	500		
Stock (Madras)	9,000		
Stock (Madurai)	8,000		
Stock (Mayuram)	7,000		
Sundry Debtors	6,250		
Cas at Bank	2,000		
	71,750		71,750

They agreed to dissolve the firm on December 31, 2004, on the following terms:

(1) The freehold property was sold and realised Rs 25,000; the investments realised Rs 3,750; debtors Rs 5,750; and office furniture Rs 300.

(2) Ishwar retired from the business altogether.

(3) Isaac took over the Madurai business and the assets in connection therewith at book values, goodwill being valued at Rs 5,000.

(4) Ibrahim took over the Mayuram business and the corresponding assets at book values, goodwill being valued at Rs 2,500.

(5) The Madras stock was taken over by Isaac and Ibrahim equally at book value.

(6) The partners—Ishwar, Isaac and Ibrahim—shared in the ratio of 3 : 1 : 1.

(7) There was an unrecorded liability of Rs 400.

Show the Realisation Account, the Partners' Capital Accounts and the Bank Account, assuming that each partner finally settled his account with the firm. (*B.Com., Madurai*)

[**Ans:** Profit on Realisation: Rs 9,650 i.e., Rs 5,790 to Ishwar, Rs 1,930 to Isaac and Rs 1,930 to Ibrahim. Final Settlement: Isaac brings in Rs 570; Ibrahim brings in Rs 3,070 and Ishwar gets Rs 30,790]

14. Black, White and Green were partners sharing profits and losses in the ratio of 4 : 3 : 3. Their Balance Sheet as on 31st December, 2004 was as follows:

Liabilities	*Rs*	*Assets*	*Rs*
Creditors	10,000	Cash	3,000
Bills Payable	6,000	Stock	10,000
Black's Loan	3,000	Debtors	5,000
Employee's Provident Fund	1,000	Furniture	7,000
General Reserve	4,000	Building	20,000
Provisions for Depreciation	2,000	Green's Current Account	2,500
Contingency Reserve	5,000	Goodwill	4,500
Current Accounts:		Profit & Loss Account	6,000
Black	3,000		
White	2,000		
Capital Account			
Black	10,000		
White	8,000		
Green	4,000		
	58,000		58,000

On 1st January, 2005 the firm was dissolved. Assets were realised as follows—Stock Rs 12,000, Debtors Rs 3,000. Building Rs 11,000. Furniture was taken over by Black. Creditors agreed to accept 75 paise in a rupee. The winding up expenses amounted to Rs 2,500. There was a Joint Life Policy of Rs 10,000 which was surrendered to Life Insurance Corporation for Rs 3,000.

Prepare necessary accounts to close the books of the firm. *(B.Com., Madurai)*

[**Ans:** Loss on Realisation Rs 8,500 i.e., Rs 3,400 to Black; Rs 2,550 to white Rs 2,550 to Green. Final settlement: Green brings in Rs 150; Black gets Rs 3,800 and White gets Rs 8,350]

Insolvency

15. X, Y and Z are partners sharing profits and losses in the ratio of 3 : 2 : 1. The firm was dissolved on 31st December 2004 when their financial position was as under:

		Rs		Rs
Capital of	X	12,000	Land and Buildings	6,000
	Y	6,000	Plant	5,600
Creditors		10,428	Patents	2,000
			Furniture	640
			Stock	5,360
			Debtors	6,428
			Cash in hand	2,000
			Z's Capital	400
		28,428		28,428

Realisations were as follows:

Land and Buildings	4,920
Plant	4,000
Patents	Nil
Furniture	200
Stock	4,000
Debtors	5,440
Realisation Expenses	124

There was a contingent liability for Rs 400 not provided is now materialised. Mr Z is insolvent and is unable to bring anything to meet his deficiency. You are required to close the books of the firm in accordance with decision in Garner vs. Murray. (*B.Com., Madurai*)

[**Ans:** Realisation Loss Rs 7,992 i.e., Rs 3,996 to X; Rs 2,664 to Y and Rs 1,332 to Z. Deficiency of Z (Rs 1,732) met by X and in 2 : 1 ratio i.e., Rs 1,155 by X and Rs 577 by Y. Final settlement: X gets Rs 10,845 and Y gets Rs 5,423]

16. A, B and C are partners in a firm sharing profits and losses in the ratio of 30%, 40% and 30% respectively. They decided to dissolve the firm and appointed A to realise the assets. A is to receive 5% remuneration on amount realised and is to bear all expenses of realisation.

On dissolution of the firm on 31st December, 2004 the Balance Sheet was as under:

Liabilities		*Rs*	*Assets*		*Rs*
Creditors		50,000	Cash		1,500
Bills Payable		9,000	Debtors	46,000	
Capital Accounts:			Less Provision for		
A	20,000		Bad Debts	3,000	43,000
B	30,000	50,000	Stock		55,000
			Furniture		5,000
			C's Capital Overdrawn		4,500
		1,09,000			1,09,000

A reports the result of realisation as follows: Debtors Rs 38,000, Stock Rs 40,000, Furniture Rs 2,000. Goodwill is sold for Rs 2,000. Creditors were paid Rs 48,500 and Bills payable in full. Outstanding creditors of Rs 500, which were not recorded in the books were also paid. Realisation expenses amounted to Rs 800 which were met by A personally. A and B agree to receive from C Rs 3,000 in full settlement of the firm's claim against him. Garner vs. Murray rule is applicable. Prepare necessary accounts. (*B.Com., Madurai*)

[**Ans:** Realisation Loss: Rs 24,000 i.e., A Rs 7,200; B Rs 9,600 and C Rs 7,200. C's Capital Deficiency of Rs 8,700 met by A and B in their capital ratio i.e., 2 : 3. Final settlement A gets Rs 13,320 and B gets Rs 15,180]

17. Partnership of Good, Better and Best was dissolved on 1st November 2004, when their financial position was as under:

Liabilities		*Rs*	*Assets*	*Rs*
Good's Loan A/c		3,700	Cash on hand	750
Bank Loan		1,900	Furniture	4,000
Creditors	5,000		Building	1,500
Less: Reserve	250	4,750	Plant & Machinery	6,000
Capital A/c			Goodwill	3,400
Good	3,900		P & L A/c	4,000
Better	1,300			
Best	4,100	9,300		
		19,650		19,650

Furniture and Building realised for Rs 6,000.

Machinery taken over by 'Best' at agreed value of Rs 5,400. Goodwill proved valueless.

Creditors accepted Rs 5,600 in full satisfaction of debt. Other liabilities paid in full. Realisation Expenses Rs 600.

Partners share profit in the ratio of 1/10, 1/2 and 2/5. Better declared as insolvent and firm recovered Rs 75 from him. Show ledger accounts. *(B.Com., Karnataka)*

[**Ans:** Loss on Realisation: 4,950; i.e., Good Rs 495; Better Rs 2,475 and Best Rs 1,980. Deficiency of Better borne by Good Rs 1,808 and Best Rs 1,292. Final settlement: Best brings in Rs 4,192 and paid to Good Rs 1,692]

18. Raman, Krishnan and Murugan were partners in a firm. They shared profits and losses in the proportion of 4 : 3 : 3. The firm was dissolved and Krishnan was appointed to realise the assets and distribute the proceeds. Krishnan is to receive 5% commission on the amounts realised from sale of assets and is to bear all expenses of realisation.

The following was the balance sheet on the date of dissolution:

Liabilities	*Rs*	*Assets*		*Rs*
Creditors	29,500	Cash		750
Capital Accounts:		Debtors	22,750	
Raman	15,000	Less: Provision	1,250	21,500
Krishnan	10,000	Stock		30,000
		Murugan – Capital overdrawn		2,250
	54,500			54,500

Rs 17,500 was collected from debtors in full settlement. Stock realised Rs 22,500; Goodwill Rs 1,000. Creditors were paid Rs 28,750 in full settlement. In addition, outstanding creditors Rs 250 were also paid. The expenses of dissolution amounted to Rs 300.

Raman and Krishnan received Rs 1,500 from Murugan in full settlement of accounts.

Show the Realisation Account, the Cash Account and the Capital Accounts of the partners in the books of the firm. *(B.Com., Madurai; Madras)*

[**Ans:** Realisation Loss: Raman Rs 4,820, Krishnan Rs 3,615 and Murugan Rs 3,615. Murugan's Deficiency of Rs 4,365 borne by Raman and Krishnan in 3 : 2 ratio i.e. Rs 2,619 by Raman and Rs 1,746 by Krishnan. Final settlement to Raman Rs 12,381 and Krishnan Rs 10,004]

19. A, B, C and D were in partnership. Their position on 30th June 2004 was as follows:

Liabilities	*Rs*	*Assets*	*Rs*
Capital Accounts:			
A:	7,000	Sundry Assets	32,000
B:	8,000	Loss to date	15,000
C:	4,000	Current Accounts:	
D:	3,000	B:	4,000
Sundry Creditors	30,000	D:	1,000
	52,000		52,000

They shared profits and losses as 4 : 3 : 2 : 1. They decided to dissolve on this date. The assets realised Rs 27,000. A and B are both insolvent. B's private assets amount to Rs 10,000 and his private liabilities are Rs 7,000. D's private assets are Rs 7,000 and his private liabilities are Rs 6,000.

Show the accounts concerned till the final dissolution assuming all transactions are put through on 30th September 2004 and B's estate realised only Rs 4,000 and D's estate realised Rs 5,000.

(*CA Final, B.Com., MS; MK*)

[**Ans:** Realisation Loss: A—Rs 2,000; B—Rs 1,500 C—Rs 1,000; D—Rs 500 (Deficiency of A and B *i.e.*, Rs 3,000 borne by C and D in 2 : 1 ratio)]

20. The following Balance Sheet is presented to you:

Liabilities		*Rs*	*Assets*		*Rs*
Creditors		20,000	Sundry Assets		30,000
B's Loan		5,000	Cash at Bank		1,000
Capitals:			Loss		15,000
A	10,000		Drawings:		
B	6,000		B	2,000	
C	6,000		C	2,000	4,000
D	3,000	25,000			
		50,000			50,000

The partners share profits and losses at A 2/10, B 3/10, C 3/10 and D 2/10. The position of partners was as follows:

	Private Estate	Private Liabilities
	Rs	Rs
A	10,000	15,000
B	20,000	6,000
C	5,000	4,000
D	8,000	9,000

The assets realised Rs 26,000 and expenses of dissolution came to Rs 1,000. Prepare ledger accounts, giving effect to the dissolution. (*B.Com., Madurai; Mysore; Madras*)

[**Ans:** Loss on Realisation Rs 5,000. A receives Rs 4,000 The deficiency of C and D is borne by A alone as B has no credit balance.]

21. A, B, C and D were partners sharing profits and losses in the ratio of 3 : 3 : 2 : 2. Following is their Balance Sheet as on June 30, 2004.

Liabilities		*Rs*	*Assets*		*Rs*
Sundry Creditors		15,500	Cash at Bank		2,000
A's Loan		10,000	Sundry Debtors		16,000
Capital Accounts:			Less Provision for		
A	20,000		Bad Debts	500	15,500
B	15,000	35,000	Stock		10,000
			Furniture and Fittings		4,000
			Trade Marks		7,000
			Capital Accounts:		
			C	16,000	
			D	6,000	22,000
		60,500			60,500

On June 30, 2004 the firm was dissolved and B was appointed to realise the assets and pay off the liabilities. He was entitled to receive 5% commission on the amounts finally paid to other partners as capital. He was to bear the expenses of realisation. The assets realised as follows:

	Rs
Sundry Debtors	11,000
Stock	8,000
Furniture and Fittings	1,000
Trade Marks	4,000

Creditors were paid off in full; in addition, a contingent liability for Bills Receivable discounted materialised to the extent of Rs 2,500. Also there was a joint life policy for Rs 30,000. This was surrendered for Rs 3,000. Expenses of realisation amounted to Rs 500. C was insolvent but Rs 3,700 were recovered from his estate.

Write up the necessary accounts to close the books of the firm. *(B.Com., Bombay; Kerala)*

[**Ans:** Loss: A Rs 3,600; B Rs 3,600;
C Rs 2,400; D Rs 2,400
Final settlement: D brings in Rs 8,400;
A receives Rs 11,219 and B receives Rs 8581.
Deficiency of C met by A and B in 4 : 3 ratio or
Rs 8,400 by A and Rs 6,300 by B.]

22. Balance Sheet of P, Q and R as on March 31, 2004:

Liabilities	*Rs*	*Assets*	*Rs*
P's Capital A/c	25,000	Freehold property	10,000
R's Capital A/c	15,000	Furniture	5,000
P's Current A/c	1,000	Stock-in-trade	23,100
R's Current A/c	500	Debtors	30,000
Sundry Creditors	30,000	Cash	2,500
Loan on mortgage of freehold property	4,000	Q's Current A/c	4,900
	75,500		75,500

The partners shared profits and losses in the proportion of 6 : 3 : 5. It was decided to dissolve the partnership as on the date of the Balance Sheet.

The assets are realised as follows:

	Rs
Freehold property	6,000
Furniture	2,000
Stock-in-trade	15,000
Debtors	20,000

The expenses on realisation amounted to Rs 2,000. The sundry creditors agreed to take 75 paise in a rupee in full satisfaction. It was ascertained that Q was insolvent. A dividend of 60 paise in a rupee was received from the court receiver.

Write up the Realisation Account, the Bank Account, Capital and Current Accounts of the partners. Indicate the basis adopted for distributing the deficiency in the Capital Account. *(I.C.W.A.)*

[**Ans:** Realisation loss: P—Rs 8,400, Q—Rs 4,200 and R—Rs 7,000.
Q's Deficiency of Rs 3,640 is borne by P and R
in their fixed capital ratio i.e. 5 : 3.
Final Settlement: P receives Rs 23,725 and R receives Rs 14,135]

Piece-meal Distribution

23. Partners A, B and C share profits in the proportion of 1/2, 1/3 and 1/6. Their Balance Sheet is as follows:

Liabilities		*Rs*	*Assets*	*Rs*
Capital Accounts:			Assets	80,000
A	30,000			
B	30,000			
C	20,000	80,000		
		80,000		80,000

The firm is dissolved and the assets are realised as follows:

First realisation	10,000	
Second realisation	15,000	
Third and final realisation	25,000	50,000

Prepare a statement showing how the distribution should be made applying Garner vs. Murray principle. (*C.S., ICWA*)

[Ans:	A	B	C
	Rs	Rs	Rs
First Realisation	–	3,333	6,667
Second Realisation	2,500	8,334	4,166
Third Realisation	12,500	8,333	4,167
Realisation Loss	15,000	10,000	5,000

24. A, B and C were in partnership sharing profits and losses as 2 : 2 : 1. The Balance Sheet of the firm as on 30th June 2004 is as follows:

Liabilities	*Rs*	*Assets*	*Rs*
Partners Capitals:			
A:	60,000	Sundry Assets	2,64,000
B:	48,000		
C:	40,000		
Partners' advances:			
A:	20,000		
B:	16,000		
Sundry Creditors	80,000		
	2,64,000		2,64,000

Prepare a statement showing the distribution of cash among the partners as and when the assets were realised. The assets were realised as follows:

31st July	Rs 50,000
31st Aug.	Rs 98,000
30th Sept.	Rs 1,00,000

(*B.Com., Madurai, Kerala, Calcutta, Bombay*)

[Ans: Cash payments

	A	B	C
	Rs	Rs	Rs
Aug.	13,600	1,600	16,800
Sept.	40,000	40,000	20,000
Realisation Loss	6,400	6,400	3,200]

25. A, B and C were in partnership sharing profits and losses in the ratio of 2 : 1 : 1. They decided to dissolve the partnership on the basis of the following Balance Sheet:

Liabilities	*Rs*	*Assets*	*Rs*
Sundry Creditors	3,000	Premises	24,000
Loan mortgage on premises	18,000	Sundry Debtors	36,000
A's Loan	9,000	Stock	41,200
General Reserve	6,000	Cash	1,800
Capital Accounts:			
A:	30,000		
B:	24,000		
C:	13,000		
	1,03,000		1,03,000

The assets were realised as follows:

June Rs 3,000 received after meeting in full the mortgage Loan.

July Rs 9,000 from Debtors and Rs 6,000 from Stock.

Aug. Rs 12,000 from Debtors and Rs 15,000 from stock.

Sept. Rs 10,200 from Debtors and Rs 12,000 from stock.

The remaining Stock was taken over by B at an agreed value of Rs 1,800.

The Sundry Creditors were settled for Rs 2,400.

The partners decided to distribute cash as and when realised.

You are required to prepare a statement showing the distribution of cash, applying "Highest Relative Capitals" method. Also prepare Partners' Capital Accounts. (*CA Inter*)

[**Ans:** Realisation

	A	B	C
	Rs	Rs	Rs
July	–	8,400	–
Aug.	14,200	7,700	5,100
Sept.	12,000	4,200	6,000
Stock	–	1,800	–
Realisation Loss	6,800	3,400	3,400

26. Suresh, Ramesh and Girish are in partnership. The following is their Balance Sheet as on 31st December 2004, on which date they dissolve their firm. They share profits and losses in the ratio of 4 : 3 : 2.

Balance Sheet as on 31st December 2004

Liabilities	*Rs*	*Assets*	*Rs*
Sundry Creditors	9,500	Cash on hand	200
Reserve	3,600	Sundry Debtors	27,000
Capitals:		Stock-in-trade	13,000
Suresh	22,400	Furniture	15,800
Ramesh	12,900		
Girish	7,600		
	56,000		56,000

It is decided to repay the amounts due to the partners as and when the assets are realised. Assets realised as follows:

		Debtors	Stock	Furniture
		Rs	Rs	Rs
I	Instalment	2,000	1,000	300
II	Instalment	6,000	3,000	2,000
III	Instalment	10,000	6,500	5,200
IV	Instalment	6,000	1,500	6,000

Prepare a statement showing how the distribution should be made. (*B.Com., Karnataka*)

[**Ans:**

Realisation	Suresh	Ramesh	Girish
	Rs	Rs	Rs
II	5,000	–	–
III	10.200	7,500	4.000
IV	6,000	4,500	3,000
Realisation Loss	2,800	2,100	1,400]

(Based on Surplus Capital Method)

27. X, Y and Z were in partnership sharing profits and losses in the proportion of 1/2, 1/3 and 1/6 respectively. The partnership was dissolved on 30th June 2004 when the position was as follows:

Liabilities		*Rs*	*Assets*	*Rs*
Capital:			Cash in hand	28,000
X	1,40,000		Sundry Debtors	2,94,000
Y	70,000		Stock-in-trade	1,12,000
Z	14,000	2,24,000		
Creditors		2,10,000		
		4,34,000		4,34,000

There was a bill Rs 10,000 due on 30th November, 2004 under discount.

It was agreed that the net realisation should be distributed in their due order (at the end of each month) but as safety as possible. The realisation and expenses were as under:

	Stock and Debtors	Expenses
	Rs	Rs
31.7.2004	84,000	7,000
31.8.2004	1,26,000	5,400
30.9.2004	70,000	4,900
31.10.2004	77,000	3,500
30.11.2004	35,500	3,500

The stock was completel disposed of and amounts due from debtors were realised, the balance being irrecoverable. The acceptor of the bill under discount met the bill on the due date.

Set out the Cash and Capital Accounts showing the monthly distribution of cash realised.

(*B.Com., Madurai*)

[**Ans:**

Date	X receives	Y receives	Z receives
	Rs	Rs	Rs
31.8.2004	5,600	–	–
31.9.2004	50,050	15,050	–
31.10.2004	44,450	28,350	700
31.11.2004	21,000	14,000	7,000
Realisation Loss	18,900	12,600	6,300]

NOTES

NOTES

NOTES

NOTES